SMOTHERED PORK CHOPS STRIP ROAST
TEXAS MONKEY WOOD CIDER-BAKED
BREAD HAM
BARBECUED CORNELL GRILLED SKILLET
BEEF BARBECUED SALMON CHICKEN
RIBS CHICKEN DUTCH BABY PARMESAN
CRISPY STRAWBERRY ST. LOUIS–STYLE
FISH POKE PIZZA
STICKS CAKE
CHICKEN CHIMICHANGAS ALABAMA
CREOLE CINCINNATI BARBECUED
FRIED CHILI CHICKEN
CHICKEN TENNESSEE
WHISKEY
BETTER-THAN- MEMPHIS HULI PORK
THE-BOX CHOPPED HULI CHOPS
PANCAKES COLESLAW CHICKEN
BEST POTLUCK SOUTH SYRACUSE
MAC & CAROLINA
PULLED SALT POTATOES
CHEESE PORK NASHVILLE HOT FRIED
CHICKEN
WHOOPIE PIES COLD-OVEN POUND GRILLED POTATO
CAKE HOBO PACK
SWEET CAT DUCHESS POTATO
CORN HEAD TEXAS SHEET CAKE
SPOONBREAD BISCUITS
GRILLED STEAKHOUSE STEAK TIPS

ALSO BY THE EDITORS AT AMERICA'S TEST KITCHEN

The Complete Slow Cooker

The Complete Make-Ahead Cookbook

The Complete Mediterranean Cookbook

The Complete Vegetarian Cookbook

The Complete Cooking for Two Cookbook

What Good Cooks Know

Cook's Science

The Science of Good Cooking

The Perfect Cookie

Bread Illustrated

Master of the Grill

Kitchen Smarts

Kitchen Hacks

100 Recipes: The Absolute Best Ways to Make the True Essentials

The New Family Cookbook

The America's Test Kitchen Cooking School Cookbook

The Cook's Illustrated Meat Book

The Cook's Illustrated Baking Book

The Cook's Illustrated Cookbook

The New Best Recipe

Soups, Stews, and Chilis

The America's Test Kitchen Quick Family Cookbook

The America's Test Kitchen Healthy Family Cookbook

The America's Test Kitchen Family Baking Book

The Best of America's Test Kitchen (2007–2018 Editions)

The Complete America's Test Kitchen TV Show Cookbook 2001–2018

Food Processor Perfection

Pressure Cooker Perfection

Vegan for Everybody

Naturally Sweet

Foolproof Preserving

Paleo Perfected

The How Can It Be Gluten-Free Cookbook: Volume 2

The How Can It Be Gluten-Free Cookbook

The Best Mexican Recipes

Slow Cooker Revolution Volume 2: The Easy-Prep Edition

Slow Cooker Revolution

The Six-Ingredient Solution

The America's Test Kitchen D.I.Y. Cookbook

Pasta Revolution

THE COOK'S ILLUSTRATED ALL-TIME BEST SERIES

All-Time Best Holiday Entertaining

All-Time Best Sunday Suppers

All-Time Best Soups

All-Time Best Appetizers

COOK'S COUNTRY TITLES

One-Pan Wonders

Cook It in Cast Iron

Cook's Country Eats Local

FOR A FULL LISTING OF ALL OUR BOOKS

CooksCountry.com

AmericasTestKitchen.com

PRAISE FOR AMERICA'S TEST KITCHEN TITLES

"Another winning cookbook from ATK. . . . The folks at America's Test Kitchen apply their rigorous experiments to determine the facts about these pans."
Booklist on *Cook It in Cast Iron*

"An exceptional resource for novice canners, though preserving veterans will find plenty here to love as well."
Library Journal (starred review) on *Foolproof Preserving*

"This book upgrades slow cooking for discriminating, 21st-century palates—that is indeed revolutionary."
The Dallas Morning News on *Slow Cooker Revolution*

"The 21st-century *Fannie Farmer Cookbook* or *The Joy of Cooking*. If you had to have one cookbook and that's all you could have, this one would do it."
CBS San Francisco on *The New Family Cookbook*

"The sum total of exhaustive experimentation . . . anyone interested in gluten-free cookery simply shouldn't be without it."
Nigella Lawson on *The How Can It Be Gluten-Free Cookbook*

"The go-to gift book for newlyweds, small families or empty nesters."
Orlando Sentinel on *The Complete Cooking for Two Cookbook*

"A one-volume kitchen seminar, addressing in one smart chapter after another the sometimes surprising whys behind a cook's best practices. . . . You get the myth, the theory, the science and the proof, all rigorously interrogated as only America's Test Kitchen can do."
NPR on *The Science of Good Cooking*

"A beautifully illustrated, 318-page culinary compendium showcasing an impressive variety and diversity of authentic Mexican cuisine."
Midwest Book Review on *The Best Mexican Recipes*

"A terrifically accessible and useful guide to grilling in all its forms that sets a new bar for its competitors on the bookshelf. . . . Packed with practical advice, simple tips, and approachable recipes to ensure that grill enthusiasts are able to get the most out of their grills and ingredients."
Publisher's Weekly (starred review) on *Master of the Grill*

"This book is a comprehensive, no-nonsense guide . . . a well-thought-out, clearly explained primer for every aspect of home baking."
The Wall Street Journal on *The Cook's Illustrated Baking Book*

"Buy this gem for the foodie in your family, and spend the extra money to get yourself a copy too."
The Missourian on *The Best of America's Test Kitchen 2015*

"Some 2,500 photos walk readers through 600 painstakingly tested recipes, leaving little room for error."
Associated Press on *The America's Test Kitchen Cooking School Cookbook*

"Cook-friendly and kitchen-oriented, illuminating the process of preparing food instead of mystifying it . . . . the perfect kitchen home companion."
The Wall Street Journal on *The Cook's Illustrated Cookbook*

"There are pasta books . . . and then there's this pasta book. Flip your carbohydrate dreams upside down and strain them through this sieve of revolutionary, creative, and also traditional recipes."
San Francisco Book Review on *Pasta Revolution*

"Further proof that practice makes perfect, if not transcendent. . . . If an intermediate cook follows the directions exactly, the results will be better than takeout or Mom's."
The New York Times on *The New Best Recipe*

10TH ANNIVERSARY EDITION

The Complete
Cook's Country
TV Show Cookbook

Every Recipe and Every Review
From All Ten Seasons

THE EDITORS AT AMERICA'S TEST KITCHEN

Copyright © 2017 by the Editors at America's Test Kitchen

All rights reserved. No part of this book may be reproduced or transmitted in any manner whatsoever without written permission from the publisher, except in the case of brief quotations embodied in critical articles or reviews.

Photo, far right on page 279: Shutterstock

America's Test Kitchen
21 Drydock, Suite 201E
Boston, MA 02210

The Complete Cook's Country 10th Anniversary Cookbook
Every Recipe and Every Review From All Ten Seasons

ISBN 978-1-940352-93-0 (paperback edition)
ISBN 978-1-945256-34-9 (hardcover edition)
ISSN 2330-5762

Manufactured in the United States of America
10 9 8 7 6 5 4 3 2 1

Distributed by Penguin Random House Publisher Services
tel: 800-733-2000

- facebook.com/americastestkitchen
- twitter.com/TestKitchen
- youtube.com/AmericasTestKitchen
- instagram.com/TestKitchen
- pinterest.com/TestKitchen
- americastestkitchen.tumblr.com
- google.com/+AmericasTestKitchen

Chief Creative Officer Jack Bishop
Editorial Director, Books Elizabeth Carduff
Senior Managing Editor Debra Hudak
Assistant Editor Samantha Ronan
Editorial Assistant Alyssa Langer
Design Director Carole Goodman
Deputy Art Director Jen Kanavos Hoffman
Graphic Designer Katie Barranger
Production Designer Reinaldo Cruz
Photography Director Julie Bozzo Cote
Photography Producer Mary Ball
Feature Photography Keller + Keller
Senior Staff Photographer Daniel J. van Ackere
Additional Photography Carl Tremblay
Cover Photo Carl Tremblay
Staff Photographer Steve Klise and Kevin White
Food Stylists Daniel Cellucci, Isabelle English, Catrine Kelty, Monica Mariano, Kendra McKnight, Marie Piraino, Mary Jane Sawyer, Elle Simone Scott, and Sally Staub
Photoshoot Kitchen Team
  Senior Editor Chris O'Connor
  Lead Cook Daniel Cellucci
  Assistant Test Cooks Mady Nichas and Jessica Rudolph
Production Director Guy Rochford
Senior Production Manager Jessica Lindheimer Quirk
Production Manager Christine Walsh
Imaging Manager Lauren Robbins
Production and Imaging Specialists Heather Dube, Dennis Noble, and Jessica Voas
Historical Researcher Meg Ragland
Copyeditor Cheryl Redmond
Proofreader Amanda Poulsen Dix
Indexer Elizabeth Parson

CooksCountry.com
AmericasTestKitchen.com

contents

Welcome to Cook's Country viii

CHAPTER 1 **As Good as Grandma's** 1
CHAPTER 2 **Fork-in-the-Road Favorites** 49
CHAPTER 3 **Steakhouse Specials** 117
CHAPTER 4 **Our Sunday Best** 159
CHAPTER 5 **Tex-Mex Favorites** 233
CHAPTER 6 **Everybody Loves Italian** 271
CHAPTER 7 **The State of Grilling** 311
CHAPTER 8 **Rise-and-Shine Breakfast and Breads** 421
CHAPTER 9 **Great American Cakes and Cookies** 475
CHAPTER 10 **Old-Fashioned Fruit Desserts and Puddings** 537
CHAPTER 11 **Save Room for Pie** 561

Shopping for Equipment 596

Stocking Your Pantry 626

Episode Directory 651

Conversions and Equivalents 658

Index 661

welcome to cook's country

Where are you from?
Time was, this was an easy question to answer. The place where you lived was just down the road from where you were born. Its land and weather and people and rhythms wound themselves into you, deepening over the course of a lifetime. You ate the foods your parents, and grandparents, and great-grandparents did, and while they were similar to the foods eaten on the other side of the state, they were different, too. Everyone had a turkey on Thanksgiving, but where your family served cracker stuffing, another family had cornbread dressing or rice casserole or enchiladas. Local twists on morning biscuits or Sunday dinner helped define who you were.

But in America today, "Where are you from?" is an increasingly complicated question. Fewer and fewer of us live as adults in the same town where we were raised. We are a mobile, peripatetic people. As each generation reaches further afield, its tether to its roots frays a little. We pass on fewer traditions these days. We carry less of our history into our future. Our children know little about our own childhoods. And yet, even as we move from house to house, and city to city, we still long for something we call home.

Look at it through another lens and you'll see something hopeful: All this moving around may just be the thing that keeps a place's traditions vital and alive. Because when we travel, our traditions—especially our food traditions—travel with us.

A young woman moves from Georgia to Pittsburgh and yearns for the biscuits of her youth. She sends up a flare for a family recipe, which is by her grandmother, then uses the Internet to order the special

Southern flour she needs to get the biscuit just tender enough, in the perfect shade of gold. She brings a batch to a party and, suddenly, she's the most popular brunch guest in town. A few years on, she's teaching her son how to make them, too.

A professor relocates from Annapolis to Tacoma, and enters a seafood cooking competition at a college fundraiser. He chooses the Chesapeake crab cake recipe scrawled on a 3x5 card stuck in an old family cookbook, adapts it to a local Pacific crustacean, and wins the grand prize. By the next semester, the dining hall is serving the professor's "famous" Chesapeake crab cakes every other week.

And when each of these people returns to Georgia or to Annapolis for a visit, they seek out and re-connect with the original dishes. With their history. With home.

There are so many different kinds of "American" food, and here at Cook's Country, we celebrate them all. We look at rural foods, from low country grits to high desert tacos. We look at city foods, from New Orleans gumbo to New York cheesecake. We search high, low, and in between for recipes from every community in the country, the old ones and the new, from centuries-old switchel to modern-day monkey bread.

It's been ten years since Cook's Country presented its first recipe. Since then, our hard-working crew of test cooks, editors, and instructors have carried on the mission to find these recipes and work hard to perfect them. We look for ways to refine the ingredients and techniques to jive with contemporary cooking habits, while zealously maintaining the integrity and spirit of the originals. It can take weeks of experimentation, tinkering with seasoning amounts and cooking times until we get things just right. And we don't stop there. These recipes inspire brand-new ideas for simple, straightforward, easy meals that mix time-tested knowledge with fresh discoveries.

Our goal is to produce recipes that are easy, clear, and rewarding enough that you'll want to make them too. We work to clarify concepts, streamline processes, and shorten the distance from hunger pang to dinner time. Over the past decade, we've been proud to share thousands of recipes with you. And as we look ahead to our second decade, we've added to our cast of characters. These new faces, in our test kitchen and on our TV show and website, represent a whole new set of cooking traditions to explore.

It can take us weeks, or maybe months, to produce even a simple, two-step recipe. But it's worth it. Because by getting these dishes from our kitchens to your table, we believe we're helping to preserve, and expand, our shared American recipe book.

It's a big country, Cook's Country, and there's no better time to celebrate America's incredibly rich, incredibly broad, and incredibly deep cooking traditions. There's plenty of room in the kitchen, no matter where you're from.

Welcome home. Now, grab an apron. Let's cook.

Tucker Shaw
Executive Editor
Cook's Country magazine

This book has been tested, written, and edited by the folks at America's Test Kitchen. Located in Boston's Seaport District in the historic Innovation and Design Building, it features 15,000 square feet of kitchen space including photography and video studios. It is the home of *Cook's Illustrated* and *Cook's Country* magazines and is the Monday-through-Friday destination for more than 60 test cooks, editors, and cookware specialists. Our mission is to test recipes over and over again until we understand how and why they work and until we arrive at the "best" version.

Filmed in a rustic farmhouse kitchen, *Cook's Country from America's Test Kitchen* features the best regional home cooking in the country and relies on the same practical, no-nonsense approach to cooking that has made *Cook's Country* magazine so successful.

Bridget Lancaster and Julia Collin Davison are the hosts of the show and ask the questions you might ask. It's the job of our chefs, Ashley Moore, Bryan Roof, and Christie Morrison, to demonstrate our recipes. The chefs show Bridget and Julia what works and what doesn't, and they explain why. In the process, they discuss (and show you) the best examples from our development process as well as the worst. Jack Bishop challenges Bridget and Julia to live tastings of kitchen staples like hot dogs, apple cider vinegar, fettuccine, and sauerkraut, while Adam Ried reveals the test kitchen's top choices for equipment, including kitchen timers, Dutch ovens, cast-iron skillets, and more.

Although just seven cooks and editors appear on the television show, dozens more worked to make the show a reality. Executive producer Mary Mullaney conceived and developed each episode along with producer Kaitlin Keleher, associate producer Shan Shan Tam, and production assistant

The Complete Cook's Country TV Show Cookbook

Sara Joyner. Meg Ragland and Cara Eisenpress assisted with all the historical recipe research. Debby Paddock assisted with photography research.

Along with the on-air crew, executive chefs Erin McMurrer, Dan Zuccarello, and Morgan Bolling helped plan and organize the 13 television episodes shot in November 2016 and ran the "back kitchen," where all the food that appeared on camera originated. Lauren Savoie, Kate Shannon, Miye Bromberg, and Carolyn Grillo organized the tasting and equipment segments.

During filming, chefs Allison Berkey, Lyndsay Burginger, Steve Dunn, Matthew Fairman, Eric Haessler, Andrew Janjigian, Cecelia Jenkins, Lawman Johnson, Lan Lam, Katie Leaird, Timothy McQuinn, Anne Petito, Stephanie Pixley, and Anne Wolf cooked all the food needed on set. Kitchen assistants Ena Gudiel and Jarod Torres also worked long hours. Chefs Allison Berkey, Daniel Cellucci, Leah Colins, Afton Cyrus, Joseph Gitter, Sara Mayer, and Katherine Perry helped coordinate the kitchen with the television set by readying props, equipment, and food. Assistant test kitchen director Leah Rovner, test kitchen manager Alexxa Benson, lead senior kitchen assistant Meridith Lippard, and senior kitchen assistant Taylor Pond were charged with making sure all the ingredients and kitchen equipment we needed were on hand.

Special thanks to director and editor Herb Sevush and director of photography Stephen Hussar. We also appreciate the hard work of the video production team, including Scott Brawn, Wilson Chao, Joe Cristofori, Peter Dingle, Eric Fisher, Ken Fraser, Erik Freitas, Bob Hirsch, Jim Hirsch, Sue Willard Kiess, Joe McCleish, Gilles Morin, Tom Robertson,

and Phil Teves. Thanks also to Nick Dakoulas and Conor Olmstead, our second unit camera department. We also would like to thank Judy Barlow at American Public Television, which presents the show.

Blue Apron, DCS by Fisher & Paykel, Holland America Line, and Valley Fig Growers sponsored the show, and we thank them for their support. We also thank Deborah Fagone, Christine Anagnostis, and Kate Zebrowski for serving our sponsors.

Aprons were made by Crooked Brook. Thanks to music supervisor Christopher Sabec, Aaron Redner, and the band Hot Buttered Rum.

We also thank Dona Neely from Devens Eco-Efficiency Center, Transitions at Devens, Veterans, Inc., Roche Bros, Whole Foods, Westerman Store & Restaurant Equipment Inc., Suburban Supply, T.F. Kinnealey & Co., Sid Wainer & Son, and Michael's Movers.

as good as grandma's

3	Macaroni and Cheese with Tomatoes	24	Frosted Meatloaf
4	Best Potluck Macaroni and Cheese	27	Meatloaf with Mushroom Gravy
6	Classic Tomato Soup	28	Bacon-Wrapped Meatloaf
9	Creamy Cheese Grits	31	Swiss Steak with Tomato Gravy
10	Roasted Green Beans with Goat Cheese and Hazelnuts	33	Salisbury Steak
		34	Milk-Can Supper
13	Green Goddess Dressing	36	Pan-Fried Pork Chops
14	Classic Tuna Salad	39	Smothered Pork Chops
16	Chicken Florentine	41	Cider-Braised Pork Chops
19	Chicken Divan	42	Crispy Fish Sticks with Tartar Sauce
21	Southern-Style Smothered Chicken	44	Strawberry Pretzel Salad
22	Glazed Meatloaf	47	Slow-Cooker Chicken Stock

Why This Recipe Works To pack our mac and cheese with bright tomato flavor, we discovered that undercooking the pasta and adding petite canned diced tomatoes with their juices to the drained macaroni allowed the macaroni to soak up more of the tomato flavor. Returning the pasta to the heat afterward allowed the noodles to absorb some of the tomato juice. Finally, to avoid a curdled sauce, we added fat in the form of half-and-half (cut with some chicken broth) and a mix of sharp and mild cheddar cheeses.

MACARONI AND CHEESE WITH TOMATOES

SERVES 8 TO 10

Let the finished dish rest for 10 to 15 minutes before you serve it; otherwise, it will be soupy.

- 1 pound elbow macaroni
- Salt and pepper
- 1 (28-ounce) can petite diced tomatoes
- 6 tablespoons unsalted butter
- ½ cup all-purpose flour
- ¼ teaspoon cayenne pepper
- 4 cups half-and-half
- 1 cup chicken broth
- 1 pound mild cheddar cheese, shredded (4 cups)
- 8 ounces sharp cheddar cheese, shredded (2 cups)

1. Adjust oven rack to middle position and heat oven to 400 degrees. Bring 4 quarts water to boil in large Dutch oven. Add macaroni and 1 tablespoon salt and cook, stirring often, until just al dente, about 6 minutes. Drain pasta and return to pot. Pour diced tomatoes with their juices over pasta and stir to coat. Cook over medium-high heat, stirring occasionally, until most of liquid is absorbed, about 5 minutes. Set aside.

2. Meanwhile, melt butter in medium saucepan over medium heat. Stir in flour and cayenne and cook until golden, about 1 minute. Slowly whisk in half-and-half and broth until smooth. Bring to boil, reduce heat to medium, and simmer, stirring occasionally, until mixture is slightly thickened, about 15 minutes. Off heat, whisk in cheeses, 1 teaspoon salt, and 1 teaspoon pepper until cheeses melt. Pour sauce over macaroni and stir to combine.

3. Scrape mixture into 13 by 9-inch baking dish set in rimmed baking sheet and bake until top begins to brown, 15 to 20 minutes. Let sit for 10 to 15 minutes before serving.

To Make Ahead The macaroni and cheese can be made in advance through step 2. Scrape mixture into 13 by 9-inch baking dish, cool, lay plastic wrap directly on surface of pasta, and refrigerate for up to 2 days. When ready to bake, remove plastic, cover with aluminum foil, and bake for 30 minutes. Uncover and bake until top is golden brown, about 15 minutes. Let sit for 10 to 15 minutes before serving.

An Automat Classic

Home cooks have long put their stamp on plain-Jane macaroni and cheese, stirring in such items as hot dogs or diced ham and peas. One appealing, old-fashioned variation, however, is practically endangered: baked macaroni and cheese with tomatoes. The genius in the recipe is that the bright acid of the tomato cuts the richness of the cheese. Today, people of a certain age remember tomato mac and cheese fondly from Horn and Hardart's automats.

Automats started in Germany in 1896 as a way to quickly feed hundreds of thousands of workers during their lunch hour. The idea was very much like a vending machine. Rather than ordering their meals through a server, patrons would drop coins into a slot to open a glass door in front of a compartment holding a menu item. Frank Hardart brought back the automat idea after a visit to Germany. Hardart, along with his partner, Joseph B. Horn, hired an engineer to further simplify the German system so they could transform their traditional lunch counter into an automat in 1902.

As for one of their most popular menu items, macaroni and cheese with tomatoes, most of us have never heard of it, much less tasted it. Automats may be a thing of the past, but a good recipe for macaroni and cheese shouldn't be.

BEST POTLUCK MACARONI AND CHEESE

SERVES 8 TO 10

Block American cheese from the deli counter is best here, as prewrapped singles result in a drier macaroni and cheese.

- 4 slices hearty white sandwich bread, torn into quarters
- 4 tablespoons unsalted butter, melted, plus 4 tablespoons unsalted butter
- ¼ cup grated Parmesan cheese
- 1 pound elbow macaroni
  Salt
- 5 tablespoons all-purpose flour
- 3 (12-ounce) cans evaporated milk
- 2 teaspoons hot sauce
- 1 teaspoon dry mustard
- ⅛ teaspoon ground nutmeg
- 8 ounces extra-sharp cheddar cheese, shredded (2 cups)
- 5 ounces American cheese, shredded (1¼ cups)
- 3 ounces Monterey Jack cheese, shredded (¾ cup)

1. Adjust oven rack to middle position and heat oven to 350 degrees. Pulse bread, melted butter, and Parmesan in food processor until ground to coarse crumbs, about 8 pulses. Transfer to bowl.

2. Bring 4 quarts water to boil in large pot. Add macaroni and 1 tablespoon salt and cook, stirring often, until just al dente, about 6 minutes. Reserve ½ cup macaroni cooking water, then drain and rinse macaroni in colander under cold running water. Set aside.

3. Melt remaining 4 tablespoons butter in now-empty pot over medium-high heat. Stir in flour and cook, stirring constantly, until mixture turns light brown, about 1 minute. Slowly whisk in evaporated milk, hot sauce, mustard, nutmeg, and 2 teaspoons salt and cook until mixture begins to simmer and is slightly thickened, about 4 minutes. Off heat, whisk in cheeses and reserved cooking water until cheese melts. Stir in macaroni until completely coated.

4. Transfer mixture to 13 by 9-inch baking dish and top evenly with bread-crumb mixture. Bake until cheese is bubbling around edges and top is golden brown, 20 to 25 minutes. Let sit for 5 to 10 minutes before serving.

To Make Ahead The macaroni and cheese can be made in advance through step 3. Increase amount of reserved macaroni cooking water to 1 cup. Scrape mixture into 13 by 9-inch baking dish, cool, lay plastic wrap directly on surface of pasta, and refrigerate for up to 1 day. Bread-crumb mixture may be refrigerated for up to 2 days. When ready to bake, remove plastic, cover with aluminum foil, and bake for 30 minutes. Uncover, sprinkle bread crumbs over top, and bake until topping is golden brown, about 20 minutes longer. Let sit before serving.

Keeping It Together

Using already stabilized ingredients like American cheese and evaporated milk ensures that this cheesy sauce doesn't break in the oven.

Why This Recipe Works Unlike many macaroni and cheese recipes, our Best Potluck Macaroni and Cheese is creamy, sturdy, and rich. We prevented the sauce from separating and clumping when baked by using evaporated milk and American cheese—the stabilizers in these ingredients kept the sauce from breaking, so that it emerged from the oven satiny smooth. Homemade bread crumbs, enriched with melted butter and Parmesan cheese, created a flavorful, crisp topping.

CLASSIC TOMATO SOUP

SERVES 6 TO 8

Use unseasoned canned tomatoes.

- 2 (28-ounce) cans diced tomatoes
- ¾ cup low-sodium chicken broth
- 3 tablespoons unsalted butter
- 1 onion, chopped
- 1 bay leaf
- 1 teaspoon brown sugar
- 2 tablespoons tomato paste
- 2 tablespoons all-purpose flour
- ½ teaspoon baking soda
- Salt and pepper
- ½ cup heavy cream

1. Drain tomatoes in colander set over large bowl, pressing lightly to release juices. Transfer tomato juice and chicken broth to large measuring cup (mixture should measure about 4 cups); reserve.

2. Melt butter in Dutch oven over medium heat. Add onion and cook until softened, about 5 minutes. Add two-thirds of drained tomatoes, bay leaf, and brown sugar and cook, stirring occasionally, until tomatoes begin to brown, about 15 minutes.

3. Add tomato paste and flour to pot and cook, stirring frequently, until paste begins to darken, 1 to 2 minutes. Slowly stir in reserved tomato juice–broth mixture, remaining tomatoes, baking soda, and ½ teaspoon salt and bring to boil. Reduce heat to medium-low and simmer until slightly thickened, about 5 minutes. Remove from heat.

4. Discard bay leaf. Puree soup in batches. Return pureed soup to pot and stir in cream. Season with salt and pepper. Serve. (Soup can be refrigerated for 3 days.)

Are You Kidding Me?

You can use it to brush your teeth, scrub your counters, or make your refrigerator smell better. Still, we were shocked at the difference that a mere ½ teaspoon of baking soda made in our Classic Tomato Soup. It neutralized some of the acid in the tomatoes for a perfect sweet-tart balance. And its sodium ions weakened the pectin in the cells of the tomatoes, allowing them to puree into a silken soup.

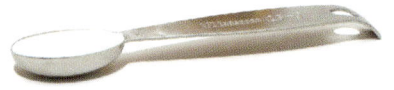

Bay Leaves

Bay leaves are a standard addition to soups, stews, and bean dishes. We prefer dried bay leaves to fresh; they work just as well in long-cooked recipes, are cheaper, and will keep for months in the freezer. We prefer Turkish bay leaves to those from California. The California bay leaf has a medicinal and potent flavor, like something you'd put in a cough drop. The Turkish bay leaf has a mild, green, and slightly clove-like flavor.

Why This Recipe Works We were shocked that the key to a satiny, well-balanced classic tomato soup turned out to be just ½ teaspoon of baking soda, which also helped neutralize the metallic taste and acidity of the canned tomatoes. To enhance the tomatoes' complexity, we browned most of them in a Dutch oven to concentrate their flavor, and saved some to add at the end of cooking to keep the soup fresh. We were tempted to add a variety of classic seasonings, but found they made the soup taste like marinara sauce. Tasters were most satisfied with a single bay leaf, chicken broth, and the richness of heavy cream.

Why This Recipe Works Grits are a southern staple, but their appeal can be lost in bland, gluey incarnations. To take this down-home dish from dull to delicious, we needed to work on both texture and flavor. Replacing some of the cooking water with milk gave a creamy sweetness to the unadorned grits. As for the cheese, we found that a combination of Monterey Jack and sharp cheddar lent both smoothness and pronounced cheesy flavor. To give the dish more depth, we sautéed scallion whites and added real pureed corn for an extra boost of corn flavor.

CREAMY CHEESE GRITS

SERVES 4 TO 6

The grits are ready when they are mostly creamy but still retain a little bite. If the grits get too thick, whisk in a little water. If you are using frozen corn, thaw it first.

- ½ cup fresh or frozen corn kernels
- 3½ cups water
- 4 tablespoons unsalted butter
- 4 scallions, white parts minced, green parts sliced thin
- 1 cup milk
- ½ teaspoon hot sauce
- Salt and pepper
- 1 cup old-fashioned grits
- 4 ounces Monterey Jack cheese, shredded (1 cup)
- 4 ounces sharp cheddar cheese, shredded (1 cup)

1. Puree corn and ¼ cup water in blender until smooth, about 1 minute; set aside. Melt 2 tablespoons butter in medium saucepan over medium heat. Add scallion whites and cook until softened, about 2 minutes. Stir in remaining 3¼ cups water, milk, hot sauce, ½ teaspoon salt, and ½ teaspoon pepper and bring to boil.

2. Slowly whisk grits into saucepan until no lumps remain. Reduce heat to low and cook, stirring frequently, until thick and creamy, about 15 minutes.

3. Off heat, stir in Monterey Jack, cheddar, pureed corn, and remaining 2 tablespoons butter until incorporated. Season with salt and pepper to taste. Serve sprinkled with scallion greens.

Know Your Corn

Cornmeal Cornmeal is corn kernels that are dried and ground to a powder.

Grits Grits are cornmeal, but the name also refers to the cooked porridge popular in the South.

Hominy Grits Hominy grits are corn kernels with the hull and bran removed before grinding.

Polenta Polenta is cornmeal, but the name also refers to the cooked Italian porridge, which is traditionally enriched with butter and Parmesan.

Weighing Cheese

Our recipes specify cup amounts of cheese to reflect the habits of the typical home cook. But cheese is sold by weight, so it can be hard to determine how much to buy. Also, one person's measure may not precisely equal another's. To complicate matters, we classify cheese into three categories: hard, such as Parmesan and Pecorino Romano; semisoft, such as cheddar and Monterey Jack; and soft, such as feta, blue, and fresh goat cheeses. Each packs into cup measures differently. To develop a standard weight for each cheese category, we gathered 10 test cooks and had each weigh out 1-cup samples of each type. We averaged the weights to account for the heavy and light hands of different individuals. We found that 1 cup of grated hard cheese equals about 2 ounces, while the same measure of soft and semisoft is about 4 ounces. And remember, when measuring cheese, lightly pack measuring cups meant for dry ingredients; don't use liquid measuring cups, which will give you an inaccurate measurement for dry ingredients.

ROASTED GREEN BEANS WITH GOAT CHEESE AND HAZELNUTS

SERVES 4 TO 6

To trim green beans quickly, line up a handful so the stem ends are even and then cut off the stems with one swipe of the knife.

- 1½ pounds green beans, trimmed
- 5½ tablespoons extra-virgin olive oil
- ¾ teaspoon sugar
- Kosher salt and pepper
- 2 garlic cloves, minced
- 1 teaspoon grated orange zest plus 2 teaspoons juice
- 2 teaspoons lemon juice
- 1 teaspoon Dijon mustard
- 2 tablespoons minced fresh chives
- 2 ounces goat cheese, crumbled (½ cup)
- ¼ cup hazelnuts, toasted, skinned, and chopped

1. Adjust oven rack to lowest position and heat oven to 475 degrees. Combine green beans, 1½ tablespoons oil, sugar, ¾ teaspoon salt, and ½ teaspoon pepper in bowl. Evenly distribute green beans on rimmed baking sheet.

2. Cover sheet tightly with aluminum foil and roast for 10 minutes. Remove foil and continue to roast until green beans are spotty brown, about 10 minutes longer, stirring halfway through roasting.

3. Meanwhile, combine garlic, orange zest, and remaining ¼ cup oil in medium bowl and microwave until bubbling, about 1 minute; let steep for 1 minute. Whisk orange juice, lemon juice, mustard, ¼ teaspoon salt, and ¼ teaspoon pepper into garlic mixture.

4. Transfer green beans to bowl with dressing, add chives, and toss to combine. Transfer to serving platter and sprinkle with goat cheese and hazelnuts. Serve.

ROASTED GREEN BEANS WITH ALMONDS AND MINT
Omit orange zest and juice, substitute with 1 teaspoon grated lime zest and 4 teaspoons lime juice; ¼ cup torn fresh mint leaves for chives; and ¼ cup whole blanched almonds, toasted and chopped, for hazelnuts. Omit goat cheese.

ROASTED GREEN BEANS WITH PECORINO AND PINE NUTS
Omit orange zest and juice, substitute with 1 teaspoon grated lemon zest and 4 teaspoons lemon juice; 2 tablespoons chopped fresh basil for chives; 1½ ounces Pecorino Romano cheese, shredded, for goat cheese; and ¼ cup pine nuts, toasted, for hazelnuts.

Steam and Then Roast Uncovered
For tender green beans with a hint of flavorful browning, we found that a hybrid moist-then-dry roasting method worked best. First we roast the beans covered with foil, which traps steam and helps them cook through quickly. Then we remove the foil to allow the beans to brown in the dry heat.

Why This Recipe Works For tender green beans with a hint of flavorful browning, we developed a hybrid method—first steaming the beans under a foil cover and then removing the foil and allowing them to roast. Adding a bit of sugar to the beans promoted the browning and blistering we wanted in the oven's high heat. Tossing the beans with a light citrus dressing and goat cheese brightened their flavor, while toasted hazelnuts provided a welcome crunch.

Why This Recipe Works Too often a bright, crisp romaine salad is weighed down by an overly heavy dressing, so we set out to make a light and flavorful green goddess dressing. We achieved this by using three kinds of herbs: tarragon, parsley, and chives. To discreetly add depth, we used a single anchovy fillet, and for the creamiest texture, we used mayo and sour cream and prepared the dressing in a blender. While modern versions of green goddess dressing often contain avocado, the original version, credited to chef Philip Roemer of the Palace Hotel in San Francisco in the 1920s, does not, so we skipped it.

GREEN GODDESS DRESSING

MAKES 1¼ CUPS; ENOUGH FOR 6 WEDGES OF LETTUCE

To appreciate the full flavor of this rich dressing, drizzle it over chilled wedges of mild iceberg lettuce or romaine lettuce leaves. A blender yields a brighter, slightly more flavorful dressing, but a food processor will work, too.

- 2 teaspoons dried tarragon
- 1 tablespoon lemon juice
- 1 tablespoon water
- ¾ cup mayonnaise
- ¼ cup sour cream
- ¼ cup coarsely chopped fresh parsley
- 1 garlic clove, chopped
- 1 anchovy fillet, rinsed and dried
- ¼ cup chopped chives
  Salt and pepper

1. Combine tarragon, lemon juice, and water in small bowl and let sit for 15 minutes.

2. Blend tarragon mixture, mayonnaise, sour cream, parsley, garlic, and anchovy in blender until smooth, scraping down sides as necessary. Transfer to medium bowl, stir in chives, and season with salt and pepper. Chill until flavors meld, about 1 hour. (Dressing can be covered and refrigerated for up to 1 day.)

Don't Fear the Fish

The single anchovy fillet we call for in this recipe may seem superfluous, but it adds savory depth to the dressing (without tasting like fish). Try adding a minced anchovy to your next batch of beef stew or tomato sauce—it will boost the flavor considerably. Anchovies are sold jarred or canned. Extra jarred anchovies can be refrigerated right in the jar according to package directions. But extra canned anchovies should be transferred to a nonreactive airtight container, covered with oil, and refrigerated for up to 2 weeks.

Juicing Lemons

We squeezed a dozen lemons—cold, rolled, and warm—and found that each yielded the same amount of juice. The only difference was that warm and room-temperature lemons were softer and therefore easier to squeeze than the cold lemons. When you use a tool like a reamer or juicer, this doesn't come into play as much, but if you're juicing by hand, we recommend room-temperature lemons. To quickly warm a cold lemon, you can heat it in the microwave until it is warm to the touch.

To quickly juice a lemon, we prefer a wooden reamer with a sharp tip that can easily pierce the flesh. Plastic reamers with rounded tips didn't work as well in our tests. Plastic and glass juicers (which sit on the counter and collect juice) are better suited to oranges and grapefruits than lemons. When purchasing lemons at the supermarket, choose large ones that give to gentle pressure; hard lemons have thicker skin and yield less juice.

CLASSIC TUNA SALAD

MAKES 2 CUPS; ENOUGH FOR 4 SANDWICHES

For slightly milder salads, use an equal amount of shallot instead of onion.

- ¼ cup finely chopped onion
- 2 tablespoons olive oil
- 3 (5-ounce) cans solid white tuna in water
- ½ cup plus 2 tablespoons mayonnaise
- 1 celery rib, minced
- 2 teaspoons lemon juice
- ½ teaspoon sugar
- Salt and pepper

1. Combine onion and oil in small bowl and microwave until onion begins to soften, about 2 minutes. Let onion mixture cool for 5 minutes. Place tuna in fine-mesh strainer and press dry with paper towels. Transfer tuna to medium bowl and mash with fork until finely flaked.

2. Stir mayonnaise, celery, lemon juice, sugar, ½ teaspoon salt, ½ teaspoon pepper, and onion mixture into tuna until well combined. Season with salt and pepper to taste. Serve. (Salad can be refrigerated for up to 24 hours.)

TUNA SALAD WITH HARD-COOKED EGGS, RADISHES, AND CAPERS

Substitute 2 tablespoons extra-virgin olive oil for olive oil and 6 tablespoons extra-virgin olive oil for mayonnaise. Add 2 thinly sliced hard-cooked eggs; 2 trimmed, halved, and thinly sliced radishes; and ¼ cup capers, minced, to salad.

TUNA SALAD WITH APPLE, WALNUTS, AND TARRAGON

Add 1 apple, cored and cut into ½-inch pieces; ½ cup walnuts, toasted and chopped coarse; and 1 tablespoon minced fresh tarragon to salad.

TUNA SALAD WITH CORNICHONS AND WHOLE-GRAIN MUSTARD

Add ¼ cup finely chopped cornichons, 1 tablespoon minced fresh chives, and 1 tablespoon whole-grain mustard to salad.

TUNA SALAD WITH CURRY AND GRAPES

Add 1 teaspoon curry powder to bowl with onion and oil before microwaving. Add 1 cup green grapes, halved, to salad.

Draining Tuna

Place tuna in fine-mesh strainer and press dry with paper towels to remove excess moisture and prevent watery tuna salad. Once drained, transfer to medium bowl and mash with fork until finely flaked.

Why This Recipe Works A classic lunchbox staple, tuna salad too often turns out watery, chalky, and/or bland. It may sound odd, but the key to great tuna salad is to first thoroughly drain chunked tuna and dry it with paper towels. Mashing the dried tuna with a fork made for a nice, uniform consistency. To moisten the salad, we quickly infused olive oil with chopped onion in the microwave and added it to the tuna, along with a bit of sugar, lemon juice, and mayo to round out the flavor. We tasted every variety of canned tuna and the runaway winner was solid white tuna packed in water.

CHICKEN FLORENTINE

SERVES 4 TO 6

We like tender, quick-cooking bagged baby spinach here; if using curly-leaf spinach, chop it before cooking.

- 2 tablespoons vegetable oil
- 12 ounces (12 cups) baby spinach
- 4 (6-ounce) boneless, skinless chicken breasts, trimmed
- Salt and pepper
- 1 shallot, minced
- 2 garlic cloves, minced
- 1¼ cups chicken broth
- 1¼ cups water
- 1 cup heavy cream
- 6 tablespoons grated Parmesan cheese
- 1 teaspoon grated lemon zest plus 1 teaspoon juice

1. Adjust oven rack to upper-middle position and heat broiler. Heat 1 tablespoon oil in 12-inch skillet over medium-high heat until shimmering. Add spinach and cook, stirring occasionally until wilted, 1 to 2 minutes. Transfer spinach to colander set over bowl and press with spoon to release excess liquid. Discard liquid.

2. Pat chicken dry with paper towels and season with salt and pepper. Wipe out pan and heat remaining 1 tablespoon oil over medium-high heat until just smoking. Cook chicken on both sides until golden, 4 to 6 minutes. Add shallot and garlic to skillet and cook until fragrant, about 30 seconds. Stir in broth, water, and cream and bring to boil.

3. Reduce heat to medium-low and simmer until chicken is cooked through, about 10 minutes; transfer chicken to plate and tent with aluminum foil. Continue to simmer sauce until reduced to 1 cup, about 10 minutes. Off heat, stir in 4 tablespoons Parmesan and lemon zest and juice.

4. Cut chicken crosswise into ½-inch-thick slices and arrange on broiler-safe platter. Scatter spinach over chicken and pour sauce over spinach. Sprinkle with remaining Parmesan and broil until golden brown, 3 to 5 minutes. Serve.

Draining Spinach

As it cooks, spinach releases a lot of moisture, which can make dishes like our Chicken Florentine watery. To prevent that, we transferred the spinach to a colander and pressed the leaves with a spoon to force the liquid out. We drained nearly ¼ cup of liquid from the 12 ounces of spinach used in this recipe.

Enchanting Chicken—Without A Wand

The idea of chicken Florentine as a dish made from chicken, spinach, and a cheesy cream sauce appeared in print as early as 1931, when *The Lowell (Mass.) Sun* breathlessly described Chicken Mornay Florentine as served at the Manhattan restaurant, Divan Parisien: "They make magic passes over spinach, then cover it with breasts of chicken and a Mornay sauce." In the "Tables for Two" column of *The New Yorker*, April 25, 1931, the Divan Parisien was described as "a quiet and extremely civilized restaurant with an assorted clientele. . . ." What a shame then, that one of their most popular dishes morphed to a 1960s casserole (made with frozen spinach, margarine, packaged bread crumbs, and condensed soups) and then to wedding banquet fare in the 1970s and '80s (breasts stuffed with spinach, rolled, fried, and served with a cheesy sauce). We wanted to deconstruct the casserole, unroll the spirals, and return chicken Florentine to its earliest version: a bright, elegant, streamlined sauté with a pan sauce. No magic passes involved.

Why This Recipe Works To restore chicken Florentine to its elegant roots, we started with fresh spinach. To prevent the water from the spinach from washing out the other flavors in the dish, we drained excess liquid from the cooked spinach by pressing the leaves with the back of a spoon in a colander. For flavor, we seared the chicken breasts first and then poached them in the sauce before broiling. We used cream to make the sauce silky and built volume with equal amounts of chicken broth and water. We also added a squeeze of lemon juice and a hit of zest, along with Parmesan cheese for its nutty, savory punch.

Why This Recipe Works Once-trendy chicken Divan's original recipe calls for many different components and even more cooking steps. We wanted to stay true to the original flavor of the dish but streamline the cooking process. To do this, we batch-cooked the broccoli first, then the chicken. While the broccoli and chicken rested, we used the same pan to prepare our sauce. And instead of making a separate hollandaise sauce, like the traditional chicken Divan recipes demand, we whisked egg yolks and lemon juice together, then tempered the mixture with the hot pan sauce, and whisked in butter at the end.

CHICKEN DIVAN

SERVES 4

Use one small onion instead of the shallots, if desired.

- 3 tablespoons vegetable oil
- 1 pound broccoli florets, cut into 1-inch pieces
- 2½ cups chicken broth
- ¼ cup all-purpose flour
- 4 (6-ounce) boneless, skinless chicken breasts, trimmed
- Salt and pepper
- 2 shallots, minced
- 1 cup heavy cream
- ½ cup dry sherry
- 2 teaspoons Worcestershire sauce
- 3 ounces Parmesan cheese, grated (1½ cups)
- 3 large egg yolks
- 1 tablespoon lemon juice
- 3 tablespoons unsalted butter

1. Adjust oven rack to lower-middle position and heat broiler. Heat 1 tablespoon oil in large skillet over medium-high heat until just smoking. Add broccoli and cook until spotty brown, about 1 minute. Add ½ cup broth, cover, and steam until just tender, about 1½ minutes. Remove lid and cook until liquid has evaporated, about 1 minute. Transfer broccoli to plate lined with paper towels; rinse and wipe out skillet.

2. Heat remaining 2 tablespoons oil in now-empty skillet over medium-high heat until smoking. Meanwhile, place flour in shallow dish. Season chicken with salt and pepper and dredge in flour to coat. Cook chicken until golden brown on both sides, 4 to 6 minutes. Transfer chicken to plate.

3. Add shallots to skillet and cook until just softened, about 1 minute. Add remaining 2 cups broth and cream and scrape browned bits from bottom of pan. Return chicken to skillet and simmer over medium-high heat until cooked through, about 10 minutes. Transfer chicken to clean plate and continue to simmer sauce until reduced to 1 cup, about 10 minutes. Add sherry and Worcestershire and simmer until reduced again to 1 cup, about 3 minutes. Stir in 1 cup Parmesan.

4. Whisk egg yolks and lemon juice in small bowl, then whisk in about ¼ cup sauce. Off heat, whisk egg yolk mixture into sauce in skillet, then whisk in butter.

5. Cut chicken into ½-inch-thick slices and arrange on broiler-safe platter. Scatter broccoli over chicken and pour sauce over broccoli. Sprinkle with remaining ½ cup Parmesan and broil until golden brown, 3 to 5 minutes. Serve.

Broccoli Makes It to the Big Time

It can seem hard to believe today, but broccoli, a key ingredient in chicken Divan, an elegant chicken dish from Manhattan's Divan Parisien restaurant (see page 16), was a relative latecomer to the American diet. This headline from *The New York Times* in 1926 attests to its arrival on the scene: "New Vegetables Vary our Menus: Broccoli, Artichoke, and Avocado Naturalized, and Fennel Enters Under Foreign Name—Homely Carrot Is Still in Demand." Broccoli aside, the restaurant's recipe required a whole poached chicken and a sauce made with béchamel, hollandaise, Parmesan cheese, and whipped cream. The ingredients were combined *à la minute* (just before being plated) and broiled to perfection. Sounds good, but if we're counting right, that's at least five pots, four recipes, and more time than we'd care to spend in the kitchen. No wonder most "modern" recipes rely on canned soup. We wanted to bring Divan into the 21st century without compromising the flavors of the original dish.

Why This Recipe Works Our take on smothered chicken had two goals: big chicken flavor and weeknight ease. For perfectly tender, evenly cooked southern-style smothered chicken, we started with chicken parts rather than a whole bird. We browned the pieces and then shallow-braised them in a savory gravy built from pantry ingredients: chicken broth, flour, sautéed onions, celery, garlic, and dried sage. We found that we needed just 2 tablespoons of flour to thicken the gravy to a rich—but not stodgy—consistency. A splash of cider vinegar brightened the sauce and helped the chicken's flavor shine.

SOUTHERN-STYLE SMOTHERED CHICKEN

SERVES 4

This dish is best served with rice, but it's also good with potatoes. You may substitute ground sage for the dried sage leaves, but decrease the amount to ¼ teaspoon.

- 3 pounds bone-in chicken pieces (split breasts cut in half crosswise, drumsticks, and/or thighs), trimmed
- Salt and pepper
- ½ cup plus 2 tablespoons all-purpose flour
- ¼ cup vegetable oil
- 2 onions, chopped fine
- 2 celery ribs, chopped fine
- 3 garlic cloves, minced
- 1 teaspoon dried sage leaves
- 2 cups chicken broth
- 1 tablespoon cider vinegar
- 2 tablespoons minced fresh parsley

1. Pat chicken dry with paper towels and season with salt and pepper. Spread ½ cup flour in shallow dish. Working with 1 piece at a time, dredge chicken in flour, shaking off excess, and transfer to plate.

2. Heat oil in Dutch oven over medium-high heat. Add half of chicken to pot, skin side down, and cook until deep golden brown, 4 to 6 minutes per side; transfer to plate. Repeat with remaining chicken, adjusting heat if flour begins to burn.

3. Pour off all but 2 tablespoons fat and return pot to medium heat. Add onions, celery, 1 teaspoon salt, and ½ teaspoon pepper and cook until softened, 6 to 8 minutes. Stir in garlic, sage, and remaining 2 tablespoons flour and cook until vegetables are well coated with flour and garlic is fragrant, about 1 minute. Whisk in broth, scraping up any browned bits.

4. Nestle chicken into sauce, add any accumulated juices from plate, and bring to boil. Reduce heat to low, cover, and simmer until breasts register 160 degrees and drumsticks/thighs register 175 degrees, 30 to 40 minutes.

5. Transfer chicken to serving dish. Stir vinegar into sauce and season with salt and pepper to taste. Pour sauce over chicken, sprinkle with parsley, and serve.

How to Split and Trim Breasts

1. With whole breast skin side down on cutting board, center knife on breastbone, then apply pressure to cut through and separate breast into two halves.

2. Using kitchen shears, trim off rib section from each breast, following vertical line of fat from tapered end of breast up to socket.

3. Using chef's knife or kitchen shears, trim excess fat and skin from breasts.

GLAZED MEATLOAF

SERVES 6 TO 8

Both ground sirloin and ground chuck work well here, but avoid ground round—it is gristly and bland.

Glaze
- 1 cup ketchup
- ¼ cup packed brown sugar
- 2½ tablespoons cider vinegar
- ½ teaspoon hot sauce

Meatloaf
- 2 teaspoons vegetable oil
- 1 onion, chopped fine
- 2 garlic cloves, minced
- 17 square or 19 round saltines
- ⅓ cup whole milk
- 1 pound 90 percent lean ground beef
- 1 pound ground pork
- 2 large eggs plus 1 large yolk
- ⅓ cup finely chopped fresh parsley
- 2 teaspoons Dijon mustard
- 2 teaspoons Worcestershire sauce
- ½ teaspoon dried thyme
- Salt and pepper

1. For the Glaze Whisk all ingredients in saucepan until sugar dissolves. Reserve ¼ cup glaze mixture, then simmer remaining glaze over medium heat until slightly thickened, about 5 minutes. Cover and keep warm.

2. For the Meatloaf Line rimmed baking sheet with aluminum foil and coat lightly with vegetable oil spray. Heat oil in nonstick skillet over medium heat until shimmering. Cook onion until golden, about 8 minutes. Add garlic and cook until fragrant, about 30 seconds. Transfer to large bowl.

3. Process saltines and milk in food processor until smooth, about 30 seconds. Add beef and pork and pulse until well combined, about 10 pulses. Transfer meat mixture to bowl with cooled onion mixture. Add eggs and yolk, parsley, mustard, Worcestershire, thyme, 1 teaspoon salt, and ¾ teaspoon pepper to bowl and mix with hands until combined.

4. Adjust 1 oven rack to middle position and second rack 4 inches from broiler element; heat broiler. Transfer meat mixture to prepared baking sheet and shape into 9 by 5-inch loaf. Broil on upper rack until well browned, about 5 minutes. Brush 2 tablespoons unreduced glaze over top and sides of loaf and then return to oven and broil until glaze begins to brown, about 2 minutes.

5. Transfer meatloaf to lower rack and brush with remaining unreduced glaze. Reduce oven temperature to 350 degrees and bake until meatloaf registers 160 degrees, 40 to 45 minutes. Transfer to cutting board, tent with foil, and let rest for 20 minutes. Slice and serve, passing remaining reduced glaze at table.

Ketchup—The Truffle Oil Of The '20s?

Say "meatloaf" and most Americans think 1950s comfort food and Mom, but this humble recipe has surprisingly elegant roots in a now-forgotten dish called "cannelon." A typical cannelon recipe from the original *Boston Cooking-School Cookbook* calls for chopping and seasoning beef, shaping it into a log, and basting it with melted butter as it bakes. The wide availability of meat grinders and the advent of reliable refrigeration made ground beef a household staple in the early 20th century and meatloaf recipes gained wide circulation. As a topping, butter was usurped by tomato sauce until ketchup became popular in the 1920s. The Heinz company created a "House of Heinz" campaign to tout the gourmet appeal their products gave to everyday dishes such as meatloaf. Along with their ketchup, Heinz suggested incorporating other Heinz products, such as beefsteak sauce, chili sauce, and olives into meatloaf, or serving cubes of meatloaf with pickle slices for an easy hors d'oeuvre. For our meatloaf, we skipped the gourmet aspirations and unnecessary mix-ins for a stellar version of the 1950s favorite.

Why This Recipe Works For our old-fashioned meatloaf, we cut ground beef with an equal portion of sweet ground pork for better flavor. As for seasoning, we stuck with tradition: salt, pepper, Dijon mustard, Worcestershire sauce, thyme, parsley, sautéed onion, and garlic. To add moisture and structure, we used a panade (paste) of milk and saltines. Combining the panade in a food processor and then pulsing it with the meat gave the loaf the most cohesive, tender structure. To evaporate the surface moisture that was inhibiting the formation of a crust, we broiled the loaf prior to baking and glazing.

AS GOOD AS GRANDMA'S

FROSTED MEATLOAF

SERVES 6 TO 8

If you don't have a ricer or a food mill, just mash the potatoes thoroughly.

¼	cup ketchup
1	tablespoon packed light brown sugar
1	tablespoon cider vinegar
½	teaspoon hot sauce
8	tablespoons unsalted butter
1	onion, chopped fine
3	garlic cloves, minced
17	square or 19 round saltines, crushed (⅔ cup)
1	cup whole milk
1	pound ground pork
2	large eggs plus 1 large yolk
⅓	cup minced fresh parsley
2	teaspoons Dijon mustard
2	teaspoons Worcestershire sauce
	Salt and pepper
½	teaspoon dried thyme
1	pound 90 percent lean ground beef
2	pounds russet potatoes, peeled and cut into 1-inch pieces

1. Adjust oven racks to upper-middle and lower-middle positions and heat broiler. Line rimmed baking sheet with aluminum foil, set wire rack in sheet, and place 14 by 6-inch piece of foil in center of rack. Whisk ketchup, sugar, vinegar, and hot sauce together in bowl; set aside glaze.

2. Melt 2 tablespoons butter in 10-inch skillet over medium heat. Add onion and cook until just softened, 3 to 5 minutes. Add garlic and cook until fragrant, about 30 seconds. Set aside off heat.

3. Combine saltines and ⅓ cup milk in large bowl and mash with fork until chunky paste forms. Add pork, eggs and yolk, parsley, mustard, Worcestershire, 1 teaspoon salt, ¾ teaspoon pepper, thyme, and onion mixture and knead with your hands until mostly combined. Add beef and knead until combined.

4. Transfer meat mixture to foil rectangle on wire rack and form into 9 by 6-inch loaf. Broil on upper-middle oven rack until well browned, 5 to 7 minutes. Brush glaze over top and sides of meatloaf, return to upper-middle rack, and broil until glaze begins to brown, 3 to 5 minutes. Move meatloaf to lower-middle oven rack, adjust oven temperature to 350 degrees, and bake until meatloaf registers 160 degrees, 40 to 45 minutes. Remove from oven.

5. Meanwhile, bring potatoes and 2 quarts water to boil in Dutch oven over high heat. Reduce heat to medium-low and simmer until potatoes are tender, 20 to 25 minutes; drain potatoes thoroughly in colander. Set ricer or food mill over now-empty pot and press or mill potatoes into pot. Stir 1 teaspoon salt, remaining 6 tablespoons butter, and remaining ⅔ cup milk into potatoes until combined.

6. Using offset spatula, spread mashed potatoes evenly over top and sides of meatloaf. Heat broiler and return meatloaf to lower-middle oven rack. Broil until potatoes are browned, about 15 minutes. Using foil as sling, transfer meatloaf to carving board and let rest for 15 minutes. Slice and serve.

Reviving Comfort Food
During World War II, meat was rationed. Americans were encouraged to extend short supplies through many means, boosting meatloaf's popularity. In the '50s, this classic was reinvented as a centerpiece for entertaining, topped with garnishes, glazes, sauces, and, of course, mashed potatoes.

Why This Recipe Works Meatloaf and potatoes are an unbeatable combination, so frosted meatloaf—meatloaf coated in a layer of mashed potatoes—was an idea we could get behind. To perfect this nearly forgotten 1950s classic, we found that we had to broil the meatloaf in stages to keep the potatoes from slipping off: First, it was broiled to create a crust and then coated with a tangy, ketchup-based glaze for flavor and broiled again. After cooking through, the meatloaf was frosted with creamy mashed potatoes and broiled for a final stint to turn the fluffy crown of potatoes beautifully brown.

Why This Recipe Works As much as we love classic meatloaf, a recipe for a rustic meatloaf with a deep brown crust and hearty mushroom gravy piqued our interest. Sliced button mushrooms plus minced porcini gave the gravy an earthy richness. To further boost the flavor of the meatloaf itself, we added the porcini soaking liquid and more button mushrooms, which we ground in a food processor and sautéed. To keep the procedure simple, we baked the meatloaf in the same skillet. Then, while the loaf was resting, we used the skillet and the meat drippings to build our gravy.

MEATLOAF WITH MUSHROOM GRAVY

SERVES 8

If you're short the 2 tablespoons of meatloaf drippings needed to make the gravy, supplement the drippings with melted butter or vegetable oil.

- 1 cup water
- ¼ ounce dried porcini mushrooms, rinsed
- 16 square or 18 round saltines
- 10 ounces white mushrooms, trimmed
- 1 tablespoon vegetable oil
- 1 onion, chopped fine
- Salt and pepper
- 4 garlic cloves, minced
- 1 pound ground pork
- 2 large eggs
- 1 tablespoon plus ¾ teaspoon Worcestershire sauce
- 1 pound 85 percent lean ground beef
- ¾ teaspoon minced fresh thyme
- ¼ cup all-purpose flour
- 2½ cups chicken broth

1. Adjust oven rack to middle position and heat oven to 375 degrees. Microwave water and porcini in covered bowl until steaming, about 1 minute. Let sit until softened, about 5 minutes. Strain porcini through fine-mesh strainer lined with coffee filter, reserving liquid. Mince and reserve porcini.

2. Process saltines in food processor until finely ground, about 30 seconds; transfer to large bowl and reserve. Pulse 5 ounces of white mushrooms in processor until finely ground, 8 to 10 pulses.

3. Heat oil in 12-inch nonstick oven-safe skillet over medium-high heat until shimmering. Add onion and cook until browned, 6 to 8 minutes. Stir in processed mushrooms and ¼ teaspoon salt and cook until liquid evaporates and mushrooms begin to brown, about 5 minutes. Add garlic and cook until fragrant, about 30 seconds. Transfer to bowl with saltines and let cool to room temperature, about 15 minutes. Wipe out skillet with paper towels.

4. Add pork, ¼ cup reserved porcini liquid, eggs, 1 tablespoon Worcestershire, 1 teaspoon salt, and ¾ teaspoon pepper to cooled mushroom-saltine mixture and knead gently until nearly combined. Add beef and knead until well combined. Transfer meat mixture to now-empty skillet and shape into 10 by 6-inch loaf. Bake until meatloaf registers 160 degrees, 45 to 55 minutes. Transfer meatloaf to carving board and tent loosely with aluminum foil.

5. Slice remaining 5 ounces white mushrooms. Discard any solids in skillet and pour off all but 2 tablespoons fat. Heat fat over medium-high heat until shimmering. Add sliced mushrooms and reserved porcini and cook, stirring occasionally, until deep golden brown, 6 to 8 minutes. Stir in thyme and ¼ teaspoon salt and cook until fragrant, about 30 seconds. Add flour and cook, stirring frequently, until golden, about 2 minutes. Slowly whisk in broth, ½ cup reserved porcini liquid, and remaining ¾ teaspoon Worcestershire, scraping up any browned bits, and bring to boil. Reduce heat to medium and simmer, whisking occasionally, until thickened, 10 to 15 minutes. Season with salt and pepper to taste. Slice meatloaf and serve with gravy.

One Skillet, Start to Finish

ON THE STOVE
We brown the onion and ground mushrooms for robust flavor.

INTO THE OVEN
We shape and bake the meatloaf in the same skillet.

BACK TO THE STOVE
While the meatloaf rests, we use its drippings to make the gravy.

BACON-WRAPPED MEATLOAF

SERVES 6 TO 8

Bull's-Eye Original is our favorite barbecue sauce. Do not use thick-cut bacon for this recipe, as the package will yield fewer strips for wrapping the meatloaf. Oscar Mayer Naturally Hardwood Smoked Bacon is our favorite thin-sliced bacon.

- ¼ cup barbecue sauce, plus extra for serving
- 1 tablespoon cider vinegar
- 1 tablespoon Worcestershire sauce
- 1 tablespoon spicy brown mustard
- 17 square or 19 round saltines, crushed (⅔ cup)
- 4 slices coarsely chopped bacon, plus 8 whole slices
- 1 onion, chopped coarse
- 3 garlic cloves, minced
- ⅓ cup whole milk
- 2 large eggs plus 1 large yolk
- ⅓ cup minced fresh parsley
- ¾ teaspoon salt
- ½ teaspoon pepper
- 1½ pounds 90 percent lean ground beef

1. Adjust oven rack to upper-middle position and heat oven to 375 degrees. Line rimmed baking sheet with aluminum foil and set wire rack in sheet. Whisk barbecue sauce, vinegar, Worcestershire, and mustard together in bowl; set glaze aside.

2. Process saltines in food processor until finely ground, about 30 seconds; transfer to large bowl. Pulse chopped bacon and onion in now-empty processor until coarsely ground, about 10 pulses. Transfer bacon mixture to 10-inch nonstick skillet and cook over medium heat until onion is soft and translucent, about 5 minutes. Add garlic and cook until fragrant, about 30 seconds. Set aside off heat.

3. Add milk, eggs and yolk, parsley, salt, pepper, and 2 tablespoons glaze to saltines and mash with fork until chunky paste forms. Stir in bacon mixture until combined. Add the beef and knead with your hands until combined.

4. Lightly spray 8½ by 4½-inch loaf pan with vegetable oil spray. Line pan with large sheet of plastic wrap, with extra plastic hanging over edges of pan. Push plastic into corners and up sides of pan. Line pan crosswise with remaining 8 bacon slices, overlapping them slightly and letting excess hang over edges of pan (you should have at least ½ inch of overhanging bacon). Brush bacon with 3 tablespoons glaze. Transfer meatloaf mixture to bacon-lined pan and press mixture firmly into pan. Fold bacon slices over mixture.

5. Using metal skewer or tip of paring knife, poke 15 holes in one 14 by 3-inch piece of foil. Center foil rectangle on top of meatloaf. Carefully flip meatloaf onto wire rack so foil is on bottom and bacon is on top. Gripping plastic, gently lift and remove pan from meatloaf. Discard plastic. Gently press meatloaf into 9 by 5-inch rectangle.

6. Bake until bacon is browned and meatloaf registers 150 degrees, about 1 hour. Remove from oven and heat broiler. Brush top and sides of meatloaf with remaining 2 tablespoons glaze. Broil meatloaf until glaze begins to char and meatloaf registers 160 degrees, 3 to 5 minutes. Using foil as sling, transfer meatloaf to carving board and let rest for 15 minutes. Slice and serve, passing extra barbecue sauce.

That's a Wrap

Invert the foil-topped loaf, bacon and all, onto a wire rack set in a baking sheet, remove the loaf pan and plastic, press the meatloaf into shape, and bake.

Why This Recipe Works What's even better than a bacon-wrapped meatloaf? A bacon-wrapped meatloaf that also has chopped bacon added to the ground beef inside. To make shaping easy, we lined a loaf pan with plastic wrap and then shingled slices of bacon in the pan. After pressing the meatloaf mixture into the pan, we turned it out onto a piece of foil set on a wire rack inside a rimmed baking sheet. This allowed the fat from the meat to drain away from the loaf as it cooked. A pass under the broiler ensured that the bacon was crisp and that the spicy-sweet glaze caramelized to perfection.

Why This Recipe Works The point of Swiss steak is to transform a tough, inexpensive cut of meat into a delicate meal so tender you can almost eat it with a spoon. Many recipes called for tenderizing the meat by pounding it before cooking, but we know from experience that pounding meat does nothing to tenderize it. Instead we relied on a slow braise to create the ideal texture. To flavor the Swiss steak gravy, we found a combination of sautéed onion, diced tomatoes, and sun-dried tomatoes was ideal.

SWISS STEAK WITH TOMATO GRAVY

SERVES 6 TO 8

Top blade roast may also be labeled chuck roast first cut, top chuck roast, flat iron roast, or simply blade roast.

- 1 (3½- to 4-pound) boneless top blade roast, trimmed
- Salt and pepper
- 2 tablespoons vegetable oil
- 1 onion, halved and sliced thin
- 2 tablespoons tomato paste
- 1 tablespoon all-purpose flour
- 3 garlic cloves, minced
- ½ teaspoon dried thyme
- 1 (14.5-ounce) can diced tomatoes
- 1½ cups chicken broth
- 1 tablespoon sun-dried tomatoes packed in oil, rinsed, patted dry, and minced
- 1 tablespoon minced fresh parsley

1. Adjust oven rack to middle position and heat oven to 300 degrees. Cut roast crosswise into quarters and remove center line of gristle from each quarter to yield 8 steaks.

2. Pat steaks dry with paper towels and season lightly with salt and pepper. Heat 1 tablespoon oil in Dutch oven over medium-high heat just until smoking. Brown 4 steaks on both sides, about 6 minutes. Transfer to plate and repeat with remaining oil and steaks.

3. Add onion to empty pot and cook until softened, about 5 minutes. Add tomato paste, flour, garlic, and thyme and cook until fragrant, about 1 minute. Stir in diced tomatoes and broth and bring to boil.

4. Return steaks and any accumulated juices to pan. Cover, transfer to oven and cook until steaks are fork-tender, about 2 hours. Transfer steaks to platter, tent with aluminum foil, and let rest for 5 minutes. Skim fat from sauce. Stir in sun-dried tomatoes and parsley. Season with salt and pepper to taste. Pour sauce over steaks. Serve.

Preparing Blade Roast for Swiss Steak

Top blade roast, a shoulder cut with great flavor, has a pesky line of gristle that runs horizontally through its center. Follow these simple steps to remove it and cut perfect Swiss steaks.

1. Place roast on cutting board and cut crosswise into 4 even pieces.

2. One piece at a time, turn meat on its side to expose line of gristle that runs through its center.

3. Remove by slicing through meat on either side of gristle to yield 2 "steaks."

Why This Recipe Works We wanted to rescue this American classic from the frozen foods aisle for a great weeknight option. We started by mixing a panade (a milk and bread paste) into ground beef to help bind the meat and preserve moisture, but this trick made the dish taste too much like meatloaf. On a lark, we added mashed potatoes as seen in one recipe and were impressed with the silky texture and great flavor of the patties. To make the dish easier, we swapped in instant potato flakes. We browned the patties on both sides and let them finish cooking in the extra-rich mushroom and onion sauce, which kept the beef tender.

SALISBURY STEAK

SERVES 4

When shaping the patties in step 1, be sure to wet your hands to prevent sticking. Tawny port or dry sherry can be substituted for the ruby port. Do not use potato granules, which add an off-flavor.

- ½ cup milk
- 7 tablespoons instant potato flakes
- 1 pound 90 percent lean ground beef
- Salt and pepper
- 4 tablespoons unsalted butter
- 1 onion, halved and sliced thin
- 1 pound white mushrooms, trimmed and sliced thin
- 1 tablespoon tomato paste
- 2 tablespoons all-purpose flour
- 1¾ cups beef broth
- ¼ cup ruby port

1. Whisk milk and potato flakes in large bowl. Add beef, ½ teaspoon salt, and ½ teaspoon pepper and knead until combined. Shape into four ½-inch-thick oval patties and transfer to parchment paper–lined plate. Refrigerate for at least 30 minutes or up to 4 hours.

2. Melt 1 tablespoon butter in 12-inch nonstick skillet over medium-high heat. Cook patties until well browned on each side, about 10 minutes. Transfer to plate.

3. Add onion and remaining 3 tablespoons butter to now-empty skillet and cook until onion is softened, about 5 minutes. Add mushrooms and ½ teaspoon salt and cook until liquid has evaporated, 5 to 7 minutes. Stir in tomato paste and flour and cook until browned, about 2 minutes. Slowly stir in broth and port and bring to simmer. Return patties to skillet, cover, and simmer over medium-low heat until cooked through, 12 to 15 minutes. Season sauce with salt and pepper to taste. Serve.

Take 2 Aspirin—or Have Some Salisbury Steak

It's hard to imagine that chopped steak could be considered health food, but that's just what Dr. James Henry Salisbury had in mind when he invented his eponymous dish as a "meat cure" for wounded and ill Civil War soldiers (who were instructed to eat it three times a day—with no vegetables allowed). Some 60 years later, during the period of World War I food rations, restaurateurs ground up their lean beef scraps, shaped them into patties, dressed the cooked patties with a rich mushroom cream sauce, and called it Salisbury steak. Around this time, recipes for Salisbury steak began showing up in cookbooks, but with a nod toward the original recipe, instructions indicated that invalids should skip the sauce. During World War II, Salisbury steak again enjoyed popularity because it was a great way to stretch meat: cream of wheat, oats, and soy grits were common fillers. And in 1965, Salisbury steak really hit the big time when Swanson introduced it in a special three-course TV dinner. Impressed by its storied past, we couldn't resist resurrecting this American classic.

MILK-CAN SUPPER

SERVES 6 TO 8

If your Dutch oven is slightly smaller than 8 quarts, the lid may not close all the way when you start cooking. But as the contents of the pot cook, they will decrease in volume, so you'll soon be able to clamp on the lid. Use small red potatoes, measuring 1 to 2 inches in diameter. Light-bodied American lagers, such as Budweiser, work best in this recipe.

- 1 tablespoon vegetable oil
- 2½ pounds bratwurst (10 sausages)
- 2 pounds small red potatoes, unpeeled
- 1 head green cabbage (2 pounds), cored and cut into 8 wedges
- 3 ears corn, husks and silk removed, ears cut into 3 pieces
- 6 carrots, peeled and cut into 2-inch pieces
- 1 onion, halved and cut through root end into 8 wedges
- 4 garlic cloves, peeled and smashed
- 10 sprigs fresh thyme
- 2 bay leaves
- Salt and pepper
- 1½ cups beer
- 2 green bell peppers, stemmed, seeded, and cut into 1-inch-wide strips

1. Heat oil in 8-quart Dutch oven over medium heat until shimmering. Add bratwurst and cook until browned all over, 6 to 8 minutes. Remove pot from heat. Transfer bratwurst to cutting board and halve crosswise.

2. Place potatoes in single layer in now-empty Dutch oven. Arrange cabbage wedges in single layer on top of potatoes. Layer corn, carrots, onion, garlic, thyme, bay leaves, 1 teaspoon salt, and ½ teaspoon pepper over cabbage. Pour beer over vegetables and arrange browned bratwursts on top.

3. Bring to boil over medium-high heat (wisps of steam will be visible). Cover, reduce heat to medium, and simmer for 15 minutes. Add bell peppers and continue to simmer, covered, until potatoes are tender, about 15 minutes. (Use long skewer to test potatoes for doneness.)

4. Transfer bratwurst and vegetables to large serving platter (or roasting pan, if your platter isn't large enough); discard thyme sprigs and bay leaves. Pour 1 cup cooking liquid over platter. Season with salt and pepper to taste. Serve, passing remaining cooking liquid separately.

Trail Talk

Food often outlasts the culture that created it. Milk-can supper, for example, originated as a way of feeding cowhands after a long day of work. It is still popular in parts of the West and upper Midwest, but the food lingo of the cowboys who once ate this dish has faded away. Some names for individual dishes, such as calf slobber (for meringue), reflected the coarseness of trail language. Perhaps most revealing was the name for the 5- or 10-gallon can that served as an all-purpose cooking utensil throughout a thousand-mile cattle drive: It was called the squirrel can, the uncomplimentary moniker coming from the idea that it was never emptied during the course of the entire drive but instead became the receptacle for whatever the cook found to add to it. In her 1933 article "Ranch Diction of the Texas Panhandle," author Mary Dale Buckner declared, "It is true that when a spoon, cup, dipper or some small object was dropped into [the squirrel can], usually no one bothered to remove it." We'll stick with the milk can.

Why This Recipe Works Traditionally, cowboys layered vegetables and meat (usually sausage) into a giant milk can, then cooked it over an open fire to feed large groups of cowhands. To bring this all-in-one dish into the home kitchen, we opted to use a Dutch oven but keep the basic technique of layering ingredients according to cooking time. Browning the Bratwurst first created flavorful fond. We lined the bottom of the pot with sturdy red potatoes to protect the other vegetables from burning, and we added the quick-cooking green bell peppers halfway through cooking. Traditional lager as a cooking liquid gave our meat-and-potatoes meal toasty depth.

PAN-FRIED PORK CHOPS

SERVES 4

Chops between ¾ and 1 inch thick will work in this recipe.

- 1 teaspoon garlic powder
- ½ teaspoon paprika
- ½ teaspoon salt
- ½ teaspoon pepper
- ¼ teaspoon cayenne pepper
- 1 cup all-purpose flour
- 4 (8- to 10-ounce) bone-in pork rib or center-cut chops, about ¾ inch thick, trimmed
- 3 slices bacon, chopped
- ½ cup vegetable oil

1. Combine garlic powder, paprika, salt, pepper, and cayenne in bowl. Place flour in shallow dish. Pat chops dry with paper towels. Cut 2 slits about 2 inches apart through fat and connective tissue on edge of each chop. Season both sides of chops with spice mixture, then dredge chops lightly in flour (do not discard flour). Transfer to plate and let rest for 10 minutes.

2. Meanwhile, cook bacon in 12-inch nonstick skillet over medium heat until fat renders and bacon is crisp, 5 to 7 minutes. Using slotted spoon, transfer bacon to paper towel–lined plate and reserve for another use. Do not wipe out pan.

3. Add oil to fat in pan and heat over medium-high heat until just smoking. Return chops to flour dish and turn to coat chops again. Cook chops until well browned on each side, 6 to 8 minutes. Serve.

BBQ PAN-FRIED PORK CHOPS
Replace first 5 ingredients with 3 tablespoons light brown sugar, 1 teaspoon chili powder, 1 teaspoon paprika, ½ teaspoon salt, ½ teaspoon dry mustard, ¼ teaspoon ground cumin, and ¼ teaspoon cayenne pepper.

HERBED PAN-FRIED PORK CHOPS
Replace first 5 ingredients with ½ teaspoon dried marjoram, ½ teaspoon dried thyme, ¼ teaspoon dried basil, ¼ teaspoon dried rosemary (crumbled), ¼ teaspoon dried sage, pinch ground fennel, and ½ teaspoon salt.

Preventing Curly Chops

Pork chops—especially thin-cut chops—have a tendency to curl as they cook. When exposed to the high heat of the pan, the ring of fat and connective tissue that surrounds the exterior tightens, causing the meat to buckle and curl. To prevent it, we cut two slits about 2 inches apart through the fat and connective tissue on each chop.

BUCKLED CHOP
No slits

FLAT CHOP
Slits cut

Why This Recipe Works Not all pork chops are created alike—for pan-frying, we found that center-cut or bone-in pork chops worked best. The bone added valuable flavor to the meat and prevented it from drying out. Simply dredging the pork chops in flour, as most recipes instructed, produced a spotty, insubstantial crust that wouldn't stay put. We have had success letting floured chicken rest before re-dredging and frying, and we wondered if the same treatment would work for pork. Sure enough, our double-dipped chops emerged from the pan with a hefty, crisp, golden-brown crust.

Why This Recipe Works Bone-in chops were a must for smothered pork chops, because the bone kept the meat moist and added flavor to the sauce. Caramelizing the onions made the sauce too sweet and took almost an hour. We had better luck cooking them in butter until they were lightly browned. We swapped out chicken broth in favor of meatier beef broth, which greatly improved the flavor of our sauce. Adding dried thyme, a bay leaf, and cider vinegar bumped up the flavor even more. To thicken our broth, we made a cornstarch-and-broth slurry. The results? A silky sauce that clung to our chops.

SMOTHERED PORK CHOPS

SERVES 4

Chops thicker than ½ inch won't be fully tender in the allotted cooking time.

- 1 teaspoon onion powder
- ½ teaspoon paprika
- Salt and pepper
- ¼ teaspoon cayenne pepper
- 4 (8- to 10-ounce) bone-in blade-cut pork chops, about ½ inch thick, trimmed
- 1½ tablespoons vegetable oil
- 1 tablespoon unsalted butter
- 2 onions, halved and sliced ¼ inch thick
- 2 garlic cloves, minced
- ¼ teaspoon dried thyme
- ¾ cup plus 1 tablespoon beef broth
- 1 bay leaf
- 1 teaspoon cornstarch
- 1 teaspoon cider vinegar

1. Adjust oven rack to middle position and heat oven to 300 degrees. Combine onion powder, paprika, ½ teaspoon salt, ½ teaspoon pepper, and cayenne in small bowl. Pat chops dry with paper towels. Cut 2 slits about 2 inches apart through fat and connective tissue on edge of each chop. Rub chops with spice mixture.

2. Heat oil in large skillet over medium-high heat until just smoking. Brown chops on both sides, 6 to 8 minutes, and transfer to plate. Melt butter in now-empty skillet over medium heat. Cook onions until browned, 8 to 10 minutes. Add garlic and thyme and cook until fragrant, about 30 seconds. Stir in ¾ cup broth and bay leaf, scraping up any browned bits, and bring to boil. Return chops and any accumulated juices to pan, cover, and transfer to oven. Cook until chops are completely tender, about 1½ hours.

3. Transfer chops to platter and tent with aluminum foil. Discard bay leaf. Strain contents of skillet through fine-mesh strainer into large liquid measuring cup; reserve onions. Let liquid settle, then skim fat. Return 1½ cups defatted pan juices to now-empty skillet and bring to boil. Reduce heat to medium and simmer until sauce is reduced to 1 cup, about 5 minutes.

4. Whisk remaining 1 tablespoon broth and cornstarch in bowl until no lumps remain. Whisk cornstarch mixture into sauce and simmer until thickened, 1 to 2 minutes. Stir in reserved onions and vinegar. Season with salt and pepper to taste. Serve.

Pork Chop Perfection

You might think smothered pork chops were born in a diner somewhere. You'd be wrong. "Smother" is an English term that refers to a method of cooking meat, poultry, or game slowly in a covered vessel. This method, essentially a braise, goes back at least to the 16th century. Recipes for smothers first came to the United States from England during the Revolutionary War. Amelia Simmons's *American Cookery*, written in 1796, includes a recipe for smothering a chicken with oysters, though onions are the most common smothering agent. It is believed onions in smothers were used to tone down the gaminess of meat or hide off-flavors. Sailors smothered their salt beef and salt pork rations with onions and potatoes when out to sea. Regional variations soon developed throughout the country: New Englanders often made smothers with fresh pork; in the South, Creole cooking advised against smothering pork, but recommended it for beef, chicken, and veal; and while other traditions in the Deep South did smother pork, it was more typically tails, chitterlings, or other tough or gamy parts—the parts of the pig most available to African-American slaves. Eventually, pork chops did make it into the pot, and we're glad they did.

Why This Recipe Works The apple flavor in cider-braised pork chops can be fleeting. We wanted tender, juicy chops infused with deep, rich cider flavor. Tasters preferred 1-inch blade chops for their heft, silky meat, and rich taste. Patting the chops dry before adding them to the heated Dutch oven helped them develop a flavorful crust. Apple cider lent both sweetness and tartness to the braising mixture and sauce, while a bit of fresh thyme provided a heady herbal component. Jarred apple butter added further apple flavor, and its natural pectin gave the sauce a thick, glossy consistency. A splash of cider vinegar provided brightness.

CIDER-BRAISED PORK CHOPS

SERVES 6

Do not use chops thinner than 1 inch. In step 3, a fat separator makes quick work of defatting the sauce.

- 6 (8- to 10-ounce) bone-in blade-cut pork chops, about 1 inch thick, trimmed
- Salt and pepper
- 2 tablespoons vegetable oil
- 1 onion, chopped
- ¼ cup apple butter
- 2 tablespoons all-purpose flour
- 3 garlic cloves, minced
- 1 cup apple cider
- 1 sprig fresh thyme
- 1 teaspoon cider vinegar
- 1 tablespoon finely chopped fresh parsley

1. Adjust oven rack to lower-middle position and heat oven to 300 degrees. Pat chops dry with paper towels. Cut 2 slits about 2 inches apart through fat and connective tissue on edge of each chop. Season chops with salt and pepper. Heat oil in Dutch oven over medium-high heat until just smoking. Brown 3 chops on each side, about 8 minutes; transfer to plate, and then repeat with remaining 3 chops.

2. Pour off all but 1 tablespoon fat from pot and cook onion over medium heat until softened, about 5 minutes. Stir in 2 tablespoons apple butter, flour, and garlic and cook until onion is coated and mixture is fragrant, about 1 minute. Stir in cider and thyme, scraping up any browned bits with wooden spoon, and bring to boil. Add browned chops and any accumulated juices to pot, cover, and transfer to oven. Braise until chops are completely tender, about 1½ hours.

3. Transfer chops to serving platter. Strain sauce, then skim off fat. Whisk in vinegar, parsley, and remaining 2 tablespoons apple butter. Season with salt and pepper to taste. Serve, passing sauce at table. (Pork chops and sauce can be refrigerated separately for up to 2 days. To serve, reheat sauce and chops together over medium heat until chops are warmed through.)

Three Keys to Better Apple Flavor
Cider alone won't provide much apple flavor. To pack the taste of apples into our pork chops, we settled on a triple helping of apple products.

APPLE BUTTER
Apple butter provides intense apple and warm spice flavor. It also helps thicken the sauce.

CIDER VINEGAR
Finishing with a splash of cider vinegar adds brightness and complexity to the sauce.

CIDER
Sweet-tart cider provides most of the liquid for the braising mixture and sauce.

CRISPY FISH STICKS WITH TARTAR SAUCE

SERVES 4

Be sure to rinse the capers, otherwise the tartar sauce will be too salty. Halibut, haddock, or catfish can be substituted for the cod.

- 4 slices hearty white sandwich bread, torn into quarters
- 16 square or 18 round saltines
- ½ cup all-purpose flour
- 2 large eggs
- 1 cup mayonnaise
- 2 pounds skinless cod, cut into 1-inch-thick strips
  Salt and pepper
- ¼ cup finely chopped dill pickles, plus 1 tablespoon pickle juice
- 1 tablespoon capers, rinsed and minced
- 1 cup vegetable oil

1. Adjust oven rack to middle position and heat oven to 200 degrees. Pulse bread and saltines in food processor to fine crumbs, about 15 pulses; transfer to shallow dish. Place flour in second shallow dish. Beat eggs with ¼ cup mayonnaise in third shallow dish.

2. Pat fish dry with paper towels and season with salt and pepper. One at a time, coat fish strips lightly with flour, dip in egg mixture, and then dredge in crumbs, pressing on both sides to adhere. Transfer breaded fish to plate. Combine remaining ¾ cup mayonnaise, pickles, pickle juice, and capers in small bowl and set aside.

3. Heat ½ cup oil in large 12-inch nonstick skillet over medium heat until just smoking. Fry half of fish strips until deep golden and crisp on both sides, about 4 minutes. Drain on paper towel–lined plate and transfer to oven to keep warm. Discard oil, wipe out skillet, and repeat with remaining ½ cup oil and remaining fish. Serve with tartar sauce.

Fish Sticks—Pioneering the Frozen Food Landscape

Commercial freezing brought fish to the people, but it was the fish stick, introduced in 1953 by Birds Eye, that got them interested in eating fish. Why? Fish sticks have always appealed on a few levels. The breading helps prevent the fish from sticking to the pan; their mild flavor and crunchy crust appeal to children; and conveniently, fish sticks require minimal cleanup. Over the years, neither the expanded market created by freezing nor the wild popularity of fish sticks did much to boost the nation's overall fish consumption. But fish sticks did fire up the frozen foods market, both in terms of the creativity of producers and the enthusiasm of consumers for new, convenient heat-and-eat food products. Before fish sticks went commercial in the frozen foods industry, they were found at fish markets and delis along the East Coast. And of course, they were made at home. Homemade might not be as convenient as the frozen type, but we still aimed for a recipe that was easy enough for a weeknight.

Why This Recipe Works Forget the boxed varieties in the frozen foods aisle—our homemade fish sticks are fresh and crisp, and fry up in just minutes. Our recipe calls for cod, but halibut, haddock, and catfish are all worthy substitutes. Eggs beaten with mayonnaise helped our coating of crisp saltines and fresh bread crumbs adhere to the fish. We pan-fried the fish in two batches to ensure they cooked up even and crisp.

STRAWBERRY PRETZEL SALAD

SERVES 10 TO 12

For a sturdier crust, use (thinner) pretzel sticks not (fatter) rods. Thaw the strawberries in the refrigerator the night before you begin the recipe. You'll puree 2 pounds of the strawberries and slice the remaining 1 pound.

- 6½ ounces pretzel sticks
- 2¼ cups (15¾ ounces) sugar
- 12 tablespoons unsalted butter, melted and cooled
- 8 ounces cream cheese
- 1 cup heavy cream
- 3 pounds (10½ cups) frozen strawberries, thawed
- ¼ teaspoon salt
- 4½ teaspoons unflavored gelatin
- ½ cup cold water

1. Adjust oven rack to middle position and heat oven to 400 degrees. Spray 13 by 9-inch baking pan with vegetable oil spray. Pulse pretzels and ¼ cup sugar in food processor until coarsely ground, about 15 pulses. Add melted butter and pulse until combined, about 10 pulses. Transfer pretzel mixture to prepared pan. Using bottom of measuring cup, press crumbs into bottom of pan. Bake until crust is fragrant and beginning to brown, about 10 minutes, rotating pan halfway through baking. Set aside crust, letting it cool slightly, about 20 minutes.

2. Using stand mixer fitted with whisk, whip cream cheese and ½ cup sugar on medium speed until light and fluffy, about 2 minutes. Increase speed to medium-high and, with mixer still running, slowly add cream in steady stream. Continue to whip until soft peaks form, scraping down bowl as needed, about 1 minute longer. Spread whipped cream cheese mixture evenly over cooled crust. Refrigerate until set, about 30 minutes.

3. Meanwhile, process 2 pounds strawberries in now-empty food processor until pureed, about 30 seconds. Strain mixture through fine-mesh strainer set over medium saucepan, using underside of small ladle to push puree through strainer. Add remaining 1½ cups sugar and salt to strawberry puree in saucepan and cook over medium-high heat, whisking occasionally, until bubbles begin to appear around sides of pan and sugar is dissolved, about 5 minutes; remove from heat.

4. Sprinkle gelatin over water in large bowl and let sit until gelatin softens, about 5 minutes. Whisk strawberry puree into gelatin. Slice remaining strawberries and stir into strawberry-gelatin mixture. Refrigerate until gelatin thickens slightly and starts to cling to sides of bowl, about 30 minutes. Carefully pour gelatin mixture evenly over whipped cream cheese layer. Refrigerate salad until gelatin is fully set, at least 4 hours or up to 24 hours. Serve.

Salad Days

Baked beans, marshmallows, fruit cocktail, flavored gelatin, grated American cheese, ginger ale, sauerkraut . . . Do the words "salad fixings" spring to mind? Probably not, but then you aren't a well-bred, middle-class lady living in the first half of the 20th century. Had you been reared on the tenets of the domestic science movement that dominated American cooking at that time, such a list would indeed have suggested salad. As a "progressive housekeeper," you would have cringed at the very idea of what we call salad today. As culinary historian Laura Shapiro has detailed in *Perfection Salad: Women and Cooking at the Turn of the Century*, vegetables had to be tamed, and the very best way to render untidy raw vegetables harmless was to encase them in gelatin. After molding and chilling her salad, she could gild the lily with a few stuffed prunes, rococo swirls of thinned mayonnaise, and a carved tomato tulip. Pretzel salad is a direct descendent of such "Festive for Special Occasions Salads," as Betty Crocker's *New Picture Cook Book* grouped similar concoctions as late as 1961. Even today, despite the Cool Whip and the strawberry Jell-O, pretzel salad is not dessert—it's a salad.

Why This Recipe Works This tri-layer Midwestern specialty doesn't much resemble salad, but the sweet-salty, creamy-crunchy combination grabbed our attention. We knew we could make this slightly offbeat potluck favorite shine with some home-made elements. We replaced the "whipped topping" with real cream, which we whipped into softened cream cheese with some sugar for a tangy, not-too-sweet middle layer. The top layer, traditionally made from boxed Jell-O, got an upgrade to plain gelatin flavored with real pureed strawberry juice and sliced frozen berries. The time it took to make these elements from scratch was well worth the extra effort.

Why This Recipe Works Homemade stock tastes a lot better than even the best store-bought broths. While it's not complicated to make, it does require some babysitting on the stovetop, so instead, we turned to our slow cooker. We piled vegetables and leftover cooked chicken bones in cold water, added seasonings, and set it on high. The slow cooker prevented evaporation so the bones remained submerged, which is often a challenge with stovetop stock recipes. Refrigerating the strained stock allowed the fat to rise to the top and solidify, making it easy to discard. This rich, savory stock is remarkably easy—and thrifty too.

SLOW-COOKER CHICKEN STOCK

MAKES ABOUT 3 QUARTS

This stock is great to use in any of our recipes calling for chicken broth. You can freeze chicken carcasses one at a time until you have the 2½ pounds needed for this recipe; three to four rotisserie chicken carcasses or one 6-pound roaster carcass will weigh about 2½ pounds. This recipe was developed using bones from cooked chicken.

- 3 quarts water
- 2½ pounds roasted chicken bones
- 1 onion, chopped
- 2 carrots, peeled and cut into 1-inch chunks
- 2 celery ribs, chopped
- 1 teaspoon black peppercorns
- 1 teaspoon salt
- 1 bay leaf

1. Place all ingredients in slow cooker. Cover and cook on high for 8 to 10 hours.

2. Let stock cool slightly, then strain through fine-mesh strainer set over large bowl. Use immediately or let cool completely, then refrigerate until cold. (When cold, surface fat will solidify and can be easily removed with spoon. Stock will keep, refrigerated, for up to 5 days, or frozen for up to 2 months).

Stock Storage

Frozen homemade chicken stock lasts for up to two months. Freeze small and medium amounts in ice cube trays or muffin tins; once frozen, pop out the stock blocks and keep them in zipper-lock bags for easy access when making pan sauces or gravy. Freeze larger amounts in plastic quart containers or zipper-lock bags, which are easy to stack in crowded freezers.

Celery

Buy loose celery heads, not bagged celery heads (with clipped leaves) or bagged celery hearts. Loose celery heads tend to be fuller and fresher. Look for glossy green stalks without brown edges or yellowing leaves. Revive limp celery stalks by cutting off about 1 inch from both ends and submerging the stalks in a bowl of ice water for 30 minutes. The best way to store celery is to wrap it in foil and store it in the refrigerator. It will keep for several weeks.

Carrots

Buy fresh carrots with greens attached for the best flavor. If buying bagged carrots, check that they are evenly sized and firm (they shouldn't bend). Don't buy extra-large carrots, which are often woody and bitter. To prevent shriveling, store carrots in the crisper drawer in a partially open zipper-lock bag or in their original plastic bag. Before storing green-topped carrots, remove and discard the greens or the carrots will become limp. Both bagged and fresh carrots will keep for several weeks.

SMALL AMOUNTS   MEDIUM AMOUNTS   LARGE AMOUNTS

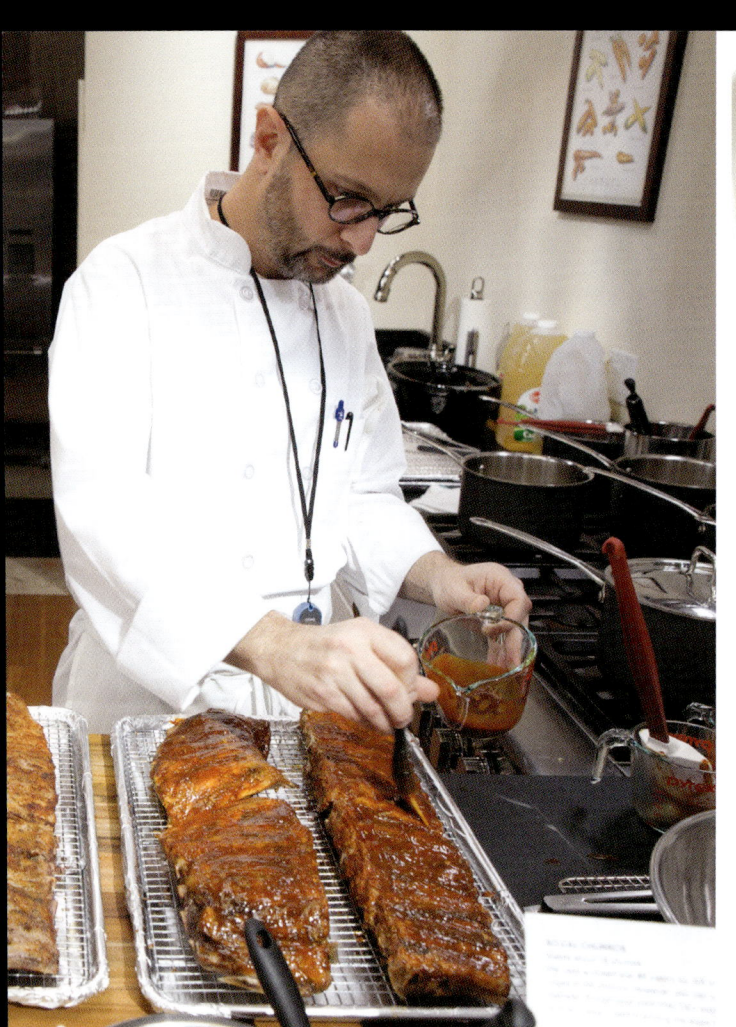

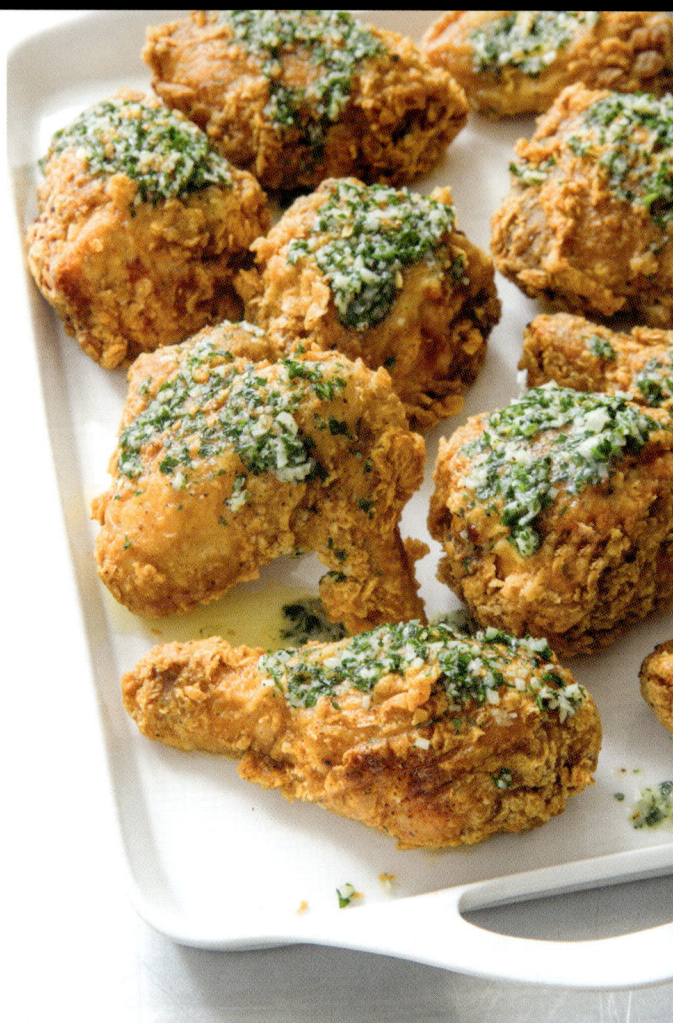

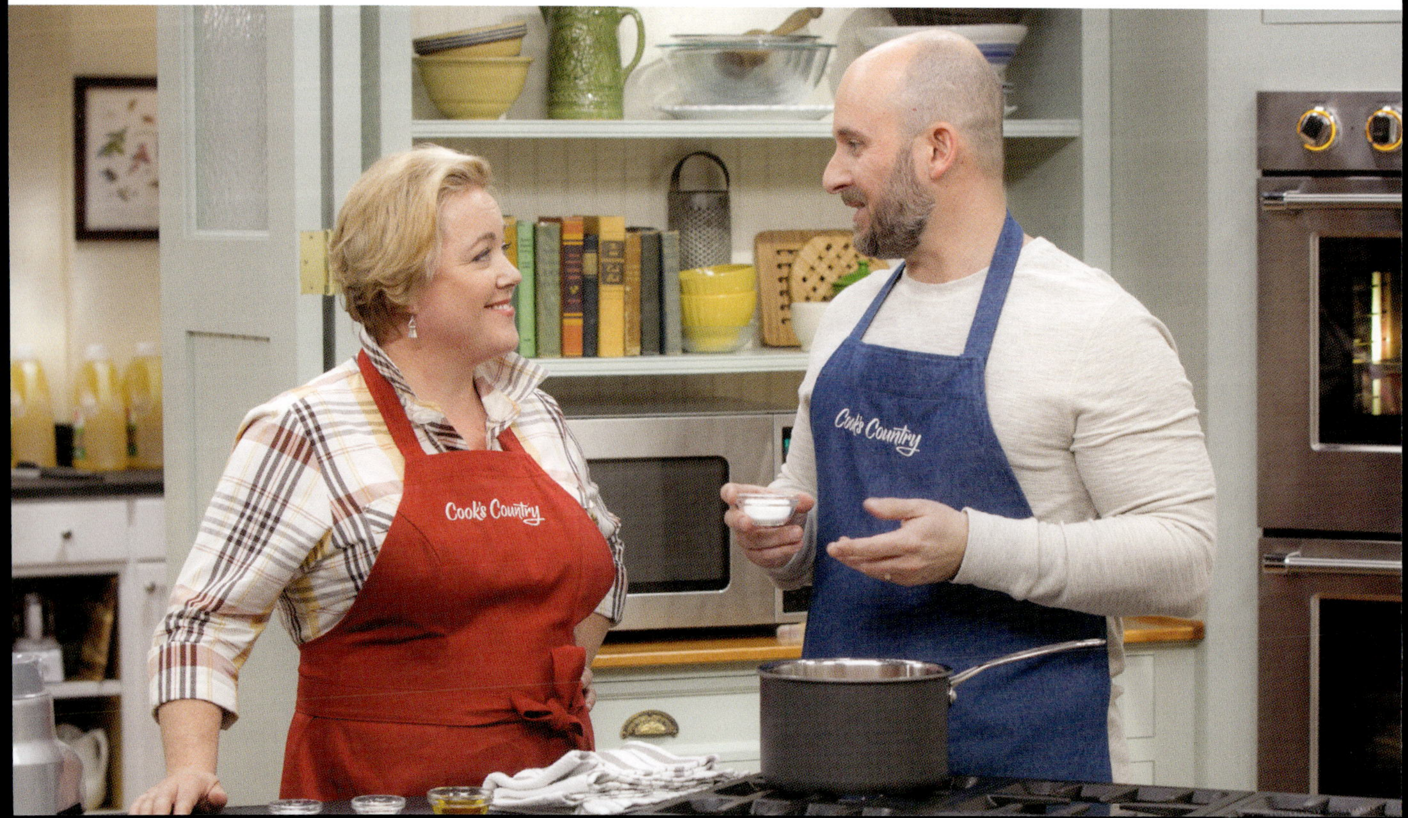
Cook's Country
Cook's Country

fork-in-the-road favorites

- 51 Batter-Fried Chicken
- 53 Honey Fried Chicken
- 54 Creole Fried Chicken
- 57 Garlic Fried Chicken
- 58 Extra-Crunchy Fried Chicken
- 60 Nashville Hot Fried Chicken
- 63 Ranch Fried Chicken
- 65 Chicken Nuggets
- 66 Delta Hot Tamales
- 69 Gumbo
- 70 New Orleans Barbecue Shrimp
- 72 Shrimp and Grits
- 75 Charleston Shrimp Perloo
- 77 New Orleans Muffulettas
- 78 Chinese Chicken Salad
- 81 Chicken Chow Mein
- 82 Slow-Cooker Chinese Barbecued Pork
- 84 Patty Melts
- 87 Oklahoma Fried Onion Burgers
- 89 Atlanta Brisket
- 90 Slow-Cooker BBQ Beef Brisket
- 93 Tennessee Whiskey Pork Chops
- 94 Memphis-Style Wet Ribs for a Crowd
- 96 Slow-Cooker Memphis-Style Wet Ribs
- 99 Baltimore Pit Beef
- 101 Cincinnati Chili
- 102 Colorado Green Chili
- 105 Natchitoches Meat Pies
- 106 St. Louis–Style Pizza
- 108 Potato-Cheddar Pierogi
- 111 Crunchy Potato Wedges
- 113 Crispy Potato Tots
- 114 Beer-Battered Onion Rings

Why This Recipe Works The old-fashioned method of batter-fried chicken calls for dipping chicken parts in a batter not unlike pancake batter before frying. For juicy meat, we brined our chicken. To ensure a crisp crust, we replaced the milk in our initial batters with plain old water. With milk, the sugars in the milk solids browned too fast and produced a soft crust. Using equal parts cornstarch and flour in the batter also helped ensure a crisp crust on the chicken. And baking powder added lift and lightness without doughiness.

BATTER-FRIED CHICKEN

SERVES 4 TO 6

You will need at least a 6-quart Dutch oven for this recipe.

Brine and Chicken
- ¼ cup salt
- ¼ cup sugar
- 4 pounds bone-in chicken pieces (breasts halved crosswise and leg quarters separated into drumsticks and thighs), trimmed

Batter
- 1 cup all-purpose flour
- 1 cup cornstarch
- 5 teaspoons pepper
- 2 teaspoons baking powder
- 1 teaspoon salt
- 1 teaspoon paprika
- ½ teaspoon cayenne pepper
- 1¾ cups cold water
- 3 quarts peanut or vegetable oil

1. For the Brine and Chicken Dissolve salt and sugar in 1 quart cold water in large container. Submerge chicken in brine, cover, and refrigerate for 30 minutes or up to 1 hour.

2. For the Batter Meanwhile, combine flour, cornstarch, pepper, baking powder, salt, paprika, and cayenne in large bowl, add water, and whisk until smooth. Refrigerate batter while chicken is brining.

3. Set wire rack in rimmed baking sheet. Add oil to large Dutch oven until it measures about 2 inches deep and heat over medium-high heat to 350 degrees. Using tongs, remove chicken from brine and pat dry with paper towels. Rewhisk batter. Transfer half of chicken to batter and turn to coat. Remove chicken from batter, 1 piece at a time, allowing excess to drip back into bowl, and transfer to oil. Fry chicken, adjusting burner as necessary to maintain oil temperature between 300 and 325 degrees, until deep golden brown and breasts register 160 degrees and thighs and drumsticks register 175 degrees, 12 to 15 minutes. Drain chicken on prepared baking sheet. Return oil to 350 degrees and repeat with remaining chicken. Serve.

Keys to Best Batter-Fried Chicken

1. Whisk together flour, cornstarch, baking powder, spices, and water to make thin batter for crisp crust.

2. After dipping chicken in batter, let excess drip off (back into bowl) to avoid doughy coating.

3. To prevent chicken pieces from sticking together in oil, don't crowd pot. Fry chicken in 2 batches.

Why This Recipe Works Really good honey fried chicken is juicy and tender on the inside with a crispy, sticky, honey-flavored coating. To keep the meat moist, we brined the chicken first. For the coating, we dusted the chicken in cornstarch and dipped it in a thin cornstarch-and-water batter. The hardest part was glazing the fried chicken in honey without making the crust soggy. We found that the key was to double-fry the chicken: We partially fried the chicken, let it rest to allow moisture from the skin to evaporate, then fried it again for an incredibly crunchy crust that stayed crispy when dunked in a glaze of warm honey and hot sauce.

HONEY FRIED CHICKEN

SERVES 4

If using kosher chicken, do not brine. You will need at least a 6-quart Dutch oven for this recipe.

Brine and Chicken
- ½ cup salt
- ½ cup sugar
- 3 pounds bone-in chicken pieces (breasts halved crosswise and leg quarters separated into drumsticks and thighs), trimmed

Batter
- 1½ cups cornstarch
- ¾ cup cold water
- 2 teaspoons pepper
- 1 teaspoon salt
- 3 quarts peanut or vegetable oil

Honey Glaze
- ¾ cup honey
- 2 tablespoons hot sauce

1. For the Brine and Chicken Dissolve salt and sugar in 2 quarts cold water in large container. Submerge chicken in brine, cover, and refrigerate for 30 minutes to 1 hour.

2. For the Batter While chicken is brining, whisk 1 cup cornstarch, water, pepper, and salt together in large bowl until smooth. Refrigerate batter.

3. Set wire rack inside rimmed baking sheet. Sift remaining ½ cup cornstarch into shallow bowl. Remove chicken from brine and dry thoroughly with paper towels. Working with 1 piece at a time, coat chicken thoroughly with cornstarch, shaking to remove excess; transfer to platter.

4. Add oil to large Dutch oven until it measures about 2 inches deep and heat over medium-high heat to 350 degrees. Whisk batter to recombine. Using tongs, transfer half of chicken to batter and turn to coat. Remove chicken from batter, 1 piece at a time, allowing excess to drip back into bowl, and transfer to hot oil. Fry chicken, stirring to prevent pieces from sticking together, until slightly golden and just beginning to crisp, 5 to 7 minutes. Adjust burner, if necessary, to maintain oil temperature between 325 and 350 degrees. (Chicken will not be cooked through at this point.) Transfer parcooked chicken to platter. Return oil to 350 degrees and repeat with remaining raw chicken and batter. Let each batch of chicken rest for 5 to 7 minutes.

5. Return oil to 350 degrees. Return first batch of chicken to oil and fry until breasts register 160 degrees and thighs/drumsticks register 175 degrees, 5 to 7 minutes. Transfer to prepared baking sheet. Return oil to 350 degrees and repeat with remaining chicken.

6. For the Honey Glaze Combine honey and hot sauce in large bowl and microwave until hot, about 1½ minutes. Add chicken pieces to honey mixture, one at a time, and turn to coat. Return to baking sheet, skin side up, to drain. Serve.

Making a Beeline West

The common honeybee (*Apis mellifera L.*) is not native to North America. British settlers bound for Virginia brought hives aboard ships, along with peacocks, pigeons, and rabbits, as the author of a letter from the Virginia Company recorded in 1621. During the next 200 years, the bee population slowly rolled westward, pollinating the prairies and the settlers' crops and providing pioneers with honey, wax, candles, and medicine. Native Americans called the honeybee the "white man's fly," and they saw the bees that swarmed ahead of the settlers as a threat. "The Indians . . . consider them the harbinger of the white man," Washington Irving wrote as he traveled through the Oklahoma Territory in 1832. "As the bee advances, the Indian and the buffalo retire." Similarly, after visiting members of the Osage tribe in the Missouri Territory in 1836, writer Alphonso Wetmore reported that "the Indians held a day of mourning because a swarm of bees had been found."

CREOLE FRIED CHICKEN

SERVES 4 TO 6

In step 1, do not soak the chicken longer than 8 hours, or it will be too salty. You will need at least a 6-quart Dutch oven for this recipe.

Seasoned Brine and Chicken
- ¼ cup sugar
- 3 tablespoons Worcestershire sauce
- 3 tablespoons hot sauce
- 2 tablespoons salt
- 1 tablespoon garlic powder
- 4 pounds bone-in chicken pieces (breasts halved crosswise and leg quarters separated into drumsticks and thighs), trimmed

Creole Seasoning
- 1 tablespoon pepper
- 1 tablespoon dried oregano
- 1 tablespoon garlic powder
- 2 teaspoons onion powder
- 2 teaspoons cayenne pepper
- 1 teaspoon white pepper
- 1 teaspoon celery salt
- 2 cups all-purpose flour
- 3 quarts peanut or vegetable oil

1. For the Seasoned Brine and Chicken Dissolve sugar, Worcestershire, hot sauce, salt, and garlic powder in 1 quart cold water in large container. Submerge chicken in brine, cover, and refrigerate for 1 hour or up to 8 hours.

2. For the Creole Seasoning Combine pepper, oregano, garlic powder, onion powder, cayenne, white pepper, and celery salt in large bowl; reserve ¼ cup spice mixture. Add flour to bowl with remaining spice mixture and stir to combine. Set wire rack in rimmed baking sheet.

3. Remove chicken from brine and pat dry with paper towels. Sprinkle chicken with 3 tablespoons reserved spice mixture and toss to coat. Dredge chicken pieces in flour mixture. Shake excess flour from chicken and transfer to wire rack. (Do not discard flour mixture.)

4. Adjust oven rack to middle position and heat oven to 200 degrees. Set second wire rack in second rimmed baking sheet. Add oil to large Dutch oven until it measures about 2 inches deep and heat over medium-high heat to 375 degrees. Return chicken pieces to flour mixture and turn to coat. Fry half of chicken, adjusting burner as necessary to maintain oil temperature between 300 and 325 degrees, until deep golden brown and breasts register 160 degrees and thighs and drumsticks register 175 degrees, 10 to 12 minutes. Transfer chicken to prepared baking sheet and place in oven. Return oil to 375 degrees and repeat with remaining chicken. Sprinkle crisp chicken with remaining 1 tablespoon spice mixture. Serve.

Secrets to Boldly Flavored Creole Fried Chicken

1. Soaking chicken in brine of sugar, Worcestershire, hot sauce, salt, and garlic powder seasons chicken fully.

2. After brining, home-made Creole seasoning adds flavor without dusty saltiness of packaged spice blends.

3. The homemade Creole seasoning also lends potent punch to chicken's flour coating.

4. For peppery finish, sprinkle hot chicken with more homemade Creole seasoning when it comes out of oil.

Why This Recipe Works Creole fried chicken recipes should turn out meat that is deeply seasoned with the complex, lively heat of black, white, and cayenne peppers. We built depth of flavor in our fried chicken with a three-step approach: After brining the chicken, we sprinkled it with homemade Creole seasoning for added flavor without the dusty saltiness of packaged spice blends. We also added seasoning to the chicken's flour coating to lend a potent punch. And for a peppery finish, we sprinkled the hot chicken with more seasoning when it came out of the oil.

Why This Recipe Works For fried chicken loaded with garlic flavor, we started by tossing a mix of chicken pieces in a marinade chock-full of both fresh and granulated garlic. We further reinforced our key flavor by dipping the parts in beaten egg whites and dredging them in flour boosted with more granulated garlic. After frying the chicken in peanut oil, we created a potent garlic-parsley butter that took the chicken's flavor right over the top.

GARLIC FRIED CHICKEN

SERVES 4

You will need at least a 6-quart Dutch oven for this recipe. Mince the garlic with a knife rather than with a garlic press.

Chicken
- 3 tablespoons extra-virgin olive oil
- 2 tablespoons granulated garlic
- 5 garlic cloves, minced
- Kosher salt and pepper
- 3 pounds bone-in chicken pieces (split breasts cut in half crosswise, drumsticks, thighs, and/or wings), trimmed
- 2 cups all-purpose flour
- 4 large egg whites
- 3 quarts peanut or vegetable oil

Garlic Butter
- 8 tablespoons unsalted butter, softened
- 2 tablespoons minced fresh parsley
- ¼ teaspoon kosher salt
- ¼ teaspoon pepper
- 8 garlic cloves, minced
- 1 tablespoon water

1. For the Chicken Combine olive oil, 1 tablespoon granulated garlic, minced garlic, 2 teaspoons salt, and 2 teaspoons pepper in large bowl. Add chicken and toss to thoroughly coat with garlic mixture. Cover with plastic wrap and refrigerate for at least 1 hour or up to 24 hours.

2. Set wire rack in rimmed baking sheet. Whisk flour, remaining 1 tablespoon granulated garlic, 2 teaspoons salt, and 2 teaspoons pepper together in separate bowl. Lightly beat egg whites together in shallow dish.

3. Remove chicken from marinade and brush away any solidified clumps of oil with paper towels. Working with 1 piece at a time, dip chicken into egg whites to thoroughly coat, letting excess drip back into dish; then dredge in flour mixture, pressing firmly to adhere. Transfer chicken to prepared wire rack and refrigerate, uncovered, for at least 30 minutes or up to 2 hours.

4. Set second wire rack in second rimmed baking sheet and line with triple layer of paper towels. Add peanut oil to large Dutch oven until it measures about 2 inches deep and heat over medium-high heat to 325 degrees. Add half of chicken to hot oil and fry until breasts register 160 degrees and drumsticks/thighs register 175 degrees, 13 to 16 minutes. Adjust burner, if necessary, to maintain oil temperature between 300 and 325 degrees. Transfer to paper towel–lined rack, return oil to 325 degrees, and repeat with remaining chicken.

5. For the Garlic Butter While chicken rests, combine 7 tablespoons butter, parsley, salt, and pepper in bowl; set aside. Melt remaining 1 tablespoon butter in 8-inch nonstick skillet over medium heat. Add garlic and water and cook, stirring frequently, until garlic is softened and fragrant, 1 to 2 minutes. Add hot garlic mixture to butter-parsley mixture and whisk until well combined.

6. Transfer chicken to platter and spoon garlic butter over top. Serve.

On the Road: Basque Cooking in California

Though it might seem out of place, Basque food is as comfortable in California as any other cuisine. Immigrants from the Basque lands—primarily the Pyrenees Mountains separating Spain and France—flooded California during the Gold Rush in the mid-19th century; when gold proved elusive, they turned to agriculture and shepherding in and around Bakersfield, California, which boasts one of the largest Basque populations in the United States.

During our visit to this region, we were struck by how the vibrant fare at the Pyrenees Cafe stands firmly against the city's ever-present heat. There we feasted on plates of garlic fried chicken, Basque-style green beans, cabbage and bean soup dotted with spicy salsa, thin slices of pickled veal tongue, and a few glasses of chilled house wine, before enjoying the customary Basque dessert: vanilla ice cream doused with red wine. Unusual, yes, but there are certainly worse ways to end a meal.

EXTRA-CRUNCHY FRIED CHICKEN

SERVES 4

Keeping the oil at the correct temperature is essential to producing crunchy fried chicken that is neither too brown nor too greasy. You will need at least a 6-quart Dutch oven for this recipe. If you want to produce a slightly lighter version of this recipe, you can remove the skin from the chicken before soaking it in the buttermilk. The chicken will be slightly less crunchy.

- 2 tablespoons salt
- 2 cups plus 6 tablespoons buttermilk
- 1 (3½-pound) whole chicken, cut into 8 pieces and trimmed (4 breast pieces, 2 drumsticks, 2 thighs), wings discarded
- 3 cups all-purpose flour
- 2 teaspoons baking powder
- ¾ teaspoon dried thyme
- ½ teaspoon pepper
- ¼ teaspoon garlic powder
- 1 quart peanut or vegetable oil

1. Dissolve salt in 2 cups buttermilk in large container. Submerge chicken in brine, cover, and refrigerate for 1 hour.

2. Whisk flour, baking powder, thyme, pepper, and garlic powder together in large bowl. Add remaining 6 tablespoons buttermilk; with your fingers rub flour and buttermilk together until buttermilk is evenly incorporated into flour and mixture resembles coarse, wet sand. Set wire rack inside rimmed baking sheet.

3. Dredge chicken pieces in flour mixture and turn to coat thoroughly, gently pressing flour mixture onto chicken. Shake excess flour from each piece of chicken and transfer to prepared baking sheet.

4. Line platter with triple layer of paper towels. Add oil to large Dutch oven until it measures about ¾ inch deep and heat over medium-high heat to 375 degrees. Place chicken pieces skin side down in oil, cover, and fry until deep golden brown, 8 to 10 minutes. Remove lid after 4 minutes and lift chicken pieces to check for even browning; rearrange if some pieces are browning faster than others. Adjust burner, if necessary, to maintain oil temperature between 300 and 315 degrees. Turn chicken pieces over and continue to fry, uncovered, until chicken pieces are deep golden brown on second side and breasts register 160 degrees and thighs and drumsticks register 175 degrees, 6 to 8 minutes. Using tongs, transfer chicken to prepared platter; let stand for 5 minutes. Serve.

EXTRA-SPICY, EXTRA-CRUNCHY FRIED CHICKEN

Add ¼ cup hot sauce to buttermilk-salt mixture in step 1. Replace dried thyme and garlic powder with 2 tablespoons cayenne pepper and 2 teaspoons chili powder in step 2.

Steps to an Extra-Crunchy Coating

1. Soak chicken in buttermilk-salt mixture.

2. Coat chicken with buttermilk-moistened flour.

3. Add chicken to hot oil and cover pot to capture steam.

4. Use tongs to flip chicken and finish cooking with cover off.

Why This Recipe Works For well-seasoned, extra-crunchy fried chicken we started by brining the chicken in heavily salted buttermilk. For the crunchy coating, we combined flour with a little baking powder, then added buttermilk to make a thick slurry, which clung tightly to the meat. Frying the chicken with the lid on the pot for half the cooking time contained the spatter-prone oil and kept it hot.

NASHVILLE HOT FRIED CHICKEN

SERVES 4 TO 6

Chicken quarters take longer to cook than smaller pieces. To ensure that the exterior doesn't burn before the inside cooks through, keep the oil temperature between 300 and 325 degrees while the chicken is frying. You will need at least a 6-quart Dutch oven for this recipe. Serve the chicken as they do in Nashville, on white bread with pickles.

Brine and Chicken
- ½ cup hot sauce
- ½ cup salt
- ½ cup sugar
- 1 (3½- to 4-pound) whole chicken, quartered

Coating
- 3 quarts peanut or vegetable oil
- 1 tablespoon cayenne pepper
- ½ teaspoon paprika
- ½ teaspoon sugar
- ¼ teaspoon garlic powder
-   Salt and pepper
- 2 cups all-purpose flour

1. For the Brine and Chicken Dissolve hot sauce, salt, and sugar in 2 quarts cold water in large container. Submerge chicken in brine, cover, and refrigerate for 30 minutes or up to 1 hour.

2. For the Coating Heat 3 tablespoons oil in small saucepan over medium heat until shimmering. Add cayenne, paprika, sugar, garlic powder, and ½ teaspoon salt and cook until fragrant, about 30 seconds. Transfer to small bowl.

3. Set wire rack in rimmed baking sheet. Remove chicken from brine and pat with paper towels. Combine flour, ½ teaspoon salt, and ½ teaspoon pepper in large bowl. Dredge chicken pieces two at a time in flour mixture. Shake excess flour from chicken and transfer to prepared baking sheet. (Do not discard seasoned flour.)

4. Adjust oven rack to middle position and heat oven to 200 degrees. Set second wire rack in second rimmed baking sheet. Add remaining oil to large Dutch oven until it measures about 2 inches deep and heat over medium-high heat to 350 degrees. Return chicken pieces to flour mixture and turn to coat. Fry half of chicken, adjusting burner as necessary to maintain oil temperature between 300 and 325 degrees, until deep golden brown and breast meat registers 160 degrees and legs register 175 degrees, 20 to 25 minutes. Drain chicken on prepared baking sheet and place in oven. Return oil to 350 degrees and repeat with remaining chicken. Stir spicy oil mixture to recombine and brush over both sides of chicken. Serve.

NASHVILLE EXTRA-HOT FRIED CHICKEN

For spiced oil in step 2, increase oil to ¼ cup, cayenne to 3½ tablespoons, and sugar to ¾ teaspoon and add 1 teaspoon dry mustard. Continue with recipe as directed.

Quartering a Chicken

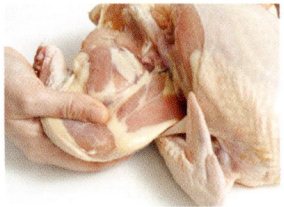

1. Slice between drumstick and breast. Use hands to bend back leg and pop out joint.

2. Cut through leg joint. Do not separate thigh from drumstick. Repeat steps 1 and 2 for other leg quarter.

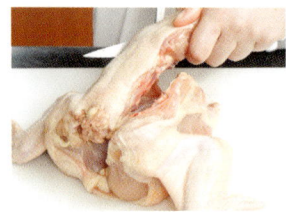

3. To separate breast from backbone, cut through ribs with kitchen shears on each side of backbone.

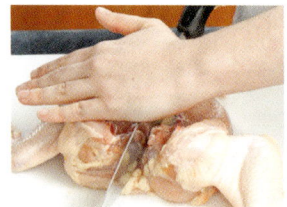

4. Cut through breastbone to separate breast and wing section into halves.

Why This Recipe Works Mimicking the heat of this Nashville hot fried chicken was harder than we anticipated. We created a spicy exterior to the chicken by "blooming" the spices (cooking them in oil for a short period) to create a complex yet still lip-burning spicy flavor. We also added a healthy amount of hot sauce to our brine to inject spicy flavor into the chicken, making the flavor more than skin deep.

Why This Recipe Works Hot oil is the key to crunchy fried chicken, but it can be deadly to fresh herbs. To get the flavors to last throughout the frying process, the key was to fry for as little time as possible. Thin boneless chicken thighs took half the time to fry than bone-in chicken parts required, which allowed the fresh herb flavors to flourish. Also, thighs are cheaper to purchase. After a few tests, we settled on a three-part technique for the chives, dill, and cilantro; we added them to the tangy buttermilk dip, the flour coating, and the dipping sauce. This triple punch provided the classic aroma and flavor we know and love as "ranch."

RANCH FRIED CHICKEN

SERVES 4 TO 6

You will need at least a 6-quart Dutch oven for this recipe.

Chicken
- 8 (5- to 7-ounce) boneless, skinless chicken thighs, trimmed
- Salt and pepper
- 2 quarts peanut or vegetable oil

Buttermilk Mixture
- 1 cup buttermilk
- 2 tablespoons minced fresh chives
- 2 tablespoons minced fresh cilantro
- 2 teaspoons minced fresh dill
- 2 teaspoons distilled white vinegar
- 1 garlic clove, minced
- ½ teaspoon salt
- Pinch cayenne pepper

Coating
- 1¼ cups all-purpose flour
- ½ cup cornstarch
- 3 tablespoons minced fresh chives
- 3 tablespoons minced fresh cilantro
- 1 tablespoon minced fresh dill
- 1½ teaspoons garlic powder
- 1½ teaspoons salt
- ¾ teaspoon pepper

Ranch Sauce
- ½ cup mayonnaise
- Salt and pepper

1. For the Chicken Pat chicken dry with paper towels and season with salt and pepper.

2. For the Buttermilk Mixture Whisk all ingredients together in bowl. Set aside ¼ cup buttermilk mixture for ranch sauce.

3. For the Coating Whisk all ingredients together in large bowl.

4. Set wire rack in rimmed baking sheet. Set second wire rack in second rimmed baking sheet and line half of rack with triple layer of paper towels.

5. Working with 1 piece at a time, dip chicken in remaining buttermilk mixture to coat, letting excess drip back into bowl; then dredge in coating, pressing to adhere. Transfer chicken to first wire rack (without paper towels). (At this point, coated chicken may be refrigerated, uncovered, for up to 2 hours.)

6. Heat oil in large Dutch oven over medium-high heat until it reaches 350 degrees. Add half of chicken to hot oil and fry until golden brown and registers 175 degrees, 7 to 9 minutes. Adjust burner, if necessary, to maintain oil temperature between 325 and 350 degrees.

7. Transfer chicken to paper towel–lined side of second wire rack to drain on each side for 30 seconds, then move to unlined side of rack. Return oil to 350 degrees and repeat with remaining chicken.

8. For the Ranch Sauce Whisk mayonnaise into reserved buttermilk mixture. Season with salt and pepper to taste.

9. Transfer chicken to platter and serve with ranch sauce.

Key Ingredients: Three Herbs, Three Ways

We use the defining herbs of ranch flavor—dill, chives, and cilantro—in three ways for this chicken: in the buttermilk dip, in the flour coating, and in the serving sauce.

Why This Recipe Works Some chicken nuggets recipes take the least desirable parts of the chicken and put them through a grinder. We opted for boneless, skinless chicken breasts. Brining the chicken prevented it from drying out, and seasoning the breast meat combated its inherently bland flavor. Ground-up panko (Japanese-style bread crumbs) combined with flour and a pinch of baking soda provided a crispy brown exterior for our nuggets. Using whole eggs to adhere the coating made the nuggets too eggy. Egg whites alone didn't have enough binding power, but we found that resting the nuggets before frying solved the problem.

CHICKEN NUGGETS

SERVES 4 TO 6

Do not brine the chicken longer than 30 minutes or it will be too salty. To crush the bread crumbs, place them inside a zipper-lock bag and lightly beat it with a rolling pin. You will need at least a 6-quart Dutch oven for this recipe. This recipe doubles easily and freezes well.

- 4 (6-ounce) boneless, skinless chicken breasts, trimmed
- 2 cups water
- 2 tablespoons Worcestershire sauce
  Salt and pepper
- 1 cup all-purpose flour
- 1 cup panko bread crumbs, crushed
- 2 teaspoons onion powder
- ½ teaspoon garlic powder
- ½ teaspoon baking soda
- 3 large egg whites
- 1 quart peanut or vegetable oil
- 1 recipe dipping sauce (recipes follow)

1. Cut each chicken breast diagonally into thirds, then cut each third diagonally into ½-inch-thick pieces. Whisk water, Worcestershire, and 1 tablespoon salt in large bowl until salt dissolves. Add chicken pieces, cover, and refrigerate for 30 minutes.

2. Remove chicken from brine and pat dry with paper towels. Combine flour, panko, onion powder, 1 teaspoon salt, ¾ teaspoon pepper, garlic powder, and baking soda in shallow dish. Whisk egg whites in second shallow dish until foamy. Coat half of chicken with egg whites and dredge in flour mixture, pressing gently to adhere. Transfer to plate and repeat with remaining chicken (don't discard flour mixture). Let sit for 10 minutes.

3. Adjust oven rack to middle position and heat oven to 200 degrees. Set wire rack in rimmed baking sheet. Add oil to large Dutch oven until it measures about ¾ inch deep and heat over medium-high heat to 350 degrees. Return chicken pieces to flour mixture and turn to coat, pressing flour mixture gently to adhere. Fry half of chicken until deep golden brown, about 3 minutes, turning halfway through cooking. Transfer chicken to prepared baking sheet and place in oven. Return oil to 350 degrees and repeat with remaining chicken. Serve with dipping sauce.

To Make Ahead Let fried nuggets cool, transfer to zipper-lock bag, and freeze for up to 1 month. To serve, adjust oven rack to middle position and heat oven to 350 degrees. Place nuggets on rimmed baking sheet and bake, flipping once, until heated through, about 15 minutes.

HONEY-MUSTARD SAUCE
MAKES ¾ CUP

- ½ cup yellow mustard
- ⅓ cup honey
  Salt and pepper

Whisk mustard and honey in medium bowl until smooth. Season with salt and pepper to taste.

SWEET AND SOUR SAUCE
MAKES ¾ CUP

- ¾ cup apple, apricot, or hot pepper jelly
- 1 tablespoon white vinegar
- ½ teaspoon soy sauce
- ⅛ teaspoon garlic powder
  Pinch ground ginger
  Pinch cayenne pepper
  Salt and pepper

Whisk jelly, vinegar, soy sauce, garlic powder, ginger, and cayenne in medium bowl until smooth. Season with salt and pepper to taste.

DELTA HOT TAMALES

SERVES 6 TO 8

Use a saucepan that holds 4 quarts or more, with at least 5-inch sides. Corn husks can be found in the international aisle of grocery stores.

- 24 corn husks
- 1½ tablespoons chili powder
- 1 tablespoon paprika
- 1 tablespoon salt
- 2 teaspoons ground cumin
- 2 teaspoons sugar
- ¾ teaspoon pepper
- ¾ teaspoon cayenne pepper
- 2½ cups (12½ ounces) yellow cornmeal
- 1 tablespoon baking powder
- 12 tablespoons unsalted butter, cut into 12 pieces
- ½ teaspoon baking soda
- 1 pound 85 percent lean ground beef
- 2 garlic cloves, minced
- 2 tablespoons cornstarch combined with 2 tablespoons cold water

1. Place husks in large bowl and cover with hot water; soak until pliable, about 30 minutes. Combine chili powder, paprika, salt, cumin, sugar, pepper, and cayenne in bowl.

2. Pulse cornmeal and baking powder in food processor until combined, about 3 pulses. Add butter and 1½ tablespoons spice mixture and pulse to chop butter into small pieces, about 8 pulses. Add 1¼ cups water and process until dough forms, about 30 seconds. Reserve ½ cup cornmeal mixture. Divide remaining cornmeal mixture into 24 equal portions, about 1½ tablespoons each, and place on plate.

3. Dissolve baking soda in 2 tablespoons water in large bowl. Add beef, garlic, reserved ½ cup cornmeal mixture, and 1½ tablespoons spice mixture and knead with your hands until thoroughly combined. Divide meat mixture into 24 equal portions, about 1½ tablespoons each, and place on plate.

4. Remove husks from water and pat dry with dish towel. Working with 1 husk at a time, lay husk on counter, smooth side up, with long side parallel to counter edge and wide end oriented toward right. Using small offset spatula, spread 1 portion of cornmeal mixture in 3½-inch square over lower right corner of husk, flush to bottom edge but leaving ¼-inch border on right edge.

5. Place 1 portion of meat mixture in log across center of cornmeal (end to end), parallel to long side of husk. Roll husk away from you and over meat mixture so cornmeal mixture surrounds meat and forms cylinder; continue rolling to complete tamale. Fold tapered end (left side) of tamale up leaving top open. Using scissors, trim tapered end of tamale to align with filled end (if tapered end hangs over). Set tamales aside seam side down.

6. Stack tamales on their sides in groups of 6 and tie into bundles with kitchen twine. Add remaining 2 tablespoons spice mixture to large saucepan. Stand tamales, open ends up, in pot (walls of pot should clear tops of tamales). Add about 5½ cups water to pot to come within 1 inch of tops of tamales, being careful not to pour water into tamales.

7. Bring tamales to boil. Cover, reduce heat to low to maintain gentle simmer, and cook until tamales are firm and beginning to pull away from husks, about 30 minutes. Using tongs and slotted spoon, carefully transfer tamales to serving platter and remove twine.

8. Return liquid to simmer over medium heat. Whisk in cornstarch slurry and cook until slightly thickened, about 1 minute. Serve sauce with tamales.

Cooking with Corn Husks

Cooking the tamales in corn husks—which are available in most supermarkets near the dried chiles—adds a subtle depth of flavor. Working with the husks is actually quite easy, as they become pliable when soaked in hot water.

Why This Recipe Works Hot tamales—rich, spicy meat wrapped in flavorful corn dough—are a favorite in the Mississippi delta. A bit of this cornmeal mixture stirred into the uncooked ground beef kept the filling moist and baking soda was the trick for a more tender bite. We used butter instead of the traditional lard with coarsely ground cornmeal for a more balanced taste. We cooked the tamales in groups of six for more stability in the pot and made a spicy, glazy sauce with the seasoned stewing liquid and a cornstarch slurry. This was as close as we could come to being in the delta without a plane ticket.

Why This Recipe Works Our biggest challenge in making gumbo was finding an easier way to prepare the dark brown roux, the fat and flour paste that thickens the stew and adds flavor. We created a relatively hands-off roux by toasting the flour on the stovetop, adding the oil, and finishing the roux in the oven. For the soup base, we started by making our own shrimp stock, but the process was time-consuming. Instead, we switched to store-bought chicken broth fortified with fish sauce. Tasters preferred meaty chicken thighs to breasts because they had more flavor.

GUMBO

SERVES 6 TO 8

A heavy cast-iron Dutch oven yields the fastest oven roux. If a lightweight pot is all you've got, increase the oven time by 10 minutes. The chicken broth must be at room temperature to prevent lumps from forming. Fish sauce lends an essential savory quality. Since the salt content of fish sauce varies among brands, taste the finished gumbo before seasoning with salt.

- ¾ cup plus 1 tablespoon all-purpose flour
- ½ cup vegetable oil
- 1 onion, chopped fine
- 1 green bell pepper, stemmed, seeded, and chopped
- 1 celery rib, chopped fine
- 5 garlic cloves, minced
- 1 teaspoon minced fresh thyme
- ¼ teaspoon cayenne pepper
- 1 (14.5-ounce) can diced tomatoes, drained
- 3¾ cups chicken broth, room temperature
- ¼ cup fish sauce
- 2 pounds bone-in chicken thighs, skin removed, trimmed
  Salt and pepper
- 8 ounces andouille sausage, halved lengthwise and sliced thin
- 2 cups frozen okra, thawed (optional)
- 2 pounds extra-large shrimp (21 to 25 per pound), peeled and deveined

1. Adjust oven rack to lowest position and heat oven to 350 degrees. Toast ¾ cup flour in Dutch oven over medium heat, stirring constantly, until just beginning to brown, about 5 minutes. Off heat, whisk in oil until smooth. Cover, transfer pot to oven, and cook until mixture is deep brown and fragrant, about 45 minutes. (Roux can be refrigerated for 1 week. To use, heat in Dutch oven over medium-high heat, whisking constantly, until just smoking, and continue with step 2.)

2. Transfer Dutch oven to stovetop and whisk cooked roux to combine. Add onion, bell pepper, and celery and cook over medium heat, stirring frequently, until vegetables are softened, about 10 minutes. Stir in remaining 1 tablespoon flour, garlic, thyme, and cayenne and cook until fragrant, about 1 minute. Add tomatoes and cook until dry, about 1 minute. Slowly whisk in broth and fish sauce until smooth. Season chicken with pepper. Add chicken to vegetable mixture and bring to boil.

3. Reduce heat to medium-low and simmer, covered, until chicken is tender, about 30 minutes. Skim fat and transfer chicken to plate. When chicken is cool enough to handle, cut into bite-size pieces and return to pot; discard bones.

4. Stir in sausage and okra, if using, and simmer until heated through, about 5 minutes. Add shrimp and simmer until cooked through, about 5 minutes. Season with salt and pepper to taste. Serve. (Gumbo can be refrigerated for 1 day.)

To Make Ahead Gumbo can be made through step 3 and refrigerated for 3 days. To serve, bring gumbo to simmer, covered, in Dutch oven. Remove lid and proceed with recipe as directed.

Newcomer to the Bayou

Asian fish sauce? Admittedly, it's an unconventional idea. And here's the cool part: New Orleans has a well-established Vietnamese community; it began after the fall of Saigon. As far as we know, we're the first to put fish sauce in gumbo, but there's no question that these new immigrants to New Orleans are having an impact on the city's storied food traditions: They've tossed lemon grass into crawfish boils, organized a farmers' market with such exotic items as *ngo gai* (an herb), banana buds, and longan fruit, and put the *banh mi* sandwich on the city's must-eat food list, right there next to the city's signature po' boys.

NEW ORLEANS BARBECUE SHRIMP

SERVES 4

Although authentic barbecue shrimp is always made with shell-on shrimp, peeled and deveined shrimp may be used. Light- or medium-bodied beers work best here. Serve with Tabasco sauce and French bread, if desired.

- 2 pounds extra-large (21 to 25 per pound) shrimp
- ½ teaspoon salt
- ½ teaspoon cayenne pepper
- 2 tablespoons vegetable oil
- 6 tablespoons unsalted butter, cut into 6 pieces
- 2 teaspoons all-purpose flour
- 1 teaspoon tomato paste
- 1 teaspoon minced fresh rosemary
- 1 teaspoon minced fresh thyme
- ½ teaspoon dried oregano
- 3 garlic cloves, minced
- ¾ cup bottled clam juice
- ½ cup beer
- 1 tablespoon Worcestershire sauce

1. Pat shrimp dry with paper towels and sprinkle with salt and cayenne. Heat 1 tablespoon oil in large skillet over medium-high heat until just smoking. Cook half of shrimp, without moving, until spotty brown on one side, about 1 minute; transfer to large plate. Repeat with remaining oil and shrimp.

2. Melt 1 tablespoon butter in empty skillet over medium heat. Add flour, tomato paste, rosemary, thyme, oregano, and garlic and cook until fragrant, about 30 seconds. Stir in clam juice, beer, and Worcestershire, scraping up any browned bits, and bring to boil. Return shrimp and any accumulated juices to skillet. Reduce heat to medium-low and simmer, covered, until shrimp are cooked through, about 2 minutes. Off heat, stir in remaining butter until incorporated. Serve.

Not Your Average Barbecue Sauce

Barbecue sauce conjures up an image of a thick, sticky tomato-based mop, but New Orleans Barbecue Shrimp is bathed in a spicy herbed butter sauce made with these ingredients.

CLAM JUICE
The briny bite makes a simple replacement for fish stock.

BEER
The mellow, slightly hoppy bitterness balances the rich butter.

WORCESTERSHIRE
Often used to add bold, ultrasavory flavor to dishes.

BUTTER
Adding butter twice makes a rich, satiny sauce.

Why This Recipe Works Named for the "barbecue" color rather than the cooking method, this New Orleans skillet shrimp dish relies on a velvety, butter-based sauce to flavor shell-on shrimp. To achieve perfectly cooked shrimp, we started by searing them first to partially cook them and then later returned the shrimp to the finished sauce to gently cook through. By using a roux to thicken the sauce and sautéing the aromatics with tomato paste, we were able to create a silky, flavorful sauce that clung perfectly to the shrimp. We replaced time-consuming seafood stock with bottled clam juice, a technique the test kitchen has used before.

SHRIMP AND GRITS

SERVES 4

We prefer untreated shrimp—those without added sodium or preservatives like sodium tripolyphosphate. Most frozen E-Z peel shrimp have been treated (the ingredient list should tell you). If you're using treated shrimp, do not add the salt in step 4. If you use our winning grits (Anson Mills Pencil Cob) or other fresh-milled grits, you will need to increase the simmering time by 25 minutes.

Grits
- 3 tablespoons unsalted butter
- 1 cup grits
- 2¼ cups whole milk
- 2 cups water
- Salt and pepper

Shrimp
- 3 tablespoons unsalted butter
- 1½ pounds extra-large shrimp (21 to 25 per pound), peeled and deveined, shells reserved
- 1 tablespoon tomato paste
- 2¼ cups water
- 3 slices bacon, cut into ½-inch pieces
- 1 garlic clove, minced
- Salt and pepper
- 2 tablespoons all-purpose flour
- 1 tablespoon lemon juice
- ½ teaspoon Tabasco sauce, plus extra for serving
- 4 scallions, sliced thin

1. For the Grits Melt 1 tablespoon butter in medium saucepan over medium heat. Add grits and cook, stirring often, until fragrant, about 3 minutes. Add milk, water, and ¾ teaspoon salt. Increase heat to medium-high and bring to boil. Reduce heat to low, cover, and simmer, whisking often, until thick and creamy, about 25 minutes. Remove from heat, stir in remaining 2 tablespoons butter, and season with salt and pepper to taste. Cover and keep warm.

2. For the Shrimp Meanwhile, melt 1 tablespoon butter in 12-inch nonstick skillet over medium heat. Add shrimp shells and cook, stirring occasionally, until shells are spotty brown, about 7 minutes. Stir in tomato paste and cook for 30 seconds. Add water and bring to boil. Reduce heat to low, cover, and simmer for 5 minutes.

3. Strain shrimp stock through fine-mesh strainer set over bowl, pressing on solids to extract as much liquid as possible; discard solids. You should have about 1½ cups stock (add more water if necessary to equal 1½ cups). Wipe out skillet with paper towels.

4. Cook bacon in now-empty skillet over medium-low heat until crisp, 7 to 9 minutes. Increase heat to medium-high and stir in shrimp, garlic, ½ teaspoon salt, and ½ teaspoon pepper. Cook until edges of shrimp are just beginning to turn pink, but shrimp are not cooked through, about 2 minutes. Transfer shrimp mixture to bowl.

5. Melt 1 tablespoon butter in now-empty skillet over medium-high heat. Whisk in flour and cook for 1 minute. Slowly whisk in shrimp stock until incorporated. Bring to boil, reduce heat to medium-low, and simmer until thickened slightly, about 5 minutes.

6. Stir in shrimp mixture, cover, and cook until shrimp are cooked through, about 3 minutes. Off heat, stir in lemon juice, Tabasco, and remaining 1 tablespoon butter. Season with salt and pepper to taste. Serve over grits, sprinkled with scallions, and passing extra Tabasco.

Fresh versus Frozen
Just because shrimp are raw at the store doesn't mean they're fresh; roughly 90 percent of the shrimp sold in the United States comes from outside the country. So unless you live near a coastal area, you can bet the shrimp you're seeing were frozen and then defrosted. The problem is, once shrimp have been defrosted, their quality deteriorates quickly—and there is no way of telling how long they've been sitting in the case. We prefer to buy frozen shrimp and defrost them ourselves.

Why This Recipe Works Many modern versions of this Carolina favorite add too many frills. We set out to bring it back to basics: tender shrimp, silky sauce, and creamy grits. To avoid overcooking the shrimp, we lightly sautéed them in rendered bacon fat and set them aside while creating a flavorful sauce in the same skillet. We used the shrimp shells to make the stock that formed the base of our sauce. To finish cooking, we added the shrimp back into the sauce. Toasting the grits in butter helped coax the most corn flavor out of them before we added more-than-usual liquid. A sprinkle of chopped scallions added a fresh finish to the dish.

Why This Recipe Works Perloo (pronounced "PUHR-low"), a staple in South Carolina's Low Country, is a tomatoey rice dish simmered in broth. To start, we went the classic route and used reserved shrimp shells to create and flavor shrimp stock, which is surprisingly easy and practical to make from scratch. For the rice, we stuck to the traditional flavor base of onions, celery, and bell pepper. Sautéing the rice with the vegetables firmed up the grains' exterior and prevented mushiness. Just before removing the rice from the heat, we folded in the shrimp and let them rest, covered, for perfectly cooked shrimp and tender rice in a delicious one-pot meal.

CHARLESTON SHRIMP PERLOO

SERVES 4 TO 6

After adding the shrimp to the pot, fold it in gently; stirring the rice too vigorously will make it mushy. Any extra stock can be refrigerated for 3 days or frozen for up to 1 month. Serve with hot sauce.

- 5 tablespoons unsalted butter
- 1½ pounds extra-large shrimp (21 to 25 per pound), peeled and deveined, shells reserved
- 2 onions, chopped
- 4 celery ribs, chopped
- Salt
- 4 cups water
- 1 tablespoon peppercorns
- 5 sprigs fresh parsley
- 2 bay leaves
- 1 green bell pepper, stemmed, seeded, and chopped
- 2 cups long-grain white rice
- 2 garlic cloves, minced
- 1 teaspoon minced fresh thyme
- ¼ teaspoon cayenne pepper
- 1 (14.5-ounce) can diced tomatoes

1. Melt 1 tablespoon butter in large saucepan over medium heat. Add shrimp shells, 1 cup onion, ½ cup celery, and 1 teaspoon salt and cook, stirring occasionally, until shells are spotty brown, about 10 minutes. Add water, peppercorns, parsley, and bay leaves. Increase heat to high and bring to boil. Reduce heat to low, cover, and simmer for 30 minutes. Strain shrimp stock through fine-mesh strainer set over large bowl, pressing on solids to extract as much liquid as possible; discard solids.

2. Melt remaining 4 tablespoons butter in Dutch oven over medium heat. Add bell pepper, remaining onion and celery, and ½ teaspoon salt and cook until vegetables are beginning to soften, 5 to 7 minutes. Add rice, garlic, thyme, and cayenne and cook until fragrant and rice is translucent, about 2 minutes. Stir in tomatoes and their juice and 3 cups shrimp stock (reserve remainder for another use) and bring to boil. Reduce heat to low, cover, and cook for 20 minutes.

3. Gently fold shrimp into rice until evenly distributed, cover, and continue to cook 5 minutes longer. Remove pot from heat and let sit, covered, until shrimp are cooked through and all liquid is absorbed, about 10 minutes. Serve.

Peeling and Deveining Shrimp

1. Break shell under swimming legs, which will come off as shell is removed. Leave tail intact if desired, or tug tail to remove shell.

2. Use paring knife to make shallow cut along back of shrimp to expose vein. Use tip of knife to lift out vein. Discard vein by wiping blade against paper towel.

Why This Recipe Works This Italian sandwich is a New Orleans classic, and we wanted to do it justice. We started by inspecting Central Grocery's famous olive salad. Then we got to work on our own version and found that combining olives, capers, giardiniera, garlic, herbs, and spices gave us the salty, tangy mixture we wanted. We baked store-bought pizza dough into perfect puffy rounds, which we sprinkled with sesame seeds. Alternating layers of meats and cheese gave our sandwich stability, making it easier to eat. Lastly, we pressed the assembled sandwiches for an hour to allow the olive salad to properly soak into the bread.

NEW ORLEANS MUFFULETTAS

SERVES 8

You will need one 16-ounce jar of giardiniera to yield 2 cups drained; our favorite brand is Pastene. If you like a spicier sandwich, increase the amount of pepper flakes to ½ teaspoon.

- 2 (1-pound) balls pizza dough
- 2 cups drained jarred giardiniera
- 1 cup pimento-stuffed green olives
- ½ cup pitted kalamata olives
- 2 tablespoons capers, rinsed
- 1 tablespoon red wine vinegar
- 1 garlic clove, minced
- ½ teaspoon dried oregano
- ¼ teaspoon red pepper flakes
- ¼ teaspoon dried thyme
- ½ cup extra-virgin olive oil
- ¼ cup chopped fresh parsley
- 1 large egg, lightly beaten
- 5 teaspoons sesame seeds
- 4 ounces thinly sliced Genoa salami
- 6 ounces thinly sliced aged provolone cheese
- 6 ounces thinly sliced mortadella
- 4 ounces thinly sliced hot capicola

1. Form dough balls into 2 tight round balls on oiled baking sheet, cover loosely with greased plastic wrap, and let sit at room temperature for 1 hour.

2. Meanwhile, pulse giardiniera, green olives, kalamata olives, capers, vinegar, garlic, oregano, pepper flakes, and thyme in food processor until coarsely chopped, about 6 pulses, scraping down sides of bowl as needed. Transfer to bowl and stir in oil and parsley. Let sit at room temperature for 30 minutes. (Olive salad can be refrigerated for up to 1 week.)

3. Adjust oven rack to middle position and heat oven to 425 degrees. Keeping dough balls on sheet, flatten each into 7-inch disk. Brush tops of disks with egg and sprinkle with sesame seeds. Bake until golden brown and loaves sound hollow when tapped, 18 to 20 minutes, rotating sheet halfway through baking. Transfer loaves to wire rack and let cool completely, about 1 hour. (Loaves can be wrapped in plastic and stored at room temperature for up to 24 hours.)

4. Slice loaves in half horizontally. Spread one-fourth of olive salad on cut side of each loaf top and bottom, pressing firmly with rubber spatula to compact. Layer 2 ounces salami, 1½ ounces provolone, 3 ounces mortadella, 1½ ounces provolone, and 2 ounces capicola in order on each loaf bottom. Cap with loaf tops and individually wrap sandwiches tightly in plastic.

5. Place baking sheet on top of sandwiches and weigh down with heavy Dutch oven or two 5-pound bags of flour or sugar for 1 hour, flipping sandwiches halfway through pressing. Unwrap and slice each sandwich into quarters and serve. (Pressed, wrapped sandwiches can be refrigerated for up to 24 hours. Bring to room temperature before serving.)

A Weighty Solution

If you don't have a heavy Dutch oven, use two 5-pound bags of flour or sugar to weigh down the wrapped muffulettas.

Pressing the assembled sandwiches for an hour helps the olive salad properly soak into the bread.

CHINESE CHICKEN SALAD

SERVES 6

You can substitute 1 minced clove of garlic and ¼ teaspoon of cayenne pepper for the Asian chili-garlic sauce.

- 2 oranges
- ¼ cup rice vinegar
- ¼ cup soy sauce
- 3 tablespoons grated fresh ginger
- 3 tablespoons sugar
- 1 tablespoon Asian chili-garlic sauce
- 3 tablespoons vegetable oil
- 2 tablespoons toasted sesame oil
- 4 (6- to 8-ounce) boneless, skinless chicken breasts, trimmed
- 2 romaine lettuce hearts (12 ounces), sliced thin
- ½ small head napa cabbage, cored and sliced thin (6 cups)
- 2 red bell peppers, stemmed, seeded, and cut into 2-inch-long matchsticks
- 1 cup fresh cilantro leaves
- 1 cup salted, dry-roasted peanuts, chopped
- 6 scallions, sliced thin

1. Cut thin slice from top and bottom of each orange, exposing fruit. Slice off rind and pith, cutting from top to bottom. Working over bowl, cut orange segments from thin membrane and transfer segments to second bowl; set aside. Squeeze juice from membrane into first bowl (juice should measure ¼ cup).

2. Combine orange juice, vinegar, soy sauce, ginger, sugar, and chili-garlic sauce in bowl. Transfer ½ cup of orange juice mixture to 12-inch skillet. Slowly whisk vegetable oil and sesame oil into remaining orange juice mixture to make vinaigrette; set aside.

3. Bring orange juice mixture in skillet to boil. Add chicken, reduce heat to medium-low, cover, and simmer until meat registers 160 degrees, 10 to 15 minutes, flipping halfway through cooking. Transfer chicken to plate and let rest for 5 to 10 minutes.

4. Meanwhile, boil pan juices until reduced to ¼ cup, 1 to 3 minutes, and set aside. Using 2 forks, shred chicken into bite-size pieces. Off heat, add chicken, any accumulated juices, and 2 tablespoons vinaigrette to skillet. Toss to coat and let sit for 10 minutes.

5. Toss lettuce, cabbage, bell peppers, cilantro, peanuts, and scallions with remaining vinaigrette in large bowl. Transfer to serving platter and top with chicken and oranges. Serve.

Shopping for Aromatic Asian Ingredients

Consider keeping these three versatile ingredients on hand to add authentic Asian flavor to a variety of dishes, including our Chinese Chicken Salad.

RICE VINEGAR
This Japanese vinegar is sweet and mild.

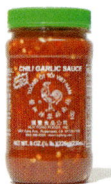

ASIAN CHILI-GARLIC SAUCE
If you like garlic and heat, you'll reach for this bottle often.

TOASTED SESAME OIL
This aromatic, boldly flavored oil is made from roasted sesame seeds. Its flavor doesn't hold up to cooking, so add it off heat.

Why This Recipe Works We aimed to give this stale chain restaurant classic a fresh makeover. The salad-bar pile ons, from chow mein noodles to snow peas to water chestnuts, got the ax. Instead, we started with crisp romaine lettuce, napa cabbage, bell peppers, cilantro, and scallions. To keep the chicken from tasting like an afterthought, we eschewed rotisserie chicken. We poached boneless, skinless chicken breasts in a flavorful mixture of soy sauce, orange juice, rice vinegar, and ginger, setting aside some of the mixture to whisk with sesame and vegetable oils for a bold dressing. We finished the dish with fresh oranges and roasted peanuts.

Why This Recipe Works Like many dishes you'll find in America's Chinese restaurants, chow mein has deep roots in China, where chao mian ("fried noodles") has been around for centuries. But this takeout standard often features dry meat and a bland, pasty sauce. To help the chicken retain moisture, we soaked sliced chicken in water and baking soda followed by a quick soak in Chinese rice wine and cornstarch. For the chow mein's sauce, oyster sauce added meaty notes, and more rice wine added sweet brightness. To avoid a gloppy sauce, we used just a bit of cornstarch as thickener then added plenty of bean sprouts for fresh crunch.

CHICKEN CHOW MEIN

SERVES 4

Purchase thin, round fresh Chinese egg noodles, not flat and/or dried noodles, or substitute 6 ounces of dried chow mein, ramen, or wheat vermicelli.

- 1 (9-ounce) package fresh Chinese noodles
- 1 tablespoon toasted sesame oil
- 1 teaspoon baking soda
- 2 (6-ounce) boneless, skinless chicken breasts, trimmed and cut crosswise into $\frac{1}{4}$-inch-thick slices
- 3 tablespoons Chinese rice wine or dry sherry
- 1 tablespoon cornstarch
- $\frac{1}{2}$ cup chicken broth
- 3 tablespoons soy sauce
- 3 tablespoons oyster sauce
- $\frac{1}{4}$ teaspoon white pepper
- 2 tablespoons vegetable oil
- 6 ounces shiitake mushrooms, stemmed and sliced thin
- 1 carrot, peeled and cut into 2-inch matchsticks
- 2 celery ribs, cut on bias into $\frac{1}{4}$-inch-thick slices
- 4 scallions, white and green parts separated and sliced thin
- 3 garlic cloves, minced
- 1 tablespoon grated fresh ginger
- 4 ounces (2 cups) mung bean sprouts

1. Bring 4 quarts water to boil in large pot. Add noodles to boiling water and cook until tender, 2 to 4 minutes. Drain noodles, rinse thoroughly with cold water, then drain again. Toss noodles with sesame oil in bowl; set aside.

2. Meanwhile, dissolve baking soda in $\frac{1}{2}$ cup cold water in bowl. Add chicken and let sit at room temperature for 15 minutes. Drain chicken, rinse under cold water, then drain again. Pat chicken dry with paper towels. Combine 1 tablespoon rice wine, 2 teaspoons cornstarch, and chicken in bowl; set aside.

3. Whisk broth, soy sauce, oyster sauce, pepper, remaining 2 tablespoons rice wine, and remaining 1 teaspoon cornstarch together in bowl; set aside.

4. Heat oil in 12-inch nonstick skillet over high heat until just smoking. Add chicken and cook, stirring frequently, until opaque, about 2 minutes. Add mushrooms and carrot and cook, stirring frequently, until tender, about 2 minutes. Add celery and cook until crisp-tender, about 1 minute. Add scallion whites, garlic, and ginger and cook until fragrant, about 30 seconds.

5. Whisk broth mixture to recombine, then add to skillet and cook until thickened and chicken is cooked through, about 2 minutes. Add bean sprouts and noodles and toss until sauce evenly coats noodles, about 1 minute. Transfer to platter and sprinkle with scallion greens. Serve.

Fresh Egg Noodles

You'll find chow mein in Chinese restaurants prepared with wheat noodles, Italian pastas, ramen noodles, or egg noodles. But our tasters preferred fresh Chinese egg noodles, available in the Asian section of most grocery stores.

SLOW-COOKER CHINESE BARBECUED PORK

SERVES 8

Pork butt roast is often labeled Boston butt in the supermarket. Look for five-spice powder and hoisin sauce in the international aisle at your supermarket.

- 1½ teaspoons salt
- 1½ teaspoons five-spice powder
- ½ teaspoon pepper
- 1 (5- to 6-pound) boneless pork butt roast, trimmed and sliced crosswise into 1-inch-thick steaks
- ⅓ cup hoisin sauce
- ⅓ cup honey
- ¼ cup sugar
- ¼ cup soy sauce
- ¼ cup ketchup
- 2 tablespoons dry sherry
- 1 tablespoon toasted sesame oil
- 1 tablespoon grated fresh ginger
- 2 garlic cloves, minced

1. Combine salt, ¾ teaspoon five-spice powder, and pepper in bowl. Rub spice mixture all over pork and transfer to slow cooker. Cover and cook on low until pork is just tender, 5 to 6 hours.

2. When pork is nearly done, combine hoisin, honey, sugar, soy sauce, ketchup, sherry, oil, ginger, garlic, and remaining ¾ teaspoon five-spice powder in bowl. Set wire rack inside aluminum foil–lined rimmed baking sheet. Pour 1 cup water into sheet. Adjust oven rack 4 inches from broiler element and heat broiler.

3. Using tongs, transfer pork from slow cooker to prepared wire rack in single layer. Brush pork with one-third of hoisin mixture and broil until lightly caramelized, 5 to 7 minutes. Flip pork, brush with half of remaining hoisin mixture, and broil until lightly caramelized on second side, 5 to 7 minutes. Brush pork with remaining hoisin mixture and broil until deep mahogany and crispy around edges, about 3 minutes. Transfer to carving board and let rest for 10 minutes. Slice crosswise into thin strips. Serve.

Pork Butt (Blade Shoulder)

This large, flavorful cut (often labeled Boston butt or pork shoulder at supermarkets) can weigh as much as 8 pounds when sold with the bone in. Many markets take out the bone and sell this cut in smaller chunks, often wrapped in netting to hold the roast together. This cut is ideal for slow roasting, barbecuing, stewing, or braising.

Why This Recipe Works Unlike what we typically think of as barbecue, Chinese barbecued pork is made neither on a grill nor in a smoker: It's usually cooked (and then glazed) in an oven. But we made this dish even more convenient—by adapting it to the slow cooker. Boneless pork butt renders lots of flavorful fat and pork juices as it cooks. Because this fat diluted any sauce we tried, we instead used a dry rub and then cooked the pork with a glazy sauce under the broiler. The finished "barbecued" pork was tender with a shiny, slightly charred exterior that tasted even better than it looked, earning it the nickname "meat candy" in the test kitchen.

PATTY MELTS

SERVES 4

To make sure the melts hold together, use rye bread that's sliced about ½ inch thick.

- 10 slices hearty rye sandwich bread
- 2 tablespoons whole milk
- ¾ teaspoon onion powder
-    Salt and pepper
- 1½ pounds 85 percent lean ground beef
- 3 tablespoons unsalted butter
- 2 onions, halved and sliced thin
- 8 ounces Swiss cheese, shredded (2 cups)

1. Adjust oven rack to middle position and heat oven to 200 degrees. Tear 2 pieces of bread into ½-inch pieces. Using potato masher, mash torn bread, milk, onion powder, ¾ teaspoon salt, and ½ teaspoon pepper in large bowl until smooth. Add beef and gently knead until well combined. Divide meat into 4 equal portions. Shape each portion into 6 by 4-inch oval.

2. Melt 1 tablespoon butter in 12-inch nonstick skillet over medium-high heat. Cook 2 patties until well browned on first side, about 5 minutes. Transfer to large plate, browned side up, and repeat with remaining 2 patties.

3. Pour off all but 1 teaspoon fat from pan. Add onions and ½ teaspoon salt and cook, stirring occasionally, until golden brown, 5 to 7 minutes. Arrange patties, browned side up, on top of onions, pouring any accumulated juices into pan. Reduce heat to medium and cook, shaking pan occasionally, until onions are tender and burgers are cooked through, about 5 minutes.

4. Divide 1 cup cheese among 4 slices bread. Top with patties, onions, remaining cheese, and remaining bread. Wipe out skillet with paper towels. Melt 1 tablespoon butter in now-empty skillet over medium heat. Cook 2 sandwiches until golden brown and cheese is melted, 3 to 4 minutes per side. Transfer to rimmed baking sheet and keep warm in oven. Repeat with remaining 1 tablespoon butter and remaining 2 sandwiches. Serve.

Heyday of the Sandwich

When it comes to inventive sandwiches, you can't top 1920s America. Just a decade earlier, New Yorkers were said to eat only six types of sandwich: sardine, tongue, roast beef, Swiss cheese, liverwurst, and egg, according to William Grimes's book *Appetite City: A Culinary History of New York*. But three factors—Prohibition, the newfound popularity of automobiles, and women's increasing independence—had created a tearoom craze across the country, making sandwiches so popular that one New Yorker counted nearly 1,000 different types. In these newly minted salons of sandwiches, customers chose among dubious combinations like cheese-ketchup, lemon-prune, and baked bean–celery. Cookbooks reflected the trend, offering other odd partnerships, such as peanut butter and chili sauce, not to mention shredded coconut, cucumber, and mayonnaise. Makes Elvis's prized sandwich of fried peanut butter, banana, and bacon sound almost tame.

Why This Recipe Works Because the ground beef patty for patty melts is traditionally cooked twice—browned once in butter and a second time while the sandwich is griddled—many recipes produce something resembling dried-out hockey pucks. To solve the problem, we incorporated a panade (a paste of bread and milk) into the meat. To bump up the flavor of our burgers, we used rye bread and onion powder in the panade. Covering the cooking onions with the patties trapped some of the steam and helped the onions to soften quicker. This also allowed the flavors of the meat to seep into the onions and vice versa.

Why This Recipe Works This Oklahoma specialty features a thin patty of ground beef topped with a crispy crust of caramelized onions cooked on a griddle. Served on a buttery grilled bun with yellow mustard, dill pickles, and a slice of American cheese, this exceptional burger is well worth a road trip. To make them at home, we sliced and salted the onions, then squeezed out their excess moisture so they'd brown quickly and stick to the burgers. We mashed the onions into the burgers, then put the burgers on a buttered skillet onion side down to brown the onions. Then we flipped the burgers and turned up the heat to finish cooking and get a nice sear.

OKLAHOMA FRIED ONION BURGERS

SERVES 4

A mandoline makes quick work of slicing the onion thinly. Squeeze the salted onion slices until they're as dry as possible, or they won't adhere to the patties. These burgers are traditionally served with yellow mustard and slices of dill pickle.

- 1 large onion, halved and sliced ⅛ inch thick
  Salt and pepper
- 12 ounces 85 percent lean ground beef
- 1 tablespoon unsalted butter
- 1 teaspoon vegetable oil
- 4 slices American cheese (4 ounces)
- 4 hamburger buns, buttered and toasted

1. Combine onion and 1 teaspoon salt in bowl and toss to combine. Transfer to colander and let sit for 30 minutes, tossing occasionally. Using tongs, transfer onion to clean dish towel, gather edges, and squeeze onion dry. Sprinkle with ½ teaspoon pepper.

2. Divide onion mixture into 4 separate mounds on rimmed baking sheet. Form beef into 4 lightly packed balls and season with salt and pepper. Place beef balls on top of onion mounds and flatten beef firmly so onion adheres and patties measure 4 inches in diameter.

3. Melt butter with oil in 12-inch nonstick skillet over medium heat. Using spatula, transfer patties to skillet, onion side down, and cook until onion is deep golden brown and beginning to crisp around edges, 6 to 8 minutes. Flip burgers, increase heat to high, and cook until well browned on second side, about 2 minutes. Place 1 slice cheese on each bottom bun. Place burgers on buns, add desired toppings, and serve.

Keys to Fried Onion Burgers

A few tricks helped the onions adhere to the burgers and caramelize rather than burn.

1. After salting and squeezing onions dry, divide into four piles, place beef balls on top, and press.

2. Brown onion side over medium heat, then flip burgers and turn up heat to sear beef side.

Why This Recipe Works Atlanta brisket is a southern braise featuring onion soup mix, ketchup, and Atlanta's own Coca-Cola. We wanted to keep the regional charm but update the convenience-product flavor. To season the brisket, we pierced it with a fork, salted it, and let it sit overnight. For a great crust, we seared the brisket weighed down with a heavy pot. Finally, for the characteristic braising liquid, we mixed cola and ketchup and replaced the artificial-tasting soup mix with our own blend of sautéed onions, onion and garlic powders, brown sugar, and dried thyme. The mixture both flavored the meat and became a sweet, tangy sauce for serving.

ATLANTA BRISKET

SERVES 6

Parchment paper provides a nonreactive barrier between the cola-based braising liquid and the aluminum foil. A whole brisket is comprised of two smaller roasts: the flat cut and the point cut. For this recipe, we prefer the flat cut, which is rectangular in shape and leaner than the knobby, well-marbled point cut. The flat cut is topped with a thick fat cap; make sure that the fat cap isn't overtrimmed.

- 1 (3½ pound) beef brisket, flat cut, fat trimmed to ¼ inch thick
- Salt and pepper
- 4 teaspoons vegetable oil
- 1 pound onions, halved and sliced ½ inch thick
- 2 cups cola
- 1½ cups ketchup
- 4 teaspoons onion powder
- 2 teaspoons packed dark brown sugar
- 1 teaspoon garlic powder
- 1 teaspoon dried thyme

1. Using fork, poke holes all over brisket. Rub entire surface of brisket with 1 tablespoon salt. Wrap brisket in plastic wrap and refrigerate for at least 6 or up to 24 hours.

2. Adjust oven rack to lower-middle position and heat oven to 325 degrees. Pat brisket dry with paper towels and season with pepper. Heat 2 teaspoons oil in 12-inch nonstick skillet over medium-high heat until just smoking. Place brisket fat side down in skillet; weigh down brisket with heavy Dutch oven or cast-iron skillet and cook until well browned on bottom, about 4 minutes. Remove pot, flip brisket, and replace pot on top of brisket. Cook on second side until well browned, about 4 minutes longer. Transfer brisket to plate.

3. Heat remaining 2 teaspoons oil in now-empty skillet over medium heat until shimmering. Add onions and cook, stirring occasionally, until soft and golden brown, 10 to 12 minutes. Transfer onions to 13 by 9-inch baking dish and spread out in even layer.

4. Combine cola, ketchup, onion powder, sugar, garlic powder, thyme, 1 teaspoon salt, and 1 teaspoon pepper in bowl. Place brisket fat side up on top of onions and pour cola mixture over brisket. Place parchment paper over brisket and cover dish tightly with aluminum foil. Bake until tender and fork slips easily in and out of meat, 3½ to 4 hours. Let brisket rest in liquid, uncovered, for 30 minutes.

5. Transfer brisket to carving board. Skim any fat from top of sauce with large spoon. Slice brisket against grain into ¼-inch-thick slices and return to baking dish. Serve brisket with sauce.

To Make Ahead Follow recipe through step 4. Allow brisket to cool in sauce, cover, and refrigerate overnight or up to 24 hours. To serve, slice brisket, return to sauce, and cover with parchment paper. Cover baking dish with aluminum foil and cook in 350-degree oven until heated through, about 1 hour.

Getting a Great Sear

Brisket is a flat cut of meat that curls up when you try to sear it. We fixed this problem by weighing down the brisket with a heavy Dutch oven (wrapped in foil to make cleanup easier) to ensure a more even sear.

SLOW-COOKER BBQ BEEF BRISKET

SERVES 8 TO 10

Scoring the fat on the brisket at ½-inch intervals will allow the rub to penetrate the meat. Two disposable aluminum loaf pans stacked inside one another can be substituted for the metal loaf pan.

Spice Rub and Brisket
- ½ cup packed dark brown sugar
- 2 tablespoons minced canned chipotle chile in adobo sauce
- 1 tablespoon ground cumin
- 1 tablespoon paprika
- 2 teaspoons pepper
- 1 teaspoon salt
- 1 (4- to 5-pound) brisket roast, fat trimmed to ¼ inch thick and scored lightly

Aromatics and Sauce
- 3 tablespoons vegetable oil
- 1 onion, chopped fine
- 2 tablespoons tomato paste
- 1 tablespoon chili powder
- 1 tablespoon minced canned chipotle chile in adobo sauce
- 2 garlic cloves, minced
- ½ cup water, plus extra as needed
- ¼ cup ketchup
- 1 tablespoon cider vinegar
- ¼ teaspoon liquid smoke
- Salt and pepper

1. For the Spice Rub and Brisket Combine sugar, chipotle, cumin, paprika, pepper, and salt in bowl. Rub sugar mixture all over brisket. Cover with plastic wrap and let sit at room temperature for 1 hour or refrigerate for up to 24 hours.

2. For the Aromatics and Sauce Heat oil in 12-inch skillet over medium-high heat until shimmering. Cook onion until softened, about 5 minutes. Add tomato paste and cook until beginning to brown, about 1 minute. Stir in chili powder, chipotle, and garlic and cook until fragrant, about 30 seconds. Mound onion mixture in center of slow cooker, arrange inverted metal loaf pan over onion mixture, and place brisket fat side up on top of loaf pan. Add water to slow cooker, cover, and cook on high until fork inserted in brisket can be removed with no resistance, 7 to 8 hours (or cook on low for 10 to 12 hours).

3. Transfer brisket to 13 by 9-inch baking dish, cover with aluminum foil, and let rest for 30 minutes. Carefully remove loaf pan from slow cooker. Pour onion mixture and accumulated juices into large bowl and skim fat. (You should have about 2 cups defatted juices; if you have less, supplement with water.)

4. Transfer brisket to carving board, slice thin against grain, and return to baking dish. Pour 1 cup reserved defatted juices over sliced brisket. Whisk ketchup, vinegar, and liquid smoke into remaining juices. Season with salt and pepper to taste. Serve, passing sauce at table.

To Make Ahead In step 3, wrap brisket tightly in foil and refrigerate for up to 3 days. (Refrigerate juices separately.) To serve, transfer foil-wrapped brisket to baking dish and heat in 350-degree oven until brisket is heated through, about 1 hour. Reheat juices in microwave or saucepan set over medium heat. Continue with recipe as directed.

Preventing Waterlogged Brisket
To minimize the moisture absorbed by the brisket, we place the meat on top of a loaf pan. The juices exuded by the meat are drawn under the pan by a vacuum effect, creating less moisture directly below the meat.

1. Pile onion mixture under inverted loaf pan and place brisket on top.

2. After cooking, release juices from loaf pan and reserve for use in barbecue sauce.

Why This Recipe Works Barbecued brisket in the slow cooker? You bet. To minimize the moisture absorbed by the brisket (which traditionally isn't cooked directly in liquid), we came up with an unorthodox solution: elevating the meat off the bottom of the slow cooker with an inverted loaf pan. The liquid exuded from the meat during cooking was drawn under the loaf pan by a vacuum effect, which meant that the slow cooker more closely mimicked the dry heat of real barbecue. To bump up the flavor of this liquid, we added sautéed onion, garlic, tomato paste, and chipotle chiles.

Why This Recipe Works We wanted a foolproof recipe for this southern specialty. We started by making a whiskey-flavored marinade, then steeped the chops in it for at least one hour prior to cooking. We cooked the chops in a hot skillet and then used the same pan to prepare the glaze—browned bits left behind by the chops in the pan added deep, meaty flavor. Allowing the cooked chops to sit in the pan in the glaze for a few minutes before serving helped ensure it clung to the meat.

TENNESSEE WHISKEY PORK CHOPS

SERVES 4

Bourbon tastes fine, but we think it's worth purchasing the real deal—Jack Daniel's Tennessee Whiskey—for this recipe. Watch the glaze closely during the last few minutes of cooking—the bubbles become very small as it approaches the right consistency.

- ½ cup Jack Daniel's Tennessee Whiskey or bourbon
- ½ cup apple cider
- 2 tablespoons packed light brown sugar
- 4 teaspoons cider vinegar
- 1 tablespoon Dijon mustard
- ½ teaspoon vanilla extract
- ⅛ teaspoon cayenne pepper
- 4 (8- to 10-ounce) bone-in, center-cut pork chops, about 1 inch thick, trimmed
- 2 teaspoons vegetable oil
- Salt and pepper
- 1 tablespoon unsalted butter

1. Whisk whiskey, cider, sugar, 2 teaspoons vinegar, mustard, vanilla, and cayenne together in bowl. Transfer ¼ cup whiskey mixture to 1-gallon zipper-lock bag, add pork chops, press air out of bag, and seal. Turn bag to coat chops with marinade and refrigerate 1 to 2 hours. Reserve remaining whiskey mixture separately.

2. Remove chops from bag, pat dry with paper towels, and discard marinade. Heat oil in 12-inch skillet over medium-high heat until just beginning to smoke. Season chops with salt and pepper and cook until well browned on both sides and a peek into thickest part of a chop using paring knife yields still-pink meat ¼ inch from surface, 6 to 8 minutes, flipping chops halfway through cooking. Transfer chops to plate and cover tightly with aluminum foil.

3. Add reserved whiskey mixture to skillet and bring to boil, scraping up any browned bits with wooden spoon. Cook until reduced to thick glaze, 3 to 5 minutes. Reduce heat to medium-low and, holding on to chops, tip plate to add any accumulated juices back to skillet. Add remaining 2 teaspoons vinegar, whisk in butter, and simmer glaze until thick and sticky, 2 to 3 minutes. Remove pan from heat.

4. Return chops to skillet and let rest in pan, turning chops occasionally to coat both sides, until sauce clings to chops and meat registers 145 degrees, about 5 minutes. Transfer chops to platter and spoon sauce over. Serve.

Break Out the Good Stuff

Bourbon was fine, but we loved the deep, caramel-flavored glaze we got when using Jack Daniel's in this recipe. Tennessee whiskey differs from Kentucky bourbon because of a distiller's trick called the Lincoln County process, in which the distilled whiskey is filtered over hard maple charcoal. Then, like bourbon, it is aged in charred oak barrels, where it picks up its distinctive caramel color and smoky flavor.

MEMPHIS-STYLE WET RIBS FOR A CROWD

SERVES 8 TO 12

Spice Rub
- ¼ cup paprika
- 2 tablespoons packed brown sugar
- 2 tablespoons salt
- 2 teaspoons pepper
- 2 teaspoons onion powder
- 2 teaspoons granulated garlic

Barbecue Sauce and Mop
- 1½ cups ketchup
- 1¼ cups apple juice
- ¼ cup molasses
- ½ cup cider vinegar
- ¼ cup Worcestershire sauce
- 3 tablespoons yellow mustard
- 2 teaspoons pepper

Ribs
- 4 (2½- to 3-pound) racks St. Louis–style spareribs, trimmed, membrane removed
- 2 cups wood chips, soaked in water for 15 minutes and drained
- 1 (13 by 9-inch) disposable aluminum roasting pan (if using charcoal) or 1 (8½ by 6-inch) disposable aluminum pan (if using gas)

1. For the Spice Rub Combine all ingredients in bowl.

2. For the Barbecue Sauce and Mop Combine ketchup, ¾ cup apple juice, molasses, ¼ cup vinegar, Worcestershire, 2 tablespoons mustard, and 2 tablespoons spice rub in medium saucepan and bring to boil over medium heat. Reduce heat to medium-low and simmer until thickened and reduced to 2 cups, about 20 minutes. Off heat, stir in pepper; set barbecue sauce aside. For the mop, whisk ½ cup apple juice, ¼ cup vinegar, 1 tablespoon mustard, and ¼ cup barbecue sauce together in bowl.

3. For the Ribs Pat ribs dry with paper towels and season with remaining spice rub. Place 1 rack of ribs, meaty side down, on cutting board. Place second rack of ribs, meaty side up, directly on top of first rack, arranging thick end over tapered end. Tie racks together at 2-inch intervals with kitchen twine. Repeat with remaining 2 racks of ribs for two bundles. Using large piece of heavy-duty aluminum foil, wrap soaked chips in foil packet and cut several vent holes in top.

4A. For a Charcoal Grill Open bottom vent halfway and place disposable roasting pan on 1 side of grill. Fill pan with 2 quarts water. Arrange 3 quarts unlit charcoal briquettes on other side of grill. Light large chimney starter half filled with charcoal briquettes (3 quarts). When top coals are partially covered with ash, pour evenly over unlit coals. Place wood chip packet on coals. Set cooking grate in place, cover, and open lid vent halfway. Heat grill until hot and wood chips are smoking, about 5 minutes.

4B. For a Gas Grill Place wood chip packet and disposable pan over primary burner and fill pan with 2 cups water. Turn primary burner to high (leave other burners off), cover, and heat grill until hot and wood chips are smoking, about 15 minutes. (Adjust primary burner as needed to maintain grill temperature of 275 to 300 degrees.)

5. Clean and oil cooking grate. Place ribs on cooler side of grill and baste with one-third of mop. Cover (positioning lid vent over ribs for charcoal) and cook for 2 hours, flipping and switching positions of ribs and basting again with half of remaining mop halfway through cooking.

6. Adjust oven racks to upper-middle and lower-middle positions and heat oven to 300 degrees. Line 2 rimmed baking sheets with foil. Cut kitchen twine from racks. Transfer 2 racks, meaty side up, to each sheet. Baste with remaining mop and bake for 2 hours, switching and rotating sheets halfway through baking.

7. Remove ribs from oven and brush evenly with ½ cup barbecue sauce. Return to oven and continue to bake until tender, basting with ½ cup barbecue sauce and switching and rotating sheets twice during baking, about 45 minutes. (Ribs do not need to be flipped and should remain meaty side up during baking.) Transfer ribs to carving board. Brush evenly with remaining ½ cup barbecue sauce, tent loosely with foil, and let rest for 20 minutes. Cut ribs in between bones to separate. Serve.

Why This Recipe Works For these saucy Memphis wet ribs, a potent spice rub performs double duty, seasoning the meat and creating the backbone for our barbecue sauce. Tying two racks together allowed us to double our yield and cook four hefty racks of ribs at once. To keep the ribs moist, we grilled them over indirect heat and basted them with a traditional "mop" of juice and vinegar. After a few hours of smoking on the grill, we brushed the ribs with our flavorful barbecue sauce and transferred them to the steady, even heat of the oven to finish tenderizing.

SLOW-COOKER MEMPHIS-STYLE WET RIBS

SERVES 4 TO 6

Try to find ribs of equal shape to ensure even cooking. These ribs should be tender but not falling off the bone.

Ribs
- 2 tablespoons paprika
- 1 tablespoon packed brown sugar
- 1 tablespoon kosher salt
- 2 teaspoons pepper
- 2 teaspoons onion powder
- 2 teaspoons granulated garlic
- 2 (2½- to 3-pound) racks St. Louis–style spareribs, trimmed and each rack cut in half

Barbecue Sauce
- ¾ cup ketchup
- 6 tablespoons apple juice
- 2 tablespoons molasses
- 2 tablespoons cider vinegar
- 2 tablespoons Worcestershire sauce
- 1 tablespoon yellow mustard
- 1 teaspoon pepper
- ¼ teaspoon liquid smoke

1. For the Ribs Combine paprika, sugar, salt, pepper, onion powder, and granulated garlic in bowl. Reserve 1 tablespoon spice rub for sauce. Pat ribs dry with paper towels and coat all over with remaining 5 tablespoons rub.

2. Arrange ribs vertically with thick ends pointing down and meaty side against interior wall of slow cooker (ribs will overlap). Cover and cook until ribs are just tender, 5 to 6 hours on high or 6 to 7 hours on low.

3. For the Barbecue Sauce Meanwhile, whisk ketchup, apple juice, molasses, vinegar, Worcestershire, mustard, pepper, liquid smoke, and reserved 1 tablespoon spice rub together in medium saucepan. Bring to boil over medium heat, then reduce heat to medium-low and simmer, stirring occasionally, until thickened and reduced to 1 cup, about 10 minutes. (Sauce can be refrigerated for up to 3 days.)

4. Line rimmed baking sheet with aluminum foil and set wire rack in sheet. Using tongs, transfer ribs, meaty side up, to prepared rack. Let ribs sit for 10 minutes to allow surface to dry out.

5. Adjust oven rack 3 inches from broiler element and heat broiler. Liberally brush ribs with ½ cup sauce and broil until sauce is bubbling and beginning to char, about 4 minutes. Remove ribs from oven, brush with remaining ½ cup sauce, tent with foil, and let rest for 20 minutes. Cut ribs in between bones to separate. Serve.

How Hot is Your Broiler?

It's good to know if your broiler runs relatively hot, average, or cold. This information allows you to adjust the cooking time for this recipe (and others) accordingly. To see how your broiler stacks up, heat it on high and place a slice of white sandwich bread directly under the heating element on the upper-middle rack. If the bread toasts to golden brown in 30 seconds or less, your broiler runs very hot, and you will need to reduce the cooking time by a minute or two. If the bread toasts perfectly in one minute, your broiler runs about average. If the bread takes two minutes or longer to toast, your broiler runs cool and you may need to increase the cooking time by a minute or two.

Why This Recipe Works To serve up saucy Memphis wet ribs without ever leaving the kitchen, we turned to our slow cooker. After applying a zesty spice rub, we arranged two racks of St. Louis–style ribs in the slow cooker. The ribs cooked low and slow in their own flavorful juices, no other liquid required. Hours later, the ribs were tender and perfectly cooked. We created a thick glazy sauce and brushed it over our deeply seasoned ribs before sliding them under the broiler to create authentic "wet" barbecue ribs indoors.

Why This Recipe Works Baltimore is known for its pit beef, replete with a well-seasoned, charred crust and a rosy pink interior. The meat is shaved paper thin, piled onto a kaiser roll, topped with a horseradish-y mayo known as tiger sauce, and finally covered with sliced onions. We started by cutting a beefy top sirloin roast in half and slow-cooked the meat on the cool side of the grill—a foil shield provided maximum protection so the meat didn't dry out. Then for maximum char, we generously seared both pieces all over.

BALTIMORE PIT BEEF

SERVES 10

When shopping for the prepared horseradish, buy the brined (not creamy) variety and, if necessary, drain it.

Tiger Sauce
- ½ cup mayonnaise
- ½ cup hot prepared horseradish
- 1 teaspoon lemon juice
- 1 garlic clove, minced
- Salt and pepper

Pit Beef
- 4 teaspoons kosher salt
- 1 tablespoon paprika
- 1 tablespoon pepper
- 1 teaspoon garlic powder
- 1 teaspoon dried oregano
- ¼ teaspoon cayenne pepper
- 1 (4- to 5-pound) boneless top sirloin roast, trimmed and halved crosswise
- 10 kaiser rolls
- 1 onion, sliced thin

1. For the Tiger Sauce Whisk mayonnaise, horseradish, lemon juice, and garlic together in bowl. Season with salt and pepper to taste. (Sauce can be refrigerated for up to 2 days.)

2. For the Pit Beef Combine salt, paprika, pepper, garlic powder, oregano, and cayenne in bowl. Pat roasts dry with paper towels and rub with 2 tablespoons seasoning mixture. Wrap meat tightly with plastic wrap and refrigerate for 6 to 24 hours.

3A. For a Charcoal Grill Open bottom vent halfway. Light large chimney starter filled with charcoal briquettes (6 quarts). When top coals are partially covered with ash, pour evenly over half of grill. Set cooking grate in place, cover, and open lid vent halfway. Heat grill until hot, about 5 minutes.

3B. For a Gas Grill Turn all burners to high, cover, and heat grill until hot, about 15 minutes. Leave primary burner on high and turn other burner(s) off.

4. Clean and oil cooking grate. Unwrap roasts and place end to end on long side of 18 by 12-inch sheet of aluminum foil. Loosely fold opposite long side of foil around top of roasts. Place meat on cool part of grill with foil-covered side closest to heat source. Cover (positioning lid vent over meat if using charcoal) and cook until meat registers 100 degrees, 45 minutes to 1 hour.

5. Transfer roasts to plate and discard foil. Turn all burners to high if using gas. If using charcoal, carefully remove cooking grate and light large chimney starter three-quarters filled with charcoal briquettes (4½ quarts). When top coals are partially covered with ash, pour evenly over spent coals. Set cooking grate in place and cover. Heat grill until hot, about 5 minutes.

6. Pat roasts dry with paper towels and rub with remaining spice mixture. Place meat on hot part of grill. Cook (covered if using gas), turning occasionally, until charred on all sides and meat registers 120 to 125 degrees (for medium-rare), 10 to 20 minutes. Transfer meat to carving board, tent loosely with foil, and let rest for 15 minutes. Slice meat thin against grain. Transfer sliced beef to rolls, top with onion slices, and drizzle with sauce. Serve.

Preventing Pit Beef from Drying out

Even with indirect heat, the sides of the roasts closest to the fire can overcook. A simple foil shield protects them.

Why This Recipe Works Warm spices and unexpected garnishes lend Cincinnati chili recipes their unique flavors—but can sometimes muddle the dish. To recreate this Midwestern recipe in our own kitchen, we narrowed our ingredient list to four spices. Tomato paste added richness to our chili, while dark brown sugar gave it a sweet tang. Boiling the beef in water kept it tender during cooking—we cooked ours directly in our spices and liquid to infuse the meat with their intense flavor. Serving our chili over spaghetti, plus cheese, onions, red beans, and oyster crackers, gave us the true Cincinnati chili experience.

CINCINNATI CHILI

SERVES 6 TO 8

Use canned tomato sauce for this recipe—do not use jarred spaghetti sauce.

- 1 tablespoon vegetable oil
- 2 onions, chopped fine
- 2 tablespoons tomato paste
- 2 tablespoons chili powder
- 1 tablespoon dried oregano
- 1½ teaspoons ground cinnamon
- 1 garlic clove, minced
- Salt and pepper
- ¼ teaspoon ground allspice
- 2 cups chicken broth
- 2 cups canned tomato sauce
- 2 tablespoons cider vinegar
- 2 teaspoons packed dark brown sugar
- 1½ pounds 85 percent lean ground beef

1. Heat oil in Dutch oven over medium-high heat until shimmering. Cook onions until soft and browned around edges, about 8 minutes. Add tomato paste, chili powder, oregano, cinnamon, garlic, 1 teaspoon salt, ¾ teaspoon pepper, and allspice and cook until fragrant, about 1 minute. Stir in chicken broth, tomato sauce, vinegar, and sugar.

2. Add beef and stir to break up meat. Bring to boil, reduce heat to medium-low, and simmer until chili is deep brown and slightly thickened, 15 to 20 minutes. Season with salt to taste and serve. (Chili can be refrigerated for up to 3 days or frozen for up to 2 months.)

Five Ways to Cincinnati

Those in the know can order their chili without a second thought, but for the uninitiated, here's a quick guide to the five ways of Cincinnati chili. The chili is almost never served on its own (one-way). Just don't forget the oyster crackers!

TWO-WAY CHILI
Served over spaghetti.

THREE-WAY CHILI
Served over spaghetti and topped with cheese.

FOUR-WAY CHILI
Served over spaghetti and topped with onions and cheese.

FIVE-WAY CHILI
Served over spaghetti and topped with onions, red beans, and cheese.

COLORADO GREEN CHILI

SERVES 6

The chiles can be roasted and refrigerated up to 24 hours in advance.

- 3 pounds boneless pork butt roast, trimmed and cut into 1-inch pieces
- Salt
- 2 pounds (10 to 12) Anaheim chiles, stemmed, halved lengthwise, and seeded
- 3 jalapeño chiles
- 1 (14.5-ounce) can diced tomatoes
- 1 tablespoon vegetable oil
- 2 onions, chopped fine
- 8 garlic cloves, minced
- 1 tablespoon ground cumin
- ¼ cup all-purpose flour
- 4 cups chicken broth
- Cayenne pepper
- Lime wedges

1. Combine pork, ½ cup water, and ½ teaspoon salt in Dutch oven over medium heat. Cover and cook for 20 minutes, stirring occasionally. Uncover, increase heat to medium-high, and continue to cook, stirring frequently, until liquid evaporates and pork browns in its own fat, 15 to 20 minutes. Transfer pork to bowl and set aside.

2. Meanwhile, adjust 1 oven rack to lowest position and second rack 6 inches from broiler element. Heat broiler. Line rimmed baking sheet with aluminum foil and spray with vegetable oil spray. Arrange Anaheims, skin side up, and jalapeños in single layer on prepared sheet. Place sheet on upper rack and broil until chiles are mostly blackened and soft, 15 to 20 minutes, rotating sheet and flipping only jalapeños halfway through broiling. Place Anaheims in large bowl and cover with plastic wrap; let cool for 5 minutes. Set aside jalapeños. Heat oven to 325 degrees.

3. Remove skins from Anaheims. Chop half of Anaheims into ½-inch pieces and transfer to bowl. Process remaining Anaheims in food processor until smooth, about 10 seconds; transfer to bowl with chopped Anaheims. Pulse tomatoes and their juice in now-empty food processor until coarsely ground, about 4 pulses.

4. Heat oil in now-empty Dutch oven over medium heat until shimmering. Add onions and cook until lightly browned, 5 to 7 minutes. Stir in garlic and cumin and cook until fragrant, about 30 seconds. Stir in flour and cook for 1 minute. Stir in broth, Anaheims, tomatoes, and pork with any accumulated juices and bring to simmer, scraping up any browned bits. Cover pot, transfer to lower oven rack, and cook until pork is tender, 1 to 1¼ hours.

5. Without peeling, stem and seed jalapeños and reserve seeds. Finely chop jalapeños and stir into chili. Season chili with salt, cayenne, and reserved jalapeño seeds to taste. Serve with lime wedges.

Easier Roasted Chiles

Roasting chiles whole and then seeding them—the usual procedure—makes a mess: The wet seeds stick to everything. We halve and seed the raw Anaheims. It's neater and lets us skip the usual flipping step. We leave the jalapeños whole; they soften but don't deeply roast.

READY FOR ROASTING
Arrange the chiles head to foot for the best fit.

Why This Recipe Works This popular southwestern dish boasts rich bites of pork in a sauce dominated by green chiles. For our version, we used a combination of Anaheim and jalapeño peppers. To achieve the cohesive flavor and mild vegetal taste that we liked, we used canned, diced tomatoes and more than 2 pounds of chiles, along with 3 pounds of boneless pork butt—our preferred cut for its rich meatiness. To reduce the hands-on time, we started the pork with water in a covered pan to render the fat, then let the even heat of the oven cook the chili. Adding the jalapeños just before serving gave a fresh hit of heat.

Why This Recipe Works Similar to Latin American empanadas, these deep-fried hand pies from Louisiana are filled with savory ground meat and spices. For the filling, we used equal parts ground beef and pork along with the classic Creole combination of onions, green bell peppers, and a pinch of cayenne for heat. Chicken broth and flour made the filling cohesive. Using chicken broth rather than milk in the dough gave the crust a subtle savory flavor. After a few minutes in hot oil, they emerged with a crisp, flaky crust and piping-hot filling.

NATCHITOCHES MEAT PIES

MAKES 16 PIES

You can make the dough and the filling up to 24 hours ahead and refrigerate them separately. You can also shape and fill the pies, refrigerating them for up to 24 hours before frying. You will need at least a 6-quart Dutch oven for this recipe.

Filling
- 5 teaspoons vegetable oil
- ¾ pound 85 percent lean ground beef
- ¾ pound ground pork
- Salt and pepper
- 1 onion, chopped fine
- 1 green bell pepper, stemmed, seeded, and minced
- 6 scallions, white parts minced, green parts sliced thin
- 3 garlic cloves, minced
- ¼ teaspoon cayenne pepper
- 2 tablespoons all-purpose flour
- 1 cup chicken broth

Dough
- 4 cups (20 ounces) all-purpose flour
- 2 teaspoons salt
- 1 teaspoon baking powder
- 8 tablespoons vegetable shortening, cut into ½-inch pieces
- 1 cup chicken broth
- 2 large eggs, lightly beaten
- 1 quart vegetable oil for frying

1. For the Filling Heat 2 teaspoons oil in 12-inch skillet over medium-high heat until just smoking. Add beef, pork, 1 teaspoon salt, and ½ teaspoon pepper and cook, breaking up pieces with spoon, until no longer pink, 8 to 10 minutes. Transfer meat to bowl.

2. Add remaining 1 tablespoon oil to now-empty skillet and heat over medium-high heat until shimmering. Add onion, bell pepper, scallion whites, ½ teaspoon salt, and ½ teaspoon pepper and cook until vegetables are just starting to brown, 3 to 5 minutes. Stir in garlic and cayenne and cook until fragrant, about 30 seconds.

3. Return meat and any accumulated juices to skillet with vegetables. Sprinkle flour over meat and cook, stirring constantly, until evenly coated, about 1 minute. Add broth, bring to boil, and cook until slightly thickened, about 3 minutes. Transfer filling to bowl and stir in scallion greens. Refrigerate until completely cool, about 1 hour. (Filling can be refrigerated for up to 24 hours.)

4. For the Dough Process flour, salt, and baking powder in food processor until combined, about 3 seconds. Add shortening and pulse until mixture resembles coarse cornmeal, 6 to 8 pulses. Add broth and eggs and pulse until dough just comes together, about 5 pulses. Transfer dough to lightly floured counter and knead until dough forms smooth ball, about 20 seconds. Divide dough into 16 equal pieces. (Dough can be covered and refrigerated for up to 24 hours.)

5. Line rimmed baking sheet with parchment paper. Working with 1 piece of dough at a time, roll into 6-inch circle on lightly floured counter. Place ¼ cup filling in center of dough round. Brush edges of dough with water and fold dough over filling. Press to seal, trim any ragged edges, and crimp edges with tines of fork. Transfer to prepared sheet. (Filled pies can be covered and refrigerated for up to 24 hours.)

6. Adjust oven rack to middle position and heat oven to 200 degrees. Set wire rack in second rimmed baking sheet. Add oil to large Dutch oven until it measures about ¾ inch deep and heat over medium-high heat to 350 degrees. Place 4 pies in oil and fry until golden brown, 3 to 5 minutes per side, using slotted spatula or spider to flip. Adjust burner, if necessary, to maintain oil temperature between 325 and 350 degrees. Transfer pies to prepared wire rack and place in oven to keep warm. Return oil to 350 degrees and repeat with remaining pies. Serve.

ST. LOUIS–STYLE PIZZA

MAKES TWO 12-INCH PIZZAS

If you can find Provel cheese, use 10 ounces in place of the American cheese, Monterey Jack cheese, and liquid smoke.

Sauce and Cheeses
- 1 (8-ounce) can tomato sauce
- 3 tablespoons tomato paste
- 2 tablespoons chopped fresh basil
- 1 tablespoon sugar
- 2 teaspoons dried oregano
- 8 ounces white American cheese, shredded (2 cups)
- 2 ounces Monterey Jack cheese, shredded (½ cup)
- 3 drops liquid smoke

Dough
- 2 cups (10 ounces) all-purpose flour
- 2 tablespoons cornstarch
- 2 teaspoons sugar
- 1 teaspoon baking powder
- 1 teaspoon salt
- ½ cup plus 2 tablespoons water
- 2 tablespoons olive oil

1. For the Sauce and Cheeses Whisk together tomato sauce, tomato paste, basil, sugar, and oregano in small bowl; set aside. Toss cheeses with liquid smoke in medium bowl; set aside.

2. For the Dough Combine flour, cornstarch, sugar, baking powder, and salt in large bowl. Combine water and olive oil in liquid measuring cup. Stir water mixture into flour mixture until dough starts to come together. Turn dough onto lightly floured surface and knead 3 or 4 times, until cohesive.

3. Adjust oven rack to lower-middle position, place baking stone (or inverted baking sheet) on rack, and heat oven to 475 degrees. Divide dough into 2 equal pieces. Working with 1 piece of dough at a time, press into small circle and transfer to parchment paper dusted lightly with flour. Using rolling pin, roll and stretch dough to form 12-inch circle, rotating parchment as needed. Lift parchment and pizza off work surface onto inverted baking sheet.

4. Top each piece of dough with half of sauce and half of cheese. Carefully pull parchment paper and pizza off baking sheet onto hot baking stone. Bake until underside is golden brown and cheese is completely melted, 9 to 12 minutes. Remove pizza and parchment from oven. Transfer pizza to wire rack and let cool briefly. Assemble and bake second pizza. Cut into 2-inch squares. Serve.

To Make Ahead The dough can be made in advance. At end of step 2, tightly wrap ball of dough in plastic wrap and refrigerate for up to 2 days.

Meet Me in St. Louis

You can make terrific pizza without yeast. It may sound crazy to most of us, but folks in St. Louis have been doing it for years. With its wafer-thin crust; thick, sweet tomato sauce; gooey Provel cheese (another local secret); and signature square slices, St. Louis–style pizza is unmistakable. Imo's, a popular local chain, is credited with creating it, and it's said that founder Ed Imo, a former tile-layer, subconsciously cut the circular pizza into tile-shaped squares (the "square beyond compare," as the jingle goes). The chain and its pizza have since crossed into Illinois and Kansas.

Why This Recipe Works With its wafer-thin crust, thick, sweet tomato sauce, and gooey Provel cheese, St. Louis–style pizza is unmistakable. Adding cornstarch to the dough absorbed moisture and allowed the crust to crisp in a conventional oven. We doctored a simple pizza sauce by adding sugar, tomato paste, dried oregano, and fresh basil. The fresh herb wasn't typical, but it gave the pizza a flavorful lift. Smoky, melty Provel cheese was difficult to find outside the St. Louis area, so we crafted a respectable substitute with American cheese, Monterey Jack, and liquid smoke.

POTATO-CHEDDAR PIEROGI

MAKES ABOUT 30 PIEROGI

When rolling the dough in step 4, be sure not to dust the top surface with too much flour, as that will prevent the edges from forming a tight seal when pinched.

Filling
- 1 pound russet potatoes, peeled and sliced ½ inch thick
- Salt and pepper
- 4 ounces sharp cheddar cheese, shredded (1 cup)
- 2 tablespoons unsalted butter

Dough
- 2½ cups (13¾ ounces) bread flour
- 1 teaspoon baking powder
- Salt
- 1 cup sour cream
- 1 large egg plus 1 large yolk

Topping
- 4 tablespoons unsalted butter
- 1 large onion, chopped fine
- ½ teaspoon salt

1. For the Filling Combine potatoes and 1 tablespoon salt in large saucepan and cover with water by 1 inch. Bring to boil over medium-high heat; reduce heat to medium and cook at vigorous simmer until potatoes are very tender, about 15 minutes.

2. Drain potatoes in colander. While still hot, combine potatoes, cheddar, butter, ½ teaspoon salt, and ½ teaspoon pepper in bowl of stand mixer. Fit mixer with paddle and mix on medium speed until potatoes are smooth and all ingredients are fully combined, about 1 minute. Transfer filling to 8-inch square baking dish and refrigerate until fully chilled, about 30 minutes, or cover with plastic wrap and refrigerate for up to 24 hours.

3. For the Dough Whisk flour, baking powder, and ½ teaspoon salt together in clean bowl of stand mixer. Add sour cream and egg and yolk. Fit mixer with dough hook and knead on medium-high speed for 8 minutes (dough will be smooth and elastic). Transfer dough to floured bowl, cover with plastic, and refrigerate until ready to assemble.

4. Line rimmed baking sheet with parchment paper and dust with flour. Roll dough on lightly floured counter into 18-inch circle, about ⅛ inch thick. Using 3-inch biscuit cutter, cut 20 to 24 circles from dough. Place 1 tablespoon chilled filling in center of each dough round. Fold dough over filling to create half-moon shape and pinch edges firmly to seal. Transfer to prepared sheet.

5. Gather dough scraps and reroll to ⅛-inch thickness. Cut 6 to 10 more circles from dough and repeat with remaining filling. (It may be necessary to reroll dough once more to yield 30 pierogi.) Cover pierogi with plastic and refrigerate until ready to cook, up to 3 hours.

6. For the Topping Melt butter in 12-inch skillet over medium-low heat. Add onion and salt and cook until onion is caramelized, 15 to 20 minutes. Remove skillet from heat and set aside.

7. Bring 4 quarts water to boil in Dutch oven. Add 1 tablespoon salt and half of pierogi to boiling water and cook until tender, about 5 minutes. Using spider or slotted spoon, remove pierogi from water and transfer to skillet with caramelized onion. Return water to boil, cook remaining pierogi, and transfer to skillet with first batch.

8. Add 2 tablespoons cooking water to pierogi in skillet. Cook over medium-low heat, stirring gently, until onion mixture is warmed through and adhered to pierogi. Transfer to platter and serve.

To Make Ahead Uncooked pierogi can be frozen for several weeks. After sealing pierogi in step 4, freeze them on baking sheet, about 3 hours. Transfer frozen pierogi to zipper-lock freezer bag. When ready to cook, extend boiling time in step 7 to about 7 minutes.

Why This Recipe Works Our take on the Polish dumplings known as *pierogi* combined potatoes and cheese tucked into a tender dough. We began by thoroughly combining boiled russet potatoes, shredded cheddar cheese, and butter in a stand mixer. The heat from the potatoes melted the butter and cheese for an even consistency. We created a pliable, rollable dough using higher-protein bread flour, sour cream, and egg. We stamped out rounds with a biscuit cutter and sealed in the filling by pinching the edges together before boiling the pierogi. A caramelized onion topping mixed with the dumplings made for an authentic sweet-savory finish.

Why This Recipe Works We wanted a recipe for fast-food-style crunchy potato wedges that we could prepare at home. Microwaving the potatoes in a tightly covered bowl helped them obtain perfectly cooked interiors and nicely crisped exteriors. For the coating, adding baking soda to buttermilk and replacing some of the flour with cornstarch resulted in crunchy, deep-golden-brown wedges. Finally, seasoning our crunchy potato wedges with a spice blend as they precooked in the microwave, then tossing the wedges in the seasonings when they came out of the oil, produced potatoes that were flavored from the inside out.

CRUNCHY POTATO WEDGES

SERVES 6

If you don't have buttermilk, substitute 1 cup milk mixed with 1 tablespoon lemon juice. Let the mixture sit 15 minutes before using. You will need at least a 6-quart Dutch oven for this recipe.

- 4 teaspoons kosher salt
- 2 teaspoons onion powder
- 1 teaspoon garlic powder
- 1 teaspoon dried oregano
- ¾ teaspoon cayenne pepper
- ½ teaspoon pepper
- 3 large russet potatoes (about 1¾ pounds), cut into ¼-inch wedges
- ¼ cup peanut or vegetable oil, plus 3 quarts for frying
- 1½ cups all-purpose flour
- ½ cup cornstarch
- 1 cup buttermilk
- ½ teaspoon baking soda

1. Combine salt, onion powder, garlic powder, oregano, cayenne, and pepper in small bowl.

2. Toss potato wedges with 4 teaspoons spice mixture and ¼ cup oil in large bowl; cover. Microwave until potatoes are tender but not falling apart, 7 to 9 minutes, shaking bowl to redistribute potatoes halfway through cooking. Uncover and drain potatoes. Arrange potatoes on rimmed baking sheet and let cool until potatoes firm up, about 10 minutes. (Potatoes can be held at room temperature for up to 2 hours.)

3. Set wire rack in rimmed baking sheet and line second baking sheet with triple layer of paper towels. Add remaining 3 quarts oil to large Dutch oven until it measures about 2 inches deep and heat over medium-high heat to 340 degrees. Meanwhile, combine flour and cornstarch in medium bowl and whisk buttermilk and baking soda together in large bowl. Working in 2 batches, dredge potato wedges in flour mixture, shaking off excess. Dip in buttermilk mixture, allowing excess to drip back into bowl, then coat again in flour mixture. Shake off excess and place on wire rack. (Potatoes can be coated up to 30 minutes in advance.)

4. When oil is ready, add half of coated wedges and fry until deep golden brown, 4 to 6 minutes. Transfer wedges to large bowl and toss with 1 teaspoon spice mixture. Drain wedges on paper towel–lined baking sheet. Return oil to 340 degrees and repeat with second batch of wedges. Serve with extra spice mixture.

To Make Ahead Our Crunchy Potato Wedges freeze very well. Follow steps 1 through 4, frying each batch of wedges until they are light golden brown, 2 to 3 minutes. Do not toss with seasoning, and drain and cool potatoes completely on baking sheet lined with paper towels. Freeze wedges on baking sheet until completely frozen, about 2 hours, then transfer potatoes to zipper-lock bag for up to 2 months. When ready to eat, heat 3 quarts oil to 340 degrees and cook in 2 batches until deep golden brown, about 3 minutes. Toss with seasonings, drain, and serve.

CREAMY BBQ SAUCE
MAKES 1¼ CUPS

Combine ¾ cup mayonnaise, ¼ cup barbecue sauce, 3 tablespoons cider vinegar, 1 minced garlic clove, ¼ teaspoon pepper, and ⅛ teaspoon salt in small bowl.

BUFFALO BLUE CHEESE SAUCE
MAKES 1½ CUPS

Combine ¾ cup mayonnaise, ¼ cup blue cheese salad dressing, 3 tablespoons hot sauce, 1 minced garlic clove, ¼ teaspoon pepper, and ⅛ teaspoon celery salt in small bowl.

CURRIED CHUTNEY SAUCE
MAKES 1¼ CUPS

Combine ¾ cup mayonnaise, ¼ cup yogurt, ¼ cup minced fresh cilantro, 3 tablespoons mango chutney, 2 teaspoons curry powder, ¼ teaspoon pepper, and ⅛ teaspoon salt in small bowl.

Why This Recipe Works Let's face it, frozen potato tots don't live up to our childhood memories. And many recipes simply mix coarsely ground potato with flour and egg, which fry up into raw, dense nuggets. We found that parcooking the chopped potato in the microwave was a step in the right direction, but the tots were still too heavy. Reducing the flour and omitting the egg helped, but they were still not light and fluffy. To minimize the gluey texture of potato starch, we tried processing the potatoes with water. Perfection. This step rinsed off the excess starch, and a small amount of salt in the mixture kept the interior downy white.

CRISPY POTATO TOTS

MAKES 48 POTATO TOTS

If any large pieces of potato remain after processing, chop them coarsely by hand. To make handling the uncooked tots easier, use a wet knife blade and wet hands. Once the tots are added to the hot oil, they may stick together; resist the temptation to stir and break them apart until after they have browned and set. You will need at least a 6-quart Dutch oven for this recipe.

- 2¼ teaspoons salt
- 2½ pounds russet potatoes, peeled and cut into 1½-inch pieces
- 1½ tablespoons all-purpose flour
- ½ teaspoon pepper
- 1 quart peanut or vegetable oil

1. Whisk 1 cup water and salt together in bowl until salt dissolves. Pulse potatoes and salt water in food processor until coarsely ground, 10 to 12 pulses, stirring occasionally. Drain mixture in fine-mesh strainer, pressing potatoes with rubber spatula until dry (liquid should measure about 1½ cups); discard liquid. Transfer potatoes to bowl and microwave, uncovered, until dry and sticky, 8 to 10 minutes, stirring halfway through cooking.

2. Stir flour and pepper into potatoes. Spread potato mixture into thin layer over large sheet of aluminum foil and let cool for 10 minutes. Push potatoes to center of foil and place foil and potatoes in 8-inch square baking pan. Push foil into corners and up sides of pan, smoothing it flush to pan. Press potato mixture tightly and evenly into pan. Freeze, uncovered, until firm, about 30 minutes.

3. Meanwhile, adjust oven rack to middle position and heat oven to 200 degrees. Set wire rack in rimmed baking sheet. Add oil to large Dutch oven until it measures about ¾ inch deep and heat over high heat until 375 degrees. Using foil overhang, lift potatoes from pan and cut into 48 pieces (5 cuts in 1 direction and 7 in other). Fry half of potato tots until golden brown and crisp, 5 to 7 minutes, stirring only after they are browned and set. Transfer to prepared baking sheet and place in oven. Return oil to 375 degrees and repeat with remaining potato tots. Serve.

To Make Ahead Let fried potato tots cool, transfer to zipper-lock bag, and freeze for up to 1 month. To serve, adjust oven rack to middle position and heat oven to 400 degrees. Place potato tots on rimmed baking sheet and bake until heated through, 12 to 15 minutes.

CRISPY POTATO TOTS FOR A CROWD

Double all ingredients for Crispy Potato Tots. Process and drain potato mixture in 2 batches. Microwave entire potato mixture for 12 to 14 minutes, stirring halfway through cooking. Spread potato mixture over large sheet of foil to cool and press into 13 by 9-inch baking pan. After freezing, cut potato rectangle in half crosswise before cutting into potato tots per recipe. Fry in 4 batches.

BACON-RANCH POTATO TOTS

Stir 1 tablespoon cider vinegar into potatoes after microwaving. Add 4 slices finely chopped cooked bacon, 1 teaspoon onion powder, ½ teaspoon garlic powder, and ½ teaspoon dried dill to potatoes with flour in step 2.

PARMESAN-ROSEMARY POTATO TOTS

Stir 2 minced garlic cloves into drained potatoes before microwaving. Add 1 cup grated Parmesan cheese and 2 tablespoons minced fresh rosemary to potatoes with flour in step 2.

SOUTHWESTERN POTATO TOTS

Add ½ cup shredded smoked gouda cheese, 3 tablespoons minced fresh cilantro, and 2 tablespoons minced jarred jalapeños to potatoes with flour in step 2.

BEER-BATTERED ONION RINGS

SERVES 4 TO 6

In step 1, do not soak the onion rounds longer than 2 hours or they will turn soft and become too saturated to crisp properly. Ordinary yellow onions will produce acceptable rings here. We like full-bodied beers like Sam Adams in this recipe. Cider vinegar can be used in place of malt vinegar. You will need at least a 6-quart Dutch oven for this recipe.

- 2 sweet onions, peeled and sliced into ½-inch-thick rounds
- 3 cups ale or lager
- 2 teaspoons malt vinegar
- Salt and pepper
- 2 quarts peanut or vegetable oil
- ¾ cup all-purpose flour
- ¾ cup cornstarch
- 1 teaspoon baking powder

1. Place onion rounds, 2 cups beer, vinegar, ½ teaspoon salt, and ½ teaspoon pepper in 1-gallon zipper-lock bag; refrigerate for 30 minutes or up to 2 hours.

2. Line rimmed baking sheet with triple layer of paper towels. Add oil to large Dutch oven until it measures about 1½ inches deep and heat over medium-high heat to 350 degrees. While oil is heating, combine flour, cornstarch, baking powder, ½ teaspoon salt, and ¼ teaspoon pepper in large bowl. Slowly whisk in ¾ cup beer until just combined (some lumps will remain). Whisk in remaining beer as needed, 1 tablespoon at a time, until batter falls from whisk in steady stream and leaves faint trail across surface of batter.

3. Adjust oven rack to middle position and heat oven to 200 degrees. Remove onions from refrigerator and pour off liquid. Pat onion rounds dry with paper towels and separate into rings. Transfer one-third of rings to batter. One at a time, carefully transfer battered rings to oil. Fry until rings are golden brown and crisp, about 5 minutes, flipping halfway through frying. Drain rings on prepared baking sheet, season with salt and pepper to taste, and transfer to oven. Return oil to 350 degrees and repeat 2 more times with remaining onion rings and batter. Serve.

Troubleshooting Onion Rings

1. To prevent raw, crunchy onions, soak rings in combination of beer, vinegar, and salt, which softens and flavors raw onion.

2. If batter is too thick, rings will be doughy; too thin and it will run off. Add beer gradually until batter falls from whisk to form ribbon trail.

3. To prevent fused rings, fry battered onion rings in small batches and transfer to hot oil one at a time so they don't stick together.

Why This Recipe Works We wanted sweet, tender onions for our beer-battered onion rings. We found that sweet onions worked best, and after testing many different batters, we settled on a beer, flour, salt, pepper, baking powder, and cornstarch batter. The beer gave the coating flavor, and the carbonation also provided lift to the batter. Baking powder yielded a coating that was thick and substantial, yet light, while cornstarch added crunch to the coating. Before frying our onion rings, we soaked the onions in a mixture of beer, malt vinegar, and salt to soften them and build flavor.

steakhouse specials

- **119** Grilled Steakhouse Steak Tips
- **121** Grilled Sugar Steak
- **122** Broiled Steaks
- **125** Char-Grilled Steaks
- **126** Grilled Cowboy-Cut Rib Eyes
- **128** Grilled Steak Burgers
- **131** Pork Grillades
- **132** Baked Stuffed Shrimp
- **134** Foolproof Chicken Cordon Bleu
- **137** Slow-Cooker French Onion Soup
- **138** Garlic Mashed Potatoes
- **141** Delmonico Potato Casserole
- **143** Crispy Parmesan Potatoes
- **144** Roasted Salt-and-Vinegar Potatoes
- **147** Super-Stuffed Baked Potatoes
- **149** Crispy Baked Potato Fans
- **150** Olive Oil Potato Gratin
- **152** Mashed Potato Cakes
- **155** Grill-Roasted Peppers
- **156** Stuffed Tomatoes

Why This Recipe Works The sizzling arrival of cast-iron plates of marinated steakhouse steak tips is often the most exciting part about them, because in reality, the first bite reveals chewy meat in an overly sweet marinade. For tender tips with great beefy flavor, we relied on sirloin steak tips. As for the marinade, we replaced the usual culprits—ketchup, barbecue sauce, and cola—with a mixture of soy sauce, oil, dark brown sugar, and tomato paste for enhanced meaty flavor and maximum char.

GRILLED STEAKHOUSE STEAK TIPS

SERVES 4 TO 6

Sirloin steak tips are often labeled "flap meat" and are sold as whole steaks, strips, and pieces. For even pieces, buy a whole steak of uniform size and cut it up yourself.

- ⅓ cup soy sauce
- ⅓ cup vegetable oil
- 3 tablespoons packed dark brown sugar
- 5 garlic cloves, minced
- 1 tablespoon tomato paste
- 1 tablespoon paprika
- ½ teaspoon pepper
- ¼ teaspoon cayenne pepper
- 2½ pounds sirloin steak tips, trimmed

1. Whisk soy sauce, oil, sugar, garlic, tomato paste, paprika, pepper, and cayenne together in bowl until sugar dissolves; transfer to zipper-lock bag. Pat beef dry with paper towels. Prick beef all over with fork and cut into 2½-inch pieces. Add meat to bag with soy sauce mixture and refrigerate for at least 2 or up to 24 hours, turning occasionally.

2A. For a Charcoal Grill Open bottom vent completely. Light large chimney starter filled with charcoal briquettes (6 quarts). When top coals are partially covered with ash, pour evenly over grill. Set cooking grate in place, cover, and open lid vent completely. Heat grill until hot, about 5 minutes. Leave burners on high.

2B. For a Gas Grill Turn all burners to high, cover, and heat grill until hot, about 15 minutes.

3. Clean and oil cooking grate. Grill beef (covered if using gas) until charred and registers 130 to 135 degrees (for medium), 8 to 10 minutes. Transfer meat to platter, tent loosely with aluminum foil, and let rest for 5 to 10 minutes. Serve.

Common Ingredients, Uncommon Results

We engineered our marinade to give the steak tips maximum meaty flavor and satisfying texture. These familiar ingredients make a strong team, each with its own part to play.

DARK BROWN SUGAR Delivers depth, complexity, and a caramelized, crusty char.

VEGETABLE OIL Distributes flavors and activates oil-soluble flavor compounds, such as those found in garlic.

TOMATO PASTE Adds background savor and enough body to help the marinade cling.

SOY SAUCE Its salt penetrates to deeply season the meat. Its glutamates boost meaty flavor.

Why This Recipe Works Adding sugar to steak may at first seem strange, but trust us, the sugar provides a hint of sweetness and helps create the ultimate charred crust. To keep the sugar-salt mixture from sliding off the steaks or melting away on the grill, we sprinkled the mixture onto the steaks, let them rest for at least an hour, and then seasoned the moist steaks again just before hitting the heat. Though we typically discourage fussing with meat once it's on the grill, in this case, moving the steaks around as they cooked minimized the hot spots and evened out the heavy browning caused by the sugar.

GRILLED SUGAR STEAK

SERVES 4 TO 6

These steaks need to sit for at least 1 hour after seasoning. You will have about 1 teaspoon of sugar mixture left over after the final seasoning of the steaks in step 3. If your steaks are more than 1 inch thick, pound them to 1 inch.

- ¼ cup sugar
- 3 tablespoons kosher salt
- 4 (9- to 11-ounce) boneless strip steaks, 1 inch thick, trimmed
- Pepper

1. Mix sugar and salt together in bowl. Pat steaks dry with paper towels and place in 13 by 9-inch baking dish. Evenly sprinkle 1½ teaspoons sugar mixture on top of each steak. Flip steaks and sprinkle second side of each steak with 1½ teaspoons sugar mixture. Cover with plastic wrap and let sit at room temperature for 1 hour or refrigerate for up to 24 hours.

2A. For a Charcoal Grill Open bottom vent completely. Light large chimney starter mounded with charcoal briquettes (7 quarts). When top coals are partially covered with ash, pour evenly over half of grill. Set cooking grate in place, cover, and open lid vent completely. Heat grill until hot, about 5 minutes.

2B. For a Gas Grill Turn all burners to high, cover, and heat grill until hot, about 15 minutes. Turn all burners to medium-high.

3. Clean and oil cooking grate. Transfer steaks to plate. (Steaks will be wet; do not pat dry.) Sprinkle steaks with 1 teaspoon sugar mixture on each side, then season with pepper.

4. Place steaks on hotter side of grill (if using charcoal) and cook (covered if using gas) until evenly charred on first side, 3 to 5 minutes, rotating and switching positions for even cooking. Flip steaks and continue to cook until meat registers 120 to 125 degrees (for medium-rare), 3 to 5 minutes, rotating and switching positions for even cooking.

5. Transfer steaks to wire rack set in rimmed baking sheet and let rest for 5 minutes. Slice and serve.

On the Road: A Denver Gem

Shaped like a circus tent, Bastien's Restaurant is a historic family-owned restaurant in Denver, Colorado, where grilled sugar steak has been the signature dish and a customer favorite for decades. The restaurant sits prominently on Colfax Avenue, a 50-odd-mile street that bisects Denver. It's a notorious street of contrasts (one stretch abuts the state capital while the next teems with unlawful trade, and gentrification mixes with grit along its entire stretch), but as Denver's defining throughway, it was granted Heritage Corridor status in the late 1990s to help protect and preserve Bastien's and many other mid-century architectural gems.

BROILED STEAKS

SERVES 4

To minimize smoking, be sure to trim as much exterior fat and gristle as possible from the steaks before cooking. Try to purchase steaks of a similar size and shape for this recipe. Note that you will need 2 cups of salt to line the roasting pan; the salt will absorb drippings from the steak and minimize smoking.

- 4 tablespoons unsalted butter, softened
- 1 teaspoon minced fresh thyme
- 1 teaspoon Dijon mustard
  Salt and pepper
- 1 (13 by 9-inch) disposable aluminum roasting pan, 3 inches deep
- 4 strip, rib-eye, or tenderloin steaks, 1 to 2 inches thick, trimmed

1. Adjust oven racks to upper-middle and lower-middle positions and heat oven to 375 degrees. Beat butter, thyme, mustard, ¼ teaspoon salt, and ¼ teaspoon pepper in bowl and refrigerate.

2. Spread 2 cups salt over bottom of aluminum pan. Pat steaks dry with paper towels, season with salt and pepper, and transfer to wire rack. Set rack over aluminum pan and transfer to lower oven rack. Cook 6 to 10 minutes, then remove pan from oven. Flip steaks, pat dry with paper towels, and let rest for 10 minutes.

3. Heat broiler. Transfer pan to upper oven rack and broil steaks, flipping every 2 to 4 minutes, until meat registers 120 to 125 degrees (for medium-rare), 6 to 16 minutes, depending on thickness of steaks (see chart). Transfer steaks to platter, top with reserved butter mixture, and tent with aluminum foil. Let rest for 5 minutes. Serve.

Perfectly Broiled Steaks

The first step to perfectly broiled steaks is knowing exactly how thick your steaks are. Using a ruler, measure each steak and then follow the guidelines below.

STEAK THICKNESS	PRECOOK	BROIL
1 inch	6 minutes	Turn steaks every 2 minutes
1½ inches	8 minutes	Turn steaks every 3 minutes
2 inches	10 minutes	Turn steaks every 4 minutes

Broiler Prep

Since oven-rack positioning varies greatly from model to model, we suggest you ensure correct positioning with a dry run before turning on your oven.

Before preheating your oven and with your oven racks adjusted to the upper-middle and lower-middle positions, place a wire rack on top of a 3-inch-deep disposable aluminum pan and place it on the upper-middle rack. Place the steaks on top of the rack and use a ruler to measure the distance between the top of the steaks and the heating element of the broiler. For optimal searing, there should be ½ inch to 1 inch of space.

If there is more than 1 inch of space, here's how to close the gap: Elevate the aluminum pan by placing it on an inverted rimmed baking sheet; use a deeper-sided disposable aluminum pan; or stack multiple aluminum pans inside one another. If there's less than ½ inch of space, adjust the oven rack or use a shallower pan.

Why This Recipe Works We usually rely on a red-hot skillet or the grill for our recipes that include putting a crusty sear on steaks, but we wondered if our oven's broiler could do the job just as well. Starting the steaks at a moderate temperature took the chill off, and letting them rest before putting them under the broiler produced evenly cooked meat. Covering the bottom of the pan with salt helped absorb the grease from the meat and greatly minimized smoking. To ensure a good sear on our steaks, we placed a wire rack over a 3-inch disposable pan, to bring the meat closer to the heating element.

Why This Recipe Works In order to achieve a respectable crust on our restaurant-style grilled steak, the exterior of the meat must be dry. After trying numerous drying-out methods, including salting and aging, we considered the freezer. The freezer's intensely dry environment sufficiently dehydrated the steaks' exteriors, and since we were only freezing them for a short time, the interiors remained tender and juicy. We rubbed the steaks with a mixture of salt and cornstarch before freezing. The salt ensured they were well seasoned, and cornstarch, a champ at absorbing moisture, allowed us to cut the freezing time in half.

CHAR-GRILLED STEAKS

SERVES 4

Serve with one of the sauces that follow, if desired.

- 1 teaspoon salt
- 1 teaspoon cornstarch
- 4 strip, rib-eye, or tenderloin steaks, about 1½ inches thick, trimmed
  Pepper
- 1 recipe steak sauce (recipes follow)

1. Combine salt and cornstarch. Pat steaks dry with paper towels and rub with salt mixture. Arrange on wire rack set in rimmed baking sheet and freeze until steaks are firm and dry to touch, at least 30 minutes or up to 1 hour.

2A. For a Charcoal Grill Open bottom vent completely. Light large chimney starter filled with charcoal briquettes (6 quarts). When top coals are partially covered with ash, pour evenly over grill. Set cooking grate in place, cover, and open lid vent completely. Heat grill until hot, about 5 minutes.

2B. For a Gas Grill Turn all burners to high, cover, and heat grill until hot, about 15 minutes. Leave burners on high.

3. Clean and oil cooking grate. Season steaks with pepper. Grill (covered if using gas) until meat registers 120 to 125 degrees (for medium-rare), 8 to 16 minutes, flipping steaks halfway through cooking. Transfer to plate, tent with aluminum foil, and let rest for 5 minutes. Serve.

CLASSIC STEAK SAUCE
MAKES 1¼ CUPS
Raisins add depth and sweetness to this sauce.

- ½ cup boiling water
- ⅓ cup raisins
- ¼ cup ketchup
- 3 tablespoons Worcestershire sauce
- 2 tablespoons Dijon mustard
- 2 tablespoons distilled white vinegar
  Salt and pepper

Combine water and raisins in bowl and let sit, covered, until raisins are plump, about 5 minutes. Puree raisin mixture, ketchup, Worcestershire, mustard, and vinegar in blender until smooth, 30 seconds to 1 minute. Season with salt and pepper to taste. (Sauce can be refrigerated for 1 week.)

SPICY RED PEPPER STEAK SAUCE
MAKES 1¼ CUPS
This peppery sauce is a simplified version of the Spanish classic, romesco.

- 1 slice hearty white sandwich bread, toasted until golden and torn into pieces
- 2 tablespoons slivered almonds, toasted
- 1 cup jarred roasted red peppers, drained
- 1 plum tomato, seeded and chopped
- 2 teaspoons red wine vinegar
- 1 garlic clove, minced
- ⅛ teaspoon cayenne pepper
- 1 tablespoon extra-virgin olive oil
  Salt

Process bread and almonds in food processor until finely ground, about 10 seconds. Add red peppers, tomato, vinegar, garlic, and cayenne and process until smooth, about 1 minute. Season with salt to taste. (Sauce can be refrigerated for 1 week.)

GARLIC-PARSLEY STEAK SAUCE
MAKES 1¼ CUPS
A little of this aromatic vinaigrette goes a long way.

- ½ cup finely chopped fresh parsley
- ¼ cup minced red onion
- ¼ cup red wine vinegar
- 2 garlic cloves, minced
- ⅛ teaspoon red pepper flakes
- ¼ cup extra virgin olive oil
  Salt and pepper

Combine parsley, onion, vinegar, garlic, and pepper flakes in bowl. Slowly whisk in oil. Season with salt and pepper to taste. (Sauce can be refrigerated for 1 week.)

GRILLED COWBOY-CUT RIB EYES

SERVES 4 TO 6

Don't start grilling until the steaks' internal temperatures have reached 55 degrees. Otherwise, the times and temperatures in this recipe will be inaccurate.

- 2 (1¼- to 1½-pound) double-cut bone-in rib-eye steaks, 1¾ to 2 inches thick, trimmed
- 4 teaspoons kosher salt
- 2 teaspoons vegetable oil
- 2 teaspoons pepper

1. Set wire rack inside rimmed baking sheet. Pat steaks dry with paper towels and sprinkle all over with salt. Place steaks on prepared rack and let stand at room temperature until meat registers 55 degrees, about 1 hour. Rub steaks with oil and sprinkle with pepper.

2A. For a Charcoal Grill Open bottom vent halfway. Arrange 4 quarts unlit charcoal briquettes in even layer over half of grill. Light large chimney starter one-third filled with charcoal briquettes (2 quarts). When top coals are partially covered with ash, pour evenly over unlit coals. Set cooking grate in place, cover, and open lid vent halfway. Heat grill until hot, about 5 minutes.

2B. For a Gas Grill Turn all burners to high, cover, and heat grill until hot, about 15 minutes. Turn primary burner to medium-low and turn off other burner(s). Adjust primary burner as needed to maintain grill temperature of 300 degrees.

3. Clean and oil cooking grate. Place steaks on cooler side of grill with bones facing fire. Cover and cook until steaks register 75 degrees, 10 to 20 minutes. Flip steaks, keeping bones facing fire. Cover and continue to cook until steaks register 95 degrees, 10 to 20 minutes.

4. If using charcoal, slide steaks to hotter part of grill. If using gas, remove steaks from grill, turn primary burner to high, and heat until hot, about 5 minutes; place steaks over primary burner. Cover and cook until well browned and steaks register 120 degrees (for medium-rare), about 4 minutes per side. Transfer steaks to clean wire rack set in rimmed baking sheet, tent loosely with foil, and let rest for 15 minutes. Transfer steaks to carving board, cut meat from bone, and slice into ½-inch-thick slices. Serve.

In Praise of Cowboy Steaks

Rib-eye steaks are deeply marbled, tender, and beefy—they're from the same part of the steer that's used for prime rib. Bone-in steaks (like these) have more flavor than boneless, and the bone protects against overcooking. Of special interest is the exterior band of fat and meat on a rib eye called the deckle; connoisseurs say it is the most flavorful part of the cow.

BIGGER IS BETTER
Cowboy-cut rib eyes are double-thick bone-in steaks. They take longer to cook than single-serving rib eyes, so they have more time to soak up smoky grill flavor.

Why This Recipe Works Oversized cowboy-cut rib eyes offer big, beefy flavor, but cooking the huge steaks all the way through while achieving a flavorful seared crust is challenging. We used a bare minimum of seasonings—salt, pepper, and oil—to highlight the flavor of the steaks. To cook them, we opted for a low and slow approach to start. To keep the fire burning long enough, we layered unlit coals under lit ones. We let the steaks come to room temperature before grilling to cut down on cooking time, and then slow-roasted the steaks on the cooler side of the grill until they were almost done. A quick sear over hot coals gave them a flavorful dark crust.

GRILLED STEAK BURGERS

SERVES 4

Use kaiser rolls or other hearty buns for these substantial burgers.

Burgers
- 8 tablespoons unsalted butter
- 2 garlic cloves, minced
- 2 teaspoons onion powder
- 1 teaspoon pepper
- ½ teaspoon salt
- 2 teaspoons soy sauce
- 1½ pounds 90 percent lean ground sirloin
- 4 hamburger buns

Steak Sauce
- 2 tablespoons tomato paste
- ⅔ cup beef broth
- ⅓ cup raisins
- 2 tablespoons soy sauce
- 2 tablespoons Dijon mustard
- 2 tablespoons balsamic vinegar
- 1 tablespoon Worcestershire sauce

1. For the Burgers Melt butter in 8-inch skillet over medium-low heat. Add garlic, onion powder, pepper, and salt and cook until fragrant, about 1 minute. Pour all but 1 tablespoon butter mixture into bowl and let cool for about 5 minutes.

2. For the Steak Sauce Meanwhile, add tomato paste to skillet and cook over medium heat until paste begins to darken, 1 to 2 minutes. Stir in broth, raisins, soy sauce, mustard, vinegar, and Worcestershire and simmer until raisins plump, about 5 minutes. Process sauce in blender until smooth, about 30 seconds; transfer to bowl.

3. Add 5 tablespoons cooled butter mixture and soy sauce to ground beef and gently knead until well combined. Shape into four ¾-inch-thick patties and press shallow divot in center of each. Brush each patty all over with 1 tablespoon steak sauce. Combine remaining 2 tablespoons cooled butter mixture with 2 tablespoons steak sauce; set aside.

4A. For a Charcoal Grill Open bottom vent completely. Light large chimney starter filled with charcoal briquettes (6 quarts). When top coals are partially covered with ash, pour evenly over grill. Set cooking grate in place, cover, and open lid vent completely. Heat grill until hot, about 5 minutes.

4B. For a Gas Grill Turn all burners to high, cover, and heat grill until hot, about 15 minutes. Leave burners on high.

5. Clean and oil cooking grate. Grill burgers (covered if using gas) until meat registers 120 to 125 degrees (for medium-rare), 3 to 4 minutes per side, or 130 to 135 degrees (for medium), 4 to 5 minutes per side. Transfer burgers to plate, tent loosely with aluminum foil, and let rest for 5 to 10 minutes. Brush cut side of buns with butter–steak sauce mixture. Grill buns, cut side down, until golden, 2 to 3 minutes. Place burgers on buns. Serve with remaining steak sauce.

Butter Makes It Better

Why are our steakhouse burgers so good? Yep, butter. Ground sirloin has great flavor, but it's a little dry: Butter helps keep the burgers moist. Butter also gives richness and body to our homemade steak sauce. And we slather butter on the buns before toasting them on the grill.

FLAVORED BUTTER
For the meat, sauce, and buns.

Why This Recipe Works We wanted a burger with the big beefy flavor and crusty char of a grilled steak. Ground sirloin, the most flavorful ground beef, was a natural choice, but unfortunately it's also quite lean. A seasoned butter added richness to the sirloin, but something was missing. Steak sauce! In about five minutes, we simmered up our own intensely flavored sauce, perfect for serving with the burger, smearing on the bun, and even mixing into the beef before cooking.

Why This Recipe Works Despite their name, grillades are not grilled; rather, they are thinly sliced cuts of meat browned and stewed in a supersavory tomato-based gravy. For consistency and ease we opted for pork blade chops (with the bones cut off) which cooked evenly and held up to stewing. When it came time to make a roux for the base of our gravy, dry-toasting the flour in a skillet in advance helped cut down on the cooking time. Adding our own Cajun seasoning spice blend, a traditional mix of vegetables, and a dash of Tabasco provided heat and complexity to this iconic Louisiana dish.

PORK GRILLADES

SERVES 6 TO 8

We prefer pork blade chops because they hold up to stewing better than loin chops. Blade chops aren't typically available boneless; ask your butcher to bone them for you. Use our Louisiana Seasoning (recipe follows) or your favorite store-bought variety.

- 1 cup all-purpose flour
- 8 (6- to 8-ounce) bone-in pork-blade-cut chops, ½ inch thick, bones discarded, and trimmed
- 2 tablespoons Louisiana Seasoning
- Salt and pepper
- ½ cup vegetable oil
- 1 onion, chopped
- 1 green bell pepper, stemmed, seeded, and chopped
- 1 celery rib, chopped
- 2 garlic cloves, minced
- 2 cups chicken broth
- 1 (14.5-ounce) can whole peeled tomatoes, crushed by hand
- 2 slices bacon
- 1 tablespoon Worcestershire sauce
- 1 bay leaf
- 1 teaspoon Tabasco sauce, plus extra for serving
- 4 cups cooked white rice
- 2 scallions, sliced thin

1. Adjust oven rack to lower-middle position and heat oven to 350 degrees. Toast ¼ cup flour in small skillet over medium heat, stirring constantly, until just beginning to brown, about 3 minutes; set aside.

2. Season chops with 1½ teaspoons Louisiana Seasoning, salt, and pepper. Whisk remaining ¾ cup flour and remaining 1½ tablespoons Louisiana Seasoning together in shallow dish. Working with 1 chop at a time, dredge in seasoned flour, shaking off excess; transfer chops to plate.

3. Heat oil in Dutch oven over medium heat until shimmering. Add 4 chops and cook until browned, 3 to 5 minutes per side; transfer to plate. Repeat with remaining 4 chops.

4. Remove all but ¼ cup oil from Dutch oven and return to medium heat. Add toasted flour to pot and cook, whisking constantly, until deep brown, about 2 minutes. Add onion, bell pepper, celery, and 1 teaspoon salt and cook, stirring often, until vegetables are just softened, about 3 minutes. Add garlic and cook until fragrant, about 30 seconds.

5. Stir in broth, tomatoes and their juice, bacon, Worcestershire, and bay leaf, scraping up any browned bits. Nestle chops into liquid and add any accumulated pork juices from plate. Bring to simmer, cover, and transfer to oven. Cook until fork slips easily in and out of pork, about 1 hour.

6. Remove grillades from oven. Discard bacon and bay leaf; stir in Tabasco. Season with salt and pepper to taste. Serve over rice, sprinkled with scallions and passing extra Tabasco.

LOUISIANA SEASONING
MAKES ABOUT ¾ CUP

- 5 tablespoons paprika
- 2 tablespoons garlic powder
- 1 tablespoon dried thyme
- 1 tablespoon cayenne pepper
- 1 tablespoon celery salt
- 1 tablespoon salt
- 1 tablespoon pepper

Combine all ingredients in bowl.

The Right Chop

The problem with buying pork chops is that markets call chops by different names. Since grillades are braised, it's important that you don't buy a lean chop, which would be better quickly grilled or sautéed. Flavorful blade chops may not look pretty, but their fat and connective tissue softens and melts out during braising.

BAKED STUFFED SHRIMP

SERVES 4 TO 6

In a pinch, chicken broth can be substituted for the clam juice. A sturdy rimmed baking sheet can be used in place of the broiler pan bottom. Shrimp that are labeled U12 contain 12 or less shrimp per pound.

- 4 slices hearty white sandwich bread, torn into quarters
- ½ cup mayonnaise
- ¼ cup bottled clam juice
- ¼ cup finely chopped fresh parsley
- 4 scallions, chopped fine
- 1 tablespoon Dijon mustard
- 2 garlic cloves, minced
- 2 teaspoons grated lemon zest plus 1 tablespoon juice
- ⅛ teaspoon cayenne pepper
  Salt
- 1¼ pounds colossal shrimp (U12), peeled and deveined

1. Adjust oven rack to upper-middle position and heat oven to 375 degrees. Pulse bread in food processor to coarse crumbs, about 10 pulses. Transfer crumbs to broiler pan bottom and bake until golden and dry, 8 to 10 minutes, stirring halfway through cooking time. Remove crumbs from oven and reduce temperature to 275 degrees.

2. Combine toasted bread crumbs, mayonnaise, clam juice, parsley, scallions, mustard, garlic, lemon zest and juice, cayenne, and ¼ teaspoon salt in bowl.

3. Pat shrimp dry with paper towels and season with salt. Grease empty broiler pan bottom. To butterfly shrimp, use sharp paring knife to cut along (but not through) vein line, then open up shrimp like a book. Using tip of paring knife, cut 1-inch opening through center of shrimp. Arrange shrimp cut side down on prepared pan. Divide breadcrumb mixture among shrimp, pressing to adhere. Bake until shrimp are opaque, 20 to 25 minutes.

4. Remove shrimp from oven and heat broiler. Broil shrimp until crumbs are deep golden brown and crispy, 1 to 3 minutes. Serve.

CREOLE BAKED STUFFED SHRIMP WITH SAUSAGE
The smoky, meaty flavor of kielbasa is a nice foil to the sweet shrimp in this variation.
Omit cayenne and add 1 teaspoon Creole seasoning in step 2. Fold 4 ounces kielbasa sausage, chopped fine, into filling and proceed as directed.

Easy Steps to Baked Stuffed Shrimp
Cutting a hole through the center of each butterflied shrimp helps the shrimp hold on to the stuffing.

1. Use paring knife to cut along but not through vein line, then open up shrimp like a book. Cut 1-inch opening all the way through center of shrimp.

2. After shrimp have been butterflied and openings have been cut, flip shrimp over onto broiler pan so that they will curl around stuffing.

3. Divide stuffing among shrimp, firmly pressing stuffing into opening and to edges of shrimp.

Why This Recipe Works There are often two problems with baked stuffed shrimp: mushy, bland stuffing and shrimp as chewy as rubber bands. We wanted a recipe that produced crisp, flavorful stuffing and perfectly cooked shrimp. For the stuffing, tasters preferred the sweet flavor of fresh bread crumbs, toasted to ensure crispness. Butterflying the shrimp allowed us to press the stuffing into the shrimp—as the shrimp contracted in the oven, the stuffing was sealed into place. To prevent overcooked shrimp, yet still achieve crisp stuffing, we cooked the shrimp for a longer time at a lower temperature.

FOOLPROOF CHICKEN CORDON BLEU

SERVES 4 TO 6

To help prevent the filling from leaking, thoroughly chill the stuffed breasts before breading. We like Black Forest ham here.

- 25 Ritz crackers (about ¾ sleeve)
- 4 slices hearty white sandwich bread, torn into quarters
- 6 tablespoons unsalted butter, melted
- 8 thin slices deli ham (8 ounces)
- 8 ounces Swiss cheese, shredded (2 cups)
- 4 (8-ounce) boneless, skinless chicken breasts, trimmed
- Salt and pepper
- 3 large eggs
- 2 tablespoons Dijon mustard
- 1 cup all-purpose flour

1. Adjust oven racks to lowest and middle positions and heat oven to 450 degrees. Pulse crackers and bread in food processor until coarsely ground, about 15 pulses. Drizzle in butter; pulse a few times to incorporate. Bake crumbs on rimmed baking sheet on middle rack, stirring occasionally, until light brown, 3 to 5 minutes. Transfer to shallow dish. Do not turn oven off.

2. Top each ham slice with ¼ cup cheese and roll tightly; set aside. Pat chicken dry with paper towels. Using paring knife, cut into thickest part of each chicken breast to create deep pocket with opening of 3 to 4 inches. Stuff each breast with 2 ham-and-cheese rolls and press closed. Season both sides of chicken with salt and pepper. Transfer chicken to plate, cover with plastic wrap, and refrigerate for at least 20 minutes.

3. Beat eggs and mustard in second shallow dish. Place flour in third shallow dish. One at a time, coat stuffed chicken lightly with flour, dip into egg mixture, and dredge in crumbs, pressing to adhere. (Breaded chicken can be refrigerated, covered, for 1 day.) Transfer chicken to clean rimmed baking sheet. Bake on lowest rack until bottom of chicken is golden brown, about 10 minutes, and then move baking sheet to middle rack and reduce oven temperature to 400 degrees. Bake until golden brown and chicken registers 160 degrees, 20 to 25 minutes. Transfer to platter, tent with aluminum foil, and let rest for 5 minutes. Serve.

Stuffing, Streamlined

1. Using paring knife, cut into thickest part of chicken breast to create deep pocket with opening of 3 to 4 inches.

2. Stuff each pocket with 2 ham-and-cheese rolls and seal. Refrigerate chicken for at least 20 minutes before breading.

Why This Recipe Works Making chicken cordon bleu can be fussy; we wanted an easier way. We found cutting a pocket into the breast to be much more efficient than the traditional method of pounding and rolling. To get the same swirl effect achieved by rolling the chicken around the ham and cheese, we simply rolled the ham slices into cylinders around shredded cheese and tucked the cylinders into each chicken breast. Adding a healthy dose of Dijon mustard to the egg wash boosted the flavor of our chicken, as did supplementing homemade bread crumbs with buttery Ritz cracker crumbs.

Why This Recipe Works It can be a hassle to stand over a pot of caramelized onions when a craving for this French classic strikes. We looked to the slow cooker for simplification. Replicating the meaty flavor of the soup was more of a challenge, as the slow, long cooking can result in washed-out flavor. We found that soy sauce, sherry, and thyme added early on helped boost flavor and the addition of beef bones to store-bought chicken and beef broths reproduced the rich meatiness of the classic. Apple butter highlighted the flavor of the onions without drawing attention to itself and also helped make for a rich, silky broth.

SLOW-COOKER FRENCH ONION SOUP

SERVES 6 TO 8

After halving the onions, slice them through the root end for hearty slices that will hold up to long cooking. Beef bones are stocked in the frozen foods aisle of most supermarkets.

Soup
- 2 pounds beef bones
- 4 tablespoons unsalted butter
- 4 pounds yellow onions, halved and sliced through root end into ¼-inch-thick slices
- Salt and pepper
- 1 tablespoon packed brown sugar
- 1 teaspoon minced fresh thyme
- ¾ cup apple butter
- ¾ cup dry sherry
- 5 tablespoons all-purpose flour
- ¼ cup soy sauce
- 2 cups chicken broth
- 2 cups beef broth

Cheese Croutons
- 1 small baguette, cut into ½-inch slices
- 10 ounces Gruyère cheese, shredded (2½ cups)

1. For the Soup Arrange beef bones on paper towel–lined plate. Microwave until well browned, 8 to 10 minutes. Meanwhile, set slow cooker to high. Add butter, cover, and cook until melted. Add onions, 2 teaspoons salt, 1 teaspoon pepper, brown sugar, and thyme. Stir apple butter, sherry, flour, and soy sauce together in small bowl until smooth. Pour over onions and toss to coat. Tuck bones under onions around edge of slow cooker. Cover and cook on high heat until onions are softened and deep golden brown, 10 to 12 hours (start checking onions after 8 hours). (Cooked onions can be refrigerated for 1 day.)

2. Remove bones from slow cooker. Heat broths in microwave until beginning to boil. Stir into slow cooker. Season with salt and pepper to taste.

3. For the Cheese Croutons Adjust oven rack to upper-middle position (about 6 inches from broiler element) and heat oven to 400 degrees. Arrange bread slices in single layer on baking sheet and bake until bread is golden at edges, about 10 minutes. Heat broiler. Divide cheese evenly among croutons and broil until melted and bubbly, 3 to 5 minutes.

4. Ladle soup into bowls and top each with 2 croutons. Serve.

Slicing Onions for French Onion Soup

For this soup, we found that cutting onions with the grain (rather than across it) yielded slices that retained their shape through 10 to 12 hours in the slow cooker.

1. Using chef's knife, trim off both ends of onion.

2. Turn onion onto cut end to steady it and slice in half, through root end.

3. Peel each half, place flat side down, and cut onion, lengthwise, into slices.

GARLIC MASHED POTATOES

SERVES 8 TO 10

Cutting the potatoes into ½-inch pieces ensures that the maximum surface area is exposed to soak up garlicky flavor.

- 4 pounds russet potatoes, peeled, quartered, and cut into ½-inch pieces
- 12 tablespoons unsalted butter, cut into pieces
- 12 garlic cloves, minced
- 1 teaspoon sugar
- 1½ cups half-and-half
- ½ cup water
- Salt and pepper

1. Place cut potatoes in colander. Rinse under cold running water until water runs clear. Drain thoroughly.

2. Melt 4 tablespoons butter in Dutch oven over medium heat. Cook garlic and sugar, stirring often, until sticky and straw colored, 3 to 4 minutes. Add rinsed potatoes, 1¼ cups half-and-half, water, and 1 teaspoon salt to pot and stir to combine. Bring to boil, then reduce heat to low and simmer, covered and stirring occasionally, until potatoes are tender and most of liquid is absorbed, 25 to 30 minutes.

3. Off heat, add remaining 8 tablespoons butter to pot and mash with potato masher until smooth. Using rubber spatula, fold in remaining ¼ cup half-and-half until liquid is absorbed and potatoes are creamy. Season with salt and pepper to taste. Serve.

Folk Remedies for Removing Garlic Odor

Garlic odor is hard to remove from your hands, but folk remedies for doing so abound, from washing with baking soda, vinegar, lemon juice, salt, or toothpaste to rubbing your hands on stainless steel. To find out if any of these tricks worked, we rubbed minced garlic on our hands and tried each method.

Washing with all of these substances lessened the odor at least a little, with baking soda and lemon juice outperforming the others, and rubbing one's hands on stainless steel succeeding just as well. Why? Some of the aromatic compounds in garlic are weak acids that can be neutralized by alkaline baking soda. Because not all aroma compounds are acidic, baking soda can't neutralize the odor 100 percent. Stainless steel removes some of the odor when iron atoms in the stainless steel exchange some of their electrons with sulfur atoms from the volatile aroma compounds, rendering them nonvolatile (nonstinky). Lemon juice contains lemon oils that dissolve the oil-soluble aroma compounds in garlic, plus its own fragrance masks the remaining odor. The bottom line? Lemon juice, baking soda, and stainless steel all help a little, but there is no magic cure for removing garlic smell from your hands.

Secrets to Great Roasted Garlic Flavor

1. To bloom garlic flavor and temper harshness, cook minced garlic and sugar in butter until garlic is sticky and straw-colored.

2. For deeply integrated garlic flavor, toss raw potatoes with garlic-butter mixture, add half-and-half and water directly to pot, cover, and gently cook until tender.

Why This Recipe Works Making mashed potatoes isn't typically a quick endeavor—add roasted garlic to the mix and you've really got a project on your hands. We wanted a streamlined recipe. We cut the potatoes into small pieces to promote even, quicker cooking. The small pieces also meant the potatoes could better soak up garlicky flavor. To mimic the flavor of roasted garlic, we sprinkled in a little sugar while sautéing the garlic. Finally, we simmered the potatoes in half-and-half, butter, and the sautéed garlic to avoid the "washing away" of flavor that can come from boiling in just water.

Why This Recipe Works To revive this classic potato dish, we first focused on how to prep the potatoes. Boiled cubed potatoes won out over shredded because they held their texture better in the casserole. Next, we sautéed onion and garlic, added cream and chicken broth (to cut the richness of the cream), and cooked the cubed potatoes in this mixture. Lemon juice and zest brought the casserole welcome brightness. For the crusty topping, we turned to an unexpected ingredient: frozen shredded hash browns. We sautéed the thawed hash browns in butter, cream, and chicken broth to enhance their flavor before topping the casserole.

DELMONICO POTATO CASSEROLE

SERVES 8 TO 10

We prefer the buttery flavor of Yukon Gold potatoes here, but all-purpose and red potatoes also work. Do not use russets—their high starch content will make the casserole gluey. For the topping, we had good results with Ore-Ida Country Style Hash Browns, available in the frozen foods aisle of most supermarkets.

- 3 tablespoons unsalted butter
- 1 onion, chopped fine
- 2 garlic cloves, minced
- 2½ cups heavy cream
- 1½ cups chicken broth
- 2½ pounds Yukon Gold potatoes, peeled and cut into ½-inch cubes
- ⅛ teaspoon ground nutmeg
- Salt and pepper
- 1 teaspoon grated lemon zest plus 2 teaspoons juice
- 5 cups frozen shredded hash brown potatoes, thawed and patted dry with paper towels
- 1½ ounces Parmesan cheese, grated (¾ cup)
- ¼ cup finely chopped fresh chives

1. Adjust oven rack to upper-middle position and heat oven to 450 degrees. Melt 1 tablespoon butter in Dutch oven over medium-high heat. Cook onion until softened, about 3 minutes. Stir in garlic and cook until fragrant, about 30 seconds. Stir in 2 cups cream, 1 cup broth, Yukon Golds, nutmeg, 2 teaspoons salt, and 1 teaspoon pepper. Bring to boil, then reduce heat to medium and simmer until potatoes are translucent at edges and mixture is slightly thickened, about 10 minutes. Off heat, stir in lemon zest and juice.

2. Transfer potato mixture to 13 by 9-inch baking dish and bake until bubbling around edges and surface is just golden, about 20 minutes. Meanwhile, melt remaining 2 tablespoons butter in 12-inch nonstick skillet over medium-high heat. Cook shredded potatoes until beginning to brown, about 2 minutes. Add remaining ½ cup cream, remaining ½ cup broth, and ½ teaspoon pepper to skillet and cook, stirring occasionally, until liquid has evaporated, about 3 minutes. Off heat, stir in ½ cup Parmesan and 2 tablespoons chives.

3. Remove baking dish from oven and top with shredded potato mixture. Sprinkle with remaining ¼ cup Parmesan and continue to bake until top is golden brown, about 20 minutes. Let cool for 15 minutes. Sprinkle with remaining 2 tablespoons chives. Serve.

To Make Ahead Prepare through step 1, let cool completely, transfer to baking dish, and refrigerate, covered with plastic wrap, for 1 day. To serve, proceed as directed in step 2, increasing baking time to 25 to 30 minutes.

Potatoes with Panache

In 1837, Delmonico's opened in lower Manhattan and a restaurant star was born. Owned by two Swiss men, the restaurant served French-style cuisine and became the model for many other fashionable restaurants of the era. Its lavish dining room served such luxurious fare as lobster Newburg, baked Alaska, and their signature potato side dish, Delmonico potatoes. The potatoes were boiled, finely shredded, and cooked with milk and heavy cream. When an order came in, a serving of potatoes was sprinkled with Parmesan cheese and "gratinéed" under the broiler. The result was a potato gratin with a creamy interior and a crusty, cheesy topping. But look up a modern recipe for this dish and you'll most likely find a casserole made of overboiled chunks of potatoes baked in a creamy cheddar sauce and topped with more cheese. We wanted to bring back the simplicity and elegance of the original dish, but make it more practical to feed a crowd.

Why This Recipe Works These crispy, cheesy Parmesan potatoes promised to be a habit-forming snack, but first we had to figure out how best to cook the potatoes and how to get the cheese to stick to them. Using thinly sliced, creamy Yukon Gold potatoes meant they wouldn't dry out during roasting. We tossed the potato slices with seasoned cornstarch to promote crisping. Parmesan, rosemary, and a little more cornstarch made for a savory coating that clung evenly to the slices. Baked in a very hot oven until golden brown and served with a cool chive sour cream, these were just the potatoes we craved.

CRISPY PARMESAN POTATOES

SERVES 6 TO 8

Try to find potatoes that are 2½ to 3 inches long. Spray the baking sheet with an aerosol (not pump) vegetable oil spray. Use a good-quality Parmesan cheese here. Serve with Chive Sour Cream (recipe follows), if desired.

- 2 pounds medium Yukon gold potatoes, unpeeled
- 4 teaspoons cornstarch
- Salt and pepper
- 1 tablespoon extra-virgin olive oil
- 6 ounces Parmesan cheese, cut into 1-inch chunks
- 2 teaspoons minced fresh rosemary

1. Adjust oven rack to lower-middle position and heat oven to 500 degrees. Spray rimmed baking sheet liberally with vegetable oil spray. Cut thin slice from 2 opposing long sides of each potato; discard slices. Cut potatoes crosswise into ½-inch-thick slices and transfer to large bowl.

2. Combine 2 teaspoons cornstarch, 1 teaspoon salt, and 1 teaspoon pepper in small bowl. Sprinkle cornstarch mixture over potatoes and toss until potatoes are thoroughly coated and cornstarch is no longer visible. Add oil and toss to coat.

3. Arrange potatoes in single layer on prepared sheet and bake until golden brown on top, about 20 minutes.

4. Meanwhile, process Parmesan, rosemary, ½ teaspoon pepper, and remaining 2 teaspoons cornstarch in food processor until cheese is finely ground, about 1 minute.

5. Remove potatoes from oven. Sprinkle Parmesan mixture evenly over and between potatoes (cheese should cover surface of baking sheet), pressing on potatoes with back of spoon to adhere. Using two forks, flip slices over into same spot on sheet.

6. Bake until cheese between potatoes turns light golden brown, 5 to 7 minutes. Transfer sheet to wire rack and let potatoes cool for 15 minutes. Using large metal spatula, transfer potatoes, cheese side up, and accompanying cheese to platter and serve.

CHIVE SOUR CREAM
MAKES ABOUT 1 CUP

This enhanced condiment makes an excellent topping for potatoes of all kinds.

- 1 cup sour cream
- ¼ cup minced fresh chives
- ½ teaspoon minced fresh rosemary
- ½ teaspoon salt
- ½ teaspoon pepper
- ½ teaspoon garlic powder
- ¼ teaspoon onion powder

Combine all ingredients in bowl. Cover and refrigerate at least 30 minutes to allow flavors to blend.

Flipping For Frico

Using 2 forks, turn each potato slice over and return it to the same spot on the sheet. As the Parmesan bakes, it will transform into crispy cheesey bits called frico.

ROASTED SALT-AND-VINEGAR POTATOES

SERVES 4

Use small red potatoes, measuring 1 to 2 inches in diameter. If you prefer to use kosher salt, you will need 1½ cups of Morton's or 2½ cups of Diamond Crystal. Cider vinegar is a good substitute for the malt vinegar.

- 6 tablespoons olive oil
- 2 pounds small red potatoes, scrubbed
- 1¼ cups salt
- 3 tablespoons malt vinegar
- Pepper

1. Adjust oven rack to upper-middle position and heat oven to 500 degrees. Set wire rack inside rimmed baking sheet. Brush second rimmed baking sheet evenly with oil. Bring 2 quarts water to boil in Dutch oven over medium-high heat. Stir in potatoes and salt and cook until just tender and paring knife slips easily in and out of potatoes, 20 to 30 minutes. Drain potatoes and transfer to wire rack; let dry for 10 minutes.

2. Transfer potatoes to oiled baking sheet. Flatten each potato with underside of measuring cup until ½ inch thick. Brush potatoes with half of vinegar and season with pepper. Roast until potatoes are well browned, 25 to 30 minutes. Brush with remaining vinegar. Transfer potatoes to platter, smashed side up. Serve.

Scrub the Potatoes

Because the skins will be in the finished dish, it's important to scrub the potatoes well before cooking.

Salt of the Earth (and Sea)

A variety of salts are available in supermarkets today: table, iodized, kosher, and sea salt. What's the difference? Table and iodized salt (simply table salt with iodine added) have fine grains and contain anticaking agents that help them flow freely. Kosher salt, so named because it is used in the koshering process, has larger crystals and typically contains no additives. Both table and kosher salts are considered "refined salts" because they are mined from rock salt deposits and then purified. Sea salt is harvested by evaporating seawater and therefore has a full, slightly mineral flavor. Though we use table salt in the vast majority of our recipes, the choice is a matter of preference—except when it comes to our Roasted Salt-and-Vinegar Potatoes. While table, kosher, and sea salts all performed equally well in this recipe, we advise against using iodized salt as it gives the potatoes a noticeably chemical flavor.

Malt Vinegar Substitutes

For our salt-and-vinegar potatoes, we raided the English larder for a beloved condiment: malt vinegar. Brits commonly douse fish and chips with it, so we knew it would be a perfect match for roasted potatoes. The vinegar, which is made from sprouted barley grains, gives the potatoes a pleasantly malty, tangy taste. But if you don't have it, cider or white wine vinegars are good substitutes. Avoid balsamic and rice vinegars, which tasters found too sweet, and red wine and distilled white vinegars, which were too harsh.

Why This Recipe Works Cooking red potatoes in a super-saturated salt solution gave them incredibly creamy, well-seasoned interiors. After the potatoes were parcooked, we smashed them to expose some of the potato flesh, brushed them with malt vinegar, and roasted them on a well-oiled baking sheet until the exposed surface was golden and crispy. A final brush with more vinegar when the potatoes came out of the oven reinforced the addictive salty-sour flavor of these spuds.

Why This Recipe Works Our Super-Stuffed Baked Potatoes feature fluffy potato, garlic, herbs, and creamy cheese in crispy potato-skin shells. Precooking the potatoes in the microwave shaved an hour off the cooking time. And while most stuffed baked potato recipes call for cutting the potato in half, we preferred to lop off just the top quarter of the potato. Prepared this way, the potato shells held more filling. But after hollowing out the potatoes, there wasn't enough stuffing to fill each one and mound the filling on top. To make the filling go further, we cooked an extra potato and used its flesh to top off the other stuffed baked potatoes.

SUPER-STUFFED BAKED POTATOES

SERVES 6

This recipe calls for seven potatoes but makes six servings; the remaining potato is used for its flesh.

- 7 large russet potatoes
- 3 tablespoons unsalted butter, melted, plus 3 tablespoons unsalted butter
- Salt and pepper
- 1 (5.2-ounce) package Boursin cheese, crumbled
- ½ cup half-and-half
- 2 garlic cloves, minced
- ¼ cup chopped fresh chives

1. Adjust oven rack to middle position and heat oven to 475 degrees. Set wire rack in rimmed baking sheet. Prick potatoes all over with fork, place on paper towel, and microwave until tender, 20 to 25 minutes, turning potatoes over after 10 minutes.

2. Slice and remove top quarter of each potato, let cool for 5 minutes, then scoop out flesh, leaving ¼-inch layer of potato on inside. Discard 1 potato shell. Brush remaining shells inside and out with 3 tablespoons melted butter and sprinkle interiors with ¼ teaspoon salt. Transfer potatoes, scooped side up, to prepared baking sheet and bake until skins begin to crisp, about 15 minutes.

3. Meanwhile, mix half of Boursin with half-and-half in bowl until blended. Cook remaining 3 tablespoons butter and garlic in saucepan over medium-low heat until garlic is straw-colored, 3 to 5 minutes. Stir in Boursin mixture until combined.

4. Set ricer or food mill over medium bowl and press or mill potatoes into bowl. Gently fold in warm Boursin mixture, 3 tablespoons chives, 1 teaspoon pepper, and ½ teaspoon salt until well incorporated. Remove potato shells from oven and fill with potato-cheese mixture. Top with remaining crumbled Boursin and bake until tops of potatoes are golden brown, about 15 minutes. Sprinkle with remaining 1 tablespoon chives. Serve.

Bigger, Better Stuffed Potatoes

During testing for our Super-Stuffed Baked Potatoes, we found that most recipes called for the baked potatoes to be cut right in half before being filled. But these skimpy spuds were far from the super-stuffed garlic potatoes we were looking for. Instead, we found the best method was to cut off only the top quarter of the potato, leaving a much more substantial spud to stuff.

1. Slice off top quarter of microwaved potato.

2. Use spoon to scoop out interior of potato, being careful to leave ¼-inch layer of potato in shell.

Why This Recipe Works For this showstopper side dish, we found that using the right kind of potato is key. The russet potato was the best choice because of its starchy flesh and fluffy texture. Taking the time to rinse the potatoes of surface starch after they were sliced prevented them from sticking together, while trimming off the end of each potato gave the remaining slices room to fan out. To prevent overcooking our spuds in the punishing oven heat, we precooked them in the microwave before baking. A topping of fresh bread crumbs, melted butter, two kinds of cheese, garlic powder, and paprika is the crowning touch.

CRISPY BAKED POTATO FANS

SERVES 4

To ensure that the potatoes fan out evenly, look for uniformly shaped potatoes.

Bread-Crumb Topping
- 1 slice hearty white sandwich bread, torn into quarters
- 4 tablespoons unsalted butter, melted
- 2 ounces Monterey Jack cheese, shredded (½ cup)
- ¼ cup grated Parmesan cheese
- 1 teaspoon paprika
- ½ teaspoon garlic powder
- Salt and pepper

Potato Fans
- 4 russet potatoes
- 2 tablespoons extra-virgin olive oil
- Salt and pepper

1. For the Bread-Crumb Topping Adjust oven rack to middle position and heat oven to 200 degrees. Pulse bread in food processor until coarsely ground, about 5 pulses. Bake bread crumbs on rimmed baking sheet until dry, about 20 minutes. Let cool for 5 minutes, then combine crumbs, butter, Monterey Jack, Parmesan, paprika, garlic powder, ¼ teaspoon salt, and ¼ teaspoon pepper in large bowl. (Bread-crumb topping can be refrigerated in zipper-lock bag for 2 days.)

2. For the Potato Fans Heat oven to 450 degrees. Cut ¼ inch from bottom and ends of potatoes, then slice potatoes crosswise at ¼-inch intervals, leaving ¼ inch of potato intact. Gently rinse potatoes under running water, let drain, and transfer, sliced side down, to plate. Microwave until slightly soft to touch, 6 to 12 minutes, flipping potatoes halfway through cooking.

3. Line rimmed baking sheet with aluminum foil. Arrange potatoes, sliced side up, on prepared baking sheet. Brush potatoes all over with oil and season with salt and pepper. Bake until skin is crisp and potatoes are beginning to brown, 25 to 30 minutes. Remove potatoes from oven and heat broiler.

4. Carefully top potatoes with stuffing mixture, pressing gently to adhere. Broil until bread crumbs are deep golden brown, about 3 minutes. Serve.

BLUE CHEESE AND BACON BAKED POTATO FANS

In step 1, substitute ⅓ cup crumbled blue cheese for Monterey Jack. In step 4, sprinkle 4 slices bacon, cooked until crisp and then crumbled, over potatoes just prior to serving.

Prepping Baked Potato Fans

These potatoes may look difficult to make, but we found a few simple tricks to ensure perfect potato fans every time.

1. Trim ¼-inch slices from bottom and ends of each potato to allow them to sit flat and to give slices extra room to fan out during baking.

2. Chopsticks provide a foolproof guide for slicing potato petals without cutting all the way through.

3. Gently flex open fans while rinsing under cold running water; this rids potatoes of excess starch that can impede fanning.

OLIVE OIL POTATO GRATIN

SERVES 6 TO 8

The test kitchen's favorite supermarket extra-virgin olive oil is California Olive Ranch Everyday. We prefer to use a mandoline to create thin, even slices of potato.

- 2 ounces Pecorino-Romano cheese, grated (1 cup)
- ½ cup extra-virgin olive oil
- ¼ cup panko bread crumbs
- Salt and pepper
- 2 onions, halved and sliced thin
- 2 garlic cloves, minced
- 1 teaspoon minced fresh thyme
- 1 cup low-sodium chicken broth
- 3 pounds Yukon Gold potatoes, peeled and sliced ⅛ inch thick

1. Adjust oven rack to upper-middle position and heat oven to 400 degrees. Grease 13 by 9-inch baking dish. Combine Pecorino, 3 tablespoons oil, panko, and ½ teaspoon pepper in bowl; set aside.

2. Heat 2 tablespoons oil in 12-inch skillet over medium heat until shimmering. Add onions, ½ teaspoon salt, and ¼ teaspoon pepper and cook, stirring frequently, until browned, about 15 minutes. Add garlic and ½ teaspoon thyme and cook until fragrant, about 30 seconds. Add ¼ cup broth and cook until nearly evaporated, scraping up any browned bits, about 2 minutes. Remove from heat; set aside.

3. Toss potatoes, remaining 3 tablespoons oil, 1 teaspoon salt, ½ teaspoon pepper, and remaining ½ teaspoon thyme together in bowl. Arrange half of potatoes in prepared dish, spread onion mixture in even layer over potatoes, and distribute remaining potatoes over onions. Pour remaining ¾ cup broth over potatoes. Cover dish tightly with aluminum foil and bake for 1 hour.

4. Remove foil, top gratin with reserved Pecorino mixture, and continue to bake until top is golden brown and potatoes are completely tender, 15 to 20 minutes. Let cool for 15 minutes. Serve.

Slicing Potatoes

A mandoline makes quick work of thinly slicing potatoes, but if you don't own one, cut a slice off of one side of each potato to create a flat, stable surface for thin slicing.

Why This Recipe Works Potato gratin is a notoriously heavy side dish, laden with cream and gooey cheese. We wanted to shift the focus of this classic side dish to the potatoes. We chose Yukon Gold potatoes for their rich flavor and moderate starch content, which helped them hold their shape when cooked. Tossing the potatoes with fruity, flavorful extra-virgin olive oil heightened the flavor of the potatoes but didn't overpower them. For a crisp, cheesy topping, we mixed more olive oil with panko bread crumbs and sprinkled the dish with sharp, salty Pecorino-Romano. For added depth, we added sautéed onions, fresh thyme, and garlic.

MASHED POTATO CAKES

SERVES 4 TO 6

Using two spatulas to flip the cakes helps prevent splattering. We like to change the oil after frying the first batch of cakes because any dark panko remnants left behind will freckle the second batch. You can strain the oil through a fine-mesh strainer if you prefer to reuse it, but be careful because it is very hot. Plan ahead: The cooked mashed potatoes need to chill in the refrigerator for 1 hour, which makes it easier to form the cakes.

- 2½ pounds russet potatoes, peeled, halved lengthwise, and sliced ¼ inch thick
- Salt and pepper
- 1 ounce Parmesan cheese, grated (½ cup)
- ¼ cup chopped fresh chives
- 1 large egg yolk plus 2 large eggs
- 2 cups panko bread crumbs
- 1 cup vegetable oil
- Sour cream

1. Place potatoes in medium saucepan and add water to cover by 1 inch, then stir in 1 tablespoon salt. Bring to boil over high heat. Reduce heat to medium-low and simmer until tip of paring knife inserted into potatoes meets no resistance, 8 to 10 minutes. Drain potatoes and return to saucepan; let cool for 5 minutes.

2. Add Parmesan, chives, egg yolk, ¾ teaspoon salt, and ¼ teaspoon pepper to cooled potatoes. Using potato masher, mash until smooth and well combined. Transfer potato mixture to bowl and refrigerate until completely cool, about 1 hour.

3. Beat remaining 2 eggs together in shallow dish. Place panko in second shallow dish. Divide potato mixture into 8 equal portions (about ½ cup each) and shape into 3-inch-diameter cakes, about ¾ inch thick. Working with 1 cake at a time, carefully dip cakes in egg mixture, turning to coat both sides and allowing excess to drip off; then coat with panko, pressing gently to adhere. Transfer to plate and let sit for 5 minutes.

4. Line large plate with paper towels. Heat ½ cup oil in 12-inch nonstick skillet over medium-high heat until shimmering. Place 4 cakes in skillet and cook until deep golden brown on first side, about 3 minutes. Using 2 spatulas, carefully flip cakes and continue to cook until deep golden brown on second side, about 2 minutes longer, gently pressing on cakes with spatula for even browning.

5. Transfer cakes to prepared plate. Discard oil and wipe out skillet with paper towels. Repeat with remaining ½ cup oil and remaining 4 cakes. Serve with sour cream.

BLUE CHEESE AND BACON MASHED POTATO CAKES

Substitute ¾ cup crumbled blue cheese for Parmesan. Stir 6 slices cooked chopped bacon into potato mixture after mashing in step 2.

CHEDDAR AND SCALLION MASHED POTATO CAKES

Substitute 1 cup shredded sharp cheddar cheese for Parmesan and sliced scallions for chives.

Why This Recipe Works Mashed potato cakes—soft, fluffy mashed potatoes coated in bread crumbs and fried—are equally welcome at suppertime next to a piece of meat or at breakfast under a poached egg. Using leftover mashed potatoes yielded mushy cakes, so we started from scratch, mashing russet potatoes with Parmesan, chives, and an egg yolk for extra richness. Chilling the mashed potatoes before forming the cakes made shaping them easier. For a golden-brown and crisp crust, we dipped the disks in beaten egg to help the coating adhere. Serving the potato cakes with a dollop of sour cream offered a cool, tangy finish.

Why This Recipe Works Roasting red peppers on the grill turns their juicy crunch smoky and tender. We tossed stemmed and cored peppers in garlic-infused olive oil, allowing the oil to soak into the interiors' exposed flesh. To prevent flare-ups, we grilled the peppers in a foil-covered disposable pan then drained them and placed them directly on the hot grates to char. After easily scraping the charred skins from the peppers, we tossed them in a vinaigrette made from the leftover oil and liquid released from the peppers. The finished peppers were tender, smoky, and infused with heady garlic flavor that complemented the intensified sweetness.

GRILL-ROASTED PEPPERS

SERVES 4

These peppers can be refrigerated for up to 5 days.

- ¼ cup extra-virgin olive oil
- 3 garlic cloves, peeled and smashed
- Salt and pepper
- 1 (13 by 9-inch) disposable aluminum pan
- 6 red bell peppers
- 1 tablespoon sherry vinegar

1. Combine oil, garlic, ½ teaspoon salt, and ¼ teaspoon pepper in disposable pan. Using paring knife, cut around stems of peppers and remove cores and seeds. Place peppers in pan and turn to coat with oil. Cover pan tightly with aluminum foil.

2A. For a Charcoal Grill Open bottom vent completely. Light large chimney starter filled with charcoal briquettes (6 quarts). When top coals are partially covered with ash, pour evenly over half of grill. Set cooking grate in place, cover, and open lid vent completely. Heat grill until hot, about 5 minutes.

2B. For a Gas Grill Turn all burners to high, cover, and heat grill until hot, about 15 minutes. Turn all burners to medium-high.

3. Clean and oil cooking grate. Place pan on grill (over hotter side for charcoal) and cook, covered, until peppers are just tender and skins begin to blister, 10 to 15 minutes, rotating and shaking pan halfway through cooking.

4. Remove pan from heat and carefully remove foil (reserve foil to use later). Using tongs, remove peppers from pan, allowing juices to drip back into pan, and place on grill (over hotter side for charcoal). Grill peppers, covered, turning every few minutes until skins are blackened, 10 to 15 minutes.

5. Transfer juices and garlic in pan to medium bowl and whisk in vinegar. Remove peppers from grill, return to now-empty pan, and cover tightly with foil. Let peppers steam for 5 minutes. Using spoon, scrape blackened skin off each pepper. Quarter peppers lengthwise, add to vinaigrette in bowl, and toss to combine. Season with salt and pepper to taste, and serve.

Steam Then Sear

We first steam the peppers in garlicky olive oil and their own juices. Then we sear the peppers and serve them with a vinaigrette made from the infused oil.

STUFFED TOMATOES

SERVES 6

Look for large tomatoes, about 3 inches in diameter.

- 6 large vine-ripened tomatoes (8 to 10 ounces each)
- 1 tablespoon sugar
- Kosher salt and pepper
- 4½ tablespoons extra-virgin olive oil
- ¼ cup panko bread crumbs
- 3 ounces Gruyère cheese, shredded (¾ cup)
- 1 onion, halved and sliced thin
- 2 garlic cloves, minced
- ⅛ teaspoon red pepper flakes
- 8 ounces (8 cups) baby spinach, chopped coarse
- 1 cup couscous
- ½ teaspoon grated lemon zest
- 1 tablespoon red wine vinegar

1. Adjust oven rack to middle position and heat oven to 375 degrees. Cut top ½ inch off stem end of tomatoes and set aside. Using melon baller, scoop out tomato pulp and transfer to fine-mesh strainer set over bowl. Press on pulp with wooden spoon to extract juice; set aside juice and discard pulp. (You should have about ⅔ cup tomato juice; if not, add water as needed to equal ⅔ cup.)

2. Combine sugar and 1 tablespoon salt in bowl. Sprinkle each tomato cavity with 1 teaspoon sugar mixture, then turn tomatoes upside down on plate to drain for 30 minutes.

3. Combine 1½ teaspoons oil and panko in 10-inch skillet and toast over medium-high heat, stirring frequently, until golden brown, about 3 minutes. Transfer to bowl and let cool for 10 minutes. Stir in ¼ cup Gruyère.

4. Heat 2 tablespoons oil in now-empty skillet over medium heat until shimmering. Add onion and ½ teaspoon salt and cook until softened, 5 to 7 minutes. Stir in garlic and pepper flakes and cook until fragrant, about 30 seconds. Add spinach, 1 handful at a time, and cook until wilted, about 3 minutes. Stir in couscous, lemon zest, and reserved tomato juice. Cover, remove from heat, and let sit until couscous has absorbed liquid, about 7 minutes.

Transfer couscous mixture to bowl and stir in remaining ½ cup Gruyère. Season with salt and pepper to taste.

5. Coat bottom of 13 by 9-inch baking dish with remaining 2 tablespoons oil. Blot tomato cavities dry with paper towels and season with salt and pepper. Pack each tomato with couscous mixture, about ½ cup per tomato, mounding excess. Top stuffed tomatoes with 1 heaping tablespoon panko mixture. Place tomatoes in prepared dish. Season reserved tops with salt and pepper and place in empty spaces in dish.

6. Bake, uncovered, until tomatoes have softened but still hold their shape, about 20 minutes. Using slotted spoon, transfer to serving platter. Whisk vinegar into oil remaining in dish, then drizzle over tomatoes. Place tops on tomatoes and serve.

STUFFED TOMATOES WITH BACON

Substitute shredded smoked cheddar for Gruyère. Stir 3 slices chopped, cooked bacon into cooked couscous mixture with cheddar in step 4.

STUFFED TOMATOES WITH CAPERS AND PINE NUTS

Substitute shredded mozzarella for Gruyère. Stir 2 tablespoons rinsed capers and 2 tablespoons toasted pine nuts into cooked couscous mixture with mozzarella in step 4.

STUFFED TOMATOES WITH CURRANTS AND PISTACHIOS

Substitute crumbled feta for Gruyère. Stir 2 tablespoons currants and 2 tablespoons chopped pistachios into cooked couscous mixture with feta in step 4.

STUFFED TOMATOES WITH OLIVES AND ORANGE

Substitute shredded Manchego for Gruyère. Substitute ¼ teaspoon grated orange zest for lemon zest. Stir ¼ cup pitted kalamata olives, chopped, into cooked couscous mixture with Manchego in step 4.

Why This Recipe Works Stuffed tomatoes always sound delicious, but too often you get tasteless tomatoes and a lackluster stuffing that falls out in a clump. To concentrate flavor and get rid of excess moisture, we seasoned hollowed-out tomato shells with salt and sugar and let them drain. Couscous proved the best base for the filling, and we rehydrated it with the reserved tomato juice, ensuring the savory tomato flavor we craved. A topping of panko bread crumbs—pretoasted for proper browning—mixed with more cheese added crunch and richness, and a drizzle of the cooking liquid mixed with red wine vinegar provided a piquant final touch.

our sunday best

- **160** Old-Fashioned Roast Turkey with Gravy
- **162** Cornbread and Sausage Stuffing
- **165** Herb Roast Chicken
- **166** Roast Lemon Chicken
- **168** Apple Cider Chicken
- **171** One-Pan Roast Chicken with Root Vegetables
- **172** Skillet-Roasted Chicken and Potatoes
- **175** Skillet-Roasted Chicken with Stuffing
- **177** Chicken Baked in Foil with Sweet Potato and Radish
- **178** Chicken and Slicks
- **180** Moravian Chicken Pie
- **183** Guinness Beef Stew
- **184** Brunswick Stew
- **187** Sunday-Best Garlic Roast Beef
- **189** Classic Roast Beef and Gravy
- **190** Herbed Roast Beef
- **192** Herb-Crusted Beef Tenderloin
- **195** Holiday Strip Roast
- **196** Deviled Beef Short Ribs
- **198** One-Pan Prime Rib and Roasted Vegetables
- **201** Prime Rib with Potatoes and Red Wine–Orange Sauce
- **203** Chuck Roast in Foil
- **204** Crown Roast of Pork
- **207** Slow-Cooker Pork Pot Roast
- **209** Old-Fashioned Roast Pork
- **210** Puerto Rican Pork Roast
- **212** Cider Braised Pork Roast
- **215** Cider-Baked Ham
- **216** Parmesan-Crusted Asparagus
- **218** Brussels Sprout Salad
- **221** Whipped Potatoes
- **223** Duchess Potatoes
- **224** Syracuse Salt Potatoes
- **227** Mashed Potato Casserole
- **228** Creamy Mashed Sweet Potatoes
- **230** Sweet Corn Spoonbread

OLD-FASHIONED ROAST TURKEY WITH GRAVY

SERVES 10 TO 12

You will need one 2-yard package of cheesecloth for this recipe. Because we layer the bird with salt pork, we prefer to use a natural turkey here; a self-basting turkey (such as a frozen Butterball) may become too salty. If using a self-basting turkey, omit the chicken broth in the gravy and increase the amount of water to 7 cups. Make sure to start the gravy as soon as the turkey goes into the oven.

Turkey
- 1 (2-yard) package cheesecloth
- 4 cups water
- 1 (12- to 14-pound) turkey, neck, giblets, and tailpiece removed and reserved for gravy
- 1 pound salt pork, cut into ¼-inch-thick slices

Gravy
- 1 tablespoon vegetable oil
- 1 onion, chopped
- 5 cups water
- 2 cups chicken broth
- 4 sprigs fresh thyme
- 1 bay leaf
- 6 tablespoons all-purpose flour
- Salt and pepper

1. For the Turkey Adjust oven rack to lowest position and heat oven to 350 degrees. Fold cheesecloth into 18-inch square, place in large bowl, and cover with water. Tuck wings behind turkey and arrange, breast side up, on V-rack set in roasting pan. Prick skin of breast and legs of turkey all over with fork, cover breast and legs with salt pork, top with soaked cheesecloth (pouring any remaining water into roasting pan), and cover cheesecloth completely with heavy-duty aluminum foil.

2. Roast turkey until breast registers 140 degrees, 2½ to 3 hours. Remove foil, cheesecloth, and salt pork and discard. Increase oven temperature to 425 degrees. Continue to roast until breast registers 160 degrees and thighs register 175 degrees, 40 minutes to 1 hour longer. Transfer turkey to carving board and let rest 30 minutes.

3. For the Gravy Meanwhile, heat oil in large saucepan over medium-high heat until shimmering. Cook turkey neck and giblets until browned, about 5 minutes. Add onion and cook until softened, about 3 minutes. Stir in water, broth, thyme, and bay leaf and bring to boil. Reduce heat to low and simmer until reduced by half, about 3 hours. Strain mixture through fine-mesh strainer into 4-cup liquid measuring cup (you should have about 3½ cups), reserving giblets if desired.

4. Carefully strain contents of roasting pan into fat separator. Let liquid settle, then skim, reserving ¼ cup fat. Pour defatted pan juices into measuring cup with giblet broth to yield 4 cups liquid.

5. Heat reserved fat in empty saucepan over medium heat until shimmering. Stir in flour and cook until golden and fragrant, about 4 minutes. Slowly whisk in giblet broth and bring to boil. Reduce heat to medium-low and simmer until slightly thickened, about 5 minutes. Chop giblets and add to gravy, if desired, and season with salt and pepper to taste. Carve turkey and serve with gravy.

Salt Pork

Covering the breast and tops of the legs of the turkey with salt pork helps to season the meat and insulate it from overcooking. Don't confuse salt pork with bacon. Although both come from the belly of the pig and are salt-cured, bacon is heavily smoked and is typically leaner and meatier. Salt pork is unsmoked and used primarily as a flavoring agent (traditionally in dishes like baked beans) and is rarely actually consumed. We recommend buying blocks of salt pork (precut slices can dry out) and portioning it as needed. Look for salt pork that has at least a few streaks of meat throughout. Salt pork can be refrigerated for up to one month.

Why This Recipe Works For a roast turkey with moist, flavorful meat, we tried a number of options until we discovered a technique used for ages: barding. Similar to larding, it is a process of wrapping strips of lard (or other animal fat) around the meat so that it slowly releases flavor and moisture throughout roasting. After piercing the skin of the turkey breast and legs with a fork, we covered it with thin slices of salt pork before layering on cheesecloth that had been soaked in water and then aluminum foil. This insulated the meat and allowed the salt pork to slowly melt in the oven, basting the turkey with rich fat.

CORNBREAD AND SAUSAGE STUFFING

SERVES 10 TO 12

We prefer spicy andouille sausage in this recipe, but chorizo or kielbasa work well, too. For the cornbread, use your favorite recipe, store-bought cornbread, or Betty Crocker Golden Corn Muffin and Bread Mix or Jiffy Corn Muffin Mix, both of which will work fine in stuffing.

- 12 cups prepared cornbread cut into ¾-inch cubes
- 1½ pounds andouille sausage, halved lengthwise and sliced into ¼-inch-thick half-moons
- 2 tablespoons unsalted butter
- 2 small onions, chopped fine
- 3 celery ribs, chopped fine
- 2 tablespoons minced fresh sage
- 3 garlic cloves, minced
- 1 teaspoon salt
- 1 teaspoon pepper
- 4 cups chicken broth

1. Adjust oven racks to upper-middle and lower-middle positions and heat oven to 400 degrees. Spread cornbread evenly over 2 rimmed baking sheets. Bake until slightly crisp, 15 to 20 minutes; let cool. Carefully remove upper-middle rack from oven.

2. Cook sausage in Dutch oven over medium-high heat until lightly browned, 5 to 7 minutes. Transfer to paper towel–lined plate and pour off fat left behind in pot. Melt butter over medium-high heat, add onions and celery, and cook until softened, about 5 minutes. Stir in sage, garlic, salt, and pepper and cook until fragrant, about 1 minute. Add broth and sausage, scraping up browned bits with wooden spoon. Add cornbread and gently stir until liquid is absorbed. Cover and set aside for 10 minutes. (Stuffing can be refrigerated for 1 day; let sit at room temperature for 30 minutes before baking.)

3. Remove lid and bake until top of stuffing is golden brown and crisp, about 30 minutes. Serve.

CORNBREAD AND BACON STUFFING

Substitute 1 pound bacon, chopped, for sausage, 3 cups fresh or frozen corn kernels for celery, and 3 thinly sliced scallions for sage.

Drying Cornbread

Although cornbread gives stuffing great flavor, it also adds a lot of moisture, making a soggy baked mess. If you have the time, cube the cornbread, spread it out on baking sheets, and let it sit overnight on the counter. If you're in a hurry (and who isn't around the holidays?), pop the baking sheets holding the cornbread into a 400-degree oven until slightly crisp, 15 to 20 minutes.

Why This Recipe Works We wanted a stuffing rich enough to stand on its own without gravy. We found our answer in cornbread and sausage. Cornbread gives the stuffing more flavor than plain white bread. We wanted plenty of stuffing, so we chose to cook it in a Dutch oven, which is large enough to accommodate 10 to 12 portions. To compensate for the loss in richness and poultry flavor we didn't just rely on any sausage—we chose spicy andouille sausage. Adding chicken broth to the stuffing further boosted the meaty flavor of our stuffing and helped keep it from drying out.

Why This Recipe Works Developing a recipe for a classic herb roast chicken proved surprisingly tricky. Stuffing the chicken with fresh herbs delivered zero flavor, herb butter melted off the chicken, and infused oil failed to really penetrate the meat. Our solution was to slather the chicken with a thick paste of fresh herbs and garlic, processed until smooth, then let it rest to develop a pronounced herbal flavor. So that there was plenty of meat to go around, we used two whole chickens instead of one. For a simple pan sauce, while the chicken rested we whisked the drippings with chicken broth, white wine, cornstarch, butter, and additional herb paste.

HERB ROAST CHICKEN

SERVES 6 TO 8

For even cooking, arrange the chickens side by side a few inches apart on the V-rack, with the legs pointing in opposite directions.

- 1 cup chopped fresh parsley
- 2 tablespoons chopped fresh thyme
- 1 tablespoon chopped fresh rosemary
- 2 garlic cloves, minced
- Salt and pepper
- 2 tablespoons olive oil
- 2 (3½- to 4-pound) whole chickens, giblets discarded
- 1 cup plus 2 tablespoons water
- 2 teaspoons cornstarch
- 1¼ cups chicken broth
- ¼ cup dry white wine
- 2 tablespoons unsalted butter, chilled

1. Process parsley, thyme, rosemary, garlic, 2 teaspoons salt, and 1 teaspoon pepper in food processor until paste forms, about 30 seconds. Reserve 1 teaspoon herb paste for sauce. Combine 2 tablespoons herb paste with oil in bowl. Set aside herb-oil paste and remaining herb paste.

2. Adjust oven rack to middle position and heat oven to 450 degrees. Pat chickens dry with paper towels. Using your fingers, gently loosen skin covering breast and thighs. Rub remaining herb paste under skin of each chicken, making sure to coat breast, thigh, and leg meat. Rub herb-oil paste over outside of each chicken. Tuck wings behind back and tie legs together with kitchen twine. Transfer chickens to platter. Cover and refrigerate 1 hour.

3. Arrange chickens 2 inches apart, breast side down, on V-rack set inside large roasting pan. Roast until thigh meat registers 135 to 140 degrees, 35 to 40 minutes. Remove chickens from oven and, using 2 bunches of paper towels, flip breast side up (meat that was facing in should now be facing out). Pour 1 cup water into roasting pan. Return chickens to oven and roast until breast registers 160 degrees and thighs register 175 degrees, 25 to 30 minutes. Transfer to carving board and let rest for 20 minutes.

4. Whisk cornstarch with remaining 2 tablespoons water in bowl until no lumps remain. Pour pan juices and any accumulated chicken juices into liquid measuring cup; skim fat. Transfer ½ cup defatted pan juices to medium saucepan. Add broth and wine and bring to boil. Reduce heat to medium-low and simmer until sauce is slightly thickened and reduced to 1¼ cups, 8 to 10 minutes. Whisk in cornstarch mixture and simmer until thickened, 3 to 5 minutes. Off heat, whisk in butter and reserved 1 teaspoon herb paste. Season with salt and pepper to taste. Carve chickens and serve, passing sauce at table.

Herb Flavor Times Three

To get deeply flavored roast chicken, we triple up on the herb paste.

1. Separate skin from meat and rub herb paste under skin.

2. Apply herb paste mixed with olive oil to exterior of each chicken.

3. Whisk teaspoon of herb paste into sauce for a fresh finish.

ROAST LEMON CHICKEN

SERVES 3 TO 4

Avoid using nonstick or aluminum roasting pans in this recipe. The former can cause the chicken to brown too quickly, while the latter may react with the lemon juice, producing off-flavors.

- 1 (3½- to 4-pound) whole chicken, giblets discarded
- 3 tablespoons grated lemon zest plus ⅓ cup juice (3 lemons)
- 1 teaspoon sugar
  Salt and pepper
- 2 cups chicken broth
  Water
- 1 teaspoon cornstarch
- 3 tablespoons unsalted butter
- 1 tablespoon finely chopped fresh parsley

1. Adjust oven rack to middle position and heat oven to 475 degrees. Pat chicken dry with paper towels. Using kitchen shears, cut along both sides of backbone to remove it. Flatten breastbone and tuck wings behind back. Using your fingers, gently loosen skin covering breast and thighs. Combine lemon zest, sugar, and 1 teaspoon salt in small bowl. Rub 2 tablespoons zest mixture under skin of chicken. Season chicken with salt and pepper and transfer to roasting pan. (Seasoned chicken can be refrigerated for 2 hours.)

2. Whisk broth, 1 cup water, lemon juice, and remaining zest mixture in 4-cup liquid measuring cup, then pour into roasting pan. (Liquid should just reach skin of thighs. If it does not, add enough water to reach skin of thighs.) Roast until skin is golden brown and breast registers 160 degrees and thighs register 175 degrees, 40 to 45 minutes. Transfer to carving board and let rest for 20 minutes.

3. Carefully pour liquid from pan, along with any accumulated chicken juices, into saucepan (you should have about 1½ cups). Skim fat, then cook over medium-high heat until reduced to 1 cup, about 5 minutes. Whisk cornstarch with 1 tablespoon water in small bowl until no lumps remain, then whisk into saucepan. Simmer until sauce is slightly thickened, about 2 minutes. Off heat, whisk in butter and parsley and season with salt and pepper. Carve chicken and serve, passing sauce at table.

More Lemon Flavor in Less Time
Butterflying the chicken may be unfamiliar, but this surprisingly simple process makes it easier to flavor the chicken with lemon—and it speeds roasting, too.

1. Use kitchen shears to cut out backbone. Flip bird over and press to flatten breastbone.

2. Carefully loosen skin, then rub zest mixture into breast, thigh, and leg meat.

3. Roast flattened chicken in lemony sauce so that its flavor can permeate meat.

Why This Recipe Works The citrus flavor in roasted lemon chicken can be harsh or, on the flip side, totally absent. To infuse the meat with bright flavor, we combined lemon zest, sugar, and salt and rubbed it into the chicken under the skin. For even more lemon flavor, we roasted the chicken in a sauce of lemon juice mixed with water, more zest, and chicken broth. Roasting the bird at a high temperature ensured that the exposed skin became crisp. Before serving, we reduced the sauce to concentrate its flavor and thickened it with butter and cornstarch for sheen, body, and richness.

APPLE CIDER CHICKEN

SERVES 3 TO 4

Plain brandy, cognac, or Calvados (a French apple brandy) can be used in place of the apple brandy.

- 3 pounds bone-in chicken pieces, (split breasts halved crosswise, legs separated into thighs and drumsticks), trimmed
  Salt and pepper
- 2 teaspoons vegetable oil
- 1 onion, chopped fine
- 2 garlic cloves, minced
- 2 teaspoons minced fresh thyme
- 2 teaspoons all-purpose flour
- 1 large Golden Delicious, Cortland, or Jonagold apple (8 ounces), peeled, cored, and cut into ¾-inch pieces
- 1 cup apple cider
- ¼ cup apple brandy
- 1 teaspoon cider vinegar

1. Adjust oven rack to middle position and heat oven to 450 degrees. Pat chicken dry with paper towels and season with salt and pepper. Heat oil in 12-inch ovenproof skillet over medium-high heat until just smoking. Cook chicken skin side down until well browned, about 10 minutes. Flip and brown on second side, about 5 minutes. Transfer to plate.

2. Pour off all but 1 tablespoon fat from skillet. Add onion and cook until softened, about 5 minutes. Stir in garlic, thyme, and flour and cook, stirring frequently, until fragrant and flour is absorbed, about 1 minute. Add apple, apple cider, and 3 tablespoons apple brandy and bring to boil.

3. Nestle chicken skin side up into sauce and roast in oven until breasts register 160 degrees and thighs/drumsticks register 175 degrees, about 10 minutes. Transfer chicken to platter. Stir vinegar and remaining 1 tablespoon brandy into sauce and season with salt and pepper to taste. Serve, passing sauce at table.

Preventing Flabby Skin
We avoid flabby skin with a hybrid technique that combines braising and pan roasting.

1. Brown chicken skin side down in skillet for 10 minutes until deep brown. Brown second side for 5 more minutes.

2. Finish chicken, skin side up and uncovered, in hot oven. Be sure liquid does not submerge chicken pieces.

Apple Cider versus Apple Juice
To make cider, apples are simply cored, chopped, mashed, and then pressed to extract their liquid. Most cider is pasteurized before sale, though unpasteurized cider is also available. To make apple juice, manufacturers follow the same steps used to make cider, but they also filter the extracted liquid to remove pulp and sediment. Apple juice is then pasteurized, and potassium sorbate (a preservative) is often mixed in to prevent fermentation. Finally, apple juice is sometimes sweetened with sugar or corn syrup. We tried using unsweetened apple juice in recipes for pork chops and glazed ham that call for cider. Tasters were turned off by excessive sweetness in the dishes made with apple juice, unanimously preferring those made with cider. This made sense: The filtration process used in making juice removes some of the complex, tart, and bitter flavors that are still present in cider. (When we tested the pH level of both liquids, the cider had a lower pH than the apple juice, confirming its higher level of acidity.) The bottom line: When it comes to cooking, don't swap apple juice for cider.

Why This Recipe Works We had a tall order with our Apple Cider Chicken: It had to taste like apples, and it had to have super-crisp skin. Cooking the chicken in a skillet, skin side down, then moving it to a hot oven kept the skin exceptionally crisp. When it came to flavor, apple cider alone didn't do the trick. We also needed fresh apples, apple brandy, and cider vinegar to flavor the chicken with apple goodness. For the sauce, Granny Smith apples were too sour, while other varieties turned to mush when cooked. In the end, we preferred Golden Delicious, Cortland, or Jonagold apples, which held their shape and offered sweet flavor.

Why This Recipe Works Cooking vegetables and chicken together in the same pan often leads to unevenly cooked chicken and greasy, soggy vegetables. To get the chicken and vegetables to cook at the same rate, we used chicken parts, which contain less overall fat than a whole chicken and don't smother the vegetables underneath, which would cause them to steam. To ensure that the delicate white meat stayed moist while the darker meat cooked through, we placed the chicken breasts in the center of the pan, with the thighs and drumsticks around the perimeter.

ONE-PAN ROAST CHICKEN WITH ROOT VEGETABLES

SERVES 4

We halve the chicken breasts crosswise for even cooking. Use Brussels sprouts no bigger than golf balls, as larger ones are often tough and woody.

- 12 ounces Brussels sprouts, trimmed and halved
- 12 ounces red potatoes, cut into 1-inch pieces
- 8 ounces shallots, peeled and halved
- 4 carrots, peeled and cut into 2-inch pieces, thick ends halved lengthwise
- 6 garlic cloves, peeled
- 4 teaspoons minced fresh thyme
- 1 tablespoon vegetable oil
- 2 teaspoons minced fresh rosemary
- 1 teaspoon sugar
- Salt and pepper
- 2 tablespoons unsalted butter, melted
- 3½ pounds bone-in chicken pieces (2 split breasts halved crosswise, 2 drumsticks, and 2 thighs), trimmed

1. Adjust oven rack to upper-middle position and heat oven to 475 degrees. Toss Brussels sprouts, potatoes, shallots, carrots, garlic, 2 teaspoons thyme, oil, 1 teaspoon rosemary, sugar, ¾ teaspoon salt, and ¼ teaspoon pepper together in bowl. Combine butter, remaining 2 teaspoons thyme, remaining 1 teaspoon rosemary, ¼ teaspoon salt, and ⅛ teaspoon pepper in second bowl; set aside.

2. Pat chicken dry with paper towels and season with salt and pepper. Place vegetables in single layer on rimmed baking sheet, arranging Brussels sprouts in center. Place chicken, skin side up, on top of vegetables, arranging breast pieces in center and leg and thigh pieces around perimeter of sheet.

3. Brush chicken with herb butter and roast until breasts register 160 degrees and thighs/drumsticks register 175 degrees, 35 to 40 minutes, rotating pan halfway through cooking. Transfer chicken to serving platter, tent loosely with aluminum foil, and let rest for 5 to 10 minutes. Toss vegetables in pan juices and transfer to platter with chicken. Serve.

ONE-PAN ROAST CHICKEN WITH FENNEL AND PARSNIPS
Replace Brussels sprouts and carrots with 1 fennel bulb, stalks discarded, bulb halved, cored, and sliced into ½-inch wedges, and 8 ounces (4 medium) parsnips, peeled and cut into 2-inch pieces.

Preparing Fennel

1. Cut off stalks and feathery fronds. Trim very thin slice from base and remove any tough or blemished outer layer.

2. Cut bulb in half through base. Use small sharp knife to remove pyramid-shaped cone.

3. Cut each half into ½-inch wedges.

SKILLET-ROASTED CHICKEN AND POTATOES

SERVES 4

Use uniform, medium potatoes.

- 3 tablespoons olive oil
- 2 teaspoons minced fresh thyme
- 1½ teaspoons smoked paprika
- 1½ teaspoons grated lemon zest, plus lemon wedges for serving
- Salt and pepper
- 1 (4-pound) whole chicken, giblets discarded
- 2 pounds Yukon Gold potatoes, peeled, ends squared off, and sliced into 1-inch-thick rounds

1. Adjust oven rack to lower middle position and heat oven to 400 degrees. Combine 2 tablespoons oil, thyme, paprika, lemon zest, 1 teaspoon salt, and ½ teaspoon pepper in bowl. Pat chicken dry with paper towels and use your fingers or handle of wooden spoon to carefully separate skin from breast. Rub oil mixture all over chicken and underneath skin of breast. Tie legs together with kitchen twine and tuck wingtips behind back.

2. Toss potatoes with remaining 1 tablespoon oil, 1½ teaspoons salt, and ½ teaspoon pepper. Arrange potatoes, flat sides down, in single layer in 12-inch ovensafe nonstick skillet. Place skillet over medium heat and cook potatoes, without moving them, until brown on bottom, 7 to 9 minutes (do not flip).

3. Place chicken, breast side up, on top of potatoes and transfer skillet to oven. Roast until breast registers 160 degrees and thighs register 175 degrees, 1 to 1¼ hours. Transfer chicken to carving board, tent loosely with aluminum foil, and let rest for 20 minutes.

4. Meanwhile, cover skillet, return potatoes to oven, and roast until tender, about 20 minutes. Carve chicken and serve with potatoes and lemon wedges.

Keys to Potatoes That Are Tender and Brown

Potatoes don't cook at the same rate as a chicken. Here's how we got the dish to work.

1. On the Stove Brown one side of potatoes on stovetop, then top spuds with chicken and roast.

2. In the Oven Once chicken is done, set aside; cover pan and return to oven to finish cooking potatoes.

Prepping Fresh Thyme

For thin-stemmed thyme, chop stems along with leaves. If stems are thick, hold sprig upright and run your thumb and forefinger along stem to release leaves.

Why This Recipe Works For this convenient, one-pan meal, we were challenged to deliver tender potatoes and moist chicken at the same time. First, we quickly browned one side of the potatoes (an entire 2 pounds of potatoes fit into a 12-inch skillet when sliced into 1-inch-thick rounds). We placed the bird on top and moved everything to the oven where flavorful juices basted the potatoes. An hour later, the chicken was golden and juicy and the potatoes had a caramelized crust on the bottom. While the chicken rested, we returned the potatoes to the oven. By the time the chicken was ready to be served, the potatoes were soft and flavorful.

Why This Recipe Works To simplify Sunday-style stuffed chicken into a one-pan meal, we sped things up by taking the stuffing out of the chicken and making the entire dish in just one skillet. First we sautéed the aromatics for the stuffing, then we placed the chicken—brushed with a flavorful herb butter—right on top. We scattered the bread cubes around the bird and moved the skillet to the oven to simultaneously roast the chicken and toast the bread. As the chicken cooked, the bread soaked up its flavorful juices. Finally, while the chicken rested, a quick stir and a splash of broth mixed up the aromatics and moistened the stuffing.

SKILLET-ROASTED CHICKEN WITH STUFFING

SERVES 4

You can find Italian bread in the bakery section of your grocery store. Take care when stirring the contents of the skillet in steps 4 and 5, as the skillet handle will be very hot.

- 1 (4-pound) whole chicken, giblets discarded
- 6 tablespoons unsalted butter
- 2 tablespoons minced fresh sage
- 2 tablespoons minced fresh thyme
- Salt and pepper
- 2 onions, chopped fine
- 2 celery ribs, minced
- 7 ounces Italian bread, cut into ½-inch cubes (6 cups)
- ⅓ cup chicken broth

1. Adjust oven rack to lower-middle position and heat oven to 375 degrees. Pat chicken dry with paper towels. Melt 4 tablespoons butter in small bowl in microwave, about 45 seconds. Stir in 1 tablespoon sage, 1 tablespoon thyme, 1 teaspoon salt, and ½ teaspoon pepper. Brush chicken with herb butter.

2. Melt remaining 2 tablespoons butter in 12-inch ovensafe skillet over medium heat. Add onions, celery, ½ teaspoon salt, and ½ teaspoon pepper and cook until softened, about 5 minutes. Add remaining 1 tablespoon sage and remaining 1 tablespoon thyme and cook until fragrant, about 1 minute. Off heat, place chicken, breast side up, on top of vegetables. Arrange bread cubes around chicken in bottom of skillet.

3. Transfer skillet to oven and roast until breasts register 160 degrees and thighs register 175 degrees, about 1 hour, rotating skillet halfway through roasting.

4. Carefully transfer chicken to plate and tent loosely with aluminum foil. Holding skillet handle with potholder (handle will be hot), stir bread and vegetables to combine, cover, and let stand for 10 minutes.

5. Add broth and any accumulated chicken juice from plate and cavity to skillet and stir to combine. Warm stuffing, uncovered, over low heat until heated through, about 3 minutes. Remove from heat, cover, and let sit while carving chicken. Transfer chicken to carving board, carve, and serve with stuffing.

Chopping Onions Finely

1. Halve onion through root end, then peel onion and trim top. Make several horizontal cuts from one end of onion to other but don't cut through root end.

2. Make several vertical cuts. Be sure to cut up to but not through root end.

3. Rotate onion so root end is in back; slice onion thinly across previous cuts. As you slice, onion will fall apart into chopped pieces.

Why This Recipe Works A quick meal of chicken and vegetables baked in foil sounded great to us, but our first attempts were not much better than an old-style TV dinner. Seasoning the chicken with salt on both sides and refrigerating it for at least an hour proved ideal, as did using sturdy vegetables which held up during cooking. Placing the potato slices under the chicken insulated the meat from the oven's direct heat, and we found that leaving plenty of headroom above the chicken within the pouch gave the steam room to circulate, ensuring even cooking. An added bonus? No pots or pans to clean.

CHICKEN BAKED IN FOIL WITH SWEET POTATO AND RADISH

SERVES 4

To ensure even cooking, cut the vegetables as directed and buy chicken breasts of the same size. Refrigerate the pouches for at least 1 hour before cooking.

- 5 tablespoons extra-virgin olive oil
- 6 garlic cloves, sliced thin
- 1 tablespoon grated fresh ginger
- ¼ teaspoon red pepper flakes
- 12 ounces sweet potatoes, peeled and sliced ¼ inch thick
- 4 radishes, trimmed and quartered
- 2 celery ribs, quartered lengthwise and cut into 2-inch lengths
- ½ large red onion, sliced ½ inch thick, layers separated
- Kosher salt and pepper
- 4 (6-ounce) boneless, skinless chicken breasts, trimmed
- 2 tablespoons rice vinegar
- 2 tablespoons minced fresh cilantro

1. Spray centers of four 20 by 12-inch sheets of heavy-duty aluminum foil with vegetable oil spray. Microwave oil, garlic, ginger, and pepper flakes in small bowl until garlic begins to brown, 1 to 1½ minutes. Combine potato slices, radishes, celery, onion, 1 teaspoon salt, and garlic oil in large bowl.

2. Pat chicken dry with paper towels. Sprinkle ⅛ teaspoon salt evenly over each side of each chicken breast, then season with pepper. Position 1 piece of prepared foil with long side parallel to counter edge. In center of foil, arrange one-quarter of potato slices in 2 rows perpendicular to counter edge. Lay 1 chicken breast on top of potato slices. Place one-quarter of vegetables around chicken. Repeat with remaining foil, potato slices, chicken, and vegetables. Drizzle any remaining oil mixture from bowl over chicken.

3. Bring short sides of foil together and crimp to seal tightly. Crimp remaining open ends of packets, leaving as much headroom as possible inside packets. Refrigerate for at least 1 hour or up to 24 hours.

4. Adjust oven rack to lowest position and heat oven to 475 degrees. Arrange packets on rimmed baking sheet. Bake until chicken registers 160 degrees, 18 to 23 minutes. (To check temperature, poke thermometer through foil and into chicken.) Let chicken rest in packets for 3 minutes.

5. Transfer chicken packets to individual dinner plates, carefully open (steam will escape), and slide contents onto plates. Drizzle vinegar over chicken and vegetables and sprinkle with cilantro. Serve.

CHICKEN BAKED IN FOIL WITH POTATOES AND CARROTS

Substitute 12 ounces Yukon Gold potatoes (unpeeled, sliced ¼ inch thick) and 2 carrots (peeled, quartered lengthwise and cut into 2-inch lengths), for sweet potatoes, radishes, and celery; lemon juice for rice vinegar. Substitute 1 teaspoon minced fresh thyme for ginger and 2 tablespoons minced fresh chives for cilantro.

CHICKEN BAKED IN FOIL WITH FENNEL AND SUN-DRIED TOMATOES

Substitute 1 fennel bulb, stalks discarded, bulb halved, cored, and cut into ½-inch-thick wedges, layers separated, for celery; balsamic vinegar for rice vinegar; and minced fresh basil for cilantro. Add ¼ cup oil-packed sun-dried tomatoes, rinsed, patted dry, and chopped fine and ¼ cup pitted kalamata olives, chopped fine, to vegetables in step 1.

CHICKEN AND SLICKS

SERVES 4 TO 6

If you're short on chicken fat at the end of step 1, supplement it with vegetable oil.

- 1½ pounds bone-in chicken thighs, trimmed
- 2 (12-ounce) bone-in split chicken breasts, halved crosswise and trimmed
- Salt and pepper
- 6 tablespoons plus 2 cups all-purpose flour
- 3 tablespoons vegetable oil
- 1 onion, chopped
- 2 teaspoons minced fresh thyme
- 7½ cups chicken broth
- 2 bay leaves
- ¼ cup chopped fresh parsley

1. Pat chicken dry with paper towels and season with salt and pepper. Toast 6 tablespoons flour in Dutch oven over medium heat, stirring constantly, until just beginning to brown, about 5 minutes. Transfer flour to medium bowl and wipe out pot. Heat 1 tablespoon oil in now-empty Dutch oven over medium-high heat until just smoking. Cook chicken until browned all over, about 10 minutes; transfer to plate. When chicken is cool enough to handle, remove and discard skin. Pour fat (you should have about 2 tablespoons) into small bowl; reserve.

2. Add onion and 1 tablespoon oil to now-empty pot and cook over medium heat until softened, about 5 minutes. Stir in thyme and cook until fragrant, about 30 seconds. Add 7 cups broth, chicken, and bay leaves and bring to boil. Reduce heat to low and simmer, covered, until breasts register 160 degrees and thighs register 175 degrees, 20 to 25 minutes. Remove from heat and transfer chicken to clean plate. When chicken is cool enough to handle, shred into bite-size pieces, discarding bones.

3. Meanwhile, combine remaining ½ cup chicken broth, reserved fat, and remaining 1 tablespoon oil in liquid measuring cup. Process remaining 2 cups flour and ½ teaspoon salt in food processor until combined. With processor running, slowly pour in broth mixture and process until mixture resembles coarse meal. Turn dough onto lightly floured surface and knead until smooth. Divide in half.

4. Roll each dough half into 10-inch square about ⅛ inch thick. Cut each square into twenty 5 by 1-inch rectangles. Place handful of noodles in single layer on parchment paper–lined plate, cover with another sheet of parchment, and repeat stacking with remaining noodles and additional parchment, ending with parchment. Freeze until firm, at least 10 minutes or up to 30 minutes.

5. Return broth to simmer and add noodles. Cook until noodles are nearly tender, 12 to 15 minutes, stirring occasionally to separate. Remove 1 cup broth from pot and whisk into reserved toasted flour. Stir broth-flour mixture into pot, being careful not to break up noodles, and simmer until slightly thickened, 3 to 5 minutes. Add shredded chicken and parsley and cook until heated through, about 1 minute. Season with salt and pepper to taste. Serve.

Making Slicks

1. Roll each dough half into 10-inch square of ⅛ inch thickness. Then, using sharp knife, cut dough into twenty 5 by 1-inch rectangles.

2. Stack slicks between layers of parchment and freeze briefly before simmering.

Why This Recipe Works A distant cousin to chicken and dumplings, chicken and slicks offers tender chicken in a rich, flavorful broth but swaps the traditional biscuit-style dumpling for a thick, chewy, noodlelike version. For a flavorful base, we browned the chicken before simmering it in the broth; bone-in pieces provided the best flavor. While authentic recipes call for lard in the slicks, we replaced it with more readily available vegetable oil, plus some of the rendered fat from our chicken. Cooking the slicks in an already thickened broth caused them to break apart, so we cooked them in the broth before adding toasted flour to thicken it.

MORAVIAN CHICKEN PIE

SERVES 8

Crust
- ½ cup sour cream, chilled
- 1 large egg, lightly beaten
- 2½ cups (12½ ounces) all-purpose flour
- 1½ teaspoons salt
- 12 tablespoons unsalted butter, cut into ½-inch pieces and chilled

Filling
- 2 (10- to 12-ounce) bone-in split chicken breasts, halved crosswise and trimmed
- 3 (5- to 7-ounce) bone-in chicken thighs, trimmed
- Salt and pepper
- 1 tablespoon vegetable oil
- 3 cups chicken broth
- 1 bay leaf
- 2 tablespoons unsalted butter
- ¼ cup all-purpose flour
- ¼ cup half-and-half
- 1 large egg, lightly beaten

1. For the Crust Combine sour cream and egg in bowl. Process flour and salt in food processor until combined, about 3 seconds. Add butter and pulse until only pea-size pieces remain, about 10 pulses. Add half of sour cream mixture and pulse until combined, 5 pulses. Add remaining sour cream mixture and pulse until dough begins to form, about 10 pulses.

2. Transfer mixture to lightly floured counter and knead briefly until dough comes together. Divide dough in half and form each half into 4-inch disk. Wrap each disk in plastic wrap and refrigerate for at least 1 hour or up to 2 days.

3. Line rimmed baking sheet with parchment paper. Remove 1 dough disk from refrigerator and let sit for 10 minutes. Working on lightly floured counter, roll into 12-inch round and transfer to 9-inch pie plate, leaving ½-inch overhang all around. Repeat with second dough disk and transfer to prepared baking sheet. Cover both dough rounds with plastic wrap and refrigerate for 30 minutes.

4. For the Filling Pat chicken dry with paper towels and season with salt and pepper. Heat oil in large Dutch oven over medium-high heat until just smoking. Cook chicken until browned, about 10 minutes; transfer to plate. Pour fat (you should have 2 tablespoons; supplement with butter if necessary) into bowl; reserve. When chicken is cool enough to handle, remove and discard skin. Add broth, chicken, and bay leaf to now-empty pot and bring to boil. Reduce heat to low and simmer, covered, until breasts register 160 degrees and thighs register 175 degrees, 14 to 18 minutes. Transfer chicken to bowl. When chicken is cool enough to handle, shred into bite-size pieces, discarding bones. Pour broth through fine-mesh strainer into second bowl and reserve (you should have about 2¾ cups); discard bay leaf.

5. Adjust oven rack to lowest position and heat oven to 450 degrees. Heat butter and reserved fat in now-empty pot over medium heat until shimmering. Add flour and cook, whisking constantly, until golden, 1 to 2 minutes. Slowly whisk in 2 cups reserved broth and half-and-half and bring to boil. Reduce heat to medium-low and simmer gravy until thickened and reduced to 1¾ cups, 6 to 8 minutes. Season with salt and pepper to taste. Combine 1 cup gravy with shredded chicken; reserve remaining gravy for serving.

6. Transfer chicken mixture to dough-lined pie plate and spread into even layer. Top with second dough round, leaving at least ½-inch overhang all around. Fold dough under so that edge of fold is flush with rim of pie plate. Flute edges using thumb and forefinger or press with tines of fork to seal. Cut four 1-inch slits in top. Brush pie with egg and bake until top is light golden brown, 18 to 20 minutes. Reduce oven temperature to 375 degrees and continue to bake until crust is deep golden brown, 10 to 15 minutes. Let pie cool on wire rack for at least 45 minutes.

7. When ready to serve, bring remaining ¾ cup reserved gravy and remaining ¾ cup reserved broth to boil in medium saucepan. Simmer over medium-low heat until slightly thickened, 5 to 7 minutes. Season with salt and pepper to taste. Serve pie with gravy.

Why This Recipe Works Protestant immigrants from the Czech province Moravia settled in Pennsylvania and later North Carolina and brought with them such homey dishes as Moravian cake, cookies, and chicken pie, a satisfying double-crusted pie filled with shredded chicken and served with a rich gravy. Searing the chicken (a mix of breasts and thighs) helped to render its fat, which we used in a roux to thicken the gravy. For moist chicken, we poached it in chicken broth and used that broth to give our gravy flavor. As for the pie crust, we found that sour cream helped make for a rich, flaky crust that was remarkably easy to roll out.

Why This Recipe Works Guinness beef stew often captures only the bitterness and none of the deep, caramelized flavors of the beer. We found the trick to rich, malty flavor was to add some of the beer at the end of cooking so that the heat didn't dull the complex flavors. We also added a little brown sugar to balance some of the bitterness. We loved the idea of just dumping the meat into the pot without searing, but the flavor was lacking. To compensate, we first browned the onions and tomato paste, then cooked the stew uncovered so that the meat could brown in the oven.

GUINNESS BEEF STEW

SERVES 6 TO 8

Use Guinness Draught, not Guinness Extra Stout, which is too bitter.

- 1 (3½- to 4-pound) boneless beef chuck-eye roast, pulled apart at seams, trimmed, and cut into 1½-inch pieces
- Salt and pepper
- 3 tablespoons vegetable oil
- 2 onions, chopped fine
- 1 tablespoon tomato paste
- 2 garlic cloves, minced
- ¼ cup all-purpose flour
- 3 cups chicken broth
- 1¼ cups Guinness Draught
- 1½ tablespoons packed dark brown sugar
- 1 teaspoon minced fresh thyme
- 1½ pounds Yukon Gold potatoes, unpeeled, cut into 1-inch pieces
- 1 pound carrots, peeled and cut into 1-inch pieces
- 2 tablespoons minced fresh parsley

1. Adjust oven rack to lower-middle position and heat oven to 325 degrees. Season beef with salt and pepper. Heat oil in Dutch oven over medium-high heat until shimmering. Add onions and ¼ teaspoon salt and cook, stirring occasionally, until well browned, 8 to 10 minutes.

2. Add tomato paste and garlic and cook until rust-colored and fragrant, about 2 minutes. Stir in flour and cook for 1 minute. Whisk in broth, ¾ cup Guinness, sugar, and thyme, scraping up any browned bits. Bring to simmer and cook until slightly thickened, about 3 minutes. Stir in beef and return to simmer. Transfer to oven and cook, uncovered, for 90 minutes, stirring halfway through cooking.

3. Stir in potatoes and carrots and continue cooking until beef and vegetables are tender, about 1 hour, stirring halfway through cooking. Stir in remaining ½ cup Guinness and parsley. Season with salt and pepper to taste and serve.

Cook It Uncovered

Most stew recipes start by searing meat in batches on the stovetop. For an easier beef stew, we skip that step but keep the flavor by cooking the stew uncovered in the oven; the open pot allows the meat on top to take on flavorful browning. In addition, the liquid reduces, concentrating in flavor and texture, while the meat cooks.

Preparing a Chuck Roast

1. Pull apart roast at major seams (marked by lines of fat and silverskin). Use knife as necessary.

2. With sharp chef's knife or boning knife, trim off thick layers of fat and silverskin. Cut meat into 1½-inch pieces.

BRUNSWICK STEW

SERVES 4 TO 6

Our favorite kielbasa is Wellshire Farms Smoked Polska Kielbasa.

- 1 tablespoon vegetable oil
- 1 onion, chopped fine
- ¾ cup ketchup
- 4 cups water
- 2 pounds boneless, skinless chicken thighs, trimmed
- 1 pound russet potatoes, peeled and cut into ½-inch chunks
- 8 ounces kielbasa sausage, sliced ¼ inch thick
- 6–8 tablespoons cider vinegar
- 2 tablespoons Worcestershire sauce
- 1 tablespoon yellow mustard
- 1 teaspoon garlic powder
- Salt and pepper
- ¼ teaspoon red pepper flakes
- 1 cup canned crushed tomatoes
- ½ cup frozen lima beans
- ½ cup frozen corn

1. Heat oil in Dutch oven over medium-high heat until shimmering. Add onion and cook until softened, 3 to 5 minutes. Add ketchup and ¼ cup water and cook, stirring frequently, until fond begins to form on bottom of pot and mixture has thickened, about 6 minutes.

2. Add chicken, potatoes, kielbasa, 6 tablespoons vinegar, 1½ tablespoons Worcestershire, mustard, garlic powder, 1 teaspoon salt, 1 teaspoon pepper, pepper flakes, and remaining 3¾ cups water and bring to boil. Reduce heat to low, cover, and simmer until potatoes are tender, 30 to 35 minutes, stirring frequently.

3. Transfer chicken to plate and let cool for 5 minutes, then shred into bite-size pieces with 2 forks. While chicken cools, stir tomatoes, lima beans, and corn into stew and continue to simmer, uncovered, for 15 minutes. Stir in shredded chicken and remaining 1½ teaspoons Worcestershire and cook until warmed through, about 2 minutes. Season with salt, pepper, and remaining vinegar (up to 2 tablespoons) to taste. Serve.

Browning Ketchup

Ketchup offers a lot of culinary bang for the buck, with sweet, tangy, and savory flavors in a single bottle. For this recipe, we cook the ketchup until it thickens and browns, making it even more complex.

Why This Recipe Works Brunswick stew is a fixture at many Southern barbecues, but because there is no definitive recipe for the stew, many cooks use it as a kitchen sink dump-all, resulting in variations that simply aren't appealing. After testing various versions, we settled on an eastern North Carolina style made with barbecue sauce for complex flavor and potatoes for thickness. We kept the meats simple, opting for tender chicken thighs and flavorful kielbasa. Because barbecue sauce flavors vary across brands, we created our own. Browning the ketchup before adding other ingredients helped to soften its raw edge and created a rich tomato base.

Why This Recipe Works Is there a more affordable roast beef alternative to pricey prime rib? One that is faster to cook and full of rich, beefy, tender flavor? In our testing, we found our answer with top sirloin. Skipping a stovetop sear, we browned the roast in the oven at a high temperature and then reduced the oven temperature to cook the roast through without losing too much moisture. And to give our roast an extra layer of savory flavor, we turned to garlic. A three-pronged attack yielded roast beef with great garlic flavor: We studded the roast beef with toasted garlic, rubbed it with garlic salt, and coated it while it cooked with a garlic paste.

SUNDAY-BEST GARLIC ROAST BEEF

SERVES 6 TO 8

Look for a top sirloin roast that has a thick, substantial fat cap still attached. The rendered fat will help to keep the roast moist. When making the jus, taste the reduced broth before adding any of the accumulated meat juices from the roast. The meat juices are well seasoned and may make the jus too salty. If you don't have a heavy-duty nonstick roasting pan, a broiler pan bottom works well, too.

Beef
- 8 large garlic cloves, unpeeled
- 1 (4-pound) top sirloin roast, fat trimmed to ¼ inch

Garlic-Salt Rub
- 3 large garlic cloves, minced
- 1 teaspoon dried thyme
- ½ teaspoon salt

Garlic Paste
- ½ cup olive oil
- 12 large garlic cloves, cut in half lengthwise
- 2 sprigs fresh thyme
- 2 bay leaves
- ½ teaspoon salt
- Pepper

Jus
- 1½ cups beef broth
- 1½ cups chicken broth

1. For the Beef Toast garlic in 8-inch skillet over medium-high heat, tossing frequently, until spotty brown, about 8 minutes. Set aside. When cool enough to handle, peel and cut into ¼-inch slivers. Using paring knife, make 1-inch-deep slits all over roast and insert toasted garlic into slits.

2. For the Garlic-Salt Rub Combine garlic, thyme, and salt in small bowl and rub all over roast. Place roast on large plate and refrigerate, uncovered, for at least 4 hours or preferably overnight.

3. For the Garlic Paste Heat oil, garlic, thyme, bay leaves, and salt in small saucepan over medium-high heat until bubbles start to rise to surface. Reduce heat to low and cook until garlic is soft, about 30 minutes. Let cool completely, then strain, reserving oil. Discard herbs and transfer garlic to small bowl. Mash garlic with 1 tablespoon garlic oil until paste forms. Cover and refrigerate paste until ready to use. Cover and reserve garlic oil.

4. Adjust oven rack to middle position, place nonstick roasting pan on rack, and heat oven to 450 degrees. Using paper towels, wipe garlic-salt rub off beef. Rub beef with 2 tablespoons reserved garlic oil and season with pepper. Transfer meat, fat side down, to preheated pan and roast, turning as needed until browned on all sides, 10 to 15 minutes.

5. Reduce oven temperature to 300 degrees. Remove pan from oven, turn roast fat side up, and, using spatula, coat top with garlic paste. Return meat to oven and roast until it registers 120 to 125 degrees (for medium-rare), 50 minutes to 1 hour, 10 minutes. Transfer to carving board, cover loosely with aluminum foil, and let rest for 20 minutes.

6. For the Jus Pour off fat from roasting pan and place pan over high heat. Add beef broth and chicken broth and bring to boil, scraping up browned bits with wooden spoon. Simmer, stirring occasionally, until reduced to 2 cups, about 5 minutes. Add accumulated juices from roast and cook for 1 minute, then pour through fine-mesh strainer. Slice roast crosswise into ¼-inch-thick slices. Serve with jus.

Why This Recipe Works For tender, juicy roast beef, we chose top sirloin roast with a thick fat cap, which rendered as the beef roasted and kept it moist. Searing each side before roasting helped to develop a flavorful crust. Though the right roasting temperature produced juicy meat (our roast having expelled very little liquid), it left precious few drippings in the roasting pan from which to make gravy. A good amount of beef broth, plus the rendered fat and fond left behind from searing the meat, provided volume and richness, while mushrooms, red wine, and Worcestershire sauce amped up the flavor.

CLASSIC ROAST BEEF AND GRAVY

SERVES 6 TO 8

For the best flavor and texture, refrigerate the roast overnight after salting. If you don't have a V-rack, cook the roast on a wire rack set inside a rimmed baking sheet.

- 1 (4-pound) top sirloin roast, fat trimmed to ¼ inch
- Salt and pepper
- 1 tablespoon vegetable oil
- 8 ounces white mushrooms, trimmed and chopped
- 2 onions, chopped fine
- 1 carrot, peeled and chopped
- 1 celery rib, minced
- 1 tablespoon tomato paste
- 4 garlic cloves, minced
- ¼ cup all-purpose flour
- 1 cup red wine
- 4 cups beef broth
- 1 teaspoon Worcestershire sauce

1. Pat roast dry with paper towels. Rub 2 teaspoons salt evenly over meat. Cover with plastic wrap and refrigerate for at least 1 hour or up to 24 hours.

2. Adjust oven rack to lower-middle position and heat oven to 275 degrees. Pat roast dry with paper towels and rub with 1 teaspoon pepper. Heat oil in Dutch oven over medium-high heat until just smoking. Brown roast all over, 8 to 12 minutes, then transfer to V-rack set inside roasting pan (do not wipe out Dutch oven). Transfer to oven and cook until meat registers 120 to 125 degrees (for medium-rare), 1½ to 2 hours.

3. Meanwhile, add mushrooms to fat left in Dutch oven and cook until golden, about 5 minutes. Stir in onions, carrot, and celery and cook until browned, 5 to 7 minutes. Stir in tomato paste, garlic, and flour and cook until fragrant, about 2 minutes. Stir in wine and broth, scraping up any browned bits with wooden spoon. Bring to boil, then reduce heat to medium and simmer until thickened, about 10 minutes. Strain gravy, then stir in Worcestershire and season with salt and pepper; cover and keep warm.

4. Transfer roast to carving board, tent with aluminum foil, and let rest for 20 minutes. Slice roast crosswise into ½-inch-thick slices. Serve with gravy.

Flavor Builders
A combination of sautéed mushrooms, tomato paste, beef broth, and Worcestershire sauce mimicked the roasted, beefy flavor of traditional gravy made with pan drippings.

Top Sirloin—The Right Cut
Through extensive testing of every cut of beef, the test kitchen has settled on top sirloin as our favorite inexpensive roast. Look for a roast with at least a ¼-inch fat cap on top; the fat renders in the oven, basting the roast and helping to keep it moist.

HERBED ROAST BEEF

SERVES 6 TO 8

For even deeper seasoning, refrigerate the roast overnight after filling it with the herb mixture in step 2.

- ⅓ cup minced fresh parsley
- 1 shallot, minced
- 2 tablespoons minced fresh thyme
- 2 tablespoons olive oil
- 1 tablespoon Dijon mustard
- 4 tablespoons unsalted butter, softened
- 1 (4-pound) top sirloin roast, fat trimmed to ¼ inch
- 1 tablespoon salt
- 1 tablespoon pepper

1. Combine parsley, shallot, and thyme in bowl. Transfer 2 tablespoons herb mixture to second bowl and stir in 1 tablespoon oil and mustard until combined; set aside. Add butter to remaining herb mixture and mash with fork until combined.

2. Butterfly roast by slicing horizontally through middle of meat, leaving about ½ inch of meat intact, and rub roast inside and out with salt and pepper. Spread herb-mustard mixture over interior of meat, fold roast back together, and tie securely with kitchen twine at 1-inch intervals. Refrigerate for at least 1 hour or up to 24 hours.

3. Adjust oven rack to middle position and heat oven to 275 degrees. Pat roast dry with paper towels. Heat remaining 1 tablespoon oil in 12-inch skillet over medium-high heat until just smoking. Brown roast all over, 8 to 12 minutes, then arrange on V-rack set inside roasting pan. Transfer to oven and roast until meat registers 120 to 125 degrees (for medium-rare), 1½ to 2 hours.

4. Transfer roast to carving board, spread with herb-butter mixture, tent with aluminum foil, and let rest for 20 minutes. Remove twine and slice roast crosswise into ¼-inch-thick slices. Serve.

Fast Sear, Slow Roast for Beef
We brown most beef roasts on the stovetop to build a flavorful crust, then roast them gently for a uniformly rosy, juicy interior.

1. Searing roast assures a flavorful, deep brown crust.

2. Roasting at a low temperature (275 degrees) keeps the meat moist and succulent.

Herbs Galore
Fresh parsley and thyme flavor both the interior and exterior of our roast.

1. Butterfly roast by slicing horizontally through middle of the meat. Leave about ½ inch of meat intact, then open it like a book.

2. After seasoning meat, spread herb-mustard mixture over interior of meat.

3. Fold meat back to its original position, then tie securely at 1-inch intervals with kitchen twine.

4. For second hit of herb flavor after roast is cooked, spread it with herb butter.

Why This Recipe Works For a roast beef dressed to impress without much effort, we turned to a swirl of herbs and mustard. To start, we combined fresh herbs with the mustard, butterflied the roast, and spread the herbs over the interior of the meat before folding it back together and securing it with twine. A simple herb butter, spread over the resting roast, melted and mingled with the natural juices of the meat, creating a flavorful sauce without the need to dirty another pan.

OUR SUNDAY BEST 191

HERB-CRUSTED BEEF TENDERLOIN

SERVES 12 TO 16

Make sure to begin this recipe 2 hours before you plan to put the roast in the oven. The tenderloin can be trimmed, tied, rubbed with the salt mixture, and refrigerated up to 24 hours in advance; make sure to bring the roast back to room temperature before putting it into the oven.

- 1 (6-pound) whole beef tenderloin, trimmed, tail end tucked, and tied at 1½-inch intervals
- Kosher salt and cracked peppercorns
- 2 teaspoons sugar
- 2 slices hearty white sandwich bread, torn into pieces
- 2½ ounces Parmesan cheese, grated (1¼ cups)
- ½ cup chopped fresh parsley
- 6 tablespoons olive oil
- 2 teaspoons plus 2 tablespoons chopped fresh thyme
- 4 garlic cloves, minced
- 1 recipe Horseradish Cream Sauce

1. Set wire rack in rimmed baking sheet. Pat tenderloin dry with paper towels. Combine 1 tablespoon salt, 1 tablespoon pepper, and sugar in small bowl and rub all over tenderloin. Transfer to prepared baking sheet and let sit at room temperature for 2 hours.

2. Meanwhile, pulse bread in food processor to fine crumbs, about 15 pulses. Transfer bread crumbs to medium bowl and toss with ½ cup Parmesan, 2 tablespoons parsley, 2 tablespoons oil, and 2 teaspoons thyme until evenly combined. Wipe out food processor with paper towels and process remaining ¾ cup Parmesan, 6 tablespoons parsley, ¼ cup oil, 2 tablespoons thyme, and garlic until smooth paste forms. Transfer herb paste to small bowl.

3. Adjust oven rack to upper-middle position and heat oven to 400 degrees. Roast tenderloin for 20 minutes and remove from oven. Using scissors, carefully cut kitchen twine and remove it. Coat tenderloin with herb paste, then bread-crumb topping. Roast until meat registers 120 to 125 degrees (for medium-rare) and topping is golden brown, 20 to 25 minutes. (If topping browns before meat reaches preferred internal temperature, lightly cover with aluminum foil for remainder of roasting time and remove while roast rests.) Let roast rest, uncovered, for 30 minutes on wire rack. Transfer to carving board and carve. Serve with Horseradish Cream Sauce.

HORSERADISH CREAM SAUCE
MAKES ABOUT 1 CUP

- ½ cup sour cream
- ½ cup heavy cream
- ¼ cup prepared horseradish, drained
- 2 teaspoons Dijon mustard
- 1 garlic clove, minced
- ¼ teaspoon sugar
- Salt and pepper

Mix all ingredients in bowl; add salt and pepper to taste. Cover and let stand at room temperature for 1 to 1½ hours to thicken. (Sauce can be refrigerated for up to 2 days.)

Preparing Herb-Crusted Beef Tenderloin

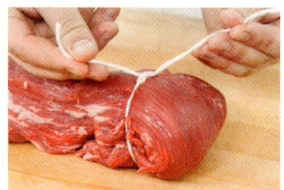 

1. To ensure even cooking, fold thin, tapered end under roast, then tie entire roast with kitchen twine every 1½ inches. Roast for 20 minutes.

2. Remove roast from oven, snip twine with scissors, and remove before adding herb paste and bread-crumb mixture. Return to oven to finish cooking.

Why This Recipe Works Though beef tenderloin offers incomparable tenderness, its flavor could often use some embellishment. To give the meat a flavor boost, we turned to a thick herbed crust. But herbs can burn easily, lose their flavor in a hot oven, or just fall off the meat. Cooking the roast in the oven at a high temperature for part of the time gave us a perfectly caramelized exterior that made applying an herb paste easy. Adding grated Parmesan cheese to the paste gave it nutty flavor and helped the paste adhere to the meat. Fresh parsley and thyme provided a flavorful coating, and for a crisp texture, we relied on bread crumbs.

Why This Recipe Works For an occasion-worthy, beefy top-loin roast, we wanted a seared crust and a perfect medium-rare throughout, but most recipes we found could only give us one or the other. Gently roasting in a low oven until the meat was almost done and then setting it under the broiler for a few minutes achieved both results without the hassle of pan-searing. Scoring the fat cap before cooking helped the fat to render and the surface to crisp. We let the meat sit overnight with a spice and herb rub (and plenty of salt) to ensure a perfectly seasoned, flavorful roast, and served it with a bright, fresh salsa verde to complement the rich meat.

HOLIDAY STRIP ROAST

SERVES 8 TO 10

Serve with Salsa Verde (recipe follows).

- 1 (5- to 6-pound) boneless top loin roast, fat trimmed to ¼ inch
- 2 tablespoons peppercorns
- 1 tablespoon coriander seeds
- 1 tablespoon yellow mustard seeds
- 3 tablespoons olive oil
- 2 tablespoons kosher salt
- 2 tablespoons chopped fresh rosemary
- 1 teaspoon red pepper flakes

1. Pat roast dry with paper towels. Using sharp knife, cut ½-inch crosshatch pattern through fat cap, ¼ inch deep. Tie kitchen twine around roast at 2-inch intervals. Grind peppercorns, coriander seeds, and mustard seeds to texture of coarse sand in spice grinder. Combine spice mixture, oil, salt, rosemary, and pepper flakes in bowl until thick paste forms. Rub paste all over roast and into crosshatch. Wrap roast with plastic wrap and refrigerate for 6 to 24 hours.

2. Set wire rack inside rimmed baking sheet. One hour before cooking, unwrap meat and place on prepared rack, fat side up. Adjust oven rack to middle position and heat oven to 275 degrees. Transfer roast to oven and cook until meat registers 115 degrees, about 90 minutes, rotating sheet halfway through cooking. Remove roast from oven and heat broiler.

3. Return roast to oven and broil on middle oven rack until fat cap is deep brown and interior of roast registers 125 degrees, 3 to 5 minutes. Transfer to carving board, tent loosely with aluminum foil, and let rest for 20 minutes. Remove twine and carve into thin slices. Serve.

SALSA VERDE

MAKES ABOUT 1½ CUPS

Mince the garlic before processing it, or it won't break down enough. This sauce can be prepared up to two days in advance and refrigerated. Before serving, bring it to room temperature and stir to recombine.

- 2 slices hearty white sandwich bread, torn into 1-inch pieces
- 1 cup extra-virgin olive oil
- ¼ cup lemon juice (2 lemons)
- 4 cups fresh parsley leaves
- ¼ cup capers, rinsed
- 4 anchovy fillets, rinsed
- 2 garlic cloves, minced
- ½ teaspoon kosher salt

Process bread, oil, and lemon juice in food processor until smooth, about 10 seconds. Add parsley, capers, anchovies, garlic, and salt and pulse until mixture is finely chopped, about 5 pulses, scraping down bowl as needed.

The Right Grind

As part of the rub for the roast, we grind peppercorns with mustard seeds and coriander seeds to the texture of coarse sand. Since these ingredients are irregularly sized and of varying densities, the texture won't be uniform, which is OK. The correct grind looks like this.

Coarse and irregular

DEVILED BEEF SHORT RIBS

SERVES 4 TO 6

English-style short ribs contain a single rib bone. For a milder sauce, use only one jalapeño and discard the seeds.

- ⅔ cup yellow mustard
- ⅓ cup orange juice
- ⅓ cup packed light brown sugar
- 1–2 jalapeño chiles, stemmed, seeds reserved, and roughly chopped
- 4 teaspoons dry mustard
- 1 tablespoon lemon juice plus 1 teaspoon grated lemon zest
- Salt and pepper
- ½ teaspoon cayenne pepper
- 5 pounds bone-in English-style short ribs, bones 4 to 5 inches long, 1 to 1½ inches of meat on top of bone, trimmed
- 2 tablespoons unsalted butter
- 1½ cups panko bread crumbs
- 1 tablespoon chopped fresh parsley

1. Adjust oven rack to middle position and heat oven to 325 degrees. Combine yellow mustard, orange juice, sugar, jalapeños and reserved seeds, dry mustard, lemon juice, and 2 teaspoons pepper in food processor and process until smooth, about 30 seconds; set aside. (Mustard mixture can be refrigerated for up to 1 week.)

2. Combine 1 tablespoon salt, 1 tablespoon pepper, and cayenne in bowl. Sprinkle ribs all over with spice mixture. Arrange ribs, meat side down, in 13 by 9-inch baking dish. Cover dish tightly with aluminum foil and roast until meat is nearly tender, about 3 hours.

3. Meanwhile, melt butter in 12-inch skillet over medium-high heat. Add panko and cook, stirring often, until golden brown, about 3 minutes. Off heat, stir in parsley and lemon zest and transfer to shallow dish.

4. Remove baking dish from oven and increase oven temperature to 425 degrees; transfer ribs to plate. Discard rendered fat and juices from dish. Brush meat (not bone) all over with one-fourth of mustard sauce and return ribs to dish, meat side up. Roast, uncovered, until beginning to brown, about 10 minutes. Brush meat again with one-third of remaining mustard sauce and continue to roast until well browned and completely tender, 10 to 15 minutes longer. Transfer ribs to serving platter, tent loosely with foil, and let rest for 15 minutes.

5. Brush meat once more with half of remaining mustard sauce and roll in panko mixture, taking care to entirely coat meat. Serve, passing remaining mustard sauce separately.

A Roasting-Braising Hybrid Method

Most short rib recipes call for searing, then braising, and finally turning the braising liquid into a sauce. For our Deviled Beef Short Ribs, we took a different road: We put the ribs in a baking dish, meat side down, and roasted them (covered) until tender, about 3 hours. The meat cooked in its own rendered fat and juices, giving us fully rendered, supertender short ribs without much hands-on work. To finish, we uncovered the ribs, brushed them with a glaze, roasted them meat side up, repeated, and then rolled them in toasted crumbs.

Why This Recipe Works "Deviling" food usually involves flavoring it with mustard, black pepper, and other seasonings, but for our deviled short ribs we really wanted to feel the heat. We first roasted the seasoned ribs meat side down in a covered baking dish, allowing the meat to cook in its own rendered fat and juices. After cranking the heat and pouring off the juices, we brushed the ribs with a spicy glaze of dry and prepared mustards, citrus, brown sugar, and pureed jalapeños. A few rounds of brushing and roasting created a browned crust, and for a crunchy finish we coated the ribs with buttery, toasted panko bread crumbs.

ONE-PAN PRIME RIB AND ROASTED VEGETABLES

SERVES 8 TO 10

The roast must be salted and then refrigerated for at least 24 hours before cooking; salting and refrigerating for the full 4 days results in the most tender, flavorful meat.

- 1 (7-pound) first-cut beef standing rib roast (3 bones), fat trimmed to ¼ inch
- Kosher salt and pepper
- Vegetable oil
- 2 pounds carrots, peeled, cut into 2-inch lengths, halved or quartered lengthwise to create ½-inch-diameter pieces
- 1 pound parsnips, peeled and sliced ½ inch thick on bias
- 1 pound Brussels sprouts, trimmed and halved
- 1 red onion, halved and sliced through root end into ½-inch wedges
- 2 teaspoons minced fresh thyme

1. Using sharp knife, cut through roast's fat cap in 1-inch crosshatch pattern, being careful not to cut into meat. Rub 2 tablespoons salt over entire roast and into crosshatch. Transfer to large plate and refrigerate, uncovered, for at least 24 hours or up to 4 days.

2. Adjust oven rack to lower-middle position and heat oven to 250 degrees. Season roast with pepper and arrange, fat side up, on V-rack set in large roasting pan. Roast until meat registers 115 degrees for rare, 120 degrees for medium-rare, or 125 degrees for medium, 3 to 3½ hours. Transfer V-rack with roast to carving board, tent loosely with aluminum foil, and let rest for about 1 hour.

3. Meanwhile, increase oven temperature to 425 degrees. Pour off all but 2 tablespoons fat from pan. (If there isn't enough fat in pan, add vegetable oil to equal 2 tablespoons.) Toss carrots, parsnips, brussels sprouts, onion, thyme, 1 teaspoon salt, and ½ teaspoon pepper with fat in pan. Roast vegetables, stirring halfway through roasting, until tender and browned, 45 to 50 minutes.

4. Remove pan from oven and heat broiler. Carefully nestle V-rack with roast among vegetables in pan. Broil roast until fat cap is evenly browned, about 5 minutes, rotating pan as necessary. Transfer roast to carving board, carve meat from bones, and cut into ¾-inch-thick slices. Season vegetables with salt and pepper to taste. Serve roast with vegetables.

Buy the Right Roast

This recipe calls for a first-cut, bone-in standing rib roast, which contains ribs 9, 10, and 11 (the ribs that are closest to the tail of the steer; butchers often label this cut "loin-end"). First-cut roasts contain the largest eye of meat. While second-cut roasts are pretty good, too, they are slightly fattier and more irregular, making them more difficult to cook evenly. Since these cuts are often priced the same, it's worth your while to ask for the superior first-cut roast.

FIRST CUT
More meat, larger eye

SECOND CUT
More fat, smaller eye (but still good)

Carving a Standing Rib Roast

To carve a bone-in rib roast, simply hold the roast in place with a carving fork and cut parallel to the rib bones to remove the meat in one big piece. Then slice and serve the meat.

Why This Recipe Works Our goal was to produce a recipe for holiday prime rib with roasted vegetables that was simple and foolproof. We scored and salted a first-cut standing rib roast and refrigerated it for 24 hours for tender beef. A low-and-slow cooking method yielded evenly red and juicy meat, and an additional stint under the broiler turned the outside crispy and golden. Instead of forcing the vegetables to work in concert with the beef, we roasted them solo in the flavorful beef fat while the prime rib was resting. It was definitely a feast fit for a holiday—with only one pan to wash.

Why This Recipe Works To ensure a juicy roast, we trimmed the excess fat, made shallow crosshatch cuts in the remaining fat cap, and rubbed the roast with salt 24 hours before cooking. We saved the trimmed fat and placed it under the roast as it cooked, creating intensely flavored drippings. To achieve a creamy interior, we pre-cooked the potatoes in the microwave before tossing them with the rendered fat and roasting them until crisp. Searing the cooked roast in a hot skillet added some last-minute browning to the roast's exterior without overcooking it. An easy red wine–orange sauce proved a bright contrast to the savory beef.

PRIME RIB WITH POTATOES AND RED WINE–ORANGE SAUCE

SERVES 8 TO 10

The roast must be salted and refrigerated for at least 24 hours before cooking. Wait until the roast is done cooking before peeling and cutting the potatoes so they don't discolor. It is crucial to use a sturdy rimmed baking sheet for this recipe. Serve with Red Wine–Orange Sauce (recipe follows).

- 1 (7-pound) first-cut beef standing rib roast (3 bones), with untrimmed fat cap Kosher salt and pepper
- 4 pounds Yukon gold potatoes, peeled and cut into 1½-inch pieces
- 1 tablespoon minced fresh rosemary
- 1 tablespoon vegetable oil

1. Using sharp knife, trim roast's fat cap to even ¼-inch-thickness; reserve and refrigerate trimmings. Cut 1-inch crosshatch pattern in fat cap, being careful not to cut into meat. Rub 2 tablespoons salt over roast and into crosshatch. Transfer to large plate and refrigerate, uncovered, for at least 24 hours or up to 4 days.

2. Adjust oven rack to lower-middle position and heat oven to 250 degrees. Cut reserved trimmings into ½-inch pieces. Place 1 cup of trimmings in rimmed baking sheet, then set wire rack in sheet. Season roast with pepper and place, fat side up, on wire rack.

3. Roast until meat registers 115 degrees for rare, 120 degrees for medium-rare, or 125 degrees for medium, 3 to 3½ hours. Transfer roast to carving board, tent with aluminum foil, and let rest for 1 hour. Carefully remove wire rack and reserve beef fat in baking sheet (there should be about ½ cup; if not, add vegetable oil).

4. Increase oven temperature to 450 degrees. Microwave potatoes, covered, in large bowl until they begin to release moisture and surfaces look wet, about 7 minutes. Pat potatoes dry with paper towels. Toss potatoes with rosemary, 2 teaspoons salt, and ½ teaspoon pepper. Transfer potatoes to baking sheet and carefully toss with reserved fat (fat may be hot). Roast until tender and browned, 35 to 40 minutes, redistributing halfway through cooking. Season potatoes with salt and pepper to taste.

5. Pat roast dry with paper towels. Heat oil in 12-inch skillet over medium-high heat until just smoking. Sear all sides until browned, 6 to 8 minutes total. Transfer roast to carving board. Carve meat from bones and cut into ¾-inch-thick slices. Serve with potatoes.

RED WINE–ORANGE SAUCE
MAKES ABOUT 1½ CUPS
Medium-bodied red wines are best for this sauce.

- 6 tablespoons unsalted butter, cut into 6 pieces and chilled
- 3 shallots, minced
- 1½ tablespoons tomato paste
- 1 tablespoon sugar
- 4 garlic cloves, minced
- 1 tablespoon all-purpose flour
- 3 cups beef broth
- 1½ cups red wine
- ⅓ cup orange juice
- 1½ tablespoons Worcestershire sauce
- 1 sprig fresh thyme
  Salt and pepper

1. Melt 2 tablespoons butter in medium saucepan over medium-high heat. Add shallots, tomato paste, and sugar and cook, stirring frequently, until deep brown, 4 to 5 minutes. Stir in garlic and flour and cook until garlic is fragrant and vegetables are well coated with flour, about 30 seconds.

2. Stir in broth, wine, orange juice, Worcestershire, and thyme, scraping up any browned bits. Bring to boil, reduce heat to medium, and cook at low boil until reduced to 2 cups, about 40 minutes.

3. Strain sauce through fine-mesh strainer set over bowl; discard solids. Return sauce to pot and place over low heat. Whisk in remaining 4 tablespoons butter, 1 piece at a time. Season with salt and pepper to taste.

Why This Recipe Works Traditionally, this lazy cook's pot roast involves rubbing a chuck roast with onion soup mix, wrapping it in foil, and cooking it in the oven until tender. While we liked the ease of this dish, we weren't fans of its artificial, salty taste. To develop oniony flavor with ease, we started with onion powder and salt, but ditched the monosodium glutamate in favor of soy sauce, which enhanced the roast's beefy flavor. Brown sugar added sweetness and depth, while a surprise ingredient, a little espresso powder, provided toasty complexity. Dividing the roast into two halves allowed us to apply more of the flavorful spice rub to its exterior.

CHUCK ROAST IN FOIL

SERVES 4 TO 6

You will need an 18-inch-wide roll of heavy-duty aluminum foil for wrapping the roast. We prefer to use small red potatoes, measuring 1 to 2 inches in diameter, in this recipe.

Rub
- 3 tablespoons cornstarch
- 4 teaspoons onion powder
- 2 teaspoons packed light brown sugar
- 2 teaspoons salt
- 1 teaspoon pepper
- 1 teaspoon garlic powder
- 1 teaspoon instant espresso powder
- 1 teaspoon dried thyme
- ½ teaspoon celery seeds

Chuck Roast
- 1 (4-pound) boneless beef chuck-eye roast, pulled apart at seams, fat trimmed to ¼ inch, and tied at 1-inch intervals
- 2 onions, peeled and quartered
- 1 pound small red potatoes, quartered
- 4 carrots, peeled and cut into 1½-inch pieces
- 2 bay leaves
- 2 tablespoons soy sauce

1. For the Rub Adjust oven rack to lower-middle position and heat oven to 300 degrees. Combine all ingredients in small bowl.

2. For the Chuck Roast Pat roast dry with paper towels. Place two 30 by 18-inch sheets of heavy-duty aluminum foil perpendicular to each other inside large roasting pan. Place onions, potatoes, carrots, and bay leaves in center of foil and drizzle with soy sauce. Set roasts on top of vegetables. Rub roasts all over with rub. Fold opposite corners of foil toward each other and crimp edges tightly to seal. Transfer pan to oven and cook until meat is completely tender, about 4½ hours.

3. Remove roasts from foil pouch and place on carving board. Tent meat with foil and let rest for 20 minutes. Remove onions and bay leaves. Using slotted spoon, place carrots and potatoes on serving platter. Strain contents of roasting pan through fine-mesh strainer into fat separator. Let liquid settle, then pour defatted pan juices into serving bowl.

4. Remove kitchen twine from roasts. Slice roasts thin against grain and transfer to platter with vegetables. Pour ½ cup pan juices over meat. Serve with remaining pan juices.

Back in Fashion

Family Circle magazine once asked Peg Bracken, author of the mega-bestselling *I Hate to Cook Book*, to select her greatest-hits list for the hate-to-cook set. Her list included such gems as Stayabed Stew ("For those days when you're en negligee, en bed, with a murder story and a box of bonbons") and the Basic I-Hate-to-Cook Muffin (made by combining beer and muffin mix). But one classic super-easy dish of the day was notably absent: chuck roast with instant onion soup. "Done to death," Bracken explained, adding, "I remember years ago when every working wife in the land was sprinkling a package of dried onion soup mix onto a chunk of chuck steak...the thing was bigger than a Hula-Hoop, and it died, of course, of over-exposure." But guess what? The hula hoop is back, and in its new incarnation, chuck roast in foil is poised for a comeback, too.

CROWN ROAST OF PORK

SERVES 10 TO 12

A crown roast is two bone-in pork loin roasts tied into a crown shape, with the rib bones frenched and chine bones removed. This can be difficult to do, so ask your butcher to make this roast for you. We wrap extra kitchen twine around the widest part of the roast to provide more support when flipping. Use potatoes that measure 1 to 2 inches in diameter.

- Kosher salt and pepper
- 3 tablespoons minced fresh thyme
- 2 tablespoons minced fresh rosemary
- 5 garlic cloves, minced
- 1 (8- to 10-pound) pork crown roast
- 2 pounds small red potatoes
- 10 ounces shallots, peeled and halved
- 2 Golden Delicious apples, peeled, cored, and halved
- 8 tablespoons unsalted butter, melted
- ½ cup apple cider
- 1 cup chicken broth

1. Combine 3 tablespoons salt, 1 tablespoon pepper, thyme, rosemary, and garlic in bowl; reserve 2 teaspoons for vegetables. Pat pork dry with paper towels and rub with remaining herb salt. Wrap kitchen twine twice around widest part of roast and tie tightly. Refrigerate roast, covered, for 6 to 24 hours.

2. Adjust oven rack to lower-middle position and heat oven to 475 degrees. Place V-rack inside large roasting pan. Toss potatoes, shallots, apples, 4 tablespoons butter, and reserved herb salt in large bowl and transfer to pan. Arrange roast bone side down in V-rack and brush with remaining 4 tablespoons butter. Roast until meat is well browned and registers 110 degrees, about 1 hour.

3. Remove roast from oven and reduce oven temperature to 300 degrees. Using 2 bunches of paper towels, flip roast bone side up. Add apple cider to pan and return to oven, rotating direction of pan. Roast until meat registers 140 degrees, 30 to 50 minutes. Place meat on carving board, tent loosely with aluminum foil, and let rest for 15 to 20 minutes.

4. Transfer apple halves to blender and potatoes and shallots to bowl. Pour pan juices into fat separator, let liquid settle for 5 minutes, then pour into blender. Add chicken broth to blender with apples and pan juices and process until smooth, about 1 minute. Transfer sauce to medium saucepan and bring to simmer over medium heat. Season with salt and pepper to taste. Cover and keep warm. Remove twine from roast and slice meat between bones. Serve with vegetables and sauce.

Cooking Crown Roast of Pork Evenly

1. Using kitchen twine, make 2 loops around widest part of roast and tie securely to help crown hold its shape when flipped.

2. Place pork bone side down on V-rack and adjust bones to steady roast. Roast about 1 hour, until meat registers 110 degrees.

3. Using paper towels to protect your hands, flip hot roast bone side up and set it back on V-rack to finish cooking in gentle oven.

Why This Recipe Works A crown roast—two bone-in pork loin roasts tied together in a round—can feed a holiday crowd and offers a dramatic presentation, but its shape presents serious challenges to even cooking. Simply roasting it yielded meat overcooked on the outside and undercooked around the inner circle. The solution? We turned the roast upside down to allow more air to circulate and to better expose the thickest part of the roast to the heat. For a side, we opted for potatoes, shallots, and apples roasted in the pan alongside the meat. Pureeing the apples into a rich pan sauce gave us both fruity flavor and a nice, thick consistency.

OUR SUNDAY BEST

Why This Recipe Works Pork shoulder's fat content and marbling mean it requires low and slow cooking to become tender—making it a natural for the slow cooker. For a full-flavored sauce, we browned the pork, then sautéed onions and garlic with tomato paste in the browned bits left behind before adding them to the slow cooker. A little instant tapioca produced just the right texture in the braising liquid. White wine added brightness and a splash of white wine vinegar, stirred in at the end of cooking, refreshed the wine flavor. Hearty root vegetables and diced tomatoes, which cooked along with the roast, balanced the flavors.

SLOW-COOKER PORK POT ROAST

SERVES 8

This roast is sometimes sold in elastic netting that must be removed before cooking. If you cannot find 2½- to 3-pound pork picnic shoulder roasts, you can substitute one 6-pound pork picnic shoulder roast; cut it into two pieces and prepare as directed.

- 2 (2½- to 3-pound) boneless pork picnic shoulder roasts, trimmed
  Salt and pepper
- 2 tablespoons vegetable oil
- 2 onions, chopped
- 6 garlic cloves, minced
- 1 tablespoon tomato paste
- ½ cup white wine
- 1 (28-ounce) can diced tomatoes, drained
- 3 tablespoons instant tapioca
- 2 teaspoons minced fresh thyme
- 1 pound carrots, peeled, halved lengthwise, and cut into 2-inch pieces
- 1 pound parsnips, peeled, halved lengthwise, and cut into 2-inch pieces
- 2 teaspoons white wine vinegar

1. Open each roast and trim any excess fat, then tie each roast with kitchen twine at 1½-inch intervals and once around length of roasts. Pat roasts dry with paper towels and season with salt and pepper. Heat 2 teaspoons oil in 12-inch skillet over medium-high heat until just smoking. Brown roasts all over, about 10 minutes. Transfer to slow cooker.

2. Add onions and 2 teaspoons oil to now-empty skillet and cook until browned, about 5 minutes. Add garlic and tomato paste and cook until fragrant, about 1 minute. Stir in wine and simmer, scraping up browned bits with wooden spoon, until thickened, about 2 minutes. Stir in tomatoes, tapioca, and thyme; transfer to slow cooker.

3. Toss carrots, parsnips, ¼ teaspoon salt, ¼ teaspoon pepper, and remaining 2 teaspoons oil in bowl until vegetables are well coated. Scatter vegetable mixture over pork. Cover and cook on low until meat is tender, 9 to 10 hours (or cook on high 4 to 5 hours).

4. Transfer roasts to carving board, tent with aluminum foil, and let rest for 10 minutes. Remove twine from roasts and cut meat into ½-inch-thick slices; transfer to serving platter. Using slotted spoon, transfer carrots and parsnips to platter with pork. Stir vinegar into sauce and season with salt and pepper to taste. Serve, passing sauce separately.

Two Roasts are Better than One

We like to use two smaller roasts for this recipe, because the meat cooks more quickly and the small roasts are easier to manage in the slow cooker—and to find in the supermarket. Most boneless pork shoulder roasts come bound in string netting, which is difficult to remove after cooking. We prefer to cut the netting off before cooking, trim the roasts, and then tie each one with kitchen twine.

 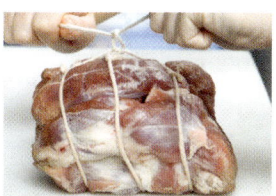

1. Remove netting from pork roasts. Open each roast and trim any excess fat.

2. Tie roasts separately. To ensure even cooking, fold smaller lobes under, then tie each roast with kitchen twine every 1½ inches around circumference and once around length.

Why This Recipe Works For this Sunday dinner–worthy pork roast, we skipped lean loins and opted for a meaty and inexpensive pork butt roast, which we flavored with a spice rub of cracked peppercorns, rosemary, sage, fennel seeds, and garlic. Cooking the roast in a low oven for seven hours rendered its fat and softened its tough connective tissue. For easy slicing, we refrigerated the cooked roast overnight until firm, then reheated it in the oven while we made a simple sauce from apple cider, apple jelly, and cider vinegar.

OLD-FASHIONED ROAST PORK

SERVES 8

A heavy roasting pan with 3-inch sides is the best choice for this recipe, but a shallow broiler pan also works well. Boneless pork butt roast is often labeled Boston butt in the supermarket.

- 6 pounds boneless pork butt roast, fat trimmed to ⅛ inch, tied lengthwise and crosswise
- 3 garlic cloves, minced
- 2 teaspoons peppercorns, cracked
- 1½ teaspoons salt
- 1 tablespoon chopped fresh rosemary
- 1 tablespoon chopped fresh sage
- 1 tablespoon fennel seeds, chopped
- 2 large red onions, cut into 1-inch wedges
- 1 cup apple cider
- ¼ cup apple jelly
- 2 tablespoons cider vinegar

1. Adjust oven rack to lower-middle position and heat oven to 300 degrees. Pat pork dry with paper towels. Combine garlic, peppercorns, salt, rosemary, sage, and fennel seeds in small bowl. Rub roast with herb mixture.

2. Transfer to roasting pan and cook for 3 hours. Scatter onion wedges around roast, tossing onions in pan drippings to coat. (If roast has not produced any juices, toss onions with 1 tablespoon vegetable oil before adding to pan.) Continue roasting until meat is extremely tender and skewer inserted in center meets no resistance, 3½ to 4 hours. (Check pan juices every hour to make sure they have not evaporated. If necessary, add 2 cups water to pan and scrape up browned bits.)

3. Transfer roast to large baking dish, place onions in medium bowl, and pour pan drippings into 2-cup liquid measuring cup, adding enough water to measure 1½ cups. Let roast, onions, and drippings cool for 30 minutes, cover each with plastic wrap, and refrigerate overnight.

4. One hour before serving, adjust oven rack to middle position and heat oven to 300 degrees. Cut meat into ¼-inch slices and overlap in large baking dish. Skim off fat from pan drippings and transfer drippings and reserved onions to medium saucepan. Add cider, jelly, and vinegar and bring to boil over medium-high heat, then reduce to simmer. Spoon ½ cup sauce over pork slices and cover baking dish with aluminum foil. Place in oven and heat until very hot, 30 to 40 minutes.

5. Just before serving, reduce sauce until dark and thickened, 10 to 15 minutes. Serve pork, spooning onion mixture over meat or passing separately.

Secrets to Old-Fashioned Flavor

1. Trim any excess fat from pork, leaving behind ⅛-inch-thick layer. Tie trimmed roast tightly into uniform shape, lengthwise and then crosswise.

2. Rub mixture of rosemary, sage, fennel seeds, garlic, salt, and pepper over roast.

3. Roast pork for 3 hours, add onion wedges, and continue to roast until meat is extremely tender, 3½ to 4 hours more.

PUERTO RICAN PORK ROAST

SERVES 8 TO 10

Depending on their size, you may need two bunches of cilantro. Crimp the foil tightly over the edges of the roasting pan in step 2 to minimize evaporation. Make sure to spray the V-rack in step 3. Serve over white rice.

- 1½ cups chopped fresh cilantro leaves and stems
- 1 onion, chopped coarse
- ¼ cup kosher salt
- ¼ cup olive oil
- 10 garlic cloves, peeled
- 2 tablespoons pepper
- 1 tablespoon dried oregano
- 1 tablespoon ground cumin
- 1 (7-pound) bone-in pork picnic shoulder
- 1 tablespoon grated lime zest plus ⅓ cup juice (3 limes)

1. Pulse 1 cup cilantro, onion, salt, oil, garlic, pepper, oregano, and cumin in food processor until finely ground, about 15 pulses, scraping down sides of bowl as needed. Pat pork dry with paper towels and rub sofrito all over. Wrap pork in plastic wrap and refrigerate for at least 12 hours or up to 24 hours.

2. Adjust oven rack to lower-middle position and heat oven to 450 degrees. Pour 8 cups water in large roasting pan. Unwrap pork and place skin side down in pan. Cover pan tightly with aluminum foil and roast for 90 minutes. Remove foil, reduce oven temperature to 375 degrees, and continue to roast for 2½ hours.

3. Remove pan from oven. Spray V-rack with vegetable oil spray. Gently slide metal spatula under pork to release skin from pan. Using folded dish towels, grasp ends of pork and transfer to V-rack, skin side up. Wipe skin dry with paper towels. Place V-rack with pork in roasting pan. If pan looks dry, add 1 cup water. Return to oven and roast until pork registers 195 degrees, about 1 hour. (Add water as needed to keep bottom of pan from drying out.)

4. Line rimmed baking sheet with foil. Remove pan from oven. Transfer V-rack and pork to prepared sheet and return to oven. Immediately increase oven temperature to 500 degrees. Cook until pork skin is well browned and crispy (when tapped lightly with tongs, skin will sound hollow), 15 to 30 minutes, rotating sheet halfway through cooking. Transfer pork to carving board and let rest for 30 minutes.

5. Meanwhile, pour juices from pan into fat separator. Let liquid settle for 5 minutes, then pour off 1 cup defatted juices into large bowl. (If juices measure less than 1 cup, make up difference with water.) Whisk remaining ½ cup cilantro and lime zest and juice into bowl.

6. Remove crispy skin from pork in 1 large piece. Coarsely chop skin into bite-size pieces and set aside. Trim and discard excess fat from pork. Remove pork from bone and chop coarse. Transfer pork to bowl with cilantro-lime sauce and toss to combine. Serve pork, with crispy skin on side.

Creating Crispy Skin

Elevating the roast on a V-rack to finish cooking crisps up the flavorful skin.

Why This Recipe Works Famous for its crispy skin, this Puerto Rican dish of long-cooked, heavily seasoned pork roast should result in flavorful meat along with its trademark crispy exterior. We rubbed a picnic shoulder with a salty sofrito (a paste of aromatics and herbs) the day before roasting, which kept the meat moist and packed a flavor punch. We then roasted the pork skin-side down, covered, which helped transform tough collagen into gelatin. Next, we removed the foil cover to ensure that our pork didn't taste steamed, and then turned the roast skin side up on a V-rack to dry the skin to prepare it for the last step—a quick roast at very high heat.

CIDER-BRAISED PORK ROAST

SERVES 8

Pork butt roast is often labeled Boston butt in the supermarket. Plan ahead: This roast needs to cure for 18 to 24 hours before cooking. If you can't find Braeburn apples, substitute Jonagold. If you don't have a fat separator, strain the liquid through a fine-mesh strainer into a medium bowl in step 4 and wait for it to settle.

- 1 (5- to 6-pound) bone-in pork butt roast
- ¼ cup packed brown sugar
- Kosher salt and pepper
- 3 tablespoons vegetable oil
- 1 onion, halved and sliced thin
- 6 garlic cloves, smashed and peeled
- 2 cups apple cider
- 6 sprigs fresh thyme
- 2 bay leaves
- 1 cinnamon stick
- 2 Braeburn apples, cored and cut into 8 wedges each
- ¼ cup apple butter
- 1 tablespoon cornstarch
- 1 tablespoon cider vinegar

1. Using sharp knife, trim fat cap on roast to ¼ inch. Cut 1-inch crosshatch pattern, 1/16 inch deep, in fat cap. Place roast on large sheet of plastic wrap. Combine sugar and ¼ cup salt in bowl and rub mixture over entire roast and into slits. Wrap roast tightly in double layer of plastic, place on plate, and refrigerate for 18 to 24 hours.

2. Adjust oven rack to middle position and heat oven to 275 degrees. Unwrap roast and pat dry with paper towels, brushing away any excess salt mixture from surface. Season roast with pepper.

3. Heat oil in Dutch oven over medium-high heat until just smoking. Sear roast until well browned on all sides, about 3 minutes per side. Turn roast fat side up. Scatter onion and garlic around roast and cook until fragrant and beginning to brown, about 2 minutes. Add 1¾ cups cider, thyme sprigs, bay leaves, and cinnamon stick and bring to simmer. Cover, transfer to oven, and braise until fork slips easily in and out of meat and meat registers 190 degrees, 2 hours 15 minutes to 2 hours 45 minutes.

4. Transfer roast to carving board, tent with aluminum foil, and let rest for 30 minutes. Strain braising liquid through fine-mesh strainer into fat separator; discard solids and let liquid settle for at least 5 minutes.

5. About 10 minutes before roast is done resting, wipe out pot with paper towels. Spoon 1½ tablespoons of clear, separated fat from top of fat separator into now-empty pot and heat over medium-high heat until shimmering. Season apples with salt and pepper. Space apples evenly in pot, cut side down, and cook until well browned on both cut sides, about 3 minutes per side. Transfer to platter and tent with foil.

6. Wipe out pot with paper towels. Return 2 cups defatted braising liquid to now-empty pot and bring to boil over high heat. Whisk in apple butter until incorporated. Whisk cornstarch and remaining ¼ cup cider together in bowl and add to pot. Return to boil and cook until thickened, about 1 minute. Off heat, add vinegar and season with salt and pepper to taste. Cover sauce and keep warm.

7. To carve roast, cut around inverted T-shaped bone until it can be pulled free from roast (use clean dish towel to grasp bone if necessary). Slice pork and transfer to serving platter with apples. Pour 1 cup sauce over pork and apples. Serve, passing remaining sauce at table.

Removing the Bone

Holding onto tip of T-shaped bone, use long knife to cut meat away from all sides of bone until bone is loose enough to pull out of roast.

Why This Recipe Works Pork and apples are a classic combination, so we paired flavorful bone-in pork butt roast with apple cider. Rubbing the meat with a brown sugar–salt mixture and refrigerating it overnight seasoned the pork and helped keep it juicy. Onions, garlic, bay leaf, cinnamon, and thyme were welcome additions that kept the clean, sweet-tart taste of cider in focus. Apple butter and cider vinegar added more apple-y punch, and a slurry of cornstarch and reserved cider thickened the braising liquid into a beautiful sauce. Apple wedges seared in flavorful pork fat united the elements of this hearty roast.

Why This Recipe Works Ham glazed with sweet apple cider certainly sounds great, but most recipes lack serious apple flavor, not to mention they call for frequent basting. For a relatively hands-off ham that was infused with lots of apple flavor, we marinated the ham in apple cider spiked with warm spices. Baking the ham in an oven bag guarded against dried-out meat. And to give our ham a crusty, spicy-sweet exterior, we rolled back the bag once the ham was heated through, slathered on reduced apple cider, pressed a mixture of brown sugar and black pepper all over, and slid it back into the oven until it caramelized.

CIDER-BAKED HAM

SERVES 16 TO 20

We prefer a bone-in, uncut, cured ham for this recipe, because the exterior layer of fat can be scored and helps create a nice crust. A spiral-sliced ham can be used instead, but there won't be much exterior fat, so skip the trimming and scoring in step 2. This recipe requires nearly a gallon of cider and a large oven bag. In step 4, be sure to stir the reduced cider mixture frequently to prevent scorching.

- 1 cinnamon stick, broken into rough pieces
- ¼ teaspoon whole cloves
- 3¼ quarts apple cider
- 8 cups ice cubes
- 1 (7- to 10-pound) cured bone-in half ham, preferably shank end
- 2 tablespoons Dijon mustard
- 1 cup packed dark brown sugar
- 1 teaspoon pepper
- Large oven bag

1. Toast cinnamon and cloves in large saucepan over medium heat until fragrant, about 3 minutes. Add 4 cups cider and bring to boil. Pour spiced cider into large stockpot or clean bucket, add 4 cups cider and ice, and stir until melted.

2. Meanwhile, remove skin from exterior of ham and trim fat to ¼-inch thickness. Score remaining fat at 1-inch intervals in crosshatch pattern. Transfer ham to container with chilled cider mixture (liquid should nearly cover ham) and refrigerate for at least 4 hours or up to 12 hours.

3. Discard cider mixture and transfer ham to large oven bag. Add 1 cup fresh cider to bag, tie securely, and cut 4 slits in top of bag. Transfer to large roasting pan and let stand at room temperature for 1½ hours.

4. Adjust oven rack to lowest position and heat oven to 300 degrees. Bake until ham registers 100 degrees, 1½ to 2½ hours. Meanwhile, bring remaining 4 cups cider and mustard to boil in saucepan. Reduce heat to medium-low and simmer, stirring often, until mixture is very thick and reduced to ⅓ cup, about 1 hour.

5. Combine sugar and pepper in bowl. Remove ham from oven and let rest for 5 minutes. Increase oven temperature to 400 degrees. Roll back oven bag and brush ham with reduced cider mixture. Using your fingers, carefully press sugar mixture onto exterior of ham. Return to oven and bake until dark brown and caramelized, about 20 minutes. Transfer ham to carving board, tent loosely with aluminum foil, and let rest for 15 minutes. Carve and serve.

Secrets to Cider-Baked Ham

1. Soaking ham in spice-infused cider lends concentrated flavor.

2. Baking ham with cider in oven bag keeps meat moist and lends even more cider flavor.

3. Brushing ham with sticky cider reduction provides big apple flavor and base for crust.

4. Pressing mixture of brown sugar and pepper onto ham gives exterior spicy-sweet, crackly crust.

PARMESAN-CRUSTED ASPARAGUS

SERVES 4 TO 6

Avoid pencil-thin asparagus for this recipe. Work quickly when tossing the asparagus with the egg whites, as the salt on the asparagus will rapidly begin to deflate the whites.

- 2 pounds (½-inch-thick) asparagus, trimmed
  Salt and pepper
- 3 ounces Parmesan cheese, grated (1½ cups)
- ¾ cup panko bread crumbs
- 1 tablespoon unsalted butter, melted and cooled
  Pinch cayenne
- 2 large egg whites
- 1 teaspoon honey

1. Adjust oven rack to middle position and heat oven to 450 degrees. Line rimmed baking sheet with aluminum foil and spray with vegetable oil spray. Using fork, poke holes up and down stalks of asparagus. Toss asparagus with ½ teaspoon salt and let stand for 30 minutes on a paper towel–lined baking sheet.

2. Meanwhile, combine 1 cup Parmesan, panko, butter, ¼ teaspoon salt, ⅛ teaspoon pepper, and cayenne in bowl. Transfer half of panko mixture to shallow dish and reserve remaining mixture. Using stand mixer fitted with whisk, whip egg whites and honey on medium-low speed until foamy, about 1 minute. Increase speed to medium-high and whip until soft peaks form, 2 to 3 minutes. Scrape into 13 by 9-inch baking dish and toss asparagus in mixture. Working with 1 spear at a time, dredge half of asparagus in panko and transfer to aluminum foil–lined baking sheet. Refill shallow dish with reserved panko mixture and repeat with remaining half of asparagus.

3. Bake asparagus until just beginning to brown, 6 to 8 minutes. Sprinkle with remaining ½ cup Parmesan and continue to bake until cheese is melted and panko is golden brown, 6 to 8 minutes. Transfer to platter. Serve.

Making the Coating Stick

1. Perforate and salt asparagus to draw out excess moisture that could saturate crumbs.

2. Whip egg whites to help crumbs adhere. Add honey for flavor and extra sticking power.

3. Work with 1 spear at a time to keep bread crumbs from clumping.

Why This Recipe Works Simply roasting asparagus and topping it with shaved Parmesan gives you limp spears and rubbery cheese. To get perfectly crisp-tender asparagus, we first salted it to rid it of excess moisture. For a cheesy coating that would stay put on the slender spears, we whipped a combination of honey and egg whites to soft peaks, dipped the asparagus in the mixture, then coated them with a mixture of bread crumbs and Parmesan. Finally, to reinforce the Parmesan flavor, we sprinkled the spears with more cheese at the end of roasting.

BRUSSELS SPROUT SALAD

SERVES 8

Slice the sprouts as thin as possible. Shred the Pecorino Romano on the large holes of a box grater.

- 3 tablespoons lemon juice
- 2 tablespoons Dijon mustard
- 1 small shallot, minced
- 1 garlic clove, minced
  Salt and pepper
- 6 tablespoons extra-virgin olive oil
- 2 pounds Brussels sprouts, trimmed, halved, and sliced very thin
- 3 ounces Pecorino Romano cheese, shredded (1 cup)
- ½ cup pine nuts, toasted

1. Whisk lemon juice, mustard, shallot, garlic, and ½ teaspoon salt together in large bowl. Slowly whisk in oil until incorporated. Toss Brussels sprouts with vinaigrette and let sit for at least 30 minutes or up to 2 hours.

2. Fold in Pecorino and pine nuts. Season with salt and pepper to taste. Serve.

BRUSSELS SPROUT SALAD WITH CHEDDAR, HAZELNUTS, AND APPLE

Substitute 1 cup shredded sharp cheddar for Pecorino and ½ cup hazelnuts, toasted, skinned, and chopped, for pine nuts. Add 1 Granny Smith apple, cored and cut into ½-inch pieces.

BRUSSELS SPROUT SALAD WITH SMOKED GOUDA, PECANS, AND DRIED CHERRIES

Substitute 1 cup shredded smoked gouda for Pecorino and ½ cup pecans, toasted and chopped, for pine nuts. Add ½ cup chopped dried cherries.

How to Slice Brussels Sprouts

You can use the slicing disk of your food processor or slice the sprouts with a chef's knife. Follow these steps to do the latter safely and quickly.

1. Trim stem end of each sprout and then cut each sprout in half through cut end.

2. With flat surface on cutting board, thinly slice each half.

Why This Recipe Works Raw Brussels sprout salad isn't as weird as it sounds: Brussels sprouts are very much like miniature cabbages in both texture and taste. To make this slaw-like salad, we thinly sliced the sprouts and tossed them with a bright, lemony vinaigrette with a touch of Dijon. We briefly marinated the salad in the vinaigrette to soften and season the sprouts. We topped the sprouts with toasted pine nuts and salty Pecorino Romano for a salad that's so delicious it can turn Brussels sprout loathers into Brussels sprout lovers.

Why This Recipe Works Conventional wisdom holds that anything but the gentlest treatment turns mashed potatoes into wallpaper paste, but we think our mixer-whipped spuds prove otherwise. For the lightest, fluffiest potatoes, we found high-starch russets worked best. Boiling the potatoes added extra water, resulting in a flat, not fluffy, finished dish. The best technique was to rinse excess starch from the raw potatoes, steam them, and then dry them in a pot on the stovetop over low heat. This process made them fluffier and better able to absorb the warm butter-and-milk mixture during whipping.

WHIPPED POTATOES

SERVES 8 TO 10

If your steamer basket has short legs (under 1¾ inches), the potatoes will sit in water as they cook and get wet. To prevent this, use balls of aluminum foil as steamer basket stilts. A stand mixer fitted with a whisk yields the smoothest potatoes, but a hand-held mixer may be used as well.

- 4 pounds russet potatoes, peeled and cut into 1-inch pieces
- 1½ cups whole milk
- 8 tablespoons unsalted butter, cut into 8 pieces
- 2 teaspoons salt
- ½ teaspoon pepper

1. Place cut potatoes in colander. Rinse under cold water until water runs clear, about 1 minute. Drain potatoes. Fill Dutch oven with 1 inch water and bring to boil. Place steamer basket in Dutch oven and fill with potatoes. Reduce heat to medium and cook, covered, until potatoes are tender, 20 to 25 minutes.

2. Heat milk, butter, salt, and pepper in small saucepan over medium-low heat, whisking until smooth, about 3 minutes; cover and keep warm.

3. Pour contents of Dutch oven into colander and return potatoes to dry pot. Stir over low heat until potatoes are thoroughly dried, about 1 minute. Using stand mixer fitted with whisk, break potatoes into small pieces on low speed, about 30 seconds. Add milk mixture in steady stream until incorporated. Increase speed to high and whip until potatoes are light and fluffy and no lumps remain, about 2 minutes. Serve.

Choosing Your Mixing Method

Don't try this recipe in your food processor—its sharp blades cut open the starch granules and turn the potatoes to glue. The beating motion of the mixer makes smooth, fluffy potatoes every time.

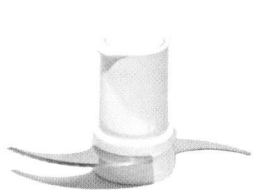

DON'T DO IT
A food processor's blade makes gluey mashed potatoes.

WHIP SMART
Use the mixer for light, fluffy whipped potatoes.

Whip It Good

In all likelihood, whipped potatoes owe their mid 20th-century fame to the Sunbeam Mixmaster. The appliance, first manufactured in 1930 and quickly enshrined as the must-have kitchen tool for American housewives, actually had a Mix-Finder Dial setting for whipped potatoes—speed 4 or 5, depending on the model. Whipping potatoes in the Mixmaster, the manufacturer claimed, saved "one-third the time usually taken by hand." But then, this machine promised time savings on just about every kitchen task. The 17 available attachments on early models included not only a slicer/shredder and an ice cream maker, but also a butter churn, a string bean slicer, and (our personal favorite) a pea sheller. It's no wonder this kitchen tool became perhaps the most famous appliance of the 20th century.

Why This Recipe Works Duchess potatoes take mashed potatoes to the next level, enriching them with egg and piping them into decorative rosettes before baking. To cook our spuds, we tried boiling, but this made them waterlogged; baking dried them out. Parcooking them in the microwave and finishing the rosettes in a hot oven proved best. For a potato mixture that was the right texture for piping, we stirred in butter, eggs, and cream while the potatoes were still hot, then added more butter once the potatoes had cooled. Baking powder ensured our picture-perfect Duchess Potatoes had the perfect airy, light texture to match.

DUCHESS POTATOES

SERVES 8

For the smoothest, most uniform texture, use a food mill or ricer to mash the potatoes. Choose potatoes of the same size so that they cook evenly.

- 3 pounds russet potatoes
- 1 cup heavy cream
- 6 tablespoons unsalted butter, cut into ¼-inch pieces and softened
- 1 large egg plus 1 large yolk, lightly beaten
- 1¼ teaspoons salt
- ½ teaspoon pepper
- ½ teaspoon baking powder
- Pinch nutmeg
- Vegetable oil spray

1. Adjust oven rack to upper-middle position and heat oven to 475 degrees. Meanwhile, prick potatoes all over with fork, place on plate, and microwave until tender, 18 to 25 minutes, turning potatoes over after 10 minutes.

2. Cut potatoes in half. When cool enough to handle, scoop flesh into large bowl and mash until no lumps remain. Add cream, 3 tablespoons butter, egg and yolk, salt, pepper, baking powder, and nutmeg and continue to mash until potatoes are smooth. Let cool to room temperature, about 10 minutes. Gently fold in remaining butter until pieces are evenly distributed.

3. Transfer potato mixture to piping bag fitted with ½-inch star tip. Pipe eight 4-inch-wide mounds of potato onto rimmed baking sheet. Spray lightly with vegetable oil spray and bake until golden brown, 15 to 20 minutes. Serve.

To Make Ahead Once piped onto baking sheet, potatoes can be covered loosely with plastic wrap and refrigerated for 24 hours. Remove plastic and spray lightly with vegetable oil spray before baking.

Two Paths to Perfect Piping

With a pastry bag fitted with a star tip, making beautiful duchess potatoes is child's play. If you don't have a pastry bag, don't worry: There's another easy way.

With Pastry Bag
Pipe 4-inch circle of potato mixture onto baking sheet. Continue to pipe upward in circles to form 3-inch-high peak.

Without Pastry Bag
Scoop potato mixture into zipper-lock bag, snip off 1 corner, and pipe as directed. Use tines of fork to create rippled surface.

Freezer Friendly

Our Duchess Potatoes freeze beautifully, which is handy, as they're ideal for a party. Pipe the mounds onto a rimmed baking sheet and then cover lightly with plastic wrap. Freeze for 2 hours until solid and transfer the potatoes to an airtight container (or leave them on the baking sheet if you've got the space). When you are ready to bake them, arrange on a rimmed baking sheet (or simply remove the plastic), spray lightly with vegetable oil spray, and bake according to our recipe. They can go straight from freezer to oven, and they won't even need any extra time.

SYRACUSE SALT POTATOES

SERVES 6 TO 8

You will need 1¼ cups of noniodized table salt, 1½ cups of Morton kosher salt, or 2½ cups of Diamond Crystal kosher salt to equal 14 ounces. We prefer to use small potatoes, measuring 1 to 2 inches in diameter, in this recipe.

- 8 cups water
- 14 ounces salt
- 3 pounds small white or red potatoes
- 8 tablespoons unsalted butter, cut into 8 pieces
- 2 tablespoons minced fresh chives
- 1 teaspoon pepper

1. Set wire rack in rimmed baking sheet. Bring water to boil in Dutch oven over medium-high heat. Stir in salt and potatoes and cook until potatoes are just tender, 20 to 30 minutes. Drain potatoes and transfer to prepared baking sheet. Let dry until salty crust forms, about 1 minute.

2. Meanwhile, microwave butter, chives, and pepper in medium bowl until butter is melted, about 1 minute. Transfer potatoes to serving bowl and serve, passing butter separately.

Salt Magic

Just out of the salty water, the potatoes will look like any other boiled potato.

One minute after they've been drained, the characteristic salt crust will appear on the potato skins.

The high salinity means the cooking water gets hotter than normal, resulting in extra-creamy potato flesh.

Selling Salt Potatoes

Salt potatoes have their origin in the mid-1800s when Irish salt workers in the Syracuse area would cook unpeeled new potatoes in huge evaporation vats filled with boiling salt water. In 1914, John Hinerwadel, owner of an eponymous central New York clambake company, began offering salt potatoes on his menu. They became so popular that Mr. Hinerwadel started selling salt potato kits—complete with a sack of small white potatoes and a packet of salt—so people could make the potatoes at home. The red and white bags of potatoes with the signature red and yellow sun are still sold in the Syracuse area.

Why This Recipe Works For Syracuse salt potatoes with a well-seasoned crust and ultra-creamy interior, we cut back on the usual 3 cups of salt, which resulted in overly salty potatoes. We found that white or red potatoes proved best, but they needed to be boiled in the salted water whole—if they were cut or peeled, they absorbed too much salt. Though these potatoes are usually served with plain melted butter for dipping, we found that adding chives and black pepper to the butter brought this dish to new heights.

Why This Recipe Works Most recipes for mashed potato casserole simply dump mashed potatoes in a baking dish and pop it in the oven, but these dishes always end up bland, gluey, and dense. We wanted a casserole that delivered fluffy, buttery, creamy potatoes nestled under a savory golden crust. Using half-and-half instead of the traditional heavy cream lightened the recipe, and cutting it with chicken broth kept the potatoes moist. Beating eggs into the potato mixture helped it achieve a fluffy, airy texture. For bold flavor, we added Dijon mustard and fresh chives.

MASHED POTATO CASSEROLE

SERVES 8

The casserole may also be baked in a 13 by 9-inch pan.

- 4 pounds russet potatoes, peeled and cut into 1-inch chunks
- 12 tablespoons unsalted butter, cut into 12 pieces
- ½ cup half-and-half
- ½ cup chicken broth
- 2 teaspoons Dijon mustard
- 1 garlic clove, minced
- 2 teaspoons salt
- 4 large eggs
- ¼ cup finely chopped fresh chives

1. Adjust oven rack to upper-middle position and heat oven to 375 degrees. Bring potatoes and water to cover by 1 inch to boil in large pot over high heat. Reduce heat to medium and simmer until potatoes are tender, about 20 minutes.

2. Heat butter, half-and-half, broth, mustard, garlic, and salt in saucepan over medium-low heat until smooth, about 5 minutes. Keep warm.

3. Drain potatoes and transfer to large bowl. Using stand mixer fitted with paddle, beat potatoes on medium-low speed, slowly adding half-and-half mixture, until smooth and creamy, about 1 minute. Scrape down bowl; beat in eggs, 1 at a time, until incorporated, about 1 minute. Fold in chives.

4. Transfer potato mixture to greased 3-quart baking dish. Smooth surface of potatoes, then use fork to make peaked design on top of casserole. Bake until potatoes rise and begin to brown, about 35 minutes. Let cool for 10 minutes. Serve.

To Make Ahead The baking dish with the potatoes can be covered with plastic and refrigerated for up to 24 hours. When ready to bake, let the casserole sit at room temperature for 1 hour. Increase baking time by 10 minutes.

Secrets to Perfect Mashed Potato Casserole

1. When poured into casserole dish, mashed potatoes will look very soupy. They will firm up and rise in oven.

2. For better browning and an impressive presentation, use fork to make peaked design on top of casserole.

Can Evaporated Milk Be Substituted for Half-and-Half?

Sorry, the answer is no. We substituted evaporated milk in a handful of recipes that call for half-and-half. The savory dishes made with evaporated milk in place of half-and-half tasted tinny, and the desserts were too sweet.

Not willing to give up, we diluted the evaporated milk with water and then used it in place of the half-and-half in our test recipes. Tasters didn't like that either, detecting a mildly cooked taste. We tried heavy cream, but its high milk-fat content muted the other flavors. Whole milk made the food less rich, but the flavors remained lively.

With heavy cream and either skim or whole milk, you can mix up a good substitute for half-and-half. If you don't mind a slightly thinner consistency and lighter flavor, whole milk will work in most recipes.

⅓ cup heavy cream + ⅔ cup skim milk =
1 cup half-and-half

¼ cup heavy cream + ¾ cup whole milk =
1 cup half-and-half

CREAMY MASHED SWEET POTATOES

SERVES 4 TO 6

This recipe can be doubled and prepared in a Dutch oven, but the cooking time will need to be doubled as well.

- 2 pounds sweet potatoes, peeled, quartered, and sliced ¼ inch thick
- 4 tablespoons unsalted butter, cut into 4 pieces
- 3 tablespoons heavy cream
- 1 teaspoon sugar
- Salt and pepper

1. Combine sweet potatoes, butter, 2 tablespoons cream, sugar, ½ teaspoon salt, and ¼ teaspoon pepper in large saucepan. Cook, covered, over low heat until potatoes are fall-apart tender, 35 to 40 minutes.

2. Off heat, add remaining 1 tablespoon cream and mash sweet potatoes with potato masher. Serve.

HERBED MASHED SWEET POTATOES WITH CARAMELIZED ONION

If you prefer, substitute ¼ teaspoon dried thyme for the thyme sprig.

Add 1 sprig fresh thyme to saucepan in step 1. While sweet potatoes are cooking, melt 1 tablespoon butter in 8-inch nonstick skillet and add 1 small onion, chopped, ¼ teaspoon sugar, and ¼ teaspoon salt. Cook over low heat until onion is caramelized, about 15 minutes. Remove thyme and mash potatoes as directed. Stir in onion and 1 tablespoon sour cream.

SMOKEHOUSE MASHED SWEET POTATOES

Add ⅛ teaspoon cayenne pepper to saucepan in step 1. Mash sweet potatoes with ½ cup shredded smoked Gouda cheese and cover with lid until cheese melts, about 1 minute. Sprinkle with 6 slices chopped cooked bacon and 1 thinly sliced scallion.

No-Boil Sweet Potatoes

Boiling sweet potatoes in lots of liquid—as you would regular potatoes—is not a good idea. Sweet potatoes will soak up too much water, and the resulting mash will be a soggy mess. Better to cook them in a small amount of liquid. Just 2 tablespoons of heavy cream (plus a little butter), along with the water released from the sweet potatoes as they cook, is enough to steam them to tenderness.

The Slice is Right

It is imperative to cut the sweet potato into thin, even slices to ensure perfect cooking.

1. Quarter each peeled sweet potato lengthwise.

2. Cut each quarter into ¼-inch slices crosswise.

Why This Recipe Works Deeply flavored, earthy, and subtly sweet, mashed sweet potatoes hardly need a layer of marshmallows to make them into a tempting side. For a silky and full-flavored mash, we found the secret was to thinly slice the potatoes and cook them covered, on the stovetop, over low heat in a small amount of butter and cream. Once the sweet potatoes were fall-apart tender, they could be mashed right in the pot—no draining, no straining, no fuss. Adding another spoonful of cream when we mashed the potatoes enriched them even more.

SWEET CORN SPOONBREAD

SERVES 6

You will need three ears of corn to yield 2 cups. Frozen corn, thawed and drained well, can be substituted for the fresh corn.

- 1 cup cornmeal
- 2¾ cups whole milk
- 4 tablespoons unsalted butter
- 2 cups fresh corn
- 1 teaspoon sugar
- 1 teaspoon salt
- ⅛ teaspoon cayenne pepper
- 3 large eggs, separated
- ¼ teaspoon cream of tartar

1. Adjust oven rack to middle position and heat oven to 400 degrees. Grease 1½-quart soufflé dish or 8-inch baking dish. Whisk cornmeal and ¾ cup milk in bowl until combined; set aside.

2. Melt butter in Dutch oven over medium-high heat. Cook corn until beginning to brown, about 3 minutes. Stir in remaining 2 cups milk, sugar, salt, and cayenne and bring to boil. Off heat, cover mixture and let steep for 15 minutes.

3. Transfer warm corn mixture to blender or food processor and puree until smooth. Return to pot and bring to boil. Reduce heat to low and add cornmeal mixture, whisking constantly, until thickened, 2 to 3 minutes; transfer to large bowl and let cool to room temperature, about 20 minutes. Once mixture is cool, whisk in egg yolks until combined.

4. Using stand mixer fitted with whisk, beat egg whites and cream of tartar on medium-low speed until foamy, about 1 minute. Increase speed to medium-high and whip until stiff peaks form, 3 to 4 minutes. Whisk one-third of whites into corn mixture, then gently fold in remaining whites until combined. Scrape mixture into prepared dish and transfer to oven. Reduce oven temperature to 350 degrees and bake until spoonbread is golden brown and has risen above rim of dish, about 45 minutes. Serve immediately.

INDIVIDUAL SPOONBREADS

To make individual spoonbreads, divide batter among 6 greased 7-ounce ramekins. Arrange ramekins on rimmed baking sheet and bake as directed, reducing cooking time to 30 to 35 minutes.

Egg Whites 101

Egg whites are most easily whipped in a very clean metal bowl with a pinch of cream of tartar, which promotes stabilization.

 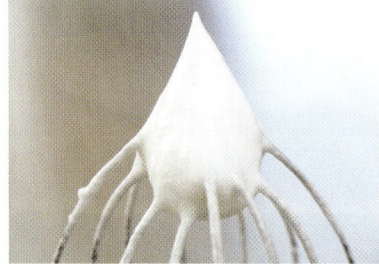 

Soft Peaks
Soft peaks will droop slightly downward from tip of whisk or beater.

Stiff Peaks
Stiff peaks will stand up tall on their own.

Overwhipped
Overwhipped egg whites will look curdled and separated; if you reach this point, start over with new whites and clean bowl.

Why This Recipe Works For a fluffy, soufflé-style sweet corn spoonbread with deep corn flavor, we focused on flavor, then texture. Sautéing the corn in butter, before steeping it in milk and pureeing it, ensured that the sweet corn flavor permeated our spoonbread. To make sure the cornmeal didn't impart a gritty texture, we soaked it in the milk beforehand. And to guarantee a stable foam and an impressive rise, we beat the egg whites with a bit of cream of tartar.

tex-mex favorites

- **235** Ultimate Spicy Beef Nachos
- **237** Ultimate Seven-Layer Dip
- **238** Chunky Guacamole
- **241** Huevos Rancheros
- **242** Arroz con Pollo
- **244** Latin Fried Chicken
- **247** California-Style Fish Tacos
- **248** Easy Chicken Tacos
- **251** Puffy Tacos
- **253** Citrus-Braised Pork Tacos
- **254** Easier Chicken Chimichangas
- **256** Smoky Salsa Verde
- **259** Tex-Mex Cheese Enchiladas
- **260** Authentic Beef Enchiladas
- **262** Chicken Chilaquiles
- **265** Easy Chili con Carne
- **267** Five-Alarm Chili
- **268** So-Cal Churros

Why This Recipe Works Too often, nacho recipes produce soggy chips loaded down with bland, greasy beef, dry beans, and cold strings of cheese. Instead, we wanted hearty nachos that are crisp, flavorful, and fresh. Boldly seasoning our beef with a mixture of spices and other flavorings caused the flavor to pop. While many nacho recipes call for cheddar cheese, we found it didn't melt nearly as well as pepper Jack, which melted smoothly and added a kick, too.

ULTIMATE SPICY BEEF NACHOS

SERVES 8

In addition to our One-Minute Salsa (recipe follows), garnish the nachos with sour cream, chopped cilantro, and diced avocado.

Refried Beans
- ½ cup canned refried beans
- 3 tablespoons shredded pepper Jack cheese
- 1 tablespoon chopped canned jalapeños

Spicy Beef
- 2 teaspoons vegetable oil
- 1 small onion, chopped fine
- 3 garlic cloves, minced
- 1 tablespoon chili powder
- 1 teaspoon ground cumin
- ½ teaspoon dried oregano
- 1 teaspoon salt
- 1 pound 90 percent lean ground beef
- 2 tablespoons tomato paste
- 1 teaspoon packed brown sugar
- 1½ teaspoons minced canned chipotle chile in adobo sauce, plus 1 teaspoon adobo sauce
- ½ cup water
- 2 teaspoons lime juice

- 1 (9.5-ounce) bag tortilla chips
- 1 pound pepper Jack cheese, shredded (4 cups)
- 2 jalapeño chiles, sliced into thin rings
- 1 recipe One-Minute Salsa

1. Adjust oven rack to middle position and heat oven to 400 degrees.

2. For the Refried Beans Pulse ingredients in food processor until smooth, about 10 pulses. Transfer to bowl and cover with plastic wrap.

3. For the Spicy Beef Heat oil in large skillet over medium heat until shimmering. Cook onion until softened, about 4 minutes. Add garlic, chili powder, cumin, oregano, and salt and cook until fragrant, about 1 minute. Add beef and cook, breaking meat into small bits with wooden spoon and scraping pan bottom to prevent scorching, until no longer pink, about 5 minutes. Add tomato paste, sugar, chipotle, and adobo sauce and cook until paste begins to darken, about 1 minute. Add water, bring to simmer, and cook over medium-low until mixture is nearly dry, 5 to 7 minutes. Stir in lime juice and transfer mixture to plate lined with several layers of paper towels. Use more paper towels to blot up excess grease.

4. Spread half of chips on large ovensafe serving platter or in 13 by 9-inch baking dish. Dollop half of bean mixture over chips, then spread evenly. Scatter half of beef mixture over beans, top with 2 cups cheese and half of jalapeños. Repeat with remaining chips, beans, beef, cheese, and jalapeños. Bake until cheese is melted and just beginning to brown, 12 to 14 minutes. Serve with salsa and other suggested garnishes.

ONE-MINUTE SALSA
MAKES ABOUT 1 CUP

Make sure to drain both the tomatoes and the jalapeños before processing. The salsa will keep for two days in the refrigerator. Season to taste before serving.

- ½ small red onion
- ¼ cup fresh cilantro leaves
- 2 tablespoons jarred jalapeños, drained
- 1 tablespoon lime juice
- 1 garlic clove, peeled
- ¼ teaspoon salt
- 1 (14.5-ounce) can diced tomatoes, drained

Pulse onion, cilantro, jalapeños, lime juice, garlic, and salt in food processor until roughly chopped, about 5 pulses. Add tomatoes and pulse until chopped, about 2 pulses. Transfer mixture to fine-mesh strainer and drain briefly. Serve.

Why This Recipe Works With bold Southwestern flavors and an appealing ingredient list, seven-layer dip recipes sound like a hit. But most versions of this party classic assume that guests won't notice the messy layers and tired flavors. In our version, canned black beans stood in for refried beans, while garlic, chili powder, and lime juice added flavor. We found that sour cream on its own quickly watered down our dip, but combining it with cheese gave this layer more structure.

ULTIMATE SEVEN-LAYER DIP

SERVES 8 TO 10

This recipe is usually served in a clear dish so you can see the layers. For a crowd, double the recipe and serve in a 13 by 9-inch glass baking dish. If you don't have time to make fresh guacamole as called for, simply mash three avocados with 3 tablespoons lime juice and ½ teaspoon salt.

- 4 large tomatoes, cored, seeded, and chopped fine
- 2 jalapeño chiles, stemmed, seeded, and minced
- 3 tablespoons chopped fresh cilantro
- 6 scallions (2 minced, 4 with green parts sliced thin and white parts discarded)
- 2 tablespoons plus 2 teaspoons lime juice (2 limes)
- Salt
- 1 (15-ounce) can black beans, drained but not rinsed
- 2 garlic cloves, minced
- ¾ teaspoon chili powder
- 1½ cups sour cream
- 1 pound pepper Jack cheese, shredded (4 cups)
- 1 recipe Chunky Guacamole (page 238)
- Tortilla chips

1. Combine tomatoes, jalapeños, cilantro, minced scallions, and 2 tablespoons lime juice in medium bowl. Stir in ⅛ teaspoon salt and let stand until tomatoes begin to soften, about 30 minutes. Strain mixture into bowl and discard liquid.

2. Pulse black beans, garlic, remaining 2 teaspoons lime juice, chili powder, and ⅛ teaspoon salt in food processor until mixture resembles chunky paste, about 15 pulses. Transfer to bowl and wipe out food processor. Pulse sour cream and 2½ cups pepper Jack until smooth, about 15 pulses. Transfer to separate bowl.

3. Spread bean mixture evenly over bottom of 8-inch square baking dish or 1-quart glass bowl. Spread sour cream mixture evenly over bean layer and sprinkle evenly with remaining 1½ cups cheese. Spread guacamole over cheese and top with tomato mixture. Sprinkle with sliced scallion greens and serve with tortilla chips. (Dip can be refrigerated for up to 24 hours. Let dip stand at room temperature for 1 hour before serving.)

ULTIMATE SMOKY SEVEN-LAYER DIP

Cook 4 slices bacon in 10-inch skillet over medium-high heat until crisp, about 8 minutes. Drain on paper towel–lined plate and crumble. Pulse 1 to 3 teaspoons minced canned chipotle chile in adobo sauce with black beans in step 2. Garnish dip with crumbled bacon along with scallions.

Processing Your Pico

Although the pico de gallo topping in our Ultimate Seven-Layer Dip adds lots of fresh flavor, chopping all the ingredients by hand takes some work. We found that a food processor gets the job done, but the texture won't be as perfectly uniform as pico made by hand. To make pico de gallo in the food processor, start by pulsing jalapeños with cilantro until finely chopped. Then add quartered, cored, and seeded tomatoes and pulse in 1-second bursts until the tomatoes are evenly chopped. Add minced scallions and lime juice. Strain as instructed.

Seeding Jalapeños

Halve pepper lengthwise. Starting at end opposite stem, use melon baller to scoop down inside of each half.

CHUNKY GUACAMOLE

MAKES ABOUT 3 CUPS

Preparing the guacamole ahead of time helps the flavors marry, but it should not be prepared more than one day in advance. To prevent the dip from turning brown, press a sheet of plastic wrap directly onto the surface and refrigerate until ready to use. We prefer pebbly Hass avocados to the smoother Fuerte variety.

- 2 scallions, green and white parts separated and sliced thin
- 1 jalapeño chile, stemmed, seeded, and minced
- 1 small garlic clove, minced
- ¼ teaspoon finely grated lime zest plus 2 tablespoons juice
- 3 avocados, halved, pitted, and cubed
- 3 tablespoons chopped fresh cilantro
- Salt

1. Combine scallion whites, jalapeño, garlic, and lime juice in large bowl. Let sit for 30 minutes.

2. Add two-thirds of avocado pieces to bowl with jalapeño mixture and mash with potato masher until smooth. Gently fold remaining avocado pieces into mashed avocado mixture. Gently stir in lime zest, scallion greens, and cilantro. Season with salt to taste. Serve.

Ripening Avocados

Avocados have a small window of perfect ripeness. To see if we could broaden this time frame, we ripened avocados four ways: on the counter or refrigerator shelf, enclosed in a paper bag, and enclosed in a paper bag with pieces of green apple (fruit gives off ethylene gas, which helps many fruits and vegetables ripen more quickly). We also tried burying the avocados at room temperature in flour and in rice. In the end, the only thing that mattered was the temperature at which the avocados were stored.

At room temperature, rock-hard avocados ripened within two days, but many of them ripened unevenly, developing soft spots and air pockets on one side just as the other side was ripening. Once ripe, they lasted two days on average if kept at room temperature (stored in the fridge after ripening, they lasted five days). Avocados ripened in the refrigerator, whether in a bag or out in the open, took around four days to soften, but did so evenly. Stored in the fridge, they lasted a full five days before starting to show signs of overripening.

The bottom line: If you need avocados to ripen sooner rather than later, keep them on the counter. Otherwise, you're better off putting them in the fridge and allowing them to ripen slowly. In either case, store the ripened fruit in the fridge to extend its shelf life.

Preparing Avocado for Guacamole

1. Halve avocado. Strike pit sharply with chef's knife. Twist blade to remove pit, then use dish towel to pull pit off blade.

2. Place avocado half on dish towel to secure it and make ½-inch crosshatch slices into flesh without cutting through skin.

3. Insert spoon between skin and flesh to separate the two. Gently scoop out avocado cubes.

Why This Recipe Works The best guacamole starts with ripe avocados, but other ingredients often overwhelm their delicate flavor. Tasters liked the flavor of minced garlic in guacamole, but thought raw onions were just too harsh. Instead, scallions lent a mellower onion flavor. Steeping them in lime juice for a few minutes before combining them with the avocados mellowed their flavor even more. To provide some textural contrast to our guacamole, we chopped the avocados and then mashed just two-thirds of the chunks.

Why This Recipe Works Huevos rancheros has made its way northward from Mexico, becoming common on breakfast menus around the United States. To make this crowd-pleasing but involved dish of fried eggs, cheese, and tomato-chile sauce manageable for a group, we roasted the sauce components to brown the vegetables and replicate the char from a cast-iron skillet. We then transferred everything to a casserole dish and nestled the eggs into the sauce so we could cook eight eggs at once. Moving this spicy dish of eggs and charred chiles to the oven gave us a perfectly timed meal that's not just for breakfast.

HUEVOS RANCHEROS

SERVES 4

Use a heavyweight rimmed baking sheet; flimsy sheets will warp. Our winning sheet is the Nordic Ware Baker's Half Sheet. Serve with refried beans and hot sauce.

- 2 (28-ounce) cans diced tomatoes
- 1 tablespoon packed brown sugar
- 1 tablespoon lime juice
- 1 onion, chopped
- ½ cup chopped canned green chiles
- ¼ cup extra-virgin olive oil
- 3 tablespoons chili powder
- 4 garlic cloves, sliced thin
- Salt and pepper
- 4 ounces pepper Jack cheese, shredded (1 cup)
- 8 large eggs
- 1 avocado, halved, pitted, and diced
- 3 scallions, sliced thin
- ⅓ cup minced fresh cilantro
- 8 (6-inch) corn tortillas, warmed

1. Adjust oven rack to middle position and heat oven to 500 degrees. Line rimmed baking sheet with parchment paper. Drain tomatoes in fine-mesh strainer set over bowl, pressing with rubber spatula to extract as much juice as possible. Reserve 1¾ cups tomato juice and discard remainder. Whisk sugar and lime juice into reserved tomato juice and set aside.

2. In separate bowl, combine onion, chiles, oil, chili powder, garlic, ½ teaspoon salt, and drained tomatoes. Transfer tomato mixture to prepared baking sheet and spread in even layer to edges of sheet. Roast until charred in spots, 35 to 40 minutes, stirring and redistributing into even layer halfway through baking. Reduce oven temperature to 400 degrees.

3. Transfer roasted tomato mixture to 13 by 9-inch baking dish and stir in tomato juice mixture. Season with salt and pepper to taste, then spread into even layer. Sprinkle pepper Jack over tomato mixture. Using spoon, hollow out 8 holes in tomato mixture in 2 rows. Crack 1 egg into each hole. Season eggs with salt and pepper.

4. Bake until whites are just beginning to set but still have some movement when dish is shaken, 13 to 16 minutes. Transfer dish to wire rack, tent loosely with aluminum foil, and let sit for 5 minutes. Spoon avocado over top, then sprinkle with scallions and cilantro. Serve with warm tortillas.

To Make Ahead The sauce can be made 24 hours in advance. Microwave until hot, about 2 minutes (stirring halfway), before transferring to baking dish and proceeding with recipe.

Roast the Vegetables, Bake the Eggs

To evoke the charred flavors in traditional huevos rancheros, we roast vegetables in a hot oven before layering them into a dish with cheese sprinkled over. Cracking eggs into wells in the mixture allows us to bake eight servings at once—no more standing at the stove frying egg after egg for an impatient crowd.

ARROZ CON POLLO

SERVES 6

Sazón is a spice blend common in Latin American cooking. We developed this recipe with Goya Sazón with Coriander and Annatto (or con Culantro y Achiote). It can be found in the international aisle of most supermarkets; however, other brands will work. (One tablespoon of Goya Sazón equals about two packets.) If you can't find sazón, use our homemade version (recipe follows). You can substitute ¾ cup of chopped green bell pepper for the Cubanelle pepper. Allow the rice to rest for the full 15 minutes before lifting the lid to check it. Long-grain rice may be substituted for medium-grain, but the rice will be slightly less creamy.

- 1 cup fresh cilantro leaves and stems, chopped
- 1 onion, chopped (1 cup)
- 1 Cubanelle pepper, stemmed, seeded, and chopped (¾ cup)
- 5 garlic cloves, chopped coarse
- 1 teaspoon ground cumin
- ½ cup mayonnaise
- 3½ tablespoons lemon juice (2 lemons), plus lemon wedges for serving
  Salt and pepper
- 6 (5- to 7-ounce) bone-in chicken thighs, trimmed
- 1 tablespoon vegetable oil
- 2 cups medium-grain rice, rinsed
- 1 tablespoon Goya Sazón with Coriander and Annatto
- 2½ cups chicken broth
- ¼ cup pimento-stuffed green olives, halved
- 2 tablespoons capers, rinsed
- 2 bay leaves
- ½ cup frozen peas, thawed (optional)

1. Adjust oven rack to middle position and heat oven to 350 degrees. Process cilantro, ½ cup onion, Cubanelle, garlic, and cumin in food processor until finely chopped, about 20 seconds, scraping down bowl as needed. Transfer sofrito to bowl.

2. Process mayonnaise, 1½ tablespoons lemon juice, ⅛ teaspoon salt, and 2 tablespoons sofrito in now-empty processor until almost smooth, about 30 seconds. Transfer mayonnaise-herb sauce to small bowl, cover, and refrigerate until ready to serve.

3. Pat chicken dry with paper towels and sprinkle with 1 teaspoon salt and ¼ teaspoon pepper. Heat oil in Dutch oven over medium heat until shimmering. Add chicken to pot skin side down and cook without moving it until skin is crispy and golden, 7 to 9 minutes. Flip chicken and continue to cook until golden on second side, 7 to 9 minutes longer. Transfer chicken to plate; discard skin.

4. Pour off all but 2 tablespoons fat from pot and heat over medium heat until shimmering. Add remaining ½ cup onion and cook until softened, 3 to 5 minutes. Stir in rice and Sazón and cook until edges of rice begin to turn translucent, about 2 minutes.

5. Stir in broth, olives, capers, bay leaves, remaining sofrito, remaining 2 tablespoons lemon juice, 1 teaspoon salt, and ½ teaspoon pepper, scraping up any browned bits. Nestle chicken into pot along with any accumulated juices and bring to vigorous simmer. Cover, transfer to oven, and bake for 20 minutes.

6. Transfer pot to wire rack and let stand, covered, for 15 minutes. Fluff rice with fork and stir in peas, if using. Discard bay leaves. Serve with mayonnaise-herb sauce and lemon wedges.

HOMEMADE SAZÓN
MAKES 1 TABLESPOON

We add paprika in place of annatto for color. In addition to flavoring our Arroz con Pollo, this blend makes a great seasoning for eggs, beans, and fish.

- 1 teaspoon garlic powder
- ¾ teaspoon salt
- ½ teaspoon paprika
- ½ teaspoon ground coriander
- ¼ teaspoon ground cumin

Combine all ingredients in bowl.

Why This Recipe Works *Arroz con pollo* is a classic Latin take on chicken and rice. To serve up an all-purpose version at home, we first created the dish's flavor backbone: a *sofrito* of onions, peppers, garlic, and spices. Next, after browning meaty skin-on chicken thighs, we used the rendered fat to soften chopped onion, toast the rice, and bloom the starring spice blend, *sazón*. We removed the skin from the thighs and finished cooking them nestled into the rice, studded with halved green olives, capers, and our zesty sofrito. We served our arroz con pollo with a drizzle of herby lemon sauce for a final punch of freshness.

LATIN FRIED CHICKEN

SERVES 4

Don't let the chicken marinate any longer than 2 hours or it will toughen from the lime juice. You will need at least a 6-quart Dutch oven for this recipe.

Marinade and Chicken

- 2 tablespoons kosher salt
- 6 garlic cloves, chopped coarse
- 1 tablespoon pepper
- 1 tablespoon ground cumin
- 2 teaspoons smoked paprika
- 2 teaspoons dried oregano
- 2 teaspoons grated lime zest plus ¼ cup juice (2 limes)
- 3 pounds bone-in chicken pieces (split breasts cut in half crosswise, drumsticks, thighs, and/or wings), trimmed

Coating

- 1¼ cups all-purpose flour
- ¾ cup cornstarch
- 1 tablespoon pepper
- 1 tablespoon granulated garlic
- 1 teaspoon baking powder
- 1 teaspoon white pepper
- 1 teaspoon kosher salt
- 1 teaspoon ground cumin
- ¼ teaspoon cayenne pepper
- 3 large egg whites, lightly beaten

- 3 quarts peanut or vegetable oil

1. For the Marinade and Chicken Combine salt, garlic, pepper, cumin, paprika, oregano, and lime zest and juice in bowl. Add chicken and turn to coat thoroughly. Cover with plastic wrap and refrigerate for at least 1 hour or up to 2 hours.

2. For the Coating Whisk flour, cornstarch, pepper, granulated garlic, baking powder, white pepper, salt, cumin, and cayenne together in bowl. Place egg whites in shallow dish.

3. Set wire rack in rimmed baking sheet. Remove chicken from marinade and scrape off solids. Pat chicken dry with paper towels. Working with 1 piece at a time, dip chicken into egg whites to thoroughly coat, letting excess drip back into dish. Dredge chicken in flour mixture, pressing to adhere. Transfer chicken to prepared wire rack and refrigerate for at least 30 minutes or up to 2 hours.

4. Add oil to large Dutch oven until it measures about 2 inches deep and heat over medium-high heat to 325 degrees. Add half of chicken to hot oil and fry until breasts register 160 degrees and drumsticks/thighs register 175 degrees, 13 to 16 minutes. Adjust burner, if necessary, to maintain oil temperature between 300 and 325 degrees. Transfer chicken to second wire rack set in second rimmed baking sheet. Return oil to 325 degrees and repeat with remaining chicken. Serve.

White Pepper

White peppercorns are fully ripe black peppercorns—the black outer husk is removed and the berries are dried. They lose much of their heat in this process but have a sharpness and a pronounced citrus flavor. Their taste is especially welcome in our spicy Latin Fried Chicken coating. Many chefs like the way that these peppercorns blend into white sauces, while Asian cooks use them in stir-fries and hot-and-sour soup.

Why This Recipe Works While each cuisine puts its own spin on the dish, Latin-style fried chicken is set apart by its garlicky-lime marinade and an extra-crunchy coating with lots of spice. Classic Latin fried chicken has a thin and crispy crust; we used a combination of flour cut with cornstarch for a nice, light coating and a little baking powder made it extra crisp. Refrigerating the marinated dredged chicken before frying made sure the coating set up nicely and thus stayed put on the chicken. Whether your idea of "South" is Savannah or San Salvador, this is one fried chicken recipe that you're definitely going to want to make.

Why This Recipe Works We wanted our California-Style fish tacos to be light, fresh, and simple, with a perfect balance of flavors and textures. An ultrathin beer batter using a combination of flour, cornstarch, and baking powder proved to be ideal for getting a light, crispy coating on the delicate white fish. Quick-pickled onions and jalapeños added tart spiciness, and tossing shredded cabbage with the pickling liquid just before serving added flavor without overcomplicating the dish. Lime juice and sour cream added tang to the traditional creamy white sauce.

CALIFORNIA-STYLE FISH TACOS

SERVES 6

Light-bodied American lagers, such as Budweiser, work best here. Cod, haddock, or halibut are good choices for the fish. Cut the fish on a slight bias if your fillets aren't quite 4 inches wide. You should end up with about 24 pieces of fish. Serve with green salsa, if desired.

Pickled Onions
- 1 small red onion, halved and sliced thin
- 2 jalapeño chiles, stemmed and sliced into thin rings
- 1 cup white wine vinegar
- 2 tablespoons lime juice
- 1 tablespoon sugar
- 1 teaspoon salt

Cabbage
- 3 cups shredded green cabbage
- ¼ cup pickling liquid from pickled onions
- ½ teaspoon salt
- ½ teaspoon pepper

White Sauce
- ½ cup mayonnaise
- ½ cup sour cream
- 2 tablespoons lime juice
- 2 tablespoons milk

Fish
- 2 pounds skinless white-flesh fish fillets, cut crosswise into 4 by 1-inch strips
- Salt and pepper
- ¾ cup all-purpose flour
- ¼ cup cornstarch
- 1 teaspoon baking powder
- 1 cup beer
- 1 quart peanut or vegetable oil

- 24 (6-inch) corn tortillas, warmed
- 1 cup fresh cilantro leaves

1. For the Pickled Onions Combine onion and jalapeños in medium bowl. Bring vinegar, lime juice, sugar, and salt to boil in small saucepan. Pour vinegar mixture over onion mixture and let sit for at least 30 minutes. (Pickled onions can be made and refrigerated up to 2 days in advance.)

2. For the Cabbage Toss all ingredients together in bowl.

3. For the White Sauce Whisk all ingredients together in bowl. (Sauce can be made and refrigerated up to 2 days in advance.)

4. For the Fish Adjust oven rack to middle position and heat oven to 200 degrees. Set wire rack inside rimmed baking sheet. Pat fish dry with paper towels and season with salt and pepper. Whisk flour, cornstarch, baking powder, and 1 teaspoon salt together in large bowl. Add beer and whisk until smooth. Transfer fish to batter and toss until evenly coated.

5. Add oil to large Dutch oven until it measures about ¾ inch deep and heat over medium-high heat to 350 degrees. Working with 5 to 6 pieces at a time, remove fish from batter, allowing excess to drip back into bowl, and add to hot oil, briefly dragging fish along surface of oil to prevent sticking. Adjust burner, if necessary, to maintain oil temperature between 325 and 350 degrees. Fry fish, stirring gently to prevent pieces from sticking together, until golden brown and crispy, about 2 minutes per side. Transfer fish to prepared wire rack and place in oven to keep warm. Return oil to 350 degrees and repeat with remaining fish.

6. Divide fish evenly among tortillas. Top with pickled onions, cabbage, white sauce, and cilantro. Serve.

EASY CHICKEN TACOS

SERVES 6

To warm the tortillas, wrap them in foil and heat them in a 350-degree oven for 15 minutes. Top the tacos with shredded lettuce, grated cheese, diced avocado, chopped tomato, and sour cream.

- 3 tablespoons unsalted butter
- 4 garlic cloves, minced
- 2 teaspoons minced canned chipotle chile in adobo sauce
- ¾ cup chopped fresh cilantro
- ½ cup orange juice
- 1 tablespoon Worcestershire sauce
- 4 (6-ounce) boneless, skinless chicken breasts, trimmed
- 1 teaspoon yellow mustard
- Salt and pepper
- 12 (6-inch) flour tortillas

1. Melt butter in large skillet over medium-high heat. Add garlic and chipotle and cook until fragrant, about 30 seconds. Stir in ½ cup cilantro, orange juice, and Worcestershire and bring to boil. Add chicken and simmer, covered, over medium-low heat until meat registers 160 degrees, 10 to 15 minutes, flipping chicken halfway through cooking. Transfer to plate and tent with aluminum foil.

2. Increase heat to medium-high and cook until liquid is reduced to ¼ cup, about 5 minutes. Off heat, whisk in mustard. Using 2 forks, shred chicken into bite-size pieces and return to skillet. Add remaining ¼ cup cilantro to skillet and toss until well combined. Season with salt and pepper to taste. Serve with tortillas.

Storing Canned Chipotle Chiles

When a recipe uses just a teaspoon or two of chipotle chiles, here's how to store the rest of the can.

Canned chipotle chiles are jalapeños that have been ripened until red, smoked, and packed in a tangy tomato-based adobo sauce. Since the size of chipotles varies, in the test kitchen we measure them by minced teaspoons. Could we store leftovers in the freezer, or would they lose their potency? To see, we pureed several cans and froze measured teaspoons on a plastic wrap–covered plate. Once our "chipotle chips" were hard, we peeled them off the plastic and transferred them to a zipper-lock freezer bag.

Weeks later we made a salsa and a casserole with the frozen chipotles and compared them with the same dishes made with chiles from a newly opened can. Most tasters couldn't tell the two apart. The chipotles will keep for up to two months in the freezer and should be thawed before you use them. The chiles will also last for two weeks in the refrigerator.

Shredding Chicken

Hold one fork in each hand, with tines facing down. Insert tines into chicken and gently pull forks away from each other, breaking meat apart and into long thin shreds.

Why This Recipe Works We like the convenience of boneless, skinless chicken breasts in tacos, but they can be dry. After trying a variety of cooking methods, we found that poaching produced meat that was tender and moist. Chipotle chiles gave our poaching liquid a smoky, full-bodied flavor and orange juice offered a touch of sweetness that tempered its vivid acidity. For more robust flavor, we called on two kitchen staples: Worcestershire mimicked the complex flavor of dark meat, and mustard added sharpness that balanced the sweet orange juice and smoky chipotle.

Why This Recipe Works San Antonio's been enjoying puffy taco shells in restaurants for years, and we were determined to re-create a similar version in the test kitchen. Instead of using the traditional *masa de maíz* (finely ground hominy), we used the more widely available masa harina (dried masa flour) for our tortilla dough. Pressing the dough with a clear pie plate allowed us to gauge the diameter and to get a consistent thickness. Using a large saucepan containing just 2 quarts of oil made our taco shell prep much easier. For a flavorful filling, picadillo made with ground beef, green bell pepper, onions, garlic, and cumin fit the bill.

PUFFY TACOS

SERVES 6 TO 8

We used Maseca Instant Masa Corn Flour for our taco shells. The dough should not be sticky and should have the texture of Play-Doh. If the dough cracks or falls apart when pressing the tortillas, just reroll and press again.

Picadillo
- 12 ounces 85 percent lean ground beef
- ½ russet potato (4 ounces), peeled and cut into ¼-inch pieces
- Salt and pepper
- 1 onion, chopped fine
- 1 small green bell pepper, stemmed, seeded, and chopped fine
- 3 garlic cloves, minced
- 1½ teaspoons ground cumin
- 2 teaspoons all-purpose flour
- ¾ cup water

Taco Shells
- 2½ cups (10 ounces) masa harina
- 1 teaspoon salt
- 1⅔ cups warm water
- 2 quarts vegetable oil

Shredded iceberg lettuce
Chopped tomato
Shredded sharp cheddar cheese
Hot sauce

1. For the Picadillo Combine beef, potato, 1 teaspoon pepper, and ¾ teaspoon salt in 12-inch nonstick skillet. Cook over medium-high heat until meat and potatoes begin to brown, 6 to 8 minutes, breaking up meat with spoon. Add onion and bell pepper and cook until softened, 4 to 6 minutes. Add garlic and cumin and cook until fragrant, about 30 seconds.

2. Stir in flour and cook for 1 minute. Stir in water and bring to boil. Reduce heat to medium-low and simmer until thickened slightly, about 1 minute. Season with salt and pepper to taste. Remove from heat, cover, and keep warm.

3. For the Taco Shells Mix masa harina and salt together in medium bowl. Stir in warm water with rubber spatula. Using your hands, knead mixture in bowl until it comes together fully (dough should be soft and tacky, not sticky), about 30 seconds. Cover dough with damp dish towel and let rest for 5 minutes.

4. Divide dough into 12 equal portions, about ¼ cup each, then roll each into smooth ball between your hands. Transfer to plate and keep covered with damp dish towel. Cut sides of 1-gallon zipper-lock bag, leaving bottom seam intact.

5. Set wire rack in rimmed baking sheet and line rack with triple layer of paper towels. Add oil to large saucepan until it measures 2½ inches deep and heat over medium-high heat to 375 degrees.

6. When oil comes to temperature, enclose 1 dough ball at a time in split bag. Using clear pie plate (so you can see size of tortilla), press dough flat into 6-inch circle (about ⅛ inch thick).

7. Carefully remove tortilla from plastic and drop into hot oil. Fry tortilla until it puffs up, 15 to 20 seconds. Using 2 metal spatulas, carefully flip tortilla. Immediately press down in center of tortilla with 1 spatula to form taco shape, submerging tortilla into oil while doing so. Using second spatula, spread top of tortilla open about 1½ inches. Fry until golden brown, about 60 seconds. Adjust burner, if necessary, to maintain oil temperature between 350 and 375 degrees.

8. Transfer taco shell to prepared rack and place upside down to drain. Return oil to 375 degrees and repeat with remaining dough balls.

9. Divide picadillo evenly among taco shells, about ¼ cup each. Serve immediately, passing lettuce, tomato, cheddar, and hot sauce separately.

Why This Recipe Works Traditional *cochinita pibil* requires a suckling pig and banana leaves. To make these richly flavored tacos at home, we replaced annatto seeds with bay leaves and tomato paste and swapped in well-marbled, collagen-rich pork butt for the pig. Our savory braising liquid delivered layers of flavor. Cooking the pork butt low and slow produced luscious meat that shredded easily with a potato masher. Served on warm tortillas with punchy quick-pickled red onions and a fiery homemade habanero sauce, our supermarket-friendly tacos tasted perfectly authentic.

CITRUS-BRAISED PORK TACOS

SERVES 6

Pork butt roast is often labeled Boston butt in the supermarket. For a spicier sauce, add an extra habanero or two; if you are spice-averse, substitute jalapeños for the habaneros. Pickled onions and habanero sauce can each be refrigerated for up to 1 week.

Pork
- 2 tablespoons vegetable oil
- 1 onion, chopped fine
- 3 garlic cloves, minced
- 1 teaspoon ground cumin
- 1 teaspoon dried oregano
- ½ teaspoon ground allspice
- ½ teaspoon ground cinnamon
- ⅓ cup tomato paste
- 1½ cups water
- ¼ cup frozen orange juice concentrate, thawed
- 3 tablespoons distilled white vinegar
- 1½ tablespoons Worcestershire sauce
- 5 bay leaves
- Salt and pepper
- 1 (2½- to 3-pound) boneless pork butt roast, trimmed and cut into 1-inch chunks

Pickled Red Onions
- 1 red onion, halved and sliced thin
- 1 cup distilled white vinegar
- ⅓ cup sugar
- ¼ teaspoon salt

Habanero Sauce
- 1 cup water
- 1 carrot, peeled and chopped
- 1 vine-ripened tomato, cored and chopped
- ¼ cup chopped onion
- ½ habanero chile, stemmed
- 1 garlic clove, smashed and peeled
- Salt and pepper
- 1 tablespoon distilled white vinegar
- 1½ teaspoons lime juice, plus lime wedges for serving

- 18 (6-inch) corn tortillas, warmed

1. For the Pork Adjust oven rack to lower-middle position and heat oven to 300 degrees. Heat oil in Dutch oven over medium heat until shimmering. Add onion and cook until lightly browned, 4 to 6 minutes.

2. Add garlic, cumin, oregano, allspice, and cinnamon and cook until fragrant, about 30 seconds. Stir in tomato paste and cook, stirring constantly, until paste begins to darken, about 45 seconds. Stir in water, orange juice concentrate, 2 tablespoons vinegar, Worcestershire, bay leaves, 2 teaspoons salt, and 1 teaspoon pepper, scraping up any browned bits.

3. Add pork and bring to boil. Transfer to oven, uncovered, and cook until pork is tender, about 2 hours, stirring once halfway through cooking.

4. For the Pickled Red Onions Meanwhile, place onion in medium bowl. Bring vinegar, sugar, and salt to simmer in small saucepan over medium-high heat, stirring occasionally, until sugar dissolves. Pour over onions and cover loosely. Let onions cool completely, about 30 minutes.

5. For the Habanero Sauce Combine water, carrot, tomato, onion, habanero, garlic, and ½ teaspoon salt in now-empty saucepan. Bring to boil over medium heat and cook until carrot is tender, about 10 minutes. Remove from heat and let carrot mixture cool slightly, about 5 minutes. Transfer carrot mixture to blender, add vinegar and lime juice, and process until sauce is smooth, 1 to 2 minutes. Season with salt and pepper to taste; set aside.

6. Transfer pot to stovetop; discard bay leaves. Using potato masher, mash pork until finely shredded. Bring to simmer over medium-high heat, then reduce heat to medium-low and cook until most of liquid has evaporated, 3 to 5 minutes.

7. Off heat, stir in remaining 1 tablespoon vinegar and season with salt and pepper to taste. Serve on tortillas with pickled red onions, habanero sauce, and lime wedges.

EASIER CHICKEN CHIMICHANGAS

SERVES 4

If using a cast-iron Dutch oven, increase the broth to 1¾ cups, adding 1¼ cups in step 2. Serve with Smoky Salsa Verde (page 256).

1¼ cups chicken broth
 1 tablespoon minced canned chipotle chile in adobo sauce
 ½ cup long-grain white rice
   Salt and pepper
 2 (6-ounce) boneless, skinless chicken breasts, trimmed
 1 tablespoon peanut or vegetable oil, plus 3 cups for frying
 1 onion, chopped fine
 2 garlic cloves, minced
 1 teaspoon chili powder
 ½ teaspoon ground cumin
 1 (15-ounce) can pinto beans, rinsed
 4 ounces sharp cheddar cheese, shredded (1 cup)
 ⅓ cup chopped fresh cilantro
 1 tablespoon all-purpose flour
 1 tablespoon water
 4 (10-inch) flour tortillas

1. Whisk broth and chipotle together in 2-cup liquid measuring cup. Combine ½ cup chipotle broth, rice, and ¼ teaspoon salt in bowl. Cover bowl and microwave until liquid is completely absorbed, about 5 minutes. Meanwhile, pat chicken dry with paper towels and season with salt and pepper.

2. Heat 1 tablespoon oil in Dutch oven over medium-high heat until just smoking. Add onion and cook until softened, about 5 minutes. Stir in garlic, chili powder, and cumin and cook until fragrant, about 30 seconds. Add remaining ¾ cup chipotle broth, parcooked rice, and beans and bring to boil.

3. Reduce heat to medium-low, add chicken, and cook, covered, until chicken registers 160 degrees and rice is tender, about 15 minutes, flipping chicken halfway through cooking. Transfer chicken to cutting board and let rest for 5 to 10 minutes. Cut chicken into ½-inch pieces and combine with rice and bean mixture, cheddar, and cilantro in large bowl. Wash now-empty pot.

4. Whisk flour and water together in small bowl. Stack tortillas on plate and microwave, covered, until pliable, about 1 minute. Working with one at a time, place one-quarter of chicken mixture in center of warm tortilla. Brush edges of tortilla with flour paste. Wrap top and bottom of tortilla tightly over filling. Brush ends of tortilla with paste and fold into center, pressing firmly to seal.

5. Set wire rack in rimmed baking sheet. Heat remaining 3 cups oil in clean pot over medium-high heat until 325 degrees. Place 2 chimichangas, seam side down, in oil. Fry, adjusting burner as necessary to maintain oil temperature between 300 and 325 degrees, until chimichangas are deep golden brown, about 4 minutes, turning them halfway through frying. Drain on prepared wire rack. Bring oil back to 325 degrees and repeat with remaining chimichangas. Serve.

Glue and Fold

The usual burrito-style wrapping method left us between the devil and the deep blue sea: Either the filling leaked out in the pot of oil or the ends of the tortilla never crisped. Our new chimichanga folding technique solves both problems.

1. Place filling in middle of tortilla. Brush tortilla's circumference with flour-and-water paste.

2. After folding opposing sides toward center and pressing to seal, brush open flaps with more paste. Fold flaps in and press firmly to seal chimichanga shut.

Why This Recipe Works Forget about tasteless fillings. We simmer the chicken and rice for our chimichangas in a chipotle broth, infusing them with a smoky bite through and through. As for construction, we noticed that the standard burrito-style wrapping method left us with doughy tortilla ends and filling that fell out. We created an easy new folding technique that kept the filling put without any floury bites.

SMOKY SALSA VERDE

MAKES 1¼ CUPS

This salsa is especially good served with our Easier Chicken Chimichangas (page 254), or try it with just about anything you'd serve salsa with, such as tortilla chips, grilled steak, or scrambled eggs.

- 1 pound tomatillos, husks and stems removed, rinsed well, and dried
- 1 small onion, quartered
- 1 jalapeño chile, stemmed, halved, and seeded
- 1 garlic clove, peeled
- 1 teaspoon olive oil
- ½ cup fresh cilantro leaves
- 1 tablespoon lime juice
    Salt

1. Adjust oven rack 5 inches from broiler element and heat broiler. Toss tomatillos, onion, jalapeño, and garlic with oil and place on aluminum foil–lined rimmed baking sheet. Broil, shaking pan occasionally, until vegetables are lightly charred, 10 to 12 minutes. Cool slightly, about 5 minutes.

2. Add vegetables, cilantro, lime juice, and ¼ teaspoon salt to food processor and pulse until coarsely ground, 5 to 7 pulses. Season with salt to taste. Serve. (Salsa can be refrigerated for up to 3 days.)

Tomatillos

Called *tomates verdes* (green tomatoes) in much of Mexico, small green tomatillos have a tangier, more citrusy flavor than true green tomatoes. When choosing tomatillos, look for pale-green orbs with firm flesh that fills and splits open the fruit's outer papery husk, which must be removed before cooking. Avoid tomatillos that are too yellow and soft, as these specimens are past their prime and will taste sour and muted.

Reviving Tired Herbs

We rarely use an entire bunch of herbs at once, and inevitably a few days later they are looking less-than-fresh and we have to throw them out and start all over. Is there a way to revive tired herbs? With a little research, we found that soaking herbs in water restores the pressure of the cell contents against the cell wall, causing them to become firmer as the dehydrated cells plump up. So, after purposely letting several bunches of parsley, cilantro, and mint sit in the refrigerator until they became limp, sorry-looking versions of their former selves, we tried bringing the herbs back to life by soaking them in tepid and cold water. We found that soaking herbs (stems trimmed) for 10 minutes in cold water perks them up better than tepid water. These herbs had a fresher look and an improved texture.

Why This Recipe Works Our recipe for *salsa verde* includes the typical ingredients: tomatillos, onions, garlic, jalapeño, and lots of cilantro. To temper their sharply acidic flavor, we broiled the tomatillos just until tender. We also broiled the other vegetables to provide subtle smokiness. Our recipe calls for a large amount of cilantro to ensure that its flavor stands out from the other ingredients.

Why This Recipe Works Tex-Mex cheese enchiladas are a wildly popular dish in the Lone Star State, beloved for their relative simplicity and their chile gravy, a red sauce that's a cross between beef gravy and Mexican enchilada sauce. We found that two toasted ancho chiles ground with a combination of spices gave the sauce smoky flavors that we brightened with a little white vinegar. We skipped frying the corn tortillas instead brushing them with oil and microwaving, resulting in soft, easy-to-roll tortillas without excess grease. For the cheesy filling, we combined sharp cheddar and Monterey Jack and used the oven to ensure melty, gooey cheese.

TEX-MEX CHEESE ENCHILADAS

SERVES 6

Dried chiles vary in size and weight. You'll get a more accurate measure if you seed and tear them first; you need about ½ cup of prepped chiles. You'll lose some flavor, but you can substitute 2 tablespoons ancho chile powder and 1 tablespoon ground cumin for the whole ancho chiles and cumin seeds, decreasing the toasting time to 1 minute.

Gravy
- 2 dried ancho chiles, stemmed, seeded, and torn into ½-inch pieces (½ cup)
- 1 tablespoon cumin seeds
- 1 tablespoon garlic powder
- 2 teaspoons dried oregano
- 3 tablespoons vegetable oil
- 3 tablespoons all-purpose flour
- Salt and pepper
- 2 cups chicken broth
- 2 teaspoons distilled white vinegar

Enchiladas
- 12 (6-inch) corn tortillas
- 1½ tablespoons vegetable oil
- 8 ounces Monterey Jack cheese, shredded (2 cups)
- 6 ounces sharp cheddar cheese, shredded (1½ cups)
- 1 onion, chopped fine

1. For the Gravy Toast chiles and cumin in 12-inch skillet over medium-low heat, stirring frequently, until fragrant, about 2 minutes. Transfer to spice grinder and let cool for 5 minutes. Add garlic powder and oregano and grind to fine powder.

2. Heat oil in now-empty skillet over medium-high heat until shimmering. Whisk in flour, ½ teaspoon salt, ½ teaspoon pepper, and spice mixture and cook until fragrant and slightly deepened in color, about 1 minute. Slowly whisk in broth and bring to simmer. Reduce heat to medium-low and cook, whisking frequently, until gravy has thickened and reduced to 1½ cups, about 5 minutes. Whisk in vinegar and season with salt and pepper to taste. Remove from heat, cover, and keep warm.

3. For the Enchiladas Adjust oven rack to middle position and heat oven to 450 degrees. Brush both sides of tortillas with oil. Stack tortillas, then wrap in damp dish towel. Place tortillas on plate and microwave until warm and pliable, about 1 minute.

4. Spread ½ cup gravy in bottom of 13 by 9-inch baking dish. Combine cheeses in bowl; set aside ½ cup cheese mixture for topping enchiladas. Sprinkle ¼ cup cheese mixture and 1 tablespoon onion across center of each tortilla. Tightly roll tortillas around filling and lay them seam side down in dish (2 columns of 6 tortillas will fit neatly across width of dish). Pour remaining 1 cup gravy over enchiladas, then sprinkle with reserved cheese mixture.

5. Cover dish with aluminum foil and bake until sauce is bubbling and cheese is melted, about 15 minutes. Let enchiladas cool for 10 minutes, then sprinkle with remaining onion. Serve.

To Make Ahead The sauce can be made up to 24 hours in advance. To reheat, add 2 tablespoons water and microwave until loose, 1 to 2 minutes, stirring halfway through microwaving.

Enchilada Orientation

After spreading ½ cup chile gravy in 13 by 9-inch baking dish, fit 12 enchiladas by creating two snug rows of six.

AUTHENTIC BEEF ENCHILADAS

SERVES 4 TO 6

Cut back on the jalapeños if you like your enchiladas on the mild side.

- 3 tablespoons chili powder
- 3 garlic cloves, minced
- 2 teaspoons ground coriander
- 2 teaspoons ground cumin
- 1 teaspoon sugar
- Salt
- 1¼ pounds top blade steaks, trimmed
- 1 tablespoon vegetable oil
- 2 onions, chopped
- 1 (15-ounce) can tomato sauce
- ½ cup water
- 8 ounces Monterey Jack or mild cheddar cheese, shredded (2 cups)
- ⅓ cup chopped fresh cilantro
- ¼ cup chopped canned jalapeños
- 12 (6-inch) corn tortillas

1. Combine chili powder, garlic, coriander, cumin, sugar, and 1 teaspoon salt in small bowl. Pat meat dry with paper towels and sprinkle with salt. Heat oil in Dutch oven over medium-high heat until shimmering. Cook meat until browned on both sides, about 6 minutes. Transfer meat to plate. Add onions to pot and cook over medium heat until golden, about 5 minutes. Stir in garlic mixture and cook until fragrant, about 1 minute. Add tomato sauce and water and bring to boil. Return meat and juices to pot, cover, reduce heat to low, and gently simmer until meat is tender and can be broken apart with wooden spoon, about 1½ hours.

2. Adjust oven rack to middle position and heat oven to 350 degrees. Strain beef mixture over medium bowl, breaking meat into small pieces; reserve sauce. Transfer meat to bowl and mix with 1 cup cheese, cilantro, and jalapeños.

3. Spread ¾ cup sauce in bottom of 13 by 9-inch baking dish. Place 6 tortillas on plate and microwave until soft, about 1 minute. Spread ⅓ cup beef mixture down center of each tortilla, roll tortillas tightly, and set in baking dish seam side down. Repeat with remaining tortillas and beef mixture (you may have to fit 2 or more enchiladas down the sides of the baking dish). Pour remaining sauce over enchiladas and spread to coat evenly. Sprinkle remaining 1 cup cheese evenly over enchiladas, wrap with aluminum foil, and bake until heated through, 20 to 25 minutes. Remove foil and continue baking until cheese browns slightly, 5 to 10 minutes. Serve.

Trimming Blade Steaks

Halve each steak lengthwise and slice away center strip of gristle.

Why This Recipe Works Traditional beef enchilada recipes require simmering steak for hours. Convenience recipes call for hamburger and canned sauce. We wanted to find a middle ground. For a deeply flavored sauce, we relied on chili powder and tomato sauce, along with onions, garlic, and spices. Slicing beefy, inexpensive blade steaks into small pieces cut our cooking time considerably. Authentic recipes fry the corn tortillas and then dip them in sauce to soften and season them. Instead, we softened the tortillas in the microwave. Once filled, topped with sauce and cheese, and baked, our enchiladas tasted like the real deal.

CHICKEN CHILAQUILES

SERVES 6

New Mexican or Anaheim chiles can be substituted for the guajillo chiles. If queso fresco is unavailable, you can substitute farmer's cheese or a mild feta. When baking the tortillas, stir them well to promote even browning.

- 16 (6-inch) corn tortillas, each cut into 8 wedges
- ¼ cup olive oil
- Salt
- 5 dried guajillo chiles, stemmed and seeded
- 1 (28-ounce) can whole peeled tomatoes
- 1 cup finely chopped onion
- 1 poblano chile, stemmed, seeded, and chopped
- 1 jalapeño chile, stemmed, seeded, and chopped
- 8 sprigs fresh cilantro, plus 2 tablespoons chopped
- 3 garlic cloves, chopped
- 1½ cups chicken broth
- 1½ pounds boneless, skinless chicken breasts, trimmed
- 4 ounces queso fresco, crumbled (1 cup)
- 1 avocado, halved, pitted, and cut into ½-inch chunks
- 2 radishes, trimmed and sliced thin
- Sour cream
- Lime wedges

1. Adjust oven racks to upper-middle and lower-middle positions and heat oven to 425 degrees. Divide tortillas evenly between 2 rimmed baking sheets and drizzle with oil and ½ teaspoon salt. Toss until tortillas are evenly coated with oil. Bake until golden brown and crisp, 15 to 20 minutes, stirring chips and switching and rotating sheets halfway through baking.

2. Toast guajillos in Dutch oven over medium heat until fragrant and slightly darkened, about 5 minutes. Transfer to blender and process until finely ground, 60 to 90 seconds, scraping down sides of blender jar as needed.

3. Add tomatoes and their juice, ¾ cup onion, poblano, jalapeño, cilantro sprigs, garlic, and ¾ teaspoon salt to guajillos and process until very smooth, 60 to 90 seconds. Transfer sauce to now-empty Dutch oven and stir in broth. Bring sauce to boil over medium-high heat. Add chicken breasts; reduce heat to low and simmer, uncovered, until chicken registers 160 degrees, 15 to 20 minutes, flipping halfway through cooking.

4. Using tongs, transfer chicken to large plate. Increase heat to medium and continue to simmer sauce until thickened and reduced to about 4½ cups, about 5 minutes longer. While sauce simmers, shred chicken into bite-size pieces using 2 forks. Return chicken to sauce and cook until warmed through, about 2 minutes.

5. Add chips to pot and toss to coat. Remove from heat and season with salt to taste. Cover and let stand for 2 to 5 minutes, depending on how soft you like your chips.

6. Transfer chilaquiles to serving dish and top with queso fresco, avocado, radishes, remaining ¼ cup onion, and chopped cilantro. Serve with sour cream and lime wedges.

Entrée-Worthy Chilaquiles

1. Use three types of chiles.

2. Make easy homemade chips.

3. Cook chicken in sauce.

4. Finish with fresh garnishes.

Why This Recipe Works *Chilaquiles* are often made from leftover meats and are considered a side dish, but we started from scratch for the best flavor and turned the dish into a meal. We began by baking our own tortilla chips. For the tomato-based red sauce, we toasted dried guajillo chiles to intensify their flavor before pureeing them with fresh poblanos, jalapeños, and other aromatic ingredients. To make the chilaquiles a complete meal, we poached boneless, skinless chicken breasts in the red sauce before shredding and mixing the tender meat back in with the chips. Finishing the dish with sour cream and queso fresco balanced the heat.

Why This Recipe Works Many chili con carne recipes call for toasting and grinding whole chiles. We wanted to create a simpler, authentic-tasting version. For the meat, we settled on beef chuck, our favorite cut for stews because its substantial marbling provides rich flavor and tender texture after prolonged cooking. To add a smoky meatiness to our chili, we browned the beef in bacon fat instead of oil. We added a jalapeño for brightness and heat and minced chipotle for smoky, spicy depth. A few tablespoons of corn muffin mix, in place of masa harina (corn flour), helped thicken our chili and gave it a silky texture.

EASY CHILI CON CARNE

SERVES 6 TO 8

If the bacon does not render a full 3 tablespoons of fat in step 1, supplement it with vegetable oil. If desired, serve chili with chopped onion, avocado, shredded cheese, lime wedges, and/or hot sauce.

- 1 (14.5-ounce) can diced tomatoes
- 2 teaspoons minced canned chipotle chile in adobo sauce
- 4 slices bacon, chopped fine
- 1 (3½- to 4-pound) boneless beef chuck-eye roast, pulled apart at seams, trimmed, and cut into 1-inch pieces
- Salt and pepper
- 1 onion, chopped fine
- 1 jalapeño chile, stemmed, seeded, and chopped fine
- 3 tablespoons chili powder
- 4 garlic cloves, minced
- 1½ teaspoons ground cumin
- ½ teaspoon dried oregano
- 4 cups water
- 1 tablespoon packed brown sugar
- 2 tablespoons yellow corn muffin mix

1. Process tomatoes and chipotle in food processor until smooth. Cook bacon in Dutch oven over medium heat until crisp, about 8 minutes. Transfer bacon to paper towel–lined plate and reserve 3 tablespoons bacon fat.

2. Pat beef dry with paper towels and season with salt and pepper. Heat 1 tablespoon reserved bacon fat in now-empty Dutch oven over medium-high heat until just smoking. Brown half of beef, about 8 minutes. Transfer to bowl and repeat with 1 tablespoon bacon fat and remaining beef.

3. Add remaining 1 tablespoon bacon fat, onion, and jalapeño to again-empty Dutch oven and cook until softened, about 5 minutes. Stir in chili powder, garlic, cumin, and oregano and cook until fragrant, about 30 seconds. Stir in water, pureed tomato mixture, bacon, browned beef, and sugar and bring to boil. Reduce heat to low and simmer, covered, for 1 hour. Skim fat and continue to simmer uncovered until meat is tender, 30 to 45 minutes.

4. Ladle 1 cup chili liquid into medium bowl and stir in muffin mix; cover with plastic wrap. Microwave until mixture is thickened, about 1 minute. Slowly whisk mixture into chili and simmer until chili is slightly thickened, 5 to 10 minutes. Season with salt and pepper to taste. Serve. (Chili can be refrigerated for up to 3 days.)

Silky Sauce

Our chili gets silky texture and a hint of corn flavor from the addition of corn muffin mix.

Why This Recipe Works As the name implies, five-alarm chili should be spicy enough to make you break a sweat—but it has to have rich, complex chile flavor as well. We used a combination of dried anchos, smoky chipotle chiles in adobo sauce, fresh jalapeños, and chili powder to create layers of spicy flavor. Ground beef added meaty bulk, and pureeing the chiles along with canned tomatoes and corn chips added extra body and another layer of flavor. Mellowed with a bit of sugar and enriched with creamy pinto beans, our chili was well balanced and spicy without being harsh.

FIVE-ALARM CHILI

SERVES 8 TO 10

Look for ancho chiles in the international aisle at the supermarket. Light-bodied American lagers, such as Budweiser, work best here. Serve chili with lime, sour cream, diced tomato, diced avocado, scallions, and cornbread.

- 2 ounces (4 to 6) dried ancho chiles, stemmed, seeded, and cut into 1-inch pieces
- 3½ cups water
- 1 (28-ounce) can whole peeled tomatoes
- ¾ cup crushed corn tortilla chips
- ¼ cup canned chipotle chile in adobo sauce plus 2 teaspoons adobo sauce
- 2 tablespoons vegetable oil
- 2 pounds 85 percent lean ground beef
- Salt and pepper
- 2 pounds onions, chopped fine
- 2 jalapeño chiles, stemmed, seeds reserved, and minced
- 6 garlic cloves, minced
- 2 tablespoons ground cumin
- 2 tablespoons chili powder
- 1 tablespoon dried oregano
- 2 teaspoons ground coriander
- 2 teaspoons sugar
- 1 teaspoon cayenne pepper
- 1½ cups beer
- 3 (15-ounce) cans pinto beans, rinsed

1. Combine anchos and 1½ cups water in bowl and microwave until softened, about 3 minutes. Drain and discard liquid. Process anchos, tomatoes and their juice, remaining 2 cups water, tortilla chips, chipotle, and adobo sauce in blender until smooth, about 1 minute; set aside.

2. Heat 2 teaspoons oil in Dutch oven over medium-high heat until just smoking. Add beef, 1 teaspoon salt, and ½ teaspoon pepper and cook, breaking up pieces with spoon, until all liquid has evaporated and meat begins to sizzle, 10 to 15 minutes. Drain in colander and set aside.

3. Heat remaining 4 teaspoons oil in now-empty Dutch oven over medium-high heat until simmering. Add onions and jalapeños and seeds and cook until onions are lightly browned, about 5 minutes. Stir in garlic, cumin, chili powder, oregano, coriander, sugar, and cayenne and cook until fragrant, about 30 seconds. Pour in beer and bring to simmer. Stir in beans, reserved chile-tomato mixture, and reserved cooked beef and return to simmer. Cover, reduce heat to low, and cook, stirring occasionally, until thickened, 50 to 60 minutes. Season with salt to taste. Serve.

Five Hits for Five-Alarm Chili

JALAPEÑO
Brings fresh vegetable flavor

CHIPOTLE IN ADOBO
Instant shortcut to smokiness

CHILI POWDER
Wouldn't be chili without it

CAYENNE
Adds raw heat

ANCHO
Adds depth, complexity, and mild heat

SO-CAL CHURROS

MAKES ABOUT 18 CHURROS

We used a closed star #8 pastry tip, ⅝ inch in diameter, to create deeply grooved ridges in the churros. However, you can use any large, closed star tip of similar diameter, though your yield may vary slightly. It's important to mix the dough for 1 minute in step 2 before adding the eggs to keep them from scrambling.

Dough
- 2 cups water
- 2 tablespoons unsalted butter
- 2 tablespoons sugar
- 1 teaspoon vanilla extract
- ½ teaspoon salt
- 2 cups (10 ounces) all-purpose flour
- 2 large eggs
- 2 quarts vegetable oil

Chocolate Sauce
- ¾ cup heavy cream
- 4 ounces semisweet chocolate chips
- Pinch salt
- ¼ teaspoon vanilla extract

Coating
- ½ cup (3½ ounces) sugar
- ¾ teaspoon ground cinnamon

1. For the Dough Line 1 rimmed baking sheet with parchment paper and spray with vegetable oil spray. Combine water, butter, sugar, vanilla, and salt in large saucepan and bring to boil over medium-high heat. Remove from heat; add flour all at once and stir with rubber spatula until well combined, with no streaks of flour remaining.

2. Transfer dough to bowl of stand mixer. Fit mixer with paddle and mix on low speed until cooled slightly, about 1 minute. Add eggs, increase speed to medium, and beat until fully incorporated, about 1 minute.

3. Transfer warm dough to piping bag fitted with ⅝-inch closed star pastry tip. Pipe 18 (6-inch) lengths of dough onto prepared sheet, using scissors to snip dough at tip. Refrigerate, uncovered, for 15 minutes to 1 hour.

4. Adjust oven rack to middle position and heat oven to 200 degrees. Set wire rack in second rimmed baking sheet and place in oven. Line large plate with triple layer of paper towels. Add oil to Dutch oven until it measures about 1½ inches deep and heat over medium-high heat to 375 degrees.

5. Gently drop 6 churros into hot oil and fry until dark golden brown on all sides, about 6 minutes, turning frequently for even cooking. Adjust burner, if necessary, to maintain oil temperature between 350 and 375 degrees. Transfer churros to paper towel–lined plate for 30 seconds to drain off excess oil, then transfer to wire rack in oven. Return oil to 375 degrees and repeat with remaining dough in 2 more batches.

6. For the Chocolate Sauce Microwave cream, chocolate chips, and salt in bowl at 50 percent power, stirring occasionally, until melted, about 2 minutes. Stir in vanilla until smooth.

7. For the Coating Combine sugar and cinnamon in shallow dish. Roll churros in cinnamon sugar, tapping gently to remove excess. Transfer churros to platter and serve warm with chocolate sauce.

Churning Out Churros

Pipe eighteen 6-inch lengths of warm dough, snipping at tip. Refrigerate 15 minutes to 1 hour to firm up before frying.

Why This Recipe Works The fried pastries known as *churros* should be crisp on the outside and soft on the inside, but piping thick *pâte à choux* dough into hot oil is no easy feat. We began by preparing a simple dough, precooking a mixture of water, butter, sugar, vanilla, and salt before stirring in flour and beating in eggs. The dough proved easier to work with when still warm, so we transferred it to a pastry bag right away. Piping the dough onto a baking sheet and frying the churros in batches made it easier to monitor when they were done. A roll in cinnamon sugar and a dip in a simple chocolate sauce made for a sweet finish.

everybody loves italian

- **273** Slow-Cooker Minestrone
- **275** Slow-Cooker Italian Sunday Gravy
- **276** Pork Ragu
- **279** Pasta with Sausage Ragu
- **280** Pasta with Roasted Garlic Sauce, Arugula, and Walnuts
- **282** Pasta with Mushroom Sauce
- **285** Fluffy Baked Polenta with Red Sauce
- **286** Meatballs and Marinara
- **289** Slow-Cooker Meatballs and Marinara
- **291** Slow-Cooker Baked Ziti
- **292** Skillet Chicken Parmesan
- **294** Skillet Lasagna
- **297** Spinach and Tomato Lasagna
- **299** Baked Manicotti with Meat Sauce
- **300** Grandma Pizza
- **303** Cast-Iron Skillet Pizza
- **304** Italian Pot Roast
- **306** Pork Chops with Vinegar Peppers
- **309** Zeppoles

Why This Recipe Works To translate a classic minestrone to the slow cooker, we needed to find a combination of vegetables that would cook through in the same amount of time. Green beans took too long to become tender. We scrapped cauliflower because its flavor overwhelmed the soup. Zucchini squash and Swiss chard won out for texture and their similar cooking times. Canned beans disintegrated in the soup, so we used dried white beans. We started cooking the beans in the soup along with some softened carrots and onions, then added the squash, chard, and pasta toward the end of cooking so they would be perfectly tender.

SLOW-COOKER MINESTRONE

SERVES 6 TO 8

We recommend using great Northern or cannellini beans here. Serve the minestrone with grated Parmesan cheese.

- 1 cup dried medium–size white beans, rinsed and picked over
- 6 tablespoons extra-virgin olive oil
- 2 onions, chopped fine
- 4 carrots, peeled and cut into ½-inch pieces
- 8 garlic cloves, minced
- 1 (28-ounce) can whole peeled tomatoes, coarsely crushed by hand
- 8 cups chicken broth
- 3 cups water
- 2 cups fresh basil leaves, chopped
- 1 teaspoon dried oregano
- ¼ teaspoon red pepper flakes
- 2 medium zucchini, quartered lengthwise, seeded, and sliced ¼ inch thick
- 8 ounces Swiss chard, stemmed and chopped
- ½ cup small dried pasta, such as ditalini, orzo, or small elbows
- Salt and pepper

1. Bring beans and enough water to cover by 1 inch to boil in medium saucepan over high heat. Reduce heat to low and simmer, covered, until beans are just beginning to soften, about 20 minutes. Drain beans and transfer to slow cooker.

2. Heat 3 tablespoons oil in Dutch oven over medium heat until shimmering. Add onions and carrots and cook until softened, about 5 minutes. Stir in garlic and cook until fragrant, about 30 seconds. Add tomatoes and their juice and cook until pan is nearly dry, 8 to 12 minutes. Stir in broth, water, ½ cup basil, oregano, and pepper flakes and bring to boil; transfer to slow cooker. Cover and cook until beans are tender, 6 to 7 hours on low or 5 to 6 hours on high.

3. Stir zucchini, Swiss chard, and pasta into slow cooker and cook on high, covered, until pasta is tender, 20 to 30 minutes. Stir in remaining 1½ cups basil and remaining 3 tablespoons oil. Season with salt and pepper to taste and serve.

To Make Ahead Recipe can be made through step 2 and refrigerated for up to 2 days. To finish, bring to boil in Dutch oven. Stir in zucchini, chard, and pasta; reduce heat to low; and simmer until pasta is tender, about 10 minutes.

Timing is Everything

First the onions, carrots, and tomatoes go into the slow cooker with the broth to create a rich, long-simmered backbone of flavor. Then we add the quick-cooking zucchini, Swiss chard, and pasta toward the end so they don't overcook.

HEAD START
Sautéed vegetables and canned whole tomatoes season the broth.

LAST MINUTE
The more delicate vegetables are added with the pasta near the end of cooking.

Why This Recipe Works We love the flavor and heartiness of Sunday gravy, but not the laundry list of ingredients or hours of monitoring the stovetop. For a streamlined recipe, we turned to our slow cooker and narrowed the meat selection down to three: flank steak, for meaty flavor; country-style spareribs, for tender, fall-off-the-bone meat; and sausage, for its spicy, sweet kick. Using the flavorful drippings left behind from browning the sausage to sauté our aromatics infused the whole dish with flavor. And a combination of drained diced tomatoes, canned tomato sauce, and tomato paste ensured a rich, thick sauce.

SLOW-COOKER ITALIAN SUNDAY GRAVY

SERVES 8 TO 10

Most sausage has enough seasoning to make extra salt unnecessary. This recipe makes enough to sauce 2 pounds of pasta. We like rigatoni, ziti, or penne with this sauce.

- 1 tablespoon vegetable oil
- 1 pound sweet Italian sausage
- 1 pound hot Italian sausage
- 2 onions, chopped
- 12 garlic cloves, minced
- 2 teaspoons dried oregano
- 1 (6-ounce) can tomato paste
- ½ cup dry red wine
- 1 (28-ounce) can diced tomatoes, drained
- 1 (28-ounce) can tomato sauce
- 2 pounds bone-in country-style pork spareribs, trimmed
- 1 (1½-pound) flank steak, trimmed
- 3 tablespoons chopped fresh basil
- Pepper

1. Heat oil in Dutch oven over medium-high heat until just smoking. Add sweet sausage and cook until well browned and fat begins to render, about 8 minutes. Using slotted spoon, transfer sausage to paper towel–lined plate to drain, then place in slow cooker. Repeat with hot sausage; transfer to slow cooker.

2. Cook onions in rendered fat over medium heat until well browned, about 6 minutes. Stir in garlic and oregano and cook until fragrant, about 1 minute. Add tomato paste and cook until it begins to brown, about 5 minutes. Stir in wine and simmer, scraping up browned bits, until wine is slightly reduced, about 3 minutes. Transfer to slow cooker. Stir in diced tomatoes and tomato sauce.

3. Submerge spareribs and steak in sauce in slow cooker. Cover and cook until meat is tender, 8 to 10 hours on low or 4 to 5 hours on high.

4. About 30 minutes before serving, remove ribs, steak, and sausages and set aside until cool enough to handle. Shred ribs and steak into small pieces, discarding excess fat and bones; slice sausages in half crosswise. Skim fat from surface of sauce, then stir sausages and shredded meat back into sauce. Stir in basil and season with pepper to taste. Serve. (Gravy can be refrigerated for up to 3 days.)

To Make Ahead Recipe can be made in advance through step 2. After stirring in diced tomatoes and tomato sauce, add browned sausages and simmer over medium-low heat until cooked through, about 12 minutes. Refrigerate sausage and sauce for up to 2 days. To cook gravy, warm sauce and sausages together over medium heat until heated through; transfer to slow cooker. Proceed with step 3.

The Meat Matters

For our easy Slow-Cooker Italian Sunday Gravy, we narrowed down the meat to the following combination, which offers the best taste and texture.

ITALIAN SAUSAGES
Browning the sausages in advance helps build deep flavor.

FLANK STEAK
This lean cut adds beefy flavor without too much grease.

COUNTRY-STYLE SPARERIBS
These meaty ribs become fall-apart tender in a slow cooker.

PORK RAGU

MAKES ABOUT 8 CUPS

This recipe makes enough sauce to coat 2 pounds of pasta. Leftover sauce may be refrigerated for up to 3 days or frozen for up to 1 month.

- 2 (2¼- to 2½-pound) racks baby back ribs, trimmed and each rack cut into fourths
- 2 teaspoons ground fennel
- Kosher salt and pepper
- 3 tablespoons olive oil
- 1 large onion, chopped fine
- 1 large fennel bulb, stalks discarded, bulb halved, cored, and chopped fine
- 2 large carrots, peeled and chopped fine
- ¼ cup minced fresh sage
- 1½ teaspoons minced fresh rosemary
- 1 cup plus 2 tablespoons dry red wine
- 1 (28-ounce) can whole peeled tomatoes, drained and chopped coarse
- 3 cups chicken broth
- 1 garlic head, outer papery skins removed and top fourth of head cut off and discarded
- 1 pound pappardelle or tagliatelle
- Grated Parmesan cheese

1. Adjust oven rack to middle position and heat oven to 300 degrees. Sprinkle ribs with ground fennel and generously season with salt and pepper, pressing spices to adhere. Heat oil in Dutch oven over medium-high heat until just smoking. Add half of ribs, meat side down, and cook, without moving them, until meat is well browned, 6 to 8 minutes; transfer to plate. Repeat with remaining ribs; set aside.

2. Reduce heat to medium and add onion, fennel, carrots, 2 tablespoons sage, rosemary, and ½ teaspoon salt to now-empty pot. Cook, stirring occasionally and scraping up any browned bits, until vegetables are well browned and beginning to stick to pot bottom, 12 to 15 minutes.

3. Add 1 cup wine and cook until evaporated, about 5 minutes. Stir in tomatoes and broth and bring to simmer. Submerge garlic and ribs, meat side down, in liquid; add any accumulated juices from plate. Cover and transfer to oven. Cook until ribs are fork-tender, about 2 hours.

4. Remove pot from oven and transfer ribs and garlic to rimmed baking sheet. Using large spoon, skim any fat from surface of sauce. Once cool enough to handle, shred meat from bones; discard bones and gristle. Return meat to pot. Squeeze garlic from its skin into pot. Stir in remaining 2 tablespoons sage and remaining 2 tablespoons wine. Season with salt and pepper to taste.

5. Meanwhile, bring 4 quarts water to boil in large pot. Add pasta and 2 tablespoons salt and cook, stirring often, until al dente. Reserve ½ cup cooking water, then drain pasta and return it to pot. Add half of sauce and toss to combine, adjusting consistency with reserved cooking water as needed. Serve, passing Parmesan separately.

Cutting Baby Back Ribs for Ragu

Before browning ribs, divide each rack into three-rib segments using a chef's knife.

Why This Recipe Works Earthy and intense, pork ragu takes pasta to a new level. Most recipes call for pork shoulder and a hard-to-find, bony cut like neck, shank, or feet. We tried using all baby back ribs and found the resulting ragu rich and meaty. For a classic Italian flavor profile, fennel took the place of celery in the ragu's base and ground fennel rubbed into the ribs echoed the anise flavor. Simmering the garlic head whole right in the sauce yielded sweeter softened cloves that we squeezed back into the sauce when tender. With fresh herbs and red wine, our ragu tasted balanced and far more complex than its simple preparation would suggest.

Why This Recipe Works For the long-cooked flavor of pork ragu in under 90 minutes, we looked to our food processor. Whirring fennel, onion, and fennel seeds together created a savory flavor base. Pulsing canned whole tomatoes created a silky tomato sauce, and processing sweet Italian sausage delivered bites of well-seasoned meat in every forkful. We cooked the components in stages, browning the sausage before softening the *soffritto* in the rendered fat. Minced garlic and dried oregano, bloomed in tomato paste, further defined the Italian flavors, and red wine offered brightness. A 45-minute simmer produced a rich ragu with the perfect consistency.

PASTA WITH SAUSAGE RAGU

SERVES 4 TO 6

For a spicier sauce, substitute hot Italian sausage for sweet. You will have 3 cups of extra sauce, which can be used to sauce 1 pound of pasta.

- ½ fennel bulb, stalks discarded, bulb cored and chopped coarse
- ½ onion, chopped coarse
- 1 tablespoon fennel seeds
- 1 (28-ounce) can whole peeled tomatoes
- 2 pounds sweet Italian sausage, casings removed
- 1 tablespoon extra-virgin olive oil, plus extra for drizzling
- Salt and pepper
- 2 tablespoons tomato paste
- 4 garlic cloves, minced
- 1½ teaspoons dried oregano
- ¾ cup red wine
- 1 pound pappardelle or tagliatelle
- Grated Parmesan cheese

1. Pulse fennel, onion, and fennel seeds in food processor until finely chopped, about 10 pulses, scraping down sides of bowl as needed; transfer to separate bowl. Process tomatoes in now-empty processor until smooth, about 10 seconds; transfer to second bowl. Pulse sausage in now-empty processor until finely chopped, about 10 pulses, scraping down sides of bowl as needed.

2. Heat oil in Dutch oven over medium-high heat until shimmering. Add sausage and cook, breaking up meat with spoon, until all liquid has evaporated and meat begins to sizzle, 10 to 15 minutes.

3. Add fennel mixture and ½ teaspoon salt and cook, stirring occasionally, until softened, about 5 minutes. (Fond on bottom of pot will be deeply browned.) Add tomato paste, garlic, and oregano and cook, stirring constantly, until fragrant, about 30 seconds.

4. Stir in wine, scraping up any browned bits, and cook until nearly evaporated, about 1 minute. Add 1 cup water and pureed tomatoes and bring to simmer. Reduce heat to low and simmer gently, uncovered, until thickened, about 45 minutes. (Wooden spoon should leave trail when dragged through sauce.) Season with salt and pepper to taste; cover and keep warm.

5. Bring 4 quarts water to boil in large pot. Add pasta and 1 tablespoon salt and cook, stirring often, until al dente. Reserve 1 cup cooking water, then drain pasta and return it to pot. Add 3 cups sauce and ½ cup reserved cooking water to pasta and toss to combine. Adjust consistency with remaining reserved cooking water as needed. Transfer to serving dish. Drizzle with extra oil, sprinkle with Parmesan, and serve. (Remaining 3 cups sauce can be refrigerated for up to 3 days or frozen for up to 1 month.)

Spotlight on Fennel

The vegetable that we slice and eat raw or cooked is Florence fennel, or *finocchio*; its bulb, stems, and feathery fronds boast a mildly sweet, faint anise flavor. Fennel seeds, which are a key part of the flavor profile of Italian sausage, come from a perennial herb called common fennel (also referred to as herb, sweet, or wild fennel) that has no bulb.

FLORENCE FENNEL
A vegetable grown for its edible bulb, stems, and fronds.

COMMON FENNEL
A perennial herb grown for its ornamental fronds and aromatic seeds.

PASTA WITH ROASTED GARLIC SAUCE, ARUGULA, AND WALNUTS

SERVES 4

It takes about four heads of garlic to yield 50 cloves, but you can use prepeeled.

- 50 garlic cloves, peeled (1 cup)
- 3 tablespoons extra-virgin olive oil, plus extra for drizzling
- 1 cup chicken broth
- 2 teaspoons balsamic vinegar
- Salt and pepper
- 1 pound spaghetti, linguine, or fettuccine
- 8 ounces (8 cups) baby arugula
- 1 cup walnuts, toasted and chopped
- Grated Pecorino Romano cheese

1. Combine garlic and oil in medium saucepan over medium-low heat. Cover and cook, stirring occasionally, until garlic is browned all over, 6 to 8 minutes. Add broth, vinegar, ¾ teaspoon salt, and ½ teaspoon pepper and bring to boil. Reduce heat to low and simmer, uncovered, until garlic is fork-tender, 5 to 7 minutes. Pour garlic mixture into food processor and process until smooth, about 1 minute.

2. Meanwhile, bring 4 quarts water to boil in large pot. Add pasta and 1 tablespoon salt and cook, stirring often, until al dente. Reserve ½ cup cooking water, then drain pasta and return it to pot. Add garlic sauce, arugula, and walnuts to pasta and toss to combine. Adjust consistency with reserved cooking water as needed. Season with salt and pepper to taste. Serve, drizzling individual servings with extra oil and passing Pecorino separately.

Speedy Stovetop "Roasting"

We love the mellow sweetness of roasted garlic, but we don't always have an hour to make it. Our stovetop method takes just 15 minutes. We sauté 50 cloves of garlic in olive oil in a covered pan for just 6 minutes or so. Later, we add balsamic vinegar, which helps mimic the complex, sweet flavor of oven-roasted garlic.

Why This Recipe Works Toasting mellows, softens, and sweetens a head of garlic. But rather than waiting the hour or more it can take to roast garlic in the oven, we set out to develop a quick pasta dish that could harness the same great flavor in short order. We browned a whopping 50 whole cloves on the stovetop, and then poached the garlic in chicken broth seasoned with sweet, tangy balsamic vinegar. After a spin in the food processor, the final result was a complex and silky sauce that we combined with walnuts and spicy arugula. The best part? The whole thing took just 15 minutes—more than enough time to cook the pasta.

PASTA WITH MUSHROOM SAUCE

SERVES 4

If you can't find shiitake mushrooms, cremini mushrooms can be substituted or white mushrooms can be used exclusively, but don't omit the dried porcini. Parmesan cheese can be substituted for the Pecorino Romano.

- 12 ounces shiitake mushrooms, stemmed
- 12 ounces white mushrooms, trimmed
- 4 tablespoons unsalted butter
- Salt and pepper
- 2 shallots, minced
- 2 tablespoons minced fresh sage
- 4 garlic cloves, minced
- ¼ ounce dried porcini mushrooms, rinsed and chopped fine
- ½ cup dry white wine
- 4 cups water plus ¼ cup hot water
- 12 ounces (3¾ cups) campanelle, penne, or fusilli
- 2 ounces Pecorino Romano cheese, grated (1 cup), plus extra for serving
- 1 tablespoon lemon juice
- 2 tablespoons minced fresh chives

1. Coarsely chop half of shiitake mushrooms and white mushrooms; then quarter remaining shiitake mushrooms and white mushrooms. Melt 2 tablespoons butter in Dutch oven over medium-high heat. Add all shiitake mushrooms and white mushrooms (both chopped and quartered) and ¾ teaspoon salt. Cover and cook until mushrooms release their liquid, about 5 minutes. Uncover and continue to cook, stirring occasionally, until all liquid has evaporated and mushrooms begin to brown, about 10 minutes.

2. Add shallots, sage, garlic, and porcini mushrooms and cook until fragrant, about 1 minute. Add wine and cook until evaporated, about 2 minutes. Stir in 4 cups water, pasta, and 1¼ teaspoons salt and bring to boil. Reduce heat to medium, cover, and cook, stirring occasionally, until pasta is tender, 12 to 15 minutes.

3. Off heat, stir in Pecorino, ¼ cup hot water, lemon juice, remaining 2 tablespoons butter, and ½ teaspoon pepper. Stir vigorously for 1 minute, until sauce is thickened. Season with salt and pepper to taste. Transfer to serving dish and sprinkle with chives. Serve, passing extra Pecorino separately.

Doubling Down for Big Impact

Chopping half the mushrooms creates more fond for a flavorful sauce; quartering the rest gives big, meaty mushroom texture.

Coarsely Chopped   **Quartered**

Why This Recipe Works In order to coax as much earthy, meaty flavor as possible from supermarket mushrooms, we used fresh shiitake and white mushrooms, plus dried porcini. We coarsely chopped half of them, providing better browning due to the increased surface area, and we quartered the rest for visual appeal and meaty texture. After deglazing the pan with wine, we added the pasta directly to the pot so it could absorb the flavorful liquid. One minute of vigorous stirring drew out the pasta's starch, adding structure to the sauce and helping it cling to the pasta. The end result? An elegant one-pot dish with deep mushroom flavor.

Why This Recipe Works We wanted a creamy, light polenta substantial enough to serve as an entrée. Cooking the cornmeal in water instead of dairy gave us clean, sweet corn flavor and an airy texture. Garlic oil boosted the dish's savory quality, and adding half-and-half and nutty Pecorino contributed some welcome richness. While the polenta chilled, we processed canned whole tomatoes into a smooth, thick puree and created a sweet-and-savory red sauce. We sliced and baked blocks of polenta long enough to brown and heat through before serving.

FLUFFY BAKED POLENTA WITH RED SAUCE

SERVES 6

We developed this recipe using Quaker Yellow Corn Meal for its desirable texture and relatively short cooking time. We recommend you use the same product for this recipe. The timing may be different for other types of cornmeal, so be sure to cook the polenta until it is thickened and tender. Whole milk can be substituted for the half-and-half. Plan ahead: The polenta needs to be cooled for at least 3 hours before being cut, baked, and served.

Polenta
- 4 tablespoons unsalted butter
- 2 tablespoons extra-virgin olive oil
- 2 garlic cloves, smashed and peeled
- 7 cups water
- 1½ teaspoons salt
- ½ teaspoon pepper
- 1½ cups cornmeal
- 3 ounces Pecorino Romano cheese, grated (1½ cups)
- ¼ cup half-and-half

Red Sauce
- 1 (14.5-ounce) can whole peeled tomatoes
- ¼ cup extra-virgin olive oil
- 1 onion, peeled and halved through root end
- 1 (15-ounce) can tomato sauce
- 1 ounce Pecorino Romano cheese, grated (½ cup)
- 1½ tablespoons sugar
- ¾ teaspoon salt
- ½ teaspoon garlic powder

1. For the Polenta Lightly grease 8-inch square baking pan. Heat butter and oil in Dutch oven over medium heat until butter is melted. Add garlic and cook until lightly golden, about 4 minutes. Discard garlic.

2. Add water, salt, and pepper to butter mixture. Increase heat to medium-high and bring to boil. Add cornmeal in slow, steady stream, whisking constantly. Reduce heat to medium-low and continue to cook, whisking frequently and scraping sides and bottom of pot, until mixture is thick and cornmeal is tender, about 20 minutes.

3. Off heat, whisk in Pecorino and half-and-half. Transfer to prepared pan and let cool completely on wire rack. Once cooled, cover with plastic wrap and refrigerate until completely chilled, at least 3 hours.

4. For the Red Sauce Process tomatoes and their juice in blender until smooth, about 30 seconds. Heat 1 tablespoon oil in large saucepan over medium heat until shimmering. Add onion, cut side down, and cook without moving until lightly browned, about 4 minutes. Add pureed tomatoes, tomato sauce, Pecorino, sugar, salt, garlic powder, and remaining 3 tablespoons oil. Bring mixture to boil, reduce heat to medium-low, and simmer until sauce is slightly thickened, about 15 minutes. Remove from heat, discard onion, cover, and keep warm.

5. Adjust oven rack to middle position and heat oven to 375 degrees. Line rimmed baking sheet with parchment paper, then grease parchment. Cut chilled polenta into 6 equal pieces (about 4 by 2⅔ inches each). Place on prepared sheet and bake until heated through and beginning to brown on bottom, about 30 minutes. Serve each portion covered with about ½ cup red sauce.

MEATBALLS AND MARINARA

SERVES 8

To keep the recipe easy and streamlined, the meatballs and sauce start with the same onion mixture. This recipe makes enough to sauce 2 pounds of pasta.

Onion Mixture
- ¼ cup olive oil
- 3 onions, chopped fine
- 8 garlic cloves, minced
- 1 tablespoon dried oregano
- ¾ teaspoon red pepper flakes

Marinara
- 1 (6-ounce) can tomato paste
- 1 cup dry red wine
- 1 cup water
- 4 (28-ounce) cans crushed tomatoes
- 1 ounce Parmesan cheese, grated (½ cup)
- ¼ cup chopped fresh basil
- Salt
- 1–2 teaspoons sugar

Meatballs
- 4 slices hearty white sandwich bread, torn into pieces
- ¾ cup milk
- 8 ounces sweet Italian sausage, casings removed
- 2 ounces Parmesan cheese, grated (1 cup)
- ½ cup chopped fresh parsley
- 2 large eggs
- 2 garlic cloves, minced
- 1½ teaspoons salt
- 2½ pounds 80 percent lean ground chuck

1. For the Onion Mixture Heat oil in Dutch oven over medium-high heat until shimmering. Cook onions until golden, 10 to 15 minutes. Add garlic, oregano, and pepper flakes and cook until fragrant, about 30 seconds. Transfer half of onion mixture to large bowl and set aside.

2. For the Marinara Add tomato paste to remaining onion mixture in pot and cook until fragrant, about 1 minute. Add wine and cook until slightly thickened, about 2 minutes. Stir in water and tomatoes and simmer over low heat until sauce is no longer watery, 45 minutes to 1 hour. Stir in Parmesan and basil and season with salt and sugar to taste.

3. For the Meatballs Meanwhile, adjust oven rack to upper-middle position and heat oven to 475 degrees. Add bread and milk to bowl with reserved onion mixture and mash together until smooth. Add sausage, Parmesan, parsley, eggs, garlic, and salt to bowl and mash to combine. Add beef and knead with hands until well combined. Lightly shape mixture into 2½-inch round meatballs (about 16 meatballs total), place on rimmed baking sheet, and bake until well browned, about 20 minutes.

4. Transfer meatballs to pot with sauce and simmer for 15 minutes. Serve. (Meatballs and marinara can be frozen for up to 1 month.)

Well-Seasoned Meatballs Without the Mess

We bypassed the messy frying step and baked our meatballs in a super-hot oven instead to ensure a nicely browned crust. Simmering the meatballs in the sauce briefly allows the sauce to season the meat, and vice versa.

1. Bake meatballs in very hot oven to ensure browned crust.

2. Simmer meatballs in sauce for 15 minutes before serving for flavorful sauce and meatballs

Why This Recipe Works Meatballs and marinara sauce are the epitome of comfort food, except when you're the cook. Frying the meatballs can be messy and take a good chunk of time when working in batches. For an easier method, we turned to the oven and roasted our meatballs at a high temperature, which ensured they developed a nice, browned crust. To keep our meatballs moist and tender, we added a panade (a paste of milk and bread). In addition to ground beef, using Italian sausage for the pork gave the meatballs a flavor boost, as did simmering them in the sauce after baking.

Why This Recipe Works To infuse our slow-cooker meatballs and marinara sauce with depth of flavor, we used lots of onion, garlic, and tomato paste and sautéed them before adding them to the slow cooker. Microwaving the meatballs before adding them to the slow cooker rendered just enough fat (which we discarded) to ensure the sauce wouldn't be greasy. To bind and moisten the meatballs, we traded in the usual panade (a paste of milk and bread), which caused them to break apart in the slow cooker, for cream and shredded mozzarella cheese.

SLOW-COOKER MEATBALLS AND MARINARA

SERVES 6

Microwave the meatballs on a large plate or in a casserole dish to contain the rendering fat. This recipe makes enough to sauce 1½ pounds of pasta.

Onion Mixture
- 2 tablespoons olive oil
- 2 onions, chopped fine
- 1 (6-ounce) can tomato paste
- 6 garlic cloves, minced
- 1 tablespoon dried oregano
- ½ teaspoon red pepper flakes
- ¼ teaspoon salt

Marinara
- ½ cup red wine
- 2 (28-ounce) cans crushed tomatoes

Meatballs
- 4 ounces Italian sausage, casings removed
- 2 ounces mozzarella cheese, shredded (½ cup)
- 1 ounce Parmesan cheese, grated (½ cup)
- 2 large eggs
- 2 garlic cloves, minced
- ¾ teaspoon salt
- 1¼ pounds 85 percent lean ground beef
- 3 tablespoons heavy cream

- 1 ounce Parmesan cheese, grated (½ cup)
- 2 tablespoons finely chopped fresh basil
- Salt

1. For the Onion Mixture Heat oil in Dutch oven over medium-high heat until shimmering. Add onions, tomato paste, garlic, oregano, pepper flakes, and salt and cook until softened and lightly browned, about 8 to 10 minutes. Transfer half of onion mixture to large bowl and set aside.

2. For the Marinara Add wine to remaining onion mixture in pot and cook until slightly thickened, about 2 minutes. Stir in tomatoes, then transfer to slow cooker.

3. For the Meatballs Add sausage, mozzarella, Parmesan, eggs, garlic, and salt to bowl with reserved onion mixture. Mash with potato masher until smooth. Add beef and cream to bowl and knead with hands until well combined. Lightly shape mixture into 2-inch round meatballs (about 12 total). Microwave meatballs on large plate until fat renders and meatballs are firm, 4 to 7 minutes. Nestle meatballs into slow cooker, discarding rendered fat. Cover and cook until meatballs are tender and sauce is slightly thickened, 4 to 5 hours on low.

4. Let meatballs and sauce settle for 5 minutes, then skim fat from surface and stir in Parmesan and basil. Season with salt to taste. Serve.

To Make Ahead Recipe can be made in advance through shaping meatballs in step 3. Uncooked meatballs and sauce can be refrigerated in separate containers for up to 24 hours. When ready to cook, add sauce to slow cooker and proceed with microwaving meatballs in step 3.

Microwaving Meatballs

Microwave meatballs uncovered until fat renders and meat is firm.

Why This Recipe Works Pasta in a slow cooker? You bet. But achieving well-cooked pasta and melty cheese in the slow cooker takes some strategy. Borrowing a technique from risotto was the key to perfect pasta—we stirred the raw pasta into the browned sausage and onion mixture, coating the starch in fat and preventing the pasta from bloating in the slow cooker. To get cheese that was evenly melted, we added it after cooking and let it sit in the residual warmth of the turned-off slow-cooker.

SLOW-COOKER BAKED ZITI

SERVES 6

Our favorite crushed tomatoes are SMT Crushed Tomatoes.

- 2 tablespoons olive oil
- 1 pound hot or sweet Italian sausage, casings removed
- 1 onion, chopped
- 3 garlic cloves, minced
- ½ teaspoon dried oregano
- ½ teaspoon salt
- ½ teaspoon pepper
- 8 ounces (2½ cups) ziti
- 1 (28-ounce) can crushed tomatoes
- 1 (15-ounce) can tomato sauce
- 8 ounces (1 cup) whole-milk ricotta cheese
- 4 ounces mozzarella cheese, shredded (1 cup)
- 2 tablespoons thinly sliced fresh basil

1. Make aluminum foil collar for slow cooker by folding 2 (18-inch-long) pieces of foil to make 2 (18 by 4-inch) strips. Line perimeter of slow cooker with foil strips and spray with vegetable oil spray.

2. Heat oil in Dutch oven over medium-high heat until just smoking. Cook sausage, breaking up pieces with spoon, until well browned, 6 to 8 minutes. Add onion and cook until lightly browned, about 5 minutes. Stir in garlic, oregano, salt, and pepper and cook until fragrant, about 1 minute.

3. Reduce heat to medium-low. Add ziti and cook, stirring constantly, until edges of pasta become translucent, about 4 minutes. Off heat, stir in crushed tomatoes and tomato sauce, scraping up any browned bits. Transfer mixture to prepared slow cooker. Cover and cook on low until pasta is tender, about 3 hours.

4. Using tongs, remove foil collar from slow cooker. Dollop ricotta over ziti and sprinkle with mozzarella. Cover and let sit for 20 minutes to let cheeses melt. Garnish with basil and serve.

Key Steps to Great Slow-Cooker "Baked" Ziti

1. To prevent burning, fold aluminum foil into two strips and use them to line perimeter of slow cooker.

2. To avoid slimy, bloated pasta, sauté it with sausage and onion.

SKILLET CHICKEN PARMESAN

SERVES 4

We like the assertive flavor of sharp provolone here, but mild provolone works well, too.

- 2 slices hearty white sandwich bread, torn into large pieces
- 3 tablespoons olive oil
- 2½ ounces Parmesan cheese, grated (1¼ cups)
- ¼ cup chopped fresh basil
- 1 (28-ounce) can crushed tomatoes
- 2 garlic cloves, minced
- Salt and pepper
- 4 (6-ounce) boneless, skinless chicken breasts, trimmed
- ½ cup all-purpose flour
- 3 tablespoons vegetable oil
- 3 ounces mozzarella cheese, shredded (¾ cup)
- 3 ounces provolone cheese, shredded (¾ cup)

1. Pulse bread in food processor to coarse crumbs, about 10 pulses. Toast bread crumbs in 12-inch nonstick skillet over medium-high heat until browned, about 5 minutes, and transfer to bowl. Toss with 1 tablespoon olive oil, ¼ cup Parmesan, and half of basil. In separate bowl, combine remaining 2 tablespoons olive oil, ¼ cup Parmesan, remaining basil, tomatoes, garlic, and salt and pepper to taste.

2. Using sharp knife, and holding chicken securely, slice each breast horizontally into 2 cutlets of even thickness. Place flour in shallow dish. Season chicken with salt and pepper and dredge in flour. Heat 2 tablespoons vegetable oil in now-empty skillet over medium-high heat until shimmering. Add 4 cutlets and cook until golden brown on both sides, about 5 minutes. Transfer to plate and repeat with remaining cutlets and remaining 1 tablespoon vegetable oil.

3. Reduce heat to medium-low and add tomato mixture to now-empty skillet. Return cutlets to pan in even layer, pressing down to cover with sauce. Sprinkle mozzarella, provolone, and remaining ¾ cup Parmesan over chicken. Cover and cook until cheese is melted, about 5 minutes. Sprinkle with bread crumb mixture and serve.

Making Cutlets from Breasts

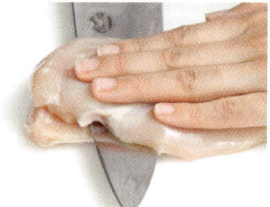

Use hand to hold breast in place, keeping fingers straight and parallel to breast. Starting at thickest end of breast, slice in half horizontally, producing 2 even cutlets.

Shredding Semisoft Cheese

To keep grater holes from clogging, lightly coat side of box grater with vegetable oil spray before shredding cheese.

Why This Recipe Works To streamline chicken Parmesan and still keep its flavors and textures intact, we browned boneless, skinless chicken breasts, which we had sliced into cutlets, in a nonstick pan, then made a simple tomato sauce and simmered the chicken right in the sauce so it could absorb the flavors. For the cheesy layer, we supplemented the traditional mozzarella with provolone (preferably the sharp variety) for a much richer flavor. And rather than breading the chicken, we sprinkled the bread crumbs, which we toasted and seasoned with Parmesan and basil, over the finished dish so they stayed ultra-crisp.

SKILLET LASAGNA

SERVES 4 TO 6

A 12-inch nonstick skillet with a tight-fitting lid works best for this recipe.

- 1 (28-ounce) can diced tomatoes
- Water
- 1 tablespoon olive oil
- 1 onion, chopped fine
- Salt and pepper
- 3 garlic cloves, minced
- ⅛ teaspoon red pepper flakes
- 1 pound meatloaf mix
- 10 curly-edged lasagna noodles, broken into 2-inch lengths
- 1 (8-ounce) can tomato sauce
- 1 ounce Parmesan cheese, grated (½ cup), plus 2 tablespoons, grated
- 8 ounces (1 cup) whole-milk or part-skim ricotta cheese
- 3 tablespoons chopped fresh basil

1. Place tomatoes in 4-cup liquid measuring cup. Add water until mixture measures 4 cups.

2. Heat oil in 12-inch nonstick skillet over medium heat until shimmering. Add onion and ½ teaspoon salt and cook until onion begins to brown, about 5 minutes. Stir in garlic and pepper flakes and cook until fragrant, about 30 seconds. Add meat and cook, breaking up meat into small pieces with wooden spoon, until it is no longer pink, about 4 minutes.

3. Scatter pasta over meat but do not stir. Pour tomato mixture and tomato sauce over pasta, cover, and bring to simmer. Reduce heat to medium-low and simmer, stirring occasionally, until pasta is tender, about 20 minutes.

4. Off heat, stir in ½ cup Parmesan and season with salt and pepper to taste. Dollop heaping tablespoons of ricotta over top, cover, and let sit for 5 minutes. Sprinkle with basil and remaining 2 tablespoons Parmesan. Serve.

SKILLET LASAGNA WITH SAUSAGE AND RED PEPPER

Substitute 1 pound Italian sausage, casings removed, for meatloaf mix. Add 1 chopped red bell pepper to skillet with onion.

Secrets to Skillet Lasagna

1. Sauté onion, garlic, and meat in skillet, then scatter broken lasagna noodles over meat.

2. Pour diced tomatoes and tomato sauce over noodles, cover, and cook until pasta is tender, about 20 minutes.

3. Stir in Parmesan and dollop with ricotta, then cover skillet and let cheese soften off heat.

Why This Recipe Works To get our lasagna fix without spending hours in the kitchen, we made the entire dish, from start to finish, in a 12-inch skillet. After sautéing aromatics, we browned our meat in the pan, then added the noodles and sauce. Meatloaf mix (a blend of ground beef, pork, and veal) contributed deep, meaty flavor. Canned diced tomatoes and tomato sauce, thinned with water, provided ample liquid to cook our noodles and thickened to just the right consistency after a brief simmer. For a rich, creamy topping, we dropped big dollops of ricotta cheese over the noodles and covered the pan so they'd melt.

Why This Recipe Works To make a spinach lasagna worthy of its name, we increased the amount of spinach. Frozen spinach tasted just as good as fresh and cut down on kitchen time. For the most even texture, we used the food processor to chop the spinach. For extra spinach flavor we included some of the drained spinach liquid (we combined it with the ricotta in the food processor) but not enough to make the lasagna watery. To keep the spinach flavor front and center, we nixed the traditional creamy béchamel in favor of a fresh, herb-flecked tomato sauce but still layered in plenty of mozzarella and Parmesan for richness.

SPINACH AND TOMATO LASAGNA

SERVES 8 TO 10

Our favorite brand of no-boil lasagna noodles is Barilla. You can thaw the spinach overnight in the refrigerator instead of microwaving it, but be sure to warm the spinach liquid to help smooth the ricotta.

- 30 ounces frozen chopped spinach
- 2 tablespoons olive oil
- 1 onion, chopped fine
- 5 garlic cloves, minced
- ⅛ teaspoon red pepper flakes
- 2 (28-ounce) cans crushed tomatoes
- Salt and pepper
- 6 tablespoons chopped fresh basil
- 1½ pounds (3 cups) whole-milk or part-skim ricotta cheese
- 3 ounces Parmesan cheese, grated (1½ cups)
- 2 large eggs
- 12 no-boil lasagna noodles
- 12 ounces whole-milk mozzarella cheese, shredded (3 cups)

1. Adjust oven rack to middle position and heat oven to 375 degrees. Microwave spinach in covered large bowl until completely thawed, about 15 minutes, stirring halfway through cooking. Squeeze spinach dry, reserving ⅓ cup liquid. Pulse spinach in food processor until ground, 8 to 10 pulses, scraping down bowl every few pulses. Wipe out large bowl with paper towels. Transfer spinach to now-empty bowl; set aside.

2. Heat oil in large saucepan over medium heat until shimmering. Add onion and cook until softened, about 5 minutes. Stir in garlic and pepper flakes and cook until fragrant, about 30 seconds. Add tomatoes, ½ cup processed spinach, 1 teaspoon salt, and ½ teaspoon pepper and cook until slightly thickened, about 10 minutes. Off heat, stir in 3 tablespoons basil; set aside.

3. Process ricotta and reserved spinach liquid in food processor until smooth, about 30 seconds. Add Parmesan, remaining 3 tablespoons basil, eggs, 1½ teaspoons salt, and ½ teaspoon pepper and process until combined. Stir ricotta mixture into remaining processed spinach.

4. Cover bottom of 13 by 9-inch baking dish with 1¼ cups sauce. Top with 3 noodles and spread one-third of ricotta mixture evenly over noodles. Sprinkle with ⅔ cup mozzarella and cover with 1¼ cups sauce. Repeat twice, beginning with noodles and ending with sauce. Top with remaining 3 noodles, remaining sauce, and remaining 1 cup mozzarella.

5. Cover pan tightly with aluminum foil sprayed with vegetable oil spray and bake until bubbling around edges, about 40 minutes. Discard foil and continue to bake until cheese is melted, about 10 minutes. Let cool on wire rack for 30 minutes. Serve.

Keys to Spinach Flavor

For lasagna that actually tastes like spinach, we took a three-pronged approach.

1. Increasing the amount of spinach to triple the amount called for in most recipes guaranteed it had a distinct presence.

2. Adding some of the spinach water, from squeezing the spinach dry to prevent a soggy lasagna, to the ricotta cheese ensured a creamy, spinach-flavored filling.

3. Chopping the spinach in the food processor produced a fine, even texture that distributed nicely in both the cheese filling and the sauce.

Why This Recipe Works For fuss-free but flavorful manicotti, we started by substituting no-boil lasagna noodles for the manicotti tubes. Briefly soaking them in hot water made them pliable and easy to roll up. Using the food processor to break down the ground beef allowed its flavor to permeate the sauce quickly so it needed just a short simmer. For even more meaty flavor, we added a popular pizza topping—pepperoni—which gave the sauce a spicy backbone. To liven up the filling, we included assertive provolone, plus a portion of the processed ground beef and pepperoni; a single egg helped to bind it all together.

BAKED MANICOTTI WITH MEAT SAUCE

SERVES 6 TO 8

You will need 16 no-boil lasagna noodles for this recipe. The test kitchen's preferred brand, Barilla, comes 16 noodles to a box, but other brands contain only 12. It is important to let the dish cool for 15 minutes after baking.

Meat Sauce
- 1 onion, chopped
- 6 ounces thinly sliced deli pepperoni
- 1 pound 85 percent lean ground beef
- 5 garlic cloves, minced
- 1 tablespoon tomato paste
- ¼ teaspoon red pepper flakes
- 2 (28-ounce) cans crushed tomatoes
- Salt and pepper

Manicotti
- 1½ pounds (3 cups) ricotta cheese
- 10 ounces mozzarella cheese, shredded (2½ cups)
- 6 ounces provolone cheese, shredded (1½ cups)
- 1 large egg, lightly beaten
- ¼ cup finely chopped fresh basil
- ½ teaspoon salt
- ½ teaspoon pepper
- 16 no-boil lasagna noodles

1. For the Meat Sauce Adjust oven rack to upper-middle position and heat oven to 375 degrees. Pulse onion and pepperoni in food processor until coarsely ground, about 10 pulses. Add beef and pulse until thoroughly combined, 5 to 8 pulses.

2. Transfer mixture to large saucepan and cook over medium heat, breaking up mixture with wooden spoon, until no longer pink, about 5 minutes. Using slotted spoon, transfer 1 cup meat mixture to paper towel–lined plate and reserve. Add garlic, tomato paste, and pepper flakes to pot and cook until fragrant, about 1 minute. Stir in tomatoes and simmer until sauce is slightly thickened, about 20 minutes. Season with salt and pepper to taste. (Meat sauce can be refrigerated for up to 3 days.)

3. For the Manicotti Combine ricotta, 2 cups mozzarella, 1 cup provolone, egg, basil, salt, pepper, and reserved meat mixture in large bowl. Pour 1 inch boiling water into 13 by 9-inch baking dish and slip noodles into water, one at a time. Let noodles soak until pliable, about 5 minutes, separating noodles with tip of knife to prevent sticking. Remove noodles from water and place in single layer on clean dish towels; discard water and dry off baking dish.

4. Spread half of meat sauce over bottom of baking dish. Spread ¼ cup ricotta mixture evenly over bottom of each noodle. Roll noodles up around filling and lay them seam side down in baking dish. Spread remaining sauce over top to cover pasta completely. Cover dish tightly with aluminum foil and bake until bubbling around edges, about 40 minutes. Remove foil and sprinkle with remaining ½ cup mozzarella and ½ cup provolone. Bake until cheese is melted, about 5 minutes. Let cool for 15 minutes. Serve.

Manicotti Made Easy

Manicotti shells are hard to fill without tearing. For easy-to-fill manicotti, we found a better solution in no-boil lasagna noodles.

1. After soaking no-boil lasagna noodles briefly in hot water, spread filling across bottom of each and roll into tube.

2. Arrange rolled manicotti seam side down over sauce in baking dish.

GRANDMA PIZZA

SERVES 4

If the dough snaps back when you press it to the corners of the baking sheet, cover it, let it rest for 10 minutes, and try again.

Dough
- 3 tablespoons olive oil
- ¾ cup water
- 1½ cups (8¼ ounces) bread flour
- 2¼ teaspoons instant or rapid-rise yeast
- 1 teaspoon sugar
- ¾ teaspoon salt

Topping
- 1 (28-ounce) can diced tomatoes
- 1 tablespoon olive oil
- 2 garlic cloves, minced
- 1 teaspoon dried oregano
- ¼ teaspoon salt
- 8 ounces mozzarella cheese, shredded (2 cups)
- ¼ cup grated Parmesan cheese
- 2 tablespoons chopped fresh basil

1. For the Dough Coat rimmed baking sheet with 2 tablespoons oil. Combine water and remaining 1 tablespoon oil in 1-cup liquid measuring cup. Using stand mixer fitted with dough hook, mix flour, yeast, sugar, and salt on low speed until combined. With mixer running, slowly add water mixture and mix until dough comes together, about 1 minute. Increase speed to medium-low and mix until dough is smooth and comes away from sides of bowl, about 10 minutes.

2. Transfer dough to greased baking sheet and turn to coat. Stretch dough to 10 by 6-inch rectangle. Cover loosely with plastic wrap and let rise in warm place until doubled in size, 1 to 1½ hours. Stretch dough to corners of pan, cover loosely with plastic, and let rise in warm place until slightly puffed, about 45 minutes. Meanwhile, adjust oven rack to lowest position and heat oven to 500 degrees.

3. For the Topping Place tomatoes in colander and drain well. Combine drained tomatoes, oil, garlic, oregano, and salt in bowl. Combine mozzarella and Parmesan in second bowl. Sprinkle cheese mixture over dough, leaving ½-inch border around edges. Top with tomato mixture and bake until well browned and bubbling, about 15 minutes. Slide pizza onto wire rack, sprinkle with basil, and let cool for 5 minutes. Serve.

Easy Rise

Our method lets the dough proof right on the sheet. Spread dough on oiled baking sheet, then cover with plastic wrap and set it aside to rise.

Where Was Grandma Pizza Born?

In a 2003 piece in the Long Island newspaper Newsday, writer Erica Marcus traced grandma pizza's origins to Umberto's Pizzeria in New Hyde Park. According to Marcus, in the early 1970s proprietor Umberto Corteo would ask his pizza man to create a simple pizza like the one his mother used to make in Italy. The Corteos opened a second pizzeria, King Umberto's, in nearby Elmont. It was later bought by two former Umberto's pizza makers, who built a best-selling item out of their former boss's favorite lunch, naming it grandma pizza sometime in the late 1980s. Within 10 years, other Long Island pizzerias were offering the pie, and a phenomenon was born.

Why This Recipe Works Grandma pizza is a thin-crust pan pizza topped with a modest amount of cheese and chunks of tomatoes. To re-create this Long Island specialty, bread flour and lengthy kneading gave us the chewy crust we wanted, but the dough was difficult to stretch thin. Proofing the dough on the same sheet pan that we used to bake the pizza let it stretch on its own as it proofed. For a fresh, easy tomato topping that wouldn't make our crust soggy, we tossed drained diced tomatoes with salt, olive oil, garlic, and oregano. Baking the pizza on the lowest rack then cooling it on a wire rack perfectly crisped the bottom crust.

Why This Recipe Works Getting crisp pizza crust from your oven can be a challenge, but with just a few tweaks and the right tools, you'll have homemade pizza that's miles better than offerings from the freezer case or the delivery guy. We started by rolling out pizza dough thinly and then gently pressing it into our cast-iron skillet. Heating the pizza dough in the skillet on the stove gave our crust a jump start before going into the oven. Once in the oven, the skillet functioned like a pizza stone and crisped up our crust in just minutes. Our simple, classic pizza toppings—pizza sauce, mozzarella cheese, and basil—allowed our crust to really shine.

CAST-IRON SKILLET PIZZA

SERVES 4

We like to use our Classic Pizza Dough and No-Cook Pizza Sauce (recipes follow); however, you can use ready-made pizza dough and sauce from the local pizzeria or supermarket.

- ¼ cup extra-virgin olive oil
- 1 pound pizza dough, room temperature
- 1 cup pizza sauce
- 12 ounces fresh mozzarella cheese, sliced ¼ inch thick
- 2 tablespoons chopped fresh basil

1. Adjust oven rack to upper-middle position and heat oven to 500 degrees. Grease 12-inch cast-iron skillet with 2 tablespoons oil.

2. Place dough on lightly floured counter, divide in half, and cover with greased plastic wrap. Press and roll 1 piece of dough (keeping remaining dough covered) into 11-inch round. Transfer dough to prepared skillet and gently push it to corners of pan. Spread ½ cup sauce over surface of dough, leaving ½-inch border around edge. Top with half of mozzarella.

3. Set skillet over medium-high heat and cook until outside edge of dough is set, pizza is lightly puffed, and bottom crust is spotty brown when gently lifted with spatula, 2 to 4 minutes. Transfer skillet to oven and bake until edge of pizza is golden brown and cheese is melted, 7 to 10 minutes.

4. Using potholders, remove skillet from oven and slide pizza onto wire rack using spatula; let cool slightly. Sprinkle with 1 tablespoon basil, cut into wedges, and serve. Being careful of hot skillet, repeat with remaining 2 tablespoons oil, dough, sauce, mozzarella, and 1 tablespoon basil. Cut into wedges and serve.

CLASSIC PIZZA DOUGH
MAKES 1 POUND

- 2 cups (11 ounces) plus 2 tablespoons bread flour
- 1⅛ teaspoons instant or rapid-rise yeast
- ¾ teaspoon salt
- 1 tablespoon olive oil
- ¾ cup warm water (110 degrees)

1. Pulse flour, yeast, and salt together in food processor to combine, about 5 pulses. With processor running, add oil, then water, and process until rough ball forms, 30 to 40 seconds. Let dough rest for 2 minutes, then process for 30 seconds longer. (If after 30 seconds dough is very sticky and clings to blade, add extra flour as needed.)

2. Transfer dough to lightly floured counter and knead by hand to form smooth, round ball, about 1 minute. Place dough in large, lightly greased bowl, cover tightly with greased plastic wrap, and let rise until doubled in size, 1 to 1½ hours. (Alternatively, dough can be refrigerated for at least 8 hours or up to 16 hours.)

NO-COOK PIZZA SAUCE
MAKES 2 CUPS

While it is convenient to use ready-made pizza sauce, we think it is a lot tastier to make your own.

- 1 (28-ounce) can whole peeled tomatoes, drained with juice reserved
- 1 tablespoon extra-virgin olive oil
- 1 teaspoon red wine vinegar
- 2 garlic cloves, minced
- 1 teaspoon dried oregano
- Salt and pepper

Process tomatoes with oil, vinegar, garlic, and oregano in food processor until smooth, about 30 seconds. Transfer mixture to 2-cup liquid measuring cup and add tomato juice until sauce measures 2 cups. Season with salt and pepper to taste. (Sauce can be refrigerated for up to 1 week or frozen for up to 1 month.)

ITALIAN POT ROAST

SERVES 4 TO 6

Start checking the roast for doneness after 2 hours; if there is a little resistance when prodded with a fork, it's done. Light, sweeter red wines, such as a Merlot or Beaujolais, work especially well with this recipe.

- 1 (3½- to 4-pound) boneless beef chuck-eye roast, trimmed, tied at 1-inch intervals
  Salt and pepper
- 2 tablespoons vegetable oil
- 1 onion, chopped
- 1 celery rib, minced
- 1 pound cremini or white mushrooms, trimmed and quartered
- 2 tablespoons tomato paste
- 1 (14.5-ounce) can diced tomatoes
- ½ cup canned tomato sauce
- ½ cup water
- 1 cup red wine
- 2 teaspoons sugar
- 1 large garlic head, outer papery skins removed, halved
- 1 sprig fresh thyme
- 1 sprig fresh rosemary

1. Adjust oven rack to middle position and heat oven to 300 degrees. Pat roast dry with paper towels and season with salt and pepper.

2. Heat oil in Dutch oven over medium-high heat until just smoking. Brown roast on all sides, 8 to 12 minutes. Transfer roast to large plate. Reduce heat to medium, add onion, celery, mushrooms, and tomato paste and cook until vegetables begin to soften, about 8 minutes. Add diced tomatoes, tomato sauce, water, ½ cup wine, sugar, garlic, and thyme. Add roast, with accumulated juices, to pot and bring to simmer over medium-high heat. Place piece of aluminum foil over pot, cover with lid, and transfer pot to oven.

3. Cook until roast is just fork-tender, 2½ to 3½ hours, turning roast after 1 hour. Remove lid and foil and let roast rest for 30 minutes, skimming fat from surface of liquid after 20 minutes. Transfer roast to carving board and tent with foil.

4. Remove and reserve garlic head and skim remaining fat. Add remaining ½ cup wine to pot, bring to boil over medium-high heat, and cook until sauce begins to thicken, about 12 minutes. Meanwhile, carefully squeeze garlic cloves from their skins and mash into paste. Add rosemary to pot and simmer until fragrant, about 2 minutes. Remove rosemary and thyme sprigs, stir in mashed garlic, and season with salt and pepper to taste.

5. Remove twine from roast and slice meat against grain into ½-inch-thick slices or pull apart into large pieces. Transfer meat to serving platter and pour ¾ cup sauce over meat. Serve, passing remaining sauce separately.

Fit To Be Tied

A tied roast will cook evenly and won't fall apart during the long cooking time. If your roast doesn't come tied, simply tie pieces of kitchen twine around it at 1-inch intervals.

Getting the Garlic Right

Here's how we tone down the garlic in our Italian Pot Roast so it offers mellow, not overpowering, flavor.

1. After slicing whole head of garlic in half, add it to pot to simmer with roast.

2. Once roast is done, squeeze garlic cloves from skins and mash garlic with fork to form paste. Stir garlic paste back into sauce.

Why This Recipe Works The bolder cousin of American-style pot roast, Italian Pot Roast trades the potatoes, carrots, and gravy for mushrooms, onion, and a thick sauce based on tomatoes, red wine, garlic, and herbs. For our version, we started with a chuck-eye roast for its beefy flavor and ample fat. Canned diced tomatoes, tomato sauce, and tomato paste gave us a thick, rich sauce; a double dose of red wine added depth and brightness. Simmering a whole head of garlic with our roast ensured the meat and sauce were infused with mellow garlic flavor.

PORK CHOPS WITH VINEGAR PEPPERS

SERVES 4

Our favorite chicken broth is Swanson Chicken Stock.

- 3 tablespoons sugar
- Salt and pepper
- 4 (8- to 10-ounce) bone-in pork rib chops, 1 inch thick, trimmed
- ⅓ cup all-purpose flour
- 2 tablespoons olive oil
- 1 onion, halved and sliced thin
- 8 garlic cloves, lightly crushed and peeled
- 2 anchovy fillets, rinsed, patted dry, and minced
- 2 cups thinly sliced sweet green vinegar peppers
- 1 sprig fresh rosemary
- 1 cup chicken broth
- ½ cup red wine vinegar
- 1 tablespoon unsalted butter

1. Dissolve sugar and 3 tablespoons salt in 1½ quarts cold water in large container. Add chops, cover, and refrigerate for 30 minutes or up to 1 hour.

2. Place flour in shallow dish. Remove chops from brine. Pat chops dry with paper towels and season with pepper. Working with 1 chop at a time, dredge both sides in flour, shaking off excess. Heat 1 tablespoon oil in 12-inch skillet over medium-high heat until just smoking. Add chops and cook until well browned on first side, 5 to 7 minutes. Flip chops and cook on second side for 1 minute; transfer to plate, browned side up.

3. Reduce heat to medium and add remaining 1 tablespoon oil, onion, garlic, and anchovies to now-empty skillet. Cook, stirring frequently, until onion is softened and golden brown, 6 to 8 minutes. Add peppers and rosemary and cook until peppers begin to caramelize, about 5 minutes. Add broth and vinegar and bring to boil.

4. Arrange chops, browned side up, in skillet and add any accumulated juices from plate. Reduce heat to low, cover, and simmer until chops register 145 degrees, 6 to 10 minutes. Transfer chops to serving platter and tent loosely with aluminum foil.

5. Increase heat to high and boil sauce until slightly thickened, about 3 minutes. Off heat, stir in butter and season with salt and pepper to taste. Stir any accumulated juices from platter into sauce. Discard rosemary and spoon sauce over chops. Serve.

Finishing a Pan Sauce with Butter

Add butter to pan sauce off heat to prevent butter from separating and leaving an oil slick on top.

Why This Recipe Works Choosing the right pork chop and the right kind of peppers was essential to getting this dish right. We decided on thick-cut, bone-in rib chops, which we brined briefly to ensure seasoned and moist meat. Jarred sweet vinegar peppers held up to braising, and had a mild tang that we liked. To give long-cooked flavor to our quick-cooked braising sauce, we added a secret ingredient—anchovy fillets—which lent savory depth but did not impart any fishy flavor. We thickened the sauce in two ways: by flouring the chops (which also aided browning) and by reducing the sauce slightly after the pork was done.

Why This Recipe Works To make zeppoles, a cross between doughnuts and fried dough, we discovered that two leaveners were better than one. Although typically used independently, in the case of these Italian fritters, a combination of baking powder and yeast created the perfect fluffy confection. We fried the wet, sticky dough at 350 degrees, which yielded a crispy exterior that didn't overcook by the time the interior had finished cooking. These light, tender zeppoles are best served warm with a dusting of powdery confectioners' sugar.

ZEPPOLES

MAKES 15 TO 18 ZEPPOLES

This dough is very wet and sticky. If you own a 4-cup liquid measuring cup, you can combine the batter in it to make it easier to tell when it has doubled in volume in step 1. Zeppoles are best served warm.

- 1⅓ cups (6⅔ ounces) all-purpose flour
- 1 tablespoon granulated sugar
- 2 teaspoons instant or rapid-rise yeast
- 1 teaspoon baking powder
- ½ teaspoon salt
- 1 cup warm water (110 degrees)
- ½ teaspoon vanilla extract
- 2 quarts peanut or vegetable oil
- Confectioners' sugar

1. Combine flour, granulated sugar, yeast, baking powder, and salt in large bowl. Whisk water and vanilla into flour mixture until fully combined. Cover tightly with plastic wrap and let rise at room temperature until doubled in size, 15 to 25 minutes.

2. Set wire rack in rimmed baking sheet and line rack with triple layer of paper towels. Adjust oven rack to middle position and heat oven to 200 degrees. Add oil to large Dutch oven until it measures about 1½ inches deep and heat over medium-high heat to 350 degrees.

3. Using greased tablespoon measure, add 6 heaping tablespoonfuls of batter to oil. (Use dinner spoon to help scrape batter from tablespoon if necessary.) Fry until golden brown and toothpick inserted in center of zeppole comes out clean, 2 to 3 minutes, flipping once halfway through frying. Adjust burner, if necessary, to maintain oil temperature between 325 and 350 degrees.

4. Using slotted spoon, transfer zeppoles to prepared wire rack; roll briefly so paper towels absorb grease. Transfer sheet to oven to keep warm. Return oil to 350 degrees and repeat twice more with remaining batter. Dust zeppoles with confectioners' sugar and serve.

Instant Yeast

Instant, or rapid-rise, yeast is much like active dry yeast, but it has undergone a gentler drying process that has not destroyed the outer cells. Instant yeast does not require proofing and can be added directly to the dry ingredients when making bread—hence the name "instant." Our recipes call for instant yeast because it's easier to use. In breads that contain butter, sugar, and other flavorings, we find virtually no difference in flavor between instant and active dry yeasts. If you have a recipe that calls for active dry yeast, you can use instant as long as you reduce the amount of yeast by 25 percent. For example if the recipe calls for 1 packet, or 2¼ teaspoons, of active dry yeast, use 1¾ teaspoons of instant yeast.

the state of grilling

313	Huli Huli Chicken	368	Chinese-Style Glazed Pork Tenderloin
314	Cornell Barbecued Chicken	371	Chinese-Style Barbecued Spareribs
316	Alabama Barbecued Chicken	373	Barbecued Country-Style Ribs
319	Classic Barbecued Chicken	374	South Dakota Corncob-Smoked Ribs
321	Smoked Bourbon Chicken	377	Grilled Mustard-Glazed Pork Loin
322	Grilled Butterflied Lemon Chicken	378	Wood-Grilled Salmon
325	Grilled Chicken Wings	380	Cedar-Planked Salmon with Cucumber-Yogurt Sauce
326	Grilled Chicken Leg Quarters		
328	BBQ Chicken Thighs	383	Grilled Salmon Steaks with Lemon-Caper Sauce
331	Grilled Chicken Diavolo		
333	Barbecued Pulled Chicken	385	Grilled Jalapeño and Lime Shrimp Skewers
334	Barbecued Burnt Ends	386	Husk-Grilled Corn
336	Grilled Bourbon Steaks	389	Grilled Corn on the Cob
339	California Barbecued Tri-Tip	391	Backyard Barbecue Beans
341	Shredded Barbecued Beef	392	California Barbecued Beans
342	Jucy Lucy Burgers	394	Grilled Potato Hobo Packs
345	Green Chile Cheeseburgers	397	Grilled Broccoli with Lemon and Parmesan
346	Chicago-Style Barbecued Ribs	398	Grilled Caesar Salad
348	Texas Barbecued Beef Ribs	401	Tangy Apple Cabbage Slaw
351	South Carolina Smoked Fresh Ham	403	Memphis Chopped Coleslaw
353	Lexington-Style Pulled Pork	404	All-American Potato Salad
354	South Carolina Pulled Pork	406	Smoky Potato Salad
356	Tennessee Pulled Pork Sandwiches	409	Amish Potato Salad
359	Hoecakes	410	Ranch Potato Salad
361	Texas Thick-Cut Smoked Pork Chops	413	Dill Potato Salad
362	Smoked Double-Thick Pork Chops	415	Texas Potato Salad
365	Grilled Thin-Cut Pork Chops	416	Smashed Potato Salad
366	St. Louis BBQ Pork Steaks	418	Lemon and Herb Red Potato Salad

Why This Recipe Works Authentic Hawaiian huli huli chicken is typically something home cooks buy instead of make. The birds are continually basted with a sticky-sweet glaze and "huli"-ed, which means "turned" in Hawaiian. For the teriyaki-like glaze, we developed a version with soy sauce, rice vinegar, ginger, garlic, chili sauce, ketchup, brown sugar, and lots and lots of pineapple juice. We boiled the sauce down until it was thick, glossy, and sweet. To mimic a Hawaiian rotisserie, we spread the coals in a single layer. The direct heat rendered the fat and crisped the skin, but the chicken was far enough from the coals to avoid burning.

HULI HULI CHICKEN

SERVES 4 TO 6

Mesquite wood chips give this recipe authentic flavor, but you can substitute another variety.

Chicken
- 2 (3½- to 4-pound) whole chickens
- 2 quarts water
- 2 cups soy sauce
- 1 tablespoon vegetable oil
- 6 garlic cloves, minced
- 1 tablespoon grated fresh ginger

Glaze
- 3 (6-ounce) cans pineapple juice
- ¼ cup packed light brown sugar
- ¼ cup soy sauce
- ¼ cup ketchup
- ¼ cup rice vinegar
- 4 garlic cloves, minced
- 2 tablespoons grated fresh ginger
- 2 teaspoons chili-garlic sauce
- 2 cups wood chips, soaked in water for 15 minutes and drained

1. For the Chicken Using kitchen shears, cut along both sides of backbone to remove it. Trim any excess fat or skin at neck. Flip chicken over and, using chef's knife, cut through breastbone to separate chicken into halves. Repeat with other chicken. Combine water and soy sauce in large bowl. Heat oil in large saucepan over medium-high heat until shimmering. Add garlic and ginger and cook until fragrant, about 30 seconds. Stir into soy sauce mixture. Add chicken and refrigerate, covered, for at least 1 hour or up to 8 hours.

2. For the Glaze Combine pineapple juice, sugar, soy sauce, ketchup, vinegar, garlic, ginger, and chili-garlic sauce in empty saucepan and bring to boil. Reduce heat to medium and simmer until thick and syrupy (you should have about 1 cup), 20 to 25 minutes. Using large piece of heavy-duty aluminum foil, wrap soaked chips in foil packet and cut several vent holes in top.

3A. For a Charcoal Grill Open bottom vent halfway. Light large chimney starter three-quarters filled with charcoal briquettes (4½ quarts). When top coals are partially covered with ash, pour evenly over grill. Place foil packet on coals. Set cooking grate in place, cover, and open lid vent halfway. Heat grill until hot and wood chips are smoking, about 5 minutes.

3B. For a Gas Grill Place wood chip packet directly on primary burner. Turn all burners to high, cover, and heat grill until hot and wood chips are smoking, about 15 minutes. Turn all burners to medium-low. (Adjust burners as needed to maintain grill temperature of 350 degrees.)

4. Clean and oil cooking grate. Remove chicken from brine and pat dry with paper towels. Place chicken skin side up on grill (do not place chicken directly above foil packet). Cover and cook chicken until well browned on bottom and thighs register 120 degrees, 25 to 30 minutes. Flip chicken skin side down and continue to cook, covered, until skin is well browned and crisp and thighs register 175 degrees, 20 to 25 minutes longer. Transfer chicken to platter, brush with half of glaze, and let rest for 5 minutes. Serve, passing remaining glaze at table.

To Make Ahead Both brine and glaze can be made ahead and refrigerated for up to 3 days. Do not brine chicken for longer than 8 hours or it will become too salty.

Huli History Lesson
In 1955, Hawaiian chicken farmer Ernie Morgado served local farmers barbecued chickens he'd made with his mom's homemade teriyaki-style sauce. They liked it so much that he launched a catering business using specially designed barbecue troughs that held chicken halves between two grates. When the chickens were ready to turn, the workers would yell "Huli!" (turn, in Hawaiian), and all the chickens would be rotated in one go. Morgado named his sauce Huli Huli.

CORNELL BARBECUED CHICKEN

SERVES 4 TO 6

Do not brine the chicken longer than 2 hours or the vinegar will turn the meat mushy. Poultry seasoning is a mix of herbs and spices that can be found in the spice aisle of most supermarkets.

Chicken
- 2 (3½- to 4-pound) whole chickens
- ¼ cup salt
- 3½ cups cider vinegar

Seasoning and Sauce
- 1 tablespoon ground poultry seasoning
- Salt and pepper
- ½ cup cider vinegar
- 3 tablespoons Dijon mustard
- 1 tablespoon chopped fresh sage leaves
- 1 tablespoon chopped fresh rosemary
- ½ cup olive oil

1. For the Chicken Using kitchen shears, cut along both sides of backbone to remove it. Trim any excess fat or skin at neck. Flip chicken over and, using chef's knife, cut through breastbone to separate chicken into halves. Repeat with other chicken. In large container, dissolve salt in vinegar and 2 quarts water. Submerge chickens in brine, cover, and refrigerate for 1 to 2 hours.

2. For the Seasoning and Sauce Combine poultry seasoning, 2 teaspoons salt, and 2 teaspoons pepper in small bowl; set aside. Process vinegar, mustard, sage, rosemary, ½ teaspoon salt, and ½ teaspoon pepper in blender until smooth, about 1 minute. With blender running, slowly add oil until incorporated. Transfer vinegar sauce to small bowl and reserve for basting chicken in steps 5 and 6.

3. Remove chickens from brine, pat dry with paper towels, and rub evenly with poultry seasoning mixture. Measure out ¾ cup vinegar sauce and set aside for cooking; reserve remaining sauce for serving.

4A. For a Charcoal Grill Open bottom vent completely. Light large chimney starter three-quarters filled with charcoal briquettes (4½ quarts). When top coals are partially covered with ash, pour evenly over grill. Set cooking grate in place, cover, and open lid vent halfway. Heat grill until hot, about 5 minutes.

4B. For a Gas Grill Turn all burners to high, cover, and heat grill until hot, about 15 minutes. Turn all burners to medium-low. (Adjust burners as needed to maintain grill temperature around 350 degrees.)

5. Clean and oil cooking grate. Place chicken skin side up on grill and brush with 6 tablespoons vinegar sauce for cooking. Cover and cook chicken until well browned on bottom and thighs register 120 degrees, 25 to 30 minutes, brushing with more sauce for cooking halfway through grilling.

6. Flip chicken skin side down and brush with remaining sauce for cooking. Cover and continue to cook chicken until skin is golden brown and crisp and breasts register 160 degrees and thighs register 175 degrees, 20 to 25 minutes longer.

7. Transfer chicken to carving board and let rest for 10 minutes. Carve chicken and serve with reserved sauce.

The Chicken Man of Cornell University

Robert Baker (1921–2006) developed the recipe for Cornell chicken while employed at Pennsylvania State University, but his recipe didn't take off until he had moved on to the Animal Sciences Department at Cornell University (his alma mater) and published it in a school journal. This vinegary chicken wasn't Dr. Baker's only contribution to the culinary world: He also had a hand in developing the vacuum packaging still used by much of the poultry industry and was the inventor of chicken nuggets, turkey ham, and chicken hot dogs.

Why This Recipe Works Invented in the 1940s by Robert Baker, a Cornell University professor, this tangy, crisp-skinned grilled chicken recipe has been a star attraction at the New York State Fair ever since. Grilling two split chickens over gentle direct heat worked best here. To crisp the skin without burning it, we started the chicken skin side up to render the fat slowly, then flipped the chicken skin side down to brown until crisp. The traditional poultry seasoning worked great as a rub but tasted dusty in the sauce, so we replaced it with fresh rosemary and sage. Dijon mustard contributed even more flavor to the sauce and thickened it perfectly.

ALABAMA BARBECUED CHICKEN

SERVES 4 TO 6

Hickory wood chips are traditional here; however, any type of wood chips will work fine. Two medium wood chunks, soaked in water for 1 hour, can be substituted for the wood chips on a charcoal grill.

Sauce
- ¾ cup mayonnaise
- 2 tablespoons cider vinegar
- 2 teaspoons sugar
- ½ teaspoon prepared horseradish
- ½ teaspoon salt
- ½ teaspoon black pepper
- ¼ teaspoon cayenne pepper

Chicken
- 1 teaspoon salt
- 1 teaspoon black pepper
- ½ teaspoon cayenne pepper
- 2 (3½- to 4-pound) whole chickens
- 2 cups wood chips, soaked in water for 15 minutes and drained
- 1 (13 by 9-inch) disposable aluminum roasting pan (if using charcoal)

1. For the Sauce Process ingredients in blender until smooth, about 1 minute. Refrigerate for at least 1 hour or up to 2 days.

2. For the Chicken Combine salt, pepper, and cayenne in small bowl. Using kitchen shears, cut along both sides of backbone to remove it. Trim any excess fat or skin at neck. Flip chicken over and, using chef's knife, cut through breastbone to separate chicken into halves. Repeat with other chicken. Pat chickens dry with paper towels and rub them evenly with spice mixture. Using large piece of heavy-duty aluminum foil, wrap soaked chips in foil packet and cut several vent holes in top.

3A. For a Charcoal Grill Open bottom vent halfway and place disposable pan in center of grill. Light large chimney starter filled with charcoal briquettes (6 quarts). When top coals are partially covered with ash, pour into 2 even piles on either side of pan. Place wood chip packet on 1 pile of coals. Set cooking grate in place, cover, and open lid vent halfway. Heat grill until hot and wood chips are smoking, about 5 minutes.

3B. For a Gas Grill Place wood chip packet directly on primary burner. Turn all burners to high, cover, and heat grill until hot and wood chips are smoking, about 15 minutes. Turn all burners to medium-low. (Adjust burners as needed to maintain grill temperature around 350 degrees.)

4. Clean and oil cooking grate. Place chicken skin side down on grill (in center of grill if using charcoal). Cover (positioning lid vent over chicken if using charcoal) and cook chicken until well browned on bottom and thighs register 120 degrees, 35 to 45 minutes.

5. Flip chicken skin side up. Cover and continue to cook chicken until skin is golden brown and crisp and breasts register 160 degrees and thighs register 175 degrees, 15 to 20 minutes longer.

6. Transfer chicken to carving board and brush with 2 tablespoons sauce. Tent chicken with foil and let rest for 10 minutes. Brush chicken with remaining sauce, carve, and serve.

Keeping BBQ in the Family
Big Bob Gibson's, famous for its white mayonnaise-based sauce, has been serving hickory-smoked barbecue in Decatur, Alabama, since 1925. Now run by Big Bob's grandchildren and great-grandchildren, the restaurant has expanded several times. The current pit smoker can cook 175 chickens, 110 slabs of ribs, and 60 whole turkeys at the same time. Although Big Bob used the sauce mostly on chicken, his grandson Don McLemore says nowadays people put it on everything from pork to potato chips.

Why This Recipe Works For Alabama-inspired barbecued chicken, we ditched the tomato and slathered a mayonnaise-based sauce on hickory-smoked chicken. Smoking generally takes hours, but our recipe expedites the process by cutting the chickens in half and cooking them in the middle of the grill, sandwiched between piles of smoking coals topped with hickory chips. We coated our chickens with the traditional Alabama mixture of seasoned mayonnaise and vinegar two times during cooking so the hot chicken absorbed the sauce and was flavored through and through.

Why This Recipe Works Despite its popularity, barbecued chicken recipes cause grillers plenty of headaches. Most recipes call for searing chicken quickly over high heat, but we found that starting the chicken over low heat slowly rendered the fat without the danger of flare-ups. Using a method called "grill roasting" ensured that we had almost completely cooked chicken before we were ready to add our sauce. We created a thick, complex layer of barbecue flavor for our grilled chicken by applying the sauce in coats and turning the chicken frequently as it cooked over moderate heat and then finishing it over higher heat

CLASSIC BARBECUED CHICKEN

SERVES 4 TO 6

Don't try to grill more than 10 pieces of chicken at a time; you won't be able to line them up on the grill as directed in step 5.

Quick Barbecue Sauce
- 3 cups store-bought barbecue sauce
- ½ cup molasses
- ½ cup ketchup
- ¼ cup cider vinegar
- 3 tablespoons brown mustard
- 2 teaspoons onion powder
- 1 teaspoon garlic powder

Chicken
- 1 teaspoon salt
- 1 teaspoon pepper
- ¼ teaspoon cayenne pepper
- 3 pounds bone-in chicken pieces, breasts halved crosswise and leg quarters separated into thighs and drumsticks, trimmed
- 1 (13 by 9-inch) disposable aluminum roasting pan (if using charcoal)

1. For the Quick Barbecue Sauce Whisk all ingredients in medium saucepan and bring to boil over medium-high heat. Reduce heat to medium and cook until sauce is thick and reduced to 3 cups, about 20 minutes. (Sauce can be refrigerated for up to 1 week.)

2. For the Chicken Combine salt, pepper, and cayenne in small bowl. Pat chicken dry with paper towels and rub evenly with spice mixture.

3A. For a Charcoal Grill Open bottom vent completely. Place disposable pan on 1 side of grill. Light large chimney starter filled with charcoal briquettes (6 quarts). When top coals are partially covered with ash, pour evenly over half of grill, opposite pan. Set cooking grate in place, cover, and open lid vent completely. Heat grill until hot, about 5 minutes.

3B. For a Gas Grill Turn all burners to high, cover, and heat grill until hot, about 15 minutes. Leave primary burner on high and turn other burner(s) off. (Adjust primary burner as needed to maintain grill temperature around 350 degrees.)

4. Clean and oil cooking grate. Place chicken, skin side down, on cool side of grill. Cover (positioning lid vent over chicken if using charcoal) and cook until chicken begins to brown, 30 to 35 minutes. Reserve 2 cups barbecue sauce for cooking; set aside remaining 1 cup sauce for serving.

5. Slide chicken into single line between hot and cool sides of grill and continue to cook, uncovered, flipping chicken and brushing with half of sauce for cooking every 5 minutes, until sticky, about 20 minutes.

6. Slide chicken to hot side of grill and continue to cook, flipping and brushing chicken with remaining sauce for cooking, until well glazed and breasts register 160 degrees and thighs/drumsticks register 175 degrees, about 5 minutes.

7. Transfer chicken to platter, tent loosely with aluminum foil, and let rest for 10 minutes. Serve with reserved sauce.

Barbecued Chicken, Slow and Low

First grill roasting, then basting over moderate heat, and finally finishing with more basting over higher heat ensures rendered, saucy, perfectly cooked chicken.

1. Cook chicken skin side down and covered on cool side of grill for about 30 minutes.

2. Move chicken into a single line near coals; baste and turn chicken. Then move pieces directly over coals to caramelize sauce.

Why This Recipe Works The combination of bourbon and smoke flavors sounded perfect, but first we had get the savory taste we wanted while keeping the chicken from drying out. The key was a mopping sauce: a sauce that is applied during long-grilling recipes to help keep the meat moist. And since smoke is attracted to moisture, keeping the chicken skin damp enhanced the smoky flavor. For even tastier chicken, we split them in half and cut slashes into the meat to create more surface area to soak up the flavor. By basting the chicken every 15 minutes, we ended up with moist, browned chicken with smokin' good bourbon taste.

SMOKED BOURBON CHICKEN

SERVES 4

Use a bourbon you'd be happy drinking. Use all the basting liquid in step 5.

- 1¼ cups bourbon
- 1¼ cups soy sauce
- ½ cup packed brown sugar
- 1 shallot, minced
- 4 garlic cloves, minced
- 2 teaspoons pepper
- 2 (3½- to 4-pound) whole chickens, giblets discarded
- 1 cup wood chips
- 4 (12-inch) wooden skewers

1. Bring bourbon, soy sauce, sugar, shallot, garlic, and pepper to boil in medium saucepan over medium-high heat and cook for 1 minute. Remove from heat and let cool completely. Set aside ¾ cup bourbon mixture for basting chicken. (Bourbon mixture can be refrigerated for up to 3 days.)

2. With chickens breast side down, using kitchen shears, cut through bones on both sides of backbones; discard backbones. Flip chickens over and, using chef's knife, split chickens in half lengthwise through centers of breastbones. Cut ½-inch-deep slits across breasts, thighs, and legs, about ½ inch apart. Tuck wingtips behind backs. Divide chicken halves between two 1-gallon zipper-lock bags and divide remaining bourbon mixture between bags. Seal bags, turn to distribute marinade, and refrigerate for at least 1 hour or up to 24 hours, flipping occasionally.

3. Just before grilling, soak wood chips in water for 15 minutes, then drain. Using large piece of heavy-duty aluminum foil, wrap soaked chips in foil packet and cut several vent holes in top. Remove chicken halves from marinade and pat dry with paper towels; discard marinade. Insert 1 skewer lengthwise through thickest part of breast down through thigh of each chicken half.

4A. For a Charcoal Grill Open bottom vent halfway. Light large chimney starter filled with charcoal briquettes (6 quarts). When top coals are partially covered with ash, pour into steeply banked pile against side of grill. Place wood chip packet on coals. Set cooking grate in place, cover, and open lid vent halfway. Heat grill until hot and wood chips are smoking, about 5 minutes.

4B. For a Gas Grill Remove cooking grate and place wood chip packet directly on primary burner. Set grate in place, turn all burners to high, cover, and heat grill until hot and wood chips are smoking, about 15 minutes. Leave primary burner on high and turn off other burners. (Adjust primary burner as needed to maintain grill temperature between 350 to 375 degrees.)

5. Clean and oil cooking grate. Place chicken halves skin side up on cooler side of grill with legs pointing toward fire. Cover and cook, basting every 15 minutes with reserved bourbon mixture, until breasts register 160 degrees and thighs register 175 degrees, 75 to 90 minutes, switching placement of chicken halves after 45 minutes. (All of bourbon mixture should be used.) Transfer chicken to carving board, tent loosely with foil, and let rest for 20 minutes. Carve and serve.

How to Cut a Chicken in Half

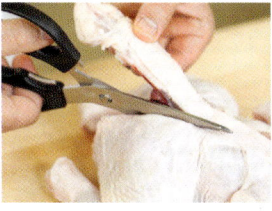 

1. Remove backbone
Using poultry shears, cut through bones on both sides of backbone; discard backbone.

2. Cut through breast
Flip chicken over and use chef's knife to halve chicken through center of breastbone.

GRILLED BUTTERFLIED LEMON CHICKEN

SERVES 8

Chicken and Rub
- 2 (3½- to 4-pound) whole chickens
- 2 teaspoons grated lemon zest (reserve lemon for vinaigrette)
- 2 teaspoons salt
- 1 teaspoon pepper
- 1 (13 by 9-inch) disposable aluminum roasting pan (if using charcoal)

Vinaigrette
- 4 lemons, halved; plus zested, halved lemon from rub
- 2 tablespoons minced fresh parsley
- 2 teaspoons Dijon mustard
- 1 garlic clove, minced
- 1 teaspoon sugar
- ½ teaspoon salt
- ½ teaspoon pepper
- ⅔ cup extra-virgin olive oil

1. For the Chicken and Rub Set wire rack in rimmed baking sheet. Using kitchen shears, cut along both sides of backbone to remove it. Flatten breastbone. Use your hands to loosen skin over breast and thighs and remove any excess fat. Repeat with other chicken. Combine lemon zest, salt, and pepper in bowl. Rub zest mixture under chicken skin and tuck wings behind back. Transfer chickens to prepared baking sheet and refrigerate, uncovered, for 30 minutes. (Chickens may be prepared up to this point 24 hours in advance; allow chickens to sit at room temperature for 30 minutes before grilling.)

2A. For a Charcoal Grill Open bottom vent completely and place disposable pan on 1 side of grill. Light large chimney starter filled with charcoal briquettes (6 quarts). When top coals are partially covered in ash, pour into steeply banked pile against side of grill (opposite disposable pan). Evenly scatter 20 unlit coals on top of hot coals. Set cooking grate in place, cover, and open lid vent completely. Heat grill until hot, about 5 minutes.

2B. For a Gas Grill Turn all burners to high, cover, and heat grill until hot, about 15 minutes. Leave primary burner on high and turn off other burner(s). (Adjust primary burner as needed to maintain grill temperature around 350 degrees.)

3. Clean and oil cooking grate. Place lemon halves, cut side down, on hot side of grill and cook until deep brown and caramelized, 5 to 8 minutes. Transfer to bowl.

4. Place chicken skin side down on cool side of grill, with legs closer to hot side. Cover (positioning lid vent over chicken if using charcoal) and cook until skin is well browned, 45 to 55 minutes.

5. Slide chicken to hot side of grill and continue to cook (covered if using gas) until deeply browned and breasts register 160 degrees and thighs register 175 degrees, about 5 minutes longer. Transfer chicken to carving board, tent loosely with aluminum foil, and let rest for 10 minutes.

6. For the Vinaigrette While chicken cooks, squeeze ⅓ cup juice from grilled lemons into bowl. Stir in parsley, mustard, garlic, sugar, salt, and pepper, then slowly whisk in oil until emulsified.

7. Carve chicken and transfer to serving platter. Pour ⅓ cup vinaigrette over chicken and serve, passing remaining vinaigrette separately.

Butterflying a Whole Chicken

1. Cut through bones on either side of backbone and trim any excess fat or skin at neck.

2. Flip chicken over and use heel of your hand to flatten breastbone.

Why This Recipe Works For perfectly grilled butterflied lemon chicken, we banked all the coals on one side of the grill, placing the chicken opposite the coals and setting the lid on the grill. This allowed the fat under the chicken's skin to render slowly and the relatively gentle heat resulted in a moister bird. Placing the chicken on the grill skin side down reduced cooking time and allowed the most fat to render—a final sear directly over the dying coals at the end of cooking crisped and browned the skin nicely. To finish the chicken with intense lemon flavor, we caramelized lemon halves over the grill and made a sauce from their juice.

Why This Recipe Works To get crisp, well-rendered chicken wings, we tossed the wings in cornstarch and pepper and grilled them over a gentle medium-low heat. We began grilling with the thicker skin side facing up so that the fat could slowly render, and then we flipped the wings at the end of cooking to crisp the skin. Also, though we normally cook white chicken meat to 160 degrees, wings are chock-full of collagen, which begins to break down upwards of 170 degrees. Cooking the wings to 180 degrees produced meltingly tender wings.

GRILLED CHICKEN WINGS

MAKES 24 WINGS

If you buy whole wings, cut them into two pieces before brining. Don't brine the wings for more than 30 minutes or they'll be too salty.

- ½ cup salt
- 2 pounds chicken wings, wingtips discarded, trimmed
- 1½ teaspoons cornstarch
- 1 teaspoon pepper

1. Dissolve salt in 2 quarts cold water in large container. Prick chicken wings all over with fork. Submerge chicken in brine, cover, and refrigerate for 30 minutes.

2. Combine cornstarch and pepper in bowl. Remove chicken from brine and pat dry with paper towels. Transfer wings to large bowl and sprinkle with cornstarch mixture, tossing until evenly coated.

3A. For a Charcoal Grill Open bottom vent completely. Light large chimney starter half filled with charcoal briquettes (3 quarts). When top coals are partially covered with ash, pour evenly over grill. Set cooking grate in place, cover, and open lid vent completely. Heat grill until hot, about 5 minutes.

3B. For a Gas Grill Turn all burners to high, cover, and heat grill until hot, about 15 minutes. Turn all burners to medium-low.

4. Clean and oil cooking grate. Grill wings (covered if using gas), thicker skin side up, until browned on bottom, 12 to 15 minutes. Flip chicken and grill until skin is crisp and lightly charred and meat registers 180 degrees, about 10 minutes. Transfer chicken to platter, tent loosely with aluminum foil, and let rest for 5 to 10 minutes. Serve.

BBQ GRILLED CHICKEN WINGS
Reduce pepper to ½ teaspoon. Add 1 teaspoon chili powder, 1 teaspoon paprika, ½ teaspoon garlic powder, ½ teaspoon dried oregano, and ½ teaspoon sugar to cornstarch mixture in step 2.

CREOLE GRILLED CHICKEN WINGS
Add ¾ teaspoon dried oregano, ½ teaspoon garlic powder, ½ teaspoon onion powder, ½ teaspoon white pepper, and ¼ teaspoon cayenne pepper to cornstarch mixture in step 2.

TANDOORI GRILLED CHICKEN WINGS
Reduce pepper to ½ teaspoon. Add 1 teaspoon garam masala, ½ teaspoon ground cumin, ¼ teaspoon garlic powder, ¼ teaspoon ground ginger, and ⅛ teaspoon cayenne pepper to cornstarch mixture in step 2.

Prepping Grilled Chicken Wings

1. Puncturing each wing with fork lets brine easily penetrate meat and helps fat render away.

2. Quick saltwater brine seasons wings and keeps them juicy.

3. Dusting wings with cornstarch and black pepper prevents sticking and encourages crisping.

GRILLED CHICKEN LEG QUARTERS

SERVES 4

A garlic press makes quick work of mincing the 6 cloves called for here. You can use 1 teaspoon of dried oregano in place of the fresh called for in the dressing. Do not (ever) use dried cilantro.

- 6 garlic cloves, minced
- 4 teaspoons kosher salt
- 1 tablespoon sugar
- 2 teaspoons grated lime zest plus 2 tablespoons juice
- 2 teaspoons plus ¼ cup extra-virgin olive oil
- 1½ teaspoons ground cumin
- 1 teaspoon pepper
- ½ teaspoon cayenne pepper
- 4 (10-ounce) chicken leg quarters, trimmed
- 2 tablespoons chopped fresh cilantro
- 2 teaspoons chopped fresh oregano

1. Combine garlic, salt, sugar, lime zest, 2 teaspoons oil, cumin, pepper, and cayenne in bowl and mix to form paste. Reserve 2 teaspoons garlic paste for dressing.

2. Position chicken skin side up on cutting board and pat dry with paper towels. Leaving drumsticks and thighs attached, make 4 parallel diagonal slashes in chicken: 1 across drumsticks, 1 across leg joints; and 2 across thighs (each slash should reach bone). Flip chicken over and make 1 more diagonal slash across back of drumsticks. Rub remaining garlic paste all over chicken and into slashes. Refrigerate chicken for at least 1 hour or up to 24 hours.

3A. For a Charcoal Grill Open bottom vent completely. Light large chimney starter filled with charcoal briquettes (6 quarts). When top coals are partially covered with ash, pour two-thirds evenly over half of grill, then pour remaining coals over other half of grill. Set cooking grate in place, cover, and open lid vent completely. Heat grill until hot, about 5 minutes.

3B. For a Gas Grill Turn all burners to high, cover, and heat grill until hot, about 15 minutes. Turn primary burner to medium and turn other burner(s) to low. (Adjust primary burner as needed to maintain grill temperature of 400 to 425 degrees.)

4. Clean and oil cooking grate. Place chicken on cooler side of grill, skin side up. Cover and cook until underside of chicken is lightly browned, 9 to 12 minutes. Flip chicken, cover, and cook until leg joint registers 165 degrees, 7 to 10 minutes.

5. Transfer chicken to hotter side of grill, skin side down, and cook (covered if using gas) until skin is well browned, 3 to 5 minutes. Flip chicken and continue to cook until leg joint registers 175 degrees, about 3 minutes longer. Transfer to platter, tent loosely with aluminum foil, and let rest for 5 to 10 minutes.

6. Meanwhile, whisk lime juice, remaining ¼ cup oil, cilantro, oregano, and reserved garlic paste together in bowl. Spoon half of dressing over chicken and serve, passing remaining dressing separately.

Making Flavorful, Well-Cooked Chicken Leg Quarters

1. Slash Make bone-deep slashes in each quarter so the seasonings can penetrate and the meat cooks more readily.

2. Rub Massage the garlicky seasoning paste into the slashes and all over the chicken and refrigerate for up to 24 hours.

Why This Recipe Works Chicken leg quarters seem like a perfect candidate for the grill—the rich leg and thigh meat has plenty of skin to crisp up. But the thick joint takes longer to cook than the rest of the leg, so grilling often results in overcooking. To remedy this, we took a two-pronged approach. To prepare the chicken, we made slashes down to the bone, a technique often used for large cuts of meat. This helped the chicken cook evenly, and also ensured deep seasoning. We then used our two-level grilling technique, starting the chicken over a low flame, then searing it over a hot fire. A citrus-y dressing provided a welcome hit of brightness.

BBQ CHICKEN THIGHS

SERVES 4 TO 6

The seasoned chicken thighs need to sit for 1 hour before grilling. We prefer Frank's RedHot Original Cayenne Pepper Sauce for this recipe. If you use Tabasco, reduce the amount to 2 teaspoons in the broth mixture and 1 teaspoon in the glaze.

- 2 tablespoons packed brown sugar
- 1 tablespoon kosher salt
- 1 tablespoon paprika
- 1 teaspoon pepper
- 1 teaspoon white pepper
- ¾ teaspoon granulated garlic
- 4 pounds bone-in chicken thighs, trimmed
- 1 (13 by 9-inch) disposable aluminum roasting pan
- ½ cup plus 2 tablespoons bottled barbecue sauce
- ½ cup chicken broth
- 7 garlic cloves (6 sliced thin, 1 minced)
- 3 tablespoons Worcestershire sauce
- 3 tablespoons hot sauce
- 2 tablespoons apple jelly
- 1½ cups wood chips

1. Combine 1 tablespoon sugar, salt, paprika, pepper, white pepper, and granulated garlic in bowl. Set aside 4 teaspoons spice mixture. Place chicken in disposable pan and season all over with remaining spice mixture. Flip chicken skin side down and let sit at room temperature for 1 hour.

2. Meanwhile, whisk ½ cup barbecue sauce, broth, sliced garlic, Worcestershire sauce, and 2 tablespoons hot sauce together in bowl; set aside. In separate bowl, microwave jelly until melted, about 30 seconds. Stir minced garlic, remaining 2 tablespoons barbecue sauce, remaining 1 tablespoon sugar, and remaining 1 tablespoon hot sauce into jelly; set glaze aside.

3. Just before grilling, soak wood chips in water for 15 minutes, then drain. Using large piece of heavy-duty aluminum foil, wrap soaked chips in foil packet and cut several vent holes in top.

4A. For a Charcoal Grill Open bottom vent completely. Light large chimney starter mounded with charcoal briquettes (7 quarts). When top coals are partially covered with ash, pour into steeply banked pile against side of grill. Place wood chip packet on coals. Set cooking grate in place, cover, and open lid vent completely. Heat grill until hot and wood chips are smoking, about 5 minutes.

4B. For a Gas Grill Remove cooking grate and place wood chip packet directly on primary burner. Set grate in place, turn all burners to high, cover, and heat grill until hot and wood chips are smoking, about 15 minutes. Leave primary burner on high and turn off other burners. (Adjust primary burner as needed to maintain grill temperature of 350 to 375 degrees.)

5. Pour broth mixture over chicken in pan. Place pan on cooler side of grill, cover (positioning lid vent over chicken for charcoal), and cook for 30 minutes (chicken will be about 140 degrees).

6. Remove pan from grill. Using tongs, transfer chicken skin side up to cooler side of grill. (Discard cooking liquid.) Brush chicken skin with half of glaze, then sprinkle with reserved spice rub. Cover and cook for 15 minutes.

7. Brush chicken skin with remaining glaze. Cover and cook until glaze has set and chicken registers 175 degrees, 25 to 30 minutes longer. Transfer chicken to platter, tent loosely with foil, and let rest for 15 minutes. Serve.

Why This Recipe Works For juicy grilled chicken thighs slick with a shiny barbecue glaze, we started by applying a sweet-meets-spicy rub. We braised spice-rubbed chicken thighs in a pan of flavorful bottled barbecue sauce and chicken broth. After 30 minutes, we poured off the cooking liquid, applied a sticky glaze and more spice rub, and arranged the thighs directly on the grill to render the skin. With a final layer of glaze and a brief rest, we had the ultimate finger-licking chicken.

Why This Recipe Works To make a chicken diavolo that was fiery and smoky, we took it to the grill. A mixture of herbs, spices, lemon, oil, sugar, and both black and red pepper performed double duty as a marinade and as a sauce. We built a two-level fire, starting the chicken on the cooler side of the grill to cook through and then searing it over the hotter side to char the outside and crisp the skin. For extra smoky flavor, we added a foil-wrapped packet of soaked wood chips. We cooked the reserved marinade mixture to mellow the garlic bite, added a shot of lemon juice, and spooned our supercharged vinaigrette over the grilled chicken.

GRILLED CHICKEN DIAVOLO

SERVES 4

If you are buying a whole chicken and cutting it into pieces yourself, reserve the backbone and wings to make stock. To use wood chunks on a charcoal grill, substitute one medium wood chunk, soaked in water for 1 hour, for the wood chip packet.

- 3 pounds bone-in chicken pieces (split breasts cut in half, drumsticks, and/or thighs), trimmed
- ½ cup extra-virgin olive oil
- 4 garlic cloves, minced
- 1 tablespoon chopped fresh rosemary
- 2 teaspoons grated lemon zest plus 4 teaspoons juice
- 2 teaspoons red pepper flakes
- 1 teaspoon sugar
- Salt and pepper
- ½ teaspoon paprika
- 1 cup wood chips

1. Pat chicken dry with paper towels. Whisk oil, garlic, rosemary, lemon zest, pepper flakes, sugar, 1 teaspoon pepper, and paprika together in bowl until combined. Reserve ¼ cup oil mixture for sauce. (Oil mixture can be covered and refrigerated for up to 24 hours.) Whisk 2¼ teaspoons salt into oil mixture remaining in bowl and transfer to 1-gallon zipper-lock bag. Add chicken, turn to coat, and refrigerate for at least 1 hour or up to 24 hours. Just before grilling, soak wood chips in water for 15 minutes, then drain. Using large piece of heavy-duty aluminum foil, wrap soaked chips in foil packet and cut several vent holes in top.

2A. For a Charcoal Grill Open bottom vent halfway. Light large chimney starter filled with charcoal briquettes (6 quarts). When top coals are partially covered with ash, pour two-thirds evenly over half of grill, then pour remaining coals over other half of grill. Place wood chip packet on larger pile of coals. Set cooking grate in place, cover, and open lid vent halfway. Heat grill until hot and wood chips are smoking, about 5 minutes.

2B. For a Gas Grill Place wood chip packet over primary burner. Turn all burners to high, cover, and heat grill until hot and wood chips are smoking, about 15 minutes. Turn primary burner to medium and turn other burner(s) to low. (Adjust primary burner as needed to maintain grill temperature of 400 to 425 degrees.)

3. Remove chicken from marinade and pat dry with paper towels. Discard used marinade. Clean and oil cooking grate. Place chicken on cooler side of grill, skin side up. Cover and cook until underside of chicken is lightly browned, 8 to 12 minutes. Flip chicken, cover, and cook until white meat registers 155 degrees and dark meat registers 170 degrees, 7 to 10 minutes.

4. Transfer chicken to hotter side of grill, skin side down, and cook (covered if using gas) until skin is well browned, about 3 minutes. Flip and continue to cook (covered if using gas) until white meat registers 160 degrees and dark meat registers 175 degrees, 1 to 3 minutes. Transfer chicken to platter, tent loosely with foil, and let rest for 5 to 10 minutes.

5. Meanwhile, heat reserved oil mixture in small saucepan over low heat until fragrant and garlic begins to brown, 3 to 5 minutes. Off heat, whisk in lemon juice and ¼ teaspoon salt. Spoon sauce over chicken. Serve.

The Right Fire

A two-level fire lets us gently cook the chicken on the cooler side and then sear it on the hotter side for flavorful char. To get good smoky flavor, we place an aluminum foil–wrapped packet of soaked wood chips on the larger pile of charcoal.

Why This Recipe Works Barbecuing is the perfect method for cooking fatty cuts of pork or beef, but relatively lean chicken is another story. For barbecued pulled chicken with a smoky flavor and moist, tender meat, we'd have to come up with some tricks. Brining the birds kept the white meat moist and juicy, and arranging the chickens on the grill with the breast meat farther from the heat source than the dark meat evened out the cooking times. We tweaked our favorite barbecue sauce to better complement the chicken, increasing the vinegar to balance the sweetness and swapping the root beer for coffee to boost the smoky flavor.

BARBECUED PULLED CHICKEN

MAKES ENOUGH FOR 8 SANDWICHES

We prefer to halve the chickens ourselves, but you may be able to buy halved chickens from your butcher.

Chicken
- 1 cup salt
- 2 (4-pound) whole chickens, giblets discarded
- Pepper
- 2 cups wood chips, soaked in water for 15 minutes and drained

Sauce
- 2 teaspoons vegetable oil
- 1 onion, chopped fine
- 4 cups chicken broth
- 1¼ cups cider vinegar
- 1 cup brewed coffee
- ¾ cup molasses
- ½ cup tomato paste
- ½ cup ketchup
- 2 tablespoons brown mustard
- 1 tablespoon hot sauce
- ½ teaspoon garlic powder
- ¼ teaspoon liquid smoke

1. For the Chicken Dissolve salt in 4 quarts cold water in large container. Remove backbones from chickens and split chickens in half lengthwise through center of breastbone. Using metal skewer, poke 20 holes all over each chicken half. Submerge chicken halves in brine, cover, and refrigerate for 1 hour. Remove chicken halves from brine, pat dry with paper towels, and season with pepper. Using large piece of heavy-duty aluminum foil, wrap soaked wood chips in foil packet and cut several vent holes in top.

2. For the Sauce Meanwhile, heat oil in Dutch oven over medium-high heat until shimmering. Add onion and cook until softened, about 5 minutes. Whisk in broth, vinegar, coffee, molasses, tomato paste, ketchup, mustard, hot sauce, and garlic powder and bring to boil. Reduce heat to medium-low and simmer until mixture is thick and reduced to 4 cups, about 65 to 75 minutes. Stir in liquid smoke; reserve 1 cup sauce for serving. (Sauce can be refrigerated for up to 2 days.)

3A. For a Charcoal Grill Open bottom vent halfway. Light large chimney starter filled with charcoal briquettes (6 quarts). When top coals are partially covered with ash, pour into steeply banked pile against side of grill. Place wood chip packet on coals. Set cooking grate in place, cover, and open lid vent halfway. Heat grill until hot and wood chips are smoking, about 5 minutes.

3B. For a Gas Grill Place wood chip packet over primary burner. Turn all burners to high, cover, and heat grill until hot and wood chips are smoking, about 15 minutes. Leave primary burner on high and turn off other burner(s).

4. Clean and oil cooking grate. Place chicken halves skin side up on cool side of grill with legs closest to heat source. Cover and cook until breasts register 160 degrees and thighs register 175 degrees, 75 to 85 minutes. Transfer chicken to carving board, tent loosely with foil, and let rest until cool enough to handle, about 15 minutes. Remove and discard skin. Pull meat off bones, separating dark and light meat. Roughly chop dark meat into ½-inch pieces. Shred white meat into thin strands.

5. Add chicken to pot with sauce and cook over medium-low heat until chicken is warmed through, about 5 minutes. Serve on hamburger rolls, passing reserved sauce separately.

BARBECUED BURNT ENDS

SERVES 8 TO 10

Look for a brisket with a significant fat cap. This recipe takes about 8 hours to prepare. The meat can be brined ahead of time, transferred to a zipper-lock bag, and refrigerated for up to a day. If you don't have ½ cup of juices from the rested brisket, supplement with beef broth.

Brisket and Rub
- 2 cups plus 1 tablespoon kosher salt
- ½ cup granulated sugar
- 1 (5- to 6-pound) beef brisket, flat cut, untrimmed
- ¼ cup packed brown sugar
- 2 tablespoons pepper
- 4 cups wood chips
- 1 (13 by 9-inch) disposable aluminum roasting pan (if using charcoal) or 2 (8½ by 6-inch) disposable aluminum pans (if using gas)

Barbecue Sauce
- ¾ cup ketchup
- ¼ cup packed brown sugar
- 2 tablespoons cider vinegar
- 2 tablespoons Worcestershire sauce
- 2 teaspoons granulated garlic
- ¼ teaspoon cayenne pepper

1. For the Brisket and Rub Dissolve 2 cups salt and granulated sugar in 4 quarts cold water in large container. Slice brisket with grain into 1½-inch-thick strips. Add brisket strips to brine, cover, and refrigerate for 2 hours. Remove brisket from brine and pat dry with paper towels.

2. Combine brown sugar, pepper, and remaining 1 tablespoon salt in bowl. Season brisket all over with rub. Just before grilling, soak wood chips in water for 15 minutes, then drain. Using 2 large pieces of heavy-duty aluminum foil, wrap soaked chips in 2 foil packets and cut several vent holes in tops.

3A. For a Charcoal Grill Open bottom vent halfway and place disposable pan filled with 2 quarts water on one side of grill, with long side of pan facing center of grill. Arrange 3 quarts unlit charcoal briquettes on opposite side of grill and place 1 wood chip packet on coals. Light large chimney starter filled halfway with charcoal briquettes (3 quarts). When top coals are partially covered with ash, pour evenly over unlit coals and wood chip packet. Place remaining wood chip packet on lit coals. Set cooking grate in place, cover, and open lid vent halfway. Heat grill until hot and wood chips are smoking, about 5 minutes.

3B. For a Gas Grill Add ½ cup ice cubes to 1 wood chip packet. Remove cooking grate and place both wood chip packets directly on primary burner; place disposable pans each filled with 2 cups water directly on secondary burner(s). Set grate in place, turn all burners to high, cover, and heat grill until hot and wood chips are smoking, about 15 minutes. Leave primary burner on high and turn off other burner(s). (Adjust primary burner as needed to maintain grill temperature of 275 to 300 degrees.)

4. Clean and oil cooking grate. Arrange brisket on cooler side of grill as far from heat source as possible. Cover (positioning lid vent over brisket for charcoal) and cook without opening for 3 hours.

5. Adjust oven rack to middle position and heat oven to 275 degrees. Remove brisket from grill and transfer to rimmed baking sheet. Cover sheet tightly with foil. Roast until fork slips easily in and out of meat and meat registers 210 degrees, about 2 hours. Remove from oven, leave covered, and let rest for 1 hour. Remove foil, transfer brisket to carving board, and pour accumulated juices into fat separator.

6. For the Barbecue Sauce Combine ketchup, sugar, vinegar, Worcestershire, granulated garlic, cayenne, and ½ cup defatted brisket juices in medium saucepan. Bring to simmer over medium heat and cook until slightly thickened, about 5 minutes.

7. Cut brisket strips crosswise into 1- to 2-inch chunks. Combine brisket chunks and barbecue sauce in large bowl and toss to combine. Serve.

Why This Recipe Works Real burnt ends are all about moist meat and plenty of flavorful, charred bark, but most pit masters use fatty point-cut brisket. To make the leaner (and more widely available) flat-cut brisket work, we cut it into strips and brine it for maximum moisture and flavor. Three hours of smoke on the grill—with a water pan for more moisture—followed by a few more hours in a low oven ensures fully tender brisket with plenty of char. We cut the meat into cubes before tossing it with a flavorful, homemade sauce. Home pit masters, take note.

GRILLED BOURBON STEAKS

SERVES 6 TO 8

Use a bourbon you'd be happy drinking. Plan ahead: These steaks need to marinate for at least 4 hours before grilling.

- 1 cup bourbon
- 1 cup Worcestershire sauce
- 1 shallot, minced
- 2 garlic cloves, minced
- Kosher salt and pepper
- 4 (1-pound) boneless rib-eye steaks, 1 to 1½ inches thick, trimmed
- 2 tablespoons vegetable oil

1. Whisk bourbon, Worcestershire, shallot, garlic, 2 teaspoons salt, and 2 teaspoons pepper together in bowl. Place 2 steaks in each of two 1-gallon zipper-lock bags and divide bourbon mixture between bags, about 1 cup each. Seal bags, turn to distribute marinade, and refrigerate for at least 4 hours or up to 24 hours, flipping occasionally.

2. Remove steaks from marinade and pat dry with paper towels; discard marinade. Brush steaks all over with oil and season liberally with salt and pepper.

3A. For a Charcoal Grill Open bottom vent completely. Light large chimney starter filled with charcoal briquettes (6 quarts). When top coals are partially covered with ash, pour evenly over grill. Set cooking grate in place, cover, and open lid vent completely. Heat grill until hot, about 5 minutes.

3B. For a Gas Grill Turn all burners to high, cover, and heat grill until hot, about 15 minutes. Turn all burners to medium-high. (Adjust burners as needed to maintain grill temperature between 350 and 400 degrees.)

4. Clean and oil cooking grate. Place steaks on grill and cook (covered if using gas) until well charred and meat registers 125 degrees (for medium-rare), 6 to 8 minutes per side.

5. Transfer steaks to wire rack set in rimmed baking sheet, tent with aluminum foil, and let rest for 10 minutes. Serve.

The World of Whiskey

The word whiskey comes from the Celtic *uisqebaugh* (whis-kee-BAW), meaning "water of life." It is traditionally made from barley, corn, rye, wheat, or oats, but artisanal makers now incorporate everything from buckwheat to farro to spelt.

A whiskey's distinct flavor is determined by a number of factors including the type of grain used, the aging time, the type of wood in which it is stored, and the distillation method. There are many types of whiskey, but American, Irish, Canadian, and Scotch are the most widely consumed. (Scotch and Canadian whiskys drop the e.)

AMERICAN

- Bourbon is the most popular form of American whiskey.
- It must contain at least 51 percent corn.
- It must be aged in charred new oak barrels for two years.
- Bourbon can't go into the barrel for aging at higher than a 62.5-percent alcohol level.

IRISH

- Irish whiskey is made from a blend of malted barley (grain that's been germinated or sprouted, which converts its starch to sugar) and unmalted barley.
- It's aged in wood for a minimum of three years.
- Often, it is triple-distilled, so it's extra-smooth.

CANADIAN

- Canadian whisky is typically made from a base whisky (usually a mix of grains but predominantly corn) and a flavoring whisky (often rye).
- Fifty-one percent of each batch must be aged in wood for three years.

SCOTCH

- Single-malt scotches are made from malted barley.
- Blends are made from a mix of single malt(s) and grain whisky made from various unmalted grains.
- Scotch whisky is usually distilled twice and is aged in oak for three years.

Why This Recipe Works Why marinate rib eyes in bourbon? The bourbon not only enhances the beef's meatiness, it also increases the char. To maximize the steaks' flavor, we soaked four hefty rib eyes in a mixture of bourbon, Worcestershire, shallot, and garlic. After marinating the meat for four hours, we fired up the grill, brushed the steaks with oil and a liberal dose of salt and pepper, and cooked them to a juicy medium-rare. The boozy marinade really delivered, giving us sweet-savory flavors and perfect char.

Why This Recipe Works Unlike other barbecue recipes, California barbecued tri-tip recipes call for cooking the meat (bottom sirloin roast) over high heat and seasoning it only with salt, pepper, garlic, and the sweet smoke of the grill. This consistently produces a charred exterior and very rare center—but we wanted the outside cooked less and the inside cooked more. To achieve this, we pushed all the coals in our grill to one side, which created a hot zone for cooking and a cooler one for finishing the meat slowly. To prevent the meat from tasting too smoky, we held off on the wood chips until after we'd seared the meat.

CALIFORNIA BARBECUED TRI-TIP

SERVES 4 TO 6

If you can't find tri-tip, bottom round steak will also work. Two medium wood chunks, soaked in water for 1 hour, can be substituted for the wood chips on a charcoal grill. Serve with Santa Maria Salsa (recipe follows) and California Barbecued Beans (page 392). We prefer this roast cooked medium-rare.

- 6 garlic cloves, minced
- 2 tablespoons olive oil
- ¾ teaspoon salt
- 1 (2-pound) tri-tip roast, trimmed
- 1 teaspoon pepper
- ¾ teaspoon garlic salt
- 2 cups wood chips, soaked in water for 15 minutes and drained

1. Combine garlic, oil, and salt in bowl. Pat meat dry with paper towels, poke it about 20 times on each side with fork, and rub it evenly with garlic mixture. Wrap meat in plastic wrap and let sit at room temperature for at least 1 hour or refrigerate for up to 24 hours. (If refrigerated, let sit at room temperature for 1 hour before grilling.) Before cooking, unwrap meat, wipe off garlic paste using paper towels, and rub it evenly with pepper and garlic salt. Using large piece of heavy-duty aluminum foil, wrap soaked chips in foil packet and cut several vent holes in top.

2A. For a Charcoal Grill Open bottom vent completely. Light large chimney starter filled with charcoal briquettes (6 quarts). When top coals are partially covered with ash, pour evenly over half of grill. Set cooking grate in place, cover, and open lid vent completely. Heat grill until hot, about 5 minutes.

2B. For a Gas Grill Turn all burners to high, cover, and heat grill until hot, about 15 minutes.

3. Clean and oil cooking grate. Grill meat on hot side of grill until well browned on both sides, about 10 minutes. Transfer meat to plate.

4. Place wood chip packet directly on coals or primary burner. If using gas, leave primary burner on high and turn other burner(s) off.

5. Place meat on cool side of grill. Cover (positioning lid vent over meat if using charcoal) and cook until meat registers 120 to 125 degrees (for medium-rare), about 20 minutes.

6. Transfer meat to carving board, tent loosely with aluminum foil, and let rest for 20 minutes. Slice meat thin against grain and serve.

SANTA MARIA SALSA
MAKES ABOUT 4 CUPS

The distinct texture of each ingredient is part of this salsa's identity and appeal, so we don't recommend using a food processor.

- 2 pounds tomatoes, cored and chopped
- 2 teaspoons salt
- 2 jalapeño chiles, stemmed, seeded, and chopped fine
- 1 small red onion, chopped fine
- 1 celery rib, chopped fine
- ¼ cup lime juice (2 limes)
- ¼ cup chopped fresh cilantro
- 1 garlic clove, minced
- ⅛ teaspoon dried oregano
- ⅛ teaspoon Worcestershire sauce

1. Place tomatoes in strainer set over bowl and sprinkle with salt; drain for 30 minutes. Discard liquid. Meanwhile, combine jalapeños, onion, celery, lime juice, cilantro, garlic, oregano, and Worcestershire in large bowl.

2. Add drained tomatoes to jalapeño mixture and toss to combine. Cover with plastic wrap and let stand at room temperature for 1 hour before serving. (Salsa can be refrigerated for up to 2 days.)

Why This Recipe Works For our Shredded Barbecued Beef, we cut a chuck roast into quarters. The smaller pieces of beef absorbed more smoke flavor and cooked much faster. After cooking the meat in a disposable roasting pan on the cooler side of the grill for a few hours, we flipped all 4 pieces, wrapped the pan in foil, and placed the roast in the oven to finish cooking. For a barbecue sauce with richer flavor, we sautéed the onions in beef fat from the pan. Chili powder and pepper added bite, while ketchup, vinegar, coffee, Worcestershire sauce, brown sugar, and the beef juices rounded out the flavors.

SHREDDED BARBECUED BEEF

SERVES 8 TO 10

If you prefer a smooth barbecue sauce, strain the sauce before tossing it with the beef in step 5. We like to serve this beef on white bread with plenty of pickle chips. Three medium wood chunks, soaked in water for 1 hour, can be substituted for the wood chips on a charcoal grill.

- 1 tablespoon salt
- 1 tablespoon pepper
- 1 teaspoon cayenne pepper
- 1 (5- to 6-pound) boneless beef chuck-eye roast, trimmed and quartered
- 1 (13 by 9-inch) disposable aluminum roasting pan
- 3 cups wood chips, soaked in water for 15 minutes and drained
- 1 onion, chopped fine
- 4 garlic cloves, minced
- ½ teaspoon chili powder
- 1¼ cups ketchup
- ¾ cup brewed coffee
- ½ cup cider vinegar
- ½ cup packed brown sugar
- 3 tablespoons Worcestershire sauce
- ½ teaspoon pepper

1. Combine salt, pepper, and cayenne in small bowl. Pat meat dry with paper towels and rub evenly with spice mixture. Wrap meat in plastic wrap and let sit at room temperature for at least 1 hour or refrigerate up to 24 hours. (If refrigerated, let sit at room temperature for 1 hour before grilling.) Before cooking, unwrap meat and transfer to disposable pan. Using 2 large pieces of heavy-duty aluminum foil, wrap soaked chips in 2 foil packets and cut several vent holes in tops.

2A. For a Charcoal Grill Open bottom vent completely. Light large chimney starter half filled with charcoal briquettes (3 quarts). When top coals are partially covered with ash, pour into steeply banked pile against 1 side of grill. Place wood chip packets on coals. Set cooking grate in place, cover, and open lid vent halfway. Heat grill until hot and wood chips are smoking, about 5 minutes.

2B. For a Gas Grill Place wood chip packets directly on primary burner. Turn all burners to high, cover, and heat grill until hot and wood chips are smoking, about 15 minutes. Leave primary burner on high and turn other burner(s) off. (Adjust primary burner as needed to maintain grill temperature between 250 and 300 degrees.)

3. Place pan of meat on cool side of the grill. Cover (positioning lid vent over meat if using charcoal) and cook until meat is deep red, about 2 hours. During final 20 minutes of grilling, adjust oven rack to lower-middle position and heat oven to 300 degrees.

4. Flip meat over in pan, cover pan tightly with foil, and roast beef in oven until fork slips easily in and out of beef, 2 to 3 hours.

5. Transfer meat to large bowl, tent loosely with foil, and let rest for 30 minutes. While meat rests, skim fat from accumulated juices in pan; reserve 2 tablespoons fat. Strain defatted juices; reserve ½ cup juice. Combine onion and reserved fat in medium saucepan and cook over medium heat until onion has softened, about 10 minutes. Add garlic and chili powder and cook until fragrant, about 30 seconds. Stir in ketchup, coffee, vinegar, sugar, Worcestershire, pepper, and any accumulated meat juices and simmer until thickened, about 15 minutes. Using 2 forks, pull meat into shreds, discarding any excess fat or gristle. Toss meat with ½ cup barbecue sauce. Serve, passing remaining sauce separately.

JUCY LUCY BURGERS

SERVES 4

Buy the American cheese from the deli counter, and ask them to slice it into a ½-inch slab from which you can cut four big cubes to fill the center of the burgers. One or two percent low-fat milk can be substituted for the whole milk. The cheesy center of these burgers is molten hot when first removed from the grill, so be sure to let the burgers rest for at least 5 minutes before serving.

- 2 slices hearty white sandwich bread, torn into 1-inch pieces
- ¼ cup whole milk
- 1 teaspoon garlic powder
- ¾ teaspoon salt
- ½ teaspoon pepper
- 1½ pounds 85 percent lean ground beef
- 1 slice deli American cheese (½-inch-thick), quartered

1. In large bowl using potato masher, mash bread, milk, garlic powder, salt, and pepper into smooth paste. Add beef and lightly knead mixture until well combined.

2. Divide meat into 4 equal portions. Using half of each portion of meat, encase cheese to form mini burger patty. Mold remaining half-portion of meat around mini patty and seal edges to form ball. Flatten ball with palm of your hand, forming ¾-inch-thick patty. Cover and refrigerate patties for at least 30 minutes or up to 24 hours.

3A. For a Charcoal Grill Open bottom vent completely. Light large chimney starter half filled with charcoal briquettes (3 quarts). When top coals are partially covered with ash, pour evenly over grill. Set cooking grate in place, cover, and heat grill until hot, about 5 minutes.

3B. For a Gas Grill Turn all burners to high, cover, and heat grill until hot, about 15 minutes. Turn all burners to medium.

4. Clean and oil cooking grate. Lay burgers on grill and cook, without pressing on them, until well browned on both sides and cooked through, 12 to 16 minutes, flipping burgers halfway through grilling. Transfer burgers to platter, tent loosely with aluminum foil, and let rest for 5 minutes before serving.

How to Form a Jucy Lucy
To avoid a burger blowout, it's essential to completely seal in the cheese.

1. Using half of each portion of meat, encase cheese to form mini burger patty.

2. Mold remaining half-portion of meat around mini patty and seal edges to form a ball and flatten to form ¾-inch patty.

The Great Lucy Debate
A debate still rages as to where the Jucy Lucy was created. Two Minnesota taverns, Matt's Bar and the 5–8 Club, claim to have created the burger in the 1950s. As the story goes, a customer requested a burger with the cheese sealed in the middle. When he bit in, the hot cheese spurted out and he exclaimed, "That's one juicy Lucy!" As for the unusual spelling, that's still a mystery.

Why This Recipe Works Minneapolis taverns are famous for the Jucy Lucy, a moist beef burger stuffed with American cheese. Replicating the Jucy Lucy seemed easy enough—but our burgers, cooked to well-done to melt the cheese inside, were dry and tough or the cheese melted through the meat, leaving an empty cavern where the cheese had been. To keep the cheese in place, we created a double-sealed pocket by wrapping the cheese inside a small beef patty and then molding a second patty around it. Adding a mixture of bread and milk, mashed into a paste, to the ground beef kept the burgers moist and juicy.

Why This Recipe Works For our version of New Mexico's green chile cheeseburgers—ground beef patties grilled to a crusty brown and topped with chopped fire-roasted chiles and a slice of cheese—we preferred the flavor and fat of 85 percent lean ground beef. For the topping, we used mild Anaheim chiles and spicy jalapeños for a complex chile flavor. We grilled the chiles with onions, then quickly chopped them with fresh garlic in the food processor. For even more chile flavor, we pureed some of the chile topping into a smooth paste and mixed it into the raw ground beef. This gave us burgers with satisfying heat through and through.

GREEN CHILE CHEESEBURGERS

SERVES 4

In step 3, you may need to add a teaspoon or two of water to the food processor to help process the chile mixture. Pressing a shallow divot in the center of each burger patty keeps the burgers flat during grilling.

- 3 Anaheim chiles, stemmed, halved, and seeded
- 3 jalapeño chiles, stemmed, halved, and seeded
- 1 onion, sliced into ½-inch-thick rounds
- 1 garlic clove, minced
- Salt and pepper
- 1½ pounds 85 percent lean ground beef
- 4 slices deli American cheese

1A. For a Charcoal Grill Open bottom vent completely. Light large chimney starter filled with charcoal briquettes (6 quarts). When top coals are partially covered with ash, pour evenly over grill. Set cooking grate in place, cover, and open lid vent completely. Heat grill until hot, about 5 minutes.

1B. For a Gas Grill Turn all burners to high, cover, and heat grill until hot, about 15 minutes.

2. Clean and oil cooking grate. Place Anaheims, jalapeños, and onion on grill, cover, and cook until vegetables are lightly charred and tender, 4 to 6 minutes, flipping halfway through cooking. Transfer vegetables to bowl, cover, and let cool 5 minutes. Remove skins from chiles and discard; separate onion rounds into rings.

3. Transfer chiles and onion to food processor, add garlic, and pulse until coarsely chopped, about 5 pulses. Transfer all but ¼ cup chopped chile mixture to empty bowl and season with salt and pepper; set aside. Process remaining mixture until finely chopped, about 45 seconds, scraping down bowl as needed.

4. Combine beef, finely chopped chile mixture, ½ teaspoon salt, and ¼ teaspoon pepper in large bowl and lightly knead until well combined. Shape into four ¾-inch-thick patties and press shallow depression in center of each.

5. Place burgers on grill, cover, and cook until well browned on first side, 3 to 5 minutes. Flip burgers, top with reserved coarsely chopped chile mixture and cheese, and continue to cook, covered, until cheese is melted and burgers are cooked to desired doneness, 3 to 5 minutes. Serve.

Chile Pinch Hitter

For complex green chile flavor outside of New Mexico, we found that a combination of mild Anaheims and spicy jalapeños has a nice peppery balance.

MILD HEAT
Anaheim chiles add a mildly sweet, grassy flavor.

SPICE IS NICE
Jalapeño chiles have just enough heat to stand up to the beefiness of the burger.

CHICAGO-STYLE BARBECUED RIBS

SERVES 4 TO 6

The dry spices are used to flavor both the rub and the barbecue sauce. One medium wood chunk, soaked in water for 1 hour, can be substituted for the wood chips on a charcoal grill. When removing the ribs from the oven, be careful to not spill the hot water in the bottom of the baking sheet.

Spice Rub and Ribs
- 1 tablespoon dry mustard
- 1 tablespoon paprika
- 1 tablespoon packed dark brown sugar
- 1½ teaspoons garlic powder
- 1½ teaspoons onion powder
- 1½ teaspoons celery salt
- 1 teaspoon cayenne pepper
- ½ teaspoon ground allspice
- 2 racks baby back ribs (about 1½ pounds each), trimmed
- 1 cup wood chips, soaked in water for 15 minutes and drained
- 1 (13 by 9-inch) disposable aluminum roasting pan

Sauce
- 1¼ cups ketchup
- ¼ cup molasses
- ¼ cup cider vinegar
- ¼ cup water
- ⅛ teaspoon liquid smoke

1. For the Spice Rub and Ribs Combine dry mustard, paprika, sugar, garlic powder, onion powder, celery salt, cayenne, and allspice in bowl. Measure out and reserve 2 tablespoons spice mixture for sauce. To remove chewy membrane from ribs, loosen it with tip of paring knife and, with aid of paper towel, pull it off slowly in 1 big piece. Pat ribs dry with paper towels and rub evenly with spice mixture. Wrap meat in plastic wrap and let sit at room temperature for at least 1 hour or refrigerate for up to 24 hours. (If refrigerated, let sit at room temperature for 1 hour before grilling.)

2. For the Sauce Whisk all ingredients with reserved 2 tablespoons spice rub in bowl. Using large piece of heavy-duty aluminum foil, wrap soaked chips in foil packet and cut several vent holes in top.

3A. For a Charcoal Grill Open bottom vent completely. Light large chimney starter filled with charcoal briquettes (6 quarts). Add 2 cups water to disposable pan and place it on 1 side of grill. When top coals are partially covered with ash, pour into steeply banked pile against other side of grill, opposite pan of water. Place wood chip packet on coals. Set cooking grate in place, cover, and open lid vent completely. Heat grill until hot and wood chips are smoking, about 5 minutes.

3B. For a Gas Grill Place wood chip packet directly on primary burner. Add 2 cups water to disposable pan and place it on secondary burner. Turn all burners to high, cover, and heat grill until hot and wood chips are smoking, about 15 minutes. Turn primary burner to medium and turn other burner(s) off. (Adjust primary burner as needed to maintain grill temperature around 325 degrees.)

4. Clean and oil cooking grate. Place ribs meat side down on grill over water-filled pan; ribs may overlap slightly. Cover (positioning lid vent over meat if using charcoal) and cook until ribs are deep red and smoky, about 1½ hours, flipping and rotating racks halfway through grilling. During final 20 minutes of grilling, adjust oven rack to middle position and heat oven to 250 degrees.

5. Set wire rack in rimmed baking sheet and add just enough water to cover pan bottom. Transfer ribs to rack and cover tightly with foil. Continue to cook ribs in oven until fork slips easily in and out of meat, 1½ to 2 hours.

6. Remove ribs from oven, tent with foil, and let rest for 30 minutes. Brush ribs evenly with half of sauce. Slice ribs between bones and serve with remaining sauce.

Why This Recipe Works Chicago-style barbecued ribs recipes typically call for smoking the ribs at about 200 degrees for at least 8 hours. This slow-and-low cooking method delivers the moist, tender meat that defines Chicago ribs. We wanted to replicate the same method at home. To shorten cooking time, we started our recipe on the grill—where the ribs picked up good color and smoke flavor—and finished them in the oven. Placing pans of water on the grill and in the oven steamed the ribs, making them extra moist and tender. For Chicago-style barbecue sauce, we used celery salt, allspice, and plenty of cayenne pepper.

TEXAS BARBECUED BEEF RIBS

SERVES 4

Beef ribs are sold in slabs with up to seven bones, but slabs with three to four bones are easier to manage on the grill. If you cannot find ribs with a substantial amount of meat on the bones, don't bother making this recipe. One medium wood chunk, soaked in water for 1 hour, can be substituted for the wood chips on a charcoal grill.

Texas Barbecue Sauce
- 2 tablespoons unsalted butter
- ½ small onion, chopped fine
- 2 garlic cloves, minced
- 1½ teaspoons chili powder
- 1½ teaspoons pepper
- ½ teaspoon dry mustard
- 2 cups tomato juice
- 6 tablespoons distilled white vinegar
- 2 tablespoons Worcestershire sauce
- 2 tablespoons packed brown sugar
- 2 tablespoons molasses
- Salt

Ribs
- 3 tablespoons packed brown sugar
- 4 teaspoons chili powder
- 1 tablespoon salt
- 2 teaspoons pepper
- ½ teaspoon cayenne pepper
- 3–4 beef rib slabs (3 to 4 ribs per slab, about 5 pounds total), trimmed
- 1 cup wood chips, soaked in water for 15 minutes and drained

1. For the Texas Barbecue Sauce Melt butter in medium saucepan over medium heat. Add onion and cook until softened, about 5 minutes. Stir in garlic, chili powder, pepper, and dry mustard and cook until fragrant, about 30 seconds. Stir in tomato juice, vinegar, Worcestershire, sugar, and molasses and simmer until sauce is reduced to 2 cups, about 20 minutes. Season with salt to taste. (Sauce can be refrigerated for 1 week.)

2. For the Ribs Combine sugar, chili powder, salt, pepper, and cayenne in bowl. Pat ribs dry with paper towels and rub them evenly with spice mixture. Cover ribs with plastic wrap and let sit at room temperature for 1 hour.

3. Adjust oven rack to middle position and heat oven to 300 degrees. Set wire rack in rimmed baking sheet and add just enough water to cover pan bottom. Arrange ribs on rack and cover tightly with aluminum foil. Bake until fat has rendered and meat begins to pull away from bones, about 2 hours. Using large piece of heavy-duty foil, wrap soaked chips in foil packet and cut several vent holes in top.

4A. For a Charcoal Grill Open bottom vent halfway. Light large chimney starter filled with charcoal briquettes (6 quarts). When top coals are partially covered with ash, pour into steeply banked pile against 1 side of grill. Place wood chip packet on coals. Set cooking grate in place, cover, and open lid vent halfway. Heat grill until hot and wood chips are smoking, about 5 minutes.

4B. For a Gas Grill Place wood chip packet directly on primary burner. Turn all burners to high, cover, and heat grill until hot and wood chips are smoking, about 15 minutes. Leave primary burner on high and turn other burner(s) off. (Adjust primary burner as needed to maintain grill temperature between 250 and 300 degrees.)

5. Clean and oil cooking grate. Place ribs meat side down on cool side of grill; ribs may overlap slightly. Cover (positioning lid vent over meat if using charcoal) and cook until ribs are lightly charred and smoky, about 1½ hours, flipping and rotating racks halfway through grilling. Transfer to cutting board, tent with foil, and let rest for 10 minutes. Serve with barbecue sauce.

Why This Recipe Works Traditional Texas barbecued beef ribs are placed in pits for up to 10 hours. The smoke slowly permeates the meat, melting away fat, building flavor, and creating an unforgettable crust. We wanted a streamlined recipe. To speed things up, we first turned to steaming the ribs in the oven on a tray of water covered with aluminum foil, which tenderized the ribs. We then moved the ribs to the grill, where we smoked them over indirect heat (banking all the coals to one side of the grill and placing the ribs on the empty side) using wood chips. The surface of the meat dried and formed a spicy, crusty bark.

Why This Recipe Works For a new take on pulled pork, we started with a shank-end fresh ham. We rubbed it with only salt to keep the flavor pure and let it rest overnight for deeply seasoned, juicy meat. To speed up the usually long cooking time, we smoked the ham on the grill to infuse it with flavor before covering it with foil and transferring it to the oven. For crisp and crackling skin, we removed the skin when the meat hit 200 degrees and roasted it separately. From there, we chopped the ham, stirring in the crisp bits of skin and the flavorful rendered juices, and served it on soft buns with a smear of tangy mustard sauce.

SOUTH CAROLINA SMOKED FRESH HAM

SERVES 8 TO 10

Plan ahead: The ham must be salted at least 18 hours before cooking. You'll have about 2½ cups of mustard sauce.

Ham
- 1 (6- to 8-pound) bone-in, skin-on shank-end fresh ham
- Kosher salt
- 2 cups wood chips

Mustard Sauce
- 1½ cups yellow mustard
- ½ cup cider vinegar
- 6 tablespoons packed brown sugar
- 2 tablespoons ketchup
- 2 teaspoons hot sauce
- 2 teaspoons Worcestershire sauce
- 1 teaspoon pepper

Hamburger buns

1. For the Ham Pat ham dry with paper towels. Place ham on large sheet of plastic wrap and rub all over with 2 tablespoons salt. Wrap tightly in plastic and refrigerate for 18 to 24 hours.

2. Just before grilling, soak wood chips in water for 15 minutes, then drain. Using large piece of heavy-duty aluminum foil, wrap soaked chips in 8 by 4½-inch foil packet. (Make sure chips do not poke holes in sides or bottom of packet.) Cut 2 evenly spaced 2-inch slits in top of packet.

3A. For a Charcoal Grill Open bottom vent completely. Light large chimney starter three-quarters filled with charcoal briquettes (4½ quarts). When top coals are partially covered with ash, pour evenly over half of grill. Place wood chip packet on coals. Set cooking grate in place, cover, and open lid vent completely. Heat grill until hot and wood chips are smoking, about 5 minutes.

3B. For a Gas Grill Remove cooking grate and place wood chip packet directly on primary burner. Set cooking grate in place, turn all burners to high, cover, and heat grill until hot and wood chips are smoking, about 15 minutes. Turn primary burner to medium-high and turn off other burner(s). (Adjust primary burner as needed to maintain grill temperature of 300 degrees.)

4. Clean and oil cooking grate. Unwrap ham and place flat side down on cooler side of grill. Cover grill (position lid vent directly over ham if using charcoal) and cook for 2 hours. Thirty minutes before ham comes off grill, adjust oven rack to middle position and heat oven to 300 degrees.

5. For the Mustard Sauce Meanwhile, whisk all ingredients together in bowl. (Sauce can be refrigerated for up to 1 week.)

6. Transfer ham to 13 by 9-inch baking pan, flat side down. Cover pan tightly with foil. Transfer to oven and roast until fork inserted in ham meets little resistance and meat registers 200 degrees, about 2½ hours.

7. Remove ham from oven and increase oven temperature to 400 degrees. Line rimmed baking sheet with foil. Using tongs, remove ham skin in 1 large piece. Place skin fatty side down on prepared sheet. Transfer to oven and roast until skin is dark and crispy and sounds hollow when tapped with fork, about 25 minutes, rotating sheet halfway through roasting. Tent ham with foil and let rest while skin roasts.

8. Transfer ham to carving board. Strain accumulated juices from pan through fine-mesh strainer set over bowl; discard solids. Trim and discard excess fat from ham. Remove bone and chop meat into bite-size pieces; transfer to large bowl.

9. When cool enough to handle, chop skin fine. Rewarm reserved ham juices in microwave for 1 minute. Add juices and chopped skin to ham and toss to combine. Season with salt to taste. Serve on buns, topped with mustard sauce.

Why This Recipe Works Traditional vinegar-based Lexington-style pulled pork recipes take hours to prepare. We wanted to simplify this recipe without sacrificing flavor. To do so, we used a combination of grilling and oven roasting to reduce the cooking time from all day to just a few hours. To infuse our Lexington-style pulled pork with ample smoke flavor despite the abbreviated cooking time, we doubled the amount of wood chips we used.

LEXINGTON-STYLE PULLED PORK

SERVES 8

Boneless pork butt (also labeled Boston butt) is often wrapped in elastic netting; be sure to remove the netting before rubbing the meat with the spices in step 1. Four medium wood chunks, soaked in water for 1 hour, can be substituted for the wood chips on a charcoal grill.

Spice Rub and Pork
- 2 tablespoons paprika
- 2 tablespoons pepper
- 2 tablespoons packed brown sugar
- 1 tablespoon salt
- 1 (4- to 5-pound) boneless pork butt roast, trimmed
- 4 cups wood chips, soaked in water for 15 minutes and drained

Lexington Barbecue Sauce
- 1 cup water
- 1 cup cider vinegar
- ½ cup ketchup
- 1 tablespoon granulated sugar
- ¾ teaspoon salt
- ½ teaspoon pepper
- ½ teaspoon red pepper flakes

1. For the Spice Rub and Pork Combine paprika, pepper, sugar, and salt in bowl. Pat meat dry with paper towels and rub it evenly with spice mixture. Wrap meat in plastic wrap and let sit at room temperature for at least 1 hour or refrigerate for up to 24 hours. (If refrigerated, let sit at room temperature for 1 hour before grilling.) Using 2 large pieces of heavy-duty aluminum foil, wrap soaked chips in 2 foil packets and cut several vent holes in tops.

2A. For a Charcoal Grill Open bottom vent halfway. Light large chimney starter half filled with charcoal briquettes (3 quarts). When top coals are partially covered with ash, pour into steeply banked pile against 1 side of grill. Place wood chip packets on coals. Set cooking grate in place, cover, and open lid vent halfway. Heat grill until hot and wood chips are smoking, about 5 minutes.

2B. For a Gas Grill Place wood chip packets directly on primary burner. Turn all burners to high, cover, and heat grill until hot and wood chips are smoking, about 15 minutes. Turn primary burner to medium and turn other burner(s) off. (Adjust primary burner as needed to maintain grill temperature around 275 degrees.)

3. Clean and oil cooking grate. Place meat on cool side of grill. Cover (positioning lid vent over meat if using charcoal) and cook until pork has dark, rosy crust, about 2 hours. During final 20 minutes of grilling, adjust oven rack to lower-middle position and heat oven to 325 degrees.

4. Transfer pork to large roasting pan, cover pan tightly with foil, and roast pork in oven until fork slips easily into and out of meat, 2 to 3 hours. Remove pork from the oven and let rest, still covered with foil, for 30 minutes.

5. For the Lexington Barbecue Sauce Whisk together all ingredients until sugar and salt are dissolved. When cool enough to handle, unwrap pork and pull meat into thin shreds, discarding excess fat and gristle. Toss pork with ½ cup barbecue sauce, serving remaining sauce at table.

North Carolina Barbecue Battle
In the eastern part of North Carolina, it's just not barbecue unless it's a whole hog. Known as a pig pickin', this type of barbecue starts with a split hog and ends with succulent meat and crackling-crisp skin. The meat is then literally picked from the bones and lightly seasoned with a thin vinegar and pepper sauce. Western Carolinians eschew the whole hog and go straight for the pork shoulder—the most marbled and meatiest chunk of the animal. The pork shoulder is cooked just like the whole hog, but the sauce is enriched with just enough ketchup and sugar to take the edge off the acidity.

SOUTH CAROLINA PULLED PORK

SERVES 8

Boneless pork butt (also labeled Boston butt) is often wrapped in elastic netting; be sure to remove the netting before rubbing the meat with the spices in step 1. The cooked meat can be shredded or chopped. Four medium wood chunks, soaked in water for 1 hour, can be substituted for the wood chip packet on a charcoal grill.

Spice Rub and Pork

- 3 tablespoons dry mustard
- 2 tablespoons salt
- 1½ tablespoons packed light brown sugar
- 2 teaspoons pepper
- 2 teaspoons paprika
- ¼ teaspoon cayenne pepper
- 1 (4- to 5-pound) boneless pork butt roast, trimmed
- 4 cups wood chips, soaked in water for 15 minutes and drained

Mustard Barbecue Sauce

- ½ cup yellow mustard
- ½ cup packed light brown sugar
- ¼ cup distilled white vinegar
- 2 tablespoons Worcestershire sauce
- 1 tablespoon hot sauce
- 1 teaspoon salt
- 1 teaspoon pepper

1. For the Spice Rub and Pork Combine dry mustard, salt, sugar, pepper, paprika, and cayenne in bowl. Pat meat dry with paper towels and rub it evenly with spice mixture. Wrap meat in plastic wrap and let sit at room temperature for at least 1 hour or refrigerate up to 24 hours. (If refrigerated, let sit at room temperature for 1 hour before grilling.) Using 2 large pieces of heavy-duty aluminum foil, wrap soaked chips in 2 foil packets and cut several vent holes in tops.

2A. For a Charcoal Grill Open bottom vent completely. Light large chimney starter half filled with charcoal briquettes (3 quarts). When top coals are partially covered with ash, pour into steeply banked pile against 1 side of grill. Place wood chip packets on coals. Set cooking grate in place, cover, and open lid vent halfway. Heat grill until hot and wood chips are smoking, about 5 minutes.

2B. For a Gas Grill Place wood chip packets directly on primary burner. Turn all burners to high, cover, and heat grill until hot and wood chips are smoking, about 15 minutes. Turn primary burner to medium-high and turn other burner(s) off. (Adjust primary burner as needed to maintain grill temperature around 325 degrees.)

3. Clean and oil cooking grate. Place meat on cool side of grill. Cover (positioning lid vent over meat if using charcoal) and cook until pork has dark, rosy crust, about 2 hours. During final 20 minutes of grilling, adjust oven rack to lower-middle position and heat oven to 325 degrees.

4. For the Mustard Barbecue Sauce Whisk yellow mustard, sugar, vinegar, Worcestershire, hot sauce, salt, and pepper in bowl until smooth. Measure out ½ cup sauce and set aside for cooking, reserving remaining sauce for serving.

5. Transfer pork to roasting pan and brush evenly with sauce for cooking. Cover pan tightly with foil and roast pork in oven until fork slips easily in and out of meat, 2 to 3 hours.

6. Remove pork from oven and let rest, still covered with foil, for 30 minutes. When cool enough to handle, unwrap pork and pull meat into thin shreds, discarding excess fat and gristle. Toss pork with reserved sauce and serve.

Why This Recipe Works This regional recipe, nicknamed Carolina Gold, demands more than just a last-minute dose of bold flavors. A combination of grilling and oven roasting reduces the cooking time from all day to just four or five hours. We used a spice rub, which included dry mustard to jump-start the mustard flavor of the sauce. Most South Carolina barbecue sauce recipes use yellow mustard, which our tasters praised for its bright tang. Brushing the pork with the sauce before it went into the oven produced a second hit of mustard flavor; tossing the shredded pork with the remaining sauce gave the meat a final layer of mustard flavor.

TENNESSEE PULLED PORK SANDWICHES

SERVES 8 WITH LEFTOVERS

In step 8, shred the pork while it's still hot. Leftover pork can be refrigerated for up to three days.

Pork
- 1 (5- to 6-pound) bone-in pork butt roast, trimmed
- Kosher salt
- 2 cups wood chips
- 1 (13 by 9-inch) disposable aluminum roasting pan

Barbecue Sauce
- 1 cup ketchup
- ¼ cup cider vinegar
- ¼ cup water
- 2 tablespoons yellow mustard
- 1 tablespoon Worcestershire sauce
- 1 teaspoon granulated garlic
- 1 teaspoon pepper

- 1 recipe Hoecakes (page 359)
- Dill pickle chips
- Coleslaw

1. For the Pork Using sharp knife, cut 1-inch crosshatch pattern about ¼ inch deep in fat cap of roast, being careful not to cut into meat. Pat roast dry with paper towels. Place roast on large sheet of plastic wrap and rub 2 tablespoons salt over entire roast and into slits. Wrap tightly with plastic and refrigerate for 18 to 24 hours.

2. Just before grilling, soak wood chips in water for 15 minutes, then drain. Using large piece of heavy-duty aluminum foil, wrap soaked chips in foil packet and cut several vent holes in top.

3A. For a Charcoal Grill Open bottom vent completely. Light large chimney starter three-quarters filled with charcoal briquettes (4½ quarts). When top coals are partially covered with ash, pour evenly over half of grill. Place wood chip packet on coals. Set cooking grate in place, cover, and open lid vent completely. Heat grill until hot and wood chips are smoking, about 5 minutes.

3B. For a Gas Grill Remove cooking grate and place wood chip packet directly on primary burner. Set cooking grate in place, turn all burners to high, cover, and heat grill until hot and wood chips are smoking, about 15 minutes. Turn primary burner to medium-high and turn off other burner(s). (Adjust primary burner as needed to maintain grill temperature of 300 degrees.)

4. Unwrap pork and place fat side down in disposable pan. Place disposable pan on cooler side of grill. Cover grill (with lid vent directly over pork for charcoal) and cook until pork registers 120 degrees, about 2 hours. Thirty minutes before pork comes off grill, adjust oven rack to middle position and heat oven to 300 degrees.

5. Transfer disposable pan from grill to rimmed baking sheet. Cover pan tightly with foil and transfer to oven (still on sheet). Cook until fork inserted in pork meets little resistance and meat registers 210 degrees, about 3 hours.

6. For the Barbecue Sauce Meanwhile, combine all ingredients in medium saucepan and bring to boil over medium-high heat. Reduce heat to medium-low and simmer, whisking constantly, until slightly thickened, about 3 minutes. Transfer sauce to bowl and let cool completely.

7. Carefully remove foil from disposable pan (steam will escape). Remove blade bone from roast using tongs. Immediately transfer hot pork to bowl of stand mixer fitted with paddle attachment. Strain accumulated juices from pan through fine-mesh strainer set over separate bowl; discard solids.

8. Mix pork on low speed until meat is finely shredded, about 1½ minutes. Whisk pork juices to recombine, if separated, and add 1½ cups juices to shredded pork. Continue to mix pork on low speed until juices are incorporated, about 15 seconds longer. Season with salt to taste, adding more pork juices if desired. Serve pork on hoecakes with barbecue sauce, pickles, and coleslaw.

Why This Recipe Works Inspired by a central Tennessee sandwich of pulled pork on cornmeal griddle cakes called hoecakes, we wanted pork shredded so finely that it resembled pâté. A combination of grill smoking and oven roasting brought our meat to a higher temperature for a softer pork butt roast. Instead of hand-shredding the meat, we used a stand mixer fitted with a paddle attachment to handily get a superfine shred. To keep the meat moist, we returned some of the pork juices to the shredded meat and served our sandwich with barbecue sauce just like they do at Papa KayJoe's (see "A 30-Year Journey to Pulled Pork Perfection," page 359).

Why This Recipe Works To fully recreate our Papa KayJoe's experience in Centerville, Tennessee, we felt obligated to serve our Tennessee pulled pork on hoecakes. These cornmeal griddle cakes can be served on their own (with butter and syrup) or, in this case, as the perfect vehicle for a delicious barbecue sandwich. A loose batter with plenty of tangy buttermilk flavor gives the hoecakes a light texture, and the cornmeal makes them sturdy enough to hold up to a sandwich filling. Frying them in bacon fat adds a nice hit of smoky pork richness. Although our pulled pork is great on hamburger buns, we prefer to serve it on hoecakes.

HOECAKES

MAKES 16 HOECAKES

Papa KayJoe's makes their hoecakes with bacon fat.

- 3 cups (15 ounces) white cornmeal
- 2 tablespoons sugar
- 2 teaspoons baking powder
- 1½ teaspoons salt
- 2 cups buttermilk
- 2 large eggs
- 2 tablespoons bacon fat or vegetable oil

1. Adjust oven rack to middle position and heat oven to 200 degrees. Set wire rack in rimmed baking sheet and place in oven. Whisk cornmeal, sugar, baking powder, and salt together in large bowl. Beat buttermilk and eggs together in separate bowl. Whisk buttermilk mixture into cornmeal mixture until combined.

2A. For a Skillet Heat 1 teaspoon fat in 12-inch nonstick skillet over medium heat until shimmering. Using level ¼-cup dry measuring cup, drop 3 evenly spaced scoops of batter into skillet, smoothing tops slightly if necessary.

2B. For a Griddle Heat 1 tablespoon fat on 400-degree nonstick griddle until shimmering. Using level ¼-cup dry measuring cup, drop 8 evenly spaced scoops of batter onto griddle, smoothing tops slightly if necessary.

3. Cook until small bubbles begin to appear on surface of cakes and edges are set, about 2 minutes. Flip and cook until second side is golden brown, about 2 minutes longer. Transfer hoecakes to prepared sheet in oven. Repeat with remaining fat and batter: 5 additional batches for skillet or 1 additional batch for griddle. Serve.

A 30-Year Journey to Pulled Pork Perfection

Papa KayJoe's in Centerville, Tennessee, is a gray wooden building with a red tin roof at the end of a steep driveway. In the dining room, patrons tuck into Papa KayJoe's for their signature sandwiches—pulled pork on cornmeal griddle cakes—and share local news. Each morning owner Devin Pickard feeds armloads of hickory sticks into an outdoor furnace, where they slowly burn down to coals. Pickard then carries the hot embers to a nearby dirt-floored barbecue shack where a pair of cinder block pits sit waiting. At 11 a.m., Pickard lines up 24 heavily salted pork butts on the thick, black metal grate that sits over the pit and covers them with sheets of corrugated steel to trap the heat. The pork spends 6 to 8 hours on the grill, picking up the woodsy aroma of the smoldering hickory. After a day on the grill, the pork butts are packed into large aluminum roasting pans and transferred to a low oven where they'll spend the night. The next morning, Pickard slips on a pair of thick fireproof rubber gloves, picks out a pork butt, removes the blade bone and attacks the meat. In a clapping motion, he brings his fingertips together, pinching the pork; in less than a minute, the pork is in tiny shreds. He works in cupfuls of the juices that have accumulated in the roasting pan, moistening the pork with its own essence. Inside, Pickard's mother (Debbie) and daughter (Ruby) help pile the pork onto hot cornmeal griddle cakes (hoecakes) made to order with buttermilk and bacon fat. They'll produce dozens of these sandwiches today, and every day—including one for Pickard. "I would eat a barbecue sandwich every day of my life, that's how much I love it."

Why This Recipe Works Big chops demand big flavor. Soaking thick pork chops in a salt and sugar brine promised juicy, seasoned meat that would brown beautifully on the grill. For authentic Hill Country flavor, we applied a rub of kosher salt, pepper, onion powder, and granulated garlic and smoked the chops over mesquite chips. Before firing up the grill, we readied a kicked-up barbecue sauce, rendering strips of bacon and stirring in grated onion and cider vinegar for a pop of acidity; liquid smoke added extra flavor and hot sauce introduced some heat. Brushing the chops with some sauce before serving doubled down on the pork's smoky goodness.

TEXAS THICK-CUT SMOKED PORK CHOPS

SERVES 8

Each chop can easily serve two people. Grate the onion for the sauce on the large holes of a box grater. Our preferred hot sauce is Frank's RedHot Original Cayenne Pepper Sauce. If you'd like to use wood chunks instead of wood chips when using a charcoal grill, substitute two medium chunks, soaked in water for 1 hour, for the wood chip packet.

Pork
Kosher salt and pepper
3 tablespoons sugar
4 (18- to 20-ounce) bone-in pork rib chops, 2 inches thick
2 teaspoons onion powder
2 teaspoons granulated garlic
2 cups mesquite wood chips

Barbecue Sauce
2 slices bacon
¼ cup grated onion
Kosher salt and pepper
¾ cup cider vinegar
1¼ cups chicken broth
1 cup ketchup
2 tablespoons hot sauce
½ teaspoon liquid smoke

1. For the Pork Dissolve 6 tablespoons salt and sugar in 1½ quarts cold water in large container. Submerge chops in brine, cover, and refrigerate for 1 hour. Combine onion powder, granulated garlic, 1½ tablespoons salt, and 2 tablespoons pepper in bowl; set aside.

2. For the Barbecue Sauce Cook bacon in medium saucepan over medium heat until fat begins to render and bacon begins to brown, 4 to 6 minutes. Add onion and ¼ teaspoon salt and cook until softened, 2 to 4 minutes. Stir in vinegar, scraping up any browned bits, and cook until slightly thickened, about 2 minutes.

3. Stir in broth, ketchup, hot sauce, liquid smoke, and ¼ teaspoon pepper. Bring to simmer and cook until slightly thickened, about 15 minutes, stirring occasionally. Discard bacon and season with salt and pepper to taste. Remove from heat, cover, and keep warm.

4. Just before grilling, soak wood chips in water for 15 minutes, then drain. Using large piece of heavy-duty aluminum foil, wrap soaked chips in 8 by 4½-inch foil packet. (Make sure chips do not poke holes in sides or bottom of packet.) Cut 2 evenly spaced 2-inch slits in top of packet. Remove chops from brine and pat dry with paper towels. Season chops all over with reserved spice mixture.

5A. For a Charcoal Grill Open bottom vent completely. Light large chimney starter three-quarters filled with charcoal briquettes (4½ quarts). When top coals are partially covered with ash, pour evenly over half of grill. Place wood chip packet on coals. Set cooking grate in place, cover, and open lid vent completely. Heat grill until hot and wood chips are smoking, about 5 minutes.

5B. For a Gas Grill Remove cooking grate and place wood chip packet directly on primary burner. Set grate in place, turn all burners to high, cover, and heat grill until hot and wood chips are smoking, about 15 minutes. Leave primary burner on medium-high and turn off other burner(s). (Adjust primary burner as needed to maintain grill temperature around 325 degrees.)

6. Clean and oil cooking grate. Arrange chops on cooler side of grill with bone ends toward fire. Cook, covered (positioning lid vent over chops if using charcoal), until chops register 140 degrees, 45 to 50 minutes, flipping halfway through cooking.

7. Transfer chops to platter, tent with foil, and let rest for 10 minutes. Brush chops generously with warm sauce and serve, passing remaining sauce separately.

SMOKED DOUBLE-THICK PORK CHOPS

SERVES 6 TO 8

We prefer blade chops, which have more fat to prevent drying out on the grill, but leaner loin chops will also work. Two medium wood chunks, soaked in water for 1 hour, can be substituted for the wood chips on a charcoal grill. These chops are huge. You may want to slice the meat off the bone before serving.

- ¼ cup packed dark brown sugar
- 1 tablespoon ground fennel
- 1 tablespoon ground cumin
- 1 tablespoon ground coriander
- 1 tablespoon paprika
- 1 teaspoon salt
- 1 teaspoon pepper
- 4 (1¼- to 1½-pound) bone-in blade-cut pork chops, about 2 inches thick, trimmed
- 2 cups wood chips, soaked in water for 15 minutes and drained

1. Combine sugar, fennel, cumin, coriander, paprika, salt, and pepper in bowl. Pat pork chops dry with paper towels and rub them evenly with spice mixture. Wrap chops in plastic wrap and refrigerate for at least 1 hour or up to 24 hours. Using large piece of heavy-duty aluminum foil, wrap soaked chips in foil packet and cut several vent holes in top.

2A. For a Charcoal Grill Open bottom vent halfway. Light large chimney starter filled with charcoal briquettes (6 quarts). When top coals are partially covered with ash, pour into pile on 1 side of grill. Place wood chip packet on coals. Set cooking grate in place, cover, and open lid vent halfway. Heat grill until hot and wood chips are smoking, about 5 minutes.

2B. For a Gas Grill Place wood chip packet directly on primary burner. Turn all burners to high, cover, and heat grill until hot and wood chips are smoking, about 15 minutes. Turn primary burner to medium and turn other burner(s) off. (Adjust primary burner as needed to maintain grill temperature around 275 degrees.)

3. Clean and oil cooking grate. Place pork chops on cool side of grill with bone sides facing hot side of grill. Cover (positioning lid vent over pork if using charcoal) and cook until meat registers 145 degrees, 50 minutes to 1 hour. Slide chops directly over fire (hot side on gas grill) and cook, uncovered, until well browned, about 4 minutes, flipping chops halfway through grilling. Transfer to platter and let rest for 20 minutes. Serve.

Cutting Your Own Double-Thick Pork Chops

We like juicy blade-end chops that are at least 2 inches thick for our Smoked Double-Thick Pork Chops recipe. If you can't find them prepackaged at your grocery store, just buy a 4½- to 5-pound bone-in blade roast and cut it into 2-inch portions yourself. If cutting your own chops, ask your butcher or meat department manager if the chine bone (a part of the backbone) has been removed from the base of the roast—this thick bone can make carving difficult. If the chine bone has not been removed, ask the butcher to cut the chops for you.

Why This Recipe Works Most grilled double-thick pork chop recipes result in a charred exterior and raw meat, or gray meat that tastes steamed. We wanted our pork chops to have great taste and tenderness. Cooking our pork chops over indirect heat made for juicy and tender meat. We used wood chips on the grill to infuse the pork with a nice level of smoke flavor. Coating the double-thick pork chops with a rub of brown sugar and potent herbs and spices helped produce a flavorful crust, and quick grilling over hot coals at the end of cooking gave the crust a crisp texture and rich mahogany color.

Why This Recipe Works Usually, by the time thin-cut pork chops pick up char on the grill, the insides have dried out. To ensure that our pork chops would brown quickly, we partially froze them to eliminate excess moisture from the exterior. Salting them first prevented them from drying out and allowed us to skip brining. A combination of softened butter and brown sugar spread over the chops resulted in a flavorful golden-brown crust when they came off the grill. And a chive-mustard butter added even more flavor to the finished chops.

GRILLED THIN-CUT PORK CHOPS

SERVES 4 TO 6

To prevent the chops from curling, cut two slits about 2 inches apart through the fat around the outside of each raw chop.

- 6 bone-in rib or center-cut pork chops, about ½ inch thick, trimmed
- ¾ teaspoon salt
- 4 tablespoons unsalted butter, softened
- 1 teaspoon packed brown sugar
- ½ teaspoon pepper
- 1 teaspoon minced fresh chives
- ½ teaspoon Dijon mustard
- ½ teaspoon grated lemon zest

1. Set wire rack in rimmed baking sheet. Pat chops dry with paper towels. Cut 2 slits, about 2 inches apart, through outer layer of fat and silverskin on each chop. Rub chops with salt. Arrange on prepared rack and freeze until chops are firm, at least 30 minutes but no more than 1 hour. Combine 2 tablespoons butter, sugar, and pepper in small bowl; set aside. Mix remaining 2 tablespoons butter, chives, mustard, and zest in second small bowl and refrigerate until firm, about 15 minutes. (Butter-chive mixture can be refrigerated, covered, for 1 day.)

2A. For a Charcoal Grill Open bottom vent completely. Light large chimney starter filled with charcoal briquettes (6 quarts). When top coals are partially covered with ash, pour evenly over grill. Set cooking grate in place, cover, and open lid vent completely. Heat grill until hot, about 5 minutes.

2B. For a Gas Grill Turn all burners to high, cover, and heat grill until hot, about 15 minutes.

3. Pat chops dry with paper towels. Spread softened butter-sugar mixture evenly over both sides of each chop. Grill, covered, over hot fire until well browned and meat registers 145 degrees, 6 to 8 minutes, flipping chops halfway through grilling. Transfer chops to platter and top with chilled butter-chive mixture. Tent with aluminum foil and let rest for 5 minutes. Serve.

SPICY THAI GRILLED THIN-CUT PORK CHOPS
Substitute 1½ teaspoons Asian chili-garlic sauce, 1 teaspoon minced fresh cilantro, and ½ teaspoon grated lime zest for chives, mustard, and lemon zest.

CARIBBEAN GRILLED THIN-CUT PORK CHOPS
Substitute 1 teaspoon grated fresh ginger, ½ teaspoon minced fresh thyme, and ½ teaspoon grated orange zest for chives, mustard, and lemon zest.

MEDITERRANEAN GRILLED THIN-CUT PORK CHOPS
Substitute 1½ teaspoons black olive tapenade and ½ teaspoon minced fresh oregano for chives and mustard.

Thin Is the New Thick

For juicy, nicely charred chops, try our method: salting, freezing, and brushing with softened butter before grilling. Salting ensures juicy chops; freezing promotes crust formation by drying the exterior and adding valuable minutes to the cooking time; and butter accelerates browning and adds richness to the lean meat.

WOULD YOU EAT THIS? Grilled straight from the package, this chop is dry, pale, and bland.

NOW WE'RE TALKING Salted, frozen, buttered, then grilled, this chop is juicy, browned, and flavorful.

ST. LOUIS BBQ PORK STEAKS

SERVES 4

Boneless pork butt is also labeled Boston butt. If pork steaks are available, use them and increase the cooking time in the sauce to 1 to 1½ hours. We use Budweiser in this recipe, since it's made in St. Louis, but any mild-tasting beer will do.

Spice Rub and Pork Steaks
- 1 tablespoon packed brown sugar
- 1 tablespoon paprika
- 2 teaspoons dry mustard
- 2 teaspoons pepper
- 1 teaspoon onion powder
- 1 teaspoon garlic powder
- 1 teaspoon ground cumin
- 1 teaspoon salt
- ¼ teaspoon cayenne pepper
- 1 (5- to 6-pound) boneless pork butt roast, sliced crosswise, trimmed, and each half cut into three or four 1-inch-thick steaks

Barbecue Sauce
- 2 cups beer
- 1½ cups ketchup
- ¼ cup Heinz 57 Steak Sauce
- ¼ cup packed dark brown sugar
- 2 tablespoons cider vinegar
- 2 tablespoons Worcestershire sauce
- 1 teaspoon garlic powder
- 1 teaspoon hot sauce
- 1 teaspoon liquid smoke
- 1 (13 by 9-inch) disposable aluminum roasting pan

1. For the Spice Rub and Pork Steaks Combine sugar, paprika, dry mustard, pepper, onion powder, garlic powder, cumin, salt, and cayenne in bowl. Pat pork steaks dry with paper towels and rub them evenly with spice mixture. Wrap pork in plastic wrap and refrigerate for at least 1 hour or up to 24 hours.

2. For the Barbecue Sauce Whisk all ingredients together in bowl and transfer to disposable pan.

3A. For a Charcoal Grill Open bottom vent halfway. Light large chimney starter filled with charcoal briquettes (6 quarts). When top coals are partially covered with ash, pour evenly over grill. Set cooking grate in place, cover, and open lid vent halfway. Heat grill until hot, about 5 minutes.

3B. For a Gas Grill Turn all burners to high, cover, and heat grill until hot, about 15 minutes. Leave primary burner on high and turn other burner(s) off. (Adjust primary burner as needed to maintain grill temperature around 350 degrees.)

4. Clean and oil cooking grate. Place pork steaks on hot side of grill. Cook (covered if using gas) until well browned on both sides, about 10 minutes, flipping steaks halfway through grilling.

5. Transfer pork steaks to sauce in pan and coat thoroughly. Cover pan with aluminum foil and place on grill. Cover (positioning lid vent over pan if using charcoal) and cook steaks until fork-tender and they register 190 degrees, 45 minutes to 1 hour. Remove steaks from pan and grill until lightly charred around edges, 4 to 8 minutes, flipping steaks halfway through grilling.

6. Transfer steaks to serving platter, tent loosely with foil, and let rest for 10 minutes. Skim excess fat from sauce and serve with steaks.

Making Pork Steaks

1. Slice pork crosswise in half and remove any large pieces of fat.

2. Rotate and stand each half of pork butt on its cut end and cut each half into three or four 1-inch-thick steaks.

Why This Recipe Works St. Louis BBQ pork steaks are little-known in other parts of America, but in St. Louis, they are so popular that pork steaks are on permanent sale in family packs at the supermarket. We found there was no substitute for pork steak, so the only option was to cut our own. We ordered a boneless Boston butt and cut it in half crosswise, then turned each piece on end to slice 1-inch-thick steaks. Inspired by a test kitchen recipe for brats and beer, we used a method of sear, simmer, sear again. This untraditional process gives the steaks a nice char, candy-like edges, and succulent, slightly chewy interiors.

CHINESE-STYLE GLAZED PORK TENDERLOIN

SERVES 4 TO 6

Leftover pork makes an excellent addition to fried rice or noodle soup.

- 2 (12- to 16-ounce) pork tenderloins, trimmed
- ½ cup soy sauce
- ½ cup apricot preserves
- ¼ cup hoisin sauce
- ¼ cup dry sherry
- 2 tablespoons grated fresh ginger
- 1 tablespoon toasted sesame oil
- 2 garlic cloves, minced
- 1 teaspoon five-spice powder
- 1 teaspoon pepper
- ¼ cup ketchup
- 1 tablespoon molasses
- 2 teaspoons vegetable oil

1. Lay tenderloins on cutting board with long side running parallel to counter edge. Cut horizontally down length of each tenderloin, stopping ½ inch from edge so tenderloin remains intact. Working with one at a time, open up tenderloins, place between 2 sheets of plastic wrap, and pound to ¾-inch thickness.

2. Combine soy sauce, preserves, hoisin, sherry, ginger, sesame oil, garlic, five-spice powder, and pepper in bowl. Reserve ¾ cup marinade. Place pork in large zipper-lock bag and pour remaining marinade into bag with pork. Seal bag, turn to coat, and refrigerate for at least 30 minutes or up to 4 hours.

3. Combine reserved marinade, ketchup, and molasses in small saucepan. Cook over medium heat until syrupy and reduced to ¾ cup, 3 to 5 minutes. Reserve ¼ cup glaze for glazing cooked pork.

4A. For a Charcoal Grill Open bottom vent completely. Light large chimney starter filled with charcoal briquettes (6 quarts). When top coals are partially covered with ash, pour evenly over grill. Set cooking grate in place, cover, and open lid vent completely. Heat grill until hot, about 5 minutes.

4B. For a Gas Grill Turn all burners to high, cover, and heat grill until hot, about 15 minutes. Turn all burners to medium-high.

5. Clean and oil cooking grate. Pat pork dry with paper towels, then rub with vegetable oil. Grill pork (covered if using gas) until lightly charred on first side, about 2 minutes. Flip and brush grilled side of pork evenly with 2 tablespoons glaze. Continue grilling until lightly charred on second side, about 2 minutes. Flip and brush evenly with 2 more tablespoons glaze. Repeat flipping and glazing twice more, until pork registers 140 degrees and is thickly glazed, about 4 minutes longer. Transfer pork to cutting board and brush with reserved glaze. Tent loosely with aluminum foil and let rest for 5 minutes. Slice and serve.

Preparing the Tenderloins

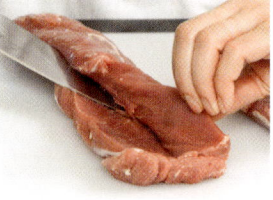 

1. Place tenderloins on cutting board and slice each down side, leaving ½ inch of meat uncut. Open each tenderloin like a book.

2. Place each butterflied tenderloin between two sheets of plastic wrap. Using meat pounder, pound each to ¾-inch thickness.

Why This Recipe Works For an easy take on Chinese-style glazed and charred pork, we turned to the grill and opted for pork tenderloin, which cooks quickly over a hot fire. Butterflying and pounding the meat gave us maximum surface area for our glaze. A combination of thick, sweet apricot preserves and ketchup flavored with hoisin, fresh ginger, sesame oil, sherry, garlic, and five-spice powder gave us a salty-sweet sauce that acted as both marinade and glaze. Continuously flipping and glazing the pork creates a charred, caramelized—but not burnt—exterior.

Why This Recipe Works We began our Chinese-Style Barbecue Spareribs by removing the tough membrane on the underside of the ribs. Instead of cooking the ribs on the grill the entire time, we found that cooking them in the sauce in the oven and then finishing them on the grill allowed for deeply seasoned Chinese-style ribs and eliminated the need to marinate them. Since the smoke from wood chips was overpowering, we replaced the wood chips with orange spice or Earl Grey tea bags soaked in water, wrapped in foil, and placed on the hot coals for a mellow, smoky flavor that complemented the Asian seasonings.

CHINESE-STYLE BARBECUED SPARERIBS

SERVES 6

Full-size spareribs are fatty, plus they're too large to fit on the grill. If you can't find St. Louis–style spareribs (which have been trimmed of the brisket bone and surrounding meat), substitute baby back ribs and begin to check for doneness after 1 hour on the grill. Cover the edges of the ribs loosely with foil if they begin to burn while grilling.

- 2 (2½ to 3 pound) racks St. Louis style spareribs, trimmed
- 8 black tea bags, preferably orange spice or Earl Grey
- 1½ cups ketchup
- 1 cup soy sauce
- 1 cup hoisin sauce
- 1 cup sugar
- ½ cup dry sherry
- 6 garlic cloves, minced
- 2 tablespoons grated fresh ginger
- 2 teaspoons toasted sesame oil
- 1½ teaspoons cayenne pepper
- 1 (13 by 9-inch) disposable aluminum roasting pan
- 1 cup red currant jelly

1. To remove chewy membrane from ribs, loosen it with tip of paring knife and, with aid of paper towel, pull it off slowly in 1 big piece. Cut rib racks in half. Cover tea bags with water in small bowl and soak for 5 minutes. Squeeze water from tea bags. Using large piece of heavy-duty aluminum foil, wrap tea bags in foil packet and cut several vent holes in top.

2. Adjust oven rack to middle position and heat oven to 300 degrees. Whisk 1 cup ketchup, soy sauce, hoisin sauce, sugar, sherry, garlic, ginger, sesame oil, and cayenne in large bowl; reserve ½ cup for glaze. Arrange ribs, meaty side down, in disposable pan and pour remaining ketchup mixture over ribs. Cover pan tightly with foil and cook until fat has rendered and meat begins to pull away from bones, 2 to 2½ hours. Transfer ribs to large plate. Pour pan juices into fat separator. Let liquid settle and reserve 1 cup defatted pan juices.

3. Simmer reserved pan juices in medium saucepan over medium-high heat until reduced to ½ cup, about 5 minutes. Stir in jelly, reserved ketchup mixture, and remaining ½ cup ketchup and simmer until reduced to 2 cups, 10 to 12 minutes. Reserve one-third of glaze for serving.

4A. For a Charcoal Grill Open bottom vent completely. Light large chimney starter filled with charcoal briquettes (6 quarts). When top coals are partially covered with ash, pour evenly over half of grill. Place tea packet on coals. Set cooking grate in place, cover, and open lid vent completely. Heat grill until hot and tea is smoking, about 5 minutes.

4B. For a Gas Grill Place tea packet directly on primary burner. Turn all burners to high, cover, and heat grill until hot and tea is smoking, about 15 minutes. Leave primary burner on high and turn other burner(s) off.

5. Clean and oil cooking grate. Arrange ribs, meaty side down, on cool side of grill and cook, covered, until ribs are smoky and edges begin to char, about 30 minutes.

6. Brush ribs with glaze, flip, rotate, and brush again. Cover and cook, brushing with glaze every 30 minutes, until ribs are fully tender and glaze is browned and sticky, 1 to 1½ hours. Transfer ribs to cutting board, tent with foil, and let rest for 10 minutes. Serve with reserved glaze.

To Make Ahead Ribs and glaze can be prepared through step 3 up to 2 days in advance. Once ribs are cool, wrap tightly in foil and refrigerate. Transfer glaze to microwave-safe bowl, cover with plastic wrap, and refrigerate. Before proceeding with step 4, allow ribs to stand at room temperature for 1 hour. Before proceeding with step 6, microwave glaze until warm, about 1 minute.

Why This Recipe Works Boneless country-style ribs present several cooking challenges. Each piece not only varies wildly from the next, but is also a mishmash of lean white meat and rich dark meat. Unfortunately, if the ribs are cooked to optimize the white meat, then the dark meat stays tough, and if they are cooked to optimize the dark meat, the white meat turns dry. To even out the cooking, we brined the ribs so that the white meat would stay juicy and pounded the ribs to an even ¾-inch thickness to "break down" the fattier dark meat. As for flavor, a double layer of barbecue spice and sauce and a quick smoke on the grill worked wonders.

BARBECUED COUNTRY-STYLE RIBS

SERVES 4 TO 6

For easier pounding, cut any ribs that are longer than 5 inches in half crosswise.

- 1 tablespoon salt
- 2 pounds boneless country-style pork ribs, trimmed
- ¾ cup packed dark brown sugar
- 2 tablespoons chili powder
- 2 tablespoons paprika
- 1 tablespoon dry mustard
- 1 tablespoon onion powder
- ¾ teaspoon pepper
- ¼ teaspoon cayenne pepper
- 6 tablespoons ketchup
- 1 tablespoon cider vinegar
- ¼ cup wood chips, soaked in water for 15 minutes and drained

1. Dissolve salt in 2 cups cold water in large container. Place ribs, cut side down, between 2 sheets of plastic wrap and pound to ¾ inch thickness. Submerge pork in brine, cover, and refrigerate for 30 minutes to 1 hour.

2. Combine sugar, chili powder, paprika, dry mustard, onion powder, pepper, and cayenne in shallow dish. Transfer half of mixture to bowl and stir in ketchup and vinegar; set aside.

3. Remove pork from brine and pat dry with paper towels. Dredge pork in remaining spice mixture and transfer to plate. Using large piece of heavy-duty aluminum foil, wrap soaked chips in foil packet and cut several vent holes in top.

4A. For a Charcoal Grill Open bottom vent halfway. Light large chimney starter filled with charcoal briquettes (6 quarts). When top coals are partially covered with ash, pour evenly over half of grill. Place wood chip packet on coals. Set cooking grate in place, cover, and open lid vent halfway. Heat grill until hot and wood chips are smoking, about 5 minutes.

4B. For a Gas Grill Place wood chip packet directly on primary burner. Turn all burners to high, cover, and heat grill until hot and wood chips are smoking, about 15 minutes. Leave primary burner on high and turn other burner(s) off.

5. Clean and oil cooking grate. Place pork on cool side of grill, cover (positioning lid vent over meat if using charcoal), and cook until meat registers 125 degrees, 3 to 5 minutes. Brush pork with ketchup mixture and grill, brushed side down, over hot side of grill until lightly charred, 2 to 3 minutes. Brush second side of pork, flip, and grill until lightly charred and meat registers 145 degrees, 2 to 3 minutes. Transfer pork to platter, tent loosely with foil, and let rest for 5 to 10 minutes. Serve.

Country-Style Ribs

Country-style ribs aren't ribs at all. They're well-marbled pork chops cut from the blade end of the loin. We bought dozens of these chops while testing this recipe and found that they were inconsistently shaped and sized. What's more, these "ribs" had widely varying proportions of light and dark meat. To help level the culinary playing field and ensure even cooking, we pounded each piece into an even ¾ inch thickness.

MISMATCHED MEAT
Each "rib" contains both light and dark meat.

Ensuring Even Cooking

The white and dark meat in country-style ribs cook at different rates—the white meat cooks quickly, while the dark meat is slower to tenderize. To equalize them, we brined and pounded. Brining kept the white meat from drying out, while pounding the ribs thin let them cook faster, helpful since long cooking times accentuate differences in cooking. Think of a fast car and a slow car starting from a stoplight at the same time: 30 seconds after the light turns green, the two cars won't be far apart, but after 10 minutes, they will be.

SOUTH DAKOTA CORNCOB-SMOKED RIBS

SERVES 4 TO 6

A gas grill can't do these corncob ribs justice, so please use charcoal. The test kitchen's favorite ketchup is Heinz Organic. To use up some of the leftover corn, try our recipe for Sweet Corn Spoonbread (page 230).

Sauce
- 1 cup ketchup
- ¼ cup water
- 1 tablespoon pepper
- 1 tablespoon onion powder
- 1 tablespoon Worcestershire sauce
- 1 tablespoon light corn syrup
- 1 tablespoon granulated garlic
- 2 teaspoons celery seeds
- ½ teaspoon liquid smoke

Ribs
- 5 tablespoons packed light brown sugar
- 1 teaspoon salt
- ½ teaspoon pepper
- 2 (2½- to 3-pound) racks baby back pork ribs, trimmed and membrane removed
- 1 cup cornmeal
- 6 corncobs, kernels removed and reserved for another use
- 1 (13 by 9-inch) disposable aluminum roasting pan

1. For the Sauce Whisk all ingredients together in medium bowl; set aside.

2. For the Ribs Combine sugar, salt, and pepper in bowl. Pat ribs dry with paper towels and rub with sugar mixture; set aside. Using large piece of heavy-duty aluminum foil, wrap cornmeal in foil packet and cut several vent holes in top.

3. Open bottom vents of charcoal grill halfway. Place disposable pan on 1 side of grill and fill pan with 2 quarts water. Arrange 3 quarts unlit charcoal briquettes on opposite side of grill. Place cobs on top of unlit briquettes. Light large chimney starter filled halfway with charcoal briquettes (3 quarts). When top coals are partially covered with ash, pour over cobs and unlit briquettes. Place cornmeal packet on coals. Set cooking grate in place, cover, and open lid vent halfway. Heat grill until hot and cornmeal is smoking, about 5 minutes.

4. Clean and oil cooking grate. Place ribs, meat side up, on cool part of grill opposite coals. Cover, positioning lid vent over ribs, and cook until ribs are deep red and tender, 3½ to 4 hours, rotating and switching ribs every hour. (Do not flip ribs.) During last 30 minutes of cooking, baste ribs every 10 minutes, rotating and switching ribs each time. Transfer ribs to carving board, tent loosely with foil, and let rest for 15 to 20 minutes. Cut ribs in between bones. Serve, passing remaining sauce separately.

Failed Corncob Tests

In South Dakota, bushels of dried, stripped corncobs impart a special flavor to ribs. To replicate it, we left no kernel unturned. It was A for effort, but these attempts were a bust.

SOOTY Unhusked ears of corn. | **SOOTY** Husked ears with the corn intact. | **TOO MUCH WORK** Husked, stripped, and oven-dried. | **BURNT TASTE** Popped popcorn.

Why This Recipe Works Corncob-smoking, a South Dakota specialty, may seem odd, but it gives meat a subtle smokiness hardwoods can't match. For barbecued ribs with mild, nutty sweetness, but without the complicated barbecuing rig, we layered charcoal on our grill with fresh corncobs (with the kernels removed) and a foil packet of cornmeal. The cornmeal gave the ribs an initial blast of smoky flavor, and the fresh cobs offered long-lasting smoke and a nutty aroma. We basted the ribs with a simple ketchup-based barbecue sauce with plenty of garlic and some celery seeds for sticky, sweet ribs that we couldn't get enough of.

Why This Recipe Works Two surefire ways to dress up a pork roast are to give it a flavorful, deeply caramelized crust on the grill and serve it with a savory-sweet mustard glaze. Our mustard-glazed pork loin has the best of both worlds. Leaving our roast untrimmed added moisture and flavor—and scoring the fat kept it from tasting too fatty. For the mustard glaze, apple jelly was a perfect complement to the spicy crunch of grainy mustard, and both married well with the other glaze ingredients—brown sugar, garlic, and fresh thyme. To fully infuse our pork loin with mustard flavor, we applied the glaze before, during, and after grilling.

GRILLED MUSTARD-GLAZED PORK LOIN

SERVES 6 TO 8

Dijon and yellow mustards also work well in the glaze, but make certain to use apple jelly, not apple butter. Look for a pork roast with about ¼ inch of fat on top and tie the roast at 1-inch intervals to ensure an even shape.

- ½ cup whole-grain mustard
- 6 tablespoons apple jelly
- 2 tablespoons packed dark brown sugar
- 2 tablespoons extra-virgin olive oil
- 1 large garlic clove, minced
- 2 teaspoons minced fresh thyme
- ¾ teaspoon pepper
- ½ teaspoon salt
- 1 boneless pork loin roast (2½ to 3 pounds), fat scored lightly, tied at 1-inch intervals

1. Whisk mustard, jelly, sugar, oil, garlic, thyme, pepper, and salt together in bowl. Measure out ⅔ cup sauce and set aside for cooking; reserve remaining sauce for serving. Before grilling, pat pork loin dry with paper towels and coat it evenly with ⅓ cup sauce for cooking.

2A. For a Charcoal Grill Open bottom vent halfway. Light large chimney starter filled with charcoal briquettes (6 quarts). When top coals are partially covered with ash, pour evenly over half of grill. Set cooking grate in place, cover, and open lid vent halfway. Heat grill until hot, about 5 minutes.

2B. For a Gas Grill Turn all the burners to high, cover, and heat grill until hot, about 15 minutes. Leave primary burner on high and turn other burner(s) off. (Adjust primary burner as needed to maintain grill temperature around 350 degrees.)

3. Clean and oil cooking grate. Place pork loin on hot side of grill. Cook (covered if using gas) until well browned on all sides, 12 to 15 minutes, turning as needed.

4. Flip pork loin fat side up and slide to cool side of grill. Brush pork with 2 tablespoons sauce for cooking. Cover (positioning lid vent over pork if using charcoal) and continue to cook until meat registers 140 degrees, 25 to 40 minutes longer, brushing every 10 minutes with remaining sauce for cooking.

5. Transfer pork loin to carving board, tent loosely with aluminum foil, and let rest for 15 minutes. Remove twine, cut meat into ¼-inch-thick slices, and transfer to serving platter. Whisk any accumulated juices into reserved sauce, spoon over meat, and serve.

The Benefits of Scoring

Gently scoring the fat helps it render (basting the meat and keeping it moist as it cooks) and creates an uneven surface that holds the glaze.

WOOD-GRILLED SALMON

SERVES 4

Any variety of wood chips will work here, but aromatic woods such as cedar and alder give the most authentic flavor.

- 1½ teaspoons sugar
- ½ teaspoon salt
- ¼ teaspoon pepper
- 4 (6- to 8-ounce) skin-on salmon fillets, about 1¼ inches thick
- 1 tablespoon olive oil
- 2 cups wood chips, soaked in water for 15 minutes and drained

1. Combine sugar, salt, and pepper in bowl. Pat salmon fillets dry with paper towels, then brush flesh sides with oil and rub evenly with sugar mixture. Using 4 large sheets of heavy-duty aluminum foil, crimp edges of each sheet to make 4 trays, each measuring 7 by 5 inches. Perforate bottom of each tray with tip of paring knife. Divide wood chips among trays and lay 1 fillet skin side down on top of wood chips in each tray.

2A. For a Charcoal Grill Open bottom vent completely. Light large chimney starter filled with charcoal briquettes (6 quarts). When top coals are partially covered with ash, pour evenly over grill. Set cooking grate in place, cover, and open lid vent completely. Heat grill until hot, about 5 minutes.

2B. For a Gas Grill Turn all burners to high, cover, and heat grill until hot, about 15 minutes.

3. Clean and oil cooking grate. Place trays on grill. Cook (covered if using gas) until center is still translucent when checked with tip of paring knife and registers 125 degrees (for medium-rare), about 10 minutes.

4. Transfer trays to wire rack, tent loosely with foil, and let rest for 5 minutes. Slide metal spatula between skin and flesh of fish, transfer fish to platter, and serve.

BARBECUED WOOD-GRILLED SALMON
Add ¾ teaspoon chili powder and ¼ teaspoon cayenne pepper to sugar mixture and substitute 1 tablespoon Dijon mustard mixed with 1 tablespoon maple syrup for oil in step 1.

LEMON-THYME WOOD-GRILLED SALMON
Add 2 teaspoons minced fresh thyme and 1½ teaspoons grated fresh lemon zest to sugar mixture and substitute 2 tablespoons Dijon mustard for oil in step 1.

An Easier Way to Planked Salmon
Cooking salmon on a cedar plank infuses it with gentle wood flavor rather than overwhelming smokiness. Here's how to get the same great taste, minus the mail-order plank.

1. Crimp 4 sheets of foil to make trays. Using paring knife, poke small slits in bottom of trays.

2. Place soaked wood chips in foil trays and arrange salmon skin side down directly on top of wood chips.

3. Once salmon is cooked, slide metal spatula between flesh and skin; fish should release easily.

Why This Recipe Works To create the flavor of cedar planks in our wood-grilled salmon (without having to mail-order them), we settled on wood chips and made individual aluminum foil trays to hold the chips and salmon. To prevent the salmon from sticking to the wood chips, we left the skin on, which easily separated from the cooked fish. Poking a few slits in the bottom of the foil allowed more heat to reach the wood chips, which caused them to release more of their woodsy—but not overly smoky—flavor. Coating each fillet with a thin layer of olive oil and a light sprinkling of granulated sugar produced a golden, mildly sweet exterior.

CEDAR-PLANKED SALMON WITH CUCUMBER-YOGURT SAUCE

SERVES 4

Be sure to buy an untreated cedar plank specifically intended for cooking. To ensure uniform pieces of fish, we prefer to purchase a whole center-cut salmon fillet and cut it into four equal pieces. Note that the seasoned fillets must be refrigerated for at least 1 hour before grilling. When preheating the cedar plank, you will know it's ready when it is just giving off wisps of smoke. It should not ignite. Serve with lemon wedges and our Cucumber-Yogurt Sauce (recipe follows).

- 1 (2-pound) center-cut, skinless salmon fillet, about 1½ inches thick
- 2 tablespoons packed brown sugar
- 1½ tablespoons kosher salt
- 1 tablespoon chopped fresh dill
- 1 teaspoon pepper
- 1 (16 by 7-inch) cedar plank
- 1 teaspoon vegetable oil
- Lemon wedges

1. Cut salmon crosswise into 4 equal fillets and pat dry with paper towels. Combine sugar, salt, dill, and pepper in bowl. Sprinkle salmon all over with sugar mixture, place on plate, and refrigerate, uncovered, for at least 1 hour or up to 24 hours. One hour before grilling, soak cedar plank in water for 1 hour (or according to manufacturer's directions).

2A. For a Charcoal Grill Open bottom vent completely. Light large chimney starter filled with charcoal briquettes (6 quarts). When top coals are partially covered with ash, pour evenly over grill. Set cooking grate in place. Place cedar plank in center of grill. Cover and open lid vent completely. Heat grill until plank is lightly smoking and crackling (it should not ignite), about 5 minutes.

2B. For a Gas Grill Place cedar plank in center of grill. Turn all burners to medium-low, cover, and heat grill until plank is smoking and crackling (it should not ignite), about 15 minutes. Leave all burners on medium-low. Adjust burners as needed to maintain grill temperature between 300 and 325 degrees.

3. Brush 1 side of salmon fillets with oil, then place oiled side down on plank. Cover grill and cook until center of salmon is translucent when checked with tip of paring knife and registers 125 degrees (for medium-rare), 12 to 15 minutes. Using tongs, transfer plank with salmon to baking sheet, tent with aluminum foil, and let rest for 5 minutes. Serve with lemon wedges.

CUCUMBER-YOGURT SAUCE
MAKES ABOUT ¾ CUP
A spoon makes easy work of removing the cucumber seeds. Using Greek yogurt here is key; don't substitute regular plain yogurt, or the sauce will be very watery.

- ½ cucumber, peeled, halved lengthwise, and seeded
- ½ cup plain whole-milk Greek yogurt
- 1 tablespoon extra-virgin olive oil
- 1 tablespoon chopped fresh mint
- 1 tablespoon chopped fresh dill
- 1 small garlic clove, minced
- ¼ teaspoon pepper
- ⅛ teaspoon salt

Shred cucumber on large holes of box grater. Combine yogurt, oil, mint, dill, garlic, pepper, salt, and shredded cucumber in bowl. Cover and refrigerate until chilled, about 20 minutes. Serve.

Why This Recipe Works Our smoky, succulent salmon is surprisingly easy to make. Grilling the delicate fish on a cedar plank prevented it from sticking to the grill and provided subtle smoky flavor while keeping the grill grates pristine. While the plank soaked in water, we seasoned the salmon with a simple "cure" of brown sugar, kosher salt, fresh dill, and pepper. We preheated the plank on the grill before adding the salmon to get just the right woodsy flavor that wouldn't overwhelm the fish. Opting for skinless fillets allowed just enough cedar flavor to permeate the salmon. A Greek yogurt–cucumber tzatziki sauce balanced the salmon's smoky richness.

Why This Recipe Works Salmon steaks are a common choice for grilling: Their bone and thickness make them a far sturdier cut than a fillet. But the steak's thickness can also work against it, making it difficult for the interior and exterior to finish cooking at the same time. We began by tucking the belly flaps in toward the center of the steak and tying them to create medallions that would cook evenly and be easily maneuvered. To make sure our steaks were packed with flavor, we finished cooking them in a pan of zesty sauce on the cooler part of the grill. When they were done, our salmon steaks were flavorful, juicy, and moist.

GRILLED SALMON STEAKS WITH LEMON-CAPER SAUCE

SERVES 4

Before eating, lift out the small circular bone from the center of each steak.

- 4 (10-ounce) salmon steaks, 1 to 1½ inches thick
- Salt and pepper
- 2 tablespoons olive oil
- 1 teaspoon grated lemon zest and 6 tablespoons juice (2 lemons)
- 1 shallot, minced
- 3 tablespoons unsalted butter, cut into 3 pieces
- 1 tablespoon capers, rinsed
- 2 tablespoons minced fresh parsley
- 1 (13 by 9-inch) disposable aluminum pan

1. Pat salmon steaks dry with paper towels. Working with 1 steak at a time, carefully trim 1½ inches of skin from 1 tail. Tightly wrap other tail around skinned portion and tie steaks with kitchen twine. Repeat with remaining salmon steaks. Season salmon steaks with salt and pepper and brush both sides with oil. Combine lemon zest, lemon juice, shallot, butter, capers, and ⅛ teaspoon salt in disposable pan.

2A. For a Charcoal Grill Open bottom vent completely. Light large chimney starter filled with charcoal briquettes (6 quarts). When top coals are partially covered with ash, pour evenly over half of grill. Set cooking grate in place, cover, and open lid vent completely. Heat grill until hot, about 5 minutes.

2B. For a Gas Grill Turn all burners to high, cover, and heat grill until hot, about 15 minutes. Leave primary burner on high and turn off other burner(s).

3. Clean and oil cooking grate. Place salmon medallions on hot part of grill. Cook until browned, 2 to 3 minutes per side. Meanwhile, set pan on cool part of grill and cook until butter has melted, about 2 minutes. Transfer medallions to pan and gently turn to coat. Cook (covered if using gas) until center is still translucent when checked with tip of paring knife and registers 125 degrees (for medium-rare), 6 to 14 minutes, flipping salmon and rotating pan halfway through grilling. Remove twine and transfer salmon to platter. Off heat, whisk parsley into sauce and drizzle sauce over salmon. Serve.

Prepping Salmon Medallions

1. For salmon steaks sturdy enough to grill easily, remove 1½ inches of skin from one tail of each steak.

2. Tuck skinned portion into center of steak, wrap other tail around it, and tie with kitchen twine.

Why This Recipe Works We wanted tender, juicy, shrimp with a smoky, charred crust and chile flavor that was more than just superficial. To achieve this, we sprinkled one side of the shrimp with sugar to promote browning and cooked the shrimp sugar side down over the hot side of the grill for a few minutes. We then flipped the skewers to gently finish cooking on the cool side of the grill. Creating a flavorful marinade that doubled as a sauce gave our shrimp skewers a spicy, assertive kick. And butterflying the shrimp before marinating and grilling them opened up more shrimp flesh for the marinade and finishing sauce to flavor.

GRILLED JALAPEÑO AND LIME SHRIMP SKEWERS

SERVES 4

We prefer flat metal skewers that are at least 14 inches long for this recipe.

Marinade
- 1–2 jalapeño chiles, stemmed, seeded, and chopped
- 3 tablespoons olive oil
- 6 garlic cloves, minced
- 1 teaspoon grated lime zest plus 5 tablespoons juice (3 limes)
- ½ teaspoon ground cumin
- ¼ teaspoon cayenne pepper
- ½ teaspoon salt

Shrimp
- 1½ pounds extra-large shrimp (21 to 25 per pound), peeled and deveined
- ½ teaspoon sugar
- 1 tablespoon minced fresh cilantro

1. For the Marinade Process all ingredients in food processor until smooth, about 15 seconds. Reserve 2 tablespoons marinade; transfer remaining marinade to medium bowl.

2. For the Shrimp Pat shrimp dry with paper towels. To butterfly shrimp, use paring knife to make shallow cut down outside curve of shrimp. Add shrimp to bowl with marinade and toss to coat. Cover and refrigerate for 30 minutes to 1 hour.

3A. For a Charcoal Grill Open bottom vent completely. Light large chimney starter filled with charcoal briquettes (6 quarts). When top coals are partially covered with ash, pour evenly over half of grill. Set cooking grate in place, cover, and open lid vent completely. Heat grill until hot, about 5 minutes.

3B. For a Gas Grill Turn all burners to high, cover, and heat grill until hot, about 15 minutes.

4. Clean and oil cooking grate. Thread marinated shrimp on skewers. (Alternate direction of each shrimp as you pack them tightly on skewer to allow about a dozen shrimp to fit snugly on each skewer.) Sprinkle 1 side of skewered shrimp with sugar. Grill shrimp, sugared side down, over hot side of grill (covered if using gas), until lightly charred, 3 to 4 minutes. Flip skewers and move to cool side of grill (if using charcoal) or turn all burners off (if using gas), and cook, covered, until other side of shrimp is no longer translucent, 1 to 2 minutes. Using tongs, slide shrimp into clean medium bowl and toss with reserved marinade. Sprinkle with cilantro and serve.

GRILLED RED CHILE AND GINGER SHRIMP SKEWERS

Replace marinade with 1 to 3 seeded and chopped small red chiles (or jalapeños), 1 minced scallion, 3 tablespoons rice vinegar, 2 tablespoons soy sauce, 1 tablespoon toasted sesame oil, 1 tablespoon grated fresh ginger, 2 teaspoons sugar, and 1 minced garlic clove. Prepare and grill shrimp as directed. Replace cilantro with 1 thinly sliced scallion and serve with lime wedges.

GRILLED CARIBBEAN SHRIMP SKEWERS

Replace marinade with 1 to 2 seeded and chopped habanero or serrano chiles, ¼ cup pineapple juice, 2 tablespoons olive oil, 1 tablespoon white wine vinegar, 3 minced garlic cloves, 1 teaspoon grated fresh ginger, 1 teaspoon packed brown sugar, 1 teaspoon dried thyme, ½ teaspoon salt, and ¼ teaspoon ground allspice. Prepare and grill shrimp as directed. Replace cilantro with 1 tablespoon minced fresh parsley.

How to Skewer Shrimp

1. Make shallow cut down outside curve of shrimp to open up flesh.

2. Alternate direction of each shrimp as you pack them tightly on skewer.

HUSK-GRILLED CORN

SERVES 6

The flavored butter can be made ahead and refrigerated for up to three days; bring it to room temperature before using. Set up a cutting board and knife next to your grill to avoid traveling back and forth between the kitchen and grill.

- 6 ears corn (unshucked)
- 6 tablespoons unsalted butter, softened
- ½ teaspoon salt
- ½ teaspoon pepper

1. Cut and remove silk protruding from top of each ear of corn. Combine butter, salt, and pepper in bowl. Fold one 14 by 12-inch piece heavy-duty aluminum foil in half to create 7 by 12-inch rectangle; then crimp into boat shape long and wide enough to accommodate 1 ear of corn. Transfer butter mixture to prepared foil boat.

2A. For a Charcoal Grill Open bottom vent completely. Light large chimney starter mounded with charcoal briquettes (7 quarts). When top coals are partially covered with ash, pour evenly over half of grill. Set cooking grate in place, cover, and open lid vent completely. Heat grill until hot, about 5 minutes.

2B. For a Gas Grill Turn all burners to high, cover, and heat grill until hot, about 15 minutes.

3. Clean and oil grate. Place corn on grill (over coals, with stem ends facing cooler side of grill, for charcoal). Cover and cook, turning corn every 3 minutes, until husks have blackened all over, 12 to 15 minutes. (To check for doneness, carefully peel down small portion of husk. If corn is steaming and bright yellow, it is ready.) Transfer corn to cutting board. Using chef's knife, cut base from corn. Using dish towel to hold corn, peel away and discard husk and silk with tongs.

4. Roll each ear of corn in butter mixture to coat lightly and return to grill (over coals for charcoal). Cook, turning as needed to char corn lightly on each side, about 5 minutes total. Remove corn from grill and roll each ear again in butter mixture. Transfer corn to platter. Serve, passing any remaining butter mixture.

HUSK-GRILLED CORN WITH MUSTARD-PAPRIKA BUTTER

Stir 2 tablespoons spicy brown mustard and 1 teaspoon smoked paprika into butter mixture in step 1.

HUSK-GRILLED CORN WITH CILANTRO-LIME BUTTER

Stir ¼ cup minced fresh cilantro, 2 teaspoons grated lime zest plus 1 tablespoon juice, and 1 minced small garlic clove into butter mixture in step 1.

HUSK-GRILLED CORN WITH ROSEMARY-PEPPER BUTTER

Increase pepper to 1 teaspoon. Stir 1 tablespoon minced fresh rosemary and 1 minced small garlic clove into butter mixture in step 1.

HUSK-GRILLED CORN WITH BROWN SUGAR-CAYENNE BUTTER

Stir 2 tablespoons packed brown sugar and ¼ teaspoon cayenne pepper into butter mixture in step 1.

Why This Recipe Works Corn is the perfect vegetable to grill because its sweet flavor loves a smoky accent and it's large enough not to fall through the grate. But grilled corn seldom tastes as good as it sounds. Our goal was to prevent the corn from drying out while achieving a classic char. To keep the kernels moist, we found that initially cooking the ears of corn within their husks worked best. We then shucked the hot corn, rolled the ears in seasoned butter, and returned them to the grill to caramelize. This way, the kernels achieved a good char but weren't on the grill long enough to dry out. One last roll in the butter and our corn was ready.

Why This Recipe Works Grilling corn sounds like a simple proposition—but our research found dozens of variations on the cooking method for this classic summer vegetable. For a recipe that produced corn with a distinctly grilled taste and lightly charred kernels, we grilled the corn unhusked. The grill imparted great flavor to our grilled corn, but also made the kernels tough and dry. To avoid this, we soaked the husked corn in salted water before grilling, which kept the kernels moist and seasoned them as well.

GRILLED CORN ON THE COB

SERVES 4 TO 6

If your corn isn't as sweet as you'd like, stir ½ cup of sugar into the water along with the salt. Avoid soaking the corn for more than 8 hours, or it will become overly salty.

- Salt and pepper
- 8 ears corn, husks and silks removed
- 8 tablespoons unsalted butter, softened, or 1 recipe flavored butter (recipes follow)

1. In large pot, stir ½ cup salt into 4 quarts cold water until dissolved. Add corn and let soak for at least 30 minutes or up to 8 hours.

2A. For a Charcoal Grill Open bottom vent completely. Light large chimney starter filled with charcoal briquettes (6 quarts). When top coals are partially covered with ash, pour evenly over grill. Set cooking grate in place, cover, and open lid vent completely. Heat grill until hot, about 5 minutes.

2B. For a Gas Grill Turn all burners to high, cover, and heat grill until hot, about 15 minutes.

3. Clean and oil cooking grate. Grill corn, turning every 2 to 3 minutes, until kernels are lightly charred all over, 10 to 14 minutes. Remove corn from grill, brush with softened butter, and season with salt and pepper. Serve.

CHESAPEAKE BAY BUTTER
MAKES ABOUT ½ CUP

Using fork, beat 8 tablespoons softened, unsalted butter with 1 tablespoon hot sauce, 1 teaspoon Old Bay seasoning, and 1 minced garlic clove.

LATIN-SPICED BUTTER
MAKES ABOUT ½ CUP

Using fork, beat 8 tablespoons softened, unsalted butter with 1 teaspoon chili powder, ½ teaspoon ground cumin, ½ teaspoon grated lime zest, and 1 minced garlic clove. (Sprinkle cobs with ½ cup grated Parmesan, if desired.)

BASIL PESTO BUTTER
MAKES ABOUT ½ CUP

Using fork, beat 8 tablespoons softened, unsalted butter with 1 tablespoon basil pesto and 1 teaspoon lemon juice.

BARBECUE-SCALLION BUTTER
MAKES ABOUT ½ CUP

Using fork, beat 8 tablespoons softened, unsalted butter with 2 tablespoons barbecue sauce and 1 minced scallion.

A Good Soak

The grill imparts great flavor but can make corn tough and dry. Soaking the husked corn in salted water keeps the kernels moist and seasons them, too.

Why This Recipe Works For a standout backyard barbecue side, we turned canned beans into a savory showstopper. Baked beans gave us an easy starting point, and mixing in pinto and cannellini beans built a multifaceted bean base. We boosted the beans' flavor with an easy pantry sauce made with cider vinegar, granulated garlic, cayenne, and liquid smoke for that off-the-grill flavor. Browned bratwurst gave the sauce some meaty heft. We stirred the beans into this rich mixture, arranged bite-size pieces of bacon over the surface, and baked, allowing the bacon to render, crisp, and infuse the dish with its smoky flavor.

BACKYARD BARBECUE BEANS

SERVES 12 TO 16

Be sure to use a 13 by 9-inch metal baking pan; the volume of the beans is too great for a 13 by 9-inch ceramic baking dish, and it will overflow. We found that Bush's Original Recipe Baked Beans are the most consistent product for this recipe. Our favorite supermarket barbecue sauce is Bull's-Eye Original Barbecue Sauce.

- ½ cup barbecue sauce
- ½ cup ketchup
- ½ cup water
- 2 tablespoons spicy brown mustard
- 2 tablespoons cider vinegar
- 1 teaspoon liquid smoke
- 1 teaspoon granulated garlic
- ¼ teaspoon cayenne pepper
- 1¼ pounds bratwurst, casings removed
- 2 onions, chopped
- 2 (28-ounce) cans baked beans
- 2 (15-ounce) cans pinto beans, drained
- 2 (15-ounce) cans cannellini beans, drained
- 1 (10-ounce) can Ro-Tel Original Diced Tomatoes and Green Chilies, drained
- 6 slices thick-cut bacon, cut into 1-inch pieces

1. Adjust oven rack to middle position and heat oven to 350 degrees. Whisk barbecue sauce, ketchup, water, mustard, vinegar, liquid smoke, granulated garlic, and cayenne together in large bowl; set aside.

2. Cook bratwurst in 12-inch nonstick skillet over medium-high heat, breaking up into small pieces with spoon, until fat begins to render, about 5 minutes. Stir in onions and cook until sausage and onions are well browned, about 15 minutes.

3. Transfer bratwurst mixture to bowl with sauce. Stir in baked beans, pinto beans, cannellini beans, and tomatoes. Transfer bean mixture to 13 by 9-inch baking pan and place pan on rimmed baking sheet. Arrange bacon pieces in single layer over top of beans.

4. Bake until beans are bubbling and bacon is rendered, about 1½ hours. Let cool for 15 minutes. Serve.

To Make Ahead At end of step 3, beans can be wrapped in plastic and refrigerated for up to 24 hours. Proceed with recipe from step 4, increasing baking time to 1¾ hours.

Best for Baking

We tried several varieties of baked beans and found that firm, creamy **Bush's Original Recipe Baked Beans** held their shape best in this recipe. Plus, their meaty flavor is ideal for doctoring.

CALIFORNIA BARBECUED BEANS

SERVES 4 TO 6

If you can find them, pinquito beans (a variety grown in the Santa Maria Valley) are traditional in this dish. Bottled taco sauce is available in the Mexican aisle of most grocery stores. Don't add the tomato puree, taco sauce, brown sugar, and salt before the beans have simmered for an hour; they will hinder the proper softening of the beans.

- 4 slices bacon, chopped fine
- ½ pound deli ham, chopped fine
- 1 onion, chopped fine
- 4 garlic cloves, minced
- 1 pound pink kidney beans, soaked in 6 cups water overnight and drained
- 6 cups water
- 1 cup canned tomato puree
- ½ cup bottled taco sauce
- 5 tablespoons packed light brown sugar
- 1 tablespoon dry mustard
- Salt
- ¼ cup chopped fresh cilantro
- 2 tablespoons cider vinegar

1. Cook bacon and ham in Dutch oven over medium heat until fat renders and bacon and ham are lightly browned, 5 to 7 minutes. Add onion and cook until softened, about 5 minutes. Stir in garlic and cook until fragrant, about 30 seconds. Add beans and water and bring to simmer. Reduce heat to medium-low, cover, and cook until beans are just soft, about 1 hour.

2. Stir in tomato puree, taco sauce, sugar, dry mustard, and 2 teaspoons salt. Continue to simmer, uncovered, until beans are completely tender and sauce is thickened, about 1 hour. (If mixture becomes too thick, add water.) Stir in cilantro and vinegar and season with salt. Serve. (Beans can be refrigerated for up to 4 days.)

Sorting Dried Beans

It is important to rinse and pick over dried beans to remove any stones or debris before cooking. To make the task easier, sort dried beans on a large white plate or on a white, rimmed cutting board. The neutral background makes any unwanted matter a cinch to spot and discard.

Quick-Soaking Beans

If you don't want to soak the beans overnight, there is a faster way. Simply cover the beans with water in a Dutch oven, bring them to a boil over high heat, and let them boil for 5 minutes. Remove the beans from the heat and allow them to sit, covered, in the hot water for 1 hour. Drain the beans and proceed with the recipe as directed. The quick-soaked beans taste just as good as beans that are soaked overnight.

Why This Recipe Works California barbecued beans recipes use a bean variety and chili sauce rarely found outside of California. We wanted to re-create this recipe with nationally available supermarket ingredients. Pink kidney beans proved to be a good stand-in for the hard-to-find pinquito beans. Some recipes suggest using jarred taco sauce alone if the original recipe's requisite red chili sauce can't be found, but we found its taste and texture too thin. Instead, augmenting the sauce with a combination of fried bacon, ham, onion, and garlic with tomato puree, brown sugar, and dry mustard perfectly captured the chili sauce's bite.

GRILLED POTATO HOBO PACKS

SERVES 4

To keep the packs from tearing, use heavy-duty aluminum foil or two layers of regular foil. Also, scrape the cooking grate clean before grilling.

- 2 pounds Yukon Gold potatoes (about 3 large), scrubbed
- 1 tablespoon olive oil
- 2 garlic cloves, peeled and chopped
- 1 teaspoon minced fresh thyme
- 1 teaspoon salt
- ½ teaspoon pepper

1. Cut each potato in half crosswise, then cut each half into 8 wedges. Place potatoes in large bowl and wrap tightly with plastic wrap. Microwave until edges of potatoes are translucent, 4 to 7 minutes, shaking bowl (without removing plastic) to redistribute potatoes halfway through cooking. Carefully remove plastic and drain well. Gently toss potatoes with oil, garlic, thyme, salt, and pepper.

2. Cut four 14 by 10-inch sheets of heavy-duty aluminum foil. Working with 1 at a time, spread one-quarter of potato mixture over half of foil, fold foil over potatoes, and crimp edges tightly to seal.

3A. For a Charcoal Grill Open bottom vent completely. Light large chimney starter filled with charcoal briquettes (6 quarts). When top coals are partially covered with ash, pour evenly over grill. Set cooking grate in place, cover, and open lid vent completely. Heat grill until hot, about 5 minutes.

3B. For a Gas Grill Turn all burners to medium-high, cover, and heat grill until hot, about 15 minutes.

4. Grill hobo packs over hot fire, covered, until potatoes are completely tender, about 10 minutes, flipping packs halfway through cooking. Cut open foil and serve.

SPANISH-STYLE GRILLED POTATO HOBO PACKS
Prepare Grilled Potato Hobo Packs, adding 6 ounces thinly sliced cured chorizo sausage, 1 seeded and chopped red bell pepper, and 1 teaspoon paprika to cooked potatoes as they are tossed in step 1.

VINEGAR AND ONION GRILLED POTATO HOBO PACKS
Prepare Grilled Potato Hobo Packs, microwaving 1 halved and thinly sliced small onion with potatoes in step 1. Add 2 tablespoons white wine or red wine vinegar to cooked potatoes as they are tossed in step 1.

SPICY HOME FRY GRILLED POTATO HOBO PACKS
Prepare Grilled Potato Hobo Packs, omitting chopped garlic. Add 1 teaspoon paprika, ½ teaspoon garlic powder, ½ teaspoon onion powder, and ¼ teaspoon cayenne pepper to cooked potatoes as they are tossed in step 1.

Making Potato Hobo Packs

1. Microwave potatoes first to help them cook quickly on grill.

2. Arrange microwaved potatoes on foil, fold over, and crimp.

3. Flip packs halfway through grilling for evenly charred potatoes.

Why This Recipe Works We wanted to rescue this campfire classic, which too often results in unevenly cooked spuds. After multiple tests, we found that Yukon Golds were preferred to starchy, mealy russets and "slippery" red potatoes. To ensure evenly grilled potatoes, we cut them into evenly sized wedges and microwaved them for a few minutes before grilling them. Tossing the potatoes with a little oil prevented them from sticking to the foil.

Why This Recipe Works Steaming or sautéing broccoli is fine, but if you want vivid green florets with flavorful char, there's no beating the grill. To avoid toughness, we peeled the stalks with a vegetable peeler and cut the head into spears small enough to cook quickly but large enough to grill easily. Since grilling alone would yield dry broccoli, we tossed the spears in olive oil and water and steamed them in sealed foil packets on the grill. As soon as the stems and florets were evenly cooked, we placed them directly on the grill to give them plenty of char. A squeeze of grilled lemon and a sprinkling of Parmesan sealed the deal.

GRILLED BROCCOLI WITH LEMON AND PARMESAN

SERVES 4

To keep the packs from tearing, use heavy-duty aluminum foil. Use the large holes of a box grater to shred the Parmesan.

- ¼ cup extra-virgin olive oil, plus extra for drizzling
- 1 tablespoon water
- Salt and pepper
- 2 pounds broccoli
- 1 lemon, halved
- ¼ cup shredded Parmesan cheese

1. Cut two 26 by 12-inch sheets of heavy-duty aluminum foil. Whisk oil, water, ¾ teaspoon salt, and ½ teaspoon pepper together in large bowl.

2. Trim stalk ends so each entire head of broccoli measures 6 to 7 inches long. Using vegetable peeler, peel away tough outer layer of broccoli stalks (about ⅛ inch). Cut stalks in half lengthwise into spears (stems should be ½ to ¾ inch thick and florets 3 to 4 inches wide). Add broccoli spears to oil mixture and toss well to coat.

3. Divide broccoli between sheets of foil, cut side down and alternating direction of florets and stems. Bring short sides of foil together and crimp tightly. Crimp long ends to seal packs tightly.

4A. For a Charcoal Grill Open bottom vent completely. Light large chimney starter filled with charcoal briquettes (6 quarts). When top coals are partially covered with ash, pour evenly over half of grill. Set cooking grate in place, cover, and open lid vent completely. Heat grill until hot, about 5 minutes.

4B. For a Gas Grill Turn all burners to high, cover, and heat grill until hot, about 15 minutes. Turn all burners to medium-high. (Adjust burners as needed to maintain grill temperature around 400 degrees.)

5. Clean and oil cooking grate. Arrange packs evenly on grill (over coals if using charcoal), cover, and cook for 8 minutes, flipping packs halfway through cooking.

6. Transfer packs to rimmed baking sheet and, using scissors, carefully cut open, allowing steam to escape away from you. (Broccoli should be bright green and fork inserted into stems should meet some resistance.)

7. Discard foil and place broccoli and lemon halves cut side down on grill (over coals if using charcoal). Grill (covered if using gas), turning broccoli about every 2 minutes, until stems are fork-tender and well charred on all sides, 6 to 8 minutes total. Transfer broccoli to now-empty sheet as it finishes cooking. Grill lemon halves until well charred on cut side, 6 to 8 minutes.

8. Transfer broccoli to cutting board and cut into 2-inch pieces; transfer to platter. Season with salt and pepper to taste. Squeeze lemon over broccoli to taste, sprinkle with Parmesan, and drizzle with extra oil. Serve.

GRILLED BROCCOLI WITH ANCHOVY-GARLIC BUTTER

Omit lemon and Parmesan cheese. In step 1, whisk together 4 tablespoons melted unsalted butter, 3 rinsed and minced anchovy fillets, 1 minced garlic clove, 1 teaspoon lemon juice, ¼ teaspoon red pepper flakes, ½ teaspoon salt, and ⅛ teaspoon pepper. Set aside, then rewarm in step 8 and drizzle over broccoli before serving.

GRILLED BROCCOLI WITH SWEET CHILI SAUCE

Omit lemon and Parmesan cheese. In step 1, whisk together 4 teaspoons toasted sesame oil, 1 teaspoon distilled white vinegar, 2½ teaspoons sugar, 2 teaspoons Asian chili-garlic sauce, and ¼ teaspoon salt. Set aside, then drizzle over broccoli before serving.

GRILLED CAESAR SALAD

SERVES 6

Our favorite Parmesan cheese is Boar's Head Parmigiano-Reggiano.

Dressing
- 1 tablespoon lemon juice
- 1 garlic clove, minced
- ½ cup mayonnaise
- ½ ounce Parmesan cheese, grated (¼ cup)
- 1 tablespoon white wine vinegar
- 1 tablespoon Worcestershire sauce
- 1 tablespoon Dijon mustard
- 2 anchovy fillets, rinsed
- ½ teaspoon salt
- ½ teaspoon pepper
- ¼ cup extra-virgin olive oil

Salad
- 1 (12-inch) baguette, cut on bias into 5-inch-long, ½-inch-thick slices
- 3 tablespoons extra-virgin olive oil
- 1 garlic clove, peeled
- 3 romaine lettuce hearts (18 ounces), halved lengthwise through cores
- ½ ounce Parmesan cheese, grated (¼ cup)

1. For the Dressing Combine lemon juice and garlic in bowl and let stand for 10 minutes. Process mayonnaise, Parmesan, lemon-garlic mixture, vinegar, Worcestershire, mustard, anchovies, salt, and pepper in blender for about 30 seconds. With blender running, slowly add oil. Reserve 6 tablespoons dressing for brushing romaine.

2A. For a Charcoal Grill Open bottom vent completely. Light large chimney starter filled with charcoal briquettes (6 quarts). When top coals are partially covered with ash, pour evenly over half of grill. Set cooking grate in place, cover, and open lid vent completely. Heat grill until hot, about 5 minutes.

2B. For a Gas Grill Turn all burners to high, cover, and heat grill until hot, about 15 minutes. Leave all burners on high.

3. For the Salad Clean and oil cooking grate. Brush bread with oil and grill (over coals if using charcoal), uncovered, until browned, about 1 minute per side. Transfer to platter and rub with garlic clove. Brush cut sides of romaine with reserved dressing; place half of romaine, cut side down, on grill (over coals if using charcoal). Grill, uncovered, until lightly charred, 1 to 2 minutes. Move to platter with bread. Repeat. Drizzle romaine with remaining dressing. Sprinkle with Parmesan. Serve.

Salad Prep for Grilled Caesar
We get twice the flavor by using the dressing before and after grilling.

1. Brush homemade Caesar dressing onto halved romaine hearts before grilling.

2. Grill dressed romaine halves on just one side to keep lettuce from wilting.

3. Once charred lettuce comes off grill, finish with more Caesar dressing.

Why This Recipe Works Grilled salad may seem like an oxymoron, but we were intrigued by the idea of the flavors of a classic Caesar salad enriched with the smoky char of the grill. We found that compact romaine hearts held their shape better than whole heads. We halved them lengthwise to increase their surface area, making sure to keep the core intact so the leaves didn't fall apart on the grill. To prevent sticking, we brushed the leaves with dressing. Just 1 to 2 minutes over a hot grill gave us a smoky and charred (not wilted) exterior. To keep things simple, we replaced the croutons with slices of crusty bread grilled alongside the lettuce.

Why This Recipe Works We wanted to discover the secrets to tender cabbage, crunchy apples, and the sweet and spicy dressing that brings them together in this Southern barbecue side dish. Because cabbage is relatively watery, we salted the cut cabbage to draw out excess moisture before dressing it, which prevented moisture from diluting the dressing later and leaving us with a watery slaw. Granny Smith apples work best in this slaw recipe—tasters loved their sturdy crunch and tart bite. Cider vinegar gave the dressing a fruity flavor, while red pepper flakes, chopped scallions, and mustard added some punch.

TANGY APPLE CABBAGE SLAW

SERVES 6 TO 8

In step 1, the salted, rinsed, and dried cabbage can be refrigerated in a zipper-lock bag for up to 24 hours. To prep the apples, cut the cored apples into ¼-inch-thick planks, then stack the planks and cut them into thin matchsticks.

- 1 medium head green cabbage (2 pounds), cored and chopped fine (12 cups)
- 2 teaspoons salt
- 2 Granny Smith apples, cored and cut into thin matchsticks
- 2 scallions, sliced thin
- 6 tablespoons vegetable oil
- ½ cup cider vinegar
- ½ cup sugar
- 1 tablespoon Dijon mustard
- ¼ teaspoon red pepper flakes

1. Toss cabbage and salt in colander set over medium bowl. Let stand until wilted, about 1 hour. Rinse cabbage under cold water, drain, dry well with paper towels, and transfer to large bowl. Add apples and scallions and toss to combine.

2. Bring oil, vinegar, sugar, mustard, and pepper flakes to boil in saucepan over medium heat. Pour over cabbage mixture and toss to coat. Cover with plastic wrap and refrigerate at least 1 hour or up to 1 day. Serve.

Cutting Apples for Slaw

1. Cut each side of apple squarely away from core and cut each piece into ¼-inch-thick slices.

2. Stack planks and cut them into thin matchsticks.

Vinegar Primer

Although cider vinegar and white vinegar are made by the same process, the similarities end there. Vinegar is made by turning fermented liquid into acetic acid by adding certain bacteria to the liquid. Cider and distilled vinegars are made by the same process but start with different liquids: Cider vinegar begins with apple cider and distilled vinegar with ethyl alcohol (also known as grain alcohol). Although both vinegars are commonly used in pickle recipes (and are often substituted for each other), they do have distinctly different flavors. We like to use sweeter cider vinegar in sweet pickles, reserving white vinegar for applications such as sour pickles, where we want acidity without added flavor. While cider vinegar is fine in a sweet salad dressing, we don't think distilled vinegar adds much to any dressing. In general, we find that vinegars that start with wine are the best choice for salad dressings.

CIDER VINEGAR
Sweet cider vinegar begins with apple cider.

DISTILLED VINEGAR
Acidic distilled vinegar begins with ethyl alcohol.

Why This Recipe Works The high water content of cabbage is typically to blame for watery slaws. We salted our cabbage to draw out the excess moisture. Memphis Chopped Coleslaw is usually studded with celery seeds and crunchy green peppers and tossed with an unapologetically sugary mustard dressing that's balanced by a bracing hit of vinegar. To ensure our slaw boasted brash, balanced flavor, we quickly cooked the spicy dressing to meld the flavors and tossed the hot dressing with the cabbage. The salted cabbage absorbed the dressing and became seasoned inside and out.

MEMPHIS CHOPPED COLESLAW

SERVES 8 TO 10

In step 1, the salted, rinsed, and dried cabbage mixture can be refrigerated in a zipper-lock bag for up to 24 hours.

- 1 head green cabbage (2 pounds), cored and chopped fine (12 cups)
- 1 jalapeño chile, stemmed, seeded, and minced
- 1 carrot, peeled and shredded on box grater
- 1 small onion, peeled and shredded on box grater
- 2 teaspoons salt
- ¼ cup yellow mustard
- ¼ cup chili sauce
- ¼ cup mayonnaise
- ¼ cup sour cream
- ¼ cup cider vinegar
- 1 teaspoon celery seeds
- ⅔ cup packed light brown sugar

1. Toss cabbage, jalapeño, carrot, onion, and salt in colander set over medium bowl. Let stand until wilted, about 1 hour. Rinse cabbage mixture under cold water, drain, dry well with paper towels, and transfer to large bowl.

2. Bring mustard, chili sauce, mayonnaise, sour cream, vinegar, celery seeds, and sugar to boil in saucepan over medium heat. Pour over cabbage and toss to coat. Cover with plastic wrap and refrigerate 1 hour or up to 1 day. Serve.

How to Chop Cabbage

1. Cut cabbage into quarters, then trim and discard hard core.

2. Separate cabbage into small stacks of leaves that flatten when pressed.

3. Cut each stack of cabbage leaves into ¼-inch strips.

4. Cut strips into ¼-inch pieces.

ALL-AMERICAN POTATO SALAD

SERVES 4 TO 6

Make sure not to overcook the potatoes or the salad will be quite sloppy. Keep the water at a gentle simmer and use the tip of a paring knife to judge the doneness of the potatoes. If the knife inserts easily into the potato pieces, they are done.

- 2 large eggs
- Salt
- 2 pounds Yukon Gold potatoes, peeled and cut into ¾-inch cubes
- 3 tablespoons dill pickle juice, plus ¼ cup finely chopped dill pickles
- 1 tablespoon yellow mustard
- ¼ teaspoon pepper
- ½ teaspoon celery seeds
- ½ cup mayonnaise
- ¼ cup sour cream
- ½ small red onion, chopped fine
- 1 celery rib, chopped fine

1. Bring eggs, 1½ teaspoons salt, and 1 quart water to boil in small saucepan. Remove pan from heat, cover and let sit for 10 minutes. Transfer eggs to bowl filled with ice water and let cool for 5 minutes, then peel and chop coarse.

2. Place potatoes in large saucepan with cold water to cover by 1 inch. Bring to boil over high heat, add 1 teaspoon salt, reduce heat to medium-low, and simmer until potatoes are tender, 10 to 15 minutes.

3. Drain potatoes thoroughly, then spread out on rimmed baking sheet. Mix 2 tablespoons pickle juice and mustard together in small bowl, drizzle pickle juice mixture over hot potatoes, and toss until evenly coated. Refrigerate until cooled, about 30 minutes.

4. Mix remaining tablespoon pickle juice, chopped pickles, ½ teaspoon salt, pepper, celery seeds, mayonnaise, sour cream, red onion, and celery in large bowl. Toss in cooled potatoes, cover, and refrigerate until well chilled, about 30 minutes. (Salad can be refrigerated for up to 2 days.) Gently stir in eggs, just before serving.

Don't Throw Out the Juice

Pickle juice tossed with just-cooked potatoes gives them a tangy flavor that's not as harsh as straight vinegar and has a gentle sweetness, too.

Why This Recipe Works For flavorful all-American potato salad, we decided to use firm-textured Yukon Gold potatoes because they hold their shape after cooking and won't turn mushy in the salad. Our recipe benefited from the sweetness of an unexpected ingredient: pickle juice. We drizzled the still-warm potatoes with a mixture of pickle juice and mustard. The hot potatoes easily absorbed the acidic liquid and tasted seasoned through to the middle. A combination of mayonnaise and sour cream formed the base of our creamy dressing, seasoned with classic additions like celery seeds, celery, and chopped hard-cooked eggs.

SMOKY POTATO SALAD

SERVES 8

Use small red potatoes 1½ to 2 inches in diameter. If you don't have 2 tablespoons of fat in the skillet after frying the bacon, add olive oil to make up the difference.

- 6 slices bacon
- 3 tablespoons red wine vinegar
- 2 tablespoons mayonnaise
- 2 teaspoons minced canned chipotle chile in adobo sauce
- Salt and pepper
- 3 tablespoons olive oil, plus extra for brushing
- 3 pounds small red potatoes, unpeeled, halved
- 1 large onion, sliced into ½-inch-thick rounds
- 4 scallions, sliced thin

1. Cook bacon in 12-inch skillet over medium heat until crisp, 7 to 9 minutes; transfer to paper towel–lined plate. Set aside 2 tablespoons bacon fat. When cool enough to handle, crumble bacon and set aside. Whisk vinegar, mayonnaise, chile, ½ teaspoon salt, and ½ teaspoon pepper together in large bowl. Slowly whisk in 3 tablespoons oil until combined; set aside.

2A. For a Charcoal Grill Open bottom vent completely. Light large chimney starter three-quarters filled with charcoal briquettes (4½ quarts). When top coals are partially covered with ash, pour evenly over grill. Set cooking grate in place, cover, and open lid vent completely. Heat grill until hot, about 5 minutes.

2B. For a Gas Grill Turn all burners to high, cover, and heat grill until hot, about 15 minutes. Turn all burners to medium.

3. Clean and oil cooking grate. Toss potatoes with reserved bacon fat and ½ teaspoon salt. Push a toothpick horizontally through each onion round to keep rings intact while grilling. Brush onion rounds lightly with extra oil and season with salt and pepper. Place potatoes, cut side down, and onion rounds on grill and cook, covered, until charred on first side, 10 to 14 minutes.

4. Flip potatoes and onion rounds and continue to cook, covered, until well browned all over and potatoes are easily pierced with tip of paring knife, 10 to 16 minutes longer. Transfer potatoes and onion rounds to rimmed baking sheet and let cool slightly.

5. When cool enough to handle, halve potatoes; remove toothpicks and coarsely chop onion rounds. Add potatoes, onion, scallions, and bacon to dressing and toss to combine. Season with salt and pepper to taste. Serve warm or at room temperature.

Why This Recipe Works For a summery potato salad cooked on the grill from start to finish featuring smoky, tender potatoes with crispy outsides, we began with halved, unpeeled red potatoes: The skin helped them to stay intact, and their firm, waxy texture stood up to the heat of the grill. Prior to grilling, we coated the potatoes with flavorful bacon fat. For even more smokiness, we grilled rounds of onions along with the potatoes. A spicy, smoky vinaigrette with a touch of mayo, chipotle, and crumbled bacon was the perfect match for this backyard-ready potato salad.

Why This Recipe Works Amish potato salad is distinct for its creamy cooked dressing and sweet-and-sour flavor. We modernized this recipe by ditching the labor-intensive dressing, which is traditionally enriched with eggs and gently cooked over a double-boiler. To keep the rich taste with less work, we processed a hard-cooked egg yolk into the dressing base of vinegar and sugar. Sprinkling a few tablespoons of the tangy dressing over the hot potatoes infused them with flavor. Then we tossed the cooled potatoes with the rest of the dressing, enriched with sour cream, for a cool, creamy potato salad with great old-fashioned flavor.

AMISH POTATO SALAD

SERVES 8

You can substitute an equal amount of celery salt for the celery seed, but if you do, eliminate the table salt from the dressing. Make sure to use sturdy Yukon Golds here; fluffy russets will fall apart in the salad.

- 3 pounds Yukon Gold potatoes, peeled and cut into ¾-inch chunks
- Salt and pepper
- ⅓ cup cider vinegar
- ¼ cup sugar
- 2 tablespoons yellow mustard
- 4 large hard-cooked eggs, peeled (recipe follows)
- ½ teaspoon celery seeds
- ¾ cup sour cream
- 1 celery rib, chopped fine

1. Bring potatoes, 1 tablespoon salt, and enough water to cover by 1 inch to boil in large pot over high heat. Reduce heat to medium and simmer until potatoes are just tender, about 10 minutes.

2. Meanwhile, microwave vinegar and sugar in small bowl until sugar dissolves, about 30 seconds. Process vinegar mixture, mustard, 1 hard-cooked egg yolk (reserve white), celery seeds, and ½ teaspoon salt in food processor until smooth, about 30 seconds. Transfer to medium bowl.

3. Drain potatoes thoroughly and transfer to large bowl. Drizzle 2 tablespoons dressing over hot potatoes and, using rubber spatula, gently toss until evenly coated. Refrigerate until cooled, at least 30 minutes, stirring gently once to redistribute dressing.

4. Whisk sour cream into remaining dressing. Add reserved egg white and 3 hard-cooked eggs to dressing and, using potato masher, mash until only small pieces remain. Add dressing and celery to cooled potatoes, tossing gently to combine. Cover and refrigerate until chilled, about 30 minutes. Season with salt and pepper to taste. Serve. (Salad can be refrigerated for up to 2 days.)

FOOLPROOF HARD-COOKED EGGS
MAKES 4 EGGS

You can double or triple this recipe as long as you use a pot large enough to hold the eggs in a single later, covered by an inch of water.

- 4 large eggs

Bring eggs and enough water to cover by 1 inch to boil in medium saucepan over high heat. Remove pan from heat, cover, and let sit 10 minutes. Meanwhile, fill medium bowl with 4 cups water and 1 tray of ice cubes. Transfer eggs to ice water bath with slotted spoon; let sit for 5 minutes. Peel eggs.

Sweet on Sweet-and-Sour

Like most other resourceful Colonial Americans, the Amish turned to pickling as a way to preserve fruits and vegetables for long (prerefrigeration) winters. It wasn't just practicality that drove them to pickling, however. The Amish people's penchant for these sweet-and-sour flavors is also rooted in the group's native Germany, where rich dishes are often finished with a splash of vinegar or served with vinegar-spiked sides, such as sauerkraut. The Amish table, it's said, is incomplete without "seven sweets and seven sours." A cornucopia of delicious foods reflects this Amish predilection, from watermelon rind and cantaloupe pickles to chow chow, pickled beets and eggs, and Amish potato salad, which is seasoned with plenty of vinegar and sugar.

RANCH POTATO SALAD

SERVES 6 TO 8

We prefer white wine vinegar here, but white and cider vinegars are acceptable substitutes.

- 3 pounds red potatoes, peeled and cut into ¾-inch chunks
- Salt
- ¾ cup mayonnaise
- ½ cup buttermilk
- ¼ cup white wine vinegar
- ¼ cup drained jarred roasted red peppers, chopped fine
- 3 tablespoons finely chopped fresh cilantro
- 3 scallions, chopped fine
- 1 garlic clove, minced
- ⅛ teaspoon dried dill
- 2 teaspoons pepper
- 2 tablespoons Dijon mustard

1. Bring potatoes, 1 tablespoon salt, and enough water to cover potatoes by 1 inch to boil in large pot over high heat. Reduce heat to medium and simmer until potatoes are just tender, about 10 minutes. While potatoes simmer, whisk mayonnaise, buttermilk, 2 tablespoons vinegar, red peppers, cilantro, scallions, garlic, dill, 1 teaspoon salt, and pepper in large bowl.

2. Drain potatoes thoroughly, then spread out on rimmed baking sheet. Whisk mustard and remaining vinegar in small bowl. Drizzle mustard mixture over hot potatoes and toss until evenly coated. Refrigerate until cooled, about 30 minutes.

3. Transfer cooled potatoes to bowl with mayonnaise mixture and toss to combine. Cover and refrigerate until well chilled, about 30 minutes. Serve. (Salad can be refrigerated for up to 2 days.)

Better Potato Texture, and Faster, Too

We discovered some interesting information about boiling potatoes while developing our recipe for Ranch Potato Salad. Most recipes for boiled potatoes call for starting the spuds in cold water so that they will come up to temperature slowly and cook evenly throughout. In an attempt to shorten the cooking time, we tried letting the water boil before adding the potatoes. In a side-by-side test, we weren't surprised that tasters preferred the potatoes started in cold water for their uniformly creamy texture. We were surprised, however, to find that the total cooking time for potatoes started in cold water was less than for those started in boiling water.

Hidden Valley Ranch Dressing

The original ranch dressing first became popular at the Hidden Valley Guest Ranch near Santa Barbara, Calif., in the late 1950s. It began as a dried herb mixture that Steve Henson, the ranch's owner, combined with mayonnaise and buttermilk to make a creamy, tangy dressing for the ranch's house salad. It was so well received that guests clamored for bottles of the dressing to take home with them. Recognizing the potential of his concoction, Henson began marketing the mix in small packets, and the rest is culinary history. The little packets are still around, but the dressing really took off in 1983 when manufacturers figured out how to bottle this creamy dressing in a shelf-stable format.

Why This Recipe Works Bottled ranch dressing sounds like a quick way to dress up potato salad, but many recipes are surprisingly dull and bland. We found that peeling the potatoes (we liked red spuds) allowed them to absorb more dressing. For the dressing, we doubled the amount of cilantro used in most recipes and added fresh garlic and scallions for a welcome bite. Dijon mustard and vinegar provided acidity and bite, while chopped roasted red peppers made a sweet counterpoint. To better season the potatoes, we tossed the hot spuds first with just the Dijon mustard and vinegar. And just a dash of dried dill lent more herb flavor.

Why This Recipe Works We wanted potato salad with vibrant dill flavor through and through. To do so, we seasoned our potato salad with three rounds of dill: first as an herb sachet while the potatoes simmered, next as a piquant dill vinegar, and finally as a fresh sprinkle. A dressing based on a combination of creamy mayonnaise and tangy sour cream, accented with Dijon mustard, provided the perfect backdrop for our dill flavor to shine.

DILL POTATO SALAD

SERVES 8

Use both dill stems and chopped leaves (sometimes called fronds) in the herb sachet. Trois Petits Cochons is our favorite brand of Dijon mustard.

- ¼ cup white wine vinegar
- 3 tablespoons minced fresh dill, plus ½ cup leaves and stems, chopped coarse
- 3 pounds Yukon Gold potatoes, peeled and cut into ¾-inch pieces
- Salt and pepper
- ½ cup mayonnaise
- ¼ cup sour cream
- 1 tablespoon Dijon mustard
- 3 scallions, green parts only, sliced thin

1. Combine vinegar and 1 tablespoon minced dill in bowl and microwave until steaming, 30 to 60 seconds. Set at room temperature until cool, 15 to 20 minutes.

2. Meanwhile, place chopped dill inside disposable coffee filter and tie closed with kitchen twine. Bring potatoes, dill sachet, 1 tablespoon salt, and enough water to cover potatoes by 1 inch to boil in large pot over high heat. Reduce heat to medium and simmer until potatoes are just tender, about 10 minutes.

3. Drain potatoes thoroughly, then transfer to large bowl; discard sachet. Drizzle 2 tablespoons dill vinegar over hot potatoes and gently toss until evenly coated. Refrigerate until cooled, about 30 minutes, stirring once.

4. Whisk mayonnaise, sour cream, remaining dill vinegar, mustard, ½ teaspoon salt, and ¼ teaspoon pepper together until smooth. Add dressing to cooled potatoes. Stir in scallions and remaining 2 tablespoons minced dill. Cover and refrigerate to let flavors meld, about 30 minutes. Season with salt and pepper to taste. Serve. (Salad can be refrigerated for up to 2 days.)

Dill Three Ways

Three rounds of fresh dill season our Dill Potato Salad.

Infuse
We add a packet of chopped dill to the water in which the potatoes simmer.

Marinate
We steep vinegar with minced dill and use it to dress the hot potatoes.

Mince
We sprinkle extra minced dill over the dressed potato salad.

Why This Recipe Works Texans take their potato salad up a notch with plenty of mustard and spicy chopped jalapeños. For our version, we started with classic potato salad, using firm Yukon Gold potatoes, which have a rich earthy flavor and hold their shape after cooking, and a mayonnaise-based dressing seasoned with onion, celery seeds, and dill pickles. To this we added plenty of bold yellow mustard and spicy jalapeños. We tempered the jalapeños' raw bite by quick-pickling them in a mixture of vinegar, sugar, and mustard seeds. We used the leftover pickling solution to flavor the hot potatoes. A pinch of cayenne added extra kick.

TEXAS POTATO SALAD

SERVES 8

Annie's Naturals Organic Yellow Mustard is our favorite brand of yellow mustard.

- ½ cup red wine vinegar
- 1½ tablespoons sugar
- Salt and pepper
- 1 teaspoon yellow mustard seeds
- ½ small red onion, sliced thin
- 2 jalapeño chiles (1 sliced into thin rings; 1 stemmed, seeded, and minced)
- 3 pounds Yukon Gold potatoes, peeled and cut into ¾-inch pieces
- 6 tablespoons mayonnaise
- 6 tablespoons yellow mustard
- ¼ teaspoon cayenne pepper
- 2 large hard-cooked eggs, cut into ¼-inch pieces
- 1 celery rib, minced

1. Combine vinegar, sugar, 1½ teaspoons salt, and mustard seeds in bowl and microwave until steaming, about 2 minutes. Whisk until sugar and salt are dissolved. Add onion and jalapeños and set aside until cool, 15 to 20 minutes. Strain onion and jalapeños through fine-mesh strainer set over bowl. Reserve pickled vegetables and vinegar mixture separately.

2. Meanwhile, combine potatoes, 8 cups water, and 1 tablespoon salt in Dutch oven and bring to boil over high heat. Reduce heat to medium and simmer until potatoes are just tender, 10 to 15 minutes.

3. Drain potatoes thoroughly, then transfer to large bowl. Drizzle 2 tablespoons reserved vinegar mixture over hot potatoes and toss gently until evenly coated. (Reserve remaining vinegar mixture for another use.) Refrigerate until cool, about 30 minutes, stirring once halfway through chilling.

4. Whisk mayonnaise, mustard, ½ teaspoon pepper, and cayenne together in bowl until combined. Add mayonnaise mixture, reserved pickled vegetables, eggs, and celery to potatoes and stir gently to combine. Season with salt and pepper to taste. Cover and refrigerate to let flavors blend, about 30 minutes. Serve. (Salad can be refrigerated for up to 2 days.)

Keeping Potato Salad Safe

Though mayonnaise is often blamed for spoiled potato salads, it is rarely the problem. In fact, it's the potatoes that are more likely to go bad. The bacteria usually responsible for spoiled potato salad is found in soil and dust, and it thrives on starchy foods like potatoes. No matter what kind of dressing you use, don't leave any potato salad out for more than 2 hours (1 hour if the temperature is above 90 degrees), and promptly refrigerate any leftovers in a covered container.

SMASHED POTATO SALAD

SERVES 8 TO 10

Use the tip of a paring knife to judge the doneness of the potatoes. If the tip inserts easily into the potato pieces, they are done. Hellmann's Real Mayonnaise is our favorite nationally available mayonnaise. Note that the salad needs to be refrigerated for about 2 hours before serving.

- 3 pounds Yukon Gold potatoes, unpeeled, cut into 1-inch chunks
- Salt and pepper
- 2 tablespoons distilled white vinegar
- 1 cup mayonnaise
- 3 tablespoons yellow mustard
- ¼ teaspoon cayenne pepper
- 3 hard-cooked large eggs, chopped
- 3 scallions, sliced thin
- ½ cup chopped sweet pickles
- ½ cup finely chopped celery
- ¼ cup finely chopped onion

1. Combine potatoes, 8 cups water, and 1 tablespoon salt in Dutch oven and bring to boil over high heat. Reduce heat to medium and cook at vigorous simmer until potatoes are tender, 14 to 17 minutes.

2. Drain potatoes in colander. Transfer 3 cups potatoes to large bowl, add 1 tablespoon vinegar, and coarsely mash with potato masher. Transfer remaining potatoes to rimmed baking sheet, drizzle with remaining 1 tablespoon vinegar, and toss gently to combine. Let cool completely, about 15 minutes.

3. Whisk mayonnaise, ½ cup water, mustard, cayenne, 1 teaspoon salt, and 1 teaspoon pepper together in bowl. Stir mayonnaise mixture into mashed potatoes. Fold in eggs, scallions, pickles, celery, onion, and remaining potatoes until combined. (Mixture will be lumpy.)

4. Cover and refrigerate until fully chilled, about 2 hours. Season with salt and pepper to taste. Serve.

Mayo Showdown

Commercial mayonnaise is one of the most hotly debated ingredients out there, with impassioned salad- and sandwich-makers insisting that only their favorite will do. Here are three of the most well-loved mayos.

HELLMANN'S
(Sold as Best Foods west of the Rockies) The most popular brand in the U.S., Hellmann's accounts for about half of all mayonnaise sales.

DUKE'S
This spread is made with cider vinegar, which gives it a sharp flavor. It has ardent fans in many Southern states.

BLUE PLATE
The test kitchen's favorite mayo is made with egg yolks, not whole eggs. It must be mail-ordered in most of the country.

Why This Recipe Works For our take on this Southern picnic staple, wanted both the creamy texture of mashed potatoes and the tender chunks of traditional potato salad. Yukon Gold potatoes worked best—their soft skins cooked up tender and saved us from peeling. For a mix of textures, we smashed a third of the boiled spuds with some vinegar before tossing the mashed portion with the cubes. Yellow mustard contributed some extra bite, which we balanced with chopped sweet pickles, and a touch of cayenne gave. Hard-cooked eggs, scallions, celery, and onion added even more textural variety to finish off our smooth-yet-chunky potato salad.

LEMON AND HERB RED POTATO SALAD

SERVES 8

To rinse the onion, place it in a fine-mesh strainer and run it under cold water. This removes some of the onion's harshness. Drain, but do not rinse, the capers here.

- 3 pounds red potatoes, unpeeled, cut into 1-inch chunks
- 2 tablespoons distilled white vinegar
- Salt and pepper
- 2 teaspoons grated lemon zest plus 3 tablespoons juice
- ⅓ cup extra-virgin olive oil
- ½ cup finely chopped onion, rinsed
- 3 tablespoons minced fresh tarragon
- 3 tablespoons minced fresh parsley
- 3 tablespoons minced fresh chives
- 2 tablespoons capers, minced

1. Combine potatoes, 8 cups water, vinegar, and 2 tablespoons salt in Dutch oven and bring to boil over high heat. Reduce heat to medium and cook at strong simmer until potatoes are just tender, 10 to 15 minutes.

2. Meanwhile, whisk lemon zest and juice, 1 teaspoon salt, and ½ teaspoon pepper together in large bowl. Slowly whisk in oil until emulsified; set aside.

3. Drain potatoes thoroughly, then transfer to rimmed baking sheet. Drizzle 2 tablespoons dressing over hot potatoes and toss gently until evenly coated. Let potatoes cool, about 30 minutes, stirring once halfway through cooling.

4. Whisk dressing to recombine and stir in onion, tarragon, parsley, chives, and capers. Add cooled potatoes to dressing and stir gently to combine. Season with salt and pepper to taste. Serve warm or at room temperature.

Capers 101

Capers are actually pickles made from the unopened flower buds of the *Capparis spinosa* shrub, which grows in the Mediterranean. In France, Italy, and Spain, the shrubs are cultivated for capers, and Roquevaire, in Provence, is known as the "caper capital." Capers are never used fresh, and are preserved one of two ways: in a salt and water brine, sometimes with added vinegar, or in salt. More often, the flower buds are soaked in saltwater, then packed in brine or a mixture of brine and vinegar. This is how capers are sold in most supermarkets. The other option is to cure them with salt. This kind of caper costs more and is available only in specialty markets. Capers also vary in size, from the tiny non-pareilles to surfines, capucines, fines, and capotes—increasing in size and decreasing in value.

Why This Recipe Works Too often potato salad is weighed down by a heavy mayonnaise-based dressing; we sought a lighter alternative. We used waxy red potatoes, as they are lower in starch than russets and more colorful than Yukon Golds. To prevent them from breaking down too much, we added vinegar to the cooking water, giving us tender but firm potatoes that held their shape. A mixture of capers, olive oil, and lemon juice and zest complemented the potatoes' earthiness, while tarragon, parsley, and chives provided freshness. Adding some of the herbed vinaigrette while the potatoes were still hot ensured they best absorbed all of its flavor.

rise-and-shine breakfast and breads

- 423 Fluffy Diner-Style Cheese Omelet
- 425 "Impossible" Ham-and-Cheese Pie
- 426 Breakfast Pizza
- 429 Homemade Breakfast Sausage
- 430 Short-Order Home Fries
- 432 Better-Than-the-Box Pancake Mix
- 435 Fluffy Cornmeal Pancakes
- 437 Dutch Baby
- 438 Beignets
- 441 Cornmeal Biscuits
- 442 Cat Head Biscuits
- 444 Mixed Berry Scones
- 447 Southern-Style Skillet Cornbread
- 449 Spicy Cheese Bread
- 450 Perfect Popovers
- 452 Whole-Wheat Blueberry Muffins
- 455 Morning Glory Muffins
- 456 Muffin Tin Doughnuts
- 458 Ultimate Cinnamon Buns
- 461 Quicker Cinnamon Buns
- 463 Morning Buns
- 464 Kolaches
- 466 Monkey Bread
- 469 English Muffin Bread
- 471 Brown Soda Bread
- 472 Dakota Bread

Why This Recipe Works For a tall, fluffy diner-worthy omelet, we ditched the whisk for an electric mixer, which helped us incorporate air into the eggs. Cream added richness, but when we added it to the whipped eggs, the omelet lost its fluffiness. Combining the cream and eggs before whipping didn't work either—the fat in the cream made it impossible to whip air into the eggs. Instead, we whipped the dairy first, then folded it into the whipped eggs. After letting the bottom of the omelet set on the stovetop, we popped the skillet into a preheated oven, and just six minutes later had a puffy, fluffy omelet, cooked to perfection.

FLUFFY DINER-STYLE CHEESE OMELET

SERVES 2

Although this recipe will work with a stand mixer, a hand-held mixer makes quick work of whipping such a small amount of cream. To make two omelets, double this recipe and cook the omelets simultaneously in two skillets. If you have only one skillet, prepare a double batch of ingredients and set half aside for the second omelet. Be sure to wipe out the skillet in between omelets.

- 3 tablespoons heavy cream, chilled
- 5 large eggs, room temperature
- ¼ teaspoon salt
- 2 tablespoons unsalted butter
- 2 ounces sharp cheddar cheese, shredded (½ cup)
- 1 recipe omelet filling (optional) (recipes follow)

1. Adjust oven rack to middle position and heat oven to 400 degrees. Using stand mixer fitted with whisk, whip cream on medium-low speed until foamy, about 1 minute. Increase speed to high and whip until soft peaks form, 1 to 3 minutes. Set whipped cream aside. Using dry, clean bowl and whisk attachment, whip eggs and salt on high speed until frothy and eggs have tripled in size, about 2 minutes. Gently fold whipped cream into eggs.

2. Melt butter in ovensafe 10-inch nonstick skillet over medium-low heat, swirling pan to coat bottom and sides. Add egg mixture and cook until edges are nearly set, 2 to 3 minutes. Sprinkle with ¼ cup cheddar and half of omelet filling, if using, and transfer to oven. Bake until eggs are set and edges are beginning to brown, 6 to 8 minutes.

3. Carefully remove pan from oven (handle will be very hot), sprinkle eggs with remaining ¼ cup cheddar and remaining omelet filling, if using, and let sit, covered, until cheese begins to melt, about 1 minute. Tilt pan and, using rubber spatula, push half of omelet onto cutting board, then fold omelet over itself to form half-moon shape. Cut omelet in half and serve.

SAUSAGE AND PEPPER FILLING
MAKES ABOUT 1 CUP

- 4 ounces hot or sweet Italian sausage, casings removed
- 1 tablespoon unsalted butter
- 1 small onion, chopped
- ½ red bell pepper, chopped
- Salt and pepper

Cook sausage in 10-inch nonstick skillet over medium heat, breaking up clumps with wooden spoon, until browned, about 6 minutes. Transfer to paper towel–lined plate. Add butter, onion, and bell pepper to now-empty skillet and cook until softened, about 10 minutes. Stir in sausage and season with salt and pepper to taste.

LOADED BAKED POTATO FILLING
MAKES ABOUT 1 CUP

- 1 large Yukon Gold potato, peeled and cut into ½-inch pieces
- 4 slices bacon, chopped
- 2 scallions, sliced thin
- Salt and pepper

Microwave potato, covered, in large bowl until just tender, 2 to 5 minutes. Cook bacon in 10-inch nonstick skillet over medium heat until crisp, about 8 minutes. Transfer bacon to paper towel–lined plate; pour off all but 1 tablespoon bacon fat. Add potato to skillet and cook until golden brown, about 6 minutes. Transfer potato to bowl, add cooked bacon, and stir in scallions. Season with salt and pepper to taste.

Why This Recipe Works "Impossible" pie is a 1970s phenomenon that promises a pie "crust" without rolling out finicky dough. Traditionally, a simple Bisquick batter was whisked with eggs and poured over vegetables, meat, and cheese and baked. To give our "crust" a crispy, browned exterior, we buttered the pie dish and coated it with Parmesan cheese. We replaced the Bisquick with a simple batter of flour, baking powder, eggs, and creamy half-and-half. Doubling the number of eggs made for a richer, custardy pie. For the filling, we chose ingredients that required a minimum of prep work: scallions, diced deli ham, and Gruyère cheese.

"IMPOSSIBLE" HAM-AND-CHEESE PIE

SERVES 8

Use a rasp-style grater or the smallest holes on a box grater for the Parmesan.

- 1 tablespoon unsalted butter, softened, plus 2 tablespoons melted
- 3 tablespoons finely grated Parmesan cheese
- 8 ounces Gruyère cheese, shredded (2 cups)
- 4 ounces thickly sliced deli ham, chopped
- 4 scallions, minced
- ½ cup (2½ ounces) all-purpose flour
- ¾ teaspoon baking powder
- ½ teaspoon pepper
- ¼ teaspoon salt
- 1 cup half-and-half
- 4 large eggs, lightly beaten
- 2 teaspoons Dijon mustard
- ⅛ teaspoon ground nutmeg

1. Adjust oven rack to lowest position and heat oven to 350 degrees. Grease 9-inch pie plate with softened butter, then coat plate evenly with Parmesan.

2. Combine Gruyère, ham, and scallions in bowl. Sprinkle cheese-and-ham mixture evenly in bottom of prepared pie dish. Combine flour, baking powder, pepper, and salt in now-empty bowl. Whisk in half-and-half, eggs, melted butter, mustard, and nutmeg until smooth. Slowly pour batter over cheese-and-ham mixture in pie dish.

3. Bake until pie is light golden brown and filling is set, 30 to 35 minutes. Let cool on wire rack for 15 minutes. Slice into wedges. Serve warm.

Finger Food

To serve our "Impossible" Ham-and-Cheese Pie as an hors d'oeuvre at your next party, forgo the pie plate and instead bake it in an 8-inch square baking dish. Slice it into 1-inch squares and serve warm or at room temperature.

Grating Hard Cheese

Using a rasp-style grater to grate hard cheeses like Parmesan produces lighter, fluffier shreds that melt seamlessly into all kinds of dishes.

BREAKFAST PIZZA

SERVES 6

Small-curd cottage cheese is sometimes labeled "country-style." Room-temperature dough is much easier to shape than cold, so pull the dough from the fridge about 1 hour before you start cooking.

- 3 tablespoons extra-virgin olive oil, plus extra for drizzling
- 6 slices bacon
- 8 ounces mozzarella cheese, shredded (2 cups)
- 1 ounce Parmesan cheese, grated (½ cup)
- 4 ounces (½ cup) small-curd cottage cheese
- ¼ teaspoon dried oregano
- Salt and pepper
- Pinch cayenne pepper
- 1 pound store-bought pizza dough, room temperature
- 6 large eggs
- 2 scallions, sliced thin
- 2 tablespoons minced fresh chives

1. Adjust oven rack to lowest position and heat oven to 500 degrees. Grease rimmed baking sheet with 1 tablespoon oil.

2. Cook bacon in 12-inch skillet over medium heat until crisp, 7 to 9 minutes. Transfer to paper towel–lined plate; when cool enough to handle, crumble bacon. Combine mozzarella and Parmesan in bowl; set aside. Combine cottage cheese, oregano, ¼ teaspoon pepper, cayenne, and 1 tablespoon oil in separate bowl; set aside.

3. Press and roll dough into 15 by 11-inch rectangle on lightly floured counter, pulling on corners to help make distinct rectangle. Transfer dough to prepared sheet and press to edges of sheet. Brush edges of dough with remaining 1 tablespoon oil. Bake dough until top appears dry and bottom is just beginning to brown, about 5 minutes.

4. Remove crust from oven and, using spatula, press down on any air bubbles. Spread cottage cheese mixture evenly over top, leaving 1-inch border around edges. Sprinkle bacon evenly over cottage cheese mixture.

5. Sprinkle mozzarella mixture evenly over pizza, leaving ½-inch border. Create 2 rows of 3 evenly spaced small wells in cheese, each about 3 inches in diameter (6 wells total). Crack 1 egg into each well, then season each with salt and pepper.

6. Return pizza to oven and bake until crust is light golden around edges and eggs are just set, 9 to 10 minutes for slightly runny yolks or 11 to 12 minutes for soft-cooked yolks, rotating sheet halfway through baking.

7. Transfer pizza to wire rack and let cool for 5 minutes. Transfer pizza to cutting board. Sprinkle with scallions and chives and drizzle with extra oil. Slice and serve.

SMOKED SALMON BREAKFAST PIZZA

In step 7, after cooling, omit scallions and top pizza with ¼ cup sliced red onion, 3 ounces sliced smoked salmon (cut into thin strips), and ¼ cup sour cream. Sprinkle with chives and 1 tablespoon chopped fresh dill and drizzle with extra oil.

SAUSAGE AND RED BELL PEPPER BREAKFAST PIZZA

Substitute 6 ounces bulk breakfast sausage for bacon and extra-sharp cheddar for mozzarella. Combine sausage; 1 stemmed, seeded, and chopped red bell pepper; 1 chopped onion; and ¼ teaspoon salt in 12-inch skillet. Cook over medium heat, breaking up sausage with spoon, until sausage begins to brown and bell pepper and onion are translucent, about 6 minutes. Transfer to paper towel–lined plate. Let mixture cool completely before proceeding.

CHORIZO AND MANCHEGO BREAKFAST PIZZA

Substitute 6 ounces chorizo sausage, halved lengthwise and cut into ½-inch slices, for bacon and 1 cup shredded Manchego cheese for Parmesan. Cook chorizo in 12-inch skillet over medium heat until lightly browned, 7 to 9 minutes. Let cool completely before proceeding.

Why This Recipe Works Eggs and bacon on a cheese pizza? Sounded like an excellent breakfast to us. Our challenge was to achieve a crisp, golden-brown crust without overcooking the eggs. We gave the crust a head start by parbaking it for 5 minutes. The remaining oven time cooked the eggs and other toppings to perfection. To keep the eggs in place while they cooked, we created wells in the cheese. Though we initially used ricotta, it became dry and grainy in the oven. Then we tried cottage cheese and were pleasantly surprised to find the curds melted in the oven, leaving a creamy, silky cheese layer that tied everything together.

Why This Recipe Works Commercially made breakfast sausage always disappoints when it comes to flavor, tasting either too sweet or salty, or too bland or highly seasoned, so we decided to make our own. We started with ground pork with some fat in it (lean meat was neither fatty nor flavorful enough) and amped up its mild flavor with classic breakfast sausage flavors: garlic, sage, thyme, and cayenne pepper. A spoonful of maple syrup sweetened the patties nicely. To combine the meat mixture, we kneaded it gently with our hands, but were careful not to overmix it, which would toughen the meat.

HOMEMADE BREAKFAST SAUSAGE

MAKES 16 PATTIES

Avoid lean or extra-lean ground pork; it makes the sausage dry, crumbly, and less flavorful.

- 2 pounds ground pork
- 1 tablespoon maple syrup
- 1 garlic clove, minced
- 2 teaspoons dried sage
- 1½ teaspoons pepper
- 1 teaspoon salt
- ½ teaspoon dried thyme
- ⅛ teaspoon cayenne pepper
- 2 tablespoons unsalted butter

1. Combine pork, maple syrup, garlic, sage, pepper, salt, thyme, and cayenne in large bowl. Gently mix with hands until well combined. Using greased ¼-cup measure, divide mixture into 16 patties and place on rimmed baking sheet. Cover patties with plastic wrap, then gently flatten each one to ½-inch thickness.

2. Melt 1 tablespoon butter in 12-inch nonstick skillet over medium heat. Cook half of patties until well browned and cooked through, 6 to 10 minutes. Transfer to paper towel–lined plate and tent with aluminum foil. Wipe out skillet. Repeat with remaining butter and patties. Serve.

To Make Ahead Follow recipe through step 1. Refrigerate uncooked patties for up to 1 day or freeze for up to 1 month. To serve, proceed as directed in step 2, increasing cooking time to 14 to 18 minutes.

Dried Herbs

We use plenty of dried herbs in the test kitchen, but we don't use every dried herb. Delicate leafy herbs, such as basil, parsley, chives, mint, and cilantro become stale-tasting when dried. Heartier herbs, such as oregano, sage, and thyme, dry well and are good substitutes for fresh in most recipes—especially those in which the herbs will cook in liquid. We've found that tarragon and dill fall into a middle category: They do add flavor in their dried form, but that flavor is more muted than that provided by other dried herbs.

A few general rules: Use only half as much dried herbs as fresh, and add them at the same time as you would add fresh. Dried herbs lose potency 6 to 12 months after opening; you can test dried herbs for freshness by rubbing them between your fingers—if they don't smell bright, throw them away.

OREGANO
Great in tomato sauces, chili, Mexican and Latin dishes, and sprinkled on pizza. Dried does not have the same sharp bite as fresh, but it does have a distinct and recognizable floral element.

SAGE
We prefer rubbed (or finely crumbled) sage to the ground or chopped kinds. Use with poultry, stuffings, pork, full-flavored vegetables (like squash), and in butter sauces.

ROSEMARY
Works well in long-cooked dishes like soups, stews, and braises. Too much dried rosemary can turn a dish bitter, so use sparingly.

THYME
Good for long-cooked soups and stews and roasted meats and poultry; pairs well with mustard and lemon flavors.

SHORT-ORDER HOME FRIES

SERVES 4

Although we prefer the sweetness of Yukon Gold potatoes, other medium-starch potatoes, such as red potatoes, can be substituted. If you want to spice things up, add a pinch of cayenne pepper.

- 1½ pounds Yukon Gold potatoes, cut into ¾-inch pieces
- 4 tablespoons unsalted butter
- 1 onion, chopped fine
- ½ teaspoon garlic salt
- ½ teaspoon salt
- Pepper

1. Place potatoes and 1 tablespoon butter in large bowl and microwave, covered, until edges of potatoes begin to soften, 5 to 7 minutes, stirring halfway through cooking.

2. Meanwhile, melt 1 tablespoon butter in 12-inch nonstick skillet over medium heat. Add onion and cook until softened and golden brown, 8 to 10 minutes. Transfer to small bowl.

3. Melt remaining 2 tablespoons butter in now-empty skillet over medium heat. Add potatoes and pack down with spatula. Cook, without moving, until bottoms of potatoes are brown, 5 to 7 minutes. Turn potatoes, pack down again, and continue to cook until well browned and crisp, 5 to 7 minutes. Reduce heat to medium-low and continue to cook until potatoes are crusty, 9 to 12 minutes, stirring occasionally. Stir in onion, garlic salt, and salt and season with pepper to taste. Serve.

GREEK DINER-STYLE HOME FRIES
Omit garlic salt and add 1 tablespoon lemon juice, 2 minced garlic cloves, and ½ teaspoon dried oregano to potatoes along with onion in step 3.

HOME FRIES WITH FRESH HERBS
Add 1 teaspoon each chopped fresh basil, parsley, thyme, and tarragon to potatoes along with onion in step 3.

The Right Spuds for Home Fries
High-starch, low-moisture potatoes, such as russets, may be great for baking and mashing, but when it comes to home fries, they are not the best choice. The fluffy flesh of these potatoes breaks down in the skillet, leaving nothing but a greasy pool of stodgy spuds. For tender tubers that retain their texture, we prefer medium-starch varieties, such as Yukon Gold and red potatoes. They hold their shape in the skillet, develop a great crust, and fry up to a beautiful golden brown.

RUSSET POTATOES
A falling-apart mess

YUKON GOLD POTATOES
Intact, crisp, and browned

Why This Recipe Works Though a commercial-grade griddle helps our local diner serve up home fries with a perfectly crispy exterior, the real secret is precooking the potatoes. Roasting or boiling our spuds took too much time for a quick breakfast side, so we turned to the microwave to jump-start their cooking before frying them in a large skillet. We found that packing the potatoes down with a spatula and cooking them a few minutes before turning them and then repeating these steps ensured they were evenly browned and extra-crunchy. Finally, we stirred in some sautéed onion and garlic salt to give our home fries a deep, savory flavor.

RISE-AND-SHINE BREAKFAST AND BREADS

BETTER-THAN-THE-BOX PANCAKE MIX

MAKES ABOUT 6 CUPS; ENOUGH FOR 24 PANCAKES

Malted milk powder might seem odd here, but it gives the pancakes a deeper, more complex flavor.

- 2 cups (10 ounces) all-purpose flour
- 2 cups (8 ounces) cake flour
- 1 cup (3 ounces) nonfat dry milk powder
- ¾ cup (3⅓ ounces) malted milk powder
- ⅓ cup (2⅓ ounces) sugar
- 2 tablespoons baking powder
- 1 teaspoon baking soda
- 1 tablespoon salt
- 12 tablespoons unsalted butter, cut into ½-inch pieces

Process all ingredients in food processor until no lumps remain and mixture resembles wet sand, about 2 minutes. (Pancake mix can be frozen for up to 2 months.)

BETTER-THAN-THE-BOX PANCAKES

To make 8 pancakes, whisk 2 cups Better-Than-the-Box Pancake Mix, 2 lightly beaten large eggs, and ½ cup buttermilk in large bowl until smooth. Using ¼-cup measure, portion batter into lightly oiled 12-inch nonstick skillet or griddle in 4 places and cook over medium-low heat until golden brown, about 2 minutes per side. Repeat with remaining batter. Serve. (If you don't have buttermilk, whisk 1½ teaspoons lemon juice or white vinegar into ½ cup whole or low-fat milk and let sit until slightly thickened, about 10 minutes.)

Not Just for Milkshakes

To give our pancakes complexity and depth, we added malted milk powder to the mix. This product is made from malted barley that has been evaporated and pulverized, and sometimes includes flour or evaporated milk powder. Though it is more commonly used to make milkshakes, we found it added a sweet, nutty flavor to the pancakes made from our Better-Than-the-Box Pancake Mix.

Is the Pan Ready for Pancakes?

A properly heated pan or griddle is essential to making perfect, golden-brown, fluffy pancakes. A skillet that has not been properly heated and is too cool will produce pale, gummy pancakes. Here's a test to make sure your pan is hot enough: Drop a tablespoon of batter in its center. If, after one minute, the pancake is golden brown on the bottom, the pan is ready. If it remains blond—or is close to burning—adjust the heat accordingly.

PALE, GUMMY PANCAKE

PERFECT, FLUFFY PANCAKE

Why This Recipe Works For our take on pancake mix that delivers both store-bought ease and from-scratch taste, we combined all-purpose flour with cake flour; this duo yielded sturdy yet tender cakes. To give pancakes made from our mix complexity and depth, we added an unusual ingredient, malted milk powder, which imparted a sweet, nutty flavor. Though most mixes call for shortening, we opted for butter, which gave us moister, more flavorful pancakes. Using buttermilk instead of milk when mixing the batter gave us high-rising pancakes—the acid of the buttermilk reacts with the baking soda, causing the batter to bubble and rise.

Why This Recipe Works Getting the height and lightness of traditional pancakes with the robust flavor and texture of cornmeal pancakes is tougher than it seems. Coarsely ground cornmeal can be sandy, and it lacks the gluten necessary to support a fluffy internal structure. We found that we could use more cornmeal by heating it with some of the buttermilk to soften it first. Soaking the cornmeal also thickened the batter, helping it ride higher in the pan instead of spreading out. Letting the batter sit for a few minutes before griddling the cakes allowed the buttermilk to react with the baking soda, which resulted in fluffier, airier pancakes.

FLUFFY CORNMEAL PANCAKES

MAKES ABOUT 15 (4-INCH) PANCAKES

Our favorite cornmeal is Arrowhead Mills Organic Yellow Cornmeal.

- 1¾ cups buttermilk
- 1¼ cups (6¼ ounces) cornmeal
- 2 tablespoons unsalted butter, cut into ¼-inch pieces
- ¾ cup (3¾ ounces) all-purpose flour
- 2 tablespoons sugar
- 1¾ teaspoons baking powder
- ½ teaspoon baking soda
- ½ teaspoon salt
- 2 large eggs
- 2½ teaspoons vegetable oil

1. Adjust oven rack to middle position and heat oven to 200 degrees. Set wire rack inside rimmed baking sheet and place in oven. Whisk 1¼ cups buttermilk and cornmeal together in medium bowl. Stir in butter, cover, and microwave until slightly thickened around edges, about 90 seconds, stirring once halfway through cooking. Let sit, covered, for 5 minutes.

2. Whisk flour, sugar, baking powder, baking soda, and salt in large bowl. Beat eggs and remaining ½ cup buttermilk together in 1-cup liquid measuring cup. Whisk egg mixture into cornmeal mixture. Whisk cornmeal mixture into flour mixture. Let sit for 10 minutes.

3. Heat ½ teaspoon oil in 12-inch nonstick skillet over medium-low heat until shimmering. Using paper towels, carefully wipe out oil, leaving thin film on bottom of pan. Using level ¼-cup measure for each pancake, drop batter for 3 pancakes into pan. Cook until edges are set and bubbles begin to form on tops of pancakes, about 90 seconds. Flip, then cook until second side is golden brown, about 2 minutes longer. Transfer to prepared baking sheet in oven, cover loosely with aluminum foil, and repeat with remaining oil and batter. Serve.

The Virtues of Pancake Patience

For the fluffiest pancakes, let the finished batter sit for 10 minutes before griddling the cakes. The rest gives the baking soda extra time to react and form large air bubbles, lightening the batter, ergo the pancakes. With a hearty whole grain like cornmeal, you want all the lift you can get. This trick works with any pancake batter made with whole grains.

Choosing the Right Cornmeal

Cornmeal, or ground processed corn kernels, is available in all manner of sizes for use in different applications. In most cases, we recommend choosing stone-ground over commercially produced cornmeal on two counts: First of all, stone-ground cornmeal has a more rustic texture because of the stone's rough grinding surface (companies like Quaker use smooth steel rollers that produce very fine, uniform cornmeal). And secondly, stone-ground cornmeal has a fuller flavor because it contains both the hull and oil-rich germ of the corn kernel, which commercial producers extract for better shelf life.

Why This Recipe Works A big, puffy pancake, a Dutch baby puffs and rises as it bakes, then falls in the center a few minutes out of the oven, resulting in a bowl-shaped breakfast treat with crisp sides and a thin, custardy bottom. For our version we started with a 12-inch skillet; its gently sloping walls promoted an even rise. Brushing the pan with oil and preheating it in the oven helped ensure the sides had the texture we wanted and jump-started the pancake's rise. Since fats tend to make baked goods tender rather than crisp, we used skim milk in our batter. For even more crispness, we replaced some of the flour with cornstarch.

DUTCH BABY

SERVES 4

You can use whole or low-fat milk instead of skim, but the texture won't be as crisp. Serve with an assortment of berries and lightly sweetened whipped cream, if desired.

- 2 tablespoons vegetable oil
- 1 cup (5 ounces) all-purpose flour
- ¼ cup cornstarch
- 2 teaspoons grated lemon zest plus 2 tablespoons juice
- 1 teaspoon salt
- 3 large eggs
- 1¼ cups skim milk
- 1 tablespoon unsalted butter, melted and cooled
- 1 teaspoon vanilla extract
- 3 tablespoons confectioners' sugar

1. Adjust oven rack to middle position and heat oven to 450 degrees. Brush bottom and sides of 12-inch skillet with oil. Heat skillet in oven until oil is shimmering, about 10 minutes.

2. Meanwhile, combine flour, cornstarch, lemon zest, and salt in large bowl. Whisk eggs in second bowl until frothy and light, about 1 minute. Whisk milk, butter, and vanilla into eggs until incorporated. Whisk one-third of milk mixture into flour mixture until no lumps remain, then slowly whisk in remaining milk mixture until smooth.

3. Carefully pour batter into skillet and bake until edges are deep golden brown and crisp, about 20 minutes. Transfer skillet to wire rack, sprinkle pancake with lemon juice and confectioners' sugar, and cut into wedges. Serve.

Easy Steps to Making a Dutch Baby

1. Brush bottom and sides of pan with vegetable oil to guarantee crisp exterior.

2. Heat greased pan before carefully pouring in batter to initiate rise.

3. Bake in 450-degree oven to ensure high rise.

4. Sprinkle deflated pancake with lemon juice and confectioners' sugar before serving.

BEIGNETS

MAKES 24 BEIGNETS

This dough is very wet and sticky, so flour the counter and baking sheet generously. You'll need at least a 6-quart Dutch oven for this recipe.

- 1 cup water, heated to 110 degrees
- 3 tablespoons granulated sugar
- 1 tablespoon instant or rapid-rise yeast
- 3 cups (15 ounces) all-purpose flour
- ¾ teaspoon salt
- 2 large eggs
- 2 tablespoons plus 2 quarts vegetable oil
  Confectioners' sugar

1. Combine water, 1 tablespoon granulated sugar, and yeast in large bowl and let sit until foamy, about 5 minutes. Combine flour, remaining 2 tablespoons granulated sugar, and salt in second bowl. Whisk eggs and 2 tablespoons oil into yeast mixture. Add flour mixture and stir vigorously with rubber spatula until dough comes together. Cover bowl with plastic wrap and refrigerate until nearly doubled in size, about 1 hour.

2. Set wire rack inside rimmed baking sheet. Line second sheet with parchment paper and dust generously with flour. Place half of dough on well-floured counter and pat into rough rectangle with floured hands, flipping to coat with flour. Roll dough into ¼-inch-thick rectangle (roughly 12 by 9 inches). Using pizza wheel, cut dough into twelve 3-inch squares and transfer to floured baking sheet. Repeat with remaining dough.

3. Add remaining oil to large Dutch oven until it measures about 1½ inches deep and heat over medium-high heat to 350 degrees. Fry 6 beignets, adjusting burner as necessary to maintain oil temperature between 325 and 350 degrees, until golden brown, about 3 minutes, flipping halfway through frying. Using slotted spoon or tongs, transfer beignets to prepared baking sheet. Return oil to 350 degrees and repeat with remaining beignets. Dust beignets with confectioners' sugar and serve immediately.

Forming Beignets

This dough is very wet, which allows a network of delicate holes to develop in the beignets. However, wet dough can be tricky to work with. Here's how to easily shape and cut the beignets:

1. Dust counter and rolling pin generously with flour before you roll out chilled beignet dough.

2. Cut 3-inch squares with pizza wheel.

A Faster Way to Flavor

Starting with a full tablespoon of yeast and proofing it in warm water jump-starts the fermentation process, giving our beignets complex flavor after just a 1-hour rise.

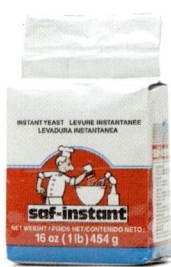

Why This Recipe Works To replicate the crisp, airy texture and tangy flavor of these classic New Orleans doughnuts, we began by using plenty of yeast, kick-starting it with warm water and sugar to develop its flavor. We added extra water for a super-hydrated dough, so that as soon as the wet dough hits the hot oil, it created lots of steam, giving our beignets an open, honeycombed structure. Since wet dough is tricky to roll out, we let it rise in the refrigerator to firm it up. A few minutes of frying and a shower of powdered sugar, and our beignets were ready to be enjoyed, Big Easy style.

Why This Recipe Works A good cornmeal biscuit combines the tender, fluffy crumb of a traditional biscuit with the distinct cornmeal flavor of cornbread. To make the dough, we used a food processor to cut chilled butter quickly into our dry ingredients. So our biscuits would taste like cornmeal, but wouldn't have its dry, gritty texture, we soaked the cornmeal in buttermilk; just 10 minutes was enough to soften it. A bit of honey provided a subtle sweetness that drew out the corn flavor even more. Kneading the dough briefly prior to cutting out rounds ensured evenly textured biscuits that rose to an impressive height.

CORNMEAL BISCUITS

MAKES 12 BISCUITS

If you don't have buttermilk, you can substitute clabbered milk; whisk 1 tablespoon lemon juice into 1¼ cups of milk and let the mixture sit until slightly thickened, about 10 minutes. Avoid coarsely ground cornmeal, which makes gritty biscuits.

- 1 cup (5 ounces) cornmeal
- 1¼ cups buttermilk
- 1 tablespoon honey
- 2 cups (10 ounces) all-purpose flour
- 1 tablespoon baking powder
- ½ teaspoon baking soda
- 1 teaspoon salt
- 12 tablespoons unsalted butter, cut into ½-inch pieces and chilled

1. Adjust oven rack to middle position and heat oven to 450 degrees. Line rimmed baking sheet with parchment paper. Whisk cornmeal, buttermilk, and honey together in large bowl; let sit for 10 minutes.

2. Pulse flour, baking powder, baking soda, and salt in food processor until combined, about 3 pulses. Scatter butter evenly over top and continue to pulse until mixture resembles coarse meal, about 15 pulses. Add flour mixture to buttermilk mixture and stir until dough forms.

3. Turn dough out onto lightly floured counter and knead until smooth, 8 to 10 times. Pat dough into 9-inch circle, about ¾ inch thick. Using 2½-inch biscuit cutter dipped in flour, cut out rounds and transfer to prepared baking sheet, dipping cutter in flour after each cut. Pat remaining dough into ¾-inch-thick circle, cut rounds from dough, and transfer to baking sheet.

4. Bake until biscuits begin to rise, about 5 minutes, then reduce oven temperature to 400 degrees and bake until golden brown, 8 to 12 minutes longer, rotating baking sheet halfway through baking. Let biscuits cool on baking sheet for 5 minutes, then transfer to wire rack. Serve warm or let cool to room temperature. (Biscuits can be stored at room temperature for up to 2 days.)

Steps to Tender, Fluffy Cornmeal Biscuits

Our Cornmeal Biscuits have the moist, flavor-packed crumb of cornbread and the fluffy stature of a stamped biscuit.

1. Soak cornmeal in buttermilk for soft crumb without too much cornmeal grit before mixing with dough.

2. Transfer dough to lightly floured counter and knead briefly before patting into 9-inch circle.

3. Use biscuit cutter to cut dough into rounds, dipping cutter into flour between cuts.

CAT HEAD BISCUITS

MAKES 6 BISCUITS

If you don't have buttermilk, you can substitute clabbered milk; whisk 1 tablespoon lemon juice into 1¼ cups milk and let the mixture sit until slightly thickened, about 10 minutes. The recipe will also work with 3 cups White Lily flour in place of both the all-purpose and cake flours.

- 1½ cups (7½ ounces) all-purpose flour
- 1½ cups (6 ounces) cake flour
- 1 tablespoon baking powder
- ½ teaspoon baking soda
- 1 teaspoon salt
- 8 tablespoons unsalted butter, cut into ½-inch pieces and softened
- 4 tablespoons vegetable shortening, cut into ½-inch pieces
- 1¼ cups buttermilk

1. Adjust oven rack to upper-middle position and heat oven to 425 degrees. Grease 9-inch round cake pan. Combine all-purpose flour, cake flour, baking powder, baking soda, and salt in large bowl. Using fingertips, rub butter and shortening into flour mixture until mixture resembles coarse meal. Stir in buttermilk until combined.

2. Using greased ½-cup measure or large spring-loaded ice cream scoop, transfer 6 heaping portions of dough into prepared pan, placing five around edge and one in center.

3. Bake until puffed and golden brown, 20 to 25 minutes, rotating pan halfway through baking. Let biscuits cool in pan for 10 minutes, then transfer to wire rack. Serve. (Biscuits can be stored at room temperature for up to 2 days.)

Forming Cat Head Biscuits
Instead of kneading, rolling, and stamping, Cat Head Biscuits are scooped.

Scoop dough and nestle biscuits in cake pan using spring-loaded ice cream scoop.

Flour Mixology
Southern bakers swear by White Lily all-purpose flour, which they say makes biscuits soft and downy, exactly the texture we sought for our Cat Head Biscuits. We found we could replicate it by combining equal amounts of all-purpose flour and cake flour.

ALL-PURPOSE FLOUR
Contributes structure

CAKE FLOUR
Contributes softness

WHITE LILY
The soft and fluffy standard-bearer

Why This Recipe Works As big as a cat's head, these tender, moist biscuits that originated in the Appalachian region boast a golden-brown, craggy top and downy, soft sides. Many Southern bakers rely on White Lily flour to ensure a tender texture, but since this flour isn't readily available everywhere, we substituted an equal mix of cake flour and all-purpose flour. For biscuits with a fluffy texture, we relied on softened butter and shortening, worked in with warm hands. Scooping the dough into a round cake pan, so the mounds were touching, gave us baked biscuits with tender, soft sides.

MIXED BERRY SCONES

MAKES 8 SCONES

Work the dough as little as possible, just until it comes together. Work quickly to keep the butter and berries as cold as possible for the best results. Note that the butter is divided in this recipe. An equal amount of frozen blueberries, raspberries, blackberries, or strawberries (halved) can be used in place of the mixed berries.

Scones
- 1¾ cups (8¾ ounces) frozen mixed berries
- 3 tablespoons confectioners' sugar
- 3 cups (15 ounces) all-purpose flour
- 12 tablespoons unsalted butter, cut into ½-inch pieces, chilled
- ⅓ cup (2⅓ ounces) granulated sugar
- 1 tablespoon baking powder
- 1¼ teaspoons salt
- ¾ cup plus 2 tablespoons whole milk
- 1 large egg plus 1 large yolk

Glaze
- 2 tablespoons unsalted butter, melted
- 1 tablespoon honey

1. For the Scones Adjust oven rack to upper-middle position and heat oven to 425 degrees. Line rimmed baking sheet with parchment paper. (If your berry mix contains strawberries, cut them in half.) Toss berries with confectioners' sugar in bowl; freeze until needed.

2. Combine flour, 6 tablespoons butter, granulated sugar, baking powder, and salt in food processor and process until butter is fully incorporated, about 15 seconds. Add remaining 6 tablespoons butter and pulse until butter is reduced to pea-size pieces, 10 to 12 pulses. Transfer mixture to large bowl. Stir in berries.

3. Beat milk and egg and yolk together in separate bowl. Make well in center of flour mixture and pour in milk mixture. Using rubber spatula, gently stir mixture, scraping from edges of bowl and folding inward until very shaggy dough forms and some bits of flour remain. Do not overmix.

4. Turn out dough onto well-floured counter and, if necessary, knead briefly until dough just comes together, about 3 turns. Using your floured hands and bench scraper, shape dough into 12 by 4-inch rectangle, about 1½ inches tall. Using knife or bench scraper, cut dough crosswise into 4 equal rectangles. Cut each rectangle diagonally into 2 triangles (you should have 8 scones total). Transfer scones to prepared sheet. Bake until scones are lightly golden on top, 16 to 18 minutes, rotating pan halfway through baking.

5. For the Glaze While scones bake, combine melted butter and honey in small bowl.

6. Remove scones from oven and brush tops evenly with glaze mixture. Return scones to oven and continue to bake until golden brown on top, 5 to 8 minutes longer. Transfer scones to wire rack and let cool for at least 10 minutes before serving.

To Make Ahead Unbaked scones can be frozen for several weeks. After cutting scones into triangles in step 4, freeze them on baking sheet. Transfer frozen scones to zipper-lock freezer bag. When ready to bake, heat oven to 375 degrees and extend cooking time in step 4 to 23 to 26 minutes. Glaze time in step 6 will remain at 5 to 8 minutes.

Why This Recipe Works A random stop at a rural Massachusetts antique store—which had a coffee shop attached—provided the inspiration for these berry-filled scones. To recreate them, we discovered that treating the butter in two different ways was key: We processed half the cold butter to fully incorporate it into the dough, then we pulsed in the remaining butter, processing it to pea-size pieces that created pockets of steam as the scones baked. Adding confectioners' sugar to the frozen berries counteracted their tartness and helped control them from "bleeding" into the dough. A simple glaze added a nice sheen and sweet finish.

Why This Recipe Works Savory skillet-baked Southern-style cornbread should boast hearty corn flavor, a sturdy, moist crumb, and a dark brown crust. For the right texture, we used finely ground cornmeal. Toasting it in the oven for a few minutes intensified the corn flavor. Buttermilk added a sharp tang that worked well with the corn, and soaking the cornmeal in the buttermilk helped to soften it so our cornbread was moist and tender. When it came to the fat, a combination of butter (for flavor) and vegetable oil (which can withstand high heat without burning) worked best, and greasing the pan with both delivered the crisp crust we were after.

SOUTHERN-STYLE SKILLET CORNBREAD

SERVES 12

If you don't have buttermilk, you can substitute clabbered milk; whisk 2 tablespoons lemon juice into 2 cups of milk and let the mixture sit until slightly thickened, about 10 minutes. We prefer a cast-iron skillet here, but any ovensafe 10-inch skillet will work fine. Avoid coarsely ground cornmeal, as it will make the cornbread gritty.

- 2¼ cups (11¼ ounces) cornmeal
- 2 cups buttermilk
- ¼ cup vegetable oil
- 4 tablespoons unsalted butter, cut into 4 pieces
- 2 large eggs
- 1 teaspoon baking powder
- 1 teaspoon baking soda
- ¾ teaspoon salt

1. Adjust oven racks to lower-middle and middle positions and heat oven to 450 degrees. Heat 10-inch cast-iron skillet on middle rack for 10 minutes. Spread cornmeal over rimmed baking sheet and bake on lower-middle rack until fragrant and color begins to deepen, about 5 minutes. Transfer hot cornmeal to large bowl and whisk in buttermilk; set aside.

2. Carefully add oil to hot skillet and continue to bake until oil is just smoking, about 5 minutes. Remove skillet from oven and add butter, carefully swirling pan until butter is melted. Pour all but 1 tablespoon oil mixture into cornmeal mixture, leaving remaining oil mixture in pan. Whisk eggs, baking powder, baking soda, and salt into cornmeal mixture.

3. Pour cornmeal mixture into hot skillet and bake until top begins to crack and sides are golden brown, 12 to 16 minutes, rotating pan halfway through baking. Let cornbread cool in pan for 5 minutes, then turn out onto wire rack. Serve.

Secrets to Savory Southern-Style Skillet Cornbread

1. Toast cornmeal to give bread richer corn flavor.

2. Soak cornmeal in buttermilk to soften cornmeal and ensure tender yet sturdy crumb.

3. Grease and thoroughly heat skillet to create crisp crust.

Why This Recipe Works Stella's Bakery in Madison, Wisconsin, is known for its spicy cheese bread. One challenge we had while trying to recreate this addictive bread was finding a way to incorporate the cheese without stunting the dough's rise. We found the key was to make sure the cheese cubes came to room temperature before adding them to the dough. To help keep its shape, we baked the bread in a cake pan. An egg wash and a generous sprinkle of red pepper flakes finished off the loaf. A final brush of melted butter helped the crust stay supple and gave it a nice shine.

SPICY CHEESE BREAD

MAKES 1 LOAF

Take the cheese out of the refrigerator when you start the recipe to ensure that it comes to room temperature by the time you need it. Cold cheese will retard rising. The dough needs to rise for several hours before baking.

Bread
- 3¼ cups (16¼ ounces) all-purpose flour
- ¼ cup (1¾ ounces) sugar
- 1 tablespoon instant or rapid-rise yeast
- 1½ teaspoons red pepper flakes
- 1¼ teaspoons salt
- ½ cup warm water (110 degrees)
- 2 large eggs plus 1 large yolk
- 4 tablespoons unsalted butter, melted
- 6 ounces Monterey Jack cheese, cut into ½-inch cubes (1½ cups), room temperature
- 6 ounces provolone cheese, cut into ½-inch cubes (1½ cups), room temperature

Topping
- 1 large egg, lightly beaten
- 1 teaspoon red pepper flakes
- 1 tablespoon unsalted butter, melted

1. For the Bread Whisk flour, sugar, yeast, pepper flakes, and salt together in bowl of stand mixer. Whisk warm water, eggs and yolk, and melted butter together in liquid measuring cup. Add egg mixture to flour mixture. Fit stand mixer with dough hook and knead on medium speed until dough clears bottom and sides of bowl, about 8 minutes.

2. Transfer dough to unfloured counter, shape into ball, and transfer to greased bowl. Cover with plastic wrap and let rise in warm place until doubled in size, 1½ to 2 hours.

3. Grease 9-inch round cake pan. Transfer dough to unfloured counter and press to deflate. Roll dough into 18 by 12-inch rectangle with long side parallel to counter's edge. Distribute Monterey Jack and provolone evenly over dough, leaving 1-inch border around edges. Starting with edge closest to you, roll dough into log. Pinch seam and ends to seal, then roll log so seam side is down. Roll log back and forth on counter, applying gentle, even pressure, until log reaches 30 inches in length. If any tears occur, pinch to seal.

4. Starting at one end, wind log into coil; tuck end underneath coil. Place loaf in prepared cake pan and cover loosely with clean dish towel. Let rise in warm place until doubled in size, 1 to 1½ hours. Adjust oven rack to lower-middle position and heat oven to 350 degrees.

5. For the Topping Brush top of loaf with egg, then sprinkle with pepper flakes. Place cake pan on rimmed baking sheet. Bake until loaf is golden brown, about 25 minutes. Rotate loaf, tent with aluminum foil, and continue to bake until loaf registers 190 degrees, 25 to 30 minutes longer.

6. Transfer pan to wire rack and brush bread with butter. Let cool for 10 minutes. Run knife around edge of pan to loosen bread. Slide bread onto wire rack, using spatula as needed for support. Let cool for 30 minutes before slicing. Serve warm.

PERFECT POPOVERS

MAKES 6 POPOVERS

Greasing the pan with shortening ensures the best release, but vegetable oil spray may be substituted; do not use butter. Bread flour makes for the highest and sturdiest popovers, but 2 cups (10 ounces) of all-purpose flour may be substituted.

- 3 large eggs
- 2 cups 1 percent or 2 percent low-fat milk, heated to 110 degrees
- 3 tablespoons unsalted butter, melted and cooled
- 2 cups (11 ounces) bread flour
- 1 teaspoon salt
- 1 teaspoon sugar

1. Adjust oven rack to lower-middle position and heat oven to 450 degrees. Grease 6-cup popover pan with shortening, then flour pan lightly. Whisk eggs until light and foamy in medium bowl. Slowly whisk in milk and butter until incorporated.

2. Combine flour, salt, and sugar in large bowl. Whisk three-quarters of milk mixture into flour mixture until no lumps remain, then whisk in remaining milk mixture. Transfer batter to 4-cup liquid measuring cup, cover with plastic wrap, and let sit at room temperature for 1 hour. (Alternatively, batter can be refrigerated for up to 1 day. Bring to room temperature before proceeding.)

3. Whisk batter to recombine, then pour into prepared pan (batter will not reach top of cups). Bake until just beginning to brown, about 20 minutes. Without opening oven door, decrease oven temperature to 300 degrees and continue to bake until popovers are golden brown, 35 to 40 minutes longer. Poke small hole in top of each popover with skewer and continue to bake until deep golden brown, about 10 minutes longer. Transfer pan to wire rack, poke popovers again with skewer, and let cool for 2 minutes. Remove from pan and serve.

To Make Ahead Cooled popovers can be stored at room temperature for up to 2 days. To serve, adjust oven rack to middle position and heat oven to 400 degrees. Heat popovers on rimmed baking sheet until crisp and heated through, 5 to 8 minutes.

MUFFIN TIN POPOVERS

If you don't have a popover pan, you can bake the popovers in a 12-cup muffin tin—with a sacrifice in stature. To ensure even cooking, use only the outer 10 cups of the tin.

Grease and flour outer 10 cups of muffin tin, then fill ¼ inch from the top (you may have some batter left over). Reduce initial baking time in step 3 to 15 minutes, and reduce secondary baking time to 20 to 25 minutes after oven temperature has been lowered. Poke popovers as directed and continue to bake for another 10 minutes.

Popovers Gone Wrong

POP NEVER

Short, squat popovers occur when the recipe calls for cake flour, which doesn't provide enough structure to the batter. Using too little batter can also make for squat popovers, as can an oven that's not hot enough.

POP UNDER

Deflated popovers occur when they aren't baked long enough to set up properly or aren't poked during baking to allow the steam to escape.

POP UGLY

Misshapen popovers are caused by using a preheated, oiled pan. The batter that first hits the pan immediately rises up through the wet batter, resulting in an ugly shape.

Why This Recipe Works For golden-brown popovers that really popped, we used bread flour instead of all-purpose flour in the batter—the bread flour's higher protein content ensured the highest rise and crispiest crust. Resting the batter before baking prevented the popovers from setting up too quickly. We first baked our popovers at a high temperature to jump-start the initial rise, then turned the oven down so they would cook through evenly. To let steam escape (which can cause popovers to collapse), we poked a hole in the top of each one when they were almost done baking, and then again as they cooled.

WHOLE-WHEAT BLUEBERRY MUFFINS

MAKES 12 MUFFINS

Do not overmix the batter. You can substitute frozen (unthawed) blueberries for fresh in this recipe.

Streusel
- 3 tablespoons granulated sugar
- 3 tablespoons packed brown sugar
- 3 tablespoons whole-wheat flour
- Pinch salt
- 2 tablespoons unsalted butter, melted

Muffins
- 3 cups (16½ ounces) whole-wheat flour
- 2½ teaspoons baking powder
- ½ teaspoon baking soda
- 1 teaspoon salt
- 1 cup (7 ounces) granulated sugar
- 2 large eggs
- 4 tablespoons unsalted butter, melted
- ¼ cup vegetable oil
- 1¼ cups buttermilk
- 1½ teaspoons vanilla extract
- 7½ ounces (1½ cups) blueberries

1. For the Streusel Combine granulated sugar, brown sugar, flour, and salt in bowl. Add melted butter and toss with fork until evenly moistened and mixture forms large chunks with some pea-size pieces throughout; set aside.

2. For the Muffins Adjust oven rack to middle position and heat oven to 400 degrees. Spray 12-cup muffin tin, including top, generously with vegetable oil spray. Whisk flour, baking powder, baking soda, and salt together in large bowl. Whisk sugar, eggs, melted butter, and oil together in separate bowl until combined, about 30 seconds. Whisk buttermilk and vanilla into sugar mixture until combined.

3. Stir sugar mixture into flour mixture until just combined. Gently stir in blueberries until incorporated. Using a heaping ¼-cup dry measuring cup, divide batter evenly among prepared muffin cups (cups will be filled to rim); sprinkle evenly with streusel.

4. Bake until golden brown and toothpick inserted in center comes out with few crumbs attached, 18 to 20 minutes, rotating muffin tin halfway through baking. Let muffins cool in muffin tin on wire rack for 5 minutes. Remove muffins from muffin tin and let cool 5 minutes longer. Serve.

Don't Make this Mistake: Heavy and Dense Muffins

You can't simply swap whole-wheat flour into any muffin recipe and expect it to work. But if you know the science behind baking and account for the variables, you can make great blueberry muffins using 100 percent whole-wheat flour.

Why This Recipe Works When it comes to baking with whole wheat, the benefits—added fiber, bran, and nutty sweetness—are often trumped by the drawbacks: dense texture and squat appearance. To use one hundred percent whole wheat, we had to revise our standard blueberry muffin recipe. The resulting whole-wheat muffins were light and tender thanks to two leaveners and several high-moisture ingredients (buttermilk, eggs, blueberries, melted butter, and oil). As a final step we added a crumbly streusel topping to round out our now light and delicate muffins with hearty whole-wheat flavor.

Why This Recipe Works Morning glory muffins are chock-full of nuts, fruit, carrots, and spices. But all these tempting add-ins can make for heavy, dense muffins, so our first move was to strain the fruit and press out the extra juice to prevent our muffins from being soggy. To keep the bright, fruity flavor intact, we simply saved the released fruit juice, reduced it on the stovetop, and added the concentrated syrup back to the batter. To keep the nuts and coconut from becoming mealy or soggy in the finished muffins, we toasted and processed them. At last, our muffins were truly glorious.

MORNING GLORY MUFFINS

MAKES 12 MUFFINS

Though we prefer golden raisins here, ordinary raisins will work, too.

- ¾ cup (2¼ ounces) sweetened shredded coconut, toasted
- ½ cup walnuts, toasted
- 2¼ cups (11¼ ounces) all-purpose flour
- ¾ cup (5¼ ounces) sugar
- 1½ teaspoons baking soda
- ½ teaspoon baking powder
- 1 teaspoon ground cinnamon
- ¾ teaspoon salt
- 1 (8-ounce) can crushed pineapple
- 1 Granny Smith apple, peeled, cored, and shredded
- 8 tablespoons unsalted butter, melted
- 3 large eggs
- 1 teaspoon vanilla extract
- 1½ cups shredded carrots (2 to 3 carrots)
- 1 cup golden raisins

1. Adjust oven rack to middle position and heat oven to 350 degrees. Spray 12-cup muffin tin with vegetable oil spray. Process coconut and walnuts in food processor until finely ground, 20 to 30 seconds. Add flour, sugar, baking soda, baking powder, cinnamon, and salt and pulse until combined. Transfer mixture to large bowl.

2. Place pineapple and shredded apple in fine-mesh strainer set over liquid measuring cup. Press fruit dry (you should have about 1 cup juice). Bring juice to boil in 12-inch skillet over medium-high heat and cook until reduced to ¼ cup, about 5 minutes. Let cool slightly. Whisk melted butter, cooled juice, eggs, and vanilla together until smooth. Stir wet mixture into dry mixture until combined. Stir in pineapple-apple mixture, carrots, and raisins.

3. Divide batter evenly among muffin cups. Bake until toothpick inserted in center comes out clean, 24 to 28 minutes, rotating pan halfway through baking. Let muffins cool in muffin tin on wire rack for 10 minutes. Remove muffins from tin and let cool for at least 10 minutes before serving. (Muffins can be stored at room temperature for up to 3 days.)

Secrets to Glorious Morning Glory Muffins

1. Toasting the coconut and walnuts heightens their flavor, and processing them in a food processor until finely ground prevents soggy, stringy coconut and mealy nuts.

2. Pressing the juice out of the shredded apple and pineapple before stirring them into the batter keeps the muffins from being gummy and wet.

3. Reducing the released fruit juice on the stovetop (down from 1 cup to ¼ cup) and adding the syrup to the batter provides a bright, fruity flavor without adding too much moisture.

MUFFIN TIN DOUGHNUTS

MAKES 12 DOUGHNUTS

In step 3, brush the doughnuts generously, using up all the melted butter. Use your hand to press the cinnamon sugar onto the doughnuts to coat them completely.

Doughnuts
- 2¾ cups (13¾ ounces) all-purpose flour
- 1 cup (7 ounces) sugar
- ¼ cup cornstarch
- 1 tablespoon baking powder
- 1 teaspoon salt
- ½ teaspoon ground nutmeg
- 1 cup buttermilk
- 8 tablespoons unsalted butter, melted
- 2 large eggs plus 1 large yolk

Coating
- 1 cup sugar
- 2 teaspoons ground cinnamon
- 8 tablespoons unsalted butter, melted

1. For the Doughnuts Adjust oven rack to middle position and heat oven to 400 degrees. Spray 12-cup muffin tin with vegetable oil spray. Whisk flour, sugar, cornstarch, baking powder, salt, and nutmeg together in bowl. Whisk buttermilk, melted butter, and eggs and yolk together in separate bowl. Add wet ingredients to dry ingredients and stir with rubber spatula until just combined.

2. Scoop batter into prepared tin. Bake until doughnuts are lightly browned and toothpick inserted in center comes out clean, 19 to 22 minutes. Let doughnuts cool in tin for 5 minutes.

3. For the Coating Whisk sugar and cinnamon together in bowl. Remove doughnuts from tin. Working with 1 doughnut at a time, brush all over with melted butter, then roll in cinnamon sugar, pressing lightly to adhere. Transfer to wire rack and let cool for 15 minutes. Serve.

Brush with Butter

We brush the warm muffins liberally with melted butter before rolling them in the cinnamon sugar. The butter helps the coating stick and makes the muffins taste more fried.

Why This Recipe Works To capture the best of breakfast baking, we set out to create a muffin that tasted like a cake doughnut in disguise with a tender crumb, a crisp exterior, and a buttery spiced coating. Adding an extra yolk and cutting all-purpose flour with cornstarch gave the muffins a tender crumb that wouldn't break apart. To replicate a fried exterior, we turned up the oven temperature, which crisped the crust nicely. Lastly we brushed the muffins with butter and rolled them in cinnamon sugar. From coating to crumb, these doughnut muffins combined the essence of a doughnut and the ease of a muffin (without a deep fryer in sight).

ULTIMATE CINNAMON BUNS

MAKES 8 BUNS

For smaller cinnamon buns, cut the dough into 12 pieces in step 3.

Dough
- ¾ cup whole milk, heated to 110 degrees
- 2¼ teaspoons instant or rapid-rise yeast
- 3 large eggs, room temperature
- 4¼ cups (21¼ ounces) all-purpose flour
- ½ cup cornstarch
- ½ cup (3½ ounces) granulated sugar
- 1½ teaspoons salt
- 12 tablespoons unsalted butter, cut into 12 pieces and softened

Filling
- 1½ cups packed (10½ ounces) light brown sugar
- 1½ tablespoons ground cinnamon
- ¼ teaspoon salt
- 4 tablespoons unsalted butter, softened

Glaze
- 1½ cups confectioners' sugar
- 4 ounces cream cheese, softened
- 1 tablespoon whole milk
- 1 teaspoon vanilla extract

1. For the Dough Make foil sling for 13 by 9-inch baking pan by folding 2 long sheets of aluminum foil; first sheet should be 13 inches wide and second sheet should be 9 inches wide. Lay sheets of foil in pan perpendicular to each other, with extra foil hanging over edges of pan. Push foil into corners and up sides of pan, smoothing foil flush to pan. Grease foil. Whisk milk and yeast together in liquid measuring cup until yeast dissolves, then whisk in eggs.

2. Adjust oven rack to middle position and place loaf or cake pan on bottom of oven. Using stand mixer fitted with dough hook, mix flour, cornstarch, sugar, and salt on low speed until combined. Add warm milk mixture in steady stream and mix until dough comes together, about 1 minute. Increase speed to medium and add butter, 1 piece at a time, until incorporated. Continue to mix until dough is smooth and comes away from sides of bowl, about 10 minutes (if dough is still wet and sticky, add up to ¼ cup flour, 1 tablespoon at a time, until it releases from bowl). Turn dough out onto counter and knead to form smooth, round ball. Transfer dough to medium greased bowl, cover with plastic wrap, and transfer to middle rack of oven. Pour 3 cups boiling water into loaf pan in oven, close oven door, and let dough rise until doubled in size, about 2 hours.

3. For the Filling Combine sugar, cinnamon, and salt in small bowl. Remove dough from oven and turn out onto lightly floured counter. Roll dough into 18-inch square and, leaving ½-inch border around edges, spread with butter, then sprinkle evenly with sugar mixture and lightly press sugar mixture into dough. Starting with edge closest to you, roll dough into tight cylinder, pinch lightly to seal seam, and cut into 8 pieces. Transfer pieces, cut side up, to prepared pan. Cover with plastic and let rise in oven until doubled in size, about 1 hour.

4. For the Glaze Remove buns and water pan from oven and heat oven to 350 degrees. Whisk all glaze ingredients together in medium bowl until smooth. Remove plastic and bake buns until deep golden brown and filling is melted, 35 to 40 minutes, rotating pan halfway through baking. Transfer to wire rack, top buns with ½ cup glaze, and let cool for 30 minutes. Using foil overhang, lift buns from pan and top with remaining glaze. Serve.

To Make Ahead Follow recipe through step 3, skipping step of letting buns rise. Place buns in pan, cover with plastic wrap, and refrigerate for up to 1 day. To bake, let sit at room temperature for 1 hour. Remove plastic and proceed with step 4.

Why This Recipe Works Gooey softball-size cinnamon buns are the ultimate breakfast treat. For the base of ours, we turned to a buttery, tender brioche dough. Adding cornstarch to the all-purpose flour in the dough made the buns especially tender. For a filling with great flavor, we combined a good amount of cinnamon—no other spices necessary—with brown sugar. Softened butter helped keep the filling from spilling out as we rolled up the dough. Baked together, the butter and cinnamon sugar turned into a rich, gooey filling. A thick, tangy glaze of cream cheese, confectioners' sugar, and milk ensured our buns really looked the part.

Why This Recipe Works Rich, gooey, homemade cinnamon buns can take upwards of 3 hours to prepare. We wanted the same tender, yeasty results in half the time. For a quicker rise, we supplemented the yeast (which we proofed in warm milk for extra speed) with baking powder. A mere 2 minutes of hand-kneading and a single 30-minute rise were enough to give us the flavor and texture we were looking for. We used a cooler-than-normal oven to give the yeast time to rise and develop flavor before the tops of the buns set. Brown sugar and butter in the filling and a touch of vanilla in our tangy cream cheese glaze made these buns ultra-rich and indulgent.

QUICKER CINNAMON BUNS

MAKES 8 BUNS

Since the filling, dough, and glaze all require melted butter, it's easier to melt all 10 tablespoons in a liquid measuring cup and divvy it up as needed. Stir the melted butter before each use to redistribute the milk solids. We developed this recipe using a dark cake pan, which produces deeply caramelized buns. If your cake pan is light-colored, adjust the oven rack to the lowest position, heat the oven to 375 degrees, and increase the baking time to 29 to 32 minutes.

Filling
- ¾ cup packed (5¼ ounces) light brown sugar
- ¼ cup (1¾ ounces) granulated sugar
- 1 tablespoon ground cinnamon
- ⅛ teaspoon salt
- 2 tablespoons unsalted butter, melted
- 1 teaspoon vanilla extract

Dough
- 1¼ cups whole milk, room temperature
- 4 teaspoons instant or rapid-rise yeast
- 2 tablespoons granulated sugar
- 2¾ cups (13¾ ounces) all-purpose flour
- 2½ teaspoons baking powder
- ¾ teaspoon salt
- 6 tablespoons unsalted butter, melted

Glaze
- 3 ounces cream cheese, softened
- 2 tablespoons unsalted butter, melted
- 2 tablespoons whole milk
- ½ teaspoon vanilla extract
- ⅛ teaspoon salt
- 1 cup (4 ounces) confectioners' sugar, sifted

1. For the Filling Combine brown sugar, granulated sugar, cinnamon, and salt in bowl. Stir in melted butter and vanilla until mixture resembles wet sand; set aside.

2. For the Dough Grease dark 9-inch round cake pan, line with parchment paper, and grease parchment. Pour ¼ cup milk in small bowl and microwave until 110 degrees, 15 to 20 seconds. Stir in yeast and 1 teaspoon sugar and let sit until mixture is bubbly, about 5 minutes.

3. Whisk flour, baking powder, salt, and remaining 5 teaspoons sugar together in large bowl. Stir in 2 tablespoons butter, yeast mixture, and remaining 1 cup milk until dough forms (dough will be sticky). Transfer dough to well-floured counter and knead until smooth ball forms, about 2 minutes.

4. Roll dough into 12 by 9-inch rectangle, with long side parallel to counter edge. Brush dough all over with 2 tablespoons butter, leaving ½-inch border on far edge. Sprinkle dough evenly with filling, then press filling firmly into dough. Using bench scraper or metal spatula, loosen dough from counter. Roll dough away from you into tight log and pinch seam to seal.

5. Roll log seam side down and cut into 8 equal pieces. Stand buns on end and gently re-form ends that were pinched during cutting. Place 1 bun in center of prepared pan and others around perimeter of pan, seam sides facing in. Brush tops of buns with remaining 2 tablespoons butter. Cover buns loosely with plastic wrap and let rise for 30 minutes. Adjust oven rack to middle position and heat oven to 350 degrees.

6. Discard plastic and bake buns until edges are well browned, 23 to 25 minutes. Loosen buns from sides of pan with paring knife and let cool for 5 minutes. Invert large plate over cake pan. Using potholders, flip plate and pan upside down; remove pan and parchment. Reinvert buns onto wire rack, set wire rack inside parchment-lined rimmed baking sheet, and let cool for 5 minutes.

7. For the Glaze Place cream cheese in large bowl and whisk in butter, milk, vanilla, and salt until smooth. Whisk in sugar until smooth. Pour glaze evenly over tops of buns, spreading with spatula to cover. Serve.

Why This Recipe Works Morning buns rely on a complicated croissant-like dough that requires both substantial effort and time. For an easier path, we switched to a quick dough closer to puff pastry. Instead of rolling the butter into the dry ingredients on the counter, we moved it all to a zipper-lock bag and rolled everything right in the bag. To produce multiple layers in this rich pastry, we rolled the dough into a rectangle, then into a cylinder, and gently patted it flat. A blend of brown and white sugar added a subtle molasses flavor to the filling, while orange zest instilled it with bright citrus notes.

MORNING BUNS

MAKES 12 BUNS

If the dough becomes too soft to work with at any point, refrigerate it until it's firm enough to easily handle.

Dough
- 3 cups (15 ounces) all-purpose flour
- 1 tablespoon sugar
- 2¼ teaspoons instant or rapid-rise yeast
- ¾ teaspoon salt
- 24 tablespoons (3 sticks) unsalted butter, cut into ¼-inch-thick slices and chilled
- 1 cup sour cream, chilled
- ¼ cup orange juice, chilled
- 3 tablespoons ice water
- 1 large egg yolk

Filling
- ½ cup (3½ ounces) granulated sugar
- ½ cup packed (3½ ounces) light brown sugar
- 1 tablespoon grated orange zest
- 2 teaspoons ground cinnamon
- 1 teaspoon vanilla extract

1. For the Dough Combine flour, sugar, yeast, and salt in large zipper-lock bag. Add butter to bag, seal, and shake to coat. Press air out of bag and reseal. Roll over bag several times with rolling pin, shaking bag after each roll, until butter is pressed into large flakes. Transfer mixture to large bowl and stir in sour cream, orange juice, water, and egg yolk until combined.

2. Turn dough onto floured counter and knead briefly to form smooth, cohesive ball. Roll dough into 20 by 12-inch rectangle. Starting with short edge, roll dough into tight cylinder. Pat cylinder flat to 12 by 4-inch rectangle and transfer to parchment paper–lined rimmed baking sheet. Cover with plastic wrap and freeze for 15 minutes.

3. For the Filling Line 12-cup muffin tin with paper or foil liners and spray with vegetable oil spray. Combine granulated sugar, brown sugar, orange zest, cinnamon, and vanilla in medium bowl. Remove dough from freezer and place on lightly floured counter. Roll dough into 20 by 12-inch rectangle and sprinkle evenly with filling, leaving ½-inch border around edges. Starting at long edge, roll dough into tight cylinder and pinch lightly to seal seam. Trim ½ inch dough from each end and discard. Cut dough into 12 pieces and transfer, cut side up, to prepared tin. Cover loosely with plastic and refrigerate for at least 4 hours or up to 1 day.

4. Adjust oven rack to middle position and place loaf or cake pan on bottom of oven. Remove plastic from buns and place in oven. Pour 3 cups boiling water into loaf pan in oven, close oven door, and let buns rise until puffed and doubled in size, 20 to 30 minutes. Remove buns and water pan from oven and heat oven to 425 degrees. Bake until buns begin to rise, about 5 minutes, then reduce oven temperature to 325 degrees. Bake until deep golden brown, 40 to 50 minutes, rotating pan halfway through baking. Let buns cool in muffin tin on wire rack for 5 minutes, then transfer to wire rack and discard liners. Serve warm.

To Make Ahead Follow recipe through step 3, skipping step of refrigerating buns. Freeze buns, in muffin tin, until firm, about 30 minutes. Transfer buns, with liners, to zipper-lock bag and freeze for up to 1 month. To bake, return buns to muffin tin, cover with plastic, and refrigerate for at least 8 hours or up to 1 day. Proceed with step 4.

Key Steps to Flaky Pastry

1. Flatten flour-coated butter into long flakes by pressing air out of bag, sealing it, and rolling over it a few times with rolling pin.

2. Add butter-flour mixture to bowl and stir in sour cream, orange juice, water, and egg yolk. Then mix and knead briefly before rolling dough.

KOLACHES

MAKES 16 KOLACHES

Do not use nonfat ricotta cheese in this recipe. In step 1, if the dough hasn't cleared the sides of the bowl after 12 minutes, add more flour, 1 tablespoon at a time, up to 2 tablespoons. In step 6, to prevent sticking, reflour the bottom of the measuring cup (or drinking glass) after making each indentation.

Dough
- 1 cup whole milk
- 10 tablespoons unsalted butter, melted
- 1 large egg plus 2 large yolks
- 3½ cups (17½ ounces) all-purpose flour
- ⅓ cup (2⅓ ounces) sugar
- 2¼ teaspoons instant or rapid-rise yeast
- 1½ teaspoons salt

Cheese Filling
- 6 ounces cream cheese, softened
- 3 tablespoons sugar
- 1 tablespoon all-purpose flour
- ½ teaspoon grated lemon zest
- 6 ounces (¾ cup) whole-milk or part-skim ricotta cheese

Streusel
- 2 tablespoons plus 2 teaspoons all-purpose flour
- 2 tablespoons plus 2 teaspoons sugar
- 1 tablespoon unsalted butter, cut into 8 pieces and chilled

- 1 large egg beaten with 1 tablespoon milk

1. For the Dough Grease large bowl. Whisk milk, melted butter, and egg and yolks together in 2-cup liquid measuring cup (butter will form clumps). Whisk flour, sugar, yeast, and salt together in bowl of stand mixer. Fit stand mixer with dough hook, add milk mixture to flour mixture, and knead on low speed until no dry flour remains, about 2 minutes. Increase speed to medium and knead until dough clears sides of bowl but still sticks to bottom, 8 to 12 minutes.

2. Transfer dough to greased bowl and cover with plastic wrap. Adjust oven racks to upper-middle and lower-middle positions. Place dough on lower-middle rack and place loaf pan on bottom of oven. Pour 3 cups boiling water into loaf pan, close oven door, and let dough rise until doubled, about 1 hour.

3. For the Cheese Filling Using stand mixer fitted with paddle, beat cream cheese, sugar, flour, and lemon zest on low speed until smooth, about 1 minute. Add ricotta and beat until just combined, about 30 seconds. Transfer to bowl, cover with plastic, and refrigerate until ready to use.

4. For the Streusel Combine flour, sugar, and butter in bowl and rub between fingers until mixture resembles wet sand. Cover with plastic and refrigerate until ready to use.

5. Line 2 rimmed baking sheets with parchment paper. Punch down dough and place on lightly floured counter. Divide into quarters and cut each quarter into 4 equal pieces. Form each piece into rough ball by pulling dough edges underneath so top is smooth. On unfloured counter, cup each ball in your palm and roll into smooth, tight ball. Arrange 8 balls on each prepared sheet and cover loosely with plastic. Place sheets on oven racks. Replace water in loaf pan with 3 cups boiling water, close oven door, and let dough rise until doubled, about 90 minutes.

6. Remove sheets and loaf pan from oven. Heat oven to 350 degrees. Grease and flour bottom of ⅓-cup measuring cup (or 2¼-inch-diameter drinking glass). Make deep indentation in center of each dough ball by slowly pressing until cup touches sheet. (Perimeter of balls may deflate slightly.)

7. Gently brush kolaches all over with egg-milk mixture. Divide filling evenly among kolaches (about 1½ tablespoons per kolache) and smooth with back of spoon. Sprinkle streusel over kolaches, avoiding filling. Bake until golden brown, about 25 minutes, switching and rotating sheets halfway through baking. Let kolaches cool on pans for 20 minutes. Serve warm.

Why This Recipe Works Brought to Texas by Czech immigrants, kolaches are palm-size rounds of sweetened bread with dollops of sweet cheese or fruit filling in the center and a streusel topping. We discovered that long mixing with a dough hook developed plenty of stretchy gluten, making the finished pastries light and pleasantly chewy. For a Texas-style filling, a combination of tangy cream cheese and milkier, slightly salty ricotta created a perfect base, while a little sugar and lemon zest balanced the flavor. At the end of the day, our kolaches were subtly sweet, tender, buttery, and . . . gone.

MONKEY BREAD

SERVES 6 TO 8

Make sure to use light brown sugar in the coating mix; dark brown sugar has a stronger molasses flavor that can be overwhelming. After baking, don't let the bread cool in the pan for more than 5 minutes or it will stick to the pan and come out in pieces. Monkey bread is best served warm.

Dough
- 2 tablespoons unsalted butter, softened, plus 2 tablespoons melted
- 1 cup milk, heated to 110 degrees
- ⅓ cup water, heated to 110 degrees
- ¼ cup (1¾ ounces) granulated sugar
- 2¼ teaspoons instant or rapid-rise yeast
- 3¼ cups (16¼ ounces) all-purpose flour
- 2 teaspoons salt

Brown Sugar Coating
- 1 cup packed (7 ounces) light brown sugar
- 2 teaspoons ground cinnamon
- 8 tablespoons unsalted butter, melted

Glaze
- 1 cup (4 ounces) confectioners' sugar
- 2 tablespoons milk

1. For the Dough Grease 12-cup nonstick Bundt pan with softened butter; set aside. Combine milk, water, melted butter, sugar, and yeast in 2-cup liquid measuring cup.

2. Adjust oven rack to middle position and place loaf or cake pan on bottom of oven. Using stand mixer fitted with dough hook, mix flour and salt on low speed. Slowly add milk mixture and mix until dough comes together (if dough is too wet and doesn't come together, add up to 2 tablespoons more flour). Increase speed to medium and knead until dough is shiny and smooth, 6 to 7 minutes. Turn dough onto lightly floured counter and knead briefly to form smooth, round ball. Place dough in large greased bowl, coat surface with vegetable oil spray, and transfer to oven. Pour 3 cups boiling water into loaf pan in oven, close oven door, and let dough rise until doubled in size, 50 minutes to 1 hour.

3. For the Brown Sugar Coating While dough rises, combine sugar and cinnamon in small bowl. Place melted butter in second bowl. Set aside.

4. Gently remove dough from bowl and pat into rough 8-inch square. Using bench scraper or knife, cut square into quarters, then cut each quarter into 16 pieces. Roll each piece of dough into a ball. Working with one at a time, dip each ball in melted butter, allowing excess butter to drip off, then roll in sugar mixture. Layer dough balls in prepared pan, staggering seams where dough balls meet. Cover pan tightly with plastic wrap, transfer to oven, and let rest until dough balls are puffy and have risen 1 to 2 inches from top of pan, 50 minutes to 1 hour, 10 minutes.

5. Remove Bundt pan and water pan from oven; adjust oven rack to medium-low position and heat oven to 350 degrees. Remove plastic and bake until top of dough is deeply browned and caramel begins to bubble around edges, 30 to 35 minutes, rotating pan halfway through baking. Let monkey bread cool in pan for 5 minutes, then turn out on platter and let cool slightly, about 10 minutes.

6. For the Glaze Meanwhile, whisk sugar and milk together in small bowl until smooth. Using whisk, drizzle glaze over warm monkey bread, letting it run over top and sides of bread. Serve warm.

Forming Monkey Bread

After forming dough balls, dip each one in melted butter and sugar and then place in greased Bundt pan, staggering seams where dough balls meet.

Why This Recipe Works It might have a funny name, but monkey bread is a soft, sweet, sticky, ultra-cinnamony treat (its moniker probably refers to how it's pulled apart and stuffed into eager mouths). To expedite the rising and proofing of the dough, and ensure our bread had plenty of yeasty flavor, we used a good amount of instant yeast. Butter and milk helped keep the dough rich and moist, and a little sugar made the bread sweet enough to eat on its own. A dip in butter and cinnamon sugar gave the monkey bread a thick, caramel-like coating after its stint in the oven. And a drizzle of a simple glaze finished it off.

Why This Recipe Works With their chewy interiors, crunchy crusts, and craggy texture, English muffins are a treat—but they're also a lot of work. For a no-fuss recipe without the kneading, rolling, cutting, or griddling, we made a simple loaf bread with the flavor and texture of English muffins. Protein-rich bread flour gave the loaf a chewy yet light consistency, and baking soda created the all-important honeycombed texture. Heating the milk before mixing the dough activated the yeast and shortened the rising time. We simply mixed the dough, let it rise, then baked it in loaf pans until the crust was well browned and the interior was perfectly craggy.

ENGLISH MUFFIN BREAD

MAKES 2 LOAVES

Serve this bread with butter and jam.

    Cornmeal
5 cups (27½ ounces) bread flour
4½ teaspoons instant or rapid-rise yeast
1 tablespoon sugar
2 teaspoons salt
1 teaspoon baking soda
3 cups whole milk, heated to 120 degrees

1. Grease two 8½ by 4½-inch loaf pans and dust with cornmeal. Combine flour, yeast, sugar, salt, and baking soda in large bowl. Stir in hot milk until combined, about 1 minute. Cover dough with greased plastic wrap and let rise in warm place for 30 minutes, or until dough is bubbly and has doubled.

2. Stir dough and divide between prepared loaf pans, pushing into corners with greased rubber spatula. (Pans should be about two-thirds full.) Cover pans with greased plastic and let dough rise in warm place until it reaches edges of pans, about 30 minutes. Adjust oven rack to middle position and heat oven to 375 degrees.

3. Discard plastic and transfer pans to oven. Bake until loaves are well browned and register 200 degrees, about 30 minutes, rotating and switching pans halfway through baking. Turn loaves out onto wire rack and let cool completely, about 1 hour. Slice, toast, and serve.

Tricks to the Right Texture

To give our English Muffin Bread the proper chew and porous texture, we needed a few tricks. High-protein bread flour allows more gluten to develop in the batter for a satisfyingly chewy loaf. Stirring baking soda in with the other dry ingredients gives the bread extra rise for an appropriately coarse, honeycombed texture.

A Well-Dressed Table

By the end of the 19th century, the English were losing their taste for English-style muffins, but in the U.S. they had become such a popular breakfast bread that the properly set breakfast table required special dishes for serving them. Victorians, of course, were ardent believers that the correct home environment shaped correct behavior; proper dining and tableware, especially, equated with proper civilization. So wealthy families had specific dishware for everything, from glass or silver vases for celery to custom dishes to hold bananas to specialized vessels and utensils for serving sardines. And don't forget asparagus forks.

Why This Recipe Works For a brown soda bread with good wheaty flavor but without a gummy, dense texture, we started by finding the right ratio of whole-wheat to all-purpose flour. Toasted wheat germ played up the sweet, nutty flavor of the whole wheat. To keep the texture light, we needed plenty of leavening; baking soda alone gave the bread a soapy taste, so we used a combination of baking soda and baking powder. Just a touch of sugar and a few tablespoons of butter kept our bread wholesome but not "health foody," and brushing a portion of the melted butter on the loaf after baking gave it a rich crust.

BROWN SODA BREAD

MAKES 1 LOAF

Toasted wheat germ is sold in jars at well-stocked supermarkets.

- 2 cups (10 ounces) all-purpose flour
- 1½ cups (8¼ ounces) whole-wheat flour
- ½ cup toasted wheat germ
- 3 tablespoons sugar
- 1½ teaspoons salt
- 1 teaspoon baking powder
- 1 teaspoon baking soda
- 1¾ cups buttermilk
- 3 tablespoons unsalted butter, melted

1. Adjust oven rack to lower-middle position and heat oven to 400 degrees. Line rimmed baking sheet with parchment paper. Whisk all-purpose flour, whole-wheat flour, wheat germ, sugar, salt, baking powder, and baking soda together in large bowl. Combine buttermilk and 2 tablespoons melted butter in 2-cup liquid measuring cup.

2. Add wet ingredients to dry ingredients and stir with rubber spatula until dough just comes together. Turn out dough onto lightly floured counter and knead until cohesive mass forms, about 8 turns. Pat dough into 7-inch round and transfer to prepared baking sheet. Using sharp serrated knife, make ¼-inch-deep cross about 5 inches long on top of loaf. Bake until skewer inserted in center comes out clean and loaf registers 195 degrees, 45 to 50 minutes, rotating baking sheet halfway through baking.

3. Remove bread from oven. Brush with remaining 1 tablespoon melted butter. Transfer loaf to wire rack and let cool for at least 1 hour. Serve.

BROWN SODA BREAD WITH CURRANTS AND CARAWAY

Add 1 cup dried currants and 1 tablespoon caraway seeds to dry ingredients in step 1.

Fastest Bread Ever

No yeast, no rise time, and almost no kneading or shaping.

Measure and whisk dry ingredients	5 minutes
Measure and combine wet ingredients	2 minutes
Stir wet into dry	1 minute
Knead briefly	1 minute
Shape simply	1 minute
Total work time	10 minutes

Mimicking Whole-Meal Flour

Brown Irish soda bread boasts a delicious wheaty sweetness. Traditionally, this bread adds whole-meal flour to the all-purpose flour used in the more familiar Irish soda bread to get that uniquely wheaty flavor. Many recipes simply substitute ordinary whole-wheat flour, while others skip the white flour entirely, combining the whole-wheat flour with practically the entire contents of a natural foods store. The former produced bland loaves while the latter offered great taste but crumbly textures.

For our recipe, we tried various ratios of all-purpose and whole-wheat flours until we landed on 2 cups of white flour combined with 1½ cups of whole-wheat. To play up the toasty, nutty flavor, we tried adding by turns wheat germ, wheat bran, and oatmeal. All of them gave our loaf complex wheatiness, but the bran required a trip to a specialty store and the oats required toasting and processing. Toasted wheat germ comes in convenient jars at the supermarket, so that's what we used.

A combination of whole-wheat flour, toasted wheatgerm, and all-purpose flour gives our loaf both robust flavor and tender, moist texture.

DAKOTA BREAD

MAKES ONE 10-INCH LOAF

In step 2, if the dough is still sticking to the sides of the mixing bowl after 2 minutes, add more flour 1 tablespoon at a time, up to 3 tablespoons. Be sure to use hot cereal mix, not boxed cold breakfast cereals, which may also be labeled "seven-grain."

- 2 cups warm water (110 degrees)
- 1½ cups (7½ ounces) seven-grain hot cereal mix
- 2 tablespoons honey
- 2 tablespoons vegetable oil
- 3½ cups (19¼ ounces) bread flour
- 1¾ teaspoons salt
- 1 teaspoon instant or rapid-rise yeast
- 3 tablespoons raw, unsalted pepitas
- 3 tablespoons raw, unsalted sunflower seeds
- 1 teaspoon sesame seeds
- 1 teaspoon poppy seeds
- 1 large egg, lightly beaten

1. Grease large bowl. Line rimmed baking sheet with parchment paper. In bowl of stand mixer, combine water, cereal, honey, and oil and let sit for 10 minutes.

2. Add flour, salt, and yeast to cereal mixture. Fit stand mixer with dough hook and knead on low speed until dough is smooth and elastic, 4 to 6 minutes. Add 2 tablespoons pepitas and 2 tablespoons sunflower seeds to dough and knead for 1 minute longer. Turn out dough onto lightly floured counter and knead until seeds are evenly distributed, about 2 minutes.

3. Transfer dough to greased bowl and cover with plastic wrap. Let dough rise at room temperature until almost doubled in size and fingertip depression in dough springs back slowly, 60 to 90 minutes.

4. Gently press down on center of dough to deflate. Transfer dough to lightly floured counter and shape into tight round ball. Place dough on prepared sheet. Cover dough loosely with plastic and let rise at room temperature until almost doubled in size, 60 to 90 minutes.

5. Adjust oven racks to upper-middle and lowest positions and heat oven to 425 degrees. Combine remaining 1 tablespoon pepitas, remaining 1 tablespoon sunflower seeds, sesame seeds, and poppy seeds in small bowl. Using sharp knife, make ¼-inch-deep cross, 5 inches long, on top of loaf. Brush loaf with egg and sprinkle seed mixture evenly over top.

6. Place 8½ by 4½-inch loaf pan on lowest oven rack and fill with 1 cup boiling water. Place baking sheet with dough on upper-middle rack and reduce oven to 375 degrees. Bake until crust is dark brown and bread registers 200 degrees, 40 to 50 minutes. Transfer loaf to wire rack and let cool completely, about 2 hours. Serve.

The Right Mix

Our Dakota Bread recipe calls for bread flour (for an appropriately chewy texture) supplemented with seven-grain hot cereal mix, which provides the bread with nutty depth. Don't confuse seven-grain hot cereal with seven-grain cold cereal; the latter will harm the texture of the loaf.

HOT TO TROT
Seven-grain hot cereal

Why This Recipe Works This hearty loaf from the breadbasket of America usually contains a daunting variety of flours and seeds. We shortened the ingredient list by using seven-grain cereal mix. This easy addition gave our loaf hearty texture and complex flavor. To round it out, we stirred some seeds into the batter and sprinkled more on top of the loaf. Starting the bread in a hot oven created an initial "spring," giving the loaf a lighter crumb, then lowering the temperature prevented the seeds from burning. High-protein bread flour allowed our loaf to rise high, and a pan of water in the oven prevented the crust from setting before the bread had fully risen.

great american cakes and cookies

476	Red Velvet Cake	**507**	Cream Cheese Pound Cake
478	Chocolate Blackout Cake	**508**	Cold-Oven Pound Cake
481	Tunnel of Fudge Cake	**511**	Chocolate Cream Cupcakes
483	Lane Cake	**513**	Hot Fudge Pudding Cake
484	Strawberry Dream Cake	**514**	Lemon Pudding Cake
487	Strawberry Poke Cake	**516**	Lemon Icebox Cheesecake
488	Texas Sheet Cake	**519**	Milk Chocolate Cheesecake
490	Chocolate Éclair Cake	**520**	Chocolate Chip Skillet Cookie
493	Magic Chocolate Flan Cake	**523**	Melting Moments
495	Tres Leches Cake	**525**	Slice-and-Bake Cookies
496	Swiss Hazelnut Cake	**526**	Fairy Gingerbread
499	Blitz Torte	**528**	Joe Froggers
501	Angel Food Cake	**531**	Black and White Cookies
502	Chiffon Cake	**532**	Whoopie Pies
504	Italian Cream Cake	**535**	Basic Chocolate Truffles

RED VELVET CAKE

SERVES 12

This recipe must be prepared with natural cocoa powder. Dutch-processed cocoa will not yield the proper color or rise.

Cake
- 2¼ cups (11¼ ounces) all-purpose flour
- 1½ teaspoons baking soda
- Pinch salt
- 1 cup buttermilk
- 2 large eggs
- 1 tablespoon distilled white vinegar
- 1 teaspoon vanilla extract
- 2 tablespoons cocoa powder
- 2 tablespoons (1 ounce) red food coloring
- 12 tablespoons unsalted butter, softened
- 1½ cups (10½ ounces) granulated sugar

Frosting
- 16 tablespoons unsalted butter, softened
- 4 cups (16 ounces) confectioners' sugar
- 16 ounces cream cheese, cut into 8 pieces, softened
- 1½ teaspoons vanilla extract
- Pinch salt

1. For the Cake Adjust oven rack to middle position and heat oven to 350 degrees. Grease two 9-inch round cake pans, line with parchment paper, grease parchment, then flour pans. Whisk flour, baking soda, and salt in medium bowl. Whisk buttermilk, eggs, vinegar, and vanilla in 4-cup liquid measuring cup. Mix cocoa with food coloring in small bowl until smooth paste forms.

2. Using stand mixer fitted with paddle, beat butter and sugar together on medium-high speed until pale and fluffy, about 3 minutes. Reduce speed to medium-low and add flour mixture in 3 additions, alternating with buttermilk mixture in 2 additions, scraping down bowl as needed. Add cocoa mixture and beat on medium speed until completely incorporated, about 30 seconds. Give batter final stir by hand. Scrape batter into prepared pans and bake until toothpick inserted in center comes out clean, about 25 minutes. Let cakes cool in pans on wire rack for 10 minutes. Remove cakes from pans, discarding parchment, and let cool completely on rack, about 2 hours. (Cooled cakes can be wrapped tightly in plastic wrap and kept at room temperature for up to 1 day.)

3. For the Frosting Using stand mixer fitted with paddle, beat butter and sugar on medium-high speed until pale and fluffy, about 2 minutes. Add cream cheese, 1 piece at a time, and beat until incorporated, about 30 seconds. Beat in vanilla and salt. Refrigerate until ready to use.

4. When cakes are cooled, cover edges of cake platter with strips of parchment. Place 1 cake layer on platter. Spread 2 cups frosting evenly over top, right to edge of cake. Top with second cake layer, press lightly to adhere, then spread remaining frosting evenly over top and sides of cake. Carefully remove parchment strips before serving. (Cake can be refrigerated for up to 3 days.)

Lost and Found
Red velvet cake fell out of fashion in the 1970s amidst health scares relating to red dye #2 (a similar fate befell red M&Ms, even though the candies never contained the dye in question). Once consumers were convinced that other red dyes were safe, red candies made it back into the M&Ms assortment (in 1987) and red velvet cakes started a comeback in bakeries.

Why This Recipe Works Although the exact origins of this cake are muddled, the appeal of a tender, shockingly bright red cake swathed in fluffy cream cheese frosting is undeniable. For a cake with an extra-tender crumb, we used two unexpected ingredients: buttermilk and vinegar. They reacted with our recipe's baking soda to create a fine, tender crumb. We also zeroed in on the perfect amount of cocoa that would add a dark hue to our cake as well as lending it a pleasant cocoa flavor.

CHOCOLATE BLACKOUT CAKE

SERVES 10 TO 12

Be sure to give the pudding and the cake enough time to cool or you'll end up with runny pudding and gummy cake.

Pudding
- 1¼ cups (8¾ ounces) granulated sugar
- ¼ cup cornstarch
- ½ teaspoon salt
- 2 cups half-and-half
- 1 cup whole milk
- 6 ounces unsweetened chocolate, chopped
- 2 teaspoons vanilla extract

Cake
- 1½ cups (7½ ounces) all-purpose flour
- 2 teaspoons baking powder
- ½ teaspoon baking soda
- ½ teaspoon salt
- 8 tablespoons unsalted butter
- ¾ cup (2¼ ounces) Dutch-processed cocoa powder
- 1 cup brewed coffee
- 1 cup buttermilk
- 1 cup packed (7 ounces) light brown sugar
- 1 cup (7 ounces) granulated sugar
- 2 large eggs
- 1 teaspoon vanilla extract

1. For the Pudding Whisk sugar, cornstarch, salt, half-and-half, and milk in large saucepan. Set pan over medium heat. Add chocolate and whisk constantly until chocolate melts and mixture begins to bubble, 2 to 4 minutes. Stir in vanilla and transfer pudding to large bowl. Place plastic wrap directly on surface of pudding and refrigerate until cold, at least 4 hours or up to 1 day.

2. For the Cake Adjust oven rack to middle position and heat oven to 325 degrees. Grease two 8-inch round cake pans, line with parchment paper, grease parchment, then flour pans. Whisk flour, baking powder, baking soda, and salt in bowl.

3. Melt butter in large saucepan over medium heat. Stir in cocoa and cook until fragrant, about 1 minute. Off heat, whisk in coffee, buttermilk, brown sugar, and granulated sugar until dissolved. Whisk in eggs and vanilla, then slowly whisk in flour mixture.

4. Divide batter evenly between prepared pans and bake until toothpick inserted in center comes out clean, 30 to 35 minutes. Let cakes cool in pans on wire rack for 15 minutes. Remove cakes from pans, discarding parchment, and let cool completely on wire rack, about 2 hours.

5. Working with 1 cake layer at a time, cut cakes horizontally into 2 layers using long, serrated knife. Crumble 1 cake layer into medium crumbs and set aside. Cover edges of cake platter with strips of parchment. Place 1 cake layer on platter. Spread 1 cup pudding over top, right to edge of cake. Top with second layer; press lightly to adhere. Repeat with 1 cup pudding and last cake layer. Spread remaining pudding evenly over top and sides of cake. Sprinkle cake crumbs evenly over top and sides of cake, pressing lightly to adhere crumbs. Carefully remove parchment strips before serving. (Cake can be refrigerated for up to 2 days.)

Lost Icon

Ebinger's Baking Company opened in 1898 on Flatbush Avenue in Brooklyn and grew into a chain of more than 60 stores before going bankrupt in 1972. Started by Arthur Ebinger, a baker who emigrated from Germany with a vast collection of recipes, the business grew to include his wife and their three sons. During its heyday, Ebinger's was a point of bragging rights for Brooklynites, as celebrities and the well-to-do from Manhattan never went to Brooklyn without taking home a cake or one of Ebinger's other specialties, which included challah, rye bread, pumpkin pie, Othellos (filled mini sponge cakes covered in chocolate), and crumb buns.

Why This Recipe Works Chocolate blackout cake, a tender chocolate layer cake sandwiched together with a puddinglike filling and covered with cake crumbs, was created by the now-shuttered Ebinger's bakery in Brooklyn. We set out to create our own version. We started by adding cocoa powder to the butter we were already melting for the cake. Heating the cocoa in the butter produced a cake that was dark and rich. And to complement the chocolate flavor of the cake, we made a chocolaty, dairy-rich pudding with a combination of milk and half-and-half, which gave it a velvety, lush quality.

Why This Recipe Works We wanted to resurrect the classic childhood favorite tunnel of fudge cake without the benefit of a prepackaged cake mix. Dutch-processed cocoa gave our cake deep chocolate flavor. Adding melted chocolate to the batter made our cake moister and contributed more chocolate punch. Slightly underbaking the cake was the first step toward achieving the ideal consistency for the tunnel. Replacing some of the granulated sugar with brown sugar and cutting back on the flour and butter provided the perfect environment for the fudgy interior to form.

TUNNEL OF FUDGE CAKE

SERVES 12 TO 14

For an accurate measurement of boiling water, bring a full kettle of water to a boil, then measure out the desired amount. Do not use a cake tester, toothpick, or skewer to test the cake—the fudgy interior won't give an accurate reading. Instead, remove the cake from the oven when the sides just begin to pull away from the pan and the surface of the cake springs back when pressed gently with your finger.

Cake
- ¾ cup (2¼ ounces) Dutch-processed cocoa powder, plus extra for dusting pan
- ½ cup boiling water
- 2 ounces bittersweet chocolate, chopped
- 2 cups (10 ounces) all-purpose flour
- 2 cups pecans or walnuts, chopped fine
- 2 cups (8 ounces) confectioners' sugar
- 1 teaspoon salt
- 5 large eggs, room temperature
- 1 tablespoon vanilla extract
- 20 tablespoons (2½ sticks) unsalted butter, softened
- 1 cup (7 ounces) granulated sugar
- ¾ cup packed (5¼ ounces) light brown sugar

Chocolate Glaze
- ¾ cup heavy cream
- ¼ cup light corn syrup
- 8 ounces bittersweet chocolate, chopped
- ½ teaspoon vanilla extract

1. For the Cake Adjust oven rack to lower-middle position and heat oven to 350 degrees. Grease 12-cup Bundt pan and dust with cocoa powder. Pour boiling water over chocolate in medium bowl and whisk until smooth. Let cool to room temperature. Whisk cocoa, flour, pecans, confectioners' sugar, and salt in large bowl. Whisk eggs and vanilla in 4-cup liquid measuring cup.

2. Using stand mixer fitted with paddle, beat butter, granulated sugar, and brown sugar on medium-high speed until light and fluffy, about 2 minutes. On low speed, add egg mixture until combined, about 30 seconds. Add chocolate mixture and beat until incorporated, about 30 seconds. Beat in flour mixture until just combined, about 30 seconds.

3. Scrape batter into prepared pan, smooth batter, and bake until edges are beginning to pull away from pan, about 45 minutes. Let cool in pan on wire rack for 1½ hours, then invert onto serving plate and let cool completely, at least 2 hours.

4. For the Chocolate Glaze Heat cream, corn syrup, and chocolate in small saucepan over medium heat, stirring constantly, until smooth. Stir in vanilla and set aside until slightly thickened, about 30 minutes. Drizzle glaze over cake and let set for at least 10 minutes. Serve. (Cake can be stored at room temperature for up to 2 days.)

Birth of the Bundt Pan
Metallurgical engineer H. David Dalquist invented the Bundt pan in 1950 at the request of bakers in Minneapolis who were using old-fashioned ceramic pans of the same design. Dalquist turned to cast aluminum to produce a pan that was much lighter and easier to use. Sales of his Bundt pan (a name he trademarked) were underwhelming until Ella Helfrich's Tunnel of Fudge Cake made its debut in 1966. The Pillsbury Company quickly received over 200,000 requests for the pan, and to meet demand Dalquist's company, Nordic Ware, went into 24-hour production. Over 50 million Bundt pans have been sold worldwide.

Why This Recipe Works Lane cake is a tall, fluffy, snow white cake filled with a rich, sweet mixture of egg whites, butter, raisins, and "a wineglass full of good whiskey." Our simplified recipe capped the number of layers at two, and using a food processor streamlined much of the tedious prep work. Replacing sugar with boiled corn syrup in our frosting quickly brought the whipped egg whites to a safe temperature without resorting to a candy thermometer or complicated (and unreliable) guesswork.

LANE CAKE

SERVES 10 TO 12

Cake
- 1 cup whole milk, room temperature
- 6 large egg whites, room temperature
- 2 teaspoons vanilla extract
- 2¼ cups (9 ounces) cake flour
- 1¾ cups (12¼ ounces) sugar
- 4 teaspoons baking powder
- 1 teaspoon salt
- 12 tablespoons unsalted butter, cut into 12 pieces and softened

Filling
- 5 tablespoons bourbon
- 1 tablespoon heavy cream
- 1 teaspoon cornstarch
- Pinch salt
- ⅓ cup sweetened shredded coconut
- ¾ cup pecans
- ¾ cup golden raisins
- 4 tablespoons unsalted butter
- ¾ cup sweetened condensed milk
- ½ teaspoon vanilla extract

Frosting
- 2 large egg whites, room temperature
- ¼ teaspoon cream of tartar
- ¼ cup (1¾ ounces) sugar
- ⅔ cup light corn syrup
- 1 teaspoon vanilla extract

1. For the Cake Adjust oven rack to middle position and heat oven to 350 degrees. Grease two 9-inch round cake pans, line with parchment paper, grease parchment, then flour pans. Whisk milk, egg whites, and vanilla in 4-cup liquid measuring cup. Using stand mixer fitted with paddle, mix flour, sugar, baking powder, and salt on low speed until combined. Add butter, 1 piece at a time, and beat until only pea-size pieces remain. Add half of milk mixture, increase speed to medium-high, and beat until light and fluffy, about 1 minute. Reduce speed to medium-low, add remaining milk mixture, and beat until incorporated, about 30 seconds. Give batter final stir by hand.

2. Scrape batter into prepared pans and bake until toothpick inserted in center comes out clean, 20 to 25 minutes. Let cakes cool in pans on wire rack for 10 minutes. Remove cakes from pans, discarding parchment, and let cool completely on racks, about 2 hours. (Cooled cakes can be tightly wrapped in plastic wrap and stored at room temperature for up to 2 days.)

3. For the Filling Whisk bourbon, cream, cornstarch, and salt in bowl until smooth. Process coconut in food processor until finely ground, about 15 seconds. Add pecans and raisins and pulse until coarsely ground, about 10 pulses. Melt butter in large skillet over medium-low heat. Add processed coconut mixture and cook, stirring occasionally, until golden brown and fragrant, about 5 minutes. Stir in bourbon mixture and bring to boil. Remove from heat and add condensed milk and vanilla. Transfer to medium bowl and let cool to room temperature, about 30 minutes. (Filling can be refrigerated for 2 days. Bring filling to room temperature before using.)

4. For the Frosting Using stand mixer fitted with whisk, whip egg whites and cream of tartar on medium-high speed until frothy, about 30 seconds. With mixer running, slowly add sugar and whip until soft peaks form, about 2 minutes; set aside. Bring corn syrup to boil in small saucepan over medium-high heat and cook until large bubbles appear around perimeter of pan, about 1 minute. With mixer running, slowly pour hot syrup into whites (avoid pouring syrup onto beaters or it will splash). Add vanilla and beat until mixture has cooled and is very thick and glossy, 3 to 5 minutes.

5. Cover edges of cake platter with strips of parchment. Place 1 cake layer on platter. Spread filling over cake, then top with second cake layer, pressing lightly to adhere. Spread remaining frosting evenly over top and sides of cake. Carefully remove parchment strips before serving. (Cake can be refrigerated for up to 2 days.)

STRAWBERRY DREAM CAKE

SERVES 8 TO 10

Be sure to allow the cream cheese to soften so that it blends into a smooth frosting.

Cake
- 10 ounces frozen whole strawberries (2 cups)
- ¾ cup whole milk, room temperature
- 6 large egg whites, room temperature
- 2 teaspoons vanilla extract
- 2¼ cups (9 ounces) cake flour
- 1¾ cups (12¼ ounces) granulated sugar
- 4 teaspoons baking powder
- 1 teaspoon salt
- 12 tablespoons unsalted butter, cut into 12 pieces and softened

Frosting
- 10 tablespoons unsalted butter, softened
- 2¼ cups (9 ounces) confectioners' sugar
- 12 ounces cream cheese, cut into 12 pieces and softened
- Pinch salt
- 8 ounces fresh strawberries, hulled and sliced thin (about 1½ cups)

1. For the Cake Adjust oven rack to middle position and heat oven to 350 degrees. Grease two 9-inch round cake pans, line with parchment paper, grease parchment, then flour pans.

2. Transfer strawberries to bowl, cover, and microwave until strawberries are soft and have released their juices, about 5 minutes. Place in fine-mesh strainer set over small saucepan. Firmly press fruit dry (juice should measure at least ¾ cup); reserve strawberry solids. Bring juice to boil over medium-high heat and cook, stirring occasionally, until syrupy and reduced to ¼ cup, 6 to 8 minutes. Whisk milk into juice until combined.

3. Whisk strawberry-milk mixture, egg whites, and vanilla in bowl. Using stand mixer fitted with paddle, mix flour, sugar, baking powder, and salt on low speed until combined. Add butter, 1 piece at a time, and mix until only pea-size pieces remain, about 1 minute. Add half of milk mixture, increase speed to medium-high, and beat until light and fluffy, about 1 minute. Reduce speed to medium-low, add remaining milk mixture, and beat until incorporated, about 30 seconds. Give batter final stir by hand.

4. Scrape batter into prepared pans and bake until toothpick inserted in center comes out clean, 20 to 25 minutes, rotating pans halfway through baking. Let cakes cool in pans on wire rack for 10 minutes. Remove cakes from pans, discarding parchment, and let cool completely on rack, about 2 hours. (Cooled cakes can be tightly wrapped with plastic wrap and stored at room temperature for up to 2 days.)

5. For the Frosting Using stand mixer fitted with paddle, mix butter and sugar on low speed until combined, about 30 seconds. Increase speed to medium-high and beat until pale and fluffy, about 2 minutes. Add cream cheese, 1 piece at a time, and beat until incorporated, about 1 minute. Add reserved strawberry solids and salt and mix until combined, about 30 seconds. Refrigerate until ready to use, up to 2 days.

6. Pat strawberries dry with paper towels. Cover edges of cake platter with strips of parchment. Place 1 cake layer on platter. Spread ¾ cup frosting evenly over top, right to edge of cake. Press 1 cup strawberries in even layer over frosting and cover with additional ¾ cup frosting. Top with second cake layer, press lightly to adhere, then spread remaining frosting evenly over top and sides of cake. Garnish with remaining strawberries. Carefully remove parchment strips before serving. (Cake can be refrigerated for up to 2 days.)

Why This Recipe Works Strange as it may seem, the vast majority of existing strawberry cake recipes turn to strawberry Jell-O for flavor. Hoping to avoid this artificial solution, we performed test after test to figure out the best way to flavor our cake with actual strawberries. Any strawberry solids wreaked havoc on the tender cake, but strained and reduced strawberry juices kept our cake light and packed a strawberry punch. Not to be left behind, the reserved strawberry solids enriched the frosting with more berry flavor.

Why This Recipe Works Strawberry poke cake was invented in 1969 as a way to increase Jell-O sales. It quickly became popular thanks to its festive look and easy assembly. But we encountered two problems: dull strawberry flavor and soggy box mix cake. For a sturdier cake that would hold up to hot gelatin, we opted to make our own white cake from scratch. And to improve the strawberry flavor of the Jell-O, we combined it with the juice from cooked strawberries. Making a homemade "jam" from the berry solids and spreading the mixture on top of the cake gave our cake an extra layer of flavor.

STRAWBERRY POKE CAKE

SERVES 12

The top of the cake will look slightly overbaked—this keeps the crumb from becoming too soggy after the gelatin is poured on top.

Cake
- 2¼ cups (11¼ ounces) all-purpose flour
- 4 teaspoons baking powder
- 1 teaspoon salt
- 1 cup whole milk
- 2 teaspoons vanilla extract
- 6 large egg whites
- 12 tablespoons unsalted butter, softened
- 1¾ cups (12¼ ounces) sugar

Syrup and Topping
- 4 cups frozen strawberries
- ½ cup water
- 6 tablespoons (2⅔ ounces) sugar
- 2 tablespoons orange juice
- 2 tablespoons strawberry-flavored gelatin
- 2 cups heavy cream, chilled

1. For the Cake Adjust oven rack to middle position and heat oven to 350 degrees. Grease 13 by 9-inch baking pan, line with parchment paper, grease parchment, then flour pan. Whisk flour, baking powder, and salt in bowl. Whisk milk, vanilla, and egg whites in 4-cup liquid measuring cup.

2. Using stand mixer fitted with paddle, beat butter and sugar on medium-high speed until pale and fluffy, about 2 minutes, scraping down bowl as needed. Reduce speed to low and add flour mixture in 3 additions, alternating with milk mixture in 2 additions, beating after each addition until combined, about 30 seconds each time, scraping down bowl as needed. Give batter final stir by hand. Scrape into prepared pan and bake until toothpick inserted in center comes out clean, about 35 minutes. Let cake cool completely in pan, at least 1 hour. (Once cool, cake can be wrapped in plastic wrap and kept at room temperature for up to 2 days.)

3. For the Syrup and Topping Heat 3 cups strawberries, water, 2 tablespoons sugar, and orange juice in medium saucepan over medium-low heat. Cover and cook until strawberries are softened, about 10 minutes. Strain liquid into bowl, reserving solids, then whisk gelatin into liquid. Let cool to room temperature, at least 20 minutes.

4. Meanwhile, poke 50 deep holes all over top of cake with skewer, taking care not to poke through to dish bottom and twisting skewer to enlarge holes. Pour cooled liquid over top of cake. Wrap with plastic wrap and refrigerate until gelatin is set, at least 3 hours or up to 2 days.

5. Pulse reserved strained strawberries, 2 tablespoons sugar, and remaining 1 cup strawberries in food processor until mixture resembles strawberry jam, about 15 pulses. Spread mixture evenly over cake. Using stand mixer fitted with whisk, whip cream with remaining 2 tablespoons sugar on medium-low speed until foamy, about 1 minute. Increase speed to high and whip until soft peaks form, 1 to 3 minutes. Spread cream over strawberries. Serve. (Cake can be refrigerated for up to 2 days.)

Perfecting the Poke

Finding the right poking device wasn't as simple as you might think. Toothpicks were too small, while straws, handles of wooden spoons, pencils, and fingers were too big. A wooden skewer finally did the trick. But just poking didn't create a large enough hole for the liquid to seep into. In order to create deep lines of red color against the white crumb, we had to poke and then twist the skewer to really separate the crumb.

1. Using skewer, poke about 50 deep holes over cake, being careful not to poke through to bottom. Twist skewer to enlarge holes.

2. Slowly pour cooled gelatin mixture evenly over surface of cake and it will slowly soak into cake.

TEXAS SHEET CAKE

SERVES 24

Toast the pecans in a dry skillet over medium heat, shaking the pan occasionally, until golden and fragrant, about 5 minutes.

Cake
- 2 cups (10 ounces) all-purpose flour
- 2 cups (14 ounces) granulated sugar
- ½ teaspoon baking soda
- ½ teaspoon salt
- 2 large eggs plus 2 large yolks
- ¼ cup sour cream
- 2 teaspoons vanilla extract
- 8 ounces semisweet chocolate, chopped
- ¾ cup vegetable oil
- ¾ cup water
- ½ cup (1½ ounces) Dutch-processed cocoa powder
- 4 tablespoons unsalted butter

Chocolate Icing
- 8 tablespoons unsalted butter
- ½ cup heavy cream
- ½ cup (1½ ounces) Dutch-processed cocoa powder
- 1 tablespoon light corn syrup
- 3 cups (12 ounces) confectioners' sugar
- 1 tablespoon vanilla extract
- 1 cup pecans, toasted and chopped

1. For the Cake Adjust oven rack to middle position and heat oven to 350 degrees. Grease 18 by 13-inch rimmed baking sheet. Combine flour, sugar, baking soda, and salt in large bowl. Whisk eggs and yolks, sour cream, and vanilla in another bowl until smooth.

2. Heat chocolate, oil, water, cocoa, and butter in large saucepan over medium heat, stirring occasionally, until smooth, 3 to 5 minutes. Whisk chocolate mixture into flour mixture until incorporated. Whisk egg mixture into batter, then pour into prepared baking pan. Bake until toothpick inserted into center comes out clean, 18 to 20 minutes. Transfer to wire rack.

3. For the Chocolate Icing About 5 minutes before cake is done, heat butter, cream, cocoa, and corn syrup in large saucepan over medium heat, stirring occasionally, until smooth. Off heat, whisk in sugar and vanilla. Spread warm icing evenly over hot cake and sprinkle with pecans. Let cake cool to room temperature on wire rack, about 1 hour, then refrigerate until icing is set, about 1 hour longer. Cut into 3-inch squares. Serve. (Cake can be refrigerated for up to 2 days.)

Timing Is Everything

The key to perfectly moist Texas sheet cake is to let the warm icing soak into the hot cake. As soon as the cake comes out of the oven, pour the warm icing over the cake and use a spatula to spread the icing to the edges of the cake. This creates the fudgy layer between the icing and the cake.

Why This Recipe Works Texas sheet cake is a huge, pecan-topped chocolate-glazed cake. For the cake, we relied on a combination of butter and vegetable oil, which produced a dense, brownielike texture. To increase the fudgy chocolate flavor, we used both cocoa powder and melted semisweet chocolate. Replacing milk with heavy cream gave the icing more body, while adding corn syrup produced a lustrous finish. The key to creating the signature fudgy layer between cake and icing was to let the warm icing soak into the hot cake. We poured the icing over the sheet cake straight out of the oven and smoothed it with a spatula.

CHOCOLATE ÉCLAIR CAKE

SERVES 15

Six ounces of finely chopped semisweet chocolate can be used in place of the chips.

1¼	cups (8¾ ounces) sugar
6	tablespoons cornstarch
1	teaspoon salt
5	cups whole milk
4	tablespoons unsalted butter, cut into 4 pieces
5	teaspoons vanilla extract
1¼	teaspoons unflavored gelatin
2	tablespoons water
2¾	cups heavy cream, chilled
14	ounces graham crackers
1	cup semisweet chocolate chips
5	tablespoons light corn syrup

1. Combine sugar, cornstarch, and salt in large saucepan. Whisk milk into sugar mixture until smooth and bring to boil, scraping bottom of pan with heatproof rubber spatula, over medium-high heat. Immediately reduce heat to medium-low and cook, continuing to scrape bottom, until thickened and large bubbles appear on surface, 4 to 6 minutes. Off heat, whisk in butter and vanilla. Transfer pudding to large bowl and place plastic wrap directly on surface of pudding. Refrigerate until cool, about 2 hours.

2. Sprinkle gelatin over water in bowl and let sit until gelatin softens, about 5 minutes. Microwave until mixture is bubbling around edges and gelatin dissolves, 15 to 30 seconds. Using stand mixer fitted with whisk, whip 2 cups cream on medium-low speed until foamy, about 1 minute. Increase speed to high and whip until soft peaks form, 1 to 3 minutes. Add gelatin mixture and whip until stiff peaks form, about 1 minute.

3. Whisk one-third of whipped cream into chilled pudding, then gently fold in remaining whipped cream, 1 scoop at a time, until combined. Cover bottom of 13 by 9-inch baking dish with layer of graham crackers, breaking crackers as necessary to line bottom of pan. Top with half of pudding–whipped cream mixture (about 5½ cups) and another layer of graham crackers. Repeat with remaining pudding–whipped cream mixture and remaining graham crackers.

4. Microwave chocolate chips, remaining ¾ cup cream, and corn syrup in bowl, on 50 percent power, stirring occasionally, until smooth, 1 to 2 minutes. Let glaze cool to room temperature, about 10 minutes. Cover graham crackers with glaze and refrigerate cake for 6 to 24 hours. Serve. (Cake can be refrigerated for up to 2 days.)

The Worst College Food Ever

The Reverend Sylvester Graham, the inventor of the graham cracker, wasn't quite as much fun as that crisp treat might have you believe. In fact, he was a food zealot, convinced that a diet of nothing but water and graham crackers—originally a "health food" made from whole-wheat flour and honey—would turn you into a better person. Some 170 years ago, the administrators at Oberlin College, a small liberal arts school in Ohio, grew enamored of Graham's ideas and decided to feed students according to his principles. (And you think your college food was bad?) Oberlin students were encouraged to abstain from consuming meat, tea, and coffee—except for "crust coffee" made from toast and boiled water. They were discouraged from eating butter and pastries and even from seasoning their food. (As legend has it, a professor actually lost his job for bringing a pepper shaker to the dining hall.) Oberlin students complained so vociferously that the college was forced to abandon its dining plan, and the Graham diet (if not his eponymous cracker) faded into culinary history.

Why This Recipe Works This no-bake dessert is typically made by layering a mixture of instant vanilla pudding and Cool Whip between graham crackers and topping it with chocolate frosting. We loved the convenience of these store-bought items, but our enthusiasm waned when confronted by their flavor. With a couple of easy techniques (a quick stovetop pudding, whipped cream, and a microwave-and-stir glaze) and very little active time, we produced a from-scratch version that easily trumped its inspiration.

Why This Recipe Works This unique dessert combines a layer of fudgy chocolate cake and a layer of rich, caramel-coated flan that "magically" switch places as they bake. We started with an easy dump-and-stir cake recipe. The cake's flavor was great, but it was soggy due to the moisture from the flan. Cutting some of the buttermilk and sugar from the cake batter did the trick. To help our flan firm up, we swapped some of the egg yolks for whole eggs and added cream cheese. The cream cheese also lent the flan a tanginess that offset its sweetness. Convenient store-bought caramel sauce topped it all off.

MAGIC CHOCOLATE FLAN CAKE

SERVES 16

It's worth using good-quality caramel sauce, such as Fat Toad Farm Goat's Milk Caramel. If your blender doesn't hold 2 quarts, process the flan in two batches. The cake needs to chill for at least 8 hours before you can unmold it.

Cake
- ½ cup caramel sauce or topping
- ½ cup plus 2 tablespoons (3⅛ ounces) all-purpose flour
- ⅓ cup (1 ounce) cocoa powder
- ½ teaspoon baking soda
- ⅛ teaspoon salt
- 4 ounces bittersweet chocolate, chopped
- 6 tablespoons unsalted butter
- ½ cup buttermilk
- ½ cup (3½ ounces) sugar
- 2 large eggs
- 1 teaspoon vanilla extract

Flan
- 2 (14-ounce) cans sweetened condensed milk
- 2½ cups whole milk
- 6 ounces cream cheese
- 6 large eggs plus 4 large yolks
- 1 teaspoon vanilla extract

1. For the Cake Adjust oven rack to middle position and heat oven to 350 degrees. Grease 12-cup nonstick Bundt pan. Microwave caramel until easily pourable, about 30 seconds. Pour into pan to coat bottom. Combine flour, cocoa, baking soda, and salt in bowl; set aside. Combine chocolate and butter in large bowl and microwave at 50 percent power, stirring occasionally, until melted, 2 to 4 minutes. Whisk buttermilk, sugar, eggs, and vanilla into chocolate mixture until incorporated. Stir in flour mixture until just combined. Pour batter over caramel in pan.

2. For the Flan Process all ingredients in blender until smooth, about 1 minute. Gently pour flan over cake batter and place Bundt pan in large roasting pan. Place roasting pan on oven rack and pour warm water into roasting pan until it reaches halfway up side of Bundt pan. Bake until toothpick inserted in cake comes out clean and flan registers 180 degrees, 75 to 90 minutes. Transfer Bundt pan to wire rack. Let cool to room temperature, about 2 hours, then refrigerate until set, at least 8 hours. (Remove roasting pan from oven once water has cooled.)

3. Place bottom third of Bundt pan in bowl of hot tap water for 1 minute. Invert completely flat cake platter, place platter over top of pan, and gently turn platter and pan upside down. Slowly remove pan, allowing caramel to drizzle over top of cake. Serve.

Modulate the Heat

A water bath, or bain-marie, makes for a more even, temperate baking environment. Simply place your baking vessel in a larger vessel (we use a roasting pan) and partially fill the latter with water.

Why This Recipe Works A great tres leches cake—a sponge cake soaked with a mixture of "three milks" (heavy cream, evaporated milk, and sweetened condensed milk)—should be moist but not mushy and sweet but not sickeningly so. For an ideal version, we needed to make our cake sturdy enough to handle the milk mixture, so we used whipped whole eggs instead of the usual egg whites. Although some tres leches recipes use equal amounts of evaporated milk, sweetened condensed milk, and cream, we found that cutting back on the cream produced a thicker mixture that didn't oversaturate the cake.

TRES LECHES CAKE

SERVES 12

The cake is best frosted right before serving.

Milk Mixture
- 1 (14-ounce) can sweetened condensed milk
- 1 (12-ounce) can evaporated milk
- 1 cup heavy cream
- 1 teaspoon vanilla extract

Cake
- 2 cups (10 ounces) all-purpose flour
- 2 teaspoons baking powder
- 1 teaspoon salt
- ½ teaspoon ground cinnamon
- 8 tablespoons unsalted butter
- 1 cup whole milk
- 4 large eggs, room temperature
- 2 cups (14 ounces) sugar
- 2 teaspoons vanilla extract

Topping
- 1 cup heavy cream
- 3 tablespoons corn syrup
- 1 teaspoon vanilla extract

1. For the Milk Mixture Pour condensed milk into large bowl. Microwave covered at 50 percent power, stirring every 3 to 5 minutes, until slightly darkened and thickened, 9 to 15 minutes. Remove from microwave and slowly whisk in evaporated milk, cream, and vanilla. Let cool to room temperature.

2. For the Cake Adjust oven rack to middle position and heat oven to 325 degrees. Grease and flour 13 by 9-inch baking dish. Whisk flour, baking powder, salt, and cinnamon in bowl. Heat butter and milk in small saucepan over low heat until butter is melted; remove from heat and set aside.

3. Using stand mixer fitted with whisk, whip eggs on medium speed until foamy, about 30 seconds. Slowly add sugar and continue to whip until fully incorporated, 5 to 10 seconds. Increase speed to medium-high and whip until mixture is thick and glossy, 5 to 7 minutes. Reduce speed to low, add milk-butter mixture and vanilla, and mix until combined, about 15 seconds. Add flour mixture in 3 additions, mixing on medium speed after each addition and scraping down bowl as needed, until flour is fully incorporated, about 30 seconds. Using rubber spatula, scrape batter into prepared dish. Bake until toothpick inserted in center comes out clean, 30 to 35 minutes. Transfer cake to wire rack and let cool for 10 minutes.

4. Using skewer, poke holes at ½-inch intervals in top of cake. Slowly pour milk mixture over cake until completely absorbed. Let sit at room temperature for 15 minutes, then refrigerate, uncovered, for 3 hours or up to 24 hours.

5. For the Topping Remove cake from refrigerator 30 minutes before serving. Using stand mixer fitted with whisk, whip cream, corn syrup, and vanilla on medium-low speed until foamy, about 1 minute. Increase speed to high and whip until soft peaks form, 1 to 3 minutes. Spread over cake and cut into 3-inch squares. Serve.

SWISS HAZELNUT CAKE

SERVES 12 TO 16

We toast and grind the hazelnuts with their skins for better color and flavor. When working with the marshmallow crème, grease the inside of your measuring cup and spatula with vegetable oil spray to prevent sticking. You may use a vegetable peeler or the large holes of a box grater to shave the chocolate.

Cake
- ½ cup (2 ounces) skin-on hazelnuts, toasted and cooled
- 1¼ cups (5 ounces) cake flour
- 1 cup (7 ounces) granulated sugar
- 1½ teaspoons baking powder
- ½ teaspoon salt
- ½ cup vegetable oil
- ¼ cup water
- 3 large egg yolks, plus 5 large whites
- 2½ teaspoons vanilla extract
- ¼ teaspoon cream of tartar

Frosting
- 24 tablespoons (3 sticks) unsalted butter, softened
- ¼ teaspoon salt
- 1¾ cups (7 ounces) confectioners' sugar
- 12 ounces (2⅔ cups) Fluff brand marshmallow crème
- 2 tablespoons hazelnut liqueur
- 6 ounces bittersweet chocolate

1. For the Cake Adjust oven rack to middle position and heat oven to 350 degrees. Line the bottoms of 2 light-colored 9-inch round cake pans with parchment paper; grease parchment but not pan sides.

2. Process hazelnuts in food processor until finely ground, about 30 seconds. Whisk flour, sugar, baking powder, salt, and ground hazelnuts together in large bowl. Whisk oil, water, egg yolks, and vanilla together in separate bowl. Whisk egg yolk mixture into flour mixture until smooth batter forms.

3. Using stand mixer fitted with whisk, whip egg whites and cream of tartar on medium-low speed until foamy, about 1 minute. Increase speed to medium-high and whip until soft peaks form, 2 to 3 minutes. Gently whisk one-third of whipped egg whites into batter. Using rubber spatula, gently fold remaining egg whites into batter until incorporated.

4. Divide batter evenly between prepared pans and gently tap pans on counter to release air bubbles. Bake until tops are light golden brown and cakes spring back when pressed lightly in center, 25 to 28 minutes, rotating pans halfway through baking.

5. Let cakes cool in pans for 15 minutes. Run knife around edges of pans; invert cakes onto wire rack. Discard parchment and let cakes cool completely, at least 1 hour. (To prepare to make chocolate shavings, place food processor shredding disk and chocolate in freezer.)

6. For the Frosting Using clean stand mixer fitted with whisk, whip butter and salt on medium speed until smooth, about 1 minute. Reduce speed to low and slowly add sugar. Increase speed to medium and whip until smooth, about 2 minutes, scraping down sides of bowl as needed. Add marshmallow crème, increase speed to medium-high, and whip until light and fluffy, 3 to 5 minutes. Reduce speed to low, add hazelnut liqueur, return speed to medium-high, and whip to incorporate, about 30 seconds.

7. Line rimmed baking sheet with parchment paper. Fit food processor with chilled shredding disk. Turn on processor and feed chocolate through hopper. Transfer shaved chocolate to prepared baking sheet and spread into even layer. Place in freezer to harden, about 10 minutes.

8. Place 1 cake layer on cake stand. Spread 2 cups frosting evenly over top, right to edge of cake. Top with second cake layer, pressing lightly to adhere. Spread remaining 2 cups frosting evenly over top and sides of cake.

9. Fold 16 by 12-inch sheet of parchment paper into 6 by 4-inch rectangle. Using parchment rectangle, scoop up half of chocolate shavings and sprinkle over top of cake. Once top of cake is coated, scoop up remaining chocolate shavings and press gently against sides of cake to adhere, scooping and reapplying as needed. Serve.

Why This Recipe Works This sweet, nutty cake is famous in Philadelphia, but when the Swiss Haus pastry chef wouldn't disclose the recipe, we played detective. We settled on a chiffon base, knowing that the beaten egg whites would give the cake a fluffy texture. For full hazelnut flavor, we ground the nuts in a food processor, then substituted this hazelnut "flour" for a portion of the cake flour. Since meringue buttercream frosting is a project, we found an excellent shortcut using marshmallow crème. To prevent the chocolate from melting, we froze it before and after shaving and used parchment paper to gently press the curls into the frosting.

Why This Recipe Works The beauty of blitz torte is that you get five impressive layers—cake, meringue, fruit-and-cream filling, more cake, and more meringue—for about the same amount of work as a two-layer cake. That's because the recipe is incredibly clever: Each meringue layer is baked directly atop the yellow cake batter. The recipe is also pleasingly symmetrical: The egg yolks go into the cake, while the whites go into the meringue. For our filling, we mimicked the rich egginess of custard by folding store-bought lemon curd into whipped cream, stabilizing it with gelatin, and layering it with raspberries. Bliss torte is more like it!

BLITZ TORTE

SERVES 8 TO 10

If your pans are dark, reduce the baking time in step 6 to 30 to 35 minutes.

Filling
- 1 teaspoon unflavored gelatin
- 2 tablespoons water
- 1 cup heavy cream, chilled
- 1 teaspoon vanilla extract
- ½ cup lemon curd
- 10 ounces (2 cups) raspberries
- 2 tablespoons orange liqueur
- 1 tablespoon sugar

Cake
- ½ cup whole milk
- 4 large egg yolks
- 1½ teaspoons vanilla extract
- 1¼ cups (5 ounces) cake flour
- 1 cup (7 ounces) sugar
- 1½ teaspoons baking powder
- ½ teaspoon salt
- 12 tablespoons unsalted butter, cut into 12 pieces and softened

Meringue
- 4 large egg whites
- ¼ teaspoon cream of tartar
- ¾ cup (5¼ ounces) sugar
- ½ teaspoon vanilla extract
- ½ cup sliced almonds

1. For the Filling Sprinkle gelatin over water in small bowl and let sit until gelatin softens, about 5 minutes. Microwave until mixture is bubbling around edges and gelatin dissolves, 15 to 30 seconds. Using stand mixer fitted with whisk, whip cream and vanilla on medium-low speed until foamy, about 1 minute. Increase speed to medium-high and whip until soft peaks form, about 2 minutes. Add gelatin mixture and whip until firm, stiff peaks form, about 1 minute.

2. Whisk lemon curd in large metal bowl to loosen. Fold whipped cream mixture into curd. Refrigerate cream filling for 1½ to 3 hours.

3. For the Cake Meanwhile, adjust oven rack to middle position and heat oven to 325 degrees. Grease 2 light-colored 9-inch round cake pans, line with parchment paper, grease parchment, and flour pans.

4. Beat milk, yolks, and vanilla together with fork. Using stand mixer fitted with paddle, mix flour, sugar, baking powder, and salt on low speed until combined, about 5 seconds. Add butter, 1 piece at a time, and mix until only pea-size pieces remain, about 1 minute. Add half of milk mixture, increase speed to medium-high, and beat until light and fluffy, about 1 minute. Reduce speed to medium-low, add remaining milk mixture, and beat until incorporated, about 30 seconds. Give batter final stir by hand. Divide batter evenly between prepared pans and spread into even layer using small offset spatula.

5. For the Meringue Using clean, dry stand mixer fitted with a whisk, whip egg whites and cream of tartar on medium-low speed until foamy, about 1 minute. Increase speed to medium-high and whip whites to soft, billowy mounds, 1 to 3 minutes. Gradually add sugar and whip until glossy, stiff peaks form, 3 to 5 minutes. Add vanilla and whip until incorporated.

6. Divide meringue evenly between cake pans and spread evenly over cake batter to edges of pan. Use back of spoon to create peaks in meringue. Sprinkle meringue with almonds. Bake cakes until meringue is golden and has pulled away from sides of pan, 50 to 55 minutes, switching and rotating pans halfway through baking. Let cakes cool completely in pans on wire rack. (Cakes can be baked up to 24 hours in advance and stored, uncovered, in pans at room temperature.)

7. To finish filling, 10 minutes before assembling cake, combine raspberries, liqueur, and sugar in bowl.

8. Gently remove cakes from pans, discarding parchment. Place 1 cake layer on platter, meringue side up. Spread half of cream filling evenly over top. Using slotted spoon, spoon raspberries evenly over filling. Gently spread remaining cream filling over raspberries, covering raspberries completely. Top with second cake layer, meringue side up. Serve cake within 2 hours of assembly.

Why This Recipe Works The key to angel food cake is voluminous, stable egg whites. A mere speck of yolk precludes them from whipping to peaks. We had equal success with both cold and room-temperature egg whites. Cold whites achieved the same volume as room-temperature whites; they just took a few minutes longer. Cream of tartar offered some insurance against deflated whites because its acidity helped stabilize the egg whites. Cake flour was also important—all-purpose flour produced a chewy, gummy cake.

ANGEL FOOD CAKE

SERVES 10 TO 12

Do not use all-purpose flour in this recipe as it will give the cake a breadlike texture. You will need a 12-cup tube pan with a removable bottom for this recipe. If your pan has "feet" that rise above the top edge of the pan, let the cake cool upside down; otherwise, invert the tube pan over a large metal kitchen funnel or the neck of a sturdy bottle. Cake can be served plain or dusted with confectioners' sugar.

- 1 cup plus 2 tablespoons (4½ ounces) cake flour
- ¼ teaspoon salt
- 1¾ cups (12¼ ounces) sugar
- 12 large egg whites
- 1½ teaspoons cream of tartar
- 1 teaspoon vanilla extract

1. Adjust oven rack to lower-middle position and preheat oven to 325 degrees. Whisk flour and salt in bowl. Process sugar in food processor until fine, about 1 minute. Reserve half of sugar in small bowl. Add flour mixture to food processor with remaining sugar and process until aerated, about 1 minute.

2. Using stand mixer fitted with whisk, whip egg whites and cream of tartar on medium-low speed until foamy, about 1 minute. Increase speed to medium-high. Slowly add reserved sugar and whip until soft peaks form, about 6 minutes. Add vanilla and mix until incorporated.

3. Sift flour-sugar mixture over egg whites in 3 additions, folding gently with rubber spatula after each addition until incorporated. Scrape mixture into 12-cup ungreased tube pan.

4. Bake until skewer inserted into center comes out clean and cracks in cake appear dry, 40 to 45 minutes. Let cool, inverted, to room temperature, about 3 hours. To unmold, run knife along interior of pan. Turn out onto platter. Serve.

CHOCOLATE-ALMOND ANGEL FOOD CAKE

Replace ½ teaspoon vanilla extract with ½ teaspoon almond extract in step 2. Fold 2 ounces finely grated bittersweet chocolate into batter following flour in step 3.

CAFÉ AU LAIT ANGEL FOOD CAKE

Add 1 tablespoon instant coffee or espresso powder to food processor along with flour in step 1. Replace ½ teaspoon vanilla with 1 tablespoon coffee liqueur in step 2.

Key Steps to Angel Food Cake

1. Grind Sugar Process granulated sugar in food processor until powdery. It'll be fine, light, and won't deflate egg whites.

2. Stabilize Egg Whites Add cream of tartar to egg whites at start of whipping. Once whites become foamy, add half of sugar—gradually.

3. Sift Flour in Batches Gently sift flour-sugar mixture over beaten egg whites in batches to avoid deflating whites.

4. Cool Upside Down Invert cake until it is completely cool, about 3 hours. If you don't have pan with feet, invert it over neck of sturdy bottle.

CHIFFON CAKE

SERVES 10 TO 12

Separate the eggs when they're cold; it's easier. You will need a 16-cup tube pan with a removable bottom for this recipe. If your pan has "feet" that rise above the top edge of the pan, let the cake cool upside down; otherwise, invert the tube pan over a large metal kitchen funnel or the neck of a sturdy bottle.

- 5 large eggs, separated
- 1 teaspoon cream of tartar
- 1½ cups (10½ ounces) sugar
- 1⅓ cups (5⅓ ounces) cake flour
- 2 teaspoons baking powder
- ½ teaspoon salt
- ¾ cup water
- ½ cup vegetable oil
- 1 tablespoon vanilla extract

1. Adjust oven rack to lower-middle position and heat oven to 325 degrees. Using stand mixer fitted with whisk, whip egg whites and cream of tartar on medium-high speed until soft peaks form, about 2 minutes. With mixer running, slowly add 2 tablespoons sugar and whip until just stiff and glossy, about 1 minute; set aside.

2. Combine flour, remaining sugar, baking powder, and salt in large bowl. Whisk water, oil, egg yolks, and vanilla in medium bowl until smooth. Whisk wet mixture into flour mixture until smooth. Whisk one-third whipped egg whites into batter, then gently fold in remaining whites, 1 scoop at a time, until well combined. Scrape mixture into 16-cup ungreased tube pan.

3. Bake until skewer inserted into center comes out clean and cracks in cake appear dry, 55 minutes to 1 hour, 5 minutes. Let cool, inverted, to room temperature, about 3 hours. To unmold, turn pan right side up and run flexible knife around tube and outer edge. Use tube to pull cake out of pan and set it on inverted baking pan. Cut bottom free. Invert cake onto serving plate and gently twist tube to remove. Serve.

ORANGE CHIFFON CAKE

Reduce total sugar to 1¼ cups. Replace water with ¾ cup orange juice and add 1 tablespoon grated orange zest along with vanilla in step 2. For glaze, whisk 3 tablespoons orange juice, 2 tablespoons softened cream cheese, and ½ teaspoon grated orange zest in medium bowl until smooth. Add 1½ cups confectioners' sugar and whisk until smooth. Pour glaze over cooled cake. Let glaze set for 15 minutes. Serve.

Let Me Outta Here!
Like angel food cake, chiffon cake is baked in an ungreased pan. Why? The stiffly beaten egg whites need to cling to the pan to rise. If the pan were greased, they couldn't. Here's how to remove it from the pan.

1. When cake is cool, turn pan right side up and run flexible knife around tube and outer edge.

2. Use tube to pull cake out of pan and set it on inverted baking pan. Cut bottom free.

3. Invert cake onto serving plate and gently twist tube to remove.

Why This Recipe Works Chiffon cake should have the airy height of angel food cake with the richness of pound cake. For our chiffon cake recipe, we eliminated the unnecessary step of sifting the dry ingredients. We also perfected the method for beating our egg whites—slowly adding sugar once the eggs had been beaten to soft peaks and then continuing to beat them until just stiff and glossy—to avoid little pockets of cooked egg whites.

ITALIAN CREAM CAKE

SERVES 8 TO 10

Toast the coconut and nuts in a 350-degree oven until golden brown, 10 to 12 minutes. Watch carefully and stir occasionally to prevent burning.

Cake
- 1½ cups sweetened shredded coconut, toasted
- 1 cup buttermilk, room temperature
- 2 teaspoons vanilla extract
- 2½ cups (10 ounces) cake flour
- 2 teaspoons baking powder
- ¾ teaspoon salt
- ½ teaspoon baking soda
- 12 tablespoons unsalted butter, cut into 12 pieces and softened
- 4 tablespoons shortening, cut into 4 pieces
- 1¾ cups (12¼ ounces) sugar
- 5 large eggs, room temperature
- 2 cups (8 ounces) pecans, toasted and chopped

Frosting
- 12 tablespoons unsalted butter, softened
- 2¼ cups (9 ounces) confectioners' sugar
- ½ cup cream of coconut
- ½ teaspoon vanilla extract
- Pinch salt
- 16 ounces cream cheese, cut into 8 pieces and softened

1. For the Cake Adjust oven rack to middle position and heat oven to 350 degrees. Grease two 9-inch round cake pans, line with parchment paper, grease parchment, then flour pans. Process coconut in food processor until finely ground, about 1 minute. Combine coconut, buttermilk, and vanilla in 2-cup liquid measuring cup and let sit until coconut is slightly softened, about 10 minutes; reserve.

2. Combine flour, baking powder, salt, and baking soda in bowl. Using stand mixer fitted with paddle, beat butter, shortening, and sugar on medium-high speed until pale and fluffy, about 3 minutes. Add eggs, one at a time, and beat until combined. Reduce speed to low and add flour mixture in 3 additions, alternating with 2 additions of reserved coconut-buttermilk mixture, scraping down bowl as needed. Add ¾ cup pecans and give batter final stir by hand.

3. Scrape equal amounts of batter into prepared pans and bake until toothpick inserted in center comes out clean, 28 to 32 minutes. Cool cakes in pans on wire rack for 10 minutes. Remove cakes from pans, discarding parchment, and cool completely, about 2 hours. (Cooled cakes can be wrapped with plastic wrap and stored at room temperature for up to 2 days.)

4. For the Frosting Using stand mixer fitted with paddle, mix butter and sugar on low speed until combined, about 30 seconds. Increase speed to medium-high and beat until pale and fluffy, about 2 minutes. Add cream of coconut, vanilla, and salt and beat until smooth, about 30 seconds. Add cream cheese, one piece at a time, and beat until incorporated, about 1 minute. Refrigerate until ready to use.

5. When cakes are cooled, spread 1½ cups frosting over 1 cake round. Top with second cake round and spread remaining frosting evenly over top and sides of cake. Press remaining pecans onto sides of cake. Serve. (Cake can be refrigerated for up to 2 days. Bring to room temperature before serving.)

Coconut: Toast, Grind, Soak

To bring out the flavor of the shredded coconut, we toast it in a 350-degree oven until it is golden brown (about 10 minutes). To help the coconut flavor permeate the cake, we grind it to meal in the food processor. But toasted, ground coconut is hard and dry, a real problem in such a deliciously soft, moist cake. To moisten and soften the coconut meal, we soak it in buttermilk before adding it to the cake batter.

Why This Recipe Works Although the name is a mystery (there's nothing Italian about this cake), the appeal of this Southern specialty is obvious: tender yellow cake with coconut and pecans, doused in tangy cream cheese frosting. But the recipes we found produced gummy cakes with weak coconut flavor. Cake flour made a more tender crumb, and heat-activated baking powder ensured the cake would rise evenly in the oven. To boost coconut flavor, we added it twice—pulverized, toasted coconut added flavor to the cake without drying it out, and cream of coconut amped up the frosting. Finally, we coated the sides in a blanket of toasted pecans.

Why This Recipe Works In this delicious variation on classic pound cake, we added cream cheese for richness, tangy flavor, and an especially velvety texture. We let the pure flavors of eggs, butter, and the cream cheese take center stage, adding only a few teaspoons of vanilla and a moderate amount of sugar. To achieve a tight, fine crumb and a velvety texture, we left the leavener out altogether and used lower-protein cake flour. Extra egg yolks kept the cake moist and tender. Finally, a low oven took a little longer, but it produced a perfect golden-brown crust and a moist, tender interior.

CREAM CHEESE POUND CAKE

SERVES 12 TO 14

If you do not have cake flour on hand, you can substitute ⅞ cup all-purpose flour and 2 tablespoons cornstarch for each cup of flour. Serve with Strawberry-Rhubarb Compote (recipe follows).

- 3 cups (12 ounces) cake flour
- 1 teaspoon salt
- 4 large eggs plus 2 large yolks, room temperature
- ¼ cup milk
- 2 teaspoons vanilla extract
- 3 cups (21 ounces) sugar
- 24 tablespoons (3 sticks) unsalted butter, softened
- 6 ounces cream cheese, softened

1. Adjust oven rack to middle position and heat oven to 300 degrees. Grease and flour 12-cup nonstick Bundt pan. Combine flour and salt in bowl. Whisk eggs and yolks, milk, and vanilla together in 2-cup liquid measuring cup.

2. Using stand mixer fitted with paddle, beat sugar, butter, and cream cheese on medium-high speed until pale and fluffy, about 3 minutes. Reduce speed to low and very slowly add egg mixture, mixing until incorporated (batter may look slightly curdled). Add flour mixture in 3 additions, scraping down bowl as needed. Give batter final stir by hand.

3. Scrape batter into prepared pan and gently tap pan on counter to release air bubbles. Bake until toothpick inserted in center comes out clean, 80 to 90 minutes, rotating pan halfway through baking. Cool cake in pan on wire rack for 15 minutes. Remove cake from pan and cool completely, about 2 hours. Serve. (Cake can be stored, wrapped in plastic wrap, at room temperature for 3 days.)

STRAWBERRY-RHUBARB COMPOTE
MAKES 4 CUPS

The compote can be refrigerated for up to one week. It's delicious drizzled on Cream Cheese Pound Cake or ice cream or stirred into yogurt or oatmeal.

- 1 pound strawberries, hulled and chopped (3 cups)
- 1 cup (7 ounces) sugar
- 1 tablespoon lemon juice
- 1 pound rhubarb, sliced ¼-inch thick
- Pinch salt

1. Toss strawberries with ½ cup sugar and lemon juice in medium bowl. Transfer strawberry mixture to fine-mesh strainer set over medium saucepan and let stand, stirring occasionally, for 30 minutes. Do not wash bowl.

2. Return strawberries to bowl. Add rhubarb, remaining ½ cup sugar, and salt to strawberry juices in pan and bring to boil over medium-high heat. Reduce heat to medium-low and cook, stirring occasionally, until rhubarb is soft and liquid has thickened, 6 to 8 minutes.

3. Stir strawberries into pan and remove from heat. Transfer compote to bowl and let cool to room temperature, about 45 minutes. Serve.

Preparing a Bundt Pan

To ensure a clean release, apply paste of 1 tablespoon melted butter and 1 tablespoon flour to pan using pastry brush.

COLD-OVEN POUND CAKE

SERVES 12

You'll need a 16-cup tube pan for this recipe; if not using a nonstick pan, make sure to thoroughly grease a traditional pan. In step 2, don't worry if the batter looks slightly separated.

- 3 cups (12 ounces) cake flour
- ½ teaspoon baking powder
- 1 teaspoon salt
- 1 cup whole milk
- 2 teaspoons vanilla extract
- 20 tablespoons (2½ sticks) unsalted butter, softened
- 2½ cups (17½ ounces) sugar
- 6 large eggs

1. Adjust oven rack to lower-middle position. Grease and flour 16-cup tube pan. Combine flour, baking powder, and salt in bowl. Whisk milk and vanilla in measuring cup.

2. Using stand mixer fitted with paddle, beat butter and sugar on medium-high speed until light and fluffy, about 2 minutes. Beat in eggs, one at a time, until combined. Reduce speed to low and add flour mixture in 3 additions, alternating with milk mixture in 2 additions, scraping down bowl as needed. Mix on low until smooth, about 30 seconds. Give batter final stir by hand.

3. Pour batter into prepared pan and smooth top. Place cake in cold oven. Adjust oven temperature to 325 degrees and bake, without opening oven door, until cake is golden brown and skewer inserted in center comes out clean, 1 hour, 5 minutes to 1 hour, 20 minutes.

4. Let cake cool in pan on wire rack for 15 minutes. Remove cake from pan and let cool completely on rack about 2 hours. Serve. (Cake can be stored at room temperature for up to 2 days.)

A Cold Oven Really Makes a Difference

Curiosity led us to try baking our Cold-Oven Pound Cake in a preheated oven. The cake baked more quickly (no surprise), but it was squat and lacked the thick crust we'd come to expect. Evidently, the hot oven stopped the small amount of leavener in our recipe before its work was done. And it turns out the crust on our Cold-Oven Pound Cake is formed by moisture in the oven reacting with starch in the batter. A hot oven is drier than a cold oven (heat evaporates moisture), so there wasn't enough moisture in the preheated oven to form a nice, thick crust.

SQUAT CAKE
A preheated oven produces a squat, crustless cake with this recipe.

PERFECT CAKE
In contrast, a cold oven produces a high rise and a thick crust.

Why Pay for Preheating?

Gas ovens became widely available in the United States during the first decades of the 20th century. Because these ovens were more expensive than their wood- and coal-fired counterparts, gas companies had to get creative in marketing them. One popular tactic was to develop and promote recipes started in a cold oven, with the hook that consumers could save money in their gas ovens by not paying for "needless" preheating. Hence: cold-oven pound cake.

Why This Recipe Works This thrifty pound cake, which was designed to save on gas by not requiring a preheated oven, is an especially tall cake and boasts a crisp crust. To create a light crumb, we used leaner whole milk instead of the heavy cream called for in most recipes. Swapping out all-purpose flour for cake flour yielded an even finer, more delicate crumb for our pound cake. We also used baking powder, which produced carbon dioxide bubbles that gave our cake its rise. Putting the pound cake into a cold oven, as is tradition, gave the carbon dioxide more time to produce greater rise.

Why This Recipe Works Packaged chocolate cream cupcakes are a childhood treat. But try one today and you're met with wan chocolate cake encasing salty whipped vegetable shortening. We knew we could do better. Blooming cocoa powder in boiling water and adding chocolate chips and espresso powder gave our cupcakes plenty of chocolate depth. Combining marshmallow crème and the right amount of gelatin gave us the perfect creamy filling. To fill our cupcakes without a pastry bag, we used a paring knife to cut inverted cones from the tops of the cupcakes, added the frosting, and plugged the holes.

CHOCOLATE CREAM CUPCAKES

MAKES 12 CUPCAKES

To ensure an appropriately thick filling, be sure to use marshmallow crème (such as Fluff), not marshmallow sauce. For an accurate measurement of boiling water, bring a full kettle of water to a boil, then measure out the desired amount.

Cupcakes
- 1 cup (5 ounces) all-purpose flour
- ½ teaspoon baking soda
- ¼ teaspoon salt
- ½ cup boiling water
- ⅓ cup (1 ounce) cocoa powder
- ⅓ cup (2 ounces) semisweet chocolate chips
- 1 tablespoon instant espresso powder
- ¾ cup (5¼ ounces) sugar
- ½ cup sour cream
- ½ cup vegetable oil
- 2 large eggs
- 1 teaspoon vanilla extract

Filling
- ¾ teaspoon unflavored gelatin
- 3 tablespoons water
- 4 tablespoons (½ stick) unsalted butter, softened
- 1 teaspoon vanilla extract
- Pinch salt
- 1¼ cups marshmallow crème

Glaze
- ½ cup semisweet chocolate chips
- 3 tablespoons unsalted butter

1. For the Cupcakes Adjust oven rack to middle position and heat oven to 325 degrees. Spray 12-cup muffin tin with vegetable oil spray and flour. Combine flour, baking soda, and salt in bowl. Whisk water, cocoa, chocolate chips, and espresso powder in large bowl until smooth. Add sugar, sour cream, oil, eggs, and vanilla and mix until combined. Whisk in flour mixture until incorporated. Divide batter evenly among muffin cups. Bake until toothpick inserted in center comes out with few dry crumbs attached, 18 to 22 minutes. Let cupcakes cool in tin on wire rack for 10 minutes, then turn out onto wire rack and let cool completely.

2. For the Filling Sprinkle gelatin over water in large bowl and let sit until gelatin softens, about 5 minutes. Microwave until mixture is bubbling around edges and gelatin dissolves, about 30 seconds. Stir in butter, vanilla, and salt until combined. Let mixture cool until just warm to touch, about 5 minutes, then whisk in marshmallow crème until smooth; refrigerate until set, about 30 minutes. Transfer ⅓ cup marshmallow mixture to pastry bag fitted with small plain tip; reserve remaining mixture for filling cupcakes.

3. For the Glaze Microwave chocolate and butter in small bowl, stirring occasionally, until smooth, about 30 seconds. Let glaze cool to room temperature, about 10 minutes.

4. Insert tip of paring knife at 45-degree angle and about ¼ inch from edge of cupcake, cut cone from top of each cupcake, and cut off all but top ¼ inch of cone, leaving circular disk of cake. Fill cupcakes with 1 tablespoon filling each. Replace tops, frost with 2 teaspoons cooled glaze, and let sit 10 minutes. Using pastry bag, pipe curlicues across glazed cupcakes. Serve. (Cupcakes can be stored at room temperature for up to 2 days.)

Filling the Cupcakes

1. Insert tip of paring knife at 45-degree angle about ¼ inch from edge of cupcake. Cut out and remove cake cone. Cut off all but top ¼ inch of cone, leaving circular disk of cake.

2. Using spoon, fill each cupcake with marshmallow mixture and then top with reserved cake "plug." The glaze and the curlicues will hide your handiwork.

Why This Recipe Works Most hot fudge pudding cakes end up looking rich and fudgy but have very little chocolate flavor. For chocolate pudding cake that tasted as good as it looked, we folded semisweet chocolate chips into the batter, which added another layer of chocolate flavor and ensured plenty of gooey pockets in the baked cake. Vegetable oil, which most recipes call for, was flavorless, and we found substituting melted butter improved our pudding cake's flavor. Using Dutch-processed cocoa, which is less acidic than natural cocoa powder, produced a richer chocolate taste.

HOT FUDGE PUDDING CAKE

SERVES 6 TO 8

For an accurate measurement of boiling water, bring a full kettle of water to a boil, then measure out the desired amount. Do not overbake this cake or the pudding sauce will burn in the pan and the cake will be dry, not fudgy. Store leftovers, covered with plastic wrap, in the refrigerator. Reheat individual servings in a microwave on high power until hot (about 1 minute).

- 1 cup (7 ounces) sugar
- ½ cup (1½ ounces) Dutch-processed cocoa powder
- 1 cup (5 ounces) all-purpose flour
- 2 teaspoons baking powder
- ¼ teaspoon salt
- ½ cup milk
- 4 tablespoons unsalted butter, melted
- 1 large egg yolk
- 2 teaspoons vanilla extract
- ½ cup semisweet chocolate chips
- 1 cup boiling water
- Vanilla ice cream or whipped cream

1. Adjust oven rack to middle position and heat oven to 350 degrees. Spray 8-inch square baking pan with vegetable oil spray. Whisk ½ cup sugar with ¼ cup cocoa in small bowl.

2. Whisk flour, remaining ½ cup sugar, remaining ¼ cup cocoa, baking powder, and salt in large bowl. Whisk milk, butter, egg yolk, and vanilla in medium bowl until smooth. Stir milk mixture into flour mixture until just combined. Fold in chocolate chips (batter will be stiff).

3. Using rubber spatula, scrape batter into prepared pan and spread into corners. Sprinkle reserved cocoa mixture evenly over top. Gently pour boiling water over cocoa. Do not stir.

4. Bake until top of cake looks cracked, sauce is bubbling, and toothpick inserted into cakey area comes out with moist crumbs attached, about 25 minutes. Let cool in pan on wire rack for at least 10 minutes. To serve, scoop warm cake into individual serving bowls and top with vanilla ice cream or whipped cream.

BABY PUDDING CAKES

Put a fancy spin on this homey recipe by baking up individual pudding cakes.

Spray eight 6-ounce ovenproof ramekins or coffee cups with vegetable oil spray. Fill each with 2 tablespoons batter. Top each with 1½ tablespoons cocoa mixture, followed by 2 tablespoons boiling water. Arrange cups on rimmed baking sheet and bake until tops are just cracked, 20 to 25 minutes.

Is It Done Yet?

This highly unconventional cake breaks most of the usual rules, including how to judge when it's ready to come out of the oven.

 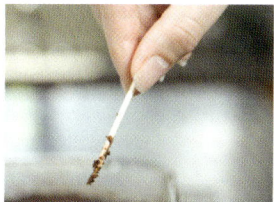

1. Start testing for doneness when top is crackled like a brownie and sauce is bubbling up from bottom. Insert toothpick close to the edge, where the cake is firmest. (Don't insert the toothpick in center, where cake should be gooey.)

2. Toothpick should have large, moist crumbs—but no gooey batter—attached. Check at least two spots to be certain that what's sticking to toothpick isn't just melted chocolate.

LEMON PUDDING CAKE

SERVES 8

This dessert is best served warm or at room temperature the same day it is made.

- ¼ cup (1¼ ounces) all-purpose flour
- 2 teaspoons cornstarch
- 1¼ cups (8¾ ounces) sugar
- 5 tablespoons unsalted butter, softened
- 2 tablespoons grated zest and ½ cup juice from 4 lemons
- 5 large eggs, separated
- 1¼ cups whole milk, room temperature
- 2 quarts boiling water

1. Adjust oven rack to lowest position and heat oven to 325 degrees. Grease 8-inch square baking dish. Whisk flour and cornstarch in bowl. Using stand mixer fitted with paddle, beat ½ cup sugar, butter, and lemon zest on medium-high speed until light and fluffy, about 2 minutes. Beat in egg yolks, 1 at a time, until incorporated. Reduce speed to medium-low. Add flour mixture and mix until incorporated. Slowly add milk and lemon juice, mixing until just combined.

2. Using clean bowl and whisk attachment, beat egg whites on medium-high speed until soft peaks form, about 2 minutes. With mixer running, slowly add remaining ¾ cup sugar until whites are firm and glossy, about 1 minute. Whisk one-third of whites into batter, then gently fold in remaining whites, 1 scoop at a time, until well combined.

3. Place clean dish towel in bottom of roasting pan and arrange prepared baking dish on towel. Spoon batter into prepared dish. Carefully place pan on oven rack and pour boiling water into pan until water comes halfway up sides of baking dish. Bake until surface is golden brown and edges are set (center should jiggle slightly when gently shaken), about 1 hour. Transfer dish to wire rack and let cool for at least 1 hour. To serve, scoop warm cake into individual serving bowls.

Using a Water Bath

The water lowers the temperature surrounding the baking dish for gentle, even cooking.

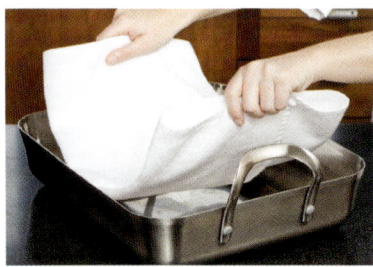

1. To prevent baking dish from sliding, line bottom of roasting pan with clean dish towel and place baking dish on top.

2. Set roasting pan on oven rack and carefully pour boiling water into pan, halfway up sides of baking dish.

3. After baking, promptly remove baking dish from water. Let water cool before moving water bath.

Why This Recipe Works For the brightest lemon flavor in our lemon pudding cake, we used a half cup of lemon juice. To coax even more flavor from the lemons, we creamed a bit of grated zest with the butter and sugar. A bit of cornstarch gently firmed the pudding layer without muddying the lemon flavor. To prevent the top layer of the cake from deflating, we beat sugar into the egg whites. This stabilized the whites and resulted in a high, golden, and fluffy cake. For the creamiest texture, it was important to bake the cake in a water bath. The hot water protected the pudding from cooking too quickly.

LEMON ICEBOX CHEESECAKE

SERVES 12 TO 16

Let the dissolved gelatin mixture cool down for a few minutes, or the gelatin will seize before combining with the filling. We tested our cheesecake with several store brands of lemon sandwich cookies; all worked well.

Crust
- 10 lemon sandwich cookies, broken into pieces (about 1¼ cups)
- 2 tablespoons unsalted butter, melted
- 1 teaspoon grated lemon zest

Curd
- ¼ cup (1¾ ounces) sugar
- 1 large egg plus 1 large yolk
- Pinch salt
- 2 tablespoons lemon juice
- 1 tablespoon unsalted butter
- 1 tablespoon heavy cream

Filling
- 2¾ teaspoons unflavored gelatin
- ¼ cup lemon juice (2 lemons)
- 1½ pounds cream cheese, cut into 1-inch pieces and softened
- ¾ cup (5¼ ounces) sugar
- Pinch salt
- 1¼ cups heavy cream, room temperature

1. For the Crust Adjust oven rack to middle position and heat oven to 350 degrees. Process cookies in food processor until finely ground, about 30 seconds. Add butter and zest and pulse until combined, about 10 pulses. Press mixture into bottom of 9-inch springform pan. Bake until lightly browned and set, about 10 minutes. Let cool completely on wire rack, at least 30 minutes.

2. For the Curd While crust is cooling, whisk sugar, egg and yolk, and salt together in small saucepan. Add lemon juice and cook over medium-low heat, stirring constantly, until thick and puddinglike, about 3 minutes. Remove from heat and stir in butter and cream. Press through fine-mesh strainer into small bowl and refrigerate lemon curd until needed.

3. For the Filling Sprinkle gelatin over lemon juice in small bowl and let stand until gelatin softens, about 5 minutes. Microwave until mixture is bubbling around edges and gelatin dissolves, about 30 seconds. Set aside.

4. Using stand mixer fitted with paddle beat cream cheese, sugar, and salt on medium speed until smooth and creamy, scraping down sides of bowl as needed, about 2 minutes. Slowly add cream and beat until light and fluffy, about 2 minutes. Add gelatin mixture and ¼ cup curd, increase speed to medium-high, and beat until smooth and airy, about 3 minutes.

5. Pour filling into cooled crust and smooth top. Pour thin lines of remaining curd on top of cake and lightly drag paring knife or skewer perpendicularly through lines to create marbled appearance. Refrigerate until set, at least 6 hours. Remove sides of pan. Serve. (Cheesecake can be refrigerated for up to 3 days.)

Swirl Showstopper

Making a swirl with the lemon curd on top of the cheesecake is absurdly easy and awfully impressive.

1. Use measuring cup to pour curd in 4 thin lines on top of cheesecake.

2. Drag paring knife or skewer perpendicularly through lines to create marbled design.

Why This Recipe Works In a baked cheesecake, tart lemon juice is mellowed by the heat of the oven. For our icebox version of lemon cheesecake, we needed to dial back the lemon juice to compensate for the lack of baking. Lemon curd, a rich, tangy spread made from eggs, butter, cream, sugar, and lemon juice, added crisp lemon flavor without the undesirable chewiness of zest or the processed flavor of lemon extract. Using lemon cookies instead of graham crackers for the crust created an additional layer of lemon flavor.

Why This Recipe Works Too often, chocolate's bitter side can clash with the tangy flavor of cream cheese, but we were determined to create a fluffy chocolate cheesecake without the bitterness. After making dozens of versions, we figured out that switching from dark to mild-mannered milk chocolate was the secret to a sweet, creamy cheesecake. Adding cocoa powder added depth and rounded out the chocolate flavor. Unlike traditional cheesecake that is baked in a water bath, we simplified our recipe by baking it in a low 250-degree oven. For an easy and crunchy, chocolaty crust, we used Oreo cookies processed with butter and a bit of sugar.

MILK CHOCOLATE CHEESECAKE

SERVES 12

Our favorite milk chocolate is Dove Silky Smooth Milk Chocolate. For the crust, use the entire Oreo cookie, filling and all. The cheesecake needs to be refrigerated for at least 8 hours before serving.

- 16 Oreo sandwich cookies, broken into rough pieces
- 1 tablespoon sugar plus ½ cup (3½ ounces)
- 2 tablespoons unsalted butter, melted
- 8 ounces milk chocolate, chopped
- ⅓ cup heavy cream
- 2 tablespoons unsweetened cocoa powder
- ¼ teaspoon salt
- 1½ pounds cream cheese, softened
- 4 large eggs, room temperature
- 2 teaspoons vanilla extract

1. Adjust oven rack to middle position and heat oven to 350 degrees. Grease bottom and sides of 9-inch nonstick springform pan.

2. Process cookies and 1 tablespoon sugar in food processor until finely ground, about 30 seconds. Add melted butter and pulse until combined, about 6 pulses. Transfer crumb mixture to prepared pan and press firmly with bottom of dry measuring cup into even layer in bottom of pan. Bake until fragrant and set, about 10 minutes. Let cool completely on wire rack.

3. Reduce oven temperature to 250 degrees. Combine 6 ounces chocolate and cream in medium bowl and microwave at 50 percent power, stirring occasionally, until melted and smooth, 60 to 90 seconds. Let cool for 10 minutes. In small bowl, whisk cocoa, salt, and remaining ½ cup sugar until no lumps remain.

4. Using stand mixer fitted with paddle, beat cream cheese and cocoa mixture on medium speed until creamy and smooth, about 3 minutes, scraping down bowl as needed. Reduce speed to medium-low, add chocolate mixture, and beat until combined. Gradually add eggs, one at a time, until incorporated, scraping down bowl as needed. Add vanilla and give batter final stir by hand until no streaks of chocolate remain.

5. Pour cheesecake mixture into cooled crust and smooth top with spatula. Tap cheesecake gently on counter to release air bubbles. Cover pan tightly with aluminum foil (taking care not to touch surface of cheesecake with foil) and place on rimmed baking sheet. Bake for 1 hour, then remove foil. Continue to bake until edges are set and center registers 150 degrees and jiggles slightly when shaken, 30 to 45 minutes. Let cool completely on wire rack, then cover with plastic wrap and refrigerate in pan until cold, about 8 hours. (Cake can be refrigerated for up to 4 days.)

6. To unmold cheesecake, remove sides of pan, slide thin metal spatula between crust and pan bottom to loosen, and slide cake onto serving platter. Microwave remaining 2 ounces chocolate in small bowl at 50 percent power, stirring occasionally, until melted, 60 to 90 seconds. Let cool for 5 minutes. Transfer to small zipper-lock bag, cut small hole in corner, and pipe chocolate in thin zigzag pattern across top of cheesecake. Let cheesecake stand at room temperature for 30 minutes. Using warm, dry knife, cut into wedges and serve.

Melt Milk Chocolate Carefully

Because milk chocolate contains milk solids, its protein content is generally higher than that of dark chocolate. The extra protein means that milk chocolate melts at a slightly lower temperature than dark; what's more, when you add heat to protein and sugar, new molecules may form, introducing unwelcome scorched or burned flavors. Microwaves are generally gentle, but notoriously inconsistent, so choose 50 percent power, keep a close eye on the chocolate, and give it a stir every 15 seconds.

CHOCOLATE CHIP SKILLET COOKIE

SERVES 8

Top with ice cream for an extra-decadent treat.

- 12 tablespoons unsalted butter
- ¾ cup packed (5¼ ounces) dark brown sugar
- ½ cup (3½ ounces) granulated sugar
- 2 teaspoons vanilla extract
- 1 teaspoon salt
- 1 large egg plus 1 large yolk
- 1¾ cups (8¾ ounces) all-purpose flour
- ½ teaspoon baking soda
- 1 cup (6 ounces) semisweet chocolate chips

1. Adjust oven rack to upper-middle position and heat oven to 375 degrees. Melt 9 tablespoons butter in 12-inch cast-iron skillet over medium heat. Continue to cook, stirring constantly, until butter is dark golden brown, has nutty aroma, and bubbling subsides, about 5 minutes; transfer to large bowl. Stir remaining 3 tablespoons butter into hot butter until completely melted.

2. Whisk brown sugar, granulated sugar, vanilla, and salt into melted butter until smooth. Whisk in egg and yolk until smooth, about 30 seconds. Let mixture sit for 3 minutes, then whisk for 30 seconds. Repeat process of resting and whisking 2 more times until mixture is thick, smooth, and shiny.

3. Whisk flour and baking soda together in separate bowl, then stir flour mixture into butter mixture until just combined, about 1 minute. Stir in chocolate chips, making sure no flour pockets remain.

4. Wipe skillet clean with paper towels. Transfer dough to now-empty skillet and press into even layer with spatula. Transfer skillet to oven and bake until cookie is golden brown and edges are set, about 20 minutes, rotating skillet halfway through baking. Using potholders, transfer skillet to wire rack and let cookie cool for 30 minutes. Slice cookie into wedges and serve.

Making a Skillet Cookie

To ensure a uniformly baked cookie, transfer dough to skillet and press into even layer with spatula.

Seasoning Your Skillet

1. While the skillet is still warm, wipe it clean with paper towels to remove excess food bits and oil.

2. Rinse the skillet under hot running water, scrubbing with a brush or nonabrasive scrub pad to remove traces of food. Use a small amount of soap if you like, but make sure to rinse it all off.

3. Dry the skillet thoroughly (do not let it drip-dry) and put it back on the burner over medium-low heat until all traces of moisture disappear (this keeps rusting at bay). Never put a wet cast-iron skillet away or stack anything on top of a skillet that hasn't been properly dried.

4. Add ½ teaspoon of vegetable oil to the warm, dry skillet and wipe the interior with a wad of paper towels until it is lightly covered with oil.

5. Continue to rub oil into the skillet, replacing the paper towels as needed, until the skillet looks dark and shiny and does not have any remaining oil residue.

6. Turn off the heat and allow the skillet to cool completely before putting it away.

A well-seasoned skillet should have a smooth, dark black, semiglossy finish.

Why This Recipe Works A cookie in a skillet? Unlike baking a traditional batch of cookies, a skillet cookie can go straight from the oven to the table for a fun, hands-on dessert. This scaled-up cookie benefits from the hot bottom and tall sides of a well-seasoned cast-iron pan to create a great crisp crust. Reeling in the butter and chocolate chips from our usual cookie dough recipe allowed our oversized cookie to bake through in the middle while staying perfectly chewy. We increased the baking time to accommodate the giant size, but otherwise this recipe was simpler and faster than baking regular cookies.

Why This Recipe Works These delicate butter cookies literally melt in your mouth, thanks to the generous amount of cornstarch in the dough. Unfortunately, the cornstarch leaves behind a chalky residue with each bite. After settling on the maximum amount of cornstarch we could use without detection, we scoured supermarket shelves in search of other low-protein dry ingredients to replace the remainder. We replaced all-purpose flour with cake flour and chose confectioners' sugar over granulated, but we still needed more bulk. The solution? Rice Krispies! The ground cereal added the volume we were looking for without toughening the crumb.

MELTING MOMENTS

MAKES ABOUT 70 COOKIES

If the dough gets too soft to slice, return it to the refrigerator to firm up.

- ½ cup Rice Krispies cereal
- 16 tablespoons unsalted butter, cut into 16 pieces and softened
- 3 tablespoons heavy cream
- 1 teaspoon vanilla extract
- 1¼ cups (5 ounces) cake flour
- ¼ cup (1¼ ounces) cornstarch
- ⅛ teaspoon salt
- ⅔ cup (2⅔ ounces) confectioners' sugar

1. Process Rice Krispies in blender until finely ground, about 30 seconds. Combine 4 tablespoons butter and cream in large bowl and microwave until butter is melted, about 30 seconds. Whisk in processed Rice Krispies and vanilla until combined. Let cool slightly, 5 to 7 minutes.

2. Combine flour, cornstarch, and salt in medium bowl; reserve. Whisk sugar into cooled butter mixture until incorporated. Add remaining 12 tablespoons butter, whisking until smooth. Stir in flour mixture until combined.

3. Working with half of dough at a time, dollop dough into 8-inch strip down center of 14 by 12-inch sheet of parchment paper. Fold 1 long side of parchment over dough. Using ruler, press dough into tight 1-inch-wide log. Repeat with remaining dough and another sheet of parchment. Refrigerate dough until firm, about 1 hour. (Dough can be wrapped in plastic wrap and aluminum foil and frozen for up to 1 month.)

4. Adjust oven racks to upper-middle and lower-middle positions and heat oven to 300 degrees. Line 2 baking sheets with parchment. Cut dough into ¼-inch slices and place 1 inch apart on prepared baking sheets. Bake until set but not brown, 18 to 22 minutes, switching and rotating baking sheets halfway through baking. Let cool completely on sheets, about 15 minutes. Repeat with remaining dough. Serve. (Cookies can be stored at room temperature for up to 2 days.)

CRESCENT COOKIES
After step 2, transfer dough to pastry bag fitted with ½-inch star tip. Pipe 1½-inch-long crescents onto prepared baking sheets. Refrigerate dough until firm, about 30 minutes. Bake as directed.

JAM THUMBPRINT COOKIES
After step 2, transfer dough to pastry bag fitted with ½-inch plain tip. Pipe 1-inch-wide and ½-inch-high dough rounds onto prepared baking sheets. Using back of ¼-teaspoon measuring spoon dipped in water, make indentation in center of each round. Refrigerate dough until firm, about 30 minutes. Bake until set, 18 to 20 minutes, switching and rotating sheets halfway through baking. Fill each dimple with ½ teaspoon jam and bake for 5 minutes.

ROUND SPRITZ COOKIES
After step 2, transfer dough to pastry bag fitted with ½-inch star tip. Pipe 1-inch-wide and ½-inch-high dough rounds onto prepared baking sheets. Refrigerate dough until firm, about 30 minutes. Bake as directed.

Handling Soft Dough
The high proportion of butter to flour makes the dough for these cookies very soft and challenging to handle. With this technique, you can easily roll it into a log.

1. Dollop half of dough in strip down center of sheet of parchment.

2. Pulling parchment taut, use ruler to press dough into tight log

Why This Recipe Works We set out to create a slice-and-bake cookie recipe that would combine both crispness and rich butter and vanilla flavors—in effect, shortbread shaped into a convenient slice-and-bake log. Using both granulated sugar and light brown sugar gave the cookies a richness and complexity that tasters liked. We used the food processor to combine our recipe ingredients quickly without whipping in too much air—our cookies had the fine, shortbreadlike texture we were after.

SLICE-AND-BAKE COOKIES

MAKES ABOUT 40 COOKIES

Be sure that the cookie dough is well chilled and firm so that it can be uniformly sliced.

- ⅓ cup (2⅓ ounces) granulated sugar
- 2 tablespoons packed light brown sugar
- ½ teaspoon salt
- 12 tablespoons unsalted butter, cut into pieces and softened
- 2 teaspoons vanilla extract
- 1 large egg yolk
- 1½ cups (7½ ounces) all-purpose flour

1. Process granulated sugar, brown sugar, and salt in food processor until no lumps of brown sugar remain, about 30 seconds. Add butter, vanilla, and yolk and process until smooth and creamy, about 20 seconds. Scrape down sides of bowl, add flour, and pulse until dough forms, about 15 seconds.

2. Turn out dough onto lightly floured counter and roll into 10-inch log. Wrap tightly with plastic wrap and refrigerate until firm, at least 2 hours or up to 3 days. (Dough can be wrapped in foil and frozen for up to 1 month.)

3. Adjust oven racks to upper-middle and lower-middle positions and heat oven to 350 degrees. Line 2 baking sheets with parchment paper. Slice chilled dough into ¼-inch rounds and place 1 inch apart on prepared baking sheets. Bake until edges are just golden, about 15 minutes, switching and rotating baking sheets halfway through baking. Let cool 10 minutes on sheets, then transfer to wire rack and let cool completely. Repeat with remaining dough. (Cookies can be stored at room temperature for up to 1 week.)

COCONUT-LIME COOKIES
In step 1, add 2 cups sweetened shredded coconut and 2 teaspoons grated lime zest to food processor along with sugars and salt.

WALNUT–BROWN SUGAR COOKIES
In step 1, add 2 more tablespoons brown sugar and 1 cup chopped walnuts to food processor along with sugars and salt.

ORANGE–POPPY SEED COOKIES
In step 1, add ¼ cup poppy seeds and 1 tablespoon grated orange zest to food processor along with sugars and salt.

Glaze Me
We love the simplicity of our Slice-and-Bake Cookies, but a confectioners' sugar glaze is an easy way to dress them up. If the glaze is too thick to spread, thin it with 1 tablespoon water. Each glaze makes enough for 1 recipe Slice-and-Bake Cookies.

Ginger-Lime Glaze Whisk 1 tablespoon softened cream cheese, 1 teaspoon ground ginger, and 2 tablespoons lime juice in medium bowl until combined. Whisk in 1½ cups confectioners' sugar until smooth.

Malted Milk Glaze Whisk 1 tablespoon softened cream cheese, 1 tablespoon malted milk powder, 1 teaspoon vanilla extract, and 2 tablespoons milk in medium bowl until combined. Whisk in 1½ cups confectioners' sugar until smooth.

Cappuccino Glaze Whisk 1 tablespoon softened cream cheese, 1 tablespoon instant espresso powder, and 2 tablespoons milk in medium bowl until combined. Whisk in 1½ cups confectioners' sugar until smooth.

Peanut Butter and Jelly Glaze Whisk 1 tablespoon creamy peanut butter, 2 tablespoons strawberry jelly, and 1 tablespoon water in medium bowl until combined. Whisk in 1½ cups confectioners' sugar until smooth.

FAIRY GINGERBREAD

MAKES 60 COOKIES

Use cookie or baking sheets that measure at least 15 by 12 inches. Don't be disconcerted by the scant amount of batter: You really are going to spread it very thin. Use the edges of the parchment paper as your guide, covering the entire surface thinly and evenly. For easier grating, freeze a 2-inch piece of peeled ginger for 30 minutes, then use a rasp-style grater.

- 1½ teaspoons ground ginger
- ¾ cup plus 2 tablespoons (4⅜ ounces) all-purpose flour
- ½ teaspoon baking soda
- ¼ teaspoon salt
- 5 tablespoons unsalted butter, softened
- 9 tablespoons (4 ounces) packed light brown sugar
- 4 teaspoons grated fresh ginger
- ¾ teaspoon vanilla extract
- ¼ cup whole milk, room temperature

1. Adjust oven racks to upper-middle and lower-middle positions and heat oven to 325 degrees. Spray 2 rimless baking sheets (or inverted rimmed baking sheets) with vegetable oil spray and cover each with 15 by 12-inch sheet parchment paper. Heat ground ginger in small skillet over medium heat until fragrant, about 1 minute. Combine flour, toasted ginger, baking soda, and salt in medium bowl.

2. Using stand mixer fitted with paddle, beat butter and sugar on medium-high speed until light and fluffy, about 2 minutes. Add fresh ginger and vanilla and mix until incorporated. Reduce speed to low and add flour mixture in 3 additions, alternating with milk in 2 additions; scrape down bowl as needed.

3. Evenly spread ¾ cup batter to cover parchment on each prepared sheet (batter will be very thin). Bake until deep golden brown, 16 to 20 minutes, switching and rotating baking sheets halfway through baking. Immediately score cookies into 3 by 2-inch rectangles. Let cool completely, about 20 minutes. Using tip of paring knife, separate cookies along score marks. (Cookies can be stored at room temperature for 3 days.)

Making Fairy Gingerbread

While making several dozen batches of Fairy Gingerbread, we had time to perfect our technique. The cookies are made with an unusual method we'd never encountered before. Here's how:

1. To form cookies of requisite thinness, use small offset spatula to spread batter to edges of 15 by 12-inch sheet of parchment paper.

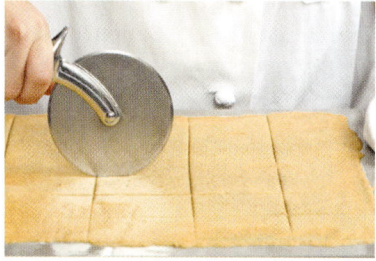

2. Immediately after removing cookies from oven, use chef's knife or pizza wheel to score 3 by 2-inch rectangles. Work quickly to prevent breaking.

3. Once cookies are cool, trace over scored lines with paring knife and gently break cookies apart along lines.

Why This Recipe Works Original recipes for fairy gingerbread, a cookie popular in the 19th century, melted in our mouths but were also severely lacking in flavor. A bit of vanilla extract and salt helped boost the flavor. Doubling the ginger added a much-needed kick, but without any competing flavors it was overwhelming. We cut back a little and toasted the ground ginger to bring out its natural flavor. Grating fresh ginger straight into the batter added even more intense ginger flavor. Switching from bread flour to all-purpose flour made the batter slightly easier to spread. A little baking soda helped retain the cookies' airy crispness.

JOE FROGGERS

MAKES 24 COOKIES

Place only six cookies on each baking sheet—they will spread. If you don't own a 3½-inch cookie cutter, use a drinking glass. Use mild (not robust or blackstrap) molasses. Make sure to chill the dough for a full 8 hours or it will be too hard to roll out.

- ⅓ cup dark rum (such as Myers's)
- 1 tablespoon water
- 1½ teaspoons salt
- 3 cups (15 ounces) all-purpose flour
- ¾ teaspoon ground ginger
- ½ teaspoon ground allspice
- ¼ teaspoon ground nutmeg
- ⅛ teaspoon ground cloves
- 1 cup molasses
- 1 teaspoon baking soda
- 8 tablespoons unsalted butter, softened but still cool
- 1 cup (7 ounces) sugar

1. Stir rum, water, and salt in small bowl until salt dissolves. Whisk flour, ginger, allspice, nutmeg, and cloves in medium bowl. Stir molasses and baking soda in liquid measuring cup (mixture will begin to bubble) and let sit until doubled in volume, about 15 minutes.

2. Using stand mixer fitted with paddle, beat butter and sugar on medium-high speed until fluffy, about 2 minutes. Reduce speed to medium-low and gradually beat in rum mixture. Add flour mixture in 3 additions, beating on medium-low until just incorporated, alternating with molasses mixture in 2 additions, scraping down sides of bowl as needed. Give dough final stir by hand (dough will be extremely sticky). Cover bowl with plastic wrap and refrigerate until stiff, at least 8 hours or up to 3 days.

3. Adjust oven racks to upper-middle and lower-middle positions and heat oven to 375 degrees. Line 2 baking sheets with parchment paper. Working with half of dough at a time on heavily floured counter, roll out to ¼-inch thickness. Using 3½-inch cookie cutter, cut out 12 cookies. Transfer 6 cookies to each baking sheet, spacing cookies about 1½ inches apart. Bake until cookies are set and just beginning to crack, about 8 minutes, switching and rotating baking sheets halfway through baking time. Let cookies cool on sheets on wire rack 10 minutes, then transfer cookies to rack to cool completely. Repeat with remaining dough. (Cookies may be stored for up to 1 week.)

Salty History

Joe froggers date back more than 200 years to Black Joe's Tavern, located in Marblehead, Massachusetts, a seaside town north of Boston. A freed slave and Revolutionary War veteran, Joseph Brown (known as Old Black Joe), and his wife, Lucretia (affectionately known as Auntie Cresse), opened the tavern in a part of Marblehead called Gingerbread Hill. Besides serving drinks (mostly rum), Joe and Auntie Cresse baked cookies: large, moist molasses and rum cookies made salty by the addition of Marblehead seawater. These cookies were popular sustenance on long fishing voyages, as they had no dairy to spoil and the combination of rum, molasses, and seawater kept them chewy for weeks.

According to Samuel Roads Jr.'s *History and Traditions of Marblehead*, published in 1879, the funny name for these cookies referred to the lily pads (similar in size and shape to the cookies) and large croaking frogs that would fill the pond behind Joe's tavern. Thus the cookies became known as Joe froggers.

Why This Recipe Works Joe froggers, from a recipe that dates back more than 200 years, are incredibly moist, spicy, slightly salty cookies, found in bakeries along the North Shore of Massachusetts. We wanted to develop our own recipe. Dissolving salt into our recipe's rum and water gave the cookie its distinctive salty flavor. Ginger, allspice, nutmeg, and cloves contributed warm spice flavor. Many recipes we found in our research called for lard, but we found that using butter made for a more flavorful cookie.

Why This Recipe Works These cakey cookies are a deli favorite in New York, but rarely do they live up to the hype. We wanted to improve upon the classic chocolate-vanilla combination. To get the "cookie" just right, we made several small but high-impact adjustments. We dialed back the amount of baking soda and baking powder to get rid of unwanted air bubbles, added more vanilla extract to heighten the flavor, and used just enough sour cream to make the cookies tender but not sticky. Corn syrup made the glaze thick and shiny, while milk made it creamy and spreadable. Cocoa powder kept the chocolate glaze flavorful and simple.

BLACK AND WHITE COOKIES

MAKES 12 COOKIES

Twelve cookies doesn't sound like much, but these cookies are huge. You'll get neater cookies if you spread on the vanilla glaze first. This recipe provides a little extra glaze, just in case.

Cookies
- 1¾ cups (8¾ ounces) all-purpose flour
- ½ teaspoon baking powder
- ¼ teaspoon baking soda
- ⅛ teaspoon salt
- 10 tablespoons unsalted butter, softened
- 1 cup (7 ounces) granulated sugar
- 1 large egg
- 2 teaspoons vanilla extract
- ⅓ cup sour cream

Glaze
- 5 cups (20 ounces) confectioners' sugar, sifted
- 7 tablespoons whole milk
- 2 tablespoons corn syrup
- 1 teaspoon vanilla extract
- ½ teaspoon salt
- 3 tablespoons Dutch-processed cocoa powder, sifted

1. For the Cookies Adjust oven racks to upper-middle and lower-middle positions and heat oven to 350 degrees. Line 2 baking sheets with parchment paper. Combine flour, baking powder, baking soda, and salt in bowl.

2. Using stand mixer fitted with paddle, beat butter and sugar on medium-high speed until pale and fluffy, about 2 minutes. Add egg and vanilla and beat until combined. Reduce speed to low and add flour mixture in 3 additions, alternating with 2 additions of sour cream, scraping down bowl as needed. Give dough final stir by hand.

3. Using greased ¼-cup measure, drop cookie dough 3 inches apart onto prepared baking sheets. Bake until edges are lightly browned, 15 to 18 minutes, switching and rotating sheets halfway through baking. Let cookies cool on sheets for 5 minutes, then transfer to wire rack to cool completely, about 1 hour.

4. For the Glaze Whisk sugar, 6 tablespoons milk, corn syrup, vanilla, and salt together in bowl until smooth. Transfer 1 cup glaze to small bowl; reserve. Whisk cocoa and remaining 1 tablespoon milk into remaining glaze until combined.

5. Working with 1 cookie at a time, spread 1 tablespoon vanilla glaze over half of underside of cookie. Refrigerate until glaze is set, about 15 minutes. Cover other half of cookies with 1 tablespoon chocolate glaze and let cookies sit at room temperature until glaze is firm, at least 1 hour. Serve. (Cookies can be stored at room temperature for up to 2 days.)

Glazing Black and White Cookies

1. Using butter knife or offset mini spatula, glaze half of underside of each cookie with vanilla glaze. Chill cookies in refrigerator for 15 minutes so glaze can start to harden.

2. Glaze other half of each cookie with chocolate glaze, and let cookies sit until glaze sets, about 1 hour.

WHOOPIE PIES

MAKES 6 PIES

Don't be tempted to bake all the cakes on one baking sheet; the batter needs room to spread in the oven.

Cakes
- 2 cups (10 ounces) all-purpose flour
- ½ cup (1½ ounces) Dutch-processed cocoa powder
- 1 teaspoon baking soda
- ½ teaspoon salt
- 8 tablespoons unsalted butter, softened but still cool
- 1 cup packed (7 ounces) light brown sugar
- 1 large egg, room temperature
- 1 teaspoon vanilla extract
- 1 cup buttermilk

Filling
- 12 tablespoons unsalted butter, softened but still cool
- 1¼ cups (5 ounces) confectioners' sugar
- 1½ teaspoons vanilla extract
- ⅛ teaspoon salt
- 2½ cups marshmallow crème

1. For the Cakes Adjust oven racks to upper-middle and lower-middle positions and heat oven to 350 degrees. Line 2 baking sheets with parchment paper. Whisk flour, cocoa, baking soda, and salt in medium bowl.

2. Using stand mixer fitted with paddle, beat butter and sugar on medium-high speed until fluffy, about 4 minutes. Beat in egg until incorporated, scraping down sides of bowl as necessary, then beat in vanilla. Reduce speed to low and beat in flour mixture in 3 additions, alternating with buttermilk in 2 additions. Give batter final stir by hand.

3. Using ⅓-cup measure, scoop 6 mounds of batter onto each baking sheet, spacing mounds about 3 inches apart. Bake until cakes spring back when pressed, 15 to 18 minutes, switching and rotating baking sheets halfway through baking. Let cool completely on baking sheets, at least 1 hour.

4. For the Filling Using stand mixer fitted with paddle, beat butter and sugar on medium speed until fluffy, about 2 minutes. Beat in vanilla and salt. Beat in marshmallow crème until incorporated, about 2 minutes. Refrigerate filling until slightly firm, about 30 minutes. (Bowl can be wrapped and refrigerated for up to 2 days.)

5. Dollop ⅓ cup filling on center of flat side of 6 cakes. Top with flat side of remaining 6 cakes and gently press until filling spreads to edges of cakes. Serve. (Whoopie pies can be refrigerated for up to 3 days.)

What's Up, Whoopie Pie?

Where did whoopie pies originate? Both Maine and Pennsylvania—the Pennsylvania Dutch of Lancaster County, to be specific—claim whoopie pies as their own. Maine's earliest claim dates back to 1925, when Labadie's Bakery in Lewiston first sold whoopie pies to the public. Some research showed that the Berwick Cake Company began manufacturing Whoopie! Pies (the exclamation point was part of the name) in 1927. These sources claim that whoopie pies were named after the musical *Whoopie*; *Whoopie* had its debut in Boston in 1927. In addition, Marshmallow Fluff, a key ingredient in many whoopie pie recipes, had been invented in nearby Lynn seven years earlier.

What about Pennsylvania's claim on whoopie pies? We found an article in a copy of the *Gettysburg Times* from 1982 that spoke of a chocolate cake sandwich with a fluffy cream center. These sandwiches were called gobs and were sold by the Dutch Maid Bakery of Geistown. While the name was different, the description (and a huge picture) showed that these were no doubt whoopie pies. The Dutch Maid Bakery purchased the rights to the gob in 1980 from the Harris and Boyer Baking Company, also of Pennsylvania, which had started manufacturing gobs in 1927. Maine might have a few years on Pennsylvania when it comes to whoopie pies, but who's to know for sure?

Why This Recipe Works We wanted a light, airy cake for our whoopie pies, so we used the creaming mixing method—blending the butter and sugar with a mixer until fluffy and nearly white in color. We also used lots of Dutch-processed cocoa powder and vanilla in our recipe for full flavor and a deep, dark-colored crumb. And for a cleaner, fuller flavor, we replaced the shortening (or lard) found in most recipes with butter.

Why This Recipe Works Chocolate truffles are often reserved for special occasions because they can be laborious to make. We wanted a streamlined, foolproof recipe, making the process as simple as possible. We utilized the microwave to melt the chocolate and cream ganache base, stirred the mixture with a rubber spatula (a whisk incorporates too much air), and chilled it. Rolling truffles can get messy, so we wore disposable gloves for easy clean up. A dusting of cocoa powder and confectioners' sugar keeps the truffles from sticking together during chilling and storing.

BASIC CHOCOLATE TRUFFLES

MAKES 24 TRUFFLES

Wear latex gloves when forming the truffles to keep your hands clean.

- ¼ cup (¾ ounce) unsweetened cocoa powder
- 1 tablespoon confectioners' sugar
- 8 ounces bittersweet chocolate, chopped fine
- ½ cup heavy cream
- Pinch salt

1. Sift cocoa and sugar through fine-mesh strainer into pie plate. Microwave chocolate, cream, and salt in bowl at 50 percent power, stirring occasionally with rubber spatula, until melted, about 1 minute. Stir truffle mixture until fully combined; transfer to 8-inch square baking dish and refrigerate until set, about 45 minutes.

2. Using heaping teaspoon measure, scoop truffle mixture into 24 portions, transfer to large plate, and refrigerate until firm, about 30 minutes. Roll each truffle between your hands to form uniform balls (balls needn't be perfect).

3. Transfer truffles to cocoa mixture and roll to evenly coat. (Coated truffles can be refrigerated along with excess cocoa mixture for up to 1 week.) Lightly shake truffles in your hand over pie plate to remove excess coating; transfer to platter. Refrigerate for 30 minutes. Let sit at room temperature for 10 minutes before serving.

CHOCOLATE-ALMOND TRUFFLES
Substitute 1 cup sliced almonds, toasted and chopped fine, for cocoa mixture coating. Add ½ teaspoon almond extract to chocolate mixture before microwaving in step 2.

CHOCOLATE-CINNAMON TRUFFLES
Sift ¼ teaspoon ground cinnamon with cocoa powder and sugar for coating. Add 1 teaspoon ground cinnamon and ⅛ teaspoon cayenne pepper to chocolate mixture before microwaving.

CHOCOLATE-GINGER TRUFFLES
Add 2 teaspoons ground ginger to chocolate mixture before microwaving.

CHOCOLATE-LEMON TRUFFLES
Add 1 teaspoon grated lemon zest to chocolate mixture before microwaving.

No-Stick Solution

The best way to store chocolate truffles is in the cocoa mixture you dredged them in. This keeps the chocolates from sticking and avoids the need to use more cocoa to touch them up.

old-fashioned fruit desserts and puddings

539 Baked Apple Dumplings
541 Apple Fritters
542 Apple Pandowdy
544 Cranberry-Apple Crisp
547 Maine Blueberry Grunt
548 Skillet Peach Cobbler

550 Dakota Peach Kuchen
553 Banana Pudding
555 New Orleans Bourbon Bread Pudding
556 Summer Berry Pudding
559 Old-Fashioned Vanilla Frozen Custard

Why This Recipe Works Apple dumplings are a homespun combination of warm pastry, concentrated apple flavor, raisins, butter, and cinnamon, but too often the apples turn too soft or are unevenly baked. The pastry can also turn gummy from the apples' juices. We found that biscuit dough was easier to work with than pie dough and did a great job of absorbing the liquid from the apples without getting mushy. Rather than baking the dumplings in syrup as some recipes instruct, we served our sauce on the side, which preserved the dumplings' texture.

BAKED APPLE DUMPLINGS

MAKES 8 DUMPLINGS

Use a melon baller or a metal teaspoon measure to core the apples. Serve warm, with Cider Sauce (recipe follows).

Dough
- 2½ cups (12½ ounces) all-purpose flour
- 3 tablespoons sugar
- 2 teaspoons baking powder
- ¾ teaspoon salt
- 10 tablespoons unsalted butter, cut into ½-inch pieces and chilled
- 5 tablespoons vegetable shortening, cut into ½-inch pieces and chilled
- ¾ cup cold buttermilk

Apple Dumplings
- 6 tablespoons (2⅔ ounces) sugar
- 1 teaspoon ground cinnamon
- 3 tablespoons unsalted butter, softened
- 3 tablespoons golden raisins, chopped
- 4 Golden Delicious apples
- 2 egg whites, lightly beaten

1. For the Dough Process flour, sugar, baking powder, and salt in food processor until combined, about 15 seconds. Scatter butter and shortening over flour mixture and pulse until mixture resembles wet sand, about 10 pulses; transfer to bowl. Stir in buttermilk until dough forms. Turn out onto lightly floured work surface and knead briefly until dough is cohesive. Press dough into 8 by 4-inch rectangle. Cut in half, wrap each half tightly in plastic wrap, and refrigerate until firm, about 1 hour.

2. For the Apple Dumplings Adjust oven rack to middle position and heat oven to 425 degrees. Combine sugar and cinnamon in small bowl. In second bowl, combine butter, raisins, and 3 tablespoons cinnamon sugar mixture. Peel apples and halve through equator. Remove core and pack butter mixture into each apple half.

3. On lightly floured counter, roll each dough half into 12-inch square. Cut each 12-inch square into four 6-inch squares. Working with one at a time, lightly brush edges of dough square with egg white and place apple, cut side up, in center of each square. Gather dough 1 corner at a time on top of apple, crimping edges to seal. Using paring knife, cut vent hole in top of each dumpling.

4. Line rimmed baking sheet with parchment paper. Arrange dumplings on prepared baking sheet, brush tops with egg white, and sprinkle with remaining cinnamon sugar. Bake until dough is golden brown and juices are bubbling, 20 to 25 minutes. Let cool on baking sheet for 10 minutes. Serve.

CIDER SAUCE
MAKES ABOUT 1½ CUPS

- 1 cup apple cider
- 1 cup water
- 1 cup (7 ounces) sugar
- ½ teaspoon ground cinnamon
- 2 tablespoons unsalted butter
- 1 tablespoon lemon juice

Bring cider, water, sugar, and cinnamon to simmer in small saucepan and cook over medium-high heat until thickened and reduced to 1½ cups, about 15 minutes. Off heat, whisk in butter and lemon juice. Drizzle over dumplings to serve.

Wrapping Dumplings

1. Fold corners of dough up to enclose apple halves, overlapping and crimping to seal.

2. Arrange dumplings on baking sheet, brush with egg white, and sprinkle with cinnamon sugar.

Why This Recipe Works Apple fritters should be crisp on the outside, moist within, and sing out apple flavor. Too often, recipes for fritters produce leaden, soggy pastries with undercooked interiors. We found that the best solution was to dry the apples with paper towels and mix them with the dry ingredients. The dry ingredients absorbed the moisture that would otherwise have leached out during frying. As for the batter, we found that replacing the milk with apple cider reinforced the sweet apple flavor. And a quick glaze, spiked with more cider and warm spices and spooned over the warm fritters, added another layer of apple flavor.

APPLE FRITTERS

MAKES 10 FRITTERS

We like Granny Smith apples in these fritters because they are tart and crisp. Apple juice doesn't have enough flavor—you really do need the cider.

Fritters
- 2 Granny Smith apples, peeled, cored, and cut into ¼-inch pieces
- 2 cups (10 ounces) all-purpose flour
- ⅓ cup (2⅓ ounces) granulated sugar
- 1 tablespoon baking powder
- 1 teaspoon salt
- 1 teaspoon ground cinnamon
- ¼ teaspoon ground nutmeg
- ¾ cup apple cider
- 2 large eggs, lightly beaten
- 2 tablespoons unsalted butter, melted
- 3 cups peanut or vegetable oil

Glaze
- 2 cups (8 ounces) confectioners' sugar
- ¼ cup apple cider
- ½ teaspoon ground cinnamon
- ¼ teaspoon ground nutmeg

1. For the Fritters Spread prepared apples in single layer on paper towel–lined baking sheet and pat thoroughly dry with paper towels. Combine flour, sugar, baking powder, salt, cinnamon, and nutmeg in large bowl. Whisk cider, eggs, and melted butter in medium bowl until combined. Stir apples into flour mixture. Stir in cider mixture until incorporated.

2. Set wire rack in rimmed baking sheet. Heat oil in Dutch oven over medium-high heat to 350 degrees. Use ⅓-cup measure to transfer 5 heaping portions of batter to oil. Press batter lightly with back of spoon to flatten. Fry, adjusting burner as necessary to maintain oil temperature between 325 and 350 degrees, until deep golden brown, 2 to 3 minutes per side. Transfer fritters to prepared wire rack. Bring oil back to 350 degrees and repeat with remaining batter. Let fritters cool for 5 minutes.

3. For the Glaze While fritters cool, whisk sugar, cider, cinnamon, and nutmeg in medium bowl until smooth. Top each fritter with 1 heaping tablespoon glaze. Let glaze set for 10 minutes. Serve.

Forming Fritters

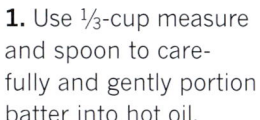

1. Use ⅓-cup measure and spoon to carefully and gently portion batter into hot oil.

2. Use spoon to gently press on each fritter. Flattened shape helps interior cook through.

APPLE PANDOWDY

SERVES 6

Disturbing the crust, or "dowdying," allows juices from the filling to rise over the crust and caramelize as the dessert continues to bake. Removing the skillet from the oven allows you to properly press down on the crust. Do not use store-bought pie crust in this recipe; it yields gummy results.

Pie Dough
- 3 tablespoons ice water
- 1 tablespoon sour cream
- ⅔ cup (3⅓ ounces) all-purpose flour
- 1 teaspoon granulated sugar
- ½ teaspoon salt
- 6 tablespoons unsalted butter, cut into ¼-inch pieces and frozen for 15 minutes

Filling
- 2½ pounds Golden Delicious apples, peeled, cored, halved, and cut into ½-inch-thick wedges
- ¼ cup packed (1¾ ounces) light brown sugar
- ½ teaspoon ground cinnamon
- ¼ teaspoon salt
- 3 tablespoons unsalted butter
- ¾ cup apple cider
- 1 tablespoon cornstarch
- 2 teaspoons lemon juice

Topping
- 1 tablespoon granulated sugar
- ¼ teaspoon ground cinnamon
- 1 large egg, lightly beaten

Vanilla ice cream

1. For the Pie Dough Combine ice water and sour cream in bowl. Process flour, sugar, and salt in food processor until combined, about 3 seconds. Add butter and pulse until size of large peas, 6 to 8 pulses. Add sour cream mixture and pulse until dough forms large clumps and no dry flour remains, 3 to 6 pulses, scraping down sides of bowl as needed.

2. Form dough into 4-inch disk, wrap tightly in plastic wrap, and refrigerate for 1 hour. (Wrapped dough can be refrigerated for up to 2 days or frozen for up to 1 month. If frozen, let dough thaw completely on counter before rolling.)

3. Adjust oven rack to middle position and heat oven to 400 degrees. Let chilled dough sit on counter to soften slightly, about 5 minutes, before rolling. Roll dough into 10-inch circle on lightly floured counter. Using pizza cutter, cut dough into four 2½-inch-wide strips, then make four 2½-inch-wide perpendicular cuts to form squares. (Pieces around edges of dough will be smaller.) Transfer dough pieces to parchment paper–lined baking sheet, cover with plastic, and refrigerate until firm, at least 30 minutes.

4. For the Filling Toss apples, sugar, cinnamon, and salt together in large bowl. Melt butter in 10-inch skillet over medium heat. Add apple mixture, cover, and cook until apples become slightly pliable and release their juices, about 10 minutes, stirring occasionally.

5. Whisk cider, cornstarch, and lemon juice in bowl until no lumps remain; add to skillet. Bring to simmer and cook, uncovered, stirring occasionally, until sauce is thickened, about 2 minutes. Off heat, press lightly on apples to form even layer.

6. For the Topping Combine sugar and cinnamon in small bowl. Working quickly, shingle dough pieces over filling until mostly covered, overlapping as needed. Brush dough pieces with egg and sprinkle with cinnamon sugar.

7. Bake until crust is slightly puffed and beginning to brown, about 15 minutes. Remove skillet from oven. Using back of large spoon, press down in center of crust until juices come up over top of crust. Repeat four more times around skillet. Make sure all apples are submerged and return skillet to oven. Continue to bake until crust is golden brown, about 15 minutes longer.

8. Transfer skillet to wire rack and let cool for at least 20 minutes. Serve with ice cream, drizzling extra sauce over top.

Why This Recipe Works Unlike traditional skillet pie, apple pandowdy's crust is gently pressed into the filling (or "dowdied") during baking so the juices flood the top and caramelize in the oven. We tossed wedges of buttery Golden Delicious apples in cinnamon and brown sugar for sweet-spiced flavor and partially cooked them before simmering in an apple cider–lemon juice slurry to thicken the filling. Topping the apples with squares of dough allowed steam to escape during baking, preventing the apples from overcooking. Dowdying the crust partway through created the dessert's sweet finish.

CRANBERRY-APPLE CRISP

SERVES 8 TO 10

If you can't find Braeburn apples, Golden Delicious will work. Serve with vanilla ice cream or whipped cream.

Topping
- ¾ cup (3¾ ounces) all-purpose flour
- ½ cup packed (3½ ounces) light brown sugar
- ½ cup (3½ ounces) granulated sugar
- 1 teaspoon ground cinnamon
- 12 tablespoons unsalted butter, cut into ½-inch pieces and chilled
- ¾ cup (2¼ ounces) old-fashioned rolled oats

Filling
- 1 pound (4 cups) fresh or frozen cranberries
- 1¼ cups (8¾ ounces) granulated sugar
- ¼ cup water
- 2½ pounds Granny Smith apples, peeled, cored, halved, and cut into ½-inch pieces
- 2½ pounds Braeburn apples, peeled, cored, halved, and cut into ½-inch pieces
- 1 cup dried sweetened cranberries
- 3 tablespoons instant tapioca

1. For the Topping Adjust oven rack to middle position and heat oven to 400 degrees. Pulse flour, brown sugar, granulated sugar, cinnamon, and butter in food processor until mixture has texture of coarse crumbs (some pea-size pieces of butter will remain), about 12 pulses. Transfer to medium bowl, stir in oats, and use fingers to pinch topping into peanut-size clumps. Refrigerate while preparing filling.

2. For the Filling Bring fresh cranberries, ¾ cup sugar, and water to simmer in Dutch oven over medium-high heat and cook until cranberries are completely softened and mixture is jamlike, about 10 minutes. Scrape mixture into bowl. Add apples, remaining ½ cup sugar, and dried cranberries to now-empty Dutch oven and cook over medium-high heat until apples begin to release their juices, about 5 minutes.

3. Off heat, stir cranberry mixture and tapioca into apple mixture. Pour into 13 by 9-inch baking dish set in rimmed baking sheet and smooth surface evenly with spatula.

4. Mound topping over filling in center of dish, then use your fingers to rake topping out toward edges of dish and bake until juices are bubbling and topping is deep golden brown, about 30 minutes. (If topping is browning too quickly, loosely cover with piece of aluminum foil.) Let cool on wire rack for 10 minutes. Serve.

To Make Ahead After pinching topping into small clumps in step 1, transfer mixture to zipper-lock bag and refrigerate for up to 5 days or freeze for up to 1 month. The cooked filling can be refrigerated for up to 2 days. To bake, sprinkle chilled topping evenly over chilled filling, loosely cover with foil, and bake for 20 minutes. Uncover and bake until juices are bubbling and topping is deep golden brown, 15 to 20 minutes longer.

Crisp Essentials

1. Cook cranberries, sugar, and water until mixture is thick and jammy.

2. Mound topping in center of dish, then use your fingers to rake topping out toward edges of dish.

Why This Recipe Works Although it's hard to imagine that apple crisp needs much improving upon, we liked the tartness and texture that cranberries added to one of our favorite standard dessert recipes. Raw cranberries proved too bitter, but we found dried cranberries and cooked fresh berries made cranberry-apple crisp with the best taste and texture. And we used tapioca to thicken the fruit juices instead of cornstarch or flour.

Why This Recipe Works This 19th-century fruit dessert boasts sweetened stewed berries covered with drop biscuit dough that is covered to steam and cook through. We found the idea of a simple stovetop fruit dessert appealing, but standard recipes produced washed-out fruit and a soggy topping. To improve the recipe, we cooked down half of the berries until jammy, and then stirred in the remaining berries. A bit of cornstarch further thickened the filling. For a fluffy biscuit topping, we placed a dish towel under the lid during cooking to absorb condensation. A sprinkle of cinnamon sugar over the finished dessert provided sweet crunch.

MAINE BLUEBERRY GRUNT

SERVES 12

Do not use frozen blueberries here, as they will make the filling watery. You will need a clean dish towel for this recipe.

Filling
- 2½ pounds (8 cups) blueberries
- ½ cup (3½ ounces) sugar
- ½ teaspoon ground cinnamon
- 2 tablespoons water
- 1 teaspoon grated lemon zest plus 1 tablespoon juice
- 1 teaspoon cornstarch

Topping
- ¾ cup buttermilk
- 6 tablespoons unsalted butter, melted and cooled slightly
- 1 teaspoon vanilla extract
- 2¼ cups (11¼ ounces) all-purpose flour
- 1½ teaspoons baking powder
- ½ teaspoon baking soda
- ½ teaspoon salt
- ½ cup (3½ ounces) sugar
- ½ teaspoon ground cinnamon

1. For the Filling Cook 4 cups blueberries, sugar, cinnamon, water, and lemon zest in Dutch oven over medium-high heat, stirring occasionally, until mixture is thick and jamlike, 10 to 12 minutes. Whisk lemon juice and cornstarch in small bowl, then stir into blueberry mixture. Add remaining 4 cups blueberries and cook until heated through, about 1 minute; remove pot from heat, cover, and keep warm.

2. For the Topping Combine buttermilk, butter, and vanilla in 2-cup liquid measuring cup. Whisk flour, baking powder, baking soda, salt, and 6 tablespoons sugar in large bowl. Slowly stir buttermilk mixture into flour mixture until dough forms.

3. Using small ice cream scoop or 2 large spoons, spoon golf ball–size dough pieces on top of warm berry mixture (you should have 14 pieces). Wrap lid of Dutch oven with clean dish towel (keeping towel away from heat source) and cover pot. Simmer gently until biscuits have doubled in size and toothpick inserted in center comes out clean, 16 to 22 minutes.

4. Combine remaining 2 tablespoons sugar and cinnamon in small bowl. Remove lid and sprinkle biscuit topping with cinnamon sugar. Serve immediately.

Secrets to Great Grunt

1. Use small ice cream scoop to drop evenly sized balls of biscuit dough over warm filling.

2. A clean dish towel beneath lid absorbs condensation during cooking, keeping biscuit topping light and fluffy.

3. A sprinkling of cinnamon sugar adds crunchy contrast to steamed biscuits.

SKILLET PEACH COBBLER

SERVES 6 TO 8

You can substitute 4 pounds of frozen sliced peaches for fresh; there is no need to defrost them. Start step 2 when the peaches are almost done.

Filling
- 4 tablespoons unsalted butter
- 5 pounds peaches, peeled, halved, pitted, and cut into ½-inch wedges
- 6 tablespoons (2⅔ ounces) sugar
- ⅛ teaspoon salt
- 1 tablespoon lemon juice
- 1½ teaspoons cornstarch

Topping
- 1½ cups (7½ ounces) all-purpose flour
- 6 tablespoons (2⅔ ounces) sugar
- 1½ teaspoons baking powder
- ¼ teaspoon baking soda
- ¼ teaspoon salt
- ¾ cup buttermilk
- 4 tablespoons unsalted butter, melted and cooled
- 1 teaspoon ground cinnamon

1. For the Filling Adjust oven rack to middle position and heat oven to 425 degrees. Melt butter in 12-inch ovensafe nonstick skillet over medium-high heat. Add two-thirds of peaches, sugar, and salt and cook, covered, until peaches release their juices, about 5 minutes. Remove lid and simmer until all liquid has evaporated and peaches begin to caramelize, 15 to 20 minutes. Add remaining peaches and cook until heated through, about 5 minutes. Whisk lemon juice and cornstarch in small bowl, then stir into peach mixture. Cover skillet and set aside off heat.

2. For the Topping Meanwhile, whisk flour, 5 tablespoons sugar, baking powder, baking soda, and salt in medium bowl. Stir in buttermilk and butter until dough forms. Turn dough out onto lightly floured work surface and knead briefly until smooth, about 30 seconds.

3. Combine remaining 1 tablespoon sugar and cinnamon. Break dough into rough 1-inch pieces and space them about ½ inch apart on top of hot peach mixture. Sprinkle with cinnamon sugar and bake until topping is golden brown and filling is thickened, 18 to 22 minutes. Let cool on wire rack for 10 minutes. Serve.

Peeling Peaches

1. With paring knife, score small X at base of each peach.

2. Lower peaches into boiling water and simmer until skins loosen, 30 to 60 seconds.

3. Transfer peaches immediately to ice water and let cool for about 1 minute.

4. Use paring knife to remove strips of loosened peel, starting at X on base of each peach.

Why This Recipe Works We wanted a peach cobbler that avoided a watery filling and soggy topping. To do this, we turned to a skillet and concentrated the peach flavor by first sautéing the peaches in butter and sugar to release their juices, then cooking them down until all the liquid had evaporated. To keep the filling from being too mushy, we withheld some of the peaches from sautéing, adding them just before baking. We also made the biscuits sturdy enough to stand up to the fruit by mixing melted butter rather than cold butter into the dry ingredients.

DAKOTA PEACH KUCHEN

MAKES TWO 9-INCH KUCHENS

The dough will need 2 hours to rise plus 1 hour to chill in the refrigerator. We developed this recipe using dark cake pans; if your pans are light, increase the baking time in step 7 to 55 to 60 minutes.

Crust
- ½ cup whole milk
- 2 large eggs
- 2½ cups (12½ ounces) all-purpose flour
- 1 tablespoon sugar
- 2 teaspoons instant or rapid-rise yeast
- ½ teaspoon salt
- 8 tablespoons unsalted butter, cut into 8 pieces and softened

Fruit and Custard
- 1 pound fresh peaches, peeled, halved, pitted, and cut into ½-inch wedges or 12 ounces frozen sliced peaches, thawed
- 2 tablespoons plus ¾ cup (5¼ ounces) sugar
- 1 large egg plus 1 large yolk
- ¼ teaspoon salt
- 1¼ cups heavy cream
- 4 tablespoons unsalted butter, cut into 4 pieces
- ½ teaspoon vanilla extract
- ¼ teaspoon ground cinnamon

1. For the Crust Grease large bowl. Whisk milk and eggs in 2-cup liquid measuring cup until combined. Using stand mixer fitted with dough hook, mix flour, sugar, yeast, and salt on medium-low speed until combined, about 5 seconds. With mixer running, slowly add milk mixture and knead until dough forms, about 1 minute.

2. With mixer still running, add butter 1 piece at a time until incorporated. Continue kneading until dough clears sides of bowl but still sticks to bottom, 8 to 12 minutes (dough should be soft and sticky).

3. Transfer dough to greased bowl, cover with plastic wrap, and let rise on counter until doubled in size, about 1 hour. Punch down dough and divide into 2 equal balls. Wrap each ball in plastic, transfer to refrigerator, and let rest for at least 1 hour or up to 24 hours.

4. Grease 2 dark-colored 9-inch round cake pans. Roll each chilled dough balls into a 9-inch disk on lightly floured counter. Transfer to prepared pans, pushing dough to edges of pans. Cover pans loosely with plastic and let rise on counter until puffy, about 1 hour. Adjust oven rack to middle position and heat oven to 350 degrees.

5. For the Fruit and Custard Meanwhile, toss peaches with 2 tablespoons sugar in bowl, then transfer to colander set in sink; let sit for 25 minutes. Whisk remaining ¾ cup sugar, egg and yolk, and salt in medium bowl until combined. Heat cream in medium saucepan over medium heat until just beginning to simmer.

6. Slowly whisk hot cream into egg mixture. Transfer cream mixture back to saucepan and cook over medium-low heat, stirring constantly, until mixture thickens and coats back of spoon, 3 to 5 minutes. Strain custard through fine-mesh strainer set over medium bowl. Whisk in butter and vanilla and transfer to refrigerator to cool until dough is ready. (Custard can be made up to 24 hours in advance but does not need to be fully chilled before going into crust.)

7. Leaving 1-inch border all around, press down centers of doughs with bottom of dry measuring cup to deflate and create wells for peaches and custard. Arrange peaches, evenly spaced, in circular pattern in depressed dough, avoiding border. Pour custard evenly over peaches in each pan, about 1 cup per pan (you may have a few tablespoons extra). Sprinkle with cinnamon. Bake until crusts are golden brown and centers jiggle slightly when shaken, 35 to 40 minutes, switching and rotating pans halfway through baking. Let cool completely. Remove kuchens from pans using flexible spatula. Slice and serve.

Why This Recipe Works Kuchen, the official state dessert of South Dakota, features a tender yeasted dough, peaches full of flavor, and a layer of smooth, delicately sweet custard. We created a buttery crust by slowly adding softened butter to the dough, letting the dough rise and then rest in the fridge. An extra egg yolk made our custard thick and rich, without the eggy flavor found in egg whites. Finally, to ready the peaches, we sprinkled them with sugar and let them sit in a colander to pull out their excess juice and prevent the kuchen from becoming soggy. This dessert might come from South Dakota, but it felt right at home in our kitchen.

Why This Recipe Works We wanted our banana pudding to be rich and creamy, so we opted for half-and-half instead of milk in the pudding component. Roasting the bananas intensified their flavor and helped break them down so we could incorporate them more easily into the pudding. Adding a squeeze of lemon juice to the roasted bananas prevented them from browning in the refrigerator. Even whole cookies became sodden and pasty when layered with hot pudding. We solved the problem by simply waiting for the pudding to cool a little before assembling the dessert.

BANANA PUDDING

SERVES 12

If your food processor bowl holds less than 11 cups, puree half the pudding with the roasted bananas and lemon juice in step 3, transfer it to a large bowl, and whisk in the rest of the pudding.

Pudding
- 7 slightly underripe large bananas (2½ pounds), unpeeled
- 1½ cups (10½ ounces) sugar
- 8 large egg yolks
- 6 tablespoons cornstarch
- 6 cups half-and-half
- ½ teaspoon salt
- 3 tablespoons unsalted butter
- 1 tablespoon vanilla extract
- 3 tablespoons lemon juice
- 1 (12-ounce) box vanilla wafers

Whipped Topping
- 1 cup heavy cream, chilled
- 1 tablespoon sugar
- ½ teaspoon vanilla extract

1. For the Pudding Adjust oven rack to upper-middle position and heat oven to 325 degrees. Place 3 unpeeled bananas on baking sheet and bake until skins are completely black, about 20 minutes. Let cool for 5 minutes.

2. Meanwhile, whisk ½ cup sugar, egg yolks, and cornstarch in medium bowl until smooth. Bring half-and-half, remaining 1 cup sugar, and salt to simmer over medium heat in large saucepan. Whisk ½ cup simmering half-and-half mixture into egg yolk mixture to temper. Slowly whisk tempered yolk mixture into saucepan. Cook, whisking constantly, until mixture is thick and large bubbles appear at surface, about 2 minutes. Remove from heat and stir in butter and vanilla.

3. Transfer pudding to food processor. Add warm peeled roasted bananas and 2 tablespoons lemon juice and process until smooth. Scrape into large bowl and place plastic wrap directly on surface of pudding. Refrigerate until slightly cool, about 45 minutes.

4. Peel and cut remaining bananas into ¼-inch slices and toss in bowl with remaining 1 tablespoon lemon juice. Spoon one-quarter of pudding into 3-quart trifle dish and top with layer of cookies, layer of sliced bananas, and another layer of cookies. Repeat twice, ending with pudding. Place plastic wrap directly on surface of pudding and refrigerate until wafers have softened, at least 8 hours or up to 2 days.

5. For the Whipped Topping Using stand mixer fitted with whisk, whip cream, sugar, and vanilla on medium-low speed until foamy, about 1 minute. Increase speed to high and whip until stiff peaks form, 1 to 3 minutes. (Whipped cream can be refrigerated for 4 hours.) Top banana pudding with whipped cream. Serve.

TOASTED COCONUT BANANA PUDDING
Replace 2 cups half-and-half with one 16-ounce can unsweetened coconut milk in step 2. Sprinkle ¼ cup toasted sweetened shredded coconut over whipped cream–topped pudding before serving.

PEANUT-Y BANANA PUDDING
In step 4, sandwich 2 vanilla wafers around 1 banana slice and ½ teaspoon creamy peanut butter (you'll need ½ cup total). Assemble by alternating layers of pudding and cookie-banana sandwiches, ending with pudding. Sprinkle ¼ cup chopped salted dry-roasted peanuts over whipped cream–topped pudding before serving.

Why This Recipe Works The best bourbon bread pudding is a rich, "scoopable" custard that envelops the bread with a balance of sweet spiciness and robust bourbon flavor. Tearing a crusty baguette into ragged pieces, then toasting them, gave the pudding a rustic look and kept the bread from turning soggy in the custard. We used a mixture of 3 parts cream to 1 part milk and replaced the whole eggs with yolks for a rich, creamy custard that didn't curdle. Once the custard set up in the oven, we sprinkled cinnamon, sugar, and butter on top and let it bake until the topping was caramelized.

NEW ORLEANS BOURBON BREAD PUDDING

SERVES 8 TO 10

This bread pudding is great on its own, but for a little more punch, drizzle Bourbon Sauce over individual servings (recipe follows). A bakery-quality French baguette makes this dish even better.

- 1 (18- to 20-inch) baguette, torn into 1-inch pieces (10 cups)
- 1 cup golden raisins
- ¾ cup bourbon
- 6 tablespoons unsalted butter, cut into 6 pieces and chilled, plus extra for baking dish
- 8 large egg yolks
- 1½ cups packed (10½ ounces) light brown sugar
- 3 cups heavy cream
- 1 cup whole milk
- 1 tablespoon vanilla extract
- 1½ teaspoons ground cinnamon
- ¼ teaspoon nutmeg
- ¼ teaspoon salt
- 3 tablespoons granulated sugar

1. Adjust oven rack to middle position and heat oven to 450 degrees. Arrange bread in single layer on baking sheet and bake until crisp and browned, about 12 minutes, turning pieces over and switching baking sheets halfway through baking. Let bread cool. Reduce oven temperature to 300 degrees.

2. Meanwhile, heat raisins with ½ cup bourbon in small saucepan over medium-high heat until bourbon begins to simmer, 2 to 3 minutes. Strain mixture, reserving bourbon and raisins separately.

3. Butter 13 by 9-inch broiler-safe baking dish. Whisk egg yolks, brown sugar, cream, milk, vanilla, 1 teaspoon cinnamon, nutmeg, and salt together in large bowl. Whisk in reserved bourbon plus remaining ¼ cup bourbon. Add toasted bread and toss until evenly coated. Let mixture sit until bread begins to absorb custard, about 30 minutes, tossing occasionally. If majority of bread is still hard, continue to soak for 15 to 20 minutes.

4. Pour half of bread mixture into prepared baking dish and sprinkle with half of raisins. Pour remaining bread mixture into dish and sprinkle with remaining raisins. Cover with aluminum foil and bake for 45 minutes.

5. Meanwhile, mix granulated sugar and remaining ½ teaspoon cinnamon in small bowl. Using your fingers, cut 6 tablespoons butter into sugar mixture until size of small peas. Remove foil from pudding, sprinkle with butter mixture, and bake, uncovered, until custard is just set, 20 to 25 minutes. Remove pudding from oven and heat broiler.

6. Once broiler is heated, broil pudding until top forms golden crust, about 2 minutes. Transfer to wire rack and cool at least 30 minutes or up to 2 hours. Serve.

BOURBON SAUCE
MAKES ABOUT 1 CUP

- 1½ teaspoons cornstarch
- ¼ cup bourbon
- ¾ cup heavy cream
- 2 tablespoons sugar
- Pinch salt
- 2 teaspoons unsalted butter, cut into 8 pieces

Whisk cornstarch and 2 tablespoons bourbon in small bowl until well combined. Heat cream and sugar in small saucepan over medium heat until sugar dissolves. Whisk in cornstarch mixture and bring to boil. Reduce heat to low and cook until sauce thickens, 3 to 5 minutes. Off heat, stir in salt, butter, and remaining 2 tablespoons bourbon. Drizzle warm sauce over individual servings. (Sauce can be refrigerated for up to 5 days.)

SUMMER BERRY PUDDING

SERVES 6

Fill in any gaps in pudding crusts with toast trimmings.

- 8 (¼-inch-thick) slices challah, crusts removed
- 12 ounces strawberries, hulled and chopped (2 cups)
- 8 ounces blackberries, halved (1½ cups)
- 8 ounces (1½ cups) blueberries
- 5 ounces (1 cup) raspberries
- ½ cup (3½ ounces) granulated sugar
- 1 teaspoon unflavored gelatin
- 2 tablespoons cold water
- ½ cup (5½ ounces) apricot preserves
- 1 cup heavy cream, chilled
- 1 tablespoon confectioners' sugar

1. Adjust oven rack to middle position and heat oven to 350 degrees. Line 8½ by 4½-inch loaf pan with plastic wrap, pushing plastic into corners and up sides of pan and allowing excess to overhang long sides. Make cardboard cutout just large enough to fit inside pan.

2. Place challah on wire rack set in rimmed baking sheet. Bake until dry, about 10 minutes, flipping challah and rotating sheet halfway through baking. Let challah cool completely.

3. Combine strawberries, blackberries, blueberries, and raspberries in bowl. Transfer half of mixture to medium saucepan, add granulated sugar, and bring to simmer over medium-low heat, stirring occasionally. Reduce heat to low and continue to cook until berries release their juices and raspberries begin to break down, about 5 minutes. Off heat, stir in remaining berries. After 2 minutes, strain berries through fine-mesh strainer set over medium bowl for 10 minutes, stirring berries once halfway through straining (do not press on berries). Reserve berry juice. (You should have ¾ to 1 cup.)

4. Sprinkle gelatin over water in bowl and let sit until gelatin softens, about 5 minutes. Microwave until mixture is bubbling around edges and gelatin dissolves, about 30 seconds. Whisk preserves and gelatin mixture together in large bowl. Fold in strained berries.

5. Trim 4 slices of challah to fit snugly side by side in bottom of loaf pan (you may have extra challah). Dip slices in reserved berry juice until saturated, about 30 seconds per side, then place in bottom of pan. Spoon berry mixture over challah. Trim remaining 4 slices of challah to fit snugly side by side on top of berries (you may have extra challah). Dip slices in reserved berry juice until saturated, about 30 seconds per side, then place on top of berries. Cover pan loosely with plastic and place in 13 by 9-inch baking dish. Place cardboard cutout on top of pudding. Top with 3 soup cans to weigh down pudding. Refrigerate pudding for at least 8 hours or up to 24 hours.

6. Using stand mixer fitted with whisk, whip cream and confectioners' sugar on medium-low speed until foamy, about 1 minute. Increase speed to high and whip until soft peaks form, 1 to 3 minutes. Transfer to serving bowl. Remove cans, cardboard, and plastic from top of pudding. Loosen pudding by pulling up on edges of plastic. Place inverted platter over top of loaf pan and flip platter and pan upside down to unmold pudding. Discard plastic. Slice pudding with serrated knife and serve with whipped cream.

Constructing Summer Berry Pudding

1. Saturate dried, trimmed challah with reserved berry juices and place in bottom of plastic wrap–lined pan.

2. Spoon sweetened four-berry mixture over challah, and top with four more slices of saturated challah.

Why This Recipe Works Although our initial tests of this traditional British "pudding" were fairly disastrous, we knew that good bread and fresh summer berries could make a delicious dessert. The rectangular shape of a loaf pan proved a more stable mold than traditional round bowls. We staled challah bread (our top choice for its flavor and texture) in the oven for added support. Since the moisture content of fresh berries can vary, we strained the juice from the filling and dipped the bread in it ourselves. Cooking only half of the berries and mixing the rest in later brightened the filling, and apricot preserves and gelatin helped the pudding keep its shape.

Why This Recipe Works There's nothing like a cone of creamy frozen custard on a hot summer day—or really any day. While stores use industrial condensers to produce the consistency we know and love, we set out to find a way to achieve super smooth custard at home without a machine. After combining our heated cream and egg yolk mixtures, we strained the custard to remove any pieces of cooked egg. To achieve the smoothest possible custard, we cooled the mixture on ice, let it chill in the refrigerator, then whipped it in a stand mixer to add air. This prevented ice crystals from building up and made the final texture silky and creamy.

OLD-FASHIONED VANILLA FROZEN CUSTARD

MAKES ABOUT 1 QUART

One teaspoon of vanilla extract can be substituted for the vanilla bean; stir the extract into the strained custard in step 3. Use an instant-read thermometer for the best results.

- 6 large egg yolks
- ¼ cup (1¾ ounces) sugar
- 2 tablespoons nonfat dry milk powder
- 1 cup heavy cream
- ½ cup whole milk
- ⅓ cup light corn syrup
- ⅛ teaspoon salt
- 1 vanilla bean

1. Whisk egg yolks, sugar, and milk powder in bowl until smooth, about 30 seconds; set aside. Combine cream, milk, corn syrup, and salt in medium saucepan. Cut vanilla bean in half lengthwise. Using tip of paring knife, scrape out vanilla seeds and add to cream mixture, along with vanilla bean. Heat cream mixture over medium-high heat, stirring occasionally, until it steams steadily and registers 175 degrees, about 5 minutes. Remove saucepan from heat.

2. Slowly whisk heated cream mixture into yolk mixture to temper. Return cream-yolk mixture to saucepan and cook over medium-low heat, stirring constantly, until mixture thickens and registers 180 degrees, 4 to 6 minutes.

3. Immediately pour custard through fine-mesh strainer set over large bowl; discard vanilla bean. Fill slightly larger bowl with ice and set custard bowl in bowl of ice. Transfer to refrigerator and let chill until custard registers 40 degrees, 1 to 2 hours, stirring occasionally.

4. Transfer chilled custard to stand mixer fitted with whisk and whip on medium-high speed for 3 minutes, or until mixture increases in volume to about 3¾ cups. Pour custard into airtight 1-quart container. Cover and freeze until firm, at least 6 hours, before serving. (Frozen custard is best eaten within 10 days.)

OLD-FASHIONED CHOCOLATE FROZEN CUSTARD
Omit vanilla bean. Add ½ ounce finely chopped 60 percent cacao bittersweet chocolate and 1 tablespoon Dutch-processed cocoa powder to cream mixture in step 1 before cooking. Add ½ teaspoon vanilla extract to strained custard in step 3.

Steps to Smooth Frozen Custard

1. TEMPER Heating cream mixture before slowly adding it to cold yolk mixture prevents eggs from curdling.

2. STRAIN Pouring warm custard through strainer removes any pieces of cooked egg.

3. CHILL Cooling custard on ice primes it for adding air.

4. WHIP Whipping cooled custard adds air to make final texture especially creamy.

save room for pie

- **562** Double-Crust Pie Dough
- **562** Classic Single-Crust Pie Dough
- **563** No-Fear Single-Crust Pie Dough
- **565** Shaker Lemon Pie
- **567** Sour Orange Pie
- **568** Peaches and Cream Pie
- **570** Fried Peach Hand Pies
- **573** Apple Pie with Cheddar Crust
- **574** Apple Slab Pie
- **576** Old-Fashioned Pecan Pie
- **579** Sweet Potato Pie
- **581** French Coconut Pie
- **582** Icebox Key Lime Pie
- **585** Mile-High Lemon Meringue Pie
- **586** Raspberry Chiffon Pie
- **588** Icebox Strawberry Pie
- **591** French Silk Chocolate Pie
- **592** Chocolate Angel Pie
- **594** Mississippi Mud Pie

DOUBLE-CRUST PIE DOUGH

MAKES ENOUGH FOR ONE 9-INCH PIE

- 2½ cups (12½ ounces) all-purpose flour
- 2 tablespoons sugar
- 1 teaspoon salt
- 8 tablespoons vegetable shortening, cut into ¼-inch pieces and chilled
- 12 tablespoons unsalted butter, cut into ¼-inch pieces and chilled
- 6–8 tablespoons ice water

1. Process flour, sugar, and salt in food processor until combined, about 5 seconds. Scatter shortening over top and process until mixture resembles coarse cornmeal, about 10 seconds. Scatter butter over top and pulse until mixture resembles coarse crumbs, about 10 pulses. Transfer to bowl.

2. Sprinkle 6 tablespoons water over flour mixture. Using rubber spatula, stir and press dough until it sticks together. If dough does not come together, stir in remaining water, 1 tablespoon at a time, until it does.

3. Divide dough into 2 even pieces and flatten each into 4-inch disk. Wrap disks tightly in plastic wrap and refrigerate for 1 hour. Let chilled dough soften slightly on counter before rolling.

CLASSIC SINGLE-CRUST PIE DOUGH

MAKES ENOUGH FOR ONE 9-INCH PIE

- 1¼ cups (6¼ ounces) all-purpose flour
- 1 tablespoon sugar
- ½ teaspoon salt
- 4 tablespoons vegetable shortening, cut into ¼-inch pieces and chilled
- 6 tablespoons unsalted butter, cut into ¼-inch pieces and chilled
- 3–4 tablespoons ice water

1. Process flour, sugar, and salt in food processor until combined, about 5 seconds. Scatter shortening over top and process until mixture resembles coarse cornmeal, about 10 seconds. Scatter butter over top and pulse until mixture resembles coarse crumbs, about 10 pulses. Transfer to bowl.

2. Sprinkle 3 tablespoons water over flour mixture. Using rubber spatula, stir and press dough until it sticks together. If dough does not come together, add remaining 1 tablespoon water. Flatten dough into 4-inch disk, wrap tightly in plastic wrap, and refrigerate for 1 hour.

3. Let chilled dough soften slightly. Lightly flour counter, then roll dough into 12-inch circle and fit it into 9-inch pie plate. Trim, fold, and crimp edges of dough. Wrap dough-lined pie plate in plastic and place in freezer until dough is fully chilled and firm, about 30 minutes, before using.

Rolling and Fitting Pie Dough

1. Roll dough outward from its center into 12-inch circle. Between every few rolls, give dough quarter turn.

2. Toss additional flour underneath dough as needed to keep dough from sticking to counter.

3. Loosely roll dough around rolling pin, then gently unroll it over pie plate.

4. Lift dough and gently press it into pie plate, letting excess hang over plate.

NO-FEAR SINGLE-CRUST PIE DOUGH

MAKES ENOUGH FOR ONE 9-INCH PIE

Anyone can make this pat-in-the-pan pie dough—no rolling or transferring of dough to the dish required. Cream cheese helps make this dough easy to handle and helps ensure a tender crust. Make sure you press the dough evenly into a glass pie plate; if you hold the dough-lined plate up to the light, you will be able to clearly see any thick or thin spots.

- 1¼ cups (6¼ ounces) all-purpose flour
- 2 tablespoons sugar
- ¼ teaspoon salt
- 8 tablespoons unsalted butter, softened but still cool
- 2 ounces cream cheese, softened but still cool

1. Lightly coat 9-inch Pyrex pie plate with vegetable oil spray. Whisk flour, sugar, and salt together in bowl.

2. Using stand mixer fitted with paddle, beat butter and cream cheese on medium-high speed until completely homogeneous, about 2 minutes, stopping once or twice to scrape down beater and sides of bowl. Add flour mixture and mix on medium-low speed until mixture resembles coarse cornmeal, about 20 seconds. Scrape down sides of bowl. Increase mixer speed to medium-high and beat until dough begins to form large clumps, about 30 seconds. Reserve 3 tablespoons of dough. Turn remaining dough onto lightly floured counter, gather into ball, and flatten into 6-inch disk. Transfer disk to greased pie plate.

3. Press dough evenly over bottom of pie plate toward sides, using heel of your hand. Hold plate up to light to ensure that dough is evenly distributed. With your fingertips, continue to work dough over bottom of plate and up sides until evenly distributed.

4. On floured counter, roll reserved dough into 12-inch rope. Divide into 3 pieces and roll each piece into 8-inch rope. Arrange ropes, evenly spaced, around top of pie plate, pressing and squeezing to join them with dough in plate and form uniform edge. Use your fingers to flute edge of dough. Wrap dough-lined pie plate in plastic wrap and place in freezer until dough is fully chilled and firm, about 30 minutes, before using.

No-Fear Pie Dough

1. Hold pie plate up to light to check thickness of dough; it should be translucent, not opaque. Pay attention to curved edges.

2. Roll reserved dough into three 8-inch ropes. Arrange ropes around perimeter of pie plate, leaving small (about 1-inch) gaps between them.

3. Squeeze ropes together.

4. Create a fluted edge, dipping your fingers in flour if dough is sticky.

Why This Recipe Works Most Shaker lemon pie recipes mix lemon slices—peel and all—with sugar and eggs to form a custardy filling. But unless we macerated the lemon slices for 24 hours, the pie turned out bitter. We wanted to speed up this recipe for modern times. First, we squeezed the seeded lemon slices and reserved the juice for the filling. Then, we simmered the slices and then added them to the filling with the uncooked juice for bright lemon flavor without any macerating time.

SHAKER LEMON PIE

SERVES 8

Have an extra lemon on hand in case the three sliced lemons do not yield enough juice. See page 562 for more information on rolling and fitting pie dough.

- 1 recipe Double-Crust Pie Dough (page 562)
- 3 large lemons, sliced thin and seeded
- 1¾ cups (12¼ ounces) sugar
- ⅛ teaspoon salt
- 1 tablespoon cornstarch
- 4 large eggs
- 1 tablespoon heavy cream

1. Roll 1 disk of dough into 12-inch circle on lightly floured counter, then fit it into 9-inch pie plate, letting excess dough hang over edge; cover with plastic wrap and refrigerate for 30 minutes. Roll other disk of dough into 12-inch circle on lightly floured counter, then transfer to parchment paper–lined baking sheet; cover with plastic and refrigerate for 30 minutes.

2. Adjust oven rack to lowest position and heat oven to 425 degrees. Squeeze lemon slices in fine-mesh strainer set over bowl; reserve juice (you should have 6 tablespoons). Bring drained slices and 2 cups water to boil in saucepan, then reduce heat to medium-low and simmer until slices are softened, about 5 minutes. Drain well and discard liquid. Combine softened lemon slices, sugar, salt, and ¼ cup reserved lemon juice in bowl; stir until sugar dissolves.

3. Whisk cornstarch and remaining 2 tablespoons lemon juice in large bowl. Whisk eggs into cornstarch mixture, then slowly stir in lemon slice mixture until combined. Pour into chilled pie shell. Brush edges of dough with 1 teaspoon cream. Loosely roll second piece of dough around rolling pin then gently unroll it over pie. Trim, fold, and crimp edges, and cut 4 vent holes in top. Brush top with remaining 2 teaspoons cream.

4. Bake until light golden, about 20 minutes, then decrease oven temperature to 375 degrees and continue to bake until golden brown, 20 to 25 minutes. Let pie cool on wire rack for at least 1 hour. Serve. (Pie can be refrigerated for 2 days.)

Building Bold, Not Bitter, Lemon Flavor

Using sliced whole lemons, pith and all, can produce an overwhelmingly bitter filling. We found a few tricks to create bright lemon flavor while tempering the bitterness of the pith.

1. Squeeze seeded lemon slices and reserve juice for filling.

2. Simmer slices to mellow bitterness of pith and then add them to filling with uncooked juice.

Shaker Cooking

The Shakers' food was never ornate and was always healthy and hearty enough to support their industrious, hard-working lifestyle. Shakers scrubbed—rather than peeled—their vegetables (and, in the case of Shaker Lemon Pie, their citrus fruit) to minimize waste. They were also pioneers in using exact measurements in cooking at a time when many recipes called for a "dash," "glob," or "handful" of something.

The Slice is Right

While developing our recipe for Shaker Lemon Pie, we found that cutting the lemons into paper-thin slices was a difficult and time-consuming task. We had better results with a mandoline (or V-slicer), which produced perfectly thin slices in no time at all. If you don't have a mandoline, another piece of kitchen equipment will make the process easier: the freezer. Freezing the lemons for about 30 minutes firms them up for better hand slicing, which is best accomplished with a serrated knife.

Why This Recipe Works Think of sour orange pie as Northern Florida's answer to Key lime: Its custard-like filling is made with the juice of wild sour oranges. Since fresh sour oranges are hard to source, we re-created their ultrasour taste with frozen orange juice concentrate, lemon juice, and orange and lemon zests. We mixed the juice with sweetened condensed milk for sweetness and egg yolks for structure. Slightly sweet animal crackers made a crunchy crust to contrast the tart filling. Chilled and topped with orange-flavored whipped cream, this sunny pie was bright and refreshing.

SOUR ORANGE PIE

MAKES ONE 9-INCH PIE

If sour oranges are available, use ¾ cup strained sour orange juice in place of the lemon juice and orange juice concentrate in the filling.

Crust
- 5 ounces animal crackers
- 3 tablespoons sugar
- Pinch salt
- 4 tablespoons unsalted butter, melted

Filling
- 1 (14-ounce) can sweetened condensed milk
- 6 tablespoons thawed orange juice concentrate
- 4 large egg yolks
- 2 teaspoons grated lemon zest plus 6 tablespoons juice (2 lemons)
- 1 teaspoon grated orange zest
- Pinch salt

Whipped Cream
- ¾ cup heavy cream, chilled
- 2 tablespoons sugar
- ½ teaspoon grated orange zest

1. For the Crust Adjust oven rack to middle position and heat oven to 325 degrees. Process crackers, sugar, and salt in food processor until finely ground, about 30 seconds. Add melted butter and pulse until combined, about 8 pulses. Transfer crumbs to 9-inch pie plate.

2. Using bottom of dry measuring cup, press crumbs firmly into bottom and up sides of pie plate. Bake until fragrant and beginning to brown, 12 to 14 minutes. Cool to room temperature, about 30 minutes.

3. For the Filling When crust is cool, whisk condensed milk, orange juice concentrate, egg yolks, lemon zest and juice, orange zest, and salt together in bowl until fully combined. Pour filling into cooled crust.

4. Bake until center of pie jiggles slightly when shaken, 15 to 17 minutes. Cool to room temperature, then refrigerate until fully chilled, at least 3 hours; or cover with greased plastic wrap and refrigerate for up to 24 hours.

5. For the Whipped Cream Whisk cream, sugar, and orange zest together in medium bowl until stiff peaks form, 2 to 4 minutes.

6. Slice chilled pie and serve with whipped cream.

No Sour Oranges? No Problem.

Since fresh sour oranges can be hard to find, we recreated their ultrasour, slightly bitter taste by combining thawed frozen orange juice concentrate with fresh lemon juice and bolstering the mixture with lots of orange and lemon zest.

FRESH LEMON JUICE
Provides plenty of sourness

ORANGE JUICE CONCENTRATE
Adds potent orange flavor

SOUR ORANGE
Intense tartness

PEACHES AND CREAM PIE

SERVES 8

Keep an eye on the peaches at the end of their baking time to ensure that they don't scorch. You can use Classic Single-Crust Pie Dough (page 562) or No-Fear Single-Crust Pie Dough (page 563) for this pie.

- 1 recipe single-crust pie dough, fitted into 9-inch pie plate and chilled
- 2 pounds ripe but firm peaches, peeled, halved, and pitted
- 2 tablespoons plus ½ cup (4⅓ ounces) sugar
- 3 tablespoons all-purpose flour
- ¼ teaspoon salt
- ⅓ cup heavy cream
- 2 large egg yolks
- ½ teaspoon vanilla extract

1. Adjust oven racks to upper-middle and lower-middle positions and heat oven to 375 degrees. Line chilled crust with double layer of aluminum foil and fill with pie weights.

2. Place peach halves cut side up on foil-lined rimmed baking sheet and sprinkle with 2 tablespoons sugar. Bake peaches on upper-middle rack until softened and juice is released, about 30 minutes, flipping halfway through baking.

3. After 30 minutes, place crust on lower-middle rack and, while peaches continue to roast, bake until edges are lightly browned, about 15 minutes. Remove crust from oven and carefully remove foil and weights. Continue to bake until bottom of crust is light golden brown and peaches are caramelized, about 5 minutes longer. Cool crust and peaches for 15 minutes.

4. Reduce oven temperature to 325 degrees. Cut peach halves lengthwise into quarters. Arrange peaches in single layer over crust. Combine remaining ½ cup sugar, flour, and salt in bowl. Whisk in cream, egg yolks, and vanilla until smooth. Pour cream mixture over peaches. Bake until filling is light golden brown and firm in center, 45 to 55 minutes. Cool pie on wire rack for at least 3 hours. Serve.

Twice-Baked Peaches
Eat a peach out of hand, and its juiciness is no small part of what makes it so good. But cook the fruit, and that same high water content can ruin peach pie, especially when coupled with cream. To evaporate the peach juices and concentrate the peach flavor, we roasted the fruit before filling the pie. A sprinkle of sugar helps the peach halves caramelize. Plus, to save time, while you're roasting the fruit on one rack of the oven, you can prebake the crust on another.

Blind Baking a Pie Crust
The crusts for many pies and tarts are baked before filling (this is called blind baking) so that they stay golden brown, crisp, and flaky once filled.

1. Line chilled pie crust with double layer of aluminum foil, fill crust with pie weights or pennies, and bake until lightly browned, about 15 minutes.

2. Remove pie weights and foil and continue to bake until light golden brown, about 5 minutes longer.

Why This Recipe Works Old-fashioned recipes for this pie call for simply arranging peaches in a pie crust, dousing them with fresh cream, and baking. But today's commercial cream gave us a milky, lumpy, and bland puddle rather than a rich filling. To thicken the cream, we whisked in a little flour and two egg yolks. But the juicy peaches wreaked watery havoc on our custardy pie filling. Roasting them in the oven evaporated their excess liquid, and a dusting of sugar encouraged caramelizing for even more flavor. Prebaking the crust ensured it would stay crisp and flaky after the roasted fruit and filling were added.

FRIED PEACH HAND PIES

MAKES 8 HAND PIES

If using frozen peaches, purchase a no-sugar-added product; we prefer Earthbound Farm or Cascadian Farm frozen peaches. There is no need to thaw the frozen peaches, but they will take longer to cook; times for both fresh and frozen are given in step 1. Use a Dutch oven that holds 6 quarts or more for frying. The assembled pies can be refrigerated for up to 24 hours before frying.

- 4 ripe peaches, peeled, halved, pitted, and cut into ½-inch wedges, or 20 ounces frozen peaches
- ½ cup (3½ ounces) sugar
- Salt
- 2 teaspoons lemon juice
- 2 cups (10 ounces) all-purpose flour
- 2 teaspoons baking powder
- 6 tablespoons unsalted butter, melted and cooled
- ½ cup whole milk
- 2 quarts peanut or vegetable oil

1. Combine peaches, sugar, and ⅛ teaspoon salt in medium saucepan. Cover and cook over medium heat, stirring occasionally and breaking up peaches with spoon, until tender, about 5 minutes for fresh peaches and 16 to 19 minutes for frozen peaches.

2. Uncover and continue to cook, stirring and mashing frequently with potato masher to coarse puree, until mixture is thickened and measures about 1⅔ cups, 7 to 13 minutes. Remove from heat, stir in lemon juice, and let cool completely. (Filling can be refrigerated for up to 3 days.)

3. Line rimmed baking sheet with parchment paper. Pulse flour, baking powder, and ¾ teaspoon salt in food processor until combined, about 3 pulses. Add melted butter and pulse until mixture resembles wet sand, about 8 pulses, scraping down sides of bowl as needed. Add milk and process until no floury bits remain and dough looks pebbly, about 8 seconds.

4. Turn dough onto lightly floured counter, gather into disk, and divide into 8 equal pieces. Roll each piece between your hands into ball, then press to flatten into round. Place rounds on prepared sheet, cover with plastic wrap, and refrigerate for 20 minutes.

5. Working with 1 piece of dough at a time, roll into 6- to 7-inch circle about ⅛ inch thick on lightly floured counter. Place 3 tablespoons filling in center of circle. Brush edges of dough with water and fold dough over filling to create half-moon shape, lightly pressing out air at seam. Trim any ragged edges and crimp edges with tines of fork to seal. Return pies to prepared sheet, cover with plastic, and refrigerate until ready to fry, up to 24 hours.

6. Line platter with triple layer of paper towels. Add oil to large Dutch oven until it measures about 1½ inches deep and heat over medium-high heat to 375 degrees. Gently place 4 pies in hot oil and fry until golden brown, about 1½ minutes per side, using slotted spatula or spider to flip. Adjust burner, if necessary, to maintain oil temperature between 350 and 375 degrees. Transfer to prepared platter. Return oil to 375 degrees and repeat with remaining 4 pies. Let cool for 10 minutes before serving.

On the Road: Peach Park

The massive, peach-shaped water tower looming over Clanton, Alabama, heralds Peach Park, a roadside retail attraction and restaurant that serves as the spiritual center of Alabama's peach-producing region. Out front, an open-air market sells fresh produce (peaches, mostly) and peach-based pantry products; inside, a long cafeteria case houses meat-and-three fare (preludes, perhaps, to peach ice cream and peach cobbler). Portraits of the reigning Miss Peach and her younger counterparts Junior Miss Peach, Young Miss Peach, and Little Miss Peach honor their regal stone-fruit court.

But the best reason to visit Peach Park is the fried peach hand pies. Rumor has it these sweet, warm pies were created as a way to use up overripe peaches, too soft and ugly to sell as is but still full of peach flavor. At Peach Park, we left no leftovers.

Why This Recipe Works These hand pies have it all: A crust that is delicate and tender but crumbly and a filling that's pure peach flavor. Starting with the filling, we cooked peeled, sliced peaches with sugar and a pinch of salt on the stovetop before gently mashing the fruit and letting it thicken. A bit of lemon juice added vibrancy. For the crust, we created a soft dough using melted butter and flour. Adding baking powder and milk created the dainty crumble we wanted. We divided, rolled out, and filled the dough, sealing in the filling before frying the pies in a Dutch oven, achieving peachy little pie perfection in minutes.

Why This Recipe Works Apple pie and cheddar cheese share a history, and we wanted to incorporate this sweet-savory pairing into a single recipe. For a flaky crust infused with cheesy flavor, extra-sharp cheddar and a teaspoon of dry mustard amped up the crust's savory qualities. Traditional apple filling got a kick from some cayenne, and precooking the filling allowed us to cram in twice as many apples. Starting with a hotter oven browned the bottom crust, and then reducing the heat kept the top from burning. The result: a moist, sweet-tart filling that perfectly complemented our flaky, cheesy crust.

APPLE PIE WITH CHEDDAR CRUST

SERVES 8

For the best flavor, be sure to use extra-sharp cheddar here. Freezing the butter for 15 minutes promotes flakiness in the crust—do not skip this step.

Crust
- 2½ cups (12½ ounces) all-purpose flour
- 1 tablespoon granulated sugar
- 1 teaspoon salt
- 1 teaspoon dry mustard
- ⅛ teaspoon cayenne pepper
- 8 ounces extra-sharp cheddar cheese, shredded (2 cups)
- 8 tablespoons unsalted butter, cut into ¼-inch pieces and frozen for 15 minutes
- ⅓ cup ice water, plus extra as needed

Filling
- 2 pounds Granny Smith, Empire, or Cortland apples, peeled, cored, halved, and sliced ¼-inch thick
- 2 pounds Golden Delicious, Jonagold, or Braeburn apples, peeled, cored, halved, and sliced ¼-inch thick
- 6 tablespoons (2⅔ ounces) granulated sugar
- ¼ cup packed (1¾ ounces) light brown sugar
- ½ teaspoon grated lemon zest plus 1 tablespoon juice
- ¼ teaspoon salt
- ⅛ teaspoon ground cinnamon

1. For the Crust Process flour, sugar, salt, mustard, and cayenne in food processor until combined, about 5 seconds. Scatter cheddar and butter over top and pulse until butter is size of large peas, about 10 pulses.

2. Pour half of ice water over flour mixture and pulse until incorporated, about 3 pulses. Repeat with remaining ice water. Pinch dough with your fingers; if dough feels dry and does not hold together, sprinkle 1 to 2 tablespoons extra ice water over mixture and pulse until dough forms large clumps and no dry flour remains, 3 to 5 pulses.

3. Divide dough in half and form each half into 4-inch disk. Wrap disks tightly in plastic wrap and refrigerate for 1 hour. Let chilled dough sit on counter to soften slightly, about 10 minutes, before rolling. (Wrapped dough can be refrigerated for up to 2 days or frozen for up to 1 month. If frozen, let dough thaw completely on counter before rolling.)

4. For the Filling Stir apples, granulated sugar, brown sugar, lemon zest, salt, and cinnamon together in Dutch oven. Cover and cook over medium heat, stirring frequently, until apples are just tender but still hold their shape, 10 to 15 minutes. Off heat, stir in lemon juice. Spread apple mixture on rimmed baking sheet and let cool completely, about 30 minutes. (Filling can be refrigerated for up to 24 hours.)

5. Roll 1 disk of dough into 12-inch circle between 2 sheets of parchment paper or plastic. Loosely roll dough around rolling pin and gently unroll it onto 9-inch pie plate, letting excess dough hang over edge. Ease dough into plate by gently lifting edge of dough with your hand while pressing into plate bottom with your other hand. Trim overhang to ½ inch beyond lip of pie plate. Wrap dough-lined pie plate loosely in plastic and refrigerate until dough is firm, about 15 minutes.

6. Adjust oven rack to lowest position and heat oven to 425 degrees. Fill pie shell with apple mixture. Roll other disk of dough into 12-inch circle between 2 sheets of parchment or plastic. Loosely roll dough around rolling pin and gently unroll it onto filling.

7. Trim overhang to ½ inch beyond lip of pie plate. Pinch edges of top and bottom crusts firmly together. Tuck overhang under itself; folded edge should be flush with edge of pie plate. Crimp dough around edge of pie plate using your fingers. Cut four 2-inch slits in top of dough.

8. Set pie on foil or parchment-lined baking sheet and bake for 20 minutes. Reduce oven temperature to 375 degrees and continue to bake until crust is deep golden brown and filling is bubbling, 35 to 45 minutes. Transfer pie to wire rack and let cool for at least 1½ hours. Serve.

APPLE SLAB PIE

SERVES 18 TO 20

We prefer an 18 by 13-inch nonstick rimmed baking sheet for this pie. If using a conventional baking sheet, coat it lightly with vegetable oil spray.

Pie

- 3½ pounds Granny Smith apples, peeled, cored, halved, and sliced thin
- 3½ pounds Golden Delicious apples, peeled, cored, halved, and sliced thin
- 1½ cups (10½ ounces) granulated sugar
- ½ teaspoon salt
- 1½ cups (4 ounces) animal crackers
- 2 (16-ounce) boxes refrigerated pie dough
- 4 tablespoons unsalted butter, melted and cooled
- 6 tablespoons instant tapioca
- 2 teaspoons ground cinnamon
- 3 tablespoons lemon juice

Glaze

- ¾ cup reserved apple juice (from filling)
- 2 tablespoons lemon juice
- 1 tablespoon unsalted butter, softened
- 1¼ cups (5 ounces) confectioners' sugar

1. For the Pie Combine apples, 1 cup sugar, and salt in colander set over large bowl. Let sit, tossing occasionally, until apples release their juices, about 30 minutes. Press gently on apples to extract liquid and reserve ¾ cup juice. Adjust oven rack to lower-middle position and heat oven to 350 degrees.

2. Pulse crackers and remaining ½ cup sugar in food processor until finely ground, about 20 pulses. Dust counter with cracker mixture, brush half of 1 pie round with water, overlap with second pie round, and dust top with cracker mixture. Roll out dough to 19 by 14 inches and transfer to rimmed baking sheet. Brush dough with butter, cover loosely with plastic wrap and refrigerate.

3. Roll remaining 2 dough rounds together with remaining cracker mixture to a 19 by 14-inch rectangle.

4. Toss drained apples with tapioca, cinnamon, and lemon juice and arrange evenly over bottom crust, pressing lightly to flatten. Brush edges of bottom crust with water and arrange top crust on pie. Press crusts together. Use paring knife to trim any excess dough. Use fork to crimp and seal outside edge of pie and then pierce top of pie at 2-inch intervals. Bake until pie is golden brown and juices are bubbling, about 1 hour. Let pie cool on wire rack for 1 hour.

5. For the Glaze While pie is cooling, simmer reserved apple juice in saucepan over medium heat until syrupy and reduced to ¼ cup, about 6 minutes. Stir in lemon juice and butter and let cool to room temperature. Whisk in sugar and brush glaze evenly over warm pie. Let pie cool completely, at least 1 hour longer. Serve. (Pie can be refrigerated for up to 1 day.)

How to Make Apple Slab Pie

1. Use water to "glue" together 2 store-bought pie crusts.

2. Add flavor to the bottom crust by rolling it out in mixture of crushed cookie crumbs and sugar.

3. After transferring bottom crust to baking dish, brush with melted butter for extra richness.

4. Top filled pie with second "double" crust and use fork to tightly seal edges of crust.

Why This Recipe Works Unlike a traditional apple pie, a slab pie is prepared in a baking sheet and can feed up to 20 people. Its filling is thickened to ensure neat slicing, and its crust is topped with a sugary glaze. But rolling out the dough for this mammoth pie proved problematic, as did making the filling thick enough to hold up to slicing. Gluing two sturdy store-bought crusts together with water and then rolling the dough into a large rectangle allowed us to get the crust into the large pan without a tear. To give the crust a sweet, buttery flavor, we rolled it in crushed animal crackers. Tapioca thickened the filling well without making it starchy.

OLD-FASHIONED PECAN PIE

SERVES 8 TO 10

Serve with Bourbon Whipped Cream (recipe follows), if desired. You can use Classic Single-Crust Pie Dough (page 562) or No-Fear Single-Crust Pie Dough (page 563) for this pie.

- 1 cup maple syrup
- 1 cup packed (7 ounces) light brown sugar
- ½ cup heavy cream
- 1 tablespoon molasses
- 4 tablespoons unsalted butter, cut into ½-inch pieces
- ½ teaspoon salt
- 6 large egg yolks, lightly beaten
- 1½ cups (6 ounces) pecans, toasted and chopped
- 1 recipe single-crust pie dough, fitted into 9-inch pie plate and chilled

1. Adjust oven rack to lowest position and heat oven to 450 degrees. Heat syrup, sugar, cream, and molasses in saucepan over medium heat, stirring occasionally, until sugar dissolves, about 3 minutes. Remove from heat and let cool for 5 minutes. Whisk butter and salt into syrup mixture until combined. Whisk in egg yolks until incorporated.

2. Scatter pecans in pie shell. Carefully pour filling over. Place pie in oven and immediately reduce oven temperature to 325 degrees. Bake until filling is set and center jiggles slightly when pie is gently shaken, 45 minutes to 1 hour. Let pie cool on rack for 1 hour, then refrigerate until set, about 3 hours or up to 1 day. Bring to room temperature before serving.

BOURBON WHIPPED CREAM
MAKES ABOUT 2 CUPS

Although any style of whiskey will work here, we like the smokiness of bourbon.

- 1 cup heavy cream
- 2 tablespoons bourbon
- 1½ tablespoons packed light brown sugar
- ½ teaspoon vanilla extract

Using stand mixer fitted with whisk, whip cream, bourbon, sugar, and vanilla on medium-low speed until foamy, about 1 minute. Increase speed to high and whip until stiff peaks form, about 2 minutes. (Whipped cream can be refrigerated for 4 hours.)

Move Over, Karo

Before cloying Karo syrup monopolized the market, pies were made with many other, less processed types of syrup, including sorghum (made from a cereal grass) and cane (made from the boiled-down juice of the sugarcane plant). These syrups still exist, and you can mail-order them, or travel to places like Louisiana or Kentucky to find them. We tasted a range of such syrups, including Steen's 100% Pure Cane Syrup and Townsend's Sweet Sorghum, then tried to duplicate their complex flavors from products we could buy at the supermarket. In the end, a combination of three ordinary sweeteners created an old-fashioned flavor that easily bested Karo.

Molasses brings a robust, slightly bitter quality.

Light brown sugar adds warmth and caramel tones.

Maple syrup adds delicate complexity.

Why This Recipe Works The pecan pies of today bear little resemblance to their 19th-century inspiration. Could we re-create old-fashioned pecan pie without using modern-day processed corn syrup? Many traditional syrups (cane, sorghum) produced a great pie, but we had to mail away for those ingredients. In the end, combining maple syrup with brown sugar and molasses replicated the old-fashioned versions perfectly. We started the pie at a high oven temperature to ensure the bottom crust was crisp and golden brown and then dropped the temperature to finish baking.

Why This Recipe Works Hoping to streamline this holiday dessert, we started by "baking" whole sweet potatoes in the microwave. A food processor made quick work of pureeing the flesh and lent a super-smooth texture. Sour cream added subtle tang while smoothing out the custard even more, and supplementing whole eggs with extra yolks added richness and helped with sliceability. We heated the spices in butter to intensify (or bloom) their flavor before adding them, along with some bourbon and vanilla, to the filling. First we sprinkled brown sugar onto the crust, which melted into a gooey faux caramel and took this pie to the next level.

SWEET POTATO PIE

SERVES 8

The best pies use homemade crust. You can use Classic Single-Crust Pie Dough (page 562) or No-Fear Single-Crust Pie Dough (page 563) for this pie. If you're pressed for time, try our favorite store-bought crust, Wholly Wholesome 9" Certified Organic Traditional Bake at Home Rolled Pie Dough. Choose sweet potatoes that are about the same size so that they'll cook evenly. Serve with Bourbon Whipped Cream (page 576), if desired.

- 1 (9-inch) single-crust pie dough
- 1¼ cups packed (8¾ ounces) light brown sugar
- 1¾ pounds sweet potatoes, unpeeled
- ½ teaspoon salt
- 4 tablespoons unsalted butter
- ½ teaspoon ground cinnamon
- ¼ teaspoon ground nutmeg
- 1 cup sour cream
- 3 large eggs plus 2 large yolks
- 2 tablespoons bourbon (optional)
- 1 teaspoon vanilla extract

1. Adjust oven rack to middle position and heat oven to 375 degrees. Roll dough into 12-inch circle on lightly floured counter. Loosely roll dough around rolling pin and gently unroll it onto 9-inch pie plate, letting excess dough hang over edge. Ease dough into plate by gently lifting edge of dough with your hand while pressing into plate bottom with your other hand. Trim overhang to ½ inch beyond lip of pie plate. Tuck overhang under itself; folded edge should be flush with edge of pie plate. Crimp dough evenly around edge of pie using your fingers. Wrap dough-lined pie plate loosely in plastic and freeze until dough is firm, about 15 minutes.

2. Line chilled pie shell with two 12-inch squares of parchment paper, letting parchment lie over edges of dough, and fill with pie weights. Bake until lightly golden around edges, 18 to 25 minutes. Carefully remove parchment and weights, rotate crust, and continue to bake until center begins to look opaque and slightly drier, 3 to 6 minutes. Remove from oven. Let crust cool completely. Sprinkle ¼ cup sugar over bottom of crust; set aside. Reduce oven temperature to 350 degrees.

3. Meanwhile, prick potatoes all over with fork. Microwave on large plate until potatoes are very soft and surface is slightly wet, 15 to 20 minutes, flipping every 5 minutes. Immediately slice potatoes in half to release steam. When cool enough to handle, scoop flesh into bowl of food processor. Add salt and remaining 1 cup sugar and process until smooth, about 60 seconds, scraping down sides of bowl as needed. Melt butter with cinnamon and nutmeg in microwave, 15 to 30 seconds; stir to combine. Add spiced butter, sour cream, eggs and yolks, bourbon, if using, and vanilla to potatoes and process until incorporated, about 10 seconds, scraping down sides of bowl as needed.

4. Pour potato mixture into prepared pie shell. Bake until filling is set around edges but center registers 165 degrees and jiggles slightly when pie is shaken, 35 to 40 minutes. Let pie cool completely on wire rack, about 2 hours. Serve.

Why This Recipe Works French coconut pie, a southern favorite, is a coconut-custard pie that is often too eggy, too sweet, or lacking in coconut flavor. We set out to tackle all of these issues. First, we found that two whole eggs plus one extra yolk provided just the right amount of richness. To better control the sweetness, we tried unsweetened shredded coconut which also intensified the coconut flavor. Since the dried coconut was not fully softening as the pie baked, we soaked it in buttermilk and vanilla before adding it to the filling. The finished pie was golden brown—from the pie crust to the lovely sugar crust that formed on top of the custard.

FRENCH COCONUT PIE

SERVES 8 TO 10

Look for shredded unsweetened coconut, about ¼ inch in length, in the natural foods section of the supermarket. It sometimes goes by the name "coconut flakes." Do not use large flaked coconut in this recipe. Our favorite shredded unsweetened coconut is NOW Real Food Organic Unsweetened Coconut, Shredded.

- 1 (9-inch) store-bought pie dough round
- 1¼ cups (3¾ ounces) unsweetened shredded coconut
- ½ cup buttermilk
- 1 teaspoon vanilla extract
- 1 cup (7 ounces) sugar
- 8 tablespoons unsalted butter, melted and cooled
- 2 large eggs plus 1 large yolk
- 2 tablespoons all-purpose flour
- ¼ teaspoon salt

1. Adjust oven rack to lower-middle position and heat oven to 325 degrees. Roll dough into 12-inch circle on lightly floured counter. Loosely roll dough around rolling pin and gently unroll it onto 9-inch pie plate, letting excess dough hang over edge. Ease dough into plate by gently lifting edge of dough with your hand while pressing into plate bottom with your other hand.

2. Trim overhang to ½ inch beyond lip of plate. Tuck overhang under itself; folded edge should be flush with edge of plate. Crimp dough evenly around edge of plate using your fingers. Wrap dough-lined plate loosely in plastic wrap and freeze until dough is firm, about 15 minutes.

3. Discard plastic wrap and line chilled pie shell with two 12-inch squares of parchment paper, letting parchment lie over edges of dough, and fill with pie weights. Bake until lightly golden around edges, 18 to 25 minutes. Transfer to wire rack and carefully remove parchment and weights. (Pie shell needn't cool completely before proceeding.)

4. Meanwhile, combine coconut, buttermilk, and vanilla in bowl. Cover with plastic and let sit for 15 minutes.

5. Whisk sugar, butter, eggs and yolk, flour, and salt together in large bowl. Stir in coconut mixture until fully incorporated. Pour filling into warm pie shell. Bake until custard is set and golden-brown crust forms on top of pie, 40 to 55 minutes.

6. Transfer pie to wire rack and let cool completely, about 4 hours. Serve at room temperature. (Cooled pie can be covered with plastic and refrigerated for up to 2 days. Let come to room temperature before serving.)

Crimping a Single Crust Pie Shell
Our easy crimping technique makes a decorative, sturdy edge.

1. Use scissors to trim overhanging dough to uniform ½ inch.

2. Tuck dough under to form thick, even edge on lip of pie plate.

3. Use both hands to pinch dough into ridges, working around perimeter.

ICEBOX KEY LIME PIE

SERVES 8 TO 10

Use instant pudding, which requires no stovetop cooking, for this recipe. Do not be tempted to use bottled lime juice, which lacks depth of flavor.

Crust
- 8 whole graham crackers, broken into small pieces
- 2 tablespoons sugar
- 5 tablespoons unsalted butter, melted

Filling
- ¼ cup (1¾ ounces) sugar
- 1 tablespoon grated lime zest plus 1 cup juice (8 limes)
- 8 ounces cream cheese, softened
- 1 (14-ounce) can sweetened condensed milk
- ⅓ cup instant vanilla pudding mix
- 1¼ teaspoons unflavored gelatin
- 1 teaspoon vanilla extract

1. For the Crust Adjust oven rack to middle position and heat oven to 350 degrees. Process crackers and sugar in food processor until finely ground, about 30 seconds. Add melted butter in steady stream while pulsing until crumbs resemble damp sand. Sprinkle mixture into 9-inch pie plate and use bottom of dry measuring cup to press crumbs firmly into bottom and sides. Bake until fragrant and browned around edges, 12 to 14 minutes. Let cool completely.

2. For the Filling Process sugar and zest in clean food processor until sugar turns bright green, about 30 seconds. Add cream cheese and process until combined, about 30 seconds. Add condensed milk and pudding mix and process until smooth, about 30 seconds. Scrape down sides of bowl. Sprinkle gelatin over 2 tablespoons lime juice in small bowl and let sit until gelatin softens, about 5 minutes. Heat in microwave for 15 seconds; stir until dissolved. With processor running, pour in gelatin mixture, remaining lime juice, and vanilla and mix until thoroughly combined, about 30 seconds.

3. Pour filling into cooled crust, cover with plastic wrap, and refrigerate for at least 3 hours or up to 2 days. To serve, let pie sit at room temperature for 10 minutes before slicing.

Bigger Limes = Less Work

When developing our recipe for Icebox Key Lime Pie, we found the flavor of Key limes and regular supermarket limes (called Persian limes) to be almost identical in our pie recipe. But there was a big difference in squeezing time.

KEY LIMES
We had to squeeze 40 Key limes to yield 1 cup of juice.

PERSIAN LIMES
Just six to eight Persian limes gave us all the juice we needed.

A Mystery of Pie History

Before Gail Borden invented sweetened condensed milk in 1856, drinking milk was a health risk, as there was no pasteurization or refrigeration for fresh milk. The shelf-stability and safety of sweetened condensed milk made it especially popular in areas like the Florida Keys, where the hot climate promoted rapid spoilage of anything perishable. Like many of our iconic foods, no one knows for sure when or by whom the first Key lime pie was made, but with canned milk in every pantry by the 1870s and an abundance of tiny Key limes throughout the area, it was only a matter of time. Most food historians trace the history of this pie back to the 1890s, but there are those—especially in the Keys—who claim the recipe is decades older.

Why This Recipe Works Authentic Key lime pie recipes used to be simple and uncooked—but they contained raw eggs, a no-no in modern times. We wanted to develop an eggless Key lime pie recipe as bright and custardy as the original. In lieu of using egg yolks, we found the right ratio of instant vanilla pudding, gelatin, and cream cheese to thicken our Icebox Key Lime Pie's filling into a perfect, smooth consistency. A full cup of fresh lime juice produced a pie with bracing lime flavor. Lime zest added another layer of flavor, and processing the zest with a little sugar offset its sourness and eliminated the annoying chewy bits.

Why This Recipe Works We wanted a lemon meringue pie with an impressively tall and fluffy topping, so we made the meringue with a hot sugar syrup and added a bit of cream of tartar to the egg whites as we beat them. This ensured that the meringue was cooked through and stable enough to be piled high on top of the filling. For our pie's bright citrus flavor, we flavored the filling with lemon zest and lemon juice and then, to ensure the filling was silky smooth, we strained out the zest.

MILE-HIGH LEMON MERINGUE PIE

SERVES 8 TO 10

You can use Classic Single-Crust Pie Dough (page 562) or No-Fear Single-Crust Pie Dough (page 563) for this pie. This pie is best served on the day it's made.

- 1 recipe single-crust pie dough, fitted into 9-inch pie plate and chilled

Lemon Filling
- 1¼ cups (8¾ ounces) sugar
- 1 cup lemon juice plus 2 tablespoons grated zest (5 lemons)
- ½ cup water
- 3 tablespoons cornstarch
- ¼ teaspoon salt
- 8 large egg yolks
- 4 tablespoons unsalted butter, cut into 4 pieces and softened

Meringue
- 1 cup (7 ounces) sugar
- ½ cup water
- 4 large egg whites
- Pinch salt
- ½ teaspoon cream of tartar
- ½ teaspoon vanilla extract

1. Adjust oven rack to middle position and heat oven to 375 degrees. Line chilled crust with double layer of aluminum foil and fill with pie weights. Bake until pie dough looks dry and is light in color, 25 to 30 minutes. Remove weights and foil and continue to bake crust until deep golden brown, 10 to 12 minutes longer. Let crust cool on wire rack to room temperature.

2. For the Lemon Filling Whisk sugar, lemon juice, water, cornstarch, and salt together in large saucepan until cornstarch is dissolved. Bring to simmer over medium heat, whisking occasionally until mixture becomes translucent and begins to thicken, about 5 minutes. Whisk in egg yolks until combined. Stir in lemon zest and butter. Bring to simmer and stir constantly until mixture is thick enough to coat back of spoon, about 2 minutes. Strain through fine-mesh strainer into cooled pie shell and scrape filling off underside of strainer. Place plastic wrap directly on surface of filling and refrigerate until set and well chilled, at least 2 hours or up to 1 day.

3. For the Meringue Adjust oven rack to middle position and heat oven to 400 degrees. Combine sugar and water in small saucepan. Bring to vigorous boil over medium-high heat. Once syrup comes to rolling boil, cook 4 minutes (mixture will become slightly thickened and syrupy). Remove from heat and set aside while beating whites.

4. Using stand mixer fitted with whisk, whip egg whites in large bowl at medium-low speed until frothy, about 1 minute. Add salt and cream of tartar and whip, gradually increasing speed to medium-high, until whites hold soft peaks, about 2 minutes. With mixer running, slowly pour hot syrup into whites (avoid pouring syrup onto whisk or it will splash). Add vanilla and whip until meringue has cooled and becomes very thick and shiny, 5 to 9 minutes.

5. Using rubber spatula, mound meringue over filling, making sure meringue touches edges of crust. Use spatula to create peaks all over meringue. Bake until peaks turn golden brown, about 6 minutes. Let pie cool on wire rack to room temperature. Serve.

Making a Meringue Mountain

1. Use rubber spatula to press meringue onto edge of pie crust. This will keep meringue from shrinking.

2. Use spatula to make dramatic peaks and swirls all over meringue.

RASPBERRY CHIFFON PIE

SERVES 8 TO 10

You can use Classic Single-Crust Pie Dough (page 562) or No-Fear Single-Crust Pie Dough (page 563) for this pie. The raspberry-flavored gelatin is important for the color and flavor of the chiffon layer; do not substitute unflavored gelatin. For an accurate measurement of boiling water, bring a full kettle of water to a boil, then measure out the desired amount.

- 1 recipe single-crust pie dough, fitted into 9-inch pie plate and chilled

Fruit
- 12 ounces (2½ cups) frozen raspberries
- 3 tablespoons pectin (Sure-Jell)
- 1½ cups (10½ ounces) sugar
- Pinch salt
- 5 ounces (1 cup) fresh raspberries

Chiffon
- 3 tablespoons raspberry-flavored gelatin
- 3 tablespoons boiling water
- 3 ounces cream cheese, softened
- 1 cup heavy cream, chilled

Topping
- 1¼ cups heavy cream, chilled
- 2 tablespoons sugar

1. Adjust oven rack to middle position and heat oven to 375 degrees. Line chilled crust with double layer of aluminum foil and fill with pie weights. Bake until pie dough looks dry and is light in color, 25 to 30 minutes. Remove weights and foil and continue to bake crust until deep golden brown, 10 to 12 minutes longer. Let crust cool on wire rack to room temperature.

2. For the Fruit Cook frozen berries in medium saucepan over medium-high heat, stirring occasionally, until berries begin to give up their juices, about 3 minutes. Stir in pectin and bring to full boil, stirring constantly. Stir in sugar and salt and return to full boil. Cook, stirring constantly, until slightly thickened, about 2 minutes. Pour through fine-mesh strainer into medium bowl, pressing on solids to extract as much puree as possible. Scrape puree off underside of strainer into bowl.

3. Transfer ⅓ cup raspberry puree to small bowl and let cool to room temperature. Gently fold fresh raspberries into remaining puree. Spread fruit mixture evenly over bottom of cooled pie shell and set aside.

4. For the Chiffon Dissolve gelatin in boiling water in bowl of stand mixer. Fit stand mixer with paddle, add cream cheese and reserved ⅓ cup raspberry puree, and beat on high speed, scraping down bowl once or twice, until smooth, about 2 minutes. Add cream and beat on medium-low speed until incorporated, about 30 seconds. Scrape down bowl. Increase speed to high and beat until cream holds stiff peaks, 1 to 2 minutes. Spread evenly over fruit in pie shell.Cover pie with plastic wrap. Refrigerate until set, at least 3 hours or up to 2 days.

5. For the Topping When ready to serve, fit stand mixer with whisk and whip cream and sugar on medium-low speed until foamy, about 1 minute. Increase speed to high and whip until stiff peaks form, 1 to 3 minutes. Spread or pipe over chilled filling. Serve.

Two Layers, Two Thickeners

For the Fruit Layer
For the bottom layer, we used Sure-Jell (pectin) to achieve a concentrated raspberry flavor and texture. There are two formulations of Sure-Jell. We found that the original formula made the smoothest, thickest bottom layer of fruit.

For the Chiffon Layer
A few tablespoons of raspberry gelatin made for great stability and color in the creamy chiffon layer and reinforced the berry flavor.

Why This Recipe Works Raspberry chiffon pie can often be weak on berry flavor. We wanted to produce an intensely flavored pie, so we included a layer of sweetened, thickened fruit on the crust and beneath the chiffon. We also stiffened our recipe's chiffon filling by using extra gelatin and a little cream cheese, which enabled it to hold additional raspberry puree for even more flavor.

ICEBOX STRAWBERRY PIE

SERVES 8

You can use Classic Single-Crust Pie Dough (page 562) or No-Fear Single-Crust Pie Dough (page 563) for this pie. In step 2, it is imperative that the cooked strawberry mixture measure 2 cups; any more and the filling will be loose. If your fresh berries aren't fully ripe, you may want to add extra sugar to taste in step 3.

- 1 recipe single-crust pie dough, fitted into 9-inch pie plate and chilled

Filling
- 2 pounds (7 cups) frozen strawberries
- 1 tablespoon unflavored gelatin
- 2 tablespoons lemon juice
- 2 tablespoons water
- 1 cup (7 ounces) sugar
  Pinch salt
- 1 pound fresh strawberries, hulled and sliced thin

Topping
- 4 ounces cream cheese, softened
- 3 tablespoons sugar
- ½ teaspoon vanilla extract
- 1 cup heavy cream

1. Adjust oven rack to middle position and heat oven to 375 degrees. Line chilled crust with double layer of aluminum foil and fill with pie weights. Bake until pie dough looks dry and is light in color, 25 to 30 minutes. Remove weights and foil and continue to bake crust until deep golden brown, 10 to 12 minutes longer. Let crust cool to room temperature on wire rack.

2. For the Filling Cook frozen berries in large saucepan over medium-low heat until berries begin to release juice, about 3 minutes. Increase heat to medium-high and cook, stirring frequently, until thick and jamlike, about 25 minutes (mixture should measure 2 cups).

3. Sprinkle gelatin over lemon juice and water in small bowl. Let stand until gelatin is softened and mixture has thickened, about 5 minutes. Stir gelatin mixture, sugar, and salt into cooked berry mixture and return to simmer, about 2 minutes. Transfer to bowl and cool to room temperature, about 30 minutes.

4. Fold fresh berries into filling. Spread evenly in pie shell and refrigerate until set, about 4 hours. (Filled pie can be refrigerated for 24 hours.)

5. For the Topping Using stand mixer fitted with whisk, beat cream cheese, sugar, and vanilla on medium speed until smooth, about 30 seconds. With mixer running, add cream and whip until stiff peaks form, about 2 minutes. Dollop individual slices of pie with topping and serve.

Don't Make This Mistake

In step 2, be sure to accurately measure the reduced strawberry mixture: You'll need exactly 2 cups. Scrape the strawberry mixture into a large liquid measuring cup. If it measures more than 2 cups, return it to the pan to cook down. It may seem fussy to stop to measure, but the pie will not set or slice properly if you have more than 2 cups of the strawberry mixture.

Why This Recipe Works Frozen strawberries, which are great for cooking, form the base of our strawberry pie. We cooked them down in a dry saucepan until they released their juice and the mixture was thick, concentrated, and flavorful. Because strawberries are low in pectin, the natural thickener found in citrus fruits and many other plants, we added some lemon juice, which perked up the flavor and tightened the texture of the filling a little. To thicken the filling further, we added a bit of unflavored gelatin. Then we mixed in fresh strawberries for a fresh finish with big berry flavor.

Why This Recipe Works This prize-winning icebox pie with a sophisticated name originally called for raw eggs. Testing showed that we could cook the eggs with sugar on the stovetop, almost like making a custard. Once the egg and sugar mixture was light and thick, we removed it from the heat and continued whipping it until it was fully cooled. Bittersweet chocolate folded into the cooled egg and sugar mixture made for a pie with more intense chocolate flavor. And to lighten the filling's texture, we incorporated whipped cream.

FRENCH SILK CHOCOLATE PIE

SERVES 8 TO 10

You can use Classic Single-Crust Pie Dough (page 562) or No-Fear Single-Crust Pie Dough (page 563) for this pie. Serve with lightly sweetened whipped cream.

- 1 recipe single-crust pie dough, fitted into 9-inch pie plate and chilled
- 1 cup heavy cream, chilled
- 3 large eggs
- ¾ cup (5¼ ounces) sugar
- 2 tablespoons water
- 8 ounces bittersweet chocolate, melted and cooled
- 1 tablespoon vanilla extract
- 8 tablespoons unsalted butter, cut into ½-inch pieces and softened

1. Adjust oven rack to middle position and heat oven to 375 degrees. Line chilled crust with double layer of aluminum foil and fill with pie weights. Bake until pie dough looks dry and is light in color, 25 to 30 minutes. Remove weights and foil and continue to bake crust until deep golden brown, 10 to 12 minutes longer. Let crust cool on wire rack to room temperature.

2. Using stand mixer fitted with whisk, whip cream on medium-low speed until foamy, about 1 minute. Increase speed to high and whip until stiff peaks form, 1 to 3 minutes. Transfer whipped cream to small bowl and refrigerate.

3. Combine eggs, sugar, and water in large heatproof bowl set over medium saucepan filled with ½ inch barely simmering water (don't let bowl touch water). Using hand-held mixer set at medium speed, beat egg mixture until thickened and registers 160 degrees, 7 to 10 minutes. Remove bowl from heat and continue to beat egg mixture until fluffy and cooled to room temperature, about 8 minutes.

4. Add chocolate and vanilla to cooled egg mixture and beat until incorporated. Beat in butter, few pieces at a time, until well combined. Using spatula, fold in whipped cream until no streaks of white remain. Scrape filling into pie shell and refrigerate until set, at least 3 hours or up to 24 hours. Serve.

Whisking Chocolate into Silk

1. Beat eggs and sugar together in double boiler to incorporate air for filling with light, ethereal texture. Remove from heat when egg mixture reaches 160 degrees; it will be very thick.

2. Continue beating egg mixture until fluffy and cool. Add melted chocolate and beat in softened butter for rich flavor and silky-smooth texture.

The Pillsbury Bake-Off

In 1949, General Mills launched the "Grand National Recipe and Baking Contest" (later known as the Pillsbury Bake-Off). It was held at the posh Waldorf-Astoria Hotel in New York. The grand-prize winner (for No-Knead Water Rising Twists) brought home $50,000; Eleanor Roosevelt was one of the luminaries on hand to present the awards. Since then, many prize-winning Pillsbury recipes have become part of our culinary heritage, among them French Silk Chocolate Pie (the exotic name reflects the international curiosity of postwar America), Open Sesame Pie (which caused a run on sesame seeds nationwide), and Peanut Blossom Cookies (with a Hershey's Kiss in the middle).

CHOCOLATE ANGEL PIE

SERVES 8 TO 10

Serve the assembled pie within 3 hours of chilling.

Filling
- 9 ounces milk chocolate, chopped fine
- 5 ounces bittersweet chocolate, chopped fine
- 3 large egg yolks
- 1½ tablespoons granulated sugar
- ½ teaspoon salt
- ½ cup half-and-half
- 1¼ cups heavy cream, chilled

Meringue Crust
- 1 tablespoon cornstarch, plus extra for pie plate
- ½ cup (3½ ounces) granulated sugar
- 3 large egg whites
- Pinch cream of tartar
- ½ teaspoon vanilla extract

Topping
- 1⅓ cups heavy cream, chilled
- 2 tablespoons confectioners' sugar
- Unsweetened cocoa powder

1. For the Filling Microwave milk chocolate and bittersweet chocolate in large bowl at 50 percent power, stirring occasionally, until melted, 2 to 4 minutes. Whisk egg yolks, sugar, and salt together in medium bowl until combined, about 1 minute. Bring half-and-half to simmer in small saucepan over medium heat. Whisking constantly, slowly add hot half-and-half to egg yolk mixture in 2 additions until incorporated. Return half-and-half mixture to now-empty saucepan and cook over low heat, whisking constantly, until thickened slightly, 30 seconds to 1 minute. Stir half-and-half mixture into melted chocolate until combined. Let cool slightly, about 8 minutes.

2. Using stand mixer fitted with whisk, whip cream on medium-low speed until foamy, about 1 minute. Increase speed to high and whip until soft peaks form, 1 to 3 minutes. Gently whisk one-third of whipped cream into cooled chocolate mixture. Fold in remaining whipped cream until no white streaks remain. Cover and refrigerate for at least 3 hours, or until ready to assemble pie. (Filling can be made up to 24 hours in advance.)

3. For the Meringue Crust Adjust oven rack to lower-middle position and heat oven to 275 degrees. Grease 9-inch pie plate and dust well with extra cornstarch, using pastry brush to distribute evenly. Combine sugar and 1 tablespoon cornstarch in bowl. Using stand mixer fitted with whisk, whip egg whites and cream of tartar on medium-low speed until foamy, about 1 minute. Increase speed to medium-high and whip whites to soft, billowy mounds, 1 to 3 minutes. Gradually add sugar mixture and whip until glossy, stiff peaks form, 3 to 5 minutes. Add vanilla to meringue and whip until incorporated.

4. Spread meringue into prepared pie plate, following contours of plate to cover bottom, sides, and edges. Bake for 1½ hours. Rotate pie plate, reduce oven temperature to 200 degrees, and bake until completely dried out, about 1 hour longer. (Shell will rise above rim of pie plate; some cracking is OK.) Let cool completely, about 30 minutes.

5. For the Topping Spoon cooled chocolate filling into cavity of pie shell, distributing evenly. Using stand mixer fitted with whisk, whip cream and sugar on medium-low speed until foamy, about 1 minute. Increase speed to high and whip until stiff peaks form, 1 to 3 minutes. Spread whipped cream evenly over chocolate. Refrigerate until filling is set, about 1 hour. Dust with cocoa. Slice with sharp knife and serve.

Busted Crust
The egg white crust is part of what distinguishes angel pie. To avoid a sticky, broken meringue shell, we added cornstarch to the whites, and we greased the pie plate and dusted it with more cornstarch.

MERINGUE MESS
Don't let this happen to you.

Why This Recipe Works Chocolate angel pie is a lavish version of chocolate cream pie with creamy chocolate mousse, fluffy whipped cream, and an airy meringue crust. For a light, crisp crust, 2½ hours in a low oven was necessary. To prevent the crust from sticking to the pan, we relied on cornstarch, both in the egg whites and dusted over the pie plate. We loaded nearly a pound of chocolate into the filling by making a cooked custard. Using two kinds of chocolate lent depth and complexity. To finish, we topped the pie with lightly sweetened whipped cream and a sprinkling of cocoa powder for a decadent, supremely chocolaty dessert.

MISSISSIPPI MUD PIE

SERVES 8 TO 12

This recipe takes at least 5 hours from start to finish. We used Nabisco Famous Chocolate Wafers in this recipe. Be sure to use milk chocolate in the mousse, as bittersweet chocolate will make the mousse too firm. Do not begin making the mousse until the brownie layer is fully chilled.

Crust
- 25 chocolate wafer cookies (5½ ounces), broken into coarse pieces
- 4 tablespoons unsalted butter, melted

Brownie Layer
- 4 ounces bittersweet chocolate, chopped fine
- 3 tablespoons unsalted butter
- 3 tablespoons vegetable oil
- 1½ tablespoons Dutch-processed cocoa powder
- ⅔ cup packed (4⅔ ounces) dark brown sugar
- 2 large eggs
- 2 teaspoons vanilla extract
- ¼ teaspoon salt
- 3 tablespoons all-purpose flour

Topping
- 10 chocolate wafer cookies (2 ounces)
- 2 tablespoons confectioners' sugar
- 1 tablespoon Dutch-processed cocoa powder
- ⅛ teaspoon salt
- 2 tablespoons unsalted butter, melted

Mousse
- 6 ounces milk chocolate, chopped fine
- 1 cup heavy cream, chilled
- 2 tablespoons Dutch-processed cocoa powder
- 2 tablespoons confectioners' sugar
- ⅛ teaspoon salt

1. For the Crust Adjust oven rack to middle position and heat oven to 325 degrees. Process cookie pieces in food processor until finely ground, about 30 seconds. Add melted butter and pulse until combined, about 6 pulses. Using bottom of dry measuring cup, press crumbs firmly into bottom and up sides of 9-inch pie plate. Bake until fragrant and set, about 15 minutes. Transfer to wire rack.

2. For the Brownie Layer Combine chocolate, butter, oil, and cocoa in bowl and microwave at 50 percent power, stirring often, until melted, about 1½ minutes. In separate bowl, whisk sugar, eggs, vanilla, and salt until smooth. Whisk in chocolate mixture until incorporated. Whisk in flour until just combined.

3. Pour brownie batter into crust (crust needn't be cool at this point). Bake pie until edges begin to set and toothpick inserted in center comes out with thin coating of batter attached, about 15 minutes. Transfer to wire rack and let cool for 1 hour, then refrigerate until fully chilled, about 1 hour longer.

4. For the Topping Meanwhile, line rimmed baking sheet with parchment paper. Place cookies in zipper-lock bag, press out air, and seal bag. Using rolling pin, crush cookies into ½- to ¾-inch pieces. Combine sugar, cocoa, salt, and crushed cookies in bowl. Stir in melted butter until mixture is moistened and clumps begin to form. Spread crumbs in even layer on prepared sheet and bake until fragrant, about 10 minutes, shaking sheet to break up crumbs halfway through baking. Transfer sheet to wire rack and let cool completely.

5. For the Mousse Once brownie layer has fully chilled, microwave chocolate in large bowl at 50 percent power, stirring often, until melted, 1½ to 2 minutes. Let cool until just barely warm and registers between 90 and 100 degrees, about 10 minutes.

6. Microwave 3 tablespoons cream in small bowl until it registers 105 to 110 degrees, about 15 seconds. Whisk in cocoa until homogeneous. Combine cocoa-cream mixture, sugar, salt, and remaining cream in bowl of stand mixer. Fit mixer with whisk and whip cream mixture on medium speed until beginning to thicken, about 30 seconds, scraping down bowl as needed. Increase speed to high and whip until soft peaks form, 30 to 60 seconds.

7. Using whisk, fold one-third of whipped cream mixture into melted chocolate to lighten. Using rubber spatula, fold in remaining whipped cream mixture until no dark streaks remain. Spoon mousse into chilled pie and spread evenly from edge to edge. Sprinkle with cooled topping and refrigerate for at least 3 hours or overnight. Serve.

Why This Recipe Works This pie is so named because its chocolate layers are reminiscent of the Mississippi River's silty bottom, but there's nothing muddy about its flavor. To simplify each layer of the pie, we started with a press-in chocolate wafer cookie crust. For a perfectly soft, chewy middle layer, we created a brownie-like batter and underbaked it slightly. Once this layer was fully chilled, we spread on a simple milk chocolate mousse and sprinkled on a crunchy chocolate cookie topping to finish off our striated chocolate showstopper.

SHOPPING FOR EQUIPMENT

With a well-stocked kitchen, you'll be able to take on any recipe. But there's so much equipment out there on the market, how do you figure out what's what? Price often correlates with design, not performance. Over the years, our test kitchen has evaluated thousands of products. We've gone through copious rounds of testing and have identified the most important attributes in every piece of equipment, so when you go shopping you'll know what to look for. And because our test kitchen accepts no support from product manufacturers, you can trust our ratings. Prices in this chart are based on shopping at online retailers and will vary. See AmericasTestKitchen.com for updates to these testings.

KNIVES AND MORE	ITEM	WHAT TO LOOK FOR	TEST KITCHEN FAVORITES
MUST-HAVE ITEMS	CHEF'S KNIFE	• High-carbon stainless steel knife • Thin, curved 8-inch blade • Lightweight • Comfortable grip and nonslip handle	**Victorinox Swiss Army Fibrox Pro 8-Inch Chef's Knife** $39.95
	PARING KNIFE	• 3- to 3½-inch blade • Thin, flexible blade with pointed tip • Comfortable grip	**Victorinox Swiss Army Fibrox Pro 3¼-Inch Spear Point Paring Knife** $9.47
	SERRATED KNIFE	• 10-inch blade • Fewer broader, deeper, pointed serrations • Thinner blade angle • Comfortable, grippy handle • Medium weight	**Mercer Culinary Millenia 10" Wide Bread Knife** $22.10
	SLICING KNIFE	• Tapered 12-inch blade for slicing large cuts of meat • Oval scallops (called a granton edge) carved into blade • Fairly rigid blade with rounded tip	**Victorinox Swiss Army Fibrox Pro 12-Inch Granton Edge Slicing/Carving Knife** $54.65
	STEAK KNIVES	• Super-sharp, straight-edged blade • Sturdy, not wobbly, blade	**Victorinox Swiss Army 6-Piece Rosewood Steak Set, Spear Point, Straight Edge** $170.74 for a set of six Best Buy: **Chicago Cutlery Walnut Tradition 4-Piece Steak Knife Set** $17.95 for a set of four

KNIVES AND MORE	ITEM	WHAT TO LOOK FOR	TEST KITCHEN FAVORITES
	SANTOKU KNIFE	• 6½-inch blade • Narrow, curved, and short blade • Comfortable grip	**MAC Superior Santoku Knife** $74.95
	BONING KNIFE	• 6-inch blade • Narrow, highly maneuverable and razor-sharp blade • Comfortable grip and nonslip handle	**Victorinox 6-Inch Fibrox Pro Flexible Boning Knife** $27.20
	MEAT CLEAVER	• Razor-sharp blade • Balanced weight between handle and blade • Comfortable grip	**Global 6-Inch Meat Cleaver** $144.95 Best Buy: **LamsonSharp 7-Inch Meat Cleaver** $48
	HYBRID CHEF'S KNIFE	• High-carbon stainless steel knife • Lightweight • Thin blade that tapers from spine to cutting edge and from handle to tip	**Masamoto VG-10 Gyutou, 8.2 Inches** $136.50
	MANDOLINE	• Razor-sharp blade(s) • Hand guard to shield fingers • Gripper prongs to grasp food • Measurement-marked dial for precision cuts • Storage for extra blades	**Swissmar Börner Original V-Slicer Plus Mandoline** $29.99
	CARVING BOARD	• Trenches can contain ½ cup of liquid • Large and stable enough to hold large roasts • Midweight for easy carrying, carving, and cleaning	**J.K. Adams Maple Reversible Carving Board** $69.95
MUST-HAVE ITEM	CUTTING BOARD	• Roomy work surface at least 20 by 15 inches • Teak board for minimal maintenance • Durable edge-grain construction (wood grain runs parallel to surface of board)	**Proteak Edge Grain Teak Cutting Board** $84.99 Best Buy: **OXO Good Grips Carving and Cutting Board** $21.99

KNIVES AND MORE	ITEM	WHAT TO LOOK FOR	TEST KITCHEN FAVORITES
MUST-HAVE ITEM	KNIFE SHARPENER	• Diamond abrasives and a spring-loaded chamber to precisely guide blade • Quickly removes nicks in blades • Can convert a 20-degree edge to a sharper 15 degrees	Electric: **Chef'sChoice Trizor XV Knife Sharpener, Model #15** $149.99 Electric, Best Buy: **Chef'sChoice Diamond Sharpener for Asian Knives, Model #316** $79.99 Manual: **Chef'sChoice Pronto Manual Diamond Hone Asian Knife Sharpener** $49.99

POTS AND PANS	ITEM	WHAT TO LOOK FOR	TEST KITCHEN FAVORITES
MUST-HAVE ITEM	TRADITIONAL SKILLET	• Stainless steel interior and fully clad for even heat distribution • 12-inch diameter and flared sides • Comfortable, ovensafe handle • Tight-fitting lid included	**All-Clad 12-inch Stainless Steel Fry Pan with Lid** $96.85
	INEXPENSIVE SKILLET	• Could fit 8 pieces of chicken • Helper handle eased moving the hefty pan in and out of the oven	**Cuisinart 12-Inch Multiclad Pro Skillet** $69.95
MUST-HAVE ITEM	NONSTICK SKILLET	• Dark, nonstick surface • 12- or 12½-inch diameter, thick bottom • Comfortable, ovensafe handle • Cooking surface of at least 9 inches	**OXO Good Grips Non-Stick 12-Inch Open Frypan** $39.99
	CAST-IRON SKILLET	• Thick bottom and straight sides • Roomy interior (cooking surface of 9¼ inches or more) • Preseasoned	**Lodge Classic 12-Inch Cast Iron Skillet** $33.31

POTS AND PANS	ITEM	WHAT TO LOOK FOR	TEST KITCHEN FAVORITES
MUST-HAVE ITEMS	CAST-IRON SKILLET, ENAMELED	• Boasts flaring sides, an oversize helper handle, wide pour spouts, satiny interior, and balanced weight	Le Creuset Signature 11¾" Iron Handle Skillet $179.95 Best Buy: Mario Batali by Dansk 12" Open Sauté Pan $59.95
	DUTCH OVEN	• Enameled cast iron or stainless steel • Capacity of at least 6 quarts • Diameter of at least 9 inches • Tight-fitting lid • Wide, sturdy handles	Heavier: Le Creuset 7¼-Quart Round French Oven $349.95 Lighter: All-Clad Stainless 8-Quart Stockpot $279.95 Best Buy: Cuisinart 7 Qt. Round Covered Casserole $121.94
	SAUCEPAN	• Large saucepan with 3- to 4-quart capacity and small nonstick saucepan with 2- to 2½-quart capacity • Tight-fitting lids • Pans with rounded corners that a whisk can reach into • Long, comfortable handles that are angled for even weight distribution	Large: All-Clad Stainless 4-Quart Saucepan with Lid and Loop $224.95 Best Buy: Cuisinart MultiClad Unlimited 4-Quart Saucepan $69.99 Small: Calphalon Contemporary Nonstick 2½-Quart Shallow Saucepan $39.95
	RIMMED BAKING SHEET	• Light-colored surface (heats and browns evenly) • Thick, sturdy pan • Dimensions of 18 by 13 inches • Good to have at least two	Nordic Ware Baker's Half Sheet $14.97
	SAUTÉ PAN	• Aluminum core surrounded by layers of stainless steel • Hefty but well-balanced pan • 9½- to 10-inch diameter • Helper handle and tight-fitting lid	All-Clad Stainless Steel 3-Quart Tri-Ply Sauté Pan $224.95 Best Buy: Cuisinart MultiClad Pro Stainless 3½-Quart Sauté Pan with Helper and Cover $78.13

SHOPPING FOR EQUIPMENT

POTS AND PANS	ITEM	WHAT TO LOOK FOR	TEST KITCHEN FAVORITES
	OMELET PAN	• Gently sloped sides for easy turning and rolling of omelets • Nonstick finish • Heavy construction for durability and even heat distribution • 8-inch size for French omelets	**Original French Chef Omelette Pan** $139.95
	STOCKPOT	• 12-quart capacity • Thick bottom to prevent scorching • Wide body for easy cleaning and storage • Flat or round handles that extend at least 1¾ inches	**All-Clad Stainless 12-Quart Stock Pot** $389.95 Best Buy: **Cuisinart Chef's Classic Stainless 12-Quart Stock Pot** $69.99
MUST-HAVE ITEM	ROASTING PAN	• At least 15 by 11 inches • Stainless steel interior with aluminum core for even heat distribution • Upright handles for easy gripping • Light interior for better food monitoring	**Calphalon Contemporary Stainless Roasting Pan with Rack** $99.99 Best Buy: **Calphalon Commercial Hard-Anodized Roasting Pan with Nonstick Rack** $59.99
	ROASTING RACK	• Fixed, not adjustable, to provide sturdiness • Tall, vertical handles positioned on long side of rack	**All-Clad Nonstick Large Rack** $24.95
	COOKWARE SET	• Fully clad stainless steel with aluminum core for even heat distribution • Moderately heavy, durable construction • Lids included • Ideal mix of pans includes 12-inch skillet, 10-inch skillet, 2-quart saucepan, 4-quart saucepan, 8-quart stockpot	**All-Clad Stainless Steel Cookware Set, 10-Piece** $799.95 Best Buy: **Tramontina 18/10 Stainless Steel TriPly-Clad Cookware Set, 8-piece** $144.97

The Complete Cook's Country TV Show Cookbook

	HANDY TOOLS	ITEM	WHAT TO LOOK FOR	TEST KITCHEN FAVORITES
MUST-HAVE ITEMS		KITCHEN SHEARS	• Take-apart scissors (for easy cleaning) • Super-sharp blades • Sturdy construction • Work for both right- and left-handed users	**Kershaw 1120M Taskmaster Shears/Shun Multipurpose** $49.95 Best Buy: **J.A. Henckels International Kitchen Shears—Take Apart** $14.95
		TONGS	• Scalloped edges • Slightly concave pincers • Length of 12 inches (to keep your hand far from the heat) • Open and close easily	**OXO Good Grips 12-Inch Locking Tongs** $12.09
		WOODEN SPOON	• Slim yet broad bowl • Stain-resistant bamboo • Comfortable handle	**SCI Bamboo Wood Cooking Spoon** $2.40
		SLOTTED SPOON	• Wide, shallow, thin bowl • Long, hollow, comfortable handle • Steep, ladle-like angle between handle and bowl	**Cuisinart Stainless Steel Slotted Spoon** $9.12
		BASTING SPOON	• Thin, shallow bowl • Handle at least 9 inches in length • Slight dip from handle to bowl	**Rösle Basting Spoon with Hook Handle** $28.95
MUST-HAVE ITEMS		ALL-AROUND SPATULA	• Head about 3 inches wide and 5½ inches long • 11 inches in length (tip to handle) • Long, vertical slots • Good to have a metal spatula to use with traditional cookware and plastic for nonstick cookware	Metal: **Wüsthof Gourmet Turner/Fish Spatula** $44.95 Plastic: **Matfer Bourgeat Pelton Spatula** $8.23
		SILICONE SPATULA	• Firm, wide blade ideal for efficient scraping and scooping • All-silicone design made for easy cleanup	**Di Oro Seamless Silicone Spatula—Large** $10.97

SHOPPING FOR EQUIPMENT

HANDY TOOLS	ITEM	WHAT TO LOOK FOR	TEST KITCHEN FAVORITES
MUST-HAVE ITEMS	OFFSET SPATULA	• Flexible blade offset to a roughly 30-degree angle • Enough usable surface area to frost the radius of a 9-inch cake • Comfortable handle	Large: **OXO Good Grips Bent Icing Knife** $9.99 Small: **Wilton 9-inch Angled Spatula** $4.79
	COOKIE SPATULA	• Small, silicone blade with thin, flexible edge • Angled handle	**OXO Good Grips Cookie Spatula** $6.99
	ALL-PURPOSE WHISK	• At least 10 wires • Wires of moderate thickness • Comfortable rubber handle • Balanced, lightweight feel	**OXO Good Grips 11-Inch Balloon Whisk** $9.99
	PEPPER MILL	• Easy-to-adjust, clearly marked grind settings • Efficient, comfortable grinding mechanism • Generous capacity	**Cole and Mason Derwent Gourmet Precision Pepper Mill** $40
	ONE-HANDED PEPPER MILL	• Grinds quickly and easily • Accurately grinds in five textures from fine to coarse • Long-lasting rechargeable battery	**Peppermills Supreme Electric Pepper Mill** $39.95
	SUGAR SHAKER	• Mesh head that produces a fine, even dusting • Narrow cylinder that fits comfortably in your hand	**Ateco Stainless Steel Fine Mesh Shaker** $3.88
MUST-HAVE ITEM	LADLE	• Stainless steel • Hook handle • Pouring rim to prevent dripping • Handle 9 to 10 inches in length	**Rösle Ladle with Pouring Rim** $34 Best Buy: **OXO Good Grips Brushed Stainless Steel Ladle** $9.99

HANDY TOOLS	ITEM	WHAT TO LOOK FOR	TEST KITCHEN FAVORITES
MUST-HAVE ITEM	CAN OPENER	• Intuitive and easy to attach • Smooth turning motions • Dishwasher safe	**Fissler Magic Smooth-Edge Can Opener** $29
	JAR OPENER	• Strong, sturdy clamp grip • Adjusts quickly to any size jar	**Amco Swing-A-Way Comfort Grip Jar Opener** $5.99
MUST-HAVE ITEM	GARLIC PRESS	• Conical holes that press garlic through efficiently • Solid, stainless steel construction • Comfortable handle • Easy to clean	**Kuhn Rikon Stainless Steel Epicurean Garlic Press** $39.95
	GARLIC PEELER	• Thick, comfortable silicone sleeve • Removes skins without bruising • Easy to wash	**Zak! Designs E-Z Rol Garlic Peeler** $8.79
	SERRATED FRUIT PEELER	• Comfortable grip and nonslip handle • Sharp blade	**Messermeister Serrated Swivel Peeler** $5.50
MUST-HAVE ITEM	VEGETABLE PEELER	• Sharp, carbon steel blade • 1-inch space between blade and peeler to prevent jamming • Lightweight and comfortable	**Kuhn Rikon Original Swiss Peeler** $3.50
	RASP GRATER	• Sharp teeth (require little effort or pressure when grating) • Maneuverable over round shapes • Comfortable handle	**Microplane Classic Zester Grater** $12.35
MUST-HAVE ITEM	GRATER	• Paddle-style grater • Sharp, extra-large holes and generous grating plane • Rubber-lined feet for stability • Comfortable handle	**Rösle Coarse Grater** $35.95
	ROTARY GRATER	• Barrel at least 2 inches in diameter • Classic turn-crank design • Comfortable handle • Simple to disassemble for easy cleanup	**Zyliss All Cheese Grater** $19.95

SHOPPING FOR EQUIPMENT

HANDY TOOLS	ITEM	WHAT TO LOOK FOR	TEST KITCHEN FAVORITES
	MANUAL JUICER	• Directs juice in a steady stream with no splattering or overflowing • Large, rounded handles that are easy to squeeze	**Chef'n FreshForce Citrus Juicer** $23.04
	ICE CREAM SCOOP	• Forms perfectly round orbs that release easily • Wide, comfortable handle contains heat-conductive fluid that warms up instantly when a hand grips the exterior and also warms the bowl, making scooping easy	**Zeroll Original Ice Cream Scoop** $18.44
	MEAT POUNDER	• At least 1½ pounds in weight • Vertical handle for better leverage and control	**Norpro Grip-EZ Meat Pounder** $17.50
	BENCH SCRAPER	• Sturdy blade • Beveled edge for easy cutting and scraping • Comfortable handle with plastic, rubber, or nylon grip	**Dexter-Russell 6" Dough Cutter/Scraper–Sani-Safe Series** $7.01
	BOWL SCRAPER	• Curved shape with comfortable grip • Rigid enough to move dough but flexible enough to scrape up batter • Thin, straight edge doubles as dough cutter or bench scraper	**iSi Basics Silicone Scraper Spatula** $5.99
MUST-HAVE ITEMS	ROLLING PIN	• Moderate weight (1 to 1½ pounds) • 19-inch straight barrel • Slightly textured wooden surface to grip dough for easy rolling	**J.K. Adams Plain Maple Rolling Dowel** $13.95
	MIXING BOWLS	• Good to have both stainless steel and glass (for mixing, microwaving, and holding prepped ingredients) • Sets of 6 to 9 nesting bowls ranging in capacity from about 1¼ ounces to 4 quarts (for glass) and 2 cups to 8 quarts (for stainless steel)	Stainless Steel: **Vollrath Economy Stainless Steel Mixing Bowls** $2.90–$6.90 Glass: **Pyrex Smart Essentials with Colored Lids** $27.98 for 4-bowl set

HANDY TOOLS	ITEM	WHAT TO LOOK FOR	TEST KITCHEN FAVORITES
MUST-HAVE ITEM	MINI PREP BOWLS	• Wide, shallow bowls • Easy to hold, fill, empty, and clean • Microwave-safe and oven-safe	**Anchor Hocking 6-Piece Nesting Prep Bowl Set** $11
	OVEN MITT	• Form-fitting and not overly bulky for easy maneuvering • Machine washable • Flexible, heat-resistant material	**Kool-Tek 15-Inch Oven Mitt by KatchAll** $44.95 each
	INNOVATIVE POT HOLDER	• Combines cotton for flexibility with grippy silicone for high-heat protection • Superior maneuverability	**OXO Good Grips Silicone Pot Holder with Magnet** $9.99
	COOKIE CUTTERS	• Metal cutters • Thin, sharp cutting edge and round or rubber-grip top • Depth of at least 1 inch	**Little difference among various brands**
	PASTRY BRUSH	• Silicone bristles (heat-resistant, durable, and easy to clean) • Perforated flaps (to trap liquid) • Angled head to reach tight spots • Comfortable handle	**OXO Good Grips Silicone Pastry Brush** $6.99
	BOUILLON STRAINER/ CHINOIS	• Conical shape • Depth of 7 to 8 inches • At least one hook on rim for stability	**Winco Reinforced Extra Fine Mesh Bouillon Strainer** $33.78
MUST-HAVE ITEMS	COLANDER	• 4- to 7-quart capacity • Metal ring attached to bottom for stability • Many holes for quick draining • Small holes so pasta doesn't slip through	**RSVP International Endurance Precision Pierced 5-Qt. Colander** $25.99
	FINE-MESH STRAINER	• Stiff, tightly woven mesh • Capacity of at least 5 cups with large, durable hooks for support over bowls and pots	**Rösle Fine-Mesh Strainer, Round Handle, 7.9 inches, 20 cm** $45

SHOPPING FOR EQUIPMENT

HANDY TOOLS	ITEM	WHAT TO LOOK FOR	TEST KITCHEN FAVORITES
	FOOD MILL	• Sturdy but lightweight plastic construction • Easy to turn	**RSVP Classic Rotary Food Mill** $24.95
	FAT SEPARATOR	• Bottom-draining model • Detachable bowl for easy cleaning • Strainer for catching solids	**Cuisipro Fat Separator** $33.95
	SPLATTER SCREEN	• At least 13-inches wide with a small handle • Fits over a range of pans • Minimized mess	**HIC Stainless Steel Splatter Screen** $9.99
MUST-HAVE ITEMS	POTATO MASHER	• Solid mashing disk with many small holes • Comfortable grip • Long handle	**Zyliss Stainless Steel Potato Masher** $12.99
	SALAD SPINNER	• Ergonomic and easy-to-operate hand pump • Wide base for stability • Flat lid for easy cleaning and storage	**OXO Good Grips Salad Spinner** $29.99
	STEAMER BASKET	• Collapsible stainless steel basket with feet • Adjustable and removable center rod for easy removal from pot and easy storage	**OXO Good Grips Pop-Up Steamer** $16.99
	MORTAR AND PESTLE	• Heavy, stable base with tall, narrow walls • Rough interior to help grip and grind ingredients • Comfortable, heavy pestle	**Frieling "Goliath" Mortar and Pestle Set** $49.95

MEASURING EQUIPMENT	ITEM	WHAT TO LOOK FOR	TEST KITCHEN FAVORITES
MUST-HAVE ITEMS	DRY MEASURING CUPS	• Accurate measurements • Easy-to-read measurement markings • Durable measurement markings • Stable when empty and filled • Strong and durable design • Handles perfectly flush with cups • Stacks and stores neatly	**OXO Good Grips Stainless Steel Measuring Cups** $19.99
	LIQUID MEASURING CUP	• Crisp, unambiguous markings that include ¼ and ⅓ cup measurements • Heatproof, sturdy cup with handle • Good to have in a variety of sizes (1, 2, and 4 cups)	**Pyrex 2-Cup Measuring Cup** $5.99
	ADJUSTABLE MEASURING CUP	• Plungerlike bottom (with a tight seal between plunger and tube) that you can set to correct measurement, then push up to cleanly extract sticky ingredients (such as shortening or peanut butter) • 1- or 2-cup capacity • Dishwasher-safe	**KitchenArt Pro Adjust-A-Cup Professional Series** $12.95
MUST-HAVE ITEMS	MEASURING SPOONS	• Long, comfortable handles • Rim of bowl flush with handle (makes it easy to "dip" into a dry ingredient and "sweep" across the top for accurate measuring) • Slim design	**Cuisipro Stainless Steel Measuring Spoons Set** $11.95
	KITCHEN RULER	• Stainless steel and easy to clean • 18 inches in length • Large, easy-to-read markings	**Empire 18-Inch Stainless Steel Ruler** $8.49
	DIGITAL SCALE	• Easy-to-read display not blocked by weighing platform • At least 7-pound capacity • Accessible buttons • Gram-to-ounce conversion feature • Roomy platform	**OXO Good Grips 11 lb. Food Scale with Pull Out Display** $49.99 Best Buy: **Ozeri Pronto Digital Multifunction Kitchen and Food Scale** $11.79

	ITEM	WHAT TO LOOK FOR	TEST KITCHEN FAVORITES
THERMOMETERS AND TIMERS			
MUST-HAVE ITEMS	INSTANT-READ THERMOMETER	• Display auto-rotates • Lights up in low light • Wakes up when unit is picked up • Takes a single AAA alkaline battery • Water resistant	**ThermoWorks Thermapen Mk4** $99 Best Buy: **ThermoWorks ThermoPop** $29
	OVEN THERMOMETER	• Wide, sturdy base • Clear temperature markings • Fairly easy to read	**CDN Pro Accurate Oven Thermometer** $8.70
	MEAT PROBE/ CANDY/ DEEP-FRY THERMOMETER	• Digital model • Easy-to-read console • Mounting clip (to attach probe to the pan)	**ThermoWorks ChefAlarm** $59 Best Buy: **Polder Classic Digital Thermometer/Timer** $24.99
	BARBECUE THERMOMETER	• Simultaneously checks food and grill temperature • Easy to read • Heatproof finger-grip • Dishwasher-safe	**Polder Dual Sensor Meat and Oven Thermometer** $10
	REFRIGERATOR/ FREEZER THERMOMETER	• Large, easy-to-read display • Accurate, and carefully monitors fluctuations in temperature	**ThermoWorks Fridge/ Freezer Alarm** $22
	REMOTE THERMOMETER	• Bluetooth device connects quickly to smart phones and delivers accurate temperature readouts • Easy to use	**iDevices Kitchen Thermometer** $78

THERMOMETERS AND TIMERS	ITEM	WHAT TO LOOK FOR	TEST KITCHEN FAVORITES
	KITCHEN TIMER	• Lengthy time range (1 second to at least 10 hours) • Able to count up after alarm goes off • Easy to use and read • Able to track multiple events	**OXO Good Grips Triple Timer** $19.99
	WEARABLE KITCHEN TIMER	• Combines a clock, timer, and stopwatch • Vertical orientation fits comfortably in hand and pockets • 38-inch lanyard is comfortable and long enough to slip overhead	**ThermoWorks TimeStick** $25

BAKEWARE		ITEM	WHAT TO LOOK FOR	TEST KITCHEN FAVORITES
MUST-HAVE ITEM		GLASS BAKING DISH	• Dimensions of 13 by 9 inches • Lightweight with large handles for easy grip and maneuvering	**Pyrex Easy Grab 3-Quart Oblong Baking Dish** $7.29
		BROILER-SAFE BAKING DISH	• Large, easy-to-grip handles • Straight sides for easy serving • Lightweight porcelain	**HIC Porcelain Lasagna Baking Dish** $29.95
MUST-HAVE ITEMS		METAL BAKING PAN	• Dimensions of 13 by 9 inches • Straight sides • Nonstick coating for even browning and easy release of cakes and bar cookies	**Williams-Sonoma Goldtouch Nonstick Rectangular Cake Pan, 9" x 13"** $32.95
		SQUARE BAKING PAN	• Straight sides • Light gold or dark nonstick surface for even browning and easy release of cakes • Good to have both 9-inch and 8-inch square pans	**Williams-Sonoma Goldtouch Nonstick Square Cake Pan, 8"** $21

BAKEWARE	ITEM	WHAT TO LOOK FOR	TEST KITCHEN FAVORITES
MUST-HAVE ITEMS	ROUND CAKE PAN	• Best for cake • Straight sides • Light finish for tall, even baking • Nonstick surface for easy release	Best All-Around: **Nordic Ware Naturals Nonstick 9-inch Round Cake Pan** $14.32
		• Dark finish is ideal for pizza and cinnamon buns • Nonstick	Best for Browning: **Chicago Metallic Non-Stick 9" Round Cake Pan** $10.97
	PIE PLATE	• Glass promotes even browning and allows progress to be monitored • ½-inch rim (makes it easy to shape decorative crusts) • Shallow angled sides prevent crusts from slumping • Good to have two	**Pyrex Bakeware 9 Inch Pie Plate** $8.16
	LOAF PAN	• Light gold or dark nonstick surface for even browning and easy release • Good to have both 8½ by 4½-inch and 9 by 5-inch pans	**Williams-Sonoma Nonstick Goldtouch Loaf Pan** $21 Best Buy: **Baker's Secret 9 x 5-Inch Nonstick Loaf Pan** $5
	SPRINGFORM PAN	• Tall sides make for an easy grip • Gold-toned pan produces evenly-baked crusts • Wide, raised base provides support	**Williams-Sonoma Goldtouch Springform Pan, 9"** $49.95 Best Buy: **Nordic Ware 9" Leakproof Springform Pan** $16.22
	COOKIE SHEET	• Thick aluminum heats and browns evenly • Won't warp with repeated use • Raised edges for easy maneuvering • Nonstick, spacious surface	**Vollrath Wear-Ever Cookie Sheet (Natural Finish)** $15.99

BAKEWARE	ITEM	WHAT TO LOOK FOR	TEST KITCHEN FAVORITES
MUST-HAVE ITEMS	MUFFIN TIN	• Gold nonstick surface for perfect browning and easy release • Wide, extended rims and raised lip for easy handling	**OXO Good Grips Non-Stick 12-Cup Muffin Pan** $24.99
	COOLING RACK	• Grid-style rack with tightly woven, heavy-gauge bars • Should fit inside a standard 18 by 13-inch rimmed baking sheet • Dishwasher-safe	**CIA Bakeware 12-Inch x 17-Inch Cooling Rack** $15.95
	BAKER'S COOLING RACK	• Sturdy rack • Four collapsible shelves • Unit folds down for easy storage	**Linden Sweden Baker's Cooling Rack** $17.99
	BISCUIT CUTTERS	• Sharp edges • A set with a variety of sizes	**Ateco 5357 11-Piece Plain Round Cutter Set** $14.95
	BUNDT PAN	• Heavyweight cast aluminum • Thick, easy-to-grip handles • Clearly defined ridges for elegant cakes • 15-cup capacity	**Nordic Ware Anniversary Bundt Pan** $30.99
	TART PAN	• Nonstick mold released tarts more readily than traditional finish • Deep grooves for impressive edges • Dark surface for deeply, evenly browned edges	**Matfer Steel Non-Stick Fluted Tart Mold** $27
	TUBE PAN	• Heavy pan (at least 1 pound) • Heavy bottom for leak-free seal • Dark nonstick surface for even browning and easy release • 16-cup capacity • Feet on rim	**Chicago Metallic Professional Nonstick Angel Food Cake Pan with Feet** $19.95

SHOPPING FOR EQUIPMENT

BAKEWARE	ITEM	WHAT TO LOOK FOR	TEST KITCHEN FAVORITES
	PULLMAN LOAF PAN	• Squared-off pan (4 by 4 inches) • Nonstick aluminized steel for easy cleanup • Light surface for even browning	USA Pan 13 by 4-inch Pullman Loaf Pan & Cover $33.95
	BAKER'S EDGE PAN	• Attached cutting grid • Dark nonstick surface for easy release	Baker's Edge Brownie Pan $34.95
	RAMEKINS	• Sturdy, high-fired porcelain (chip-resistant and safe for use in oven, broiler, microwave, and dishwasher) • For one all-purpose set, capacity of 6 ounces and diameter of 3 inches	Apilco 6-Ounce Ramekins $29 for a set of four
	BAKING STONE	• Substantial but not too heavy to handle • Dimensions of 16 by 14 inches • Clay, not cement, for evenly browned crusts	Old Stone Oven Pizza Baking Stone $59.95

SMALL APPLIANCES	ITEM	WHAT TO LOOK FOR	TEST KITCHEN FAVORITES
MUST-HAVE ITEM	FOOD PROCESSOR	• 14-cup capacity • Sharp and sturdy blades • Wide feed tube • Should come with basic blades and discs: steel blade, dough blade, shredding/slicing disc	Cuisinart Custom 14-Cup Food Processor $199.99 Mini Food Processor: Cuisinart Elite Collection 4-Cup Chopper/Grinder $59.95
	STAND MIXER	• Planetary action (stationary bowl and single mixing arm) • Powerful motor • Bowl size of at least 4½ quarts • Slightly squat bowl to keep ingredients in beater's range • Should come with basic attachments: paddle, dough hook, metal whisk	Kitchen-Aid Pro Line Series 7-Qt Bowl Lift Stand Mixer $549.95 Best Buy: KitchenAid Classic Plus Series 4.5-Quart Tilt-Head Stand Mixer $199.99

SMALL APPLIANCES	ITEM	WHAT TO LOOK FOR	TEST KITCHEN FAVORITES
MUST-HAVE ITEMS	HAND-HELD MIXER	• Lightweight model • Slim wire beaters without central post • Variety of speeds	**KitchenAid 5-Speed Ultra Power Hand Mixer** $69.99 Best Buy: **Cuisinart PowerSelect 3-Speed Hand Mixer** $26.77
	BLENDER	• Mix of straight and serrated blades at different angles • Jar with curved base • At least 44-ounce capacity • Heavy base for stability	**Vitamix 5200** $449 Best Buy: **Breville The Hemisphere Control** $199.99
	IMMERSION BLENDER	• Easy to maneuver and lightweight with a slim, grippy body • Well-designed blade and cage • Detachable handle for easy cleanup	**Braun Multiquick 5** $59.99
	ELECTRIC GRIDDLE	• Large cooking area (about 21 by 12 inches) • Attached pull-out grease trap (won't tip over) • Nonstick surface for easy cleanup	**BroilKing Professional Griddle** $99.99
	ELECTRIC JUICER	• Ideal for making a large amount of fruit or vegetable juice • Centrifugal, not masticating, model for fresher-tasting juice • 3-inch-wide feed tube • Easy to assemble and clean	**Breville Juice Fountain Plus** $149.99

SMALL APPLIANCES	ITEM	WHAT TO LOOK FOR	TEST KITCHEN FAVORITES
	ELECTRIC KETTLE	• Heats water rapidly • Secure base and wide comfortable handle • Removable filter in spout	**OXO On Clarity Cordless Glass Electric Kettle** $89.95 Best Buy: **Capresso Silver H2O Electric Kettle** $55.69
	COFFEE MAKER	• Thermal carafe that keeps coffee hot and fresh with capacity of at least 10 cups • Short brewing time (6 minutes is ideal) • Copper, not aluminum, heating element • Easy-to-fill water tank • Clear, intuitive controls	**Technivorm Moccamaster 10-Cup Coffee Maker with Thermal Carafe** $299 Best Buy: **Bonavita 8-Cup Coffee Maker with Thermal Carafe** $189.99
	MEAT GRINDER	• Grinds pounds of meat easily, even on older KitchenAid stand mixers • Mostly dishwasher safe	**KitchenAid Food Grinder Attachment** $48.74
	PORTABLE INDUCTION BURNER	• Large cooking surface for even heating of pans • Basic push buttons and dial controls for ease of use	**Max Burton Induction Cooktop** $124.25
	ICE CREAM MAKER	• Simple to use and very compact • Modestly priced • Made ice cream that rivaled the smooth texture of our favorite store-bought ice creams	**Cuisinart Automatic Frozen-Yogurt, Ice Cream & Sorbet Maker** $49.95

SMALL APPLIANCES	ITEM	WHAT TO LOOK FOR	TEST KITCHEN FAVORITES
	STOVETOP PRESSURE COOKER	• Stainless steel rather than aluminum for more durable construction that doesn't react to acidic foods • Stovetop model with low sides and wide base for easy access and better browning and heat retention • Pressure indicator that is easy to see and interpret at a glance	**Fissler Vitaquick 8 ½-Quart Pressure Cooker** $279.95 Best Buy: **Fagor Duo 8-Quart Stainless Steel Pressure Cooker** $109.95
	SLOW COOKER	• At least 6-quart capacity (4-quart capacity for small slow cookers) • Insert handles • Clear lid to see progress of food • Dishwasher-safe insert • Intuitive controls with programmable timer and warming mode	**KitchenAid 6-Quart Slow Cooker with Solid Glass Lid** $99.99
	TWO-SLOT TOASTER	• Quartz heating element for even heating • Clear window to monitor browning • Ample room for large or thick bread slices or bagels	**Magimix by Robot-Coupe Vision Toaster** $249.95
	TOASTER OVEN	• Quartz heating elements for steady, controlled heat • Roomy but compact interior • Simple to use	**The Smart Oven by Breville** $249.95 Best Buy: **Hamilton Beach Set & Forget Toaster Oven with Convection Cooking** $99.99
	TABLETOP GRILL	• Large grilling area • Easy to clean	**Delonghi Alfredo Healthy Indoor Grill** $53.99
	WAFFLE IRON	• Indicator lights and audible alert • Makes two waffles at a time • Six-point dial for customizing waffle doneness	**Cuisinart Double Belgian Waffle Maker** $99.95

SHOPPING FOR EQUIPMENT

GRILLING EQUIPMENT	ITEM	WHAT TO LOOK FOR	TEST KITCHEN FAVORITES
	GAS GRILL	• Large main grate • Built-in thermometer • Two burners for varying heat levels (three is even better) • Made of thick, heat-retaining materials such as cast aluminum and enameled steel	**Weber Spirit E-310 Gas Grill** $499
	CHARCOAL GRILL	• Sturdy construction to efficiently maintain heat • Well-designed cooking grate, handles, lids, and wheels • Generous cooking surface • Large charcoal capacity • Well-positioned air vents • Gas ignition to instantly and easily light coals • Ash catcher for easy cleanup	**Weber Performer Deluxe Charcoal Grill** $349 Best Buy: **Weber Original Kettle Premium Charcoal Grill, 22-Inch** $149
	PORTABLE CHARCOAL GRILL	• Ample cooking surface with raised lip • Cover that can be secured for travel • Lightweight but durable	**Weber Smokey Joe Gold Portable Charcoal Grill** $34.70
	SMOKER	• Large cooking area • Water pan • Multiple vents for precise temperature control	**Weber Smokey Mountain Cooker Smoker, 18"** $298.95
	CHIMNEY STARTER	• 6-quart capacity • Holes in canister so air can circulate around coals • Sturdy construction • Heat-resistant handle • Dual handle for easy control	**Weber Rapidfire Chimney Starter** $14.99

GRILLING EQUIPMENT	ITEM	WHAT TO LOOK FOR	TEST KITCHEN FAVORITES
	GRILL TONGS	• 16 inches in length • Scalloped, not sharp and serrated, edges • Open and close easily • Lightweight • Moderate amount of springy tension	**OXO Good Grips 16-Inch Locking Tongs** $14.99
	GRILL BRUSH	• Long handle • Replaceable, long-lasting steel pads for scrubbing	**Grill Wizard 18-inch China Grill Brush** $31.50
	GRILL SPATULA	• Handle at least 12 inches in length • Sharp cutting edge	**Weber Original Stainless Steel Spatula** $14.99
	BARBECUE BASTING BRUSH	• Silicone bristles • Angled brush head • Handle between 8 and 13 inches • Heat-resistant	**Elizabeth Karmel's Super Silicone Angled Barbecue Brush** $9.16
	GRILL GLOVES	• Excellent heat protection • Gloves, rather than mitts, for dexterity • Long sleeves to protect forearms	**Steven Raichlen Ultimate Suede Grilling Gloves** $29.99 per pair
	SKEWERS	• Flat and metal • 3/16 inch thick	**Norpro 12-Inch Stainless Steel Skewers** $6.85 for a set of 6
	RIB RACK	• Sturdily supports six racks of ribs • Doubles as roasting rack (when flipped upside down) • Nonstick coating for easy cleanup	**Charcoal Companion Reversible Rib Rack** $14.95
	GRILL LIGHTER	• Flexible neck • Refillable chamber with large, easy-to-read fuel window • Comfortable grip	**Zippo Flexible Neck Utility Lighter** $18.35

GRILLING EQUIPMENT	ITEM	WHAT TO LOOK FOR	TEST KITCHEN FAVORITES
	ELECTRIC CHARCOAL STARTER	• Long, offset heating element • Quick-to-heat	**Grill Dome Rapid-Lite Electric Charcoal Starters** $34.95
	OUTDOOR GRILL PAN	• Narrow slits and raised sides so food can't fall through or off • Sturdy construction with handles	**Weber Professional-Grade Grill Pan** $19.99
	SMOKER BOX	• Cast iron for slow heating and steady smoke • Easy to fill, empty, and clean	**GrillPro Cast Iron Smoker Box by Onward Manufacturing Company** $12.79
	WOOD, FOR SMOKING	• Hickory wood for bold, smoky flavor • Long-lasting chunks for charcoal grills • Wood chips for gas grills	**Little difference among various brands**
	VERTICAL ROASTER	• Helps poultry cook evenly • 8-inch shaft keeps chicken above fat and drippings in pan • Attached basin catches drippings for pan sauce • Sturdy construction	**Vertical Roaster with Infuser by Norpro** $22.11 Best Buy: **Elizabeth Karmel's Grill Friends Porcelain Chicken Sitter** $11.99
	PROPANE INDICATOR	• Easy-to-read dial • Accurately measures propane by weight	**Grill Gauge Propane Tank Scale** $13.99
	GRILL LIGHT	• Bright, even, wide spread of warm light • Stood freely on side tables and clipped to handles	**Ivation Multipurpose Gooseneck 7-LED Dimmable Clip Light** $24.99

SPECIALTY PIECES	ITEM	WHAT TO LOOK FOR	TEST KITCHEN FAVORITES
	APPLE CORER	• Comfortable grip with offset handle • Sharp teeth • Wide blade diameter	**CuisiPro Apple Corer** $9.95
	APPLE SLICER	• Sharp, serrated corer with 1-inch diameter • Ability to cut 8 or 16 slices • Comfortable handle	**Williams-Sonoma Dial-a-Slice Apple Divider** $19.95
	CORN STRIPPER	• Safer than using chef's knife • Attached cup to catch kernels • Comfortable grip and sharp blade	**OXO Good Grips Corn Stripper** $11.99
	TOMATO CORER	• Sharp teeth make easy, clean cuts • Lightweight, rounded-off plastic handle • Comfortable head-handle combination	**Norpro Tomato Core It** $2.99
	NUT CHOPPER	• Sharp, sturdy stainless steel chopping tines • Dishwasher-safe	**Progressive International Heavy Duty Nut Chopper** $8.89
	GRILL PAN	• Cast-iron pan with enamel coating for heat retention and easy cleanup • Tall ridges (4 to 5.5 mm high) to keep food above rendered fat • Generous cooking area	**Staub 12-Inch American Square Grill Pan and Press** $219.95 Best Buy: **Lodge Pre-Seasoned Square Grill Pan & Ribbed Panini Press** $18.97 (press sold separately for $14.58)

SHOPPING FOR EQUIPMENT

SPECIALTY PIECES	ITEM	WHAT TO LOOK FOR	TEST KITCHEN FAVORITES
	STOVETOP GRIDDLE	• Anodized aluminum for even heating • Nonstick coating • Lightweight (about 4 pounds) • Heat-resistant loop handles • At least 17 by 9 inches (large enough to span two burners) • Pour spout for draining grease	**Anolon Advanced Double Burner Griddle** $48.95
	OYSTER KNIFE	• Sturdy, flat blade with slightly curved tip for easy penetration • Slim, nonstick handle for secure, comfortable grip	**R. Murphy New Haven Oyster Knife** $16.65
	SEAFOOD SCISSORS	• Curved blade neatly snips off shells • Tidy removal of shrimp vein	**RSVP International Endurance Seafood Scissors** $14.99
	SILICONE MICROWAVE LID	• Thin, silicone round to cover splatter-prone food during microwave heating • Easy to clean • Doubles as jar opener	**Piggy Steamer** $18
	PIPING SET	• Contains all of the essentials: twelve 16-inch pastry bags; four plastic couplers; and the following Wilton tips: #4 round, #12 round, #70 leaf, #103 petal, #2D large closed star, #1M open star • All parts available at most crafts stores	**Test Kitchen Self-Assembled à La Carte Decorating Set** $12.20
	CHEESE WIRE	• Comfortable plastic handles • Narrow wire	**Fante's Handled Cheese Wire** $2.99
	PIZZA WHEEL	• Clear plastic wheel to prevent damage to pans • Comfortable, soft-grip handle	**OXO Good Grips 4-Inch Pizza Wheel** $12.99
	POTATO RICER	• Large hopper that can hold 1¼ cups sliced potatoes • Interchangeable fine and coarse disks • Sturdy, ergonomic handles	**RSVP International Potato Ricer** $13.95

SPECIALTY PIECES	ITEM	WHAT TO LOOK FOR	TEST KITCHEN FAVORITES
	TORTILLA WARMER	• Triple-layered sides with two layers of fabric around sheet of insulating plastic • 12-inch diameter to fit large wraps	**IMUSA 12-Inch Cloth Tortilla Warmer** $5.99
	INSULATED FOOD CARRIER	• Keeps food piping hot for over 3 hours • Fits two 13 by 9-inch baking dishes • Handy zippered pocket holds serving utensils	**Rachael Ray Expandable Lasagna Lugger** $26.95
	CUPCAKE AND CAKE CARRIER	• Fits both round and square cakes and cupcakes • Snap locks • Nonskid base • Collapses for easy storage	**Progressive Collapsible Cupcake and Cake Carrier** $29.95
	CAKE LIFTER	• Sturdy but small and slightly flexible • Rounded corners for visibility • Comfortable offset handle	**Fat Daddio's Cake Lifter** $11.88
	CAKE STAND	• Elevated rotating stand so you can hold the spatula steady for easy frosting • Solid, light construction	**Winco Revolving Cake Decorating Stand** $29.98
	CREAM WHIPPER	• Responsive lever better control and easy piping • Grips on handle and neck for easy refilling and cleanup	**iSi Gourmet Whip** $99.27
	SPICE/COFFEE GRINDER	• Electric, not manual, grinders • Deep bowl to hold ample amount of coffee beans • Good to have two, one each for coffee grinding and spice grinding	**Krups Fast-Touch Coffee Mill, Model 203** $19.99

SHOPPING FOR EQUIPMENT

SPECIALTY PIECES	ITEM	WHAT TO LOOK FOR	TEST KITCHEN FAVORITES
	INNOVATIVE TEAPOT	• Contained ultrafine-mesh strainer keeps tea leaf dregs separate • One-piece design for easy cleaning	**Adagio Teas IngenuiTEA** $14.95
	TRAVEL MUG	• Simple, leakproof lid design • Good heat retention • Easy-to-clean and dishwasher safe	**Timolino Icon 16-Ounces Signature Vacuum Travel Mug** $28
	WATER BOTTLE	• Clear plastic sides makes it easy to fill • Bi-level twist-on lid for easy sipping • Handy carrying loop	**Nathan LittleShot** $11.99
	WINE OPENER	• Durable design • Teflon-coated worm	**Pulltap's Classic Evolution Corkscrew by Pulltex** $39.95
	ELECTRIC WINE OPENER	• Sturdy, quiet corkscrew • Broad base that rests firmly on bottle	**Cuisinart Cordless Wine Opener with Vacuum Sealer** $39.95
	WINE AERATOR	• Long, tubelike design that exposes wine to air as it is being poured • Neat, hands-free aerating	**Nuance Wine Finer** $19.95

The Complete Cook's Country TV Show Cookbook

SPECIALTY PIECES	ITEM	WHAT TO LOOK FOR	TEST KITCHEN FAVORITES
	COCKTAIL SHAKER	• Holds at least 18 ounces to make one or two cocktails at once • Comfortable carafe-like shape • Wide mouth for easy filling, muddling, and cleaning	Cobbler Style: **Tovolo Stainless Steel 4-in-1 Cocktail Shaker** $29.99 Boston Style: **The Boston Shaker Professional Boston Shaker, Weighted** $14.50
	BEER SAVERS	• Fit both glass and plastic bottles • Preserves carbonation for up to 2 days	**Savebrands Beer Savers** $6.99 for six-pack
	COOLER	• Insulating layer of plastic lining • Lightweight, durable, sturdy, and easy to move, even when full • Easy to clean	**California Cooler Bags T-Rex Large Collapsible Rolling Cooler** $75
	SELTZER MAKER	• Easy to use and easy to control level of fizz • CO_2 canisters are long lasting and convenient to exchange at retail stores	**SodaStream Source Starter Kit** $99.95
	VACUUM SEALER	• Countertop, heat-sealed model • Works well with wide variety of bags, canisters, and rolls	**Weston Professional Advantage Vacuum Sealer** $189.99
	COMPOST BUCKET	• Plastic pail to collect food scraps for composter • Carbon filter prevents odors from escaping and allows oxygen to enter so decomposition can occur • Easy to open lid that latches securely in place • 2.4-gallon capacity	**Exaco Trading Kitchen Compost Waste Collector** $19.98

SPECIALTY PIECES	ITEM	WHAT TO LOOK FOR	TEST KITCHEN FAVORITES
MUST-HAVE ITEM	FIRE EXTINGUISHER	• Fast and effective • Intuitive to use and easy to lift • Powerful spray worked well on grease fire and burning fabric	**Kidde ABC Multipurpose Home Fire Extinguisher** $25.99

KITCHEN SUPPLIES	ITEM	WHAT TO LOOK FOR	TEST KITCHEN FAVORITES
MUST-HAVE ITEMS	PARCHMENT PAPER	• Sturdy paper for heavy doughs • Easy release of baked goods • At least 14 inches wide	**Little difference among various brands**
	PLASTIC WRAP	• Clings tightly and resticks well • Packaging with sharp teeth that aren't exposed (to avoid snags on clothing and skin) • Adhesive pad to hold cut end of wrap	**Glad Cling Wrap Clear Plastic** $1.20 per 100 square feet
	BUTTER SAVER	• Fits the end of standard-size stick of butter • Kept butter from picking up off-flavors for more than a week • Measures 1 tablespoon	**Savebrands Butter Saver** $4.99
	PAPER PLATES	• Roomy eating surface with steep lip • Thick paper holds up to 2 pounds of food	**Hefty Super Strong Paper Plates** $2.99 for 16 plates
	PLASTIC FOOD STORAGE CONTAINER	• Snap-style seal with ridge on underside to ensure tight seal • Low, flat rectangle for easy storage and more efficient heating and chilling • Made of plastic free of BPA (bisphenol-A)	**Snapware Airtight** $7.99 for 8-cup rectangle

KITCHEN SUPPLIES	ITEM	WHAT TO LOOK FOR	TEST KITCHEN FAVORITES
	DISH TOWEL	• Thin cotton for absorbency and flexibility • Dries glassware without streaks • Washes clean without shrinking	**Williams-Sonoma Striped Towels** $19.95 for set of four
	APRON	• Adjustable neck strap and long strings • Full coverage; chest area reinforced with extra layer of fabric • Stains wash out completely	**Bragard Travail Bib Apron** $27.95
	LIQUID DISH DETERGENT	• High concentration of surfactants to wash away oil • Clean scent	**Mrs. Meyer's Clean Day Liquid Dish Soap, Lavender** $3.99 for 16 fluid ounces
	DISH DRYING RACK	• Two roomy utensil holders • Seven-slot knife block • Ledge that can hang four wineglasses upside down for spot-free drying • Raised feet to hold it up off the counter	Innovative, Large: **Simple Human Steel Frame Dishrack** $63.57
		• Readily fits smaller items • Folds flat for easy storage • Best choice for small spaces or light loads	Innovative, Small: **Progressive Prepworks Collapsible Over-The-Sink Dish Drainer** $24.99
		• Fits dishes for a family of four • Angled mat tidily drains off water	Traditional/Best Buy: **Rubbermaid Antimicrobial Sink Drainer, Large, and Antimicrobial Drain Board, Large** $10.99 for basket, $7.38 for mat

SHOPPING FOR EQUIPMENT

STOCKING YOUR PANTRY

Using the best ingredients is one way to guarantee success in the kitchen. But how do you know what to buy? Shelves are filled with a dizzying array of choices—and price does not equal quality. Over the years, the test kitchen's blind tasting panels have evaluated thousands of ingredients, brand by brand, side by side, plain and in prepared applications, to determine which brands you can trust and which brands to avoid. In the chart that follows, we share the results, revealing our top-rated choices and the attributes that made them stand out among the competition. And because our test kitchen accepts no support from product manufacturers, you can trust our ratings. See AmericasTestKitchen.com for updates to these tastings.

TEST KITCHEN FAVORITE	WHY WE LIKE IT	RUNNERS-UP
ANCHOVIES King Oscar Anchovies–Flat Fillets in Olive oil	• Right amount of salt • Savory without being fishy • Firm, meaty texture • Minimal bones • Aged 4 to 6 months	Ortiz Anchovies in Olive Oil
APPLESAUCE Musselman's Lite	• An unusual ingredient, sucralose, sweetens this applesauce without overpowering its fresh, bright apple flavor • Pinch of salt boosts flavor above weak, bland, and too-sweet competitors • Coarse, almost chunky texture, not slimy like applesauces sweetened with corn syrup	Musselman's Home Style
BACON, SUPERMARKET Farmland Thick Sliced Bacon and Plumrose Premium Thick Sliced	• Good balance of saltiness and sweetness • Smoky and full flavored, not one-dimensional • Very meaty, not too fatty or insubstantial • Crisp yet hearty texture, not tough or dry	Boar's Head Brand Naturally Smoked Sliced and Hormel Black Label Original
BARBECUE SAUCE Bull's-Eye Original	• Spicy, fresh tomato taste • Good balance of tanginess, smokiness, and sweetness • Robust flavor from molasses • Sweetened with sugar and molasses, not high-fructose corn syrup, which caramelizes and burns quickly	
BEANS, CANNED BAKED B&M Vegetarian	• Firm and pleasant texture with some bite • Sweetened with molasses for complexity and depth	Bush's Best Original and Van Camp's Original

TEST KITCHEN FAVORITE	WHY WE LIKE IT	RUNNERS-UP
BEANS, CANNED BLACK **Bush's Best**	• Clean, mild, and slightly earthy flavor • Firm, almost al dente texture, not mushy or pasty • Good amount of salt	Goya and Progresso
BEANS, CANNED CHICKPEAS **Pastene**	• Firm yet tender texture bests pasty and dry competitors • Clean chickpea flavor • Enough salt to enhance but not overwhelm the flavor	Goya
BEANS, CANNED RED KIDNEY **Goya**	• Sweet with strong bean flavor • Beautiful red, plump beans • Smooth, creamy texture, not mushy, chalky, or too firm • Flavor boost from added sugar and salt	S&W
BEANS, CANNED WHITE **Goya**	• Clean, earthy flavor • Smooth, creamy interior with tender skins • Not full of broken beans like some competitors	Bush's Best Cannellini Beans White Kidney Beans
BREAD, MULTIGRAIN **Nature's Own Specialty 12 Grain**	• Substantial, chewy slices • Nutty, hearty seeds throughout and topped with rolled oats • Uses no white flour	Arnold 12 Grain and Pepperidge Farm 15 Grain
BREAD, WHITE SANDWICH **Arnold Country Classics**	• Subtle sweetness, not tasteless or sour • Perfect structure, not too dry or too soft	Pepperidge Farm Farmhouse Hearty White
BREAD, WHOLE-WHEAT SANDWICH **Arnold Whole Grains 100% Whole Wheat Bread**	• Mild nuttiness with clean wheat flavor and a touch of sweetness • Tender and chewy with crunchy flecks of bulgur on the crust	Pepperidge Farm Farmhouse 100% Whole Wheat Bread
BREAD CRUMBS, PANKO **Ian's Panko Breadcrumbs, Original Style**	• Crisp, with a substantial crunch • Not too delicate, stale, sandy, or gritty • Oil-free and without seasonings or undesirable artificial flavors	

TEST KITCHEN FAVORITE	WHY WE LIKE IT	RUNNERS-UP
BROTH, BEEF **Better Than Bouillon Roasted Beef Base**	• Contains good amount of salt and multiple powerful flavor enhancers • Paste is economical, stores easily, and dissolves quickly in hot water	
BROTH, CHICKEN **Swanson Chicken Stock**	• Strong chicken flavor, not watery, beefy, or vegetal • Hearty and pleasant aroma • Roasted notes, not sour, rancid, or salty like some competitors • Flavor-boosting ingredients include carrots, celery, and onions	Better Than Bouillon Chicken Base
BROTH, VEGETARIAN **Orrington Farms Vegan Chicken Flavored Broth Base & Seasoning**	• Savory depth without off-tasting vegetable undertones • Easy to store • Yeast extract adds depth and richness	Swanson Certified Organic Vegetable Broth
BROWNIE MIX **Ghirardelli Chocolate Supreme and Barefoot Contessa Outrageous Brownie Mix**	• Rich, balanced chocolate flavor from both natural and Dutch-processed cocoa powders • Moist, chewy, and fudgy with perfect texture	
BUTTER, UNSALTED **Plugrá European-Style**	• Sweet and creamy • Complex tang and grassy flavor • Moderate amount of butterfat so that it's decadent and glossy but not so rich that baked goods are greasy	Land O'Lakes and Vermont Creamery European-Style
BUTTER, SALTED **Lurpak Slightly Salted Butter**	• Made with cultured cream • Rich, creamy texture	Kate's Homemade, Plugrá European-Style, Land O'Lakes, Kerrygold Pure Irish, Challenge, and Organic Valley
CHEESE, AMERICAN, PRESLICED **Boar's Head**	• Strong cheesy flavor, unlike some competitors • Higher content of cheese culture contributes to better flavor	Kraft Deli Deluxe
CHEESE, ASIAGO **BelGioioso**	• Sharp, tangy, and complex flavor, not mild • Firm and not too dry • Melts, shreds, and grates well	

TEST KITCHEN FAVORITE	WHY WE LIKE IT	RUNNERS-UP
CHEESE, BLUE **Stella**	• Milder cheese is better for dressings • Crumbly texture • Nicely balanced flavor with mild sweetness	Danish Blue
CHEESE, CHEDDAR, SHARP **Cabot Vermont Sharp Cheddar**	• Buttery, creamy texture • Nutty, complex sharpness	Tillamook, Cracker Barrel, Kraft Natural, Kerrygold Aged, and Sargento Tastings Aged Wisconsin
CHEESE, CHEDDAR, EXTRA-SHARP **Cabot Private Stock**	• Balance of salty, creamy, and sweet flavors • Considerable but well-rounded sharpness, not overwhelming • Firm, crumbly texture, not moist, rubbery, or springy • Aged at least 12 months for complex flavor	Cabot Extra-Sharp Cheddar
CHEESE, CHEDDAR, PRESLICED **Tillamook Presliced Sharp**	• Slightly crumbly, not rubbery or processed, texture characteristic of block cheddar • Strong, tangy, and salty flavor, not bland or too mild	Cabot All Natural Sharp and Cracker Barrel Natural Sharp
CHEESE, CHEDDAR, ARTISINAL **Milton Creamery Prairie Breeze**	• Earthy complexity with nutty, buttery, and fruity flavors • Dry and crumbly with crystalline crunch, not rubbery or overly moist • Aged no more than 12 months to prevent overly sharp flavor	Cabot Cellars at Jasper Hill Clothbound Cheddar
CHEESE, CHEDDAR, LOW-FAT **Cracker Barrel Reduced Fat Sharp**	• Ample creaminess • Strong cheesy flavor • Good for cooking	
CHEESE, COTTAGE **Hood Country Style**	• Rich, well-seasoned, and buttery flavor • Velvety, creamy texture • Pillowy curds	Friendship 4% California Style and Breakstone's 4% Small Curd
CHEESE, CREAM **Philadelphia Cream Cheese Brick Original**	• Rich, tangy, and milky flavor • Thick, creamy texture, not pasty, waxy, or chalky	Philadelphia Cream Cheese Spreads Original
CHEESE, FETA **Mt. Vikos Traditional Feta**	• Strong tangy, salty flavor • Creamy, dense texture • Pleasing crumbly texture	Valbreso Feta

TEST KITCHEN FAVORITE	WHY WE LIKE IT	RUNNERS-UP
CHEESE, FONTINA For eating out of hand: **Fontina Val d'Aosta**	• Strong, earthy aroma • Somewhat elastic texture with small irregular holes • Grassy, nutty flavor—but can be overpowering in cooked dishes	
For cooking: **Italian Fontina**	• Semisoft, super-creamy texture • Mildly tangy, nutty flavor • Melts well	
CHEESE, GOAT **Laura Chenel's Chèvre**	• Rich-tasting, grassy, tangy flavor • Smooth and creamy both unheated and baked • High salt content	Vermont Creamery, Chevrion, and Cypress Grove
CHEESE, GRUYÈRE **1655 Le Gruyère**	• Aged between 12 and 14 months • Crystalline structure with dense, fudgy texture • Deeply aged, caramelized, grassy flavors shine through even when cooked	Mifroma Le Gruyère Cavern Reserve
CHEESE, MOZZARELLA **Polly-O Whole Milk Mozzarella Cheese**	• Creamy, rich flavor with a hint of salt reminiscent of fresh mozzarella • Elastic but not gooey when melted	Galbani Whole Milk Mozzarella
CHEESE, PARMESAN, SUPERMARKET **Boar's Head Parmigiano-Reggiano**	• Rich and complex flavor balances tanginess and nuttiness • Dry, crumbly texture yet creamy with a crystalline crunch, not rubbery or dense • Aged a minimum of 12 months for better flavor and texture	Il Villagio Parmigiano-Reggiano 18 Month and Sarvecchio Parmesan
CHEESE, PARMESAN PRESHREDDED **Sargento Artisan Blends Shredded Parmesan Cheese**	• Mix of small and large shreds • Blend of 10- and 18-month-aged Parmesan • Rich, nutty flavor	Kraft Natural
CHEESE, PEPPERJACK **Boar's Head Monterey Jack Cheese with Jalapeño**	• Buttery, tangy cheese • Clean, balanced flavor with assertive spice	Tillamook Pepper Jack Cheese

TEST KITCHEN FAVORITE	WHY WE LIKE IT	RUNNERS-UP
CHEESE, PROVOLONE **Provolone Vernengo**	• Bold, nutty, and tangy flavor, not plasticky or bland • Firm, dry texture	
CHEESE, RICOTTA **Belgioioso Ricotta Con Latte Whole Milk Ricotta Cheese**	• Rich, dense consistency • Slight sweetness thanks to sweet whey and small amount of milk	Galbani Whole Milk Ricotta Cheese and Calabro Whole Milk Ricotta Cheese
CHEESE, SWISS For eating out of hand: **Edelweiss Creamery Emmenthaler**	• Subtle flavor with sweet, buttery, nutty, and fruity notes • Firm yet gently giving texture, not rubbery • Aged longer for better flavor, resulting in larger eyes • Mildly pungent yet balanced	Emmi Kaltbach
For cooking: **Boar's Head Gold Label Switzerland Swiss Cheese**	• Mildly nutty flavor • Smooth texture when melted	
For eating out of hand or cooking: **Emmi Emmenthaler Cheese AOC**	• Creamy texture • Salty mildness preferable for grilled cheese sandwiches	
CHICKEN, WHOLE **Mary's Free Range Air-Chilled**	• Great, savory chicken flavor • Very tender • Air-chilled for minimum water retention and cleaner flavor	Bell & Evans Air-Chilled Premium Fresh
CHICKEN, BREASTS, BONELESS SKINLESS **Bell & Evans Air-Chilled Boneless, Skinless**	• Juicy and tender with clean chicken flavor • Not salted or brined • Air-chilled • Aged on bone for at least six hours after slaughter for significantly more tender meat	Springer Mountain Farms and Eberly's Free Range Young Organic
CHILI POWDER **Morton & Bassett**	• Bold, full-flavored heat • Multidimensional flavor from a blend of cayenne and other chiles • Spices that complement but don't overwhelm the chiles	Penzeys Spices

TEST KITCHEN FAVORITE	WHY WE LIKE IT	RUNNERS-UP
CHOCOLATE, DARK **Ghirardelli 60% Cacao Bittersweet Chocolate Premium Baking Bar**	• Creamy texture, not grainy or chalky • Complex flavor with notes of cherry and wine with slight smokiness • Balance of sweetness and bitterness	Callebaut Intense Dark L-60-40NV (60% Cacao)
CHOCOLATE, MILK **Dove Silky Smooth**	• Intense, full, rich chocolate flavor • Super-creamy texture from abundant milk fat and cocoa butter • Not overwhelmingly sweet	Endangered Species All-Natural Smooth and Green & Black's Organic
CHOCOLATE, DARK CHIPS **Ghirardelli 60% Cacao Bittersweet**	• Intense, complex flavor beats one-dimensional flavor of competitors • Low sugar content highlights chocolate flavor • High amount of cocoa butter ensures creamy, smooth texture, not gritty or grainy • Wider, flatter shape and high percentage of fat help chips melt better in cookie	Hershey's Special Dark Mildly Sweet
CHOCOLATE, MILK CHIPS **Hershey's**	• Bold chocolate flavor outshines too-sweet, weak chocolate flavor of other chips • Complex with caramel and nutty notes • Higher fat content makes texture creamier than grainy, artificial competitors	
CHOCOLATE, UNSWEETENED **Hershey's Unsweetened Baking Bar**	• Well-rounded, complex flavor • Assertive chocolate flavor and deep notes of cocoa	Valrhona Cacao Pate Extra 100% and Scharffen Berger Unsweetened Dark
CHOCOLATE, WHITE CHIPS **Guittard Choc-Au-Lait**	• Creamy texture, not waxy or crunchy • Silky smooth meltability from high fat content • Complex flavor like high-quality real chocolate, no artificial or off-flavors	Ghirardelli Classic White
CIDER, HARD **Angry Orchard Crisp Apple Hard Cider**	• Crisp and refreshing • Strong apple sweetness • Juicy complexity	Strongbow Gold Apple and Woodchuck Amber
CINNAMON **Morton & Bassett Spices Ground Cinnamon**	• The perfect balance of sweet and spicy • Mellow in baked applications	Penzeys Vietnamese Cinnamon Ground and McCormick Ground Cinnamon

TEST KITCHEN FAVORITE	WHY WE LIKE IT	RUNNERS-UP
COCOA POWDER **Hershey's Natural Unsweetened**	• Full, strong chocolate flavor • Complex flavor with notes of coffee, cinnamon, orange, and spice	Droste
COCONUT MILK **Aroy-D**	• Velvety, luxurious, and not overly thick texture • Balanced, clean coconut flavor	Goya Coconut Milk (Leche de Coco)
COCONUT, SHREDDED **Now Real Food Organic Unsweetened Coconut, Shredded**	• Nutty, tropical flavor • Fluffy, crisp texture	Woodstock Foods Organic
COFFEE, WHOLE BEAN, SUPERMARKET, Dark Roast: **Millstone Colombian Supremo**	• Deep, complex, and balanced flavor without metallic, overly acidic, or otherwise unpleasant notes • Smoky and chocolaty with a bitter, not burnt, finish	Starbucks Coffee House Blend
Medium Roast: **Peet's Coffee Café Domingo**	• Extremely smooth but bold-tasting with a strong finish • Rich chocolate and toast flavors • Few defective beans, low acidity, and optimal moisture	Millstone Breakfast Blend
COFFEE, DECAF **Maxwell House Decaf Original Roast**	• Smooth, mellow flavor without being acidic or harsh • Complex, with a slightly nutty aftertaste • Made with only flavorful Arabica beans	Peet's Decaf House Blend Ground and Starbucks Coffee Decaf House Blend
CORNMEAL **Arrowhead Mills Organic Yellow**	• Clean, pure corn flavor comes from using whole-grain kernels • Ideal texture resembling slightly damp, fine sand, not too fine or too coarse	

STOCKING YOUR PANTRY

TEST KITCHEN FAVORITE	WHY WE LIKE IT	RUNNERS-UP
CREOLE SEASONING Tony Chachere's Original Creole Seasoning	• Strong garlic and red pepper notes • Vibrant and zesty with a punch of heat	McCormick Perfect Pinch Cajun Seasoning
CURRY POWDER Penzeys Sweet	• Balanced, neither too sweet nor too hot • Complex and vivid earthy flavor, not thin, bland, or one-dimensional NOTE: Available through mail order, 800-741-7787 or penzeys.com	
DINNER ROLLS, FROZEN Pepperidge Farm Stone Baked Artisan French Dinner Rolls	• Tender on the inside with crispy crust • Has only seven ingredients • Tastes homemade, with a hint of salt	
EGG WHITES, PROCESSED Eggology 100% Egg Whites	• Works well in egg white omelets • Pasteurized; safe for use in uncooked applications • Make satisfactory baked goods	
FIVE-SPICE POWDER Frontier Natural Products Co-op	• Nice depth, not one-dimensional • Balanced heat and sweetness	Dynasty Chinese Five Spices, McCormick Gourmet Collection Chinese Five Spice, Dean & DeLuca Five Spice Blend, and Morton & Bassett Chinese Five Spice
FLOUR, ALL-PURPOSE King Arthur Unbleached Enriched	• Fresh, toasty flavor • No metallic taste or other off-flavors • Consistent results across recipes • Made tender, flaky pie crust, hearty biscuits, crisp cookies, and chewy, sturdy bread	Gold Medal Enriched Bleached Presifted, Gold Medal Unbleached, and Heckers/Ceresota Unbleached Enriched Presifted
Pillsbury Unbleached Enriched	• Clean, toasty, and hearty flavor • No metallic or other off-flavors • Consistent results across recipes • Made flaky pie crust, chewy cookies, and tender biscuits, muffins, and cakes	
FLOUR, WHOLE-WHEAT King Arthur Premium 100%	• Finely ground for hearty but not overly coarse texture in bread and pancakes • Sweet, nutty flavor	Bob's Red Mill Organic

TEST KITCHEN FAVORITE	WHY WE LIKE IT	RUNNERS-UP
FRENCH FRIES, FROZEN **Alexia Organic Yukon Select Fries**	• Crispy exteriors with fluffy, creamy interiors • Earthy, potato-y flavor	Ore-Ida Golden Fries
GIARDINIERA **Pastene**	• Sharp, vinegary tang • Crunchy mix of vegetables • Mellow heat that's potent but not overpowering	Scala Hot
GNOCCHI **Gia Russa Gnocchi with Potato**	• Tender, pillowlike texture • Nice potato flavor • Slightly sour taste that disappears when paired with tomato sauce	De Cecco
GRITS **Anson Mills**	• Full, ripe, fresh corn flavor • Nice chew while still thick and creamy	Arrowhead Mills and Bob's Red Mill
HAM, BLACK FOREST DELI **Dietz & Watson**	• Good texture • Nice ham flavor	
HAM, COUNTRY **Harper's Grand Champion Whole Country Ham**	• Aged 3 to 6 months • Porky and complex, with robust flavor and balanced salt levels • Available online or in some southern supermarkets	Burgers' Smokehouse Ready to Cook Country Ham and Edwards Virginia Traditions Uncooked Virginia Ham
HAM, SPIRAL-SLICED, BONE-IN **Johnston County Spiral-Sliced Smoked Ham**	• Tender and moist • Nice smokiness and just enough sweetness	Burgers' Smokehouse Spiral-Sliced City Ham and Applewood Farms Spiral-Sliced Ham

STOCKING YOUR PANTRY

TEST KITCHEN FAVORITE	WHY WE LIKE IT	RUNNERS-UP
HOISIN SAUCE **Kikkoman**	• Balances sweet, salty, pungent, and spicy flavors • Initial burn mellows into harmonious and aromatic blend without bitterness	
HONEY **Nature Nate's 100% Pure Raw and Unfiltered Honey**	• Bold notes of citrus, clover, and anise • Mild sweetness and slight acidity	Aunt Sue's Raw-Wild Honey and Sue Bee Clover Honey
HORSERADISH **Boar's Head Pure Horseradish**	• No preservatives, just horseradish, vinegar, and salt (found in refrigerated section) • Natural flavor and hot without being overpowering	Ba-Tampte Prepared Horseradish
HOT DOGS **Nathan's Famous Skinless Beef Franks**	• Meaty, robust, and hearty flavor, not sweet, sour, or too salty • Juicy but not greasy • Firm, craggy texture, not rubbery, mushy, or chewy	Kayem Skinless Beef Hot Dogs
HOT FUDGE SAUCE **Hershey's Hot Fudge Topping**	• True fudge flavor, not weak or overly sweet • Thick, smooth, and buttery texture	
HOT SAUCE **Huy Fong Sriracha Hot Chili Sauce and Frank's RedHot Original**	• Right combination of punchy heat, saltiness, sweetness, and garlic • Full, rich flavor • Mild heat that's not too hot	Original Louisiana and Tapatio Salsa Picante
ICE CREAM BARS **Dove Bar Vanilla Ice Cream with Milk Chocolate**	• Rich, prominent chocolate flavor • Thick, crunchy chocolate coating • Dense, creamy, ice cream with pure vanilla flavor • Milk chocolate, not coconut oil, listed first in coating ingredients	Häagen-Dazs Vanilla Milk Chocolate All Natural, Blue Bunny Big Alaska, and Good Humor Milk Chocolate
ICE CREAM CONES **Joy Classic Waffle Cones**	• Lightly sweet, with vanilla, toasty, and nutty flavors • Crunchy and crisp but not overly hard • Individual paper jackets keep things neat	Joy Sugar Cones, Keebler Waffle Cones, Keebler Sugar Cones, and Comet (Nabisco) Sugar Cones

TEST KITCHEN FAVORITE	WHY WE LIKE IT	RUNNERS-UP
ICE CREAM, CHOCOLATE **Friendly's Rich & Creamy Classic Chocolate**	• Ultra-creamy texture • Classic chocolate taste	Edy's Grand Rich & Creamy Chocolate
ICE CREAM, VANILLA **Ben & Jerry's**	• Complex yet balanced vanilla flavor from real vanilla extract • Sweetness solely from sugar, rather than corn syrup • Creamy richness from both egg yolks and small amount of stabilizers	Häagen-Dazs Vanilla
ICED TEA Loose leaf: **Tazo Iced Black Tea**	• Distinctive flavor with herbal notes • Balanced level of strength and astringency	Luzianne and Tetley Premium Blend
Bottled, with lemon: **Lipton PureLeaf**	• Bright, balanced, and natural tea and lemon flavors • Uses concentrated tea leaves to extract flavor	Gold Peak
JUICE, GRAPEFRUIT **Natalie's 100% Florida Grapefruit Juice**	• Balanced and bright flavor, not too sweet • Clean and refreshing crispness	Florida's Natural Ruby Red Grapefruit Juice
JUICE, ORANGE **Natalie's 100% Florida Orange Juice**	• Blend of Hamlin, Pineapple, and Valencia oranges • Fresh, sweet, and fruity flavor without overly acidic, sour, or from-concentrate taste • Gentler pasteurization helps retain fresh-squeezed flavor • Pleasant amount of light pulp	Tropicana Pure Premium 100% Pure and Natural with Some Pulp
JUICE, FROZEN ORANGE CONCENTRATE **Minute Maid Original Frozen Concentrated Orange Juice**	• Full-bodied orange flavor • Good texture, includes some pulp	Tropicana 100% Juice Frozen Concentrated Orange Juice
KETCHUP **Heinz Organic**	• Clean, pure sweetness from sugar, not high-fructose corn syrup • Bold, harmonious punch of saltiness, sweetness, tang, and tomato flavor	Hunt's and Simply Heinz

TEST KITCHEN FAVORITE	WHY WE LIKE IT	RUNNERS-UP
LEMONADE Natalie's Natural Lemonade	• Natural-tasting lemon flavor from 20 percent real lemon juice, without artificial flavors or off-notes • Perfect balance of tartness and sweetness, unlike many overly sweet competitors	Simply Lemonade and Minute Maid Premium Frozen Concentrate
MACARONI & CHEESE Kraft Homestyle Macaroni & Cheese Classic Cheddar Cheese Sauce	• Reinforces flavor with blue and cheddar cheeses • Uses creamy, clingy liquid cheese sauce • Dry noodles, rather than frozen, for substantial texture and bite • Crunchy, buttery breadcrumb topping	Kraft Velveeta Original
MAPLE SYRUP Uncle Luke's Pure Maple Syrup, Grade A Dark Amber	• Inexpensive • Dark, molasses-y color • Rich caramel flavor that tastes pleasantly toasty in pie	Highland Sugarworks, Coombs Family Farms, Anderson's, Maple Grove Farms, Maple Gold, Spring Tree, and Camp Pure
MAYONNAISE Blue Plate Real Mayonnaise	• Great balance of taste and texture • Tastes close to homemade NOTE: While it's one of the top-selling brands in the country, you'll have to mail-order it unless you live in the South or Southeast	Hellmann's Real Mayonnaise, Hellmann's Light Mayonnaise, Spectrum Organic Mayonnaise, and Duke's Mayonnaise
MAYONNAISE, LIGHT Hellmann's Light	• Bright, balanced flavor close to full-fat counterpart, not overly sweet • Not as creamy as full-fat but passable texture NOTE: Hellmann's is known as Best Foods west of the Rocky Mountains	Hellmann's Canola Cholesterol Free
MIRIN (JAPANESE RICE WINE) Mitoku Organic Mikawa Mirin Sweet Rice Seasoning	• Roasted flavor that is caramel-like and rich • Subtle salty-sweet and balanced flavor	Sushi Chef Mirin Sweetened Sake and Kikkoman Aji-Mirin Sweet Cooking Rice Seasoning

TEST KITCHEN FAVORITE	WHY WE LIKE IT	RUNNERS-UP
MOLASSES **Brer Rabbit All Natural Unsulphured Mild Flavor**	• Acidic yet balanced • Strong and straightforward raisin-y taste • Pleasantly bitter bite	Plantation Barbados Unsulphured and Grandma's Molasses Unsulphured Original
MUSTARD, BROWN **Gulden's Spicy Brown Mustard**	• Complex flavor with both heat and gentle tang • Smooth, creamy texture that goes perfectly with hot dogs	French's Spicy Brown Mustard and Beaver Deli Mustard
MUSTARD, COARSE-GRAIN **Grey Poupon Harvest Coarse Ground and Grey Poupon Country**	• Spicy, tangy burst of mustard flavor • High salt content amplifies flavor • Contains no superfluous ingredients that mask mustard flavor • Big, round seeds add pleasant crunch • Just enough vinegar, not too sour or thin	
MUSTARD, DIJON **Trois Petits Cochons Moutarde de Dijon**	• Potent, bold, and very hot, not weak or mild • Good balance of sweetness, tanginess, and sharpness • Not overly acidic, sweet, or one-dimensional like competitors	Maille Dijon Originale Traditional and Roland Extra Strong
MUSTARD, YELLOW **Annie's Naturals Organic**	• Lists mustard seeds second in the ingredients for rich mustard flavor • Good balance of heat and tang • Relatively low salt content	Gulden's, French's Classic, and Westbrae Natural
OATS, ROLLED **Bob's Red Mill Old Fashioned Rolled Oats**	• Toasty flavor, even in cookies • Tender texture with just the right amount of chew • Hearty, tender texture and nutty flavor in oatmeal	Bob's Red Mill Extra Thick Rolled Oats
OATS, STEEL-CUT **Bob's Red Mill Organic**	• Rich and complex oat flavor with buttery, earthy, nutty, and whole-grain notes • Creamy yet toothsome texture • Moist but not sticky NOTE: Not recommended for baking	Arrowhead Mills Organic Hot Cereal, Country Choice Organic, and Hodgson's Mill Premium

TEST KITCHEN FAVORITE	WHY WE LIKE IT	RUNNERS-UP
OLIVE OIL, SUPERMARKET **California Olive Ranch Everyday**	• Fruity, fragrant, and fresh with a complex finish • Flavor rivals winning high-end extra-virgin oil	Lucini Premium Select
OLIVE OIL, EXTRA-VIRGIN, PREMIUM **Gaea Fresh Extra Virgin Olive Oil**	• Smooth, buttery, and balanced flavor • Sweet olive fruitiness with peppery aftertaste	Casa de Santo Amaro Selection Extra Virgin Olive Oil
PANCAKE MIX **Hungry Jack Buttermilk Pancake and Waffle Mix**	• Flavorful balance of sweetness and tang well-seasoned with sugar and salt • Light, extra fluffy texture • Requires vegetable oil (along with milk and egg) to reconstitute the batter	Aunt Jemima Original
PAPRIKA, SWEET **The Spice House Hungarian Sweet**	• Complex flavor with earthy, fruity notes • Bright and bold, not bland and boring • Rich, toasty aroma NOTE: Available only through mail order, 312-274-0378 or thespicehouse.com	Penzeys Hungary Sweet NOTE: Available through mail order, 800-741-7787 or penzeys.com
PASTA, CHEESE RAVIOLI **Rosetto**	• Creamy, plush, and rich blend of ricotta, Romano, and Parmesan cheeses • Pasta with nice, springy bite • Perfect dough-to-filling ratio	Buitoni Four Cheese and Celentano
PASTA, CHEESE TORTELLINI **Barilla Three Cheese**	• Robustly flavored filling from combination of ricotta, Emmentaler, and Grana Padano cheeses • Tender pasta that's sturdy enough to withstand boiling but not so thick that it becomes doughy	Seviroli and Buitoni Three Cheese
PASTA, EGG NOODLES **Pennsylvania Dutch Wide Egg Noodles**	• Balanced, buttery flavor with no off-flavors • Light and fluffy texture, not gummy or starchy	De Cecco Egg Pappardelle and Light 'n Fluffy Egg Noodles, Wide

TEST KITCHEN FAVORITE	WHY WE LIKE IT	RUNNERS-UP
PASTA, ELBOW MACARONI **Barilla**	• Rich flavor from egg yolks • Firm, chewy bite • Wide corkscrew shape	Mueller's
PASTA, FETTUCCINE **Garofalo Fettuccine**	• Wide, thick noodles that cook up plump and springy with mild, clean flavor • Retained perfect chew when tossed with sauce	De Cecco Fetuccine
PASTA, FRESH **Contadina Buitoni Fettuccine**	• Firm but yielding, slightly chewy texture, not too delicate, gummy, or heavy • Faint but discernible egg flavor with no chemical, plasticky, or otherwise unpleasant flavors • Rough, porous surface absorbs sauce better than dried pasta	
PASTA, LASAGNA NOODLES No-boil: **Barilla No-Boil**	• Taste and texture of fresh pasta • Delicate, flat noodles	Ronzoni and Pasta DeFino
Whole-wheat: **Bionatura Organic 100% Whole Wheat**	• Complex nutty, rich wheat flavor • Substantial chewy texture without any grittiness	DeLallo 100% Organic
PASTA, PENNE **Mueller's Penne Rigate**	• Hearty texture, not insubstantial or gummy • Wheaty, slightly sweet flavor, not bland	Benedetto Cavalieri Penne Rigate and De Cecco
PASTA, SPAGHETTI **De Cecco Spaghetti No. 12**	• Rich, nutty, wheaty flavor • Firm, ropy strands with good chew, not mushy, gummy, or mealy	Rustichella D'Abruzzo Pasta Abruzzese di Semola di Grano Duro, Garofalo, and DeLallo Spaghetti No. 4
PASTA, SPAGHETTI, GLUTEN-FREE **Jovial Organic Gluten-Free Brown Rice**	• High in fiber and protein with springy and clean taste • No gumminess or off-flavors as experienced with other brands	Andean Dream Gluten & Corn Free Quinoa Pasta

TEST KITCHEN FAVORITE	WHY WE LIKE IT	RUNNERS-UP
PASTA, SPAGHETTI, WHOLE-WHEAT **Bionaturae Organic 100% Whole Wheat**	• Chewy, firm, and toothsome, not mushy or rubbery • Full and nutty wheat flavor	Barilla PLUS Multigrain
PASTA SAUCE **Bertolli Tomato & Basil**	• Fresh-cooked, balanced tomato flavor, not overly sweet • Pleasantly chunky, not too smooth or pasty • Not overseasoned with dry herbs like competitors	Francesco Rinaldi Traditional Marinara, Prego Marinara Italian, and Barilla Marinara
PASTA SAUCE, PREMIUM **Victoria Marinara Sauce**	• Nice, bright acidity that speaks of real tomatoes • Robust flavor comparable to homemade	Classico Marinara with Plum Tomatoes and Olive Oil
PEANUT BUTTER, CREAMY **Skippy**	• Smooth, creamy, and spreadable • Good balance of sweet and salty flavors	Jif Natural and Reese's
PEPPERCORNS, BLACK **Kalustyan's Indian Tellicherry**	• Enticing and fragrant, not musty, aroma with flavor to back it up and moderate heat • Fresh, complex flavor at once sweet and spicy, earthy and smoky, fruity and floral NOTE: Available only by mail order, 800-352-3451 or kalustyans.com	Morton & Bassett Organic Whole
PEPPERONI, SLICED **Margherita Italian Style**	• Nice balance of meatiness and spice • Tangy, fresh flavor with hints of fruity licorice and peppery fennel • Thin slices with the right amount of chew	Boar's Head
PEPPERS, ROASTED RED **Dunbars Sweet**	• Balance of smokiness and sweetness • Mild, sweet, and earthy red pepper flavor • Firm texture, not slimy or mushy • Packed in simple yet strong brine of salt and water without distraction of other strongly flavored ingredients	Cento

TEST KITCHEN FAVORITE	WHY WE LIKE IT	RUNNERS-UP
PICKLES, BREAD-AND-BUTTER **Bubbies**	• Subtle, briny tang • All-natural solution that uses real sugar, not high-fructose corn syrup	
PICKLES, WHOLE KOSHER DILL **Boar's Head**	• Authentic, garlicky flavor and firm, snappy crunch • Balanced salty, sour, and garlic flavors • Fresh and refrigerated, not processed and shelf-stable	Claussen
PIE CRUST, READY-MADE **Wholly Wholesome 9" Certified Organic Traditional Bake at Home Rolled Pie Dough**	• Palm oil gives it a tender, flaky texture without artificial taste • Sold in sheets so you can use your own pie plate • Slightly sweet, rich flavor	
PIZZA, PEPPERONI, FROZEN **Pizzeria! by DiGiorno Primo Pepperoni**	• Thick, crisp, and airy crust with a browned and charred bottom • Herby, zesty sauce • Very meaty pepperoni	Freschetta Brick Oven Crust Pepperoni and Italian Style Cheese and Red Baron Fire Baked Pepperoni Pizza
POPCORN, BAGGED **Cape Cod Sea Salt Popcorn**	• Nutty, toasty corn flavor and well-calibrated salt • Hearty, puffy kernels that are crisp and crunchy on the outside with a tender interior	Smartfood Delight Sea Salt Popcorn
PORK, PREMIUM **Snake River Farms American Kurobuta Berkshire Pork**	• Deep pink tint, which indicates higher pH level and more flavorful meat • Tender texture and juicy, intensely pork-y flavor	D'Artagnan Berkshire Pork Chops (Milanese-Style Cut)
POTATO CHIPS **Lay's Kettle Cooked Original**	• Big potato flavor, no offensive off-flavors • Perfectly salted • Slightly thick chips that aren't too delicate or brittle • Not too greasy	Herr's Crisp 'N Tasty and Utz

TEST KITCHEN FAVORITE	WHY WE LIKE IT	RUNNERS-UP
POTATO CHIPS, REDUCED FAT **Cape Cod 40% Reduced Fat**	• Real potato flavor with excellent crunch and texture • Contains only potatoes, canola oil, and salt • With less sodium than many competitors, they have just the right balance of salt	Lay's Kettle Cooked Reduced Fat Extra Crunchy
PRESERVES, PEACH **American Spoon Red Haven Peach Preserves**	• Bold, ripe peach taste and balanced sweetness • Loose and spreadable texture, similar to homemade preserves	Bonne Maman Peach Preserves and Smucker's Peach Preserves
PRESERVES, RASPBERRY **Smucker's**	• Clean, strong raspberry flavor, not too tart or sweet • Not overly seedy • Ideal, spreadable texture, not too thick, artificial, or overprocessed	Trappist Red Raspberry Jam
PRESERVES, STRAWBERRY **Welch's**	• Big, distinct strawberry flavor • Natural-tasting and not overwhelmingly sweet • Thick and spreadable texture, not runny, slimy, or too smooth	Smucker's and Smucker's Simply Fruit Spreadable Fruit
RELISH, SWEET PICKLE **Cascadian Farm**	• Piquant, sweet flavor, lacks out-of-place flavors such as cinnamon and clove present in competitors • Fresh and natural taste, free of yellow dye #5 and high-fructose corn syrup • Good texture, not mushy like competitors	Heinz Premium
RICE, ARBORIO **RiceSelect**	• Creamier than competitors • Smooth grains • Characteristic good bite of Arborio rice in risotto where al dente is ideal	Riso Baricella and Rienzi
RICE, BASMATI **Tilda Pure**	• Very long grains expand greatly with cooking, a result of being aged for a minimum of one year, as required in India • Ideal, fluffy texture, not dry, gummy, or mushy • Nutty taste with no off-flavors • Sweet aroma	Kohinoor Super

TEST KITCHEN FAVORITE	WHY WE LIKE IT	RUNNERS-UP
RICE, BROWN **Lundberg Organic Long Grain Brown**	• Firm yet tender grains • Bold, toasty, nutty flavor • Works with a range of cooking methods • Includes the best instructions	Riceland Extra Long Grain Natural, Carolina Whole Grain, and Goya
RICE, LONG-GRAIN WHITE **Lundberg Organic Long Grain White Rice**	• Nutty, buttery, and toasty flavor • Distinct, smooth grains that offer some chew without being overly chewy	Carolina Enriched Extra Long-Grain and Canilla Extra Long-Grain Enriched
RICE, READY **Minute Ready to Serve White Rice**	• Parboiled long-grain white rice that is ready in less than 2 minutes • Toasted, buttery flavor • Firm grains with al dente bite	
SALSA, JARRED GREEN **Frontera Tomatillo Salsa**	• Sweet and nuanced flavor with a roasted, smoky taste from charred tomatillo skins • A good amount of heat • Has no preservatives or stabilizers	Ortega Salsa Verde, Medium
SALSA, HOT **Pace Hot Chunky**	• Good balance of bright tomato, chile, and vegetal flavors • Chunky, almost crunchy texture, not mushy or thin • Spicy and fiery but not overpowering	Newman's Own All Natural Chunky Hot and Herdez Hot Salsa Casera
SALSA, MEDIUM **Chi-Chi's Medium Thick & Chunky Salsa**	• Fresh, balanced flavor; vegetables are firm and crunchy • Jalapeño chiles for medium-level heat	
SALSA, MILD **Chi-Chi's Mild Thick & Chunky Salsa**	• Hint of heat with good balance and sweet, satisfying tomato flavor • Thick, smooth base fortified with concentrated crushed tomatoes and chunks of vegetables	
SALT **Maldon Sea Salt**	• Light and airy texture • Delicately crunchy flakes • Not so coarse as to be overly crunchy or gritty nor so fine as to disappear	Fleur de Sel de Camargue, Morton Coarse Kosher, and Diamond Crystal Kosher

STOCKING YOUR PANTRY

TEST KITCHEN FAVORITE	WHY WE LIKE IT	RUNNERS-UP
SAUERKRAUT **Eden Organic Sauerkraut**	• Slight sweetness and subtle zing, bright tanginess • Small, soft shreds with just enough chew	Libby's Sauerkraut
SAUSAGE, BREAKFAST **Jimmy Dean Fully Cooked Original Pork Sausage Links**	• Big pork flavor, not bland or overly spiced • Good balance of saltiness and sweetness with pleasantly lingering spiciness • Tender, super-juicy meat, not rubbery, spongy, or greasy	
SOUP, CANNED CHICKEN NOODLE **Muir Glen Organic**	• Organic chicken and vegetables and plenty of seasonings give it a fresh taste and spicy kick • Firm, not mushy, vegetables and noodles • No off-flavors	Progresso Traditional
SOUP, CANNED TOMATO **Progresso Vegetable Classics Hearty**	• Includes fresh, unprocessed tomatoes, not just tomato puree like some competitors • Tangy, slightly herbaceous flavor • Balanced seasoning and natural sweetness • Medium body and slightly chunky texture	Imagine Organic Vine Ripened
SOY SAUCE **Kikkoman Soy Sauce**	• Good salty-sweet balance • Long fermentation (6 to 8 months) • Simple ingredient list (wheat, soybeans, water, and salt) with no added sugar or flavor enhancers	
STEAK SAUCE **Heinz 57 Sauce**	• Mellow, restrained flavor that doesn't overpower the meat • Fruity, sweet, and tangy flavor with hints of heat and smoke • Smooth texture with enough body to cling to steak without being gluey	Lea & Perrins
SWEETENED CONDENSED MILK **Borden Eagle Brand and Nestlé Carnation**	• Made with whole milk; creamier in desserts and balances more assertive notes from other ingredients	Nestlé Carnation
TARTAR SAUCE **Legal Sea Foods**	• Creamy, nicely balanced sweet/tart base • Lots of vegetable chunks	McCormick Original

TEST KITCHEN FAVORITE	WHY WE LIKE IT	RUNNERS-UP
TEA, BLACK For plain tea: **Twinings English Breakfast**	• Bright, bold, and flavorful yet not too strong • Fruity, floral, and fragrant • Smooth, slightly astringent profile preferred for tea without milk	Lipton Black Tea
With milk and sugar: **Tetley British Blend**	• Boasts caramel notes and full, deep, smoky flavors • Bold, fruity flavor	Celestial Seasonings English Breakfast Estate Tea
TERIYAKI SAUCE **Annie Chun's All Natural**	• Distinct teriyaki flavor without offensive or dominant flavors, unlike competitors • Smooth, rich texture, not too watery or gluey	
TOMATOES, CANNED CRUSHED **SMT Crushed Tomatoes**	• Bright, clear tomato flavor • Crushed tomatoes in liquid contribute thick, hearty texture	Red Pack Crushed Tomatoes in Puree
TOMATOES, CANNED DICED **Hunt's**	• Bright, fresh tomato flavor that balances sweet and tart • Firm yet tender texture	Muir Glen Organic Diced Tomatoes
TOMATOES, CANNED PUREED **Muir Glen Organic Tomato Puree**	• Full tomato flavor without any bitter, sour, or tinny notes • Pleasantly thick, even consistency, not watery or thin	Hunt's, Progresso, and Cento
TOMATOES, CANNED WHOLE **Muir Glen Organic**	• Pleasing balance of bold acidity and fruity sweetness • Firm yet tender texture, even after hours of simmering	Hunt's
TOMATO PASTE **Goya**	• Bright, robust tomato flavors • Balance of sweet and tart flavors	Pastene and Contadina

TEST KITCHEN FAVORITE	WHY WE LIKE IT	RUNNERS-UP
TORTILLA CHIPS **On the Border** **Café Style**	• Traditional, buttery sweetness and bright corn flavor • The perfect counterpart to salsa • Light, crisp exterior	Tostitos Original Restaurant Style and Santitas White Corn
TORTILLAS, CORN **Maria and Ricardo's Handmade Style Soft Corn Tortillas, Yellow**	• Soft and pliable, don't crack when rolled up • Light, cornlike sweetness with a hint of nuttiness • Wheat gluten added to dough makes tortilla more cohesive and elastic	Mission White Corn Tortillas, Restaurant Style, Guerrero White Corn Tortillas, and La Banderita Corn Tortillas, White
TORTILLAS, FLOUR **Old El Paso 6-Inch Flour Tortillas**	• Thin and flaky texture, not doughy or stale • Made with plenty of fat and salt	Mission
TOSTADAS, CORN **Mission Tostadas Estilo Casero**	• Crisp, crunchy texture • Good corn flavor • Flavor and texture that are substantial enough to stand up to hearty toppings	Charras
TUNA, CANNED **Wild Planet Wild Albacore**	• Rich, fresh-tasting, and flavorful, but not fishy • Hearty, substantial chunks of tuna	American Tuna Pole Caught Wild Albacore and Starkist Selects Solid White Albacore
TUNA, CANNED PREMIUM **Nardin Bonito Del Norte Ventresca Fillets**	• Creamy, delicate meat and tender yet firm fillets • Full, rich tuna flavor	Tonnino Tuna Ventresca Yellowfin in Olive Oil
TURKEY, WHOLE **Empire Kosher**	• Moist and dense texture without being watery, chewy, or squishy • Meaty, full turkey flavor • Buttery white meat • Koshering process renders brining unnecessary	Good Shepherd Ranch Heritage NOTE: Available through mail order, 785-227-5149 or reeseturkeys.net

The Complete Cook's Country TV Show Cookbook

TEST KITCHEN FAVORITE	WHY WE LIKE IT	RUNNERS-UP
VANILLA BEANS **McCormick Madagascar**	• Moist, seed-filled pods • Complex, robust flavor with caramel notes	Spice Islands Bourbon
VANILLA EXTRACT **McCormick Pure**	• Strong, rich vanilla flavor where others are weak and sharp • Complex flavor with spicy, caramel notes and a sweet undertone	Rodelle Pure and Gold Medal Imitation by C.F. Sauer Co.
VEGETABLE OIL, ALL-PURPOSE **Crisco Natural Blend Oil**	• Unobtrusive, mild flavor for stir-frying and sautéing and for use in baked goods and in uncooked applications such as mayonnaise and vinaigrette • Neutral taste and absence of fishy or metallic flavors when used for frying	Mazola Canola Oil
VINEGAR, APPLE CIDER **Heinz Filtered Apple Cider Vinegar**	• Good balance of sweet and tart • Distinct apple flavor with a floral aroma and assertive, tangy qualities	
VINEGAR, BALSAMIC **Bertolli Balsamic Vinegar of Modena**	• Tastes of dried fruit like figs, raisins, and prunes • Tastes pleasantly sweet once reduced or whisked into vinaigrette	Monari Federzoni of Modena, Colavita, Ortalli of Modena, Bellino, and Lucini Aged
VINEGAR, RED WINE **Laurent du Clos**	• Crisp red wine flavor balanced by stronger than average acidity and subtle sweetness • Complex yet pleasing taste from multiple varieties of grapes	Pompeian Gourmet and Spectrum Naturals Organic

STOCKING YOUR PANTRY

TEST KITCHEN FAVORITE	WHY WE LIKE IT	RUNNERS-UP
VINEGAR, WHITE WINE **Napa Valley Naturals Organic White Wine Vinegar**	• Balanced sweetness and acidity • Fruity and vibrant in vinaigrettes • Floral and aromatic notes with robust acidity in pickled vegetables	Star White Wine Vinegar
WHIPPED TOPPING **Cool Whip Extra Creamy**	• Thick, silky, and luscious • Excellent, fresh cream flavor and just enough sweetness	Land O' Lakes Whipped Heavy Cream
WORCESTERSHIRE SAUCE **Lea & Perrins Original Worcestershire Sauce**	• Balanced notes of vinegar, pepper, and tamarind • Distinctly punchy, bright tanginess in marinades	French's Worcestershire Sauce and Annie's Organic Vegan Worcestershire Sauce
YOGURT, GREEK WHOLE MILK **Fage Total Classic**	• High in protein with no added stabilizers or thickeners • Rich, creamy, dense, faintly sweet flavor • Holds its own against garlicky sharpness of tzatziki sauce	Dannon Oikos Traditional and Wallaby Organic
YOGURT, WHOLE-MILK **Brown Cow Cream Top Plain**	• Rich, well-rounded flavor, not sour or bland • Especially creamy, smooth texture, not thin or watery • Higher fat content contributes to flavor and texture	Stonyfield Farm Organic Plain

EPISODE DIRECTORY

2008
season one

episode 101
Forgotten Cakes
Strawberry Poke Cake 487
Chocolate Blackout Cake 478

episode 102
Sunday Dinner
Sunday-Best Garlic Roast Beef 187
Mashed Potato Casserole 227

episode 103
Feeding a Crowd, Italian-Style
Slow-Cooker Italian Sunday Gravy 275
Meatballs and Marinara 286

episode 104
Southern Regional Recipes
Lexington-Style Pulled Pork 353
Memphis Chopped Coleslaw 403

episode 105
Autumn Supper
Old-Fashioned Roast Pork 209
Cranberry-Apple Crisp 544

episode 106
All-American Picnic
Extra-Crunchy Fried Chicken 58
All-American Potato Salad 404

episode 107
Easy as Pie
Raspberry Chiffon Pie 586
No-Fear Single-Crust Pie Dough 563

episode 108
Steakhouse Favorites
Broiled Steaks 122
Super-Stuffed Baked Potatoes 147

episode 109
Barbecued Chicken
Classic Barbecued Chicken 319
Best Potluck Macaroni and Cheese 4

episode 110
Regional Chops
Tennessee Whiskey Pork Chops 93
Smoked Double-Thick Pork Chops 362

episode 111
Midwestern Favorites
Chicago-Style Barbecued Ribs 346
Cincinnati Chili 101

episode 112
California Grilling
California Barbecued Tri-Tip 339
California Barbecued Beans 392
Santa Maria Salsa 339

episode 113
Diner Favorites
Fluffy Diner-Style Cheese Omelet 423
Short-Order Home Fries 430

2009
season two

episode 201
Old-Fashioned Roast Beef Dinner
Classic Roast Beef and Gravy 189
Perfect Popovers 450

episode 202
Pucker-Up Pies
Mile-High Lemon Meringue Pie 585
Icebox Key Lime Pie 582

episode 203
Rise and Shine
Ultimate Cinnamon Buns 458
Better-Than-the-Box Pancake Mix 432

episode 204
Surefire Seafood
Wood-Grilled Salmon 378
Baked Stuffed Shrimp 132
Grilled Jalapeño and Lime Shrimp Skewers 385

episode 205
Fudgy Cakes
Tunnel of Fudge Cake 481
Hot Fudge Pudding Cake 513

episode 206
Texas Chili
Easy Chili Con Carne 265
Southern-Style Skillet Cornbread 447

episode 207
Southern BBQ
Alabama Barbecued Chicken 316
Tangy Apple Cabbage Slaw 401

episode 208
Fail-Safe Thanksgiving
Old-Fashioned Roast Turkey with Gravy 160
Garlic Mashed Potatoes 138

episode 209
Fried Chicken Dinner
Creole Fried Chicken 54
Grilled Corn on the Cob 389

episode 210
Ranch-Style Barbecue
Shredded Barbecued Beef 341
Ranch Potato Salad 410

episode 211
Stovetop Desserts
Skillet Peach Cobbler 548
Maine Blueberry Grunt 547

episode 212
Perfect Pork
Grilled Mustard-Glazed Pork Loin 377
Cider-Braised Pork Chops 41

episode 213
Historical Cakes
Red Velvet Cake 476
Cold-Oven Pound Cake 508

2010 season three

episode 301
Two Perfect Pies
Shaker Lemon Pie 565
Icebox Strawberry Pie 588

episode 302
Family Dinner Favorites
Glazed Meatloaf 22
Crunchy Potato Wedges 111

episode 303
Old-Fashioned Pork
Pan-Fried Pork Chops 36
Slow-Cooker Pork Pot Roast 207
Creamy Mashed Sweet Potatoes 228

episode 304
Southern Comfort Food
Batter-Fried Chicken 51
Sweet Corn Spoonbread 230

episode 305
Beef Meets Grill
Texas Barbecued Beef Ribs 348
Char-Grilled Steaks 125

episode 306
Everybody Loves Chocolate
Chocolate Cream Cupcakes 511
Texas Sheet Cake 488

episode 307
Hearty Italian Meals
Italian Pot Roast 304
Baked Manicotti with Meat Sauce 299

episode 308
Northern Cookout
Cornell Barbecued Chicken 314
Syracuse Salt Potatoes 224
Jucy Lucy Burgers 342

episode 309
The Chemistry of Cakes
Lemon Pudding Cake 514
Angel Food Cake 501

episode 310
Southwestern Suppers
Authentic Beef Enchiladas 260
Easy Chicken Tacos 248

episode 311
Breakfast Showstoppers
Monkey Bread 466
Dutch Baby 437

episode 312
Chicken Two Ways
Roast Lemon Chicken 166
Skillet Chicken Parmesan 292

episode 313
Ultimate Ham Dinner
Cider-Baked Ham 215
Delmonico Potato Casserole 141
Cornmeal Biscuits 441

2011
season four

episode 401
Roast Beef Dinner
Herbed Roast Beef 190
Whipped Potatoes 221

episode 402
Icebox Desserts
Lemon Icebox Cheesecake 516
French Silk Chocolate Pie 591

episode 403
Fancy Chicken
Foolproof Chicken Cordon Bleu 134
Apple Cider Chicken 168

episode 404
Tropical Barbecue
Huli Huli Chicken 313
Chinese-Style Barbecued Spareribs 371

episode 405
Southern Classics
Gumbo 69
Lane Cake 483

episode 406
Retro Desserts
Banana Pudding 553
Chiffon Cake 502

episode 407
Family Favorites
Swiss Steak with Tomato Gravy 31
Crispy Baked Potato Fans 149

episode 408
Not Just for Kids
Chicken Nuggets 65
Macaroni and Cheese with Tomatoes 3

episode 409
Fried Chicken and Biscuits
Nashville Hot Fried Chicken 60
Cat Head Biscuits 442

episode 410
Road Food at Home
Slow-Cooker BBQ Beef Brisket 90
Beer-Battered Onion Rings 114

episode 411
Autumn Desserts
Baked Apple Dumplings 539
Old-Fashioned Pecan Pie 576

episode 412
Grilling
Grilled Thin-Cut Pork Chops 365
Grilled Potato Hobo Packs 394
Grilled Butterflied Lemon Chicken 322

episode 413
St. Louis Cooking
St. Louis–Style Pizza 106
St. Louis BBQ Pork Steaks 366

2012
season five

episode 501
Hearty Autumn Dinner
Smothered Pork Chops 39
Apple Fritters 541

episode 502
Breakfast Breads
Morning Glory Muffins 455
Morning Buns 463

episode 503
Dixie Chicken
Chicken and Slicks 178
Moravian Chicken Pie 180

episode 504
Italian Favorites Revisited
Slow-Cooker Meatballs and Marinara 289
Spinach and Tomato Lasagna 297

episode 505
Simple Summer Supper
Grilled Steakhouse Steak Tips 119
Dill Potato Salad 413

episode 506
Fun Modern Cakes
Strawberry Dream Cake 484
Chocolate Éclair Cake 490

episode 507
Upscale Meat and Potatoes
Herb-Crusted Beef Tenderloin 192
Duchess Potatoes 223

2013 season six

episode 508
Thrill of the Grill
Grilled Chicken Wings 325
South Carolina Pulled Pork 354

episode 509
Forgotten Cookies
Melting Moments 523
Fairy Gingerbread 526

episode 510
Super-Easy Comfort Food
Slow-Cooker French Onion Soup 137
Chuck Roast in Foil 203

episode 511
Chicken for Everyone!
One-Pan Roast Chicken with Root Vegetables 171
Easier Chicken Chimichangas 254
Smoky Salsa Verde 256

episode 512
Great American Cookout
Baltimore Pit Beef 99
Barbecued Country-Style Ribs 373

episode 513
Dinner at the Diner
Patty Melts 84
Crispy Potato Tots 113

episode 601
Picnic in the Country
Honey Fried Chicken 53
Amish Potato Salad 409

episode 602
Company's Coming
Crown Roast of Pork 204
Parmesan-Crusted Asparagus 216

episode 603
Old-Fashioned Sweet Endings
Peaches and Cream Pie 568
Cream Cheese Pound Cake 507

episode 604
Great American Meat and Potatoes
Atlanta Brisket 89
Roasted Salt-and-Vinegar Potatoes 144

episode 605
Italian Made Easy
Grandma Pizza 300
Slow-Cooker Minestrone 273

episode 606
Backyard Barbecue
Barbecued Pulled Chicken 333
South Dakota Corncob-Smoked Ribs 374

episode 607
Homespun Breakfast Treats
Fluffy Cornmeal Pancakes 435
English Muffin Bread 469

episode 608
Irish Country Cooking
Guinness Beef Stew 183
Brown Soda Bread 471

episode 609
Sweet on Texas
Tres Leches Cake 495
Magic Chocolate Flan Cake 493

episode 610
Get Your Chile Fix
Green Chile Cheeseburgers 345
Five-Alarm Chili 267

episode 611
Dessert on Bourbon Street
New Orleans Bourbon Bread Pudding 555
Beignets 438

episode 612
Favorites with a Chinese Accent
Chinese-Style Glazed
Pork Tenderloin 368
Chinese Chicken Salad 78

episode 613
Comfort Food Classics
Meatloaf with Mushroom Gravy 27
Herb Roast Chicken 165

2014
season seven

episode 701
Short-Order Breakfast Classics
Quicker Cinnamon Buns 461
"Impossible" Ham-and-Cheese
Pie 425

episode 702
Dressing Up Meat and Potatoes
Holiday Strip Roast 195
Olive Oil Potato Gratin 150

episode 703
Black and White Desserts
Chocolate Angel Pie 592
Black and White Cookies 531

episode 704
Fresh and Spicy Spins to Pork Roast and Tacos
Puerto Rican Pork Roast 210
California-Style Fish Tacos 247

episode 705
Old-Fashioned Sunday Suppers
Skillet-Roasted Chicken
with Stuffing 175
Pork Chops with Vinegar
Peppers 306

episode 706
Steakhouse Specials Off the Grill
Grilled Cowboy-Cut Rib Eyes 126
Grilled Caesar Salad 398

episode 707
Dinner from the Prairie
Milk-Can Supper 34
Dakota Bread 472

episode 708
Memphis Ribs and Pretzel Salad
Memphis-Style Wet Ribs
for a Crowd 94
Strawberry Pretzel Salad 44

episode 709
Sweet Endings from the Icebox
Italian Cream Cake 504
Summer Berry Pudding 556

episode 710
New Orleans Shrimp and Creamy Grits
New Orleans Barbecue Shrimp 70
Creamy Cheese Grits 9

episode 711
Great Grilled Chicken and Texas Potato Salad
Grilled Chicken Leg Quarters 326
Texas Potato Salad 415

episode 712
Oklahoma Onion Burgers and Louisiana Meat Pies
Oklahoma Fried Onion Burgers 87
Natchitoches Meat Pies 105

episode 713
Colorado Chili and Slow Cooker Baked Ziti
Colorado Green Chili 102
Slow-Cooker Baked Ziti 291

2015
season eight

episode 801
American Classics with a Twist
Frosted Meatloaf 24
Apple Pie with Cheddar Crust 573

episode 802
Muffins and Doughnuts Get a Makeover
Muffin Tin Doughnuts 456
Whole-Wheat Blueberry Muffins 452

episode 803
Pasta for Every Plate
Pork Ragu 276
Pasta with Roasted Garlic Sauce, Arugula, and Walnuts 280

episode 804
Grilled and Smoked
Barbecued Burnt Ends 334
Smoky Grilled Potato Salad 406

episode 805
Bringing Home Tex-Mex Enchiladas
Tex-Mex Cheese Enchiladas 259
Huevos Rancheros 241

episode 806
Southern Comfort
Delta Hot Tamales 66
Charleston Shrimp Perloo 75

episode 807
A Hearty Fall Dinner
Skillet-Roasted Chicken and Potatoes 172
Brussels Sprout Salad 218

episode 808
Simplified Showstoppers
One-Pan Prime Rib and Vegetables 198
Blitz Torte 499

episode 809
Chinese Comes Home
Slow-Cooker Chinese Barbecued Pork 82
Chicken Chow Mein 81

episode 810
All-American Sweet Dough Desserts
Dakota Peach Kuchen 550
Kolaches 464

episode 811
Fried Chicken and Grilled Peppers
Latin Fried Chicken 244
Grill-Roasted Peppers 155

episode 812
Break Out the Bourbon
Smoked Bourbon Chicken 321
Sweet Potato Pie 579

episode 813
Grilled Salmon and Stuffed Tomatoes
Grilled Salmon Steaks with Lemon-Caper Sauce 383
Stuffed Tomatoes 156

2016 season nine

episode 901
Badger State Favorites
Spicy Cheese Bread 449
Old-Fashioned Vanilla Frozen Custard 559

episode 902
Picnic Gamechangers
Ranch Fried Chicken 63
Husk-Grilled Corn 386
Classic Tuna Salad 14

episode 903
Sweet Indulgences
Milk Chocolate Cheesecake 519
Swiss Hazelnut Cake 496
Basic Chocolate Truffles 535

episode 904
Surf and Turf Goes Regional
Cedar-Planked Salmon with Cucumber-Yogurt Sauce 380
Grilled Sugar Steak 121
Lemon and Herb Red Potato Salad 418

episode 905
Big Family Breakfast
Mixed Berry Scones 444
Breakfast Pizza 426

episode 906
A Taste of Tennessee
Tennessee Pulled Pork Sandwiches 356
Hoecakes 359
French Coconut Pie 581

episode 907
The Devil Made Me Do It
Deviled Beef Short Ribs 196
Grilled Chicken Diavolo 331

episode 908
Latin Heat
Puffy Tacos 251
Chicken Chilaquiles 262

episode 909
All Wrapped Up
Bacon-Wrapped Meatloaf 28
Chicken Baked in Foil with Sweet Potato and Radish 177

episode 910
Southern Stews
Brunswick Stew 184
Shrimp and Grits 72

episode 911
Biting into the Big Easy
Pork Grillades 131
New Orleans Muffulettas 77

episode 912
Prime Rib with All the Fixings
Prime Rib with Potatoes and Red Wine–Orange Sauce 201
Roasted Green Beans with Goat Cheese and Hazelnuts 10
Green Goddess Dressing 13

episode 913
Big Flavors from Little Italy
Zeppoles 309
Pasta with Mushroom Sauce 282
Slow-Cooker Chicken Stock 47

2017 season ten

episode 1001
Pork and Pierogi
Cider-Braised Pork Roast 212
Potato-Cheddar Pierogi 108

episode 1002
Spicy and Sour for Supper
Arroz Con Pollo 242
Sour Orange Pie 567

episode 1003
Smoky Barbecue Favorites
Texas Thick-Cut Smoked Pork Chops 361
Backyard Barbecue Beans 391

episode 1004
Smothered and Dowdied
Southern-Style Smothered Chicken 21
Apple Pandowdy 542

episode 1005
BBQ Thighs and Fried Peach Pies
BBQ Chicken Thighs 328
Fried Peach Hand Pies 570

episode 1006
Ribs and Mashed Potatoes Revisited
Slow-Cooker Memphis-Style Wet Ribs 96
Mashed Potato Cakes 152

episode 1007
Bourbon and Broccoli Hit the Grill
Grilled Bourbon Steaks 336
Grilled Broccoli with Lemon and Parmesan 397

episode 1008
Straight from So-Cal
Citrus-Braised Pork Tacos 253
So-Cal Churros 268

episode 1009
Southern Discoveries
South Carolina Smoked Fresh Ham 351
Smashed Potato Salad 416

episode 1010
Cast Iron Comforts
Cast-Iron Skillet Pizza 303
Chocolate Chip Skillet Cookie 520

episode 1011
Plenty of Garlic and Parm
Garlic Fried Chicken 57
Crispy Parmesan Potatoes 143

episode 1012
When Only Chocolate Will Do
Mississippi Mud Pie 594
Whoopie Pies 532

episode 1013
The Italian-American Kitchen
Pasta with Sausage Ragu 279
Fluffy Baked Polenta with Red Sauce 285

CONVERSIONS AND EQUIVALENTS

SOME SAY COOKING IS A SCIENCE AND AN ART. WE would say that geography has a hand in it, too. Flour milled in the United Kingdom and elsewhere will feel and taste different from flour milled in the United States. So we cannot promise that the loaf of bread you bake in Canada or England will taste the same as a loaf baked in the States, but we can offer guidelines for converting weights and measures. We also recommend that you rely on your instincts when making our recipes. Refer to the visual cues provided. If the bread dough hasn't "come together in a ball," as described, you may need to add more flour—even if the recipe doesn't tell you to. You be the judge.

The recipes in this book were developed using standard U.S. measures following U.S. government guidelines. The charts below offer equivalents for U.S., metric, and imperial (U.K.) measures. All conversions are approximate and have been rounded up or down to the nearest whole number.

EXAMPLE:
- 1 teaspoon = 4.9292 milliliters, rounded up to 5 milliliters
- 1 ounce = 28.3495 grams, rounded down to 28 grams

VOLUME CONVERSIONS

U.S.	METRIC
1 teaspoon	5 milliliters
2 teaspoons	10 milliliters
1 tablespoon	15 milliliters
2 tablespoons	30 milliliters
¼ cup	59 milliliters
⅓ cup	79 milliliters
½ cup	118 milliliters
¾ cup	177 milliliters
1 cup	237 milliliters
1¼ cups	296 milliliters
1½ cups	355 milliliters
2 cups (1 pint)	473 milliliters
2½ cups	591 milliliters
3 cups	710 milliliters
4 cups (1 quart)	0.946 liter
1.06 quarts	1 liter
4 quarts (1 gallon)	3.8 liters

WEIGHT CONVERSIONS

OUNCES	GRAMS
½	14
¾	21
1	28
1½	43
2	57
2½	71
3	85
3½	99
4	113
4½	128
5	142
6	170
7	198
8	227
9	255
10	283
12	340
16 (1 pound)	454

CONVERSIONS FOR INGREDIENTS COMMONLY USED IN BAKING

Baking is an exacting science. Because measuring by weight is far more accurate than measuring by volume, and thus more likely to achieve reliable results, in our recipes we provide ounce measures in addition to cup measures for many ingredients. Refer to the chart below to convert these measures into grams.

INGREDIENT	OUNCES	GRAMS
1 cup all-purpose flour*	5	142
1 cup whole-wheat flour	5½	156
1 cup granulated (white) sugar	7	198
1 cup packed brown sugar (light or dark)	7	198
1 cup confectioners' sugar	4	113
1 cup cocoa powder	3	85
4 tablespoons butter† (½ stick or ¼ cup)	2	57
8 tablespoons butter† (1 stick or ½ cup)	4	113
16 tablespoons butter† (2 sticks or 1 cup)	8	227

* U.S. all-purpose flour, the most frequently used flour in this book, does not contain leaveners, as some European flours do. These leavened flours are called self-rising or self-raising. If you are using self-rising flour, take this into consideration before adding leavening to a recipe.

† In the United States, butter is sold both salted and unsalted. We generally recommend unsalted butter. If you are using salted butter, take this into consideration before adding salt to a recipe.

OVEN TEMPERATURES

FAHRENHEIT	CELSIUS	GAS MARK (IMPERIAL)
225	105	¼
250	120	½
275	135	1
300	150	2
325	165	3
350	180	4
375	190	5
400	200	6
425	220	7
450	230	8
475	245	9

CONVERTING TEMPERATURES FROM AN INSTANT-READ THERMOMETER

We include doneness temperatures in many of the recipes in this book. We recommend an instant-read thermometer for the job. Refer to the above table to convert Fahrenheit degrees to Celsius. Or, for temperatures not represented in the chart, use this simple formula:

Subtract 32 degrees from the Fahrenheit reading, then divide the result by 1.8 to find the Celsius reading.

EXAMPLE:
"Roast chicken until thighs register 175 degrees."
To convert:

175°F − 32 = 143°
143° ÷ 1.8 = 79.44°C, rounded down to 79°C

index

Note: Page references in *italics* indicate photographs.

A

Alabama Barbecued Chicken, 316, *317*
All-American Potato Salad, 404, *405*
Almond(s)
 -Chocolate Truffles, 535
 and Mint, Roasted Green Beans with, 10
American cheese
 Best Potluck Macaroni and Cheese, 4, *5*
 Jucy Lucy Burgers, 342, *343*
 St. Louis–Style Pizza, 106, *107*
American whiskey, about, 336
Amish Potato Salad, *408,* **409**
Anchovy(ies)
 about, 13
 -Garlic Butter, Grilled Broccoli with, 397
 Green Goddess Dressing, *12,* 13
 Grilled Caesar Salad, 398, *399*
 Salsa Verde, 195

Angel Food Cake, *500,* **501**
 Café au Lait, 501
 Chocolate-Almond, 501
Appetizers
 Chunky Guacamole, 238, *239*
 Smoky Salsa Verde, 256, *257*
 Ultimate Seven-Layer Dip, *236,* 237
 Ultimate Smoky Seven-Layer Dip, 237
 Ultimate Spicy Beef Nachos, *234,* 235
Apple cider. *See* **Cider**
Apple(s)
 Apple Cider Chicken, 168, *169*
 Cabbage Slaw, Tangy, *400,* 401
 Cheddar, and Hazelnuts, Brussels Sprout
  Salad with, 218
 Cider-Braised Pork Roast, 212, *213*
 -Cranberry Crisp, 544, *545*

Apple(s) *(cont.)*
    Dumplings, Baked, *538,* 539
    Fritters, *540, 541*
    Morning Glory Muffins, *454,* 455
    Pandowdy, 542, *543*
    Pie with Cheddar Crust, *572,* 573
    Slab Pie, 574, *575*
    Walnuts, and Tarragon, Tuna Salad with, 14
Appliances, small, ratings of, 612–15
Arroz con Pollo, 242, *243*
Arugula, Roasted Garlic Sauce, and Walnuts, Pasta with, 280, *281*
Asparagus, Parmesan-Crusted, 216, *217*
Atlanta Brisket, *88,* **89**
Authentic Beef Enchiladas, 260, *261*
Avocados
    Chicken Chilaquiles, 262, *263*
    Chunky Guacamole, 238, *239*
    Huevos Rancheros, *240,* 241
    removing flesh from, 238
    ripening, 238
    storing, 238
    Ultimate Seven-Layer Dip, *236,* 237
    Ultimate Smoky Seven-Layer Dip, 237

B

Baby Pudding Cakes, 513
Backyard Barbecued Beans, *390,* **391**
Bacon
    Backyard Barbecued Beans, *390,* 391
    and Blue Cheese Baked Potato Fans, 149
    and Blue Cheese Mashed Potato Cakes, 152
    Breakfast Pizza, 426, *427*
    and Cornbread Stuffing, 162
    Loaded Baked Potato Omelet Filling, 423

Bacon *(cont.)*
    -Ranch Potato Tots, 113
    Smoked Salmon Breakfast Pizza, 426
    Smokehouse Mashed Sweet Potatoes, 228
    Smoky Potato Salad, 406, *407*
    Stuffed Tomatoes with, 156
    Ultimate Smoky Seven-Layer Dip, 237
    -Wrapped Meatloaf, 28, *29*
Baked Apple Dumplings, *538,* **539**
Baked Manicotti with Meat Sauce, *298,* **299**
Baked Stuffed Shrimp, 132, *133*
Bakeware, ratings of, 609–12
Baltimore Pit Beef, *98,* **99**
Banana Pudding, *552,* **553**
    Peanut-y, 553
    Toasted-Coconut, 553
Barbecued Burnt Ends, 334, *335*
Barbecued Country-Style Ribs, *372,* **373**
Barbecued Pulled Chicken, *332,* **333**
Barbecued Wood-Grilled Salmon, 378
Barbecue Sauces, 94, 96, 334, 356, 361, 366
    Chicago-Style, 346
    Creamy BBQ, 111
    Lexington, 353
    Mustard, 354
    Quick, 319
    Texas, 348
Barbecue-Scallion Butter, 389
Barbecue Shrimp, New Orleans, 70, *71*
Basic Chocolate Truffles, *534,* **535**
Basil Pesto Butter, 389
Batter-Fried Chicken, *50,* **51**
Bay leaves, about, 6
BBQ Beef Brisket, Slow-Cooker, 90, *91*
BBQ Chicken Thighs, 328, *329*
BBQ Grilled Chicken Wings, 325
BBQ Pan-Fried Pork Chops, 36

Beans

Backyard Barbecued, *390,* 391
Brunswick Stew, 184, *185*
California Barbecued, *392,* 393
dried, quick-soaking, 392
dried, sorting, 392
Easier Chicken Chimichangas, 254, *255*
Five-Alarm Chili, *266,* 267
Green, Roasted
    with Almonds and Mint, 10
    with Goat Cheese and Hazelnuts, 10, *11*
    with Pecorino and Pine Nuts, 10
Slow-Cooker Minestrone, *272,* 273
Ultimate Seven-Layer Dip, *236,* 237
Ultimate Smoky Seven-Layer Dip, 237
Ultimate Spicy Beef Nachos, *234,* 235

Beef

Atlanta Brisket, *88,* 89
Bacon-Wrapped Meatloaf, 28, *29*
Baked Manicotti with Meat Sauce, *298,* 299
Baltimore Pit, *98,* 99
Barbecued Burnt Ends, 334, *335*
blade steaks, trimming, 260
Brisket, Slow-Cooker BBQ, 90, *91*
Broiled Steaks, 122, *123*
California Barbecued Tri-Tip, *338,* 339
Char-Grilled Steaks, *124,* 125
chuck roast, preparing, 183
Chuck Roast in Foil, *202,* 203
Cincinnati Chili, *100,* 101
Classic Roast, and Gravy, *188,* 189
Delta Hot Tamales, 66, *67*
Easy Chili con Carne, *264,* 265
Enchiladas, Authentic, 260, *261*
Five-Alarm Chili, *266,* 267
Frosted Meatloaf, 24, *25*
Garlic Roast, Sunday-Best, *186,* 187

Beef *(cont.)*

Glazed Meatloaf, 22, *23*
Green Chile Cheeseburgers, *344,* 345
Grilled Bourbon Steaks, 336, *337*
Grilled Cowboy-Cut Rib Eyes, 126, *127*
Grilled Steak Burgers, 128, *129*
Grilled Steakhouse Steak Tips, *118,* 119
Grilled Sugar Steak, *120,* 121
Herbed Roast, 190, *191*
Holiday Strip Roast, *194,* 195
Italian Pot Roast, 304, *305*
Jucy Lucy Burgers, 342, *343*
Meatballs and Marinara, 286, *287*
Meatloaf with Mushroom Gravy, *26,* 27
Nachos, Ultimate Spicy, *234,* 235
Natchitoches Meat Pies, *104,* 105
Oklahoma Fried Onion Burgers, *86,* 87
One-Pan Prime Rib and Roasted
    Vegetables, 198, *199*
Patty Melts, 84, *85*
Prime Rib with Potatoes and Red Wine–Orange
    Sauce, *200,* 201
Puffy Tacos, *250,* 251
Ribs, Texas Barbecued, 348, *349*
Salisbury Steak, *32,* 33
Short Ribs, Deviled, 196, *197*
Shredded Barbecued, *340,* 341
Skillet Lasagna, 294, *295*
Slow-Cooker Italian Sunday Gravy, *274,* 275
Slow-Cooker Meatballs and Marinara, *288,* 289
standing rib roast, buying, 198
standing rib roast, carving, 198
steaks, broiling times for, 122
Stew, Guinness, *182,* 183
Swiss Steak with Tomato Gravy, *30,* 31
Tenderloin, Herb-Crusted, 192, *193*
top blade roast, removing gristle from, 31

Beer
-Battered Onion Rings, 114, *115*
Guinness Beef Stew, *182,* 183
Milk-Can Supper, 34, *35*

Beignets, 438, *439*

Berry(ies)
Cranberry-Apple Crisp, 544, *545*
Icebox Strawberry Pie, 588, *589*
Maine Blueberry Grunt, *546,* 547
Mixed, Scones, 444, *445*
Raspberry Chiffon Pie, 586, *587*
Strawberry Dream Cake, 484, *485*
Strawberry Poke Cake, *486,* 487
Strawberry Pretzel Salad, 44, *45*
Strawberry-Rhubarb Compote, 507
Summer, Pudding, 556, *557*
Whole-Wheat Blueberry Muffins, 452, *453*

Best Potluck Macaroni and Cheese, 4, *5*
Better-Than-the-Box Pancake Mix, 432
Better-Than-the-Box Pancakes, 432, *433*

Biscuits
Cat Head, 442, *443*
Cornmeal, *440,* 441

Black and White Cookies, *530,* **531**
Blitz Torte, *498,* **499**

Blueberry(ies)
Grunt, Maine, *546,* 547
Muffins, Whole-Wheat, 452, *453*
Summer Berry Pudding, 556, *557*

Blue Cheese
and Bacon Baked Potato Fans, 149
and Bacon Mashed Potato Cakes, 152
Sauce, Buffalo, 111

Bourbon
about, 336
Bread Pudding, New Orleans, *554,* 555
Chicken, Smoked, *320,* 321
Lane Cake, *482,* 483
Sauce, 555

Bourbon *(cont.)*
Steaks, Grilled, 336, *337*
Whipped Cream, 576

Bread Pudding
New Orleans Bourbon, *554,* 555
Summer Berry Pudding, 556, *557*

Breads
Brown Soda, *470,* 471
Brown Soda, with Currants and Caraway, 471
Cat Head Biscuits, 442, *443*
Cheese, Spicy, *448,* 449
Cornmeal Biscuits, *440,* 441
Dakota, 472, *473*
English Muffin, *468,* 469
Kolaches, 464, *465*
Mixed Berry Scones, 444, *445*
Monkey, 466, *467*
Morning Buns, *462,* 463
Morning Glory Muffins, *454,* 455
Muffin Tin Popovers, 450
Perfect Popovers, 450, *451*
Quicker Cinnamon Buns, *460,* 461
Southern-Style Skillet Cornbread, *446,* 447
Ultimate Cinnamon Buns, 458, *459*
Whole-Wheat Blueberry Muffins, 452, *453*
see also Tortillas

Breakfast Pizza, 426, *427*
Chorizo and Manchego, 426
Sausage and Red Bell Pepper, 426
Smoked Salmon, 426

Broccoli
Chicken Divan, *18,* 19
Grilled
with Anchovy-Garlic Butter, 397
with Lemon and Parmesan, *396,* 397
with Sweet Chili Sauce, 397

Broiled Steaks, 122, *123*

Broilers, cooking with, 122
Brown Soda Bread, *470*, 471
Brown Soda Bread with Currants and Caraway, 471
Brown Sugar–Cayenne Butter, 386
Brunswick Stew, 184, *185*
Brussels Sprout(s)
    One-Pan Prime Rib and Roasted Vegetables, 198, *199*
    One-Pan Roast Chicken with Root Vegetables, *170*, 171
    Salad, 218, *219*
    Salad with Cheddar, Hazelnuts, and Apple, 218
    Salad with Smoked Gouda, Pecans, and Dried Cherries, 218
    slicing, 218
Buffalo Blue Cheese Sauce, 111
Burgers
    Green Chile Cheeseburgers, *344*, 345
    Grilled Steak, 128, *129*
    Jucy Lucy, 342, *343*
    Oklahoma Fried Onion, *86*, 87
    Patty Melts, 84, *85*
Butter, flavored
    Barbecue-Scallion, 389
    Basil Pesto, 389
    Brown Sugar–Cayenne, 386
    Chesapeake Bay, 389
    Cilantro-Lime, 386
    Latin-Spiced, 389
    Mustard-Paprika, 386
    Rosemary-Pepper, 386

C

Cabbage
    Apple Slaw, Tangy, *400*, 401
    California-Style Fish Tacos, *246*, 247
    Chinese Chicken Salad, 78, *79*
    chopping, 403
    Memphis Chopped Coleslaw, *402*, 403
    Milk-Can Supper, 34, *35*
Caesar Salad, Grilled, 398, *399*
Café au Lait Angel Food Cake, 501
Cakes
    Angel Food, *500*, 501
        Café au Lait, 501
        Chocolate-Almond, 501
    Baby Pudding, 513
    Blitz Torte, *498*, 499
    Chiffon, 502, *503*
    Chiffon, Orange, 502
    Chocolate Blackout, 478, *479*
    Chocolate Cream Cupcakes, *510*, 511
    Chocolate Éclair, 490, *491*
    Hot Fudge Pudding, *512*, 513
    Italian Cream, 504, *505*
    Lane, *482*, 483
    Lemon Icebox Cheesecake, 516, *517*
    Lemon Pudding, 514, *515*
    Magic Chocolate Flan, *492*, 493
    Milk Chocolate Cheesecake, *518*, 519
    Pound, Cold-Oven, 508, *509*
    Pound, Cream Cheese, *506*, 507
    Red Velvet, 476, *477*
    Strawberry Dream, 484, *485*

Cakes *(cont.)*
    Strawberry Poke, *486,* 487
    Swiss Hazelnut, 496, *497*
    Texas Sheet, 488, *489*
    Tres Leches, *494,* 495
    Tunnel of Fudge, *480,* 481

California Barbecued Beans, 392, *393*
California Barbecued Tri-Tip, *338,* 339
Canadian whisky, about, 336
Caper(s)
    about, 418
    Hard-Cooked Eggs, and Radishes, Tuna Salad with, 14
    -Lemon Sauce, Grilled Salmon Steaks with, *382,* 383
    and Pine Nuts, Stuffed Tomatoes with, 156

Cappuccino Glaze, 525
Caribbean Grilled Thin-Cut Pork Chops, 365
Carrots
    buying and storing, 47
    Chuck Roast in Foil, *202,* 203
    Guinness Beef Stew, *182,* 183
    Milk-Can Supper, *34,* 35
    Morning Glory Muffins, *454,* 455
    One-Pan Prime Rib and Roasted Vegetables, 198, *199*
    One-Pan Roast Chicken with Root Vegetables, *170,* 171
    and Potatoes, Chicken Baked in Foil with, 177
    Slow-Cooker Pork Pot Roast, *206,* 207

Cast-Iron Skillet Pizza, *302,* 303
Cat Head Biscuits, 442, *443*
Cedar-Planked Salmon with Cucumber-Yogurt Sauce, 380, *381*
Celery, buying and storing, 47
Charleston Shrimp Perloo, *74,* 75

Cheddar (cheese)
    Authentic Beef Enchiladas, 260, *261*
    Best Potluck Macaroni and Cheese, 4, *5*
    Creamy Cheese Grits, *8,* 9
    Crust, Apple Pie with, *572,* 573
    Easier Chicken Chimichangas, 254, *255*
    Fluffy Diner-Style Cheese Omelet, *422,* 423
    Hazelnuts, and Apple, Brussels Sprout Salad with, 218
    Macaroni and Cheese with Tomatoes, *2,* 3
    -Potato Pierogi, 108, *109*
    Sausage and Red Bell Pepper Breakfast Pizza, 426
    and Scallion Mashed Potato Cakes, 152
    Stuffed Tomatoes with Bacon, 156
    Tex-Mex Cheese Enchiladas, *258,* 259

Cheese
    -and-Ham Pie, "Impossible," *424,* 425
    Apple Pie with Cheddar Crust, *572,* 573
    Authentic Beef Enchiladas, 260, *261*
    Baked Manicotti with Meat Sauce, *298,* 299
    Blue, and Bacon Baked Potato Fans, 149
    Blue, and Bacon Mashed Potato Cakes, 152
    Blue, Sauce, Buffalo, 111
    Bread, Spicy, *448,* 449
    Breakfast Pizza, 426, *427*
    Brussels Sprout Salad, 218, *219*
    Brussels Sprout Salad with Cheddar, Hazelnuts, and Apple, 218
    Brussels Sprout Salad with Smoked Gouda, Pecans, and Dried Cherries, 218
    Cast-Iron Skillet Pizza, *302,* 303
    Cheddar and Scallion Mashed Potato Cakes, 152
    Chicken Divan, *18,* 19
    Chorizo and Manchego Breakfast Pizza, 426
    Crispy Baked Potato Fans, *148,* 149

Cheese *(cont.)*
    Crispy Parmesan Potatoes, *142,* 143
    Delmonico Potato Casserole, *140,* 141
    Easier Chicken Chimichangas, 254, *255*
    Enchiladas, Tex-Mex, *258,* 259
    Fluffy Baked Polenta with Red Sauce, *284,* 285
    Foolproof Chicken Cordon Bleu, 134, *135*
    Goat, and Hazelnuts, Roasted Green Beans with, 10, *11*
    Grandma Pizza, 300, *301*
    Green Chile Cheeseburgers, *344,* 345
    Grilled Broccoli with Lemon and Parmesan, *396,* 397
    Grilled Caesar Salad, 398, *399*
    Grits, Creamy, *8,* 9
    Herb-Crusted Beef Tenderloin, 192, *193*
    Huevos Rancheros, *240,* 241
    Jucy Lucy Burgers, 342, *343*
    Kolaches, 464, *465*
    Macaroni and, Best Potluck, 4, *5*
    Macaroni and, with Tomatoes, *2,* 3
    Mashed Potato Cakes, 152, *153*
    New Orleans Muffulettas, *76,* 77
    Olive Oil Potato Gratin, 150, *151*
    Omelet, Fluffy Diner-Style, *422,* 423
    Parmesan-Crusted Asparagus, 216, *217*
    Parmesan-Rosemary Potato Tots, 113
    Pasta with Mushroom Sauce, 282, *283*
    Patty Melts, 84, *85*
    Potato-Cheddar Pierogi, 108, *109*
    Roasted Green Beans with Pecorino and Pine Nuts, 10
    Sausage and Red Bell Pepper Breakfast Pizza, 426
    semisoft, shredding, 292

Cheese *(cont.)*
    Skillet Chicken Parmesan, 292, *293*
    Skillet Lasagna, 294, *295*
    Skillet Lasagna with Sausage and Peppers, 294
    Slow-Cooker Baked Ziti, *290,* 291
    Slow-Cooker French Onion Soup, *136,* 137
    Smoked Salmon Breakfast Pizza, 426
    Smokehouse Mashed Sweet Potatoes, 228
    Southwestern Potato Tots, 113
    Spinach and Tomato Lasagna, *296,* 297
    St. Louis–Style Pizza, 106, *107*
    Stuffed Tomatoes, 156, *157*
    Stuffed Tomatoes with Bacon, 156
    Stuffed Tomatoes with Capers and Pine Nuts, 156
    Stuffed Tomatoes with Currants and Pistachios, 156
    Stuffed Tomatoes with Olives and Orange, 156
    Super-Stuffed Baked Potatoes, *146,* 147
    Ultimate Seven-Layer Dip, *236,* 237
    Ultimate Smoky Seven-Layer Dip, 237
    Ultimate Spicy Beef Nachos, *234,* 235
    weighing, for recipes, 9
    see also Cream Cheese

Cheesecake
    Lemon Icebox, 516, *517*
    Milk Chocolate, *518,* 519

Cherries, Dried, Smoked Gouda, and Pecans, Brussels Sprout Salad with, 218

Chesapeake Bay Butter, 389

Chicago-Style Barbecued Ribs, 346, *347*

Chicken
    Apple Cider, 168, *169*
    Arroz con Pollo, 242, *243*

Chicken *(cont.)*
- Baked in Foil
  - with Fennel and Sun-Dried Tomatoes, 177
  - with Potatoes and Carrots, 177
  - with Sweet Potato and Radish, *176,* 177
- Barbecued
  - Alabama, 316, *317*
  - Classic, *318,* 319
  - Cornell, 314, *315*
  - Pulled, *332,* 333
- breasts, preparing cutlets from, 292
- breasts, splitting and trimming, 21
- Brunswick Stew, 184, *185*
- Chilaquiles, 262, *263*
- Chimichangas, Easier, 254, *255*
- Chow Mein, *80,* 81
- Cordon Bleu, Foolproof, 134, *135*
- Diavolo, Grilled, *330,* 331
- Divan, *18,* 19
- Florentine, 16, *17*
- Fried
  - Batter-, *50,* 51
  - Creole, 54, *55*
  - Extra-Crunchy, 58, *59*
  - Extra-Spicy, Extra-Crunchy, 58
  - Garlic, *56,* 57
  - Honey, *52,* 53
  - Latin, 244, *245*
  - Nashville Extra-Hot, 60
  - Nashville Hot, 60, *61*
  - Ranch, *62,* 63
- Gumbo, *68,* 69
- Huli Huli, *312,* 313
- Leg Quarters, Grilled, 326, *327*
- Lemon, Grilled Butterflied, 322, *323*
- Nuggets, *64,* 65
- Parmesan, Skillet, 292, *293*
- Pie, Moravian, 180, *181*

Chicken *(cont.)*
- and Potatoes, Skillet-Roasted, 172, *173*
- Roast
  - with Fennel and Parsnips, One-Pan, 171
  - Herb, *164,* 165
  - Lemon, 166, *167*
  - with Root Vegetables, One-Pan, *170,* 171
- Salad, Chinese, *78,* 79
- shredding, 248
- Skillet-Roasted, with Stuffing, *174,* 175
- and Slicks, 178, *179*
- Smoked Bourbon, *320,* 321
- Smothered, Southern-Style, *20,* 21
- Stock, Slow-Cooker, *46,* 47
- Tacos, Easy, 248, *249*
- Thighs, BBQ, 328, *329*
- whole
  - butterflying, 322
  - cutting in half, 321
  - cutting into quarters, 60
- Wings, Grilled, *324,* 325
  - BBQ, 325
  - Creole, 325
  - Tandoori, 325

Chiffon Cake, 502, *503*
Chiffon Cake, Orange, 502
Chilaquiles, Chicken, 262, *263*
Chile peppers
- Chicken Chilaquiles, 262, *263*
- Colorado Green Chili, 102, *103*
- Easy Chicken Tacos, 248, *249*
- Easy Chili con Carne, *264,* 265
- Five-Alarm Chili, *266,* 267
- Green Chile Cheeseburgers, *344,* 345
- Grilled Shrimp Skewers
  - Caribbean, 385
  - Jalapeño and Lime, *384,* 385
  - Red Chile and Ginger, 385

Chile peppers *(cont.)*
    Habanero Sauce, *252,* 253
    Huevos Rancheros, *240,* 241
    One-Minute Salsa, 235
    Pickled Onions, *246,* 247
    Santa Maria Salsa, 339
    seeding jalapeños, 237
    Smoky Salsa Verde, 256, *257*
    storing canned chipotles, 248
    Texas Potato Salad, *414,* 415
    Tex-Mex Cheese Enchiladas, *258,* 259
    Ultimate Seven-Layer Dip, *236,* 237
    Ultimate Smoky Seven-Layer Dip, 237
    Ultimate Spicy Beef Nachos, *234,* 235

Chili
    Cincinnati, *100,* 101
    Colorado Green, 102, *103*
    con Carne, Easy, *264,* 265
    Five-Alarm, *266,* 267

Chimichangas, Easier Chicken, 254, *255*
Chinese Chicken Salad, 78, *79*
Chinese-Style Barbecued Spareribs, *370,* 371
Chinese-Style Glazed Pork Tenderloin, 368, *369*
Chive Sour Cream, *142,* 143

Chocolate
    -Almond Angel Food Cake, 501
    Baby Pudding Cakes, 513
    Black and White Cookies, *530,* 531
    Blackout Cake, 478, *479*
    Chip Skillet Cookie, 520, *521*
    Cream Cupcakes, *510,* 511
    Éclair Cake, 490, *491*
    Flan Cake, Magic, *492,* 493
    Frozen Custard, Old-Fashioned, *558,* 559
    Hot Fudge Pudding Cake, *512,* 513
    Milk, Cheesecake, *518,* 519
    Mississippi Mud Pie, 594, *595*

Chocolate *(cont.)*
    Pie, Angel, 592, *593*
    Pie, French Silk, *590,* 591
    Sauce, 268, *269*
    Texas Sheet Cake, *488,* 489
    Truffles, Basic, *534,* 535
        -Almond, 535
        -Cinnamon, 535
        -Ginger, 535
        -Lemon, 535
    Tunnel of Fudge Cake, *480,* 481
    Whoopie Pies, 532, *533*

Chorizo and Manchego Breakfast Pizza, 426
Chow Mein, Chicken, *80,* 81
Chuck Roast in Foil, *202,* 203
Chunky Guacamole, 238, *239*
Churros, So-Cal, *268,* 269

Cider
    Apple Cider Chicken, 168, *169*
    -Baked Ham, *214,* 215
    -Braised Pork Chops, *40,* 41
    -Braised Pork Roast, 212, *213*
    compared to apple juice, 168
    Sauce, 539

Cilantro
    Easy Chicken Tacos, 248, *249*
    -Lime Butter, 386
    One-Minute Salsa, 235
    Puerto Rican Pork Roast, 210, *211*
    Smoky Salsa Verde, 256, *257*
    tired, reviving, 256

Cincinnati Chili, *100,* 101

Cinnamon
    Buns, Quicker, *460,* 461
    Buns, Ultimate, 458, *459*
    -Chocolate Truffles, 535

Cinnamon *(cont.)*
    Monkey Bread, 466, *467*
    Morning Buns, *462*, 463
    Muffin Tin Doughnuts, 456, *457*
Citrus-Braised Pork Tacos, *252*, 253
Classic Barbecued Chicken, *318*, 319
Classic Pizza Dough, 303
Classic Roast Beef and Gravy, *188*, 189
Classic Single-Crust Pie Dough, 562
Classic Steak Sauce, 125
Classic Tomato Soup, 6, *7*
Classic Tuna Salad, 14, *15*
Coconut
    Italian Cream Cake, 504, *505*
    Lane Cake, *482*, 483
    -Lime Cookies, 525
    Morning Glory Muffins, *454*, 455
    Pie, French, *580*, 581
    Toasted, Banana Pudding, 553
Coffee
    Café au Lait Angel Food Cake, 501
    Cappuccino Glaze, 525
Cold-Oven Pound Cake, 508, *509*
Colorado Green Chili, 102, *103*
Cookies
    Black and White, *530*, 531
    Chocolate Chip Skillet, 520, *521*
    Coconut-Lime, 525
    Crescent, *522*, 523
    Fairy Gingerbread, 526, *527*
    Jam Thumbprint, *522*, 523
    Joe Froggers, 528, *529*
    Melting Moments, *522*, 523
    Orange–Poppy Seed, *524*, 525
    Round Spritz, *522*, 523
    Slice-and-Bake, *524*, 525
    Walnut–Brown Sugar, 525
    Whoopie Pies, 532, *533*

Corn
    Brunswick Stew, 184, *185*
    on the Cob, Grilled, *388*, 389
    Cornbread and Bacon Stuffing, 162
    Creamy Cheese Grits, *8*, 9
    Husk-Grilled, 386, *387*
        with Brown Sugar–Cayenne Butter, 386
        with Cilantro-Lime Butter, 386
        with Mustard-Paprika Butter, 386
        with Rosemary-Pepper Butter, 386
    Individual Spoonbreads, 230
    Milk-Can Supper, 34, *35*
    Sweet, Spoonbread, 230, *231*
Cornbread
    and Bacon Stuffing, 162
    and Sausage Stuffing, 162, *163*
    Southern-Style Skillet, *446*, 447
Corncob-Smoked Ribs, South Dakota, 374, *375*
Cornell Barbecued Chicken, 314, *315*
Corn husks
    Delta Hot Tamales, 66, *67*
    working with, 66
Cornichons and Whole-Grain Mustard, Tuna Salad with, 14
Cornmeal
    about, 9
    Biscuits, *440*, 441
    Delta Hot Tamales, 66, *67*
    Fluffy Baked Polenta with Red Sauce, *284*, 285
    Hoecakes, *358*, 359
    Individual Spoonbreads, 230
    Pancakes, Fluffy, *434*, 435
    Southern-Style Skillet Cornbread, *446*, 447
    Sweet Corn Spoonbread, 230, *231*

Cottage cheese
    Breakfast Pizza, 426, *427*
    Chorizo and Manchego Breakfast Pizza, 426
    Sausage and Red Bell Pepper Breakfast Pizza, 426
    Smoked Salmon Breakfast Pizza, 426

Couscous
    Stuffed Tomatoes, 156, *157*

Cranberry-Apple Crisp, 544, *545*

Cream Cheese
    Icebox Key Lime Pie, 582, *583*
    Italian Cream Cake, 504, *505*
    Kolaches, 464, *465*
    Lemon Icebox Cheesecake, 516, *517*
    Magic Chocolate Flan Cake, *492,* 493
    Milk Chocolate Cheesecake, *518,* 519
    Pound Cake, *506,* 507
    Red Velvet Cake, 476, *477*
    Strawberry Dream Cake, 484, *485*
    Strawberry Pretzel Salad, 44, *45*

Creamy BBQ Sauce, 111
Creamy Cheese Grits, *8,* **9**
Creamy Mashed Sweet Potatoes, 228, *229*
Creole Baked Stuffed Shrimp with Sausage, 132
Creole Fried Chicken, 54, *55*
Creole Grilled Chicken Wings, 325
Crescent Cookies, *522,* **523**
Crispy Baked Potato Fans, *148,* **149**
Crispy Fish Sticks with Tartar Sauce, 42, *43*
Crispy Parmesan Potatoes, *142,* **143**
Crispy Potato Tots, *112,* **113**
Crispy Potato Tots for a Crowd, 113
Crown Roast of Pork, 204, *205*
Crunchy Potato Wedges, *110,* **111**
Cucumber-Yogurt Sauce, 380

Cupcakes, Chocolate Cream, *510,* **511**
Currants and Caraway, Brown Soda Bread with, 471
Currants and Pistachios, Stuffed Tomatoes with, 156
Curried Chutney Sauce, 111
Curry and Grapes, Tuna Salad with, 14
Custard, Frozen
    Old-Fashioned Chocolate, *558,* 559
    Old-Fashioned Vanilla, *558,* 559

D

Dakota Bread, 472, *473*
Dakota Peach Kuchen, 550, *551*
Delmonico Potato Casserole, *140,* **141**
Delta Hot Tamales, 66, *67*
Desserts
    Apple Fritters, *540,* 541
    Apple Pandowdy, 542, *543*
    Baked Apple Dumplings, *538,* 539
    Banana Pudding, *552,* 553
        Peanut-y, 553
        Toasted-Coconut, 553
    Chocolate Truffles, Basic, *534,* 535
        -Almond, 535
        -Cinnamon, 535
        -Ginger, 535
        -Lemon, 535
    Cranberry-Apple Crisp, 544, *545*
    Dakota Peach Kuchen, 550, *551*
    Maine Blueberry Grunt, *546,* 547
    New Orleans Bourbon Bread Pudding, *554,* 555
    Old-Fashioned Chocolate Frozen Custard, *558,* 559

Desserts *(cont.)*
    Old-Fashioned Vanilla Frozen Custard, 558, *559*
    Skillet Peach Cobbler, 548, *549*
    So-Cal Churros, 268, *269*
    Summer Berry Pudding, 556, *557*
    Zeppoles, *308,* 309
    see also Cakes; Cookies; Pies (sweet)
Deviled Beef Short Ribs, 196, *197*
Dill Potato Salad, *412*, 413
Dips
    Buffalo Blue Cheese Sauce, 111
    Chive Sour Cream, *142,* 143
    Chunky Guacamole, 238, *239*
    Creamy BBQ Sauce, 111
    Curried Chutney Sauce, 111
    Honey-Mustard Sauce, 65
    One-Minute Salsa, 235
    Santa Maria Salsa, 339
    Seven-Layer, Ultimate, *236,* 237
    Seven-Layer, Ultimate Smoky, 237
    Smoky Salsa Verde, 256, *257*
    Sweet and Sour Sauce, 65
Double-Crust Pie Dough, 562
Doughnuts
    Beignets, 438, *439*
    Muffin Tin, 456, *457*
Dressing, Green Goddess, *12,* 13
Duchess Potatoes, *222,* 223
Dumplings
    Baked Apple, *538,* 539
    Potato-Cheddar Pierogi, 108, *109*
Dutch Baby, *436,* 437

E

Easier Chicken Chimichangas, 254, *255*
Easy Chicken Tacos, 248, *249*
Easy Chili con Carne, *264,* 265
Eggs
    Breakfast Pizza, 426, *427*
    Chorizo and Manchego Breakfast Pizza, 426
    Fluffy Diner-Style Cheese Omelet, *422,* 423
    Foolproof Hard-Cooked, 409
    Hard-Cooked, Radishes, and Capers, Tuna Salad with, 14
    Huevos Rancheros, *240,* 241
    Sausage and Red Bell Pepper Breakfast Pizza, 426
    Smoked Salmon Breakfast Pizza, 426
Enchiladas
    Beef, Authentic, 260, *261*
    Cheese, Tex-Mex, *258,* 259
English Muffin Bread, *468,* 469
Equipment, ratings of
    bakeware, 609–12
    grilling equipment, 616–18
    handy tools, 601–6
    kitchen supplies, 624–25
    knives and more, 596–98
    measuring equipment, 607–9
    pots and pans, 598–600
    small appliances, 612–15
    specialty pieces, 619–24
    thermometers and timers, 607–9
Extra-Crunchy Fried Chicken, 58, *59*
Extra-Spicy, Extra-Crunchy Fried Chicken, 58

F

Fairy Gingerbread, 526, *527*
Fennel
    common, about, 279
    Florence, about, 279
    and Parsnips, One-Pan Roast Chicken with, 171
    Pasta with Sausage Ragu, *278,* 279
    preparing, 171
    and Sun-Dried Tomatoes, Chicken Baked in Foil with, 177
Fish
    Sticks, Crispy, with Tartar Sauce, 42, *43*
    Tacos, California-Style, *246,* 247
    see also Anchovy(ies); Salmon; Tuna
Five-Alarm Chili, *266*, 267
Fluffy Baked Polenta with Red Sauce, *284,* 285
Fluffy Cornmeal Pancakes, *434,* 435
Fluffy Diner-Style Cheese Omelet, *422,* 423
Foolproof Chicken Cordon Bleu, 134, *135*
Foolproof Hard-Cooked Eggs, 409
French Coconut Pie, *580,* 581
French Onion Soup, Slow-Cooker, *136,* 137
French Silk Chocolate Pie, *590,* 591
Fried Peach Hand Pies, 570, *571*
Fritters
    Apple, *540,* 541
    Zeppoles, *308,* 309
Frosted Meatloaf, 24, *25*
Frozen Custard
    Old-Fashioned Chocolate, *558,* 559
    Old-Fashioned Vanilla, *558,* 559

G

Garlic
    -Anchovy Butter, Grilled Broccoli with, 397
    Fried Chicken, *56,* 57
    Mashed Potatoes, 138, *139*
    odor, removing from hands, 138
    -Parsley Steak Sauce, 125
    Roast Beef, Sunday-Best, *186,* 187
    Roasted, Sauce, Arugula, and Walnuts, Pasta with, 280, *281*
Ginger
    -Chocolate Truffles, 535
    Fairy Gingerbread, 526, *527*
    Joe Froggers, 528, *529*
    -Lime Glaze, 525
Glazed Meatloaf, 22, *23*
Glazes
    Cappuccino, 525
    Ginger-Lime, 525
    Malted Milk, 525
    Peanut Butter and Jelly, 525
Goat Cheese and Hazelnuts, Roasted Green Beans with, 10, *11*
Gouda cheese
    Smokehouse Mashed Sweet Potatoes, 228
    Southwestern Potato Tots, 113
Graham crackers
    Chocolate Éclair Cake, 490, *491*
    Icebox Key Lime Pie, 582, *583*
Grains
    Creamy Cheese Grits, *8,* 9
    Dakota Bread, 472, *473*

Grains *(cont.)*
  grits, about, 9
  hominy grits, about, 9
  polenta, about, 9
  Shrimp and Grits, 72, *73*
  see also Cornmeal; Rice
Grandma Pizza, 300, *301*
Grapes and Curry, Tuna Salad with, 14
Gravy
  Classic Roast Beef and, *188,* 189
  Mushroom, Meatloaf with, *26,* 27
  Old-Fashioned Roast Turkey with, 160, *161*
Greek Diner-Style Home Fries, 430
Green Beans
  Roasted, with Almonds and Mint, 10
  Roasted, with Goat Cheese and Hazelnuts, 10, *11*
  Roasted, with Pecorino and Pine Nuts, 10
Green Chile Cheeseburgers, *344,* 345
Green Goddess Dressing, *12,* 13
Greens
  Chicken Florentine, 16, *17*
  Chinese Chicken Salad, 78, *79*
  Grilled Caesar Salad, 398, *399*
  Pasta with Roasted Garlic Sauce, Arugula, and Walnuts, 280, *281*
  Slow-Cooker Minestrone, 272, *273*
  Spinach and Tomato Lasagna, *296,* 297
  Stuffed Tomatoes, 156, *157*
  see also Cabbage
Grilled dishes
  Alabama Barbecued Chicken, 316, *317*
  Baltimore Pit Beef, *98,* 99
  Barbecued Burnt Ends, 334, *335*
  Barbecued Country-Style Ribs, *372,* 373
  Barbecued Pulled Chicken, *332,* 333
  BBQ Chicken Thighs, 328, *329*

Grilled dishes *(cont.)*
  California Barbecued Beans, 392, *393*
  California Barbecued Tri-Tip, *338, 339*
  Cedar-Planked Salmon with Cucumber-Yogurt Sauce, 380, *381*
  Char-Grilled Steaks, *124,* 125
  Chicago-Style Barbecued Ribs, 346, *347*
  Chinese-Style Barbecued Spareribs, *370,* 371
  Chinese-Style Glazed Pork Tenderloin, 368, *369*
  Classic Barbecued Chicken, *318,* 319
  Cornell Barbecued Chicken, 314, *315*
  Green Chile Cheeseburgers, *344,* 345
  Grilled Bourbon Steaks, 336, *337*
  Grilled Broccoli
    with Anchovy-Garlic Butter, 397
    with Lemon and Parmesan, *396,* 397
    with Sweet Chili Sauce, 397
  Grilled Butterflied Lemon Chicken, 322, *323*
  Grilled Caesar Salad, 398, *399*
  Grilled Chicken Diavolo, *330,* 331
  Grilled Chicken Leg Quarters, 326, *327*
  Grilled Chicken Wings, *324,* 325
    BBQ, 325
    Creole, 325
    Tandoori, 325
  Grilled Corn on the Cob, *388,* 389
  Grilled Cowboy-Cut Rib Eyes, 126, *127*
  Grilled Mustard-Glazed Pork Loin, *376,* 377
  Grilled Potato Hobo Packs, 394
    Spanish-Style, 394, *395*
    Spicy Home Fry, 394
    Vinegar and Onion, 394
  Grilled Salmon Steaks with Lemon-Caper Sauce, *382,* 383
  Grilled Shrimp Skewers
    Caribbean, 385
    Jalapeño and Lime, *384,* 385
    Red Chile and Ginger, 385

Grilled dishes *(cont.)*
   Grilled Steak Burgers, 128, *129*
   Grilled Steakhouse Steak Tips, *118,* 119
   Grilled Sugar Steak, *120,* 121
   Grilled Thin-Cut Pork Chops, *364,* 365
      Caribbean, 365
      Mediterranean, 365
      Spicy Thai, 365
   Grill-Roasted Peppers, *154,* 155
   Huli Huli Chicken, *312,* 313
   Husk-Grilled Corn, 386, *387*
      with Brown Sugar–Cayenne Butter, 386
      with Cilantro-Lime Butter, 386
      with Mustard-Paprika Butter, 386
      with Rosemary-Pepper Butter, 386
   Jucy Lucy Burgers, 342, *343*
   Lexington-Style Pulled Pork, *352,* 353
   Memphis-Style Wet Ribs for a Crowd, 94, *95*
   Shredded Barbecued Beef, *340,* 341
   Smoked Bourbon Chicken, *320,* 321
   Smoked Double-Thick Pork Chops, 362, *363*
   Smoky Potato Salad, 406, *407*
   South Carolina Pulled Pork, 354, *355*
   South Carolina Smoked Fresh Ham, *350,* 351
   South Dakota Corncob-Smoked Ribs, 374, *375*
   St. Louis BBQ Pork Steaks, 366, *367*
   Tennessee Pulled Pork Sandwiches, 356, *357*
   Texas Barbecued Beef Ribs, 348, *349*
   Texas Thick-Cut Smoked Pork Chops, *360,* 361
   Wood-Grilled Salmon, 378, *379*
      Barbecued, 378
      Lemon-Thyme, 378
Grilling equipment, ratings of, 616–18
Grits
   about, 9
   Cheese, Creamy, *8,* 9
   Shrimp and, 72, *73*

Gruyère cheese
   "Impossible" Ham-and-Cheese Pie, *424,* 425
   Slow-Cooker French Onion Soup, *136,* 137
   Stuffed Tomatoes, 156, *157*
Guacamole
   Chunky, 238, *239*
   Ultimate Seven-Layer Dip, *236,* 237
   Ultimate Smoky Seven-Layer Dip, 237
Guinness Beef Stew, *182,* 183
Gumbo, *68,* 69

H

Habanero Sauce, *252,* 253
Half-and-half, substitutes for, 227
Ham
   -and-Cheese Pie, "Impossible," *424,* 425
   California Barbecued Beans, 392, *393*
   Cider-Baked, *214,* 215
   Foolproof Chicken Cordon Bleu, 134, *135*
   Fresh, South Carolina Smoked, *350,* 351
Handy tools, ratings of, 601–6
Hazelnut(s)
   Cake, Swiss, 496, *497*
   Cheddar, and Apple, Brussels Sprout Salad with, 218
   and Goat Cheese, Roasted Green Beans with, 10, *11*
Herb(ed)
   -Crusted Beef Tenderloin, 192, *193*
   dried, cooking with, 429
   and Lemon Red Potato Salad, 418, *419*
   Mashed Sweet Potatoes with Caramelized Onion, 228
   Pan-Fried Pork Chops, 36

Herb(ed) *(cont.)*
   Ranch Fried Chicken, *62,* 63
   Roast Beef, 190, *191*
   Roast Chicken, *164,* 165
   tired, reviving, 256
   see also specific herbs
Hoecakes, *358,* 359
Holiday Strip Roast, *194,* 195
Home Fries with Fresh Herbs, 430
Homemade Breakfast Sausage, *428,* 429
Homemade Sazón, 242
Hominy grits, about, 9
Honey
   Fried Chicken, *52,* 53
   -Mustard Sauce, 65
Horseradish
   Cream Sauce, 192
   Tiger Sauce, 99
Hot Fudge Pudding Cake, *512,* 513
Huevos Rancheros, *240,* 241
Huli Huli Chicken, *312,* 313
Husk-Grilled Corn, *386,* 387
   with Brown Sugar–Cayenne Butter, 386
   with Cilantro-Lime Butter, 386
   with Mustard-Paprika Butter, 386
   with Rosemary-Pepper Butter, 386

I

Icebox Key Lime Pie, 582, *583*
Icebox Strawberry Pie, 588, *589*
"Impossible" Ham-and-Cheese Pie, *424,* 425
Individual Spoonbreads, 230
Ingredients, tastings of, 626–50
   anchovies, 626
   applesauce, 626
   bacon, 626
   barbecue sauce, 626
   beans, canned, 626–27
   bread crumbs, panko, 627
   breads, 627
   broths, 628
   brownie mix, 628
   butter, 628
   cheeses, 628–31
   chicken, 631
   chili powder, 631
   chocolate and chocolate chips, 632
   cider, hard, 632
   cinnamon, 632
   cocoa powder, 633
   coconut, shredded, 633
   coconut milk, 633
   coffee, 633
   cornmeal, 633
   Creole seasoning, 634
   curry powder, 634
   dinner rolls, frozen, 634
   egg whites, processed, 634
   five-spice powder, 634
   flours, 634
   French fries, frozen, 635
   giardiniera, 635
   gnocchi, 635

Ingredients, tastings of *(cont.)*
    grits, 635
    ham, 635
    hoisin sauce, 636
    honey, 636
    horseradish, 636
    hot dogs, 636
    hot fudge sauce, 636
    hot sauce, 636
    ice cream, 636–37
    ice cream cones, 636
    iced tea, 637
    juice, grapefruit, 637
    juice, orange, 637
    ketchup, 637
    lemonade, 638
    macaroni and cheese, 638
    maple syrup, 638
    mayonnaise, 638
    mirin, 638
    molasses, 639
    mustard, 639
    oats, 639
    olive oils, 640
    pancake mix, 640
    paprika, 640
    pastas, 640–42
    pasta sauces, 642
    peanut butter, 642
    peppercorns, 642
    pepperoni, 642
    peppers, roasted red, 642
    pickles, 643
    pie crust, ready-made, 643
    pizza, frozen, 643
    popcorn, 643
    pork, premium, 643
    potato chips, 643–44
    preserves, 644
    relish, 644
    rice, 644–45
    salsa, 645
    salt, 645
    sauerkraut, 646
    sausages, 646
    soups, canned, 646
    soy sauce, 646
    steak sauce, 646
    sweetened condensed milk, 646
    tartar sauce, 646
    tea, 647
    teriyaki sauce, 647
    tomatoes, canned, 647
    tortilla chips, 648
    tortillas, 648
    tostadas, 648
    tuna, canned, 648
    turkey, 648
    vanilla beans and extract, 649
    vegetable oil, 649
    vinegars, 649–50
    whipped topping, 650
    Worcestershire sauce, 650
    yogurts, 650
Irish whiskey, about, 336
Italian Cream Cake, 504, *505*
Italian Pot Roast, 304, *305*

J

Jam Thumbprint Cookies, *522*, 523
Joe Froggers, 528, *529*
Jucy Lucy Burgers, 342, *343*

K

Kitchen supplies, ratings of, 624–25
Knives and more, ratings of, 596–98
Kolaches, 464, *465*

L

Lane Cake, *482*, 483
Lasagna
    Skillet, 294, *295*
    Skillet, with Sausage and Peppers, 294
    Spinach and Tomato, *296*, 297
Latin Fried Chicken, 244, *245*
Latin-Spiced Butter, 389
Lemon(s)
    -Caper Sauce, Grilled Salmon Steaks with, *382*, 383
    Chicken, Grilled Butterflied, 322, *323*
    Chicken, Roast, 166, *167*
    -Chocolate Truffles, 535
    and Herb Red Potato Salad, 418, *419*
    Icebox Cheesecake, 516, *517*
    juicing, 13
    Meringue Pie, Mile-High, *584*, 585
    Pie, Shaker, *564*, 565
    Pudding Cake, 514, *515*
    Salsa Verde, 195
    -Thyme Wood-Grilled Salmon, 378
Lettuce
    Chinese Chicken Salad, 78, *79*
    Grilled Caesar Salad, 398, *399*
Lexington Barbecue Sauce, 353
Lexington-Style Pulled Pork, *352*, 353
Lime
    -Coconut Cookies, 525
    -Ginger Glaze, 525
    Key, Pie, Icebox, 582, *583*
Loaded Baked Potato Omelet Filling, 423
Louisiana Seasoning, 131

M

Macaroni
    and Cheese, Best Potluck, 4, *5*
    and Cheese with Tomatoes, *2*, 3
Magic Chocolate Flan Cake, *492*, 493
Maine Blueberry Grunt, *546*, 547
Malted Milk Glaze, 525
Manchego and Chorizo Breakfast Pizza, 426
Manicotti, Baked, with Meat Sauce, *298*, 299
Marshmallow crème
    Chocolate Cream Cupcakes, *510*, 511
    Swiss Hazelnut Cake, 496, *497*
    Whoopie Pies, 532, *533*
Masa harina
    Puffy Tacos, *250*, 251
Mashed Potato Cakes, 152, *153*
    Blue Cheese and Bacon, 152
    Cheddar and Scallion, 152
Mashed Potato Casserole, *226*, 227
Measuring equipment, ratings of, 607–9
Meat
    scoring fat on, 377
    see also Beef; Pork
Meatballs and Marinara, 286, *287*

678   *The Complete Cook's Country TV Show Cookbook*

Meatballs and Marinara, Slow-Cooker, *288*, 289
Meatloaf
    Bacon-Wrapped, 28, *29*
    Frosted, 24, *25*
    Glazed, 22, *23*
    with Mushroom Gravy, *26*, 27
Mediterranean Grilled Thin-Cut Pork Chops, 365
Melting Moments, *522*, 523
Memphis Chopped Coleslaw, *402*, 403
Memphis-Style Wet Ribs for a Crowd, 94, *95*
Mile-High Lemon Meringue Pie, *584*, 585
Milk-Can Supper, 34, *35*
Milk Chocolate Cheesecake, *518*, 519
Minestrone, Slow-Cooker, *272*, 273
Mint
    and Almonds, Roasted Green Beans with, 10
    tired, reviving, 256
Mississippi Mud Pie, 594, *595*
Mixed Berry Scones, 444, *445*
Monkey Bread, 466, *467*
Monterey Jack cheese
    Authentic Beef Enchiladas, 260, *261*
    Best Potluck Macaroni and Cheese, 4, *5*
    Creamy Cheese Grits, *8*, 9
    Crispy Baked Potato Fans, *148*, 149
    Spicy Cheese Bread, *448*, 449
    St. Louis–Style Pizza, 106, *107*
    Tex-Mex Cheese Enchiladas, *258*, 259
Moravian Chicken Pie, 180, *181*
Morning Buns, *462*, 463
Morning Glory Muffins, *454*, 455
Mozzarella
    Baked Manicotti with Meat Sauce, *298*, 299
    Breakfast Pizza, 426, *427*
    Cast-Iron Skillet Pizza, *302*, 303

Mozzarella *(cont.)*
    Chorizo and Manchego Breakfast Pizza, 426
    Grandma Pizza, 300, *301*
    Skillet Chicken Parmesan, 292, *293*
    Slow-Cooker Baked Ziti, *290*, 291
    Smoked Salmon Breakfast Pizza, 426
    Spinach and Tomato Lasagna, *296*, 297
    Stuffed Tomatoes with Capers and Pine Nuts, 156
Muffins
    Morning Glory, *454*, 455
    Whole-Wheat Blueberry, 452, *453*
Muffin Tin Popovers, 450
Mushroom(s)
    Classic Roast Beef and Gravy, *188*, 189
    Gravy, Meatloaf with, *26*, 27
    Italian Pot Roast, 304, *305*
    Salisbury Steak, *32*, 33
    Sauce, Pasta with, 282, *283*
Mustard
    Barbecue Sauce, 354
    Deviled Beef Short Ribs, 196, *197*
    -Glazed Pork Loin, Grilled, *376*, 377
    -Honey Sauce, 65
    -Paprika Butter, 386
    Sauce, 351
    Whole-Grain, and Cornichons, Tuna Salad with, 14

N

Nachos, Ultimate Spicy Beef, *234,* 235
Nashville Extra-Hot Fried Chicken, 60
Nashville Hot Fried Chicken, 60, *61*
Natchitoches Meat Pies, *104,* 105
New Orleans Barbecue Shrimp, 70, *71*
New Orleans Bourbon Bread Pudding, *554,* 555
New Orleans Muffulettas, *76,* 77
No-Cook Pizza Sauce, 303
No-Fear Single-Crust Pie Dough, 563
Noodles
    Chicken and Slicks, 178, *179*
    Chicken Chow Mein, *80,* 81
Nuts
    Brussels Sprout Salad, 218, *219*
    Brussels Sprout Salad with Cheddar, Hazelnuts, and Apple, 218
    Chocolate-Almond Truffles, 535
    Pine, and Capers, Stuffed Tomatoes with, 156
    Pine, and Pecorino, Roasted Green Beans with, 10
    Roasted Green Beans with Almonds and Mint, 10
    Roasted Green Beans with Goat Cheese and Hazelnuts, 10, *11*
    Stuffed Tomatoes with Currants and Pistachios, 156
    Swiss Hazelnut Cake, 496, *497*
    see also Pecan(s); Walnut(s)

O

Oklahoma Fried Onion Burgers, *86,* 87
Old-Fashioned Chocolate Frozen Custard, *558,* 559
Old-Fashioned Pecan Pie, 576, *577*
Old-Fashioned Roast Pork, *208,* 209
Old-Fashioned Roast Turkey with Gravy, 160, *161*
Old-Fashioned Vanilla Frozen Custard, *558,* 559
Olive Oil Potato Gratin, 150, *151*
Olives
    New Orleans Muffulettas, *76,* 77
    and Orange, Stuffed Tomatoes with, 156
One-Minute Salsa, 235
One-Pan Prime Rib and Roasted Vegetables, 198, *199*
One-Pan Roast Chicken with Fennel and Parsnips, 171
One-Pan Roast Chicken with Root Vegetables, *170,* 171
Onion(s)
    Caramelized, Herbed Mashed Sweet Potatoes with, 228
    chopping finely, 175
    Fried, Burgers, Oklahoma, *86,* 87
    Patty Melts, 84, *85*
    Pickled, *246,* 247
    Red, Pickled, *252,* 253
    Rings, Beer-Battered, 114, *115*
    Smothered Pork Chops, *38,* 39
    Soup, French, Slow-Cooker, *136,* 137
Orange(s)
    Chiffon Cake, 502
    Chinese Chicken Salad, 78, *79*
    and Olives, Stuffed Tomatoes with, 156
    –Poppy Seed Cookies, *524,* 525
    –Red Wine Sauce, 201
    Sour, Pie, 566, *567*

P

Pancake(s)
    Better-Than-the-Box, 432, *433*
    Dutch Baby, *436,* 437
    Fluffy Cornmeal, *434,* 435
    Hoecakes, *358,* 359
    Mix, Better-Than-the-Box, 432

Pandowdy, Apple, 542, *543*

Pan-Fried Pork Chops, 36, *37*
    BBQ, 36
    Herbed, 36

Paprika
    Louisiana Seasoning, 131

Parmesan
    Blue Cheese and Bacon Baked Potato Fans, 149
    Chicken Divan, *18,* 19
    Crispy Baked Potato Fans, *148,* 149
    -Crusted Asparagus, 216, *217*
    Delmonico Potato Casserole, *140,* 141
    Grilled Caesar Salad, 398, *399*
    Herb-Crusted Beef Tenderloin, 192, *193*
    and Lemon, Grilled Broccoli with, *396,* 397
    Mashed Potato Cakes, 152, *153*
    Potatoes, Crispy, *142,* 143
    -Rosemary Potato Tots, 113
    Skillet Chicken, 292, *293*
    Skillet Lasagna, 294, *295*
    Skillet Lasagna with Sausage and Peppers, 294
    Spinach and Tomato Lasagna, *296,* 297

Parsley
    -Garlic Steak Sauce, 125
    Green Goddess Dressing, *12,* 13
    Salsa Verde, 195
    tired, reviving, 256

Parsnips
    and Fennel, One-Pan Roast Chicken with, 171
    One-Pan Prime Rib and Roasted Vegetables, 198, *199*
    Slow-Cooker Pork Pot Roast, *206,* 207

Pasta
    Baked Manicotti with Meat Sauce, *298,* 299
    Best Potluck Macaroni and Cheese, 4, *5*
    Chicken and Slicks, 178, *179*
    Cincinnati Chili, *100,* 101
    Macaroni and Cheese with Tomatoes, *2, 3*
    with Mushroom Sauce, 282, *283*
    Pork Ragu, 276, *277*
    with Roasted Garlic Sauce, Arugula, and Walnuts, *280, 281*
    with Sausage Ragu, *278,* 279
    Skillet Lasagna, 294, *295*
    Skillet Lasagna with Sausage and Peppers, 294
    Slow-Cooker Baked Ziti, *290,* 291
    Slow-Cooker Minestrone, *272,* 273
    Spinach and Tomato Lasagna, *296,* 297
    Stuffed Tomatoes, 156, *157*

Patty Melts, 84, *85*

Peach(es)
    Cobbler, Skillet, 548, *549*
    and Cream Pie, 568, *569*
    Hand Pies, Fried, 570, *571*
    Kuchen, Dakota, 550, *551*
    peeling, 548

Peanut Butter
    and Jelly Glaze, 525
    Peanut-y Banana Pudding, 553

Pecan(s)
    Italian Cream Cake, 504, *505*
    Lane Cake, *482,* 483

Pecan(s) *(cont.)*
   Pie, Old-Fashioned, 576, *577*
   Smoked Gouda, and Dried Cherries, Brussels Sprout Salad with, 218
   Texas Sheet Cake, 488, *489*
   Tunnel of Fudge Cake, 480, *481*

Pecorino Romano cheese
   Fluffy Baked Polenta with Red Sauce, 284, *285*
   Pasta with Mushroom Sauce, 282, *283*
   Roasted Green Beans with Pecorino and Pine Nuts, 10

Pepper Jack cheese
   Huevos Rancheros, *240*, 241
   Ultimate Seven-Layer Dip, *236*, 237
   Ultimate Smoky Seven-Layer Dip, 237
   Ultimate Spicy Beef Nachos, *234*, 235

Pepper(s)
   Grill-Roasted, *154*, 155
   Milk-Can Supper, 34, *35*
   Red, Steak Sauce, Spicy, 125
   Red Bell, and Sausage Breakfast Pizza, 426
   and Sausage Omelet Filling, 423
   and Sausages, Skillet Lasagna with, 294
   Vinegar, Pork Chops with, 306, *307*
   see also Chile peppers

Perfect Popovers, 450, *451*
Perloo, Charleston Shrimp, 74, *75*
Pesto, Basil, Butter, 389
Pickled Onions, *246*, 247
Pickled Red Onions, *252*, 253
Pie Dough
   blind baking, 568
   Double-Crust, 562
   rolling and fitting, 562
   Single-Crust, Classic, 562
   single-crust, crimping edge, 581
   Single-Crust, No-Fear, 563

Pierogi, Potato-Cheddar, 108, *109*
Pies (savory)
   "Impossible" Ham-and-Cheese, *424*, 425
   Moravian Chicken, 180, *181*
   Natchitoches Meat, *104*, 105

Pies (sweet)
   Apple, with Cheddar Crust, *572*, 573
   Apple Slab, 574, *575*
   Chocolate Angel, 592, *593*
   Coconut, French, *580*, 581
   French Silk Chocolate, *590*, 591
   Fried Peach Hand, 570, *571*
   Icebox Key Lime, 582, *583*
   Icebox Strawberry, 588, *589*
   Lemon Meringue, Mile-High, *584*, 585
   Mississippi Mud, 594, *595*
   Peaches and Cream, 568, *569*
   Pecan, Old-Fashioned, 576, *577*
   Raspberry Chiffon, 586, *587*
   Shaker Lemon, *564*, 565
   Sour Orange, *566*, 567
   Sweet Potato, *578*, 579

Pineapple
   Huli Huli Chicken, *312*, 313
   Morning Glory Muffins, *454*, 455

Pine Nuts
   Brussels Sprout Salad, 218, *219*
   and Capers, Stuffed Tomatoes with, 156
   and Pecorino, Roasted Green Beans with, 10

Pistachios and Currants, Stuffed Tomatoes with, 156
Pit Beef, Baltimore, *98*, 99
Pizza
   Breakfast, 426, *427*
      Chorizo and Manchego, 426
      Sausage and Red Bell Pepper, 426
      Smoked Salmon, 426

Pizza *(cont.)*
    Cast-Iron Skillet, *302,* 303
    Dough, Classic, 303
    Grandma, 300, *301*
    Sauce, No-Cook, 303
    St. Louis–Style, 106, *107*

Polenta
    about, 9
    Fluffy Baked, with Red Sauce, *284,* 285

Popovers
    Muffin Tin, 450
    Perfect, 450, *451*

Pork
    Barbecued Country-Style Ribs, *372,* 373
    butt, about, 82
    Chicago-Style Barbecued Ribs, 346, *347*
    Chinese Barbecued, Slow-Cooker, 82, *83*
    Chinese-Style Barbecued Spareribs, *370,* 371
    Chops
        BBQ Pan-Fried, 36
        Cider-Braised, *40,* 41
        cooking tip, 36
        Grilled Thin-Cut, *364,* 365
        Grilled Thin-Cut, Caribbean, 365
        Grilled Thin-Cut, Mediterranean, 365
        Grilled Thin-Cut, Spicy Thai, 365
        Herbed Pan-Fried, 36
        Pan-Fried, 36, *37*
        Smoked Double-Thick, *362,* 363
        Smothered, *38,* 39
        Tennessee Whiskey, *92,* 93
        Texas Thick-Cut Smoked, *360,* 361
        with Vinegar Peppers, *306,* 307
    Citrus-Braised, Tacos, *252,* 253
    Colorado Green Chili, 102, *103*
    country-style ribs, about, 373
    Crown Roast of, 204, *205*

Pork *(cont.)*
    Frosted Meatloaf, 24, *25*
    Glazed Meatloaf, 22, *23*
    Grillades, *130,* 131
    Homemade Breakfast Sausage, *428,* 429
    Loin, Grilled Mustard-Glazed, *376,* 377
    Memphis-Style Wet Ribs for a Crowd, 94, *95*
    Natchitoches Meat Pies, *104,* 105
    Pot Roast, Slow-Cooker, *206,* 207
    Pulled, Lexington-Style, *352,* 353
    Pulled, South Carolina, 354, *355*
    Pulled, Tennessee, Sandwiches, 356, *357*
    Ragu, 276, *277*
    Roast, Cider-Braised, 212, *213*
    Roast, Old-Fashioned, *208,* 209
    Roast, Puerto Rican, 210, *211*
    salt, about, 160
    scoring fat on, 377
    Skillet Lasagna, 294, *295*
    Slow-Cooker Italian Sunday Gravy, *274,* 275
    Slow-Cooker Memphis-Style Wet Ribs, 96, *97*
    South Dakota Corncob-Smoked Ribs, 374, *375*
    Steaks, St. Louis BBQ, 366, *367*
    Tenderloin, Chinese-Style Glazed, 368, *369*
    see also Bacon; Ham; Sausage(s)

Potato(es)
    Baked
        Fans, Blue Cheese and Bacon, 149
        Fans, Crispy, *148,* 149
        Super-Stuffed, *146,* 147
    Brunswick Stew, 184, *185*
    and Carrots, Chicken Baked in Foil with, 177
    Casserole, Delmonico, *140,* 141
    -Cheddar Pierogi, 108, *109*
    and Chicken, Skillet-Roasted, 172, *173*
    Chuck Roast in Foil, *202,* 203

Potato(es) *(cont.)*
    Crispy Parmesan, *142,* 143
    Crown Roast of Pork, 204, *205*
    Duchess, *222,* 223
    Frosted Meatloaf, 24, *25*
    Gratin, Olive Oil, 150, *151*
    Greek Diner-Style Home Fries, 430
    Guinness Beef Stew, *182,* 183
    Hobo Packs, Grilled, 394
        Spanish-Style, 394, *395*
        Spicy Home Fry, 394
        Vinegar and Onion, 394
    Home Fries with Fresh Herbs, 430
    Loaded Baked, Omelet Filling, 423
    Mashed, Cakes, 152, *153*
        Blue Cheese and Bacon, 152
        Cheddar and Scallion, 152
    Mashed, Casserole, *226,* 227
    Mashed, Garlic, 138, *139*
    Milk-Can Supper, 34, *35*
    One-Pan Roast Chicken with Fennel and Parsnips, 171
    One-Pan Roast Chicken with Root Vegetables, *170,* 171
    and Red Wine–Orange Sauce, Prime Rib with, *200,* 201
    Roasted Salt-and-Vinegar, 144, *145*
    Salad
        All-American, 404, *405*
        Amish, *408,* 409
        Dill, *412,* 413
        Ranch, 410, *411*
        Red, Lemon and Herb, 418, *419*
        Smashed, 416, *417*
        Smoky, 406, *407*
        Texas, *414,* 415
    Short-Order Home Fries, 430, *431*
    Syracuse Salt, 224, *225*

Potato(es) *(cont.)*
    Tots
        Bacon-Ranch, 113
        Crispy, *112,* 113
        Crispy, for a Crowd, 113
        Parmesan-Rosemary, 113
        Southwestern, 113
    Wedges, Crunchy, *110,* 111
    Whipped, *220,* 221
    see also Sweet Potato(es)
Pots and pans, ratings of, 598–600
Pretzel Strawberry Salad, 44, *45*
Prime Rib with Potatoes and Red Wine–Orange Sauce, *200,* 201
Provolone cheese
    Baked Manicotti with Meat Sauce, *298,* 299
    New Orleans Muffulettas, *76,* 77
    Skillet Chicken Parmesan, 292, *293*
    Spicy Cheese Bread, *448,* 449
Pudding
    Banana, *552,* 553
    Banana, Peanut-y, 553
    Banana, Toasted-Coconut, 553
    Bread, New Orleans Bourbon, *554,* 555
    Summer Berry, 556, *557*
Puerto Rican Pork Roast, 210, *211*
Puffy Tacos, *250,* 251

Quick Barbecue Sauce, 319
Quicker Cinnamon Buns, *460,* 461

R

Radish(es)
    Hard-Cooked Eggs, and Capers, Tuna Salad with, 14
    and Sweet Potato, Chicken Baked in Foil with, *176*, 177

Raisins
    Classic Steak Sauce, 125
    Lane Cake, *482*, 483
    Morning Glory Muffins, *454*, 455
    New Orleans Bourbon Bread Pudding, *554*, 555
    Steak Sauce, 128

Ranch Fried Chicken, *62*, 63
Ranch Potato Salad, 410, *411*

Raspberry(ies)
    Blitz Torte, *498*, 499
    Chiffon Pie, 586, *587*
    Summer Berry Pudding, 556, *557*

Recipe and culinary history
    Basque cooking in California, 57
    Bastien's Restaurant, 121
    Big Bob Gibson's restaurant, 316
    Bundt pans, 481
    chicken Divan, 19
    chicken Florentine, 16
    chuck roast in foil, 203
    cold-oven recipes, 508
    Cornell chicken, 314
    cowboy food lingo, 34
    Delmonico potatoes, 141
    Delmonico's restaurant, 141
    Divan Parisien restaurant, 16, 19
    Ebinger's Baking Company, 478
    frozen fish sticks, 42
    gelatin-based salads, 44

Recipe and culinary history *(cont.)*
    grandma pizza, 300
    Heinz ketchup, 22
    Hidden Valley Ranch Dressing, 410
    honeybees in America, 53
    Horn and Hardart's automats, 3
    "huli"-ed chicken, 313
    Joe froggers, 528
    Jucy Lucy burgers, 342
    macaroni and cheese, 3
    meatloaf, 22, 24
    New Orleans Vietnamese community, 69
    North Carolina barbecue, 353
    Oberlin College dining plan, 490
    Papa Kay Joe's, 359
    Peach Park, 570
    Pillsbury Bake-Off, 591
    proper dining and tableware, 469
    Salisbury steak, 33
    sandwiches, 84
    Shaker Lemon Pie, 565
    smothered pork chops, 39
    St. Louis–style pizza, 106
    Sunbeam Mixmaster, 221
    sweet-and-sour flavors, 409
    sweetened condensed milk, 582
    Syracuse salt potatoes, 224
    whoopie pies, 532

Red Velvet Cake, 476, *477*
Red Wine–Orange Sauce, 201
Rhubarb-Strawberry Compote, 507

Rice
    Arroz con Pollo, 242, *243*
    Charleston Shrimp Perloo, *74*, 75
    Easier Chicken Chimichangas, 254, *255*

Ricotta cheese
    Baked Manicotti with Meat Sauce, 298, *299*
    Kolaches, 464, *465*
    Skillet Lasagna, 294, *295*
    Skillet Lasagna with Sausage and Peppers, 294
    Slow-Cooker Baked Ziti, *290,* 291
    Spinach and Tomato Lasagna, *296,* 297

Roasted Green Beans
    with Almonds and Mint, 10
    with Goat Cheese and Hazelnuts, 10, *11*
    with Pecorino and Pine Nuts, 10

Roasted Salt-and-Vinegar Potatoes, 144, *145*

Roast Lemon Chicken, 166, *167*

Rosemary
    -Parmesan Potato Tots, 113
    -Pepper Butter, 386

Round Spritz Cookies, 522, *523*

Rum
    Joe Froggers, 528, *529*

S

Salads
    Brussels Sprout, 218, *219*
        with Cheddar, Hazelnuts, and Apple, 218
        with Smoked Gouda, Pecans, and Dried Cherries, 218
    Chinese Chicken, 78, *79*
    Grilled Caesar, 398, *399*
    Memphis Chopped Coleslaw, *402,* 403
    Potato
        All-American, 404, *405*
        Amish, *408,* 409
        Dill, *412,* 413
        Ranch, 410, *411*

Salads, Potato *(cont.)*
    Red, Lemon and Herb, 418, *419*
    Smashed, 416, *417*
    Smoky, 406, *407*
    Texas, *414,* 415
    Strawberry Pretzel, 44, *45*
    Tangy Apple Cabbage Slaw, *400,* 401
    Tuna
        with Apple, Walnuts, and Tarragon, 14
        Classic, 14, *15*
        with Cornichons and Whole-Grain Mustard, 14
        with Curry and Grapes, 14
        with Hard-Cooked Eggs, Radishes, and Capers, 14

Salisbury Steak, *32, 33*

Salmon
    Cedar-Planked, with Cucumber-Yogurt Sauce, 380, *381*
    Smoked, Breakfast Pizza, 426
    Steaks, Grilled, with Lemon-Caper Sauce, *382,* 383
    Wood-Grilled, 378, *379*
        Barbecued, 378
        Lemon-Thyme, 378

Salsa
    One-Minute, 235
    Santa Maria, 339
    Verde, 195
    Verde, Smoky, 256, *257*

Salt-and-Vinegar Potatoes, Roasted, 144, *145*

Salt pork, about, 160

Salt Potatoes, Syracuse, 224, *225*

Sandwiches
    Baltimore Pit Beef, *98,* 99
    Barbecued Pulled Chicken, *332,* 333
    New Orleans Muffulettas, *76,* 77

Sandwiches *(cont.)*
    Patty Melts, 84, *85*
    Tennessee Pulled Pork, 356, *357*
    see also Burgers; Tuna Salad
Santa Maria Salsa, 339
Sauces
    Bourbon, 555
    Buffalo Blue Cheese, 111
    Chocolate, 268, *269*
    Cider, 539
    Cucumber-Yogurt, 380
    Curried Chutney, 111
    Habanero, *252*, 253
    Honey-Mustard, 65
    Horseradish Cream, 192
    Meatballs and Marinara, 286, *287*
    Mustard, 351
    One-Minute Salsa, 235
    Pizza, No-Cook, 303
    Pork Ragu, 276, *277*
    Red, *284*, 285
    Red Wine–Orange, 201
    Salsa Verde, 195
    Santa Maria Salsa, 339
    Slow-Cooker Italian Sunday Gravy, *274*, 275
    Slow-Cooker Meatballs and Marinara, *288*, 289
    Smoky Salsa Verde, 256, *257*
    Steak, 128
        Classic, 125
        Garlic-Parsley, 125
        Spicy Red Pepper, 125
    Sweet and Sour, 65
    Tartar, Crispy Fish Sticks with, 42, *43*
    Tiger, 99
    White, 247
    see also Barbecue Sauces

Sausage(s)
    Backyard Barbecued Beans, *390*, 391
    Baked Manicotti with Meat Sauce, *298*, 299
    Brunswick Stew, 184, *185*
    Chorizo and Manchego Breakfast Pizza, 426
    and Cornbread Stuffing, 162, *163*
    Creole Baked Stuffed Shrimp with, 132
    Gumbo, *68*, 69
    Meatballs and Marinara, 286, *287*
    Milk-Can Supper, 34, *35*
    New Orleans Muffulettas, *76*, 77
    and Pepper Omelet Filling, 423
    and Peppers, Skillet Lasagna with, 294
    Ragu, Pasta with, *278*, 279
    and Red Bell Pepper Breakfast Pizza, 426
    Slow-Cooker Baked Ziti, *290*, 291
    Slow-Cooker Italian Sunday Gravy, *274*, 275
    Slow-Cooker Meatballs and Marinara, *288*, 289
    Spanish-Style Grilled Potato Hobo Packs, 394, *395*
Sazón, Homemade, 242
Scones, Mixed Berry, 444, *445*
Scotch whisky, about, 336
Seasonings
    Homemade Sazón, 242
    Louisiana, 131
Shaker Lemon Pie, *564*, 565
Shellfish. *See* **Shrimp**
Sherry
    Chicken Divan, *18*, 19
Short-Order Home Fries, 430, *431*
Shredded Barbecued Beef, *340*, 341
Shrimp
    Baked Stuffed, 132, *133*
    Baked Stuffed, Creole, with Sausage, 132
    frozen, buying, 72
    and Grits, 72, *73*

Shrimp *(cont.)*
    Gumbo, *68,* 69
    New Orleans Barbecue, 70, *71*
    peeling and deveining, 75
    Perloo, Charleston, *74,* 75
    skewering, 385
    Skewers, Grilled
        Caribbean, 385
        Jalapeño and Lime, *384,* 385
        Red Chile and Ginger, 385
Skillet Chicken Parmesan, 292, *293*
Skillet Lasagna, 294, *295*
Skillet Lasagna with Sausage and Peppers, 294
Skillet Peach Cobbler, 548, *549*
Skillet-Roasted Chicken and Potatoes, 172, *173*
Skillet-Roasted Chicken with Stuffing, *174,* **175**
Slab Pie, Apple, 574, *575*
Slaws
    Memphis Chopped Coleslaw, *402,* 403
    Tangy Apple Cabbage, *400,* 401
Slice-and-Bake Cookies, *524,* **525**
Slow-Cooker Baked Ziti, 290, *291*
Slow-Cooker BBQ Beef Brisket, 90, *91*
Slow-Cooker Chicken Stock, 46, *47*
Slow-Cooker Chinese Barbecued Pork, 82, *83*
Slow-Cooker French Onion Soup, *136,* **137**
Slow-Cooker Italian Sunday Gravy, 274, *275*
Slow-Cooker Meatballs and Marinara, 288, *289*
Slow-Cooker Memphis-Style Wet Ribs, 96, *97*
Slow-Cooker Minestrone, *272,* **273**
Slow-Cooker Pork Pot Roast, 206, *207*
Smashed Potato Salad, 416, *417*
Smoked Bourbon Chicken, 320, *321*
Smoked Double-Thick Pork Chops, 362, *363*
Smoked Gouda, Pecans, and Dried Cherries, Brussels Sprout Salad with, 218

Smoked Salmon Breakfast Pizza, 426
Smokehouse Mashed Sweet Potatoes, 228
Smoky Potato Salad, 406, *407*
Smoky Salsa Verde, 256, *257*
Smothered Pork Chops, *38,* **39**
So-Cal Churros, 268, *269*
Soups
    French Onion, Slow-Cooker, *136,* 137
    Minestrone, Slow-Cooker, *272,* 273
    Tomato, Classic, 6, *7*
    see also Stews
Sour Cream, Chive, *142,* **143**
Sour Orange Pie, *566,* **567**
South Carolina Pulled Pork, 354, *355*
South Carolina Smoked Fresh Ham, *350,* **351**
South Dakota Corncob-Smoked Ribs, 374, *375*
Southern-Style Skillet Cornbread, *446,* **447**
Southern-Style Smothered Chicken, 20, *21*
Southwestern Potato Tots, 113
Spanish-Style Grilled Potato Hobo Packs, 394, *395*
Specialty pieces, ratings of, 619–24
Spicy Cheese Bread, *448,* **449**
Spicy Home Fry Grilled Potato Hobo Packs, 394
Spicy Red Pepper Steak Sauce, 125
Spicy Thai Grilled Thin-Cut Pork Chops, 365
Spinach
    Chicken Florentine, 16, *17*
    Stuffed Tomatoes, 156, *157*
    and Tomato Lasagna, *296,* 297
Spoonbread, Sweet Corn, 230, *231*
Spoonbreads, Individual, 230
Squash
    Slow-Cooker Minestrone, *272,* 273
St. Louis BBQ Pork Steaks, 366, *367*
St. Louis–Style Pizza, 106, *107*

Steak Sauce, 128
   Classic, 125
   Garlic-Parsley, 125
   Spicy Red Pepper, 125

Stews
   Brunswick, 184, *185*
   Guinness Beef, *182*, 183
   Gumbo, *68*, 69
   see also Chili

Stock
   Chicken, Slow-Cooker, *46*, 47
   storing, 47

Strawberry(ies)
   Dream Cake, 484, *485*
   Pie, Icebox, 588, *589*
   Poke Cake, *486*, 487
   Pretzel Salad, 44, *45*
   -Rhubarb Compote, 507
   Summer Berry Pudding, 556, *557*

Stuffed Tomatoes, 156, *157*
   with Bacon, 156
   with Capers and Pine Nuts, 156
   with Currants and Pistachios, 156
   with Olives and Orange, 156

Stuffing
   Cornbread and Bacon, 162
   Cornbread and Sausage, 162, *163*
   Skillet-Roasted Chicken with, *174*, 175

Summer Berry Pudding, 556, *557*
Sunday-Best Garlic Roast Beef, *186*, 187
Super-Stuffed Baked Potatoes, *146*, 147
Sweet and Sour Sauce, 65
Sweet Chili Sauce, Grilled Broccoli with, 397
Sweet Corn Spoonbread, 230, *231*
Sweet Potato(es)
   Herbed Mashed, with Caramelized Onion, 228
   Mashed, Creamy, 228, *229*
   Pie, *578*, 579
   and Radish, Chicken Baked in Foil with, *176*, 177
   Smokehouse Mashed, 228

Swiss cheese
   Foolproof Chicken Cordon Bleu, 134, *135*
   Patty Melts, 84, *85*

Swiss Hazelnut Cake, 496, *497*
Swiss Steak with Tomato Gravy, *30*, 31
Syracuse Salt Potatoes, 224, *225*

T

Tacos
   Chicken, Easy, 248, *249*
   Citrus-Braised Pork, *252*, 253
   Fish, California-Style, *246*, 247
   Puffy, *250*, 251

Tamales, Delta Hot, 66, *67*
Tandoori Grilled Chicken Wings, 325
Tangy Apple Cabbage Slaw, *400*, 401
Tarragon, Apple, and Walnuts, Tuna Salad with, 14
Tartar Sauce, Crispy Fish Sticks with, 42, *43*
Tennessee Pulled Pork Sandwiches, 356, *357*
Tennessee Whiskey
   about, 93
   Pork Chops, *92*, 93

Texas Barbecued Beef Ribs, 348, *349*
Texas Barbecue Sauce, 348
Texas Potato Salad, *414*, 415
Texas Sheet Cake, 488, *489*
Texas Thick-Cut Smoked Pork Chops, *360*, 361
Tex-Mex Cheese Enchiladas, *258*, 259
Thermometers and timers, ratings of, 607–9
Thyme, prepping, 172
Tiger Sauce, 99
Toasted-Coconut Banana Pudding, 553
Tomatillos
   about, 256
   Smoky Salsa Verde, 256, *257*

Tomato(es)
    Baked Manicotti with Meat Sauce, *298, 299*
    Chicken Chilaquiles, *262, 263*
    Grandma Pizza, 300, *301*
    Gravy, Swiss Steak with, *30*, 31
    Huevos Rancheros, *240, 241*
    Macaroni and Cheese with, *2*, 3
    Meatballs and Marinara, *286, 287*
    No-Cook Pizza Sauce, 303
    One-Minute Salsa, 235
    Pasta with Sausage Ragu, *278*, 279
    Pork Grillades, *130*, 131
    Pork Ragu, 276, *277*
    Red Sauce, *284*, 285
    Santa Maria Salsa, 339
    Skillet Chicken Parmesan, 292, *293*
    Skillet Lasagna, 294, *295*
    Skillet Lasagna with Sausage and Peppers, 294
    Slow-Cooker Baked Ziti, *290*, 291
    Slow-Cooker Italian Sunday Gravy, *274, 275*
    Slow-Cooker Meatballs and Marinara, *288*, 289
    Soup, Classic, 6, *7*
    and Spinach Lasagna, *296, 297*
    Stuffed, 156, *157*
        with Bacon, 156
        with Capers and Pine Nuts, 156
        with Currants and Pistachios, 156
        with Olives and Orange, 156
    Sun-Dried, and Fennel, Chicken Baked in Foil with, 177
    Ultimate Seven-Layer Dip, *236*, 237
    Ultimate Smoky Seven-Layer Dip, 237
Tools, handy, ratings of, 601–6

Tortillas
    Authentic Beef Enchiladas, 260, *261*
    California-Style Fish Tacos, *246*, 247
    Chicken Chilaquiles, *262, 263*
    Citrus-Braised Pork Tacos, *252*, 253
    Easier Chicken Chimichangas, 254, *255*
    Easy Chicken Tacos, 248, *249*
    Huevos Rancheros, *240, 241*
    Tex-Mex Cheese Enchiladas, *258*, 259
    Ultimate Spicy Beef Nachos, *234*, 235
Tres Leches Cake, *494*, 495
Truffles
    Chocolate, Basic, *534*, 535
    Chocolate-Almond, 535
    Chocolate-Cinnamon, 535
    Chocolate-Ginger, 535
    Chocolate-Lemon, 535
Tuna Salad
    with Apple, Walnuts, and Tarragon, 14
    Classic, 14, *15*
    with Cornichons and Whole-Grain Mustard, 14
    with Curry and Grapes, 14
    with Hard-Cooked Eggs, Radishes, and Capers, 14
Tunnel of Fudge Cake, *480*, 481
Turkey, Old-Fashioned Roast, with Gravy, 160, *161*

U

Ultimate Cinnamon Buns, 458, *459*
Ultimate Seven-Layer Dip, *236*, 237
Ultimate Smoky Seven-Layer Dip, 237
Ultimate Spicy Beef Nachos, *234*, 235

V

Vanilla Frozen Custard, Old-Fashioned, *558*, 559
Veal
    Skillet Lasagna, 294, *295*
Vegetables
    Root, One-Pan Roast Chicken with, *170,* 171
    Slow-Cooker Minestrone, *272,* 273
    see also specific vegetables
Vinegar
    and Onion Grilled Potato Hobo Packs, 394
    primer on, 401

W

Walnut(s)
    Apple, and Tarragon, Tuna Salad with, 14
    –Brown Sugar Cookies, 525
    Morning Glory Muffins, *454,* 455
    Roasted Garlic Sauce, and Arugula, Pasta with, 280, *281*
    Tunnel of Fudge Cake, *480,* 481

Whipped Cream, Bourbon, 576
Whipped Potatoes, *220,* 221
Whiskey, about, 336
White Sauce, 247
Whole-Wheat Blueberry Muffins, 452, *453*
Whoopie Pies, 532, *533*
Wine, Red, –Orange Sauce, 201
Wood-Grilled Salmon, 378, *379*
    Barbecued, 378
    Lemon-Thyme, 378

Y

Yeast, instant (rapid-rise), about, 309
Yogurt-Cucumber Sauce, 380

Z

Zeppoles, *308,* 309
Ziti, Slow-Cooker Baked, *290,* 291
Zucchini
    Slow-Cooker Minestrone, *272,* 273

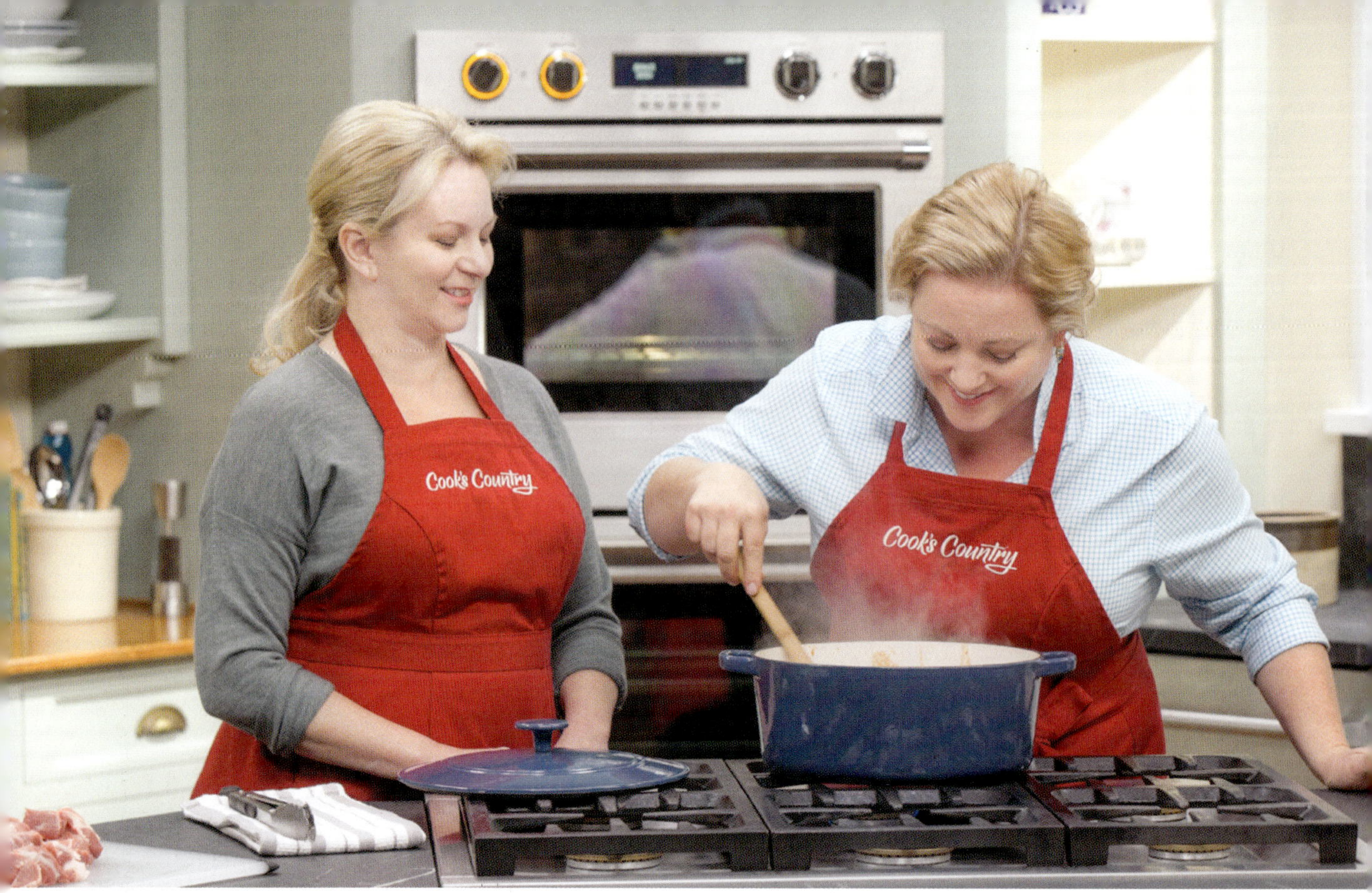
Cook's Country
Cook's Country

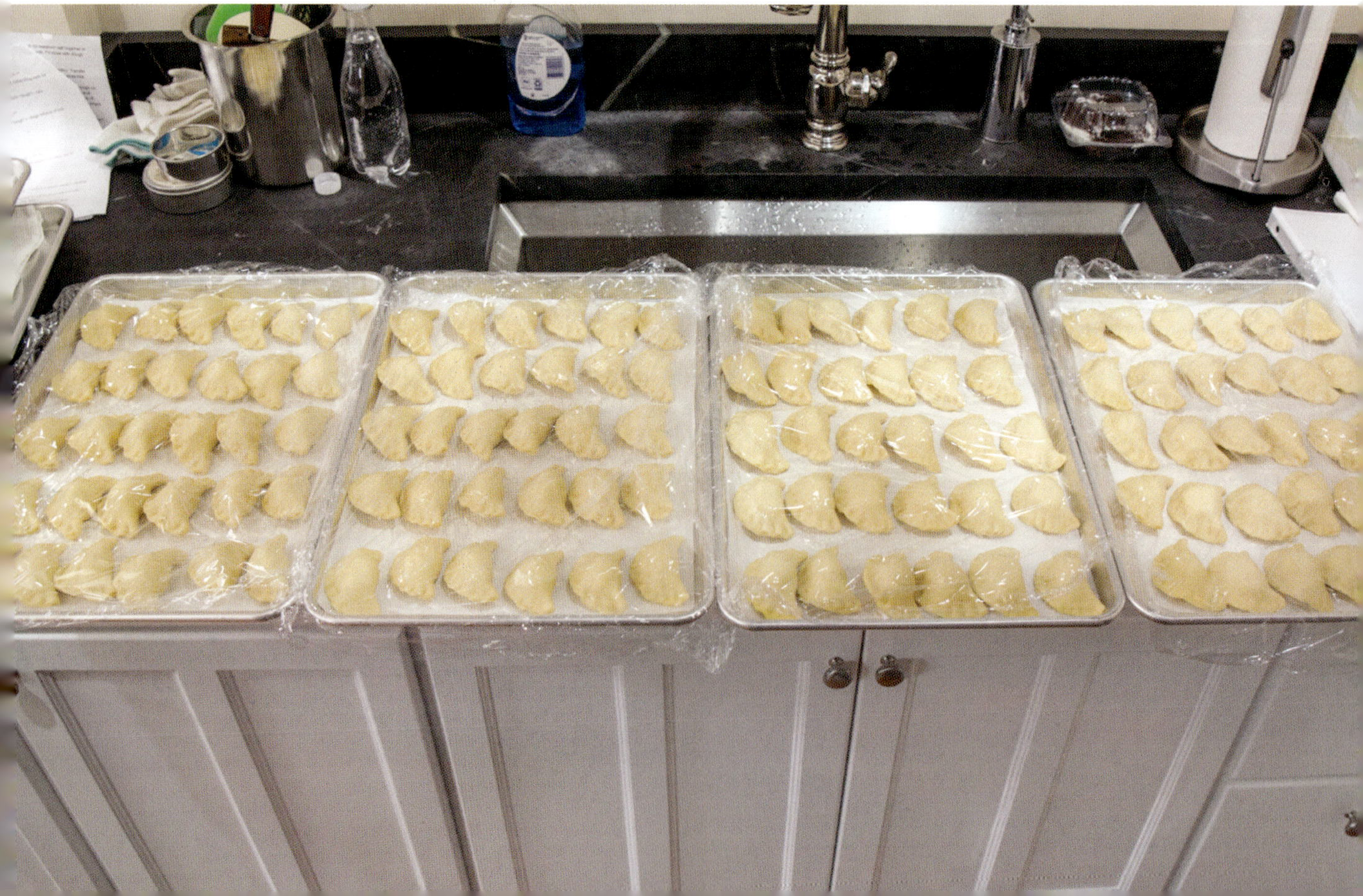

FRENCH SILK
CHOCOLATE PIE

BALTIMORE
PIT BEEF

FAIRY
GINGERBREAD

MAINE BLUEBERRY GRUNT

ALABAMA
BARBECUED
CHICKEN

TENNESSEE
WHISKEY
PORK
CHOPS

JUCY LUCY
BURGERS

MORAVIAN CHICKEN PIE

GRILLED POTATO
HOBO PACKS

SKILLET
CHICKEN
PARMESAN

Retailing Today
AN INTRODUCTION

DON L. JAMES
Fort Lewis College

BRUCE J. WALKER
Arizona State University

MICHAEL J. ETZEL
University of Kentucky

Retailing Today

AN INTRODUCTION

HARCOURT BRACE JOVANOVICH, INC.
New York   Chicago   San Francisco   Atlanta

© 1975 by Harcourt Brace Jovanovich, Inc.

All rights reserved. No part of this publication may be reproduced or transmitted in any form or by any means, electronic or mechanical, including photocopying, recording, or any information storage and retrieval system, without permission in writing from the publisher.

ISBN: 0-15-576670-8

Library of Congress Catalog Card Number: 74-34526

Printed in the United States of America

Photo and cartoon credits appear on page 642.

Preface

Since retailing includes all the activities associated with the sale of products and services to ultimate consumers, it encompasses many decision-making areas. The purpose of this book is to help students not only to become familiar with the decisions that retail managers must make but also to learn how to approach those decisions systematically. Retailing is a complex and challenging field of business. It is also an exciting and satisfying field, especially for those who enter it with the proper knowledge and skills.

As marketing and retailing instructors, we have observed two trends in the teaching of college-level retailing courses. First, there is a stronger orientation toward the decision-making tasks of middle management and less emphasis on the strategy planning of top management and the daily activities of hourly employees. Second, there is greater concern with the firm's environment—not only consumers and competitors, but also governmental bodies, the consumerism movement, and the economic problems of supply and distribution of resources.

These two trends have guided us in developing both our general approach and the particular contents of *Retailing Today: An Introduction*. We have sought to help the student

- become familiar with fundamental retailing concepts and practices
- appreciate the importance of basic managerial skills, and develop those skills
- understand the various types of decisions a retail manager must make and learn how to proceed systematically in making them
- become acquainted with important institutional aspects of retailing
- become aware of and appreciate the environmental forces that affect decisions.

To sum up, we have sought to introduce the student to the challenging, exciting world of retailing today.

To allow a systematic treatment of the basic elements of the retailing mix—offerings, physical facilities, prices, and promotion—we have grouped the twenty-six chapters into eight parts:

1. Retailing Today: Perspectives and Planning
2. Initial Considerations and Decisions
3. Merchandise Management
4. The Pricing Function
5. The Promotion Function
6. Financial and Information Management
7. Special Topics
8. Beyond In-Store Retailing Today

The first two chapters provide a general introduction to retailing. The remainder of the book's contents, as they relate to managerial decisions involved in developing the retailing mix, are outlined in Chapter 2.

Throughout the book we have relied on succinct coverage of practical, decision-oriented material, aided by figures, photographs, and cartoons that illustrate key concepts and practices. Numerous examples of actual retailing activities make the chapters interesting as well as realistic.

To present a complete learning package, each chapter contains:

- Several Review Boxes that contain fill-in questions to check comprehension and retention of material just read (Answers are given at the end of the chapter.)
- A Spotlight that describes a retailing situation or practice with specific and interesting insights for the chapter
- A point-by-point Chapter Summary
- Questions and Assignments that review material covered in the chapter and also motivate the student to venture into the "real" world of retailing.

Two Retailing Decisions are placed at the end of Parts 2 through 7. Each decision situation provides the student with an opportunity to develop or select a course of action related to a decision area discussed in preceding chapters or to evaluate a decision made by a retail manager.

A Glossary of all major terms appears at the back of the book.

Many retailing executives and journal and magazine writers and publishers provided us with materials and ideas that helped make this truly a book on retailing today. In addition, many students at Southern Illinois University and the University of Kentucky assisted in the classroom testing of the manuscript, and we are grateful for their contributions to its development. Special thanks go to Professors Joseph Kilpatrick of California State University at Sacramento, Raymond Tewell of American River College, and Orville Walker of the University of Minnesota, who evaluated our concept of a learning package, reviewed the manuscript, and provided much valuable feedback. Finally, we acknowledge with gratitude the many hours of manuscript typing by Judy Holladay, Patricia Scott, Kathy Clayton, and Virginia Scott at the University of Kentucky; Sue Hoefle at Arizona State University; Jan Crandall at Fort Lewis College; and Brenda Rubach at Southern Illinois University.

For shortcomings and errors in the book, we accept all responsibility. In this regard, we encourage our readers—both students and instructors—to write us with criticisms as well as recommendations for future editions.

Our families have made vital contributions of patience and encouragement throughout the project. In appreciation, we dedicate this book to our wives—Helen James, Pam Walker, Chris Etzel and to our children—Dan, Jennifer, and Darla James; Therese, Stephen, and Scott Walker; and Gretchen and Katy Etzel.

Don L. James
Bruce J. Walker
Michael J. Etzel

Contents

PART ONE *Retailing Today: Perspectives and Planning*

1 RETAILING YESTERDAY AND TODAY 4

Retailing and Retailers 4
The Need for Retailing 5
 The Consumer and Retailing   The Manufacturer and Retailing
The Scope of Retailing 6
Classification of Retail Businesses 7
 In-Store Retailing   Non-Store Retailing
External Forces Affecting Retailers 14
 Societal Forces   Economic Forces   Technological Forces
 Governmental Forces   *Spotlight*
The Evolution of Retailing in the United States 23
 Stage I: The Availability of Products   Stage II: The Availability of Roads   Stage III: The Availability of Mail Service   Stage IV: The Availability of Consumer Transportation   More Recent Developments
Chapter Summary 26

2 RETAIL OPERATIONS PLANNING 29

Programming Retail Operations 30
 Decisions in Programming
Steps in Operations Planning 33
 Assess the Environment   Identify Target Markets   Formulate Desired Image   *Spotlight*   Design a Retailing Mix
Chapter Summary 51

PART TWO *Initial Considerations and Decisions*

3 ANALYZING CONSUMER BEHAVIOR 56

Before the Purchase 56
Needs   Self-Concept   *Spotlight*   Social Class   Life Cycle
During the Purchase 67
Price   Loyalty
After the Purchase 73
Expected Benefits   Post-Purchase Doubt
Chapter Summary 75

4 STORE LOCATION 78

Factors in Store Location 78
Types of Location   Location Objectives
Location Analysis 83
General Area Analysis   Specific Site Analysis   *Spotlight*   Data Sources for Area and Specific Site Analyses
Chapter Summary 91

5 STORE LAYOUT AND DESIGN 93

Store Layout 93
Layout Alternatives   Space Allocation   Merchandise Placement
Store Design 100
The Objectives of Design   *Spotlight*   Design Basics
Chapter Summary 108

6 ORGANIZATIONAL STRUCTURE IN RETAILING 111

Organization and Organizing 111
The Need for Organizing   *Spotlight*   Formal and Informal Organizations

Large and Small Stores 116
  Small Store Organization   Large Store Organization
Organization for Merchandise Management 123
  Combined Buying and Selling Responsibilities   Centralized Buying
Organization of Non-Merchandising Activities in Department Stores 127
  Store Operations Division   Control Division   Promotion Division   Personnel Division
Current Trends in Store Organization 132
  Separation of Buying and Selling   The Changing Role of Retail Selling   Top Management   Customer Relations
Chapter Summary 135

7 STAFFING THE RETAIL ORGANIZATION 138

Good People are Hard to Find 138
  What Are the Problems?   Is There an Answer?
Selection and Training of Employees 143
  Manpower Planning and Recruiting   Selection and Hiring   Training   *Spotlight*
Motivating Employees 156
  Compensation   Fringe Benefits   Managers and Motivation
Chapter Summary 162
  RETAILING DECISIONS: *Riser's Department Store* 166
                          Goldberg Department Store 167

PART THREE *Merchandise Management*

8 MERCHANDISE PLANNING 170

Planning for Consumer Wants 170
  Merchandise Assortments   Product Life Cycle   Market Segmentation   Sources of Information on Consumer Wants   *Spotlight*
Stock Turnover and Merchandise Planning 180
  Ascertaining Turnover Rate   Stockturn and Profitability
Budgeting 183
  Sales Budget   Merchandise Budget
Programmed Merchandising 193
Chapter Summary 194

9 BUYING PRACTICES AND RELATIONSHIPS WITH SUPPLIERS 198

The Buying Task 198
  Buying versus Purchasing   *Spotlight*   Store Policies and Buying
The Selection of Merchandise Resources 203
  Wholesalers   Manufacturers   Other Retailers   Central Markets
Methods of Buying 209
  Cooperative Buying   Centralized Buying   Committee Buying   Consignment and Memo Buying   Leased Departments
Merchandise Pricing by Resources 212
  Negotiating with Resources   Terms of Sale
Relationships with Resources 222
  The Store Order   Order Cancellations and Returns   Split Shipments and Back Orders   The Need for Cooperation
Chapter Summary 225

10 MERCHANDISE CONTROL 228

Controlling Inventory Levels 228
  Dollar Control   Unit Control
Identifying and Minimizing Merchandise Shrinkage 233
  Shoplifting   *Spotlight*   Employee Theft   Employee Errors   Obsolescence and Spoilage
A Positive Approach to Shrinkage Control 246
  Educating Consumers   Employee Training and Supervision   Prosecution
Chapter Summary 248
  RETAILING DECISIONS: *Campus Cobbler* 252
  Shipley's Clothing Store 253

PART FOUR *The Pricing Function*

11 A FOUNDATION FOR RETAIL PRICING 256

General Pricing Essentials 257
  Price: Its Meaning and Importance   *Spotlight*   Demand-Oriented Pricing   Relationships Between Prices and Profits
Markup: Types and Arithmetic 263
  The Basic Relationship   Markup Distinctions
Chapter Summary 269

12 PRICING METHODS 272

A Pricing Decision Sequence 272
    Variations in Complexity   Overview of the Sequence   Pricing Responsibility

Individual Steps in the Sequence 275
    Relating Price to Retail Operations Planning   Determining Who Controls Prices and What Competition is Doing   Selecting a Price-Level Strategy   *Spotlight*   Calculating Planned Initial Markup Price and Store Policies   Price and Nature of the Offering   Price and Other Environmental Influences   Establishing an Original Price

Chapter Summary 294

13 PRICE ADJUSTMENTS 298

Additional Markups 298

Employee and Customer Discounts 299

Markdowns 299
    A Decision Sequence   Causes of Markdowns   *Spotlight* Timing and Size   Establishing the Markdown Price   Tracking Markdowns

Chapter Summary 309

RETAILING DECISIONS: *The Nifty-Thrifty-50 Minute Laundry and Dry Cleaning Service* 312

Main Street Boutique 313

PART FIVE *The Promotion Function*

14 THE PROMOTION BLEND AND SUPPORTIVE METHODS 316

Nature and Purposes of Promotion 316
    Definition of Promotion   Purposes of Promotion

The Basics of Promotion 318
    Selected Prerequisites   The Fundamental Tasks   Responsibility for Promotion   Developing the Promotion Blend

        Supportive Promotion Methods   *325*
            Display   Special Sales   Other Supportive Methods   *Spotlight*
        Chapter Summary   *340*

15 PERSONAL SELLING 344

        The Nature of Personal Selling   *344*
            Criticism of Personal Selling   Its Relative Importance   Self-Service Operations
        Fundamentals of Personal Selling   *348*
            Basic Selling Procedure   Adaptive Formula Selling   Types of Personal Selling
        Management of Retail Salespeople   *353*
            Responsibility for Sales Management   Tasks of Sales Management   Improving Retail Selling   *Spotlight*
        Chapter Summary   *362*

16 ADVERTISING 366

        The Nature of Advertising   *366*
            Purposes and Limitations   Expenditures and Organizational Arrangements
        Types of Retail Advertising   *371*
            What is Featured   Payment Arrangements
        Developing an Advertising Program   *379*
            Set Specific Objectives   Identify a Buying Theme   Establish a Budget   Allocate the Budget
        Selecting Suitable Media   *385*
            Media Profiles   The Selection Decision   *Spotlight*
        Preparation and Assessment   *392*
        Chapter Summary   *393*

17 CREDIT AND OTHER SUPPLEMENTARY SERVICES 397

        The Development of Supplementary Services   *398*
            Their Attraction   The Decision to Offer a Supplementary Service   The Life of Supplementary Services
        The Management of Supplementary Services   *402*
            Periodic Evaluation of Services   Special Supplementary Service Problems

Retail Credit 405
  Types of Retail Credit *Spotlight* The Decision to Offer Credit The Management of an Internal Credit Plan Capitalizing on Credit Accounts The Consumer and Credit
Chapter Summary 418
  RETAILING DECISIONS: *The Hawthorne Road Plaza* 420
    Classic Clothes 421

PART SIX *Financial and Information Management*

18 INFORMATION FOR RETAILING DECISIONS 424

The Value of Information 424
Putting Information to Work 425
  Planning Operating Evaluating
The Research Process 428
  Defining the Research Problem Setting a Research Objective Facilitating Research
Internal Sources of Information 430
  Employee Feedback Machine-Generated Information *Spotlight*
External Information Sources 434
  Trade Associations Government Sources Suppliers Publications Consumers
Information Management 441
  The Owner-Manager The Research Department The Consultant
Chapter Summary 442

19 FINANCIAL AND ACCOUNTING CONCEPTS 445

Financing the Retail Enterprise 445
  Long-Term Financing Intermediate-Term Financing Short-Term Financing The Importance of Financing
Financial Statements 450
  The Balance Sheet The Income Statement *Spotlight*
Inventory Valuation 460
  The Cost Method The Retail Method
Chapter Summary 470

20 EXPENSE CONTROL 474

Classification of Expenses 475
  Natural Classification   Functional Classification   Expense Center Accounting
Expense Allocation 482
  Types of Expenses   Methods of Allocating Expenses
Expense Budgets 487
  The Purpose of Expense Budgeting   Expense Budgets in Smaller Stores   Expense Budgets in Large Stores   *Spotlight*
Chapter Summary 496
  RETAILING DECISIONS: *Ace Hardware* 500
                          The Newton Store 501

PART SEVEN Special Topics

21 THE IMPACT OF CONSUMERISM 504

The Evolution of Consumerism 505
The Present Consumer Movement 506
  The Role of Retailing   The Role of Government
Retailing and the Challenge of Consumerism 509
  Be Honest with the Consumer   Provide Adequate Information   Listen to Customers
Legislative and Judicial Effects of Consumerism 512
  Truth-in-Packaging   Truth-in-Lending   Class Action Suits
Voluntary Actions by Retailers 515
  Unit Pricing   *Spotlight*   Open Dating
The Answer to Consumerism 519
  Posting of Prescription Prices   Other Initiating Actions
Chapter Summary 521

22 RETAILING AND RACIAL MINORITIES 524

Retailing to Minorities 524
  General Characteristics of Minority Groups   Is There a Minority Market?   *Spotlight*   Problems of Minority Consumers

Retailing by Minorities   533
Historical Perspective   The Current Scope   Efforts to Increase Minority Involvement   Prospects for the Future
Chapter Summary   537

23 FRANCHISE OPERATIONS   541

The Development of Franchising   542
Present Significance   Types of Franchising   The Boom and Bust
Franchisor's Viewpoint   547
Relative Merits of Retailing Through Franchises   Major Feature of Franchise Operations   *Spotlight*
Franchisee's Viewpoint   552
Relative Merits of Business Ownership Through Franchising   Guidelines on Purchasing a Franchise
Retail Manager's Viewpoint   555
Chapter Summary   557

24 RETAILING OF PRIMARY SERVICES   561

The Nature and Growth of Primary Services   561
A Definition and Some Distinctions   Growth of Services
Shortcomings in Services Retailing   564
Incompetent Performance   Misapplication of the Marketing Concept   The Communications Gap
Distinctive Features of Services Retailing   568
Characteristics of Services   Characteristics of Service Establishments
Improvements in Services Retailing   571
Elimination of Shortcomings   *Spotlight*
Chapter Summary   576
RETAILING DECISIONS: *Friendly Supermarkets, Inc.*   580
TLC Auto Repair   581

PART EIGHT   Beyond In-Store Retailing Today

25 NON-STORE RETAILING   584

Personal, Non-Store Retailing   584
Telephone Sales   In-Home Retailing   *Spotlight*

Non-Personal, Non-Store Retailing 591
    Mail Order Sales   Catalog Sales   Vending
Chapter Summary 602

26 RETAILING TOMORROW 605

Careers in Retailing 605
    Entrepreneur or Employee   The Road to the Executive Suite
The Future of Retailing 612
    External Changes   Internal Changes   *Spotlight*

GLOSSARY 627

INDEX 643

Retailing Today
AN INTRODUCTION

PART ONE

Retailing Today: Perspectives and Planning

1 Retailing Yesterday and Today

What is retailing? You already know part of the answer because you have been making retail purchases most of your life. Ever since you bought your first piece of penny candy you have had frequent contact with retailers and retailing.

You know one side of retailing—the consumer's side of the counter—but what of the other side? How does a retailer decide what to sell and where to locate a store? How should merchandise be arranged and displayed, prices set, customers attracted? These and many more questions make up the side of retailing most people know little about. This book is intended to show you how retailing works, and how retail managers make their decisions.

RETAILING AND RETAILERS

Two concepts—retailing and retailers—are central to this book. The first and most basic concept is *retailing*, which can be defined as all the activities associated with the sale of offerings for final consumption. Besides "sale," the key terms in this definition are "activities," "offerings," and "final consumption."

Pricing, advertising, record keeping, maintaining inventory, and many other things are "activities" that are critical parts of the retailing process. Thus, the definition must cover more than just selling. The term "offering" indicates that retailing includes the sale of both *products* (such as shoes) and *services* (such as shoe repair). In a society in which services are so important, it is vital to remember that not only products are retailed. "Final consumption," the last term in the definition, indicates that the offering is consumed or used up by consumers. The housewife buying potatoes for her family, for example, is buying for final consumption. However, the potato chip manufacturer buys potatoes to produce another product, so his purchase is not part of the retailing process.

Any business can engage in retailing, but not all businesses are retailers. *Retailers* are firms engaged primarily in retailing. In this second concept, the key term is "primarily." For example, many breweries sell kegs of beer directly to consumers. However, because a brewery is *primarily* engaged in manufacturing, it is not considered a retailer. We have already mentioned the exception of manufacturers who sell directly to consumers and who are considered retailers: the firms that produce services. Barbers, beauticians, restaurants, and dry cleaners all "manufacture" and sell their offerings directly to consumers. Some wholesalers or middlemen also make a limited number of sales to consumers. However, only firms that generate over half their total income from sales to consumers for final consumption can legitimately be called retailers. Note also that the existence of a retailer does not always mean the existence of a store. Door-to-door selling, vending, catalog sales, and telephone sales are all forms of non-store retailing.

The concepts of retailing and retailers can be easily distinguished by thinking of retailing as a *process* and a retailer as a *business*. To repeat: Any business can engage in retailing, but not all businesses are retailers.

THE NEED FOR RETAILING

Retailing meets a variety of needs of the two groups that come into contact with the retailer—consumers and manufacturers.

The Consumer and Retailing

Retailing benefits consumers by providing them with an assortment of goods and services from which to choose at the time and at the place they want to buy them.

Consumers want to be able to compare the prices, quality, and features of the various brands of the products they wish to buy. They can do this in two ways. Consumers can visit several retailers who carry at least one brand of the desired product, or they can visit one retailer who carries many brands. (Most consumers probably do both.) Without retailers, consumers would be forced to visit manufacturers all over the country to make these comparisons. Obviously they cannot do this.

A second benefit to consumers is being able to buy a product or service when and where it is needed or wanted with little or no delay. The presence of a large number of retailers in most neighborhoods, each trying to satisfy the consumers' desires, virtually assures the constant availability of products when they are needed. When a housewife needs an extra quart of milk, when a handyman needs a new blade for his power saw, when a child wants a battery for an electric toy, they take it for granted that these and thousands of other things are only a few minutes away at a retail store.

The Manufacturer and Retailing

Manufacturers benefit from retailing in two related ways. First, retailing allows manufacturers to sell their products to consumers all over the country. Second, it makes mass production possible.

So that customers can have an assortment from which to choose, most retailers stock their shelves with the offerings of many manufacturers. Likewise, manufacturers sell their offerings to many retailers. As a result, no matter where their factories are, manufacturers can sell their products to consumers everywhere.

The second benefit of retailing to manufacturers is that it makes mass production possible. The ability to produce 2000 can openers a day, for example, is of no value unless there is an efficient method for getting the can openers into the hands of consumers. The nearly 2 million retailers in the United States provide that efficient method. In the absence of a strong retail network, the manufacturer would be forced to locate near consumers, building many small manufacturing facilities in numerous areas around the country to produce just enough can openers for each area. Of course this would mean a loss of the efficiencies of mass production and a large increase in the cost of the product.

THE SCOPE OF RETAILING

Supplying the needs and wants of consumers is big business. Total retail sales in 1973 were $514 billion[1] and are estimated to be $720 billion by 1980.[2] Behind these enormous figures lie a variety of other figures that provide an interesting view of retailing today. For instance, of the nearly 1.7 million retail firms in the United States, nearly one-half have sales of less than $50,000 per year. In contrast, slightly over 6 percent of the retail firms account for 57 percent of all retail sales.[3] Thus, the retailing industry consists of a large number of small firms, a somewhat smaller number of medium-sized firms, and a handful of giants. Figure 1-1 indicates this inverse relationship between the number of firms and their total sales.

It is also interesting to note that the number of retail outlets has not increased significantly since 1948. The number has remained around 1.7

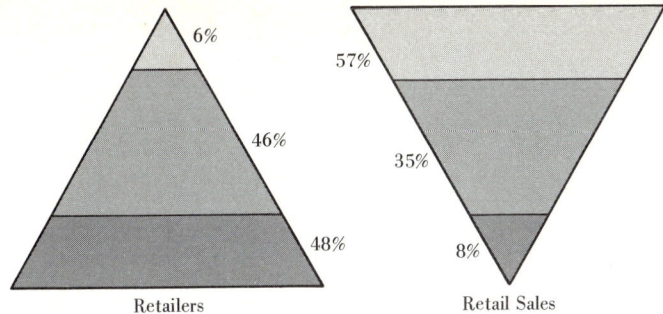

FIGURE 1-1

The relationship between the number of retail firms and total retail sales

million.[4] Yet the number of retail employees has increased by 3.5 million in the same period, and sales have more than doubled. These figures indicate a trend toward bigness in retailing. Competing with large retailers has always been a problem for the small retailer—a problem that seems likely to continue.

Finally, of the nearly 12 million retail employees in the United States during 1972, nearly one-half were women. Retailing is one business area in which women have advanced into management in significant numbers, and the opportunities in retailing's future appear to be excellent for both men and women.

CLASSIFICATION OF RETAIL BUSINESSES

The 1.7 million retail operations in the United States come in a wide variety of forms. The classification of retail businesses shown in Figure 1-2 and described in this section indicates this great diversity—a reflection of the efforts of retailers to respond to the needs of consumers.

Our classification first divides retailers according to where the consumer is when the sale takes place—in a store or away from a store. It then lists the unique operating features of in-store retailing and the method of contact for non-store retailing. Finally, the classification describes specific methods of retailing for both in-store and non-store retailers.

In-Store Retailing

In-store retailing consists of sales in which the consumer visits the seller's place of business to make a purchase. At the present time the majority of

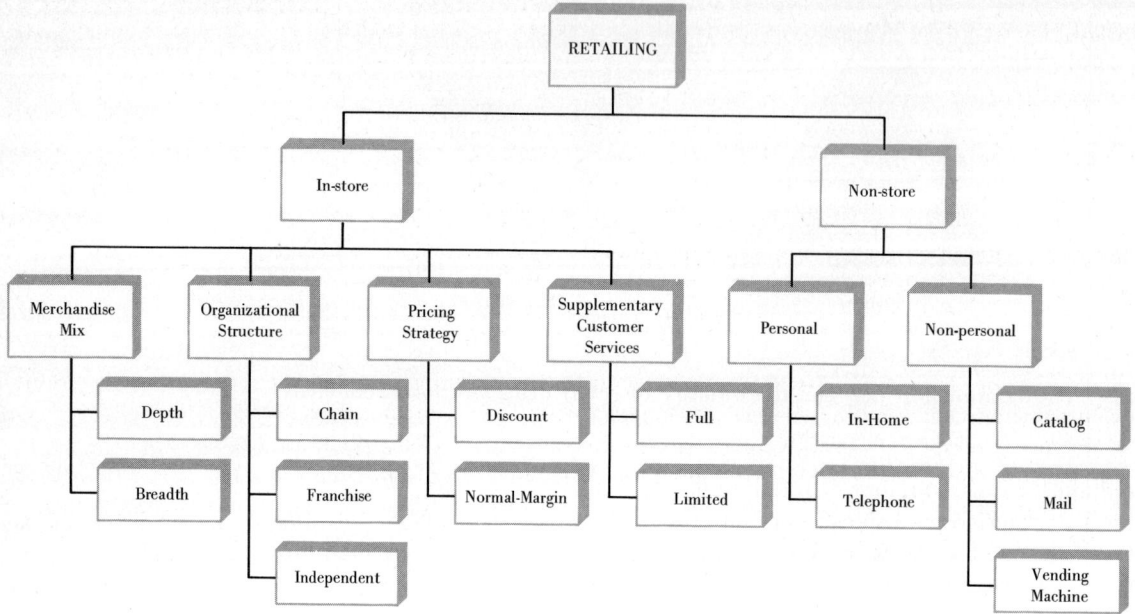

FIGURE 1-2

Classification of retail businesses by type

retail sales are in-store. Within this category we will distinguish retail operations by:

1. merchandise mix (what is offered for sale)
2. organizational structure (independent, chain, or franchise)
3. pricing strategy (normal margin or discount)
4. supplementary customer services (full or limited)

MERCHANDISE MIX

In developing a merchandise mix the retailer must decide what potential customers desire and what he can capably sell. In some product lines, for example, women's dresses or shoes, customers expect a wide selection of alternatives from which to choose. In others, like bicycles, considerably less variety is needed. In addition to customer expectations the retailer must consider his financial resources, store space, and product knowledge in developing the mix. The nature of a merchandise mix can be described in terms of its breadth and depth.[5]

Breadth. Breadth refers to the number of non-competing merchandise lines in a store. Non-competing lines are products that satisfy different needs. For example, a drug store may carry cosmetics and school supplies. A very broad mix would be found in a department store where a wide range of merchandise is available. In contrast, a retailer with a narrow line would be providing only a few different products. For example, a men's tie shop with only ties would be a single-line outlet, while a lamp store with lighting fixtures and accessories would be considered a limited-line establishment.

Depth. One measure of the depth of a store's merchandise mix is the number of different brands of any one product it routinely stocks. For example, a men's clothing store may offer five or six brands of suits, or a discount store may offer several brands of portable TV sets. These businesses are described as offering a deep line.

Other measures of a store's depth include the number of different prices, levels of quality, and styles or fashions its customers can choose from. A shallow product line usually involves offering only one or two products. Many fast food franchises like McDonald's and Arby's began this way. It is interesting to note how their product lines deepen over time. McDonald's now offers a wide variety of hamburgers and Arby's has added turkey, ham, and ham and cheese sandwiches to their original one-sandwich menu.

	Shallow	*Deep*
Broad	Hardware store Variety store	Department store Sporting goods store Men's or women's clothing store
Narrow	Gas station Fast food outlet	Hosiery store Tobacco store Book store

DEPTH (column header), BREADTH (row header)

FIGURE 1-3

Classification of retail businesses by breadth and depth

Figure 1-3 classifies various types of firms according to the breadth and depth of their normal merchandise mix. The figure indicates that a department store offers both a broad and deep product selection. In contrast, the product mix of a gas station is both narrow and shallow.

In making merchandise mix decisions, a retailer must decide on both breadth and depth. Some factors influencing the decision are the target market, the offerings of competitors, consumer expectations (what merchandise the consumer expects to find in a particular kind of store), resources of the firm, the physical space available, and the retailer's expertise in various product lines.

ORGANIZATIONAL STRUCTURE

Virtually all types of retail operations can be categorized as independents, chain stores, or franchises. Each category is described below.

Independents. An independent retail operation consists of a single shop or store unaffiliated with any other retail units in the same or similar lines of trade. An independent can be large (a department store) or small (a shoe repair shop), and it can sell products or services. The great majority of retail organizations fall into the independent category.

Chain Stores. A chain store is a retail organization consisting of two or more units with common ownership. Chains exist in a considerable variety of forms. Some chains—including A & P, Safeway, Woolworth's, and W. T. Grant's—are national in scope; others—including Kroger's, Gimbel's, Nordstrom-Best, and City Stores—are regional. The type of ownership may also differ, as in the Firestone chain of retail stores. Some are wholly owned by Firestone, while others are jointly owned by Firestone and the individual store operators. Finally, in some chains all the units have the same name, but in other chains the stores (or "sub-chains") have different names. For example, the Federated chain includes among its 18 divisions Abraham & Straus, Burdine's, Foley's, Levy's, I. Magnin's, and Shillito's.

Franchising. Franchised outlets have become very common, particularly for travel, entertainment, and other service businesses. In a franchise arrangement the franchisor provides the franchisee with an established name and various kinds of operating assistance. The nature of the licensing agreements between franchisors and franchisees varies widely. The franchisor may provide an operating program complete in every detail, including such things as operating hours and color of uniforms, or the agreement may specify only that the franchisor will provide merchandise for the franchisee to sell. Franchising falls between chain stores and independent organizations because franchisees own their businesses, but the similarity of franchise outlets makes the public think they are a chain. For example, many consumers do not know that Holiday Inns and Midas Muffler Shops are franchise operations.

For small businessmen, the main advantage of franchising is that it provides them with the sophisticated help necessary to compete. Yet they own their businesses, and the net profits belong to them.

PRICING STRATEGY

Price is often the determining factor in many consumer purchases, and the amount retailers earn on sales largely dictates their operating policy. The question of what pricing strategy retailers choose is therefore a significant classification variable. We will discuss two pricing strategies—normal margin and discounting—one or the other of which is adopted by virtually all retailers.

Normal-Margin Pricing. A store that operates with a normal price margin offers merchandise at prices comparable to those of the majority of other retailers in the same line of trade and does not use price as a primary selling point. Though normal-margin retailers may have occasional sales or specials in which reduced prices are featured, most of their sales are made on the basis of service, merchandise selection, or convenient location rather than price. Of course, the profit gained from normal-margin pricing helps to make these other features possible.

Discount Pricing. A retail store with a discount pricing strategy usually offers a broad but relatively shallow product line, incorporates the self-service features of supermarket operations, and emphasizes low prices as the main selling point.

The discounters of the late 1940s were significantly different from the discount stores of today. The earlier version offered only nationally branded durable goods like furniture and appliances in unadorned, low-rent locations. They provided no services and frequently carried no inventory beyond display merchandise. In contrast, the majority of today's discounters offer a wide variety of clothing and other soft goods along with durables, often including grocery items. Most discounters carry private brands as well as national brands, their facilities and locations have improved to the point that they often compare favorably to those of normal-margin retailers, and many of them now offer credit payment plans. Finally, today's discounter advertises more heavily than did his earlier counterpart. The only apparent similarities between old and new are an emphasis on low price as the chief selling feature and the presence of few customer services.

Several well-known retailers now operate both normal-margin and discount outlets. For example, Federated Department Stores has established Gold Circle as its discount outlet. Dayton-Hudson Corporation has a Target discount chain, May Company has Venture Stores, and Kresge's has K-Mart.

SUPPLEMENTARY CUSTOMER SERVICES

Closely related to the pricing strategy of a retail operation are the types and amount of service provided. Consumers who pay higher prices expect more service, while those who pay lower prices are usually willing to do without service. Among the common supplementary services in retailing are credit, return privileges, and delivery.

Full Service. A full-service retailer is one that offers all the services normally associated with that particular type of business. For example, Montgomery Ward and Sears Roebuck & Co. offer the full variety of customer services associated with department stores, and national brand gas stations such as Shell or Exxon also offer a full line of services.

Limited Service. In exchange for lower prices, some retailers offer few if any supplementary services. Supermarkets with cash-only policies, with pre-packaged meat and vegetables, but with carry-out service and check cashing would be considered limited-service retailers. On the other hand, an independent gasoline station that requires self-service, has no service bays, and does not offer windshield washing or oil checks would be a no-service retailer.

REVIEW BOX 1:1

1. Retailing is a _____, while retailers are _____.
2. Retailing benefits the consumer by providing an assortment of offerings from which to choose and _____.
3. Retail businesses can be divided into two major classifications according to where the consumer is when the sale takes place: _____ and _____.

Non-Store Retailing

The second major category of retailing is non-store, in which final sales take place without consumers visiting the store or premise of the seller. Although it accounts for a small percentage of retail sales—probably less than 20 percent—non-store retailing is growing in importance. In our classification, non-store retailing is divided into sales with personal contact and those without any personal contact.

PERSONAL SALES
In non-store personal retailing the consumer does not visit the premises of the seller but has some personal contact with the retailer either through a home visit or by telephone.

In-Home Retailing. All types of sales in which the transaction occurs in a consumer's home are termed in-home retailing. These include door-to-door (Avon), party selling (Tupperware), route sales (milk and newspapers), and custom selling (lawn care, storm gutters). Many firms have found this to be an effective method of retailing because it permits extensive, personal demonstration of the product or service and offers unparalleled convenience to the customer.

Telephone Retailing. Telephone retailing is the sale of products or services over the telephone. The contact is initiated either by the seller calling the potential buyer or by the buyer calling the seller in response to hearing or seeing advertising. This classification requires two qualifications. First, it does not include telephone orders from catalogs. Because catalog orders can be placed by mail, by phone, or in person, they are discussed separately. Second, calls by consumers to retail stores for information would not qualify as telephone sales. A telephone sale, as defined here, takes place entirely — it is begun and completed — over the telephone.

Although this kind of retailing accounts for only a small segment of total retail sales now, it is growing. More and more products and services are advertised in classified newspaper sections and on radio and television, inviting consumers to place telephone orders. As new communication equipment such as picture telephones and two-way communication via cable television becomes available, this method of retailing will expand.

NON-PERSONAL SALES

A retail sale in which the consumer does not visit the premises of the seller *and* in which there is no personal contact between buyer and seller is classified as non-store, non-personal retailing. This type of retailing is divided into three categories: catalog, mail order, and vending.

Catalog Retailing. This category is self-explanatory: A retail firm provides the consumer with a catalog of available merchandise and information on how to order. Some catalog sellers like Sears also have facilities for telephone and in-person orders. However, the majority of catalog retailers, especially those selling specialty and novelty items, still rely almost exclusively on mail orders in which there is no personal contact between buyer and seller.

Mail Order Retailing. Substantial sales are also made through the mail as the result of direct mail advertising or advertisements on radio and TV and in newspapers and magazines. As in the earlier discussion of telephone sales, mail order retailing excludes catalog sales.

Mail order offers cover a wide range of products and services and appear in a variety of forms. Many popular magazines (*Good Housekeeping*, *Field and Stream*, etc.) contain a large number of mail order advertisements, often in the form of classified ads in the back of the magazine. Business offices are besieged with mail order offers of office equipment and supplies, and most homeowners receive at least one or two direct mail advertisements a week for magazines, insurance, investment opportunities, or some other product or service.

Vending. Some products and services are sold directly from a machine to the consumer. Vending ranges from the simple gum ball machine to sophisticated equipment providing complete meals. Among the products and services commonly vended are cigarettes, newspapers, food and drinks, stamps, bank services (cash advances), shoe shines, and many, many others.

Classification of Retail Businesses

Although most retail sales are made in stores, non-store retailing has become a significant method of purchasing for many consumers. Consistent with the proportion of sales in each category, the primary emphasis in this book is on in-store retailing. However, Chapter 25 deals with non-store retailing in greater detail.

EXTERNAL FORCES AFFECTING RETAILERS

Various external forces over which the retailer has no control significantly affect operations. Figure 1-4 shows how the retailer is influenced by four types of forces — societal, economic, technological, and governmental — and how, in turn, the firm must accommodate these forces in making decisions which form a retail operations plan.

Societal Forces

POPULATION Retailers must first consider the nature and number of potential customers. They must rely on knowledge of a specific community and its needs, and must make use of government studies of population growth and distribution. For example, according to recent estimates, total United States population will continue to grow but at a slower annual rate, about $1\frac{1}{4}$–$1\frac{1}{2}$ percent.[6] Continued promotion of the notions of ZPG (zero population growth) and planned parenthood will contribute to the slowdown. Growth rates in different geographic areas will not be uniform, of course. For example, Arizona, California, Connecticut, Delaware, Florida, and Nevada will grow quite rapidly, at an annual rate of $1\frac{3}{4}$ percent or more. In contrast, some states including Idaho, Kansas, Montana, North Dakota, and South Dakota can expect declining or constant population.

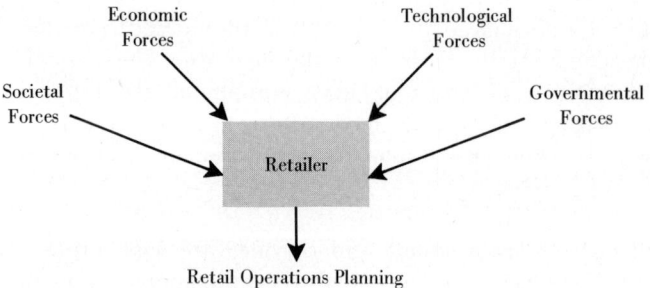

FIGURE 1-4

Environmental forces influencing the retailer

The statistics also indicate substantially more families. Combined with a projected lower birth rate, this means smaller families. This trend is reflected in a decision by Lane Bryant, Inc., a $304 million a year retailer with over 150 stores, to omit maternity departments from new stores.[7] Although the company was founded on maternity fashions in 1900, the decline in pregnancies has gradually led to a shift to other specialty styles such as clothes for the tall or large woman.

The number of working women will also increase. Whereas 46 percent of all women over age 16 worked in 1970, the proportion is expected to jump to 60 percent by 1980.[8] Obviously, employment of both parents means a boost in family income. Beyond that, an employed wife is more likely to patronize outlets which offer convenience products and services, such as dry cleaners, beauty salons, and family restaurants.

Although these national figures in themselves are of little value to the individual retailer, they indicate the dynamic nature of the population and how a retailer needs to monitor changes.

VALUES

Every generation reflects values that are somewhat different from those of their parents. For example, the youth of the 1970s might be described as more open-minded and less status conscious than their parents. In areas directly related to retailing, there is evidence of other value shifts.

Consumer Credit. The tremendous growth in the use of consumer credit reflects a move away from the Protestant ethic of saving for a rainy day and enjoying only those things that can be presently afforded. In October 1973 consumer credit outstanding (excluding home mortgages) amounted to $174 billion. This is an increase of over 800 percent above the $21 billion in credit extended in 1950.[9] In an Institute for Social Research study, it was found that one-half of all American families use at least one credit card.[10]

Credit has clearly become an acceptable method of purchasing for most consumers and a competitive necessity for the majority of retailers. This value shift has created both opportunities and responsibilities for retailers. Credit offers an avenue for increased sales, but because misuse of credit and overspending by consumers can lead to hardship and bankruptcy, retailers have a responsibility for exercising caution in extending credit and establishing credit limits.

Quality of Life. Today's consumer has become more concerned about the quality of life. People are questioning the value of a plastic and tin "throw away" society where objects are quickly consumed and convenience is given a higher priority than quality and durability. The consumer is also concerned about the effects of business and industry on our natural resources. The convenience of a proposed shopping center is likely today to be weighed against the effects of that center on the character of the area to be developed.

"I found a credit card we hadn't used yet!"

Seeman-Rothco

This change of values affects retailing two ways. First, it has produced organized efforts to create change, generally lumped under the label consumerism. Examples of this are the volunteer groups that conduct price comparisons among grocery stores in an area and publish their findings to help consumers find the best prices, and state governments that offer consumer protection "hot line" services to make it possible for consumers to immediately register complaints against businesses.

Second, consumers are demonstrating their concern through choices in the marketplace. This is reflected in the popularity of organic foods. As early as 1971, stores such as Safeway, Montgomery Ward, Walgreen's, Rich's, and Lord and Taylor were offering a line of organic or natural foods in response to consumer demand.[11]

Crime. Crimes such as vandalism, theft by employees, and shoplifting, are increasing. Whether the increase stems from relaxed moral standards or increased attention to more critical social ills, these crimes lead to millions of dollars in losses to retailers. For protection, retailers have been forced to reconsider store layout, design, and merchandise displays as well as institute greater surveillance.

Economic Forces

COMPETITION

Competition in retailing is increasing. The actual number of retail outlets has not increased significantly; however, competition has intensified. Manufacturers and wholesalers such as Sherwin-Williams and Hart, Schaffner and Marx are establishing retail sales facilities *(forward integration)* in order to achieve direct contact with the consumer and to gain greater control over distribution. Other retailers are expanding the variety of merchandise they offer *(scrambled merchandising)*, so much so that the distinction between types of retailers is becoming increasingly blurred. Drug stores now carry food items, variety stores offer patent medicines, and supermarkets provide many non-food items formerly found only in drug and variety stores.

UNIONIZATION

Because of a history in retailing of low wages for non-management personnel and arbitrary decisions by management, the unionization of retail employees is on the increase. Unionization can affect many practices that have been common among retailers. For example:[12]

Working hours
- Retailers have normally rearranged employees' working hours to meet peak demand. Split schedules (four hours in the morning and four in the evening) are often prescribed.

- Sunday openings are common in many states.

Jobs
- Retailers have moved clerks from department to department to meet seasonal demand or staff special sales.
- Sales clerks have often been expected to maintain stock, check in deliveries, and mark merchandise as well as sell.
- Department managers (supervisory personnel) have long engaged in selling.
- Representatives of suppliers frequently maintain inventory and stock shelves, particularly in supermarkets.

Seniority and job security
- Retailers have generally been able to discharge employees at will.
- Rather than give preference to seniority, many retailers provide preferential treatment to employees who can best accommodate the store's needs.

Widespread unionization could alter or eliminate all of these practices. Although such changes would likely benefit most retail employees, they would disrupt the operating procedures of many retailers and require higher prices to cover increased costs.

DISRUPTION OF NORMAL BUSINESS

Retailers are frequently affected by events that take place in other firms. If a source of supply were to go out of business, raise prices, or significantly change its product, the retailer depending upon that supplier would be affected quite drastically. Since all retailers are dependent upon other firms, they must find ways to ensure that the decisions or ill fortune of other businesses will not spell disaster for them. Retailers must remain as flexible as possible and anticipate the need for alternatives.

The Detroit newspaper strike of 1967 provides an example of retailers' use of alternatives. Newspapers are the major medium for local retail advertising, yet for 267 days Detroit had no daily newspapers because of a strike. The adjustments that retailers made indicate the need for flexibility.[13] J. L. Hudson Co., the city's largest department store, did little advertising immediately after the strike began, but soon used increased amounts of radio and television advertising and moved heavily into suburban weekly newspapers. Allied Supermarkets, no longer able to run large weekly spreads in the papers, began using handbills and direct mail advertising. United Detroit Theatres were forced to move their advertising to television, radio, and suburban newspapers. Facing a problem that eliminated their primary means of reaching consumers, these firms adapted by identifying alternative media and creating appropriate advertisements for these media. Other firms, less flexible and responsive, did not fare as well during the Detroit strike.

External Forces Affecting Retailers

Technological Forces

Two areas of technology have implications for retailing. First, there is the technology related to internal operations such as merchandise handling, sales recording, record keeping, and credit checking. Second, there is external technology such as the supply of raw materials and the manufacture of goods.

INTERNAL TECHNOLOGY

The single largest impact on internal retail operations has come from the computer. A device that can handle information at tremendous speeds, the computer is being used by retailers to solve their information-handling problems: the time lags that occur between an event — a request for credit, a payment, a stock depletion, or an order, for example — and a reaction. Using a computer, store personnel can check a customer's credit within seconds of a request, they can credit payments immediately, they can take daily inventories, and they can process orders as they come in.

In using computers, retailers have run into two problems. First, the advances are coming so quickly it is difficult to select a system and keep

Point-of-purchase terminals are replacing cash registers in the modern supermarket

it up to date. An example of this is the point-of-purchase terminal. (In simpler days it was called a cash register!) Using these terminals, a large supermarket can get information from each checkout station on sales by product category, merchandise returns, sales coupons used, and bottle deposits. In the near future a sales clerk may not have to ring-up purchases for any merchandise. It will all be done automatically as the items pass over a scanner.

Second, although retailers may have the capability to collect the necessary information, some still have a difficult problem getting it into the right person's hands at the right time. Consumer complaints about inefficient billing and ordering procedures stem from this problem.

Other internal technological developments include sophisticated monitoring systems to control shoplifting, computer programs to aid in store design and layout plans, and special electronic recording equipment for taking physical inventory.

EXTERNAL TECHNOLOGY

Retailers depend upon the availability of resources and technological advances for new products, for building new outlets, for advertising, and for providing consumers with transportation to stores. Unfortunately, the serious shortages of raw materials over the past few years are having an adverse effect on these areas of retail operations. Take for example the shortage of fossil fuels. Since oil, a fossil fuel, is an ingredient in plastics and many synthetic fibers, a shortage reduces the availability of some products. A shortage of coal affects public utilities, creating problems with lighting, heating, and air conditioning. A gasoline shortage makes it difficult for consumers to visit stores, particularly suburban shopping sites.

The list could go on and on. The point is that resources can no longer be taken for granted, and a short-run strategy has been adopted by some retailers. In a suburban Denver mall, for example, retailers are concentrating their advertising in the nearby area to encourage local shopping, rather than advertising in the *Denver Post* to try to attract shoppers from all over the city. Bullock's in California is encouraging telephone shopping, and Boston's Natick Mall is running a door-ro-door minibus for shoppers for a round trip fare of $2.[14] Eventually, however, retailers must consider more permanent solutions to these shortages, since it appears that they are more than temporary. For example, some chains are once again looking to the central business district as a possible location because of the availability of mass transportation.

Governmental Forces

The government's activities in regulating retailing can only be described as growing. At all levels — federal, state, and local — government is taking a closer look at the relationships among retailers and between retailers and consumers. We shall deal first with federal forces regulating retailing and then with state and local regulation.

FEDERAL REGULATION

Federal legislation affecting retailers began with the antimonopoly laws. The Sherman Antitrust Act of 1890, the Clayton Act of 1914 (amended by the Robinson-Patman Act), and the Federal Trade Commission Act of 1914 were all designed to protect against monopoly in business and unfair methods of competition. These laws make it illegal for competitors to agree on what prices to charge or to agree on how to divide the market. In addition, these laws specify that it is illegal to charge different prices to different customers without justification and to create mergers that significantly lessen competition. The rationale for these laws is the desire to maintain a high degree of competition among firms so that consumers are charged the lowest prices possible.

Although antitrust laws have an indirect effect upon consumers, more recent federal legislation has been directed specifically to the relationship between retailers and consumers. For example, the Federal Trade Commission (FTC), Food and Drug Administration (FDA), Federal Communications Commission (FCC), and the Federal Aviation Agency (FAA) have all become more active in scrutinizing advertising claims, promotions, prices and fares, and product safety as they relate directly to the consumer.

Some recent federal legislation that affects retailers include:

1. *The Automobile Information Disclosure Act of 1958.* This requires auto manufacturers to attach a label to new cars providing a suggested retail price including the price of specific options. The purpose of the law is to aid consumers in making comparisons between models and brands.
2. *The Fair Packaging and Labeling Act of 1966.* In retailing this affects only firms that sell private brand goods. The law stipulates that labels specify a product's identity, the name and location of the manufacturer, the quantity, and the ingredients. The law also prohibits non-functional slackfilling (having a package look bigger but not filling it entirely). Although these regulations might sound like common sense, the fact that a law was needed indicates that some firms were not providing consumers with this basic information.
3. *The Consumer Credit Protection Act of 1968.* Also known as the truth-in-lending law, it is intended to ensure that consumers are provided with all the relevant facts when making purchases on credit. A credit grantor must describe all finance charges in writing and express the total cost of the credit as an annual percentage rate.

These are just a sample of recent federal laws that are forcing retailers to exert greater care in the conduct of their businesses.

STATE AND LOCAL REGULATION

Most state and local governments have shown their concern about the retailer-consumer relationship by passing laws dealing with specific practices. For example, some states have already approved and others are considering the establishment of a maximum rate of interest a creditor can charge customers.

Another credit issue being debated in many states involves the repeal of the holder-in-due-course doctrine. Under holder-in-due-course, a retailer can sell merchandise to a consumer on credit, then sell the debt to a credit company. The consumer then owes the debt to the credit company and has no recourse to the retailer if something is wrong with the merchandise. These laws were originally designed to protect the credit company, but the problems they can cause for consumers are as obvious as the opportunity they provide the unscrupulous retailer.

Several states, the first of which was Massachusetts, have a unit pricing law. This law requires food retailers to post shelf tags indicating a price per measure (i.e., cents per ounce or another standard unit). Consumers can then make price comparisons without first making detailed computations.

"Cooling-off" legislation is another example of state consumer protection laws. Under these laws, consumers have a specified time period (usually one to three days) to back out of a purchase when the sale is made in the consumer's home. These laws protect consumers from high pressure in-home sales tactics by providing some time to think about the decision, investigate alternatives, and discuss the purchase with others before it is final. These and other issues related to the protection of the consumer are described in Chapter 21, Consumerism.

Clearly, all levels of government are accelerating efforts to guarantee fuller protection of consumers. Whether this movement continues depends, in part at least, on the willingness of retailers to regulate themselves and operate with integrity.

REVIEW BOX 1:2

1. Catalog, mail order, and vending are the three types of _____, non-store retailing.
2. External forces affecting retail operations can be categorized as *societal, economic, technological,* and _____.
3. These external forces must be accommodated as the retailer develops a _____.

External Forces Affecting Retailers

SPOTLIGHT

How fast can a retailer grow?

This highlight history of J. C. Penney Co. illustrates the dynamic nature of retailing.

1902 On an April morning in 1902, a young man opened the doors of his Golden Rule store in Kemmerer, Wyoming. Later that day, James C. Penney and his wife counted the first day's sales receipts—$166.59, a modest beginning for the future chain of stores which were to spread throughout the nation.

1903 A second store and a third were opened. Mr. Penney introduced the partnership principle by offering store managers in each new store a partnership in that store.

1911 Twenty-two more stores were established, and sales reached the first $1 million.

1913 The chain of Golden Rule stores was incorporated as the J. C. Penney Company, Inc.

1914 Penney's headquarters were moved from Salt Lake City to New York City to be closer to the sources of supply for its nationally known soft goods.

1918 Brand names for Penney's merchandise, such as "Pay Day" work clothes, were developed.

1924 This year marked the opening of the 500th store in Hamilton, Missouri. This store was not only a milestone in the Company's growth, but served as a reminder of the Horatio Alger story by its location in James Penney's birthplace.

1926 Sales increased to more than $100 million, and Penney's was moved into larger executive and buying headquarters on 34th Street in New York City.

1927 Ninety-one stores were purchased, and the first store in a suburban shopping center was opened four miles from Portland, Oregon.

1930 Penney's opened its Merchandise Testing Center which has established quality standards for a broad range of merchandise from textiles to tape recorders.

1951 Company sales soared to a record $1 billion.

1960s Innovations in this decade included catalog sales and the installation of catalog desks in many of the stores; new Penney's stores opened in Hawaii and Alaska, with a planned installation in Puerto Rico. New lines—appliances, cosmetics, gasoline, furniture, tires, batteries, and automotive accessories—were being offered in larger shopping center stores. Sales reached $2.25 billion in the mid-1960s.

1970 Annual sales pass the $4 billion mark.

1973 At year end the company operated 2,053 retail units including more than 300 full line department stores and auto centers. Corporation achieved its first billion dollar month in December as total annual sales pass $6 billion.

Source: Abstracted from J. C. Penney News Release, Public Information Department, J. C. Penney Company, Inc.

THE EVOLUTION OF RETAILING IN THE UNITED STATES

In just 175 years, retailing has evolved from simple bartering between families to the sophisticated variety of the shopping center. Changes in society as well as developments in pricing, promotion, offerings, and selling techniques created an environment that demanded new approaches and new techniques of distribution and service. At the same time, the basic task of retailing—satisfying consumers' needs at a profit to the businessman—remained constant. To describe briefly the evolution of retailing in the United States, we have selected four developments—availability of products, roads, mail service, and consumer transportation—as basic catalysts of major changes.

Stage I: The Availability of Products

By the mid-1700s, the population along the Eastern United States shore had grown large enough to be an attractive market for imported products from Europe. Consumer goods, arriving through the ports of New York, Boston, and Philadelphia, led to the growth of small shops that bought imports and resold them to city residents. At the same time, colonial craftsmen were expanding their operations, adding employees, and developing the first factories. For the sale of these products *small specialty shops* were established. As enough products became available, the first true retailers came into being.

Because many early settlers were living in rural areas and pioneers were constantly moving westward, it was difficult for them to visit stores to buy items they could not make. Thus the forerunner of the traveling salesman, the *peddler* or trader, arrived on the scene. Such small items as patent medicine, thread, scissors, hand mirrors, and small tools were carried to rural areas by peddlers traveling on foot or by horseback. The limited amount of settled area made it possible for peddlers to travel from homestead to homestead with their precious cargo, although the small amount they could carry made this an inefficient method of distribution.

Stage II: The Availability of Roads

As the population continued to grow and the frontier was extended further west, a network of roads was developed. During the period between roughly 1800 and 1850, two new forms of retailing flourished: the *general store* and the *wagon peddler*.

The Evolution of Retailing in the United States 23

Because goods could be transported in large quantities over passable roads, general stores were opened in small communities and rural areas. These stores provided a full line of staple goods such as flour, sugar, coffee, crackers, dried meat, tobacco, medicines, nails, tools, rope, cloth, gun powder, lamp oil, and whiskey. In addition to providing much-needed merchandise to rural families, the general store often served as a post office, meeting hall, and social center where families could catch up on local gossip and discuss politics.

The wagon peddler, who also appeared around this time, was simply a more advanced version of the earlier peddlers. The presence of roads made it possible for "traveling stores" to carry more merchandise and travel greater distances in supplying the needs of the sparsely settled frontier.

Stage III: The Availability of Mail Service

During the 1800s, the young U.S. Government worked hard to establish a reasonably efficient mail service, and by the latter part of the century, the system was developed enough to support *mail order* retailing. In 1872 Montgomery Ward began selling by mail, followed in 1886 by Sears Roebuck & Co. The early mail order sellers used both catalogs and advertisements in newspapers and magazines to generate business. By 1900 the arrival of a new catalog had become something of a social event. Particularly in rural areas where many of the items were not available in stores, adults and children alike spent many hours examining pictures of the wide variety of merchandise offered.

The advent of mail order selling proved to be a damaging blow to the general store. Greater selection of merchandise, coupled with lower prices, helped mail order houses put the general store out of business.

Stage IV: The Availability of Consumer Transportation

Because no method of mass transportation existed until the mid-1880s, retailers had become highly concentrated near the majority of consumers in the city center. The resulting vigorous competition led to various attempts by retailers to create differences that would attract customers. One strategy was to expand product lines, and, as product lines grew and stores increased their shopping space, the *department store* was born. Among the early department stores were Wanamaker's in New York, Filene's in Boston, L. S. Ayer's in Indianapolis, Dayton's in Minneapolis, and Meier and Frank's in Portland.

A significant change in city life that had both positive and negative effects on department stores was the introduction of the streetcar or trolley about 1875. The streetcar made it easier for some consumers to visit downtown areas and shop in the department stores. However, it also eliminated the necessity of living within walking distance of work and shopping. People began moving out of the downtown area, and cities began to expand physically. With the movement of customers to the suburbs, some retailers followed, and the *suburban shopping area,* an unplanned collection of small stores usually along a major street, developed.

At about this same time, another form of retail expansion occurred. As transportation and communication improved, retailers began capitalizing on their operating experience by opening additional stores in other locations. Initially, many firms experimented with suburban locations. If these were successful, they expanded their operations to other cities and eventually all across the country. This marked the beginning of the *chain store.* One of the first true chains, the Great Atlantic and Pacific Tea Company (A & P), began about 1860. Other pioneer chains include Woolworth's, Kresge's, and J. C. Penney, all beginning in the late 1800s and early 1900s.

A second form of consumer transportation, the automobile, became available around the turn of the century. However, the depression and World War II restricted its early growth, and it was not until the late 1940s that the automobile began to revolutionize retailing. Most downtown areas were not designed to accommodate automobiles. As a result, the traffic, congestion, and parking problems made downtown shopping unattractive. In response, the planned suburban *shopping centers* that offered a variety of retail firms in one location with adequate parking were designed and built. Seeing the growth in suburban retailing, some retailers moved out of the downtown areas; many of those that stayed did little to modernize or improve their operations. Thus, the downtown area of many cities began to deteriorate.

More Recent Developments

Two other developments of great significance to retailing occurred between 1920 and 1950. The *supermarket* had its beginning in California between 1920 and 1930. The earliest versions relied on low prices (made possible by self-service, low-rent facilities, inexpensive fixtures, and cash-and-carry selling terms) to appeal to the depression-weary consumers. Though still relying on self-service, today's supermarket scarcely resembles its predecessor. Improved locations, expanded product offerings, attractive decor and surroundings, and specialty departments such as bakeries and delicatessens are now commonplace.

Shortly after World War II, the *discount house,* offering nationally branded merchandise at lower than normal prices became popular. Discount houses offered a wide variety of merchandise including large and small

The Evolution of Retailing in the United States

appliances, furniture, sporting goods, clothing, and sometimes food and drugs. These stores reduced prices by relying on self-service, little or no inventory (in many discount houses customers placed orders and picked up merchandise when it was delivered to the store), plain facilities, and no credit or delivery service.

Today's discount houses are significantly different from their earlier counterparts. Although they still rely heavily on self-service, most are in new and more accessible locations with attractive facilities and some customer services. However, by offering a mixture of national and private brands, and some lower quality merchandise, they have maintained a low price image.

Obviously this is a very brief history of retailing. However, it serves the purpose of demonstrating the tremendous changes that have taken place in retailing and the need for flexibility on the part of retailers in responding to the needs of consumers.

This chapter has introduced you to the retailer's side of retailing. It offered definitions of some basic concepts and described the role and scope of retailing in our business system. In addition, we have considered the external forces that play a large part in shaping the direction of retailing. Finally, the diverse and dynamic nature of the industry was indicated in the classification of retailers and the evolution of the industry. From this base you can begin to explore in the following chapters the decision making sequence and the great variety of decisions the successful retailer must make.

REVIEW BOX 1:3

1. The four developments that influenced the evolution of retailing are the availability of *products*, *roads*, *mail service*, and _____.

2. The two most recent retailing innovations discussed in the evolution are the supermarket and _____.

CHAPTER SUMMARY

- Retailing can be defined as all the activities associated with the sale of offerings for final consumption, while retailers are firms engaged primarily in retailing.
- Retailing benefits the consumer by providing an assortment of offerings, when and where they are wanted.
- The manufacturer benefits from retailing through the exposure of products to a widely dispersed population and the need for mass production.

- Retailing today is more than a $500 billion industry. Most firms are small, yet a few firms account for nearly 60 percent of all retail sales. Almost one-half of all retail employees are women.
- Retail businesses can be classified as either in-store or non-store. In-store retailing can be classified by merchandise mix, type of organization, price strategy, and services offered. Non-store retailing is either personal or non-personal.
- Type of retailing and retail operations are largely determined by uncontrollable forces: societal, economic, technological, and governmental.
- Retailing in the United States has been greatly influenced by the availability of products, roads, mail service, and consumer transportation.

CHAPTER NOTES

[1] "1974 Survey of Buying Power," *Sales Management*, July 8, 1974, p. B-6.
[2] U.S. Department of Commerce, *U.S. Industrial Outlook 1973*, Washington, D.C., 1973, p. 397.
[3] U.S. Bureau of the Census, *Statistical Abstract of the U.S.: 1973*, 94th ed., Washington, D.C., 1973, p. 744.
[4] This figure and the figure below on the number of retail employees comes from U.S. Bureau of the Census, *Statistical Abstract of the United States: 1973*, 94th ed., Washington, D.C., 1973, p. 740–741.
[5] A similar method of classifying the product lines of retailers is presented by Philip Kotler, *Marketing Management: Analysis, Planning, and Control*, 2nd ed. (Englewood Cliffs, N.J.: Prentice-Hall, Inc.), 1972, p. 439.
[6] These growth rates and those below for individual states were computed from projections in *1972 Obers Projections; Regional Activity in U.S.* (Washington, D.C.: U.S. Water Resources Council, 1972).
[7] "Marketing Observer," *Business Week*, June 1, 1974, p. 67.
[8] Donald B. Miller and Lois I. McLaughlin, "Markets Today—Gone Tomorrow: Customer Profile Is Changing," *Direct Marketing*, March, 1972, p. 40.
[9] Board of Governors, *Federal Reserve Bulletin*, December, 1973, p. A-54.
[10] Lewis Mandell, *Credit Card Use in the United States* (Ann Arbor, Michigan: Institute for Social Research, 1972), p. 6.
[11] "Organic Shops Move into the Big Stores," *Business Week*, July 10, 1971, pp. 76–77.
[12] This list is summarized from Ronald D. Michman, "Union Impact on Retail Management," *Business Horizons*, Spring 1967, pp. 79–84.
[13] Stanley H. Brown, "267 Days Without a Newspaper," *Fortune*, November, 1968, pp. 154 f.
[14] "Suburban Malls Are Trying Harder," *Business Week*, March 9, 1974, p. 53.

QUESTIONS AND ASSIGNMENTS

1. Distinguish between retailing and retailers.
2. Explain how retailing benefits the large automobile manufacturer located in Detroit.
3. What type of manufacturers always sell directly to consumers? Give some

examples of product manufacturers in your area that sell directly to final consumers.

4. Assume for a moment that you wanted to buy a watch but there were no retailers. What would you have to do to get a watch? What benefits does retailing provide the consumer?
5. What were the four developments influencing the evolution of retailing? What do you think will be the next major factor to produce a change in retailing?
6. What is suggested by the increase in retail sales and retail employees combined with the constant number of retail outlets? Is "bigness" in retailing good or bad?
7. Select a retail store in your community and classify it according to the information in Figure 1-1. Examine merchandise mix, organization, price, and service. Which of these does the store emphasize?
8. Taking the types of non-store retailing discussed in the chapter, describe the conveniences each provides the consumer.
9. Do you think the volume of non-store retailing will increase or decrease? Why?
10. In what areas have changing consumer values affected retailing? Think about the dress habits of the people you know. Do you see changes and differences that might influence retailers? How have clothing retailers responded?
11. Ask a local retailer for a copy of his retail credit agreement. Read the agreement carefully. Do you think most consumers would read and understand this agreement? Why or why not?

ANSWERS TO REVIEW BOX QUESTIONS

Box 1:1

1. process
   businesses
2. providing offerings when and where they are wanted
3. in-store
   non-store

Box 1:2

1. non-personal
2. governmental
3. retail operation plan

Box 1:3

1. consumer transportation
2. discount house

Retail Operations Planning

2

When a retail firm develops the general courses of action that will be followed to achieve desired goals, this is known as retail operations planning. This concept can be illustrated by examining decisions made by executives of the Korvettes chain. Started in 1948, Korvettes was successful for many years as a discount operation but lost $3.7 million in 1970. Arlen Corporation acquired the $600 million, 51-store chain in 1971.[1] After reviewing overall operations, Arlen management made a series of strategic decisions which illustrate retail operations planning:

- Arlen spent $1 million on research to determine what kind of consumer Korvettes should be aiming at. Korvettes' president concluded that customers were not nearly as price-conscious as they've been in the past.
- Previously a discounter, Korvettes was redefined as "a promotional department store," aiming at a higher-income market than it did previously.
- Special attention was directed at restoring Korvettes' image as a store which offers good value for its prices.
- New Korvettes stores, it was decided, would be built only as part of large shopping centers rather than as free-standing units.
- Additional emphasis was given to fashion wear, sporting goods, and cameras.
- Prices "somewhere in between" discount houses and conventional department stores plus heavy promotion were decided upon.

Arlen's decisions illustrate retail operations planning in relatively large, ongoing retail firms. However, such decisions can and must also be made by new firms and by relatively small retailers.

PROGRAMMING RETAIL OPERATIONS

Before looking closely at operations planning, we should understand how this activity fits into the overall function of retail management. In a very real way, retail management is similar to computer programming since both involve first deciding on the desired results, then the general approach and necessary procedures. Also, like a computer programmer, a retail executive is seeking productive, efficient operations. A final similarity is in the computer programming expression "Garbage In, Garbage Out" (GIGO), which means that when inaccurate data or incorrect procedures are fed into a computer, useless results are produced. The same is true for retail management; effective programming of operations depends upon accurate information and sound procedures.

Decisions in Programming

Programming retail operations entails setting objectives, planning strategies, and developing policies and methods. Objectives involve *what* is to be accomplished, while strategies, policies, and methods relate to *how* objectives will be accomplished.

SETTING OBJECTIVES

An organization's *objectives*, or *goals*, constitute its reasons for being in existence. If we define *objective* as a desired result, then it is obvious that retailing objectives must be related to profit making. A business firm cannot survive—much less prosper—without profits. Two basic types of business objectives are *charter objectives* and *performance objectives*.

Charter Objectives. A business's general scope is defined in its charter objectives. For example, a charter objective for a clothing retailer might be:

> This company will sell value-priced clothing for all members of middle- and lower-income families in communities with populations of 50,000 or less.

Top management of the Sizzler family steak house chain stated its charter objective as follows:

> We are a family-oriented steak house, featuring high quality red-meat dinner and luncheon entrees, offering extraordinary value in super-clean locations—all targeted at the middle-demographics mass market.[2]

In practice, "these policies 'chart' the future character and philosophy of an enterprise by specifying guides to action and constraints on the range of action permissible."[3]

The scope of a retailer's activities can be defined in terms of the kinds of offerings to be sold and locations. This pair of decisions must be based on a merchant's resources and interests. A *prospective* retailer usually considers interests first, since most people who contemplate opening a retail outlet want to engage in a specific line of trade—for example, the clothing business or a lawn-and-garden center. Even entrepreneurs primarily interested in "making big profits" have some ideas as to which lines of trade or geographic areas would suit their interests. A sports enthusiast, for example, might want a business somehow tied to sports—perhaps a golf driving range.

Resources such as financial capital, experience in a line of trade, knowledge about a geographic area, and reputation have to be considered by the prospective retailer. Consider a merchant-to-be who is employed by a large grocery chain but wants to open his own retail grocery business. Even though he may have experience, knowledge, and a favorable reputation in an area of the community, if he has limited capital he obviously cannot open a supermarket. However, a convenience-type grocery store may be feasible.

Performance Objectives. This type of objective specifies desired financial performance within a certain time period. For example, a retail chain may state its goals for the current operating year as:

Achieve after-tax profits of 4 percent of net sales.
Become the second largest store of this kind by surpassing the sales level of two competitors.

The time frame for some performance objectives may be longer than one year.

Some objectives *directly* mention profits. Those which do *not* should indicate the *means* by which profits (the *end*) will be sought. The means ordinarily refer to satisfying certain groups of consumers in specific ways. Mentioning profits and consumer satisfaction in objectives—even building objectives around these two factors—clearly is consistent with the marketing concept.

Established firms, as well as new or prospective retailers, need to set objectives. Naturally, setting objectives is going to be a less involved task for an established enterprise. Of primary concern to established retailers is periodic updating of annual, intermediate, and long-run performance objectives. In addition, occasional review—and appropriate modification—of charter objectives is advisable.

PLANNING STRATEGIES

Once objectives are set, steps must be taken to achieve them. The first step is to plan strategies, which represent the ways in which a firm's resources are deployed in order to surpass competitors or to seize opportunities.

Strategy should not be confused with tactics. While objectives outline where a company wants to go, strategy is the road that will be followed, and tactics are the vehicles that will be used. To illustrate, consider the various economy motel chains designed to appeal to price-conscious travelers along interstate highways. Underpricing other motels is their strategy, or intended route to desired profit levels. To increase revenues, these chains use the tactic of putting pay television in the rooms. Tactics to reduce costs include using plastic cups rather than glasses, and not putting dresser drawers in the rooms since "most travelers don't use them, and they take time to dust."[4]

In short, tactics follow from and are more specific than strategy. Furthermore, strategic decision-making generally occurs at a higher level of management than does the tactical type. Used here, the term *tactics* is largely synonymous with the *policies* and *methods* discussed below.

DEVELOPING POLICIES AND METHODS

Methods are specific actions aimed at a particular purpose, whereas *policies* are guidelines which indicate appropriate methods in different situations. As such, the terms are distinct. Basically, some methods are arrived at by referring to the firm's policies, while others have to be decided on a situation-by-situation basis.

When no relevant policies are available, individual methods must be decided upon. This can occur (1) when the particular category of decisions is insignificant or is made so infrequently that developing a policy would not be worthwhile, (2) when the situation surrounding a particular decision changes so frequently that generalizing about it would be dangerous, or (3) when the firm has not previously faced decisions of this type. An example of this last instance would be decisions arising from the energy shortage which began to affect retailers in various ways in late 1973. Initial decisions in such a situation are especially important since they may guide subsequent decisions.

Policies flow from specific strategies. Hence, a retail firm may have numerous policies to guide daily decision-making. In fact, it usually will have policies in all areas of operations. For example, a clothing store's merchandising strategy may be to offer name brands at "prestige" prices. Appropriate policies for this store might be:

> Only nationally advertised brands which are among the five best selling brands in a product category will be stocked.
> Merchandise will be priced at a 50 percent retail markup as long as the retail price is within 10 percent of competitors' prices.
> No brand carried by a local discount house will be carried.

When a manufacturer's salesman suggests a new line of clothing, these policies guide a departmental buyer in purchase decisions.

The main advantage of policies is that they simplify and frequently improve decision-making. Policies can speed decision-making, for example, since one category of decisions, such as brand selection, is examined very carefully at one time rather than being thought through each time such a decision must be made. To be useful and effective, a policy must be clearly stated in writing and should be communicated to all those to whom it applies.

STEPS IN OPERATIONS PLANNING

A complete strategy for a retail firm results from a four-step process:

1. Assess the environment.
2. Identify target market(s).
3. Formulate desired image and differential advantage.
4. Design retailing mix.

Each step produces operating plans which are general and strategic in nature. Overall, these plans represent a store's attempt to appeal to—and try to satisfy—certain consumers in order to make profits.

The Greeks, who developed the word, considered *strategy* "the art of generalship."[5] In business, this would suggest that strategies are designed at the upper management levels. Thus, in a small retail outlet, the owner-manager would be the main strategist. In a retail chain, most strategy-making occurs at corporate headquarters, although store managers and direct subordinates often need to develop local strategies.

Periodic review of the overall approach to operations is commonplace in relatively large retail firms since they have enough executive personnel so that planning specialists or top-management committees can be assigned this task. On the other hand, such reviews are too infrequent in many small retail businesses. The owner-manager and his assistant manager can become so tied up with daily operations that planning is neglected. However, operations planning is so significant to the firm's future success that sufficient time for reviews must be set aside. For example, a shop owner who is extremely busy purchasing new merchandise, updating display windows, and scheduling employees, might not notice changes in consumer shopping patterns. As a result, the firm may lose customers or miss an opportunity to capture additional customers. Daily activities will be relatively ineffective until the shop owner reviews his operating plans and makes appropriate revisions.

Time spent examining strategies is worthwhile even when the review confirms the soundness of present strategies. In such a case, a merchant can aggressively and confidently attempt to produce customer satisfaction and profits.

Operations planning is most critical for merchants-to-be. In many respects, a new, small retailer is at a disadvantage in competing against large, established retailers' financial power and reputations. The disadvantage cannot be overcome without sound operating plans. Since most new retail firms do not have an abundance of capital, a merchant-to-be has to do it right the first time. Limited capital prohibits second chances!

We are not saying the Goliaths of retailing always stomp all over the Davids. Instead, the point is that David (a new, small firm) has to plan how to avoid battling Goliath (the giant firm) or, if confrontation is necessary, which weapons (merchandise, price, and promotion) might be successful.

Since planning is the foundation for all types of retail businesses, each of the four steps in operations planning will be examined separately below. Although the focus is on starting a retail business, remember that established firms also need to review their operating procedures.

REVIEW BOX 2:1

1. Programming retail operations involves setting objectives, planning strategy, and _____.
2. An objective is defined as a _____.
3. The level in a retail firm at which strategies are designed is _____.

Assess the Environment

Charter policies indicate the area of retailing in which a firm will operate. Knowing this, a strategist's first task is to look at the environment: societal forces, economic forces, technology, and government regulation. In planning operations, a retailer seeks to identify relevant environmental factors, their likely impact on his type of business, and the courses of action he might take to avoid threats *and* seize opportunities presented by these factors.

The task can be illustrated by considering an entrepreneur who intends to operate family-oriented movie theaters in the Northeast. He has long felt that a growing number of families desire and can afford entertainment which they can enjoy together. Furthermore, he thinks that too few theaters cater to this audience. He recognizes that general observations are not a sufficient basis for deciding whether to proceed, and thus his first step must be a careful look at the environment. Some relevant factors he identifies are:

    Rising disposable income
    Large numbers of middle- and upper-middle-income families in the
        suburbs

Movie projection equipment which reduces the number of employees needed to operate a theater

On the average, one of every six movies shown rated "G" (for general patronage)

Whereas the first three factors are encouraging, the fourth one concerns him. It may be that "G" movies are available but are not being leased by theaters. If theaters have determined that consumers will not patronize family-oriented movies, he would have to rethink his intentions. If, on the other hand, they simply have not recognized the potential of these movies, he faces an opportunity. Another unfavorable possibility would be limited production of these movies, which would mean minimum selection.

Identify Target Markets

The strategist's next task is to pinpoint one or more markets on which he will concentrate. A *market* consists of a group of people with needs to satisfy, money to spend, and a willingness to spend. The term *needs* is used in a broad sense here, referring to the lack of anything that is required, desired, or useful.[6]

Identification of target markets requires analysis of consumers in terms of population characteristics, income levels and distribution (which suggests purchasing power), and buying behavior (which reflects unsatisfied needs and consumers' willingness to spend).

MARKET ANALYSIS

Population Characteristics. Since population shifts vary in different geographic areas, national population figures are of value only to national retailers such as Western Auto, Richman Brothers men's clothing stores, or Penney's department stores. For this reason, most retail strategists need to assemble population statistics for a particular community or region.

Tracking down these statistics, doing any research in fact, can be difficult, but it should not be avoided just for that reason. Sources of population figures for local retailers include the Chamber of Commerce, *Sales Management* magazine's annual "Survey of Buying Power," and the bureau of business research at a university.

Income Factors. To be a worthwhile target, a market not only has to contain sufficient people, but these people also must have adequate purchasing power. This is why a strategist next examines income levels and distribution.

Before looking at income statistics, we must distinguish among three types of income:

Steps in Operations Planning

> *Personal income*—the amount earned from a job (wages or salary), a business or farm (profits), rents, and dividends.
>
> *Disposable personal income*—basically, the amount available for spending or saving after tax and nontax payments to the government are deducted.
>
> *Discretionary personal income*—the amount left after essential purchases (food, clothing, utilities) and fixed payments (rent or mortgage, installment purchases, insurance).

Type of income is significant because each type is a good indicator of likely demand for some products and services but a poor indicator with respect to other offerings. For example, a store retailing non-essentials is most interested in discretionary income levels.

In addition, each type above can be stated in terms of real income. *Money income* is the actual cash or checks received as personal income. *Real income* goes a step further, taking inflation into account; thus it indicates purchasing power. When annual inflation is 6 percent, your money income has to increase by more than that percentage for your purchasing power to grow.

Again, a strategist should accept *overall* money income figures only as general indicators. Informed selection of one or more target markets requires statistics on *real income for areas* under consideration.

Consumer Behavior. The final step in market analysis involves identifying unsatisfied consumer needs and attempting to learn how and why shoppers behave in certain purchase situations. Information gained from this analysis suggests consumers' willingness to purchase the offerings to be sold.

A starting point for this analysis is a proper perspective on products and services. Rather than thinking of them as provided and sold by business firms, a retailer should view these offerings as need-satisfying purchases of consumers. This viewpoint, part of the marketing concept, assures that a retailer evaluates the attractiveness of his offerings *to consumers* rather than to the firm or to himself.

A second key point is that products or services satisfy psychological needs as well as basic needs like hunger and protection. Psychologists have suggested that needs for friendship, self-respect, and accomplishment become prominent once all physical needs are satisfied. Thus, a retail strategist must recognize these unsatisfied psychological needs and be prepared to develop offerings to satisfy them.

MARKET SEGMENTATION

No retailer can effectively deal with the *total* United States market. Charter objectives, as indicated, ordinarily specify the geographic scope of the business. But since each person has somewhat different individual needs and purchasing power, further subdivision of geographic areas almost always is necessary. Retailers simply do not have the capability of satisfying one or more needs of everyone in an area. Even Sears, with its tremendous consumer following, is not patronized by everyone. Thus, further subdivision —for example, according to income levels or family size—is necessary.

Subdivision—or *market segmentation*—involves identifying a reasonably similar group of consumers who are not fully satisfied with present offerings and then developing a more satisfying mix (including merchandise, promotion, price, and location) for them. One or more such segments will become a firm's target markets.

Colonial Stores grocery chain is one of many retailers which have successfully employed this technique. In Atlanta, for example, this grocery chain directs distinct offerings at three segments.[7] For consumers primarily interested in location convenience and wide assortment of goods along with weekend price specials, it has conventional supermarkets. For very price-conscious shoppers, Colonial has discount-price stores, and, for consumers interested in low prices but desiring a fancy shopping atmosphere, it operates grocery departments in Rich's department stores.

Segmentation Bases. We have already mentioned geographic location, income level, and family size as possible bases for segmenting a market. Other demographic characteristics also can be used:

Age
Level of education
Social class, which combines income, education, and occupation
Type of residence
Sex
Race
Marital status
Stage in life cycle, which combines age and marital status

Subdivision according to people's attitudes and behavior also has been employed by some marketers. This category of characteristics includes:

Life style (for example, structured vs. "free-form")
Interest in different activities (sports, "do-it-yourself" projects)
Patterns of usage (for example, heavy vs. light users)
Status and price consciousness, which are related characteristics
Mobility (extent of travel, frequency of change in residence)

Some of these characteristics, especially those in the first list, can be readily measured because they are statistical in nature. These are the characteristics retailers most commonly rely on for market segmentation. Others are more difficult to gauge, perhaps requiring specially developed measures and extensive research.

A combination of characteristics—rather than a single one—frequently

Steps in Operations Planning

is used by a strategist in isolating feasible target markets. For example, the entrepreneur planning theaters may use geographic location, stage in life cycle, and price consciousness to segment the market. The target he eventually selects is suburban families which have young children and are interested in obtaining "good buys."

Important Segments. Different market segments are more important to some kinds of retailers than to others, of course. However, certain segments have grown to the point where any retail strategist would be well-advised to consider them as possible targets. Among these important segments are employed women, teenagers, young marrieds, and blacks.

Another segmentation base is *community size*. Many retail firms concentrate on large cities and metropolitan areas, preferring to go after a piece of a giant "pie." As a result, smaller cities and towns may have substantial untapped potential. This appears to be true in the restaurant business:

> With a couple of notable exceptions, most fast food franchisors have completely missed the boat by failing to penetrate a wide-open market in cities and towns of 5,000 to 40,000 populations.[8]

A successful exception among fast-food franchisors is Tastee-Freez. With most systems targeting their efforts at large metropolitan areas, Tastee-Freez is concentrating on towns of 1,500 to 10,000 persons. The firm's vice-president has explained the rationale:

> While we have aimed at smaller communities, most of our competitors have become fixtures on 'franchise rows.' In effect these outlets, although in heavily populated areas, have created small market segments with a final consumer potential similar in size to what we seek for our stores.[9]

We are not saying that all big cities are saturated and would be poor target markets. On the contrary, the point is that *both* big cities and small towns should be considered. Since many smaller communities are not serviced by large chains, they may have strong potential as targets for a retailer's efforts.

A final segment that should be considered by retailers is *mobile families*. About 20 percent of the population changes residences yearly, and one-third of these movers relocate in a different county or state. Changing residences requires purchases of certain products and services, such as carpet cleaning, professional moving services or truck rental, and perhaps temporary lodging in a motel. After moving, families have to select new suppliers of products and services. Because distinctive buying behavior is associated with moving, mobile families (or newcomers) represent a possible target market for most retailers.

Why and how the mobile segment should be cultivated was suggested in a recent study:

Retailing organizations capable of delineating this target market for successful promotion will have a distinct initial advantage over competitors in winning the loyalty of newcomers . . . Attempting to reach mobiles only through existing programs may be insufficient.[10]

The key to special retailing programs is reaching people as soon as possible after their arrival, since people tend to select new suppliers rather quickly. For example, a favorite supermarket is chosen in around three weeks, a favorite beauty salon in seven weeks, a bank in less than two weeks. Possible incentives to attract newcomers' patronage include: check cashing or credit privileges, a gift delivered to the home, a coupon which may be redeemed in the sponsoring outlet, or a special price reduction on a purchase in the outlet.

This discussion has been based on the premise that feasible target markets can be pinpointed. But an entrepreneur may not find a feasible target through this analysis. When this occurs, the problem may lie in the definition of the business's scope plus the competitive situation and consumer behavior. Redefining the scope may open up other possible target markets. For example, a charter objective may specify "donut shop" as the line of trade. If the ensuing search for feasible target markets is unproductive, the line of trade might be broadened to "full-line bakery" and another search undertaken.

> **REVIEW BOX 2:2**
>
> 1. A group of people with needs to satisfy, money to spend, and the willingness to spend is a _____.
> 2. The second step in market segmentation is developing a more satisfying mix; the *first* step consists of _____.
> 3. Certain segments have grown so large that just about any retailer might consider them a possible target; two of these segments are _____ and _____.

Formulate Desired Image

Next, a retail strategist must decide how he would like his firm to be viewed by the target market. What image does he want to project? For example, does he want shoppers to think of the store as offering really low prices and adequate merchandise, but no "extra" services? Or, would it be better to be viewed as the friendly, convenient store which carries most popular items?

There are two ways of viewing a store's image. To a retailer, image is the overall picture a firm tries to project to target consumers. To a consumer, store image is his or her set of attitudes toward a particular outlet.

This distinction suggests two points that a strategist must keep in mind: First, "an image is acquired through experience and thus is learned."[11] Hence, a totally new store has no image in consumers' minds until it communicates with consumers in some way, such as through advertising or its exterior appearance. Likewise, a new resident has no images of the area's retailers, assuming no prior experience with or talk about them. Second, as with any communication, the image *sent* to target consumers by a retail firm may not be the image *received* (or perceived) by them. Consequently, a retailer should periodically check the store's image among target consumers rather than simply assuming that the image intended is the one consumers perceive.

Store image contains many components. In a study of department store images, 99 percent of consumers' attitudes about three firms fell into one of twelve categories:

1. Price of merchandise
2. Quality of merchandise
3. Assortment of merchandise
4. Fashion of merchandise
5. Sales personnel
6. Location convenience
7. Other convenience factors (parking, store layout, hours of operation)
8. Services (credit, delivery, restaurant)
9. Sales promotions (special sales, trading stamps, special events such as fashion shows)
10. Advertising
11. Store atmosphere (decor, displays, congestion, types of customers)
12. Reputation on adjustments

Image components naturally vary across lines of trade. Some components of department store image would not apply to barber shops, drug stores, repair firms, or restaurants. For example, in the case of restaurants, speed of service and cleanliness might be added and several categories above dropped as inappropriate.

Furthermore, all image components are not of equal importance to consumers. In the study discussed above, four components emerged as most important to the charge-account customers of three Phoenix department stores: quality of merchandise, store atmosphere, sales personnel, and assortment of merchandise. Of course, since relative importance varies according to type of store, it would be dangerous to generalize about which components are most important.

The study also found that various demographic groups interpret a store's image in different ways. Thus, a retailer using demographic segmentation would have to take great care in creating an image that appeals to the chosen targets.

All retail firms differ in some ways. At the least, name, location, or sales personnel will vary from one store to the next. We refer to these variations as a business's *competitive differential*.

DIFFERENTIAL ADVANTAGE

At first glance, some differences may appear minor but, in fact, be quite important. For instance, have you noticed that most fast-food outlets are on the same side of heavily travelled streets leading to suburban residential areas? This suggests that fast-food firms feel that the two sides are not equal in drawing power. Two aspects of consumer behavior largely account for this location preference. First, many fast-food purchases are made on the way home from work. Second, consumers—especially when tired from work—desire convenience. For these reasons, the outlets ordinarily locate on the "outbound" side so that a prospective customer is very likely to notice the outlet and will not have to cross against heavy traffic to get there. Thus, if two fast-food outlets were on opposite sides of a street, a competitive differential would probably exist. According to the reasoning suggested above, one would have an advantage and the other would be at a disadvantage.

In designing a store image, a strategist seeks features that will cause target consumers to shop at his outlet rather than at a competing store. If he is successful in doing this, he has created a *differential advantage*—a crucial aspect of operating plans. An effective differential advantage has permanency. It is not just something offered during an introductory period such as special price reductions.

Any image component might be developed as a differential advantage. Consider, as an example, a car wash outlet. Potential advantages include convenient location, quality of work, a special spray-wax option, or some combination of these features. The effectiveness of a potential differential advantage is estimated by judging how important these elements are *to consumers* and what competitors are doing along these lines. If the elements are important *and* are better than what similar outlets offer, a strategist has what should be an effective differential advantage. If the elements are unimportant or identical to those of competitors, it's time to try again!

A differential advantage is supposed to be somewhat permanent, and some firms are fortunate enough to achieve this. McDonald's is a prime example among nationwide retailers. Major elements of McDonald's differential advantage seem to be quality food, reasonable prices, and speedy service. Also, some local independent merchants build and maintain a solid advantage over competitors.

Frequently, however, a differential advantage winds up being temporary. This happens when the importance to consumers of the differential elements diminishes. For example, a supermarket's combination of high quality foods and fast, friendly service might serve well as an effective differential advantage. But when food prices rise sharply, shoppers may become concerned about supermarket prices, thereby neutralizing the original advantage.

In addition, when direct competitors imitate a successful retailer or even try to go one step beyond his strategy, they diminish his differential ad-

Steps in Operations Planning

vantage. In the car wash example, a competing firm may open up nearby and offer quality work and spray wax *plus* reduced-price gasoline when a wash is purchased. The original firm's differential advantage has just evaporated.

Just as a firm may create a differential advantage, it may also unintentionally create a differential *disadvantage*. An image component may be so poor that consumers are repelled rather than attracted. Such disadvantages could include inaccessible or distant location, lack of credit, too little (or in other cases, too much) merchandise selection, and prices which are perceived as very high. A differential disadvantage can result from an incorrect strategic decision or from a failure on the part of management to carefully implement operating plans.

The struggle among competing retail firms for differential advantage is continuous. As in the car wash situation, a firm will profit from its differential advantage until target customers' attitudes change or competitors retaliate. When either occurs, a strategist has to create a new differential advantage to neutralize a substantial advantage of a competitor, such as the reduced-price gas, and regain its drawing power. As long as firms base their differential advantages on satisfaction of customer needs, this continuous battle among retailers benefits consumers.

An example from the supermarket field can be used to relate the concept of differential advantage to the broader notion of formulating a desired store image and the previous steps of assessing the environment and identifying one or more target markets. Grocery retailing in suburban areas has become highly competitive in recent years:

> Even the best sites now are within hailing distance of at least one or two well-established food outlets. And a new supermarket, more often than not, must draw much of its traffic past the doors of competitors' stores to meet projected sales goals.[12]

Curtis supermarkets of Massachusetts recognized this environment as it started to plan a new outlet for the coastal town of Hingham. The Curtis strategist decided on two primary target markets: the town's residents, relatively affluent people, and summer tourists, mostly from a resort town seven miles away. A secondary target was middle-income families residing in another nearby town. The president described the store image designed for these markets:

> To develop a following in this market, we have to compete on price. But the key to our success with the affluent, sophisticated consumers in this area is our strong service image. I would say that's our top drawing card.

Curtis, then, sought to avoid a *price disadvantage*, and based its *differential advantage* on various services. Machine-aided check approval, a weather station (weather conditions are especially important to coastal residents), and specialty departments (delicatessen, bakery, hot carry-out foods, and specialty cheeses) are some of Curtis's featured services.

Once a prospective merchant formulates a store image, he has to go to work on creating that favorable initial image among target consumers. Even an established merchant still needs to enhance or maintain store image. In both cases, effective communication of the image is essential.

As we discussed above, a consumer acquires an image of a store through experience, which can include actual shopping and perhaps purchases in the outlet, seeing its exterior and signs while passing by, hearing about it from friends, and seeing or hearing its advertising. Therefore, every aspect of a retail firm says something about it: location; appearance; type of merchandise; price levels; number, kind, knowledgeability, and friendliness of sales personnel; and amount and type of advertising.

To attract customers, a new retail enterprise usually relies heavily on promotion to communicate its desired image. Many retailers launch their business with a grand opening in order to attract first-time customers. However, even a grand opening can damage a firm's image if its atmosphere is inconsistent with the store's normal operating plans. For example, price reductions during a grand opening would be inappropriate if a store's desired image is focused upon personal attention, extra services, and regular prices. A grand opening can also be harmful if it attracts customers but they leave the outlet with an undesirable image of the firm. This problem is probably most common with fast-food restaurant openings. Heavy advertising and an attractive coupon may attract so many customers that ingredients for certain menu items are depleted, or new employees are so pressed that they treat some customers shabbily.

Obviously, the key to continued success in retailing is developing *regular* customers. Thus the initial impression must be such that first-time customers have the desired image of the store *after* their first visit and purchase. Recognizing this, some retailers forgo a splashy grand opening. Others delay the grand opening until the outlet has been open *and operating smoothly* for a couple of weeks.

Special in-store events can also be used by established retailers who want to enhance an image. In fact, this has been a recent trend:

> While retail management recognizes the soundness of the concept that a store's personality is built by its everyday performance, there is evidence of a creeping impatience with this philosophy. A growing number of merchants are asking: "In the ferocity of today's competition would it be sounder strategy to punctuate the process of gradual image building with more potent and more frequent promotions of the *block buster* type?"[13]

Some special events used by retailers, primarily department stores, to make an impact on consumers include: a "Groove-In" promotion to attract teenagers, a "Shops of Europe" event aimed especially at sophisticated shoppers, and a "Salute to America" featuring United States history and finely crafted products.

CREATING AND ENHANCING AN IMAGE

Steps in Operations Planning

SPOTLIGHT

How do a Fortnight, submarines, and His and Her camels enhance a retailer's image?

Neiman-Marcus is a chain of about eight department stores, most of which are in Texas. It has acquired an image—known almost worldwide—as *the* prestige retailer of fine merchandise.

Since its first day of operation in 1907, Neiman-Marcus has worked at creating and maintaining its prestige image. In fact, an opening-day ad expressed the intended image: "Neiman-Marcus will bring to the Southwest the finest assortments of ready-to-wear from all parts of the world," and "they will be sold with the highest degree of personalized service ever offered."

While the Neiman-Marcus merchandise offerings have expanded considerably since 1907, their image has been maintained by an emphasis on high-quality merchandise and by prices that shoppers do not mistake for discount prices. The image has been further enhanced by some novel merchandising activities. One is the annual Christmas catalog, which not only features the chain's regular merchandise but also exotic and expensive original gifts for "the person who has everything." Included in recent catalogs have been an aquarium that substituted real pearls for the sand, working miniature submarines, a live steer plus a silver serving cart, and His and Her camels.

Neiman-Marcus also uses an annual special event in the main Dallas store to enhance its image. Each October, its renowned Fortnight (a two-week period) spotlights the culture and merchandise of a foreign country. The 1973 Fortnight, for example, honored England, and Neiman-Marcus's first floor was redecorated to resemble the quadrangle of Cambridge University. Moreover, a candy-maker from Brighton created authentic British sweets in the store, while British celebrities, diplomats, and trade representatives made appearances.

When the Fortnight concept was initiated in 1957, Stanley Marcus explained, "It seemed a good way to bridge the gap between the end of the fall shopping season and the beginning of Christmas." The Fortnight requires a real flare for showmanship and is costly. The biggest expense is for the special merchandise for which the store sends 35 buyers abroad every spring. According to the Fortnight director, "Imports enable us to maintain our standard of quality without getting into exhorbitant prices. Exclusives [items not available in any other United States store] give us another handle to talk about in our advertising."

What have such innovative merchandising activities done for the chain's image? Perhaps one incident illustrates, better than anything else, how attractive the Neiman-Marcus name and image are: During one Christmas rush period, a gift wrapper accidentally substituted her lunch (ham sandwich and an orange) for the expensive gift she was supposed to be wrapping. When the wrapper reported the mistake, her boss decided to wait and see what happened. Weeks passed, and no one voiced a complaint. "Our theory is," said one N-M executive, "that whoever got the lunch figured that no matter what it was, if it came from Neiman-Marcus, it just had to be special."

Sources: Background material supplied by Neiman-Marcus plus: Stanley Marcus, "While We Were Watching the Store, The State of Texas Grew Up," *Saturday Evening Post*, Winter, 1971, p. 46; and Pauline Neff, "Neiman-Marcus Fortnight Spectacular," *Sky* Magazine October 1973, pp. 36 and 38.

Once a store is established, a retail strategist should occasionally evaluate the soundness of its desired image, considering changing market conditions in particular. If the image is judged unsound, modification is called for. A program for evaluating and modifying store image is presented in Figure 2-1. Basically, this program seeks to determine in sequence all target and actual market segments, specific image requirements of such segments, and a program to serve these segments in an effective way.[14] One complicating factor not evident in Figure 2-1 is the fact that it may not be possible to satisfy both

EVALUATING AN IMAGE

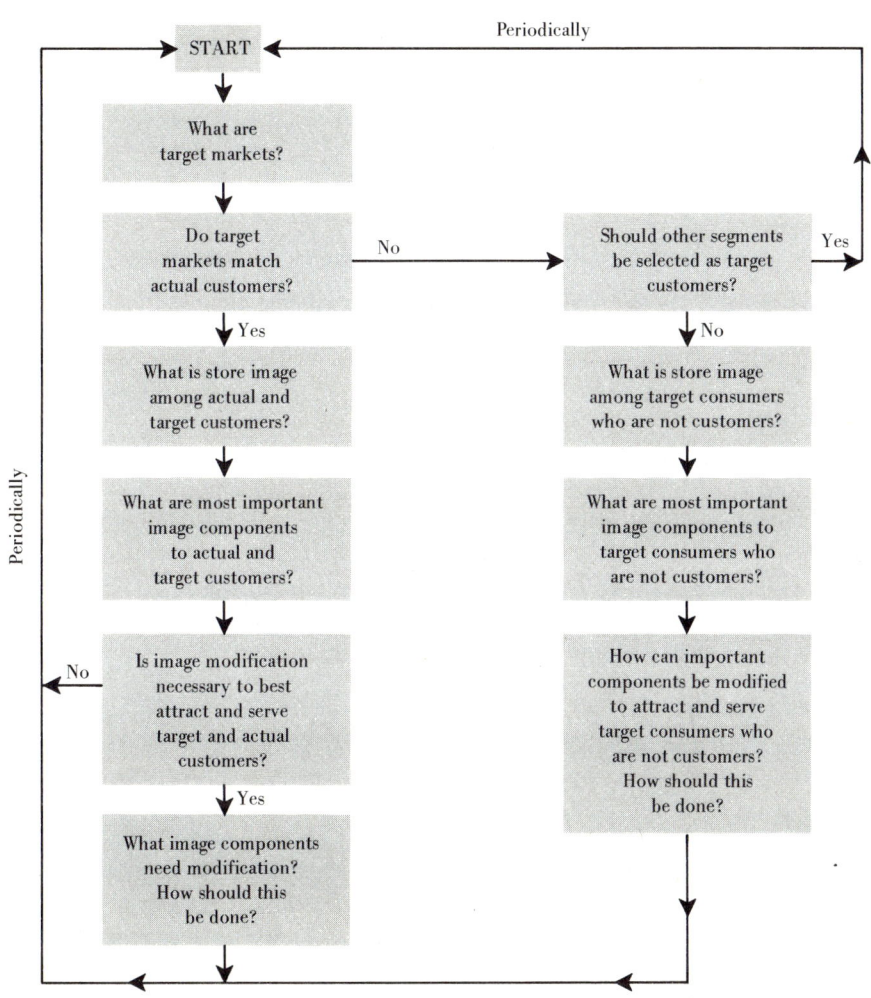

FIGURE 2-1

Store image evaluation and modification program

Source: Based on Leonard L. Berry, "The Components of Department Store Image: A Theoretical and Empirical Analysis," *Journal of Retailing*, Spring 1969, p. 18.

Steps in Operations Planning **45**

actual and target customers at the same time. To continue the present mode of operations which apparently pleases present customers may preclude attracting consumers in the target market. On the other hand, to modify operations so as to attract target consumers may jeopardize the patronage of present customers.

An interesting part of this program is the implied suggestion that efforts should be concentrated on upgrading particularly important image components. These extra efforts may be at the expense of attention to relatively less important components. In the department store study, for example, sales personnel emerged as extremely important to one store's image. Thus, according to this program, this store's efforts to retain present customers and attract additional target consumers should concentrate on sales personnel selection, training, and motivation.

REVIEW BOX 2:3

1. From a retailer's viewpoint, an image can be defined as ——————.

2. In designing a store image, a strategist tries to set his firm apart from competitors in a favorable way—that is, to come up with a ——————.

Design a Retailing Mix

After dealing as well as possible with uncontrollable factors and making certain strategic decisions, a retail executive must proceed to consideration of a more specific, controllable factor: the retailing mix. In the remainder of this book we shall examine both the strategic and tactical decisions connected with retail operations.

NATURE AND COMPONENTS

A retail strategist formulating a desired image for a firm plans to highlight certain factors (perhaps low prices and broad assortment of merchandise) and de-emphasize others (perhaps the outlet's location and number of sales personnel). In the fourth step in operations planning, a merchant specifically considers each factor that might be utilized. He plans how low the "low prices" will be, where the outlet will be located, what its exterior appearance will be, and so on. In other words, the retailer decides the *what* or *how much* of each factor and relates each factor to the others. This process is called designing a retailing mix.

The term *retailing mix* refers to a combination of offerings, physical facilities, prices, and promotion used by a retailer in attempting to satisfy target consumers and achieve performance objectives. For some merchants a retailing mix just "happens." With little if any planning, a location is arranged, merchandise is purchased and priced for resale, and so on. Of course, this is totally unsatisfactory and likely to accomplish only one thing: to add the firm to the long roster of retailing fatalities.

Much more desirable is a *systematic* approach which carefully considers environmental factors and takes into account earlier strategic decisions. Also, in light of earlier decisions, each retailing mix element should have a logical rationale. Finally, the whole mix is not firmed up until after deliberation on how the various elements affect each other and how they can best be blended.

A retailing mix has four basic elements—offerings, physical facilities, prices, and promotion—which are described below.

Offerings. Retail firms sell products (groceries, clothing, hardware items) or services (entertainment, dry cleaning, hair cuts), or both. In addition, they often provide additional services to customers, such as credit, delivery, and alterations. Services of the first type are termed *primary* since they represent the primary reason for a purchase. Those of the second type are called *supplementary* since they help sell the primary product or service.

A retailer's charter objectives, which indicate a line of trade such as clothing or women's hair care, narrow the range of decisions that must be made about offerings. But the retailer who sells a product still must decide which, if any, primary services should be offered. For example, should a men's clothing store provide a tuxedo rental service? Would this service produce customer satisfaction and profits? Likewise, a services establishment must decide whether to offer products. For example, should a beauty parlor sell hair spray?

Merchandise management, covered in Part Three, involves planning and controlling an assortment of products. Chapter 8 deals with the first task, merchandise planning. Then Chapter 9 examines a related task, buying practices and relationships with suppliers; the chapter considers what must be done to translate a merchandise *plan* into *actual* merchandise, purchased and received by the store and ready to be priced for resale. Chapter 10 looks at merchandise control, the joint task of assuring that proper inventories of merchandise are maintained and protecting merchandise against various types of loss.

Much of the material in this book applies to *both* merchandise (products) and services retailing. In addition, primary services receive special treatment in Chapter 24 because consumers are spending increasing amounts on such services and because there are some necessary differences between services retailing and merchandise retailing.

Physical Facilities. Retail firms that conduct in-store retailing rather than non-store retailing face decisions on three aspects of physical facilities: location, design, and layout. *Location*, the physical site of a business, should be chosen first. Considerations such as surroundings, amount of traffic, and cost determine where a merchant will locate. Store location is the subject of Chapter 4. *Design* of the outlet, the second facilities decision, refers to exterior and interior appearance. Store *layout*, although usually third among facilities decisions, definitely affects, and is affected by, location and design decisions. Determining retail layout requires decisions about various means used to present merchandise to shoppers, including a floor plan of display tables and racks, specific location of various types of merchandise, and amount of space allocated to various items. Design and layout decisions are examined in Chapter 5.

Prices. The third element of a retailing mix is price, the amount of money and perhaps something else of value (such as trade-ins), that a consumer needs in order to purchase a retailer's offering. The concepts of demand, cost, and markup form the foundation for effective pricing. These concepts are described in Chapter 11.

Building on this foundation, a retail manager then actually establishes retail prices. In other words, when a retailer makes a decision on whether, say, a man's suit would produce optimum sales and profits at a $79.95 or $90 price, he must consider consumer demand, the wholesale cost to him, and the amount he should add onto the wholesale price in order to show a profit. Establishing an original retail price requires a sequence of steps, which are presented in Chapter 12.

Ideally, all offerings will sell at original prices. But since retailers operate in a real rather than ideal world, adjustments sometimes are necessary. Price adjustments, the most common being markdowns, are the subject of Chapter 13 which concludes Part Four.

Promotion. Usually the last element a retailer develops is promotion, which involves communicating with target consumers as well as with shoppers in the outlet. In general, all promotion is aimed at fulfilling the retailer's basic objective: producing profits for the firm. However, promotion also has a variety of more specific purposes: informing consumers of the firm's existence, attracting them to the outlet, building the firm's image, persuading consumers to make purchases, serving shoppers in the outlet, and periodically reminding consumers about the firm and its offerings.

Three kinds of communication form a promotion blend: advertising, personal selling, and supportive methods. The first chapter in Part Five, Chapter 14, overviews the concept of a promotion blend and considers what are called supportive methods of promotion, such as display, special sales, and trading stamps. Chapter 15 deals with personal selling, the activities of retail sales employees in helping shoppers buy satisfying offerings. Chapter 16 deals with the other major form of promotion, advertising, the activities involved in communicating to consumers a nonpersonal but sponsored and paid-for message. Supplementary services, viewed as one way of promoting sales, are discussed in Chapter 17.

Obviously, a retail firm does not operate in a vacuum. Rather it is part of a larger arena in which many forces interact and numerous parties engage in various business activities. This larger arena is called a *retail system* and consists of (1) consumers, (2) uncontrollable factors which affect or might affect the retailer's line of trade or geographic area, (3) operating strategies, policies, and methods, including a retailing mix, and (4) enabling elements of the firm (explained below).

POSITION WITHIN A RETAIL SYSTEM

Figure 2-2 illustrates a retail system with a retailing mix positioned within it. The small circle in the middle represents target consumers to emphasize that all retail operations should be directed toward satisfying specified consumers' needs. This viewpoint is consistent with the marketing concept and reflects the second step in retail operations planning, identification of one or more target markets.

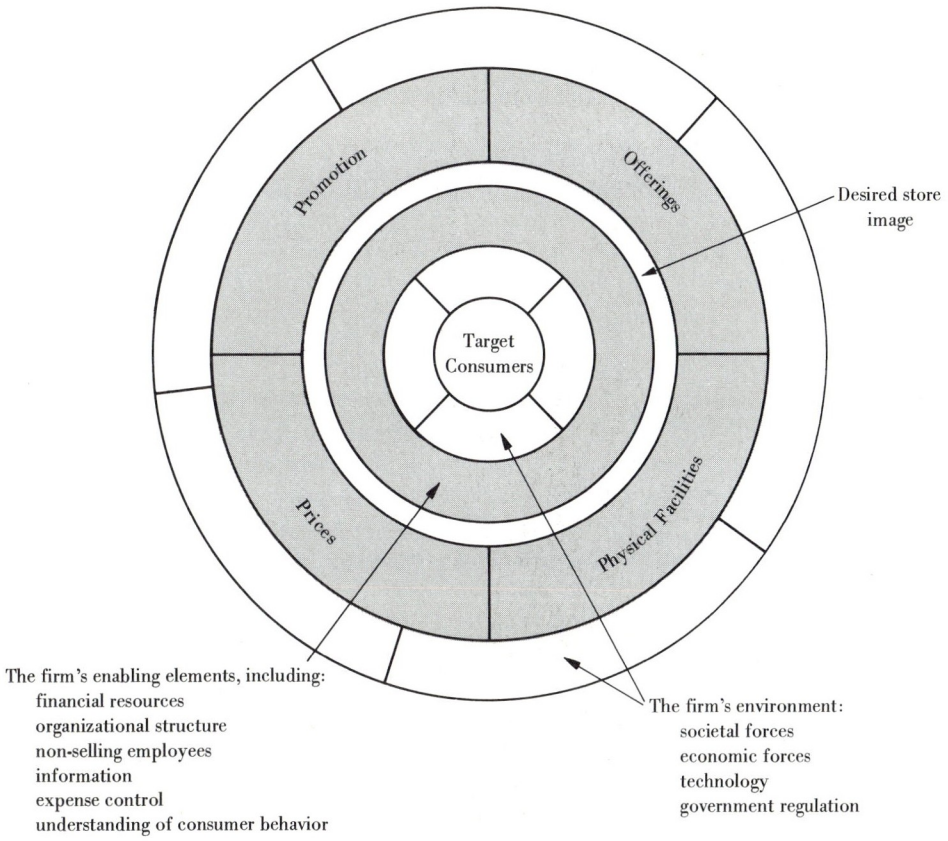

FIGURE 2-2

A retail system showing the position of a retailing mix

Steps in Operations Planning

Both the innermost and outermost rings represent the five components of a firm's environment. The environment is positioned next to target consumers, since environmental factors restrict what can be done to satisfy consumers (and make a profit) and affect the impact of the retailer's efforts on consumers. For example, laws restrict a retailer's activities while competitors' activities may neutralize a firm's offerings or, by comparison, make them quite attractive. On the other hand, the environment is also positioned as the system's boundary since it limits the nature of activities in a certain line of trade. Recall that the environment is assessed in the initial step of retail operations planning. A firm's environment was overviewed in Chapter 1, and a prominent environmental factor—consumerism—is the subject of Chapter 21.

The innermost shaded ring represents a firm's enabling elements. Although a retailing mix is the direct means of satisfying consumers, a firm also needs certain elements that will result in both an effective and efficient mix. These enabling elements include:

Financial resources and management, discussed in Chapter 19.
Organizational structure, Chapter 6.
Non-selling employees, Chapter 7.
Understanding of consumer behavior, Chapter 3.
Information for decision-making, Chapter 18.
Measures to control expenses, Chapter 20.

The relative adequacy of a firm's enabling elements either helps or hinders a firm's efforts to satisfy target consumers at a profit.

An understanding of consumer behavior includes an appreciation of any distinctive behavior of significant market segments. Consequently, the first part of Chapter 22 presents information on the dimensions and purchase behavior of minority groups. Finally, distinctive organizational arrangements sometimes are necessary or are consistent with a firm's charter objectives or target markets. Thus two such arrangements, ownership or management by minority-group members and franchise operations, are discussed in the second part of Chapter 22 and in Chapter 23, respectively.

Between the enabling elements and retailing mix is the desired store image, the third step in retail operations planning. This position indicates that an image is largely based on elements within the retailing mix but is also related to a firm's enabling elements. Finally, the retailing mix is shown by the outer shaded ring and is subdivided into its four main elements: offerings, physical facilities, prices, and promotion. The point expressed by Figure 2-2 is that a retailing mix is one part of a larger retail system but an integral part of a retail firm's operations. Given the importance of a firm's retailing mix and enabling elements, Parts Two through Six examine and relate these two parts of retail operations.

REVIEW BOX 2:4

1. The third step in retail operations planning is to _____.
2. A retailing mix contains a combination of _____, physical facilities, prices, and promotion.
3. A retail firm operates as part of a _____.

CHAPTER SUMMARY

- The function of retail management is similar to programming a computer in that it involves three basic tasks: setting objectives, planning strategies, and developing policies and methods.
- A retail firm must specify its objectives or desired results. Charter objectives define a business's general scope with respect to the kinds of offerings and locations. Performance objectives specify desired financial results within a certain time period.
- Planning strategies are the ways in which a firm's resources are deployed in order to surpass competitors or to seize opportunities.
- Specific actions aimed at a particular purpose are methods. Policies, guidelines which indicate appropriate methods in different situations, are important in retailing management since they often simplify and improve decision-making.
- A complete retail strategy results from a four-step process: (1) assess the environment, (2) identify target markets, (3) formulate desired image and differential advantage, and (4) plan retailing mix. Each step produces operating plans, which are general and strategic in nature.
- Identification of target markets requires analysis of consumers in terms of population characteristics, income levels and distribution, and buying behavior.
- Market segmentation, necessary for almost all retailers, involves identifying a reasonably similar group of consumers with unsatisfied needs and then developing a more satisfying offering for them. Markets can be subdivided according to demographic characteristics or people's attitudes and behavior.
- The third step in retail operations planning is to formulate a desired image for the firm. To a merchant, an image is the overall picture a firm tries to project to target consumers. To a consumer, store image is the set of attitudes he or she has toward a particular outlet.
- In designing a store image, a strategist tries to set his firm apart from competitors in a favorable way—that is, to come up with a differential advantage.

- A retailer should periodically evaluate the soundness of its desired image in light of changing market conditions, and modify it if it is unsound.
- Designing a retailing mix—a combination of offerings, physical facilities, prices, and promotion used by a retailer in an attempt to satisfy target consumers and achieve performance objectives—is the fourth step in operations planning. A retailing mix should result from a systematic procedure, rather than just "happen."
- A retail firm is part of a retail system which consists of (1) consumers; (2) uncontrollable factors affecting the line of trade; (3) operating strategies, policies, and methods, including a retailing mix; and (4) enabling elements of the firm. Among a retail outlet's enabling elements are its resources, non-selling employees, and information. Adequate enabling elements help a firm to satisfy target consumers.

CHAPTER NOTES

[1] This example is drawn from "Korvettes Tries for a Little Chic," *Business Week*, May 12, 1973, pp. 124–126.
[2] John Steven Klein, "Ad Clinic: Sizzler Sticks to 'Basics' in Its Advertising," *Restaurant Business*, June, 1974, p. 42.
[3] David J. Luck and Arthur E. Prell, *Market Strategy* (New York: Appleton-Century-Crofts, 1968), pp. 4–9; several other points in this section are also based on Luck and Prell's discussion.
[4] Urban C. Lehner, "Economy Motels Lure Travelers with Prices as Low as $6 a Room," *Wall Street Journal*, December 26, 1972, p. 11.
[5] Luck and Prell, *op. cit.*, p. 2.
[6] These concise definitions were suggested by William J. Stanton, *Fundamentals of Marketing*, 3rd ed. (New York: McGraw-Hill Book Company, 1971), p. 76.
[7] "The Pragmatic Supermarketer," *Dun's Review*, June, 1971, p. 62.
[8] "Small Towns Hunger for Fast Food," *Franchise Journal*, January, 1972, p. 10.
[9] "Invading Small Town, USA," *Fast Food*, April, 1972, p. 79.
[10] This paragraph is based on the excellent study conducted by James E. Bell, Jr., "Mobiles—A Possible Segment for Retailer Cultivation," *Journal of Retailing*, Fall, 1970, pp. 1–15.
[11] This quotation as well as the list of image components in the next paragraph come from Leonard L. Berry, "The Components of Department Store Image: A Theoretical and Empirical Analysis," *Journal of Retailing*, Spring, 1969, pp. 5, 7–9.
[12] The quotations in this paragraph as well as the strategy of Curtis supermarkets are contained in "Programmed Service Builds Competitive Edge," *Progressive Grocer*, September, 1972, pp. 62–68 ff at pp. 62 and 64.
[13] "More Retailers Stress 'Impact' as Image Builder," *Grey Matter* (retail edition), November, 1967.
[14] This paragraph and the following one are based on Berry, *op. cit.*, p. 17.

QUESTIONS AND ASSIGNMENTS

1. What kind of new retail firm would you like to own or work for? Develop an appropriate charter objective for this firm.
2. Is there a difference between objectives and goals? Between strategy and tactics? Between policies and methods?

3. An entrepreneur who plans to open a chain of dry cleaning outlets is assessing the environment. What environmental factors affect—or might affect—this area of retailing?
4. Which population characteristics of your community should a clothing retailer consider?
5. Use the technique of market segmentation to identify one or more feasible target markets for a new restaurant in your community. This means you have to (a) subdivide the total market according to certain factors which affect consumer behavior and then (b) tentatively suggest a retailing mix which would appeal to these consumers.
6. Review the components of department store image, as discussed in this chapter. Which components would also apply to a TV or auto repair firm? What other components, not listed for department stores, would be part of a repair firm's image? Which are the *most important* component(s) in the list you have developed for repair firms? Explain.
7. What is the difference between an outlet's competitive differential and its differential advantage? For a variety store, which would prices represent?
8. One part of the image evaluation and modification program discussed in the text is the idea that efforts should be concentrated on upgrading important image components. Could this approach, in fact, wind up hurting the firm's image rather than improving it? Why or why not?
9. What are two reasons why a retailing mix just "happens" in the case of some retailers? In other words, why is it not carefully planned?
10. What three elements can be contained in the offerings element of a retailing mix? Which one is sometimes given free to customers?

ANSWERS TO REVIEW BOX QUESTIONS

Box 2:1

1. developing policies and methods
2. desired result
3. upper management

Box 2:2

1. market
2. identifying a reasonably similar group of consumers who are not fully satisfied with present offerings
3. two of the following: employed women, teenagers, young marrieds, blacks, small communities, and mobile families

Box 2:3

1. the overall picture the store tries to project to target consumers
2. differential advantage

Box 2:4

1. formulate desired image and differential advantage
2. offerings
3. retail system

PART TWO

Initial Considerations and Decisions

Analyzing Consumer Behavior

Basically, consumers buy products and services in order to fill physical needs. They buy food for nutrition and strength, housing for shelter, clothes for protection of the body, and medical care to maintain or improve health. However, a few moments of thought indicate that other things besides physical needs are being satisfied in the purchase and consumption of retailers' offerings. First, consider the great variety of products and services available. The choices in most product categories—for example, cars or clothing—go far beyond what would be needed to satisfy basic physical needs. Second, if the only value in products were their physical function, they would be designed only to satisfy that function. For example, clothes would be made for maximum comfort and protection, all food would be highly nutritional, and cars would be strictly functional. Since this obviously is not always the case, it is apparent that more occurs in the purchase and consumption process than the satisfaction of physical needs. Behavioral or psychological factors also play a role in retailing.

A large body of literature has been developed in the field of consumer behavior.[1] Using concepts and findings from economics, psychology, sociology, and anthropology, retailers have studied and tried to explain why consumers behave as they do. These efforts have produced a wide variety of results from simple relationships such as "awareness of a product must occur before desire," to complex theories of individual and group behavior.

BEFORE THE PURCHASE

Consumers come to retail outlets with established needs and attitudes. For this reason, it is important for retailers to recognize the general needs that people have and seek to satisfy. On this basis they can then make operational plans that will respond to consumer behavior.

Needs

Psychologists have identified several classifications of needs. However, for our purposes the generally accepted five-level hierarchy developed by Maslow will be sufficient.[2]

According to Maslow's theory, all behavior is the result of unsatisfied needs which create tension and, in turn, activity to satisfy the needs. The five levels of need are:

1. *Physiological needs*—the most basic needs, necessary to sustain life and well-being. For example, hunger and thirst are physiological needs.
2. *Safety needs*—the needs for physical and mental security and for protection from the world around us. The desire to have a fair chance in life.
3. *Social needs*—the needs for love, friendship, companionship, and acceptance by others.
4. *Esteem needs*—the needs for recognition, self-confidence, self-respect, and appreciation.
5. *Self-actualization needs*—the need to fulfill one's potential in life, to become what one is capable of becoming.

Figure 3-1 shows how these needs vary according to their importance to an individual (from the bottom to the top) and the degree to which they are normally satisfied (the area within the triangle). To illustrate, physiological needs are at the bottom of the pyramid because they are the most basic. In

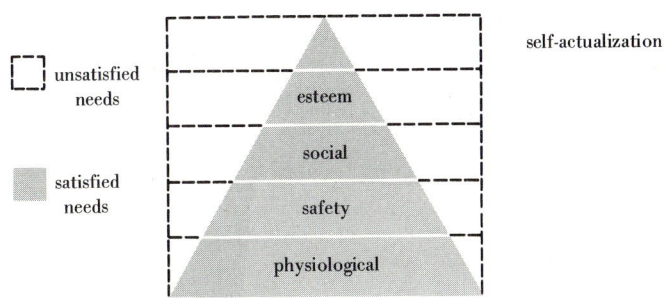

FIGURE 3-1

The hierarchy of needs

addition, they take up the greatest portion of the pyramid to indicate that they are usually the most satisfied needs. Moving up the figure, notice the order in which the needs act as motivators and the smaller degree of satisfaction a person normally experiences at each level. Also note the amount of unsatisfied need (the areas enclosed by broken lines) at each level.

There are three additional points to remember about needs:

1. Satisfied needs do not influence behavior. This explains why in our society, where physiological needs are generally well satisfied, retailers seldom direct advertising appeals at this level.
2. Needs at one level must be *reasonably* satisfied before the next level begins to influence behavior.
3. Several need levels can operate at the same time. When a need level reaches a tolerable degree of satisfaction, the next level becomes a motivator. For example, at a point in time an individual may have 90 percent of his physiological needs satisfied, 70 percent of his safety needs, 50 percent of his social needs, 30 percent of his esteem needs, and 5 percent of his self-actualization needs.

Unfortunately there is no formula to indicate a person's level of need deprivation or the amount of satisfaction provided by shopping or purchasing. However, it is clear that the offerings we buy can satisfy needs at a variety of levels. For example, food can contribute to the satisfaction of physiological needs (milk for nutrition), social needs (pizza on a date), and esteem needs (steak at a dinner party). In addition, the same product can appeal to different needs for different people. Beer, for example, may be consumed to satisfy thirst or to meet a social need.

The retailer must consider the strength as well as the existence of needs. The *more important the need* to the individual and the *greater the deprivation* (no food for two days, for example), the more effort the individual will expend to find satisfaction. Thus, in some situations (strong need and large deprivation) the consumer need only be *told* of an offering's availability. An example might be a social club for a lonely person. On the other hand, situations exist (weak need and reasonable satisfaction) in which a high level of persuasion is required to convince the consumer to buy the product. Trying to sell a new 23-inch color TV to someone who has a reasonably good 17-inch set might be an example of such a situation. Thus the task of the retailer is to identify the needs people have and evaluate their strength and then to relate products or services to those needs through adjustment of personal selling efforts, prices, and promotion.

IDENTIFICATION OF NEEDS

In order to appeal to consumers' unsatisfied needs (a subject in the chapters on promotion) the retailer must first determine what they are. Although there is no set method for identifying the existence of a need, there are some considerations which suggest which level of needs is motivating a shopper's activities.

Functional Aspects. Consider a product objectively and ask *what function* it serves. For example, an automobile provides transportation. Second, consider how efficiently the product provides that function. In the case of the automobile, is it economical and easy to maintain? Does it provide adequate usable space? If the product is inefficient in terms of providing its functional benefits, then almost certainly its purchase will have been influenced by higher level needs.

Product Use. Second, consider *how* the product is used. Is it consumed publicly or privately? A product that will be consumed in public (a suit) has important social and esteem significance for the user. On the other hand, a product used privately (a toothbrush) is normally purchased for its functional aspects.

For publicly consumed products, the type of alternatives available will suggest the needs being satisfied. For example, a man may buy a $17.95 pair of tennis shoes for casual wear to satisfy his need for esteem as well as a physiological need when a $4.95 alternative is available. However, the man who buys an electrical lawn edger for $19.95 when a manual clipper is available for $3.98 may be thinking only of his blistered hands and sore back (physiological needs).

National Advertising Themes. Manufacturers of most nationally distributed products conduct advertising centered around some particular theme. The advertisement for a brand of toothpaste might, for example, appeal to a physiological need (fewer cavities) or a social need (whiter teeth). These themes are usually based on a considerable amount of research that has identified a target market with an unfilled need. The retailer, then, can take a cue from the manufacturer and use the same theme in promotion and personal selling efforts.

STRENGTH OF NEEDS

The strength of a person's need for an offering is a critical bit of information for a seller as a potential buyer moves toward the purchase. A premature attempt to close a sale or a delay in seeking to close when the customer is ready can result in lost business. Thus, it is important to consider some indications of need strength.

Postponable. If the purchase can be postponed (shopping for a new refrigerator when the old one still works), the consumer's needs are usually not too strong. On the other hand, when the product is a necessity in the consumer's view and the need cannot be satisfied by an available alternative, the purchase is not postponable, and the need is strong.

Shopping Behavior. Except in the case of a major purchase such as a home or an automobile, the more comparisons among products and retail outlets that the consumer engages in, the weaker the need. A consumer who

Before the Purchase

looks at the product in many stores over a period of time comparing price, product features, and guarantees is looking for the ideal purchase situation and probably has a weak need.

Dollar Amount of the Purchase. If the purchase price of the product is large relative to the consumer's income level, then desire or need for the product is usually quite strong. For example, people do not ordinarily buy color TV sets or automobiles casually.

All of these indicators of need strength can be discovered by the seller through careful listening and skillful questioning of potential customers. Once the customer's need strength has been evaluated, the seller can gear selling efforts to the particular situation.

REVIEW BOX 3:1

1. Although several need levels can operate at the same time, a satisfied need is a _____.
2. It is useful for a retailer to *identify* unsatisfied needs and also to know their _____.
3. If the purchase can be postponed, the consumer's need is usually not very _____.

Self-Concept

To understand better how needs are satisfied, we must look at some of the factors that make people different. One such factor is self-concept, which deals with how an individual views himself and how he thinks others view him. It includes the kind of personality, appearance, and intelligence a person feels he possesses. To appreciate self-concept, think for a moment about yourself. How do you see yourself? Are you shy or friendly, generous or stingy? Second, how would you *like to be?* What things would you like to change to improve yourself? Finally, what opinion do you feel others have of you? Do people see you as cheerful, self-assured, and pleasant to be with? In order to distinguish among these types of self-concept, three categories have been developed:[3]

1. *Self-image*—the way an individual sees himself
2. *Ideal self*—the way an individual would like to be
3. *Looking-glass self*—the way an individual thinks others regard him.

Beginning in childhood a person recognizes his or her strengths and weaknesses through experiences in play and school, observation of older brothers and sisters, parents, teachers, and others engaged in various roles,

SPOTLIGHT

Have women, who comprise the majority of the shopping public, been ignored by store designers?

Thelma Cupino, head of corporate design for First National Stores, thinks that all too often the answer is yes, they have. In the following interview, excerpted from an article in *Chain Store Age*, Miss Cupino expresses her views on this subject.

Interviewer: Is there really such a thing as a feminine approach to store planning?

Miss Cupino: Definitely, although it doesn't necessarily mean that a man can't design a store that will appeal to women. It's just that their approach tends to be different. A man tends to work too hard at trying to keep construction costs to a minimum, often to the detriment of the store's customer appeal. A woman would not be as willing to sacrifice good decor to cut construction costs.

Interviewer: Why not?

Miss Cupino: For one, a woman isn't afraid to be a woman and think like one. Design work is, after all, an expression of an individual's personality and most men would not want their work to be considered "feminine." Yet they are trying to appeal to feminine personalities — or at least should be.

For another, I doubt if any male store planners actually shop in the stores they design. I do. I think they'd look at things differently if they did. For instance, something as basic as the female's generally shorter height isn't considered very often. Standard refrigeration cases are so high that some women shoppers can't easily reach them.

Interviewer: What you've said about costs sounds like a situation comedy in which the wife spends and spends and the husband sits home counting bills.

Miss Cupino: Not at all. I'm in favor of keeping costs to a minimum and, like any other planner, I have a budget I must adhere to. But you can also reach a point where you cut and cut and fail to do the job you started out to do — attract women shoppers. What's the sense of building a store that doesn't attract any customers?

Interviewer: But decor is a cost factor, isn't it? And low-margin supers in a highly competitive industry just can't afford too much of it.

Miss Cupino: Contrary to what some store planners seem to think, designing a store for women doesn't mean tacking on unnecessary frills. It means quite the opposite. It's designing basic store elements to not only perform their function, but to enhance decor.

Signing is an example. It need not be the cut and dried formula favored by many supermarkets. Use it to sell the merchandise and add decor at the same time. If you're selling a luxury item like wine, spell out the letters in script to indicate luxury. Even better, you can let the product sell itself and add decor. The only signing on the flower shop I'm designing is a bold, bright flower. The merchandise is arranged in such a fashion — on a circular display stand — so as to suggest a giant bouquet. The product itself acts as a sign and adds to store decor.

Or take the checkout counter area. The signs sitting on poles over each checkout denoting its number are often a visual sorepoint because they clutter up the storefront. I've replaced these with single oblong signs hanging from the ceiling over checkout areas. They serve the same purpose but avoid the visual clutter.

The point is, decor need not and should not be an extraneous afterthought, a veneer. It should be integral to the store's design and function. Most important, it should work to organize the store.

Interviewer: Organize the store?

Miss Cupino: Yes! I think this is of primary importance. Stores have to have a clean, organized, appearance if they're going to pull women shoppers. If you wanted to tack a label on it, I'd call it planned simplicity. An average supermarket handles and displays over 12,000 items in groceries alone. If these products aren't presented in an organized, orderly fashion, they won't sell. I think neatness is a recognized female characteristic. And if the female shopper is presented with visual clutter, she'll go somewhere else to shop.

Interviewer: But some say a cluttered look can suggest "lower prices" to a shopper, after the fashion of a warehouse outlet.

Miss Cupino: It's a mistake to think women shop in a given store for price alone. I make it a point to regularly shop both our own stores and the competition's, and casually chat with customers to get their opinions. As far as they know, I'm just another customer so their comments are honest. I think you'd be surprised how much customers are concerned with store design. I even get letters from them. Just the other day, an irate customer wrote me to say we had lost three customers—herself, her sister and mother—because they didn't like going to the center of the aisle to read directories there. She suggested we put a small directory on each shopping cart—not such a bad idea.

I've also found color coordination to be very important to customers. Even supermarket workers I've talked to sometimes complain about the lack of it. Color, in fact, is a major tool in designing and organizing clean-looking stores. I'm using it on floors as well as walls to color-code various departments.

Source: "You're Not Designing Stores for Women Shoppers," *Chain Store Age*, July 1973, pp. E28–9.

and training at home and in school. All of these activities—experiences, observation, and training—blend together to form an individual's view of self. For most people the self-concept is established at a relatively early age and remains basically the same for life.

SELF-CONCEPT IN PURCHASING

There are several indications that self-concept plays an important role in the choice of products, brands, and retail stores. One research study found that a man's self-image is very similar to the image he has of the car he owns.[4] In another study it was found that a greater degree of similarity exists between an individual's self-image and preferred brands of products than between self-image and least preferred brands.[5] These findings and others not described here indicate that one purchases products and brands supportive of one's self-image.

In addition to products and brands, retail outlets are selected on the basis of the images they project. We all have been in retail stores where we felt uncomfortable because we didn't "belong." Either the merchandise was not the type we would buy, the prices were too high or too low, or some other factor made the situation disconcerting. An explanation for this type of occurrence is that the image the store presents is different from our self-image. An interesting example of this phenomenon was given by a research study that found that, depending on their political allegiance, consumers discriminated between two neighboring book stores during the 1968 presidential election because one was named "Kennedy's" and the other "Wallace's."[6]

As discussed in Chapter 2, a retailer must be concerned with creating an image that is consistent with, and therefore appealing to, the target market. The importance of this is indicated by the experience of Montgomery Ward's in trying to change an image. Following World War II, Sears and J. C. Penney's expanded extensively while Wards did not. As a result, Wards developed a conservative image that has not yet been overcome. A Ward's public relations man recently said: "The company has a stodgy old image compared to Sear's and Penney's. We're fighting tooth and nail to get rid of it."[7]

Social Class

All societies have some sort of class system. Each social class within a society is made up of people with similar ambitions, values, and behavior patterns. A class system may be either closed or open. A closed system, such as exists in India, restricts an individual to the class in which he is born. In contrast, an open system permits movement between classes. This type of system, which exists in the United States, has produced the "rags to riches" social dream—that an individual through his own efforts can climb the social class ladder.

The classic description of social class structure in the United States was provided by W. Lloyd Warner in 1949.[8] Warner's system, consisting of six classes, places individuals in a particular class on the basis of four criteria: source of income, type of occupation, type of house, and location of house. The six classes he described are:

1. *Upper-upper*—The wealthy established families whose wealth has been passed down through inheritance. Don't need to work though frequently found at the head of a large family business or in public service. Usually educated at the most prominent schools. Includes about 1 percent of the United States population.

Before the Purchase

2. *Lower-upper*—Includes the newly rich whose wealth has been accumulated by the present generation. Made up of highly successful professionals (doctors, lawyers) and some businessmen. Accounts for about 2 percent of the population.
3. *Upper-middle*—People with above average incomes often from professional fees and salaries. Includes successful, medium-sized business owners, C.P.A.s, college professors. Usually hold college degrees. About 10 percent of the population is in this class.
4. *Lower-middle*—White collar, salaried, middle managers and supervisors. Middle-income groups including bank tellers, insurance agents, small business owners. Usually have some college training. Consists of about 32 percent of the population.
5. *Upper-lower*—Blue collar, skilled, and semi-skilled working class. Includes policemen, sales clerks, construction workers, repairmen. Hold high school diploma. This is the largest population class, about 40 percent.
6. *Lower-lower*—Unskilled, uneducated, holders of menial jobs. Includes dishwashers, janitors, service station attendants. Also includes unemployed and welfare recipients. Includes about 15 percent of the population.

Stratifying people by social class does not constitute an evaluation. That is, one class is not necessarily made up of better people than any other class. What it does make possible is the identification of people who may see the world in the same way and react to it in a similar fashion.

SOCIAL CLASS AND RETAILING

The effect of social class on consumers' choice of products and retail stores has been rather thoroughly studied. Over 15 years ago Martineau concluded:

> The lower-status woman is completely aware that, if she goes into high-status department stores, the clerks and the other customers in the store will punish her in various subtle ways.[9]

Since Martineau's pioneering study, a variety of generalizations have been developed concerning the preferences and behavior of social class members. Findings of importance to retailing are summarized below.[10]

Lower-Lower Class. Members of this class require more credit to buy than other classes, and they are often the least qualified for credit. Their need for credit is partly the result of low income, but it also stems from a desire for immediate gratification. People of this class are prone to impulse purchasing because their income is insecure and they have very short planning horizons.

The primary media exposure for the lower-lower class is television. Many people in this social class either lack the ability to read well or they do not enjoy it. Talking to others is a very important source of information, and many conclusions about products, brands, and retailers are based on the opinions of friends and relatives.

Upper-Lower Class. Members of the upper-lower class strive to make themselves different from the lower-lower class and often use their homes as a means to do it. Because the home is a noticeable reflection of the owner's values, members of this social class spend considerable time and money making it attractive. For the upper-lower class, ownership of major durable items is considered an important symbol of success. Because members of this class lack confidence in their shopping ability, they prefer to shop where they are known, often in neighborhood stores.

Lower-Middle Class. Lower-middle class members are characterized by the need for approval of their purchases by friends and relatives. As a result, they are very conscious of brands and stores. They want to buy the "correct" or accepted products and shop in the "right" stores. In product areas where they feel they have adequate knowledge based on experience and national advertising (for example, washing machines) they will go to a discount store and buy major brands. However, for less frequently advertised products such as furniture, the lower-middle class member will select a store with an established image rather than trust his own judgment. Mothers in this class are very child centered, wanting their children to have every opportunity for education and social improvement.

Upper-Middle Class. The upper-middle class is made up of moderately successful professional people. The fact that these people are ambitious is reflected in their achievement of professional status. This ambition results in "conspicuous consumption" or the purchase of obviously expensive products that reflect the higher-than-average income of the owner At the same time, members of this class are capable of making independent decisions, often leading in the purchase of new products. For example, it was the upper-middle class that began purchasing small foreign cars in the mid-1950s and provided the initial market for the imports. Members of the upper-middle class tend to read more than do the lower classes and watch television less.

The other social classes, the lower-upper and upper-upper are not discussed because they are not of great concern to most retailers (although they do provide the market for certain prestige, specialty stores).

How can the retailer make use of social class as an indicator of behavior? First, the social class of actual (or desired) customers must be evaluated using the descriptions given. This awareness will help the retailer to know the types of merchandise he should carry, the importance of stocking na-

APPLICATION OF SOCIAL CLASS CONCEPTS

tionally advertised brands, what the best medium for advertising is likely to be, and what types of advertising and sales messages are likely to influence the target market.

An application of the social class concept in retailing is Broadway-Hale Stores, Inc.[11] The company appeals to different social classes with three distinct operations in San Francisco. The flagship chain is the 32-unit Broadway stores, fashion-oriented department stores designed to appeal to the contemporary consumer. In contrast, the Emporium Capwell Division is a very traditional department store. Although critics suggest that its "archaic" style has led to the entrance of Bullock's (an upper-middle class retailer) into the Bay area, Edward Carter, Chairman of Broadway-Hale, says: "Emporium Capwell is one of the most profitable department stores in the nation. . . . This indicates that the company's merchandising philosophy is well-attuned to the demands of its customers."[12] Finally, Broadway-Hale has acquired Neiman-Marcus and New York's posh Bergdorf Goodman to appeal to the higher social classes.

> **REVIEW BOX 3:2**
>
> 1. The largest portion of the U.S population is in the _____ social class.
> 2. Primary information sources for the lower classes are _____ and _____.

Life Cycle

From childhood until retirement an individual passes through distinctive stages of life. In each life-cycle stage the individual's responsibilities, commitments, and aspirations change, and these changes in turn produce changes in purchasing behavior.

STAGES IN THE LIFE CYCLE

Though there is not total agreement on the number of stages in the cycle, we shall discuss the purchasing characteristics of five: teenage, young adulthood, middle years, free years, and senior citizens.[13] This five-stage approach to life cycle was chosen because the stages are easily identifiable and each represents a significant portion of the total market. As in the discussion of social class, remember that these generalizations are true for many people but not for all people in a category.

Teenagers. Increases in the number of teenagers and their spending power have made this an important market segment in recent years. Estimates indicate that over 20 million teenagers spend in excess of $12 billion a year—hardly a figure to treat lightly. Retailers' awareness of the potential of this market is reflected in specialty stores designed almost exclusively for this group, teen boutiques in department stores, teen fashion boards, and special promotions designed for the young.

Probably the most distinctive features of this market are the apparently contradictory desire for independence and "compulsive conformity."[14] Most young people want to establish their independence from parental authority and direction. At the same time, however, they feel a strong need to be socially accepted by other young people. As a result, they copy the behavior (clothing, hair styles, mannerisms) of individuals whom they feel have established their independence. The results of this process are that teenagers strictly conform to the standards of their peer group, and these standards are often distasteful to parents and the older generation generally.

Young people have recently had a major influence in establishing new styles and trends. The social leaders among the teenagers try new things (long hair, bib overalls, health foods, oriental religions) and are quickly followed by others. These trends spread quickly among teenagers who are enjoying freedom for the first time in their lives with very little responsibility—no possessions to maintain, no family to support—but enough money to indulge in new trends.

Young Adulthood. From age twenty to thirty-five, a person usually establishes independence and self-reliance. Marriage ordinarily occurs, a career is chosen, and child rearing begins. During this period a man is usually very job-oriented. He is engrossed in his job in order to learn and advance, and he is very conscious of the "correct" behavior for someone in his position. Living in the right neighborhood, driving the proper car, dressing and entertaining appropriately are all important in creating the desired impression. Thus, he is influenced by image-oriented appeals by retailers.

The young mother is preoccupied with the home and children. Because furnishing and decorations are a reflection of her taste, and since she lacks experience and often has a limited budget for such decisions, her behavior is very deliberate. In shopping she relies on numerous sources of information, asks the advice of others, and probably spreads her furnishing and decorating purchases over several months or years.

Child rearing is important at this stage. During this period parents, particularly mothers, are concerned about such things as nutrition and health, education, and training in the social graces for the children. Products such as enriched foods, vitamins, educational toys, and services such as nursery school and dancing lessons are appealing at this stage.

The Middle Years. During the middle years—from about age thirty-five to fifty—the status of the family is established, career objectives and aspirations are blended with reality, and the family "settles down." Friendships, community position, club memberships, and church interests attain

Before the Purchase

greater importance. Because the wage earner is at or near peak income, the family is usually able to indulge in some luxuries. Parents are attempting to cope with their children's teenage dilemmas and are beginning to plan for their free years.

The Free Years. Ages fifty to sixty-five are described as the free years. Children are usually grown up and gone, often to distant parts of the country. The husband is still working and is usually very secure in his position because of seniority and acquired skills. The wife must find alternative outlets for her time, and hobbies, such as gardening or golf, often become an important part of her life. During this stage people travel more, and many of them move to a smaller home, an apartment, or a condominium. Grandchildren also become an important part of their lives.

Senior Citizens. Around age sixty-five, most people retire and attain the status of "senior citizen." Retirement income forces a reduction in spending. However, since few fixed obligations remain (the home is usually paid for), money is sometimes available for luxury-type purchases.

At this stage, health maintenance becomes a major concern, and keeping physically active is important. Just as the wife had to find alternative activities during the free years, the husband must find them in this stage. Thus, a potential market develops for non-strenuous recreational products and services. Fishing tackle, gardening equipment, and home workshop equipment are attractive to this market.

APPLICATION OF THE LIFE CYCLE CONCEPT

To simplify the explanation, each stage in the life cycle was associated with an age range. However, you should take care not to assume that age is the primary factor in determining life cycle stages. The life cycle concept describes several distinct *periods* common to most people's lives. In each stage needs, desires, obligations, and responsibilities differ, and related to these changes are reasonably predictable differences in family size, income, and age. Thus, in applying this concept, the retailer should use as much information as possible (including such things as appearance, style of dress, marital status, presence of children, and shopping behavior) in evaluating the life cycle stage of a potential customer.

As an indication of how life cycle differences should influence a retailer's offering and sales approach, consider this prospective appliance sale. In shopping for a refrigerator, the young housewife will want considerable information, will probably buy a nationally advertised brand because of her lack of experience, will want a relatively large refrigerator to accommodate a growing family, and will be likely to respond to a price appeal. In contrast, a woman in the middle years has more confidence in her judgment and will make a decision more quickly. She may be interested in convenience features related to entertaining (such as an ice dispenser). Finally, a woman in the middle years may be interested in a larger machine to meet the needs of teenagers and be more concerned about labor-saving, convenience features (automatic defroster) than price.

One additional note. Markets change over time. An area made up of predominantly young adults today could be almost entirely populated by retirees in twenty years. Though such an evolution is a slow process, the retailer should be aware of the possibility and be prepared to respond to it.

Numerous other behavioral concepts such as personality, reference groups, attitudes, and learning have been shown to affect purchasing behavior in certain situations. However, the influence of these factors is not easily identifiable, nor can they be measured by the retailer. The four concepts presented here—needs, self-concept, social class, and life cycle—are related to consumer purchasing behavior and can frequently be determined by a careful observer.

OTHER PREPURCHASE CONCEPTS

REVIEW BOX 3:3

1. In identifying an individual's stage in the life cycle the easiest but most often misleading indicator is _____.
2. All of the prepurchase concepts discussed—needs, self-concept, social class, and life cycle—have a predictable _____ and are _____.

DURING THE PURCHASE

A person's needs, self-concept, social class, and life cycle stage are established before he or she enters a store. However, in the actual purchase situation such factors as location and appearance of the store, the salespeople, prices, and store loyalty come into play. Two of these factors—price and loyalty—are discussed here because they have significant behavioral meaning.

Price

Price is usually thought of in terms of dollars and cents. However, there is a behavioral side of pricing that results in its having a variety of meanings to consumers. Several examples of the behavioral meaning of price are discussed below.

ODD-ENDING PRICES

For many years retailers have set prices that end in "odd" amounts—$.98 or $1995—rather than even figures such as $1.00, $5.00, or $500. These odd prices were introduced years ago, probably to force salespeople to make change for most purchases, thereby making it difficult to pocket the proceeds of a sale. This rationale has little application today, since the existence of sales tax and sophisticated controls reduce the likelihood of theft.

More recently, attempts have been made to attribute a psychological significance to odd prices. The argument is that consumers subconsciously feel that $1.99 is a reduction from $2.00 or that $1995 is significantly less than $2,000. To put it another way, even though the difference between the odd and even prices is small, it is thought by some retailers to be psychologically appealing. However, research has indicated that odd prices have little effect upon sales and therefore may be an unnecessary tradition.[15]

A decision on whether to use odd-ending prices should be based on the desired store image. These prices are more advisable for retail firms aiming for a low-price image, while even-ending prices are consistent with a high-quality image. But if a price-setter has no reason to believe that an odd-ending price will have a positive effect on sales, then a slightly lower odd ending should not be picked over an even ending. This is especially true for outlets where profit as a percent of sales is narrow, the best example being the supermarket. When a 29¢ price is selected over a 30¢ one just because odd-ending prices are traditional, the difference may not seem like much, but over the course of a year, pennies or nickels lost through odd endings (or saved through even endings) can have a tremendous impact on what is most important—*profit*.

QUALITY-RELATED PRICES

One common but often illogical consumer use of price is as an indicator of quality. When faced with choosing from among alternative products that appear to be quite similar except for price, consumers frequently select the more expensive product, assuming that it must be better because it costs more.

Price is used to judge quality when the consumer has limited knowledge about a product because of its complexity and/or lack of previous experience with it, and when the prices of alternative products are far enough apart to indicate that differences probably exist. Studies indicate that the price-quality association is made by men and women and that it is not related to age or education.[16]

For the retailer, carrying a line of products at various prices is an effective application of the price-quality relationship. Consumers, in considering the full line, will be more inclined to "trade-up" and buy a more expensive item when there is a selection of price ranges.

The tactic of pricing a product at a relatively high level to enhance its quality image should be considered when an offering sells poorly at a legitimately low price or one which is below the normal price. Possibly the low price suggests inadequate quality, and a higher price may make it more salable. Higher pricing should also be considered when the offering is a luxury product or service. For certain offerings—jewelry, country club services, perfume, liquor, and perhaps restaurants—some people feel that quality increases with price. In both of these situations, because price suggests quality *and* quality is an important purchase criterion, a higher price may produce greater sales than would a low one.

For some products, consumers have established price expectations.[17] A package of chewing gum was 5 sticks for 5¢ for over 70 years, and a change (7 to 8 sticks for 10¢) required heavy promotion by manufacturers. For other products the "traditional price" is actually a range. "Good" men's suits may be visualized in a range from $90 to $125, and prices outside this range might be viewed as sub-par (below) or fancy (above).

CUSTOMARY PRICES

The quality of a product is sometimes based more on the prices and quality of surrounding products than on the product being considered for purchase. For example, an entire grocery store may be evaluated on the quality of the meat or produce departments. Economically priced, high quality meat may be so important to the housewife that she does all her grocery shopping in a store that offers it and ignores higher prices or poorer selection of other items. The same "aura" can be achieved in many types of stores by using prestigious brands, frequent sales, or low-priced lead items.

PRICE-AURA EFFECT

A supermarket advertises lettuce at 49¢ a head or two heads for 95¢ and Campbell's Soup at 34¢, three for 99¢; a clothing store prices men's shirts at $5.95 apiece or three for $17.50. Giving a special price when two or more units of the same offering are purchased together is called *multiple-unit pricing*. The special price ordinarily reflects what amounts to a quantity discount.

    This tactic is intended to create the impression of low prices and to encourage shoppers to purchase in larger quantities. However, multiple-unit prices can backfire; some customers may be angered because they feel the special price "forces" them to buy more of an offering than they desire at that time. Thus, two guidelines on multiple-unit pricing can be suggested: They should be restricted to items which consumers can logically buy in larger quantities, and reasonable size groups should be used, considering the item involved. For example, a group of 10 probably would be reasonable for candy bars but not for shirts.

MULTIPLE-UNIT PRICING

    The reason for concern about odd-ending prices, price-quality relations, customary prices, price-aura effects, and multiple-unit pricing is that con-

During the Purchase

sumers see much more in price than the dollars and cents. Thus, it is important to the retailer in setting and evaluating price to look beyond the standard factors of competition and cost and consider the psychological side as well.

REVIEW BOX 3:4

1. A price of $23.95 is called _____.
2. Consumers often judge _____ from price.

Loyalty

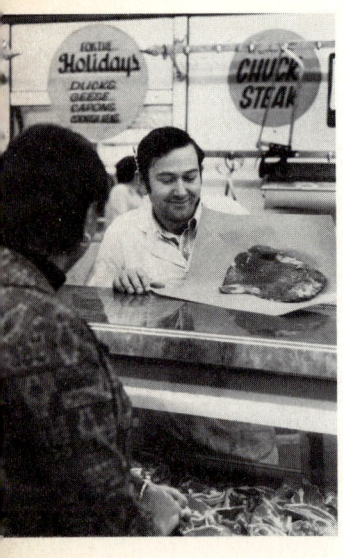

Every retailer would like to develop a highly loyal group of customers who prefer to buy from him rather than from his competitors. Using factors such as convenient location, price, quality and assortment of merchandise, and decor, the retailer tries to build an image that is consistent with the criteria (called *customer patronage motives*) used by his target market to select a store. Thus, retail image and customer patronage motives are two ways of viewing the same things.

Patronage motives can be subdivided according to the degree of positive feelings the consumer has toward an outlet. The consumer who buys from a service station only because he passes it on the way home from work is displaying no loyalty. This is called simple *patronage*. A second level, called *preference*, is exemplified by the consumer who notices he needs gas but decides to try to wait until he can visit his regular station. Unlike the first example, he prefers a particular outlet. Though the consumer with a preference for a particular outlet will usually buy there, the appearance of an important patronage motive, lower prices or greater convenience, for example, will cause him to stop elsewhere.

The highest level of patronage motives is *loyalty*. The loyal consumer will make a concerted effort to buy from a favorite outlet. In the case of the gasoline purchase, the loyal consumer will go out of his way to trade at "his" station and will make virtually all his gasoline purchases there.

Certainly this highest degree of positive feeling is what all retailers desire, but, in reality, preference is about all that most retailers can hope to achieve. Loyalty is difficult to produce for two reasons. First, the proliferation of outlets in most lines of trade with the resulting competitive pressure on prices, assortments, and services offer the consumer many nearly identical alternatives. Second, the mobility of today's consumers makes it possible for them to shop in a wide variety of stores. This was

Ch. 3 *Analyzing Consumer Behavior*

supported in a shopping study[18] which revealed that 9 out of every 10 supermarket shoppers studied visited an average of 2.8 stores for their purchases. In addition, it was found that 4 out of 5 read advertisements for 2 or more different food stores, and more than half compared prices between stores.

The implication here is not that attempts to create loyalty should be avoided. On the contrary, the retailer should assess his business and his customers to determine what degree of patronage is possible and then work hard to create an image that effectively differentiates his store from those of competitors.

AFTER THE PURCHASE

An important part of every sale takes place *after* the actual transaction has been completed. The amount of satisfaction the consumer realizes from the purchase and consumption of the offering will determine whether the purchase will be a one-time experience or whether the person will become a regular customer. Satisfaction can be divided into two types: receiving the expected benefits from consuming the product, and feeling that the decision to purchase was a correct one.

Expected Benefits

A consumer buying a product has certain expectations about what benefits the product should provide. Based upon the price, reputation of the manufacturer and the retailer, and several other factors, minimum performance expectations are established. Expectations may differ among people and for various products. For example, all automobiles are expected to provide transportation, but not all are expected to offer economical operation, ownership status, or riding comfort.

Two areas of retailing in which false expectations are frequently stimulated are personal selling and advertising. Advertising plays a major role in creating expectations by describing product features and making performance claims. In fact, advertising can do too good a job, as in the case of a classic product failure, the Edsel. Because of Ford's early publicity and extreme secrecy in regard to the car, "The public was getting to be hysterical to see our [Edsel] car, figuring it was going to be some kind of dream car—like nothing they'd ever seen."[19] As a result, thousands of consumers visited showrooms when the car was introduced, but most were disappointed and did not become buyers.

In the case of personal selling, the enthusiastic salesman may deliberately or unintentionally exaggerate product qualities or features. Although these practices may produce a single sale, it is unlikely that they will con-

"Could you tell us something about performance, design, engineering workmanship, safety, and service?"

Drawing by Koren
© 1973 The New Yorker Magazine, Inc.

tribute to the mainstay of a business—regular, repeat customers. From the retailer's point of view, it is important to create enough desire and interest to stimulate sales but to avoid producing expectations that will lead to disappointments.

Post-Purchase Doubt

It is quite common for a consumer to doubt the wisdom of his choice shortly after making a purchase decision, particularly if the item purchased is expensive. Even though the chosen alternative appeared to be the best at the time of the decision, the items that were not selected often increase in attractiveness later. This situation is based on a concept called cognitive dissonance.[20]

Two things can result from the arousal of post-purchase doubt. If the consumer has bought a product that is capable of meeting his expectations, he may either find reasons for increasing his doubts (possibly by establishing new or revised expectations) and eventually become dissatisfied with the product, or overcome his doubts and be satisfied with the product.

The retailer need not sit passively by while this process occurs. Two studies, one dealing with the purchase of automobiles[21] and the other with major appliances,[22] have shown that the retailer can work actively to reduce post-purchase doubt. Between the time a car is purchased and the consumer takes delivery, weeks or even months may go by. When salesmen telephoned buyers during the period between purchase and delivery and provided favorable information about the choice, the researchers in the study mentioned above were able to show that significantly fewer buyers changed their minds and backed out of the purchase.

In the appliance study the researcher arranged to have refrigerator purchasers contacted by the store following a sale. He found that consumers who received letters praising their decisions had more favorable attitudes toward the store and had stronger intentions of making future purchases there than consumers who received no contact.

Both of these studies indicate the value of following a sale with supportive information (positive reinforcement) to help the consumer overcome doubt. Although this is a simple procedure with proven results, surprisingly few retailers make use of it.

REVIEW BOX 3:5

1. Satisfaction in a purchase results from feeling the choice made was correct and _____.
2. A proven post-purchase doubt reducing device is _____.

CHAPTER SUMMARY

- Products and services offer more than functional benefits. They provide satisfaction for a number of behavioral needs.
- Human needs can be divided into five categories or levels—physiological, safety, social, esteem, and self-actualization. The role a need plays in purchasing depends upon its importance and upon the level of deprivation.
- The needs an offering may satisfy can be identified by considering the functional efficiency of the offering, how it is consumed, and the advertising theme employed by the manufacturer.
- Strength of needs is reflected in whether or not the purchase is postponable, the amount of shopping the consumer undertakes, and the dollar amount of the purchase.
- Self-concept includes self-image, ideal self, and looking-glass self.
- Consumers buy products and services and shop in stores with images similar to their self-images or ideal self.
- A social-class system roughly divided into six classes exists in the United States. The social classes have very different approaches to life, and therefore their shopping behavior differs significantly.
- Life cycle concept describes the various stages of life people commonly pass through. Purchasing behavior differs in different stages of the life cycle.
- Five behavioral interpretations of price were discussed. These include odd-ending pricing, quality-related pricing, customary prices, price-aura effect, and multiple-unit pricing.
- The reasons consumers choose to shop in a particular store are called customer patronage motives. Store choice can be subdivided into patronage, preference, and loyalty.
- Satisfaction following a purchase can be subdivided into feeling that the decision to purchase was a correct one, and receiving the expected benefits from consuming the product.
- The retailer can help the consumer achieve satisfaction from an offering through personal contact and careful consideration of the level of expectation created.

CHAPTER NOTES

[1] For a complete treatment of the subject of consumer behavior see: James F. Engel, David T. Kollat, and Roger D. Blackwell, *Consumer Behavior*, 2nd ed. (New York: Holt, Rinehart and Winston, 1973) or James A. McNeal, *An Introduction to Consumer Behavior* (New York: Wiley, 1973).

[2] Abraham H. Maslow, *Motivation and Personality* (New York: Harper and Row, 1954).
[3] George A. Field, John Douglas, and Lawrence X. Tarpey, *Marketing Management: A Behavioral Systems Approach* (Columbus, Ohio: Merrill, 1966), p. 105.
[4] Al E. Birdwell, "A Study of the Influence of Image Congruence on Consumer Choice," *Journal of Business*, January, 1968, pp. 76–88.
[5] Ira J. Dolich, "Congruence Relationships between Self-Image and Product Brands," *Journal of Marketing Research*, February, 1970, pp. 11–13.
[6] Terance A. Shimp, James H. Donnelly, and John M. Ivancevich, "Study of Consumer Political Orientations and Store Patronage," *Journal of Applied Psychology*, October, 1970, pp. 470–72.
[7] Ellen Hume, "Montgomery Ward's, Now on Expansion Path, Fights 'Stodgy' Image," *Lexington Leader*, May 10, 1974, p. 15.
[8] W. Lloyd Warner, Marchia Meeker, and Kenneth Eels, *Social Class in America* (Chicago: Science Research Associates, 1949).
[9] Pierre Martineau, "Social Class and Spending Behavior," *Journal of Marketing*, October, 1958, pp. 121–30.
[10] Based on a review article by Kim B. Rotzoll, "The Effect of Social Stratification on Market Behavior," *Journal of Advertising Research*, March, 1967, pp. 22–27.
[11] "Broadway-Hale's Elegant Growth Plan," *Business Week*, April 15, 1972, p. 90–98.
[12] Ibid., p. 95.
[13] The four adult stages are discussed in Harold D. Meyer, "The Adult Cycle," *The Annals of the American Academy of Political and Social Science*, Vol. 313, September, 1957, pp. 58–67.
[14] The teenage stage is based on a discussion in James H. Meyers and William H. Reynolds, *Consumer Behavior and Marketing Management* (Boston: Houghton Mifflin Co., 1967), pp. 250–56.
[15] Andre Gabor and C. W. J. Granger, "Price Sensitivity and the Consumer," *Journal of Advertising Research*, December, 1964, pp. 40–44.
[16] Donald S. Tull, R. A. Boring, and M. H. Gonsier, "A Note on the Relationship of Price and Imputed Quality," *Journal of Business*, April, 1964, pp. 186–91.
[17] Customary prices and "price aura" are described in Chester R. Wasson, *Product Management* (St. Charles, Ill.: Challenge Books, 1971), pp. 88–96.
[18] "Is Loyalty Dead?" *Progressive Grocer*, February, 1972, p. 30.
[19] John Brooks, "Annals of Business, The Edsel," *The New Yorker*, November 26, 1960, p. 90.
[20] Leon Festinger, *A Theory of Cognitive Dissonance* (Evanston, Ill.: Row, Peterson, 1957).
[21] James H. Donnelly, Jr. and John M. Ivancevich, "Post-Purchase Reinforcement and Back-Out Behavior," *Journal of Marketing Research*, August, 1970, pp. 399–400.
[22] Shelby D. Hunt, "Post-Transaction Communications and Dissonance Reduction," *Journal of Marketing*, July, 1970, pp. 46–51.

QUESTIONS AND ASSIGNMENTS

1. Give examples of several products in which the *functional* benefits of ownership are fewer than the *behavioral* benefits.
2. Into what general categories would you place the following needs:
   a. hunger pangs just before lunch time
   b. a dry throat after a tennis match
3. If the basic needs in the question above were satisfied with a. pizza, and b. beer, what needs might the individual be attempting to satisfy?
4. Give an example of:
   a. important need and great deprivation
   b. important need and little deprivation
   For which of these is the individual more likely to seek satisfaction?
5. Describe how the needs which motivate a shopper may be *identified* by the retailer.

6. What methods might a retailer use to determine the *strength* of a customer's need?
7. Define the three components of self-concept.
8. Describe a store in which you would feel uncomfortable because the image it creates is different from your self-concept.
9. Describe as many characteristics as you can of the largest social class in the United States.
10. What indicators can the retailer use to determine an individual's social class?
11. How would a retailer of color TV sets change his sales approach from talking to a couple in the young adulthood stage to a couple in the middle years stage of the life cycle?
12. Describe a purchase you have made in which you inferred *quality* from *price*.
13. Using the definition in the chapter, are you *loyal* to any retailer? If you are, explain why.
14. Write a brief letter designed to reduce the dissonance of a consumer who recently purchased a dishwasher from the store you manage.

ANSWERS TO REVIEW BOX QUESTIONS

Box 3:1

1. motivator
2. strength
3. strong

Box 3:2

1. upper-lower
2. television and word of mouth

Box 3:3

1. age
2. predictable effect, observable

Box 3:4

1. odd-ending price
2. quality

Box 3:5

1. receiving the expected benefits from consuming the product
2. contacting the consumer after the purchase

4 *Store Location*

Basic to the success or failure of any retail firm are decisions about location and appearance. An outlet can have quality offerings, excellent personnel, and competitive prices but fail because it is not conveniently located or because its appearance creates an unfavorable impression in the minds of potential customers. Unfortunately, these factors are frequently overlooked, particularly by the small merchant hurrying to "open the doors and make the first sale." Finding an empty building with a reasonable rent may be the extent of his location analysis. However, it is indicative of the importance of these factors that large department stores and supermarket chains frequently invest a year or more and many thousands of dollars in planning the location and appearance of an outlet.[1]

Location, design, and layout are closely related factors, since design and layout decisions depend to some extent on where the business will be located. By the same token, a location should not be selected without some idea of the proposed design and layout. These three topics are discussed in this chapter, where location is considered, and the next chapter, which covers design and layout.

FACTORS IN STORE LOCATION

The physical site of a retail business is called its store location. It may be leased space, a building the retailer purchases, or a new structure built to specification. In choosing a site, the retailer must consider several factors: Will he be better off in the downtown area or in a suburban shopping center?

Should his store be free standing or a part of a cluster of stores? All of these decisions will have to be based on specific objectives that the retailer has set.

Types of Locations

CENTRAL BUSINESS DISTRICT

The central business district (CBD) is the downtown area of a town or city. In this traditional location for retail establishments, we normally find large department stores and specialty outlets as well as a limited number of convenience outlets.

The economic decline of many CBDs in recent years has generated both concern and controversy among merchants, local politicians, and other citizens about the future of retailing in downtown areas. As more and more middle- and upper-income consumers move to the suburbs to avoid congestion, pollution, crime, and high taxes, many retailers follow them. One study reported that in 1958 close to 42 percent of total retail sales were made by suburban stores. In 1963 the figure had risen to 49.5 percent, and in 1967 it was 52.8 percent.[2] Now many department store chains do 60 percent or more of their total business in locations away from CBDs.

Although the CBD of many cities may appear to be an undesirable location for retailers, that may not be the case. E. B. Weiss has shown that pedestrian and auto traffic in the downtown area of most cities is increasing.[3] Thus, the problem is not a shortage of shoppers but a failure of merchants to adapt their merchandising methods to a changing audience. For example, CBDs may be good locations for discount operations. Another option is to make the CBD attractive enough to bring back the consumers who have fled. Denver's Larimer Square, Riverfront Plaza in Louisville, and Underground Atlanta are all examples of successful efforts to give new life to unproductive downtown areas. Confidence in the potential of the CBD is reflected in San Francisco's $75 million Broadway Plaza, a development that covers an entire city block and contains a 240,000 square-foot Broadway Store, a 32-story office building, a 500-room hotel, and a two-level shopping mall. Broadway-Hale, Inc. expects the new store to do twice the business of their old downtown store in half the space.

SHOPPING CENTER

A shopping center consists of a planned grouping of retail stores in a multi-unit structure (usually with the physical facility under single ownership) that provides a coordinated variety of outlets. There are many types of shopping centers, but they can be classified generally by the size of the center and the market they serve:

1. *Convenience center* — usually consists of three to six outlets such as

Factors in Store Location

Larimer Square, Denver, Colorado (above), and Underground Atlanta (below)

a branch bank, dry cleaner, liquor store, and service station. The major tenant and traffic generator is usually a convenience grocery store like 7-Eleven or Handy Pantry. Frequently located along a heavy traveled street.
2. *Neighborhood center*—similar to a convenience center except that the major tenant is a large supermarket. Frequently includes a drug store. Oriented toward serving a neighborhood.
3. *Community center*—a shopping center with 15 to 30 tenants usually including both a small department store and a supermarket. Often constructed around a pedestrian mall; provides considerable parking space. Draws customers from a much larger area than a neighborhood center.
4. *Regional center*—a large center that may include a hundred or more tenants. An example is Lloyd Center in Portland, Oregon with 1,200,000 square feet of floor space, pedestrian malls that are 50 feet wide, over 100 stores, a medical arts building, an outdoor skating rink, a hotel, and 9,000 parking spaces.[4]

There are other types of centers being developed that do not fit into this classification scheme. For example, a Minneapolis architectural firm is designing "mini-malls" of less than 120,000 square feet to provide the benefits of shopping centers to communities with populations under 25,000.[5] In California large centers are being developed which have no large tenants. Prune Yard in San Jose and Bird Cage in Sacramento consist of small specialty stores, restaurants, and entertainment establishments. The potential for these and other "unconventional" shopping centers will depend upon their ability to meet the changing needs of consumers.

To the retailer the shopping center offers the advantage of being located close to the consumer while providing a maximum of shopping convenience and comfort. In addition, each retailer benefits from the traffic drawn by other outlets in the center. It is unusual for a consumer to go to a shopping center and visit only one store. On the negative side, shopping centers usually charge high rents and require extended leases. Also, tenants are frequently required to contribute to a common maintenance fund.[6]

STRINGS

A group of retail outlets that have developed in an unplanned fashion along a major thoroughfare are referred to as a string location. Retailers select these locations because of their exposure to heavy auto traffic. However, because they tend to be spread out, each outlet must be able to attract its own customers. Car dealerships, auto service establishments, and fast food restaurants can be successful in string locations. On the other hand, merchants who depend upon impulse purchases and "drop-in" traffic will be likely to find such locations unsatisfactory.

CLUSTERS

Within high-density living areas such as apartment complexes, clusters of small retail specialty stores are often found. These unplanned developments depend heavily on foot traffic and must be tailored to the needs of the consumers in the immediate area. The inconvenience of driving and parking and the desire for greater service have resulted in clusters that include delicatessens, gift shops, florists, and fancy restaurants.

FREE-STANDING LOCATIONS

A single retail store, most often found along a major highway or street, is a free-standing location. Large discount chains like Korvette and K-Mart rely on this type of location. According to Harry Cunningham, chairman and chief executive officer of Kresge, "If our [K-Mart] merchandise assortment is right, we are in a position to take care of the general needs of the typical American family. So we don't need another group of stores besides us to dilute the traffic flow into our store."[7] To prosper, an outlet using a free-standing location must have easy access, adequate parking, and sufficient individual attraction to draw customers.

Location Objectives

The choice of a location for a retail outlet should be directed by predetermined objectives. Certainly an important objective is to avoid having to relocate. The retailer wants a location that will be appropriate as the community grows and the area changes. Other location objectives may be:

1. To provide for the potential of adequate sales and, therefore, profit
2. To offset gains made by a competitor's choice of location
3. To minimize the cost of preparing an outlet for operation
4. To respond to specific market or community needs (for example, locating in the ghetto, participating in urban renewal).

These objectives call for farsighted evaluation that combines facts with good judgment. Ideally the result will be sound decisions like those made by Sears, Roebuck and Co. following World War II.[8] At that time Sears chose to relocate and expand into suburban areas when large sites were readily available and inexpensive. This location decision, which has paid off handsomely, has been offered as a key reason for Sears' ability to outperform Montgomery Ward in the postwar period.

Although location objectives are sometimes easy to state, their fulfillment is frequently difficult. The following sections describe the process of selecting a location, considering both the choice of a general area and a specific site. Thus they should provide a model for accomplishing location objectives.

> **REVIEW BOX 4:1**
>
> 1. The four types of shopping centers described are convenience, neighborhood, community, and _____.
> 2. A retailer selecting a free-standing location over a shopping center location must have _____.

LOCATION ANALYSIS

Selecting a location begins with the choice of a community or area (general location within a chosen city) and may be a two-step process. A large chain store considering expansion would begin by investigating several cities and upon selecting one would consider alternative areas within that city. A small retailer may be limited to a community by family, financing, or other constraints and engage in only the second step. Selection of an area is followed by the analysis and evaluation of specific sites.

General Area Analysis

ECONOMIC CONDITIONS

The amount of income (or purchasing power) of consumers, the distribution of income among households, the sources of income in the area, and the cost of living are important economic factors that influence location choices.

The amount of income combined with cost of living figures will indicate whether an area is reasonably wealthy, poor, or something in between. By determining the distribution of income among the population, the retailer may discover that the area is made up of all middle-income families, or it may have a few very high-income and many low-income families.

Finally, the number and strength of the sources of income are an indication of economic stability. If there are several large employers in the area or community, it is less susceptible to economic collapse should one firm move, close down, or be hit by a strike.

POPULATION

Since most firms design their offerings for specific market segments, determining the patterns of age, income, education, and marital status of an area's population is important. Present statistics as well as their changes over the previous few years will indicate two critical factors:

1. The existence of market segments compatible with the firm's product or service.

2. The growth (or decline) rate of the area. Is it attracting young professionals, or is its youth leaving for better opportunities elsewhere?

Some behavioral aspects of the population are also useful in the location decision. For example, information on shopping habits (where, when, and in what quantities consumers buy) and expenditure patterns (how much they spend on various items) is highly useful. These factors indicate preferences, tastes, and attitudes of the population which should be used, for example, in deciding the amount of convenience and accessibility a location must have.

POTENTIAL COMPETITION Established firms that would be competitors should be pinpointed on an area map to determine how well they cover the market. In addition to their locations, the size, strength, and specific market appeal of these firms should be evaluated. Size can be determined by a visit to the competing outlets. Strength and market appeal can be roughly estimated by evaluating the frequency and content of local advertising, or by counting and observing the shoppers who visit these stores at various times of the day for several days.

GROWTH As mentioned earlier, a retailer is seeking long-term stability and profits; this is why location decisions must take into account the future of an area. Statistics on population change, industrial growth, and the total volume of wholesale and retail sales are good indicators of growth or decline. Also, the aggressiveness of local civic organizations and elected officials can play a significant role in growth.

Specific Site Analysis

The investigation of specific sites within an area differs from general area analysis in that it includes more factors and is slightly more detailed.

TRADING AREA The area from which the bulk of an outlet's customers come is called the *trading area*. For example, about 70 to 80 percent of the customers for a fast food outlet come from within a two-mile radius. On the other hand, a major department store may attract a significant proportion of its customers from many miles away.

A trading area is usually not circular. A freeway or river, for example, may act as a boundary to the area, discouraging people who live on the opposite side of the barrier from visiting the location.

Figure 4-1 illustrates how the trading area for a proposed supermarket

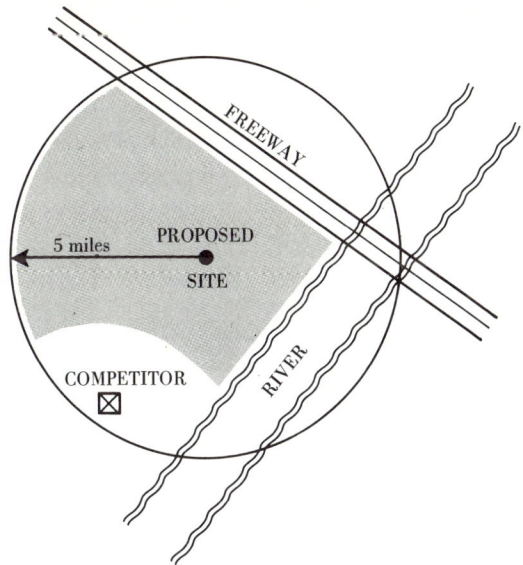

FIGURE 4-1

Identifying the trading area for a supermarket

can be estimated and sketched. First, based on industry figures and on an estimated maximum of 15 minutes driving time, the store will probably not attract a significant number of customers from beyond five miles. To reflect this, a circle with the proposed location as the center and with a radius of five miles is plotted. This circle is the *potential trading area* for the site. Then, the two major disruptive factors—physical barriers and competitors—are located. The potential trading area includes one competitor and portions of a freeway and a river. It is unlikely that the store will attract a significant number of customers from beyond the river or freeway because of the inconvenience of crossing these obstacles. Likewise, unless the store offers some significant advantage, it will not draw many customers from the proximity of the competing outlet. Thus, the *practical trading area* is the shaded portion of the diagram.

The next step is to investigate the people residing in the practical trading area. One alternative is to drive through the area identifying the type and estimated value of homes; determining the number and types of apartments, institutions, and office buildings; and gauging the apparent age distribution of the residents. A more sophisticated alternative involves personal interviews with a sample of the area's residents. In either case, the objective is to determine whether there are enough people living in the area who are among the firm's target customers.[9]

Location Analysis

PEDESTRIAN AND AUTO TRAFFIC

An important feature of any location is the volume, nature, and flow of traffic past the site. The greater the number of passers-by the better, since a convenient location ordinarily is very important to consumers. However, the nature and flow of the traffic can be as important as the volume. The *nature* of the traffic refers to its ultimate destination. For example, a site where automobile traffic consists primarily of people going to and from work would be acceptable for a gasoline station but undesirable for a laundromat. The

---

SPOTLIGHT

Could it be true that some people would rather not have Ronald McDonald in their neighborhood?

The following adaptation of a *Wall Street Journal* article points out how important evaluating surroundings can be.

On the corner of Lexington Avenue and 66th Street on the Upper East Side of New York, McDonald's, the hamburger king, bought a lot and has tried to build a restaurant. The neighborhood contains elegant townhouses, specialty shops with such names as Canine Styles, Livingston Galleries, Raphel of London, Albert's Prime Meats, and Di Pierre Corsetry, and three buildings on the corners of Lexington and 66th that have been designated New York City landmarks.

Though the McDonald's outlet would probably draw the bulk of its business from nearby Hunter College, area residents have objected strenuously to its location at the site. The arguments generally used by McDonald's to justify locating in other areas have all been rebuffed by East Side residents. To the argument that the restaurant would be architecturally compatible with the area, an architect who lives nearby responded, "... we aren't fooled. We are a little more sophisticated than that." When McDonald's claimed they provide good food, the area's city councilman commented that he was concerned about the "cancerous spread of low-quality fast-food operations into high quality neighborhoods." Finally, McDonald's called attention to the fact that they have always demonstrated community spirit and offered as proof the large number of Little League teams fed and uniformed by McDonald franchises. In an area where six-figure annual incomes are common and Little League is virtually unknown, this argument has gone practically unheard.

As an ultimate act of protest, the concerned citizens in the area formed the East Side Coalition Against McDonald's and collected over 11,000 signatures opposing the outlet. The petition containing the signatures was tied with a pink ribbon and presented to Mayor Abraham Beame.

Source: Barry Newman, "To Some New Yorkers Ronald McDonald Is an Arch Villain"; reprinted with the permission of *The Wall Street Journal*, © Dow Jones & Company, Inc. 1974.

flow of traffic refers to the speed limit (the lower the better), the congestion, presence of a stop light or sign near the site, the difficulty of making a left turn into the location, and the existence of a curve or a hill that restricts visibility near the site.

A large volume of pedestrian traffic is particularly important to outlets that depend upon impulse purchases or deal exclusively in convenience goods. Examples of such stores are florists, cigar stores, and candy stores. This explains their frequent location near large, traffic-drawing stores and in shopping centers where there is more pedestrian traffic than in isolated locations.

COMPLEMENTARY AND INDIRECTLY COMPETING OUTLETS

The presence of complementary and indirectly competitive outlets in the vicinity *can be* important location advantages. A complementary outlet is one which, because of its location, provides added customer convenience. For example, a drug store located adjacent to a supermarket will benefit from the traffic generated by the supermarket.

Indirect competitors, firms in the same general line of business but with some important product or marketing difference, can also benefit each other. It is not unusual to find a store selling a full line of shoes located near a store specializing in women's shoes or a high-priced furniture outlet near a medium-priced furniture outlet. Such locations provide two advantages for stores selling shopping goods. First, the consumer can conveniently compare merchandise and prices. Second, and more important, such locations tend to have a greater total drawing power than single outlets.

VULNERABILITY

Vulnerability refers to the existence or potential existence of direct competitors drawing from a common area. To determine whether an area has enough of a particular type of store, the retailer can check the existing outlets for sales volume. Extraordinary demand, often reflected by overcrowded stores or poorly stocked shelves, indicates the need for more outlets. Consumers can also be questioned about their satisfaction with current outlets.

A very important vulnerability consideration is the presence of other *potential* locations in the area. An outlet can be isolated if a competitor is able to open a store between the outlet and its chief source of customers. If possible, a location should be in the center of the practical trading area.

PARKING

In today's highly mobile, automobile-oriented society, a successful location must include parking facilities. However, since parking areas normally are non-revenue producing and costly, they should not be too large. A practical method of estimating how much parking to provide is to follow the lead of established, similar outlets. First, parking areas and selling space for a number of firms can be compared to determine whether some common ratio

Location Analysis

exists. Second, parking lots of similar stores can be checked during peak business hours to see if adequate space is provided.

SURROUNDINGS The area surrounding a potential site should be investigated for compatibility. The appearance of nearby buildings, types of businesses in the area (a liquor store and toy store would not make good neighbors), vacant lots and buildings, noise, dirt, heavy truck traffic, and industrial developments are examples of things to look out for. The area should be checked for these things at various times of the day and different days of the week. A neighboring motorcycle center, quiet during the week, may sponsor rallies on Saturdays that bring crowds, noise and general confusion to the area.

AREA CHANGES If the trading area has undergone any recent basic changes, these could be indicators of future developments that would alter the nature of the area completely. For example, a zoning change to accommodate low-income housing or industrial development, a moratorium on building permits, or changes in streets from two-way to one-way may all be symptoms of more significant future changes. Such developments should be investigated to determine their root cause and likely eventual result.

COST The cost of a site has been saved for last because for many retailers it is the only consideration, even though a location decision should involve considerably more than the cost of alternative sites.

A potential ideal site may be vacant simply because the owner is asking an exorbitant price. Estimates of sales and expenses including the cost of the site should be made. These can be compared to standard operating ratios, some examples of which are shown in Table 4-1. As a general rule of thumb,

TABLE 4-1

Rent as a Percent of Total Sales for Selected Types of Retailers[a]

Type of store	Rent/sales	Type of store	Rent/sales
Women's apparel	4.8	Florists	2.6
Men's apparel	4.7	Gift and novelty shops	5.6
Children's & infants' apparel	4.7	Hardware	2.4
Bookstores	4.1	Liquor	2.1
Cocktail lounges	3.2	Restaurant	3.5

[a] Figures are averages and are based on outlets of various sizes.
Source: Accounting Corporation of America, *Barometer of Small Business*, 1973, San Diego, California.

for most types of retail businesses rent should not exceed 5 percent of total expected sales.

Eight check points for evaluating a specific site have been described. In applying such a list to a site analysis, it would be unusual to give each factor equal weight. For example, trading area, parking, and vulnerability may be most important in supermarket site selection, while surroundings, traffic, and cost may be most critical to a beauty salon. Thus the nature of the proposed business must be considered in weighting the site evaluation factors.

> **REVIEW BOX 4:2**
>
> 1. Trading area, traffic, complementary and indirectly competing outlets, and vulnerability are four of the check points in specific site analysis. Two of the other four are _____ and _____.
>
> 2. The presence of indirect competitors can improve the value of a site by _____ and _____.

Data Sources for Area and Specific Site Analyses

Collecting data to conduct the area and specific site analyses outlined above requires some time and effort but it is not an impossible job. Table 4-2 describes a variety of information sources that can prove helpful. However, because available sources may not break down data finely enough for an analysis of specific sites, considerable "leg work" is often called for. Visiting the neighborhood, shopping in the stores, and talking to people, if directed toward specific objectives such as the eight factors described above, can offer useful insights. A retailer does not have to be as big as Federated Department Stores or A & P to conduct location analysis. In fact, it is probably more critical for the small business than for the giant retailer with substantial drawing power arising from an established image and heavy advertising.

It is possible to put a computer to work in analyzing sites if the hardware and appropriate data are available. In the past this luxury has largely been limited to the giants of retailing who had access to computers. However, developments in time sharing have made such analysis available to smaller retailers in at least one city.

COMPUTERIZED SITE ANALYSIS

The Detroit *News* offers current and potential advertisers free pilot retail site analysis.[10] The pilot analysis will estimate for the current year and five years in the future the number of households, total gross consumer income, and total durables market within a five-mile radius of the proposed site.

TABLE 4-2

Data Sources for General Area and Specific Site Analyses

1. Obtain several good street maps of the market area.
2. Visit local Planning Department, Chamber of Commerce, redevelopment agencies, highway departments (state, county, and city), and other agencies which provide data beneficial to an evaluation of a market. The following kinds of information should be gathered:
   a. Past population changes and those forecast for the future (often contained in planning reports and transportation studies).
   b. Direction and location of residential construction activity (building-permit data and apartment directories).
   c. Location of all major shopping centers, discount department stores, and shopping districts (existing and proposed).
   d. Location of existing industrial development and areas currently being so developed.
   e. Concentrations of office-space activity and probable areas of the future.
   f. Location of institutions, such as hospitals, high schools, and colleges.
   g. Location of major commercial streets.
   h. Existing and proposed major street and highway improvements.
   i. Traffic counts.
   j. Zoning map.
   k. Telephone directory.
   l. U.S. Department of Commerce data, Population Census, and Census of Business.

   Some of these data may be gathered by mail or phone prior to initiating this phase. State licensing agencies should be checked to ascertain the kind of information available concerning vehicle registration, sales, etc.

3. Drive around the market area and view aerial photos or any other useful device to get the "feel" for the market and its patterns of development.

Source: Robert F. Zaloudek, "Practical Location Analysis in New Market Areas," *Stores*, November, 1971, p. 15.

The data for the analysis has been gathered from a variety of sources, both state and national, and programmed by the Detroit *News* staff.

This system is designed for general use. It could not constitute a complete site analysis for a retailer. For example, not all retailers have a potential trading area with a five-mile radius. In addition, several of the factors discussed in this chapter such as competition, vulnerability, and cost of the site are not included. However, the service does provide the retailer with an initial evaluation of a site that will help in determining if further consideration is warranted. According to the research manager, the same amount of information provided by a retail consultant would cost more than $1,000. The Detroit *News* promotion and research director sums up why the service is provided by the newspaper. "We're in this business to help advertisers become successful. Our success is tied to theirs."[11]

Most major newspapers also make available a wealth of market data for their circulation areas. For example, the *Courier Journal-Louisville Times* collects extensive information on shopping centers, large department stores and discount houses, banks, supermarkets, hotels and motels, residents of the Louisville and Southern Indiana areas, and newspaper, radio, and TV audiences. This information and much more, is available free on request and can be very useful in site analysis.

CHAPTER SUMMARY

- Store location, design, and layout are interrelated decisions that have a major influence on a store's success.
- There are a variety of possible locations and types of building including the urban core, shopping center, cluster, string, and free standing. Each has its advantages and disadvantages for specific types of retailers.
- Location analysis should begin with a general area analysis including economic conditions, population, potential competition, and growth.
- Specific site selection involves the study of a trading area, traffic, complementary and competing outlets, vulnerability, parking surroundings, area changes, and cost.
- Data for location analyses can come from a wide variety of sources including government and service agencies.
- A good source of data in many cities is the local newspaper.
- Computers are now being used in preliminary location analysis.

CHAPTER NOTES

[1] Another measure of the significance of location, design, and layout is the presence of an article in nearly every issue of magazines such as *Stores*, *Progressive Grocer*, and *Chain Store Age* on one or more of these subjects.

[2] *The Suburbanization of Retail Trade: A Study of Retail Trade Dispersion in Major U.S. Markets: 1958–1967*, prepared by Spindletop Research Inc. for Columbia Broadcasting System, 1970, p. 19.

[3] E. B. Weiss, "New Store Locations in the Core City," *Stores*, May, 1972, pp. 43–44.

[4] Tom Mahoney and Leonard Sloane, *The Great Merchants* (New York: Harper and Row, 1966), p. 17.

[5] "Business Bulletin," *Wall Street Journal*, January 6, 1972, p. 1.

[6] For an interesting description of shopping center growth and development, see "Shopping Centers Grow into Shopping Cities," *Business Week*, September 4, 1972, pp. 34–38.

[7] "How Kresge Became the Top Discounter," *Business Week*, October 24, 1970, p. 62.

[8] John McDonald, "Sears Makes It Look Easy," *Fortune*, May, 1964, pp. 120–27 ff.

[9] There is no sure method of determining how many potential consumers will be "enough." Some firms, based on experience, have established rules of thumb (e.g., Cole Drug of Knoxville, Tennessee will consider a town with a population of 25,000 to 30,000 provided it is

growing). Other firms use per capita expenditure figures made available by trade publications and trade associations.

[10] Gordon Morris, "Detroit *News*' Computer Tells Retailers Where to Locate," *Editor and Publisher*, January 9, 1971, pp. 48–49.

[11] *Ibid.*, p. 49.

QUESTIONS AND ASSIGNMENTS

1. Develop a list of the advantages and disadvantages of the CBD and shopping center as location sites. Compare a furniture store, a men's shoe store, and a pet shop with each list to determine the best type of location for each.
2. Choose a retail outlet near you and discuss the good and bad points concerning its location.
3. Where would be a good site for a major department store in your city? Why?
4. How would you go about evaluating the automobile traffic going past a particular site?
5. What is the difference between general area analysis and specific site analysis?
6. Distinguish between a potential trading area and a practical trading area. What factors might limit a practical trading area?
7. Using the eight factors discussed in specific site analysis, decide the order of their importance for a liquor store and a motel.
8. What things would you look for on a walking tour of a neighborhood in which you are considering locating a convenience grocery store?

ANSWERS TO REVIEW BOX QUESTIONS

Box 4:1

1. regional
2. independent drawing power

Box 4:2

1. two of the following: parking, surroundings, area changes, and cost.
2. compare merchandise and increase drawing power

Store Layout and Design

After selecting a location, the retailer must decide how the merchandise will be presented to consumers—the layout and design of the outlet. Layout involves the placement of display tables and counters, location of various types of merchandise in the outlet, allocation of space to selling and non-selling areas, and the proportion of selling area allocated to specific items. Design consists of the exterior and interior appearance of the building including the walls, ceiling, lighting, windows, fixtures, and signs.

Clearly, location, layout, and design are related decisions. The physical features of a location will influence the layout and design, and the design of a store must complement the display.

STORE LAYOUT

The layout of a store should facilitate customer movement and present the merchandise or services in the most attractive way possible. There are three basic types of layout. The first and simplest is found in establishments where the product or service is relatively standardized and the major concern is moving customers into and out of the outlet efficiently. This layout consists of a sales counter, a cash register or drawer, and usually some directional aids to facilitate the movement of customers. It is commonly found in dry cleaners and fast food outlets.

The two layouts typical of stores selling a variety of non-standardized merchandise, and which are discussed below, are the grid and the free flow.

Virtually all other layouts are variations on these two. Finally, a layout of recent significance, the boutique, is described.

Layout Alternatives

GRID

The traditional retail layout is the *grid*. As indicated in Figure 5-1, the grid appears to be designed more for retailing efficiency than for customer convenience. Display tables and cases are set at right angles, and customer flow

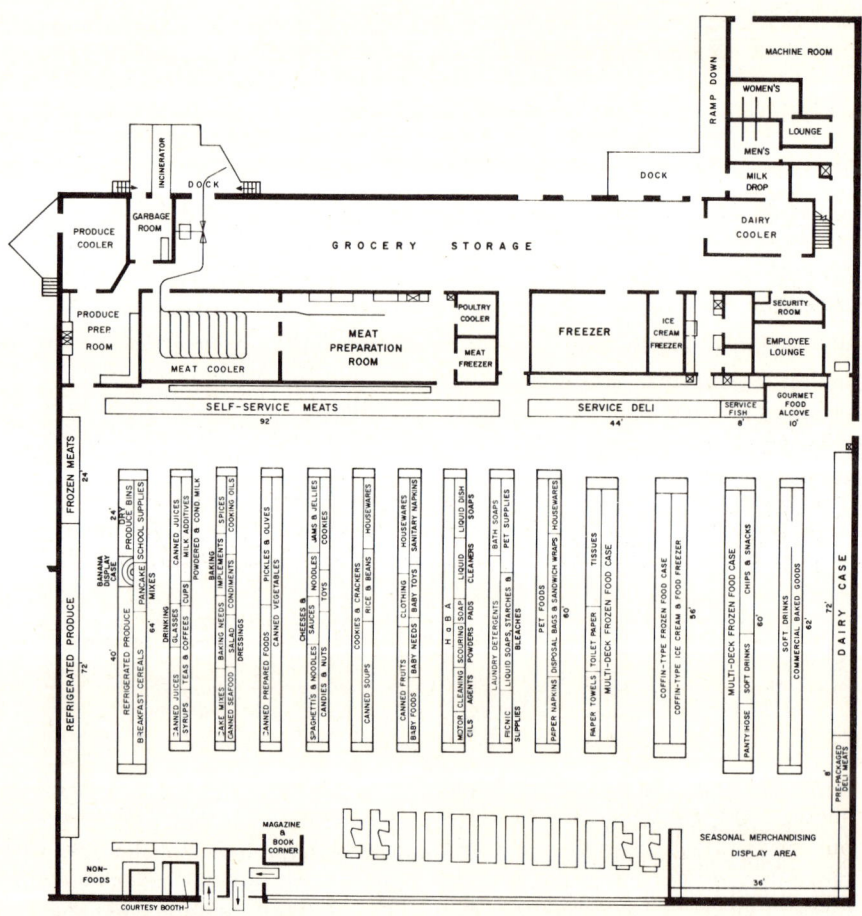

FIGURE 5-1

The grid layout

Source: "An All-Around Super for a Diverse Neighborhood," *Progressive Grocer*, February 1973, p. 120.

94   Ch. 5   *Store Layout and Design*

is more a function of physical barriers than the desire to shop for specific merchandise. This layout has three advantages: (1) it maximizes selling area by eliminating wasted space, (2) it contributes to ease of cleaning, and (3) it simplifies security. The grid design is common in older department stores and supermarkets.

The choice of the grid pattern in supermarkets is primarily a function of the need to make the best use of selling area, since a wide variety of relatively small amounts of items must be displayed. Because of its prevalence in supermarkets, this layout has been the subject of analysis that has produced some interesting results.[1] For example, customer traffic flow is concentrated along the perimeter of the stores, and short display shelves result in less store coverage by customers than would continuous shelves.

In a study by *Progressive Grocer* reported in 1960 it was found that over 80 percent of the visitors to supermarkets visit the perimeter departments, while less than 50 percent pass up and down the interior aisles.[2] This difference in store coverage can be easily explained. Supermarkets stock frequently purchased items—dairy products, meats, produce, and bakery goods—around the perimeter to maximize efficiency. These highly perishable items must be frequently restocked, which is often done from non-selling areas behind the display shelves. Perimeter locations reduce the time and disruption of stocking. In addition, most of these items require refrigeration equipment that can be most efficiently located along the perimeter.

In supermarkets the layout forces most consumers to the sides and back of the store. As they return to the front and the checkout counters, some are going to use the interior aisles, be exposed to other merchandise, and possibly make unplanned purchases. On the other hand, if the frequently purchased perishables were spread throughout the store, customer traffic would likely be more evenly dispersed.

In department and specialty stores the grid layout tends to force traffic down main aisles, with the result that merchandise along the walls is largely ignored. If a retailer chooses to use the grid, he should place the most sought-after items in locations that will draw customers away from major aisles and past other merchandise in order to stimulate unplanned purchases.

FREE FLOW

A second common layout is the free flow, or free form pattern. This layout, shown in Figure 5-2, stems from the notion that the primary objective of layout is to provide customer convenience. Thus, rather than force shoppers to move in certain directions as the grid layout does, the free flow allows movement in virtually any direction in a relaxed, almost casual atmosphere.

The free flow design is conducive to browsing, longer shopping visits, and more impulse purchases. Its chief disadvantage is that selling space is "wasted" when compared to the grid design, since more space is provided for customer movement. Also, counters and display cases are often more expensive because of their odd shapes.

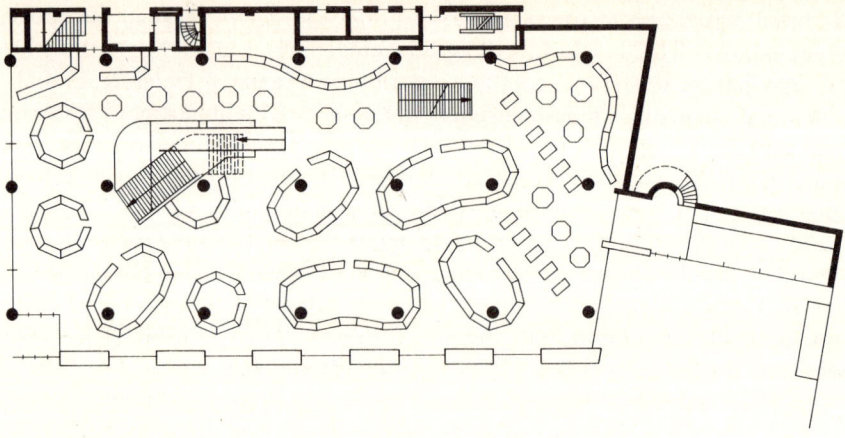

FIGURE 5-2

Model for free-flow layout

BOUTIQUE

A method of store division that became popular in department stores during the 1960s is the boutique. Instead of having separate departments within the store for various merchandise groups—such as a men's shoe department, a men's suit department, and an outerwear department—the boutique brings together complete or nearly complete offerings for a particular market in one department. For example, a "mod" boutique for the male fashionplate might include shirts, vests, sweaters, trousers, shoes, suits, coats, and accessories all in one location. The fixtures, decorations, and sales personnel are carefully selected to appeal to the target group. In effect, a specialty shop atmosphere is created.

This layout allows shoppers with a particular interest, size, or life style to shop in one location for a complete assortment of related goods in an atmosphere suited to his or her tastes. The boutique layout requires more than ordinary care in overall store design since distinct yet harmonious images must be created throughout the store.

Space Allocation

Space allocation involves two considerations. The first is the division of space in the outlet between selling and non-selling areas. The second is the allocation of space to specific items in the sales area. Both of these layout considerations will be discussed in this section.

SELLING AREA VERSUS NON-SELLING AREA

Selling area is the place where all transactions actually occur. It is commonly referred to as the "sales floor." All other space is non-selling area. The amount of space a retailer needs for non-selling activities will vary according to the type of business. For example, a restaurant with a kitchen, office, store room, walk-in refrigerator, and employee rest area requires considerable non-selling space. By the same token, an automobile parts store that maintains an extensive inventory may be located in a large building but only use a small counter near the front door for selling area. In contrast, a beauty salon or jewelry store may have almost no non-selling area.

In Table 5-1, selling space as a percent of total space is presented for department stores and specialty stores. Although these figures are for relatively large retail operations, they provide an indication that non-selling space typically ranges from 20 to 35 percent of the total area in a store.

TABLE 5-1

Selling Space as a Percent of Total Space in Department and Specialty Stores

Department Stores		Specialty Stores	
Annual sales	Ratio of selling space to total space	Annual sales	Ratio of selling space to total space
under $500,000	74%	under $1 million	78%
$500,000 to $1 million	74%	$1 to $5 million	72%
$1 to $2 million	62%	over $5 million	61%
$5 to $10 million	64%		
$20 to $50 million	65%		

Source: Jay Scher, *Department and Specialty Store Merchandise and Operation Results of 1971*, National Retail Merchants Association, 1972.

Since merchandise normally passes through the non-selling area before it reaches the selling area, retailers should give non-selling area as much consideration as they give the selling area. The retailer's first consideration should be to determine what activities will be carried out in the non-selling area and to provide adequate space for these things to be done efficiently. Second, local and state regulations concerning non-selling area should be investigated (some states require the availability of employee rest areas, for example). Finally, the appearance and cleanliness of the non-selling area should be planned to protect the merchandise and to avoid damaging the morale of employees who spend all or a great deal of their time in the non-selling area.

Store Layout

ALLOCATION OF SALES SPACE

The amount of selling area allocated to each product definitely will affect store profits. The dilemma is to provide an adequate selection of each product so the consumer can make satisfactory comparisons and evaluations but not so much that the profitability of other items is damaged because of inadequate exposure. In most lines of retailing, the merchant has a greater variety of merchandise available than the physical limits of the store will allow. In 1950, an average supermarket offered 4,000 items. By 1958 the number of items had increased to 5,000, and now the number approaches 12,000. Various space allocation methods have been applied by merchants, the degree of sophistication depending on the time and effort they can exert on the problem. The more common resources for such methods are described below.

Experience. Many small merchants, particularly in limited-line outlets, simply rely on their own personal experience and a sensitivity to customers' comments and reactions to determine space allocation. This would probably be more reliable, for example, in a specialty clothing store than in a jewelry or drug store because a smaller variety of merchandise is handled.

Trade Associations. Annual publications of many trade associations provide average industry figures for space allocation. For example, The National Retail Merchants Association's annual publication, *Merchandising and Operating Results*, provides extensive information on store operations classified by the size and type of store.[3] This information, based upon data supplied by cooperating companies, can serve as useful benchmarks for retailers in planning and evaluating their activities.

TABLE 5-2

Median Annual Sales per Square Foot of Selling Space for Selected Merchandise Lines

Merchandise	Specialty stores with sales over $1 million	Department stores with sales over $1 million
Adult female apparel	$106	$ 87
All dresses	$100	$ 90
Adult female accessories and intimate apparel	$126	$104
Adult male apparel	$127	$127
Sporting goods	—	$ 51
Televisions	—	$154
Tobacco and smoking goods	—	$294
Toys	—	$ 39
Total Company	$ 88	$ 74

Source: Jay Scher, *Department and Specialty Store Merchandise and Operating Results of 1971*, National Retail Merchants Association, 1972.

Table 5-2 presents some selected sales-per-square-foot figures for specialty and department stores. Note that the figures differ somewhat for the two kinds of stores and differ significantly for various merchandise lines.

Other associations provide similar information in various lines of trade.[4] Obviously, the use of this information must be tempered by the conditions a particular retailer faces. For example, a store specializing in conservative clothing in a retirement area might offer a different distribution of merchandise from that of a high-fashion boutique in Los Angeles.

SPACE PRODUCTIVITY

A final approach to space allocation is the evaluation of space productivity based upon sales for various products. For example, assume that industry average figures (from a trade association) indicate that men's clothing stores of a particular square footage generate $250,000 in sales per year. Also, assume that the industry average indicates that sales per square foot for dress shirts are $90 a year. Finally, consistent with other stores, assume that the store in question expects to generate 8 percent of total revenue from dress shirt sales. The amount of space allocated to shirts can be computed as follows:

(1) $250,000 (total sales) × .08 (expected share of sales generated by shirts) = $20,000 (expected shirt sales)

(2) $$\frac{\$20,000 \text{ (expected shirt sales)}}{\$90 \text{ (industry average sales per sq. ft.)}} = 222 \text{ sq. ft.}$$

This method indicates 222 square feet of shelf space should be allocated to dress shirts. (It should be noted that this method does not consider *which* 222 square feet should be allocated to shirts; nor does it take into consideration as a limiting factor the exact size of the store.) Each department or product group can be analyzed, and the total floor space allocated.

These methods can act as guides to space allocation. They are not stringent rules. Rather, they provide a reasonable estimate from which the retailer can make judgmental adjustments. The final allocation decision should also take into consideration the following three factors:

1. The contribution to profit a product can produce relative to the amount of space it occupies
2. Customer desires for availability and convenience
3. Difficulty of maintaining the display and of stocking and handling the merchandise

These factors, used to refine a general model, come only from experience and watchfulness.

Merchandise Placement

Besides the amount of space merchandise occupies, its location within the outlet is also important. Certain areas have more traffic and therefore greater sales potential. Some basic generalizations on areas within a store are:

1. Space near the front of the store is more valuable than space in the rear.
2. First-floor space is more valuable than basement or upper-floor space. The higher the floor, the lower the value of the space.
3. Space along aisles is more valuable than corner space.
4. Main or center aisles are more valuable than peripheral or side aisles.

The final decision about where to place goods is based upon two factors. The first is the merchandise itself. For example, convenience or impulse items must be readily seen. On the other hand, shopping goods (for example, most appliances) can be given secondary locations because customers interested in them will seek them out. The second factor to consider involves the store's customers. Are they in a hurry or do they browse? Are they elderly, preferring to remain on the first floor? Do they come to the store frequently for the same item? Answering these questions about the merchandise and the customers will result in more logical placement, which in turn should pay off in higher sales and profits.

REVIEW BOX 5:1

1. The basic types of layouts described in the chapter are grid, free flow, and _____.
2. Typically, non-selling area is _____ to _____ percent of a store's total area.
3. In allocating space to merchandise, a retailer should rely on three methods: experience, information from a trade association, and _____.

STORE DESIGN

The design of a store should do three things: create and convey a desired store image, facilitate customer shopping convenience, and provide for flexibility and ease of maintenance.

FIGURE 5-3

© 1974; by permission of John Hart & Field Enterprises, Inc.

The Objectives of Design

CREATE AN IMAGE

The exterior appearance of an outlet—whether highly ornate, massive and imposing, or purely functional—suggests what might be expected inside. Franchise systems such as McDonald's and Holiday Inns take care that the exteriors of all their franchise outlets are very similar. This "sameness" serves as a message to potential customers that the offering of every outlet in the system is identical. The developers of large stores and shopping centers face the problem of keeping the size of their structures from appearing threatening. As one retailer put it, "The new centers often look rather fortress-like from the exterior . . ..".[5]

Smaller retailers frequently buy or lease existing buildings. Even though this restricts their flexibility, an image can be created through the choice of a store name and the way it is displayed on the front of the outlet. "Casual Togs by Marie" written in gold scroll creates a much different image of quality and price from that of "Marie's Sportswear" in block letters. Figure 5-3 makes this point very well.

FACILITATE SHOPPING

Stores should not be designed for the sake of image alone. In other words, the design should also serve a practical purpose. The installation of air doors or curtains of air to replace conventional doors, for example, can serve the practical purpose of removing a physical barrier that discourages passers-by from entering the store as well as giving the outlet a modern image. Design should make the outlet inviting and encourage movement throughout the store.

Store Design

SPOTLIGHT

Should the entrance to a store be an important design consideration?

By controlling the flow of customer traffic, tailoring the interior of the store, and arranging the merchandise strategically, Jewelcor has experienced twice the sales that were forecast for the first year of operation. The following describes how it was done.

Everything in Jewelcor's design of its model store reflects the belief that the firm's basic business is jewelry. The entire layout of the sales area and its customer traffic flow is geared to promote

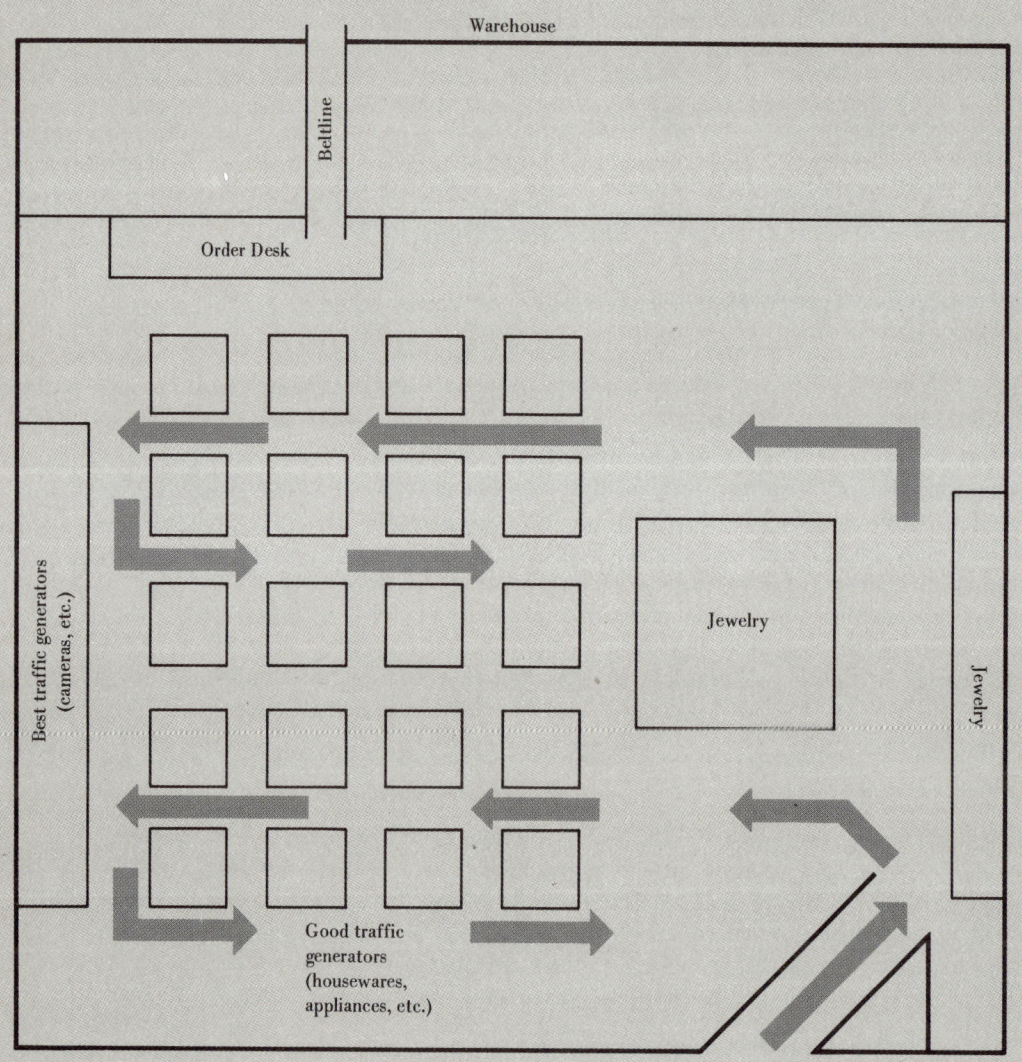

102   Ch. 5 *Store Layout and Design*

jewelry sales. So is the store's decor, both inside and out.

The first thing a customer sees upon entering a showroom is jewelry. The entranceway is designed to leave no choice, regardless of the customer's original purchase intentions.

Instead of being centrally located in the facade, as in more conventional stores, Jewelcor's entrance is set off-center, closer to a side wall of the building. Again unlike traditional entranceways, a customer isn't given a choice of directions to go once she is inside the store. Instead, Jewelcor's entranceway is set at a roughly 45-degree angle to the store facade itself, so that customers are headed toward a side of the building as they enter. That side features a large wall display of some of the highest profit merchandise in the store—diamonds.

The unique entrance also permits Jewelcor to position the customer for yet another pass-by of jewelry merchandise. "At the moment she enters the store and sees the first jewelry display, her back is to most of the other merchandise areas," notes Shendell. "She must turn around to locate whatever she originally intended to buy. And as soon as she does turn, she's facing yet another jewelry display which she must bypass to get to other areas."

The entire customer flow pattern is repeated—in reverse—as the customer leaves the store. The overall result is that the customer is exposed to jewelry displays at least four times during her stay in the store and presumably even more times than that—depending on her browsing habits.

Asserts Shendell, "The trick is to locate high turnover, low-profit items in such a way that—in order to reach them—customers have to walk by high profit merchandise." An example is the popular camera department; customers must move from the entranceway virtually the length of the store, in the process moving through many higher profit merchandise areas.

To encourage customers to browse through the store, Jewelcor's model interior presents a light, airy, relaxed atmosphere. Extensive use is made of recessed fluorescent ceiling lights over general merchandise areas. Exceptions are the jewelry departments, which use incandescents to properly highlight the quality of the jewels on display.

Jewelcor makes extensive use of silver and gold foil wallpaper with a flocked felt overlay; "This also reflects our orientation," asserts Shendell. "It's designed to say 'jewelry' to our customers."

To help motivate the customer to browse, each item on display is accompanied by a fact card which provides basic information about the merchandise "Up to and including whether or not a diamond has a fault and where the fault is located," says Shendell. He notes that this also helps reduce the need for a large staff; "Our average shift is about 20 people per store—including storage area help."

Even supporting columns within the store are enlisted to help the customer browse more easily. Each is a catalog center, with Jewelcor catalogs on display which customers may consult to find items they haven't seen on the sales floor.

Source: "Catalog Plan Designed to Direct Traffic," *Chain Store Age*, March 1973, pp. E34–5.

Store Design

MAXIMIZE FLEXIBILITY AND SIMPLIFY MAINTENANCE

Design should take into consideration the need for flexibility in retailing today and the high cost of maintenance. A recent trend in department stores is to create as many temporary or portable fixtures as possible, allowing for modifications in departments as desired. In suburban Shillito's department stores (Cincinnati, Louisville, and Lexington), for example, many interior walls can be removed and reassembled within a few hours to create new designs.

Floors and fixtures must be kept clean and attractive; walls must be painted occasionally; and mechanical equipment, such as conveyors and escalators, must be kept in good working order. These and other maintenance chores should be considered when a store is designed. For instance, carpeting may sound like a great idea until customers begin coming in with food and drinks; or a grassy, garden area in front of the store may appear to be a distinctive idea until the time comes to mow or water.

Design Basics

DISPLAY WINDOWS

The use of display windows to allow customers to see representative merchandise and look into the store from the street or sidewalk has long been a basic design feature of retail outlets. A retailer using display windows, whether large or small, must remember that the window is often all the potential customer sees before deciding whether to enter the store. Thus, it has a critical selling job. Second, the window, like the remainder of the store's exterior, contributes to the store's image. For example, a window cluttered with a wide variety of merchandise and prominently displayed price tags suggests a low-margin, high-volume outlet. The retailer should take care that the merchandise displayed and the manner of display are consistent with the desired image.

Finally, the frequency with which a display window should be changed depends on the traffic going past the store and the type of merchandise sold. If the majority of the people passing the store are the same each day, as might occur in a downtown location, displays should be changed frequently. In contrast, the display window in a resort community need only be changed occasionally, since the people passing by are different most of the time. High fashion merchandise requires frequent display changes to suggest the up-to-date nature of the outlet. A store selling more conservative clothing needs fewer display changes. The guiding principle in window display should be to use the merchandise, fixtures, and changes to create and maintain an image for the store.

INTERIOR LIGHTING

Thirty years ago retailers did not worry too much about lighting; as a result, most outlets were dimly lit. Then, fluorescent lighting became available. Due to its low cost and high output, it became very popular with retailers. According to a lighting consultant, "They [retailers] almost overlit. Everything was in bright lights and nothing looked important."[6] The major limitations of fluorescent lighting are that it cannot be effectively directed to provide emphasis and it might be described as a "harsh" light that does not always produce true colors in merchandise.

The limitations of fluorescent lighting have become more evident as designers develop alternatives. The current trend is toward flexible lighting—fluorescent lights for basic lighting and incandescent lights for emphasis. By using spotlights, lights on movable tracks, and colored lights, retailers have made lighting a merchandising tool. Figure 5-4 shows how lighting is being used by retailers to produce an almost theatrical effect. Retailers can use lights to highlight special merchandise or emphasize sales areas. At the Joseph Magnin Department Stores in Costa Mesa and Almaden, California, the atmosphere is influenced by the color of the stores' lights which are changed by means of a gel (for example, pink on Valentine's Day).[7]

When lighting is used to produce a special effect, expert planning is needed. As a result, the use of lighting as a merchandising tool has been generally limited to the larger retailers. What many small retailers have overlooked is that local electric power companies often provide free lighting plans to small retailers.

STORE EQUIPMENT

Store equipment includes all the physical objects in the store: counters and display cases, elevators and escalators, signs, and area dividers. Although these things sound very basic and functional, they can have an effect upon operations far beyond what may be apparent on the surface.

FIGURE 5-4

An example of effective use of lighting

Movable merchandise racks serve as attractive displays and flexible store dividers.

Counters and Display Cases. Although they serve the same basic functions—they display merchandise effectively and provide storage space for inventory—counters and display cases are different. A counter is an open display, while a display case is closed and may even be locked. In selecting counters and display cases, the retailer must consider whether the merchandise to be displayed will allow self-service by the consumer or will require salesperson service.

For self-service, consumers must be able to handle and evaluate the merchandise and carry it to a check-out area. A counter must offer a wide selection to permit comparisons. Durability is important since counters are subject to considerable use by consumers.

If a salesperson is involved in the merchandise selection process, counters or display cases may be used. Closed displays, of course, require the presence of a salesperson to help the customer. They are used when the merchandise is easily damaged or soiled, when having it exposed would be unsanitary (in a bakery, for example), or when the merchandise is extremely valuable and therefore subject to theft.

In many stores shoplifting has become such a serious problem that self-selection is being avoided whenever possible. Unfortunately, the protection afforded by closed displays may be offset by the increased cost of salespeople and the added inconvenience to customers. In Macy's Herald Square store, a number of former self-service items were placed in closed displays and locked cases. Though it cut shortages, there was some concern that it may also have decreased sales.[8]

Elevators and Escalators. If a store has more than one floor, an important design question is whether to include escalators or an elevator. An elevator takes up less space, is less expensive to install, provides more rapid transportation if a customer wants to go up several floors at once, and is generally preferred by the elderly and disabled. Escalators, on the other hand, involve less waiting time for the customer and offer a good view of the merchandise in the area.

In making a decision on vertical movement of customers, the important criteria include the number of people to be moved, their composition (young or old, mothers with small children), the distance they are to be moved (the number of floors), and the capacity of the alternative equipment (this can be supplied by the manufacturers).

Signs. Signs are designed to help customers find their way around a store and locate merchandise. Some signs are required by local ordinance (fire escape, exits), and others are purely functional (credit department, personnel office). Until recently, signs were not considered merchandising tools. Now the use of large, multicolored signs with fancy artwork not only inform customers but attract them as well. The growth of the shop concept (a highly specialized area within a department; for example, body suits in a hosiery department or handbags designed for young customers) has increased the importance of signs. Clever names ("Body Shop" for body suits, "Knit Nook" for knitting supplies) on highly visible signs have become important sales aids.

Signs can be used to attract attention and identify merchandise.

Retailers disagree on the impact of sign use. Some stress the functional benefits it provides consumers, while others feel it can detract from the image of the outlet. The president of Steinfeld's Men's Shops, headquartered in Tucson, explains that their store design is so effective that ". . . the lack of signing has not even been noticed by most store visitors. We leave signing to grocery stores."[9]

Store Dividers. A major concern of retailers is flexibility. Nowhere is this better demonstrated than in the move away from permanent interior walls to movable area dividers. As was mentioned earlier, it has become quite common to design interior walls that can be quickly and easily removed in order to change the design of an area. Other methods are also used. At Byck's Specialty Shop in the Oxmoor Shopping Center, Louisville, four-foot modular pods are used to create individual shops. These molded plywood shells are self-supporting and easily moved. Commenting on the flexibility the pods provide, the President of Byck's said, "After we got operating we found we were not happy with the dress area. We changed it around on our own. It took about three hours. It's real great."[10]

Another innovative device that serves as a display area for merchandise, a fixture for signing, and an area divider is described as a "tree" in the Almaden, California, Joseph Magnin Store. The trees are highly mobile and are used to define departments. The number and placement provide for flexible space allocation and the opportunity to rearrange departments easily.[11]

REVIEW BOX 5:2

1. The objectives of store design are to create and convey a desired store image, facilitate customer shopping convenience, and _____.
2. Counters are more likely to be used when the merchandise display will allow _____. Display cases require the presence of _____.

CHAPTER SUMMARY

- Store layout includes the floor plan of display tables, specific location of various types of merchandise, the allocation of space to selling and non-selling areas, and the space allocated to various items.
- Basic layout alternatives include the grid, free flow, and boutique. The division of space between selling and non-selling areas depends upon the needs of the store, the local laws, and the morale of employees.

- The allocation of selling area to merchandise can be determined through experience, with the help of trade association information, or by performing a space productivity analysis.
- The actual placement of merchandise depends upon the type of merchandise and the customers.
- Store design creates an image of the outlet in the mind of the consumer. In addition it should facilitate sales, simplify maintenance, and maximize flexibility.
- The basics of design include display windows, interior lighting, and store equipment. Major items of store equipment are counters and displays, elevators and escalators, signs, and area dividers.

CHAPTER NOTES

[1] Nick Havas and Hugh M. Smith, *Customers' Shopping Patterns in Retail Food Stores: An Exploratory Study* (Washington, D.C.: U.S. Dept. of Agriculture, 1960).
[2] "How Customers Shop the Super Market," *Progressive Grocer*, August, 1960, pp. D49–D55.
[3] Jay Scher, *Department and Specialty Store Merchandise and Operating Results of 1971*, National Retail Merchants Association, 1972. The NRMA also published *Financial and Operating Results of Department and Specialty Stores 1971*, which provides sales, merchandising, earnings, and expense data by type and size of store.
[4] See *Encyclopedia of Associations* for a complete list and description of trade associations in all lines of business.
[5] "Suburban Malls Go Downtown," *Business Week*, November 10, 1973, p. 93.
[6] "Retailers Try Out Flexible Face-Lifting," *Business Week*, January 15, 1972, p. 75.
[7] "JM: Dynamic Store, Dynamic Design," *Stores*, December, 1971, pp. 4–5.
[8] Helen Mulhern, "'Looks,' Shops and Fixtures," *Stores*, April, 1972, p. 10.
[9] "Eloquent Display Without Signing," *Stores*, February, 1972, p. 10.
[10] "Looking Ahead in Store Design: Byck's Louisville," *Stores*, August, 1971, p. 5.
[11] "JM: Dynamic Store, Dynamic Design," *Stores*, December, 1971, pp. 4–5.

QUESTIONS AND ASSIGNMENTS

1. Name a store in your city that uses a grid layout and one that uses a free flow layout. Roughly sketch out the layout of each.
2. A store will have five departments in a total floor space of 6,000 square feet. Total sales for the store are estimated at $400,000 per year. The departments have the following sales per square foot and expected contribution to revenue:
   a. $35 and 18%
   b. $67 and 14%
   c. $127 and 21%
   d. $141 and 19%
   e. $58 and 28%
   How much space should each department have using the space productivity method of space allocation?

3. Where in a book store would you place greeting cards, textbooks, sweatshirts, and razor blades? Why?
4. One of the basic functions of store design is to create and convey an image. How do many franchise outlets use design to do this?
5. If you were operating a family shoe store, would you change the window display frequently? Why?
6. Contact the local electric company in your community and find out if they provide lighting plans for small retailers. Get a sample plan including costs and present it to the class.
7. What are the advantages and disadvantages of using display cases?

ANSWERS TO REVIEW BOX QUESTIONS

Box 5:1

1. boutique
2. 20; 35
3. space productivity analysis

Box 5:2

1. provide for flexibility and ease of maintenance
2. self-service; sales people

Organizational Structure in Retailing

ORGANIZATION AND ORGANIZING

What is a retail organization? Frequently the response to this question names Sears, Marshall Field, J.C. Penney, A & P, Macy's, Montgomery Ward, or some other nationally known giant. Certainly these are examples of retail organizations, but a list of names does not tell us how to define a retail organization.

Part of the difficulty in coming up with a definition is that the term *organization* seems to have a variety of meanings. To some, the term means a number of people who belong to some group, as in political organizations, religious organizations, student organizations, and business organizations, all of which have different goals. Others view organization as the grouping and sequencing of activities to accomplish a specified task. Actually both views are correct. People are necessary and central elements in any type of organization. Furthermore, there must be some goal, objective, or purpose which unifies the people involved. An *organization*, then, can be defined as a group of people cooperating to achieve specified objectives.

A retail organization is the result of the establishment of relationships among people and other productive resources to accomplish the objective of satisfaction of consumers' wants and needs at a profit. Retail organizations are composed of people, directed by people, and have an effect on people, but the organization itself is not a person, although we often speak of it as if it were.

The Need for Organizing

Even the very smallest enterprise needs organizing efforts in order to succeed. *Organizing is the arrangement of individual effort through systematic planning and coordination.* Consider the case of a one-man retail operation, an ice cream vendor who purchases ice cream from the local dairy plant and distributes his merchandise to residential neighborhoods via a pedal three-wheeler with a cold storage box. To ensure his business success, this enterprising entrepreneur will probably engage in some organizing efforts. Perhaps by trial and error, he will determine the most productive neighborhoods to call upon and the best business hours. He will also determine what and how much stock to carry—fudge bars versus ice cream sandwiches, more ice cream bars or more ice cream cups. With this information, the entrepreneur can then *organize* his stock, *organize* his route, and *organize* his time.

In larger retail businesses, organizing is more complex and entails the additional problem of dividing the work load among employees. This involves the assignment of specific duties to specific people. In a small firm the greatest danger is *underorganizing*. Most small retail owner-managers fail to recognize the necessity for organizing efforts and tend to do too little organizing.

Usually the owners of small firms understand all aspects of their operation and feel that they can perform these tasks better than their employees. Consequently, they frequently direct employees to perform specific tasks on an hour-to-hour, day-by-day basis. The result can be disastrous: employees are uncertain of their exact duties and responsibilities and constantly rely upon the manager to direct them. This is inefficient. When the manager is busy completing a specific task or is out of the store, employees may waste a great deal of time since they are uncertain about what to do next. In addition, there is always the danger that some tasks will not be performed at all because of temporary oversight by the manager. A manager who operates on an *ad hoc* basis simply because there are few employees can greatly undermine the efficiency of the organization. Assignment of specific duties and responsibilities to employees *on a continuing basis* can overcome such problems.

Quite the opposite situation tends to exist in large retailing operations. Responsibilities may be so specifically defined through extreme job specialization that employees have little latitude in their jobs and no understanding of or interest in the overall function of the business. In such cases, employees often become bored and sometimes engage in detrimental behavior such as excessive absenteeism, tardiness, shoddy work, overindulgence in alcohol and drugs, attempts to sabotage work, and theft of money, merchandise, or supplies. Some organization behaviorists have suggested that such problems

SPOTLIGHT

What does Chairman Mao know about retailing?

"All power flows from the barrel of a gun."—*Thoughts of Chairman Mao*

But the chairman knows better. Power, at least the ability to use it, means organization. Without organization, power is merely rhetoric, wind, noise, energy.

Power means the ability to get things done. And, organization is how we do it. Want to make a profit? Got to have an organization. Want to wage a war? Got to have an organization. Write a book? Say a prayer? Make steel? Impossible without organization.

Organization is how we gather, how we collect ourselves into social machines. Organization is how we relate to each other in terms of tasks. And, it's the task nature of organizations that makes them different.

A steel company is different from a church in terms of mission—in terms of the task. And, as the task changes, so also does the organization . . . if it can.

When a steel company starts making plastics as well, its organizational structure changes. When a religious body must minister to human needs other than consolation, its organizational structure changes. When an army is given the task of keeping the peace as well as waging war, its organizational nature changes.

Simply put: as people change the tasks, as people's needs and wants change, so does the nature of the organizations they go to. After all, organizations are the various ways men and women order themselves to get things done.

Source: "Organizations: Tops, Bottoms and Turmoil," *Industry Week,* May 4, 1970, pp. 26–29. Reprinted by permission.

As with most other types of organizations, retail organizations are hierarchical in nature. They have a very narrow top and a broad bottom. Orders filter down from the top to the bottom where work gets accomplished. Such an arrangement is designed to handle tasks which are relatively constant but, being rigid, it often does not handle change well.

A major criticism of the hierarchical structure is that the men at the top are from the past while those at the bottom are now. The pressure for change comes from the bottom, while the top resists change. Perhaps this explains why retail stores in the past have resisted change so strongly. For example, department stores were very slow to accept the move to the suburbs and were adversely affected by this resistance. Many stores have been equally slow to accept changing social and economic conditions. Retailers' reactions to the consumerism movement have generally not been timely.

Perhaps what is needed is a greater willingness on the part of retail organizations to change the organizational structure to meet changes in employee needs, social changes, economic changes and so forth. Perhaps if major retailing executives were exposed to the ideas of organization theorists, adaptable retail organizations would result.

may be overcome through job enlargement—increasing the number of different tasks employees are to perform, or through job enrichment—changing the nature of the task so that it becomes more challenging and carries more responsibility.[1]

It should be evident that *overorganization* can be just as significant a problem in a large retail firm as *underorganization* is in a small firm. The key, then, is to organize enough to assure sufficient allocation of responsibility but not so much that the employee feels stifled and bored.

Formal and Informal Organizations

The discussion so far has concentrated upon *formal organization*, a division of duties and responsibilities under the direct control of the store manager in a single unit store or under the president in a multi-unit chain. Either can arrange the organizational structure as he sees fit and modify it as necessary.

The formal organization is most often depicted by an organization chart. However, this illustrates only a framework or skeleton of the organization and usually leaves a great deal to be desired. Figure 6-1, for example, represents a small to medium-size retail business. Obviously, this chart tells us little about the store. We know that the store manager has divided the store's workload into three major divisions, and we can assume that each division has a manager or a person "in charge." We do not know how many employees are in each division; nor do we know anything about their job responsibilities. Even with this information we would have little idea of the various relationships among departments or of the people in these departments.

Except in very unusual circumstances, organization charts tell us much less than we would like to know about the organization and how it functions. Primarily, they provide an idea of how the firm has divided the total store workload into divisions, departments, or other subdivisions and how the hierarchical structure is arranged.

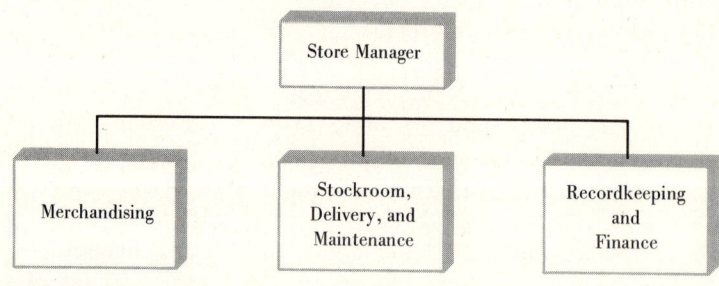

FIGURE 6-1

A small to medium-size store organization

In some cases the organization chart is supplemented by an organization manual. The manual usually spells out in more detail the specific job responsibilities of employees. Usually the purpose of indicating specific responsibilities is to prevent misunderstandings among employees about their exact duties.

A major problem with organization manuals and charts, especially in the growing firm, is keeping them up to date. Changes in responsibilities often occur because of evolving organizational needs, which bring alterations in personnel distribution and other internal changes. Unless continued effort is directed at keeping the organization chart current, it soon becomes outdated and useless.

The formal organization describes the way work *should be* accomplished. The *informal organization* is the way in which the work *actually* gets done. For example, suppose in the very simple organization depicted in Figure 6-1, a payroll clerk in the recordkeeping department has a question about the number of hours worked by a salesperson in the merchandising department. According to the organization chart, the payroll clerk should take the matter to the department manager, who would consult the merchandising manager, who would then confer with the salesperson. Common sense suggests that this is an inefficient solution to a simple problem. In reality the payroll clerk would probably go directly to the salesperson for clarification. This violates the procedure established by the organization chart, but it saves time.

Simply put, employees frequently accept directions from people who have no direct authority over them (according to the formal organization) because it often makes their job easier than would strict adherence to formal lines of authority.

> In fact, it would not, in any sense, be an exaggeration to assert that any large organization would come to a grinding halt within a month if all its members began behaving strictly in accordance with the structure of responsibility and authority defined by the formal organization chart, the position descriptions, and the formal controls.[2]

The logical question, then, is why all the concern with formal organization? A primary advantage of formal organizational structure is that it assigns *responsibility* for seeing that certain tasks are accomplished. In fact, many activities do follow the formal organization chain of command. In case of serious problems or those apt to have severe consequences, employees frequently utilize the formal organization to assure that decisions are made by those who have the responsibility for such decisions. Thus, the formal organization serves as an instrument of accountability and as a protective device for employees.

Both formal and informal organization exist in every retail enterprise, but they are not separate entities. In fact, the two may be so closely related that it is impossible to tell the difference between them. The remainder of the chapter concentrates on formal organization, but remember that in all cases informal organization exists and that performance of activities may not always be as charted.

REVIEW BOX 6:1

1. An _____ is a group of people cooperating to achieve specified objectives.
2. With respect to organizing effort, there is the danger of _____ in the large retail firm and _____ in the smaller firm.
3. The _____ organization indicates how work should be accomplished while the _____ organization is the way it is accomplished.

SMALL AND LARGE STORES

Small Store Organization

The primary difference between small and large store organization is the degree of specialization of employees. Both types have the same basic mission, buying merchandise to meet consumers' wants and needs and selling this merchandise to target consumers at a profit. Both quantity of merchandise and number of employees are smaller in the small store. The result is that small store employees usually have to be more versatile and adaptive than those in larger stores.

One major problem in talking about small stores is that there is no easy way of dividing small stores from large stores. For our purposes, we will view a store with annual volume of less than $1 million and/or fewer than 15 employees as a small retail business.

Figure 6-2 depicts a small store organization in which the owner has arranged the employee activities so that each person has a definite list of responsibilities. Although the firm is small, the chart shows evidence of organizing efforts. The major burden falls on the owner-manager, who has the assistance of various employees. Rather than develop detailed written job descriptions, an owner-manager typically assigns such responsibilities orally. Employees usually know not only their own responsibilities but also those of fellow employees.

Frequently when one employee is overburdened with work, another employee assists with the expectation of reciprocity in the future. It should be noted that the primary responsibility of almost all employees in a small firm is selling merchandise. Thus when the store is busy, each employee

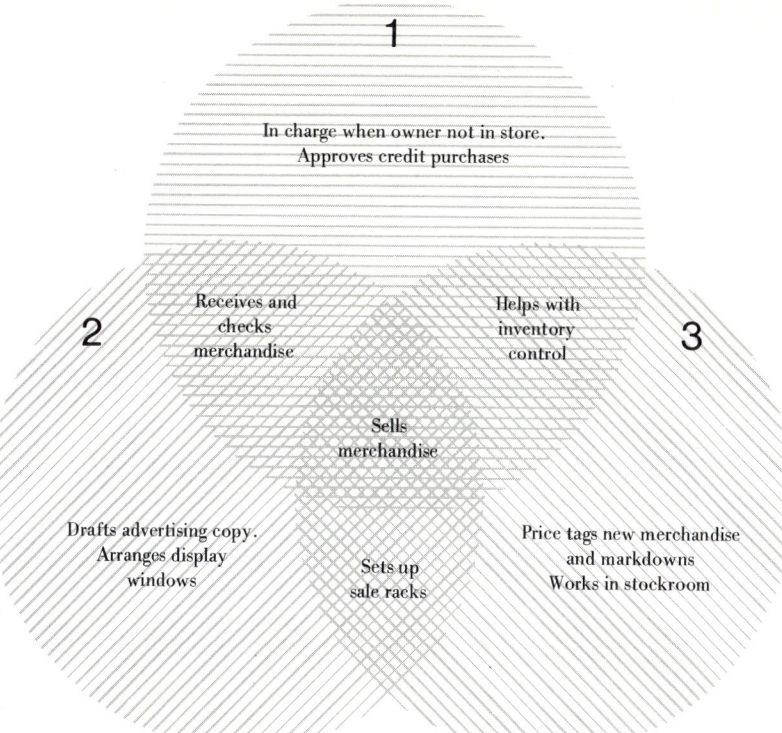

FIGURE 6-2

A small store organization—overlapping duties of 3 employees

may "put off" other duties until customers have been served. But besides selling, each small store employee is responsible for certain other tasks. In such a store, little confusion should exist concerning job duties if the manager is explicit in assigning them.

Large Store Organization

One of the major differences between small store and large store organization is degree of specialization. As a small store grows, the owner-manager cannot continue to perform all activities. As a result, he or she usually must make a decision on how to divide the work load and still get the primary mission accomplished effectively and efficiently. There are several ways to expand the organization, the most common being on the basis of *functions*, *products*, *geography*, or some *combination* of these.

One principal way organizations have expanded in the past is by organizing according to *functions*, and the traditional department store is typical of such an arrangement. The five-function organization is the most common with (1) a merchandising division, (2) a store operations division, (3) a control division, (4) a promotion division, and (5) a personnel division. The rationalization for this kind of division of responsibility is that greater expertise or specialization leads to more effective and efficient use of resources. Many large specialty stores (such as Neiman-Marcus and Saks) also use this type of organization.

A second way of organizing is on the basis of *product lines*. Many supermarkets utilize this approach with managers for groceries, meats, and produce. In this case it is thought that management may be more effective because of the specialized knowledge necessary within each general product line. Many drug stores also use this type of organization with divisions for cosmetics, pharmacy, and sundries. Usually, when merchandising activities are departmentalized, it is on the basis of products or product lines.

Retail operations which are organized *geographically* are generally limited to those which have two or more stores. Department stores with several branches are using this system of organization, as are large chains with stores in several cities.

In large stores some *combination* of the above organizations is common. For example, although a department store is basically organized by function,

FIGURE 6-3

A retail store using three bases for organizing

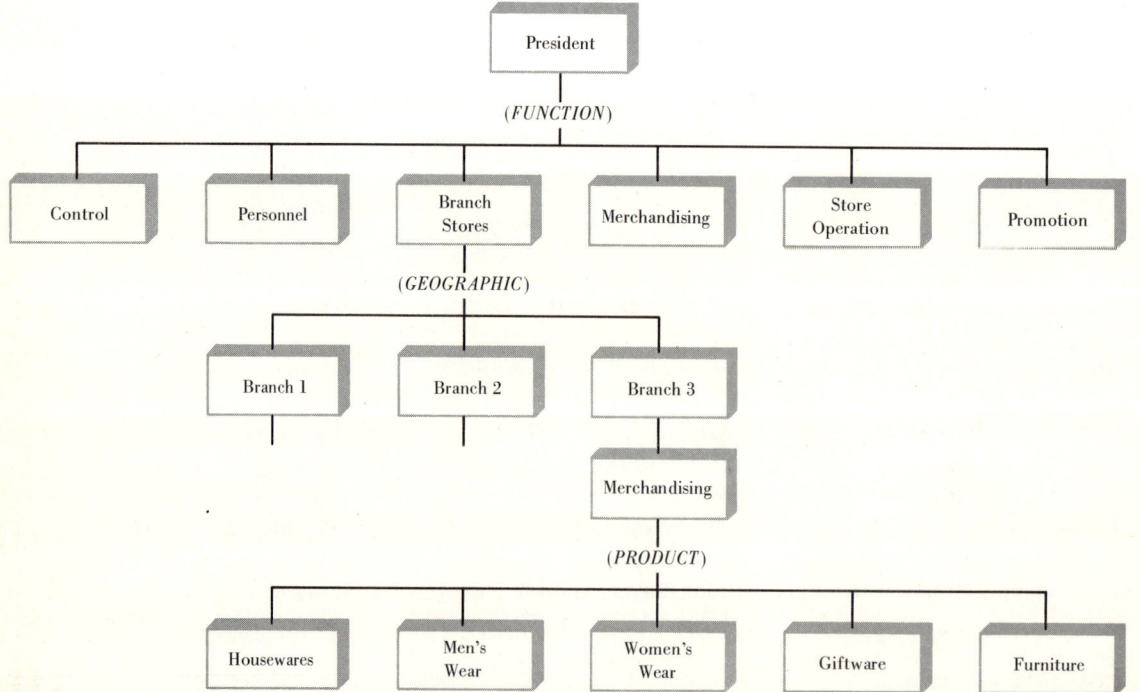

its merchandising division is usually organized by product lines. There may be a furniture department, a men's wear department, a children's department, and so forth. If the department store has branches, it may also be organized geographically. Figure 6-3 shows a combination of organizing methods.

DEPARTMENT STORE ORGANIZATION

When speaking of large store organization, we usually think of the department store since the largest *individual* retail stores are department stores. Also, this was the first form of large-scale retail organization in this country, with most of the earliest department stores being outgrowths of smaller dry goods stores.

Despite some disagreement among retail historians, it seems evident that among the first organizational changes that occurred with store growth was the division of responsibilities along product lines:

> Thus the department store, almost from the beginning, was an assemblage of shops under one roof, with the division of responsibilities running by merchandise departments; and this came to be the all-important merchandising pyramid of the organization.[3]

At the same time, in non-merchandising areas, organizational change tended to be along functional lines.

It was not until the growth of large chain stores and more recently the growth of branch department stores that much organizational division along functional lines was found in merchandising areas. This type of division involves separating buying and selling activities, a practice which is still under contention among merchandisers. Some argue that one person should be in charge of both buying and selling activities since this results in better control. Others believe that talents needed for buying are different from those needed for selling and that the two activities should be separated.

Perhaps a look at the growth of organization in one retail operation will help explain how and why certain methods of organization have come to be used.

Julius Higenbottom began his store as a one-man operation. His merchandise consisted primarily of yard goods, sewing notions, and a small line of millinery. As business prospered, he added a line of women's apparel. Before long, Julius had added four saleswomen and was stretching himself to the point that he no longer was able to keep the books, talk with all the salesmen who called on him, supervise the employees, clean the store, and price the merchandise as it came in. He delegated bookkeeping to one of the saleswomen who also sold when the store was busy and then he hired a young man to make deliveries, keep the stockroom neat and orderly, and take care of all of the store maintenance.

As the business continued to grow, he added a men's wear line. He

Small and Large Stores

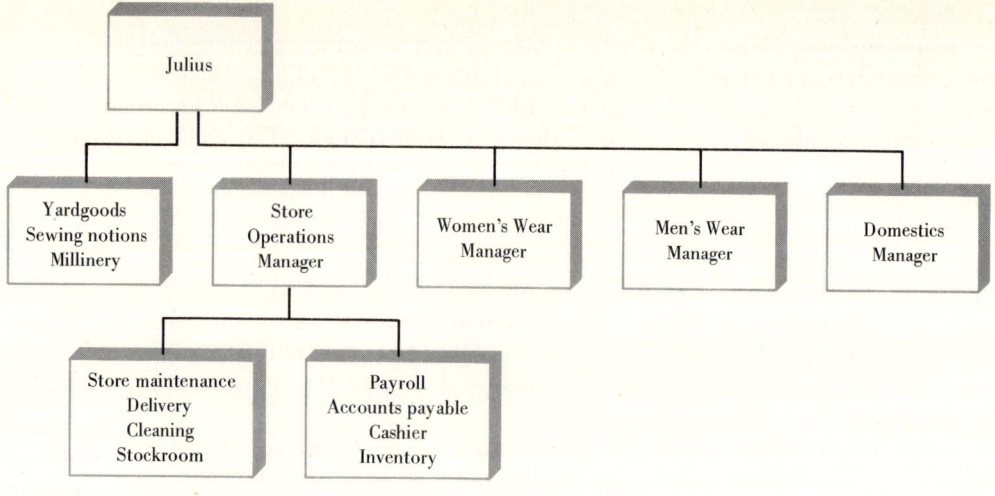

FIGURE 6-4

Higenbottom Dry Goods organization chart

FIGURE 6-5

Higenbottom Department Store organization chart

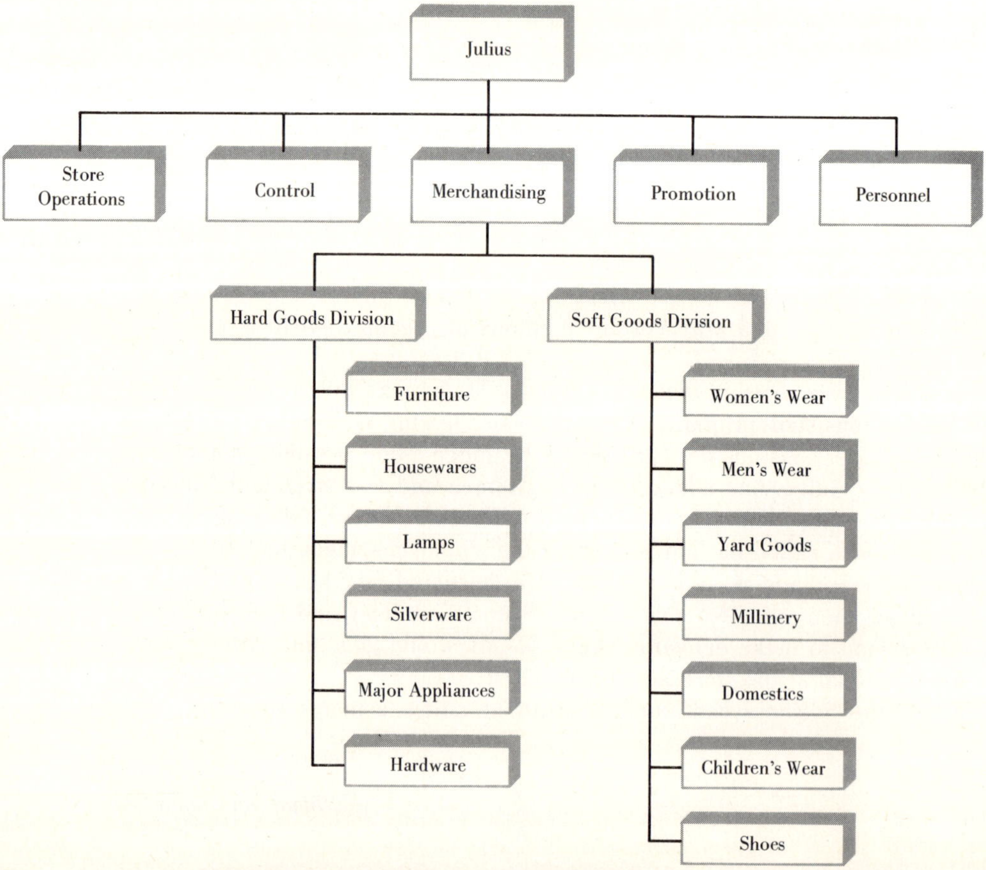

hired a wholesaler's salesman for this area, telling him that the men's department was fully his responsibility. Julius continued to buy, promote, and sell the other merchandise. Having access to the building next door, Julius expanded further by adding a line of domestics (table linens, bedding, and towels). Responsibility for operating this department was assigned to a saleswoman whom he promoted. His non-merchandising staff had grown to the point where he had to make further changes, reflected in Figure 6-4. Julius now had four merchandising departments (one of which he operated himself) and one non-merchandising department (store operations) which he put under the control of a young man hired away from the local bank. As Julius continued to expand, adding a children's department, shoes, hardware, and furniture departments, he had to expand the non-merchandising departments by forming functional divisions.

Figure 6-5 shows the result of his continued expansion. Note especially the insertion of another layer of management between the merchandising departments and Julius, that of a *hard goods* divisional manager and a *soft goods* divisional manager. (Hard goods are durable goods such as hardware and appliances as contrasted with nondurable soft goods such as textiles and clothing.) Each major non-merchandising area was also departmentalized with increased specialization, although such departmentalization is not shown.

CHAIN STORE ORGANIZATION

Chain store organization differs from department store organization in one important respect: *centralization*. Chain stores employ *centralized buying*, and their other areas of decision authority typically are also more centralized. In a centralized organization, as opposed to a decentralized one, major management decisions are made by upper-level executives. The primary reason for centralization is control. Advocates of centralization insist it is more efficient to have major decisions made by a small group of experts who are knowledgeable within their particular area.

Depending upon size, most chain stores also have more major divisions than are found in the typical department store. Generally speaking, a chain store manager is responsible for the selling function. This is typically the only decentralized function in the overall chain organization. Other operating functions such as real estate, finance, accounting and control, warehousing and transportation, buying, personnel, public relations, and store operations are typically centralized at the home office. With such centralization, elaborate systems of control through reports are necessary to ensure that the home office is always informed about happenings in the field. Figure 6-6 indicates the primary characteristics of chain store organization.

Because of the many different types of merchandise handled by some chains and because of the varying sizes of chains, no one organization chart applies to all chains. Each retail chain must organize for its own special purposes to ensure efficient performance.

Small and Large Stores

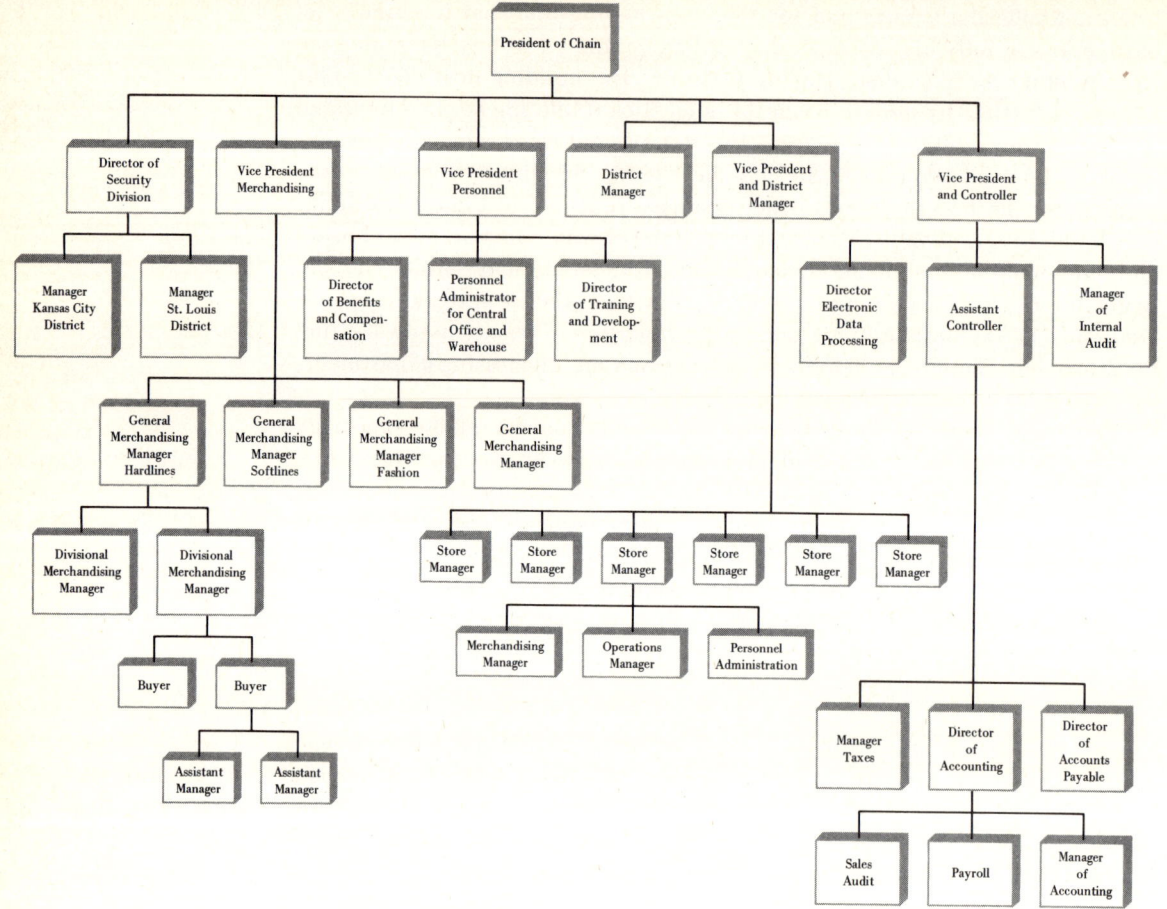

FIGURE 6-6

A chain store organization chart

(Venture Stores, a 12-store discount division of The May Company)

REVIEW BOX 6:2

1. The major difference between small and large store organization is _____.
2. The three primary ways of organizing a retail store are by _____.
3. Merchandising activities are normally subdivided according to _____.
4. Non-merchandising activities are normally subdivided according to _____.

Ch. 6 *Organizational Structure in Retailing*

ORGANIZATION FOR MERCHANDISE MANAGEMENT

Combined Buying and Selling Responsibilities

Since the primary function of retail stores is to act as purchasing agents for consumers, those activities connected with the planning and control of merchandise assortments are of major importance. All other functions of the business are dependent upon the proper selection and sale of merchandise. Therefore, the proper arrangement of merchandising activities is essential, before other activities of a firm can even be considered. This is not to say that non-merchandising activities are unimportant. It simply means that merchandising considerations should come first.

Recall that within the merchandising divisions of department stores organization normally proceeds along product lines. Such an arrangement is somewhat similar to the brand manager concept in manufacturing firms. The brand manager normally carries the full responsibility for coordinating all marketing efforts for a brand. Traditionally, a merchandise department manager of a department store or a specialty store has been responsible for profitability of each department. Although the manager is primarily concerned with acquiring and selling merchandise within a department, he or she is also responsible for coordinating efforts to see that the merchandise is delivered on time, that suppliers are paid, and that customers are properly charged for credit purchases. In a large store, many of these activities lie outside the direct control of the department manager, but it still remains his responsibility to see that the customer is properly satisfied.

Figure 6-7 indicates a fairly typical arrangement for merchandising activities in a large department store. At each lower level in the hierarchy, increased specialization with respect to specific kinds of merchandise becomes more evident. The general merchandise manager is the policy maker for total merchandise offerings and the quantity of merchandise on hand at any time. In fact, he or she is responsible for coordinating all merchandising efforts of the store. Normally, several divisional merchandise managers report to, and assist, the general merchandise manager. Divisional merchandise managers are responsible for broad divisions of merchandise. Their task is to implement merchandising policies and to work with the department managers reporting to them, assisting in assuring profitable departments. Within this area, the divisional merchandise manager sees that a proper balance between merchandise classifications is maintained.

Where there is no separation of buying and selling activities, a department manager (sometimes called a buyer) is responsible for both buying and selling activities. Supervised by a divisional merchandise manager, a department manager "runs his own little business." He or she is responsible

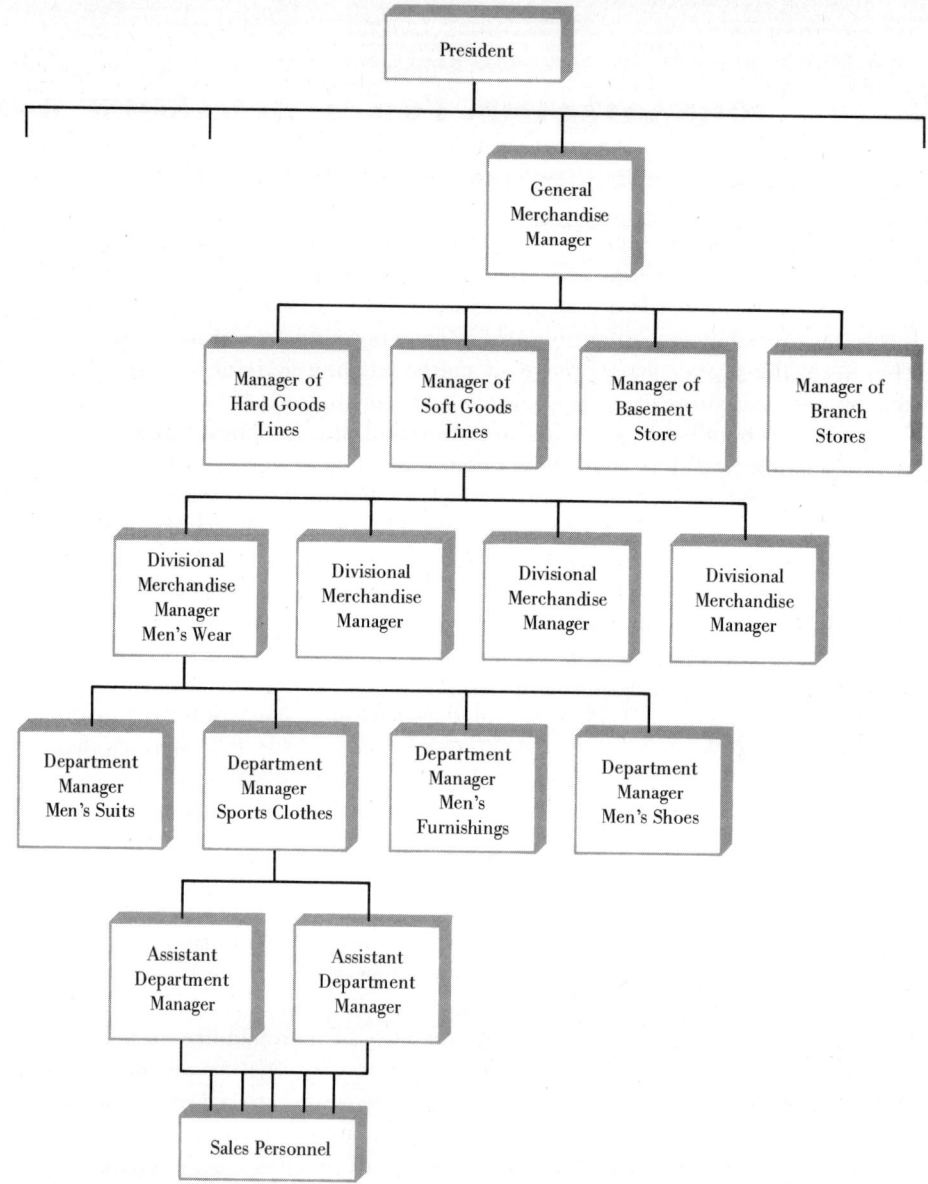

FIGURE 6-7

A typical merchandising organization for a large department store

for proper selection of merchandise and its presentation and sale. Just as the foreman is often considered the "key person" in manufacturing, the department manager is the "key person" in a department store. Usually a department manager will have one or more assistant managers. Various divisions of labor are employed with the assistant department managers, but most often they are in charge of salespersons and of maintaining stock records; they are generally in training for a department manager's position.

Departmentalized specialty stores often follow much the same method of organizing as department stores. This is especially true of independent specialty stores. The major difference is normally fewer levels of management, especially when the merchandise variety offered is more limited.

Centralized Buying

In chain stores and other types of stores (including some department stores) which have centralized buying, the merchandising arrangement differs from that of the *traditional* department store. The primary difference is that the merchandising function is separated into *buying* and *selling* functions. In a department store with a separation of buying and selling functions, the usual arrangement is a five-function organization. Separation of buying and selling activities in department stores is invariably brought about by the addition of branch stores to the extent that one department manager is no longer able to supervise the activities of the department completely and still have time to buy for and supervise the activities of several departments in the various branch stores.

FIGURE 6-8

Organization of a typical department store with several branches

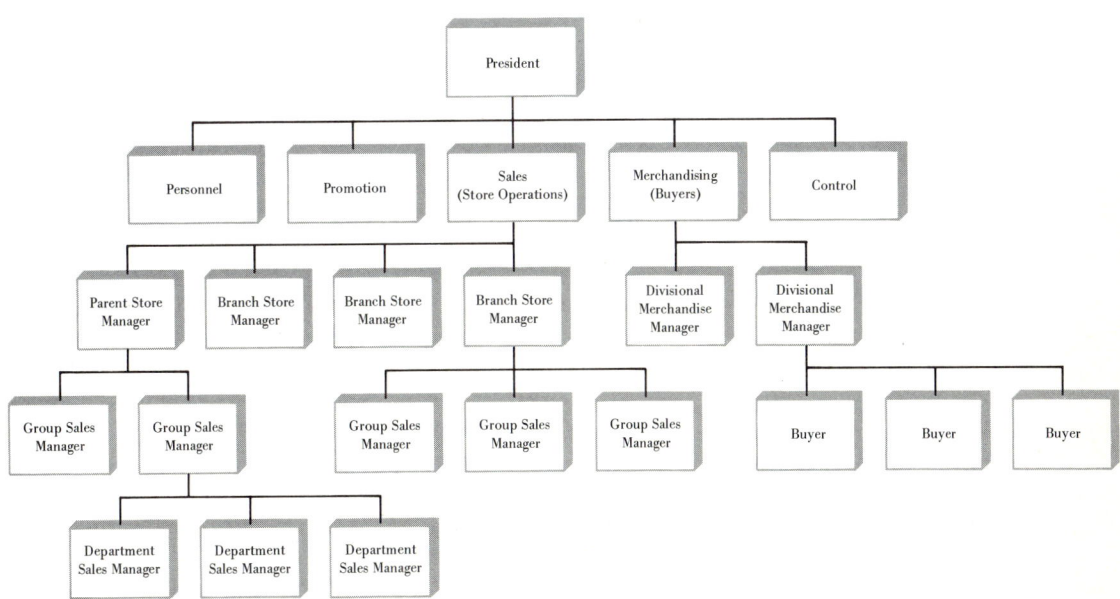

Organization for Merchandise Management

FIGURE 6-9
Merchandising organization in a large chain store

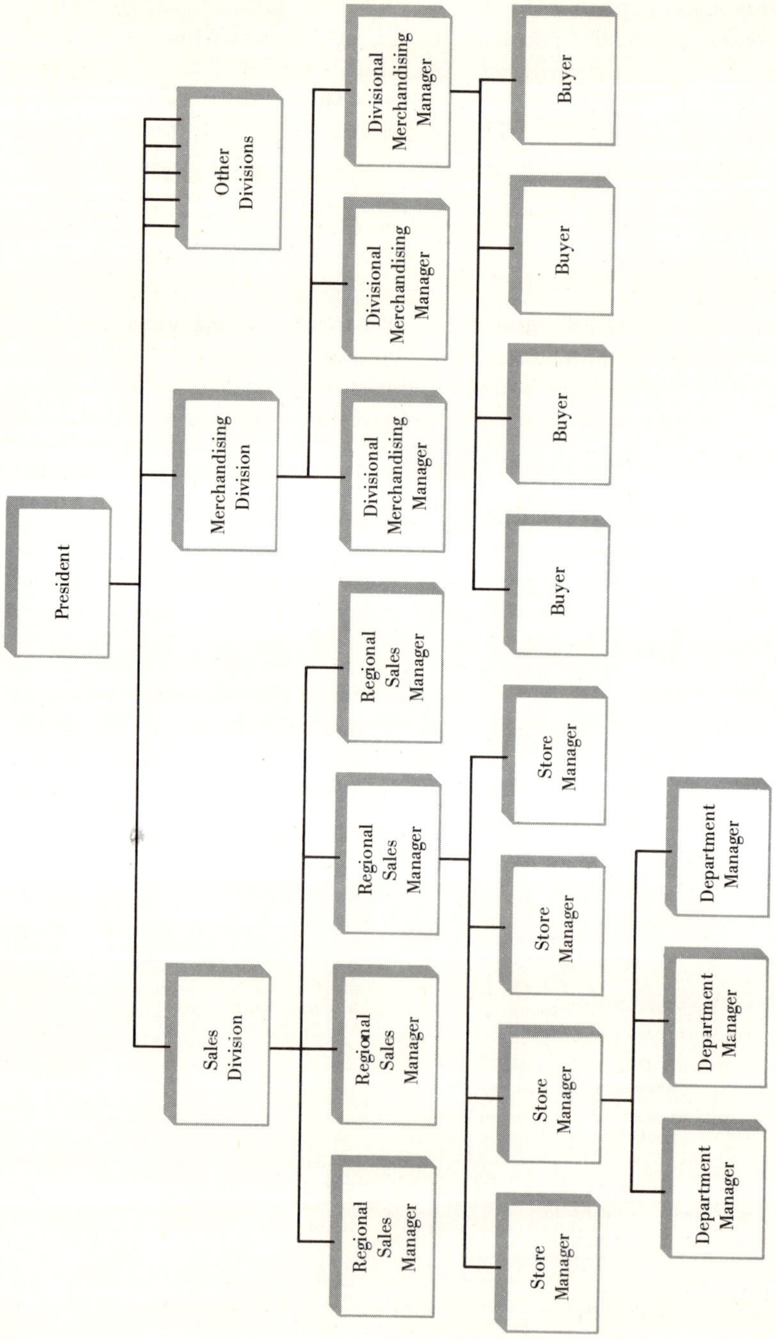

Figure 6-8 illustrates a department store organization with branch stores and separation of buying and selling. Within the sales division there are store managers reporting to the vice president of sales. Frequently they are concerned not only with the sales function but also with the operating function (non-merchandising activities). If this is the case, the operating division is combined with the sales division rather than being separate. Group sales managers within each branch store oversee the selling activities of a number of departments. This is possible because merchandise offerings are usually more restricted in branch stores than in the parent store. With less merchandise breadth and depth, the group sales manager can easily handle merchandise representing several parent store departments. Frequently, where the parent store remains dominant, separate department sales managers, rather than group sales managers, are employed in the main store. Here the merchandise assortment and sales volume are simply too large to allow for combining departments under a group sales manager. In extremely large branch stores, comparable in size to the parent store, group sales managers are often responsible for supervising several department sales managers.

Organization charts for small chain stores are very similar to those of department stores with several branches. This is logical since the department store with branch operations is really a small "chain" operation. A larger chain operation, though, may resemble Figure 6-9. The merchandising division is usually centralized at headquarters while the sales division is decentralized geographically.

REVIEW BOX 6:3

1. The "key person" in merchandising activities of a department store is _____.
2. In large department store organizations with several branch stores there may be a division of the _____ and _____ functions.

ORGANIZATION OF NON-MERCHANDISING ACTIVITIES IN DEPARTMENT STORES

In a large department store, more people are usually employed in non-merchandising divisions than in merchandising. This may seem peculiar, since the primary task of the store is merchandising, but a great deal of support is necessary to accomplish this task.

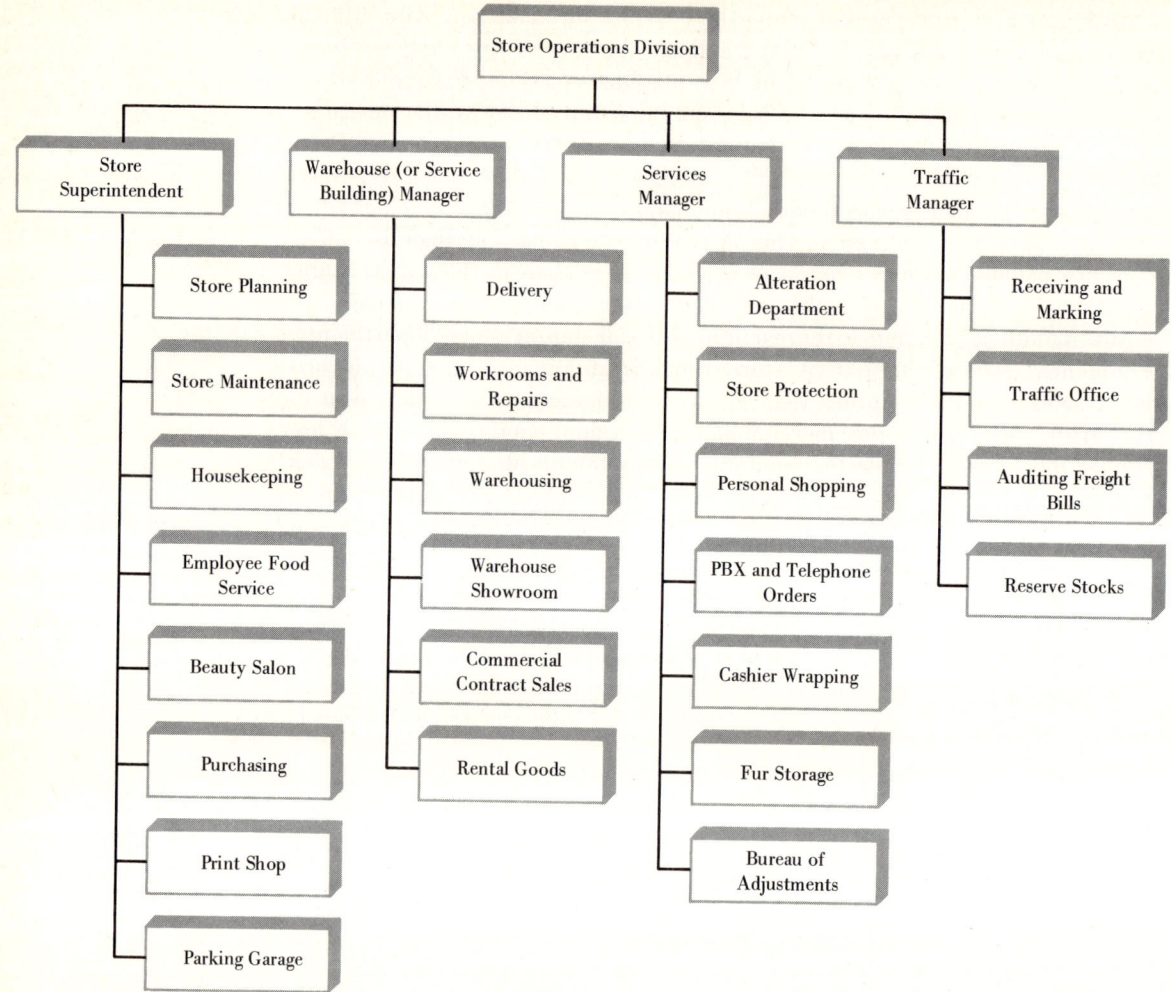

FIGURE 6-10

Organization of a store operations division of a department store

Store Operations Division

Generally this division is responsible for the physical aspects of maintaining the store — housekeeping, repairs, and security — as well as for the physical handling of all merchandise until it reaches the sales floor. The latter task includes receiving, checking, and marking merchandise. Other, often unrelated activities are also under the supervision of the store operations division. These include gift wrapping, delivery, warehousing, furniture and drapery workrooms, alterations and repair services, and purchasing of equipment and supplies.

A typical store operations divisional organization chart is shown in Figure 6-10. It is evident from the various categories listed here that the head of the store operations division must be capable of directing a number of activities and supervising a large staff. This job is one involving detail and requiring follow-up to ensure complete customer satisfaction.

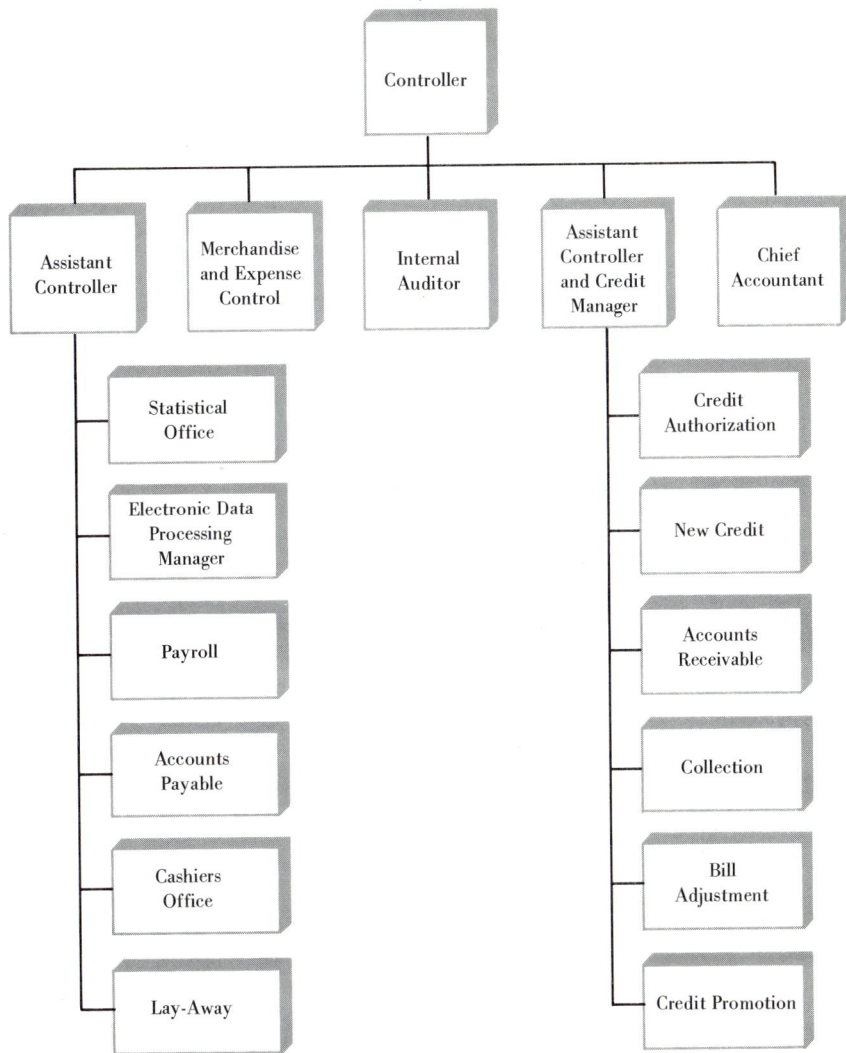

FIGURE 6-11

Organization of the control division of a department store

Control Division

The controller is the primary fiscal and accounting officer of the firm and is directly responsible for all incoming monies and all outgoing expenditures. Usually the controller has a strong accounting background and today may need to be very systems oriented to be able to supervise complete fiscal operations effectively. A computer background is desirable, if not a necessity, for most controllers today. Although arrangements vary, Figure 6-11 is fairly typical of the organization of this division.

Promotion Division

This division, often called the sales promotion or publicity division, has as its main function the creation and perpetuation of the desired store image and attraction of customers. Generally the promotion division initiates and coordinates all selling efforts of the firm with the exception of personal selling. Because of the importance of store image, the promotion manager must assure that the proper image is projected and that all the store activities reflect this image. Figure 6-12 is typical of the organization of this division.

Personnel Division

Although the personnel function is sometimes within the store operations division, it is more often a separate division. The personnel division selects and trains employees, a key asset of a retail firm, and looks after their welfare. Figure 6-13 is typical of the organization of a personnel division.

Today, hiring and retaining well-qualified personnel seems to be a special problem.[4] In fact, recruiting and hiring such personnel are often a greater problem than obtaining satisfactory merchandise. Personnel turnover is another constant problem for most stores. Furthermore, an on-going training program is needed for new employees as well as for those in the store who are being promoted to new jobs.

REVIEW BOX 6:4

1. Under a five-function organizational arrangement in department stores, the major non-merchandising divisions are (1) _____, (2) _____, (3) _____, and (4) _____.
2. In a department store the _____ division typically contains the greatest diversity of activities.

Ch. 6 *Organizational Structure in Retailing*

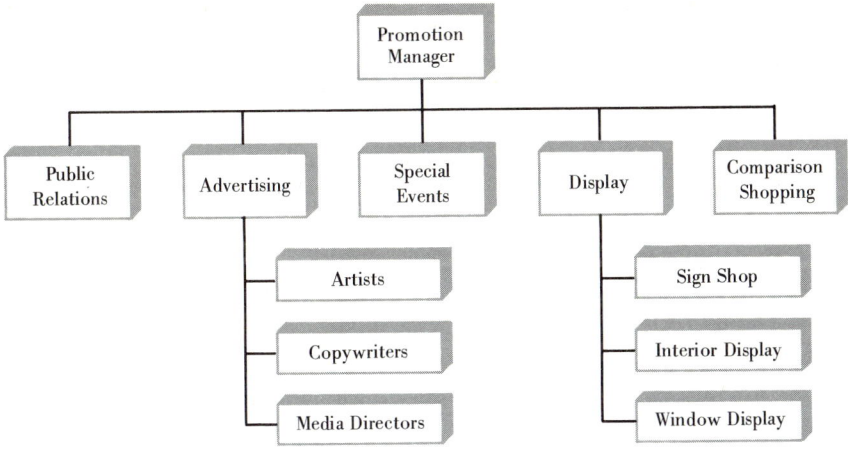

FIGURE 6-12

Organization of the promotion division of a department store

FIGURE 6-13

Organization of the personnel division of a department store

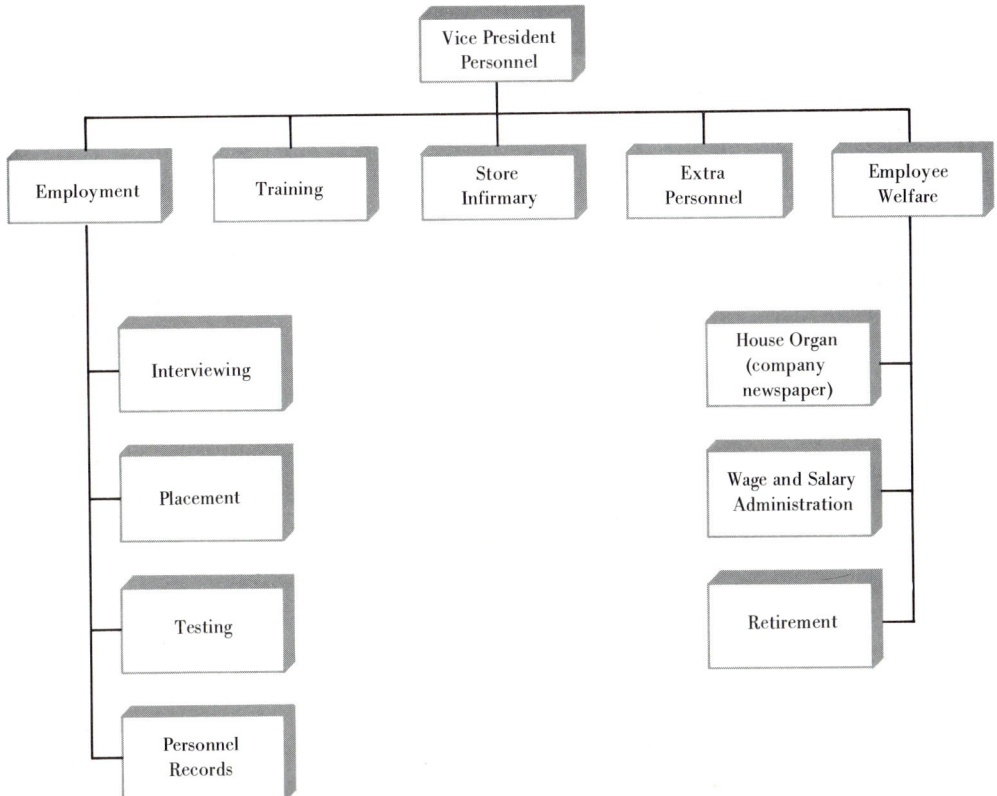

CURRENT TRENDS IN STORE ORGANIZATION

Separation of Buying and Selling

A widespread trend among large retail firms is to separate buying and selling activities. Indeed, the hallmark of chain store operations is centralized buying. In addition to getting large-quantity discounts by centralizing the buying functions, chain stores also benefit from efficiency through specialization.

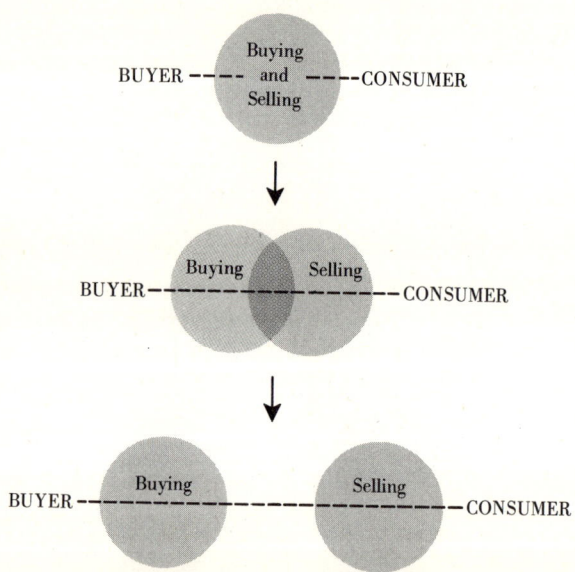

The distance between the consumer and the buyer increases as the buying and selling functions separate

With the growth in number and size of branch department stores, there is a tendency to regard each store as equal, with no store having priority over the others. At this point, buying may be separated from selling, and buyers are responsible for meeting the merchandise needs of all stores.

Buying has always been considered more important than selling in department stores. Partial evidence of this is indicated by frequent reference to department managers as buyers. However, with the two activities separated, increased attention has been given to the selling function.[5]

The Changing Role of Retail Selling

In the smaller retail store, the salesperson remains the most important link between the store and customers. However, because of the trend toward discount merchandising and its accompanying lower gross margin (the difference between wholesale price and the price for which merchandise is sold), many larger stores have reduced their sales personnel staff.

Personnel on the floor are primarily responsible for keeping the shelves well stocked and merchandise neatly arranged. Yet invariably customers have questions about merchandise or need assistance in making purchase decisions. When they ask questions about merchandise, they are often displeased with the lack of adequate information which they receive. What many consumers really want is adequate, competent sales help and discount prices. The problem for retailers is how to meet these needs with the squeeze on gross margins.

One way retailers are attempting to solve this problem is by providing employees with better training and by changing the responsibilities of store personnel. The objective is to provide floor personnel who are customer-service oriented, knowledgeable about store policies and procedures, and well informed about merchandise.

Top Management

Competition in large-scale retailing is becoming more intense. Problems such as those faced by A & P in recent years are indicative of the competitive situation. There is an obvious need for top management to engage in more long-range planning because so much is at stake in terms of dollar investment. Today many firms are questioning traditional hierarchical arrangements and are open to new ways of organizing management.

Many corporations have been re-examining the peak of the organizational pyramid. Figure 6-14 depicts the differences which exist in the types of activities at different levels. The gray area indicates the amount of time spent on the "doing" kinds of work, while the white area indicates planning, conferring, thinking kinds of work.

Top management is primarily concerned with planning and policy making. At the apex of the pyramid, chief executive officers spend virtually all of their time on such matters. Many corporations are reorganizing the chief executive's office because one person frequently is incapable of accomplishing all the planning and policy making necessary to ensure success. In some cases the president's office is shared by two or three executives who divide these responsibilities. Such an arrangement, however, does not always work satisfactorily. Many top-level executives have such

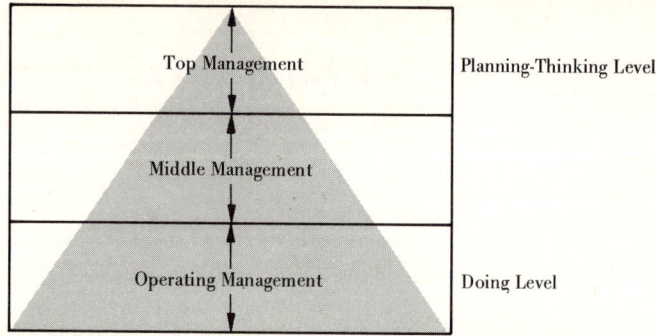

FIGURE 6-14

Types of activities at different management levels

strong personalities that they cannot share the "top rung of the ladder" with others. Other organizational arrangements at the top management level are being tried as well.⁶

Customer Relations

Some retailers, concerned with the consumerism movement, have appointed a director of consumer affairs. This position is usually within the promotion division. There is some question as to whether this is the correct location for such a function. If the responsibility of the director is to look out for consumer interests, then the director should probably report directly to the store president. Many retailers believe that their bureau of adjustments department is the logical place to handle all consumer complaints and have not made any organizational adjustments in response to the consumerism movement.

REVIEW BOX 6:5

1. With the growth in number of branch store units, there is organizationally a tendency to treat stores _____.
2. In self-service stores, customers seemed to be most displeased with _____ _____.
3. Top management spends most of its time with _____ kinds of work.

CHAPTER SUMMARY

- An organization is a group of cooperating individuals who wish to achieve specified objectives or goals.
- The primary objective of retail organizations is the satisfaction of consumers' wants and needs, at a profit.
- Organizing activity leads to efficiency of operations and greater profitability.
- All retail businesses, regardless of size, require organizing efforts. There are dangers of underorganizing in small firms and overorganizing in large firms.
- Both a formal and an informal organization exist in every retail store. Formal organizations specify how work ought to be accomplished, while informal organizations are the way work actually is accomplished.
- Specialization of employees is the primary organizational difference between small and large stores.
- The bases for organizing in large stores are functions, products, geography, or some combination thereof.
- Organization is normally arranged around products in merchandising and around functions in non-merchandising areas.
- The hallmark of chain store organization is centralized buying. Buying and selling functions are thus separated.
- The five major functional divisions in a department store are merchandising, store operations, control, promotion, and personnel.
- Current trends in store organization are a tendency toward separation of buying and selling activities, better training of sales personnel, experimentation with organizational arrangement at the top executive level, and use of a director of consumer affairs.

CHAPTER NOTES

[1] Most introductory management texts discuss these forms of despecialization. For example, see James H. Donnelly, Jr., James Gibson, and John M. Ivancevich, *Fundamentals of Management* (Austin, Texas: Business Publications, Inc., 1971), or Keith Davis, *Human Behavior at Work* (New York: McGraw-Hill, 1972).

[2] Douglas McGregor, *The Professional Manager* (New York: McGraw-Hill Book Company, 1967), p. 36.

[3] Wheelock H. Bingham and David L. Yunich, "Retail Reorganization," in John K. Ryans, Jr., James H. Donnelly, Jr., and John M. Ivancevich (eds.), *New Dimensions in Retailing: A Deci-*

sion Oriented Approach (Belmont, California: Wadsworth Publishing Company, Inc., 1970), p. 74.

[4] For specific problems as well as retail executives' comments on this matter, see "Wanted: Someone to Watch the Store," *Business Week*, September 19, 1970, pp. 52 ff.

[5] For a more thorough discussion of this organizational change, see Richard L. Lies, "Some Current Trends in Retail Organizational Thinking," *Stores*, February, 1972, pp. 14 and 31–32.

[6] Some of the types of organizational changes are illustrated by: "Up the Pyramid . . . er . . . Doughnut . . . er . . . Beehive!" *Nations Business*, January, 1972; "Is the Pyramid Crumbling?" *International Management*, July, 1971.

QUESTIONS AND ASSIGNMENTS

1. Explain what is meant by the term "retail organization."
2. Assume that a small retail store has three full-time employees and three part-timers. Explain the consequences of underorganization in the small store. Contrast with the consequences of overorganization in an extremely large store.
3. Should a store manager discourage the existence of informal organization in his store? Why or why not?
4. Assume that an automobile dealership employs 25 people. Construct an organization chart showing how you think the firm should be organized, and give a brief job description for each person. You may wish to visit a local dealership to obtain "ideas." Explain and support your organizational arrangement.
5. Indicate by means of two simplified organization charts differences in the degree of specialization for a small and a large store.
6. A large shoe store handles many types of shoes and boots for men, women, and children. Develop an organization chart for merchandising, using products or merchandise as the basis of organizing. Would such an organizational arrangement make sense to you?
7. Indicate the principal ways in which a large chain store organization differs from a large, one-unit department store organization.
8. Present arguments for a separation of the buying and selling functions in a large department store with six branch stores.
9. If two or three executives share the top position in a firm, wouldn't this simply add to the confusion? How could utter chaos be prevented?
10. Discuss what you believe should be the duties and responsibilities of a director of consumer affairs in a large department store. Is such a position necessary?

ANSWERS TO REVIEW BOX QUESTIONS

Box 6:1
1. organization
2. overorganization; underorganization
3. formal; informal

Box 6:2
1. the degree of specialization of employees
2. functions; products; geography
3. product lines
4. functions or activities

Box 6:3
1. the department manager
2. buying; selling

Box 6:4
1. (1) control (2) store operations (3) promotion (4) personnel
2. operations

Box 6:5
1. as equal in status
2. the lack of adequate merchandise information by store personnel
3. planning; thinking; conferring

Questions and Assignments

Staffing the Retail Organization

No matter how carefully a firm's organization is planned and carried out, no matter how appealing its image, design, and location, its ultimate success depends upon the people who work there. Retailing is a "people business," and, as such, it is subject to "people problems."

Well-qualified, well-trained employees are not easy to find and keep. Lack of money to add to or improve staff, weaknesses in recruitment programs and selection processes, faulty training programs, and lack of attention to motivation and leadership are some of the reasons for personnel problems in retail firms.

If a retail operation is having such problems, it must find a solution. It literally cannot *afford* to ignore the situation.[1] Not only do stores have to be concerned about sales and profits that are lost because of ineffective employees; they must also consider that their largest single expense is payroll. Depending upon the type of store, it is not at all unusual for one-third to one-half of total expenses to be payroll expenses. Obviously, this expenditure must pay off in increased sales volume and profits if a firm is to survive and prosper.

GOOD PEOPLE ARE HARD TO FIND

Small store owner-managers have frequent contact with customers. In the larger store, however, it's usually those people at the lowest level of the organization hierarchy who have the most contact with customers. A single incident of employee rudeness or unconcern can drive away a customer.

Quite possibly, unsatisfactory employee-customer relations produce more lost customers than does inadequate merchandise, as is illustrated in the incident below.

A shopper entered a department store intent upon purchasing a pair of slacks and a sport coat. One employee was assisting another customer, and two employees were chatting. After briefly examining the sport coat offerings, the potential customer chose one of a desirable style and the proper size. Taking the coat over to the pants rack, the customer sought a contrasting color. Meanwhile the two employees continued to chat and offered no help to the customer, who finally returned the coat to its proper place and left the store thinking, "They don't seem to be interested in getting my business. I'll see what the store next door has." A customer was lost, but not because of poor merchandise selection or the lack of proper size. With the intense competition facing most retailers today, a store cannot afford inattentive or apathetic employees. Customers tend to generalize on the basis of their experience. Thus, one or two experiences with poor service may convince them to avoid the store thereafter.

What Are the Problems?

With continued increases in competition, retailers have been caught in a profit squeeze. Price competition and rising costs have put increased pressure on gross margins, forcing them downward. Since all expenses and profits must be covered by gross margin, retailers have tried to curtail expenses rather than suffer lower profits. With labor costs representing the most significant expense item, profits decrease as payroll increases. Although salaries of retail personnel have risen in recent years, decreasing profits cause retailers to resist salary boosts.

PROFIT SQUEEZE

Salaries in most areas of retailing are lower than in similar jobs in wholesaling, manufacturing, transportation, and utilities. For example, the average hourly wage of nonsupervisory retail employees in 1973 was $2.87, as contrasted with $4.12 in wholesaling, $4.07 in manufacturing, and $5.04 in transportation and public utilities.[2] To increase labor rates in retailing to compete with other major industries would, in effect, force higher retail prices. With the normal demand situation, an increase in price ordinarily leads to a decrease in sales and profits.

Retailing is thus caught in a situation whereby higher salaries are needed to attract and retain more capable personnel, while increases in salaries will decrease demand and, probably, profits. Most retailers have attempted to hold the line on wages rather than risk decreased demand. In some cases, retailers have cut back on the total number of employees in order to keep labor costs constant as wages go up. This is not to say that salaries for retail employees have not been increasing—they have, and in

"Wish me luck, . . . I'm going in and ask for a raise . . ."

some cases, significantly. Indeed this is another reason for the profit squeeze in retailing.

RETAILING'S REPUTATION

How many people do you know who really want to work in retailing? Unfortunately, there probably are too few to satisfy the demand for the "right" kind of employees. Part of retailing's stigma is brought about by changing social attitudes. Retailing is largely a matter of serving consumers. As such, the retail salesperson particularly is placed in the role of serving others. Although many young people today want to "be of service," apparently they want to serve outside the business environment. Business service is viewed much less favorably than social service. As one large chain store president observed, "Everybody's an aristocrat today—nobody wants to be a servant."[3]

The life of a typical retail salesperson is not usually an easy one. The extended hours of retail stores may cause employees to work nights, Saturdays, and even Sundays. This tends to disrupt normal family life and present stresses not found with the normal 9:00 to 5:00 work day. In addition, the physical aspects of retail selling are demanding. Normally, the salesperson spends long hours standing and walking, often stooping and reaching for merchandise. Some salespeople must move merchandise from the stockroom to the sales floor, and this may be physically taxing.

Retail selling can also be emotionally fatiguing. Serving rude, overbearing customers and attempting to meet their demands can be frustrating. Under a commission or bonus compensation system, competing with other salespeople for customers forces the salesperson to always be "on his toes." Furthermore, exactness in making change, following specific instructions in writing charge sales, delivery instructions, and the like can all be emotionally tiring, especially during very busy periods.

Despite the fact that many nonsupervisory retail employees enjoy a comfortable standard of living on a middle to high five-figure income, retailing is viewed as a low-paid occupation. To a certain extent this view is correct, as we saw in the comparison of wages discussed above. Thus many people take a job in retailing until they find the job they really want. This includes students graduating from high school and college, housewives who return to the workforce, and men trained for other occupations who are "between jobs." With this situation, can there really be much doubt as to why both retailers and customers are dissatisfied with the quality of retail personnel?

FLUCTUATIONS IN SALES ACTIVITY

Sales in retail stores do not occur on a steady hour-to-hour, day-to-day, month-to-month basis. Most stores experience sales peaks and valleys. As a result, the number of employees needed also fluctuates. Thus many retailers need part-time and short-time employees.

Despite efforts to get customers to shop earlier in the week, many supermarkets find that 70 to 80 percent of their business occurs on Thursdays, Fridays, and Saturdays, with more than 50 percent occurring on Fridays and Saturdays. Some discount stores and department stores do as much as 50 percent of their annual volume between Thanksgiving and Christmas. Service stations find much of their business comes while people are on their way to and from work. Some cafeterias do 80 to 90 percent of their daily volume in three one-hour periods, while other restaurants achieve the same results from a three-hour dinner business.

The employee problems that accompany such sales fluctuations are obvious. Sufficient personnel to meet the needs of customers at peak times cannot be employed at all times. Most retailers employ extra people during maximum business periods. For example, department stores frequently double their staff during Christmas time. Although some employees are part-timers, others are more aptly called *short-timers*. These short-timers may work full time—that is, a forty-hour week—for the four- or five-week Christmas period. The store also may employ many short-timers at other busy times such as the Easter season and the back-to-school period. Using short-timers on a continuing, as-needed basis can greatly simplify a store's personnel and training requirements. Many department stores maintain a list of housewives and students for meeting their peak work load needs.

In contrast, *part-timers* usually work on a continuing basis, but work fewer hours per week or per day than regular employees. For example, supermarkets often employ high school students in the late afternoon or evening hours and on weekends. Department stores, too, employ part-time people for these shifts.

Branch department stores, discount houses, and other stores which have extended store hours well into the evening, often employ people who work evenings only. These employees are often called *LNOs*, or some similar name, to indicate that they work only on *late night open* hours. For example, a full-time bank teller may work two nights a week in the cashier's office of a department store. Such an employee is already well-trained in handling money and has only to learn the store's system of operation before becoming a valuable part-time employee.

Many stores maintain a list of "extras" who are on call, as needed, typically on an irregular basis. These people usually do not want a full-time job with the store but are willing to work occasionally as the need for extra help arises.

Is There an Answer?

A reason that small retailers frequently give for selling their business or going out of business is, "I simply can't find good, reliable employees, and I can't do all the work myself." Solutions involve either using fewer employees, continuing to try to obtain and train employees who are capable, reliable, and productive, or perhaps paying higher wages. One major reason for the rapid growth of self-service stores has been the difficulty and expense of securing adequate sales personnel.

Of course, self-service will not work for all retailers. Some customers want or need sales assistance in making purchases. In other cases the nature of the merchandise or the image of the store requires personal selling. With expensive technical products such as television sets, automobiles, or major appliances, customers often have questions they want answered before making a purchase decision. The same is true of custom-made draperies, carpeting, and certain fashion items. In addition, self-service creates a "discount aura" that would be inconsistent with the image a store might be trying to project.

It is doubtful whether retailing could ever become completely self-service. But this type of selling has been completely successful for some stores in various classes of merchandise. Simply because self-service reduces the need for personnel, it has enabled some stores to cope with the employee problem.

The remaining alternative requires retailers to do a better job of personnel management. The staffing function is so important to most retailers, who can neither go out of business nor convert to self-service, that the remainder of this chapter is devoted to the specific task of personnel management. The nature of the staffing function is essentially the same in both small and large stores. The major difference is that greater specialization is needed in the large store, while in the small store the owner-manager may carry out most of the activities personally.

REVIEW BOX 7:1

1. Retailing firms, as well as other types of businesses, suffer from "_____ problems."
2. The two key ingredients for successful merchandising are the right merchandise and _____.
3. The staffing problem of retailers has three root causes. They are: (a) the profit squeeze, (b) retailing's poor reputation, and (c) _____.
4. If a retailer can't or doesn't want to go out of business and can't switch to self-service, the only alternative remaining to overcome staffing problems is to _____.

SELECTION AND TRAINING OF EMPLOYEES

Because the success or failure of a firm is strongly related to the quality of people who work there, the finding, hiring, and training of satisfactory employees comprise one of the most important functions in any retail operation.

Manpower Planning and Recruiting

Planning for manpower needs, although essential in all types of organizations, is often neglected. Manpower planning basically involves two activities: estimating the number of people needed and setting the qualitative requirements of jobs. Manpower planning is more commonly used in large store organizations than in small ones. However, even the small retailer will find it helpful to plan ahead for peak periods or for expansion.

Since the volume of retail business fluctuates, planning to meet these fluctuations is exceedingly important. Personnel needs should be anticipated so that better employees may be obtained. Stores should prepare a *personnel budget* indicating the number and function of people to be employed per day, per week, and per season. Such planning will pay rewards through increased employee productivity and, ultimately, through higher profits.

Once personnel needs have been established, *job descriptions* should

DETERMINING THE REQUIREMENTS

be prepared. These are written summaries of specific duties, responsibilities, and relationships on the job. Job descriptions should be based upon *job analysis*, which involves studying the job to identify significant activities to be performed. Some job descriptions specifically state the traits or abilities the individual should possess to perform the job satisfactorily. Enumerating these traits or abilities is called *job specification*.

Most retail firms do not draw up job descriptions. Although many managers have had personnel courses or have been exposed to the ideas of job descriptions, they often feel too much work is involved in the development of such descriptions. In many cases these are the same managers who complain about inadequate personnel. Perhaps the problem is that the wrong type of people are being recruited and trained. Without job descriptions, it is even possible that the job may be misrepresented to potential employees. Job descriptions serve as the foundation for other staffing activities.

The story is told about an aggressive young representative of a university extension program. The young man called upon farmers to try to sell them a pamphlet published by the extension service which explained soil conservation and better farming practices. Calling upon a local farmer who was busily working on a piece of machinery, the young man proceeded to tell him all about the pamphlet and how it could contribute to more successful farming. Asked if he would like a copy, the farmer replied, "Young man, I already know how to farm better than I'm doing." Perhaps the same holds true for retail managers. Perhaps they know about job descriptions, but are not using them. It is possible that in a very small store the owner-manager has the specific duties well enough in mind that formal job descriptions are unnecessary; in larger stores, however, they are very necessary.

RECRUITING AND THE LAW

Recruiting involves activities used to attract applicants for positions in the firm. As a result of federal legislation, businesses face some constraints upon recruiting and employment practices. The laws essentially reveal a change in social attitudes toward employment practices. Retailers should be cognizant of these laws, since the penalties for noncompliance can be severe.

The *Equal Pay Act of 1963* prohibits discrimination in pay on the basis of sex. Retailers were not affected by this act until 1966 when the first court suit was filed. Although this suit was unsuccessful, several more have been filed in recent years. At the time of this writing, the appeal process is still continuing, so the effect on retailers is unknown. The implications for retailers, though, are quite clear. Great care should be taken in setting wage and salary rates so as not to discriminate against women.[4] Pay rates should be set on the basis of the job to be performed regardless of who fills the position.

Title VII of the Civil Rights Act of 1964 prohibits discrimination in employment on the basis of race, color, religion, sex, or national origin. The act created an Equal Employment Opportunity Commission to ensure compliance with the law. The law dictates that employers not only exercise care to see that discrimination on these bases does not occur, but also take steps to eliminate practices which might be interpreted as discriminatory. Special care should be taken in the wording of employment ads and in the type of information requested on employment applications.

Legislators were primarily concerned with racial discrimination in the debate which preceded the passage of the act. The so-called "sleeper" in the law was the prohibition of sex discrimination. A large number of the cases filed with the Equal Employment Opportunity Commission allege discrimination on the basis of sex. Retailers have probably employed less sex discrimination than other types of employers. There are large numbers of women executives in retailing, for example. Still, retailers must exercise care that they do not "sex type" jobs when no basis for such discrimination exists. For example, there is no reason why a repair person need be a man nor a secretary, a woman.

The *Age Discrimination in Employment Act of 1967* also affects retailers. This act was designed to protect people from age forty to sixty-five against discrimination in hiring, compensation, and firing. Since the act does not prohibit discrimination against those younger than forty or older than sixty-five, it, in effect, gives preferential treatment to the forty to sixty-five age group. The act was passed as a result of many employers refusing to hire people over a certain age, regardless of qualifications.

In addition to federal statutes, there are many state laws that prohibit certain kinds of discrimination. The retailer should be aware of all of these laws, since ignorance is seldom an adequate defense. Recruiting practices and procedures should be constantly reviewed to assure full compliance with current legislation.

Certainly most people do not question the use of ability or aptitude tests as a condition of employment. For instance, it is customary to require applicants for a typing position to take a simple typing test. Figure 7-1 is an example of a simple mathematics test given to applicants for sales positions in one store.

The use of psychological tests, however, is not nearly as well accepted. Probably the most widely used psychological test is the personality test, usually designed to measure the existence or absence of certain traits, attitudes, or behavioral characteristics. Many question the validity of such tests. Frequently, they have been developed for some purpose other than employment. Also, they may be culturally biased so that they discriminate unfairly against some applicants. Such tests should be used only if they accurately predict future job performance, and even then, invasion of privacy should be guarded against. In all cases, managers should seek professional guidance in selecting and administering such tests and in interpreting the test results.

FIGURE 7-1

A sample mathematics aptitude test

ADD:

1. $2.41
   +1.13

2. $3.25
   +1.95

SUBTRACT:

3. $1.67
   -1.46

4. $17.34
   - 7.42

MULTIPLY:

5. $2.68
   x   5

6. $8.97
   x   7

PLEASE FIGURE THE FOLLOWING TO THE NEAREST CENT:

7. What is 7% of $7.23? _____

8. What is 8% of $3.80? _____

9. A customer purchases three shirts at $7.98 each. What is the total amount of the purchase if you include 5% sales tax?

   _____

10. How much would you charge for one item if it were priced at "3 for $2.95"? (include 4% sales tax).

    _____

(Please use back of sheet for figuring)

RECRUITING SOURCES

A widely used source of retail employees for all types of stores is *walk-ins*. Larger stores with personnel departments frequently receive many voluntary applications from people who think the store would be a good place to work. In periods of relatively high unemployment, many stores are inundated with applicants. In many cases the applicants are not well qualified for vacant positions, but the general thought is that it takes no experience to sell in a retail store. Thus a large number of walk-in applicants are marginal, at best. Even if no openings exist, many stores maintain lists of the more qualified applicants for later reference.

The reception received by a walk-in applicant is extremely important to the store. This is an opportunity for effective public relations, even if the store has no openings. The way the applicant is treated is apt to have a lasting impact. Many applicants are nervous and unsure of themselves, and a brush-off or rude turn-down may drive away an existing or potential customer. A polite, friendly receptionist in the employment office can contribute favorably to a store's image.

Another source of applicants is recommendation by present employees. Although this method is widely used and recommended, some caution is necessary. The problem is that employees may be unduly influenced by friendship and may not objectively evaluate their friends. In addition, since employees may tend to recommend people like themselves, the value and ability of the present employees should be considered. Some firms have found employee recommendations to be a poor source of successful employees.

Educational institutions can be an excellent recruiting source. High schools and junior colleges with distributive education programs offer an excellent source of employees. Frequently a retail business, through cooperation with a school, can obtain part-time employees who are interested in retailing. Upon completing their studies, such students are often hired as regular, full-time employees. Many retailers rely upon colleges and universities as a source of employees for management training programs.

Both private and public employment agencies are used by some retailers in their recruiting efforts. Often employment agencies will do a certain amount of screening, thereby limiting the number of applicants the retailer needs to interview. In some large metropolitan areas, there are private employment agencies which specialize in retail and clerical recruitment.

Help-wanted advertisements are frequently used by retailers. These range all the way from advertisements for executive personnel in the *Wall Street Journal* to a sign placed in the store window. The most frequently used source is the classified section of local newspapers. This type of ad may be especially useful when a large number of employees are desired for temporary employment.

Selection and Hiring

The recruiting effort seeks applicants from which to select employees. The *selection* process is distinct from recruiting and is concerned with determining which applicants will be hired.

SELECTION

The selection process is not a precise procedure followed systematically by all stores. It may vary from a brief interview in small stores, with the hiring decision made on the spot, to a fairly extensive procedure in large stores. Whatever the procedure used, the aim is to match the talents and characteristics of an applicant with the requirements of a job.

Seldom are employees hired without a personal interview. Certain

employee characteristics, such as appearance and poise, are almost impossible to evaluate without at least a brief personal encounter. In the small store, a single interview is usually adequate. Normally, the owner-manager interviews an applicant and acquires enough information for an employment decision. If an applicant matches job requirements, the manager may make an on-the-spot decision, fill the job, and not spend time interviewing other applicants.

In large stores, the applicant is frequently interviewed more than once. When a formal employment application is used, a receptionist usually performs an initial screening. If an opening exists, and if the applicant passes the receptionist's screening, he or she is then interviewed by an employment interviewer who knows more details about job duties and responsibilities. Depending upon the nature of the position to be filled, the interviewer may either make the decision to hire the applicant or may refer him to the manager of the department that has the vacancy. In the latter case the employment interviewer performs a screening function, rejecting less desirable applicants and sending on to the department manager only those who appear to satisfy the job requirements. Thus the employment interviewer can make a negative decision on hiring in this situation but cannot make the final decision to hire.

The second most widely used selection device is the application form. The primary purpose of the application form is to secure information that will prove helpful in evaluating the applicant's qualifications. In addition to biographical information, the typical application form also contains space for the applicant's work history, educational background, and special skills. Review of the completed application blank also saves time for interviewers. They can obtain much information quickly from the application and can then ask questions about any entries or probe further for other information. If there are large numbers of applicants for limited positions, the use of application forms can create an unnecessary expense. Thus, some stores do a preliminary screening even before allowing an applicant to complete an application form.

Checking employees' references varies from extensive, formal follow-ups to a phone call or two. Although checking references is usually a good idea, the value of these checks is largely dependent upon the references themselves. Many application blanks request the name of the applicant's previous supervisors who can indicate the quality of an employee's work and the reason for his or her termination. In addition, some larger stores routinely run a police check to see if the applicant has encountered any difficulties with the law.

Physical examinations are normally limited to larger retail organizations. Even with these large stores, the extent of a physical varies from a simple examination by the store nurse to relatively thorough examinations by a doctor. Sometimes physical exams are required for certain employees such as warehouse and delivery personnel but not for clerical or sales personnel.

Two other practices, the administration of polygraph tests and various psychological tests, warrant consideration.[5] Many retailers use these tests as screening devices to ferret out what they consider undesirable employees. The polygraph, or lie detector, usually records blood pressure, heart beat, and perspiration, and is used to screen out potentially dishonest applicants. Because employee theft can be a more serious problem than shoplifting, stores use the polygraph in an attempt to spot applicants who have stolen from previous employers. Although almost one-fourth of the states prohibit a polygraph test as a condition of employment, most states allow voluntary testing. Many employees, sensing the employer's desire for testing, agree to take the test. In those stores where employees are represented by a union, lie detectors are not frequently used because of the union's stand that they constitute an invasion of privacy.

Stores wanting to use lie detectors for screening prospective employees should proceed cautiously. The first step would be to check whether present state law prohibits such testing. Second, managers should carefully contemplate whether some other means of screening will provide the same results and whether the use of a lie detector might really involve an invasion

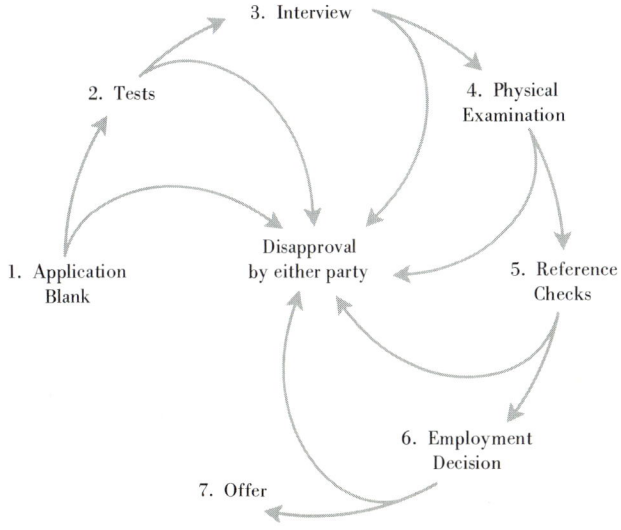

FIGURE 7-2

The selection process
Source: Wendell French, *The Personnel Management Process*, 2nd ed. (Boston: Houghton-Mifflin Company, 1970), p. 220.

Selection and Training of Employees

of privacy. Last, but certainly not least, care should be exercised in selecting a polygraph operator. There are many who profess to be competent but are not.

Just as the store may reject the applicant at any point, so too can the employee terminate the selection process. Figure 7-2 shows a typical selection process; the order of steps may vary, and all selection tools may not be used in every situation.

HIRING

The ultimate result of satisfactory selection is the decision to hire an applicant, the extension of an offer to hire, and a reaction on the part of the applicant. If not previously discussed, the offer may include a statement of the job title, specific duties, hours to be worked and salary. In many small stores the employee's acceptance is followed only by instructions about when to report to work. In large stores the new employee may be assigned an employee number and taken to the payroll department for completing tax-withholding forms. When a physical examination is not part of the selection process, the job offer may be contingent upon passing a physical exam.

Since the connection between selection and hiring is so close, some stores use one term or the other to cover both processes.

REVIEW BOX 7:2

1. _____ are summaries of the specific job duties, responsibilities, and relationships which are set forth in writing.
2. Those activities which are designed to attract applicants for job openings are referred to as _____.
3. The so-called "sleeper" in the Civil Rights Act of 1964 was the prohibition of discrimination on the basis of _____.
4. Some stores use a _____ to spot applicants who have stolen from their previous employers.
5. _____ involves determining which job applicants will be hired.

Training

Most newly hired employees require some training before they can be productive. The extent of training varies greatly among different types and sizes of stores and according to the job involved. Training programs may be either formal or informal. The tendency is for training in smaller stores to be informal while the programs in larger stores are often more formal.

A formal training program is organized and structured. It takes place according to a specific plan under a specially designated person. In contrast, informal training is largely unplanned and often occurs on a catch-as-catch-can basis. When training is informal, there is no planned program for ensuring that employees gain the knowledge needed to perform a job. Stores that claim to have no training program usually mean that their training is informal.

The distinction between centralized and decentralized training is based on how, where, and by whom the training is given. In a centralized system the responsibility for training rests with a separate department, while decentralized training takes place on the job. Centralized training is usually conducted in the training department's facilities by people who are employed only for that function. In large stores, centralized training is often used for initial training in order to ensure consistency of information concerning store policies and procedures.

CENTRALIZED OR DECENTRALIZED TRAINING

Most small stores employ decentralized training. Such training typically takes place on the job, but it may also involve home study books or tape recordings. In many cases the primary training consists of having an employee show the new employee "the ropes." In the very small store, the manager may handle this duty. To a certain extent, all retail operations employ some form of decentralized training, since some knowledge must be imparted and reinforced by a department manager or supervisor on the job.

Although there are arguments favoring both centralized and decentralized training, the preferable type is largely dependent upon the situation and the training needs. Figure 7-3 illustrates a recommended training program for a large department store. Both centralized and decentralized training are included. Note that there are four separate groups of employees to be trained: executive selling personnel, executive non-selling personnel, non-executive selling personnel, and non-executive non-selling personnel. Each group has slightly differing needs, and the training recommended recognizes these differences. Note that the training for the two non-executive groups emphasizes decentralized training more than does that for the two executive groups.

Figure 7-3 emphasizes the need for continuous employee training. Too often, only initial training is given employees. Most employees, however, need additional training to increase their productivity as well as to maintain a high level of morale. Stores which have only initial training are often neglecting an important employee need.

Training can take place on the job or in the classroom, depending upon the store's particular situation and the desired result. Some firms even prefer that employees teach themselves at home using training tapes or programmed instruction.

METHODS OF TRAINING

Selection and Training of Employees

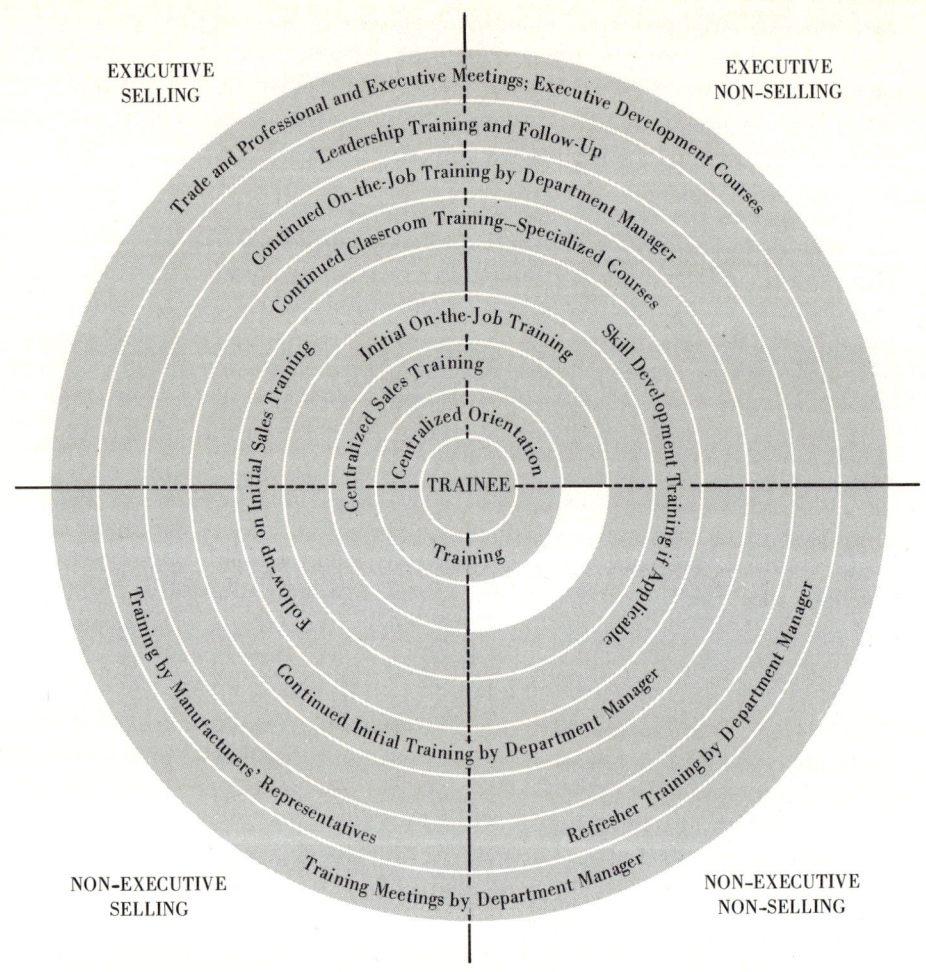

FIGURE 7-3

A recommended training program

On-the-Job. Of all methods, on-the-job training is most widely used in retailing to impart specific details of the job to the trainee. Frequently this involves little more than showing trainees how to accomplish a specific task, then letting them perform the task under the trainer's supervision. When a manager or supervisor conducts the training, the trainee usually receives adequate attention and learns the task correctly.

When an experienced employee, often called a sponsor, conducts the training, there is danger of too little specific help. This is particularly true when the sponsor is expected to take on the training in addition to a regular workload. For example, if a selling employee working on a commission is expected to continue to sell as well as train the new employee, the salesperson may neglect the training duties since such activity may reduce the opportunity for commissions. The same holds true for a non-selling employee who continues to have a production standard to meet in addition to training responsibilities. The sponsor system works best when the sponsors are re-

SPOTLIGHT

How important is a clean uniform?

Stephen Crane Associates is a management consulting company that manages specialty restaurants for Sheraton Hotel Corporation. Mr. Don Avalier is a vice-president of Stephen Crane. Here he shares some of his ideas on training and supervision:

You can't talk about productivity without talking about training. It's crucial to our business. Before we opened our restaurant in Honolulu, I spent 88 days there working with our employees. There was not a waiter, not a busboy who walked out on that floor without 30 hours of classroom training. A waiter could walk into the the kitchen blindfolded. He knew where to find the pickup area and the pantry. He knew where the drop-off area was for dirty dishes. He knew where everything was. And he could take any item on the menu and tell you how it was made. We had almost a week of classes, where we did nothing but break down the menu. We had them taste the dishes.

One year later, we had not lost one waiter. The men are making a good living. They know their jobs. Those 88 days and a considerable amount of money was time and money well spent. And once a man is on your payroll, it pays you to keep him there. We never let a man go without a termination interview. Instead of having to train new people all the time, you should take some of the money and spend it keeping your old people. If an employee leaves, there has got to be a reason. And unless you know why employees leave, and do something to correct these problems, you will always have a high turnover.

Just recently, one man was leaving us. After we talked to him, we found out that his only real complaint was the fact that he had trouble getting a clean uniform. It's a little thing. But it was important to him. This man had pride in himself, and he wouldn't work in a dirty uniform. There was a breakdown in communications between the linen room and him. It got squared away and the guy was happy to stay. He gets a clean uniform every day, and that was all he wanted. The fact that we cared enough about him to listen to him and solve his problem was important to him—and to us.

Source: Don Avalier, "The 'Ate' Theory of Productivity," *Fast Food*, February 1973, p. 80.

lieved of some other responsibilities to ensure that their income is not reduced and their workload is not unreasonable.

Unfortunately, on-the-job training sometimes involves placing new employees on the job and expecting them simply to pick up information whenever and however they can. Such a situation is inefficient and potentially disastrous. No one is aware of what the new employee has *not* learned until a crisis occurs.

On-the-job training is often used beneficially for continued training of regular employees. Such training is also widely used to describe new merchandise, upcoming special sales, changes in procedures, and fashion changes. On-the-job training may also be an integral part of supervision, with the supervisor making suggestions to individual employees that will help them increase their production or improve their skills.

Classroom. This method of formal training is centralized. It is especially useful for training groups of people at one time and is widely used as part of initial training in larger stores. The classroom method is especially effective for introducing new employees to the store. It may cover such things as store policies and organization, employee benefits, and other general information necessary to the new employee's orientation.

A training classroom with a video unit and samples of store equipment

Initial sales training is often conducted in the classroom where trainees can actually practice selling merchandise, writing saleschecks, and operating cash registers. Films, lectures, role playing, discussions, simulators, demonstrations, and case studies can be used in classroom training to facilitate learning. Different techniques may be used to accomplish different training objectives. A unique variation of classroom training is the use of videotape. In some cases the video playback units are actually placed on the selling floor for viewing by employees prior to store opening hours. The use of videotapes for imparting merchandise knowledge is becoming more widespread in chain stores and department store branches.[6]

Self-Teaching. Some firms believe that the primary responsibility for gaining necessary job knowledge rests with the employee. Such stores make materials available to the employee and recommend that he learn off the job. Some of these materials are conducive to home study, while others require the employee to use a special place in the store for studying. One chain provides audiotapes covering such items as courtesy and attention to customer needs, the techniques of suggestion selling, and trading up. New employees can conveniently take the tapes home and play them on their own recorders or on those provided by the firm.

Programmed instruction can aid certain kinds of learning. Material is typically presented in small segments, or "bits," followed by a series of questions. If responses are incorrect, further instruction is given, followed by an opportunity to "try again." A primary advantage of programmed in-

To take the register reading (x) at the close of the day,	left
a) place Salescheck Envelope _____ up on printing table	
b) move lever to the _____ and _____ to " _____ _____ " position	
c) press your assigned drawer key ___	
d) press _____ _____ to operate the register and open the _____ .	

After taking the register reading (x), move lever to the right and down to the " _____ " position.	a) face
	b) right
	    up
	    read clerks
	c) A
	d) motor bar drawer

Sample of programmed instruction for salesclerks. Answers are given next to the succeeding question.

struction is that trainees can proceed at their own pace. Although programmed instruction materials should be developed only by those who are experienced in this area, this type of instruction can be relatively inexpensive. This is especially true when the developmental cost can be spread over a large number of trainees and a long period of time; even so, programmed instruction has been adopted only by a few very large retailers.

REVIEW BOX 7:3

1. Those retail stores that claim not to have a training program usually mean that their training is _____.
2. The major distinction between centralized and decentralized training is _____.
3. The most common method of retail training is _____ training.
4. The method of training that is appropriate for large groups and is especially effective for covering such topics as store policies and procedures and store organization is _____.

MOTIVATING EMPLOYEES

Although researchers and business people have reached some understanding of what motivates employees, they have not yet reached the point where they agree on how to motivate them. Since an examination of the various theories of motivation is beyond the scope of this book, we will confine our discussion to specific ways of motivating employees: compensation, fringe benefits, and leadership style.[7]

Compensation

Many early management theorists saw motivation as being solely related to money. Generally, they believed that to get more work out of an employee it was only necessary to pay him more money. Some retailers today still seem to adhere to this method of motivation. However, enlightened managers recognize that, although money can be a motivator of desired behavior, other benefits, conditions, and attitudes are also important.

Employees view compensation not only in terms of what it will buy, but also as a measure of their worth and an indication of their status. The level of pay allows employees to quantify their apparent value to the company, and the frequency and amount of increases serve as indicators of their success or failure.

There are two primary ways to compensate retail store personnel: straight salary and straight commission. Combinations of these plans may also be used.

Straight salary is the most widely used plan of compensation. This method essentially involves "buying" an employee's time. The employee is paid a stated amount per hour, per week, or per month.

STRAIGHT SALARY

The rate of pay is based upon the general performance and qualifications of the employee. Where productivity is difficult to measure precisely or when the employee is required to perform a variety of tasks, the straight salary plan is about the only equitable method of pay. Most sales supporting personnel and executive personnel are paid a straight salary, and this plan is even used by small stores for selling personnel, since these employees are often required to perform tasks other than selling.

Under the straight commission plan the retail store "buys" employees' productivity rather than their time. Employees are paid a percentage of what they produce—most often sales. Straight commission for selling personnel has traditionally been limited to certain kinds of items, especially automobiles, boats and other expensive sporting goods, major appliances, furniture, radios and television sets, shoes, and sometimes expensive apparel items such as furs, formal wear, and better men's suits.

STRAIGHT COMMISSION

The straight commission plan provides a strong incentive for making sales, so strong in fact that employees may concentrate on "live" prospects and neglect "lookers." The net effect, of course, can be very aggressive selling techniques at the expense of the service aspect.

Straight commissions for non-selling employees are uncommon and are used only by very large retail enterprises. The difficulty involves coming up with a measurable work unit and a continuous flow of work. For example, in marking and receiving, the merchandise is not standardized, and speed can vary greatly depending on the nature of the merchandise.

Some compensation plans feature aspects of the two basic methods. Usually the objective is to take advantage of favorable attributes of straight salary while gaining additional incentive through commissions. Again, such combinations are more typical for selling employees than for those in non-selling positions.

COMBINATION PLANS

One combination plan features a straight salary plus a commission on the employee's total net sales. The amount of straight salary and the percentage commission paid are dependent upon the degree of incentive required and the nature of other activities the employee is expected to perform.

Another combination plan involves a bonus. Here the employee receives a stated salary and, in addition, a commission on all sales above a previously set quota. Most frequently quotas are determined by applying past payroll as a percent of sales to determine the sales-per-employee needed to achieve this percentage in a coming period. Sales above this level entitle the employee to a commission or bonus. For example, assume there are five employees in a department, and each one receives a salary of $100 per week. In the past, sales payroll as a percent of sales in the department has been 6 percent. Dividing $500 (five employees' salaries) by .06, we find that total departmental sales will have to be $8,333.33 per week to achieve the 6 percent figure. Thus each employee has to sell $1,666.67 worth of merchandise to "pay his own way." The department can afford to pay a bonus or commission on all sales over this amount. The commission rate may be the 6 percent to maintain the "standard" payroll expense, or it may be lower. Lower percentages are justified because even though some employees may not sell $1,666.67 in merchandise, the store must still pay their full salary, thereby incurring a higher payroll percentage expense for those employees.

Frequently, store or department managers are compensated on a bonus arrangement. The bonus may be determined by a set quota, or it can be based on the profitability of the store or department. One danger of paying a bonus on profitability is that the manager may "milk" the department or store from a short-range viewpoint rather than act to ensure long-run profitability. For example, the manager could acquire merchandise that appears to be a good bargain but will not have a long life. By the time complaints begin to be voiced, the manager has departed for greener pastures. A manager can also fail to take needed markdowns. The manager leaves the store with an inventory containing largely unsalable merchandise—unless drastic markdowns are taken. The real value of the inventory is thus much lower than shown on the books. For store or department managers, the straight salary method with frequent salary reviews to accomplish both short- and long-range goals is often used.

Fringe Benefits

There is considerable doubt as to whether fringe benefits contribute directly to motivation. Stores that have an exceptional benefits package may be known as a good place to work. Other than this, however, indications are that increased fringes do not contribute to employee motivation. This does not mean that retail stores can neglect fringe benefits, for a certain level of benefits package is necessary for the firm to attract and hold satisfactory employees. Fringe benefits are often viewed by employees as part of the total compensation package.

Fringe benefits fall into three general categories:

1. Health, disability, unemployment, and retirement plans
2. Paid vacations and holidays

3. Employee discounts and other miscellaneous services

Health, disability, and unemployment insurance plans are designed to "protect" an employee from certain of life's hazards. Most large stores offer a group hospitalization plan and an in-house health service. The health service or store hospital is usually staffed by a registered nurse.

Old age and survivors' insurance, better known as social security, requires contributions from both the employer and employee. Many firms also provide supplemental retirement plans. The plans of retailing giants such as Sears and Montgomery Ward are well known and cherished by employees of these firms.

Most stores, including small ones, offer employees paid vacations after they have worked a specified time. A typical arrangement is a one-week paid vacation after one year and two weeks off after the second year. Many stores also provide employees with a minimum of three to five paid holidays per year.

Most retail stores, with the exception of supermarkets, offer employees discounts on purchases made in the store. Discounts typically range from 10 to 20 percent. Such discounts create a favorable attitude toward the employer.

Many retailers sponsor employee activities such as bowling leagues, golf tournaments, picnics, Christmas parties, and other employee participation groups.

Most fringe benefits are not motivators so much as they are indicators of the concern and support of retailers for their employees.

Managers and Motivation

Perhaps too often management becomes so concerned with actual attempts at motivating employees to better performance that the importance of employee satisfaction as part of the motivational process is overlooked. Satisfaction results from the relative fulfillment of an individual's needs, and both compensation and fringe benefits contribute to the satisfaction of certain needs of some individuals. However, contemporary thinking indicates that most people have a whole range of needs, and the ability of these two elements to satisfy those needs is incomplete. Thus it takes more than money and fringe benefits to motivate workers.

The environment created by managers is thought to be of primary importance in motivating employees. The environment does not refer specifically to physical surroundings but more broadly to the total situation in which the employee finds himself. To a great extent, this "situation" is determined by the approach that management takes toward employees.

ASSUMPTIONS ABOUT WORKERS

Motivating Employees

Douglas McGregor identified two distinct views (or sets of assumptions) that managers can hold about workers.[8] He identified these assumptions as Theory X and Theory Y. Under Theory X, a manager assumes that:

1. The average human being has an inherent dislike of work and will avoid it if he can.
2. Because of this human characteristic of disliking work, most people must be coerced, controlled, directed, or threatened with punishment to get them to put forth adequate effort toward the achievement of organizational objectives.
3. The average human being prefers to be directed, wishes to avoid responsibility, has relatively little ambition, and wants security above all.

In contrast, a manager operating on the basis of Theory Y holds that:

1. The expenditure of physical and mental effort in work is as natural as play or rest. Depending upon controllable conditions, work may be a source of satisfaction (and will be voluntarily performed) or a source of punishment (and will be avoided if possible).
2. External control and the threat of punishment are not the only means for bringing about effort toward organizational objectives. Man will exercise self-direction and self-control in the service of objectives to which he is committed.
3. Commitment to objectives is a function of the rewards associated with their achievement. The most significant of such rewards, e.g., the satisfaction of ego and self-actualization needs, can be direct products of effort directed toward organizational objectives.
4. The average human being learns, under proper conditions, not only to accept but to seek responsibility.
5. The capacity to exercise a relatively high degree of imagination, ingenuity, and creativity in the solution of organizational problems is widely, not narrowly, distributed in the population.
6. Under the conditions of modern industrial life, the intellectual potentialities of the average human being are only partly utilized.

Theory X is consistent with the more traditional management approach, while Theory Y is more congruent with the results of recent behavioral research. Although sometimes misinterpreted, McGregor did not mean to specify that Theory X assumptions necessarily lead a manager to a "hard line" approach and Theory Y a "soft" approach. Either approach is possible under either set of assumptions.

The assumptions held by supervisors or managers do set the tone for the relationship between them and their subordinates. Managers actually create much of the work environment for the employee and determine, to a certain extent, which employee needs can be satisfied and to what extent that satisfaction may act as a motivator.

One way to view the environment created is according to leadership style. Figure 7-4 indicates possibilities for different leadership behavior based upon the use of an authoritarian versus a democratic approach. It is only logical that the manager operating with Theory X assumptions will tend toward the left of the continuum, while one making Theory Y assumptions will tend toward the right side. Tannenbaum and Schmidt suggest that before choosing a particular type of leadership behavior, managers should consider their own characteristics, those of their subordinates, and the nature of the situation.[9]

LEADERSHIP STYLE

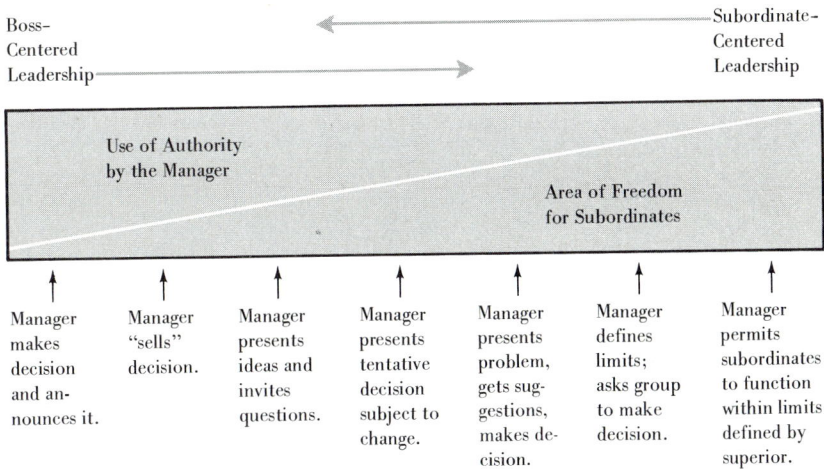

FIGURE 7-4

A leadership continuum

Source: Robert Tannenbaum and Warren H. Schmidt, "How to Choose a Leadership Pattern," *Harvard Business Review*, March–April 1958, p. 96.

Such considerations allow managers to vary their behavior, depending on conditions, from absolute direction to a high degree of freedom. One important set of variables, however, comprises the forces within subordinates. These forces are largely related to individual needs. Thus, employee needs serve a very important role in determining which leadership style will be most effective.

There is a growing body of evidence that supports the contention that employees should have a greater voice in determining how they should do their work. Generally, total freedom is not suggested or expected, for this amounts to a complete lack of leadership. Instead, what is recommended is greater freedom for subordinates to determine how work is going to be accomplished, but within the limits which have been set or defined by the superior.

Unfortunately, retailers have not made use of these and other behavioral findings to the same extent as industrial firms have. The result is that many retail employees continue to work in a very authoritarian atmosphere in which motivation comes primarily from the fear of being fired. Despite other reasons often given, this situation undoubtedly contributes to retailing's relatively high employee turnover rate and lack of increased production.

REVIEW BOX 7:4

1. Enlightened managers realize that it takes more than _____ _____ to motivate employees.
2. The most widely used method of compensating retail employees is the _____ plan.
3. Under the _____ compensation plan, a retail store "buys" an employee's productivity.
4. One of the ways managers create a work environment for employees is through _____.

CHAPTER SUMMARY

- Staffing, a major problem in retailing, includes recruiting, selecting, training, compensating, and supervising employees.
- Payroll represents the largest single expense category for most retail stores and indicates the importance of the staffing function.
- The reputation of retailing suffers from relatively low wages, a lack of understanding concerning retailing in today's society, and the type of employees attracted to retailing.
- Many stores have turned to self-service as a means of partially coping with "people problems."
- Manpower planning includes job analysis, job descriptions, and job specifications, all aimed at matching the qualifications of employees with the needs of retailers.
- Recruiting, which includes all those activities to attract applicants for jobs, must consider federal legislation which regulates recruiting and employment practices.
- Some major sources of applicants for retail jobs include "walk-ins,"

- recommendations by present employees, educational institutions, employment agencies, and advertisements.
- The selection process is concerned with deciding which people to hire from a list of applicants.
- A personal interview and an application are the two most widely used selection tools, although reference checking, physical examinations, and testing are sometimes employed.
- Formal training more precisely prescribes the content of training than does informal training.
- Decentralized training is more commonly used in retailing than centralized training. Centralized training normally concentrates the training responsibility with a separate training department within the personnel division.
- On-the-job training is the most widely used training method, although classroom training and self-teaching methods may be employed.
- Some of the factors that have an effect on employee motivation are compensation, fringe benefits, and managers' leadership styles.
- Retail employees are compensated by straight salary, straight commission, or some combination of the two.
- Fringe benefits are valuable in meeting employees' physiological and safety needs.
- Although money is important to employees, there's more to motivation than money alone.
- The work environment created by managers is an ideal way to motivate employees. Such an environment should offer employees opportunities to satisfy their higher-level needs.
- Managers need to be flexible in their leadership behavior and choose a particular pattern based upon circumstances.

CHAPTER NOTES

[1] The chief executive of an Atlanta-based apparel chain has been quoted as saying, "I would do 10% to 15% more business if I had topflight sales people right now." ("Stores Try to Crack the People Problem," *Business Week*, September 19, 1970, p. 52.)

[2] *Monthly Labor Review*, U.S. Department of Labor, August, 1974, p. 116.

[3] "Stores Try to Crack the People Problem," *Business Week*, September 19, 1970, p. 52.

[4] An interesting review of the court suits and their possible effect may be found in "Equal Pay for Women Hits Retailers," *Business Week*, January 29, 1972, pp. 76–78.

[5] Much of this discussion of lie detectors and psychological testing is based upon "Corporate Lie Detectors Come Under Fire," *Business Week*, January 13, 1973, pp. 88–90.

[6] For interesting examples of the use of video tapes, see "Lazarus Videotapes Its Own Films," *Stores*, April 1971, pp. 38 and 39; "Videotapes Help Train Staff," *Chain Store Age*, May 1969, p. 78; and "Wards Using VTR System to Build Sales Know-How," *Merchandising Weekly*, June 15, 1970, p. 4.

[7] Two widely accepted motivational theories are those of Abraham H. Maslow and Frederick Herzberg. Particulars of these theories may be found in most basic psychology texts.

[8] Douglas M. McGregor, *The Human Side of Enterprise* (New York: McGraw-Hill Book Company, 1960) pp. 33–34.
[9] Robert Tannenbaum and Warren H. Schmidt, "How to Choose a Leadership Pattern," *Harvard Business Review*, March–April 1958, p. 98.

QUESTIONS AND ASSIGNMENTS

1. How do you account for the fact that the most severe problems facing business today are human rather than technical?
2. What can the retailing industry do to correct the image that many people have of retailing as a career?
3. If a retailer is caught in the dilemma of decreasing gross margins and profits yet cannot reduce payroll costs by converting to self-service, what action can he take to increase profits?
4. Suppose that a department store with four branch stores wants to keep the branches open from 10:00 A.M. until 5:30 P.M. on Sundays. The store has a policy that none of their managerial personnel may work on Sunday. Where would you look for managers to staff the stores on Sundays?
5. Explain and illustrate the differences among job analysis, job description, and job specification.
6. Suppose a large discount house has experienced increasing losses of merchandise because of employee theft. The manager decides to subject all potential employees to a polygraph test as a part of the selection process. Assess the pros and cons of his decision and indicate whether you think he made the proper decision.
7. Assume you are the store manager of a women's ready-to-wear shop and an employee recommends a friend as a prospective employee. You have a position open, but the employee making the recommendation is your lowest producing salesperson. How would you respond to the recommendation?
8. Distinguish between the selection process and hiring.
9. Develop an outline for training employees of a drug store with twelve employees.
10. Explain how training can reduce total payroll expense as a percent of sales.
11. Discuss the merits of straight salary, straight commission, and combination compensation plans.
12. Describe how a retail store can attempt to fulfill the various categories of individual employee needs.

ANSWERS TO REVIEW BOX QUESTIONS

Box 7:1

1. people
2. sufficient qualified personnel
3. intermittent nature of sales activity
4. do a better job of personnel management

Box 7:2

1. job descriptions
2. recruiting
3. sex
4. polygraph or lie detector
5. selection

Box 7:3

1. informal
2. how, where, and by whom it is given
3. on-the-job
4. classroom training

Box 7:4

1. money
2. straight salary
3. straight commission
4. leadership style or method of supervision

RETAILING DECISION
Riser's Department Store

Riser's Department Store is a small independent outlet in a small agricultural community. Annual sales are $135,000. No other store in town offers as large a variety of merchandise. However, the town does have a family shoe store, two clothing specialty shops (one selling women's dresses and lingerie, the other women's and girls' wear), and a hardware store that could be considered competitors.

Riser's is housed in an irregularly shaped, three-story building (see diagram). The top floor is used for receiving merchandise, inventory storage, and marking. It is equipped with a wide variety of tables, shelves, and old counters, most of which have been moved up from the lower floors as they became obsolete for use there. Some merchandise has been on the third floor for as long as five years.

On the second floor, toys and housewares are displayed on a long central counter. To one side of this counter, four display tables of different sizes hold fabrics and sewing notions. On the other side of the floor are racks of men's, women's, and children's shoes.

The first floor holds men's, women's, and children's clothing departments and a luggage section. There are twelve display tables, six on each side of a main aisle. Suits, dresses, and coats are hung on racks along the walls.

There is very little storage space on either of the two selling floors, so merchandise has to be carried down from the third floor.

Although there is an elevator in Riser's, it requires an attendant, so customers are urged to use the stairs. The elevator is used almost exclusively for transporting merchandise.

The first floor has two display windows facing Main Street. At present, the Risers use them only for signs—to announce special sales or the arrival of new merchandise, for example.

Roger Riser has just inherited $25,000, and the local bank has stated it is willing to match this with a loan to improve the business.

1. How would you advise Mr. Riser to use the $50,000 to improve the store's layout and design? (See table for sales data.)

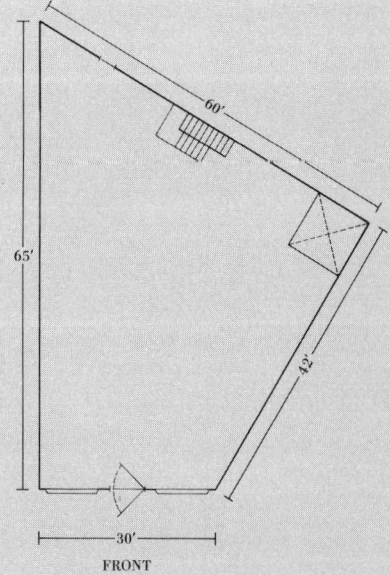

Department	Average Weekly Sales	Percent of Selling Space
First Floor		
Women's dresses and coats	$380	27
Men's casual clothes	320	22
Women's sportswear	240	15
Lingerie	200	9
Women's shoes	185	8
Men's dress clothes	145	9
Luggage and accessories (includes costume jewelery)	70	10
Second Floor		
Piece goods	$375	22
Notions	155	14
Men's and boy's shoes	215	18
Girl's and infant's shoes	185	13
Linens	150	11
Housewares	55	5
Toys	50	17

RETAILING DECISION
Goldberg Department Store

The billing and mailing section of the accounts receivable department of the Goldberg Department Store has 31 employees. The employees and their major responsibilities are indicated below:

Six pre-inspectors: check trays of accounts before they are billed to assure that all saleschecks for each account are properly filed behind that account. If sales checks are misfiled, these pre-inspectors change them to the proper account.

Ten billers: use manual billing machines to post all charges, payments, and credits to the customer accounts ledger and to mail statements to customers.

Six post-inspectors: check the accuracy of billing. Compare amounts posted against saleschecks, payment receipts, and credit slips.

One microfilm and mailing machine operator: uses high-speed microfilm and automatic feed cameras to photograph all customer statements, bills, payments, and credits. He or she also operates an automatic mailing machine that automatically inserts statements, advertising inserts, and a return envelope into a window envelope, and seals it; using a postage meter, the operator determines postage and then stacks the envelopes ready to be mailed.

Seven bill adjusters: receive customers' questions and complaints about bills both at a window and by telephone. If a mistake is discovered, they adjust customer's bill.

One reconcillation clerk: ensures that each tray of accounts is balanced on a control sheet.

Each employee in this section was hired for a specific job. However, the department manager noticed that employeees frequently traded jobs. For example, a biller would trade with a pre-inspector for a day or two at a time. Upon inquiry, the manager found that such trades were made because employees became bored with their jobs and wanted to relieve the boredom.

Construct an organization chart for the billing and mailing section of the accounts receivable department.

1. Is the work being performed in accordance with the chart?

2. What should the manager do about employees trading jobs? Allow the practice to continue? Put an immediate stop to such actions?

PART THREE

Merchandise Management

Merchandise Planning

A housewife goes to the supermarket to purchase food for the family, stops at a variety store to pick up thumb tacks and two spools of thread, then drives to the service station to get gas for the family car. Each of these transactions can be completed fairly quickly, and the shopper gives relatively little thought to the process which has preceded her purchases. She expects to find those desired items quickly and efficiently. Yet behind the scenes lie a host of activities in preparation for her visit. The merchandise planning necessary to fulfill the requirements of consumers is the subject of this chapter.

PLANNING FOR CONSUMER WANTS

Identifying *what* goods consumers will want is no easy matter. Further determination of *where* and *when* consumers will want these goods, *in what quantities* they will desire them, and *what price* they are willing to pay are all factors a retailer must consider. The planning associated with these marketing activities is referred to as *merchandising*.

Merchandise planning leads to actions designed to satisfy consumers — a difficult task. Consumers' wants and needs are constantly changing, and sometimes they are not even sure what their needs are.

Merchandise Assortments

Some confusion exists in retailing over the meaning of certain terms. Usage differs across different types or kinds of retailers. *Assortment* is one such term. There are essentially three dimensions of assortment. *Width* refers to the variety or number of different product lines a store carries. Most specialty stores such as clothing stores, shoe outlets, supermarkets, jewelry stores, and sandwich shops handle a relatively narrow assortment of merchandise. On the other hand, most department stores and large discount houses carry wide assortments. Of course, there are many variations in between.

Assortment *depth* refers to the variations available within a generic class or product line. Frequently these variations correspond to different brand names but the products may also differ by style. For example, an appliance store may carry various brands of refrigerators but also carry different sizes, colors, and styles within manufacturers' lines. Such a store would offer deep assortments. Most specialty stores mentioned above as offering relatively *narrow* assortments often carry relatively *deep* assortments.

Consistency of assortment refers to the degree to which the products carried are related. For example, in a ski shop you would expect to find not only skis and ski boots, but also ski pants and parkas, sunglasses and goggles, ski poles, after-ski boots, sweaters, and other items related to skiing and to other winter sports. A ski shop which also carries formal wear, watches, china, and draperies would not only be unusual but could be said to carry inconsistent assortments.

Certainly there is nothing inherently wrong with inconsistent assortments as long as customers know about and accept them. In small towns particularly, there are many retailers who handle inconsistent assortments and are very successful with them. There is a jewelry store in a small Colorado town which also carries ski equipment and apparel. You probably can guess this jeweler's favorite sport!

Consistency of assortment is apparently no longer as important as it once was. This is due in part to what has been called *scrambled merchandising*. Essentially, scrambling involves stocking products or product lines not traditionally carried by a particular type of store. For example, supermarkets practiced scrambled merchandising when they broadened their assortments into non-prescription drugs and other lines typically handled by drug stores. Some druggists were so concerned that they installed dairy cases in their stores and offered dairy products, bread, and other "traditional" grocery items. Such warfare was relatively short-lived, and most druggists eventually surrendered to the supermarkets, but then "raided" products—jewelry, radios, toys—from other traditional retailers.

The term scrambled merchandising may be inappropriate today, since few items seem to be "sacred" to any one particular type of store. Consumers seem to accept and perhaps even like assortment inconsistency. Note how many buy anti-freeze at the supermarket or stop by the service station to pick up a half-gallon of milk and a loaf of bread from the array of convenience goods offered by some stations.

The point is that the retailer needs to give careful consideration to the

Planning for Consumer Wants

assortment offered. This is not a one-time proposition; it must be a continuing one. An alert retailer senses the changes in consumers' needs and adjusts merchandise assortments to meet these trends.

Consider the problem of a supermarket chain which may be offered 6,000 to 7,000 new or improved items per year. This may represent as much as one-half of the number of items already carried in the average supermarket. A decision to accept a substantial number of these new offerings would result in very crowded shelves or require the elimination of an equivalent number of present items. This is a perpetual problem, not only for supermarkets but for other types of retailers as well.

Product Life Cycle

In order to make intelligent, profitable product assortment decisions, a retailer needs to understand the product life cycle. Many product classes, like old soldiers, never die; they just fade away. Knowledge of this process can prevent a retailer from making errors which might be financially disastrous.

A typical product life cycle is illustrated in Figure 8-1. Obviously, not all products follow this precise route. The curve is simply indicative of the five general phases of product life cycle:

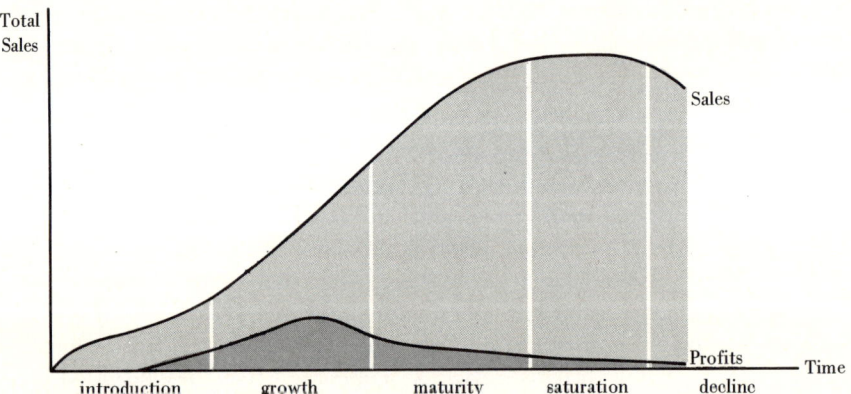

FIGURE 8-1

Product life cycle

1. *Introduction.* A product is introduced to the market. At this point, consumer awareness of the product is minimal. During this stage, heavy promotional and other introductory costs are high, resulting in little if any profit.

2. *Growth.* The results of the heavy introductory costs begin to be felt with a very rapid increase in total sales. Typically, profits reach their maximum during this stage, since margins remain relatively high and promotional costs are proportionally reduced. For some products the effects of repeat sales tend to be felt.
3. *Maturity.* By this phase the product is well known; although total sales continue to grow, they do so at a decreasing rate. Typically many competitive brands have entered the market, resulting in decreased gross margins and profits.
4. *Saturation.* A sales plateau is reached in this phase. Relatively few new customers enter the market, and some of the older customers move on to other new products. At this stage the decline of sales is relatively assured, unless new uses or new users are found for the product or unless it is substantially changed.
5. *Decline.* The decline may be very rapid — particularly when a new product dislodges the old — or it may be fairly gradual. However, once the decline begins, unless some changes are instituted in the product or the market, sales will drop continually.

It should be noted that the horizontal axis in units of time is indeterminate. Conceivably, the period involved could be as short as a few months, as with a fad, or it might be a matter of many years. The same is true with the vertical axis. Sales may reach extremely high amounts such as millions of dollars or may total only a few thousand dollars. The nature of the product under consideration is the determining factor.

When deciding to add or continue a particular item, a retailer should give attention to that product's phase in its life cycle as well as to its contribution to width, depth, and consistency of assortment. Simply because a product has reached the maturity stage is no sure indication that it should be abandoned. The major point is that consideration of the stage of the product provides more information on which to base a judgment about stocking it.

Market Segmentation

Whether intentionally or not, retailers automatically segment their market in some respects. Location of a store involves geographic segmentation, and quality of offerings and price lines further divide the total market. Neiman-Marcus, for example, has built a reputation on serving the more affluent segment of society.

Merchandise planning depends upon adequate identification of target groups of consumers before these consumers' wants and needs can be satisfied. Thus market segmentation precedes merchandise planning.

> **REVIEW BOX 8:1**
>
> 1. A store which carries only women's shoes but offers many brands and styles to choose from offers a _____ and _____ merchandise assortment.
> 2. The stocking of products "foreign" to the traditional product offerings of a store is called _____ and is contrary to the idea of consistency of assortment.
> 3. In the normal product life cycle, profits are at a maximum during the _____ stage of the cycle.

Sources of Information on Consumer Wants

Decisions on the specific merchandise to be carried must be made on the basis of target markets, stage of products in their life cycle, and assortment policies which have been developed. In addition, a retailer should examine sales data and stock lists and be alert to consumers' requests and complaints in order to judge what and how much merchandise to carry.

HISTORICAL SALES DATA

Probably the most widely used indicator of consumer wants is past sales. The assumption is that if customers have purchased a particular item in the past, they will continue to want it in the future. For some merchandise, such thinking is entirely satisfactory unless conditions change. A change in fuel supply and price, for example, would affect the demand for large and small cars. For certain classes of merchandise, however, an assumption of continuing, consistent consumer desire can be very dangerous. For example, in the fashion goods area, tastes change very rapidly, and use of historical sales data could result in merchandise inventories which will not sell without substantial markdowns.

The usefulness of historical sales data varies according to type of merchandise under consideration. A long-standing way of classifying merchandise is *staple merchandise* and *fashion merchandise*. A staple good is one in which *style* is relatively unimportant to the consumer. (Style has long been defined as "a characteristic or distinctive mode or method of expression, presentation, or conception in some field of art."[1]) Tools, hardware items, canned goods, auto batteries, and light bulbs are examples of staple goods. Consumers tend to buy these goods repeatedly, attaching little significance to style.

With today's emphasis on color and unique design, it may be difficult to draw an absolute line between staple and fashion goods. Staple items tend to change very slowly, are usually fairly standardized, and may be viewed by consumers primarily as necessities. Fashion items, on the other hand, have a shorter life span, depend less upon utilitarian functions, and are usually

SPOTLIGHT

"Don't you have anything special?"

Merchandise planning for fashion goods stores is no easy task. Offerings should be consistent with consumer wants, but in fashion it sometimes pays to be different. Consider the following:

Place: the designer department of a famous New York specialty store. Time: recently.

A woman, obviously searching for something to wear, passed from one row of racks to another. She worked her way to the back of the selling floor without pausing. She found nothing that she wanted to try on.

Then she saw a door and peered through it. A saleswoman stopped her. The customer was inadvertently heading for the stockroom.

"You can't go in there," said the saleswoman.

"Oh, is that all there is?" said the would-be customer, wistfully.

"Yes, madam, everything we have is on the floor."

The woman kept looking around restlessly, as if there just had to be something else, something that was just what she had in mind. The saleswoman was understandably puzzled by her behavior. Finally, the customer said to the saleswoman softly:

"Don't you have anything special? Don't you have anything tucked away that's really new?"

The saleswoman shook her head. The customer departed.

Was the customer capricious and unreasonable? Perhaps. But maybe she was bored by the rows of racks of look-alike clothes. Maybe she had just been in another store, where she had seen the same clothes.

When this happens, store image blurs, store loyalty erodes. Why, after all, should a customer be loyal to one store if it can't offer "something tucked away"?

That special something, with its element of surprise and delight, is part of the mystique of fashion selling.

When surprise and delight disappear, customers buy only what they need.

Store "exclusives" that used to provide special interest are sorely missed. Where did they come from? Where have they gone?

Sometimes exclusives came from a store designer or from a small, young firm that a clever buyer discovered. Sometimes they came from Europe. In this country, American designers built reputations that drew customers to stores. Their production was limited and handled on an exclusive basis.

Sometimes designers would sell different styles to a few stores in one town or city. This worked, too, as long as each store was able to create an aura of individuality.

Today, all that has changed. Store designers are vanishing. Small young firms that are discovered must grow quickly or perish. If they survive, they become big firms that sell to too many stores and the sameness sets in again. Even the best merchandise palls when it's over-exposed.

Source: Annalee Gold, "What's Happened to Exclusivity?", *Stores*, June 1973, p. 8.

Planning merchandise assortments for fashion-wear stores thus involves searching out merchandise that is different from what other stores are carrying but yet fits consumers' wants.

offered in broader assortments. Although we tend to think of women's outer apparel and accessories when we think of fashion, other merchandise is affected by fashion. In recent years, men's wear has become less staple and more fashion oriented. Also, furniture, small appliances, bed sheets, luggage, automobiles, travel, and entertainment are influenced by fashion. The more volatile the fashion, the more difficult it is to plan merchandise stocks.

BASIC STOCK LIST

Many firms maintain a *basic stock list* for staple items. The list typically shows the items carried in stock, the minimum quantity to maintain on hand, and the quantity to reorder. Most often a basic stock list is in the form of an inventory sheet, which makes counting and recording inventory levels easier. Figure 8-2 illustrates such a list.

Despite efforts to prevent such an occurrence, a store occasionally will be completely out of stock of some items. Some stores identify certain merchandise items on the basic stock list as *never outs*. The retailer feels that it is important to always have these items on hand. Usually, more frequent stock counts are made on these items to assure an adequate supply.

MODEL STOCK PLAN

A basic stock list is usually not feasible for fashion merchandise because of frequent changes in customer preferences. A *model stock plan*, while making use of historical sales data, is not as specific as a basic stock list. Typically, a model stock relies on dollar value of stock to be carried rather than upon units. A breakdown of the total stock by type, size, and perhaps source and price line is made. However, particular merchandise items cannot be precisely identified since sales of these items cannot be predetermined. Thus, dollar values and more general merchandise characteristics serve as the bases for developing the model stock.

An example of how a model stock can be developed is as follows: Assume that a men's wear retailer is interested in developing a model stock for shirts. Based upon historical sales data, the store buyer found that the total dollar volume of sales for dress shirts, sport shirts, casual shirts, and work shirts has been fairly consistent. It is found, too, that sales according to size do not vary significantly from one year to another. Further, there have been no dramatic shifts in consumer preferences for various manufacturers' brands. With this information, the retailer can develop a breakdown of the value of needed inventory according to these classifications. However, colors, collar styles, and fabrics cannot be specified since these features do not remain stable. If new colors are being introduced for the coming season, the retailer will not be able to predict consumers' reactions.

Figure 8-3 is an example of a model stock plan. Note that this retailer has planned stocks in units rather than dollars and that colors are specified. The manager apparently feels that more precise planning is possible for men's short-sleeve sport shirts.

The result is less precision in planning stocks of fashion merchandise than of staple merchandise, but it certainly provides a more sound basis for decision making than would no information at all. Thus, regardless of the type of merchandise involved, analysis of past sales data can be extremely helpful in merchandise planning.

CUSTOMER REQUESTS

Frequently, customers ask for merchandise that the store does not stock. The reply, "No, I'm sorry" is insufficient. The customer expected to find the merchandise at that store or he would not have requested it. The customer who leaves the store or department without purchasing is known as a *walkout*. A high walkout rate indicates customer dissatisfaction with the store's (or department's) offerings.

A formal method for recording customer requests is needed to provide the buyer with information for future buying. A *want slip*, used to record each unfulfilled customer inquiry, makes possible a reduction in walkout rate. An I.G.A. supermarket manager emphasizes to all personnel the necessity for telling him about all customer requests for merchandise not carried. He maintains a want book for recording such requests. Using a rule-of-thumb developed from experience, he assumes that for every request received there are five other customers who also want that item. Thus, when he receives five requests, he knows that approximately thirty customers are "speaking." If this number of customers is sufficient to warrant stocking the item, he orders it. If not, he knows that he may lose some of these customers to other supermarkets who carry the requested item.

CUSTOMER COMPLAINTS

When customers return merchandise or register a complaint, they are telling the retailer what they do *not* want. They do not want goods that fail to live up to the expectations they had when the goods were purchased. Attention to, and analysis of, returns and complaints can pinpoint problem merchandise. Again, a formal means of communicating this information to buyers for their future use in ordering merchandise is necessary. Many buyers receive copies of all complaints and returns for merchandise in their departments.

COMPARISON SHOPPING

Most retailers keep a close check on competitors' merchandise offerings. This can be accomplished either by visiting competing stores or by studying competitors' promotion. Care must be taken, though, not to interpret all of a competitor's offerings as being successful. Unless information received specifically indicates that a competitor is experiencing excellent sales from merchandise which the retailer does not stock, it may be wise to ignore the offerings. Department stores often employ comparison shoppers. They not only look at competing prices and products, but on occasion they purchase a product for a more detailed examination and comparison.

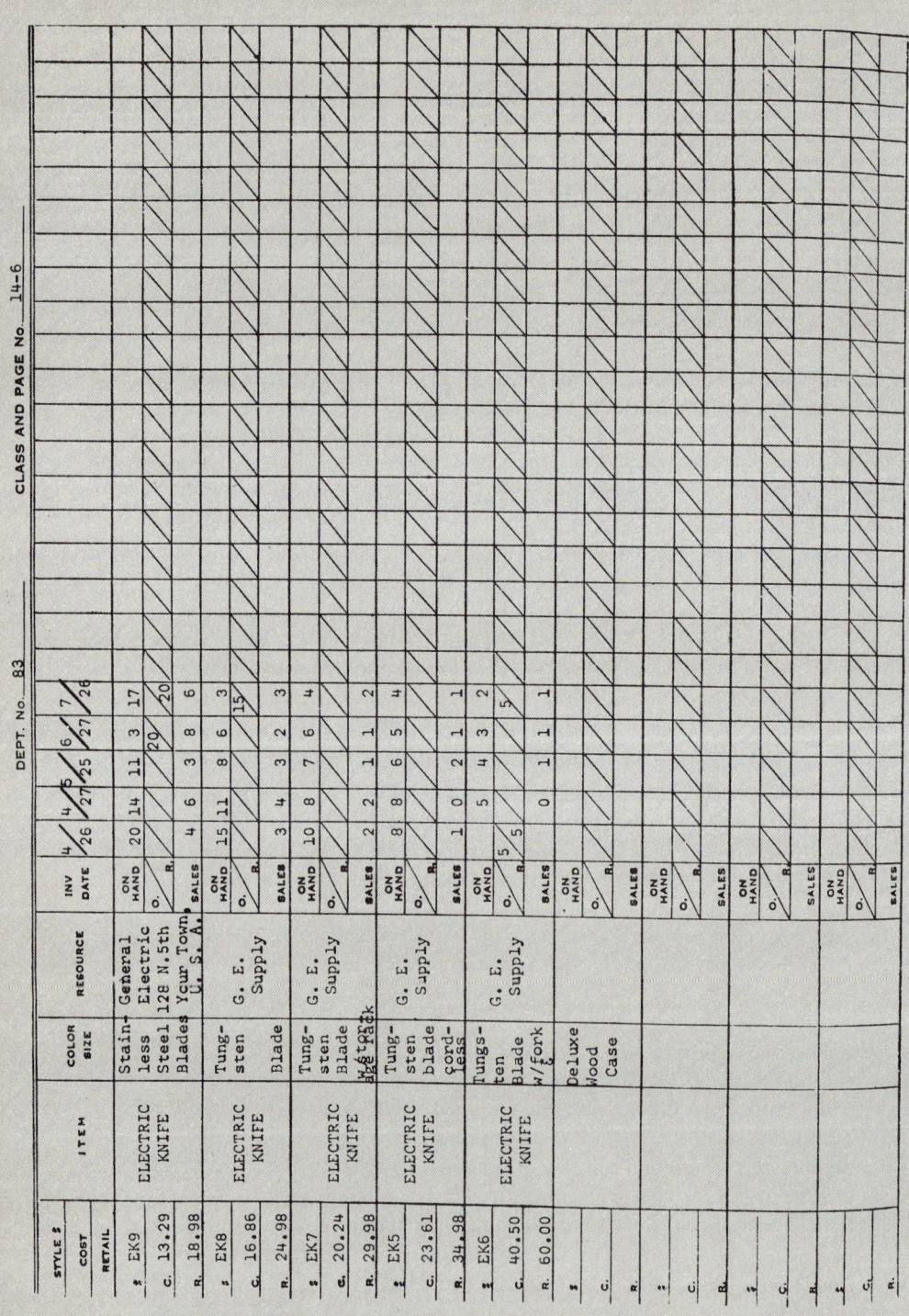

FIGURE 8-2
Example of a basic stock list

STORE	WEEKLY BI-MONTHLY **MONTHLY**	ROYAL KNIGHT MEN'S S/S SPORT SHIRT INVENTORY DEPT. 20 TYPE DACRON/COTTON PERMA PRESS								DATE APRIL 1, YR.

STYLE NO. ITEM DESCRIPTION		MEN'S S/S DACRON/COTTON PERMANENT PRESS SPORT SHIRT								TOTAL
		S	M	L	XL	CAPITAL/IMPERIAL @$24.33 DOZ				
WHITE	3 MO. PLAN SALES									200
	STOCK	10	60	30	10					110
	SALES	3	15	9	3					30
	ON O	4	20	12	4					40
	BUY	5	25	15	5					50
LIGHT BLUE	3 MO. PLAN SALES									150
	STOCK	6	30	18	6					60
	SALES	3	12	8	2					25
	ON O	5	25	15	5					50
	BUY	3	20	14	3					40
BEIGE	3 MO. PLAN SALES									150
	STOCK	8	20	12	10					50
	SALES	2	10	6	2					20
	ON O	6	30	18	6					60
	BUY	--	26	14	--					40
PEWTER	3 MO. PLAN SALES									100
	STOCK	6	20	8	6					40
	SALES	2	9	5	2					18
	ON O	2	12	12	4					30
	BUY	2	18	10	--					30
NAVY	3 MO. PLAN SALES									80
	STOCK	5	20	4	1					30
	SALES	1	6	4	1					12
	ON O	5	20	10	5					40
	BUY	-	-	10	-					10
MAIZE	3 MO. PLAN SALES									100
	STOCK	2	18	12	8					40
	SALES	1	7	5	2					15
	ON O	6	25	15	4					50
	BUY	-	-	-	-					--
TOTAL	3 MO. PLAN SALES									780
	STOCK									330
	SALES									120
	ON O									270
	BUY									170

* Show Total Sales only, not necessary to show sizes.
* Copy must be kept in departmental loose leaf book for one year.

FIGURE 8-3

Example of a model stock plan

OTHER SOURCES

Trade papers and magazines often serve as sources of information concerning new merchandise, trends, and techniques. Magazines such as *Vogue, Women's Wear Daily, Playboy, Seventeen,* and *Ebony* not only show current fashions but predict what is coming in the future. Also, consumers who read these publications will expect retailers to carry the products and styles they have seen.

Central market representatives in the major markets may be retained to keep the retailer abreast of what is happening in the market. Reports may be issued concerning new offerings by resources, shortages which appear to be developing, possible price changes, and emerging fashion trends.

Results of consumer surveys may be published by newspapers, trade associations, government agencies, and academic institutions. These survey results may aid the retailer in correctly diagnosing changes needed in merchandise assortments.

One of the most important ways of determining consumer wants is through observation and by contact with customers. Shoppers often reveal their wants and needs in very subtle ways, such as through questions or comments about merchandise. The chief executive of an ownership chain of department stores says that top retailers are good "people watchers." An astute buyer can glean much useful information simply through customer contact.

REVIEW BOX 8:2

1. For fashion goods, where a basic stock list may be inappropriate, retailers often use a _____.
2. A formal means of recording customer requests for merchandise not stocked is through the use of _____.
3. Many retailers keep track of competitors' merchandise offerings through _____.

STOCK TURNOVER AND MERCHANDISE PLANNING

Stock turnover, sometimes called stockturn, is the number of times an average inventory is sold during a stated period of time. Stockturn is usually stated as an annual rate. It has an important impact on planning and should permeate all merchandise planning activities. It provides an excellent measure of how quickly stock is moving into and out of the store. Fast turnover is ordinarily, but not always, desirable. It is sometimes possible to achieve a high turnover rate to the detriment of profits.

Ascertaining Turnover Rate

Before a turnover rate can be calculated, average inventory for the period under consideration has to be determined. Although turnover may be computed for shorter periods, annual turnover rate will be used here. *Average inventory* is the average amount of stock on hand throughout the period. Frequently, however, this figure may not be easy to obtain. Take, for example, a typical small retailer who conducts a physical inventory only once a year so that he may close his books and determine his profit for the year. Under this method it is possible to ascertain an average inventory figure but its accuracy may be questionable.

Suppose the retailer takes an inventory on December 31. This serves as the ending inventory for the current year and the beginning inventory for the coming year. Although the retailer may let ending inventory serve as an average inventory figure, it is better to average it with the ending inventory of the previous year. For example:

Ending inventory, December 31, 1974	$ 71,546
Ending inventory, December 31, 1975	93,628
	$165,174
Average inventory, 1975 ($165,174 ÷ 2)	$ 82,587

Using this method, the retailer finds that average inventory is more than $11,000 less than if the December 31, 1975, figure alone were used. Obviously, such a difference could have a considerable impact on the stockturn rate.

Even averaging the beginning and ending inventory figures may be less than satisfactory. The average figure should be representative of the "typical" amount of goods carried throughout the year. Many retailers make every effort to take a physical inventory at a time when stock on hand is at its lowest level. This greatly facilitates inventory taking, since fewer goods have to be counted. If this is true of the retailer in our example, the actual average inventory may be considerably higher than either of the year-end inventories. The net result is to overstate the rate of stock turnover.

One caution is necessary, then. Unless the average inventory figure is reasonably accurate in reflecting stock on hand throughout the year, the rate of stockturn is likely to be inaccurate to an unknown degree.

Some larger stores maintain a *perpetual book inventory system* as part of the retail inventory method of inventory valuation. Such stores are able to determine average inventory more accurately, since a book inventory figure can be calculated monthly, or even weekly, if desired.

Although we have talked in terms of a *dollar* inventory figure, it is also possible to measure turnover using average inventory *in physical units*.

Stores carrying major appliances, radios and television sets, furs, and other large unit cost items maintain a perpetual inventory in units of merchandise.

Once average inventory has been obtained, three methods of calculating stockturn rate are possible:

$$\text{stockturn rate using retail dollars} = \frac{\text{net sales}}{\text{average inventory at retail}}$$

$$\text{stockturn rate using cost dollars} = \frac{\text{cost of goods sold}}{\text{average inventory at cost}}$$

$$\text{stockturn rate using physical units} = \frac{\text{number of units sold}}{\text{average inventory in units}}$$

Provided the information necessary for calculations is correct, all these methods should result in the same turnover figure. Thus:

$$\text{stockturn rate using retail dollars} = \frac{\$122,500}{\$35,000} = 3.5$$

$$\text{stockturn rate using cost dollars} = \frac{\$73,150}{\$20,900} = 3.5$$

$$\text{stockturn rate using physical units} = \frac{455}{130} = 3.5$$

Both the numerator and the denominator must be in the same terms. For instance, in the first formula, both net sales and average inventory at retail are in terms of retail values.

Stockturn and Profitability

It might seem that an increase in stock turnover automatically means an increase in profits. While this holds true in some cases, under certain circumstances the effect may be just the opposite. For example, a jewelry store retailer experiences completely stable sales of a certain brand and style of watch at 5 per month throughout the year (somewhat far-fetched but used for illustrative purposes). Last year this retailer purchased 60 watches at the first of the year and sold them all by December 31. Average inventory was thus 30 [(60 + 0)/2], and stockturn was 2 (60 ÷ 30). This year 5 watches are ordered at the beginning of each month. The timing is such that the month's order arrives just as the last watch for the previous month is sold. Average inventory for the year is thus 5 units, and 60 watches are sold during the year. The retailer is jubilant since stockturn rate is 12 this year as compared with 2 last year. It is questionable, though, whether happiness is in order.

Watches, relatively small in size, take up little storage space. However, by ordering 60 at the beginning of the year the retailer tied funds up in inventory throughout the year. By going to the other extreme and placing monthly orders, investment in inventory was substantially reduced. However, 12 orders had to be placed, thereby increasing ordering costs by approximately 1,100 percent. Transportation costs per unit on 5 units are about 1.5 times the per-unit cost on 60 units. In addition, 12 shipments must be received and marked, again taking more time per unit than receiving and marking 60 units in one shipment. Twelve invoices must be paid, increasing bookeeping effort and postage. As a result, the retailer made less profit per unit by increasing stockturn. Although this example is extreme, it serves to indicate that increasing stockturn does not always increase profits.

The point of this example is to emphasize the necessity for planning stockturn rate so that profits are enhanced. Essentially this involves the determination of *economic order quantity* (EOQ). Inventory management recognizes two types of costs: (1) procurement or ordering costs, which include costs of a buyer's time, costs of receiving incoming merchandise, and clerical costs associated with placing orders and paying invoices; and (2) carrying costs which include storage costs, costs of funds tied up in inventory, insurance costs, and costs of obsolescence, deterioration, or spoilage. The economic order quantity is that order size which minimizes the total of these types of costs.

The nature of the merchandise carried obviously has some impact on stock turnover. Most of us would probably like to see our local supermarket have a stockturn rate of at least 52 times a year on fresh produce. If it is much lower, we might want to patronize a different store so that we can be assured of fresh produce. With merchandise which has a short shelf life, a high turnover is not only desirable but necessary to maintain a satisfactory level of profit.

REVIEW BOX 8:3

1. Probably the most difficult problem associated with accurately determining stockturn rate is arriving at an _____ _____ figure.
2. Increasing stock turnover may result in lower _____ to the retailer.

BUDGETING

Unfortunately, too many people think the primary, if not the only, purpose of budgets is to *control*. Certainly budgetary control is important, but so is

Budgeting

the planning that well-developed budgets force upon merchants. The adage "Plan your work, then work your plan" puts budgeting into its proper perspective. Budgets are plans translated into dollars and cents.

Should small retailers prepare budgets, or is it important only for large operations? Most small retailers prepare budgets only on a very informal level, and we could assume that more careful budget preparation *might* lead to greater success. However, some small retailers are so close to all facets of their business and do such a good job of planning, often on the back of an envelope, that they probably carry some form of budget in their heads. Some of these small businessmen are such good managers that they need not reduce their plans to written dollar-and-cents figures. But for many others, lack of planning often renders their spur-of-the-moment efforts ineffective.

Although we frequently speak of *the* budget, most retail firms use several budgets, each concerned with a different phase of planning.

Sales Budget

Since all other activities of a firm are dependent upon sales, it is only logical that sales must be planned before other planning can take place. Most often, sales planning is done in terms of dollars rather than units. Unfortunately, the usual guideline is to "beat last year's figures by 10 percent." Another factor is that managers are expected by top management to increase sales. Sales heads roll when increases are too modest. It is usually desirable to seek higher levels of sales, but in doing so a retail manager cannot ignore changing economic conditions, consumer tastes and preferences, competition, and other uncontrollable factors.

The most obvious starting point in planning sales is a review of past sales, especially those in the previous year. The trend of last year's sales compared to previous years may indicate the probable upward or downward movement of sales for the coming year.

Two basic approaches to sales planning may be used. In the *bottom-up* method, sales are planned by individual departments, and all departments' sales are combined to arrive at total store sales. The other method, the *top-down*, involves planning total store sales and then apportioning them to individual departments. Some stores use both approaches simultaneously and then compare the departmental budgeted sales figures.

Using bottom-up planning, a department manager plans departmental sales for the budget period, usually a year. With last year's figures at hand, usually broken down by classifications of goods, a department manager can usually predict sales with a fairly high degree of accuracy. The major problem is that managers are often by nature optimistic and believe they can greatly increase sales. On the other hand, they may feel that they will be held to the plan and therefore will be too conservative.

FIGURE 8-4

Sales planning form

Department _____

	Classification ____		Classification ____		Classification ____		Classification ____		Total		Cumulative		Cumulative
	Planned	Actual	Planned	Actual	Planned	Actual	Planned	Actual	Planned	Actual	Planned	Actual	Over/Under
197__													
January													
February													
March													
April													
May													
June													
July													
August													
September													
October													
November													
December													

Budgeting

Figure 8-4 is a sample of the sales budget used by some stores. Note that it provides four merchandise classifications within the department and space for both planned and actual sales by classification. Also included in the sales budget are cumulative planned and actual columns as well as a space for cumulative over/under planned amount.

Some stores, feeling such a form does not provide enough detail, include a cumulative column beside each planned and actual column for each merchandise classification. Some feel that monthly sales figures do not reflect enough detail and therefore budget weekly sales. Although many forms of sales budgets exist, their essential purpose is the same: they are a useful planning tool.

Merchandise Budget

Budgeted sales serve as the basis for planning merchandise requirements. A retailer needs to know when to have merchandise on hand and how much stock is necessary to achieve budgeted sales. As with a sales budget, a merchandise budget may take different forms. The following discussion concentrates upon the major variables in a merchandise budget.

PLANNING STOCKS

There are four primary methods used by retailers to plan stocks so that a satisfactory balance is achieved between stocks on hand and anticipated sales. Selecting a method is largely a matter of preference and individual circumstances.

Basic Stock Method. This method of stock planning should not be confused with the basic stock list covered earlier. Their purposes are different. The list specifies particular items to be carried in inventory, while the basic stock *method* now being discussed is a means whereby dollar value of stocks may be determined.

Merchandise classifications divide merchandise into smaller, more homogeneous groups. The nature of this division is largely dependent upon the individual situation and the type of merchandise involved. For example, in a children's store the classifications might be infants, toddlers, girls 3–6, girls 7–14, boys 3–6, boys 7–14, and shoes. The logic behind such a division is that the buyer can do more detailed planning. Using this system, a buyer can budget the level of sales for each classification and better determine the inventory levels necessary to achieve planned sales.

In a department of a large store, the classifications may be further broken down. For example, in a women's coat department in a large department store, the basis for classification might be price lines. The classifications might thus be coats priced at less than $85, from $86 to $125, from $126 to $175, and over $175. Other classification possibilities might be on

186   Ch. 8 *Merchandise Planning*

the basis of style, fabric, merchandise resource, or size (juniors or misses). The classification system used should be one that carries important distinctions for the buyer and serves as an aid in performing the merchandising function.

The basic stock method determines the beginning-of-the-month (BOM) stock necessary to meet planned sales and end the month with a basic stock inventory. The formula for determining this is:

BOM stock level = planned sales for the month
+ (average stock at retail − average monthly sales)

The formula essentially says this: There is some average amount of stock that should be carried at all times. At the beginning of a month this average stock plus anticipated sales during the month should constitute the BOM stock.

As an example, assume that a sporting goods store has determined, on the basis of experience, that an average minimum inventory level of baseball equipment for the season is two times the average monthly sales for that season. If average monthly sales are planned at $15,000, then the minimum average monthly inventory must be $30,000. If planned sales for the coming month are $18,000, then our formula shows:

BOM stock level = $18,000 + ($30,000 − $15,000)
= $18,000 + $15,000
= $33,000

In effect, planned sales for the month will determine fluctuations in BOM inventory levels as shown in Figure 8-5.

It should be noted that stock levels are at retail prices. One advantage of always using retail values when speaking of inventory values is ease of computation. It is possible, of course, to use cost values of inventory, but this necessitates converting the sales volume figure to cost.

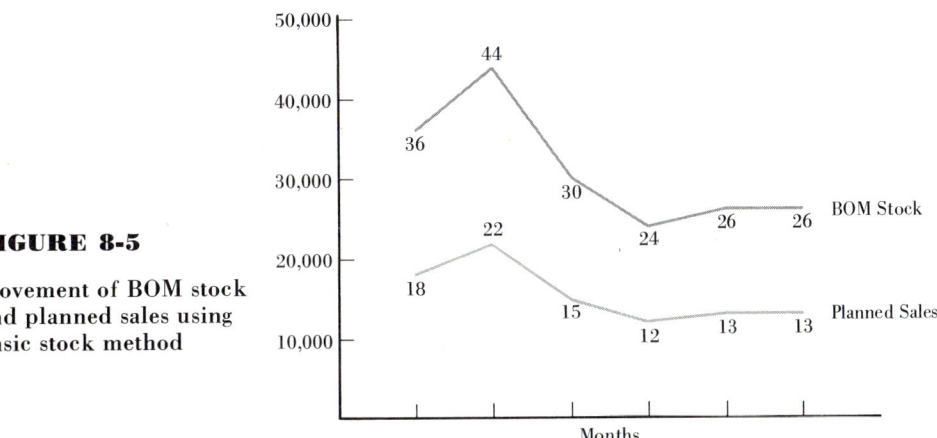

FIGURE 8-5

Movement of BOM stock and planned sales using basic stock method

Percentage Variation Method. Although the basic stock method is suitable where stockturn is less than six times per year, the percentage variation method is superior when turnover is six or greater. This method allows for the variation in stocks to be less than the variation in sales, a major difference between this and the basic stock method. The percentage variation method involves the following calculation:

$$\text{BOM stock level} = \text{average stock} \times \tfrac{1}{2}\left(1 + \frac{\text{sales for the month}}{\text{average monthly sales}}\right)$$

Assume that a housewares department has planned sales which average $24,000 per month throughout the season. On the basis of experience and desired turnover, the retailer knows that it is necessary to carry stock averaging $36,000 per month to achieve the average sales. Sales for a particular month are planned at $30,000. What should be the planned BOM stock level for this month? Using the above formula we find:

$$\begin{aligned}\text{BOM stock level} &= \$36{,}000 \times \tfrac{1}{2}\left(1 + \frac{30{,}000}{24{,}000}\right) \\ &= 36{,}000 \times \tfrac{1}{2}(1 + 1.25) \\ &= 36{,}000 \times \tfrac{1}{2}(2.25) \\ &= 36{,}000(1.125) \\ &= \$40{,}500\end{aligned}$$

For the month under consideration, it is necessary to increase BOM stocks by $4,500 to be prepared for sales $6,000 greater than average sales.

Thus, for a sales increase of 25 percent ($6,000/$24,000), it is necessary to increase stocks by 12.5 percent (4,500/36,000). That is, to achieve a stated percentage increase in sales, BOM stocks are increased by one-half of the percentage increase in sales. The reverse holds true for decreases, in that decreases in average stock should amount to one-half of the anticipated sales decrease. As you may have noticed, this method involves less fluctuation in stocks than the previous method.

Although the one-half in the formula has been used for illustration purposes, there's nothing sacred about this figure. On the basis of experience, stores are usually able to predict accurately what this fraction should be: one-third, two-thirds, or numerous other possibilities. The basic idea behind this method is that in order to increase sales by a certain percentage in a particular month, it is not necessary to increase stocks by the same percentage.

Stock-Sales Ratio Method. While the three other methods all utilize average stocks for the period and emphasize stockturn rate, the stock-sales ratio method plans for stocks on hand at specific times rather than averages. This method requires that stock-sales ratios be computed to determine monthly ratios.

Once desirable ratios have been established, then it is easy to compute needed BOM stocks. Assume that the desirable stock-sales ratio for August is determined to be three. This means that BOM stocks should equal three times the planned sales for the month. If planned sales are $10,000, then BOM stocks should be $30,000. That is:

$$\text{BOM stock level} = \text{BOM stock-sales ratio} \times \text{planned sales}$$

For initial guidance in developing stock-sales ratio, the retailer can turn to a number of sources.[2] However, caution is necessary in using these ratios. Stores vary not only by size but by philosophies, geographic area, and other factors. Ratios appropriate for one store may not be equally appropriate for another.

Weeks' Supply Method. This method is probably the weakest of the four, especially when sales fluctuate. It involves determining the number of stockturns desired, dividing that number into the stockturn period, and determining the number of weeks' supply to have on hand at the beginning of a month.

For example, assume that the stock turnover rate for a year is four times. At any given time, the stock on hand should equal 13 weeks' sales (52 weeks ÷ 4 = 13 weeks). The BOM stock level then should be equal to slightly more than the next three months' sales. With this method, the stock level varies directly and proportionately with sales. In contrast, the percentage variation method assumes that stock levels do not need to vary in direct proportion with sales.

PLANNING REDUCTIONS

Sales reduce the amount of stocks on hand. However, if daily cash register sales were totaled for a month, all reductions which have taken place would not be reflected. Other reductions include markdowns, discounts given to employees and other special groups such as nonprofit organizations, and stock shortages due to shoplifting, employee theft, and other internal factors.

Unfortunately, unlike sales, all reductions are not equally offset by cash in the register. As with sales, however, they do reduce the total value of the stock available for sale. For some stores, particularly those handling staple goods, reductions may be relatively unimportant and may be ignored in planning stocks. In many stores, though, failure to consider these reductions would result in a great deal less stock on hand than assumed. For example, in women's, misses, and junior dresses, markdowns during the month of July may run as high as 30 to 40 percent of net sales. If such reductions were ignored, the BOM stock for August would be considerably lower than expected, and August sales might be adversely affected.

An experienced retailer can plan markdowns fairly accurately if adequate records have been maintained. A fashion goods merchant knows there are going to be broken sizes and lots that have not sold at the end of a season.

Budgeting **189**

If none remain, probably too little stock was on hand and many sales were missed. Ideally, the exact amount of purchases in exactly the right colors, sizes, and styles would be purchased to match perfectly all customers' needs. Realistically, this almost never happens. Rather, even if an adequate assortment has been purchased, odds and ends will remain at the end of the season. Merchandise also becomes shopworn or contains minor flaws which require markdowns. For most stores, some markdowns are inevitable and are simply a cost of doing business. Often discounts are included as part of planned reductions. In effect, discounts may be viewed as markdowns since they represent the difference between the selling price assigned to the goods and the price actually received. Again, experience and past records allow discounts to be effectively planned.

In recent years, shortages have become increasingly difficult to plan accurately. Rapidly increasing stock shortages have forced many retailers to attempt to curtail shoplifting and employee theft. One department store personnel vice president was very proud that stock shortage in his store was only 1.5 percent of total sales. However, if sales totaled $100 million, then that shortage would represent $1.5 million annually! In planning stock shortages, about the best that a retailer can do is apply an estimated percentage to planned sales per month.

Planning markdowns per month is somewhat easier because the retailer knows when special storewide sales are planned and when the end of a season will occur. It is certain that final markdowns to clear out merchandise must be made during certain months and that markdowns for these months will be larger than for other months.

Some retail executives dislike having department managers plan reductions. They fear that needed markdowns will *not* be taken if the manager has already reached planned markdowns or that unneeded markdowns *will be* taken if markdowns are running less than those planned. If stock reductions are not planned, it is only natural that a manager will allow a "fudge factor" in planning stocks. Thus, it is better to recognize that reductions will occur and to plan ahead for them. Any misuse of planned reductions by a department manager is usually the result of a superior who believes that the budget is "law" rather than a somewhat flexible plan of action. Subordinates operating under this type of executive will take whatever steps necessary to see that actual figures are as close to planned figures as possible.

PLANNING PURCHASES

Once the foregoing items have been planned, purchases are easily calculated from the other figures. The following formula can be used to compute planned purchases:

planned purchases = planned EOM stock + planned sales
 + planned reductions − planned BOM stock

Ch. 8 *Merchandise Planning*

EOM refers to planned end-of-the-month stock, which is identical to planned BOM stock for the following month and therefore does not have to be calculated separately. Thus, April EOM stock and May BOM stock are the same figure. Suppose that planned stock for April 1 is $30,000, planned sales for the month are $20,000, planned reductions are $1,500, and planned stock for April 30 is $35,000. Applying the formula, we find:

Planned stock EOM	$35,000	
Planned April sales	20,000	
Planned April reductions	1,500	
Total merchandise needed in April		$56,500
Planned BOM stock		30,000
Planned April purchases		$26,500

As you recall, all planning figures are at retail, so it is obvious that planned purchases of $26,500 does not mean that this amount can be paid for the goods. It means that the retail value of the goods purchased is $26,500. Assume that the planned markup, the difference between cost of merchandise and retail price, is 40 percent. The cost complement of 40 percent is 60 percent, and this amount multiplied by the planned purchases at retail indicates how much can be paid for the merchandise. Thus, 60 percent of $26,500 is $15,900.

OPEN-TO-BUY

A logical extension of the merchandise budget is determination of an *open-to-buy* figure. Although open-to-buy cannot be planned as can stocks, reductions, and purchases, this figure too is a planning figure. Open-to-buy is the amount of money available during the month to spend on purchases, although it differs from the planned purchases amount. For example, assume that planned sales for the month are $50,000, planned reductions for the month (markdowns and shortages) $2,000, planned EOM stock $85,000, current inventory level $90,000, and orders placed but not yet received $30,000.

open-to-buy = planned sales + planned reductions + planned EOM stock
 − current level of stock − outstanding orders
? = $50,000 + $2,000 + $85,000 − $90,000 − $30,000
open-to-buy = $17,000 at retail

If planned markup is 40 percent, then the open-to-buy at cost is represented by the cost complement of 60 percent. Therefore $17,000 × .60 is $10,200.

To expedite such calculations, an open-to-buy sheet is often maintained by a department. Figure 8-6 is a sample form that may be used and illustrates the calculations for the example just presented. Note that all figures used in computing open-to-buy are at retail rather than cost. Further, note the ease of calculating open-to-buy in this manner, since only one conversion to cost prices needs to be made.

Department _____

Month of _____

	Planned	Actual
Sales	$ 50,000	
Reductions	2,000	
EOM stock	85,000	
Merchandise requirements	137,000	
Current inventory level	90,000	
Unfilled orders	30,000	
Merchandise available	120,000	
Open-to-buy (retail)	17,000	
(cost)	$ 10,200	

FIGURE 8-6

Open-to-buy form

"... Over buy?"

If the store utilizes the merchandise budget primarily for control rather than planning, store management may insist that no orders be placed if the department has no open-to-buy. In this situation it is possible for a department to be in desperate need of fast-moving merchandise which will assure a profit and yet be unable to buy it. For this reason, a buyer ordinarily is well advised to maintain a constant open-to-buy position so that he may take advantage of especially good buys when they are available and will also be able to purchase very popular items. Probably a more desirable situation exists when management allows a buyer to be overbought for a brief time. A buyer should not be unfairly penalized because he or she has closely adhered to the original merchandising plan. However, a buyer should not constantly be overbought.

REVIEW BOX 8:4

1. Normally, the _____ budget is prepared prior to all other budgets.
2. The _____ method of stock planning determines specific stocks to have on hand at specific times rather than averages.
3. Planned _____ allows the retailer to recognize that all goods bought will not sell at "regular" prices.
4. An _____ figure for the month represents the difference between the value of merchandise on hand plus that on order and the value of merchandise planned for that period.

PROGRAMMED MERCHANDISING

Programmed merchandising is becoming more popular, especially with larger retailers. Essentially, it involves integrated planning between a retail store and its selected key merchandise resources. Coordinated efforts can result in greater sales and profits for both parties.

Here's how the program works. Top executives of a retail store and a resource jointly develop, in writing, a merchandise plan (typically for a six-month season or even a year). Plans are specific rather than general, according to an outline by M. S. Strossner, Vice President of Famous-Barr:[3]

1. Merchandising plans
    a. Basic stocks
    b. Assortments
    c. Markon (maintained)
    d. Markdown quota
    e. Turnover
    f. Gross margin

2. Promotional program
    a. Feature promotions for flagship (main store) and each branch
    b. Secondary features
    c. Advertising
    d. Displays
    e. Departmental layout

3. Sales training
    a. Flagship store
    b. Branches — a serious problem

4. Responsibilities and due dates
    a. Who is to do what?
    b. When?
    c. How?

The obvious advantage to becoming one of a store's preferred resources is greater concentration of the store's purchases. In addition, a resource can better plan production schedules, inventory requirements, and total sales. In return for benefits received, a preferred resource is willing to concentrate on providing a store with better service and perhaps even prepackage or preticket some merchandise. With the close working relationship between retailer and resource, fewer misunderstandings develop. When problems do occur, top level executives from the two firms can confer and resolve such problems on the spot. The preferred resource will often ask his salesmen to work directly with the store in taking periodic inventories and detailing reorders.

Programmed merchandising can be initiated by either a retailer or a resource. Regardless of how it is initiated, the key to effective programmed merchandising is to get major executives from both the buying side and selling side to sit down together to refine the plan. A vice president and general merchandise manager stated:

> These men—the president, marketing vice-president or vice-president of sales—can make immediate decisions which the regional sales manager or territorial salesmen do not have the authority to make. It pays to go to the top just as it pays the vendor to go to the top in a department store, provided the program is important enough and thorough enough to demand attention.[4]

Although programmed merchandising has received widespread support from department stores, its value is not restricted to these types of stores. For many years, several large chain store operators have utilized a similar arrangement. Unfortunately, in some cases the merchandising plans have not been developed in enough detail to provide maximum benefits. Specialty stores too have started using the programmed approach. Since the benefits to be derived are substantial, there is nothing to prevent almost any type of retailer from working more closely with preferred resources to plan his merchandising efforts.

SUMMARY

- Merchandise planning involves identifying what goods consumers will want and when, where, in what quantities, and at what prices they will want them.
- Planning merchandise assortments involves three dimensions: width—variety of product lines carried; depth—number of brands and/or styles carried; and consistency—product relatedness.
- Scrambled merchandising involves increasing merchandise offerings with products not typically offered by a particular type of retailer. Scrambled merchandising results in some inconsistency of assortment.
- In merchandise planning, retailers should assess products from the standpoint of their stage in the product life cycle. The five stages in the life cycle are introduction, growth, maturity, saturation, and decline.
- Retailers practice market segmentation through their location, merchandise offerings, and price lines.
- The most widely used indicator of consumer wants is past sales data. Two means of utilizing this data are basic stock lists and model stock plans.
- Customer requests for merchandise not carried, customer complaints about merchandise they have purchased, comparison shopping of competing stores, central market representatives, and "people watching" are all valuable sources of information about what merchandise consumers want.

- Stock turnover (stockturn) refers to the number of times an average inventory is sold during a stated period of time (usually a year). Stock turnover can be determined only when both the numerator and denominator are stated in identical terms. Although increasing stock turnover rate is often the objective of retailers, too high a stockturn can result in lower profits.
- A merchandise budget, which is based upon a sales budget, is a valuable planning device to help retailers determine when and how much to buy.
- The four major methods used to plan stock levels are the basic stock method, percentage variation method, stock-sales ratio method, and the weeks' supply method. In order to plan stocks accurately, the retailer also must plan reductions and purchases. From the merchandise budget the retailer can determine, at appropriate times, his open-to-buy figure.
- Programmed merchandising involves integrated planning between a retail store and selected key merchandise resources. The result of programmed merchandising is a close working relationship between a retailer and a resource.

CHAPTER NOTES

[1] P. H. Nystrom, *Economics of Fashion* (New York: The Ronald Press, 1928), p. 3.
[2] An excellent source is *Department Store and Specialty Store Merchandising Results of 1970* (New York: Controllers Congress, National Retail Merchants Association, 1971), updated each year. Other possibilities are trade association publications and the *Survey of Current Business*.
[3] "Programmed Merchandising: The New Way to Work with Key Resources," *Department Store Economist*, October, 1964, p. 22.
[4] "How Stores Benefit from Programmed Merchandising," *Department Store Economist*, January, 1966, p. 31.

QUESTIONS AND ASSIGNMENTS

1. With respect to width and depth of assortment, indicate for each of the following types of retailers whether the assortments normally offered are wide or narrow, deep or shallow.
    a. a convenience or "quick trip" grocery store
    b. a department store
    c. a Florsheim shoe store
    d. a hardware store
    e. a McDonald's
    f. a 37-varieties ice cream shop
2. Draw a typical product life cycle curve indicating (a) the various stages of the cycle and (b) the general level of profits associated with each stage.
3. Distinguish a staple good from a fashion good. Give examples of each type.

4. Think of some types of merchandise that particular retailers would want to maintain as "never outs."
5. Indicate the turnover rate for the following:
    a. Beginning inventory at retail, $100,000; ending inventory at retail, $80,000; midyear inventory at retail, $120,000; net sales, $300,000.
    b. *Inventory in units*   *Sales in units for the year*
    January   40   482
    February   55
    March   63
    April   70
    May   73
    June   65
    July   70
    August   85
    September   74
    October   62
    November   51
    December   43
6. Discuss the utility of the merchandise budget as a planning tool as opposed to a control device.
7. Using the basic stock method, calculate BOM stock level from the following information: average minimum inventory level is 1.5 times average monthly sales; planned average sales are $30,000; planned sales for the coming month are $20,000.
8. Compare the basic stock method with the percentage variation method of stock planning.
9. Indicate the advantages of planning stock reductions in advance.
10. Explain as thoroughly as you can what is meant by the term open-to-buy. How important is this figure?
11. Given the following planned figures, calculate open-to-buy: sales, $100,000; markdowns and discounts, $1,000; EOM stock, $200,000; current inventory level, $120,000; unfilled orders, $30,000.
12. Explain the concept of programmed merchandising, indicating the benefits which accrue to both the retailer and the merchandise resource.
13. Explain the relationship between stock turnover and profitability.

ANSWERS TO REVIEW BOX QUESTIONS

Box 8:1

1. narrow; deep
2. scrambled merchandising or scrambling
3. growth

Box 8:2

1. model stock plan
2. want slips
3. comparison shopping

Box 8:3

1. average inventory
2. profit

Box 8:4

1. sales
2. stock-sales ratio
3. markdowns
4. open-to-buy

Buying Practices and Relationships with Suppliers

Merchandise planning and buying are closely related. They share the same ultimate objective: to provide consumers with merchandise that will meet their needs and make a profit for the store. Activating the merchandise plan involves both buying and selling, but buying activities must precede selling activities—and buying to meet a merchandise plan is no simple matter. Regardless of the planning involved, buying mistakes will be made. The buyer who never makes a mistake is either not honest with himself or is not attempting to maximize profits over the long run.

THE BUYING TASK

The essential task of buying is to translate the merchandise plan into products that will satisfy customers. Often the success or failure of the store is dependent upon how well the buying function is performed. Out-of-stock situations and customer walk-outs (when the store does not handle the desired merchandise) are primarily due to ineffective buying. The same is true of the constant stocking of slow-moving merchandise and excessive markdowns. Of course, these situations can never be entirely eliminated, but they must be minimized. Continued ineffective buying can lead to a loss of customers and, eventually, to financial difficulties.

Some buyers insist that buying is an art, that successful buyers are born, not made. To these people, a buyer must know intuitively what and when to buy. Certainly, imagination and intuition are important pluses, especially for a buyer of high fashion goods. However, the successful buyer relies basically on experience, on careful gathering of bits and pieces of information, and on astute observation. Most highly successful younger buyers today will admit that good buying is essentially hard work.

With the vast increase in available, up-to-date information, buying has become more complicated and more scientific. Computers, with the ability to store, summarize, and present information in the form needed, have affected the buyer's job. The problem becomes one of how to analyze and use these vast stores of information properly. For example, point-of-sale systems, such as the one pictured in Figure 9-1, transmit sales and inventory information directly into a computer as the sale is taking place. Predictions are that

FIGURE 9-1

Inventory control is greatly aided by point-of-sale terminals.

point-of-sale terminals will replace the traditional cash register because valuable information can be supplied almost instantaneously. When a transaction occurs, the dollar value and merchandise item number are recorded, while the dollar value and number of units are automatically subtracted from inventory. Thus, the buyer can conceivably know, at any given moment, the dollar volume of sales, which items are selling well, and the value and amount of inventory on hand. In the past, some of this information was not available to the buyer for weeks, and then it often was not accurate.

Although important, knowledge of what specific merchandise is selling, and how rapidly, does not solve all of the buyer's problems. Consider the comments of one men's wear buyer: "We're picking clothes eight months in advance. . . . There's no way to really know what will sell well."[1] When buying commitments must precede sales by several months, and when the public's tastes change rather rapidly as with fashions, there is no way a buyer can be right 100 percent of the time. Whether buying is an art or a science must remain essentially unanswered, for "it all depends." When reordering during a season or buying primarily staple merchandise, then a buyer can be quite scientific. However, when placing an initial order for fashion merchandise, after all pertinent available information is obtained, a buyer needs that spark of intuition—a "feel" for what will sell. At this point buying truly becomes an art.

Rather than just letting new buyers learn by making costly mistakes in the marketplace, some firms are attempting to give them "experience" in buying with no loss of profits due to mistakes. Montgomery Ward is experimenting with a computer for such buyer training.[2] The system allows buyer trainees to make realistic decisions and obtain feedback from the computer concerning the decision. The computer "talks back" to the trainee via a viewing screen with a printed analysis of the decision. Although still relatively new, such a system for training buyers seems to offer a great deal. The opportunity for buyers to make mistakes, and to learn from such mistakes at no loss to the company, may save large retailers substantial sums of money later when the decisions are "for real."

Buying versus Purchasing

Typically a large store has only one purchasing agent but several buyers. The distinction between the two is a significant one. In retailing, buyers and assistant buyers are charged with the responsibility of buying goods *for resale*. Thus, there is a buyer for each merchandising department. The purchasing department, on the other hand, normally buys all items *other* than merchandise for resale. For example, all the bags, sales books, cleaning equipment, cash registers, and other supplies and equipment are bought by the purchasing department. In this way buyers can concentrate their efforts on acquiring merchandise for resale in their departments without having to worry about operating equipment and supplies.

Note, however, that the purchasing agent may not make all decisions on what equipment and supplies to purchase. The decision, for example, to purchase a particular brand of cash register for the store may be arrived at jointly by the controller, the president, and several merchandise managers. Actual placing of the order is usually accomplished through the purchasing agent.

For control purposes it is important that these two activities be kept distinct and separate. If a buyer needs some specialized supplies for his department, he asks the purchasing agent to get them. This prevents any intermingling of equipment or supplies with merchandise.

SPOTLIGHT

What does a buyer do?

The following is a listing of the activities enumerated by a department store buyer indicating the extent of a buyer's job. Take a few minutes to read how he perceives it.

1. He must cover two shows annually of nearly 1,200 booths each and in 1,200 minutes total time, or approximately one minute per booth! He's then expected to be an expert on the relative merits of the thousands of items he shops.

2. He's asked to prepare about 30,000 inches of advertising each year and to have all of them come out crystal clear without blemish or flaw and with product results.

3. He's expected to do more and more business on less and less stock until at last, if he really reaches a state of grace, he'll be doing a great deal of volume on no stock at all.

4. He must supervise his stock so that nothing is soiled or damaged, but he's deprived by organizational structure of having any authority over the people who operate the stockroom.

5. He must be prepared to answer all questions on nondelivery or lost deliveries, or to answer any customer complaint arising in the normal course of daily business, but he's deprived of any real authority that would make it possible for him to correct the problem.

6. He must be on the floor in all branch stores (simultaneously) to talk to the customers in order to get the feel of the market.

7. He must keep the selling floor clean and orderly in all stores and present the merchandise properly organized by classification and category to maximize profit.

8. He must train the sales staffs in all stores, both day and night shifts, to sell effectively.

9. He must be in his office at all times to answer phone calls (particularly from the executive office). He must be available for price information and delivery schedules and to make sales pitches. The one thing he shouldn't do is visit manufacturers to augment his two Chicago Housewares Show trips—that's too costly and time consuming!

10. Finally, and most importantly, he must prepare promptly an endless succession of top management memos explaining why he's done such a poor job on Items 1–9.

Source: W. H. Sahloff, "Breaking Away from Yesterday," *Marketing Through Retailers* (New York: American Management Association, 1967), pp. 49–50.

Did you notice anything peculiar about the list? Not once did the buyer specifically mention buying merchandise. Do you suppose this has anything to do with the separation of buying and selling activities by some large department stores with several branches?

Store Policies and Buying

Most buyers face certain constraints which limit their freedom in buying merchandise. If buyers in a large store were given complete freedom, there would likely be duplications among various departments, inconsistencies in assortments and pricing, and no clear-cut, unified merchandising effort.

There are fewer such problems in the small, independent store. The owner or manager typically sets store objectives, develops policies, and also does the buying. In this case, the buyer *is* top management, and there should be little difficulty in buying to meet objectives. The problem in many cases is that the objectives desired are not clear; and in the role of buyer, the owner-manager may fail to consider whether buying particular merchandise is consistent with overall store objectives.

In the larger store, most objectives and buying policies are set by top management without the advice of buyers. Buyers are faced with the task of purchasing merchandise that will satisfy target markets they did not select and will fulfill an image they did not determine. All of their buying decisions must be based on management's objectives and operating plans. For example, if management determines that the store is to be a highly "promotional" store, this dictates that buyers have numerous "special sales," typically accompanied by heavy advertising. Buyers for such a store face an entirely different problem from those in a more traditional store with standardized, complete assortments, a higher gross margin, and many services.

Other types of restrictions also may limit the buyer. If management requires a certain markup percentage on all merchandise, buyers may have to forgo some "hot items," which they would have to price higher than competitors to achieve the required markup. To maintain the store image, a buyer may be unable to take advantage of bargain-priced and highly profitable merchandise buys. Many buyers have been excited by the prospects of high profits on a particular buying opportunity only to have an order rejected by a merchandise manager who believes the merchandise is in some way inappropriate for that department or store—and perhaps rightfully so.

REVIEW BOX 9:1

1. While we may not be able to state definitely whether buying is an art or a science, we can say that buying is becoming more _____.

2. In a retail firm, an individual who acquires merchandise for resale is known as a _____ while one who obtains supplies and equipment is a _____.

3. In a large store, buyers must base their decisions on _____ set by top management.

THE SELECTION OF MERCHANDISE RESOURCES

Regardless of type or size of retail store, most buyers face the problem of selecting the merchandise resources from whom they are going to buy. The task is not easy because there are usually several vendors competing for the retailer's business. In addition, most retailers must also search out sources of supply to meet their special needs.

A good starting point in some lines of trade are trade directories which list resources by lines handled and location. Some universities publish a directory of manufacturers for the state in which they are located. Local libraries often can aid the retailer in locating resource directories, and trade associations are usually happy to be of assistance. The retailer should accumulate considerable information on possible sources of supply. The problem of selecting resources from a lengthy list is much more pleasant than the one of having too few resources and inadequate merchandise choice.

Wholesalers

With the growth of large-scale retailing, we might assume that most retailers buy directly from manufacturers. However, for certain types of stores and certain classes of merchandise, buying is still done through wholesalers. Although there are various types of wholesalers, their function in retailing is generally to serve as an intermediary, or "middle man," between manufacturers and retailers. There has been much discussion about the possible elimination of wholesalers, but as long as they continue to provide a useful function, they can survive—and prosper.

For many small stores, service or *full-service wholesalers* act in the same way as retailers do for consumers. These wholesalers buy in anticipation of retailers' needs, they stock merchandise, and they usually offer delivery service and credit. They frequently have salesmen who call on retailers to solicit orders. They typically buy in large quantities and sell smaller quantities to several retailers. In many cases, the small retailer could not obtain such small quantities directly from manufacturers. Many smaller hardware, grocery, office supply, automotive supply stores, beauty shops, and gift shops rely largely on full-service wholesalers to supply their needs.

Limited-service wholesalers operate much like full-service wholesalers, except they offer fewer services. For example, one type of limited-service wholesaler, referred to as a cash-and-carry wholesaler, usually does not offer credit or delivery. Such a wholesaler might be likened to a retail self-service store in that the retailer "shops" the shelves, takes selected items to a centralized check-out and pays for them, and then loads them and transports them to the outlet. Some limited-service wholesalers provide delivery but no credit. Automotive supply houses delivering parts to service stations and small garages are one example.

A *rack jobber* is a specialized wholesaler whose function typically includes providing a merchandise display unit, selecting merchandise for the unit, and completely stocking the rack on a periodic basis. Rack jobbers originally appeared in the supermarket field and handled non-food items. The idea has spread and many other types of stores now utilize rack jobbers. The buyer's job, in this situation, is to select a rack jobber who will provide frequent service so that slow-moving merchandise is removed and out-of-stock situations are minimized. Since merchandise placed on the rack is on consignment or on a guaranteed return basis, no risk is involved. At the same time, since the rack jobber is furnishing many services, the margin is lower than if the store were merchandising the unit.

The above types of wholesalers take title to (that is, own) the merchandise that they sell to retailers. Numerous other types of wholesalers perform a service but do *not* take title. Those who do not take title are technically known as agent middlemen. They include manufacturer's representatives, brokers, and selling agents.[3]

Manufacturers

In certain lines of trade and in the case of large retailers, much merchandise is bought directly from manufacturers. Here the functions normally provided by wholesalers are taken over by either the manufacturer or the retailer, or they are divided between them. For example, time is critical with some fashion merchandise, and eliminating the wholesaler may speed delivery to the retailer. In such cases the manufacturer may decide to perform the storage and credit functions himself and may keep salesmen on the road calling on retailers. When taking over these functions, the manufacturer usually feels that he can perform them more effectively than a wholesaler could.

In some lines there are large retailers, especially chains, that purchase in larger quantities than many wholesalers. In such cases it is usually cheaper for a retailer to purchase directly from the manufacturer. Reducing the cost of merchandise enables the retailer to offer the consumer lower prices and thus gain a competitive advantage over other smaller retailers.

Retailers who purchase in large quantities directly from the manufacturer may also be able to engage in *specification buying*. That is, the retailer may specify exactly what kind of merchandise he wants manufactured. This may involve nothing more than identifying the merchandise with the retailer's brand name rather than the manufacturer's. Or the retailer may specify significant changes to clearly differentiate a product from that of the competition.

Many supermarket chains use specification buying to obtain such items as canned goods which carry their own private label. Other large chains such as Sears, Montgomery Ward, and J. C. Penney may specify exactly the type of product features desired.

Private labeling can be profitable when a retailer gains consumer acceptance. Sears has gained acceptance of its private labels, and a substantial majority of Sears sales probably involve merchandise carrying one of the Sears brand names. Pathmark, a mid-Atlantic supermarket chain, is believed to sell the highest percentage of private labels of any United States food chain. It is estimated that Pathmark sells 1,200 private-label products and that they account for 25 percent of sales.[4]

On the other hand, private labeling can backfire. Approximately 12 to 15 percent of sales of A & P are private-label merchandise. Some observers feel that a part of A & P's problems is that the chain has been unsuccessful in convincing consumers, especially young ones, that the chain's private labels are good buys.[5]

The reasons why manufacturers sell direct to retailers are sometimes difficult to analyze. Most manufacturers sell to wholesalers and also directly to retailers. If a retailer assumes the storage function, requests less liberal credit terms, and concentrates purchases with the manufacturer, then the manufacturer may have fewer expenses than when selling to wholesalers. Thus the manufacturer's profits may be greater. Manufacturers of fashion goods appreciate the need to get merchandise to retailers' shelves quickly. These manufacturers also often feel they can do a better selling job than wholesalers because of their greater merchandise knowledge. At the same time, the manufacturer benefits from a closer contact with the ultimate market. Depending upon general economic conditions and competition, manufacturers may shift their emphasis from direct selling to selling through wholesalers, and vice versa.

Other Retailers

Although not extremely important in terms of volume, more sales are made between retailers than is often recognized. It is not at all unusual for small retailers to purchase supply items on a continuing or an intermittent basis from other retailers. If, for example, paper and supplies are needed at once, the simplest thing to do is visit the closest stationery store or office supply store to acquire the needed items.

Central Markets

Although some retailers fill their merchandise needs without ever leaving their own stores, most desire a greater exposure to merchandise offerings.

Viewed broadly, a *central market* is a large collection of vendors concentrated in one geographic area. Such a collection of vendors may be concentrated under one roof, as in a merchandise mart or a show, or they may be relatively concentrated within a section of a major city. A brief investigation of kinds of central markets follows.

MERCHANDISE MARTS AND SHOWS

Large permanent buildings for the continuous showing of certain merchandise classes are located in many larger cities. Many vendors feel that retail buyers should be able to view merchandise offerings on a continuous basis in selected geographic regions. Often these marts are segregated according to lines of goods, and each showroom is staffed by a qualified vendor representative. Some have special seasonal showings which attract other vendors who do not want a continuous exhibit.

Some of these marts tend to specialize in particular lines of goods, while others attempt to attract vendors of all types of merchandise. Usually these marts are located in rather large cities such as New York, Chicago, Los Angeles, Denver, Dallas, Atlanta, and San Francisco.

Regional shows (or exhibits) are similar to merchandise marts and may even be held in these marts, but they are usually of a short duration such as a week or two. The usual objective is to bring together a large number of resources in a regional location for the convenience of small and medium-size

Merchandise marts are intended to increase both sellers' and buyers' efficiency.

retailers. Such exhibits are rather similar to the boat and travel shows often held for consumers. Retailers can compare the offerings of competing vendors in one location and thus do not have to buy without knowledge of other offerings as often happens when a salesman calls at the retailer's store.

Many retailers are especially appreciative of marts and shows and attend them faithfully. With marts, retailers can attend at their convenience and not be bound to some rigid schedule. With the shows and exhibits, as well as the marts, a retailer's travel expenses are not as great as they might be in traveling to distant manufacturers' locations.

MANUFACTURING CENTER

When buyers speak of "going to market," they usually mean visiting a manufacturing center for the type of goods they buy. Formerly, New York City represented *the* central market for many types of goods. Although New York is still generally conceded to be the *fashion* capital, other cities have come on strong as specific manufacturing centers. Although a buyer may attend one of the manufacturing center central markets alone and unaided, a more common arrangement is to make use of a resident buying office, the topic of the next section.

RESIDENT BUYING OFFICES

Within manufacturing centers, there tend to arise market specialists known as resident buyers. Although their activities, methods of operation, and ownership may vary, these offices primarily function as resident merchandise "experts." Resident buyers are continuously in contact with manufacturers and know what is happening in the market. They are usually aware not only of all resources, but of how well specific brands are selling.

Most manufacturers know the power of a resident buyer. If a particular manufacturer falls into disfavor, the resident buyer will "freeze him out" by failing to suggest his merchandise to clients. At the same time, manufacturers are extremely important to the resident buyer and are "cultivated" to provide maximum information to clients. The resident buyer thus serves as the "eyes and ears" of the retail buyer in a central market.

Figure 9-2 indicates the various kinds of resident buying offices. The major distinction between the types of resident buying offices is on the basis of control. *Independent* buying offices are just that—independent. Their relationship with stores is purely voluntary on the part of both client and representative. Independent offices are of two major types, based on their method of operation: salaried offices and merchandise brokers. The *independent, salaried office* is the most common type and is probably the best example of a true resident buying office. Frequently this type of office operates on an annual contract basis with client stores. Contract terms vary, but a monthly minimum plus a percentage of sales based upon services provided is common.

Merchandise brokers represent and are compensated by manufacturers. Even so, they may perform adequately for retailers who need only inter-

The Selection of Merchandise Resources

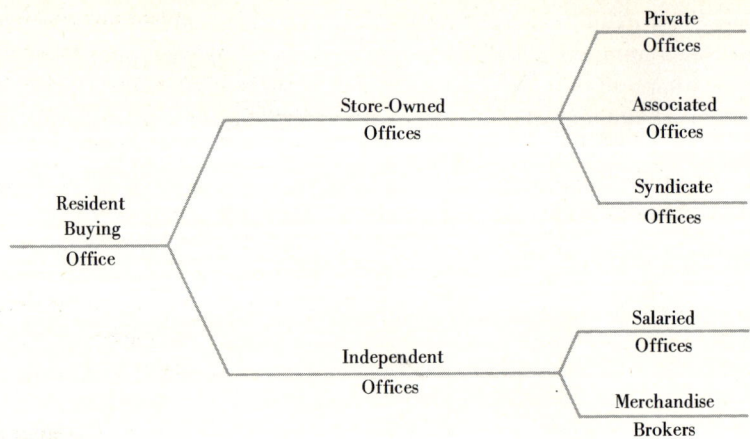

FIGURE 9-2

Types of resident buying offices

mittent assistance. Some brokers take the initiative in contacting retailers when they feel they have merchandise which would be of interest.

There are three main types of store-owned resident buying offices: the private office, the associated office, and the syndicate office. These offices are controlled by the stores which own them. Formerly, the *private resident buying office* was maintained by a single large store. Today such offices are difficult to find; most stores have found that they cannot afford to maintain them.

Today, *associated offices* are much more common. These offices are owned by several independent stores or ownership groups of stores. An outstanding example of associated offices is the Associated Merchandising Corporation, commonly known as AMC. This office is supported by Federated Department Stores plus other independent department stores. This office engages in some specification buying for the benefit of member stores, and the AMC label is well known to these stores' customers.

The *syndicate office* is slightly different from the associated office. Two major differences are that this office is typically owned by a major chain, and often the office purchases for the chain and imposes its selections on the individual stores. Thus, the syndicate office may engage in centralized buying for the chain. However, this is not always the case, and the syndicate office may act primarily in an advisory role.

Resident buying offices continue to perform a useful service for retailers, primarily through the provision of advisory and informational services. These offices vary in size from very small one-person operations to large offices with a staff of specialists. Because of the increasing complexity of merchandise offerings, these offices have become more important in certain lines of trade, and their future appears bright.

> **REVIEW BOX 9:2**
>
> 1. _____ buying allows the retailer to have goods manufactured according to his explicit needs.
> 2. A collection of vendors located in one concentrated geographic area is referred to as a _____.
> 3. Large permanent buildings for the continuous showing of vendors' merchandise are called _____.
> 4. Market specialists located in manufacturing market centers assist store buyers and are known as _____.

METHODS OF BUYING

Individual buyers usually make buying decisions. The decision may be made in the store or in a central market. The point is that the individual buyer has the decision authority and assumes responsibility for the results of that decision. Several variations of this method of buying warrant consideration. Each of these will be considered briefly.

Cooperative Buying

Although it appears in many forms, cooperative buying essentially involves group buying by independent, noncompeting stores. Often the merchandise of competing suppliers is assembled in a central market, and representatives from the allied stores meet and decide which merchandise to buy. In some cases a small representative group of buyers is elected to make buying decisions for all the stores. By combining the orders for all stores into one major order, retailers usually receive price concessions from vendors. Also, since large orders are involved, the services received may be better than normal. Thus, delivery may be more prompt, and more liberal credit terms may be granted.

An associated resident buying office often engages in this type of buying for the mutual benefit of member stores. Organizing such a group of stores to engage in cooperative buying may be difficult, despite the advantages offered. Many buyers view this as usurping their buying function, decreasing their importance. Also, despite the saying that "two heads are better than one," group decisions are not always better than individual decisions. In cases of buying errors, the effect is multiplied by the number of stores. Another limitation is that locational differences may affect merchandise salability. Merchandise that appeals to customers on the West Coast may not sell in the Midwest.

A modification of cooperative buying is the formation or purchase of a wholesale organization by a group of independent retailers. Under these circumstances a *cooperative chain* is formed. Usually, the buying responsibility is delegated to the wholesale organization and the wholesale buyers. The result may be a form of centralized buying, discussed next.

Centralized Buying

Centralized buying involves buying for more than one commonly owned retail outlet. Despite what the term suggests, all centralized (or central) buying is not done in a central market. Centralized buying simply means that buying responsibility for certain classes of goods in several commonly owned stores is vested in an individual whose sole job is buying.

Central buying is the hallmark of chain stores. Also, some department stores with many branch stores have centralized the buying responsibility. Other stores have been dissatisfied with centralized buying and have gone back to decentralized buying or have adopted some type of modified system.

One variation of centralized buying that has apparently worked well for some large chains is a requisition system. Centralized buyers acquire merchandise for all stores. Individual stores or department managers are then allowed considerable latitude in requisitioning goods from central warehouses. Thus, if a department manager finds that certain goods do not sell well in his store, he simply does not order these goods. Some stores go even further and allow managers to buy special items not bought by the centralized buyer.

Committee Buying

Committee buying attempts to capitalize upon the economies and efficiencies of centralized buying while relieving the centralized buyer of the entire buying responsibility. A buyer making decisions on merchandise to be handled in perhaps hundreds of stores (as in a large food chain) may tend to make conservative decisions, particularly after buying several items which do not move well. A buying committee thus spreads the responsibility among several executives.

Buying committees are widely used in chains handling primarily staple items such as canned goods, hardware, and variety store items. Although functions may vary, most often the committee is concerned with decisions on possible new items and discontinuance of present items. For example, in preparation for a committee meeting, a buyer may select ten items out of perhaps dozens presented by various vendors. The buyer has selected those he or she believes have the most merit, after analyzing the market, considering competitive offerings, and comparing prices and gross margins. The committee may accept or reject the recommendation of the buyer or request more information. Not infrequently, a *go* or *no go* decision is postponed until alternatives may be more precisely compared.

Frequently, acceptance of a new product must be accompanied by the elimination of another product. If this were not the case, a supermarket presently carrying 10,000 items would soon be carrying 15,000 items and could not do an adequate merchandising job within the store space available.

The composition of buying committees varies, but in addition to buyers there is usually a merchandising manager, sales promotion manager, and operations or sales managers. The buying committee usually will not meet more often than once or twice a month.

Consignment and Memo Buying

Although buying on consignment and buying by memorandum are slightly different, the effect is the same. Many vendors are so anxious to get exposure for their merchandise that they are willing to guarantee that the merchandise will sell or they will take it back. For the buyer with no open-to-buy, or one who is doubtful about whether the merchandise will sell, such an arrangement may be ideal.

Consider the situation that occurred with a gift shop in a Rocky Mountain tourist area. The shop specialized in Indian jewelry and other Indian-made handicraft items as well as some mass produced, cheaper gift items. The proprietor had completed his buying for the summer season when a vendor with a unique and attractive line of expensive Indian pottery called. Even though the shop owner thought it might sell, he was reluctant to stock the pottery line since he would be overbought by doing so. The vendor, anxious to place the pottery with reputable retailers having proven records of selling quality Indian goods, offered to leave a substantial quantity of the pottery on consignment during the three-month tourist season. In this situation, selling on consignment was beneficial to both parties. The vendor was able to place his merchandise, and the retailer was able to "test" how well the line would sell without any risk. The title remains with the vendor, and the retailer pays the vendor only for goods that are sold. The retailer thus incurs no risk in handling the merchandise other than shoplifting or in-store damage.

Memorandum buying operates much the same way, except title passes to the retailer upon acceptance of the goods. In some cases the retailer actually pays for the goods when received, while in other contractual arrangements goods are paid for only when they sell. Under memo buying, retailers price the goods as they wish. When goods are bought on consignment, the vendor typically sets retail prices, thus restricting the retailers' ability to merchandise as they see fit.

The use of rack jobbers, covered earlier in the chapter, is a form of consignment buying. Not only many of the risks, but also much of the stock work, remains the responsibility of the vendor under this arrangement.

Leased Departments

Many stores want to handle a certain class of merchandise or service but do not possess the necessary expertise. Often they lack buying ability. Thus a decision may be made to allow an outsider to operate this department. In department stores, leased departments are common in fine jewelry, shoes, rare coins, beauty salons, and restaurants. In many cases the customer is unaware that the department is operated by an outsider, since policies and procedures are usually the same as in store-owned departments.

In departments handling specialized merchandise, the leased department is a means of shifting the buying responsibility to others. This relieves the store of the danger of venturing into unknown merchandising areas where losses could be substantial.

Many discount houses originally leased several departments (camera, apparel, automotive accessories) until they were able to gain the knowledge necessary to operate the departments themselves. As they acquired knowledge, they often did not renew the lease and took over these departments themselves. As you can see, a lessee in any store always risks that the store may, at a later date, take over the operation of the department.

REVIEW BOX 9:3

1. Cooperative buying involves the placing of a single order by a group of _____, _____ stores.
2. A buyer who buys for a major department store and all of its branch stores is practicing _____ buying.
3. In order to relieve a buyer from the total responsibility for buying an item for a large number of stores, some retailers have formed _____ _____.
4. When merchandise is placed in a store by a resource who retains title to the goods and charges the retailer only for that merchandise which is sold to consumers, this is called _____ buying.

MERCHANDISE PRICING BY RESOURCES

Price amounts to more than simply so much money. For example, two vendors' offerings may involve exactly the same amount of money, yet one may seem a high price while the other may seem a low price. Perhaps in the latter case credit is extended, transportation is furnished to the buyer's store, and a liberal return policy is in effect. Thus greater value is received by the buyer and the price may be viewed as relatively low.

Negotiating with Resources

Vendors' offerings and prices may be subject to negotiation. However, far too often buyers become so concerned with negotiating price concessions that they forget their primary charge—*buying merchandise that customers want*. Obtaining low-price merchandise that does not sell is wasted effort as well as wasted money. This is not to say that price negotiations are unimportant. Rather, they are important *after* the proper merchandise has been selected.

The negotiation process is essentially a means of conflict resolution. Merchandise resources would like a high price for their products, while retail buyers seek the lowest price, considering the offerings. Sometimes relatively little negotiation takes place because of the strength or power possessed by one of the parties. If, for example, a small retailer is buying from a large manufacturer, price and offering may not be negotiable. If there is strong demand for the merchandise under consideration, the manufacturer may simply state the offering and quote a take-it-or-leave-it price.

In many cases, however, the power of participating parties is more nearly equal, and opportunities for negotiation are present. The retail buyer must evaluate the situation before negotiating. The increase in large-scale retailers has created a greater balance of power between buyers and sellers, although there are still many very small retailers.

Buyers must exercise a certain amount of caution in the negotiation process. It is possible to drive too hard a bargain and risk damage to relationships with suppliers. An overly aggressive or discourteous buyer who oversteps the bounds of common courtesy risks losing a supplier. Representatives of resources subjected to a buyer's ill treatment can hardly be expected to see that the buyer obtains prompt, fair service. Buyers can be tough negotiators, attempting to obtain concessions, without indulging in unpleasant, discourteous practices.

In price negotiations, the buyer is further limited by legal constraints. Specifically, the Robinson-Patman Act of 1936 prohibits sellers of like merchandise in like quantities from discriminating against like purchasers if the effect is to substantially lessen competition or injure competitors. The entire burden does not rest with the seller, however. A buyer who knowingly receives discriminatory price concessions is also in violation of the law. Thus, buyers should proceed with caution when negotiating for exceptionally low prices.[6]

Terms of Sale

Under terms of sale, there are three primary negotiable items: transportation charges, discounts, and dating. Although there may be other items subject to negotiation, such as timing of deliveries, methods of packaging, and the like, the three items above are those most frequently negotiated. The astute buyer should capitalize upon opportunities to negotiate, because concessions gained may well determine profitability of the enterprise. Knowledge of terms of sale allows the buyer to evaluate competing vendors' offerings more accurately.

TRANSPORTATION TERMS

Freight costs have been increasing, with the result that freight charges now represent a substantial portion of total merchandise costs. Buyers who negotiate more favorable transportation terms are thus able to reduce merchandise costs and either increase gross margin or reduce the price charged to customers. Either alternative is desirable since they both may lead to increased profits.

The seller usually quotes a selling price at a factory, warehouse, or other distribution point. The buyer is then responsible for paying all transportation charges incurred in getting the merchandise from the selling point to the store. Under this situation, transportation terms are quoted as *FOB factory* or *FOB warehouse*. The seller pays for loading the merchandise on a common carrier at the shipping point.

Under FOB (free on board) terms the buyer will be charged transportation from the point indicated. Title passes to the buyer at time of shipping, and the buyer assumes not only the shipping charges but also all risks of loss or damage to the merchandise. In the event of damage to the merchandise or even its loss, the buyer is responsible for filing a claim with the carrier. If the seller ships from only one point, *FOB shipping point* results in variations in transportation charges, depending upon how far any given retailer is from this point.

In some cases buyers may be able to negotiate *FOB destination* terms. The seller then pays the entire transportation charges to the buyer's location. In this situation, buyers all over the country would pay the same merchandise costs, but the seller would achieve varying profitability on shipments depending on the buyer's location and the amount of the freight charges involved. FOB destination terms are not common, since the seller is forced to incorporate average freight charges into the prices he quotes. When competing with other vendors, a resource may be at a disadvantage in nearby markets if competitors are offering FOB destination terms.

A common arrangement is for the seller to absorb enough of the freight charges to make him competitive with other sellers located *nearer* the buyer. For example, in Figure 9-3 resource B is located three times as far from the buyer as resource A. Let's assume that the freight costs for shipping identical merchandise amount to $50 for resource A and $100 for resource B. In order to be competitive, B decides to absorb one-half of the freight charges and quote the buyer a delivered price identical to the one A quotes. Generally, the practice is legal, as long as freight absorption is employed to meet competition, and no collusion or intent to destroy competition is involved.

Ch. 9 *Buying Practices and Relationships with Suppliers*

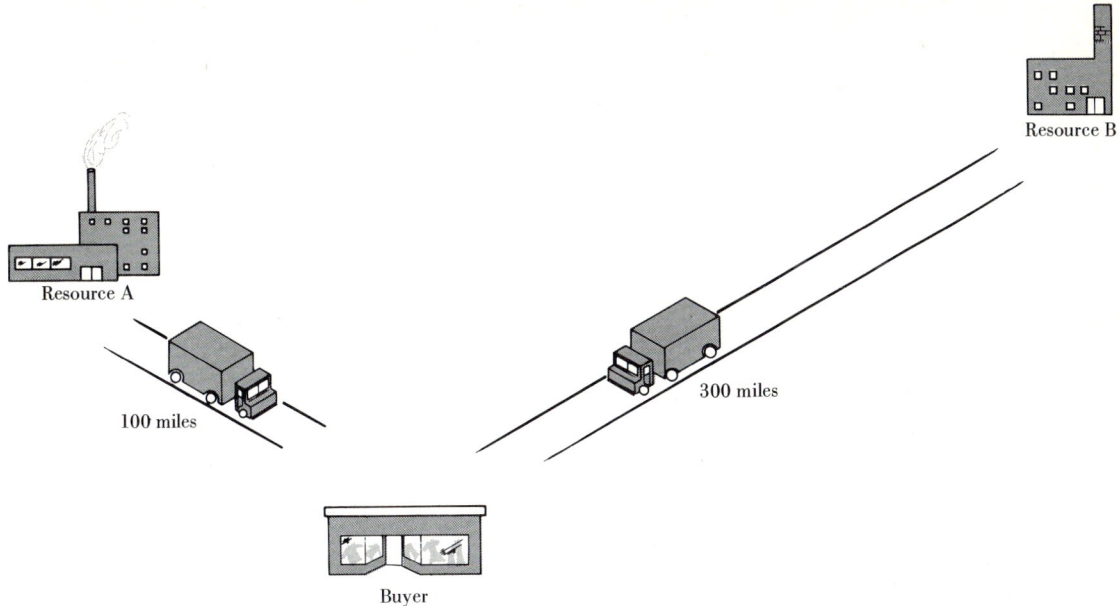

FIGURE 9-3

A situation calling for possible freight absorption

Discounts are deductions off published or stated prices which are allowed in certain circumstances. The base price from which discounts are allowed is dependent upon the type of discount under consideration. Most frequently, a discount is granted from a *list price*, which is the manufacturer's suggested retail price.

DISCOUNTS

The buyer who automatically accepts the price quoted by the vendor as the lowest possible price is doing an injustice to the firm and to its customers. Buyers for many small stores are especially naive and unfamiliar with opportunities for negotiating terms of sale.

Trade or Functional Discounts. Many manufacturers grant *trade discounts*, also called functional discounts, to compensate buyers for marketing functions performed. A full-service wholesaler might receive a discount of 45 percent, a cash-and-carry wholesaler 40 percent, and a retailer 30 percent. Both types of wholesalers receive a larger discount than the retailer because of the marketing activities which they perform. The full-service wholesaler receives a larger discount than the cash-and-carry wholesaler, because he grants credit and makes deliveries. His expenses are therefore greater than those of the limited-service wholesaler.

When manufacturers sell to different types of middlemen, *chain discounts* are rather common. When conditions warrant, the discounts may be

Merchandise Pricing by Resources

changed while the same list price is maintained. For example, a chain discount may be quoted as "list less 40-15." If the list price is $100, the wholesaler would pay $51 for the merchandise. Note that the net amount is not a 55 percent discount. Rather the net amount is computed as: $100 less 40 percent = $60 less 15 percent = $51.

Continuing our example, the wholesaler would pass on to the retailer the 40 percent discount, or $40, providing the retailer with a $60 cost. The wholesaler is thus compensated by the difference between $60 and $51, or $9, for providing the wholesaling function. For his marketing contribution the retailer receives $40, assuming the merchandise is sold at the suggested list price. Theoretically at least, discounts are provided in recognition of the functional contribution each member of the channel makes.

Quantity Discounts. Some vendors offer *quantity discounts* to encourage larger purchases. Quantity discounts take two essential forms: direct deductions from list price based upon the amount purchased *or* free goods. In the latter case, for example, liquor wholesalers often offer one free case

"... You're all heart ..."

with the purchase of a specified number of cases of liquor. The net result is identical—a reduction in the price per unit purchased.

There are two types of quantity discounts in which direct deductions are taken from the list price. *Noncumulative quantity discounts* are based upon the amount of merchandise *bought at a single time*. The discount may be allowed on the quantity of an individual item or on the total of all items included in an order. Noncumulative quantity discounts are offered when larger orders will reduce manufacturing costs, expenses connected with a salesman's call, handling and transportation expenses, and billing and credit costs. Of course, the opposite can be true. If a small manufacturer receives numerous unanticipated large orders, it may be necessary for him to pay a premium to acquire raw materials quickly. Also, costly overtime may be incurred to fill the orders. In such cases, manufacturing costs per unit may actually be increased rather than reduced. Demands for quantity discounts under these conditions may mean decreased profit if the manufacturer concedes.

Cumulative quantity discounts, also known as patronage discounts, are granted for purchases made *within a specified period of time*. The period in which the discount applies may be as short as a month for very perishable, high-volume goods to a year for more staple goods. Cumulative quantity discounts encourage a buyer to continue trading with a resource in order to qualify for larger discounts. However, they may work against the seller by encouraging the buyer to make frequent small purchases.

There is nothing illegal *per se* about quantity discounts as long as they are offered on an equal basis to all buyers. According to provisions of the Robinson-Patman Act, such discounts are to be based upon savings obtained by the seller in manufacturing and/or distribution costs. It is doubtful whether most sellers base their discount schedule upon known cost savings for varying purchase quantities. When the Federal Trade Commission contests the discount schedule, the seller must be prepared to furnish cost savings data, and such proof is difficult for cumulative quantity discounts.

Promotional Discounts. Many vendors of national brand merchandise use promotional discounts or allowances in an attempt to obtain assistance in promoting their merchandise. These allowances compensate retailers for expenses associated with promoting specific products. The vendor must provide promotional allowances on proportionally equal terms to all buyers. It is illegal to specify that promotional allowances will be granted, for example, only on orders exceeding $5,000.

Probably the most common type of promotional discount, widely used by manufacturers, is the *advertising allowance*. Two benefits accrue from the practice. First, the retailer receives financial assistance to help cover advertising expenses. Second, the manufacturer benefits not only through exposure in local media but also exposure at reduced prices. A manufacturer placing advertising in a local medium would pay a *national rate*, while a retailer placing the ad would receive a lower *local rate*.

A common means of providing advertising allowances is through *cooperative advertising programs,* which are discussed in Chapter 16. Other types of promotional allowances involve payment for point-of-purchase displays, or free merchandise, as a promotional allowance. Either must be made available on a proportional basis to all buyers.

Seasonal Discounts. Although not as widely used as the other forms of discounts, seasonal discounts are used by some vendors to level out their business peaks. For example, a ski manufacturer may offer a seasonal discount to a retailer for placing an order, and perhaps accepting delivery of merchandise, in the "off" season. Two possible advantages of seasonal discounts accrue to the manufacturer. If discounts are allowed for off-season ordering, production schedules can be leveled out. When a retailer accepts delivery in the off season, then the manufacturer's storage costs are minimized.

If a retailer is required to pay for the merchandise in the off season, then the discount must be worth the investment of funds in advance of merchandise needs. If early delivery is accepted, the discount should be large enough to compensate for storage costs as well as for the risks involved in warehousing merchandise for a lengthy period of time. Some promotional retailers take advantage of seasonal discounts and then hold a special pre-season sale offering customers substantial savings.

Cash Discounts. The most common form of discount offered to retailers is the cash discount. A *cash discount* is a deduction from the invoice price of goods which is granted if the bill is paid within a specified period of time before the net amount of the bill is due. Although this definition may seem imprecise, certainly it is more nearly correct than the statement often made that "a cash discount is granted for prompt payment." In credit management terms, any customer who pays before the expiration of the net credit period is deemed to have paid promptly. A cash discount is thus granted to encourage *early* payment of bills.

A cash discount is computed on the *net* invoice price, that is, after other discounts such as trade and quantity discounts have been deducted. Let's assume that a retail buyer has a $1,200 bill after other discounts have been deducted. How much has to be paid if the cash discount terms are 3/10, net 30? The invoice is dated May 31. If the buyer pays the invoice within 10 days (through June 10), $36 (3 percent) may be deducted from the invoice price and $1,164 paid. For payment any time after June 10 but before July 1, the net invoice price of $1,200 must be paid. After June 30 the bill is overdue and subject to an extra interest charge. Figure 9-4 illustrates the meaning of the parts of a cash discount.

Some small retailers ignore cash discounts, paying on the last net due date. Often these retailers are pressed for funds so they defer paying for merchandise as long as possible. Let's see if this is prudent management. In the above example, the retailer pays 3 percent, or $36, for the use of $1,200 *for 20 days* (after the expiration of the cash discount period until the net due date). Since there are eighteen 20-day periods in a banker's year (360 days are commonly used to determine interest rates), the annual interest rate equivalent is 54 percent (18 × 3 percent). This simple case illustrates why retailers should definitely take advantage of cash discounts even if they must pay 10 to 12 percent interest to borrow money. At 10 percent interest, it would cost the retailer $6.67 to borrow the full $1,200 for 20 days (he really need borrow only $1,164). Borrowing the money from a bank in order to take advantage of the cash discount nets the retailer $29.33 ($36.00 − $6.67). Although this savings may seem small, when it is multiplied by dozens of orders throughout the year it can amount to a substantial amount of money.

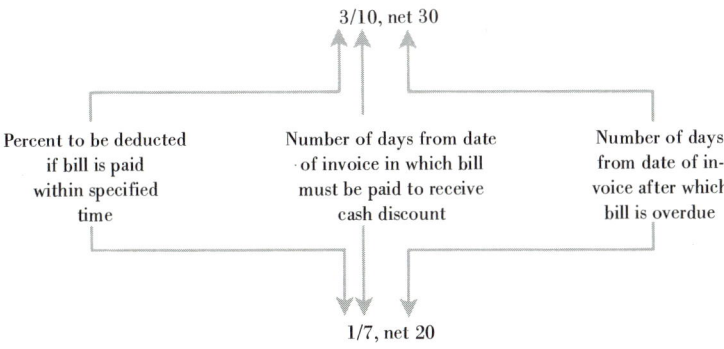

FIGURE 9-4

The parts of a cash discount

Some retailers, especially large ones, abuse the cash discount. It is a standing rule in some stores that the cash discount is to be taken even if the discount period has expired. Particularly in the case of a large important retail account, such abuse may place a small manufacturer in an untenable position. Insistence that the discount not be taken risks losing the account. Allowing the discount to be taken even though it is unearned encourages the store to continue such action in the future. If other buyers take similar action, then the purpose of the cash discount is lost. The retailer who is completely ethical and does not abuse the cash discount terms is penalized by the actions of those who are less scrupulous.

The amount of the cash discount varies among lines of trade from 1

Merchandise Pricing by Resources

to 10 percent and is usually higher where risk of physical deterioration or obsolescence is great.

Anticipation. A form of discount closely related to a cash discount is anticipation. If an invoice is paid prior to the expiration of the cash discount period, the buyer can deduct an amount equal to the going bank interest rate for the number of days of early payment. Suppose an invoice for $1,000 dated July 1 carries a cash discount of 2/10, net 30. If the bill is paid on July 5, the amount to be remitted is $978.69. This is computed as follows:

$$\$1000 - 2\% = \$980$$

$$\$980 \times 8\% \begin{pmatrix} \text{current bank} \\ \text{interest rate} \end{pmatrix} \times \frac{6}{360} \begin{pmatrix} \text{the number of days of} \\ \text{early payment divided} \\ \text{by banker's year} \end{pmatrix} = \$1.31$$

$$\$980 - \$1.31 = \$978.69$$

It is obvious that anticipation amounts to a much smaller savings than the cash discount, but it is nevertheless money to which the buyer is entitled.

DATING

Dating pertains to the amount of time allowed for the payment of invoices. Sometimes this timing is almost as important as any discounts offered. This is especially true when extremely liberal dating terms are used.

Net dating means no cash discount is allowed, and the net invoice price is due within a specified time. When a number follows the "net," it specifies the number of days before the bill becomes past due. In the absence of any number of days qualifying the net terms, it is interpreted to mean "net 30 days."

Ordinary Dating. Unless otherwise specified, the credit terms and discount period extend from the date of the invoice which is also normally the date merchandise is shipped. As generally used, ordinary dating specifies both the discount period and the net credit period from the invoice date.

Extra Dating. In some cases vendors will specify "extra" terms such as 2/10, 60X or 2/10, 60 extra. This means that the buyer has 70 days from the invoice date to take the cash discount. Primarily because of tradition, sellers use extra terms rather than state the larger period explicitly. When no net credit period is indicated, it is usually implicitly understood that 20 days after the expiration of the cash discount period will be permissible. This means, then, that the terms are in essence 2/70, net 90.

When the "extra" period becomes long, there is some question as to whether the terms really serve the purpose for which cash discounts are intended. For example, is a cash discount period of 120 days, net 140 really encouraging early payment?

End-of-Month Dating. Whereas the invoice date is normally used for calculating the cash discount and net credit period, end-of-month (EOM) dating liberalizes these terms. Under EOM terms the cash discount and the net credit period begin with the last day of the month in which the invoice was billed. For example, an invoice dated November 8 and stating terms of 3/10, net 30 EOM means that the cash discount and the net credit period are computed from November 30. Thus the buyer can take the cash discount through December 10, with the net amount due by December 30. In this case the buyer actually has 32 days after the invoice date in which to take the cash discount.

In addition to providing extended time in which the cash discount may be taken, EOM terms carry other benefits. Small buyers receiving EOM terms from all their resources can write all checks only once a month, thus saving office time. In addition, several invoices can be paid with one check, thereby reducing the number of checks written.

Most vendors granting EOM terms allow an extra month on invoices dated after the 26th of the month. For example, if an invoice is dated May 28, the buyer has until the 10th of July to take the cash discount. Note the very liberal result of 43 days after the invoice date in which the cash discount is applicable.

Middle-of-the-Month Dating. Middle-of-the-month (MOM) terms are less liberal than (EOM) terms. When MOM dating is used, there are two cutoff dates, the 15th and the last day of the month. Thus, when an invoice is dated before the 15th, the credit period extends from the 15th; but when it is dated after the 15th, the credit period begins with the last day of the month. Thus, the discount period on an invoice dated April 3 and carrying MOM terms ends on April 25. On an invoice dated April 18, the discount period ends on May 10.

Receipt of Goods and Arrival of Goods Dating. Two dating terms, receipt of goods (ROG) and arrival of goods (AOG) are aimed at creating some sort of equality for buyers located at varying distances from a seller. Under these terms the discount period begins when the goods arrive at the buyer's place of business. Suppose that two buyers, one in Seattle, Washington and the other in Jacksonville, Florida, both buy from a manufacturer in Atlanta, Georgia. It is not difficult to see that the buyer in Jacksonville has a longer time period after receiving shipment before the cash discount period expires than does the buyer in Seattle. Actually the discount period could expire before the buyer in Seattle received his merchandise. Thus, terms of 3/10, net 30 ROG treats both buyers equally with respect to the cash discount period.

REVIEW BOX 9:4

1. Bargaining between a retailer and merchandise resources is called _____.
2. FOB factory means that the _____ pays freight charges.
3. _____ are deductions which are allowed off published or list prices.
4. Trade discounts are allowed retailers for _____ _____ _____.
5. _____ quantity discounts are based upon the amount of merchandise bought at a specific time.
6. A _____ discount is a deduction granted for paying a bill within a specified period of time before the net amount is due.
7. A part of terms of sale which pertains to the time allowed for the payment of invoices is called _____.
8. With terms of 2/10, 60X, _____ dating is involved.
9. MOM dating terms are _____ liberal than EOM terms.
10. Terms which provide equal treatment in cash discount time allowed for buyers located at varying distances from the seller are called _____ or _____ dating.

RELATIONSHIPS WITH RESOURCES

Too often buyers and vendors view each other as adversaries rather than as cooperating members in a channel of distribution. In reality each is dependent upon the other in order to make a profit. Both parties must be careful to negotiate within legal and ethical constraints. However, aggressive bargaining is not the sole cause of dissension between buyers and sellers. Common courtesy and tolerance are often necessary in the relationship to perpetuate its existence.

The Store Order

One principle often advanced in retail buying is that stores should use their own order forms in placing orders for merchandise. The benefit to large retailers is that all orders are standardized, and the retail buyer can become familiar with the form. With the standardized form the buyer can readily check to see that the order is complete in every respect. Another benefit is that copies furnished for receiving and marking, accounts payable, and perhaps merchandise control do not vary in physical size and layout. An accounts payable clerk, for example, knows exactly where to look for the cash discount terms. Proper spaces are provided for approval signatures of persons other than the buyer.

A limited survey of small stores, conducted by one of the authors, indicates that many have never used their own order forms or have tried them and been dissatisfied. The expense of having forms printed is one consideration, and in some cases the forms designed were not appropriate for all classes of merchandise bought by the store. In cases where the resources require that their own order forms be used, there is a duplication of effort in that both the store's and the resource's order forms must be completed. One small men's apparel retailer stated that the order forms furnished by resources were far superior to any form the store had devised. When the buyer relies entirely upon resources to furnish order blanks, the form should be read in its entirety, since special conditions are often printed on the back of the form.

Most order forms provide for information covering:

1. Name and address of buyer and seller
2. Date of order and order number
3. Quantity, description, and price of merchandise
4. Terms (including transportation) and dating
5. Date of delivery and method of transportation
6. Special instructions for packaging and packing
7. Signature of buyer, seller, and others whose approval may be required.
8. Where appropriate, space for sizes, style numbers, and other pertinent information

Order Cancellations and Returns

Orders should not be cancelled without the consent of both parties. An exception would be when a seller cannot meet the stipulations on the order form. If the seller informs the buyer that the delivery date cannot be met or that a certain style is not available, then either party may cancel the order. But once the order is placed by the buyer and accepted by the seller, then both are contractually bound and neither can unilaterally revoke the order.

For numerous reasons, some buyers desire to return merchandise. Any returns require the approval of the vendor. In the case of defective merchandise or merchandise different from that specified on the order, the vendor will not normally object. However, some retailers attempt to return merchandise left over at the end of a season or merchandise which simply does not move. Unless a return privilege is stipulated on the order, such returns should not be made without the seller's approval. When retailers take such unjustified actions, the continued goodwill of the resource is taxed.

Split Shipments and Back Orders

When resources are unable to ship a complete order, they will often ship a partial order and "back order" the remaining merchandise for later shipment. Split shipments can be burdensome to a retailer. When the retail firm is paying transportation charges, the cost of two or more shipments can substantially increase the per-unit freight charge. If the retailer has planned a special promotion, the incomplete order may necessitate canceling of scheduled advertising. Depending upon the delay involved, merchandise may arrive too late to be sold during the season. For example, if a large back order of toys arrives at a retail outlet on the day before Christmas, it is doubtful whether the merchandise can be sold, and substantial markdowns may be necessary.

As with retailers' order cancellations, vendors' inability to fill orders can cause tensions. When resources are unable to ship complete orders, they should notify the retailer immediately so that all or part of the order may be cancelled.

The Need for Cooperation

Numerous other opportunities for misunderstanding or treatment injurious to the other party exist in a vendor-buyer relationship. The quest for cooperation between the two does not suggest "softness" in the business relationship. Rather, some empathy and understanding are needed on both sides. Honest, straightforward dealings by both parties can result in greater satisfaction and profits for both.

REVIEW BOX 9:5

1. If all the stipulations on the order can be met, neither of the parties should cancel an order without _____ _____.

2. When a resource is unable to ship a complete order and sends only a part of the order, this is called a _____.

CHAPTER SUMMARY

- Often the success or failure of a retail store depends upon effective buying. Buying is both an art and a science, but effective buying is essentially "hard work."
- Buyers buy merchandise for resale, while purchasing agents purchase supplies and equipment.
- Most buyers must operate within constraints imposed by store objectives and policies concerning store image, gross margins required, and merchandise consistency.
- Store buyers must select merchandise resources from numerous wholesalers, manufacturers, and occasionally, other retailers.
- Central markets consist of merchandise marts and shows, manufacturing centers, and resident buying offices.
- Cooperative buying, one common method of buying, involves the pooling of orders by independent, non-competing stores. The primary purpose of such buying is to obtain lower merchandise costs which allow smaller stores to compete effectively with larger stores.
- Centralized buying is practiced when a buyer buys for several stores under the same ownership.
- Committee buying spreads the buying responsibility among several executives.
- Consignment or memorandum buying allows a store to handle merchandise without risking capital on nonselling goods, since goods not sold may be returned to the vendor.
- Leasing a department allows a store to offer certain merchandise or services without the usual risk of business failure or outlays of cash.
- Terms of sale offer the retailer the opportunity to negotiate with merchandise resources for concessions.
- Negotiating lower transportation costs can aid the retailer by reducing total merchandise costs.
- Discounts are deductions allowed off published or stated prices.
- Trade discounts are allowed for marketing functions performed, while quantity discounts are price reductions based upon the amount of merchandise bought.
- Promotional discounts compensate the retailer for his persuasive efforts aimed at customers, and seasonal discounts are provided to encourage retailers to buy in the off season.
- The most common form of discount is the cash discount, which is a deduction from the invoice price if paid within a specified time before the net amount is due.
- Dating is concerned with the amount of time allowed for the pay-

ment of an invoice. Some dating variations provide a merchant with additional time in which to take a cash discount or pay the net invoice amount.
- Retailers need to maintain a cooperative relationship with suppliers based upon honest, understanding dealings by both parties.

CHAPTER NOTES

[1] David J. Elsner, "Edward Berger Discovers that Attaining Success as a Clothing Buyer is Based on Good Guesswork," *The Wall Street Journal*, March 15, 1973, p. 32.

[2] David M. Elsner, "The Mistakes of Catherine Breen Teach Montgomery Ward's Buyers to Beware," *The Wall Street Journal*, July 24, 1973, p. 10.

[3] Most basic marketing texts provide a description of the activities performed by wholesaling middlemen. For example see David J. Schwartz, *Marketing Today* (New York: Harcourt Brace Jovanovich, 1973), pp. 253–76.

[4] "How Pathmark Disarms the Crusaders," *Business Week*, May 8, 1971, p. 66.

[5] "A & P's Ploy: Cutting Prices to Turn a Profit," *Business Week*, May 20, 1972, p. 78.

[6] For a thorough discussion of the Robinson-Patman Act, see Marshall C. Howard, *Legal Aspects of Marketing* (New York: McGraw-Hill Book Co., 1964), especially Chapter 3.

QUESTIONS AND ASSIGNMENTS

1. Lost sales and loss of customer goodwill result from out-of-stock conditions and from requests for merchandise not carried by the store. What kind of a system do you think a buyer might design to reveal either condition?
2. Distinguish between a buyer and a purchasing agent.
3. How do the problems faced by a buyer for a large store differ from those of a small store buyer?
4. Explain why store management might insist that a buyer utilize a rack jobber for certain classes of merchandise.
5. Two retailers of approximately the same size and carrying the same type of merchandise are located in a city within eight blocks of each other. One uses a full-service wholesaler for a line of goods while the other uses a cash-and-carry wholesaler. How might you account for this difference?
6. Do you think a manufacturer should ever refuse to sell directly to retailers and insist that they buy through wholesalers? If so, under what conditions?
7. Distinguish between centralized buying and committee buying.
8. Is there any legal constraint which limits the ability of a buyer to negotiate lower prices on merchandise? Explain.
9. If a seller quotes all prices FOB destination, what is the effect on the seller's profit? What effect does this have on retailers?
10. An invoice for $875 dated August 5 provides terms of 4/10, net 30. If the retailer takes advantage of the cash discount, how much does he pay? When does the cash discount expire? The net credit period?
11. Explain why EOM terms are more liberal than MOM terms.
12. If an invoice provides terms of 5/15, net 30 EOM and is dated June 1, when does the cash discount expire? The net credit period?

13. An invoice is dated January 2 and specifies 4/10 MOM. When does the cash discount period expire?
14. Indicate what circumstances might prompt a buyer to request ROG dating on an invoice.
15. If merchandise is clearly defective or if many substitutes have been made, should the retailer be required to obtain the seller's permission before returning such goods? Why or why not?

ANSWERS TO REVIEW BOX QUESTIONS

Box 9:1
1. scientific
2. buyer; purchasing agent
3. policies

Box 9:2
1. specification
2. central market
3. merchandise marts
4. resident buyers

Box 9:3
1. individual, non-competing
2. centralized
3. buying committees
4. consignment

Box 9:4
1. negotiation
2. retailer
3. discounts
4. marketing functions performed
5. non-cumulative
6. cash
7. dating
8. extra
9. less
10. arrival of goods (AOG) or receipt of goods (ROG)

Box 9:5
1. mutual consent of both parties
2. split shipment

Questions and Assignments

Merchandise Control

Ten percent of employees will not steal no matter how much opportunity they are given; 80 percent will stay honest if they work under adequate controls to reduce temptation; and 10 percent will steal under any circumstances, regardless of any precautions.[1]

Several smaller retailers reported recently that they have been victimized in customer returns. Here's how it happens. A customer pays for merchandise with a worthless check, and then on the same day he or she returns the purchase. The customer has a valid receipt and is issued a complete *cash* refund.[2]

Merchandise control is an important problem for today's merchant. There are two primary elements of merchandise control: maintaining proper levels of *merchandise inventories*, and safekeeping of merchandise to regulate *merchandise shrinkage*. Problems associated with merchandise control are many and varied. However, since the annual investment in merchandise is typically the largest single asset of a retailing firm, control of this investment merits serious consideration.

CONTROLLING INVENTORY LEVELS

Merchandise budgets are used for control purposes as well as for planning. However, since the merchandise budget is derived from and dependent upon the sales budget, provision must be made for differences in actual sales and planned sales. If actual sales are either above or below planned sales, adjustments must be made in the merchandise budget.

The importance of these adjustments cannot be overemphasized. Consider what would happen if an unanticipated economic downturn occurs and sales are considerably lower than planned. If no budget adjustments are made, the buyer would continue buying merchandise in anticipation of a higher level of sales. The troublesome result: the store or department would become severely unbalanced and large inventory holding costs would result. Thus a constant review of the merchandise budget, in view of changing conditions, is a necessity. Two common forms of inventory control, dollar control and unit control, are discussed here.

Dollar Control

Dollar control essentially provides a means of regulating the amount of money invested in inventory to achieve desired sales. A merchandise budget or plan gives no assurance that all of the planned figures will be met. The purpose of dollar merchandise control is to ensure that inventory levels which deviate from planned levels are recognized and proper corrective action is taken.

Since budgets are typically stated in dollars, the budget is the most commonly used device for controlling dollar stocks. Periodic reports are usually prepared for each merchandising department. Depending upon store size and the philosophy of management, such reports may be issued weekly, monthly, or seasonally (usually quarterly). Such reports allow comparison of planned figures with actual figures.

Figure 10-1 depicts one common means of dollar inventory control. This is the same open-to-buy form we used in merchandise planning. Note that actual sales are lower than anticipated and unfilled orders are greater than planned. As a result, the buyer is overbought by $3,000. If this report were issued at the end of a month, the buyer would be faced with an upcoming month in which no additional merchandise can be bought. If merchandise on order is that needed for the *coming* month, then the buyer may suffer no more than a possible reprimand from his superior for the overbought condition. If, however, the merchandise on order simply duplicates existing inventory, then the buyer may have to negotiate with the vendors involved to cancel some orders. Such action could relieve the overbought condition and perhaps even result in a positive open-to-buy. Of course, canceling orders frequently will make vendors unhappy.

Such a report alerts not only the buyer but also upper-level management. For control purposes, the important consideration is a determination of *why* the overbought condition exists. Immediate attention to the composition of stocks and an evaluation of how the present condition was brought about are imperative for adequate control. Obviously something has happened to cause actual open-to-buy to deviate by $20,000 and result in the $3,000 overbought situation instead of the planned $17,000 open-to-buy. No

	Planned	Actual
Department _____		
Month of _____		
Sales	$ 50,000	$ 40,000
Reductions	2,000	2,000
EOM stock	85,000	95,000
Merchandise requirements	137,000	137,000
Current inventory level	90,000	95,000
Unfilled orders (merchandise ordered but not yet received)	30,000	45,000
Merchandise available	120,000	140,000
Open-to-buy	$ 17,000	($3,000)

FIGURE 10-1

An open-to-buy control form

informed corrective action can be taken until the reasons for the deviation are determined. Perhaps it is necessary to increase inventory (decrease sales-stock ratio) in order to achieve the planned level of sales.

Note that strict adherence to a budget is not the sole purpose of control. Rather, dollar merchandise control should emphasize discovering reasons for the deviations from planned figures so that necessary corrective action can be taken.

Unit Control

Whereas dollar control systems are typically used to control the actions of buyers, *unit control* is most often used by buyers to control stock assortments. Unit control maintains inventories *in terms of physical units*. A department may be meeting its dollar plan and still be missing sales opportunities because of an improper merchandise assortment. In other words, just meeting the dollar budget is not enough to ensure that sales or profits are being maximized.

Unit control is a supplement to dollar control, not a substitute for it. It has more merit for a large store than for a small one. A small merchant in daily contact with customers and merchandise can tell which merchandise is moving well, when stocks are getting low, and when sizes or colors of a particular item are unbalanced—hence unit control may not be needed. When a buyer does not have day-to-day contact with inventories or when the merchandising unit becomes large, however, some kind of unit control is necessary.

In essence, unit control provides a buyer with a periodic inventory on certain items. Maintaining a balanced inventory can be costly. On the other hand, the costs associated with lost sales because of out-of-stock conditions can also be substantial. Thus the problem becomes one of optimizing costs and minimizing the frequency of lost sales while at the same time controlling the costs of inventory investment.

STOCK-COUNT BOOKS

One method of unit control involves a physical count of the stock on hand. Stock counts are usually made on a rotating basis so that an inventory is taken on an item either weekly, biweekly, or monthly. In large fashion goods departments, a unit control clerk may be employed to continually make stock counts and update the stock-count book. Obviously, a unit control clerk's salary must be offset by the value of information provided the buyer.

In smaller departments or stores, salespeople may be responsible for stock counts. Also, in self-service stores, particularly those of the discount type, you frequently see an employee with a "black book" or clipboard making these counts. Often it is not necessary to count every separate item during the stock count. The often repeated "80-20 principle" may apply.[3] For many merchandise classifications, 80 percent of dollar sales are generated by 20 percent of the stocked goods. These so-called *important items* usually also produce the most profit and therefore require constant surveillance.[4]

Often an additional 15 percent of sales are generated by another 15 percent of stock. These *middle-value items* need less frequent stock counts and attention. The important and middle-value items account for approximately 95 percent of total dollar sales while comprising only 35 percent of the total items carried in inventory. Thus the unit control problem is greatly simplified; the retailer can identify and concentrate on the best moving items. One word of caution: Although the "80-20 principle" often holds true, important exceptions occur. Only through an investigation of stock movement and sales volume can the retailer definitely establish the principle.

SALES RECORDING SYSTEMS

Unlike a physical count of merchandise on hand, *sales recording systems* concentrate upon the recording of incoming and outgoing merchandise. Although there are variations, there are two primary methods used for sales recording systems: manual and electronic.

Manual Recording. Basically, a manual system is similar to the stock-count system. The major difference is in the way inventory levels are determined. Sales recording systems begin with a physical inventory indi-

Controlling Inventory Levels **231**

cating the number of units on hand. As merchandise is received, the units are increased, and as sales occur they are reduced. In effect a *perpetual inventory* is kept on selected items by means of unit control cards. A unit control clerk can maintain the unit control books without ever seeing the merchandise.

Invoices show the types and amounts of merchandise received. Although various methods can be used to record sales, two primary sources are common. One possibility is to use copies of handwritten sales checks. The unit control clerk uses the sales check as authorization to deduct items from inventory. This can be a rather tedious task when a store has a large volume of sales and when more than one merchandise item appears on the sales check. This procedure also requires that each item be carefully identified on each sales check.

The second method makes use of perforated price tags with half of each tag removed at the time of sale. This method is common with ready-to-wear items. The stub contains all pertinent information necessary to identify a specific item. At the end of the day the stubs are tallied and entered on appropriate unit control cards.

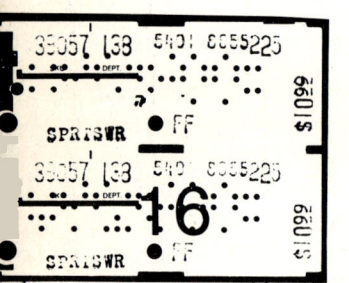

Electronic Recording. Because manual recording is cumbersome, many stores have automated their record-keeping system. A simple system uses perforated price tags which contain tiny holes representing item codes. These stubs are then automatically transferred by machine to a punched-paper tape or they are fed directly into a computer.

Point-of-sale terminals, another method, ordinarily allow the cashier to enter the information into the cash register. More advanced terminals have an optical scanner which automatically senses the information printed on price tickets and provides direct input either on a tape for further processing or into the computer.

A major shortcoming of sales recording systems is that merchandise shortages are not revealed. With stock counts, the actual amount of specific merchandise on hand is recorded. Under sales recording systems, three pieces of a specific item may be shown in stock, whereas a stock count may indicate only one piece in stock. Perhaps a shoplifter has been at work.

REVIEW BOX 10:1

1. Merchandise budgets are used for planning and _____.
2. Adjustments in the merchandise budget are primarily necessitated by deviations from planned _____.
3. _____ merchandise control emphasizes the reason for failure to meet planned figures as well as corrective actions necessary.
4. Often the unit control problem is simplified because of the _____ principle.

IDENTIFYING AND MINIMIZING MERCHANDISE SHRINKAGE

Controlling merchandise shrinkage has become a substantial problem for retailers in the 1970s. Although in most cases it is impossible to assign the exact cause to merchandise shrinkage, the problem is severe enough to warrant consideration of the possible causes. Viewed very broadly, merchandise shrinkage involves any shortage which exists when a physical inventory amount is compared with the book inventory figure.

Shoplifting

Shoplifting is the stealing of merchandise by persons other than store employees. Shoplifting is distinguished from robbery in that no force or threat is involved.

FORMS AND SEVERITY

Shoplifting takes two essential forms: either not paying for merchandise taken or paying less than the price for which the merchandise is presently selling. A shoplifter not paying for merchandise ordinarily conceals the item when leaving the store. But not always! In one case a man selected an aluminum kayak that would apparently serve his needs, lifted it above his head, and walked down six flights of stairs and out of the store. He was tying it to his car several blocks from the store when he was apprehended by a store employee.[5] Although some shoplifters probably are successful in such unorthodox methods, apprehension is often the result.

Several years ago a professor in the Rocky Mountain region was discussing the shoplifting problem with his retailing class. Pointing out local stores' inattention to merchandise control, he indicated that it would be quite easy to steal a large item from either of two local discount stores. He stated that it was only necessary to look official in removing the item. A student decided to "test the theory." He selected a large stuffed elephant and walked out of the store. Later the professor received a call from a police officer who stated that the by then arrested student reported he was simply "testing" the instructor's idea. Obviously a considerable amount of explanation and discussion was necessary before the student was released.

The moral of these two illustrations is that shoplifting motives and methods are far-ranging, which makes the situation more troublesome for retailers. As we shall see later, there are no obvious prime suspects in shoplifting.

The second form of shoplifting, paying less than the proper purchase price, usually involves switching or altering price tags. Stores that take markdowns for special sales or clearances and merely change the price tag with a pencil or perhaps a red pen are inviting trouble. Any customer with an appropriate pencil or pen can easily alter the price of an item which is not on sale. When many customers are waiting to be served, even an experienced salesperson can fail to notice that the item is not really on sale. When extra or new salespeople are involved, the probability that the error will be discovered is even less.

Stores using simple pin tags or adhesive backed tags for pricing run the risk of price tag switching. On apparel items a dishonest shopper can easily switch price tags in a dressing room. In self-service stores, when few store personnel or customers are present, the switch can be made right at the merchandise location. Many stores now use perforated price tags which cannot be removed without destroying the tag. Others use a special glue which makes the price tag almost impossible to remove without tearing it into many pieces. For many types of apparel some stores have discontinued pin tags and now use a special tagger which "shoots" a plastic string with a special tip on it through the garment. The price tag can be removed only by cutting the plastic string, which cannot then be replaced.

Supermarkets often use a stamping device to price mark merchandise. On jars with metal lids the price is normally stamped on the lid. An unusual type of price switching can occur in this situation. For example, if two sizes of bottled catsup use the same size lid, the shoplifter simply switches lids, thereby purchasing the large size for the small size price. The same can hold true for different sizes of pickles, preserves, and other goods. To attempt to eliminate this problem, supermarkets have tried, with limited success, to convince manufacturers to use non-interchangeable lids for the various sizes of containers.

Estimates of the severity of shoplifting vary. One report states that shoplifting amounts to $3.5 billion dollars annually.[6] Although in the minority, some stores report losses as high as 4 to 5 percent of sales.[7] In some cases this loss is equal to the stores' profit margins. The FBI has referred to inventory losses as "the fastest growing larceny in the nation."[8] Various studies indicate that one out of every 10 to 15 customers who enter a department store in a major metropolitan area steals something. The shoplifting problem is not limited to large stores. Small retailers, too, are experiencing substantial increases in theft by customers. Thus shoplifting is one of the most all-pervasive retailing problems.

WHO ARE TODAY'S SHOPLIFTERS?

Although we will look at various "groups" of shoplifters, we will find no simple way to categorize them. It seems that everyone's doing it! Shoplifters are not just economically deprived individuals. Various published studies as well as conversations with retailers and police officials indicate that a majority of those apprehended have enough money in their possession to purchase the stolen items.

SPOTLIGHT

Could you spot a shoplifter?

One of the major problems facing retailers is that shoplifters are not easily identified. Neither age, color, nor appearance are helpful as identifiers. Although certain merchandise is more frequently shoplifted, none seems completely immune.

One of the authors, after discussing consumer behavior, asked his class to write a paper discussing the buyer behavior exhibited in a recent purchase they had made. Imagine his surprise when one student wrote a three-page paper explaining why he never bought anything. He felt local merchants made too much profit so he stole everything he needed. Perhaps he overstated the case, but the student insisted that shoplifting is very simple if you choose the proper time and the right store.

The following profile indicates a similar situation.

A shoplifter is not necessarily unkempt, kooky-looking or badly dressed. For the most part, the shoplifter looks just like any other shopper and, in some cases, better, as this shows:

Joseph is a thief, a title he proudly bears and occasionally vaunts to anyone within hearing range, as long as they're not policemen. He says he has been a thief for three years, part-time of course, since he holds a perfectly respectable Establishment-type job five days a week, seven hours a day.

Joseph looks very "straight," very Establishment, perhaps Harvard '63, with horn-rimmed glasses and regimental stripe tie and shirt, slightly curly hair. He always wears a white shirt and tie when he goes on his forays, and he always shines his shoes because, he thinks, "Appearance is all. . . . People will stop you if you look like a freak; they'll search and, if they find something, they'll prosecute, if only to make an example of you. . . . But look straight like me. Hell, I look like a junior banking executive; I could walk off with a refrigerator and no one will try to stop me, no one. . . ."

His technique seems to work. Joseph says he hasn't bought so much as a carton of milk in the past six months. Everything he eats or feeds to his guests is stolen, even, in some cases, the shiny cooking utensils he uses.

Source: "Profile of a Shoplifter," *Modern Retailer*, June 1972, p. 15.

Unfortunately, a follow-up on these two individuals has not been conducted. It seems certain, though, that if they continue shoplifting they will eventually be caught. If convicted, they will have a police record, which seems a big risk for the gain involved.

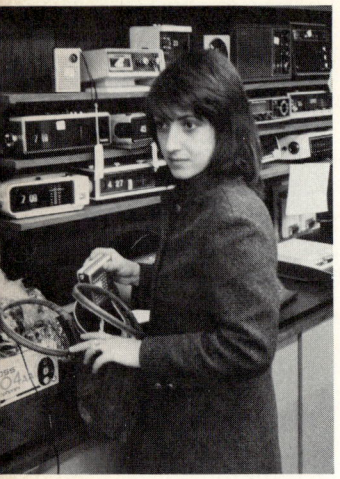

The major way to categorize shoplifters is as amateurs or professionals. Although professionals steal far more per "shopping trip," amateurs constitute the majority of shoplifters. In general, professional shoplifters are those who sell their stolen goods. Estimates are that less than 10 percent of all shoplifters are professionals. However, these estimates often fail to consider that perhaps the professionals are "smarter" and are less likely to be apprehended. Too, it is not clear whether the drug addict who shoplifts to support his daily habit is a professional or an amateur.

Considering the amateur shoplifter, the problem becomes one of attempting to analyze why the problem is a growing one. There are those who believe that shoplifting has gained a peculiar kind of legitimacy. Increased evidence of illegal activities of businesses and government officials, continued inflation, and various "permissive" approaches to life are often cited as reasons for increased shoplifting. Since "everybody's doing it," it must be okay.

Apparently both males and females engage in shoplifting to the same degree. Although more female shoplifters are usually apprehended, we must remember there are more female shoppers. One study found a slightly higher incidence of female shoplifters than males, but only four department stores in three cities were involved in the study.[9]

The same study found that age and race are not related to frequency of shoplifting. Often teenagers are identified as a major age group of shoplifters, but this is possibly due to their "peculiar" behavioral patterns as viewed by the more "adult" salespeople and a natural suspicion toward youth. This is not to minimize the youthful or teenager shoplifting problem. However, reliable nationwide data are not available on the age composition of shoplifters, and generalizing from results obtained in specific locations can be dangerous. In the previously cited study, the frequency of stealing was almost equally divided among those under twenty-one, those twenty-one to thirty-five, and those over thirty-five.

Dr. David Reuben, author of *Everything You Always Wanted to Know About Sex—But Were Afraid to Ask*, has concluded that most amateur shoplifters are married women between the ages of thirty-five and fifty-five.[10] Apparently many of these women have serious emotional conflicts such as unhappy marriages, obesity, depression, and/or unsatisfactory sexual relationships that lead them to engage in shoplifting.

ATTEMPTS TO CONTROL SHOPLIFTING

The previously mentioned methods to prevent price switching are indicative of attempts at control. However, numerous other control methods have been instituted by retail stores and range from very simple measures to those which are extremely complex and expensive.

It is estimated that stores spend $2 billion annually on security.[11] But the amounts spent to control theft vary widely according to the type and size of store. Security consultant Lincoln Zonn contends that discount stores should spend from .5 to 1 percent of total sales on the store security budget. He states that even though this sounds like a lot of money, it is not too much when compared with annual shoplifting losses.[12]

Fixtures and Layout. Planning shoplifting controls should begin prior to the opening of a new store. The store should not have walls which obstruct the view of store personnel and allow potential shoplifters a degree of privacy. Thus in full-service stores, departments divided by partitions should have at least one salesperson on the selling floor of the department at all times. In self-service stores, the trend has definitely been toward openness, with no nooks or corners which might offer shoplifters privacy.

Display cases and fixtures can also aid in control of store theft. There is a trend toward lowering the height of store display fixtures. Store fixtures of 48 inches or less allow employees visual control over the entire store. Closed display cases for small but expensive items also are becoming more popular. Normally these fixtures are well lighted and allow shoppers to inspect merchandise but prevent them from removing items without the assistance of a salesperson. Jewelry, wallets, cameras, portable electronic calculators, and stereo tapes are typical of merchandise requiring close control.

Proper merchandise placement can also assist in its control. Most stores now refrain from placing easily shoplifted items near the store entrance. In addition, the physical layout should be planned so that maximum control is assured. For example, many stores now not only limit the number of items that may be taken into a dressing room, but also provide dressing room doors or curtains which do not reach the floor and are low enough to enable salespeople to see over the closure. This provides less privacy for potential shoplifters.

Mirrors and Signs. Many smaller stores have installed circular convex mirrors at strategic locations to allow employees to check "blind spots" in the store. The effectiveness of these mirrors is not known. One school of thought contends that such mirrors allow the shoplifter a way to check whether he is being watched. The contrary argument is that mirrors act as a deterrent simply by indicating that store management is alert to the shoplifting problem.

Using signs to deter shoplifting is becoming widespread. Typically these signs say "Shoplifting is a Crime," or "Shoplifters will be Prosecuted." The ability of such signs to reduce shoplifting is unknown, but several merchants have expressed satisfaction with the results achieved.

Television Cameras, One-way Mirrors, and Peep Holes. Many stores have used these devices to spot shoplifters as well as dishonest employees. Closed circuit television enables a store security force to "patrol" various areas of the store by watching viewing screens placed in an office.

Such systems are relatively expensive, but they may reduce the need for a large security force. In some cases dummy cameras are used as a deterrent. Such dummy cameras may be used exclusively or they may be used to supplement real cameras.

Some stores have installed one-way mirrors or concealed "peep holes" in troublesome areas to allow surveillance of customers without their knowledge. When these stations are manned, use of two-way radios allows the viewer to communicate with a store detective on or near the sales floor.

Electronic Signal Devices. An increasingly popular method of control in ready-to-wear departments or stores is electronic control. Selected merchandise is marked with a special sensitized tag. If the shopper attempts to leave the store without having this tag removed or desensitized, an electronic sensor notifies store personnel by a buzzer, bell, flashing lights, or other means. The tag can be removed without damage to the article only with a special tool. In a normal sale the clerk removes the tag and the sensor is not activated as the customer leaves the store. Sales personnel must be instructed to remove every tag on garments sold to prevent valid purchasers from being unjustly embarrassed.

Security Force. Most medium-size and large stores employ a security force. A uniformed security force acts as a shoplifting deterrent, while the plainclothes force is more successful in spotting shoplifters. Since a plainclothes force cannot give complete coverage, sales employees are asked to spot suspicous looking customers. The plainclothes detective is then called to keep the suspect under surveillance. The detective usually poses as a shopper and continually circulates throughout his or her assigned area. Frequently these people do not look like store detectives. Stores with effec-

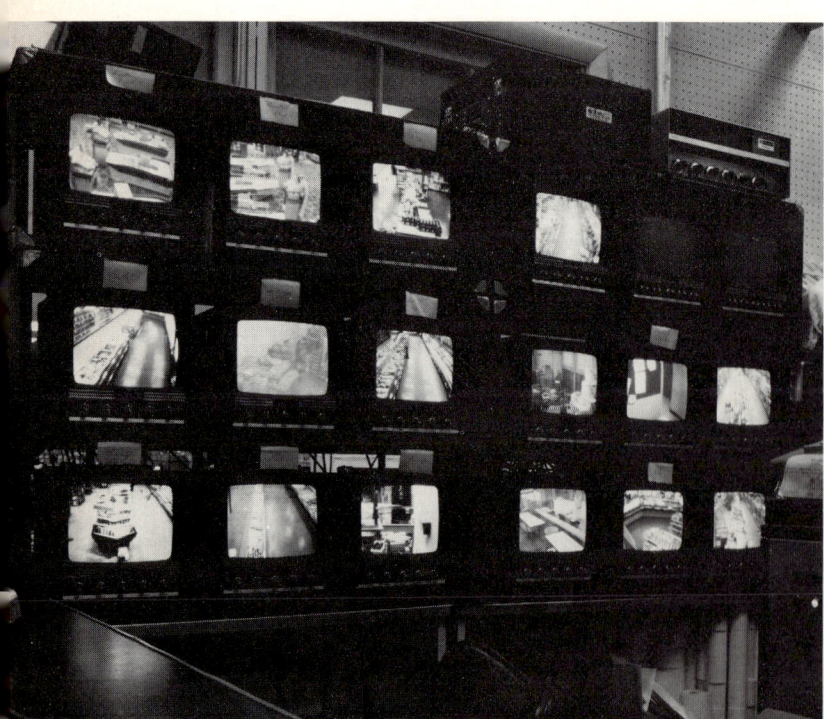

With this bank of closed-circuit television monitors, an entire store can be overseen from the manager's office.

tive forces employ both men and women of all ages. Some stores report considerable success with "teenage" detectives traveling in pairs. From all outward appearances these detectives seem to be a couple of teenagers "goofing off" and indeed may look suspicious themselves.

Regular Store Employees. Despite the advantages of the previous methods, the most effective protection against shoplifting is a well-trained, alert sales force. When a salesperson is busy with a customer, other customers should always be acknowledged. A nod, a smile, or "I'll be with you in a minute" may ward off a shoplifter who always prefers not to be noticed.

Salespeople and cashiers should be encouraged to know prices of merchandise and to be alert to altered prices or switched price tags. When ticket switching is suspected, the employee should merely indicate that he believes the merchandise is incorrectly marked. Customers should never be accused of switching unless there is proof of the accusation. Occasionally merchandise is marked incorrectly, and in other cases price tags may have been switched by a switcher who got "cold feet" and put the merchandise back. An unsuspecting customer could pick up the merchandise in good faith and become a victim of circumstances. Falsely accusing such a customer is almost assurance of losing his or her business forever.

Just as personnel need training in selling techniques, they also need training in how to spot shoplifters. They should be aware of methods used by shoplifters and trained in how to watch customers without giving the appearance of distrusting them. Alert, friendly employees can deter more shoplifters than the most sophisticated detection devices.

Employees should also be carefully instructed in the proper actions to take when shoplifting has occurred. Normally it is wise to allow only the manager, assistant manager, or a member of the security force to apprehend the shoplifter. These people should be familiar with the state law which covers shoplifting. These laws vary from one state to another, and familiarity with the applicable state law is necessary to protect the store from charges of false arrest.

Employees should be especially watchful of customers who:

Loiter in the store without buying
Carry shopping bags or large purses
Wear a raincoat or topcoat in inappropriate weather
Wear oversized, bulky clothing
Are eating popcorn or candy from a sizeable bag

These are only some of the more obvious features of shoplifters. At the same time, many of the store's customers with these characteristics will be legitimate. Thus, store personnel must exercise care not to antagonize such customers.

Only with knowledge of the methods used by shoplifters are employees able to assist in deterring and detecting them. A "booster" bag, box, or purse is fairly common. This container has a flap in the bottom. By placing it over the item to be stolen, the thief reaches a hand inside, lifts the flap, picks up the merchandise and drops it on top of the flap. The stolen merchandise holds the flap shut and the thief is off to his next "stop."

Another common tactic is for one of a pair working together to create a disturbance. Any number of actions may be taken to divert attention away from the accomplice. Loud and boisterous behavior or an argument with a salesperson or another customer may be used. Another tactic is to pretend to be ill or even fake fainting. Any of these actions divert attention away from the accomplice, who makes off with as much merchandise as possible.

REVIEW BOX 10:2

1. When the dollar value of a physical inventory is less than the book value of the inventory, this shortage is referred to as _____.
2. Price tag switching is a form of _____.
3. Ninety percent or more of all shoplifters can be classified as _____.
4. The most effective protection against shoplifting is a well-trained, _____, _____ force.

Employee Theft

Although estimates of retail inventory shrinkage vary, those knowledgeable about the subject agree that a majority of the shortage can be accounted for by employee theft. One specialist in the control of shortages claims that 70 percent of all inventory shortages are caused by employee theft, while 15 percent are due to shoplifting, with bookkeeping errors and other reasons making up the remaining 15 percent.[13] Although most retail store owners are reluctant to admit it, they do not know exactly how their merchandise shortages occur. Usually they are not even aware of the extent of merchandise shrinkage until a physical inventory is taken. With merchandise continually flowing into and out of the store, it is not convenient to do a complete inventory of a department or store at frequent intervals.

With the widespread increase in shoplifting, it is not at all unusual for retail managers to assume that merchandise shortages are due primarily to shoplifting. When and if it is discovered that employees are the major cause of shortages, merchants find it difficult to believe. This is especially true when the culprit is an old and trusted employee. In discussions with retail managers, one gets the feeling that the topic of employee theft is taboo. These managers will often brush aside or ignore questions about stealing by their employees.

MERCHANDISE THEFT

While the typical shoplifter is rushed in concealing merchandise and getting out of the store, dishonest employees normally have many opportunities, in the course of their daily routines, to pilfer merchandise. Knowledge of the store's systems allows the employee to conceal merchandise carefully, usually for later removal from the store. Even in the very small store where the manager is on hand to close the store, employee theft is possible. The employee may make a purchase at another store during the lunch hour and return with the package. During the afternoon, it may be simple to conceal some of the employer's goods in the bag and walk out innocently at closing time.

All employees who steal are not the retailer's employees. Salesmen and deliverymen who have easy access to an outlet's merchandise can also be a severe problem. Especially in a large store, deliverymen may carry in two cartons and carry another one back out. In other instances not all cartons may be unloaded.

The back door and receiving dock are crucial merchandise control areas. More employee theft probably takes place via the rear door than in any other manner. Those stores that use a closed circuit video system for shoplifting control would be well advised to place a camera near the rear entrance.

CASH THEFT AND DISCOUNTING

Whether an employee actually pockets money or allows friends special unauthorized "discounts," the results are the same—namely, a cash shortage. Employees who handle substantial sums of money day after day are often tempted to "appropriate" some of this money for themselves. To prevent detection of cash shortages, a thieving employee can under-ring a sale by the amount of the theft and then pocket the amount of the deliberate "error."

Another form of cash thievery involves unauthorized discounting. Usually this form of dishonesty involves an employee plus another employee, a relative, or a friend. It appears that this problem increases during periods of rapidly rising prices. Essentially the employee charges the "customer" less than the marked price. For example, an employee may charge another employee $19.95 for a $39.95 dress. The purchasing employee is expected to reciprocate with this type of action at a later date. Often this action is more justifiable in the mind of an employee than is outright pocketing of cash. The employee sees frequent price reductions that are designed to sell certain merchandise. The rationalization is that his or her actions are not really dishonest; they simply give a fellow employee a break, the same as customers obtain on marked-down merchandise. This, of course, is not true, since most merchandise is sold at regular rather than reduced prices.

Another type of unauthorized "discounting" may involve returned merchandise or illegal credit. The dishonest employee can refund a purchase

Identifying and Minimizing Merchandise Shrinkage

price in cash to a friend or fellow employee without receiving any merchandise in return. Where credit slips are issued, the employee may issue credit which either applies against the accomplice's account or allows him to receive a cash refund.

CONTROLLING EMPLOYEE THEFT

Just as alert employees are necessary to control shoplifting, an *alert management* is necessary to control employee theft. First and foremost, store management must set an example for employees. Complete honesty and integrity by store management are necessary before employees can be expected to follow suit. For example, if a checker in a supermarket sees the store manager remove a package of cigarettes or a candy bar from the stock without paying for it, the checker may view this action as an invitation to do likewise *or even more*. The manager who is dishonest in his dealings with merchandise resources may also be setting a poor example. Those who claim nonexistent shortages on deliveries or who make false claims of customer returns may soon find that employees too are dishonest in their work, having followed their bosses' examples.

Hiring Practices. Controlling employee dishonesty begins before the employee is hired. Some retailers are shocked to find that an employee caught stealing had been released from other firms for the same reason. Thus, adequate screening techniques should be used in hiring. Even if an applicant has an unfavorable recommendation or a conviction for theft, a retail store may hire the person. One relatively small retailer stated that he hired two employees who had been previously fired by another firm for dishonesty. He openly informed the new employees that he was aware of their previous experience but that he was willing to give them a second chance. Although one of the employees moved to another state after six months, the other has become one of the firm's best salesmen.

Training. Even though employee theft is increasing, few retailers discuss this problem openly with employees. Perhaps there is fear that employees will get ideas about stealing which they previously had never considered. Such reasoning is questionable. There is nothing wrong with a small retailer informing his employees that there are certain checks in the store system to protect merchandise and cash. Some small retailers even elicit suggestions from employees on control measures.

In larger stores, new employees should be advised of store security measures as a part of the orientation program. Exact details of these measures need not be spelled out. Employees usually respect managers who institute controls and do not view these controls as being threatening to them.

Rewards. Employee theft was such a severe problem in a large Chicago store that the store initiated a $25 reward for employees who reported thefts by other employees. Special care was taken by the security force to guard against misuse of the system. The reporting employee was quizzed about the specifics of the theft before the suspect was apprehended. Knowledge that such a system is operative may deter some internal theft.

If the store is large enough to employ a security force, an established procedure for anonymous tips concerning employee dishonesty can be successful. Even in the absence of a security force, store employees are important information sources. A *Progressive Grocer* poll revealed that 52 percent of the reporting stores pointed to employees as a source of leads on dishonest employees.[14]

REVIEW BOX 10:3

1. The greatest cause of inventory shortages is _____.
2. A form of employee theft whereby the employee may rationalize that he is doing nothing "wrong" is unauthorized "_____."
3. Just as alert employees are necessary to control shoplifting, an _____ _____ is necessary to control employee theft.

Employee Errors

Although dishonest customers and employees account for a majority of merchandise shrinkage, human fallibility produces unintentional shortages. Some of these mistakes are the result of a lack of understanding of procedures. Insufficient training underlies most such errors. In other cases employees may simply be forgetful or may not perform well during peak workload periods. Some of the more common types of errors are presented below.

PHYSICAL INVENTORY MISTAKES

Usually the extent of shortages is not discovered until a physical inventory is taken. Retailers typically maintain a book inventory in terms of dollars and compare the physical inventory value with this book figure. If the value of the physical inventory exceeds the book value, an overage exists. If the opposite is true, a shortage occurs.

Taking a physical inventory is tedious, time-consuming work. As a result, physical inventories are often not fully accurate. When substantial discrepancies are found between the book and physical inventory figures, the physical inventory may be the cause of that shortage due to:

Errors in counting merchandise
Merchandise skipped and not counted
Incorrect prices recorded on inventory sheets
Computational errors in extending and totaling inventory sheets

Identifying and Minimizing Merchandise Shrinkage

When an unusually large inventory shortage is found, many stores immediately reschedule a follow-up inventory to check on the accuracy of the first one. In some cases, errors are uncovered and no further checking is necessary.

ERRORS AT THE CASH REGISTER

The two most frequent errors made as the customer pays for merchandise are giving incorrect change and charging the wrong price. Although making change is a relatively simple operation, salespeople do make mistakes. Again, the problem with new employees may be lack of training. When an experienced employee gives incorrect change, it is likely to be due to inattention.

When a customer is short-changed, he often points this out. When he receives too much change, the probability of his pointing out this error is less. Shortages of this type are discovered when the cash register is checked out at the close of the day. One method of pinpointing the responsibility for day-end shortages is to allow only one person to make change from a particular cash drawer.

A wrong price may be charged because an employee fails to look at the price tag, thinking he knows the price, or reads the price incorrectly. Small shortages, like 10¢ or $1, may seem insignificant, but repeated several times on different items, these sums can result in a substantial shortage.

RECEIVING ERRORS

When checking incoming merchandise, employees should count individual pieces, where practical. For example, a carton containing twelve shirt boxes may be opened. The shirt boxes are marked "1/3 dozen." But two of the boxes may contain only three shirts each. Unless this mistake is detected, the store pays for 48 shirts and receives only 46. Laxness in checking incoming merchandise may mean shortages are not discovered until a physical inventory is taken.

IMPROPER MARKING

Closely related to receiving errors are mistakes made in affixing prices to merchandise, commonly referred to as *marking*. Depending upon the type of merchandise involved, two primary marking procedures are followed. The first is to mark the goods as soon as they are received. The merchandise is then ready to move to the sales floor when needed. A less frequent procedure is to mark the merchandise just before it is moved to the sales floor or to mark it on the sales floor. The latter procedure is utilized primarily by supermarkets, discount stores, and other stores selling fast turnover items which can be marked very quickly.

Consider what happens when the employee looks at the wrong line on an invoice or price sheet and mismarks the merchandise. Unless the error is discovered, and it frequently is not, the merchandise might sell at a price substantially below the intended price, cutting into store profits. The key to controlling these errors rests largely with hiring alert, conscientious employees and then training them to perform their jobs capably.

REVIEW BOX 10:4

1. When a large inventory shortage is found as a result of a physical inventory, the first step is usually to _____ _____.
2. The two most common errors made at the cash register which result in shortages are _____ and _____.
3. Two backroom errors which can cause inventory shortages are errors in _____ and errors in _____ merchandise.

Obsolescence and Spoilage

Much merchandise tends to decrease in value between the time it arrives in the store and when it leaves the store. In some cases the value may decline to zero. For example, when highly perishable goods such as produce or cut flowers are involved, they may deteriorate completely before they can be sold. When this happens, there is no alternative other than discarding the spoiled items. The result is the same as with shoplifting and employee theft. The retailer's investment in the merchandise is lost.

Another less drastic example concerns goods that become obsolete because of changing consumer wants or needs. Rapid consumer changes are prevalent in fashion goods. Some years ago the Nehru jackets and collarless blazers became relatively popular, and many men's wear retailers stocked these jackets in anticipation of widespread consumer acceptance. However, the fickle consumer soon cast aside these fashions, and retailers were unable to sell these coats at a profit. The longer they held them, the less they were able to get for them. Many retailers finally priced the coats at a fraction of what they paid for them. To a lesser extent, the same thing happened to the midi-length dress in 1971.

Both physical spoilage and style obsolescence are caused by buyer errors, which can be minimized but not completely eliminated. For example, in buying pumpkins for Halloween, a buyer must estimate demand. If too few are bought, the store loses sales, profits, and perhaps some customer goodwill. If there are too many, with virtually no demand for pumpkins after Halloween, the excess will probably have to be thrown away. Much the same problem is faced when buying high fashion goods. If too little merchandise is bought and the style is widely accepted, the buyer may be unable to obtain reorders since demand often exceeds manufacturers' capacity to produce. If the buyer buys heavily and there is no demand, the store again loses. Buying errors can be minimized by judicious buying. Basically this means the buyer must be keenly attuned to the marketplace.

Identifying and Minimizing Merchandise Shrinkage

A POSITIVE APPROACH TO SHRINKAGE CONTROL

As you can see, controlling merchandise shrinkage is no easy matter. A positive approach to the problem entails education (including training), adequate supervision, and prosecution of dishonest employees and customers.

Educating Consumers

Recognizing the widespread increase in shoplifting, merchants have begun intensive campaigns to inform consumers about the consequences of the crime. A highly successful educational campaign was launched by Philadelphia area retailers in 1971.[15] The campaign, called STEM ("Shoplifters Take Everybody's Money"), began with a committee of top retail executives and an advisory board composed of political, civic, and religious leaders. A local advertising agency prepared the advertising as a public service. The campaign stressed two major points: that shoplifting is a serious crime and that it raises prices and therefore costs everybody more money. Local advertising media donated advertising time or space valued in excess of $500,000. The initial program was so successful that it has been repeated and has served as a model for other educational campaigns across the country.

Despite the success of programs such as STEM, not enough educational effort is being undertaken. Chambers of commerce, retail merchants associations, and other concerned groups should make a concerted effort to educate consumers about shoplifting. Educational programs presented in the public schools and via the mass media can have far-reaching effects. Figure 10-2 shows an attempt by the Governor of Illinois to bring the shoplifting problem into focus for state residents.

Employee Training and Supervision

Training programs for retail employees should include information about shoplifting. For personnel who are allowed to apprehend shoplifters, training is especially needed to ensure that proper procedures are followed. Since employee theft normally constitutes the largest single cause of shortages, education and training of managers are also important.

Closely related to education and training is the need for supervision. Retail managers have many demands upon their time, but employee supervision is a necessity. The ultimate responsibility for controlling shortages rests with managers, and adequate supervision can uncover and deter employee errors and dishonesty.

FIGURE 10-2

One state's assistance to merchants in controlling shoplifting

STATE OF ILLINOIS
EXECUTIVE DEPARTMENT

Proclamation

Shoplifting, according to the Illinois Retail Merchants Association, is the nation's fastest growing crime and more than fifty percent is by teenagers. The reported value of merchandise shoplifted each year is $4.8 billion nationally and more than $800 million in Illinois. However, ninety-nine percent of the shoplifters are found to have enough money with them to pay for the merchandise they steal.

Everybody pays for shoplifting. The sales tax revenue lost can cause cutbacks in such public services as schools, street maintenance, welfare, police and fire protection, sanitation and recreation facilities. Shoplifting has forced many small merchants into bankruptcy, curtailing the flow of money to workers, banks, suppliers, transportation and utility companies.

Security guards and shoplifting prevention devices cost merchants billions of dollars annually. These costs, which must be passed on to the customer if the merchant is to stay in business, increase prices.

Yet if no one coveted his neighbors' goods, if everyone respected others' property, this shameful condition would be unknown and hundreds of young people would be spared criminal records that will handicap them all their lives.

THEREFORE I, Dan Walker, Governor of the State of Illinois, proclaim November 17-23, 1974, EVERYTHING HAS A PRICE WEEK. I appeal to parents to teach their children never to steal and to give them a good example by always showing proper regard for the property of others.

In Witness Whereof, I have hereunto set my hand and caused the Great Seal of the State of Illinois to be affixed.

Done at the Capitol, in the City of Springfield, this _eighth_ day of _November_, in the Year of Our Lord one thousand nine hundred and _seventy-four_, and of the State of Illinois the one hundred and _fifty-sixth_.

Michael J. Howlett
SECRETARY OF STATE

Dan Walker
GOVERNOR

Prosecution

Relatively few apprehended shoplifters and dishonest employees are prosecuted. Many stores apparently feel the unfavorable publicity associated with prosecution will harm the store's image. In many cases, the guilty party is allowed to return whatever is stolen, given a lecture, and released. Such activities are not particularly conducive to changing behavior, and the offense may be repeated in the future. In one reported case, for example, an employee stole merchandise and display material from the store. He was reprimanded, put back to work, and later promoted to display manager. At a later date, he was found to have stolen $150,000 in merchandise. This took place *after* his initial theft had been discovered. Although the man was prosecuted and convicted, the store's insurance was void, since there was prior knowledge of the employee's dishonesty.[16] Most blanket bonds covering employees contain a clause which limits the insurance company's liability for dishonest acts which occur after an employer discovers an incident of an employee's dishonesty. For this reason, most stores immediately terminate employees caught stealing.

One suggested remedy for customer and employee dishonesty is a "get tough" policy. If retail stores in an area undertake an educational program emphasizing that all acts of dishonesty will be prosecuted, then customers and employees alike are forewarned. Initially, merchants would experience relatively high costs in prosecution, since they would have to pay employees and managers for unproductive time spent testifying in court. If, however, a substantial reduction in store loss could be achieved, it would be worth the initial expense.

REVIEW BOX 10:5

1. Both merchandise spoilage and obsolescence are caused by _____.

2. According to the Governor of the State of Illinois, shoplifting involves costs to four persons. They are the merchant, customer, thief, and _____.

3. Three means of reducing merchandise losses are by education of consumers, training and supervising of employees, and _____.

CHAPTER SUMMARY

- The two major elements of merchandise control are the maintenance of proper levels of inventories and the safekeeping of merchandise.

- Merchandise budgets are a means of planning and controlling inventory levels.
- Dollar inventory control is a means of regulating inventory investment in line with the desired level of sales. Although the prime value of dollar control systems is to indicate deviation from planned values, the reasons for these deviations must be determined before informed corrective actions can be taken.
- Unit control systems supplement dollar control, emphasizing proper inventory levels in terms of physical units of merchandise. Unit control may be maintained either by periodic stock counts or by recording merchandise received and merchandise sold.
- Merchandise shrinkage, a major problem facing retailers, exists when the physical inventory figure is less than the book inventory figure.
- Shoplifting involves the stealing of merchandise by persons other than employees of the store. Price tag switching or alteration is a form of shoplifting.
- Contrary to popular opinion, shoplifting is not primarily limited to economically deprived individuals nor to a particular sex, race, or age group.
- Although store layout, signs, mirrors, television cameras, peep holes, electronic signal devices, and a security force can all aid in deterring shoplifting, the single most effective tool is alert, well-trained employees.
- A majority of all retail shortages, about 70 percent, are accounted for by employee theft.
- More employee theft probably occurs via the back door than by any other means. Theft of cash and unauthorized "discounting" are the two major causes of cash shortages.
- Honesty, integrity, and alertness on the part of store management are necessary to minimize employee theft. Adequate screening of applicants and informing employees of store security measures can reduce employee theft.
- Errors in taking physical inventories can indicate a shortage when none actually exists. Errors made at the cash register in giving incorrect change or charging the wrong price appear as inventory shortages.
- Failure to discover shortages when checking incoming merchandise and errors in marking merchandise also cause shortages.
- Inventory shortages caused by spoilage and obsolescence are buying errors and can only be controlled, not completely eliminated, through judicious buying.
- Educational programs to inform consumers about the consequences of shoplifting and employees about theft, followed by prosecution of offenders, must be instituted to control these forms of dishonesty.
- Training and supervision of employees aids in the control of shoplifting and employee theft.

CHAPTER NOTES

[1] Howard Haimowitz quoting a security professional in Francine Kirach, "The Independent Stores Open Forum," *Stores*, August, 1972, p. 24.
[2] Joseph Dauksys, "Washington Report," *Stores*, January 1974, p. 20.
[3] See William J. Stanton, *Fundamentals of Marketing*, 3rd ed. (New York: McGraw-Hill Book Company, 1971), pp. 638–39.
[4] This terminology and the following discussion of "middle-value" items are based on an article by John T. Padley, "Inventory Management Increases Store Profits," *Journal of Retailing*, Summer 1962, pp. 1–8.
[5] As reported in a paper by Leonard W. Prestwick, "The Shoplifting Problem in Retailing," Midwest Business Administration Association, April 21, 1972, pp. 4–5.
[6] "Foil the Shoplifters and Lure Investors," *Business Week*, December 23, 1972, p. 22.
[7] "Shoplifting: The Pinch that Hurts," *Business Week*, June 27, 1970, p. 72.
[8] *Ibid.*
[9] The frequency rate was 7.4 percent for females and 5.0 percent for males. See Saul D. Astor, "1 Customer in 15 is a Shoplifter," *Stores*, April 1971, p. 8.
[10] David Reuben, "Why So Many Women Shoplift," *McCall's*, September 1970, p. 44.
[11] "Foil the Shoplifter and Lure Investors," *Business Week*, December 23, 1972, p. 23.
[12] Lois Rosen, "Indifferent Employee Eyes Breed Shoplifting," *Modern Retailer*, June 1972, p. 18.
[13] Norman Jaspan, "Skill Can Counteract Dishonesty," *Stores*, January 1972, p. 12.
[14] "Employee Theft," *Progressive Grocer*, November 1970, p. 45.
[15] Information on the Philadelphia campaign is based on "Philadelphia's Way of Stopping the Shoplifter," *Business Week*, May 6, 1972, pp. 57–59.
[16] Norman Jaspan, "Skill Can Counteract Dishonesty," *Stores*, January 1972, p. 12.

QUESTIONS AND ASSIGNMENTS

1. Explain the two primary elements of merchandise control.
2. The controller of a medium-size store insists that the primary purpose of a merchandise budget is to force buyers to control their investment in inventory. The controller insists that store buyers "live" with their budget. Regardless of the circumstances, he insists that once the planned inventory level is reached, no further expenditures for merchandise can be made. Discuss the shortcomings of this philosophy of merchandise control.
3. Why would any store use both dollar and unit control? Explain why the use of just one means might not be satisfactory.
4. Explain the 80-20 principle, indicating what effect this principle may have on unit control.
5. Although stock counts are time consuming and expensive, they offer one distinct advantage over sales recording systems of unit control. What is it?
6. Distinguish between the two most common methods of shoplifting.
7. According to some authorities, shoplifting has achieved a peculiar kind of legitimacy. Indicate what you believe to be the major reasons for this status of shoplifting.
8. a. Assume that you are going to open a medium-size discount store. You know that shoplifting is a severe problem. Outline the steps you would take in an attempt to minimize this problem.
   b. Talk to a discount store manager about what his firm does to control shoplifting.
9. You are operating a boutique and utilize an electronic sensing device at the exit from your shop. Most merchandise is marked with special sensitized

tags. A flashing light indicates that a person has just left the store apparently without paying for some merchandise. Indicate how you would handle the situation.
10. Most retailers are apparently either unwilling to admit or unaware that a large majority of all inventory shortages are caused by employee theft. How can you account for this?
11. Three months ago you fired an employee after discovering that he was stealing merchandise. You did not prosecute him, nor did you notify the police department. In this morning's mail you receive a request for a recommendation for this employee from a store in another state. Explain what action you would take. Why?
12. Comment upon the desirability of a monetary reward system for employees who report dishonest acts of other employees. Would you turn in a dishonest co-worker? Why or why not?
13. Most stores prosecute only a minority of the shoplifters they apprehend, and an even smaller percentage of dishonest employees. How can these actions be justified?

ANSWERS TO REVIEW BOX QUESTIONS

Box 10:1
1. control
2. sales
3. Dollar
4. 80-20

Box 10:2
1. merchandise shrinkage
2. shoplifting
3. amateurs
4. alert sales

Box 10:3
1. employee theft or dishonest employees
2. "discounting"
3. alert management

Box 10:4
1. reschedule a follow-up inventory
2. giving incorrect change and charging the wrong price
3. checking; marking

Box 10:5
1. buyer errors
2. parents
3. prosecution

RETAILING DECISION
Campus Cobbler

Jim Daniels, owner and operator of a successful shoe store in College Park, Ohio, finds himself faced with an interesting decision. Over the last few years, he has been impressed by the tremendous increase in the number of bicycle riders, particularly among the students at nearby State University. At a recent Cleveland trade show, several shoe manufacturers introduced a new bicycling shoe for men and women. Designed along the lines of those worn by European bicycle racers, this shoe affords a better grip on the pedals and has an attractive, sporty appearance. With the proposed national promotion campaigns, Daniels thinks the shoes will become a popular campus fashion.

Hoping to get the jump on local competitors as he did with sandals in the 1960s and stacked heels a few years ago, he wants to place an order right away. However, the three firms from which he would consider buying offer different terms of sale. Bigelow Shoes has offered a one-year, cumulative quantity discount of 2 percent for the purchase of 500 or more pairs. Olson Shoe Company offers terms of 2/10, net 30 ROG, with anticipation of 9 percent. Finally, Fidan, a foreign firm, has offered a $200 promotional allowance at the end of a year to purchasers of at least $5,000 worth of their "bike shoes." Fidan offers no allowance on smaller sales.

All three of the manufacturers are selling the shoes at $10 a pair. Daniels has estimated that his store can sell 500 to 600 pairs in the next year.

1. Discuss the advantages and disadvantages of each offer.
2. Which offer should Daniels accept? Why?

RETAILING DECISION
Shipley's Clothing Store

Shipley's was a family-owned clothing store located in the rural town of Honeyville: population, approximately 25,000. Edgar Shipley, who had inherited the store from his father, was concerned about inventory shortages. Quarterly inventories during the past year and one-half showed inventory shortages had skyrocketed from about 1 percent of sales to well over 5 percent.

Since Honeyville was the home of a small state university, Edgar Shipley began to suspect that his shortages were being caused by "those 'long hairs' from the college and the local high school." Shipley contacted a well-known detective agency located in a nearby metropolitan city. He requested that undercover detectives be assigned to his store to control the shoplifting problem.

After three weeks of diligent efforts the detectives were able to apprehend only two shoplifters. Shipley called the head of the agency to complain about the poor surveillance his store was receiving from the detectives. Warren Tebco, the agency owner, assured Shipley that the detectives were the best available and that the inventory shortage was evidently not due to shoplifting. He suggested that the physical inventory or bookkeeping must be the cause of the shortages. Shipley arranged for an independent company to conduct the next physical inventory and for the books to be audited by a respected local C.P.A.

The outcome was still a very high shortage. As a last resort, Tebco suggested that all current employees be given a polygraph test to determine if they were stealing merchandise or money. Taking such a step was repugnant to Shipley. Most of his employees had worked at Shipley's for more than five years. Several had worked for Shipley's father before he retired.

After thinking about the problem for several days, Shipley phoned Tebco:

> Look, Mr. Tebco, I know I have a severe problem. Another year or two of continued losses as I've been experiencing will break me. I feel that I've gotten less than my money's worth from your services. I'm certain that the losses are due to shoplifting. Are you trying to give me the runaround? I'm sure that all of my employees are honest. Why, many of them have worked for the store for years. Don't you think you could use some different method to spot those thieving kids who are stealing me blind?

1. Suppose you were in Edgar Shipley's position. Do you think his course of action was the best one?
2. What do you think of Warren Tebco's suggestion of requiring employees to submit to a polygraph test?

PART FOUR

The Pricing Function

11

A Foundation for Retail Pricing

As an introduction to retail pricing, consider the following sequence of events:

On a recent buying trip, the manager of a women's sportswear department ordered an assortment of 24 double-knit pantsuits. On the invoice received with the shipment, the base price for the pantsuits was $22.00 per unit. This base price reflected a quantity discount of 2 percent, since the order was for more than a dozen units of the same style.

Because of the uniqueness of the double-knit material and the popularity of this particular sportswear brand, the buyer felt an initial markup of 45 percent, rather than the department's customary 40 percent, was in order. Twenty of the 24 pantsuits were sold at the resulting retail price of $40.95.

Toward the end of the season the pantsuits were reduced to $27.90, an off-retail markdown of approximately 33 percent, and two more were sold. Another one was sold for half price in the semi-annual clearance sale. The manager was greatly disturbed when the 24th unit could not be located and had to be recorded as a pilferage shortage.

When the manager evaluated the performance of this order, she found that merchandise costing $540.62 (which includes $12.60 for transportation charges) produced sales of $895.28. Thus, the maintained markup was $354.66. Although the pilferage had cut into the maintained markup figure, she was generally pleased with the 39.6 percent result.

These pricing events are fairly typical, although the particular details obviously vary from one situation to another. This chapter considers some general pricing essentials and the central concept of markup. Then Chapters 12 and 13 examine how to establish prices and adjust them when necessary.

GENERAL PRICING ESSENTIALS

Price: Its Meaning and Importance

In order to develop a foundation for retail pricing, we must begin with a workable definition of price. Basically, *price* is the amount of money and perhaps something else of value necessary to purchase a seller's offering of merchandise and/or services.[1] In some types of retailing, trade-ins are accepted as part of the purchase price. Appliance retailers and automobile dealers, in particular, often accept—occasionally even encourage—trade-ins. Because of trade-ins, the definition of price includes the phrase, "and perhaps something else of value."

Each year most Americans have higher incomes and more money to spend. Because of this trend, it might be thought that consumers are becoming less price conscious. But this is not necessarily true, especially in periods of severe inflation. In fact, during the 1970s various retail institutions that emphasize supposedly lower-than-normal prices have flourished. For example, "discount" pricing is quite popular in grocery retailing. In 1973 an estimated 30 percent of independent supermarkets were on a discount price policy,[2] with many others striving to stay competitive through selective price specials. These figures suggest that many consumers are quite price conscious, or they would not patronize discount-type retailers.

Because of conflicting evidence such as that above, the relative importance of price can be a confusing topic. However, successful pricing by a retailer is difficult, if not impossible, without an understanding of the importance of price in various situations.

PRICE WITHIN THE RETAILING MIX

For a sale to result, all retailing mix components must be satisfactory from the consumer's viewpoint. In other words, any unsatisfactory variable can "knock out" the possibility of a sale. A mix that is satisfactory except for the price variable is no better (nor worse) than a mix that contains an adequate price but another "knock-out" variable. So, in this sense, a retail manager should view the components of the mix as equally important.

PRICE IN PURCHASE DECISIONS

With respect to its prominence in purchase decisions, the importance of price depends on the specific offering *and* the specific individual. Quite likely, price sometimes has been the key consideration when you decided to make (or postpone) a purchase or when you selected one brand over another. But, on the other hand, you probably have disregarded price in making some decisions, even when you eventually bought the product or service.

SPOTLIGHT

Will consumers pay $6 for a T-shirt, especially when the store has the nerve to emblazon its name across the shirt?

Some retail firms seem to attract more than their share of *price-unconscious* customers. Neiman-Marcus, headquartered in Dallas, Texas, is one example. Bloomingdale's, especially its main store in New York City, is another.

Bloomingdale's 1974 offerings included not only $6 T-shirts flaunting the store's signature but also $55 jogging suits and $1 loaves of white bread. And although such prices are the rule, not the exception, at Bloomingdale's, the store is prospering. Its success is due primarily to a retailing mix that complements its price policy.

The older or more tradition-oriented customer counts on finding quality and fashion in the regular departments. The younger crowd and the "avant garde" find what they're looking for in the many boutiques throughout the store. Bloomingdale's caters to both groups with imaginative buying, attractive displays, and an immense choice of items in every category. For example, the store nurtures new designer talent so that it can spot a fashion trend in its earliest stages. Bloomingdale's also completely renovates its furniture department twice a year.

Perhaps most important is its "almost staggering breadth of selection," which means, for instance, over 100 varieties of bread in its Delicacy Shop. Finally, shopping is made even more attractive by the knowledge that a change of heart is easily forgiven—returns and exchanges are generally accepted without question.

Bloomingdale's policy of offering the newest and the "trendiest" along with the expected and established, whether in clothing, furniture, housewares, or food delicacies, has paid off. High prices? Yes, but most customers seem to get much psychological satisfaction and enjoyment from shopping along with their purchase of a shirt, a chair, a T-shirt, or whatever. Novelist Lois Gould no doubt described many Bloomingdale's customer's feelings when she described herself as a "Bloomingdale's freak—the kind who, twenty minutes late for her own wedding, would be only halfway down the aisle of the Young East Sider department, rummaging frantically for something new, something blue."

Sources: Stanley H. Slom, "To Many in New York, Trip to Bloomingdale's Is a Major Happening," *Wall Street Journal*, September 24, 1974, pp. 1 and 16; Lois Gould, "Confessions of a Bloomingdale's Addict," *New York* Magazine, March 5, 1973, p. 56.

The only generalization concerning price's importance in a purchase decision is: *It depends*. Specifically, it depends on the following factors:

Personality of the individual consumer. For various reasons, some consumers are always extremely price-conscious, while others can be termed "price-*un*conscious."

Ch. 11   A Foundation for Retail Pricing

Income level of the consumer. Generally, higher-income consumers can afford to be less concerned with price than can lower-income consumers. But there are frequent exceptions to this notion, usually involving grocery shopping.

Magnitude of the expenditure. As the amount involved increases, consumers ordinarily become more price-conscious. When purchasing a "big ticket" item, a shopper has more to gain (or lose) because of his relative awareness of and sensitivity to price.

Time pressure connected with the purchase. A consumer cannot be price-conscious when he faces an emergency. For example, if you must leave on a trip tomorrow and your car needs repairs, you do not have much time to be price-conscious. In contrast, if you convince yourself you "need" a color TV, you can shop around until you find one at the "right price."

Character of the offering. For two types of offering, numerous consumers are price-*un*conscious. *First,* if an offering becomes a *specialty good,* a brand which a consumer insists upon, then price becomes less important. Perhaps one of your friends buys only Van Heusen dress shirts because he is really impressed with their styling. There are numerous less expensive brands, of course, but he is not concerned with price when it comes to shirts. *Second,* for some products and services price is an indicator of quality or status—at least in the eyes of some consumers. A person may be price-conscious in such cases, but not in the sense of trying to be an efficient shopper. Rather he or she is conscious of prices because a higher price indicates greater quality or status. Such *prestige pricing* situations occur occasionally in the retailing of jewelry, country club services, furs, art objects, and entertainment.

The importance of price in purchase decisions varies greatly, depending upon characteristics of both the offering and the individual involved in the decision process. Thus the retail manager must appraise a specific situation in terms of these factors in order to estimate the likely impact of alternative prices on an offering's attractiveness.

REVIEW BOX 11:1

1. Price can be defined as _____ necessary to purchase a seller's offering.
2. Three of the specific factors that determine price's importance in a purchase decision are: _____, _____, and _____.

General Pricing Essentials

PRICING AS AN ART

Because pricing involves arithmetic operations and results in a dollar-and-cents figure, you might expect to find a single, precise pricing method that always, or almost always, works. Unfortunately, that is not the case. As we shall see, various equations and systematic methods are helpful in pricing. For instance, the very important concept of markup revolves around one equation: cost + markup = retail price. Furthermore, general guidelines increase the likelihood of effective pricing.

But pricing is appropriately referred to as *an art* for two reasons: Effective pricing is a managerial skill and is acquired and refined through *actual* pricing experiences. More than with any other retailing function, both a manager's judgment *and* experiments with alternatives are *key* ingredients in pricing procedures.

Recall that the sportswear department manager assessed the total situation as best she could before deciding what markup percentage to insert in the basic equation. Thus, to achieve consistently effective pricing, the retail manager not only must understand and apply pricing concepts but also must have experience and good judgment.

Demand-Oriented Pricing

Many merchants automatically add a predetermined dollar or percentage amount to the cost of all products or services to be sold. This cost-oriented method of setting price is popular because of its simplicity. However, it fails to take into account the nature and needs of the consumer. *Demand-oriented* pricing, on the other hand, is based on a determination of what and how much the consumer might want at a given price.

In general, the higher the price of a product or service, the smaller the quantity consumers will purchase. The retailer must recognize that adding 50 percent to an item such as a piece of fine jewelry may not result in sufficient profit, because the total demand for such an offering will be relatively low. What the retailer should consider, however, is that the demand might be just as great—or even greater—at a higher price. The merchant who uses demand-oriented pricing must try to determine consumer demand and then establish a price that is consistent with this demand and with the firm's image and profit objective.

DETERMINING A RANGE OF FEASIBLE PRICES

Normally the cost of an offering to a retailer represents the floor, or minimum, retail price the firm must get to make a profit. Given this floor, the retailer then must attempt to predict consumer demand at different prices. This step will establish a ceiling, or maximum, above which consumers will not buy the offering. The most difficult step is deciding which price between floor and ceiling would be best from the standpoint of achieving the firm's objectives.

Ch. 11 *A Foundation for Retail Pricing*

A profit-seeking retailer recognizes that a price is *too high* if an insufficient quantity of an offering can be sold at that price, or if a sufficient quantity can be sold, but the relatively high price might damage the firm's reputation — which over the long run would reduce sales or profits. If few retailers have a stock of antifreeze when an early freeze hits, a well-stocked retailer probably could sell this item for at least twice its regular price. But the risk is that some regular customers who purchased the antifreeze at the high price would consider it an unfair price and stop patronizing this outlet.

WHEN IS A PRICE TOO HIGH?

A price is *too low* when an amount producing greater total revenue or profits could be sold at a higher price, or when continual sales at that price level do not directly or indirectly generate profits. Occasionally, offerings called *leaders* are intentionally priced very low, perhaps at or below cost. Although not directly profitable, they can contribute to sales and profits if they accomplish their purpose of attracting extra shoppers.

WHEN IS A PRICE TOO LOW?

Relationship Between Prices and Profits

Most retailers seek either maximum long-term profits or what they consider to be a satisfactory level or profits. However, when the retailer has to set prices, there is no "sure-fire" way of achieving these profit objectives. In other words, the amount of profit that will result from different pricing strategies cannot be predicted with much certainty.

A firm's level of profits is determined by the interaction of many operating variables, such as quantity sold, merchandise cost, operating expenses, and of course price. Specifically, *profit* is the amount left after costs and expenses are deducted from total revenue. Multiplying price of the offering by quantity sold (or volume) at that price gives you total revenue.

MANY VARIABLES DETERMINE PROFITS

How numerous variables, one of which is a price, interact to determine profits can be illustrated by a hypothetical situation. An income statement for Don's Dandy Donuts is presented in Figure 11-1. With a 10¢ price for both donuts and coffee, sales totaled $250. From that figure, cost of the donuts and coffee and various expenses were subtracted. Thus, for this short time period, a profit before taxes of $65 was recorded.

What profit levels might result from different combinations of these operating variables? First, suppose that the donut shop's manager decided to advertise more. If this move stimulated sales, cost of goods sold *and* operating expenses would increase. Profits will be higher only if the sales increase exceeds the increase in costs and expenses.

WIDE-RANGING PROFIT LEVELS

General Pricing Essentials **261**

Sales:		
1,500 donuts @ 10¢	$150	
1,000 cups of coffee @ 10¢	+100	
		$250
Cost of goods sold:		
Donuts @ 3¢	$ 45	
Coffee @ 1.5¢	+ 15	
		− 60
		$190
Gross margin		
Operating expenses (manager's salary, employees' wages, rent, utilities, advertising, supplies, depreciation of equipment)		−125
Profit before taxes		$ 65

FIGURE 11-1

Income statement for Don's Dandy Donuts

Assume that after heavier advertising, sales increased to $350 and costs to $72. Expenses rose to $226, since an extra $10 in supplies were used, an additional salesperson was needed, and the advertising cost $75. In this case, the net effect on profits is undesirable. This illustrates why trying to maximize revenue does not necessarily improve the profit picture.

Lowering prices, another strategy, also can result in diverse outcomes:

- An undesirable—perhaps disastrous—outcome would be an unchanged level of sales. If donut prices were reduced to a nickel apiece and the same number were sold, profits would disappear; in fact, there would be a $10 loss for the period.
- Even if more donuts were sold at the nickel price, total revenue still might decline. For example, 2,500 donuts at a nickel and 1,000 coffees at a dime would be $225 in sales—$25 less than at the dime per donut price. Of course, costs would increase (and expenses might also), which would mean still lower profits.
- A seemingly favorable outcome would be higher total revenue. But higher profits *may not* result even then, since costs and expenses, taken together, might rise more than total revenue rises.

How raising prices affects sales depends on the importance of donut prices to consumers. Higher profits are possible but certainly not assured. The point to remember is that a retailer should not view total revenue *or* unit sales *or* price levels (or low merchandise costs or operating expenses) as desirable goals in themselves. Rather, any approach is desirable only if it leads to the ultimate goal of a merchant: maximum or satisfactory profits over the long run.

> **REVIEW BOX 11:2**
>
> 1. Even though it's difficult to do, a retailer should not set prices without first considering _____.
> 2. Normally, the *floor* retail price, if the firm is to make a profit, is indicated by _____.
> 3. Profit is what is left after _____ and _____ are deducted from _____.
> 4. Because profits are determined by the interaction of many operating variables, the effect on profits of a price raise is _____.

MARKUP: TYPES AND ARITHMETIC

A merchant attempts to make a profit by selling an offering for more than it cost. The difference between retail price and cost of the merchandise sold is termed *markup*. To a retailer, therefore, markup is "what it's all about." As such, a discussion of the various aspects of this key concept is a major component in a solid foundation for retail pricing.

The Basic Relationship

In equation form, the relationship set forth in the definition becomes:

$$\text{retail price} = \text{cost of merchandise} + \text{markup}$$

Of course, this equation can be rearranged as follows: markup = retail price − cost of merchandise, or cost = retail price − markup. The following three sub-sections go into certain characteristics of the elements in the equations as well as the arithmetic connected with markup.

DOLLAR AND PERCENTAGE MARKUP

Markup, sometimes called markon, can be expressed as a dollar amount *or* as a percent. Recall that the sportswear department manager paid $22.00 plus $.53 transportation charges[3] for each pantsuit and put them on the selling floor with $40.95 price tags. To calculate the *dollar markup*, plug the figures into the following equation:

$$\text{markup} = \text{retail price} - \text{cost}$$

$$\text{markup} = \$40.95 - \$22.53 = \$18.42$$

To calculate the *percentage markup*, the following equation is used:

$$\text{percentage markup} = \frac{\text{dollar markup}}{\text{retail price}}$$

The manager wanted to apply a 45 percent markup in this case. Let's see if she actually did:

$$\text{percentage markup} = \frac{\$18.42}{\$40.95} = 44.98 \text{ percent}$$

The buyer was close enough, since 44.98 percent rounds off to 45 percent.

COST OF MERCHANDISE SOLD

Exactly what figures make up the cost figure in the basic markup equation? *Cost of merchandise* designates the base invoice price for the merchandise *plus* any transportation charges *less* any applicable quantity, trade, and/or cash discounts.

Thus, in our example, the cost figure was obtained as follows:

$$\text{cost} = \text{billed price/unit} + \text{transportation charges} - 2\% \text{ quantity discount}$$

$$\text{cost} = \$22.45 + \$.53 - \$.45 = \$22.53/\text{unit}$$

Trade discounts come into play only when the invoice indicates a suggested retail price for the merchandise. For example, the sportswear maker could have listed the merchandise at $41.00 per unit, in which case the retailer would have deducted the agreed upon trade discount.

Another way to calculate cost is to obtain an aggregate cost figure and then divide that by the number of units purchased. If we avoid arithmetic errors, both methods will produce identical results:

$$
\begin{array}{rl}
\$538.80 & \text{(bill for merchandise)} \\
+\ 12.60 & \text{(transportation charges)} \\
\hline
551.40 & \\
-\ 10.78 & \text{(quantity discount, } .02 \times \$538.80) \\
\hline
\$540.62 &
\end{array}
$$

$$\$540.62 \div 24 = \$22.53$$

Why was retail price, rather than cost of merchandise, used in calculating percentage markup? Actually, markup can be expressed as a percent of either cost or retail price. To calculate *percentage cost markup*, we use the following equation:

TWO BASES FOR MARKUP

$$\text{percentage cost markup} = \frac{\text{dollar markup}}{\text{cost of merchandise}}$$

In our continuing example, cost markup on the pantsuits was:

$$\text{percentage cost markup} = \frac{\$18.42}{\$22.53} = 81.8\%$$

Some retailers, particularly large appliance and automobile dealers, persist in using cost as the base for percentage markup. The prevailing practice, however, is to use retail price as the base for percentage markup. A sufficient reason for basing markup on retail price (rather than on cost) is that other operating figures such as profits, expenses, and customer and employee discounts are based on retail sales rather than on costs. Throughout this book, markup is based on retail price unless otherwise noted.

In any case, every cost markup has an equivalent retail markup, so one markup figure can be converted to the other. The methods for doing this, along with other useful markup formulas, are summarized in Figure 11-3 near the end of the chapter. In actual practice, many merchants rely on conversion charts or wheels provided them free of charge by suppliers.

Based on retail price ($12.50)   *Based on cost ($10.00)*

100% { 20% { Markup (to cover expenses and profits) $2.50 } 25%

80% { Cost of merchandise (invoice price + transportation charges − applicable quantity and trade discounts) $10.00 } 100%

$$\frac{\text{percentage}}{\text{retail markup}} = \frac{\text{dollar markup}}{\text{retail price}}$$

$$= \frac{\$2.50}{\$12.50}$$

$$= 20\%$$

$$\frac{\text{percentage}}{\text{cost markup}} = \frac{\text{dollar markup}}{\text{cost of merchandise}}$$

$$= \frac{\$2.50}{\$10.00}$$

$$= 25\%$$

FIGURE 11-2

Retail and cost percentage markups for a special-ordered textbook

Two distinctions between markup types should be remembered: (1) a retail markup cannot be 100 percent (or higher), whereas a cost markup technically has no maximum; and (2) the cost percentage markup is always larger than the equivalent retail markup. Retail and cost markups are compared in Figure 11-2, showing the Cooperative Bookstore's pricing of a textbook that has been special ordered.

Markup Distinctions

Thus far, markup has been discussed only in terms of the difference between cost of *one* item and the *first* retail price applied to that item. However, no merchant deals with just one item; furthermore, few, if any, retailers maintain the first retail price *on all merchandise*. For these reasons, a retail price setter must understand additional concepts such as original price versus selling price, initial markup versus maintained markup, and the averaging of markups.

ORIGINAL PRICE VERSUS SELLING PRICE

Recall that the department manager arrived at a $40.95 *original retail price* for the pantsuits. The subsequent sales record for this order contained both good news and bad news. The good news: the *actual selling price* for 20 units was the original price. The bad (or not-as-good) news: price reductions were necessary to sell the other three units, two at $27.90 and one at $20.48.

Sometimes the original price placed on an item is the price at which the item is sold. In fact, though, the actual selling price may be either higher or lower than the original price. Strong consumer demand, for example, may permit a retailer to increase the price of an offering.

INITIAL MARKUP VERSUS MAINTAINED MARKUP

Because of price changes, there are two types of markups as well as two types of prices. *Initial markup* is the difference between merchandise cost and *original* price, while *maintained markup* is the difference between merchandise cost and *selling* price. Thus, whenever the selling price and original retail price differ, the maintained markup will be different from the initial markup.

Since maintained markup pertains to a single item as well as to groups of merchandise, there are several maintained markup figures that would apply to the pantsuits example. First, the maintained markup for the units sold at the original retail price is the same as the initial markup: 44.98 percent. Then, for each of the two units sold at $27.90, the *dollar* maintained markup is found as follows:

$$\text{dollar maintained markup} = \text{selling price} - \text{cost}$$

$$\text{dollar maintained markup} = \$27.90 - \$22.53 = \$5.37$$

For these same units, the *percentage* maintained markup can also be calculated:

$$\text{percentage maintained markup} = \frac{\text{dollar maintained markup}}{\text{selling price}}$$

$$\text{percentage maintained markup} = \frac{\$5.37}{\$27.90} = 19.25\%$$

A different pair of maintained markup figures would apply to the pantsuit sold at half price.

The *dollar* maintained markup for a *group* (or order) of merchandise is calculated by subtracting the *aggregate* cost of the merchandise from the resulting *aggregate* dollar sales. After aggregate cost is figured, the basic equation for calculating dollar maintained markup can be used. The dollar maintained markup figure of $354.66 for the entire order of pantsuits was arrived at as follows:

$$\text{cost} = \text{bill for merchandise} + \text{transportation charges} - \text{quantity discount}$$

$$\text{cost} = \$538.80 + \$12.60 - \$10.78 = \$540.62$$

$$\text{dollar maintained markup} = \text{selling price} - \text{cost}$$

$$\text{dollar maintained markup} = \$895.28 - \$540.62 = \$354.66$$

Going one step further, the *percentage* maintained markup for a merchandise group (again, the order of pantsuits) can be calculated from the available figures:

$$\text{percentage maintained markup} = \frac{\text{dollar maintained markup}}{\text{selling price}}$$

$$\text{percentage maintained markup} = \frac{\$354.66}{\$895.28} = 39.6\%$$

Two points about maintained markup should be kept in mind:

1. When the selling price is the same as the original price, dollar maintained markup equals dollar initial markup, and percentage maintained markup equals percentage initial markup.
2. When the selling price is different from the original price, maintained markup can be calculated as dollar maintained markup and percentage maintained markup for a single item *and* for a group (or order) of merchandise.

Markup: Types and Arithmetic

Given	To find	Procedure
Retail price and cost	Dollar markup	Subtract cost from retail price
Cost and dollar markup	Retail price	Add givens
Retail price and dollar markup	Cost	Subtract dollar markup from retail price
Retail price and dollar markup	Percentage markup	Divide dollar markup by retail price
Invoice price per unit of merchandise, transportation charges, quantity discount	Cost of merchandise	Add givens, except quantity discount, which is subtracted
Dollar markup and cost of merchandise	Percentage *cost* markup	Divide dollar markup by cost
Retail price and percentage markup	Cost of merchandise	Multiply retail price by (1 − percentage markup)
Retail price and cost of merchandise	Percentage markup	1. Obtain dollar markup by subtracting cost from retail price 2. Divide dollar markup by retail price
Cost and dollar markup	Percentage markup	1. Obtain retail price by adding givens 2. Divide dollar markup by retail price
Dollar markup and percentage markup	Retail price	1. Divide dollar markup by percentage markup 2. Multiply by 100
Cost of merchandise and percentage markup	Retail price	1. Divide cost by (100% − percentage markup) 2. Multiply by 100
Percentage *retail* markup	Percentage *cost* markup	Divide percentage retail markup by (100% − percentage retail markup)
Percentage *cost* markup	Percentage *retail* markup	Divide percentage cost markup by (100% + percentage cost markup)

FIGURE 11-3

Summary of markup formulas

Sometimes a retailer sets prices according to an *average markup goal*. The goal may be specified in terms of either initial markup or maintained markup. For example, a footwear department manager might aim for a 45 percent initial markup, feeling that this percentage will produce the desired level of profit. To achieve a markup goal, a retail manager must balance out markups below the goal with some above the goal.

AVERAGING MARKUPS

Figure 11-3 summarizes the procedures for calculating retail price, cost of merchandise, or markup, given certain related data.

REVIEW BOX 11:3

1. The difference between cost of merchandise sold and retail price represents _____, which can be expressed as a _____ or as a _____.
2. The cost of merchandise figure in the equation is obtained by taking the base invoice price for the merchandise and _____ any applicable quantity or trade discounts and then _____ any transportation charges.
3. To calculate percentage retail markup, dollar markup is divided by _____.
4. Because of price changes, there are two types of markups: _____ and _____.
5. The _____ markup designates the difference between cost of merchandise sold and actual selling price, while _____ markup involves _____ retail price.

CHAPTER SUMMARY

- Basically, price is the amount of money and perhaps something else of value necessary to purchase a seller's offering.
- The importance of price in purchase decisions varies greatly, depending upon characteristics of both the offering and the individual involved.
- Prices should be established only after the nature of consumer demand for the offering is considered. Normally, cost of the offering represents the floor (or minimum) retail price the firm must have to make a profit. Usually there is also a ceiling (or maximum) price above which few consumers will buy the offering.
- The retailer should view an individual outcome such as high total revenue—or high unit sales, or high or low revenue—as desirable only if it leads to maximum or satisfactory profits over the long run.

- Markup is the difference between retail price and cost of merchandise and can be expressed as a dollar amount or as a percentage. Percentage retail markup, a central concept in retail pricing, is calculated by dividing dollar markup by retail price.
- Because of price changes, there are two types of prices and two types of markups. Initial markup is the difference between merchandise cost and original price, while maintained markup is the difference between cost and sales price.
- When prices are based on an average markup goal, markups below the goal must be balanced out by some above the goal.

CHAPTER NOTES

[1] A modified version of the definition in William J. Stanton, *Fundamentals of Marketing*, 3rd ed. (New York: McGraw-Hill Book Company, 1971), p. 414.

[2] For additional details on discount grocery retailing, see "41st Annual Report of the Grocery Industry: Discounting Continues to Grow," *Progressive Grocer*, April 1974, pp. 79–80.

[3] The total transportation charges of $12.60 divided by the 24 units equals 52.5¢ per unit.

QUESTIONS AND ASSIGNMENTS

1. Define *price*. Why is the phrase "and perhaps something else of value" necessary?
2. "If there's one task I want handled by my *experienced* people, it's price setting." What can you recall from the chapter which helps explain why a store manager might make this statement?
3. Under demand-oriented pricing, what roles are played by cost and by demand?
4. When items are marked down before being sold, will maintained markup be larger or smaller than initial markup? Explain your answer, referring to the appropriate equations.
5. What are the dollar maintained markup and percentage maintained markup figures for the pantsuit which cost $22.53 and sold at $20.48 (half the original price of $40.95)?
6. In the income statement in Figure 11-1, what would the amount of profits be if sales rose to $350, costs to $72, and expenses to $226?
7. Construct a *realistic* income statement (similar to the one in Figure 11-1) which indicates a rise in total revenue *and profits* due to a price change. Explain how the profit improvement came about.
8. Don's donuts cost him 3¢ apiece, and he sold them at 10¢ apiece.
    a. What was the dollar retail markup? (Of course, since the unit value is in cents, the dollar markup will be in cents rather than dollars.)
    b. What is the percentage markup?
    c. Will the maintained markup be the same as the initial markup? Why or why not?
9. The sales representative for the Boise Boot Co. tells the Campus Shop

manager that Knockaround brand boots would be highly profitable. The Boise salesman says convincingly: "With a cost to you of $11 a pair and the suggested retail price of $16.50, that's a 50 percent markup." The manager, claiming the salesman is trying to deceive him, throws him out of the store.
  a. Is the retail markup 50 percent?
  b. Explain what might have caused the misunderstanding.
10. Wheelin' & Dealin', the local bicycle shop, foresees a tandem bicycle fad and orders 10. The invoice price is $55 each, and the transportation charges are $25. The quantity discount of 3 percent is for orders of a dozen or more. Only three of these bikes were sold at $115 before the fad fizzled. Eventually, three more were sold at $92, and another three were sold at half price. The last one was given away in a contest. Calculate the following figures for the despondent shop owner:
  a. per-unit cost of merchandise
  b. percentage initial markup on each bike
  c. percentage maintained markup on the bikes sold at $92
  d. the dollar sales produced by the order of 10 bikes
  e. the dollar maintained markup for the order
  f. the percentage maintained markup for the order

ANSWERS TO REVIEW BOX QUESTIONS

Box 11:1

1. the amount of money and perhaps something else of value
2. three of the following: the personality of the individual consumer; the income level of the consumer; the magnitude of the expenditure; the time pressure connected with the purchase; the character of the offering

Box 11:2

1. the nature of consumer demand for the offering is considered
2. cost of the offering
3. cost and expenses; total revenue
4. uncertain

Box 11:3

1. markup; dollar amount; percentage
2. subtracting; adding
3. retail price
4. initial and maintained
5. maintained; initial; original

Pricing Methods

How do you actually establish retail prices? Although this question can be simply stated, by no stretch of the imagination can it be simply answered. This does not mean, though, that setting effective retail prices should be viewed as hopeless or accidental. Rather, skillful pricing occurs when managerial experience and business judgment are combined with an understanding of certain pricing concepts. The first two qualities are acquired on the job. This chapter will help you acquire the third necessary ingredient: understanding of various pricing concepts.

A PRICING DECISION SEQUENCE

Establishing an original retail price can be visualized as a sequence, as diagrammed in Figure 12-1. Some steps are routine; others are nonroutine and can be quite difficult. At each step, the retail price setter answers a question surrounding a particular pricing situation, makes an estimate or a calculation, or judges the effect of a specific factor on a possible price.

Variations in Complexity

The process by which a price should be set is not always as complicated as Figure 12-1 suggests. Pricing is complicated when the price setter works for a new firm that is establishing its initial set of prices, for an established outlet adding a line of offerings, or for an outlet evaluating its set of prices. Pricing

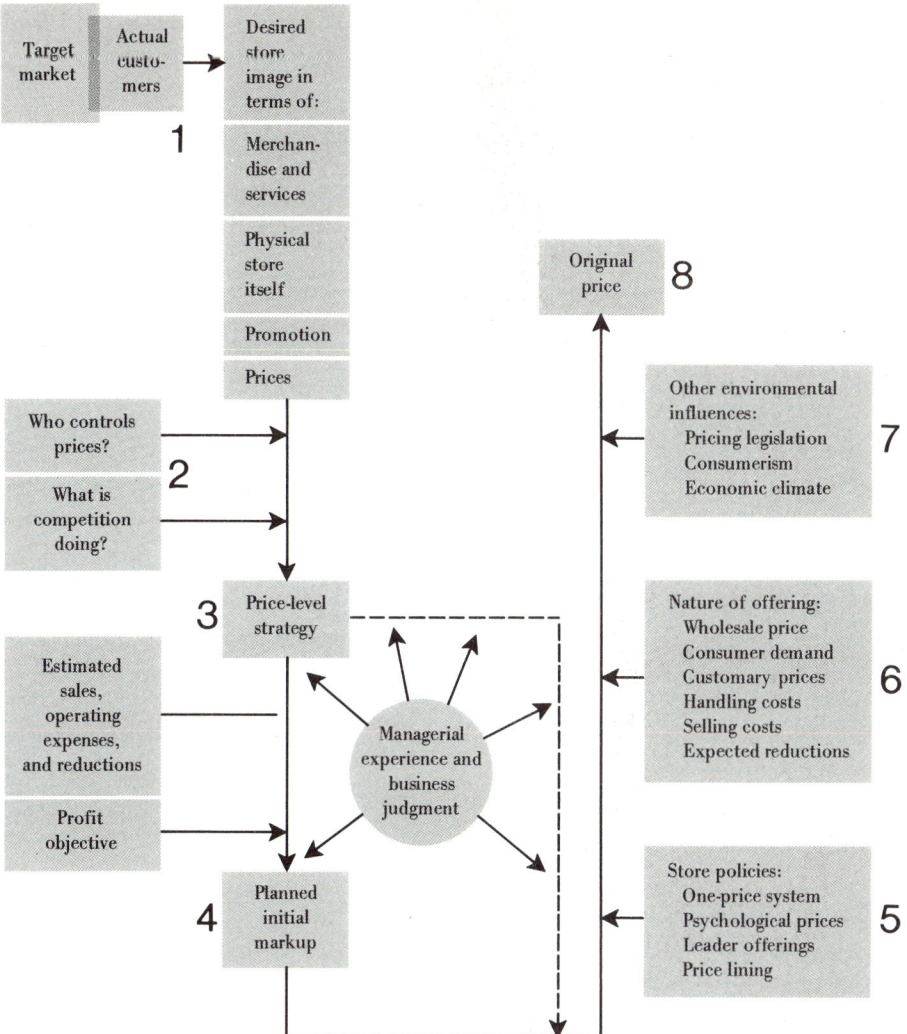

FIGURE 12-1

Pricing decision sequence

is simpler when an outlet has been in operation for some time and the offering is now sold *profitably* by the outlet. When this is true, a price setter's experience makes many steps routine.

One caution: A "routine" pricing process does not mean prices are set in a robot-like manner, without any thought about the steps or about what is going on around the firm. Skilled merchants *thoughtfully* seek profitable prices.

Overview of the Sequence

Eight specific steps comprise the pricing decision sequence:

1. Relating price to retail operations planning.
2. Determining who controls prices and what competition is doing.
3. Selecting a price-level strategy.
4. Planning initial markup.
5. Considering possible prices in relation to store policies.
6. Considering possible prices in relation to the nature of the offering.
7. Considering other environmental influences.
8. Actually establishing an original price for the offering.

Really, steps 1 through 7 are aimed at providing information which increases the likelihood of arriving at an original price that will achieve the firm's objectives.

The results of each step affect what can happen in the next step. To illustrate, consider an example involving steps 1 and 3. If a retail outlet decides upon a retailing mix featuring a variety of supplementary services to satisfy its upper-middle income target market (step 1), very low prices probably cannot be considered (in step 3). This price-level strategy would not be feasible because operating expenses will be high due to the many supplementary services.

The pricing sequence includes three key decisions. Each is examined briefly below.

PRICE-LEVEL STRATEGY

The first key decision a retailer must make is whether to price *above*, *at*, or *below* the general market level of prices for identical or comparable offerings. As Figure 12-1 indicates, this decision should be based on several preceding steps. Possible prices must be evaluated in terms of whether they would contribute to the desired store image in the minds of target and actual customers. The price setter must also answer two questions regarding control over prices and competitors' pricing activities.

PLANNED INITIAL MARKUP

Next the price setter plans initial markup. This planned figure is usually stated as a percentage figure, such as 38 or 50 percent of the retail price. If a department manager's goal is 40 percent, this indicates that the cost of the merchandise will account for 60 percent of the retail price, leaving 40 percent to cover expenses, reductions, and profit.

The dashed line that extends from the price-level strategy box in Figure 12-1 indicates that planned initial markup is occasionally omitted. Some firms simply do not take the time and effort to plan initial markup. Other merchants feel that accurate estimates of expenses or price reductions and stock shortages are not possible. This means that calculating an initial markup figure would not be sensible. *But*, if planned initial markup is relevant to the particular type of retail business *and* if expenses and reductions can be estimated, then planned initial markup should be calculated because it aids in planning a firm's or department's offerings.

Before an *original price* is established, the final step in this sequence, three groups of factors should be considered. These factors, discussed separately further on in the chapter, pertain to the store's policies related to certain pricing tactics, the nature of the offering being priced, and forces in the firm's environment that may affect possible prices. At the end of this step, the collection of possible prices should be small enough that a merchant or store employee can confidently establish an original price.

ORIGINAL PRICE

The impact of two other factors on the pricing sequence must be noted. As indicated in the center of Figure 12-1, the levels of business judgment and managerial experience possessed by a price setter play a major role in pricing. Sound judgment and experience not only will make retail pricing easier but also should result in more effective prices. These two factors are diagrammed as a sunburst because they certainly can "shed some light" on the pricing sequence.

Pricing Responsibility

Who in a retail firm participates in price setting? In most firms, top management is most likely to be involved in the early steps, particularly in deciding upon a price-level strategy and planning an initial markup. Furthermore, top management also develops certain store policies that affect pricing decisions.

Actually, pricing individual offerings is ordinarily the responsibility of buyers or department managers, who follow the guidelines laid down by top management. Buyers' or department managers' roles in pricing are not to be minimized just because they do not have *complete* pricing freedom. They must decide whether an offering should be priced precisely according to the planned initial markup or whether store policies, the nature of the offering, or some environmental force makes another price more logical. Thus their decisions on specific original prices largely determine whether an offering will be attractive to consumers and profitable to the store.

INDIVIDUAL STEPS IN THE SEQUENCE

Let us now examine in some detail the eight specific steps in the pricing decision sequence.

Relating Price to Retail Operations Planning

The first step represents a simplified version of the retail operations planning process. A retail firm narrows its scope of operations by deciding upon a general area of business and a group or groups of target customers. Then the outlet's executives must develop a retailing mix. One component, of course, is price.

Possible prices must be considered in relation to a store's overall effort to serve present customers and attract additional customers. In this step consideration is more strategic than highly specific in nature. Possible price-level strategies and initial markups will be assessed, in particular. A footwear retailer, for example, is not concerned with prices on individual pairs of shoes in this step. Rather he thinks about what particular price levels or average markups would contribute to the store's desired image.

Determining Who Controls Prices and What Competition Is Doing

Both of these concerns center around factors beyond the retail firm itself, namely, the channel of distribution and competitors. Whether channel members' and competitors' actions can be affected by a particular firm depends upon that firm's financial and market power. A large, financially strong store with a sizable consumer following no doubt will have an impact on the activities of its competitors and suppliers.

WHO CONTROLS PRICES? Even though it may seem contradictory, a retailer may not have the chance to establish retail prices on some items because of the influence of manufacturers or wholesalers. Why and how does a manufacturer or wholesaler control retail prices? The primary reason why suppliers sometimes desire to set retail prices is because they feel they can better determine what prices would be most consistent with *their* overall marketing mix. Thus the supplier is looking out for himself, first and foremost. Of course, a manufacturer or wholesaler cannot disregard retailers' interests or, eventually, they will be unwilling to sell the supplier's merchandise.

There are three methods by which a supplier can effectively establish the retail price on merchandise sold to stores. Resale price maintenance laws are a contractual means by which a supplier can control his retail prices. A second technique that can be used is for a supplier to refuse to deal with stores that do not adhere to the established retail price. The success of this method, from the supplier's standpoint, depends on how desirable the brand or line of merchandise involved is to retailers. Depending upon circumstances, this method can be illegal.

Selling on consignment is the third possible method of achieving control over retail prices. Under this arrangement, a store must comply with the suppliers' pricing instructions or be open to a court suit and a possible claim of damages.

If a manufacturer or wholesaler sets the original retail price, then the pricing sequence has a different purpose. Rather than having to establish a feasible original price, a retailer has merely to determine the acceptability of an already established price. Acceptability depends upon whether the original price set by a supplier is compatible with the store's price-level strategy and planned initial markup. Store policies, the nature of the offering, and environmental forces also need to be considered.

When a retailer accepts a supplier's retail price, it means that the firm and its competitors will have identical prices on a particular offering. Depending upon the firm's price-level strategy, this may be either advantageous or unfavorable. For example, if a store's objective is to have prices lower than those of competitors, identical prices would be unfavorable. Of course, the retailer would not have accepted the supplier's price if it were drastically out of line with the chosen price-level strategy.

Acceptance of a supplier's retail price also means a retailer has no direct control over the amount of markup on the item. On occasion, the merchant may accept retail prices that bring about smaller than normal markups, say 35 rather than 45 percent of the retail price. Under these circumstances, a department manager may attempt to lower the operating expenses and reductions usually connected with this merchandise so that a profit can still be made. For example, if a department's expenses and reductions normally run about 35 and 5 percent, respectively, the manager might strive for 30 and 2 percent results so that the supplier-priced merchandise will be profitable. However, a retailer cannot continually accept suppliers' retail prices that carry insufficient markups and still make a profit.

WHAT IS COMPETITION DOING?

Before selecting a price-level strategy (the first major pricing decision), retailers should assess competitors' prices on identical, similar, and substitute offerings. This information is necessary, since a price-level strategy should be related to the general, prevailing level of prices. Moreover, merchants must watch competitors' prices to make sure that planned prices are not drastically out of line—either much higher or much lower. If a firm has "extra high" prices *without providing extra benefits*, customers will eventually take their business elsewhere.

At the other extreme, if a firm's prices are much lower than those of competitors, problems still can arise. Some consumers might avoid the outlet because they think something has to be missing for prices to be so low—which, in fact, may not be true at all. For example, a fast-food restaurant with very low prices might be suspected of using low-quality food products. With few exceptions, a store's prices must be comparable to those of other stores *that have approximately equal retailing mixes*.

Individual Steps in the Sequence

"Their large limas are 19, make ours 17—their small peas are 2 for 19—make ours 3 for 27."

How does a retail price setter track competitors' prices? You're correct if you suggested any of the following ways: by listening to customers' comments, by reading competitors' newspaper ads, or by using comparison shoppers. Retailers who use the first two methods are simply letting the information come to them, rather than systematically gathering it. A comparison shopping staff is a more systematic method of obtaining information. Comparison shoppers check prices on designated offerings by actually going into competitors' outlets and noting prices of interest. When similar (but not identical) offerings are being compared, the shopper may actually purchase the merchandise so that quality can also be checked. Although comparison shopping is effective, its high cost limits its use to rather large stores.

REVIEW BOX 12:1

1. The result of the retail pricing decision sequence is _____ _____.
2. Actually pricing individual offerings is usually the responsibility of _____ or _____, following the guidelines laid down by _____.
3. In the second step, the price setter should answer two questions. One question is: what is competition doing? The other is: _____?

Selecting a Price-Level Strategy

The strategic decision made in step 3 is whether to aim for prices that are generally *above*, *at*, or *below* market price levels. Two special aspects of this decision are noteworthy:

1. Once a strategy has been selected for an outlet, department, or line of offerings, the decision is not remade each time through the pricing sequence. Rather, the established strategy directs the price setter toward or away from certain possible prices.
2. The resulting strategy often is stated—quite logically—in rather general terms. For example, an automobile dealer might have the following price-level strategy: "We are never knowingly undersold." A highly specific strategy may, in effect, determine the original price. This would apply in the case of the television and stereo equipment retailer with the following strategy: "We mark what we feel are our ten most popular items at 10 percent below the manufacturers' suggested price; everything else is priced as suggested

by our suppliers or at prices equal to our two main competitors." However, a very specific strategy can be dangerous because it may preclude considering other important factors in arriving at an original price.

ABOVE-THE-MARKET STRATEGY

When an outlet plans to price most, perhaps all, of its offerings higher than those of competitors, the assumption is that price is not a major concern to some shoppers because other retailing mix elements are very desirable. What extra features may make an above-the-market price strategy possible? Some combination of the following extras would be needed:

- Highly desirable offerings, which may refer to extensive assortments, exclusive products or services, or very fashionable merchandise
- Excellent supplementary services such as liberal credit, free delivery, and reliable (and perhaps free) repairs or alterations
- Extra convenience with respect to location and hours of operation
- Personable, knowledgeable sales people in adequate numbers
- Prestigious reputation, which may have evolved over the years because of the above features.

Although a combination of these features usually is needed to compensate for high prices, an abundance of one feature may be sufficient. For example, numerous independent television retailers offset their above-the-market prices with a strong service department, a feature that should always be pointed out to potential customers.

Several specific retailers and chains have prestigious reputations that permit this strategy. Certain department stores such as Neiman-Marcus (whose flagship store is in Dallas) and Saks Fifth Avenue (New York) do not compete on the basis of price because they are "standards of excellence" in their areas. Similarly, Baskin-Robbins ice cream shops have achieved success with what seem to be above-the-market prices by stressing quality and wide assortment of flavors. The rationale for Baskin-Robbins' prices is suggested by a plaque which hangs in the shops: "There is hardly anything in the world that some man cannot make a little worse and sell a little cheaper, and the people who consider price only are this man's lawful prey."

Two final points about an above-the-market strategy must be recognized by a retail price setter. First, when an above- or below-the-market strategy is adopted, a decision must be made on how much higher or lower prices generally will be. This particular decision is one in which substantial experience and judgment are especially valuable aids. Second, higher *prices* do not necessarily mean higher *profits*. The extra features that high-price stores offer their customers absorb some (maybe all) of any additional revenue brought about by this strategy.

Individual Steps in the Sequence

SPOTLIGHT

How can convenience grocery stores prosper in these days of discount prices?

Since about 1971, more and more large grocery stores have promoted discount prices as a way of appealing to consumers shocked by inflation. The smaller convenience grocery stores, on the other hand, have above-the-market price levels, running as much as 25 percent higher than nearby supermarkets.

Considering their prices, it would seem that convenience grocery stores could not compete successfully with other grocery retailers. But this clearly is not the case. In fact, in 1972, right after many grocery stores went to discount prices, the number of convenience grocery stores rose by 18 percent. Moreover, average sales per convenience store increased 7 percent.

How have convenience grocery stores achieved this outstanding record, in spite of inflation and increased price competition from supermarkets? We can look at the leading firm in this field, 7-Eleven stores operated by Southland Corporation, to obtain some answers.

Southland's president has admitted to 7-Eleven's above-the-market price strategy: "We have a reputation for being so damned high in prices that when people come in, they simply expect to pay more." But 7-Eleven offsets its prices with features not offered by supermarkets, particularly neighborhood locations and long store hours including Sunday openings. Also, consumers are offered the convenience of quick shopping. Southland feels its customers are more interested in this quick shopping feature than in low prices. As explained by a vice-president, "We had weekend specials for a while, and people started grumbling when they had to stand in line."

The results of this price-level strategy (actually, the entire retailing mix) have been impressive. Southland increased sales by more than 500 percent in a recent ten-year period. Also, Southland's after-tax profits are healthy: about 1.5 cents of each dollar of sales, which is about twice the overall average for grocery chains.

But Southland—and other convenience grocery stores—cannot afford to sit back and admire their past performance. Many supermarkets have moved to longer hours and Sunday openings, thus erasing one extra feature offered by convenience grocery stores. Furthermore, some grocery chains are experimenting with their own convenience stores, while some oil companies are retailing grocery items at their service stations. Thus the struggle for a profitable differential advantage continues.

Sources: Statistics on the number and sales of convenience grocery stores are from "3rd Annual Report of the Convenience Store Industry," *Progressive Grocer/Convenience Stores*, Fall 1973, p. 9; the profile of 7-Eleven operations is from "The Threat to Southland's Growth," *Business Week*, October 28, 1972, pp. 60 and 61.

AT-THE-MARKET STRATEGY

Marking most items with prices comparable to those of competitors is the strategy employed by the majority of retailers. They feel that this strategy enables them to appeal to most consumers. A criticism of this strategy is that it represents "an easy way out." This is a valid criticism when a price setter does not carefully consider alternative strategies. However, analysis of the overall situation may indicate that the logical decision is to match competitors' prices or to apply markups traditional in the line of trade, either of which represents an at-the-market strategy.

When a retail firm adopts either an above- or an at-the-market pricing strategy, it does not escape competition. Rather, the outlet chooses to compete on non-price factors. Management feels that customers attracted by low prices are not as loyal as those patronizing the outlet because of non-price factors, or that low prices are easier for competitors to match than are non-price factors such as excellent supplementary services and broad assortment of offerings.

BELOW-THE-MARKET STRATEGY

"Lured by a single-room rate between $6 and $9.90, bargain-hungry travelers are flocking to so-called budget or economy motel chains."[1] This recent trend illustrates the strategy in which most or all offerings are priced below prevailing market levels. Below-the-market prices are practical only when sufficient numbers of customers can be attracted by the potential savings. When this strategy is adopted, the element of low prices predominates in the retailing mix and becomes the firm's "drawing card." Also, with very few exceptions, low prices must be coupled with low operating expenses, limited assortments, and economical physical facilities if the firm is to profit.

Some firms combine below-the-market prices and reduced costs of doing business, achieved by offering fewer supplementary services. This combination is termed *discount pricing*, or sometimes low-margin retailing or simply discounting. Discount pricing is the central feature of chains such as K-Mart, Woolco, and Korvettes.[2] Over the years discount houses have been "trading up"—that is, offering additional services while raising prices. Generally, however, they are still characterized by below-the-market prices and relatively low operating costs.

PRIVATE BRANDS

Numerous retail chains have introduced private-brand merchandise, items carrying the store's or a wholesaler's name or label rather than a manufacturer's. To cite some examples, Riverside and Signature are two of Ward's own brands, Scot Lad and Top Frost are labels developed by grocery wholesalers, and Ann Page is the most familiar of A & P's many private brands. Quite often, private brands are part of a below-the-market price-level strategy.

Private brands have been gaining in popularity for several reasons. They give a retailer some pricing freedom, since they are not directly comparable to brands carried by other stores. Because private-brand merchan-

Individual Steps in the Sequence

dise usually costs a retailer less than national-brand merchandise, below-the-market prices *at normal markups* are possible. When customers view a store's private-brand merchandise as good values, they become loyal customers.

Calculating Planned Initial Markup

To this point, a price setter has chosen a price level relative to competitors' prices at which he feels his offerings will sell sufficiently well. Now he must take into account his costs of doing business and the amount of profit he is realistically seeking. *Planned initial markup,* usually stated as a percentage, helps in doing this. This markup figure can apply to an entire store, a department, or a single line of merchandise. Whichever the case, the figures pertain to a specified time period such as a three-month season or one year.

INITIAL MARKUP FORMULA

Initial markup must be high enough to cover expenses and reductions expected in selling the merchandise and also provide for some profit. Although the necessary markup can be "guestimated," it is better to use the following:

$$\text{initial markup percentage} = \frac{\text{operating expenses} + \text{reductions} + \text{profit}}{\text{net sales} + \text{reductions}}$$

The numerator indicates the necessary markup *beyond the cost of merchandise sold.* The denominator indicates the necessary original retail price of the merchandise. When they are known, two other factors are included in the numerator. Alteration costs are added in, while cash discounts obtained from suppliers are subtracted from the other factors.

To employ the formula, the price setter must estimate sales volume for the upcoming period. Of course, all estimates should be realistic—in the case of sales, high enough to be a challenge but still attainable. For example, assume that a children's shoe department anticipates annual sales of $47,000.

Next an estimate must be made of the amount of operating expenses connected with this sales volume. Assume $17,000 in expenses for the shoe department. Then the level of reductions (consisting of markdowns, stock shortages, and employee and customer discounts) must be estimated. Combining the various types, let us assume a total of $3,000 in reductions. The last figure to be inserted into the formula is a profit objective. Assume that the price setter has a $2,000 objective.

The initial markup needed to produce this amount of profit with the estimated sales, expenses, and reductions is calculated as follows:

$$\text{initial markup percentage} = \frac{\$17,000 + \$3,000 + \$2,000}{\$47,000 + \$3,000}$$

$$\text{initial markup percentage} = \frac{\$22,000}{\$50,000} = 44\%$$

While this example was based on *dollar* estimates, the formula also works with *percentage* estimates. A manager can estimate expenses, reductions, and the profit objective as percentages of sales. When this is done, sales (the figure on the left in the denominator) become 100 percent, or 1.00.

The initial markup formula can also be used to calculate any of the other four variables in the formula. For instance, the formula is sometimes used to estimate what profits will result at a certain initial markup level and selected estimates of sales, expenses, and reductions.

DEVIATIONS FROM PLANS

Some merchants, hopefully very few, take the calculated initial markup and apply it to every merchandise purchase to determine original prices. Since planned initial markup represents *an average*, however, it should not be immediately inserted into the markup formula to arrive at an original price. Deviations from the average figure may be logical for some offerings because of factors not yet considered, namely, store policies, the nature of the offering, or environmental influences.

Recognizing the limitations of an inflexible initial markup, some retailers use several initial markup figures. Some of these percentages may be higher than the planned goal, some lower. For example, a sporting goods store may apply the highest of four markup percentages to merchandise that, relatively speaking, is in great demand but has a low rate of turnover and substantial handling and selling costs. Steel-frame tennis rackets may be in this highest markup group. They are a popular item but require an extensive inventory (because of different weights and grip sizes) and skilled educational selling (because they must be shown to be an improvement over lower-priced wood-frame rackets). Consequently, steel rackets might carry a 45 percent markup rather than the average of, say, 38 percent. Of course, other offerings with different characteristics may carry markups smaller than the average.

Some price setters go even further by pricing each product and service on a completely individual basis. This approach conceivably could result in a different percentage markup for every offering.

REVIEW BOX 12:2

1. Alternative price-level strategies are pricing _____, _____, or _____ market price levels.

2. Initial markup percentage = $\dfrac{? + \text{reductions} + \text{profit}}{\text{net sales} + \text{reductions}}$

   The figure omitted from the formula used in calculating planned initial markup is _____.

Individual Steps in the Sequence

Price and Store Policies

In order to determine exactly where we are in the pricing decision sequence and what remains to be done, we will examine the decisions made by a manager in setting a price for pantsuits. Since the department was an established one, the manager did not have to calculate a markup goal; a 40 percent initial markup figure had been determined previously. Without further consideration the manager might have applied the 40 percent markup, in which case the pantsuits would have carried $37.55 price tags.

However, using good judgment, she further analyzed the situation. Apparently she concluded that the material was unique and the brand was quite popular (which suggested a strong demand for the item), and that eventual markdowns on some units were likely. Based on this analysis, a 45 percent markup—rather than the usual 40 percent—was decided upon. Since the pantsuits were eventually priced at $40.95 rather than an even $41, the manager seems also to have concluded that a price just below an even dollar amount would be more appealing to consumers. Compared to a price set at step 4, a price established after these three additional steps is more likely to be satisfactory in terms of salability of the offering *and* overall profitability.

Store policies, considered in step 5, are most commonly applied to a one-price system, psychological prices, leader items, and price-lining. Each is discussed below.

A ONE-PRICE SYSTEM

If you and a friend go into McDonald's to buy a milkshake and a Quarter-Pounder, each of you will pay the same price. However, if the two of you purchase identical portable televisions from the same dealer, you may wind up paying different prices. This is because McDonald's follows what is called a one-price system, whereas the television retailer has a negotiated price system. When prices are first set, a decision must be made on which system to use.

A *one-price system* means that the same price is charged every purchaser of a particular item. (Do not confuse a one-price system with a *single-price* system. The latter, no longer common in retailing, means that *all* of an outlet's offerings carry the same price, like 88¢ or $5. Today, some men's tie shops are perhaps the closest thing we have to a single-price outlet, but even they usually have at least several different prices.)

A merchant chooses a one-price system because it assures uniform treatment of all shoppers, at least with respect to prices. Also, the need for sales personnel is reduced or completely eliminated, since price is not only plainly marked, but inflexible as well. This second consequence permits self-service operations, as in supermarkets and discount houses. In general, most retail firms use a one-price system.

Under a *negotiated-price system*, prices are adjusted as necessary—and as feasible—to close a sale with an individual customer. For example, as part of a recent promotion, Pacific Stereo Shops in the San Francisco, Los Angeles, and Chicago areas encouraged shoppers to "haggle" over prices. The chain's ads urged stereo buffs to come in and "make a bid" on any sound system. A company spokesman explained the negotiated prices as follows:

> We find most people don't really have a concept of the normal price discounts. Most bids are close to what we would promote it for anyway.[3]

Negotiated prices are in effect in various situations, primarily when:

- Salespersons and shoppers negotiate the allowance for a trade-in, such as in the automobile and appliance businesses. In these cases, the shopper's bargaining ability may be more important than the trade-in's value in determining the final price.
- Most shoppers realize that the marked price just represents a starting point for reaching a final price. This situation prevails in new-car retailing, even when trade-ins are not involved.

The theoretical advantage of this system lies in its flexibility; a salesperson can cut price when he or she encounters price resistance on a shopper's part. On the other hand, negotiated prices have some real disadvantages: Customers may be alienated if they discover that someone else got a lower price, and more salespeople are needed because most transactions involve time-consuming negotiations.

Because of its relative merits, a one-price system is advisable for most types of retailers. However, a negotiated-price system may be a competitive necessity for stores selling durable goods such as appliances, cars, TVs, or furniture.

PSYCHOLOGICAL PRICES

As discussed in Chapter 3, certain types of prices supposedly have special psychological effects on shoppers. The main tactics used by retailers are odd-ending prices, multiple-unit prices, and quality-related prices.

Retailers deliberately use *odd-ending prices* such as 49¢, $1.98, $5.95, and $19.88, rather than even-ending prices such as 50¢ or $2.00, because they believe that they suggest low prices or bargains; even endings are thought to suggest high quality offerings.

Multiple-unit pricing means giving a special price when two or more units of the same offering are purchased together. This special price reflects what amounts to a quantity discount.

Sometimes consumers judge an offering's quality from its price. When this occurs, a higher price may sell more units than a lower price. In this case, a higher price is termed a *quality-related price*.

Individual Steps in the Sequence

LEADER OFFERINGS

When relatively low, less profitable prices are placed on selected products or services, this tactic is called *leader offerings*. Although leaders or specials may create the impression of across-the-board low prices, their primary purpose is to attract shoppers to the outlet so that they might buy more profitable offerings as well. The K-Mart ad in Figure 12-2 even tells consumers that the low-price items are intended to *lure* shoppers to that supermarket. As with other pricing tactics, the ultimate objective of leader offerings is to increase total store profits.

While individual products or services (such as TV dinners or a brake adjustment) ordinarily are selected as leader offerings, an entire line of merchandise (film or record albums) or a department (a store's cafeteria) can be used as a leader. When the offerings are deliberately sold below cost, they are referred to as *loss leaders*.

Most retailers agree that a product or service must meet certain criteria to be an effective leader offering. It must:

Be used by most people *and* be bought somewhat frequently. Accordingly, milk and soft drinks would be suitable leader offerings for grocery stores, whereas buttermilk and carrot juice would not be.

Carry a very familiar regular price, so that shoppers clearly recognize the leader as a bargain

Be a "small-ticket" item, usually under $1 in grocery stores, under $5 in discount houses and department stores. With a small-ticket item, a shopper is likely to look for additional items to make the trip to the store even more worthwhile and is also likely to have money beyond the leader's price in order to buy additional items.

In deciding how low to price a leader, the price setter should remember that a leader itself is not necessarily supposed to be profitable but definitely should generate shopper traffic. Thus being a little too low in price is preferable to being a little too high. However, the price setter must avoid violating state laws prohibiting excessively low prices, to be discussed shortly.

Bait-and-switch pricing is a deceptive variation on leader offerings. This tactic involves advertising what appears to be a bargain (the bait), but then trying to get interested shoppers to buy a higher priced, more profitable item instead (the switch). In the usual case, a salesperson combines disparaging comments about the leader offering with extra favorable remarks about the substitute—all in a high-pressure manner. While bait-and-switch pricing works for some retailers, its use is unwise. Not only is it unethical in many people's minds, it is also illegal in many instances.

PRICE LINING

This tactic consists of setting up distinct price points or zones and then pricing all offerings in a category at these points or within these zones. For instance, a men's store which sells ties only at $2.50, $5, $7.50, and $10 is

FIGURE 12-2

An advertised leader offering

practicing price lining, with four price *points* for this item. Price lining using three *zones* is illustrated by a furniture store which prices sofas only between $149.95 and $229.95, $325 and $400, and $500 and $600. As you can see, price lining limits the number of original prices. The most suitable goods for price lining are those which must be carried in large assortments because consumers want to compare them in terms of style, color, and size.

The major *advantages* of price lining include: easier consumer decision making, since there are fewer price alternatives; more complete assortments at the most popular prices; and possible simplification of managers' pricing and buying tasks since, once the price points or zones are picked, both tasks become largely a matter of finding merchandise to fit these price lines.

Somewhat offsetting the above are two disadvantages: perhaps not being able to carry some appealing merchandise because its cost means it cannot be sold at the established prices, and the difficulty of raising prices when wholesale prices rise. Problems created by these disadvantages can be minimized, however, by using zones, which provide much more flexibility than points. Another advantage of zones is that more price alternatives can be provided shoppers, but still not too many to be confusing.

What number of price points or zones is best? More than 40 years ago, Edward Filene, who started the Filene's department store chain in the East, stated that three price points are a sufficient number for a category of merchandise.[4] Today many retailers follow this same approach. They establish a low price, aimed at the price-conscious segment of shoppers; a medium price, aimed at the majority of shoppers; and a high price, aimed at the quality- or prestige-conscious. Generally speaking, specific points or zones should be selected after determining from sales records the several prices at which offerings most frequently are sold. Also, before price lines are selected, competitors' activities and target customers' desires and spending patterns should be taken into account.[5]

Thus, the output of step 5 is a set of four store pricing policies. When a price setter recognizes, for example, that the firm follows a one-price system, does not use any psychological prices or leaders, and uses price lining, he or she has greatly reduced the number of possible prices for the item and thereby moves closer to a final decision.

Price and Nature of the Offering

Next a price setter should consider how selected characteristics of a particular offering affect possible planned initial markup. Specifically, the task in this step is to compare six characteristics of a product or service to those of other offerings covered by the same planned markup.

In the following paragraphs, each characteristic is briefly discussed as to when it might justify a high markup. You will see that a condition suggesting the need for a low markup ordinarily is just the opposite of one suggesting a high markup.

Did the store get a "good deal" on this purchase relative to purchases of other merchandise? A lower-than-normal wholesale price might be obtained when a retail firm buys a large quantity and hence gets a quantity discount from the supplier, when it negotiates a special price on merchandise which is new or near the end of its selling season, or when it buys slightly imperfect goods (which must be advertised as such to consumers).
    A retailer may pass the savings from a good deal on to consumers through a lower-than-normal retail price but normal markup. A merchant may feel that the item is a suitable leader offering or that an occasional special price conveys the impression of relatively low prices throughout the outlet. On the other hand, a merchant may choose to benefit directly from the low wholesale price by putting the item out at its normal price, which would mean a markup higher than the average.

WHOLESALE PRICE

Demand for an item should always be considered in markup decisions. Offerings that are extremely popular may be given a higher markup, as may offerings that will be bought regardless of price changes.

CONSUMER DEMAND

Consumers often have a "customary" price in mind for certain items and will hesitate to spend an amount above this price. A price of 25¢ for a package of chewing gum, for example, will probably seem unreasonable. A higher-than-normal markup is advisable only if it does not produce an "uncustomary" high price for an item.

CUSTOMARY PRICES

These two costs overlap to some extent and affect markup possibilities in a similar way. An item's rate of turnover primarily determines relative handling costs, since turnover affects the amount of operating capital a retail firm must have. Handling costs are greater for slow-moving merchandise than for fast-moving merchandise (that is, items with a high turnover rate). The level of handling costs is also determined by whether unprofitable replacement parts must be stocked or the product must be assembled before being sold.
    Major factors determining the level of selling costs are the relative bulk of the product, amount of personal selling required, and need for supplementary services, such as installation or alterations, on which the firm does not profit. Selling costs are high for bulky merchandise, furniture for instance, because it requires relatively great amounts of floor space. This means that a proportionately large amount of overhead has to be covered by the "bulky" product or department.

HANDLING COSTS AND SELLING COSTS

Individual Steps in the Sequence

Higher-than-normal markups are called for when the offering being priced entails high handling *or* selling costs. Note that it is possible for relatively low handling costs to offset relatively high selling costs, or vice versa. Products with high handling and/or selling costs include window glass, children's toys, furniture, specialized hardware items, men's suits, and custom-mixed paint.

EXPECTED REDUCTIONS

The initial markup should also reflect the price setter's judgment about reasonable, expected levels of reductions. When spoilage, shoplifting, employee theft, damage, or breakage occur, the retail value becomes zero, since the merchandise is either ruined or missing. Damaged or broken merchandise sometimes can be sold through large price reductions, in which case the item is not a total loss. One type of reduction frequently taken into account by price setters is spoilage, which is inevitable in the retailing of produce and cut flowers. Markdowns, another type of reduction, are especially frequent on seasonal merchandise and fashion apparel.

When somewhat high reductions are expected, a higher-than-normal markup is called for. For example, some spoiled tomatoes have to be discarded by all produce retailers. Tomatoes will carry a higher markup than other grocery items and most produce items so that selling prices will compensate for revenue lost from unavoidable spoilage.

REVIEW BOX 12:3

1. When the same price is charged every purchaser of an item, the outlet has adopted a _____; the alternative is a _____.
2. One characteristic of products or services usually selected as leader offerings is _____.
3. An advantage of the tactic of price lining is _____; a disadvantage is _____.
4. Average or lower-than-normal markups are possible when the offering being priced has _____ handling and selling costs.

Price and Other Environmental Influences

Two environmental influences—competitors' pricing activities and the possibility of suppliers' establishing retail prices—were covered earlier in this chapter. Three additional factors in an outlet's operating environment can also have a definite impact on possible prices: pricing legislation, consumerism, and the economic climate.

A retailer's pricing may be regulated to some extent by a resale price maintenance law, called "fair-trade" laws by their backers, or by an unfair sales practices act, sometimes called sales-below-cost laws. These two forms of regulation are quite *dissimilar*, both in terms of intent and procedure.

PRICING LEGISLATION

Resale Price Maintenance Laws. These laws permit manufacturers or wholesalers to establish minimum retail prices for their brands. Under some states' laws, a supplier must get all retailers of a brand to sign a fair-trade contract if he wants to set a minimum retail price. Under other states' laws, however, all retailers must comply with the minimum established price if only one retailer signs. Currently, three-fourths of the states have some form of resale price maintenance law; those that do include California, Illinois, New Jersey, New York, and Ohio.

Backers of price maintenance laws include various manufacturers who desire control over retail prices, primarily so that price will not be cut when retail outlets engage in price competition. Among the many manufacturers employing fair-trade prices at one time or another have been Jantzen and Pendleton sportswear, General Electric and Sunbeam for their appliances, Japanese television producers, and Corning cookware. Other supporters of fair-trade laws are numerous smaller merchants who do not want to compete on a price basis.

Since about 1958, when GE first abandoned its fair-trade attempts, the practice has been on the decline. Perhaps the main reason that resale price maintenance laws have been less effective in recent years is that the manufacturers themselves must police retailers' compliance with fair-trade prices. Most manufacturers have scores or hundreds of retail dealers, making this a practically impossible task.

When a manufacturer identifies a fair-trade violation, legal action against the retailer is usually very expensive to the manufacturer in terms of money, executive time, and dealer good will. On top of this, it appears that "many judges don't care to enforce it [a resale price maintenance law] vigorously."[6] In assessing a $250 fine against one frequent violator, a New York judge called the fair-trade laws "an anachronistic leftover from . . . the 1930s" and added that "at the present time it serves primarily as an anti-consumer device." Considering that a fair-trade violation may generate a great deal of additional sales volume, a $250 fine—which is the norm in New York, at least—is hardly even a "slap on the wrist."

Many discount house chains now set their prices below the levels established by manufacturers. Perhaps the biggest violator has been JGE discount stores in the New York, Connecticut, New Jersey area. The head of JGE, Jerry Rosenberg, has even stated, "If a state where we go has a fair-trade law, we'll break it. . . . And if the fines get worse, I'll take a jail sentence."[7] Rosenberg contends that his violations of these laws has brought about lower prices on various fair-trade merchandise, thereby benefiting consumers.

Individual Steps in the Sequence

In certain other ways as well, discount chains have been thorns in the sides of manufacturers trying fair trade. Some discounters refuse to carry fair-traded items, making it difficult for manufacturers to achieve strong distribution, since discount houses are key retailers for many merchandise lines. Others have developed their own lower-price private brands, which then compete with the fair-traded brands.

Some manufacturers like Sony, Zenith, Matsushita Electric (Panasonic brand), and, in some regions, GE are somewhat aggressive in their fair-trade efforts. Still, since there are no indications that the factors mentioned above which work against manufacturers' fair-trade attempts are going to disappear, the effectiveness of resale price maintenance laws is likely to continue to decline. In turn, this will probably lead to fewer fair-trade attempts by manufacturers.

Unfair Sales Practices Acts. The majority of states have laws which specify minimum legal retail prices in relation to costs. Some states' laws pertain to specific items; others cover most kinds of merchandise. The minimum price is usually specified as either the cost of merchandise *or* merchandise cost plus a certain markup to cover operating expenses. The necessary margin is often around 6 to 8 percent. In particular, an unfair sales practices act affects grocery stores and discount houses in their pricing of leader offerings.

The rationale behind unfair sales practices acts is that they protect consumers and retailers, especially smaller retail outlets, from supposedly harmful price competition. This kind of pricing legislation is not problem-free, however. Effective enforcement represents the biggest problem, even though violations are statutory offenses and enforcement is carried out by state agencies. Agencies charged with enforcement often lack sufficient resources for the task; most states' laws encompass numerous goods, and there are many retailers to be policed.

CONSUMERISM

The consumer movement has grown out of consumers' individual and collective dissatisfaction with business practices. Consumerism can affect retail pricing in a couple of ways.

First, active (as opposed to passive) shoppers desire—or even demand—more usable information on prices. Second, many consumers are more aware of relative prices now than they were five or ten years ago. Being more price sensitive, they will shop around to obtain what they think is the "right" price.

Supermarkets have reacted to consumerism by introducing unit pricing, which is intended to make price comparisons easier. Recent evidence indicates that (a) almost two-thirds of shoppers are aware of unit pricing when supermarkets use it, (b) the majority of these "aware" shoppers use the additional information in decisions, (c) about one-third of them have switched some brands as a result, and (d) unit pricing is not very costly for supermarket chains, but can cost small stores from one-third to one-half of their average profit.[8]

Health of the economy in a retailer's area determines consumer spending power and thereby affects retail pricing. Skilled merchants appraise present and forecast economic climates and then adjust prices as warranted. This point is best explained by illustration. The manager of a supermarket in a small city recognized the economy to be depressed due to production cutbacks at a large manufacturing plant. He concluded that plant employees who were laid off or had their work weeks shortened would tend to be extremely price-conscious. Therefore, before other grocery stores had a chance to, he began a program of genuine low prices on staple items to help shoppers stretch their food dollars. The results were favorable; regular customers remained loyal, and many new customers were attracted, some of whom became regular customers.

ECONOMIC CLIMATE

In contrast, when an economy is booming, shoppers are less price-conscious. Thus a retailer can place more emphasis on discretionary or luxury-type offerings with higher-than-normal markups.

Establishing an Original Price

The pricing sequence brings about systematic pricing by specifying numerous considerations, organizing them logically, and indicating necessary intermediate decisions. Nevertheless, the price setter still must rely on managerial experience and business judgment to make the final pricing decision.

When a price setter reaches this final step, he knows the offering's cost and has decided upon an initial markup. For example, assume that the owner of a sporting goods store concluded that a 48 percent markup would be best for steel-frame tennis rackets which were purchased for $15.50 each. Original price is then determined by a three-step procedure. First, the price setter must find out what percentage of the unknown retail price is represented by the cost figure. This is determined by subtracting the percentage markup from 100 percent, which is the percentage equivalent of the unknown retail price:

$$\text{cost} = \text{retail price} - \text{markup}$$

$$\text{cost} = 100\% - 48\% = 52\%$$

The $15.50 cost of tennis rackets thus amounts to 52 percent of the unknown retail price.

Individual Steps in the Sequence

Second, the dollar cost is divided by the percentage cost to arrive at the original retail price:

$$\text{retail price} = \frac{\$15.50}{52\% \text{ (or .52)}} = \$29.80$$

Thus, the rackets should carry $29.80 price tags.

Third, the price setter must make sure that this price is compatible with any other restrictions on a possible original price. Slight modifications might have to be made so that, for example, it has an odd ending or fits into a particular price zone. Perhaps the sports store owner would modify the $29.80 price to $29.95 to obtain an odd ending.

REVIEW BOX 12:4

1. _____ legislation is one way in which manufacturers try to control retail prices for their brands.
2. When an economy is very healthy, a price setter can logically consider markups which are _____ than the planned average.
3. When the dollar cost and percentage cost are known, an original price is calculated by dividing _____ by _____.

CHAPTER SUMMARY

- Establishing an original retail price can be visualized as an eight-step sequence, some steps routine and others more difficult.
- The pricing decision sequence involves three key decisions: selecting a price-level strategy, calculating planned initial markup, and establishing an original price.
- In step 1, a retail firm considers price in relation to its overall effort to satisfy customers and make a profit.
- In step 2, a price setter answers two questions about factors generally beyond control but which affect the pricing process: Which firm in the distribution channel controls retail price? What is competition doing with respect to prices on comparable offerings?
- In step 3, a price-level strategy is selected: whether to generally aim for prices above, at, or below market price levels. A store must offer attractive extras to compensate for above-the-market prices. Most retailers aim for at-the-market prices in order to appeal to most consumers. When a retail firm uses an above- or at-the-market strategy,

- it chooses to compete on non-price factors. Below-the-market prices must be coupled with low operating expenses, limited assortments, and economical physical facilities if the firm is to profit.
- In step 4, a price setter calculates planned initial markup, taking into account costs of doing business and the amount of profit being sought. Since this percentage figure represents an average, it should not be automatically used to calculate a price but rather should serve as a guideline.
- In steps 5, 6, and 7 of the sequence, possible prices in relation to store policies, nature of the offering, and other environmental influences are considered. Store policies are most common regarding a one-price system, psychological prices, leader offerings, and price lining. Six characteristics of the offering being priced must be compared to other offerings covered by the same planned initial markup: wholesale price, consumer demand, customary prices, handling costs, selling costs, and expected reductions. Three other factors in an outlet's operating environment can have a definite impact on possible prices: pricing legislation, primarily resale price maintenance laws and unfair sales practices acts; consumerism; and the economic climate.
- In step 8, a price setter uses information acquired in the preceding steps, plus experience and judgment, to establish an original price. Basically, when an offering's cost is known and an initial markup is decided upon, original price is calculated by dividing the dollar cost by the percentage of the unknown retail price accounted for by dollar cost.

CHAPTER NOTES

[1] "Economy Motels Lure Travelers with Prices As Low as $6 a Room," *Wall Street Journal*, December 26, 1972, p. 1.

[2] The founder of Korvettes, an innovator named Eugene Ferkauf, initiated modern discounting. In 1948, in a fourth-floor store in downtown New York, he began selling name-brand appliances at drastically reduced prices. For descriptions of the different courses followed by two leading discounters, see "How Kresge Became the Top Discounter," *Business Week*, October 24, 1970, pp. 62–63ff; and "Korvettes Tries for a Little Chic," *Business Week*, May 12, 1973, pp. 124–126.

[3] "Marketing Observer," *Business Week*, November 10, 1973, p. 94.

[4] Edward A. Filene, *The Model Stock Plan* (New York: McGraw-Hill Book Co., 1930).

[5] For a step-by-step price-lining procedure, see John W. Wingate, Elmer O. Schaller, and F. Leonard Miller, *Retail Merchandise Management* (Englewood Cliffs, N.J.: Prentice-Hall, 1972), pp. 103–104.

[6] Most of this paragraph is drawn from Jonathan Kwitny, "Discounters Campaign Against Laws That Let Retail Prices Be Fixed," *Wall Street Journal*, May 10, 1974, p. 23.

[7] *Ibid.*, p. 1.

[8] These conclusions are presented in James M. Carman, "A Summary of Empirical Research on Unit Pricing in Supermarkets," *Journal of Retailing*, Winter 1972–1973, pp. 63–71.

QUESTIONS AND ASSIGNMENTS

1. Explain the difference between a price-level strategy and planned initial markup. Develop an example which indicates the basic distinction.
2. Check with a local retailer to see what proportion of his merchandise has prices established by suppliers. Does this retailer generally favor or oppose suppliers' establishing retail prices? According to this retailer, what method is most frequently used by suppliers to control retail prices on their brands?
3. Select a nearby clothing store or gas station. Which price-level strategy do you think has been selected by this outlet's owner or manager? Check with the merchant to see (a) if your impression was correct, and (b) the outlet's rationale for its price-level strategy.
4. Which price-level strategy do you feel works best for a restaurant? Support your answer with reasons.
5. In calculating planned initial markup, the children's shoe department manager mentioned in the chapter (p. 282) used dollar estimates. However, it was stated that "the formula also works with percentage estimates." Use the initial markup formula *and percentages* to calculate the department's markup goal. Is it 44 percent as when dollar estimates were used? (It should be!)
6. The owner of a sporting goods store made the following estimates for the next six months: sales $165,000, operating expenses $50,000, and reductions $10,000.
   a. If the owner is seeking a $25,000 profit for this six-month period, what planned initial markup would he need to accomplish this?
   b. If $15,000 in profits is satisfactory, what initial markup will be needed?
7. A manager is thinking about converting her department to a self-service operation. Under the new format, she estimates that expenses would run about 22 percent of sales. If she anticipates markdowns of 8 percent and retains a 40 percent initial markup, what level of profits would result?
8. Talk with a retailer who uses odd-ending prices *or* price lining. Ask why the tactic is used and whether there are any problems connected with it.
9. a. What is the resale price maintenance law? Does your state have a so-called fair-trade law? If it does, do you think it should be retained or repealed?
   b. What is an unfair sales practice act? Does your state have one? If so, what merchandise does it cover?
10. Calculate the original price for each of the following offerings:
    a. Wood-frame tennis rackets: 40 percent markup, $7 cost to retailer.
    b. Tennis balls: 20 percent markup (a leader offering), $1.20 per can purchase price for retailer.
    c. Set of three titanium-shaft golf woods: 60 percent markup (the store is the exclusive dealer in the area for this new, heavily-demanded item), purchase price to retailer of $50 per club.

ANSWERS TO REVIEW BOX QUESTIONS

Box 12:1

1. an original price for a product or service
2. buyers, department managers; top management
3. who controls retail prices

Box 12:2

1. above, at, or below
2. operating expenses

Box 12:3

1. one-price system; negotiated-price system.
2. One of the following: used by most consumers and bought somewhat frequently, a familiar regular price, a "small ticket" (a small dollar price),
3. One of the following advantages: makes consumer decision-making easier, permits more complete assortments at the most popular prices, possibly simplifies retail buying and pricing

    Either of the following disadvantages: not being able to carry some appealing merchandise whose cost does not fit price lines, difficulty of raising prices when wholesale prices rise
4. relatively low

Box 12:4

1. Resale price maintenance
2. higher
3. dollar cost; percentage cost

Questions and Assignments

Price Adjustments

Retail prices are always on trial. Special conditions sometimes require upward or downward adjustments in prices. The most common reason for adjusting price is that the offering is not selling well.

In general, price adjustments fall into one of three categories: additional markups, an upward adjustment; employee and customer discounts, a downward adjustment; and markdowns, also downward. Of the three categories, markdowns generally have the greatest impact on retail operations. They are unavoidable and can be frequent, and thus play a major role in many types of retailing.

ADDITIONAL MARKUPS

An *additional markup* is an increase in the original retail price of an offering. This upward adjustment is sensible when wholesale prices are rising, or when a relatively low-price offering is not selling well because consumers are suspicious of quality.

There really are no hard and fast guidelines that apply to additional markup decisions. Basically, when either of the above conditions arises, a merchant first must evaluate the merits of a price increase versus another alternative such as changing the level of advertising for the item or moving it to another location within the department or store. If an additional markup is decided upon, a price setter must rely on judgment, experience, and considerations from the original pricing sequence in arriving at a specific new price.

EMPLOYEE AND CUSTOMER DISCOUNTS

Except for grocery stores, most outlets give their employees price reductions. This type of discount encourages an outlet's employees to be among its customers *and* serves as a fringe benefit for employees. Ordinarily the discount is 10 percent and applies only to items on which prices have not already been reduced. However, in some cases this discount runs 20 percent or even higher. For example, some merchants permit employee purchases at cost-plus-10 percent prices.

Some outlets also give discounts to special classes of consumers. For example, various retailers such as pharmacies and movie theaters have senior citizen discounts. Also common are special prices for children and students in many types of service establishments, and lower prices for clergy in department stores. Generally, these discounts are about 10 percent in the retailing of products, but they may be substantially higher in the retailing of services. For instance, many movie theaters charge adults $2.00, and children $1.00 or less.

One caution regarding customer discounts is appropriate: They may be nothing more than a drag on profits. A price setter should establish customer discounts only when the store will benefit directly or indirectly from them. Generally, such discounts would be most suitable if they bring in new customers who would not otherwise have patronized the outlet, students for example. Another advantage is that customer discounts permit a store to be a good citizen in its dealings with senior citizens, many of whom live on a limited budget. Of course, the discount should not be so large that other customers are alienated or that the resulting sales are unprofitable for the store.

MARKDOWNS

A *markdown* is a reduction in an offering's retail price. Markdowns are inevitable and, even though this may seem contradictory, not always undesirable. Also, their significance varies greatly across merchandise lines and for different types of retailers of similar goods. For example, in department stores having at least $1 million in annual sales, markdowns range from 2 percent of net sales for books to 7 percent for towels to 20 percent for women's better dresses. As another example, men's clothing markdowns average 9 percent in department stores with greater than $50 million in annual sales, but almost 15 percent in $1 million to $5 million stores.[1]

The figures above relate the dollar total of price reductions to sales volume. The significance of markdowns might also be viewed in terms of the proportion of items on which price must be lowered. The proportion probably is greatest for fashion apparel, where consumer tastes are so fickle that a style or fabric can be popular today but unwanted tomorrow. According to one businessman, 85 percent of the ready-to-wear apparel purchased by a store buyer eventually requires markdowns.[2] The proportion of markdowns is much lower, perhaps around the 25 percent level, in almost all other categories of merchandise. Still, this figure certainly indicates that the pricing task on many items does not end when an original price is set.

A Decision Sequence

The series of decisions connected with markdowns is diagrammed in Figure 13-1. This sequence begins with the present price. Some items will be sold at that price, while others will probably remain unsold. The five general reasons why items remain unsold—buying errors, selling errors, pricing errors, uncontrollable reasons, and tactical reasons—are discussed in the next sub-section.

When a price setter decides something must be done about those offerings not sold at the present price, he has five alternatives:

1. A retailing mix element other than price can be changed. For instance, promotion levels or approaches might be modified, location of the items in the store might be changed, or different personal selling techniques might be tried.
2. The merchandise can be stored until the next selling season and then placed out for sale again. The same price may be tried once more, or price can be adjusted. Seasonal items such as winter gloves, Christmas cards, certain sporting goods, and Easter baskets (excluding the candy) are most often carried over. This alternative is appropriate when the merchandise is quite likely to be salable next year *at the present price or higher*. Nothing is gained by simply postponing markdowns until next year.
3. An additional markup can be taken, as already discussed.
4. A markdown can be taken; this alternative is considered further in the rest of this chapter.
5. The merchandise can be donated to a charitable organization or can be discarded. When other alternatives do not work, this becomes logical. In fact, admitting that merchandise is not salable is better than spending much effort on these "white elephants." A merchant should get rid of unattractive, lingering merchandise so that it does not detract from the appeal of other merchandise.

Markdowns are the most frequently used of these five alternatives.

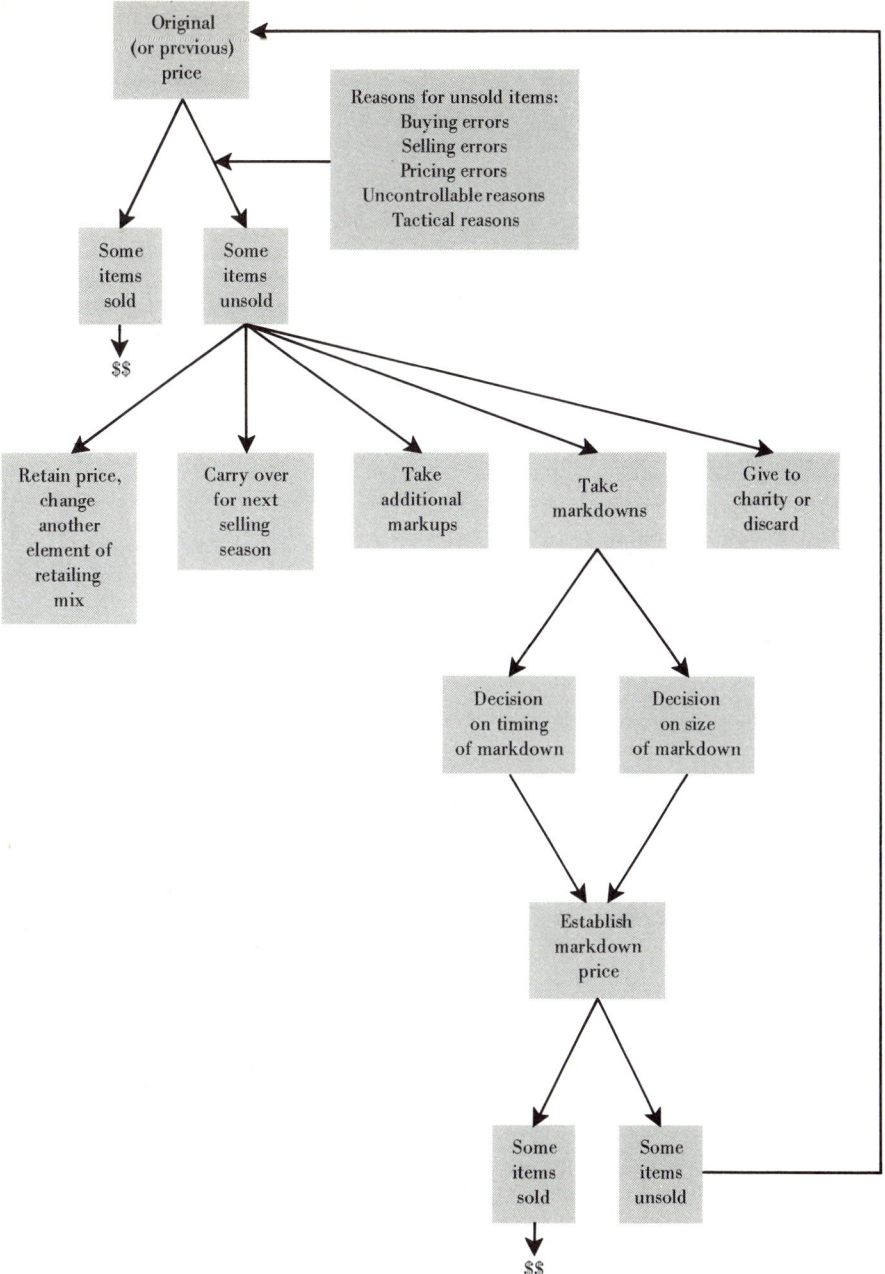

FIGURE 13-1

Markdown decision sequence

When this route is chosen, a merchant must decide on the timing and size of the markdown—that is, *when and how much* prices should be reduced. Then a price setter establishes a specific markdown price. If this downward adjustment does not sell the merchandise, the process is repeated until the remaining items are disposed of, one way or another.

Causes of Markdowns

Incorrect *but avoidable* retailing methods are often responsible for items that are not sold. When buying, selling, or pricing errors are made, markdowns are taken to bring the item's price in line with its current value in consumers' minds.

Buying errors result from a failure to match purchases with demand. Specific buying errors include poor timing, such as buying too late in a selling season; wrong assortment in terms of colors, sizes, or styles; and re-ordering too many units after the first order sells well. *Selling errors* are usually the least excusable errors. That is, they often involve careless or negligible display and selling techniques rather than incorrect decisions. *Pricing errors* simply mean that buying and selling techniques are adequate but the wrong price is selected. Price might be either too high *or* too low. Price may be out of line in relation to either consumers' expectations, such as for a new offering, or to competitors' prices, which is a prime concern with staple goods. Most often, the error involves prices that are too high.

Two other markdown causes are not considered errors, since price setters either have no control over the cause or have intentionally used merchandising tactics that may not sell all of the offerings. *Uncontrollable reasons* leading to markdowns include abnormal weather, such as a warm fall and winter which discourages winter coat purchases; a drastic change in the area's economic climate—for example, a production cutback or a strike; and unavoidable soiled merchandise and "odd sizes."

Ordinarily, uncontrollable factors such as a strike or competitors' heavier advertising and lower prices are easily recognized. Often, they hit sales "like a ton of bricks," and an item virtually stops selling. While merchants obviously cannot prevent these factors from arising, they must react accordingly with a price adjustment when they do occur.

Tactical reasons result in what amounts to a *planned* markdown. In some pricing approaches, markdowns are an essential element or at least a necessary evil. One tactic is promotional markdowns which are as significant as markdowns due to errors. The word markdown has almost a magical appeal to some shoppers. Thus most retailers occasionally take markdowns on their regular stock or on specially purchased merchandise after briefly placing it out at a "regular price." Furthermore, most outlets periodically have big promotional sales to reward present customers, attract new customers, and—in general—produce extra sales volume.

302   Ch. 13   Price Adjustments

© King Features Syndicate, Inc. 1974. World rights reserved.

FIGURE 13-2

To some consumers, any markdown indicates a
bargain that should be purchased.

Another tactic that often results in markdowns is high original price. This tactic is most often used early in a selling season or on a recently introduced, attractive offering. A retailer aims high-priced offerings at shoppers who are price-unconscious with the intention of taking markdowns later on in order to appeal to a broader group of consumers.

A final tactical reason for markdowns is that relatively complete assortments have been maintained throughout a selling season. The assumption here is that a variety of a particular offering is required to satisfy shoppers and turn them into loyal customers. Toward the end of a season, the remainder of an assortment is sold in a clearance sale.

> **REVIEW BOX 13:1**
>
> 1. Since prices are always on trial, three basic types of adjustments are used by retailers: employee and customer discounts, markdowns, and _____.
> 2. One caution regarding customer discounts is appropriate: _____.
> 3. _____ are the least excusable cause of a markdown because _____.

Markdowns

SPOTLIGHT

Can a pricing policy which includes 50 percent markdowns after 12 days be successful?

The most widely known automatic markdown policy is found in the basement store of Filene's in downtown Boston. The Filene's chain operates 10 stores in the New England area but uses automatic markdowns only in the two-floor basement area of the flagship store.

Filene's automatic markdowns work like this: The price ticket for each piece of merchandise carries the date of when it was placed on the selling floor. If the item is not sold 12 selling days later, the price is automatically reduced by 25 percent. After an additional 6 selling days, the price becomes 50 percent of the original. The Filene's price tag shown here, for example, shows that an item was placed on the selling floor May 14th and as of June 4th was marked down a total of 50 percent. If the item remains 6 more days, it is marked down 75 percent from the original price. Items unsold after a total of 30 selling days are given to charitable organizations.

Basement store merchandise includes unsold stocks from manufacturers and end-of-season merchandise purchased from various retailers including such prestigious stores as Sak's Fifth Avenue in New York and Neiman Marcus in Dallas. One reason why other stores have been unable to copy Filene's policy with the same degree of success is that Filene's has this access to desirable name-brand merchandise.

E. A. Filene, the merchant who initiated the policy in 1909, viewed this arrangement primarily as a way of selling "distress" merchandise to the benefit of consumers, suppliers, other retailers, and Filene's. It helps Filene's establish good relations with suppliers. Also, consumers who are attracted by bargains in the basement may purchase some regular-price merchandise on other floors.

Are there drawbacks to the policy? Yes, two in particular are noteworthy. As described by a Filene's employee, one problem is "the sheer physical effort required to go through the merchandise every day to check dates and see what is due to be marked down. It takes a lot of people and a lot of time to go through thousands of pieces of merchandise every day!" Second, since the markdowns are automatic and the schedule is public knowledge, some revenue may be lost due to the shoppers' delaying purchases until an additional markdown is taken.

Perhaps Sir Noel Coward, the British playwright, best summed up the feeling about the basement store and automatic markdown policy:

> For my musical comedy "Sail Away" I wrote a song with the title "The customer's always right." You know, I never really believed it until I saw Filene's Basement.

Source: Material supplied by Filene's, Boston; reprinted by permission.

Timing and Size

Decisions about timing and size are closely related in that *when* a markdown is taken affects *how much* it needs to be. Unfortunately, there is no one correct answer regarding either timing or size. Although we cannot provide a simple solution in this section, we certainly can review the basic alternatives, their relative merits, and several guidelines used by numerous retailers.

There are two basic timing possibilities: early or late. Reducing a price "early" means shortly after sales begin to lag. Early markdowns are usually taken on individual offerings as needed, rather than later during a store-wide or departmental clearance sale. A "late" markdown suggests patience—a price is retained until purchases have all but stopped or until near the end of a selling season. Some retailers combine the two approaches, marking down some merchandise early and other merchandise late depending on certain factors such as size of the initial markup or the amount remaining in stock.

Merchants favoring *early* markdowns suggest two advantages: First, more revenue is generated than with late markdowns, since an early markdown supposedly can be smaller. Second, the earlier transactions are made, the sooner this revenue or selling space can be used for better styles or a more complete assortment of other merchandise.

Several department store chains which favor early markdowns use *automatic markdowns*. Any item unsold after a certain length of time is automatically marked down a specified amount; if it does not sell at the reduced price within the next interval, additional specified markdowns are taken. Price setters and shoppers alike know that markdowns follow a predetermined schedule.

On the other side, supporters of *late* markdowns present some strong arguments. First, waiting a while before taking markdowns gives "late blooming" offerings a chance to catch on and sell at the more profitable original price. Second, customers recognize that clearances are held only infrequently and late in a season, which makes them less likely to wait for markdowns on individual items.

Ideally, the size of a markdown should be just enough to stimulate consumers to buy the unsold offerings. But what percentage markdown is "enough"? This depends on the cost of the unsold merchandise, the extent to which the outlet needs the revenue which is tied up in inventory, and the timing of markdowns. An observant price setter gradually learns the sizes of markdowns needed on different types of unsold merchandise at different times within a selling season. A guideline used by numerous retailers is that the first markdown is the cheapest for the store. The idea here is that one major reduction often produces more revenue, quicker, and with much less trouble than a series of small markdowns. However, when time is not a problem, two-stage or three-stage markdowns may produce the best results. Under this approach, the first markdown is intended to attract shoppers who "almost" bought the item at the original price. Then a second and perhaps third markdown is eventually taken on remaining items to appeal to bargain hunters.

Markdowns on price-lined merchandise represent a special situation. When specific price *points* are employed, prices are usually reduced to the next lowest point at which merchandise is selling well *or* to a point in a separate price line used only for marked-down merchandise. Thus, a men's store may have *markdown* price points of $1.66, $3.66, $5.66, and $6.66 for ties as well as *regular* $2.50, $5, $7.50, and $10 prices. Under this approach, the number of prices is still limited. Also, marked-down merchandise is readily identified, perhaps even on separate racks, so that it will not detract from original-price merchandise. Another advantage is that customers may learn that this separate price line means bargains.

When price lining by means of *zones* is used, alternative markdown procedures include establishing separate markdown zones, selecting a lower price within the same zone, or reducing the price to a figure in the next lower zone. Greater markdown flexibility without increasing the actual number of prices is one advantage of zones over specific price points.

Establishing the Markdown Price

Ordinarily, a price setter decides on the approximate dollar or percentage amount of the markdown and then calculates the new price. For instance, a sportswear department manager decided that a $33\frac{1}{3}$ percent off-retail markdown was needed to sell some remaining pantsuits.

The following formula is used in calculating the markdown price:

$$\text{markdown price} = \text{original (or previous) retail price} - \$ \text{ markdown}$$

In calculating the markdown price from the off-retail percentage, the dollar amount of the markdown must be determined first, as follows:

$$\$ \text{ markdown} = \text{off-retail percentage} \times \text{original (or previous) retail price}$$

$$\$ \text{ markdown} = .333 \times \$40.95 = \$13.64$$

Then this amount is subtracted from the original (or previous) retail price to arrive at the markdown price:

$$\text{markdown price} = \text{retail price} - \$ \text{ markdown}$$

$$\text{markdown price} = \$40.95 - \$13.64 = \$27.31$$

However, the manager decided to use a slightly different markdown price, $27.90, perhaps the price of much other marked-down merchandise.

Sometimes a retail manager will tentatively select a markdown price without first determining an off-retail percentage or a dollar markdown. In this case, the procedure involves calculating the dollar markdown and then the off-retail percentage. For example, consider a shop owner who is thinking about reducing the price of a buckskin jacket from $79 to $49. Dollar markdown is calculated as follows:

$$\text{\$ markdown} = \text{retail price} - \text{markdown price}$$

$$\text{\$ markdown} = \$79 - \$49 = \$30$$

Once dollar markdown is known, the off-retail percentage is obtained as follows:

$$\text{off-retail percentage} = \frac{\text{\$ markdown}}{\text{retail price}}$$

$$\text{off-retail percentage} = \frac{\$30}{\$79} = 38.0\%$$

The off-retail percentage represents the size of a markdown in shoppers' minds. It indicates the relative amount they are saving by buying at the reduced, rather than original, price. Thus, stores use the off-retail percentage in promoting price reductions. For example, the jackets might have been advertised as "Beautiful buckskin jackets, only 4 remain . . . Priced at $49, a markdown of more than $33\frac{1}{3}\%$!"

Tracking Markdowns

After a markdown price is established, a price setter should go one step further and keep track of the dollar amounts, percentages, and probable causes of markdowns. One reason for tracking markdowns is to improve future estimates of markdowns, used in calculating planned initial markup. Underestimating reductions will lead to an initial markup that is lower than needed to achieve the profit objective.

Another important reason for tracking markdowns is to decrease errors which necessitate price reductions. Finally, such information is useful in planning purchases. For example, two suppliers' brands of shoes may have similar purchase prices, assortments offered, and advertising support. Still, one brand may be clearly superior to the other because it seldom requires markdowns. Hence, a merchandise buyer should be able to make better purchase decisions with information on relative markdown levels for the brands being considered.

An adequate tracking procedure includes five steps:

1. Recording individual markdowns in such a way that each item is specifically identified by brand, *and* dollar and percentage amounts are listed. Many stores use standardized forms or notebooks in this task.
2. Analysis of markdown causes. Although these causes are difficult to pinpoint, a genuine effort should be made because markdowns can have such a large impact on profits. One objective is to divide markdowns into those which were error-caused, and therefore might be avoidable, versus those which were tactical or uncontrollable. As you might suspect, analysis often shows that a combination of causes, not just one, led to the markdown.
3. Evaluation of markdown levels for specific merchandise lines or an entire department. This step ordinarily includes comparing relative markdown levels for distinct brands of the same offering. Also, the actual dollar amount of markdowns in a department is compared to the planned amount. Then the meaning of any deviations, among comparable brands and between the actual and planned amounts, should be judged.
4. Development and implementation of measures aimed at reducing markdowns. The specific measures called for depend on the causes identified above. More sales training, closer control over merchandise buying, or a review of the current planned initial markup are possible measures. For a large retailer of fashion apparel, efforts might be aimed at obtaining orders of popular items more quickly. At least one distribution firm, the Nelson Corporation, assists fashion retailers in doing this.[3] For 15¢ per garment, the firm picks up fashion apparel at a manufacturer's plant, price tags the garments according to the retailer's instructions, then delivers the items to its clients, which include Sears, Bloomingdale's, and Gimbel's on the East Coast. Nelson expedites the apparel from plant to selling floor within 24 to 48 hours. As a result, the necessity for markdowns due to receiving merchandise too late to capitalize on a "hot" style, color, or fabric may be reduced.
5. Observation of the effectiveness of early versus late markdowns and markdowns of different sizes. This information would aid a price setter in making sound decisions about markdown timing and size.

No tracking procedure will completely eliminate markdowns, of course. But thousands of dollars can be saved by reducing the frequency of error-caused markdowns. To indicate the potential savings, consider a store with $10 million in annual sales (a medium-size department store, for example) and a markdown level amounting to 8 percent of sales. If the level can be reduced to 7½ percent by tracking markdowns, and no other operating figure is affected, $50,000 will be saved—which certainly would improve profits.

> **REVIEW BOX 13:2**
>
> 1. One of the two suggested advantages of *early* markdowns is _____.
> 2. To calculate _____, the dollar markdown is divided by the original (or previous) retail price.
> 3. The first step in tracking markdowns is to _____.

CHAPTER SUMMARY

- Occasionally, conditions arise which necessitate price adjustments: additional markups, an upward adjustment; employee and customer discounts, a downward adjustment; and markdowns, also downward.
- An additional markup is sensible when wholesale prices are rising or when a relatively low-price offering is not selling well because consumers are suspicious of quality.
- Most outlets—except supermarkets—give their employees price reductions as a fringe benefit and to keep them as customers. Discounts to special classes of customers should be granted only when the store will benefit directly or indirectly from them.
- When an offering's retail price is reduced, this is called a markdown. A markdown decision sequence includes several considerations. First, a method for dealing with unsold items must be selected, with markdowns being one of five alternatives. When markdowns are used, the timing and size of the price reduction must be decided upon, and the specific markdown price must be established.
- Three general causes of markdowns are due to one or more incorrect *but avoidable* retailing methods: buying, pricing, or selling errors. Two other markdown causes are not errors: uncontrollable reasons and tactical reasons.
- There are two basic timing possibilities: early markdowns or late markdowns. The size of a markdown needed to stimulate consumers to buy an unsold offering depends on the cost of the unsold merchandise, the extent to which the outlet needs revenue, and the timing of markdowns.
- The off-retail percentage, the figure promoted to shoppers, is calculated by dividing the dollar markdown amount by the original (or previous) retail price.

- Price setters should keep track of the dollar amounts, percentages, and probable causes of markdowns, primarily so that errors leading to markdowns can be minimized.

CHAPTER NOTES

[1] Jay Scher, ed., *Merchandising and Operating Results of 1972* (New York: National Retail Merchants Association, 1973). Data quoted from pp. 18, 26, 2, 166, and 78, respectively.
[2] William A. Nelson, Jr., president of a specialized distribution firm, as quoted in the "Marketing Observer" section of *Business Week*, December 15, 1973, p. 79.
[3] *Ibid.*

QUESTIONS AND ASSIGNMENTS

1. Should retail outlets grant employee discounts? Customer discounts? Explain, indicating the conditions under which they are sensible.
2. Talk to a manager in a local retail store about markdowns: frequency of markdowns on a particular type of merchandise, timing of markdowns, how he or she decides on size of markdown, what kind of tracking program is used. In the manager's opinion, what is the biggest problem connected with markdowns? In your opinion, what might be done to ease this problem?
3. The chapter states that *certain* sporting goods are not marked down (p. 300) but rather are stored until the next selling season and then placed on sale again. Specifically, which sporting goods could logically be carried over? Which should not be? Explain.
4. The size of the initial markup and the number of items remaining in stock suggest whether an early or a late markdown is called for. Would an early markdown be more appropriate for an item with a relatively large markup or one with a small markup? Would an early markdown be more sensible when there is a large number of items remaining or when there are only a few?
5. On the day before a concert, ticket prices are reduced from $5 to $3.50 (reserved seats) and from $3 to $1.50 (general admission). What is the off-retail percentage in each case?
6. A customer and a salesperson are talking about a coat which has been marked down from $75 to $50. The customer says: "That's a pretty good buy, a markdown of one-third." The salesperson replies: "It's a better buy than that since it's a 50 percent markdown." Who is correct? Could they both be? Explain.

ANSWERS TO REVIEW BOX QUESTIONS

Box 13:1

1. additional markups
2. They might be nothing more than a drag on profits. A more specific, but still correct, answer would be that the discount should not be so large that other customers are alienated or the resulting sales are unprofitable.
3. selling errors; they often involve careless or negligible efforts in the area of personal selling.

Box 13:2

1. either of the following: more revenue is generated since an early markdown can be smaller; revenue or selling space will be freed sooner for better styles or a more complete assortment of other merchandise
2. off-retail percentage
3. record individual markdowns by brand and by dollar and percentage amounts

RETAILING DECISION

The Nifty-Thrifty-50 Minute Laundry and Dry Cleaning Service

According to Gene Maynard, the general manager of Nifty-Thrifty-50 Minute Laundry and Dry Cleaning Service, "Nifty's been 'Number 1' for a long time, and we're going to stay 'Number 1' despite Top Notch's price undercutting." With this firm statement, Maynard began a meeting of Nifty executives. The meeting was called to decide what, if anything, should be done in response to the discount pricing policy now being used by a growing competitor, Top Notch Cleaners.

Three years ago, after 20 years in business, Nifty became the largest laundry and dry cleaning chain in an industrial city of 175,000. Nifty has a total of five combination dry cleaning and laundry plants. Because each plant's equipment is more than 10 years old, operating expenses have been relatively high in the past several years. In 1974, Nifty's sales increased by 2 percent, the rate of population growth in the city; profits, however, declined by 30 percent. Nifty's market share has held constant at 35 percent over the last 5 years.

Nifty's retailing efforts have always focused on upper-middle and middle income consumers. Hence, the plants are located on major streets leading to the city's better neighborhoods. A full range of laundry and dry cleaning services is offered, including fur storage, drapery cleaning, pickup and delivery, and 50-minute service. Because of its clientele, Nifty has always charged for pickup and delivery on 50-minute service. The current charge is 50¢ per order. Despite part of its name (Thrifty), the company does not compete on a price basis; in fact, its prices generally are slightly higher than competitors'. Instead, Nifty has relied on its reputation for quality work. This emphasis on quality is reflected in the company's recent advertising theme: "Nifty and thrifty because your clothing is always quality cleaned the first time."

Besides Nifty, there are three other laundry and dry cleaning chains or franchise systems operating in this city. Top Notch, one of these chains, established a discount pricing policy 18 months ago. Top Notch's market share has grown from 15 percent to 30 percent in this short period. Then last week one of the smaller chains cut all its prices 15 percent. Maynard feels that a price war, such as occasionally occur in gasoline retailing, may be forthcoming.

1. What would you recommend to Nifty's management as an appropriate pricing strategy, considering the recent move to discount pricing of competing laundry and dry cleaning services?
2. What, if any, additional information should Nifty obtain before making a final decision on pricing strategy?

RETAILING DECISION

Main Street Boutique

Liddy Austin, the owner of Main Street Boutique, was reviewing the store's performance in preparation for planning next year's business. The store featured very fashionable women's apparel and had experienced expanding sales for the five years since its opening. Ms. Austin's current concern was that profits had not increased during the past three years despite rising sales.

After a detailed examination of her records, Ms. Austin believed she had located the major problem. She noted that markdowns had skyrocketed from slightly over 5 percent of sales in the first year to almost 18 percent during the current year. Checking the figures for stores comparable in size, Ms. Austin found that markdowns averaged between 9 and 11 percent of sales.

Main Street Boutique really had no firm policy on markdowns. Ms. Austin's practice was to wait until the season was over and cut prices by 40 to 50 percent to get rid of leftover merchandise. Normally these price cuts caused the merchandise to move very quickly.

1. If you were Ms. Austin, what steps would you take to increase the boutique's profit percentage?

PART FIVE

The Promotion Function

14

The Promotion Blend and Supportive Methods

When decisions have been made on store location, design, layout, the offerings to be sold, and prices, much of the retailing mix is developed—but not all of it. Potential customers still have to be informed of the firm's existence and offerings, attracted to the outlet, persuaded to make purchases, and served when they do come in. After that, they have to be periodically reminded about the firm and its offerings. In other words, *promotion* must be added to the retailing mix. Activities ranging from network television advertising to fashion shows to advice given by highly trained "sales consultants" fall under the general category of promotion. In a sense, even services such as credit, gift wrapping, and package delivery also help in attracting and persuading customers.

This chapter first presents an overview of the promotion blend and certain tasks and arrangements connected with it. Then it briefly examines various supportive promotion methods such as display, special sales, and trading stamps.

NATURE AND PURPOSES OF PROMOTION

The term promotion and related terms are used in different ways by various persons connected with retailing. Consequently, this section explains pertinent terms and positions the promotion element within the retailing mix.

Definition of Promotion

Basically, retail *promotion* involves communication from a retailer *to* consumers or, in other situations, communication *between* a retailer's salespeople and shoppers. In fact, a classic article on the retailing mix refers specifically to communications, rather than to promotion:

> The provision of information about the retail store and the goods and services available for sale constitute the crux of the communications mix. The retailer has a variety of tools for communicating with the market place. Included among these tools are personal selling, advertising, window displays, internal displays, public relations efforts, store layouts, catalogues, and telephone sales.[1]

A *promotion blend* consists of that combination of methods used by a retailer to communicate with consumers. The methods, most of which are listed in the quote directly above, are of two major types: *personal*, in which the communication is on a face-to-face basis; and *non-personal*, communication without actual face-to-face contact, such as mail, print media, displays, and broadcast media.

Personal promotion is called either personal selling (the term used in this book) or retail salesmanship. This type of promotion is usually *between* a salesperson and a shopper. The two parties can discuss a particular offering, or the shopper can ask specific questions which, ideally, would be answered by the salesperson. On the other hand, non-personal promotion is communication from retailer *to* consumers. The primary non-personal method is advertising. Other kinds of non-personal promotion are *supportive methods* such as displays, special sales, publicity, coupons, trading stamps, and premium offers. These activities are labeled supportive because they would seldom be sufficient promotion by themselves.

Purposes of Promotion

Bringing about profitable sales volume, both in the short term *and over the long run*, is the overriding purpose of promotion. This promotion purpose really applies to any business. For a retail firm, promotion will serve three specific purposes:

- Sell specific offerings immediately or within a short time period
- Assist in creating the desired image for the outlet
- Generate shopper traffic in the outlet (on the notion that more shoppers will result in higher sales if only because of unplanned purchases by shoppers).

The order of these purposes or objectives varies from one retailer to another. Consider the viewpoint of an executive of Peck & Peck, an established specialty shop chain:

> We want to achieve three purposes: (1) build traffic, (2) reflect the personality of the whole store, (3) sell the item advertised — in that order. We have turned the old order on its head. Before, we considered the item primarily, and hoped it reflected the personality of the store and created traffic. Yet, we don't think of the current ads as being any more institutional [emphasizing the store in general] than the old; there's always an item to be bought.[2]

Whichever order is preferred, it is important to remember that each method of promotion affects the accomplishment of these purposes. For instance, you may not associate salespeople's activities with the purpose of increasing shopper traffic. But, in fact, a store's overall personal selling policy or the efforts of an individual salesperson can attract or drive away many shoppers. On the positive side, a store's policy of permitting shoppers to browse without hearing a sales pitch may bring in more shoppers than a high-pressure policy. Likewise, a shopper may come into a store because he or she knows that accurate information on a product or service can be obtained from a particular salesperson.

THE BASICS OF PROMOTION

Before beginning to develop a promotion blend, a retailer must recognize that there are various factors essential to successful promotion in general as well as to effective advertising, personal selling, and supportive methods.

Selected Prerequisites

The likelihood of effective promotion is slim unless whoever has overall responsibility for promotion in the firm has determined *what* is to be accomplished by promotion, and *why* and *how* it is to be done. Five considerations are particularly important:

The firm's desired image in relation to the target markets selected
Promotion's relationship with the other mix elements
Reach and cost of various promotion methods
Coordination at several different levels
Creativity

DESIRED IMAGE AND OTHER MIX ELEMENTS

Perhaps you noticed that the first two considerations pertain to retail operations planning. Before any mix element can be developed, a store personality, or image, must be chosen. This implies, of course, that the outlet's target markets must also be taken into account. Questions related to promotion which need answers include: To what extent do target consumers desire price information, facts about product usage and care, information about supplementary services? What are their views regarding different personal selling approaches used by retail stores? Are they interested in trading stamps?

The task is to develop a retailing mix which will create the desired image and, of course, satisfy sufficient customers at a profit to the firm. The point is that promotion must be teamed with other mix elements if retail operations planning is to be successful. Promotion cannot be developed in a vacuum, since the real measure of its effectiveness is the relative success of operations planning *in total*.

REACH AND COST

Obtaining information on the reach and cost of different forms of promotion represents a third prerequisite. An important question is: What proportion of the target market is reached by specific advertising media? Questions about promotions costs also need answers before a blend is decided upon: What is the relative cost of different advertising media such as newspapers versus television? What "out-of-pocket" expense must be incurred to utilize specific supportive methods? What would be the cost of certain selling aids or a sales training program? All these questions call for research, even if just the informal kind. Although research can be expensive and time consuming, it should not be avoided solely for these reasons since it is often the pathway to informed decision making, a key to retailing success.

COORDINATION

The need for coordinating promotion with the other mix elements has already been mentioned. In addition, a retailer's promotion efforts can be more effective if coordinated with suppliers' promotional methods and themes. For example, a display featuring the manufacturer's promotion theme could lead to increased shopper awareness of the product and, in turn, to higher sales volume. A retailer also should take advantage of any formal promotion assistance available from suppliers.

Promotion must also be coordinated within the store or chain. For maximum effectiveness, the different methods must be a unified *blend*. Promotion blend and the necessary organizational arrangements for promotion are discussed in upcoming sections.

CREATIVITY

In promotion, more than in any other aspect of retailing, creativity is a prerequisite to effectiveness. In the context of retailing, *creativity* means

The Basics of Promotion

the ability to produce promotion with *imaginative skill*. *Imaginative* implies the ability to come up with fresh, perhaps even unusual, ideas and approaches. *Skill* is what is needed to accomplish defined objectives and to relate a specific idea to the total program.

The tremendous amount of retailer-consumer communication that takes place every day makes creativity especially important in promotion. Promotion characterized by sameness and dullness is unlikely to have an impact on today's consumers who see so much advertising, encounter numerous contests and displays, and talk with so many salespeople.

As you may be thinking, creative promotion is easier to talk about than to accomplish. Nevertheless, a retailer can strive for it by seeking out personnel who have imaginative skill, by experimenting with fresh or unusual promotion ideas and approaches, and by being on the lookout for offerings, events, or techniques that might result in promotion that is lively and different.

To cite one example, a clothing shop for tall and big men might place only "tall," rectangular-shaped newspaper ads to increase reader recognition of the store's ads. This retailer also might sponsor a combined basketball discussion and very brief fashion show featuring two stars from the nearest professional team. While these two methods are not all that imaginative, they are planned attempts at creative promotion—an important first step.

The Fundamental Tasks

We have talked about what should *precede* the development of promotion to increase its effectiveness. Now we can look at the fundamental tasks to be accomplished *in* promotion for it to be effective. Promotion should

Attract *attention*
Generate *interest*
Create *desire*
Obtain *action*

As a memory aid, these tasks are identified as AIDA, formed from the first letter of each key word.

While the tasks themselves are reasonably self-explanatory, their accomplishment is not as evident. Using a newspaper ad as an example, we will explore ways to carry out AIDA. First, any retail promotion—whether a complete promotion blend, a newspaper ad, or a display window—must attract the consumer's attention. In a newspaper ad, various attention-getting devices are available. The ad's size and position within the paper or on a page will affect the amount of attention it generates. As is logical, a large ad attracts more attention than a small ad. Within an ad, whatever the size, headlines and illustrations are used to catch a reader's attention.

Once attention is attracted, interest in what is being promoted (ordinarily one or more offerings of the outlet) must be generated. Nothing generates interest better than an indication of a specific benefit that can be gained. The copy (text) in an ad ordinarily describes this benefit so as to generate reader interest.

Having generated interest, the ad—or any other kind of promotion—must create a desire for the outlet's offering. Copy in a newspaper ad, perhaps aided by an illustration, tackles this task. Ideally, the reader is convinced that the possible benefits are desirable and really can be obtained by taking the action specified. Performance claims, if believable and substantiated, or a description of "what things would be like . . ." can be convincing.

The last AIDA task is to obtain action. Most promotion seeks consumer action immediately or, in the case of an upcoming sale, quite soon. The action sought by the retailer may be to get the consumers to make a specific purchase, or it could be just to get consumers into the outlet to shop around. Some promotion emphasizes the store's reputation and general features rather than specific offerings. Even this kind of promotion seeks action, namely the consumer's regular patronage of the outlet. The last portion of the copy in a newspaper ad usually urges action.

Although commonly related only to advertising, the AIDA tasks actually apply to any type of persuasive communication. Thus we suggest AIDA as a simple, useful framework for recognizing what must be accomplished in any effective promotion.

REVIEW BOX 14:1

1. Sometimes, retail promotion consists of communication from retailers *to* consumers; other times, it involves _____.
2. There are two kinds of non-personal promotion: supportive methods and _____.
3. In determining the what, why, and how of promotion, five considerations are particularly important. One of these is the outlet's desired image; two others are _____ and _____.
4. The last of the AIDA tasks in retail promotion is to _____.

Responsibility for Promotion

Before proceeding further on what is involved in retail promotion, we must consider *who* should be responsible for this function. As you know, in large retail firms a degree of specialization is possible. For example, a relatively large department store ordinarily has a formal division which plans and

The Basics of Promotion

carries out the various activities of communicating with consumers. Generally, this division is responsible for all promotion activities except personal selling, which is supervised by either the personnel, operations, or merchandising division.

The promotion division is headed by a promotion manager or director, perhaps a vice president. Various employees under the manager supervise specific functions: advertising, comparison shopping, display, public relations (publicity), and special events (other supportive methods). Other specialists—artists, display people, copy writers, signmakers—actually create advertising or displays by writing copy, preparing illustrations, and arranging merchandise in windows.

In a small firm, however, the owner-manager is often the person who retains overall responsibility for promotion. The small store proprietor might use one employee to set up sale racks when needed (one aspect of display) and another to arrange window and interior displays as well as write advertising copy. The proprietor may take on the development of the promotion blend and handle the remaining promotion jobs such as supervision of display arrangements; determination of the amount, timing, media, and theme of the store's advertising; training of new salespeople; and the search for some free newspaper publicity.

Realize, of course, that the organizational arrangements discussed above are general examples. Organization needs vary from one firm to the next, and the appropriate organization for promotion is determined by store size, amount of promotion planned, and range of methods to be used.

Developing the Promotion Blend

Considering the firm's target markets, desired image, and other retailing mix elements, a retail manager must decide what methods will be used in communicating with consumers. Since only one method will rarely be sufficient, the manager must develop a *promotion blend*, a compatible mixture of methods that will accomplish promotion objectives. Developing a promotion blend requires a series of decisions about the relative emphasis to be given to promotion in general and methods of promotion in particular. Other components of retail operations and competitors' activities should serve as reference points for these decisions.

Factors such as attractiveness of other retailing mix elements and age of the retail firm affect the emphasis given promotion relative to other mix components. Several guidelines can be suggested regarding these factors. If other retailing mix elements are *especially* attractive, a store should not have to emphasize promotion as much as would a store with an average retailing mix. Furthermore, the promotion may be less persuasive and more informative in nature, because the other superior elements will to a large extent persuade consumers to make purchases.

The age of the firm affects promotion in that new businesses generally have to emphasize promotion more than established ones. Heavy advertising along with supportive methods such as contests, premiums, and special sales can be employed to attract first-time shoppers. Salespeople must be available to familiarize customers with the outlet as well as to make their first transaction a pleasant, satisfying experience. After that, continued advertising and supportive methods—perhaps trading stamps—are utilized to convert first-time shoppers into regular customers. Once established, a store can rely to some extent on a high level of consumer awareness and a favorable reputation to attract shoppers.

The next decision, emphasis on promotion relative to competitors, does not mean that an outlet should necessarily match whatever competition is doing. However, before deciding what might be done to get ahead of competitors, a merchant needs to know what they are doing.

Another decision involves determining the appropriate blend of personal selling, advertising, and supportive methods. Ideally, a store selects the combination of methods that, in the judgment of the promotion manager, has the greatest likelihood of attracting and satisfying target consumers and producing a satisfactory profit for the firm. In actual practice, the optimal blend can only be estimated. This decision should follow consideration of several additional factors: desired store image; type of offerings; and convenience of store location. Upcoming discussions of specific promotion methods will indicate when an emphasis on a particular method is appropriate.

This series of promotion blend decisions would be especially useful for an outlet which is just in the planning stages. However, its usefulness extends to an existing store—whether highly successful or faltering—when it is reappraising its promotion efforts.

Once these decisions are made, you might expect that retail firms would allocate a specific dollar amount as a *promotion* budget. But a *total* promotion budget is uncommon, largely because responsibility for the two main forms of promotion, personal selling and advertising, is assigned to different divisions within the firm. In the absence of such a budget, the promotion director should meet with the other managers involved to convert the general promotion blend into specific requirements. Decisions must be made, for example, on the hiring of salespeople and promotion specialists, development of sales training programs, and establishment of budgets for advertising purposes.

What is involved in developing a promotion blend can be summarized —and perhaps clarified—by following E. Z. Ryder, the proprietor of the Wheelin' & Dealin' Bicycle Shop, through the series of decisions. After one year in business, Ryder feels the soundness of his retailing mix, and promotion in particular, should be reviewed.

First, Ryder decided that promotion should be emphasized less than other mix elements, because he is now the dealer for two of the three leading bicycle brands. Furthermore, his location is another plus. The shop is

The Basics of Promotion **323**

located within a block of the college campus, which is desirable since students represent his primary target market.

As Ryder sees it, most of his direct competitors spend much more on promotion. However, this does not disturb him since all but one are located some distance from campus and must rely on heavy promotion to attract shoppers. His nearby competitor uses about the same amount of promotion as Ryder does, so promotion should not become a differential advantage for any competitor.

Ryder has reviewed the relative emphasis placed on the three forms of promotion. Two facts have caused him to consider shifting the emphasis: the successful first year of operation and the growing variety of bicycles and cycling accessories being offered to consumers. Being somewhat established, he has reduced the amount of advertising intended to inform students of the shop's location and merchandise, but he is still undecided as to whether these funds will be switched to persuasive advertising.

Because of the expanding variety of merchandise, he concludes that personal selling should receive more emphasis. In his judgment, qualified salespeople must be available to ensure that all customers find the bicycle best suited to their interests and budgets. Also, salespeople are needed to suggest possible purchases of accessories, which often have larger markups. Specifically, Ryder decides to add two more salespeople (one full time, one part time) and to have weekly sales meetings covering technical features and selling points of new merchandise.

Ryder's policy has been to use supportive methods of promotion infrequently. This includes partial sponsorship of the College Cycling Club and a semi-annual sale to move merchandise selling poorly at regular prices. Convinced that the rest of his retailing mix is quite attractive, Ryder decides to continue this policy.

Finally, Ryder compares the promotion blend for Wheelin' & Dealin' against competitors'. His conclusion: The added emphasis on personal selling just might increase the differential advantage he feels his shop enjoys over direct competitors.

Proceeding through the series of promotion blend decisions certainly does not guarantee effective promotion for Ryder or for any retailer. The resulting promotion blend may flop. However, the probability of effectiveness is increased by *systematically* developing a promotion blend. Quite simply, the approach encourages informed decision making.

REVIEW BOX 14:2

1. In a relatively large retail firm, the promotion division is usually responsible for all promotion activities except _____, which is supervised by the _____ division.
2. Developing a promotion blend involves a series of decisions, one of which is _____.

SUPPORTIVE PROMOTION METHODS

The rest of this chapter focuses on methods of retailer-consumer communication other than advertising and personal selling. Although supportive methods by themselves seldom can get the entire promotion job done, they definitely can help. Some retailers make a tremendous mistake in viewing them as leftovers in a promotion blend.

The fact that supportive methods can be an integral part of a promotion blend is illustrated by Ethan Allen furniture stores. Each of the more than 150 outlets features "a continuing schedule of activities—decorating seminars, home fashion shows, programs for art, design, and home economics students—all available free."[3] The "Ethan Allen Treasury," a 358-page book of decorating ideas and illustrations, is another supportive method used by this chain. Intended primarily to generate good will for the store, it is offered free to both customers and prospects. Ethan Allen stores use supportive promotion to sell a philosophy of service rather than products alone.

As with advertising and personal selling, supportive methods are intended to accomplish the general purposes of promotion: sell specific offerings, create the desired store image, and generate shopper traffic. In deciding whether to use supportive promotion or which method to use, a retail manager must first decide *specifically* what the promotion is to accomplish. This objective can then be evaluated against the promotion's expected cost.

The following sections look at a number of specific supportive methods. Each is examined in terms of its nature, role, types, and use considerations. The sections are written from the perspective of managers (promotion director, department head, or store owner) rather than the specialists who actually implement supportive methods. Emphasis is on appropriate use of these methods *within a promotion blend.*

Display

Display can be defined as the in-store arrangement of merchandise and information for shoppers' viewing. Of the many supportive methods, display probably is the most widely used and perhaps the most significant. As the self-service approach to retailing has grown, display's overall importance in the promotion blend has increased. Since self-service means reduced personal selling, display is expected to perform part of the selling function—in fact, a major part in most self-service stores.

TYPES OF DISPLAY

There are two types of display: display windows and interior displays. In the case of windows, the arrangement itself is in-store, although the shoppers are passing by outside the store.

Running clockwise from the top left corner, here are examples of an open assortment display, a setting display, a closed assortment display, and a merchandise display window.

Display Windows. There are three distinct kinds of display windows: merchandise, institutional, and public service. A *merchandise display* presents the store's products in either realistic or dramatic settings. *Institutional display windows* feature some aspect of the store itself, perhaps a review of its tradition of high-quality merchandise or a salute to employees' accomplishments. Whereas the merchandise kind is more oriented to selling specific items, the institutional kind is intended to improve or maintain the desired store image.

In a *public service display*, the window is related to a community event (Founder's Day), an organization (YWCA), or a charity (March of Dimes). A retailer is not seeking direct benefits with a public service window but is acting as a citizen interested in making a contribution to the community. Even in this kind of display, a retail manager must be conscious of the firm's target market and desired image and only permit displays compatible with these considerations.

Display windows are an important promotion method for stores with much pedestrian traffic passing by. This includes many downtown stores as well as ones in a shopping center mall. In fact, small retailers in shopping centers may depend greatly on windows to induce passersby on the mall to come in.

Interior Displays. This type of display is located right in a store's selling area. There are five kinds of interior displays: institutional, assortment, setting, signs, and decorations. The first kind, *institutional*, is the same as institutional display windows except for location.

In an *assortment display*, a complete merchandise assortment is presented for shoppers' viewing. You have probably noticed shelf displays in grocery stores, revolving racks for showing food items in fast-food outlets, table-top displays in department and discount stores, display cases and clothing hanger racks in many stores. Some assortment displays are stationary, others are movable.

The *open assortment* display permits shoppers to handle the merchandise, feel its texture, try it on, test how it works, or whatever is appropriate. In an open assortment display, more than in any other kind, the display (supportive promotion) substitutes for the salesperson (personal selling).

A *closed assortment* display protects merchandise in a display case which cannot be opened by shoppers. Retailers use closed displays for products susceptible to theft or damage: watches and jewelry, stereo tapes, cameras, and delicate clothing.

Setting displays show merchandise in appropriate settings. Often a group of related merchandise is displayed. For example, a family room setting may be created for various furniture and home entertainment items. In most silverware and tableware departments, dining room tables are set up to show, for instance, how certain patterns of china tableware, silverware, and glassware look together. Setting displays are supposed to encourage or help shoppers visualize how the merchandise would provide satisfaction in their lives.

Signs, the fourth kind of interior display, usually serve as selling aids by explaining prices or pointing out product features. Sometimes signs provide directions to departments or offices in the store or remind shoppers about special services or upcoming events.

". . . And I'm sick and tired of your arty meat displays."

While an employee may find it satisfying to "do his own thing," profits are made by designing a retailing mix for target consumers.

Stores use *decorations*, often very beautiful and expensive ones, to create a pleasant, appealing shopping atmosphere. Decorations, probably used most frequently by department stores and clothing retailers, are common for major holidays and the four seasons. They may also be part of special sales events. For example, "roaring twenties" decorations may highlight the annual anniversary sale of a store opened during that era.

With few exceptions, interior displays are supposed to sell specific offerings. This purpose has grown in importance as rising incomes have permitted more frequent impulse purchases by shoppers. Research findings suggest, for example, that average shoppers in a supermarket made 50.5 percent of their purchases on an unplanned basis.[4] While this figure no doubt is lower for other types of stores, the point is that many shoppers today are prone to impulse purchases. For this reason, interior displays must call attention to specific offerings and show shoppers why a purchase should be made.

Furthermore, research has demonstrated that the ways in which merchandise is displayed substantially affect sales. A *Progressive Grocer* study,[5] for example, found that:

Definite sales improvements result from stocking similar items together—for instance, all brands of canned peaches in adjacent locations, or housewares near related grocery items.

Inconvenient displays, such as placing products too high for the average female shopper, reduce sales noticeably.

Hand-lettered "As Advertised" shelf signs increase sales of specific items by 61 to 177 percent.

These findings underscore the need for increased attention to and experimenting with interior displays in retail outlets.

Point-of-Purchase Displays. Another kind of interior display, called point-of-purchase (POP) or point-of-sale, is discussed separately because it usually overlaps two or more of the five kinds discussed above. Basically, a POP display is a special arrangement set up beside the complete stock of the item—that is, in the spot where a customer makes a selection.

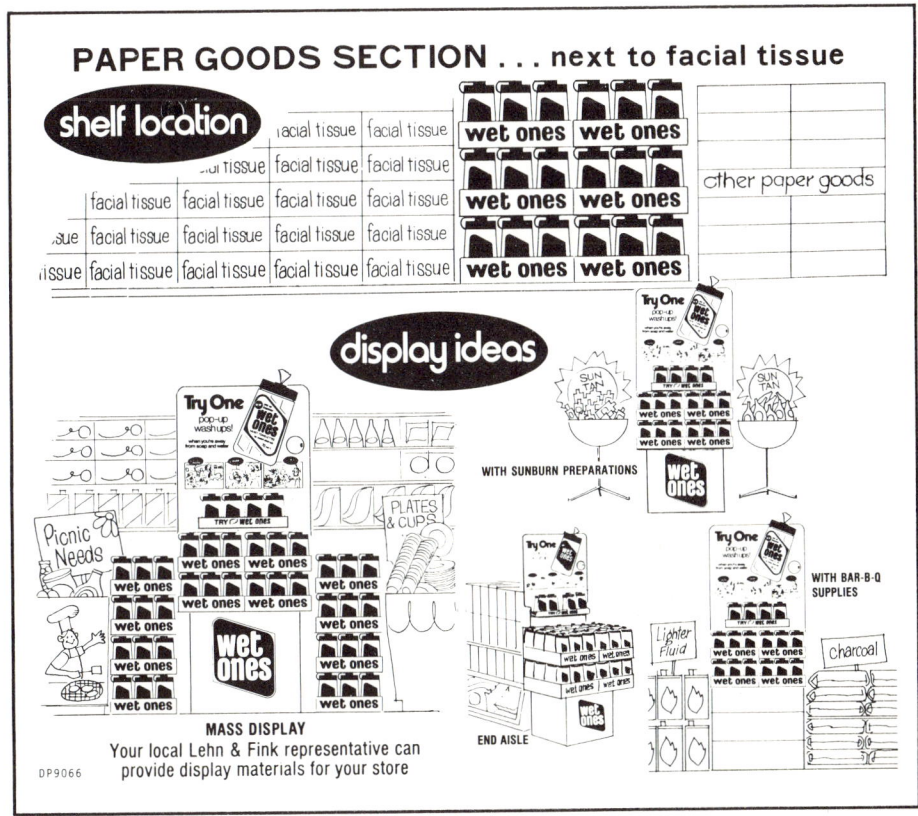

FIGURE 14-1

Display ideas and shelf location suggestions provided by a manufacturer

Supportive Promotion Methods **329**

Point-of-purchase displays often are developed by store employees. Many suppliers, convinced of the selling power of POP displays, also provide retailers with free POP materials for their brands. Figure 14-1 shows a sheet of displays ideas which one manufacturer inserted into its shipping cartons.

Suppliers' willingness to provide POP materials can be both good fortune and misfortune for a retailer. The good fortune is that the retail firm saves the time and expense of developing POP displays. The misfortune is that many merchants are swamped by suppliers' POP displays and are faced with time-consuming evaluations of the relative merits of each or outright rejection of all of them.

USE CONSIDERATIONS Most retail managers do not design the actual displays; however, they do oversee these activities or rely on the effectiveness of displays. As such, managers should be familiar with certain considerations regarding suitable display usage.

The Message. Generally speaking, a display can effectively communicate only one message. This message should relate benefits to consumers: economy, range of colors, luxury, or enjoyment, to name several possibilities.

For example, a store may feel that a dramatic display would stimulate sales of its new Formica-top children's desks. The feature of durability would be a possible selling theme—specifically, how this kind of top practically eliminates the need for repair or replacement. The actual window display might feature a desk being constantly pounded by a mechanical hammer without being damaged. The message is dramatic: the product is childproof!

Selection of Merchandise for Display. Although the requirements vary somewhat by type of store, ordinarily merchandise displayed should: (a) be an impulse item for shoppers, (b) have a relatively large margin, (c) fit into a larger group of merchandise which might be shown to increase the display's reality or impact, and (d) *not* be highly susceptible to damage or theft. Few items meet these requirements perfectly. Thus, a manager selecting display merchandise must evaluate alternatives according to how closely each meets the ideal requirements.

One requirement must be met by *all* merchandise displayed: a sufficient inventory of the item to meet anticipated demand. After seeing an item on display, customers expect to be able to purchase it.

Possible Use of Price Cards. Some retailers always indicate the price of displayed merchandise; others never do. What are the reasons for these policies? Basically, desired store image and the role of price in the retailing mix determine whether price cards should be included.

> **REVIEW BOX 14:3**
>
> 1. Methods of retailer-consumer communication other than advertising and personal selling are referred to as _____.
> 2. There are two basic types of display: _____ and _____.
> 3. One important consideration in using displays is _____.

Special Sales

Most retailers conduct at least several special sales each year. In this supportive method, merchandise with reduced prices is promoted vigorously, especially through advertising, for a limited period of time.

Some "prestige" stores shun special sales, feeling that heavy promotion or reduced prices hurt their desired image. The majority of retail outlets, however, feel that special sales contribute to their image or assist in accomplishing promotion objectives without affecting image. For example, special sales are not usually associated with automotive repair shops. Still, many such shops will feature a special low price on a tune-up, brake adjustment, or other service for a short time. Their purpose: to attract new customers, who hopefully will purchase regular-price services and become repeat customers.

TYPES

Special sales can be classified according to the number of offerings involved. Table 14-1 shows five types of special sales. The arrows pointing toward the right suggest that special sales really range in a continuum from a *single item* to *joint* (involving a group of merchants) rather than falling neatly into five categories. How frequently each promotion purpose is associated with the various types is suggested by the size of the X in the blocks. The larger the X, the more frequently the type of sale is used to accomplish that purpose.

The X sizes in Table 14-1 are open for discussion, of course. Some retailers may associate a type of special sale with a specific promotion purpose more frequently than is indicated in the table. Still, the table points out that it is an error to run a special sale just because competitors always do, or because it seems to be the thing to do at a certain time of year. Rather, it is essential to plan specifically what a special sale is to accomplish and how this will be done.

Looking at the specific types, first note that when a store places a single product or service or a limited number on sale, it is often using the technique of leader offerings. Care must be exercised in selecting specific leader offerings, since not all products or services are suitable. At other

TABLE 14-1

Special Sales Related to Promotion Purposes

Purposes of promotion	Types of Special Sales				
	Single item →	Limited number of items →	Departmental →	Store-wide →	Joint
Sell specific offerings	X	X	X	X	X
Contribute to desired image	X	X	X	X	X
Generate shopper traffic	X	X	X	X	X

times, a special sale may be run to "clear out" a few items which, in the manager's judgment, will be much less salable in the future or are detracting from the store's image.

A storewide sale does not mean that *every* offering has a reduced price and is being heavily advertised. Rather, *some* offerings from *all* merchandising units in the outlet are featured in the sale.

Joint promotions, a special sale sponsored by a group of firms rather than by a single retailer, are increasing in popularity. Merchants in large shopping centers often jointly sponsor a special sale in order to attract more shoppers to the area. As a result, retailers in downtown locations or in neighborhood shopping areas have been forced to do the same in order to compete for shoppers.

USE CONSIDERATIONS

Three factors should be considered in the use of special sales for promotion: coordination, frequency, and profitability.

Coordination. How can a special sale appear to succeed but be labeled a failure? Consider an appealing sale which is vigorously advertised and consequently attracts many shoppers. The sale will be a flop if, because of inadequate coordination, consumers find insufficient merchandise or salespeople in the store. Even though store traffic is generated by this sale, the store's image may be tarnished in the minds of many dissatisfied shoppers.

Lack of coordination between persons planning a special sale and those responsible for advertising may also doom a sale. Appropriate advertising has to be planned long before the sale dates. Naturally, coordination is needed just as much in a joint promotion as in an individual store's special sale.

Frequency. Having *too many* special sales can be as much of a mistake as having too few. You have probably noticed stores with an endless stream of storewide sales. To cite an example, in early July this kind of store has a "Get Ready for the 4th" sale, followed by a "Shoppers' Independence Day" sale on July 4, and then a "More Fireworks" sale the next week.

What's wrong with that? One undesirable possibility is that consumers may postpone purchases, waiting for the next sale and its reduced prices. Or, shoppers may come to view sale prices as the store's "normal" prices, assuming that anything not on sale is probably overpriced.

Just one special sale may be too many in some cases. This would be true if consumers purchased very large quantities of sale merchandise that a store was not really trying to clear out. Such stockpiling by consumers can reduce a retail firm's sales and profits later on. To prevent stockpiling, some outlets limit the quantity of each sale item which a shopper may purchase.

Since there is not a specific number of special sales that will be right for every store, a merchant must consider overall operating plans before deciding on the appropriate frequency. For some retail outlets, this may mean only an annual clearance sale; for others, daily single-item sales (leader offerings) and periodic departmental sales might be suitable.

Profitability. When planning a special sale, a retail manager must decide the needed profitability on sale merchandise. Reduced prices can erase profits on this particular merchandise. Still, indirect benefits from special sales, such as enhancing the store's image or clearing out old merchandise, may eventually lead to greater profits. At other times, sale merchandise can be quite profitable. This would be true when the offering has a large initial markup. Another avenue to profits is to obtain "special" reduced prices from suppliers on large orders of sale merchandise. As this suggests, sale merchandise does not have to be only items that have been in stock for a long time; on the contrary, some merchandise is bought especially for a special sale.

Other Supportive Methods

In addition to display and special sales, there are various other methods that can supplement advertising and personal selling:

Welcoming organizations, which are business firms that visit newcomers in their homes and provide information about the community as well as promotional materials, gifts, and coupons from participating retail outlets.

Sampling, which involves giving shoppers a free sample of a product or service with the aim of turning them into regular customers.

Demonstrations and fashion shows.

Spectaculars, the only appropriate name for some stores' very elaborate and expensive supportive promotions. The Thanksgiving Day parades of Macy's in New York and Hudson's in Detroit would fall in this category, as would the all-star college basketball game started in 1972 by the Pizza Hut chain.

Grand openings, which really are a mixture of several supportive promotions and heavy advertising.

Additional, commonly used supportive methods are briefly examined below.

PUBLICITY

Basically, publicity is *free promotion*. It includes those promotion activities with no out-of-pocket costs to a retailer. Usually publicity seeks to stimulate store traffic or to enhance the firm's image, rather than to sell offerings right away.

Personal appearances and news stories are the most common forms of publicity. Ordinarily, celebrities make public appearances only for a fee. Authors of new books, however, sometimes agree to free public appearances at retail stores in order to "plug" their books. An entertainer or professional athlete who is a friend of a retail manager also may agree to a free appearance. Rather than bring celebrities in, some stores occasionally send their executives out to speaking engagements.

Newspapers and broadcast stations always want interesting news stories. For this reason, retailers often can obtain publicity without too much difficulty—if in fact the story affects or appeals to the medium's audience. Media will often report a grand opening, completion of extensive store remodeling, a major change in merchandising policy, or recognition of outstanding retail employees.

A type of publicity which a retailer cannot control is *word-of-mouth publicity*. What consumers, suppliers, and other businessmen say about retail firms often plays a major role in determining where consumers shop. The main thing a retailer can do to obtain favorable word-of-mouth publicity is to provide shoppers with friendly, efficient service. Another positive step is to handle customer complaints as courteously and fairly as possible.

The major use consideration related to publicity is simply to obtain it whenever an opportunity presents itself. In fact, a retail manager should look for newsworthy offerings and events in the firm that might be converted into favorable publicity. It can be a powerful promotion tool. For example,

SPOTLIGHT

Can a basketball game in Las Vegas sell more pizza nationwide?

In 1972 the first Pizza Hut Basketball Classic, a post-season college all-star game, was held at the Las Vegas Convention Center. Details of the inaugural game provide some insights into the nature and rationale for a spectacular-type supportive promotion. Also, this particular promotion illustrates how target markets should be considered and how various methods can be blended together.

The all-star teams were chosen by a vote of basketball fans who visited one of the more than 800 Pizza Hut outlets. But why would a restaurant chain select a basketball game as a form of promotion? The president of Pizza Hut, Inc. explained:

> We feel that a college basketball game is a natural for us to sponsor. A large percentage of our customers are collegians and sports fans. And this gives us a chance through the PH Charities Foundation [which received net proceeds of the game] to benefit educational institutions.

The PH Classic originally was announced at a press conference about six weeks before the game. Until the game date, additional press conferences were called for the release of information such as the names of the coaches, interim voting tallies, and the final player selections. Why did the sponsors go to this much trouble? A prime aim of most spectacular-type promotions, including the PH Classic, is to obtain favorable publicity for the sponsoring retailer.

In an attempt to increase the likelihood of obtaining publicity, Pizza Hut sent a complete packet of data about the game to the various media in cities whose colleges had nominees. Each PH franchisee, furthermore, was furnished with copies of all press releases to tie into ads.

One PH manager near the campus of a nominated player took no chances on missing opportunities for publicity—he personally delivered each press release to his local sports editor. Then he bought quarter-page newspaper ads offering a "Monday night reduced price" and inviting students and residents of the city to vote for their player.

Special displays in the individual units were tied in with the game. A simulated backboard and basket were prominent at the counter where orders were placed.

As noted, net proceeds from the game went to Pizza Hut Charities Foundation. But the game also served the basic purposes of promotion: The attendant publicity well may have increased sales at the PH outlets, but the greatest benefits probably were in creating the desired image for the chain and individual outlets. And the carefully and vigorously promoted game certainly did generate a mountain of publicity! According to one observer, "The event drew a response of hundreds of mentions on the sports pages of the nation's newspapers, including a number of feature articles."

Source: Adapted from "Ad Clinic: Pizza Hut's 'Classic' Promotion," *Fast Food*, May 1972, pp. 48ff, by permission of *Restaurant Business* Magazine.

consider how the impact of a fashion show will be increased if the local newspaper carries an article and pictures about it. And, of course, the best part about such publicity is that it's free!

TRADING STAMPS

Another supportive promotion is to give shoppers trading stamps with each purchase, ordinarily one stamp for each 10¢ spent. Consumers can then trade accumulated stamps for merchandise at the stamp company's redemption centers. Some consumers save stamps because of the feeling of "getting something for nothing" when they visit the redemption center. Others view stamps as a painless way of saving for special items.

During the 1950s and 1960s, many retailers—especially grocery stores—used trading stamps. The first retailer to offer stamps in an area gained an advantage over competitors and thereby attracted more shoppers. Stamps also made some shoppers loyal to an outlet since they wanted to save enough of a certain kind of stamp to obtain desired merchandise.

In the last five to ten years, however, trading stamps have declined in usage. As *Business Week* observed:

> Trading stamps, which have taken a licking from both government and consumer groups that allege they contribute to high food prices, are losing some big customers. A&P eliminated E. F. MacDonald's Plaid stamps from almost all outlets in its price-cutting drive. First National Stores . . . has already phased out Sperry & Hutchinson's S&H Green stamps.[6]

With mounting inflation, many price-conscious consumers complained that trading stamps helped contribute to high prices. This is possible. Retailers must purchase stamps from a stamp company. Unless stamps attract large numbers of shoppers, thereby making a store more efficient, part or all of the stamps' cost ordinarily is passed on to consumers through somewhat higher prices.

By the 1960s, stamp plans were not attracting many extra shoppers, because numerous retail outlets were offering them. The result: many stores with the added operating expense of stamps but without a differential advantage from them abandoned this supportive promotion.

Thus the main use consideration is whether a long-standing gain can be achieved by offering stamps. If they attract new shoppers who are really pleased by the store's retailing mix *and become loyal customers*, stamps are worthwhile. Of course, new shoppers often can also be attracted by a special sale or increased advertising which runs for a limited time. Trading stamps, on the other hand, are difficult to eliminate without angering and perhaps losing some regular customers. If other retailers are likely to retaliate when stamps are added, a long-standing gain for the outlet is unlikely. Perhaps the most sensible use of trading stamps is by a store *without* them which is losing customers on a continuing basis to stores *with* stamps.

Will trading stamps continue to decline? One forecast is that "with

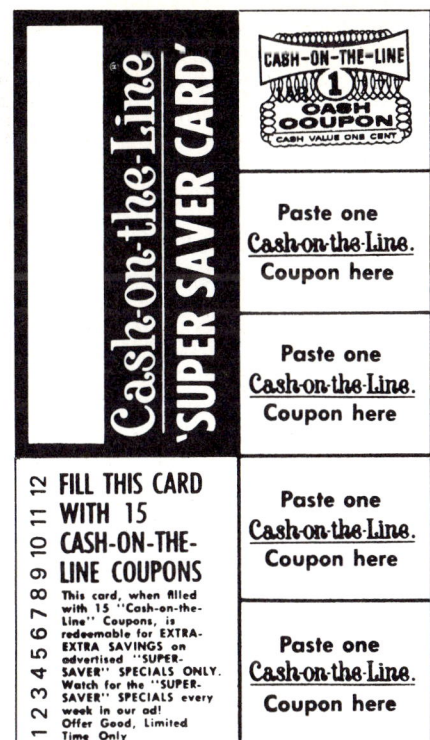

FIGURE 14-2

Sample trading stamp and card used in a new plan

the large supermarket chains well launched into a cycle of competitive discounting, the next significant upswing in the trading-stamp business seems far away indeed."[7] As this statement suggests, however, the popularity of trading stamps among consumers and retailers may be cyclical. That is, they may be valued for a while, then decline, then return, and so on.

Another possibility is that variations on normal stamp plans will be developed. Figure 14-2 shows a sample stamp and card used in a small supermarket chain's new plan. A completed card can be exchanged for special price reductions on grocery items rather than traded later for other merchandise.

PREMIUM OFFERS

In a premium offer, a product or service is given free or at a greatly reduced price with the purchase of another designated offering. For example, some service stations offer free glassware or a half-price car wash when a certain amount of gas is bought. The free or reduced-price product or service is called a premium. Like stamps, premiums appeal to many consumers because they are "something for nothing."

Premium offers can have various objectives. When only a small pur-

Supportive Promotion Methods **337**

chase is required to obtain a premium, the retailer probably is seeking to build shopper traffic. Another possible objective is to build loyal customers. This is attempted by offering a set of premiums, such as books or dishware, at one item per visit or purchase. This kind of offer does not always work. After completing a set of premiums, some (or maybe many) customers switch to competitors who also offer attractive premiums. Thus, premiums can be an expensive form of competition.

Why do numerous retail firms, notably fast-food restaurants and supermarkets, periodically use a premium offer? A Dairy Queen operator explained: "Premiums give people a reason to come in."[8] This retailer further noted that premiums may be less expensive than straight advertising in drawing new customers.

One use consideration regarding premium offers was discussed in connection with trading stamps. Before beginning a premium offer, a retail manager must decide whether a long-standing gain will be achieved. Another use consideration pertains to selection of premiums. In general, "the premium should be a product of nearly universal demand, not commonly regarded as a necessity, and be obtainable in large wholesale lots at substantial differentials from normal prices, so that the offer conveys the enticement of great value."[9] Services with the first two characteristics can also be suitable premiums.

COUPONS

This supportive method involves distributing certificates which entitle a person to buy a particular offering at a reduced price. Couponing can be initiated by both manufacturers and retailers. The number of coupons distributed by manufacturers, particularly in the food and drug industries, has mushroomed in recent years to a total of 27.6 billion in 1973. According to the Nielsen research firm, this compared with 16.4 billion cents-off coupons distributed in 1970.[10] Figure 14-3 shows the methods by which manufacturers distribute coupons and what proportion of coupons distributed in different ways are redeemed by consumers.

Manufacturers have a problem processing the tremendous number of redeemed coupons in order to reimburse retailers for the coupons' value plus handling costs. On top of this is the problem of fraudulent coupon redemption which accounts for one-third of the $300-million-a-year couponing business. Retailers are also affected by fraudulent redemption since:

> Some of the fraud takes place at the retail level when store employees pilfer a supply of coupons distributed in the store and . . . redeem them. An even more common form of illegal redemption occurs when obliging sales clerks give shoppers cash for coupons when the coupons explicitly state that they cannot be redeemed for money.[11]

The first situation is the same as outright theft since a store obviously can-

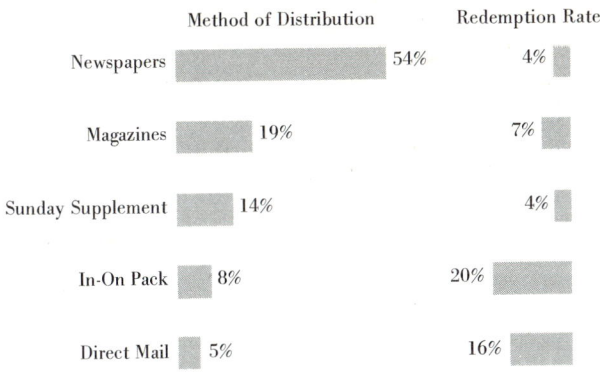

FIGURE 14-3

Distribution and redemption of manufacturers' coupons (1970 estimates)

Source of data: "NCH Study of Couponing Trends," A. C. Nielsen Co., 1972, pp. 2, 5.

not obtain reimbursement without turning in the actual coupons. Retail firms thus are forced to institute time-consuming and costly safeguards against fraudulent coupon redemption by employees.

Many retailers design and distribute their own coupons. While the most common use is by grocery stores which include coupons in their newspaper ads, service establishments and fast-food restaurants also frequently employ this method of promotion. Retailers can control the timing, number, and value of their own coupons, whereas they cannot do this with manufacturers' coupons. But, in return, retailers must absorb the full cost of their own coupons.

Again, the main use consideration regarding couponing by retailers is whether any long-standing gain will be achieved. Couponing is of little value to a retail outlet when a shopper does not buy any offerings other than those covered by coupons, and it is of little value to the manufacturer when a shopper never again buys the couponed item. Retailers may be less concerned with the direct impact of couponing when a manufacturer pays the cost. In this case, a retail manager may feel that the promotion will create good will for the store, which is a sufficient benefit.

The Fair Packaging and Labeling Act, which is enforced by the Food and Drug Administration and the Federal Trade Commission, includes regulations on "cents-off" promotions, introductory offers, and "economy size" labels. Thus, another use consideration is compliance with laws that prescribe what is permissible regarding the frequency and "cents-off" amount of coupons. For instance, it ordinarily would be illegal to use a "cents-off" coupon on a continuous basis, since this practice does away with a "regular" price.

Supportive Promotion Methods

> **REVIEW BOX 14:4**
>
> 1. One use consideration regarding special sales is profitability of sale merchandise; one of the other two considerations is _____.
> 2. Personal appearances are one common form of publicity; the other is _____.
> 3. In the last five to ten years, retail stores' usage of trading stamps has been _____.
> 4. When a retail outlet gives customers a product or service free or at a greatly reduced price with the purchase of another designated offering, this is termed a _____.
> 5. Retailers _____ the timing, number, and value of their own coupons, whereas they cannot do this with manufacturers' coupons.

CHAPTER SUMMARY

- Communication from a retailer to consumers or, in other situations, communication between a retailer's salespeople and shoppers is the promotion element of a retailing mix.
- Personal promotion, or personal selling, involves communication on a face-to-face basis. Non-personal promotion, not involving actual face-to-face contact, includes advertising and supportive methods of promotion.
- Promotion serves three major purposes in a retail firm: to sell specific offerings, to create a desired image, and to generate shopper traffic. The specific form of promotion that is used determines whether these purposes are accomplished.
- Effective promotion is based upon certain essentials: consideration of desired image in relation to target markets, promotion's relationship with other mix elements, information on reach and cost of various promotion methods, coordination, and creativity.
- For promotion to be successful, it must attract attention, generate interest, create desire, and obtain action. These are commonly referred to as the AIDA tasks. Various parts of a specific promotion are designed to accomplish each task.
- Since one promotion method seldom is sufficient, a merchant needs to develop a compatible mixture of methods, a promotion blend. This can be done through a series of decisions in which the manager

assigns a relative emphasis to promotion in general and to specific methods in particular.
- Those methods of communicating with consumers that do not fall into the advertising or personal selling categories are called supportive promotion methods. These should not be viewed as leftovers in a promotion blend, since they can play a major role in doing an effective promotion job.
- Merchants often rely on display, the in-store arrangement of merchandise and facts for shoppers' viewing. There are two types: display windows and interior displays. In addition, there are three distinct kinds of display windows and five kinds of interior displays. Retail managers should be familiar with certain considerations regarding suitable display usage: the message, selection of merchandise for display, and possible use of price cards.
- Most retailers conduct at least occasional special sales, in which merchandise with reduced prices is promoted vigorously, especially through advertising, for a limited period of time. Special sales can be classified according to the number of offerings involved, ranging from a single item placed on sale by an outlet to a joint promotion involving a group of retailers. Three considerations are particularly important in using special sales: coordination, frequency, and profitability.
- Besides display and special sales, merchants often supplement advertising and personal selling efforts with publicity, trading stamps, premium offers, and couponing.

CHAPTER NOTES

[1] William Lazer and Eugene J. Kelley, "The Retailing Mix: Planning and Management," *Journal of Retailing*, Spring 1961, p. 38.
[2] Samuel Feinberg, "From Where I Sit," *Women's Wear Daily*, November 12, 1965, p. 8.
[3] "How the Advertising of Service Can Sell Durables," *Marketing/Communications*, September 1971, p. 38.
[4] David T. Kollat and Ronald P. Willett, "Customer Impulse Purchasing Behavior," *Journal of Marketing Research*, February 1967, p. 23.
[5] "Ways to Make Every Foot of Shelf Space Pay Off," *Progressive Grocer*, March 1971, pp. 41ff.
[6] "Cancelling Stamps," *Business Week*, July 15, 1972, p. 31.
[7] "Trading Stamps: Panic at Plaidland," *Newsweek*, October 23, 1972, p. 92.
[8] "The Premium Offer—'A Reason to Come In,'" *Fast Food*, September 1971, p. 48.
[9] William R. Davidson and Alton F. Doody, *Retailing Management*, 3rd ed. (New York: Ronald Press, 1966), p. 662.
[10] A. C. Nielsen Company news release, January 16, 1974.
[11] This and the statistics above are drawn from "On the Trail of Coupon Bandits," *Business Week*, July 29, 1972, p. 48.

QUESTIONS AND ASSIGNMENTS

1. "Selling merchandise is what promotion's all about. Without sales tomorrow, you won't be around to worry about the long run. Thus, working on a store's image and traffic is like the frosting on a cake. It's real nice but without the cake it's nothing." Evaluate this statement on the basis of what you have learned in this chapter.
2. What is a promotion blend? Name at least five of its ingredients.
3. You're talking with someone about prerequisites to effective promotion. When you mention the importance of creativity, that person says: "What we need less of—not more of—is so-called creativity. There's too much weird, far-out advertising, especially on TV." Based on your reading of the chapter, how would you respond to this statement?
4. Interview the owner-manager of a small retail firm (or the head of a large retail firm's promotion division) about what promotion creativity means, how important it is, and how this manager attempts to produce creative promotion.
5. Select an actual retail ad or commercial and discuss whether—and how—each of the AIDA tasks is accomplished. Do the same for a supportive promotion conducted by a retail firm in your community. In both cases, explain which parts of the promotion carry out each task.
6. The chapter stated that display is growing in importance within the promotion blend. What factor explains this added importance? Is this true in all retail outlets?
7. Tour local retail outlets in order to locate all eight kinds of displays mentioned in the chapter. If you have a camera, take a picture of each kind. If you don't have a camera, make a rough sketch or write a one-paragraph description of each. Analyze your impression of each display.
8. Define the following supportive promotion methods: special sales, publicity, trading stamps, premium offers, and couponing. For each method, what is one specific use consideration?
9. The chapter discusses the value of publicity and how a retailer should seize opportunities for publicity. If you were the manager of a sporting goods store, what would you consider to be three possible avenues for publicity?
10. Provide a local retailer with a list of the supportive methods of promotion described in the chapter. Ask him to review what he does in each area. Which does he feel is the most important method? The least important?

ANSWERS TO REVIEW BOX QUESTIONS

Box 14:1

1. communication between a retailer's salespeople and shoppers in the outlet
2. advertising
3. Two of the following: promotion's relationship with the other mix elements, reach and cost of various promotion methods, coordination, or creativity
4. obtain action

Box 14:2

1. personal selling; personnel, operations, or merchandising
2. One of the following: the emphasis given promotion relative to other mix components; emphasis on promotion relative to competitors; or the appropriate blend of personal selling, advertising, and supportive methods

Box 14:3

1. supportive promotion methods
2. display windows and interior displays
3. One of the following: the message, selection of merchandise for display, and possible use of price cards

Box 14:4

1. coordination or frequency
2. news stories (Word-of-mouth promotion also would be a correct answer if the fact that the retailer does not control it is noted.)
3. declining
4. premium offer
5. control

Personal Selling

Most retail managers would probably agree about three things regarding personal selling. One, promotion through personal selling has been de-emphasized by many merchants because they see it as a drag on profits. Two, the quality of selling in most retail outlets leaves much to be desired—in fact, it is downright poor in many cases. Three, the effect of personal selling has a tremendous impact on most retail firms. Salespeople are also important because their wages represent as much as one-third of a retailer's operating expenses and they constitute an element by which customers can clearly distinguish an outlet from its competitors.

These points reflect the changing and complicated status of personal selling in retailing today. Accordingly, we need to look carefully at the nature of personal selling, its appropriateness in different instances, its basic requirements, considerations in sales force management, and ways of improving selling. An understanding of personal selling is necessary for all retail firms because in order to make an informed decision on the appropriate blend of personal selling, advertising, and supportive methods, a manager must know what each is and can or cannot do.

THE NATURE OF PERSONAL SELLING

Personal selling is distinguished from the other methods of communication with consumers by its face-to-face nature. This type of promotion is *between* a retailer (actually a salesperson) and a consumer rather than strictly *from* a retailer *to* consumers.

As a practical definition we may state: Personal selling is the activities of retail employees in helping shoppers buy satisfying offerings. This definition stresses a key part of the marketing concept: that a store and its employees should be geared toward satisfying consumers' needs, wants, and desires. Note that the word *sell* is not included or suggested in the definition. Instead, a consumer orientation is reflected in the words *helping shoppers buy.*

Also, the definition is broad enough to cover both direct and indirect personal selling activities. Besides talking with shoppers, showing them merchandise, and ringing up sales, salespeople perform various non-selling tasks. Probably the most frequent, and least liked, non-selling activity is restocking and straightening up merchandise displayed on tables, shelves, and racks. In addition, a salesperson may assist with recordkeeping and arranging display windows.

Criticism of Personal Selling

For a number of years, the quality of personal selling in retail outlets has been widely criticized. Even in outlets which promote this retailing mix element, personal selling has often been poor. A promotion specialist assessed the situation in department stores as follows:

> You won't get many strenuous disagreements with the assertion that, for all practical purposes, there have been relatively no changes for the better in department store selling since 1955. This places the present state of department store selling at about the time of the birth of the Model-T.[1]

After visiting England, one marketing writer blasted the quality of personal selling in the United States: "When it comes to retail salespeople—men and women—the British version is so infinitely superior to the American salesperson that there simply is no basis for comparison."[2] In fact, it has been suggested in at least two different places that only Europeans be hired (even imported!) for retail sales positions.[3]

Obviously, there is much room for improvement in the area of personal selling. The first step in the right direction is an awareness of the most common shortcomings of retail sales personnel: *lack of sales ability*, in terms of experience, knowledge of the firm's offerings, or sales closings; or *poor interpersonal skills*, in terms of personal appearance, sales tactics, or treatment of shoppers. Keep these problems in mind, because we will return to them in considering ways of improving personal selling in later sections.

Its Relative Importance

There are two ways of viewing the importance of personal selling in a retail outlet. One is that its importance varies, depending on the kind of store. The other is that personal selling is important to all retail firms, since it can distinguish an outlet from its competitors and thereby gain or lose customers. Both viewpoints will be briefly considered.

According to some retailing specialists, the planned significance of personal selling in an outlet's retailing mix can range widely, as in Figure 15-1. Outlets in which personal selling plays a very prominent role can be termed *full-service*. Besides providing salespersons to assist (and persuade) shoppers, full-service outlets ordinarily offer supplementary services such as credit, alterations, and repairs. Department stores generally rely on personal selling as a major element in their retailing mixes. Of course, some departments within department stores use reduced personal selling. Supermarkets, discount houses, and cafeteria-type restaurants—outlets in which personal selling has a minor or insignificant role—are discussed below under *self-service* retailing.

In general, three factors determine the planned significance of personal selling. First, the outlet's desired image must be taken into account. In choosing an overall strategy, a merchant may feel that profitable sales volume is most likely if the store presents itself as being willing *and able* to provide customers with wide assortments of quality merchandise and helpful salespeople. Obviously, this strategy calls for a high level of personal selling, in terms of both quantity and quality. Another retailer may examine a market situation and decide that low prices coupled with high turnover and low operating expenses would be the most profitable strategy. In this case, personal selling (a major operating expense) will be reduced to a minimum.

Nature of the offering also suggests the appropriate significance of personal selling. Quite simply, effective merchandising of some offerings requires skilled personal selling, whereas the selling of others can be done without it. A salesperson assumes a key role when (a) shoppers have little knowledge about the offering's nature or usage or about various brands' features, (b) negotiating over price is expected, (c) the offering is quite expensive, or (d) the product is technically complex and consumers might desire a demonstration of or detailed information about it. In the absence of these conditions, self-service retailing is feasible.

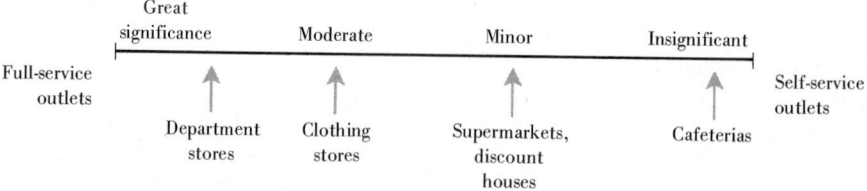

FIGURE 15-1

Personal selling related to the retailing mix

A third factor affecting the significance of personal selling is the retailer's previous experience with this form of promotion. If a retail manager has found personal selling to be effective for various offerings, he tends to favor it in other situations. However, many retailers have experienced some kind of trouble with personal selling. The natural tendency, then, is to avoid personal selling whenever possible. The first two factors—desired image and nature of the offering—certainly should be considered in planning the significance of personal selling. While the third factor, previous experience with personal selling, perhaps should not enter into the decision, it apparently does in many cases.

Another factor to keep in mind is that the quality of personal selling is as important as the quantity. However, a differential advantage might be gained by upgrading the quantity as well as the quality of personal selling. Customers may appreciate being served by knowledgeable, friendly salespeople in a situation where no sales help or low-quality selling is the rule. In fact, high-level personal selling may be a sufficient reason for some shoppers to become loyal customers. On the other hand, personal selling can handicap an outlet and drive away customers if it is much below consumers' expectations.

Self-Service Operations

"Managements of most stores have faced and continue to face unremitting pressures to adopt increasing degrees of self-service or impersonal selling."[4] Because this situation seems to hold true today, and because the concept and function of self-service are easily misunderstood, several paragraphs will be devoted here to self-service retailing.

In a store that uses self-service, shoppers examine various offerings and make their selection without assistance from a salesperson; they then take the merchandise to a check-out area to pay for it. Some self-service outlets use salespeople in certain departments where personal assistance is felt to be necessary and also have a limited number of salespeople around the store to help shoppers who request personal assistance. Also, in some self-service outlets clerks at check-out stands are encouraged to "do a little selling." For example, discount store clerks sometimes inquire whether a customer needs products connected with those selected, such as batteries for a toy or flash cubes along with film.

Self-service itself is not new. Variety stores, in particular, have used it for at least 50 years. What is new is the rush to self-service operations in the 1960s and 1970s. There are several reasons for the self-service trend. First, consumers' shopping behavior and preferences have changed dramatically in the post–World War II period. Consumers are more familiar with the merits of various offerings before they enter the outlet. Also, many are willing to serve themselves. Some shoppers even prefer the "do-it-yourself" approach in order to save money or to avoid being pressured to buy.

Second, some early self-service outlets were successful; and full-service stores which lost customers were forced to react. One reaction was to switch completely to self-service. Another was to establish a new, separate self-service section or outlet in addition to regular full-service operations.

Third, wage rates have been rising in recent years. One contributing factor has been legislation, such as Congress passed in 1974, which increases the minimum wage. As a result, some retailers have instituted self-service in which additional displays, shelves, and lighting fixtures are substituted for the greater expense of sales personnel.

The discussion above should not lead to an assumption that self-service is the answer to all of a retailer's problems. There are shortcomings in this method that must be recognized. For example, shoplifting is easier since there are fewer store employees on the selling floor. In addition, some customers who prefer personal service may shop elsewhere. Self-service operations also require careful scheduling of check-out clerks so that wage costs are kept low without creating long lines at check-out stands. Although self-service clearly is a major advantage in certain lines of retailing, it is not a cure-all.

REVIEW BOX 15:1

1. Personal selling can be defined as _____.
2. One of the two factors which definitely should be considered in planning the significance of personal selling is _____.
3. There are various pressures or reasons for the trend toward self-service retail operations. One of these is _____.

FUNDAMENTALS OF PERSONAL SELLING

The most important ingredient in personal selling is helping people to buy. Of course, persuading shoppers to make purchases cannot be neglected, but it should not be put ahead of helping shoppers in their choices. These distinct activities constitute the *service* and *selling* functions.

A retailer acts as a purchasing agent for his customers and employs salespeople to help match shoppers' needs with the outlet's offerings. But besides being a service institution, a retail firm must also be a sales institution in order to survive. This requires a reasonable amount of aggressiveness in soliciting business through planned personal selling efforts.

Below we will consider aspects of personal selling which are important not only to individual salespeople but also to retail managers who supervise or are indirectly involved with selling activities.

Basic Selling Procedure

As with other forms of promotion, personal selling techniques must accomplish the AIDA tasks to be effective. They must attract attention, generate interest, create desire, and obtain action. In the case of personal selling we can go even further and divide the function into six specific tasks or steps: approaching and greeting; determining needs; presenting the offering (explanation and demonstration); overcoming objections; closing the sale; and suggesting additional purchases. When these six steps are followed, the result is usually a purchase that is satisfying to both customer and retailer.

Neither these six steps nor the AIDA sequence is the only right procedure in personal selling. The details of each contact between salesperson and shopper determine a suitable procedure. For example, the nature of the offering and the number of shoppers waiting for service will often dictate what kind of selling procedure should be used. Because the six-step procedure is usually suitable, however, many firms instruct sales personnel in its use. The main drawback of this procedure, termed *formula selling*, can be inflexibility. A salesperson may be so intent on proceeding step by step that the shopper does not receive the help he or she wants. For example, a salesperson can literally talk a sale away by ignoring a shopper's questions or by continuing to press forward through the steps after a shopper is ready to make a purchase.

Adaptive Formula Selling

Adaptive formula selling requires knowledge and awareness on the part of salespeople. They must be attuned to situational factors which suggest the appropriate procedure. After greeting a shopper they must be able to alter their procedure in response to cues (questions, expressions, statements) they receive.

Ideally, sales employees should try to determine and understand consumers' perceptions about the outlet in general and, perhaps more important, about specific offerings. When consumer perceptions are understood, matching a shopper's needs with a specific offering is much easier. However, the findings from one study suggest that most retail employees may not be very successful at this task:

> Retailers consistently underestimate the strengths with which consumers view the importance of service and warranty, ease of use, and style in the appliance purchase decision. . . . Retailers tend to view attributes of competitive brands differently from consumers.[5]

Fundamentals of Personal Selling

One specific skill required in adaptive formula selling is answering shoppers' questions effectively.

Cartoon reproduced by permission of John Hart and Field Enterprises Inc.

One other prerequisite for effective salesmanship is familiarity with the outlet's offerings as well as those of competitors. Recall that inadequate knowledge of merchandise is a frequent criticism of personal selling efforts.

Besides the general requirements of being adaptive, aware, and knowledgeable, other essentials apply to individual steps in selling. In fact, entire books have been written on the various "musts," "shoulds," and "do's and don'ts" of selling.[6]

Considering that most retail managers do not engage in personal selling after their training periods, why do they need to be familiar with the steps and skills of personal selling? Quite simply, managers who cannot "put themselves in the salesperson's shoes" will find it difficult to supervise a salesforce effectively or to make informed decisions related to this method of promotion.

Although we cannot go into the specifics of each step, we can illustrate the skills connected with effective retail salesmanship by an analysis of the first step: the approach. This sets the tone for a shopper-salesperson relationship and is therefore very important. When a shopper is greeted in a prompt, friendly manner, a giant step toward genuine rapport has been taken.

The specific situation determines the proper approach:

> The approach is like a round of golf. You select a club depending upon the situation. You don't tee off with a nine iron on a 500-yard hole.... The salesman, like a good golfer, must appraise customer behavior [the situation] before making an approach.[7]

Being able to tell from a single observation which approach would be suitable is a skill that is developed through experience.

Let's consider three distinct approaches, each appropriate under different circumstances.

The *service approach* works well when it appears that a shopper has already made a decision to buy. In this case, the sale ordinarily can be closed simply by asking, "May I help you?" An approach intended to assess a shopper's needs or as a lead-in to presenting merchandise would be a waste of time. It might also make a shopper begin to reconsider the decision to buy. When a shopper is holding several units of the same item, he may be ready to buy once the right size or color is found. Then a suitable approach would be, "May I help you find the size or color you want?"

The *merchandise approach* is suited to situations in which a shopper seems interested in a specific offering but has not made a decision to buy. In this approach, a salesperson mentions features which may not be apparent to the shopper in order to increase the offering's appeal and move the shopper toward a purchase. For example, a wig salesperson might greet a customer with "Did you know this wig is made from 100 percent human hair?"

When a shopper has not even focused on a general offering, what might be termed the *available approach* becomes necessary. The salesperson obviously cannot close a sale yet and, in fact, does not even know what merchandise to feature. All that can be done is to let the customer know that assistance is available. This approach commonly relies on a general greeting such as "Good afternoon, Mrs. Harwood" or "How are you today?" The shopper's response suggests what the salesperson should say next. If the shopper mentions a particular offering, the merchandise approach is called for. If the response is brief but friendly, then a question like "May I help you find something in particular?" is appropriate. If the tone is less friendly, the salesperson probably should "retreat" for the time being. This can be done by saying "If you need any help, just call me over" and then moving on to another customer or a different area.

Among the more important "do's" in any approach are promptness, friendliness, courtesy, and an opening statement in line with the shopper's behavior. One "don't" apparently occurs so frequently that it must be mentioned. The greeting, "May I help you?", is suitable only when a shopper obviously has decided on the purchase. But it is widely used because it is such an easy opening. Why "May I help you?" often is *un*suitable has been explained as follows:

> For many people, the choice of saying "yes" or "no" to a purchase is the only area in which they can come close to feeling superior. . . . So what happens? A salesperson approaches the customer and says, "May I help you?" and so frustrates even this small power. Her reaction: "No thank you, I'm just looking." She will disregard the salesperson, and maybe even complain how salespeople are always so pushy . . . or say, "They never have a thing I like."[8]

It is clear that effective personal selling requires substantial motivation and abilities. One reason for low-quality retail selling may be that management ignores or is unaware of this elementary fact. As a result, programs to increase enthusiasm and skills in personal selling are too much the exception rather than the rule.

Fundamentals of Personal Selling

Types of Personal Selling

Some employees are expected only to close the sale and suggest additional purchases, while others have to cover all six steps and must possess information about the offerings along with sharp communication and persuasive skills. Note that we are only talking about *what is expected* in personal selling, not what is actually done. Some salespeople disregard necessary steps or skills regardless of whether they are expected to engage in much (or little) personal selling. Others diligently work at effective selling no matter what is expected.

TRANSACTION PROCESSING

The fewest selling steps and skills are required in transaction processing.[9] Basically, the main task is to close the sale. Retail employees assigned to this type of personal selling are commonly termed *check-out clerks* or *cashiers*.

Although this type of personal selling is the least demanding, it is by no means unimportant. This type of selling accounts for a large proportion of total volume in most stores and presents a variety of opportunities to gain good will for the store.

ROUTINE SELLING

In this type of selling, a complete procedure often must be followed, and special skills are helpful or necessary. Department store selling of non-technical lines such as children's clothing, sheets and towels, and toys usually involves routine selling. Likewise, sales attendants in discount houses cover specified areas of the store, helping shoppers find merchandise, answering questions, and mentioning selling features.

What we have labeled routine selling varies greatly across outlets in terms of the specific responsibilities assigned to salespeople. But the common characteristic of this type is that it entails communication with shoppers before purchase decisions are made, although all six selling steps and specialized information and skills may not be necessary. Most retail salespeople are engaged in either transaction processing or routine selling.

CREATIVE SELLING

Creative selling is characterized by the need for a complete procedure, the acquisition and use of various merchandise information, the ability to demonstrate expensive or technical items, and subtle persuasive skills. To emphasize the important role and expertise of employees with creative selling responsibilities, they are often called *sales consultants*.

Ethan Allen furniture stores go one step further, using the term *home planner* rather than salesperson. As the term implies, these sales personnel need to know about a prospective customer's home, family, and life style so that appropriate furniture can be suggested. The term itself also indicates what shoppers can expect from Ethan Allen employees.

As you might expect, a creative selling position ordinarily carries a higher salary than the other two types. The job is more demanding, requiring more thought and skills. Thus compensation, one aspect of managing salespeople, should vary according to the type of personal selling involved. In addition, methods used in selecting, training, and supervising salespeople (discussed below) should not be developed until the particular selling situation has been taken into account.

REVIEW BOX 15:2

1. The second of the six steps in formula selling is _____, which is the key to a real customer orientation.
2. Because details of each shopper-salesperson contact determine the appropriate selling procedure, it is preferable to rely on _____ selling.
3. *Service, merchandise,* and *available* refer to the _____ step in the selling procedure, with each alternative being appropriate under different circumstances.
4. The most demanding type of personal selling is _____ since it requires going through a complete selling procedure and also using various merchandise information, demonstration and persuasive skills.

MANAGEMENT OF RETAIL SALESPEOPLE

Sales performance is primarily a function of a person's motivation and ability. In turn, individual motivation is largely affected by type of personality and the work situation. Ability generally is thought to depend mostly on learned skills as well as on personality type.

Why are factors which affect sales performance mentioned in a section on the management of retail salespeople? Because retail managers directly or indirectly influence each of these factors — even, in one sense, personality. Granted, an individual's personality is shaped by factors beyond retail managers' control. However, retailers can try to select employees with the kinds of personalities needed in different types of personal selling.

The point is that sales management activities largely determine how effective retail salespeople are. Faced with poor-quality sales efforts, too many managers blame salespeople for being lazy or not applying any techniques covered in training sessions. Part of the blame frequently should go to retail managers, however, for failing to develop systematic programs for managing salespeople.

Responsibility for Sales Management

Before examining *what* is involved in retail sales management, we should review *who* is involved. Recall that the owner-manager of a small retail outlet is a "jack of all trades" and thus retains overall responsibility for managing sales employees. Of course, an experienced employee may be delegated tasks such as scheduling or training new salespeople.

In contrast, in large retail stores the responsibility for personal selling may be assigned to either the operations, personnel, or merchandising division. While large stores ordinarily have an overall personnel manager, relatively few have a *retail sales manager*—an employee who concentrates on managing the sales force. Instead, some sales management tasks are usually handled at the departmental level, others by the storewide division. For example, scheduling, continuing training, and supervision might be done at the departmental level, while recruiting and selection, initial training, and compensation are handled at the storewide level.

In various relatively large, departmentalized stores, *section managers* are responsible for achieving satisfactory personal selling in a specified part of the store, usually several departments. They also may handle merchandise returns, customer complaints, and approval of checks. In many department stores, one of the chief responsibilities of an *assistant manager* in a selling department is the management of sales personnel.

One barrier to better retail selling may be that sales management responsibilities are so diffuse in many firms. Various managers perform specific tasks connected with managing salespeople, but they are also responsible for other activities. Consequently, sales management does not receive anyone's full attention in most retail outlets.

Tasks of Sales Management

Regarding *what* is involved in retail sales management, we can think in terms of six general tasks: manpower planning, recruiting and selection, training, scheduling, compensation, and supervision and control.

MANPOWER PLANNING

This task should be guided by the earlier decision on the planned significance of personal selling. Specifically, whether this method of promotion is to be emphasized or minimized will affect both the number of salespeople and the type of personal selling needed.

Also, in manpower planning the characteristics of salespeople must be matched against characteristics of the outlet's target customers. For example, it would be an error for a stereo shop near a college campus to seek elderly people as sales personnel, just as it would be for a high-price furniture store to use only college students.

RECRUITING AND SELECTION

Besides the general problems retailers face in recruiting employees, they face several hurdles which pertain specifically to recruiting sales personnel. First, fewer people are interested in retail sales positions. Women today have broader employment opportunities than in the past when retail selling was *the* field for women. Second, retail sales personnel generally have to be more qualified than ever before. Reasons for this are consumerism, especially the increasing awareness and demands of shoppers, and today's more complicated offerings. This means that fewer people in the labor force qualify for some retail sales positions.

Once applicants are recruited, selection methods range from a bare minimum, such as a brief interview, to very elaborate ones which may include psychological testing of applicants. (There is some feeling, however, that the use of psychological testing is being abused.) In general, selection of sales personnel must depend on hunches and preconceived notions, since so little is actually known about the effect that education, age, family characteristics, intelligence, and sales experience have on eventual sales performance.[10]

TRAINING

The overall purpose of sales training is to increase salespeople's selling skills and knowledge about offerings in order to make them more effective. In the 1970s, sales training seems to be receiving more attention. According to a 1970 *Business Week* article, retail firms faced with an acute shortage of good salespeople "are spending more money and energy trying to turn the talent they are able to attract into a more tuned-in, inspired sales force."[11]

Currently, it appears that most retail firms have some form of new-employee training, although the programs vary greatly as to length, format, *and adequacy*. On the other hand, periodic training for continuing employees still seems to be the exception rather than the rule. This is puzzling considering that product lines change and selling skills are forgotten over time.

SCHEDULING

"One of the most perplexing problems in retail store operations today is that of maintaining a reasonable selling cost while providing a high level of service to the customer."[12] This is what scheduling is all about—balancing the level of service, which presumably grows as more salespeople are on duty, against selling costs resulting from salespeople's wages.

Systematic scheduling requires that several factors be measured. Customer *arrival patterns* provide information concerning the frequency of demand for service. *Service times* reflect the amount of time a salesperson spends in various activities—selling, stocking, recordkeeping, coffee breaks—in comparison with how much time each sales transaction takes. *Sales*

Management of Retail Salespeople **355**

volume and *number of transactions* indicate the department's (and salespeople's) output. Once this various information is known, a schedule which provides a high level of service at a reasonable cost might be set.

Of course, scheduling in this manner is not that easy. For example, accurately measuring service time requires making random observations of sales floor activity and noting what is occurring. This task is quite time-consuming. Still, the goal should be a schedule based upon arrival patterns, service times, and sales volume. Furthermore, the schedule should show the number of employees needed each hour of the day rather than just containing a budgeted number of hours per day or week for each department.

A "perfect" schedule based upon the above factors still may have to be modified. The reason: Reasonable work schedules also must be set for individual employees. For example, a retail manager obviously cannot spread a full-time employee's eight hours of work over sixteen hours just to comply with the perfect schedule. To avoid employee dissatisfaction with the work situation, the manager should consider their preferences regarding hours of work and days off. To achieve scheduling flexibility, many outlets employ some part-time salespeople.

COMPENSATION

According to various retailers and other observers, a basic cause of personal selling problems is the relatively low pay. Because of this the supply of applicants is reduced, and those who become sales employees are often poorly motivated. To offset this problem, some manufacturers and retailers finance incentive programs aimed at improving the quality of retail selling. Salespeople are offered monetary rewards beyond their normal compensation for selling certain offerings or for achieving a high level of sales performance.

Contests. Possibilities for contests are almost without end. For example, a clothing store may reward the highest-volume salesperson during a month with a substantial gift certificate. Or an outlet may give an extra vacation day to the top sales employee, as voted on by customers.

To be effective, contests—just like any management practice—must be well thought out:

> The kind of selling contest a store should have and what the salespeople should do in order to receive the prizes hinges on another question, what the contest is expected to accomplish. If the store manager wants to encourage higher sales, he should use some sales figure as a target. He should be aware that the salespeople may come to resent performing any normal non-selling duties which would take them off the selling floor.[13]

Also, when salespeople are no longer in contention for the prize, their motivation may decline.

Contests can be used to accomplish purposes other than sales performance. For example, a contest might seek to improve salespeople's merchandise knowledge or orderliness within departments.

Push Money. This form of incentive, also referred to as *PMs* or *spiffs*, is different from contests since it ordinarily applies to the sale of each unit of a designated brand or model and is often financed by a supplier. Push money is usually attached only to selected models of a product, such as "top of the line" models. Spiffs of $5 or $10 per unit are common in the case of appliances, furniture, and floor coverings. The most frequent usage of push money probably is in cosmetics retailing, although the dollar amounts of individual spiffs is not as large as in the product lines just mentioned.

Even when a manufacturer is not sharing the cost, retailers sometimes use push money in order to "give extra rewards to the salespeople for selling 'dogs', i.e., merchandise that has not lived up to expectations; or for selling merchandise that has a higher margin."[14] Push money is effective only for certain kinds of offerings and under special circumstances. To elaborate, a survey of retailers found that spiffs are moderately effective in selling slow-moving items. However, the majority of retailers felt that a spiff is no more effective than a markdown and is less effective than advertising. Even when push money is thought to be effective, problems can arise. When manufacturers pay the cost of this incentive, they sometimes feel that they should be able to dictate store policies. The potential problem is that the retailer may wind up employing practices which are out of line with the overall retailing mix or that the manufacturer may be alienated should his ideas or requests be rejected.

SUPERVISION AND CONTROL

Lack of supervision by departmental managers can lead to problems, just as can constant "over-the-shoulder" direction. The simple fact is that many salespeople, perhaps most, need frequent encouragement, praise, and reminders to get them to do their tasks well. In particular, sales employees need supervision regarding difficult or unpleasant activities, such as suggestion selling and straightening merchandise.

Sales employees should be informed of performance standards being applied. In some stores, a manager and the salespeople jointly decide and agree upon standards, usually connected with sales volume. A standard may also be a combination of factors, including number of transactions and the department manager's rating on non-selling activities, for example, in addition to sales volume. The May Company in Los Angeles began setting "customer service standards" several years ago. "Periodically, supervisors, through interviews with each sales person, evaluate how their sales force is doing on such matters as knowledge of the merchandise they sell and courtesy toward the customer."[15]

The control task is not finished until necessary corrective action aimed at improving sub-par performances is taken. Logical corrective action can range from warning or encouraging a poor performer to additional training or even replacement.

> **REVIEW BOX 15:3**
>
> 1. Sales performance is primarily a function of a person's motivation and _____.
> 2. The first of the six general tasks of sales management is _____.
> 3. Measuring customer arrival patterns and service times is necessary in the sales management task of _____.
> 4. A possible shortcoming of push money is that _____.

Improving Retail Selling

Because personal selling represents both a problem and an opportunity area for many retail firms, this chapter concludes with a discussion of several possible ways of improving personal selling. Three aspects of these recommendations should be noted:

1. Some relate to effectiveness, others to efficiency. *Effectiveness* refers to the sales output of an individual salesperson. *Efficiency* considers input as well as output, referring to the number of salespeople needed to produce a given level of sales.
2. They are management practices rather than individual actions. Sales personnel generally cannot or will not initiate improvements on their own. Thus the greatest potential lies in improving sales force management.
3. Some recommendations have been implemented by retail firms with good success; others remain either untested, or unpublicized if they have been tried by some retailers. Whichever the case, all have the potential for improving personal selling and also seem to be practical.

INCREASED ATTENTION TO INITIAL TASKS

As suggested earlier, the tasks of manpower planning, recruiting, and selecting salespeople are too often ignored or skimmed over. This is a serious mistake, just as it would be for a football coach simply to round up some bodies without considering the number and sizes of players needed, the sources of recruits, or the criteria for separating "stars," possible starters, and those with little potential.

Thus the first recommendation is a basic one — simply that the initial tasks in sales management receive greater attention. Two specific improvements can be suggested. First, job analysis should be the starting point in managing a retail salesforce. The distinct types of selling require different personalities and levels of capabilities. In addition, there may be different requirements for various merchandise. To sell cars, a salesperson has to be aggressive and seek out some prospects. In selling clothing, on the other hand, being aggressive is less important but being fashion-wise is crucial.

Second, to the extent that resources permit, research into the success requirements in retail selling should be conducted. Small retail firms cannot afford much research, but there is little evidence that large stores and chains are doing much personnel research. Without research findings, recruiting and selection decisions must be based on intuition, "rules of thumb," and general experience, all of which are too subjective or incomplete to be fully satisfactory. Thus research is necessary to develop *informed* guidelines for sales management.

RAISING PRODUCTIVITY

Sales productivity can be improved by increasing the number of transactions salespeople produce or by eliminating unnecessary salespeople. Systematic manpower planning, recruiting, and selection should raise productivity by staffing departments with the right numbers and types of sales employees.

A number of years ago, several other ways of increasing number of transactions were suggested.[16] These suggestions appear just as timely today. First, many departments can be laid out in a more efficient manner. In particular, distances should be kept to a minimum to increase speed of service and reduce employee fatigue. Also, displaying related merchandise together (for example, sheets and pillowcases of the same pattern) makes it easier for shoppers to serve themselves or for salespeople to locate desired items quickly.

Second—and the value of this recommendation varies greatly depending upon the type of store—added self-service should be installed to the extent possible. The feasibility of self-service depends primarily on whether shoppers will accept (or even prefer) "do-it-yourself" shopping.

Unnecessary salespeople can be eliminated not only through better manpower planning but also by more careful scheduling of salespeople's working hours. Varying the salesforce size is a difficult job. Regular part-time sales personnel are a partial solution. For instance, many restaurants employ students who work two to four hours daily at lunch or dinner.

Occasional temporary transfers of salespeople from an overstaffed department to a busy one is another possibility. Peak periods occur at different times of the day in various departments. Similarly, business in a particular department may be great due to a promotional event, while another department is operating as normal. Salespeople transferred must be familiar with the other department's offerings and necessary selling techniques if they are to be effective, of course. Hence, this creates the need for a special training program.

Management of Retail Salespeople

UPGRADING TRAINING

While many retail firms have excellent or at least adequate training for new, full-time salespeople, they provide little or no training for continuing sales personnel or for new part-timers. Thus the first recommendation is that added emphasis be given to improving *all* sales employees' selling skills and knowledge about product offerings.

Two training techniques particularly suitable for continuing and part-time salespeople can be recommended. Various firms have introduced instruction on tape cassettes. J.C. Penney employees, for example, listen to cassettes periodically during slack time on the selling floor. Similar, but one step further, is the videotape training program of The Higbee Company in Cleveland. For example, an eight-minute presentation was prepared in conjunction with Lenox China's representative. It was filmed "on location" in Higbee's china department. Higbee's tapes concentrate on just four selling points of a product because they are "retained much longer than if we used a 'shot gun' approach to product knowledge.... Five weeks after the program was viewed by the salespeople they could recall at least 75 percent of the product's selling points."[17]

Higbee's believes the tapes accomplish several important sales training objectives: Sales personnel are convinced that the techniques will work, since the instructional tape is filmed in an actual department, much like the one in which they work. Product information is retained better. Also, the manufacturer's representative is forced to tailor his instructional message to the store's situation.

Some retailers use role playing in their sales training programs. One salesperson acts as the customer whom the other salesperson greets and serves, using appropriate selling techniques. This form of training permits salespeople to practice newly learned techniques, and the instructor can correct errors before they undermine actual salesperson-shopper contacts. Woolworth has found role playing especially useful in training continuing employees. The salespeople act out scenes involving difficult customers. "When they see that they're not alone [in encountering shoppers who are difficult to deal with] then it's not as much of a problem," explained a Woolworth vice president.[18]

A BROADENED APPROACH TO MOTIVATION

Many retailers apparently realize that motivation (or lack of it) has a great deal to do with sales performance. However, fewer recognize that motivation results from a combination of factors, not just compensation or fear of losing a job. Compensation remains the cornerstone of motivation, but not the only building block:

> There is a small financial elite among retail sales people for whom the money rewards are great enough to be a powerful motivation. These are the specialized commission sales people, notably those in the high-ticket home furnishings de-

SPOTLIGHT

Can salespeople train each other?

Almost everyone learns better by doing, rather than by exhortation. That's the rationale behind *involvement selling*, a form of sales training which uses every salesperson as a "trainer." It is aimed at getting all salespeople more involved in learning about the merchandise in their department during slack periods.

Here's how an involvement selling program is implemented:

1. The program should start with one department, towels and bedding in a department store, for example. It is important not to move on to other departments or go storewide with the program until this department is a "success story." Thus there must be some evidence of improved performance, such as larger average purchases per customer.

2. Every salesperson is made a "sales trainer." A top-flight salesperson is asked to prepare a brief training presentation for the next departmental sales meeting on a topic such as "How to Show Quality in Towels." Can (or will) a sales employee prepare a worthwhile presentation? According to one consultant, "You'll be pleasantly surprised."

For the next meeting, another salesperson makes a presentation on a second topic such as "Suitable Gift Items, and How to Present their Benefits." This can be a continuous program if employees respond well to it, as the subjects are almost infinite.

3. In addition to the presentations of merchandise information in departmental meetings, selected salespeople are asked to plan simple interior displays on the same subjects. The display suggestion should include a small sign to convey the main selling point and should also be designed to sell related items.

4. To maintain enthusiasm for the program within the department or when it goes storewide, incentives can be used. For example, a contest might be held to identify and reward the best presentation or display suggestion during a specified period.

What are the possible benefits of an involvement selling program? For one thing, it may be a more effective form of sales training than conventional forms which ordinarily are more formal and do not permit salespeople to make use of their own ideas. Furthermore, it represents a way of increasing the motivation of salespeople. Any incentives connected with the program are a step in that direction. Involvement selling also enlarges the scope and adds a challenge to the salesperson's job, which otherwise can become quite repetitive or dull.

Source: Adapted from Ralf Shockey, "Selling Is a Science!" (Part III), *Department Store Economist*, June 1965, p. 91.

partments and stores, and in some apparel stores geared to aggressive salesmanship. . . . Money plays a much less important part in the motivation of the typical sales person who is on a straight salary.[19]

Some of the other rewards that motivate people are:

Promotion. A system of grades (or steps) within the sales force furnishes one opportunity for promotion. Another possibility open to those salespeople who are interested and qualified should be promotion to supervisory or executive positions.

Praise. Everyone needs spoken approval for good performance.

Satisfaction from the work itself. This satisfaction consists of pleasure obtained from the job and a conviction that the job has a worthwhile purpose.

Retail executives should attempt to determine the needs, interests, and attitudes of sales personnel and then assemble a package of rewards. A broadened view of motivation also includes more supervision and control of sales employees.

REVIEW BOX 15:4

1. One way of raising productivity is to increase a salesperson's number of transactions; the other is to _____
2. Salesforce size can be varied by using regular part-time sales personnel or by _____.
3. Training programs for _____ and _____ sales employees are relatively uncommon, a situation which needs to be changed.

CHAPTER SUMMARY

- Personal selling is the activities of retail employees in helping shoppers buy satisfying offerings. It is distinguished from other forms of retail promotion by the fact that it is face-to-face communication. There is substantial disagreement among retail managers as to the importance and appropriate role of personal selling in retail outlets.
- The quality of retail selling has been frequently criticized in recent years, suggesting that there is much room for improvement.
- Two factors, the outlet's desired image and nature of the offering, need to be considered before the planned significance of personal selling can be decided. Outlets which rely a great deal on personal selling are termed *full-service*. There has been a noticeable trend in recent years toward *self-service*, in which shoppers examine various offerings and make their selection without a salesperson's assistance and then take the merchandise to a check-out area to pay for it.
- Formula selling, a six-step personal selling procedure, includes ap-

proaching and greeting, determining needs, presenting the offering, overcoming objections, closing the sale, and suggesting additional purchases.
- There is no single right selling procedure. Details of each situation determine a suitable procedure. Thus *adaptive formula selling*, in which the general procedure is tailored to specific situations, is a desirable method.
- Considering the extent to which a complete selling procedure and special selling skills are required, there are three types of personal selling: *transaction processing*, *routine selling*, and *creative selling*.
- Sales performance is primarily a function of motivation and ability, with retail managers influencing both factors.
- There are six general tasks in retail sales management: manpower planning, recruiting and selection, training, scheduling, compensation, and supervision and control.
- The greatest potential for improving retail selling lies in the area of sales-force management. Possible improvements include: paying increased attention to the initial tasks of sales management; raising productivity by increasing the number of transactions salespeople produce and by eliminating unnecessary salespeople; upgrading training programs, especially those for continuing sales personnel and part-timers; and adopting a broader approach to motivation.

CHAPTER NOTES

[1] Ralf Shockey, "Selling Is a Science!" (Part X), *Department Store Economist*, January 1966, p. 40.
[2] E. B. Weiss, "Why Not Import British Salespeople?" *Stores*, July 1971, p. 32.
[3] *Ibid.*; also, "Wanted: Someone to Watch the Store," *Business Week*, September 19, 1970, p. 54.
[4] William J. Regan, "Full Cycle for Self-Service?" *Journal of Marketing*, April 1961, p. 15.
[5] Peter J. McClure and John K. Ryans, Jr., "Differences Between Retailers' and Consumers' Perceptions," *Journal of Marketing Research*, February 1968, p. 40.
[6] For an excellent, practical handbook on personal selling, see Allen E. Zimmer, *The Strategy of Successful Retail Salesmanship* (New York: McGraw-Hill Book Co., 1966).
[7] Laurence Jacobs and Dean Ellis, "How Merchandise Approach Works in Store Training," *Marketing Times*, September/October 1972, p. 18; the three types of approaches suggested below are drawn from Jacobs and Ellis' fine short article.
[8] Ben Ashell, "Let's Make Retailing More Profitable: A Salesperson's Guide to Better Selling," *Department Store Economist*, March 1966, p. 27.
[9] The terms transaction processing and creative selling were suggested by William R. Davidson and Alton F. Doody, *Retailing Management*, 3rd ed. (New York: Ronald Press Company, 1966, p. 681).
[10] James C. Cotham, III, "The Case for Personal Selling: Some Retailing Myths Exploded," *Business Horizons*, April 1968, p. 78.
[11] "Wanted: Someone to Watch the Store," *Business Week*, September 19, 1970, p. 52.
[12] Gary Johnson, "The Thinking Man's Approach to Sales-Force Scheduling," *Stores*, November 1969, p. 37; much of this section is based upon Johnson's discussion of scheduling.

[13] Laurence W. Jacobs, *Advertising and Promotion for Retailing: Text and Cases* (Glenview, Ill.: Scott, Foresman and Co., 1972), p. 198.
[14] Dale Varble and L. E. Bergerson, "The Use and Facets of PMs—A Survey of Retailers," *Journal of Retailing*, Winter 1972–73, p. 40; the findings mentioned later in the paragraph also come from this article.
[15] "Wanted: Someone to Watch the Store," *Business Week*, September 19, 1970, p. 57.
[16] Various details of this recommendation are drawn from the timeless article by Edwin W. Crooks, Jr., "Improving Department Store Selling, *Journal of Retailing*, Summer 1962, pp. 34–40.
[17] Higbee's videotape training program is described in Wayne T. Szmyt, "Selling Your Products to Your Salespeople," *Stores*, October 1971, pp. 14–15.
[18] "Wanted: Someone to Watch the Store," *Business Week*, September 19, 1970, p. 52.
[19] This statement and the following list of rewards are contained in Seymour Helfant, *Training and Motivating Retail Sales People* (New York: National Retail Merchants Association, 1969), pp. 22ff.

QUESTIONS AND ASSIGNMENTS

1. Talk with five consumers about the sales help they received when they last shopped for an item with at least a $10 price tag. Was it excellent, satisfactory, or poor? What aspects of the salespeople's efforts were generally singled out for praise or criticism?
2. Based on the small survey above and on your personal observations, do you think the quality of retail selling is good or poor? Are your observations those of a consumer or those of a potential retail manager? Might there be a difference of opinion depending on the point of view you used?
3. The chapter discusses various reasons for and shortcomings of self-service operations. Considering these, do you think the self-service trend will continue? Why or why not?
4. Visit a clothing store and an appliance outlet and ask at least one salesperson in each place whether they ordinarily rely on any kind of selling procedure such as formula selling. If so, what steps are contained in the procedure? To what extent do they adapt it to different situations?
5. What are the three types of personal selling? Which is the most demanding, and why?
6. Specifically, what offerings besides furniture ordinarily require creative selling? What special selling skills are necessary in selling each of these offerings effectively?
7. Check with a local department store and clothing store. Who in the firm has overall responsibility for personal selling? Does this arrangement coincide with what the chapter said about responsibility for personal selling in larger retail firms?
8. What two forms of incentives are used in compensating retail salespeople? Talk to two clothing retailers about whether they use either form of incentive.
9. The chapter emphasized the importance and shortcomings of retail sales training. Based on what you have read, suggest one additional way in which training of salespeople could be improved. If necessary, discuss this matter with whomever is in charge of training at a large local retail store.
10. It has been said that a basic cause of personal selling problems is low pay. Consider the following proposal: "It's not surprising that salespeople in stores aren't dedicated, considering what they are paid. If their wages

were increased by 10 percent—maybe even 25 percent—they would be more motivated. Then more transactions would result *and*, at the same time, customers would be more satisfied." Would this proposal solve the personal selling problem? Why or why not?

11. Of the various recommended ways of improving retail selling, which one would you suggest that a merchant concentrate on initially? Explain why you feel this management practice has the greatest potential?

ANSWERS TO REVIEW BOX QUESTIONS

Box 15:1

1. the activities of retail employees in helping shoppers buy satisfying offerings
2. the outlet's desired image *or* nature of the offering
3. one of the following: consumers' shopping behavior and preferences have changed since World War II; early self-service outlets were successful; or wage rates have been rising

Box 15:2

1. determining needs
2. adaptive formula
3. approaching and greeting (*first* would also be a correct answer)
4. creative selling

Box 15:3

1. ability
2. manpower planning
3. scheduling
4. one of the following: it may be less effective than emphasis on another retailing mix element; manufacturers who pay the cost may want to dictate store policies

Box 15:4

1. eliminate unnecessary salespeople
2. temporary transfer of salespeople from overstaffed to busy departments
3. continuing employees and new part-timers

Questions and Assignments

Advertising

Advertising is usually the last element to be developed in the retailing mix, because its content and approach depend on decisions regarding target markets, desired image, location, offerings, and prices. However, general advertising requirements are ordinarily considered in the early stages of putting together a retailing mix.

Because advertising is non-personal communication, it is more closely related to supportive promotion methods than to personal selling. However, criticism frequently leveled at advertising is very much like that directed at personal selling: ineffective, unimaginative, high pressure, an expense that increases prices to the consumer. Unfortunately, such criticism is often justified, and for this reason the quality of retail advertising must be a prime concern of retail firms. The first step toward improving the quality of advertising is an understanding of the purposes, limitations, and types of this form of promotion as well as who is responsible for advertising planning and control and how an advertising program is developed—all goals of this chapter.

THE NATURE OF ADVERTISING

Advertising has been defined as "any form of paid impersonal presentation of goods, services, or ideas for the purpose of inducing people to buy or to act favorably on what is called to their attention."[1] There are two key words in this definition that distinguish advertising from some other forms of promotion. Advertising is *paid*, unlike publicity; and it is *impersonal*, unlike face-to-face selling. Also important to remember is that advertising is used to promote *ideas* as well as products and services.

Purposes and Limitations

As with other forms of promotion, advertising aims to produce profitable sales volume. Advertising shares with personal selling and supportive methods the more specific purposes of promotion: to sell specific offerings, to assist in creating and sustaining the desired image, and to generate shopper traffic. It contributes to these purposes by:

- Presenting the outlet's offerings and describing their attractive features
- Reminding customers of the popular brands stocked by the store
- Telling consumers about new offerings or supplementary services
- Informing consumers of a supportive promotion such as a fashion show or contest
- Changing people's attitudes about the outlet—for example, that it has low, not high, prices
- Showing why the outlet should be the first place to shop for an offering

A retail firm's advertising often affects its employees as well as consumers. In fact, some stores deliberately seek to affect their employees with advertising. Consider the following example.[2] The slogan, "Good Ground Beef Is the Sign of a Good Store," has been promoted by Sipes Food Markets in Tulsa. The slogan was intended to reassure customers about the quality of an important item. Advertising this slogan affected the meat managers, too. It gave them pride in their work, since management publicly noted their role in the total store's success.

Although generally recognized as a powerful retailing tool, advertising has definite limitations. Specifically, advertising cannot repeatedly sell an offering which is unattractive to consumers, it cannot continually attract shoppers if they are not served well once they are in the outlet, and it cannot sell merchandise which is out of stock or not in its proper location. All of these conditions suggest that the rest of the retailing mix must complement advertising for it to be effective. Furthermore, advertising cannot accomplish much if it is used in very small amounts or sporadically. As noted by one advertising specialist, "There is a threshold level of impact for advertising, and if a store cannot afford to advertise at a sufficiently high level the manager would probably be better off putting his money in other forms of promotion."[3] This suggests the need for a definite commitment of funds to advertising and also continuity in this form of promotion.

Expenditures and Organizational Arrangements

At least $7 billion is spent annually on retail advertising.[4] Another way of looking at the magnitude of advertising expenditures is to relate them to other budget items: "In some instances, advertising is the second largest item, following salaries, in a retailer's operating budget." Even more pertinent to our study of retail management are the amounts spent by different kinds of retailers and the responsibility for these expenditures.

VARIATION BY TYPE OF RETAILER

The amount spent on advertising varies greatly according to the type and size of a retail operation. Of course, larger firms with their greater financial resources can spend more on advertising than small merchants. Still, two retailers of approximately equal size often logically spend vastly different amounts on advertising. Why? The reason is that the planned significance of advertising within the promotion blend should vary, depending on factors such as the outlet's offerings and the number and vigor of competitors.

Out of every $1 of sales revenue, how much do you think retail stores spend on advertising? An estimate ranging from nothing to 5¢ would be correct. For example, most barber shops spend relatively little on advertising — perhaps occasional small newspaper ads, maybe nothing at all. Beauty parlors, on the other hand, spend more on advertising.

The few available figures on advertising expenditures illustrate the variations across different kinds of retailers:[5]

Supermarket chains spend 1.2 percent of sales on promotional activities, almost all of which is for advertising.

Self-service discount department stores spend 2.3 percent.

Large department stores, with annual sales over $50 million, spend 2.6 percent on sales promotion for their upstairs departments, with the bulk going to advertising, and another 8.0 percent on selling salaries.

Small department stores, with annual sales in the $1 million range, spend 2.5 percent on advertising plus 8.5 percent on selling salaries.

The fact that promotion expenditures vary according to the nature of the offering is shown by the figures for department stores with annual sales of $20 to $50 million:[6]

	Sales promotion costs (primarily advertising)	Selling salaries
Adult female apparel	3.0%	6.7%
Adult male apparel	2.2	7.4
Children's clothing	2.0	8.8
Apparel fabrics	3.1	13.9
Costume jewelry	2.5	10.8
Cosmetics, toiletries	1.5	8.2
Furniture and bedding	4.1	7.9

EXPENDITURES BY SPECIFIC RETAILERS

Advertising by many retailers, notably large chains and franchise systems, runs into millions of dollars. The biggest spender among food-service systems is McDonald's, which spent $38 million in 1972, the bulk going for television advertising. Retail chains among the top 100 national advertisers include J.C. Penney, which spent $129 million in 1972, and A & P, $81 million.[7]

But the heaviest retail advertiser is Sears. Including an estimated $200 million in newspapers plus $123 million for catalogs, the largest retailer spent about $470 million in 1972, or about 4.8 percent of sales. Sears relied on *local* media and catalogs for many years. It first used *national* media in 1955 when it spent $435,000 for advertising in magazines and *farm publications* (which suggests one of Sears' target markets during the 1950s). In recent years, Sears has moved heavily into national media such as network television, particularly sports programs, and magazines such as *Sports Illustrated*.

Remember, though, that for every tremendously heavy advertiser like McDonald's, Penney's, or Sears, thousands of independent merchants spend little on advertising. They either cannot afford to spend more or choose not to.

RESPONSIBILITY

The responsibility for advertising planning and expenditures varies, depending primarily on the size and type of store. In a small outlet, the owner or manager ordinarily has this responsibility, while department stores usually have a formal promotion division which handles advertising. Retail chains often have a central advertising department which establishes strategies, serves in a staff capacity to the stores, and coordinates local programs.

While most manufacturers have advertising agencies handle their advertising, retailers generally handle it themselves. Many retail firms think the "do-it-yourself" approach is more economical. Others feel it's necessary because of the short times in which retail advertising must be developed. Retailers that advertise nationally are most likely to use advertising agencies.

What are called advertising service companies also can be useful to small independent retailers. These companies differ from agencies mainly in that they provide creative skills only, specifically sample newspaper ads and artwork for a particular type of merchandise.

Many media, especially newspapers, have advertising specialists to assist retailers who lack special skills or equipment. These artists and copywriters as well as the mat services (companies which supply molds of ads from which printing plates are made) subscribed to by many newspapers can be especially valuable to specialty shops and other small merchants.

REVIEW BOX 16:1

1. Retail advertising can be defined as _____.
2. One reason that the relative amount spent on advertising often varies from one retail firm to the next is that the firms may differ in size. Another reason is that _____.

The Nature of Advertising

FIGURE 16-1

A sample regular-price promotional ad

TYPES OF RETAIL ADVERTISING

As you see or hear retailers' ads, perhaps you notice basic differences among them. Some promote an item, while others promote an event, idea, or image. Basically, retail advertising can be categorized according to *what is featured* in the advertising and also according to *who pays for it*. Each retail ad, therefore, must be described by two labels. The ad in Figure 16-1, for example, is (1) promotional and (2) individual cooperative in nature, as we shall soon see.

What is Featured

Retail advertising can often be categorized as promotional or institutional, according to what is featured in the message. However, many advertisements fall somewhere in the middle of these classifications, being a combination of the two. Thus, there is actually a continuum of categories which can be represented as shown in Figure 16-2. In the discussion which follows, newspaper ads are used as examples because retailers spend more on advertising in newspapers than in any other medium.

Promotional	Combination of promotional and institutional	Institutional
Regular price Reduced price Clearance sale		Image Announcements Public service

FIGURE 16-2

Categorizing advertisements

PROMOTIONAL

Promotional ads feature specific offerings of the retail outlet. They are designed to create store traffic and sales immediately, or at least quite soon. To motivate consumers, prices of offerings are usually given in promotional ads. Most retail firms concentrate on promotional advertising, directing almost all of their budget to this kind. This is understandable since profits cannot result until customers are attracted to the outlet and persuaded to buy.

Promotional advertising includes three distinct types: regular price, reduced price, and clearance sale. Examples of the three types are shown in Figures 16-1, 16-3, 16-4. Regular-price advertising emphasizes the merits of the offerings themselves. A clothing store may talk about the fashionability and workmanship of the featured items; a restaurant might promote several new menu items.

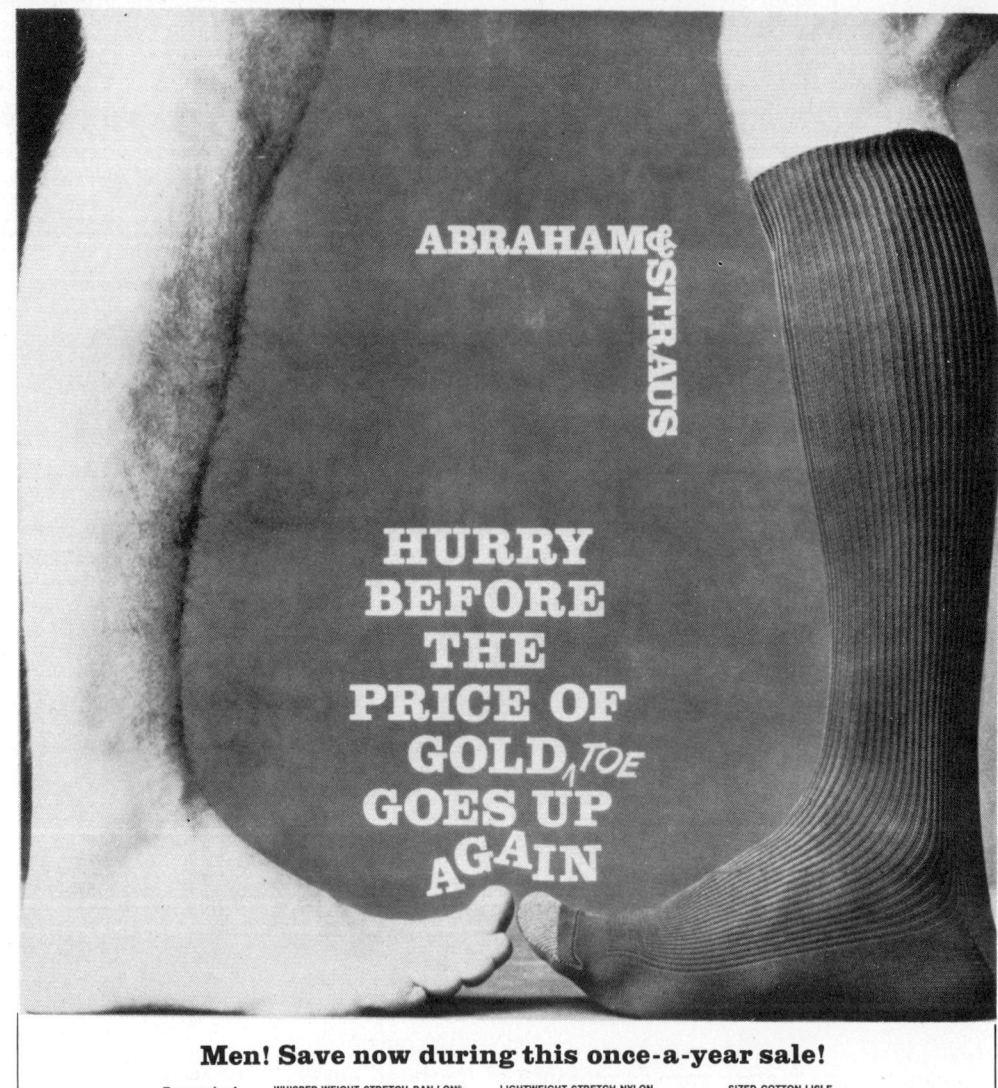

FIGURE 16-3

A sample reduced-price promotional ad

FIGURE 16-4

A sample clearance-sale promotional ad

Some stores seldom use regular-price advertising. Their strategy is to emphasize sale prices so that consumers come to think of the firm as having the lowest prices in town or bargains throughout the store. This strategy is reflected in the advertising of discount house chains such as K-Mart and Korvette.

Reduced-price and clearance-sale advertising are similar in that both feature lower-than-normal prices. However, they differ in the type of merchandise advertised. Clearance sales are run to "clear out" merchandise that is out of style or out of season, in odd sizes or colors, remnants, or that has been around too long and will be less salable in the future. Reduced-price advertising, on the other hand, features offerings which are reasonably attractive even without large price reductions, such as popular record albums or dry cleaning of men's and ladies' suits. Merchandise in reduced-price advertising ordinarily comes from the store's regular stocks or is specially purchased for a sale.

INSTITUTIONAL

In contrast to promotional advertising, the institutional type promotes aspects of the outlet itself or other facts or ideas which the retailer wants to communicate. Usually the desired payoff is profitable sales volume, although this kind seeks longer-term effects than the promotional advertising. Whereas promotional advertising is direct, institutional advertising is indirect.

Institutional advertising includes three primary types: image, announcements, and public service. The most common type of institutional ad is intended to build the outlet's image. Figure 16-5 shows one message which might accomplish this. Also the firm's large size can be stressed to remind customers that it has volume buying power or that such growth followed years of serving and satisfying the community. Or an image-type ad might present "facts and figures" on the outlet's generally low prices. Other approaches are to describe the outlet's variety of merchandise and supplementary services or how the store always obtains the latest styles.

Occasionally, announcements of changes in store policies or operations are necessary or desirable. For example, in late 1973 various grocery stores announced through advertising a switch to shorter store hours in order to conserve scarce forms of energy. Auto dealers and furniture stores often announce the addition of a salesperson who is well known in the community. This is done to attract friends and former customers of the new employee.

As Figure 16-6 illustrates, announcements are viewed by some retailers as opportunities to enhance the firm's image while informing shoppers of an important fact. This tactic is commonly used when an outlet adds a new line of offerings or a supplementary service.

There is one basic consideration in using the kinds of institutional ad-

FIGURE 16-5

A sample image-type institutional ad

FIGURE 16-6

A sample announcement-type institutional ad

FIGURE 16-7

An ad prepared and paid for under horizontal co-operative arrangements

vertising just discussed. An institutional message must tell consumers something of interest *to them*—not something of interest only to retail managers. For example, a store may announce a change in its credit plans. Without further explanation, many consumers might react with a "Who cares?" To be worthwhile, this institutional ad should explain how the new plan would reduce customers' finance charges on overdue accounts, for example.

Public service advertising, sponsored on infrequent occasions by retailers, promotes ideas or a cause which a merchant feels is in the public's best interest. Even though the ideas or cause may be unrelated to the outlet's business, this type of ad can affect the image of its sponsor. For instance, an outlet could damage its image by promoting a controversial or unpopular cause, such as building (or not building) a new civic center or Sunday closings (or openings) for retail outlets.

COMBINATION
Combination retail advertising represents a *planned* attempt to blend the institutional and promotional approaches in the same advertising. An example would be a retailer advertising with two headlines, one highlighting the several items advertised and the other making a point about the store itself. This second headline might be: ". . . More reasons why Fargo's is *your* fashion center." Or, combination advertising can be achieved by featuring a single product or service in what is primarily an institutional ad.

Payment Arrangements

Not all retail advertising is developed and paid for by individual retailers. Thus, in terms of payment arrangements, there are three kinds of advertising: individual, horizontal cooperative, and vertical cooperative.

It is fairly simple to figure out what is being featured in any ad. However, it's often impossible to pinpoint payment arrangements just by hearing or seeing the ad itself. In fact, many retailers and their suppliers prefer that the arrangements cannot be identified.

INDIVIDUAL
Individual advertising is advertising paid for entirely by the retailer. Sometimes, an individual ad is prepared with the help of an agency or mats from a service. Thus the appearance or sound of an ad does not indicate whether it is individual or cooperative. This is determined not by observing the ad but by asking the merchants whether they or a supplier paid for the ad.

HORIZONTAL COOPERATIVE
Under this arrangement, a group of retailers jointly sponsors advertising and shares its costs. The thinking behind horizontal cooperative advertising is that a greater impact can be achieved using combined funds. A sample is in

Figure 16-7. The participants also may work together in developing the advertising program.

Participants in horizontal cooperative advertising are often merchants in the same shopping center or area. They jointly sponsor advertising to attract more people to their vicinity. As the number of planned shopping centers is increasing, this kind of advertising should continue to grow.

Sometimes retailers who are in different areas of a city but sell the same lines of offerings use horizontal cooperative advertising. This advertising seeks to increase the *general* demand for the participants' products or services. This is the objective of the ad in Figure 16-7.

VERTICAL COOPERATIVE

Under vertical cooperative arrangements, part or all of the cost of specific advertising done by a retailer is paid by a supplier, usually a manufacturer. Suppliers want their merchandise lines sold at full price if at all possible. Therefore, with rare exceptions, these arrangements apply only to regular-price advertising. Figure 16-1 is a vertical cooperative ad.

Manufacturers of durable goods are most likely to reimburse retailers for advertising expenses. Vertical cooperative advertising is relatively common for "big-ticket" appliances, furniture, TVs, stereo equipment, and automobiles. In addition, some manufacturers underwrite their retail dealers' advertising for certain grocery items, clothing, cosmetics and toiletries, and athletic equipment.

Here's how vertical cooperative advertising typically works:

> Most contracts call for the manufacturer to pay, say, 50% of the retailer's advertising expenses, up to a total dollar figure equal to 3% or so of the store's purchases from the manufacturer. Thus, the more business done, the more points the retailer earns for advertising money. . . . Food companies generally don't even call their co-op programs 'advertising' at all but instead give the retailer a case allowance that may go for store displays, newspaper ads. . . . Some require evidence of where the money has been spent, perhaps an ad clipped from a newspaper, but many do not.[8]

While most manufacturers pay just part of the advertising cost, a few cover the total cost. In either case, the retailer purchases the advertising and is later reimbursed. Assistance in preparing ads is also provided by some manufacturers as part of a cooperative arrangement.

Vertical cooperative advertising provides benefits to both manufacturers and retailers. From a retail firm's standpoint, co-op arrangements increase the money available for advertising. Assume a store manager plans to spend $1,000 in advertising for a particular department or merchandise line. Under co-op arrangements with two manufacturers, he receives a $150 reimbursement. This "extra" $150 can be spent on additional advertising for this or different merchandise, or it can be used to cover other operating expenses.

Types of Retail Advertising

Furthermore, ads provided by manufacturers are often better than the merchant's own efforts. This is especially true for TV commercials. Most retailers, creating advertising strictly for their own use, ordinarily cannot afford the expense of high-caliber commercials. A manufacturer, however, will spend a substantial amount on a co-op commercial, since he knows it will be used by numerous retailers.

Vertical cooperative advertising has drawbacks from both parties' standpoints. Several in particular affect retailers. First, the ads provided by suppliers may not be in tune with the retailer's image, advertising approach, or the local situation. It would be an error to run such ads. Also, cooperative advertising funds may entice a retailer to stock merchandise which does not match the desired store image or simply duplicates merchandise already carried.

Unless they are careful, small independent stores can miss out on cooperative advertising funds. Some manufacturers would prefer to avoid co-op arrangements with small retailers, feeling that administrative troubles (such as having to then make small payments to numerous firms) exceed the benefits. However, not receiving these funds and assistance can hurt a small store's efforts to compete against sizeable stores and chains.

Under the Robinson-Patman Act, all retailers selling a line of merchandise must have an opportunity to share proportionally in a supplier's cooperative advertising program. This part of the law protects small retailers in particular. In recent years, the Federal Trade Commission has been "bearing down on marketers to make sure that they let small retailers share in co-op programs on a scale proportionate with giant chains."[9] In other words, if a manufacturer reimburses chains for advertising expenses equal to 3 percent of their sales volume in the advertised item, the same arrangements must be made available to all stores carrying the item.

Since vertical cooperative advertising can be a real bonus to a promotion budget, retail managers should seize *suitable* co-op arrangements. However, they should do so cautiously:

> Only shortsighted stores ever let themselves whore for vendor money [cooperative advertising funds]. Long-sighted stores insist on remaining ladies. They'll gladly take the vendor's money but . . . only as . . . deemed appropriate to their considered advertising image.[10]

REVIEW BOX 16:2

1. Retail advertising can be categorized according to what is featured and also according to _____.
2. Promotional advertising is designed to _____.
3. When a group of retailers jointly sponsors advertising and shares its costs, this is _____ advertising.

DEVELOPING AN ADVERTISING PROGRAM

Familiar with the general purposes, limitations, and types of retail advertising, a merchant is ready to develop an advertising program. This involves determining specific objectives, a buying theme, a total budget and its allo-

FIGURE 16-8

Diagram of a supermarket chain's objectives

Source: John O. Whitney, "Better Results from Retail Advertising," *Harvard Business Review*, May-June 1970. Reprinted by permission.

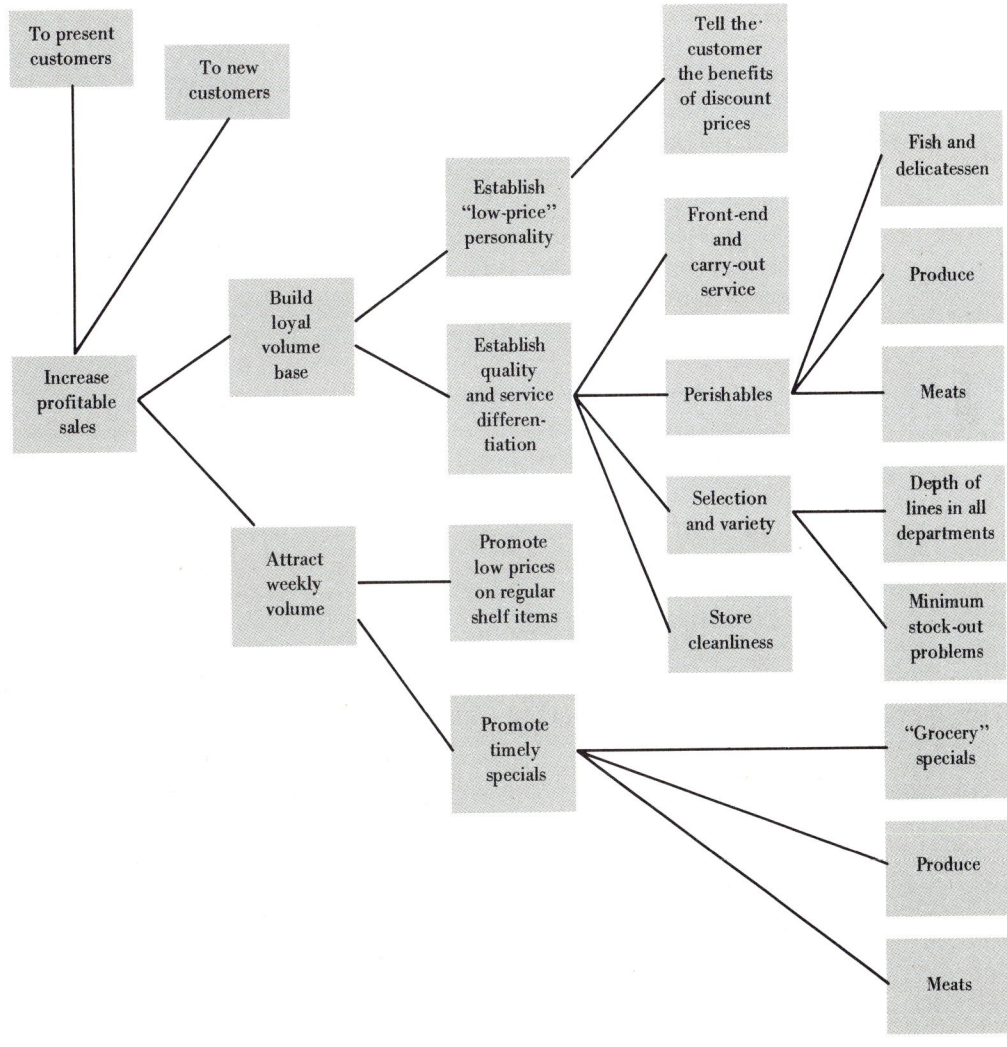

cation, and media to be used. When this is done, the merchant can prepare individual ads.

Set Specific Objectives

Advertising planning begins with a decision on specific advertising objectives. It would be foolish to plan the *how* (methods) of advertising before determining *who* is the target and *what* is to be accomplished. The nature of advertising objectives and the process of setting them can be further explained by an example. After decisions to drop trading stamps and to discount prices, a large supermarket chain stated its objectives as follows:

> At this time it is most important to communicate our new price policy to consumers. We also must simultaneously reassure our regular customers that we continue to offer the quality and service they have come to expect.[11]

A statement like this is ordinarily developed jointly by top-level executives, merchandising personnel, and the advertising staff. When agreed upon, it provides the necessary direction for advertising and other departments.

An *objectives diagram* represents an alternative to the written statement. A hierarchy of objectives as in Figure 16-8 has significant advantages. Short-range objectives (attract weekly volume) are separated from long-range ones (build loyal volume base). Since both are visible, however, discussion of one without neglecting the other is possible. While relative importance of the objectives is not indicated, the diagram provides a basis for considering their importance.

Notice that objectives must state *who* as well as *what*. Advertising's target audiences must be specified. In the example above, one objective pertains to all grocery shoppers and the other strictly to the chain's regular customers. To cite another example, in the early 1970s McDonald's decided to aim its advertising at two groups: children, with Ronald McDonald as spokesman, and adults, using the "You Deserve a Break Today..." theme.

Identify a Buying Theme

The focus now shifts to *how* the objectives can be accomplished. What we call a buying theme consists of benefits the consumer will receive by shopping at an outlet and purchasing an advertised offering. Facts alone do not form a buying theme. Thus it is not enough to promote "wide assortments" or "convenient locations." However, consumers just might notice a theme such as "WIDE, WIDE assortments so that you can find exactly what you want in style, size, and color" or "Conveniently located to save you time, which we know you have too little of." Since these statements clearly show how a customer will benefit, they are complete (but not very creative) buying themes.

Despite their importance, buying themes are often not included in advertising or are left incomplete. Another error is not reviewing buying themes periodically and updating them as necessary. As the economy fluctuates, as competitors adopt new strategies, as consumers themselves change, the benefits in last year's buying theme may lose their importance to consumers. A study several years ago showed, for example, that "two out of three leading supermarket chains switched their main advertising themes in 1971, and more than half of these changes came in response to such customer issues as ecology and product labeling."[12]

Establish a Budget

While few retail firms have a total promotion budget, many establish a specific advertising budget. A necessary step, it is also a difficult one since budgeting methods seem to be either too simple or "easier said than done." Whatever the specific approach used, the starting point is a general estimate of sales volume during the future time period under consideration. The retail manager must come up with one figure which combines how much sales *should be* and realistically *could be*.

Because of its simplicity, the most frequently used budgeting method is probably the percentage-of-sales approach. Basically, it involves two steps. First, the ratio of advertising to sales in the past is figured. Second, this ratio is applied to the sales volume estimate. Here is how a restaurant manager would use this approach to budget advertising: Last year's sales were $230,000, and advertising costs totaled just under $2,400. The advertising-to-sales ratio was approximately 1 percent. Next year the manager is aiming for $250,000 in sales, which he considers a realistic goal. When the manager calculates 1 percent of $250,000, an advertising budget of around $2,500 is established.

This method works satisfactorily when marketplace conditions are very stable. However, great stability is the exception, rather than the rule, in today's retail marketplace. For this reason, the percentage-of-sales method is too simple to be worthwhile in most situations. In addition, there is no guarantee that the past ratio of advertising to sales was correct; a different ratio might have produced better results. Also, the method does not take into account competitors' advertising levels. Don't be mistaken. A store should not base its advertising budget solely on what competitors are doing. But, as with other retailing mix decisions, competitive activities must be evaluated.

A better, but more difficult, budgeting method is the task-and-factors approach, sometimes called the objective-and-task approach. This method begins with the sales objective, the task, and then involves two related steps: First, the advertising level and approach necessary to reach the objective must be estimated. Second, the planned budget must be considered in relation to specific factors in the outlet's competitive situation. Among the factors that affect the necessary level of advertising are:

Type of offerings. For example, stores selling convenience goods ordinarily have to advertise less than stores selling shopping goods.
Convenience of location. Some stores need to advertise quite a bit to attract shoppers to free-standing or out-of-the-way locations.
Desired image. Stores employing an aggressive merchandising strategy advertise extensively.

Additional factors include length of time the outlet has been in business, size and financial resources of the outlet, and competitors' advertising levels. How much a store *should* advertise and how much it *can afford to* are two different things, however. Stores lacking adequate financial resources have to settle for an advertising level which might be less than necessary to achieve sales objectives.

Admittedly, this method is time-consuming and difficult. The main difficulty is in accurately judging the level of advertising needed to achieve an objective. Still, this general method is recommended—alone or combined with the percentage-of-sales method—because it is both systematic and sound. It considers the advertising job which must be done as well as other pertinent factors and it looks to the future rather than to the past.

Allocate the Budget

Once the total budget is established, it must be allocated with respect to lines of offerings, timing of the advertising, and media to be employed. The first two decisions are discussed here; media are discussed in a separate section.

ADVERTISING SPECIFIC LINES

Allocating the advertising budget by lines of offerings involves deciding upon the extent to which different lines (and departments) will be advertised. Two common procedures for doing this might be termed *bottom-up* and *top-down*. In the bottom-up approach, department managers develop advertising budgets for their individual departments. These budget requests are reviewed by the promotion or advertising director. Departmental budgets are adjusted, as necessary, so that they build up to the planned total budget size. An advantage of this method is that department managers' knowledge about advertising requirements for various lines of offerings is used.

In the second approach, the promotion director breaks down the total budget by departments. This often involves cooperation with merchandising personnel and department heads. The advantages of this method are that the promotion director can take an impartial view of departmental advertising requirements and can consider each department's role in the overall merchandising strategy.

A third approach, an experimental method, involves systematically testing over time different allocations to the store's merchandise divisions.[13] The divisions' resulting profits under conditions of normal, "more than normal," and "less than normal" advertising are compared to determine the best allocation.

Whichever method is used, some lines (or departments) will receive more than would appear appropriate when only sales volume is considered. Others will receive less, of course. Two factors explain such variations: (1) Because of their nature, some offerings require more advertising than others for effective merchandising. (2) The role within the overall retailing strategy can differ from one line (or department) to the next. Not only is this possible; it is also logical. For example, a family clothing store may allocate much of its advertising budget to the women's clothing division because it is viewed as the major opportunity for very profitable sales. On the other hand, the children's clothing division, not very profitable but required to satisfy customers with children, is advertised little.

TIMING OF ADVERTISING

The budget also must be divided over the entire time period. There is much disagreement among retail and advertising managers over the best timing of advertising, a situation that makes this an area where a decision-maker's judgment and experience are especially valuable.

The starting point for this decision is an analysis of *relative* monthly sales figures. Each month's proportion of total annual sales can be calculated. Outlets selling completely non-seasonal offerings would have a constant sales cycle, about 8.33 percent each month (sales for total year equal 100 percent divided by 12 months). Grocery stores, perhaps more than other retail outlets, have a constant sales cycle.

In most kinds of outlets, sales vary considerably from one month to the next. For example, the sales cycle of year-round toy stores and departments looks something like this:

	J	F	M	A	M	J	J	A	S	O	N	D
Monthly sales as percent of annual sales	3	3	5	7	5	4	4	4	4	6	15	40

Too often, monthly advertising allocations are simply set the same as the sales cycle. This approach, without modification, is inadequate because two facts are overlooked: (1) advertising is supposed to *cause* sales, and (2) there is a *time lag* between advertising and resulting purchases by consumers.

Based on the above, we can suggest a general guideline regarding timing of advertising for offerings whose sales normally vary on a monthly basis. That is, advertising should lead—rather than match—the normal sales cycle. The appropriate lead time depends on specific circumstances but ordinarily should be from one to several weeks. For example, a sporting goods department should start heavy advertising shortly before the beginning of a particular sports season. In the case of toy stores, advertising should be heavier in October and November than would be justified by sales. The reason: The store must make its bid for Christmas shoppers. As shown below, advertising may be allocated generally according to the sales cycle the rest of the year:

	J	F	M	A	M	J	J	A	S	O	N	D
Monthly sales as percent of annual sales	3	3	5	7	5	4	4	4	4	6	15	40
Monthly advertising as percent of annual advertising	2	2	8*	6*	5*	3	3	3	3	5	25	35

* slightly heavier advertising in advance of Easter and summer sports season

A much different alternative is to allocate advertising funds *opposite* the sales cycle. According to this countercyclical strategy, much advertising is run when sales normally do *not* occur, and advertising is reduced during normally big-volume months. However, this approach to allocating an advertising budget usually is criticized along the following lines:

> The underlying assumption of trying to base advertising expenditures on the sales cycle is that there are certain times of the year when customers are in a mood for buying the items carried by a store. The contra-sales-cycle [countercyclical] strategy takes dollars from a time when it is relatively easy to influence customers and spends this money at a time when most customers are not really in a buying mood. During this "off season" it will probably cost more to move a customer to action. This inefficiency of ad dollars is the biggest disadvantage.[14]

Therefore, countercyclical timing of advertising is not advisable in most situations.

REVIEW BOX 16:3

1. There are several steps involved in developing an advertising program, the first of which is to _____.
2. In the task-and-factors approach to establishing an advertising budget, one of the factors that affects the necessary level of advertising is _____.
3. To have department managers develop budgets for their individual departments is the first step in the _____ approach to allocating an advertising budget.

SELECTING SUITABLE MEDIA

The preceding sections covered *how much* to spend on advertising, *when* to spend it, and *on what* lines of offerings. This section looks at *where* to spend these funds, namely what media would be suitable.[15] Initially, we will look at individual media and then will consider the process by which media are selected.

Media Profiles

To ensure that a potentially effective medium is not overlooked, a retail manager needs to be familiar with all available media. Each medium discussed here can logically be used by retailers, depending on the circumstances of the particular advertising program.

NEWSPAPERS

Of the various media, newspapers far and away are most frequently employed by retailers. While broad statistics are not available, it is safe to say that most merchants who advertise allocate two-thirds or more of their funds to newspapers. The "average" supermarket chain, for instance, devotes 68 percent of its budget to newspapers, 8 percent to TV, 6 percent to direct mail, and the rest to other media.[16] Of course, retail firms with different objectives and finances divide their budgets differently. Sears, as mentioned earlier, puts about 40 to 45 percent of its total budget into newspapers.

Four distinct types of papers are found in large metropolitan areas: *dailies*, with morning and/or evening editions; *Sunday editions*, which have larger circulations, contain more pages and ads, and—many retailers feel—are read more thoroughly than dailies; *special-audience papers*, tailored to an ethnic group or for residents of certain areas in a city; and *shoppers' news*, usually distributed free of charge and designed specifically for retail advertising purposes.

We will focus on the relative merits of dailies, although many of these points also apply to the other types. Newspapers' first advantage is their blanket coverage of an area—most people at least glance through the daily paper. This is why retailers with broad markets, especially supermarket chains and department stores, concentrate on newspapers. Second, a newspaper ad is a relatively low-cost way of communicating a message. Of course, this depends greatly on the extent to which a retail firm's target audience matches a paper's circulation. Flexibility is the third "plus" of newspapers. Ads of various sizes and shapes can be used. Also, the time between submission of an ad and when it is run is quite short. Usually an ad submitted by noon appears in the next day's paper.

Newspapers have two notable disadvantages. First, blanket coverage is not desired by retailers, notably small firms, trying to reach a select audience. In these cases, blanket coverage would be a waste. Problems in reproducing ads in newspapers represent a second disadvantage. High-speed, rushed printing of newspapers often hurts an ad's appearance. Furthermore, color in newspaper ads is an expensive process, too expensive for most merchants.

MAGAZINES

This second print medium is not widely used by retailers. However, national chains seem to be increasing their use of magazines. As noted several years ago, "the country's two leading mass retailers—Sears, Roebuck & Company and Montgomery Ward & Company—have turned to magazine advertising to upgrade their corporate images and spur sales."[17]

National magazines offer retailers two main benefits. First, magazines are read, and perhaps re-read, over several days or weeks, whereas newspapers are thrown away more quickly. This means one magazine ad can make a repeated impression on the same reader. The possibility of high-quality, color ads is a second plus.

The main disadvantage of magazine advertising is the difficulty of matching a retail firm's target audience with a magazine's circulation. In recent years, some national magazines have developed various regional and local editions to make their medium practical for business firms that do not operate nationwide.

RADIO

While both newspapers and magazines are *print media*, radio and television are *broadcast media*. Both broadcast media sell national advertising time. Because of its broad coverage (and hence high dollar cost), only very large chains or groups of franchisees can afford national broadcast advertising. However, individual stations sell local, or spot, advertising which is practical for local retailers. The relative merits of *local* broadcast advertising are discussed below.

The first advantage of radio is that it can blanket a market, since almost everyone owns and occasionally listens to a radio. Moreover, radio reaches consumers in their cars as well as at home or work. Flexibility is a second advantage. The lead time is relatively short. Furthermore, since there are more radio stations than newspapers or TV stations in most communities, a retailer has a better chance of matching its target audience with some station's listeners. Sound is a third advantage of radio. In print media, consumers have to *read* the advertising messages. With radio, however, consumers are *told* the message by an announcer. Persuasive tones, sound effects, and music can be combined to increase a commercial's impact.

Two disadvantages of radio reduce its usefulness somewhat. First, it is the only completely nonvisual medium. This means that consumers cannot be shown the offering or the outlet. Second, a disadvantage shared with TV, radio advertising does not involve anything physical which the consumer might keep as a reminder. This drawback is serious when various features or prices or an outlet's new location and phone number must be communicated.

TELEVISION

Perhaps more than any other advertising medium, TV has the greatest impact on consumers because it combines both sight and sound. This is its foremost advantage. Hence, TV is especially appropriate for emphasizing an item's appearance or demonstrating an offering's use or performance.

Television's first disadvantage is that its messages are not physical, which makes them less permanent. A second, greater, disadvantage is cost: TV time is quite expensive, and the commercials themselves are more costly to produce than other kinds of ads. Television might be the ideal medium for a large number of retailers, but many cannot afford it.

DIRECT MAIL

This medium consists of advertising pieces — catalogs, letters, brochures, or postcards — mailed to consumers. While direct mail is the primary advertising effort for many small merchants, larger retail firms ordinarily view it as a complementary form of advertising.

Direct mail's first advantage is that, unlike other media's uncontrolled circulations, the retailer can decide who will receive the advertising. He develops and maintains the mailing list and can eliminate waste circulation. A second advantage, related to the first, is that direct mail may be the least expensive way of reaching actual or potential customers. Of course, direct mail becomes quite expensive when the costs of preparing and producing the advertising are high or waste is not eliminated.

Some consumers think of direct-mail advertising as "junk mail" and therefore do not open it. This is its first disadvantage. Direct-mail advertisers know that it is one thing to get advertising into someone's hands and quite another to get them to read it. To a large extent, this general problem of getting people to recognize and think about a specific message applies to all media. The growing number of ads "bombarding" consumers each day makes this even more difficult.

Good mailing lists are difficult and expensive to compile, a second disadvantage. A list of the firm's charge accounts is a starting point for many mailings, and additional names of shoppers can be obtained from contest entry blanks, layaway slips, and special-order forms. Newcomers' names are available from the local Chamber of Commerce, and some lists can be purchased from firms which specialize in list compilation. Naturally, whether a particular source is suitable depends on the target audience for the mailing.

OTHER MEDIA

Besides the five media mentioned above, two others are regularly used by some retailers:

Outdoor advertising is of two forms: billboards and transit advertising. In recent years, billboards have been criticized as "unsightly" and have declined in usage. Transit advertising includes signs inside or mounted on the outside of buses, taxis, commuter trains, and subway cars. Outdoor advertising may be useful in communicating a brief message, perhaps an outlet's slogan or location.

"Yellow pages" in telephone directories are useful—even crucial—to some retail firms. This medium is particularly suitable for retailers who are trying to inform newcomers about their business, sell offerings that are purchased only infrequently or in emergencies, or sell merchandise for which consumers shop around and make comparisons.

The Selection Decision

Actually selecting media for an advertising program consists of two steps: (1) determining which general medium (or media mix) would be most suitable and (2) choosing a specific vehicle from among various alternatives in the medium selected. In other words, the retail manager first decides whether to use newspapers, magazines, radio, television, direct mail, or some mix. Assume that radio is chosen as the appropriate medium. Then, since most communities have several radio stations, the manager must decide which would be most efficient. Of course, when there is only one possibility (a single newspaper or TV station in an area), this second decision is not necessary.

DETERMINING A SUITABLE MEDIUM Basically, the first step is a process of elimination. Media are reviewed in terms of the advantages and disadvantages already discussed, with unsuitable ones eliminated from consideration. In some cases, the objectives of planned advertising narrow the alternatives considerably.

Suppose, for example, an automotive repair shop wants to promote its new diagnostic equipment. The manager feels that "this equipment has to be seen in action to be believed." Given this objective and viewpoint, TV would seem suitable. Of course, if TV is ruled out by another factor such as cost, objectives will have to be revised or the manager must change his mind about how people can be told about the equipment.

The next consideration is the target audience. The question to be answered is: Which general medium's audience best matches that group of people for whom the message is intended? To answer this, a retailer first must check the number of persons in the target audience, their location within the community, and their reading, listening, and viewing habits. Research may be necessary to develop profiles of the firm's present and potential customers which can then be compared with audience breakdowns provided by various communications vehicles or by broadcast rating services such as the Nielsen Company.

SPOTLIGHT

Which media are most suitable for a $500-million retail hardware organization?

When it comes to selecting suitable advertising media and vehicles, there are innumerable possible combinations. Appreciation of the magnitude and complexity of a media mix and how different vehicles are used to reach various portions of a target audience might be gained by reviewing an actual media plan.

Cotter & Company is a national hardware wholesaler which is wholly owned by the more than 4,700 True Value Hardware Stores. During the 1973 Christmas season, Cotter & Company implemented the following media plan for True Value Hardware Stores:

SANTA'S PREVIEW
DIRECT-MAIL CATALOG
(10,000,000 distributed)

DIRECT-MAIL

64-page edition:
Toys, Giftware, Appliances, Housewares and Tools.
40-page edition:
Giftware, Appliances, Housewares and Tools.
24-page edition:
Appliances, Housewares and Tools.

MAGAZINES

MAGAZINE ADS

Better Homes and Gardens Nov.: 2 pages, gifts; 2 pages, toys (regional editions only); and 1 column, institutional; Dec.: 3 pages, gifts; and 1 column, institutional — "Happy Holidays" record album.

Family Circle Nov.: 4 pages, housewares and gifts; Dec.: 4 pages, gifts; and 2 pages, toys (regional editions only).

House & Garden Nov.: 1 column, institutional; Dec.: ½ page, gifts; and 1 column institutional — album.

Popular Science Dec.: 1 page, sporting goods.

True Dec.: 2 pages, sporting goods and bicycles.

RADIO

CBS RADIO NETWORK

RADIO

42 commercial spots per week, starting November 5, with nationally known sportscaster, PAT SUMMERALL.

NBC RADIO NETWORK

20 commercial spots per week starting November 5, with FRANK BLAIR, celebrated newsman of the "Today Show."

Regional

Extensive spot schedules on local radio stations in five major markets: Dallas—KRLD; Kansas City—WDAF; St. Louis—KMOX; Milwaukee—WTMJ; and Chicago—WGN and WBBM.

TELEVISION

National Game Shows

Starting in late October, True Value participation in 19 major network and syndicated daytime game shows:

ABC

Let's Make A Deal
Newlywed Game
Split Second
Password
The Girl In My Life

CBS

The Price Is Right
Gambit
The Joker's Wild
$10,000 Pyramid
Match Game

NBC

Hollywood Squares
Baffle
Wizard of Odds
Three On A Match
Who, What or Where

Syndicated

What's My Line
To Tell The Truth
Beat The Clock
Concentration

Regional

True Value commercial spot announcements on local television in 13 major markets: Chicago—WGN, WBBM, 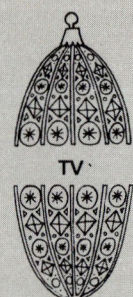 and WMAQ; Kansas City—WDAF; Milwaukee—WITI; Portland—WATU; Eugene, Ore.—KVAL; Quad Cities—WHBF; Ada, Okla.—KTEN; Green Bay—WBAY; Madison—WISC; Cedar Rapids—WMT; Rockford—WREX and WTVO; Houston—KHTV; Denver—KMGH and KWGN; and Colorado Springs—KKTV.

Regional advertising schedules in 13 major markets: Chicago Tribune, Daily News, and Sun-Times; Dallas Times Herald and Morning News; Kansas City Star; St. Louis Post-Dispatch; Milwaukee Journal and Sentinel; Lincoln Journal-Star; Detroit News and Free Press; Portland Oregonian; Seattle Times; Atlantic City Press; Madison State Journal; Fort Worth Star Telegram; and Houston Post and Chronicle.

In addition, each store was encouraged to place advertising in local media. Newspaper ad proofs and copy for radio commercials were provided by Cotter & Company.

Source: Material supplied by Cotter & Company, Chicago, and reprinted by permission.

Before deciding on a general medium or a media mix, a retailer must assemble cost information. This will indicate which media are practical within the limits of the advertising budget. Also, the efficiency of different media will be tentatively suggested. One way of determining the relative costs of different media is to consider a representative from each category. In other words, cost information is obtained for an "average" newspaper in the area, for one radio station, and so on. For direct mail, it is necessary to estimate the design, printing, paper, and mailing costs for what would be a typical direct mail effort by the retailer. Comparing these figures will indicate which media are practical from a cost standpoint.

Sample media rates are shown in Table 16-1. Note the great differences in rates between Lexington, Kentucky, a city of about 175,000, and Los Angeles, the largest metropolitan area in the United States. Merchants in either city could determine from this information which media they could afford. While the daily newspaper would be practical for many large and medium-size retail outlets in Lexington, fewer outlets of the same size in Los Angeles could afford advertising in a daily paper. These retailers would choose another medium or use a suburban newspaper.

TABLE 16-1

Sample Media Rates

Medium and vehicle	Los Angeles	Lexington, Ky.
Newspaper	*Los Angeles Times* (1,000,000+ circulation)	*Herald-Leader* (90,000 circulation)
1 page (2400 lines)	$7,080	$1,058
1000 lines	$2,950	$ 450
Radio	KFWB	WVLK
60-second commercial	$135	$24
30-second commercial	$108	$19
Television	KTTV	WKYT
60-second commercial	$1,200	$310
30-second commercial	$ 600	$155
10-second commercial	$ 300	$ 75

Note: These general figures do not reflect savings from quantity discounts for which most advertisers qualify, nor do they include the costs of producing the ads themselves.

Source: "Newspaper Rates and Data," *Standard Rates and Data*, December 15, 1973, pp. 94, 227; "Spot Radio Rates and Data," *Standard Rates and Data*, January 1, 1974, pp. 105, 322; and "Spot TV Rates and Data," *Standard Rates and Data*, December 15, 1973, pp. 57, 138.

After newspapers have been selected as the most suitable medium for certain advertising, a decision must be made as to whether the morning paper, an evening paper, or a suburban weekly will be used. Efficiency in reaching the target audience is the prime consideration. A useful figure in assessing a

CHOOSING A VEHICLE

vehicle's relative efficiency is its cost per thousand, or CPM (M is the Roman numeral for thousand). The CPM refers to viewers, listeners, or readers. Of course, other factors such as the possible impact of a medium for a certain kind of message and the extent of coverage must be taken into account as well.

Another factor is the CPM figure related to the *target audience.* Without accounting for waste circulation, a CPM figure can be misleading. If, for example, only 20 percent of a radio station's audience were among a retail firm's target consumers, then the general CPM must be multiplied by 5 to obtain a CPM that can be used in comparing different vehicles.

PREPARATION AND ASSESSMENT

Once appropriate vehicles are chosen, two steps remain in developing an advertising program: preparing individual ads and assessing the effectiveness of advertising. Because these two steps are quite technical—the work of advertising specialists and marketing researchers, ordinarily—they are only briefly noted in this chapter.

A number of separate ads form an advertising program. Preparation of each ad follows a general sequence, which is usually initiated by a department head or buyer with a request to the advertising department about two weeks before the ad will be run. The buyer or department head must provide the advertising staff with information about the offerings to be advertised and the preferred type of ad. Many stores use standardized copy fact sheets for this purpose.

Department managers and buyers become involved in ad preparation at other points in the sequence as well. For example, in the case of a newspaper ad, the manager or buyer may be called upon to review a sample of the ad as it will appear in the paper, after which the newspaper makes necessary changes or corrections. A sample of the revised ad is usually sent to the appropriate department manager or buyer as a reminder to have sufficient stock ready for sale, to tell salespeople about the advertised offerings, and to arrange special displays.

When an effort is made to measure advertising's effectiveness, a difficult task at best, a departmental manager or buyer again may be asked for reactions. Most often, sales figures for specified time periods or offerings will be requested.

In a relatively small firm, the owner-manager may actually prepare individual ads and try to assess the effectiveness of advertising. As noted, specialists normally will perform these steps in large, departmentalized stores, which means that department managers and buyers will not be as involved with these steps as in preceding ones connected with the advertising program. However, their cooperation and assessments certainly can facilitate (or impede) the specialists' efforts.

REVIEW BOX 16:4

1. The retail advertising medium most frequently employed by retailers is _____.
2. TV's growing use by retailers is due to the fact that it _____; a disadvantage of TV advertising for many retailers is _____.
3. Media selection consists of two steps, the first being to _____.
4. CPM figures can be helpful in vehicle selection if they pertain to _____.

CHAPTER SUMMARY

- Retail advertising can be defined as paid, impersonal communication that attempts to induce people to buy or to act favorably in response to the message. It is the last mix element to be developed. Decisions on target markets, desired image, offerings, and prices are necessary to advertising planning.
- Advertising shares with personal selling and supportive methods the overall purposes of promotion. It contributes to these purposes by informing consumers about the outlet's offerings and describing their attractive features.
- Some merchants spend almost nothing on advertising, while others spend 5¢ out of every $1 of sales revenue on advertising. Several factors explain why this may be logical—for example, the emphasis assigned to advertising within the promotion blend may differ. Within a store, different amounts are spent on advertising and selling various merchandise lines.
- When categorized according to what is primarily featured in the ad, There are three kinds of retail advertising: promotional, institutional, and combination. Most retail firms concentrate on promotional advertising, which features specific offerings. Most institutional advertising promotes some aspect of the store itself in order to enhance the outlet's image.
- When categorized according to payment arrangements, advertising falls into three classes: individual, horizontal cooperative, and vertical cooperative. Vertical cooperative arrangements are especially important to retail firms because they increase the money available for advertising and often include assistance in preparing ads.

- Developing an advertising program involves determining specific objectives, a buying theme, a total budget and how it should be allocated, and media to be used. Individual ads can then be prepared, and eventually an effort should be made to assess the effectiveness of the advertising.
- The simplest and most frequently used budgeting method is the percentage-of-sales approach. A better, but more difficult, budgeting method is the task-and-factors approach, which considers both what must be done to reach a sales objective and factors in the outlet's competitive situation.
- Before selecting media for an advertising program, a retail manager should be familiar with the relative merits of major ones such as newspapers, magazines, radio, television, and direct mail.
- Newspapers, the dominant retail advertising medium, achieve blanket coverage of a city at a relatively low cost per message. Radio also provides broad coverage and may be more flexible since there are more radio stations than papers or TV stations in a city. Use of magazines by national chains and use of TV by sizeable local retailers as well as by national chains has been on the rise. Direct mail, which includes catalog and single-page or several-page advertising pieces mailed to consumers, allows the retailer to decide specifically who will receive the advertising—if a good mailing list can be compiled.
- Media selection consists of two steps: (1) determining which general medium or media would be most suitable (radio or newspapers, for example) and (2) choosing a specific vehicle from among various alternatives in the medium selected (station WABC-AM or the *Daily News*, for example).

CHAPTER NOTES

[1] Ferdinand F. Mauser and David J. Schwartz, Jr., *American Business: An Introduction*, 3rd ed. (New York: Harcourt Brace Jovanovich, 1974), p. 520.

[2] This example comes from the excellent article by John O. Whitney, "Better Results from Retail Advertising," *Harvard Business Review*, May–June 1970, p. 117.

[3] Laurence W. Jacobs, *Advertising and Promotion for Retailing: Text and Cases* (Glenview, Ill.: Scott Foresman, 1972), p. 60.

[4] This estimate and the following quote introduce Whitney's article, *op. cit.*, p. 111.

[5] These figures are approximate averages for all stores of this kind. The figure for supermarkets is from "Chain Performance Reflects Heightened Competition," *Progressive Grocer*, April 1973, p. 131; the discount store figures from Earl Brown et al., *Operating Results of Self-Service Discount Department Stores, 1969–70* (Ithaca, New York: Cornell University, 1971), p. 47; and the department store figures from Jay Scher, *Department Store and Specialty Store Merchandising and Operating Results of 1972* (New York: National Retail Merchants Association, 1973), pp. 29 and 181.

[6] Scher, *op. cit.*, pp. 139, 143, 147, 151.

[7] The statistics in this paragraph and the following one are reprinted by permission from

"Advertising, Marketing Reports on the 100 Top National Advertisers," *Advertising Age*, August 27, 1973, pp. 28, 112, 134, and 146. Copyright 1973 by Crain Communications Inc.

[8] Martin Everett, "One Small Step for Co-op Advertising," *Sales Management*, April 3, 1972, p. 24.

[9] *Ibid.*, p. 23.

[10] Alan Koehler, "Beware of Seven Deadly C's of Retail Newspaper Ads," *Advertising Age*, October 26, 1970, p. 57.

[11] Adapted from Whitney, *op. cit.*, p. 115.

[12] "Supermarket Ad Budgets," *Business Week*, February 5, 1972, p. 45.

[13] Julian L. Simon, "A Scientific Approach to Dividing the Advertising Budget," *Journal of Retailing*, Fall 1969, pp. 37–45ff.

[14] Jacobs, *op. cit.*, pp. 96–97.

[15] Some ideas in this section, especially the advantages and disadvantages of different media, are drawn from Jacobs' chapter on media selection, *ibid.*, pp. 116–37.

[16] "Supermarket Ad Budgets," *loc. cit.*

[17] "Sears Moves Heavily into Magazines; Then Wards Gives It Whirl," *Advertising Age*, October 20, 1969, p. 200.

QUESTIONS AND ASSIGNMENTS

1. Early in the chapter, it was noted that the quality of retail advertising is often criticized. Do you think the quality of retail advertising is poor? Why or why not? If yes, what factors might make retailers' advertising of lower quality than that sponsored by manufacturers? If no, what do you feel is of especially high quality?

2. How does advertising differ from personal selling and supportive methods of promotion?

3. The chapter talks a lot about what retail advertising potentially can do. But what *can't* advertising do? That is, what are its limitations?

4. How does promotional advertising differ from the institutional kind? Which kind is used most by retailers? Why?

5. Scan recent issues of a local newspaper and select an ad which is clearly regular-price promotional advertising. Then select reduced-price, clearance-sale, image, and announcement ads.

6. a. Talk to the manager of a large shopping center. How frequently do the stores in the center engage in horizontal cooperative advertising? Who develops the cooperative advertising program?
   b. Do you think an individual retailer can accomplish his own objectives by jointly sponsoring advertising with other retailers? Explain.

7. An entrepreneur who is planning to open a new independent bookstore at your school seeks your advice about advertising objectives. Specifically, he asks you to develop an objectives diagram for his store. Do this after observing the present campus bookstores and talking with employees and customers.

8. What factors explain why retailers advertise more in newspapers than in any other medium? For what kinds of retail outlets would newspapers probably not be suitable? Be specific.

9. Interview the owner-manager of a specialty shop or the advertising manager of a local department store regarding how he or she develops an advertising program, focusing especially on the task of selecting suitable media. How closely does the store's advertising planning match the procedure described in the chapter? Explain the differences.

10. The manager of a soon-to-open organic foods restaurant, which will be located near your school and have a seating capacity of 60, feels that effective advertising will produce daily sales of $150 to $200 during the first year. How much should be spent on advertising during that year? Plan the media expenditures, indicating which medium or media mix would be suitable, how much of the total budget should be spent in each medium, and about how many ads this will permit in each medium employed. Explain your media plan.

ANSWERS TO REVIEW BOX QUESTIONS

Box 16:1

1. An answer which is close to the following and includes the italicized points would be suitable: any form of *paid impersonal* presentation of goods, services, or ideas for the purpose of inducing people to buy or to act favorably on what is called to their attention.
2. The planned significance of advertising within the promotion blend can vary (Although more narrow, an answer referring to differences in outlets' offerings or in the number and vigor of competitors would be correct.)

Box 16:2

1. Payment arrangements; or who pays for it
2. create store traffic and immediate sales
3. horizontal cooperative

Box 16:3

1. set specific objectives
2. Any of the following: type of offerings, convenience of location, desired image, length of time the outlet has been in business, size and financial resources of the outlet, or competitors' advertising levels
3. build-up

Box 16:4

1. newspapers
2. combines sight and sound, thereby increasing the impact on consumers; cost
3. determine which general medium (or media mix) would be most suitable
4. persons in the target audience, not just readers, listeners, or viewers in general

Credit and Other Supplementary Services

Some retailers label themselves "sales and service" outlets; others, such as telephone answering agencies, sell services independent of a product; and still other service outlets provide conveniences that are incidental to a transaction—for example, drive-up windows at a bank. Looked at from a different perspective, some services are expected (parking) while others are a pleasant surprise (a liberal merchandise return policy). Thus you can see that a discussion of services requires an explanation of the term since it has several interpretations.

To avoid confusion, services in this book are described as either primary or supplementary. *Primary services* are sold to consumers for the benefits they provide. The service itself is the object of the transaction. *Supplementary services*, discussed in this chapter, are designed to facilitate or aid in the sale of a product or primary service. By themselves, supplementary services have little or no value. Table 17-1 lists various primary and supplementary services. These lists, although not complete of course, suggest the distinction between the two types of services.

Some definitions of supplementary services include such things as window displays, convenient location, and sales personnel. However, such a broad scope includes virtually all of retailing and thus makes the concept of supplementary services nearly meaningless. Admittedly, there is a hazy line between primary and supplementary services in some cases. For example, a loan granted by a commercial bank is a primary service, while credit given by a retailer is a supplementary service. Nevertheless, this chapter deals only with services that supplement the primary objective of a retail firm. Enough examples will be used throughout the chapter to make the distinction clear.

397

TABLE 17-1

Examples of Services

Primary	Supplementary
Mass transit	Credit
Haircuts	Delivery
Dry cleaning	Gift wrapping
Movies	Check cashing
Garbage pickup	Telephone orders
Checking account	Mail orders
Repairs	Lay-away
Bowling	Evening/Sunday store hours
Car wash	Alterations
Hair styling	Drive-up windows
Taxi rides	Parking
Golf	Appliance installation
Air travel	Complaints department
Medical care	Merchandise returns

THE DEVELOPMENT OF SUPPLEMENTARY SERVICES

Although figures are not kept on the dollar value of supplementary services, you need only think about the retailers in your own city to appreciate the variety available and their importance to consumers. Consider the frequency with which you see retailers' delivery vans, and think about the number of stores with background music and check-cashing service, supermarkets with carry-out boys, stores with evening hours, liberal merchandise return policies, and stores with credit plans. The list could go on, but the point is clear—supplementary services are popular with retailers and consumers.

Their Attraction

The attractiveness of supplementary services to consumers lies in the fact that they make shopping more convenient and pleasant. In fact, due largely to services, shopping has become something of a social occasion for many people in the United States.

From a retailer's point of view, the attraction of offering supplementary services is slightly more complex. First, they can be used to *differentiate a store*. If a retailer offers a supplementary service—Sunday openings or late hours—which his competitors are unwilling or unable to duplicate, a *differ-*

ential advantage has been created. Of course, the difference must be important to consumers to be of any value.

Second, supplementary services are a form of *non-price* competition. Generally, businessmen prefer to compete on some basis other than price for several reasons: (a) It is more difficult for competitors to duplicate a service than to match a price change. (b) It is less dangerous because a mistake is easier to correct. That is, experimenting with and then eliminating a service is much easier than lowering and then raising price. (c) Price cuts can have a negative effect on consumers' attitudes. Customers who bought before the price decrease feel they were overcharged, and potential customers may feel that if the retailer can absorb a price decline, his general policy is to overcharge when possible.

Third, retailers have learned that a large percentage of consumers *want* supplementary services and are willing to pay for them. The fact is reflected in the success of many small, specialty retailers who offer a variety of services.

The Decision to Offer a Supplementary Service

In evaluating the merits of offering a particular service to consumers, a retailer should consider the cost, consumer demand, alternative sources of the service, and competition.

COST

Both the direct and indirect costs of offering a service should be evaluated. If, for example, the service under consideration is home delivery by a drug store, the retailer would have to consider the following direct costs: (a) a delivery vehicle; (b) an employee, either part-time or full-time, to make deliveries; (c) gas, oil, maintenance, repairs, and insurance on a delivery vehicle. The major indirect cost is managerial time. It is considered an indirect cost because the manager would be working in the business with or without the service. However, if the service is offered, it will require some managerial time that could be used to do other things.

DEMAND

The retailer must objectively ask himself why the supplementary service is being considered. How important is the service to the target market? If the service has been requested by only one or two customers or if the retailer feels that the service might add to the prestige of the store, then it is of dubious value. In other words, a service is worthwhile only if desired by a significant number of customers.

Although demand cannot be forecast with a great deal of accuracy, some indicators are available that will measure demand as "great," "moderate," or "slight." In the delivery service example, the drug store manager should consider the number of requests for the service from current as well as potential customers, characteristics of customers (average age, location, approximate income, mode of transportation), and the nature of the neighborhood surrounding the store. A customer or neighborhood mix that consists largely of older residents with limited access to a drugstore would indicate a need for the service.

ALTERNATIVE SOURCES

Some supplementary services can be offered by a retailer through a third party. Most medium or large cities have firms that provide local delivery for a fee. A downtown department store that wants additional parking for customers may persuade an investor to build and operate a parking garage. Small retailers frequently have outsiders handle their retail credit. All of these are examples of using an alternative source of a service.

The advantages of an alternative source are that, even though costs are involved, no investment is required by the retailer (no delivery truck, no accounts receivable), and demands on managerial time are reduced. The disadvantages include the direct cost of the service and lack of control. Since costs exist whether the service is handled internally or by an alternative source, the greatest problem is control. For example, as just one of several customers of a delivery service, a retailer would have to adjust his activities to meet the delivery schedule. Rush orders or emergencies could not be given special treatment.

Before making a selection, a retailer should investigate alternative sources according to how well the service offered meets the needs of his customers, how much the alternative would cost compared to the cost of offering the service internally, and the quality of the service provided by the alternative source.

COMPETITION

What are competitors doing, and what are they likely to do? These are important concerns to a retailer in evaluating a potential service. If one or more competitors have adopted a service that is benefiting their businesses (and therefore probably hurting the business of the decision maker), a retailer is virtually forced to duplicate the service or counteract it with an innovation of his own.

The second part of the above question—what are competitors likely to do—is more difficult to deal with. The first retailer to introduce a supplementary service is seeking an advantage. However, if the service can be quickly and easily duplicated by competitors it is of marginal value. Unfortunately, there are few services that cannot be copied, although exceptions do exist. For example, the retailer who is confident of the quality of the store's merchandise may offer a liberal return policy that cannot be matched by competitors with lower quality merchandise. The financial capabilities of competitors and their past reactions to new services are good indicators of what they are likely to do when faced with a service innovation.

> **REVIEW BOX 17:1**
>
> 1. Supplementary services are designed to facilitate or aid in the sale of a product or primary service. By themselves, supplementary services have _____.
> 2. Supplementary services are attractive to retailers because they are a type of _____ competition.
> 3. The decision to offer a service depends upon cost, demand, alternative sources, and _____.

The Life of Supplementary Services

Supplementary services tend to go through a life cycle that offers some insights into how they develop, flourish, and sometimes disappear. The cycle's five stages are:

Introduction. A supplementary service is first introduced by a retailer who feels it will help attract new customers or maintain existing ones. The retailer views the service as providing the firm with a *differential advantage.* A retailer may, for example, be the first in the trading area to open on Sunday or provide home delivery.

Duplication. If the service is popular, it will lure customers from other stores. To offset this new advantage, retailers losing customers can innovate with an attractive service of their own, or they can duplicate the originator's service. Duplication is the more likely response, because retailers have a good idea of how consumers will react to the service. Thus, competitors add the service to their offerings and its total effect is *neutralized.* Consumers can now get the service anywhere, so they usually return to shopping where they did before the service was made available.

Stalemate. At this stage all retailers have the service, but no one, except possibly the consumer, is benefiting from it. The service has become an added cost and probably an added managerial nuisance to the retailers. However, if the consumer enjoys having the service available, none of the retailers will want to eliminate it because it would put them at a *differential disadvantage.*

Institutionalization. The situation remains unchanged for some time, and consumers begin to take it for granted. New retailers coming into the market automatically include the service in their offering and, over time, it becomes *institutionalized*. That is, it becomes a basic part of the offering of that particular type of retail outlet.

Replacement. Once institutionalized, some services never disappear, while others eventually lose their attractiveness to consumers and their advantage to retailers. Needs change, shopping patterns evolve, old tasks are taken over by other types of businesses, and the service is no longer needed. Thus, some retailers drop the service. Those who retain it may be satisfying a small segment of the market that still desires the service, or they may simply not be astute enough to realize that the service is no longer valued. At this time some new service may be introduced by a retailer, beginning the cycle again.

This cyclical pattern of services has several implications for retailers. First, it suggests that services should be added cautiously, since once added they are often difficult to eliminate. Second, a retailer should watch his competitors and trade publications closely for the development and addition of services. In order to react wisely to a competitor's introduction of a new service, the retailer must be prepared to evaluate its impact quickly. Third, the retailer must avoid sentimentality when it comes to eliminating services. Services exist to improve sales and profits, and when they cannot be justified according to sales or profit criteria they should be eliminated.

THE MANAGEMENT OF SUPPLEMENTARY SERVICES

Just as in any other business function, quality must be maintained, cost controlled, and benefits evaluated in supplementary services. In this section a program for evaluating existing services and a policy for eliminating a service are discussed. Also, two special managerial problems relating to services are examined.

Periodic Evaluation of Services

On a regular basis, possibly annually or semi-annually, all supplementary services should be evaluated to determine their contribution to the business. The chief concerns in such an evaluation are costs of offering the service (Have they changed since the service was introduced? If so, by how much?) and the demand for the service (Do customers want it enough to shop elsewhere if it is not offered?). Two interesting success stories exemplify this process in action.

Kresge's management realized around 1959 that a large number of consumers were more interested in lower prices on quality merchandise than in a full line of services and merchandise. Thus, in 1962 Kresge opened the first K-mart and since then has added hundreds more. The stores have flourished using a simple combination of stocking high volume merchandise at modest prices. This has been made possible, in part, by employing few salespeople and making use of a supermarket-like checkout area.

A number of supermarket chains including Thriftmart, Penn Fruit, Acme, and A & P have introduced "warehouse markets" in formerly unprofitable traditional stores.[1] In the warehouse market, almost all services have been eliminated. Displays are usually cases (with the tops removed) stacked on pallets; produce is displayed untrimmed in the case; and meat is packaged in larger-than-normal quantities. Because customers usually purchase in large amounts, some of these stores have replaced shopping carts with flatbed hand trucks. Customers select from a slightly smaller choice of brand names and then bag and carry out their own groceries. The result is prices as much as 12 percent below those of traditional service supermarkets.

In both cases above, the retailers compared the cost of supplementary services with the demand, and they correctly concluded that there was an important segment of the market that prefers cost savings to services. The same kind of evaluation should be conducted by every retailer. Services retained should be only those which are a competitive necessity (even the warehouse markets have parking lots) or provide a competitive advantage.

Special Supplementary Service Problems

Two problems retailers have with supplementary services are charging for them and customer misuse. Both require deliberate decisions by management—decisions that can significantly influence the value of the service to the outlet.

CHARGING

Services are either paid for by some customers directly or by all customers indirectly. A service that is paid for directly is one that has a specific price; the consumer desiring it then pays that price. Gift wrapping, for which a customer pays a fee (commonly 50¢ to $1.00) is an example of this kind of arrangement.

The other arrangement, in which all customers pay for supplementary services indirectly, is frequently described as "free" service. This category would include carry-out service at the supermarket, pick-up and delivery of dry cleaning, and even a parking lot. All cost the retailer something in salaries, equipment, or property taxes, and customers—whether they use the service or not—are paying these costs in the price of the merchandise. True, each customer probably pays only a very small portion of the cost, but a large number of services can substantially raise the final price of merchandise.

This is a major factor explaining the development of discount retailing and its continued success. Many services offered by traditional retailers were eliminated by discounters who could then give customers lower prices in their place.

Whether or not a particular service should be paid for directly or indirectly depends upon the demand for the service and the behavior of the competition. If virtually all customers desire and use the service—for example, a parking lot at a suburban location—then the cost can be spread over all purchases and all customers. On the other hand, if only a few customers desire the service—delivery by a grocery store, for example—*and* their continued patronage is important to the outlet, the service should be maintained on a fee basis.

The way in which competitors handle the service should always be considered. If competitors charge, the retailer can safely charge for the service, or the retailer can eliminate the charge in the hope of creating an advantage for the outlet.

Setting a fee for a supplementary service is somewhat different from pricing merchandise. Because the service is not designed to produce a profit, the only consideration in pricing is the cost of offering the service. The retailer may even consider taking a small loss on a service if it will attract a sufficiently large amount of new business.

CUSTOMER MISUSE

There are instances when services are misused, and management should be prepared to handle such problems. For example, the liberal return policies of stores such as Sears and Montgomery Ward may encourage careless shopping or the return of merchandise purchased elsewhere. These big chains feel that the risk is worth the benefits, since the policy stimulates purchases and promotes good will. However, the cost of processing returned sales and handling returned merchandise may make this a less attractive policy for smaller retailers.

Another common misuse is ignoring interest charges on credit accounts when paying bills. Although most people would not attempt this with large retailers who will continue to add the charges and eventually take away credit privileges, many take advantage of small credit plans. The small store owner may rationalize that some customers are more important than the loss of a few cents or dollars in interest. However, over time the dollars and cents add up, and the retailer is assuming a burden that is rightfully that of the customer.

To avoid these and similar misuses, some retailers keep records on individual customers for complaints, returned merchandise, and omission of interest payments. If misuse becomes excessive, a tactful discussion or letter may be enough to correct the situation. However, if abuses continue, the retailer must decide if the customer's continued patronage is more trouble than it is worth.

> **REVIEW BOX 17:2**
>
> 1. According to the supplementary services life cycle, at introduction a service provides the retailer with a _____.
> 2. The decision to charge a fee for a supplementary service should be based on the demand for the service and _____.
> 3. Two supplementary services commonly misused are credit and _____.

RETAIL CREDIT

Retail credit merits special attention because of its growing importance in retailing. The amount of consumer credit spending is nearly 20 times greater today than it was 30 years ago. In January 1973, consumer credit outstanding totaled $157.2 billion, of which $127.4 billion was installment credit. The installment credit consisted of $44.4 billion for automobiles, $39.9 billion for other consumer goods, $36.9 billion for personal loans, and $6.2 billion for repairs and modernization loans.[2] Non-installment credit, the remaining $29.8 billion, includes single-payment loans from banks and other financial institutions and charge accounts.

Types of Retail Credit

There are several types of retail credit, and the selection of one or more by a retailer should be a carefully made decision. The simplest breakdown of credit types is internal versus external financing.

CREDIT FINANCING

Internal credit is a situation in which the retailer finances the accounts receivable. *External* credit is a plan in which some firm other than the retailer (a third party) finances the accounts receivable. Two examples will make this distinction clear.

Assume that a men's clothing retailer with an internal plan sells a $150 suit. The customer charges the suit and pays for it in six equal monthly installments of $25. To simplify the example, assume also that this is the only account the retailer has, and he charges the customer no interest on the unpaid balance. If the retailer paid the manufacturer $100 for the suit, he must wait four months (4 × $25) before he has received enough money from the customer to replace the suit in his stock, and he must wait six months to realize his full profit on the sale. Thus, in an internal plan the retailer loses the use of his money until the customer pays his bill. That is what is meant by *financing accounts receivable*.

SPOTLIGHT

What does credit mean to a young woman? (The following article offers a humorous insight.)

I did a very old-fashioned thing the other day. I sat my daughter down and told her the facts of life.

I told her about a certain time of her youth when her body would tingle with excitement and anticipation . . . when she would meet her lifelong dream (like Mommy did) and eventually sign a document and be united forever.

And then on that all-important day she would be joined in holy wedlock to . . . what? To a credit card of her very own! That's what. Together they would embark on a lifetime of charging, financing, purchasing, and paying five percent of the new balance.

There were tears in her eyes when I finished.

"Mommy was lucky," I continued. "My credit-card hand developed early. At the age of 15, it had already begun to curve into a small semicircle and the fingers had become rigid. I have every reason to believe that you will mature early too."

"But Daddy says I should wait until I have money before I buy something," she said.

"Your father," I sighed. "What does he know? He still thinks American Express is a little red wagon. I tell you, dear, money is passé. It's just something to get lost in the sofa cushions. There isn't anything for sale that you can't charge any more. I am willing to bet that I can do more with my credit cards than your father can do with a billfold full of money."

At that moment, my husband appeared. "I heard that remark," he said, "and I accept the challenge. Money is *not* obsolete, and I will prove it to you. Tonight, we will spend an evening on the town and we'll see which gets the most respect . . . charge cards or cash. I'll bet you ten dollars that money wins!"

"You're on." I smiled.

On the way to dinner, the three of us stopped off at a service station and when the attendant came to the window he said, "That'll be $5.76." My husband whipped out a $10 bill.

"I'm sorry," said the young man. "We can't take cash after eight o'clock. Too many robberies. You got a credit card?"

I smiled and etched a No. 1 in the dust on the dashboard.

We pulled into the restaurant and went in to order dinner. When it was finished my husband peeled off a $50 bill and put it on the little tray. The waiter stiffened and said, "Could you come with me, sir?"

My husband went to the cashier, who asked, "Do you have any identification?"

"For *cash?*" he gasped. "For crying out loud, don't you recognize Ulysses S. Grant when you see him?" he asked, shoving her the bill.

"I'm sorry, Mr. Grant," she said, "but I'm new and I don't know the regulars yet. We don't get many big bills and we have to be cautious. Perhaps if you had a charge card for identification. . . ."

Irritably, he started for the car then remembered he wanted to call the sitter.

He emerged from the phone booth seconds later biting his necktie in half. "Has anyone got another dime? She wants 20 cents."

"No." I smiled. "But I have a charge number that you could give."

"I don't believe any of this," he said,

leaning tiredly against the phone booth. "Money used to be next to Godliness."

"That was cleanliness," I said smugly.

"Why, I can remember once when I hoed an entire garden, washed my mother's porch down and cut a cord of wood for a shiny new dime. Do you know why?"

"Because you were an underachiever?" asked my daughter.

"Because a dime was worth a fortune in those days. It was Abe Lincoln who said, 'All I am or ever hope to be I owe to money.'"

"That was 'Mother,'" I corrected.

"I know your mother has told you the facts of life," he said, "but I feel she has dwelt on the romantic aspects of charging and not on some of the problems that you might face."

"Such as what?" asked our daughter, wide-eyed.

"Such as, did your mother tell you what to do when the bank sends you a second notice for nonpayment on your current charges?"

"Oh yes, I just charge it on my charge card."

He winced. "Did she happen to mention that when you've been unfaithful to your obligations and direct your attention to your other charge accounts, you could be sued for impersonating a good credit risk?"

"I don't understand that," she said.

"Very simply, it means you could have a future lettering license plates in prison."

"It's so confusing."

"I know, and I want you to be happy, but remember, credit cards are the root of all evil."

"That's 'money,'" I interrupted. "And don't listen to your father. Money is the Edsel of economics. You think tonight was weird? Why I could tell you stories that would make your hair stand on end."

"Like what?"

"Like a nudist camp in New Jersey that shut down because patrons complained they didn't have anyplace to carry their credit cards."

"You're kidding," said my husband.

"And the woman in Texas who went to Weight Watchers to lose 50 pounds. When she took off her credit cards to be weighed, she was hospitalized for anemia."

"I don't want to hear any more," he sulked.

"There isn't anything you cannot buy with a credit card," I insisted.

"You can't buy money," he shouted.

"In any drive-in bank," I said. "All you have to do is insert your credit card and, *voilá,* it spits out cash."

"Maybe it was happiness I was thinking about," he amended.

"Have you ever seen me cry in a department store?"

"Sex. That's it. You can't buy sex," he said.

"If you can explain the billing, I'll bet you can charge that, too."

"Health?"

"I charged my varicose veins on Blue Shield just last spring,"

"Okay," he said. "You win." He threw down a $20 bill. My daughter and I both stared at it.

She opened her purse, took out a bulky credit-card machine and said, "Sorry, we accept only Master Charge and Bank Americard."

"Our little girl is a woman!" I said, my eyes misting.

Erma Bombeck, "The Credit Card Caper." Reprinted by permission from the May 1974 issue of *Good Housekeeping Magazine.* © 1974 by the Hearst Corporation.

Now we will describe a simple *external* plan. Assume the same situation as before except that this time, after the suit is charged, the retailer sells the customer's promise to pay $150 to a third party, often called a *factor*. The retailer sells the account for $140. The customer pays six installments of $25 to the factor, who receives a total of $150 for a gross profit of $10. In the meantime, for a cost of $10 ($150 price minus $140 received from the factor), the retailer has $140 to use immediately after the sale. A third party is paid according to the amount and type of service provided. Usually the fee is based on a percentage of credit sales (frequently 4 to 9 percent) and sometimes includes an additional flat monthly fee.

In these examples, two things were oversimplified. First, a retailer makes many credit sales, and the total amount of money invested in accounts receivable can be quite large. In a clothing store, for example, it is not uncommon for half of all sales to be for credit. Second, interest charges, discussed later, were omitted.

Two particularly important external plans are bank credit cards (Master Charge and BankAmericard) and travel and entertainment cards (Diner's Club, American Express, Carte Blanche). Bank credit cards trace their origin to a New York bank that in 1951 was attempting to help small retailers accommodate customers' desire for credit. Since then the bank credit card has gone through several stages of modification and program consolidation until today there are two dominant plans—BankAmericard and Master Charge. In 1973 there were over 53 million bank credit cards in the hands of consumers, and nearly 2 million merchants honored them.[3]

The travel and entertainment (T & E) cards were designed primarily for use by travelers away from home. Accepted by restaurants, hotels and motels, airlines, and other travel-oriented businesses, they became very popular with businessmen. Within the last few years, bank credit card plans and T & E plans have become more and more alike. First the bank credit cards began signing up travel and entertainment businesses. More recently, it was announced that American Express will be accepted at Macy's department stores, the first major department store chain to honor an outside credit plan.[4] From the consumers' point of view, probably the biggest distinction between the plans has been that bank credit cards are given free, while T & E cards require an annual membership fee. Even this difference seems to be eroding as Marquette National Bank in Minneapolis announced in early 1973 that their BankAmericard holders will be required to pay a $10 annual fee.[5]

PAYMENT SCHEDULES

Both internal and external plans can be further subdivided according to the payment schedule used by the customer. Three common methods are 30-day single-payment, contract or installment, and revolving credit.

30-Day Single-Payment. Consumers use this method as a convenience rather than as a necessity. Instead of paying for a product or service at the time of purchase, the customer charges it and pays the total amount when billed, usually within 30 days. Normally there is no service charge or interest added for this type of credit. The purpose of 30-day credit is twofold. First, it relieves the consumer of the necessity of carrying cash; second, it makes it possible for the consumer to make unplanned or impulse purchases.

Installment Credit. On this type of credit plan the purchase price is divided into equal parts and spread over time, from three months to as long as five years. Since the 90-day contract in which payment is made in four parts, is quite common, it will be used as an example. One part is the down payment and is paid at the time of the purchase. The remaining three parts are spread over 90 days with payments every 30 days.

On installment credit the retailer usually charges the consumer a fee or interest for the use of the credit. The charge is usually 1 or $1\frac{1}{2}$ percent per month (depending on state legal limits) of the unpaid balance. An example will show how this works. A consumer buys a new washing machine from an appliance store for $280 and decides to use the 90-day installment plan. At the time of the purchase the customer pays $70 down ($\frac{1}{4} \times \$280$). This leaves a balance of $210 to be paid in three installments. Assume the retailers in this state are allowed to charge $1\frac{1}{2}$ percent per month interest. Thirty days from the purchase, the consumer would pay $70 + ($1\frac{1}{2}$ percent $\times$ $210), or a total of $73.15. This reduces the unpaid balance to $140. At the end of 60 days, the customer pays another bill for $70 + ($1\frac{1}{2}$ percent $\times$ $140), or $72.10. Finally, at the end of 90 days, the customer pays $70 + ($1\frac{1}{2}$ percent $\times$ $70), or $71.05. The total transaction looks like this:

price of the washing machine: $280

payments:
down payment	$70		
30 days	70	interest	$3.15
60 days	70	interest	2.10
90 days	70	interest	1.05
	$280		$6.30

total purchase price: $286.30

The consumer has paid the retailer a total of $6.30 for the privilege of spreading out the payments over a period of three months.

Revolving Credit. A revolving credit plan allows a customer to make continuous credit purchases as long as (1) a minimum amount is paid on the unpaid credit balance each month (commonly 10 percent, with a minimum of $10) and (2) the total unpaid balance remains below some specified maximum determined by the customer's ability to pay. The retailer adds an interest charge to the unpaid balance each month, again usually the legal limit of 1 to 1½ percent per month.

The Decision to Offer Credit

Almost all types of retailers are being forced to consider offering credit. To illustrate, as early as 1960, even the most traditional cash-and-carry outlet, the supermarket, was experimenting with credit.[6] The decision to offer credit depends upon consumer expectations and the image the retailer wishes to create. If consumers want to use credit and can buy comparable merchandise elsewhere on credit, the retailer has no option. Thus, in lines such as clothing, furniture and appliances, credit is an essential part of the operation.

A second factor is the retailer's desired image. A low-price, low-margin operation can sometimes justify the absence of credit and other services. For example, a men's clothing "factory outlet" advertising top quality suits and sports coats at 30 to 50 percent below traditional retail prices may not offer credit. Generally, however, the decision is beyond the control of the retailer, who must conform to the tradition in the marketplace.

SELECTING A FORM OF CREDIT

Although given little choice in whether *to offer* credit, the retailer can and should carefully *choose a particular form of credit*. The decision to employ an internal or external plan, or some combination of both will influence cost, managerial time, and the volume of credit sales. The advantages and disadvantages of the major alternatives are discussed below.

In an internal plan the retailer is responsible for the entire credit program including approving credit applications, setting credit limits, financing the accounts receivable, bad debts (losses because customers fail or refuse to pay), billing, record keeping, and collection. No fees are paid to a third party. Also, the store has access to a mailing list of interested consumers to use in special promotions. Finally, many retailers feel consumers prefer to shop where they have a credit account. On the negative side, credit management is time consuming—applications must be evaluated, credit limits set, records kept, bills sent, and collection pursued. In addition, any bad debt losses from the credit plan must be absorbed by the retailer.

Among the advantages of an external plan, the most important are freedom from credit management details and the fact that the credit program is in the hands of a specialist. As for disadvantages, the retailer loses direct contact with customers through monthly bills and loses control over the program. In addition, the retailer must pay a fee to a third party for the credit service.

Many retailers have gone to a combination of external and internal plans. Primarily because of competitive pressure, retailers with internal plans have added T & E cards or bank credit cards to their credit offerings. The major advantage of a combination of plans is that it makes credit available to a much larger potential market. In addition, the credit tasks associated with at least some credit sales are transferred to a third party. On the negative side, the retailer loses control of a portion of his credit offering and the revenue generated by interest charges on installment purchases.

> **REVIEW BOX 17:3**
>
> 1. The major difference between internal and external credit is in who finances the _____.
> 2. 30-day single-payment credit differs from installment and revolving credit in that the latter two include the addition of _____.
> 3. Although the retailer may not have much choice in offering credit, he can decide _____.

The Management of an Internal Credit Plan

The management of credit requires a variety of skills. The basic ones discussed here are credit approval, record keeping, and billing and collection.

CREDIT APPROVAL

Every credit plan, large or small, should make use of a formal application containing enough personal information to evaluate the applicant's creditworthiness and to trace the individual if necessary. Although many retailers use some rule of thumb in approving applications (such as income over a certain amount, or employed at the same job for more than five years), there are more systematic alternatives.

One such alternative is *point scoring*. Point-scoring systems, which are readily available from credit consultants, allocate points to information on an application. Points are determined through an evaluation of the information provided by former good and bad accounts. An example of a scoring system used in a bank credit card plan is shown in Figure 17-1.

Point scoring reduces but does not replace decision making. That is, individuals scoring above some specified number of points automatically qualify for credit, while people under some set figure are automatically rejected. Those scoring in the middle range require good credit judgment. Accepting potentially bad risks will raise losses, while rejecting potentially good accounts will result in fewer sales and lost profits.

Another possible aid is the local credit bureau. For a fixed annual fee and a per-request charge (usually 50¢ to $1.00), a retailer can receive a summarized credit history of an applicant. The information includes a current address, employment verification, length of time in the credit bureau file, records of credit and payments, and derogatory information such as bank-

1 CIRCLE THE ONE NUMBER IN EACH ROW OF BOXES THAT MOST CLOSELY DESCRIBES YOU AND ENTER IT IN THE CODE BOX AT THE RIGHT.

2 ADD YOUR CODE BOX SCORES INCLUDING BONUS POINTS AND ENTER THE TOTAL IN THE TOTAL SCORE BOX.

3 IF YOU HAVE SCORED 18 POINTS OR MORE, COMPLETE THE FORM ON THE RIGHT, REFOLD, SEAL AND MAIL TODAY.

A — AGE

21-25	26-36	37-50	51-65	Over 65
1	2	2	2	1

B — MARITAL STATUS

Single	Separated	Divorced	Widowed	Married
1	1	1	1	2

C — SIZE OF FAMILY (INCLUDE SELF)

1	2	3-4	5-6	7 or More
2	2	2	1	1

D — YEARS WITH PRESENT EMPLOYER

Under 1 Year	1-2 Years	3-6 Years	7-10 Years	Over 10 Years
1	2	3	4	5

E — MONTHLY INCOME (APPLICANT ONLY)

Under $400	$400-$650	$651-$900	$901-$1200	Over $1200
1	1	3	5	7

F — AMOUNT OF OTHER INCOME

$0-$75	$76-200	$201-$350	$351-$500	Over $500
1	1	2	2	3

G — YEARS AT PRESENT ADDRESS

Under 1 Year	1-2 Years	3-5 Years	6-10 Years	Over 10 Years
1	1	2	2	3

H — TYPE OF RESIDENCE

Furn. Apt.	Unfurn. Apt.	Rent House	Own: Mtg.	Own: Clear
1	2	2	3	4

I — TOTAL MONTHLY PAYMENTS (BESIDE RENT OR MORT. PYMT.)

Under $75	$75-125	$126-200	$201-300	Over $300
2	2	2	1	1

J — EDUCATION

High School or Less	High School Graduate	Attended College	College Graduate	Advanced Degree
1	1	2	3	4

K — OCCUPATION

Part-Time	Unskilled	Skilled or Equivalent	Executive or Supervisor	Professional
1	2	3	4	5

L — BONUS POINTS (CIRCLE ALL THAT APPLY AND ENTER THE TOTAL IN THE CODE BOX)

Have a Phone in Your Name	Credit With This Bank	Checking With This Bank	Local Credit Established	Savings With This Bank
1	2	1	1	1

MOTIVATIONAL SYSTEMS INC. NEW YORK N.Y. 1970

REMINDER: IF YOU SCORE 18 POINTS OR MORE MAIL TODAY!
THE RIGHT OF FINAL APPROVAL IS RESERVED BY THIS BANK.

TOTAL SCORE

FIGURE 17-1

A point-scoring application in which the credit applicant computes his own score

Source: Motivational Research Systems, Inc., 400 Madison Avenue, New York.

ruptcies or overdue accounts. For a small charge, a credit bureau will update an individual's file. This updating is done by calling various merchants in the community who share their credit information with the bureau.

The Associated Credit Bureaus, Inc. has recently established a "common language" for credit reporting to protect against confusing or misleading credit information. Figure 17-2 presents a guide for using this common lan-

YOUR GUIDE FOR USING THE COMMON LANGUAGE FOR CONSUMER CREDIT

TERMS OF SALE

Open Account (30 days or 90 days)
Revolving or Option (Open-end a/c)
Instalment (fixed number of payments)

USUAL MANNER OF PAYMENT	TYPE ACCOUNT		
	O	R	I
Too new to rate; approved but not used	0	0	0
Pays (or paid) within 30 days of billing; pays accounts as agreed	1	1	1
Pays (or paid) in more than 30 days, but not more than 60 days, or not more than one payment past due	2	2	2
Pays (or paid) in more than 60 days, but not more than 90 days, or two payments past due	3	3	3
Pays (or paid) in more than 90 days, but not more than 120 days, or three or more payments past due	4	4	4
Account is at least 120 days overdue but is not yet rated "9"	5	5	5
Making regular payments under Wage Earner Plan or similar arrangement	7	7	7
Repossession. (Indicate if it is a voluntary return of merchandise by the customer.)	8	8	8
Bad debt; placed for collection; skip	9	9	9

If Account is Disputed, indicate DISP.

Code	Kind of Business
A	Automotive
B	Banks
C	Clothing
D	Department and Variety
F	Finance
G	Groceries
H	Home Furnishings
I	Insurance
J	Jewelry and Cameras
K	Contractors
L	Lumber, Building Material, Hardware
M	Medical and Related Health
N	National Credit Card Companies and Air Lines
O	Oil Companies
P	Personal Services Other Than Medical
Q	Mail Order Houses
R	Real Estate and Public Accommodations
S	Sporting Goods
T	Farm and Garden Supplies
U	Utilities and Fuel
V	Government
W	Wholesale
X	Advertising
Y	Collection Services
Z	Miscellaneous

FIGURE 17-2

The common language used by credit bureaus

Source: Associated Credit Bureaus, Inc., Houston, Texas

guage. A typical report might include the citation: C 248 R 2. This would be interpreted as "clothing store (C) number 248 reported that the individual had a revolving account (R) which was paid in more than 30 days but not more than 60 days, or was not more than one payment past due (2)." Like point scoring, credit bureau information can be used to eliminate the obviously bad account and approve the obviously good one. However, the marginal applicant still must be evaluated. It is in these cases where experience, sound judgment, and careful control will determine whether a plan is profitable or a burden.

CREDIT RECORDS

Control was mentioned as a key factor in managing marginal accounts. The basis for control for all accounts is current, orderly records of all credit sales and payments. In any business doing more than a few credit sales a day, this means having a bookkeeper (at least part-time) and professionally designed ledger cards. With properly kept records a retailer should be able to ascertain in a short time the number of accounts that are active, inactive, behind in payments, open to buy (not as yet at their credit limit), and at their credit limit. This type of information is critical to managing credit, but many retailers do not have access to it because of poor records.

BILLING AND COLLECTION

Billing and collection have been combined because both deal with securing payment on credit accounts. However, they are very different in that one is a rather routine chore and the other is frequently a distasteful, bothersome job.

It goes without saying that statements or bills should be accurate (which depends on record keeping) and must be sent to customers on a regular basis. Although this appears to be common sense, the authors encountered a credit plan in a rural community in which no statements had been mailed in over two years! When the retailer was finally convinced to send statements, he was surprised to find that many customers had forgotten their debt but were willing to pay when reminded.

Whether to charge interest on installment or revolving accounts is a difficult decision to make. For the large retailer it is done as a matter of course and everyone accepts it. However, many small retailers have never added charges or only done so sporadically. Thus, consumers are more likely to question the charges made by the small firm. Those who argue in favor of interest charges feel that the customer owes the retailer something for the use of his capital. In addition, they feel the income from interest charges helps offset the cost of operating a credit program. Finally, adding charges to an account can spur payment. On the other side, retailers opposed to interest charges argue that they are a nuisance to compute and record; they do not amount to enough money to be worth the trouble; many customers simply ignore them and there is not much recourse for the retailer in such a situation; and finally, they create ill will among customers.

The arguments of both sides have merit. What the retailer should do is evaluate his customers' paying habits, competitors' practices, and his own preference before installing a policy of either charging or not charging interest on revolving or installment accounts.

Bad debts or uncollectable accounts are a menace to any credit program. It is generally accepted among credit grantors that no bad debts constitute a situation as unsatisfactory as too large a bad debt total. The reason is that if there are no bad debts, the credit policy may be too restrictive so that many sales are probably being lost. Table 17-2 presents average bad debt figures for various lines of trade. As the table indicates, bad debts should not exceed a very small percentage of total credit sales.

TABLE 17-2

Bad Debts as a Percentage of Total Sales, 1971

Department Stores		Specialty Stores	
Total sales	Bad debts as percent of total sales[a]	Total sales	Bad debts as percent of total sales[a]
Under $500,000	0.15	Under $1 million	0.18
$500,000 to $1 million	0.47	$1–5 million	0.27
$1–2 million	0.20	Over $5 million	0.75
$2–5 million	0.17		
$5–10 million	0.20		
$10–20 million	0.37		
$20–50 million	0.48		
Over $50 million	0.56		

[a] These are "typical figures" representing either an average for all reporting stores if 6 to 12 stores reported, or an interquartile average if the number of stores was greater than 12.
Source: Jay Scher, *Financial and Operating Results of Department and Specialty Stores of 1971* (New York: National Retail Merchants Association, 1972).

Bad debts are partially minimized through a well-managed collection program. When an account becomes overdue, a planned sequence of events designed to produce payment should begin. While customer good will should be retained if possible, it must be recognized that the good will of a customer who refuses to pay bills is of little value.

A collection program usually consists of several mailed "reminders" that the account is past due. If such notices do not produce results, the retailer should attempt to contact the customer by phone so that the retailer and customer can discuss and evaluate reasons for the delay. In addition, the retailer can explain the effect of late payment on the individual's credit record. If no satisfactory arrangement can be made, the retailer may turn the account over to a collection agency. These agencies work on a percentage of the amount collected and, because they are specialists, are frequently more successful than the retailer in securing payment.

Capitalizing on Credit Accounts

Customers who have gone to the trouble of opening an account in a store have indicated a preference for shopping there. Thus, the list of credit customers is a valuable tool for both promotion and research. Monthly statements can be used as a promotional device by including "stuffers" at a small additional cost. Second, the credit customer list can be used as a mailing list to announce special or seasonal promotions.

Often overlooked is the opportunity to use credit customers as a source of information. For example, with a simple questionnaire, credit customers can be asked about contemplated changes in store policy, services, or merchandise. Because they are interested in the store, their answers can be a useful barometer of customer sentiment.

The Computer and Credit

Because many credit chores are easily programmed, the computer has become a valuable tool in the operation of both large and small plans. Small retailers can make use of computerized billing services, and record keeping can also be done on computers, although this is limited to relatively large plans. A recent use of the computer in credit has been in transaction approval. Using a terminal at the point of sale, the clerk punches in the customer's account number. In a matter of seconds, the computer searches the customer's file and indicates whether the account is open to buy, already at the limit, or if some special problem exists requiring that the customer speak to the credit department. This type of system in a large store gives the retailer unprecedented control over stolen or misused credit cards, since the computer updates the customer's record as soon as a sale is made.

REVIEW BOX 17:4

1. Two potential aids in credit application evaluation are point scoring and _____.
2. A retailer can capitalize on credit customers in promotion and _____.

Ch. 17 *Credit and Other Supplementary Services*

CHAPTER SUMMARY

- The subject of this chapter is *supplementary services*—services that aid in the sale of a product or primary service. A *primary service* is a service that is the object of a transaction.
- Supplementary services are popular with consumers because they make shopping easier and more convenient. Retailers like them because they are a form of non-price competition.
- The decision to offer a service should include consideration of cost, demand, alternative sources, and competition.
- Supplementary services go through a five-stage cycle from introduction to replacement. The cycle reflects the ease with which services can be introduced and the difficulty of eliminating them.
- All services should be evaluated periodically to determine their contribution to the business. Services for which the costs exceed the benefits should be eliminated. Special managerial consideration should be given to charging for supplementary services and customer misuse of services.
- The volume of consumer credit singles it out as a very important supplementary service.
- Consumer credit can be subdivided according to the type of financing into internal and external credit.
- When divided according to the type of payment, credit is subdivided into 30-day single-payment, installment, and revolving.
- The decision to offer credit is largely influenced by competition. However, the type of credit offered requires careful consideration of the advantages and disadvantages of various alternatives.
- Critical aspects of an internal credit plan include credit approval, credit records, and billings and collection.
- Credit customers can be used effectively in promotions and as a source of information in retail research.
- Computers are being used in credit for record keeping, billing, and transaction approval. Their use provides the manager with unprecedented control over credit.

CHAPTER NOTES

[1] "What Makes Warehouse Markets Go," *Progressive Grocer*, August 1972, pp. 60–68.
[2] "Finance Facts," National Consumer Finance Association, April 1973.
[3] John J. Reynolds, "The Future of the Bank Card," *Credit World*, December 1973, pp. 19–21.
[4] "Macy's Opens Its Door to American Express," *Business Week*, November 11, 1972, p. 51.
[5] "The Bank Credit Card with an Annual $10 Fee," *Business Week*, March 3, 1973, p. 23.
[6] "California Grocer, Bank of America Test Credit Card," *Advertising Age*, May 2, 1960, p. 2.

QUESTIONS AND ASSIGNMENTS

1. Define supplementary services. Give two examples of services that could be either primary or supplementary depending upon the situation.
2. Why do retailers prefer non-price forms of competition?
3. Describe the stages in the services cycle. What service can you think of that has lost its usefulness but is still maintained by retailers?
4. What are the direct and indirect costs involved for a department store that has a liberal merchandise return policy?
5. Describe how you would go about evaluating the usefulness of a delivery service that your firm had put into operation a year ago.
6. Who pays for a "free" service? What are the major considerations in deciding whether to charge or offer a service at no charge?
7. Explain the difference between internal and external credit. Are bank credit cards and travel and entertainment credit plans internal or external?
8. Describe the three types of credit plans divided according to the method of payment.
9. If a customer buys a $320 refrigerator and agrees to pay for it on a 90-day installment contract of four payments, and the interest rate charged is 1 percent per month on the unpaid balance, what would be the *total cost* of the refrigerator to the customer?
10. List the advantages and disadvantages of both internal and external credit. Which type do you feel would be best for a small record shop located in the mall of a shopping center? Why?

ANSWERS TO REVIEW BOX QUESTIONS

Box 17:1
1. little or no value
2. non-price
3. competition

Box 17:2
1. differential advantage
2. competitive behavior
3. return privileges

Box 17:3
1. accounts receivable
2. interest charges
3. what form of credit to offer

Box 17:4
1. credit bureau
2. research or information gathering

Questions and Assignments

RETAILING DECISION
The Hawthorne Road Plaza

"Let's see . . . we still have to work out the details of the two commercials and have them filmed. I'll check with Ed Davis, who's a salesman at WXYZ-TV and a friend of mine, about this. Then we can meet one more time and develop a schedule of times to run the commercials. I really think this TV advertising will generate the traffic our center needs!" This is how Mike Dimay, the owner of a hobbies-and-crafts shop, wrapped up the latest meeting of the merchants in the Hawthorne Road Plaza.

Since the first store opened nine months ago, the Plaza has been modestly successful. However, it still does not have the shopper traffic most of the merchants expected. While all the outlets have advertised on an individual basis, some rather extensively, the planned TV advertising will be only their second cooperative effort.

The Plaza is one of several neighborhood shopping centers that have sprung up within the last five years in this city of 200,000. The neighborhood around this particular center contains a new car dealer, two service stations, an apartment complex of 300 units, a new development of luxury townhouses, and (a half mile down Hawthorne Road) a subdivision of new houses in the middle-price range.

The eight adjoining stores in the L-shaped plaza are a self-service laundromat, a liquor store, a convenience grocery store, a bakery, a dry cleaning outlet, a children's clothing store, a florist, and the hobbies-and-crafts shop. In addition, a bank branch is at the front of the Plaza in a separate building. Two locations in the Plaza have not yet been leased.

For the grand opening, the six merchants who were ready to open jointly sponsored a full-page ad in the afternoon newspaper, which has a larger circulation than either the local morning paper or another morning paper from a large metropolitan area about 50 miles away.

The bakery manager had an excellent response to the grand opening ad—almost too great a response. He sold 500 dozen donuts and cookies at half-price during the grand opening. The other merchants' reactions ranged from "very disappointed" to "we did OK."

In the merchants' first meeting about another cooperative advertising effort, newspapers were ruled out as a possible medium—no doubt because of the merchants' lukewarm feeling about the grand opening ad. Radio advertising was seriously considered, but the bank manager's pronouncement that radio lacks impact was convincing. Direct mail was ruled out when none of the merchants knew how they could compile a mailing list.

Television advertising was eventually decided upon because it could show the variety and attractive appearance of outlets in the Plaza and illustrate the personal service stressed by the merchants. These two features—variety and personal service—will be the theme in the first commercial. In an attempt to generate more traffic, the second will promote a contest. According to tentative plans, the contest will involve guessing the weight of a steer corraled in the bank's parking lot. First, second, and third prizes are to be different combinations of free merchandise and services.

1. Do you agree with the merchants' planned cooperative advertising? If yes, what are its strong points? If no, what would you suggest as a cooperative advertising program to increase shopper traffic?
2. Recognizing the relatively small size of the individual locations and the stores presently in the Plaza, what types of stores (with respect to line of business) should the Plaza merchants seek for the two unleased locations? Explain.

RETAILING DECISION
Classic Clothes

Upon graduating from college in 1955, John Hendricks opened a small men's clothing store, Classic Clothes, along a major thoroughfare in Lakeland, a city of 125,000 and the home of Central State University. Over the years, a formula of quality merchandise and excellent service has brought rapid growth to John's business. In 1961 he moved to a larger location in a new shopping center, and in 1965 he opened a second store across the street from the university campus. The merchandise in the campus store is more "avant garde" and less expensive than that carried in Classic Clothes.

When John began business, he used an externally financed and managed credit plan because of a lack of capital. For a charge of $1 per credit application and 3 percent of all credit sales, the factor provided a complete credit service. However, some problems developed with the quality of the factor's service regarding billing errors, and as soon as he was able John assumed the credit plan, making it totally internal. In addition to the internal plan, John also accepts Master Charge, BankAmericard, and American Express credit cards.

Recently, two problems have come up. First, several students have inquired about credit at the campus store. Due to their age and relatively small incomes, students do not qualify for the external plans like Master Charge or BankAmericard. However, John estimates that granting credit to students would increase sales 20 percent. On the other hand, he has noticed that credit management is taking more and more of his time. The stores have over 1,000 accounts, and an average of 300 statements are sent out each month. In addition, last month an amount equal to 3.5 percent of sales was written off as uncollectable bad debts, the highest monthly total in the stores' history. Since John is now considering opening a third store in a neighboring town, he is worried about his credit program.

1. What factors should John Hendricks consider in making his decision about student accounts?
2. What alternatives does he have in regard to the managerial problems of his credit program?

PART SIX

Financial and Information Management

Information for Retailing Decisions

Developing and implementing a buying plan, pricing merchandise, supervising sales personnel, and devising an advertising program all have two things in common. They are essential ingredients of a successful retail business, and they entail operating decisions the retailer must make every day. This chapter is somewhat different. It deals with what should take place prior to decision making, and how information should be used to make current operating decisions and long-range plans—aspects of retailing that are often ignored because of the pressure of daily decision making.

THE VALUE OF INFORMATION

No one would deny the importance of the retailer's involvement in daily operating problems and decisions. Unfortunately, however, attention to daily details is not enough to ensure success. Dramatic changes having a significant effect on retailing are taking place, and merchants must keep up with them.

First, the consumer is changing. People are acquiring greater spending power at a younger age, the average age for marriage (and therefore for forming households) is going up, and values dealing with such things as the environment and resources, appearance and dress, and the ownership of durable goods as status symbols are rapidly changing. Although these are just a sample of recent developments, their impact on retailing has been significant. For example, in Oregon, concern for the environment has resulted in a ban on non-returnable bottles and cans for beer and soft drinks. As a result, grocery stores and supermarkets have experienced serious problems in handling and storing empty bottles returned for credit. As another example, who would have thought a few years ago that bib overalls would one day be displayed in chic boutiques and that garments made from the scraps of old jeans would be sold in the best stores? If the past is any indication, the future seems to promise only more change in consumers.

Second, the technology of retailing is evolving very rapidly. Application of the computer to site location, inventory management, sales control, and buying has created problems but also benefits in the form of reduced operating cost and increased efficiency. Automated warehouses, price-scanning equipment, automated credit checks, retail design innovations, and closed circuit and cable television are just a few examples of the technological developments that have been applied to retailing recently.

Third, the environment in which retailers must operate is changing. The fuel shortage may significantly increase the use of mass transit but seriously hurt suburban shopping centers that depend on automobiles. Retail employees are demanding more challenging work and higher pay, and consumerism has brought pressure on hours of store operation, services, and guarantees.

Finally, in response to these developments, retailing itself has changed. Merchandise assortments have increased to the point, for example, that it is sometimes difficult to distinguish among a variety store, a drug store, and a grocery store. Major chains are opening "mini" stores in small communities and "super" stores in other areas. While these developments are going on, in-home shopping and rental of products are both increasing.

By now the point should be quite clear: retailing is a very dynamic business field! Today's retailer must adjust to the times. This chapter discusses information as a tool that can be used to develop an informed basis for decision making in this rapidly changing world.

PUTTING INFORMATION TO WORK

Today's retailer needs accurate, timely information to plan, operate, and evaluate. *Planning* includes both ongoing and new operations and encompasses market analysis, sales forecasting, and evaluation of expansion opportunities. *Operating* consists of coordinating the retailing functions and understanding the consumer. Finally, *evaluating* involves measuring performance to determine whether goals have been met.

The following description of how information can be used does not consider its sources or methods of securing it. That will be presented later. The purpose of the present section is to describe how key decisions can be improved by accurate information.

Planning

Several of the planning areas for new and ongoing businesses are the same; for example, both must forecast sales. However, this section will be directed specifically to the needs of the ongoing firm. The two areas discussed are sales forecasts and expansion decisions.

SALES FORECASTING

A sales forecast is essential to the development of effective operating plans. The establishment of a sales objective will influence such things as the amount of inventory to maintain, the number of salespeople needed, and the volume of advertising planned.

Sales forecasting methods range from "guesstimates" based on experience to sophisticated statistical projections. Whatever the method used, the basis for most forecasts is the trend in sales over the recent past adjusted by external and internal developments. For example, to make an annual forecast, the first step is to determine the difference between sales for the most recent year and the preceding year. This difference is then divided by the sales figure for the earlier year to produce the percentage change. For example, suppose sales in 19X0 were $1,640,430 and sales in 19X1 were $1,734,680. The percentage change in sales would be calculated as follows:

$$\begin{array}{lr} \text{sales for 19X1} & \$1,734,680 \\ \text{sales for 19X0} & -\$1,640,430 \\ \hline & \$94,250 \end{array}$$

$94,250 ÷ $1,640,430 = 6%, the percentage change in sales

Since sales went up, there is a percentage increase. Of course, if sales had gone down there would be a percentage decrease.

The second step is to compute the predicted sales figure for the upcoming year. This is done by multiplying the percentage change by the sales in the most recent year and adding the results to that year's sales figure. Continuing the example above, we predict sales of $1,838,760 for 19X2:

.06 × $1,734,680 = $104,080   (expected increase in sales)

$1,734,680 + $104,080 = $1,838,760   (expected total sales for 19X2)

The third and final step is to make any adjustments in the forecast based upon expected external and internal developments. The primary external considerations, those factors over which the retailer has no control, are economic conditions and competitive behavior. For example, the merchants in

Seattle were forced to revise their forecasts when Boeing laid off thousands of employees in the late 1960s. Other examples of economic factors include increases in wholesale prices that affect final prices and the loss of a supplier. Significant competitive behavior includes the arrival or departure of a competing firm in the trading area or strategy changes by one or more existing competitors.

Internal considerations, those over which the retailer has control, may be more easily identified but equally difficult to evaluate. Some common internal factors are eliminating or adding a merchandise line, increasing or decreasing advertising, losing a key employee, and redesigning or expanding the outlet.

Two things should be obvious at this point. First, sales forecasting requires the use of a considerable amount of judgment. Many factors must be considered in addition to past sales. Second, information about the outlet, the competition, and the environment plays a critical role in an accurate assessment of the future.

EXPANSION DECISIONS

An important decision every successful retailer must consider is expanding the business. Expansion can take at least three forms:

Increasing the variety of offerings available in the present outlet.
Expanding the present outlet by buying an adjoining building or constructing an addition to the present outlet.
Opening an additional outlet at another location.

Decisions on whether to expand, the type of expansion, and the amount of expansion all require a considerable amount of information. The retailer needs to know: (1) the volume of present sales and the prospects for the future; (2) the nature and extent of problems created by the existing situation (Do customers frequently request merchandise not stocked? Do you frequently run out of stock? Are customers inconvenienced by having to wait to make purchases?); (3) the nature and extent of problems created by growth (Will more personnel be needed? Will the store have to close during construction? Will it detract from the outlet's desired image?); (4) alternatives to expansion (Would greater inventory or more salespeople solve existing problems? Could the present outlet be redesigned for greater efficiency?); and (4) the cost of expansion and the availability of funds.

Operating

COORDINATION

Whether a retail business is large or small, coordination of activities will improve its efficiency. Inventories must be coordinated with actual sales to avoid stockouts or excess merchandise. Staffing, advertising, and buying must also

Putting Information to Work **427**

be coordinated with each other and with sales to avoid irritated customers and lost sales.

If you say, "This is nothing new; it is simply a way of describing the manager's job," you are correct. However, there are many retail managers who try to do their jobs without the help of important information. Recent advances in retailing have made it more possible to maintain close control over inventories, relate sales to individual buyers and sales personnel, and evaluate advertising effectiveness on at least a general scale. New electronic cash registers, mini-computers, and customer studies all can help the manager make informed coordination decisions.

KNOWING CUSTOMERS

Most retailers would like to know all about present and target customers — what they want, what causes them to buy, when they will buy, and so on. Although not every question can be answered, the consumer is an invaluable source of information frequently ignored by retailers. Among the things consumers can tell the retailer are the importance to them of the services provided, the image a store has, who the loyal customers are and why they are loyal, and what their reaction is likely to be if changes are made in the outlet or its operations.

Consumers can be observed or questioned in a variety of ways, several of which will be discussed in a later section. Although care must be taken in interpreting consumer information, it is as valuable as any other type and need not be any more expensive to collect.

Evaluating

Evaluating what has happened in the past is useful for taking any necessary corrective action. Evaluations can be divided into two categories: (1) performance relative to *internally* established standards, including meeting sales forecasts, reducing shrinkage, cutting selling expenses, or reducing employee turnover, and (2) performance relative to *external* standards including evaluating the outlet's competitive position and comparing performance to industry norms. Here, as in areas discussed earlier, information from a number of internal and external sources is necessary.

THE RESEARCH PROCESS

Information cannot be effectively gathered or incorporated in decision making without a plan. This plan, called the *research process*, includes defining the problem, setting the objectives, and facilitating performance of the research and use of the results.

Defining the Research Problem

The first step in any research project is to define the problem. Why is the information or research needed? Although this may sound like a simple task, it is complicated by the fact that problems (or opportunities) are frequently confused with symptoms. For example, declining sales, long customer waiting lines, high employee turnover, and increased shrinkage are all symptoms that indicate the existence of a problem. In order to eliminate the symptom, the retailer must solve the problem. The first task in a project may be to dig below the symptoms and identify the causes. Once this is done, information that will help solve the problem can be specified.

Setting a Research Objective

A second question that should be asked at the outset of a research project is, what is the objective? To put it another way, if something is found out, conclusions drawn, or recommendations made, what will happen? This is a critical question, since research for the sake of research is costly, time consuming, and valueless.

When research is begun, a retailer should be committed to using the results. This does not mean blindly following recommendations. If sound reasons exist, research results may be rejected. In such a case, they are being used in the sense that they are considered, evaluated, and rejected.

Facilitating Research

Because research is often employed as a last resort when all else has failed, impatience for results may overcome sound judgment. However, it must be remembered that conducting good research takes time. Thus, rather than treat research as a source of immediate answers, the retailer should anticipate information needs before decisions must be made.

Once research is completed, to be of value it must be presented in a form understood by the potential user. The language and format should be tailored to the user's level of sophistication, and a permanent record of the results should be made for future reference. Technical terms or statistical formulations are impressive but of little value to a decision maker. Rather, a summary of conclusions from the project supported by the means used to reach those conclusions will facilitate the use of the information in the decision process of the manager.

> **REVIEW BOX 18:1**
>
> 1. Information is used by retailers to plan, operate, and _____.
> 2. In the research process, a common error is to confuse symptoms with _____.

INTERNAL SOURCES OF INFORMATION

Information to aid in making the types of decisions mentioned above can be generated internally or collected from external sources. Internal information, discussed in this section, comes from two major sources: machines and employees. One source, retail employees, has always been available. To use this source the retailer must first make employees sensitive to the things that go on around them and, second, develop a method of including the information in decision making.

The second internal source, electronic data collection, is a relatively new one. Developments in the way sales are recorded have the potential of creating dramatic changes in retailing decision making.

Employee Feedback

Salespeople, checkers, cashiers, delivery men, employees receiving returned merchandise, and carry-out boys all come into direct contact with customers. They hear compliments and criticisms, they see customer pleasure and dissatisfaction, and they sometimes feel pride or embarrassment in the way things are done in the store. If retail employees are alert to these things and communicate them to management, improvement in store operations can result.

For a steady flow of information from employees to management, three things are needed. First, a method of communication is necessary. The method may be informal conversations, meetings, interviews, a suggestion box, or some other means. Choice of a method depends on the type of organization, nature of the employees, and personality of the manager.

Second, employees must feel free to express their observations and reactions without fear. For example, an employee may notice that a new merchandise arrangement developed by his boss is seriously inconveniencing customers. If he is afraid that the boss may resent or punish him for pointing out the arrangement problem, he will remain silent and the store will suffer. Simply stated, an atmosphere of trust and joint effort toward a common goal must exist between employees and managers. This atmosphere does not just happen. It develops over time as the result of managers' reactions toward employees' inputs.

Finally, employees must feel that their feedback is of some value to management. Some businesses place a dollar value on information by giving employees cash bonuses for suggestions that are used. This provides a tangible indication that feedback is valued. An intangible source of satisfaction for the employee is simply seeing a suggestion or bit of information acted upon. This is an important but frequently overlooked step in gathering information. Just as a manager wants feedback from employees about what is happening at the customer level, the employees want feedback from management on the information they provide. Acknowledging review of a suggestion and the action taken on it requires little managerial time but provides considerable satisfaction to the employee.

Machine-Generated Information

Processing sales in the store is one aspect of retailing that is experiencing rapid and significant change. In this section the impact of some of these new developments on information for decision making will be considered.

TRADITIONAL SYSTEMS

For many years retailers have relied upon either the cash register, the sales slip, or a combination of both to record sales and provide internal managerial information. Cash registers provide relatively fast, efficient customer service, a receipt for the customer, and a permanent record of sales for the store.

The sales slip usually provides more information than the cash register tape, but each sales transaction takes more time to complete. A sales slip normally includes the customer's name and address, the merchandise sold and the department from which it came, the type of sale (cash or credit), the salesperson's name and number, date of the sale, applicable taxes, and total amount of the transaction. The principal benefit of the sales slip is the information it provides. When sales slips are analyzed, sales by merchandise line and department can be evaluated, inventories can be properly controlled, and productivity of salespeople can be determined. In addition, the sales slip provides both the customer and the retailer with a detailed record of the transaction should returns or adjustments become necessary.

A retailer who wants to get decision-making information from cash register tapes or sales slips must go through the laborious task of categorizing and summarizing the information. For most outlets the time and resulting cost of such activities make them unattractive. As a result they are often left undone.

ELECTRONIC SYSTEMS

Electronic Cash Registers. The electronic cash register (ECR), the first step in the evolution of sales processing, is simply a more sophisticated version of the traditional cash register. Designed primarily for checkout systems common to supermarkets and discount stores, it still requires manual input of information through a keyboard. Depending upon the manufacturer, however, the ECR can perform a variety of valuable functions. For example, the R.C. Allen Ultra 702 can calculate and add in taxes automatically, record multiple item sales with one key, and void errors. The NCR 250 can keep track of sales for up to eleven departments, calculate trading stamps and coupons, record bottle refunds, and provide up to 51 different totals on a sales report.[1] Systems like these offer multiple benefits to the retailer. They speed up customer checkout, increase checker accuracy and efficiency, and provide a considerable amount of organized information in an immediately usable form.

Electronic Point-of-Sale Systems. When ECRs are combined with computers, an electronic point-of-sale system (POS) is the result. The ultimate POS will include a device to scan special labels on merchandise, automatically look up prices, ring up the sale, make credit approvals, make change, instantly record the sale, and provide detailed information to managers in decision-making form. The salesclerk need only pass the merchandise over the scanner, bag it, collect the customer's payment, and return the calculated change.

Franklin Stores Corporation, a New York–based specialty and discount chain, was an early POS installer, putting the system in its Barker discount division. Management reports that the stores have experienced personnel cost savings because no clerks are needed to process sales tickets in the back room. In addition, productivity of checkout clerks increased by 17 to 20 percent.[2] Another retailer, Watt and Shand in Lancaster, Pennsylvania, installed 50 terminals and achieved an immediate savings of $70,000. The system cut the credit and billing staff in half and eliminated the need for keypunching information for computer analysis.[3]

An example of POS systems in a retailing conglomerate illustrates the impact of electronic information systems on large retailers.[4] Jewel Company of Chicago has over 11 separate divisions ranging from food stores to lumber outlets. In an attempt to increase the speed and efficiency with which customers are processed and to provide management with immediate information, Jewel has installed over 600 terminals developed jointly with Nuclear Data.

In the Jewel system a register has three components: a keyboard on which the clerk inputs information, a cash drawer, and a printer that produces a receipt for the customer and control information for the store. The keyboard has only 20 keys, allowing the checker to operate it using the touch system (without looking at the keys). Once the touch system is mastered, checker productivity increases greatly. To aid the checker, taxes are computed automatically, multiple prices need only be entered once, corrections are easily made and shown on the customer's receipt, and the equipment provides special controls for handling cash, checks, and food stamps to prevent mistakes or theft by checkers.

The store manager derives useful information as well. The registers in a store can be constantly monitored from a control booth. At any given time it is possible to get departmental sales totals, store sales, customer counts, coupon redemptions, and taxable sales. Consider two specific examples of the information benefits of the system: First, by identifying the number of entries and errors by a checker over a period of time, the manager can identify peak customer loads and determine whether or not the checker needs additional training. Second, in the past it has been necessary to have someone sort, count, and total all of the Jewel and manufacturers' coupons a store received each week. With 10,000 to 12,000 coupons per week, this was a bothersome,

SPOTLIGHT

How does Sears, Roebuck satisfy its information needs? It spends $750 million on a program that ties together 30,000 registers, 640 mini-computers, and 33 large computers. *Business Week* described the Sears system as follows.

How it works: In the Sears system, as it will eventually evolve, the first step is receipt of the product from the warehouse or supplier. Say the product is a coffee pot. An automatic ticketmaker produces a ticket that indicates the coffee pot's color, price, stock number, and clerk's department number. When a customer takes the coffee pot to the register, the clerk either keys the numbers into the register or uses the reading wand.

If the customer wants to pay with a credit card, the wand picks up a magnetic code and in less than one second clears the card through the store's mini-computer. "That split second for wanding gives us the sales information for the entire inventory management system," says Thomas Wands, vice-president of operations.

The coffee pot data are stored in the mini-computer until nightfall when they are automatically transferred to one of the company's 22 regional data centers, where big IBM computers process the information. There, the customer's credit account is charged, sales and tax figures are entered into the accounting department's records, and the salesclerk's commission record is credited to the payroll department.

Sales data also enter the coffee pot department's inventory management system. If the day's coffee pot sales lower the department's inventory below a predetermined point, the computer automatically prints a purchase order, which is sent by messenger to the department manager the next morning. If the manager decides to buy more coffee pots, the reorder goes to the supplier, who fills it.

At the same time, the sales data are also channeled through the regional data center to a central data processing station in Sears' Chicago headquarters, where national unit-sale information is compiled.

Source: "How Giant Sears Grows and Grows," *Business Week*, December 16, 1972, pp. 54–55.

time-consuming task. Now, with a touch of a button, the manager gets a complete list of coupons for each register. In a matter of minutes the coupons can be bundled up and ready for shipment.

Electronic Systems and the Smaller Retailer. Small retailers cannot afford computers or even mini-computers and may have only one or two registers in their stores. Yet, they are still faced with the same needs for information. Several equipment manufacturers have responded to this situation by making full data-processing services available to small retailers. On equipment supplied by the manufacturer, point-of-sale information is stored until the end of the day. When the store closes, the information is electronically transmitted to a data center where computer reports of the day's activity are prepared and returned to the retailer by the next morning. Using, for example, an NCR system, a retailer can have a sales and inventory summary for up to 800 product classifications, a tax report, salesperson productivity figures, income statements, balance sheets, and an accounts receivable report.

REVIEW BOX 18:2

1. The two primary sources of internal information are employees and _____.
2. When electronic cash registers are combined with computers, the result is _____.

EXTERNAL INFORMATION SOURCES

Going beyond the doors of the store, the retailer has a wealth of information sources available. The most important are described below.

Trade Associations

The retailing industry has many trade associations that provide their members with a wide variety of information. One of the most prominent, the National Retail Merchants Association (NRMA) has over 23,000 members. Table 18-1 presents a list of some recent NRMA publications available to members.

A national trade association directory lists over 25 trade associations in retailing.[5] Some have broad membership, like the NRMA, and others are specialized like the Tobacconists' Association of America, Ltd. Still other associations specialize in a particular function; an example is the Retail Advertising Conference. Principal functions of trade associations include

TABLE 18-1

Examples of National Retail Merchant Association Publications

A Report of a Study of Organization in Multi-Unit Department and Specialty Stores, 1961
Housekeeping Manual for Retail Stores, 1963
Direct Mail Advertising by Retail Stores, 1967
The Branch Managers Manual, by Beatrice Judelle, 1968
Cash Management in Retail Businesses, 1968
How to Sell the Whole Store as Fashion, by Budd Gore, 1969
The Name of the Game Is Sell, by Budd Gore, 1969
A Handbook for T.V. Advertising, edited by Martin Padley, 1969
A Handbook for Radio Advertising, edited by Martin Padley, 1969
198 Ways of Controlling Markdowns, 1970
Merchandising Arithmetic of Retail Training, 1971

keeping members informed about legal, environmental, and business developments affecting the industry and acting as a spokesman for the industry.

Government Sources

Two important publications of the federal government are the *Census of Business* and *County Business Patterns*.[6] The *Census of Business* includes two volumes of particular interest to retailers, "Retail Trade-Subject Reports" and "Retail Trade-Area Statistics." These two volumes present statistics on the type, location, sales, payroll, and size of retail establishments. Although the volumes are comprehensive, they are not very timely, since there is a lag of about four years between when information is collected and when it is published. *County Business Patterns* includes total employees, total payrolls, and employees by employer size broken down by state, county, standard metropolitan statistical area, and industry. This information can be used in evaluating market potential, establishing sales expectations for particular stores, and making basic economic studies for small regions.

The Small Business Administration (SBA), an agency of the federal government, produces a wide variety of pamphlets and books that offer operating advice, comparative operating figures for various lines of business, and information on current developments of significance to small businesses. SBA publications are available at regional and district offices around the country.

State universities frequently operate business research divisions in conjunction with their colleges of business. These units conduct regional business and economic studies, publish research monographs, and often offer training and operating advice for businessmen.

Finally, at the local level many newspapers provide data on local market conditions. For example, *The Courier Journal-Louisville Times* makes available extensive market data for the Kentucky and Southern Indiana area. Included is information on consumer usage of newspapers, television, and radio; the number and location of various types of retail outlets; extensive information on shopping centers in the area; and detailed statistics on the Louisville market.

Suppliers

A retailer's suppliers can frequently serve as both formal and informal sources of valuable information. In order to merchandise their products more efficiently, manufacturers and wholesalers conduct research studies. They often share these studies with retailers who can, in turn, use the information to pinpoint target markets and direct their efforts more effectively.

A potential informal source of information is suppliers' salesmen. Most salesmen travel a territory, calling on retailers over a relatively large geographic area. A good salesman is alert to market changes, competitive developments, opportunities for growth, personnel changes, and a wide range of other facts. This is frequently described in a derogatory fashion as "trade gossip," but an alert retailer who asks the right questions can pick up important bits of information.

Publications

There are several magazines that provide useful information for retailers. Among the most prominent are:

Chain Store Age. A May issue provides a report on shopping center growth and change.

Men's Wear. The July issue presents operating ratios by type and size of men's stores and by geographic area.

Progressive Grocer. The April issue presents sales by type of grocery store, trends in grocery retailing, and operating ratios.

Sales Management. The June issue presents the "Survey of Buying Power," which includes a demographic breakdown of population estimates, effective buying power, total retail sales, and retail sales divided by type of retail outlet for a variety of geographic breakdowns. The November issue includes "Marketing on the Move," which presents metropolitan area projections, population estimates, buying power, and retail sales for counties and standard metropolitan statistical areas.

Stores. In August the sales of the 100 largest department stores, selected specialty stores, branch stores, chain stores, and discount stores are presented.

These magazines also include informative and thought-provoking articles on such topics as recent developments in store layout and design, promotional techniques, managerial practices, and legislative activity.

Several businesses publish occasional monographs, available free or for a small fee, that offer plans for controlling costs and expenses, operating ratios, and methods for evaluating efficiency. Two examples are "How to Build Profits by Controlling Costs," a Dun and Bradstreet publication, and "Expenses in Retail Business," published by National Cash Register.

Consumers

A retailer frequently would like information from customers but hesitates because of an unfamiliarity with techniques of consumer research. In addition, the retailer may fear that data collection will annoy or inconvenience customers. To some extent the retailer taking this position is probably correct. Books have been written on the proper way to do research and the problems of collecting information.[7]

It is impossible to teach research in a single section of one chapter of a retailing textbook. The objective here is less ambitious but very important: familiarization with some basics of research to help you appreciate what researchers are doing and what consumer research can do for the retailer.

The two most common research methods for consumer studies are observation and questioning. Observation consists of watching and recording a person's behavior rather than asking for information which, of course, is the questioning method.

RESEARCH METHODS

Observation. This method has the advantage of not involving the respondent. Thus, customers are not inconvenienced, and their willingness or ability to participate do not affect the research process. It is a useful technique when the researcher is *not* interested in explaining *why* people behave as they do. Because observations are subject to misinterpretation when employed to explain behavior, the method should be used with care. Take the case, for example, in which shoppers are being observed in the grocery store as they select a laundry detergent. The purpose of the study is to determine whether there is much decision making at the point of purchase. That is, do customers walk up and simply pick a brand, or do they spend time comparing prices, quantities, and contents? If a housewife picks up a box and holds it for two minutes, the observer might conclude that she is studying the package or considering alternatives. In fact, she may be thinking about the argument she had with her husband at breakfast or figuring out how she can afford a new dress. The observer, trying to explain behavior, has been misled because what goes on in a person's mind is not always obvious from behavior.

External Information Sources

Observation is appropriate when needed information can be readily observed (For example, what percentage of the people visiting this store are women?) and no attempt is to be made to explain behavior.

Observation studies take many forms, a few examples include:

Observe the route customers take through the store to determine which areas receive heavy traffic and which receive light traffic.

Check license plates in the store's parking lot to find out where customers are coming from.

Time the customer's wait at checkout stands during peak hours to evaluate the need for more or fewer checkers.

Questioning. Questioning provides more information and can contribute to explaining behavior. However, there is a price for more information. Questioning is a considerably more difficult research method. Its chief difficulties are the development of questions and interpretation of responses. Although this may sound simple, anyone experienced in developing research questions will vouch for the difficulty.

Specifically, questions must be:

Clearly stated in words understood by the person answering.

Non-technical. Words familiar to you may not be as familiar to someone else. In retailing, for example, "shrinkage," "markdowns," and "open to buy" may mean very little to the general public.

Objective. Leading questions influence answers and produce misleading results. A question such as "Do you agree with the City Council that downtown retailing should be encouraged?" will be answered according to how people feel about the City Council.

Non-sensitive. Questions on sensitive topics are often left unanswered or answered incorrectly. For example, "Have you ever stolen anything from a retail store?," even in an anonymous questionnaire, might not get truthful responses.

Easily recalled information. Questioning people about events that took place six months ago, or asking a person how many six-packs of beer he has purchased during the last twelve months will not produce good results.

A more complete explanation of the difficulties associated with writing good questions can be found in research books. This list, however, should indicate that a good questionnaire is not a simple task.

Two examples of studies using direct questioning are described below.

- A prospective retailer planning to open a clothing boutique adjacent to a college campus secured the aid of a marketing research class to survey students on the brands of sweaters, blouses, and other clothing they preferred. The students were asked to select from a list of brands their most preferred brand for each type of clothing. The retailer used the information in developing the merchandise lines for the store.

- An automobile dealer in Mayfield Heights, Ohio feels that satisfied customers are so important that he annually spends $10,000 on a study involving interviews with customers who have brought their cars in for service. The telephone interviews are taped, transcribed, and read by the owner. When problems are identified he personally makes sure they are solved. He says, "Voluntary involvement is the only way we can show the public that we are concerned. Just because we are ignorant of complaints doesn't mean they aren't there."[8]

Other studies in which direct questioning would be appropriate include: (1) a demographic profile of customers (i.e., age, sex, marital status, income, etc.) to check merchandise lines, services, prices, and personnel against customers' needs and desires; (2) consumers' awareness of the store's existence, merchandise lines, or special services; and (3) a survey of customers to determine the primary reason they visit the store.

Indirect questioning is a more subtle approach. Usually its purpose is to discover feelings or attitudes in cases where respondents might find it difficult to express their feelings directly. These techniques, borrowed from the behavioral sciences and adapted to business research, are beyond the scope of this book.[9] In retailing, indirect questioning techniques are used to determine a store's overall image, to evaluate store loyalty, and to measure consumer awareness and impressions of various facets of the store including the personnel, merchandise, advertising, and appearance.

DATA COLLECTION METHODS

Whether a researcher uses direct or indirect questioning, there are three possible methods of collecting data: face to face, mail, or telephone. Each method will be briefly discussed.

Face-to-Face Interviews. This method makes it possible to ask quite a large number of questions and to go into considerable detail. The interviewer can probe and ask for more elaboration from the respondent. In addition, because the interviewer can see the respondent, it is possible to evaluate the thoughtfulness and sincerity of the response. On the negative side, interviewers must be highly trained to ask questions properly, record answers correctly, and avoid influencing the respondent. Face-to-face interviews take a considerable amount of time to conduct, making this method the most expensive.

Mail Surveys. Sending questionnaires to people through the mail and asking them to mail back the completed response makes it possible to cover

External Information Sources

a wide geographic area at a relatively low cost. However, the questionnaire must be short, usually no more than two pages. Also, the rate of response is often very low, with as few as 10 percent of those receiving questionnaires returning them. An additional problem is that the researcher has no control over who answers the questions. The survey instructions may request that the housewife fill out the questionnaire, but the husband or a child may complete it instead.

Telephone Surveys. This is a fast and inexpensive data collection method if it is limited to the immediate telephoning area. The availability of Wide Area Telephone Service (WATS) lines has made regional or even national telephone surveys less costly. On the negative side, telephone interviews must be very short, they only reach households with phones, and they anger people who consider such a use of the phone an invasion of privacy.

You can see that each method has strengths and limitations. Unfortunately, the choice of one is often the result of compromises on cost, speed, and efficiency, when the proper criterion for selection should be the objective to be accomplished. For example, if the study requires detailed information, then personal interviews are appropriate. On the other hand, if wide geographic representation is critical, mail would be better.

SAMPLES

In a retailing study the researcher might want information from past customers, present customers, non-customers, credit customers, or from any of a hundred other defined groups. However, since it is usually impossible to collect information from all the members of a group, researchers often use a portion of the group, or a *sample*.

Selecting a sample that adequately represents the group it comes from is a delicate process. In order for the findings from a sample to hold true for the group, the sample must be *probabilistic*. Another name for a probabilistic sample is a *random sample*. Unfortunately, random sampling—ensuring that every member of the group has an equal chance of being included—is a difficult process. As an alternative, researchers often select a sample that includes a cross-section of people with the characteristics that have been judged to be important. For example, a cross-section of past customers might be used. If 70 percent of past customers were housewives, 70 percent of the sample should be housewives. If 50 percent of past customers were over forty years old, 50 percent of the sample should be over forty. Of course, the problem is in deciding which characteristics are important.[10]

Many internal and external sources of information have been described. Each has something useful to offer, and securing each requires different things of the retailer. Some sources require an investment in equipment;

Ch. 18 Information for Retailing Decisions

others require simply staying alert and listening. The problem is not the availability of information, it is the decision about what information is desired and the most efficient way to get it.

INFORMATION MANAGEMENT

If information is to be gathered and used effectively, a firm must have a system for handling it. The system can be simple, consisting only of the store owner overseeing the process, or it can be elaborate, involving a research staff receiving formal requests for research and responding with elaborate reports. Three common approaches to locating the information-gathering function—with the owner-manager, in a research department, and with consultants—are briefly discussed below.

The Owner-Manager

Small firms cannot support a research department and often cannot afford consultants. Thus, the information-gathering function usually falls to the owner-manager. The lack of funds and the time pressure common to small store operators does not mean that information gathering should be ignored. Quite the opposite is true. Because small retailers do not have the benefits of a research staff, they must assume the task themselves in order to maintain a viable competitive position. As pointed out throughout this chapter, information gathering and use need not be costly or time consuming. It only requires identifying a problem and developing an imaginative approach to investigating it. For example, using want slips is extremely simple, yet that information can tell a retailer much about the appropriateness of his merchandise and the expectations consumers have when they enter the store.

An area in which a lack of information has created problems for small to medium-size retailers is cost and expense control. As the need for new or replacement cash registers develop, the retailer should consider the information possibilities provided by new electronic equipment on the market.

The Research Department

Large retail chains are usually able to support staff research departments or divisions. Federated Department Stores, for example, has a research division available to all of the associated stores.

The decision to operate a research department depends on need. If a firm experiences a continuing need for research, then it makes sense to employ a staff of experts. Benefits of a research department are the ready availability of trained researchers, their familiarity with the business, and the opportunity to concentrate on particular problems.

The Consultant

When a firm experiences intermittent research or information needs that require skills or time not available within the firm, the answer may be to employ a consultant. Consultants can be very useful. They often bring expertise and experience beyond that of the manager. In addition, consultants can provide an independent, objective viewpoint that frequently cannot be obtained within the business. On the other hand, consultants can be expensive; they frequently have difficulty coming into a firm and quickly comprehending the problem; and, their findings often go unused, since no one is available to implement them after the consultant completes the report.

Because many retailers have had little or no experience with consultants, they avoid what may be a useful aid. If a consultant is carefully selected on the basis of skill and integrity, given adequate access to important information, and required to provide a complete explanation of his findings and conclusions, the retailer can benefit greatly.

REVIEW BOX 18:3

1. The five external information sources are trade associations, government, suppliers, publications, and _____.
2. In consumer research, the method that can be used when the researcher is not interested in explaining why people behave as they do is _____.
3. The data collection method that makes it possible to cover a wide geographical area at a relatively low cost is _____.
4. The information gathering function can be performed by the owner-manager, a research department, or _____.

CHAPTER SUMMARY

- Information for decision making is important to the retailer because of changes taking place in consumers, retailing technology, the environment, and retailing itself.
- Information can be used by the retailer to plan for the future, operate in the present, and evaluate the past. Planning for the future includes

sales forecasting and expansion decisions. Operating in the present involves coordinating retailing functions and knowing the consumer. Finally, evaluating the past involves looking at past store performance.
- The information-gathering process requires particular attention to certain activities and characteristics. Among the most important are: defining the research problem, setting a research objective, and facilitating the research process.
- Information is generated either internally or externally. Internal information comes from employees or as a result of processing sales. External information sources are trade associations, governmental sources, suppliers, publications, and consumers.
- Consumer information is collected by observation or questioning, and questioning can be either direct or indirect.
- The location of the information-gathering function is determined by the needs and resources of the firm. It may be the responsibility of the owner-manager, it may involve a research department, or it may be given to a consultant.

CHAPTER NOTES

[1] "1974: The Year of Electronics," *Progressive Grocer,* December 1973, pp. 36–52.
[2] "The Retailers Go Electronic," *Business Week,* August 19, 1972, pp. 38ff.
[3] *Ibid.*
[4] Discussion based on, "A Close-Up Look at Electronic Registers," *Progressive Grocer,* February 1973, pp. 72ff.
[5] Craig Colgate, Jr., editor, *1972 National Trade and Professional Associations of the United States* (Washington, D.C.: Columbia Books, Inc., 1972).
[6] U.S. Bureau of the Census, *Census of Business, 1967* (Washington, D.C.: U.S. Government Printing Office, 1971); and U.S. Bureau of the Census, *County Business Patterns, 1971* (Washington, D.C.: U.S. Government Printing Office, 1971).
[7] In marketing, for example, see Harper W. Boyd, Jr. and Ralph Westfall, *Marketing Research,* 3rd ed. (Homewood, Ill.: Richard D. Irwin, Inc., 1972).
[8] Peter Vanderwicken, "How Sam Marshall Makes Out with His 'Deal,'" *Fortune,* December 1972, pp. 121–30.
[9] For an introduction to indirect questioning methods see, Boyd and Westfall, *op. cit.*, pp. 322–34.
[10] For a more detailed discussion of sampling procedures see: Boyd and Westfall, Chapters 8 and 9.

QUESTIONS AND ASSIGNMENTS

1. Why is information of value to a retailer?
2. Is a decline in the number of people visiting a store a symptom or problem? Explain your answer.
3. "Information on the past is useless. I'm living today and planning for

tomorrow. Besides, you can't change what happened yesterday." Evaluate this statement.

4. Visit a local retailer and ask for examples of internal and external information used by the manager. Be specific in describing the use.
5. In order for information to flow from employees to the store manager, what three things are needed?
6. Survey several recent editions of publications on retailing (for example, *Progressive Grocer, Chain Store Age, Sales Management*) and select an article related to information gathering or use for class presentation.
7. Explain the difference between observation and questioning in data collection.
8. Discuss three approaches to the management of research, with special attention to the advantages and limitations of each.
9. Assume you are employed in a medium-size clothing store. The manager is considering opening a smaller store near your campus and has asked your opinion. Describe the research process you would use and the information you would gather.

ANSWERS TO REVIEW BOX QUESTIONS

Box 18:1

1. evaluate
2. problems

Box 18:2

1. machines
2. point-of-sale systems (POS)

Box 18:3

1. consumers
2. observation
3. mail survey

Financial and Accounting Concepts

As you are probably aware by now, successful retail operations require many talents. In large stores, with extensive specialization of labor, financial talent can usually be hired. But in the small store, financial decisions typically must be made by the store owner or manager. This does not mean that the road to success requires being a financial wizard. It does mean, though, that the owner-manager must be knowledgeable concerning financial management—able to read financial statements and to project financial needs as well as to know of sources of funds to meet these needs. The successful retailer must also wisely use the financial resources available to him. Thus, successful store operation involves obtaining and using funds intelligently and effectively, as indicated in Figure 19-1.

Note the similarity between the need for merchandise planning and the need for financial planning. Merchandise plans cannot be translated into action unless adequate financial planning assures that funds will be available when needed.

FINANCING THE RETAIL ENTERPRISE

Most retail firms require some financial assistance from outside sources. Only rarely does an individual begin a retail business with enough total funds to operate without relying to some extent on outside funding. Obviously, the nature of the financing requirements differs with the size, type, and nature of the firm.

The following brief discussion of sources of funds is divided into three

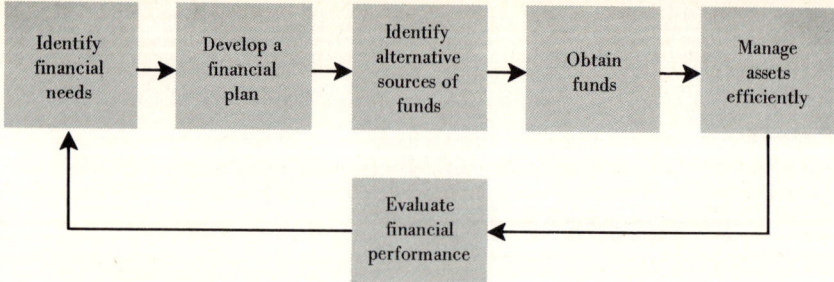

FIGURE 19-1

Steps in securing and using funds

Source: William Rudelius, W. Bruce Erickson, and William J. Bakula, Jr., *An Introduction to Contemporary Business* (New York: Harcourt Brace Jovanovich, Inc., 1973), p. 316.

classifications on the basis of the length of time for which funds are required. Long-term financing involves ten years or more, intermediate-term financing from one to ten years, and short-term financing one year or less. All three types fit the model in Figure 19-1.

Long-Term Financing

In retailing, long-term financing arrangements are primarily limited to the acquisition of land and buildings. Many retailers circumvent the need for long-term financing by leasing or renting the premises which they occupy. Some retailers, however, desire to purchase or construct a building because of:

    Unavailability of a suitable building which may be leased or rented
    Inability to negotiate a lease for the time period desired and under suitable terms
    Belief that a particular location or building offers the potential of long-term appreciation in value
    Desire for complete freedom to modify the premises in any manner desired without constraint by a landlord

Funds for long-term financing are available through either equity or debt financing. *Equity financing* represents funds furnished *by owners* of the business. For example, funds furnished by the individual operating the business as a sole proprietorship represent equity financing. In reality, an individual proprietor lends money to the business and logically expects to be paid back these funds at some future time. In a partnership, if the partners each put up a specified amount of money to purchase a building, equity financing is also involved.

A common form of equity financing involves sale of new stock by a corporation. In this case, stock purchasers are owners who furnish capital to the enterprise on a long-term basis. Under equity financing arrangements, no interest payments as such are involved, although stockholders normally expect dividends or appreciation in the stock's value as a "reward" for their investment risk.

Debt financing is more common than equity financing for most medium-size and small retailers. The most common form of debt financing is through a mortgage against the real property. Such mortgages may be held by banks, savings and loan institutions, insurance companies, private investors, friends, or relatives. Debt financing normally entails regular payments which include interest and a payback of principal. This kind of financing involves a fixed return to creditors, which distinguishes it from equity financing, where no fixed return is promised.

For larger firms the issuance of corporate bonds is a form of debt financing. Bond holders receive a promise of specific periodic interest sums and the return of principal at some specified future date. Unlike equity financing, in debt financing the lender holds no rights in conducting the business.

Intermediate-Term Financing

Financing for periods of more than one year but less than ten years is most often used to purchase equipment and fixtures, such as delivery trucks, cash registers, display cases, and office machines. Although sellers of fixtures and equipment may provide financing, a commercial bank will usually give more favorable interest rates. Other financing sources for intermediate-term credit are finance companies and the Small Business Administration.

Intermediate-term financing is used to finance those purchases which would strain the resources of the firm if short-term financing were used. At the other extreme, long-term financing is usually not available for the types of purchases indicated above, since the items purchased are usually fully depreciated (used up) within ten years or less.

Short-Term Financing

For most retail businesses, the need for short-term credit is greater than that for either long-term or intermediate-term credit. The most frequent reasons for short-term financing are to meet seasonal or unexpected needs for funds or simply to assure that cash flows are adequate. Simply because a firm shows a profit at the end of the year is no assurance that there will not be times during the year when the firm's cash balance will be inadequate to meet current bills. For example, when a new store is opened or when an existing store is expanded, the cash needed for merchandise inventory, wages and salaries, and perhaps supplies can grow faster than cash receipts from sales. In other words, a firm's cash inflow and outflow are not always balanced.

A primary form of short-term financing is *trade credit*. Any extension of time other than strict cash on delivery involves the extension of trade credit by the seller. One of the primary reasons for EOM and "extra" terms is to allow the retailer to sell some merchandise before having to pay the entire bill. However, recall that if a merchant forgoes a cash discount to use the longer net credit period, the cost of "financing" this extra period of time may be exorbitant. For example, under terms of 3/10 net 30, the annual interest rate is 54 percent.

Rather than pass up a cash discount, a retailer would be well advised to borrow money from a commercial bank at a 10 to 12 percent, or even higher, annual rate. Typically, short-term funds are borrowed from a commercial bank. Retailers often make arrangements with a bank for a line of credit to be used as needed—for seasonal loans of 30 to 90 days, for example. These loans tend to be *self-liquidating* in that the money is invested in merchandise which generates repayment funds as it sells.

Commercial banks also make loans using a retailer's accounts receivable as security. Typically such loans are made to retailers who do a substantial credit business. When credit sales are made, the investment in inventory is reduced, but there is not an immediate increase in the cash available to the business. Since some accounts may prove uncollectable, banks typically lend only a conservative percentage of the firm's outstanding receivables.

Other means of short-term financing are available to some retailers. Short-term loans may be obtained from friends or relatives. Retailers handling certain kinds of durable goods such as automobiles or major appliances may secure financing from sales finance companies or commercial banks under a *floor planning* arrangement. The lender pays for the retailer's merchandise and obtains a lien against the goods. The dealer stores and displays the merchandise. When a piece of merchandise is sold, the retailer pays the lender the merchandise cost plus any accrued interest. Since the lender has readily marketable collateral as security, floor planning usually involves a lower interest rate than the retailer might secure by other means.

As previously indicated, the need for short-term financing varies throughout the year. Figure 19-2 portrays this situation. The need for funds is represented by the sandbags which weigh the balloon down. As need increases, greater weight is added. Sales revenues and short-term financing are both needed to add buoyancy to lift the balloon over the "cash deficit hills." Sales revenues alone are frequently inadequate to meet the cash needs. Short-term financing thus serves to overcome the "deficit hills."

The Importance of Financing

This brief coverage of types of financing is not intended to play down the importance of financing. Next to the lack of adequate management, underfinancing is the most frequent reason for the failure of retail firms. Often a small retailer lacks a strong business background and fails to recognize the need for adequate financing. In studies conducted by one of the authors, inadequate financing was found to be a major reason for retail bankruptcies. The astute retailer continually assesses his financial position and projects his needs for funds in advance so that he does not experience unanticipated fund deficits.

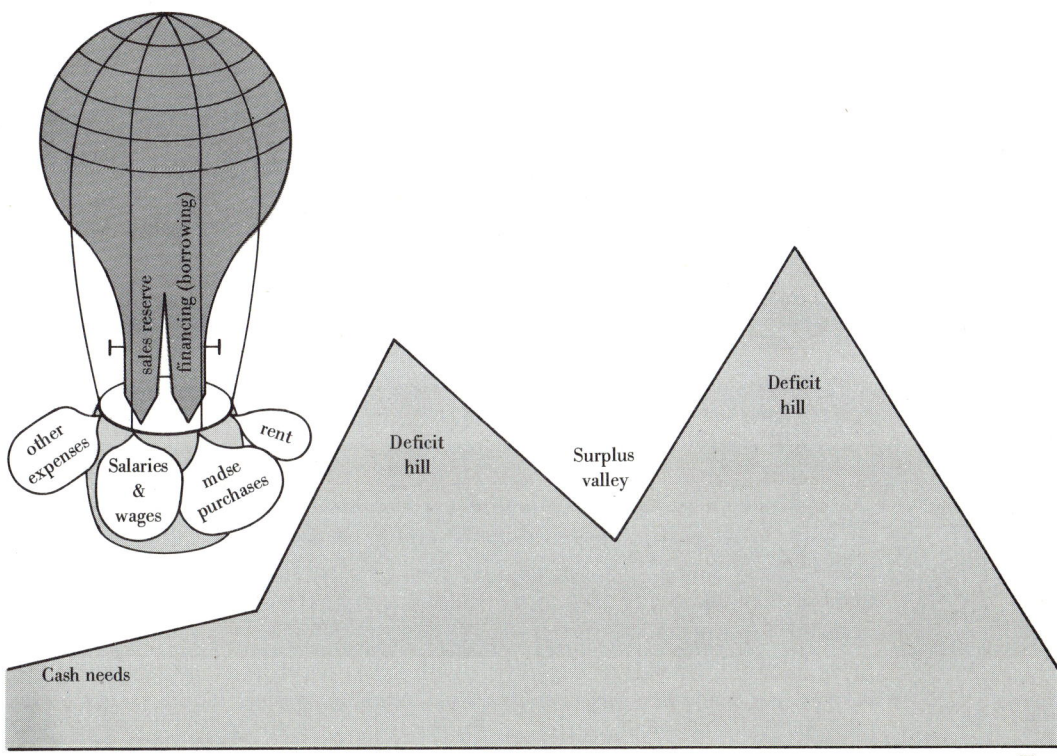

FIGURE 19-2

The cash balloon

Financing the Retail Enterprise **449**

> **REVIEW BOX 19:1**
>
> 1. _____ financing involves funds furnished by owners of the business, while _____ financing involves the loaning of funds by others.
> 2. _____ financing is most frequently used to finance the equipment and fixture needs of retailers.
> 3. An arrangement whereby finance companies or commercial banks lend money against durable goods in the retailer's possession is called _____.

FINANCIAL STATEMENTS

The accounting records (often called "books") maintained by stores serve as the basis for accounting statements, or more properly, financial statements. These statements serve several purposes:

> Determination of operating results for the accounting period just ended.
> Evidence of the soundness of the firm to creditors.
> Information necessary for filing tax returns and other government reports.

Financial statements consist of the balance sheet and the income statement. We shall examine each of these briefly.

"Oh, come, Sir! I should scarcely call $100,000.00 a glaring error."

The Balance Sheet

The balance sheet indicates the financial condition of a business at a particular point in time. It is prepared at the end of an accounting period, typically only once a year. Often the balance sheet shows the financial condition of the business as of the end of the calendar year (December 31), although a different fiscal year may be used.

A balance sheet, sometimes called a statement of net worth, has three primary components: assets, liabilities, and net worth. Total assets equal total liabilities plus net worth.

Assets include all cash and monies owed to the firm as well as all goods and other property of the firm. Typically, assets are divided into *current assets* and *fixed assets*. Current assets include cash and those items which are highly marketable and will be converted to cash within a year's time. Fixed assets include all other items of value owned by the firm but which, because of their nature, are needed by the firm on a continuing basis and will not be converted into cash within one year. For example, the store building (if it is owned by the retailer), store fixtures, delivery equipment, office furniture, and cash registers are all fixed assets.

Whereas assets represent things of value held by the firm, *liabilities* represent obligations of the firm. *Current liabilities* are those obligations due and payable within one year, while *fixed liabilities* are those obligations of a longer duration.

Since the asset portion of the balance sheet is equal to liabilities plus net worth, it is only logical that *net worth* can be ascertained by subtracting total liabilities from total assets. Net worth represents the owner's equity in the firm. Thus the owner's initial investment in the business plus any net income earned or any net loss experienced since the business was formed are reflected in the net worth section. Figure 19-3 summarizes these various components in a hypothetical balance sheet.

The Klothes Kloset
Balance Sheet
December 31, 197X

Assets		*Liabilities and Net Worth*	
Current Assets:		Current Liabilities:	
Cash on hand and in the bank	$10,000	Accounts Payable	$26,000
Accounts receivable (less		Payroll (due employees)	3,000
reserve for bad debts)	8,000	Bank Loan	2,000
Merchandise inventory	40,000	Total current liabilities	$31,000
Store supplies	2,000		
Total current assets	$60,000	Fixed Liabilities:	
		Notes payable	$10,000
Fixed Assets:		Total liabilities	$41,000
Store furniture, fixtures, and			
equipment (less reserve for			
depreciation)	$ 6,000		
Delivery equipment (less			
reserve for depreciation)	2,000		
Total fixed assets	$ 8,000	Net worth	27,000
Total Assets:	$68,000	Total Liabilities and Net Worth	$68,000

FIGURE 19-3

A sample balance sheet

The Income Statement

Although the balance sheet indicates the financial condition of a firm, it tells us almost nothing about the firm's performance. The performance feature is the keynote of the income statement. In keeping with this performance feature, the income statement is often called an *operating statement* or a *profit and loss statement*. The income statement summarizes the results of operations for a given period of time. Whereas some retailers are satisfied with a once-a-year balance sheet, most retailers desire more frequent income statements. They usually want to know at intervals throughout the year how they are progressing, whether they're making a profit or incurring a loss.

Basically there are five major components of an income statement:

```
   Sales
 − Cost of goods sold
 = Gross margin
 − Expenses
 = Net profit before taxes
```

An understanding of these components is vital to a retailer desiring to improve his profit picture. For example, utilizing this simplified income statement, the retailer can see that there are four primary ways to increase profits.

A retailer can *increase sales* with no more than a proportionate increase in Cost of goods sold and Expenses. For example, increasing advertising (an expense) can expand sales. But unless the sales increase is greater than that of expenses (and cost of goods sold), this will not increase profits. Charging a higher price for merchandise may also cause total dollar sales to grow, but only if not accompanied by a proportionate decrease in the number of units sold. Another alternative is to decrease the selling price. If the decrease results in a greater than proportional increase in the number of units sold, then total sales dollars generated are greater and profit will be increased (again with no greater than proportional increases in cost of goods sold and expenses). Of course, there are other ways of increasing the sales figure in order to generate more profit, but the above illustrations are sufficient to make the point. Unfortunately, many retailers think the only way to improve profits is to increase sales revenues.

Second, a retailer can *decrease cost of goods sold* without a proportionate decrease in sales or increase in expenses. Again there are several ways of decreasing cost of goods sold. Perhaps the major way is simply to do a better job of buying. By taking an active role in the negotiation process, the buyer may be able to reduce the price paid for merchandise. Taking advantage of discounts will also reduce merchandise costs. Reducing transportation charges, choosing cheaper transportation methods, pooling (or consolidating) shipments, and negotiating with the vendor to pay all or a part of the transportation charges are all possibilities. Although efforts to reduce cost of goods sold may seem to result in only modest gains, the impact of a concerted effort can be substantial.

Third, the retailer can *reduce expenses* without a proportionate decrease in sales or an increase in cost of goods sold. During a major economic downturn a few years ago, a large department store in the Southwest was able to generate a substantial increase in profits with a very minor increase in sales. Management was convinced that expenses were much too high. Armed with the knowledge that there would be a slowdown in the store's growth and with a directive to "cut away the fat," they achieved enviable results. Expenditures on supplies were reduced by more than $20,000, while the reduction in payroll was many times this amount. Many departments were able to reduce personnel expenses by not hiring to replace those who retired or left for other reasons.

During the energy crisis of 1973, Montgomery Ward was able to reduce the consumption of electricity 20.4 percent in its corporate headquarters building and thereby realize a significant reduction in its utility expense.[1] Incidently, Wards created a new job title of "light monitors" to aid in power conservation.

A smaller retailer may be unable to match these examples. Still, strict control over expenses (without harming the store operation) can achieve a substantial increase in profit.

Fourth, a retailer can use *a combination* of the above methods. A danger with a combination plan, of course, is that the manager may only make a half-hearted attempt, thinking that "a little improvement here, and a little there" will suffice. This may be true, but improved profits are usually the result of a determined effort to achieve the desired results.

Before leaving our simplified income statement, let's consider how a merchant might look at the five major components we have identified. Figure 19-4 indicates how little profit is left from a large sales figure. The sales figure represents 100 percent of the dollars generated by the sale of merchandise. From total sales, 65 percent of the dollars obtained is consumed by the cost of goods sold. The remaining 35 percent represents the gross margin. As shown in the bottom portion of the figure, the gross margin must be large enough to cover all expenses incurred in the operation of the store *and* any profit before taxes to the store owner. Thus:

$$\text{cost of goods sold} + \text{gross margin} = \text{sales}$$

$$\text{net profit} + \text{expenses} = \text{gross margin}$$

$$\text{net profit} + \text{expenses} + \text{cost of goods sold} = \text{sales}$$

Financial Statements

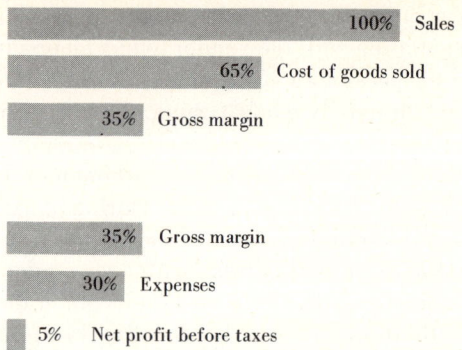

FIGURE 19-4

The major components of an income statement

Looking at the components of the income statement in this manner aids a retailer in planning his profit-seeking efforts. Both gross margin and net profit are *residuals*. That is, gross margin is what is left over after the cost of goods sold is subtracted from sales, and net profit is what is left after subtracting expenses from gross margin. However, a retailer who plans these residual figures as a percent of sales does not have to wait until the end of an accounting period with little idea of whether he has made a profit or incurred a loss.

It should be emphasized that the gross margin percentage figure actually represents the average maintained markup for all merchandise handled. Therefore, in order to achieve a gross margin of 35 percent, a retailer must make sure that the initial markup is greater than 35 percent. The reason for this is that some merchandise will be marked down before it is sold.

The retailer must also recognize that merchandise shrinkage, which is reflected in the expense portion of the income statement, may be excessive. In turn, this may cause total expenses to equal or exceed the gross margin. Obviously, when this happens, no profit is left for the retailer. The astute merchant therefore plans the major component figures in advance to ensure that he is not "surprised" by a loss at the end of the accounting period.

Now that we have examined an income statement's major components, let's look in more detail at each of these components. Figure 19-5 is a more complete income statement of the Klothes Kloset.

SALES Almost every retail store makes sales that are not permanent. *Gross sales*, however, represent all sales made to customers, even those that are tempo-

The Klothes Kloset
Income Statement
Year Ending December 31, 197X

Gross sales		$220,000
Less: Sales returns and allowances		20,000
Net sales		200,000
Less: Cost of goods sold:		
Beginning inventory, Jan. 1, 197X	$ 60,000	
Purchases	107,000	
Transportation	3,000	
Total merchandise available for sale	$170,000	
Less: Ending inventory, Dec. 31, 197X	40,000	
Cost of goods sold		130,000
Gross margin		$ 70,000
Operating expenses:		
Salaries	$ 45,000	
Rent	6,000	
Utilities	1,000	
Supplies	3,000	
Advertising	2,000	
Delivery	2,000	
Miscellaneous expenses	1,000	
Total expenses		$ 60,000
Net profit before taxes		$ 10,000

FIGURE 19-5

A sample income statement

rary. Sometimes customers return merchandise for credit or cash. In effect, this cancels the original sale. In other cases, customers want to exchange merchandise for a different style, color, size, or perhaps an entirely different item. If the value of the returned merchandise is different from the value of the new merchandise selected, sales are reduced by the value of the item exchanged and the new item is treated as another sale.

When merchandise purchased by a customer proves less satisfactory than expected, a discount may be granted. For example, if a chip, scratch, or other flaw is discovered after the customer has made a purchase, a reduction in the price paid may be allowed. This, of course, reduces sales. (In this instance an additional entry—a markdown—is required; otherwise the value of stock on hand is overstated.) In all of the above examples, the result is a reduction in amount of total sales, and an entry labeled "sales returns and allowances" is necessary to show these reductions.

Some income statements show only *net sales*. However, the sales returns and allowances figure is important for comparison with other similar types of stores. Also, showing sales returns and allowances calls attention to this figure, thereby encouraging the retailer to examine the causes of these returns and allowances. Exceptionally high returns may indicate too aggressive selling or an unsatisfactory line of merchandise.

COST OF GOODS SOLD

This section of the income statement should reflect *all* those costs associated with the acquisition of merchandise sold by the retailer. In reality this is seldom the case. Many costs associated with acquiring merchandise are actually shown in the expense portion of the income statement. This common procedure should not trouble us as long as we recognize that *all costs* are not truly reflected in the cost of goods sold figure. The difficulty arises in properly charging all costs to specific merchandise. For example, time spent by a buyer in searching out sources of supply, examining merchandise, making trips to market, and negotiating for goods are all properly *costs* of obtaining merchandise. However, the buyer's salary and travel expenses are usually classified as expenses. The same is true of the activities associated with paying invoices for merchandise. In other words, *costs* should include all monies paid for obtaining goods and getting them to the store. *Expenses* should include all monies paid to "move" merchandise out of the store and into the customers' hands. Thus the income statement actually *understates* the cost of goods sold and *overstates* expenses. Since the net result on the bottom line (profit) is the same, retailers are not generally concerned with this problem.

The cost of goods sold section of the Klothes Kloset income statement details the major costs involved in acquiring merchandise. The beginning inventory figure of $60,000 represents the cost value of that inventory. Purchases made during the year are also recorded at cost. As indicated, this figure represents the net price paid for all merchandise after all discounts have been taken. One exception to this practice is that some stores separate cash discounts earned and subtract this amount from the purchases figure to arrive at net purchases. One reason for such action is to call attention to the magnitude of cash discounts. Some stores evaluate their buyers on the amount of cash discounts received, but this can lead to manipulations by the buyer to induce vendors to overstate the purchase price and allow a larger cash discount.

The purchases figure shown in our operating statement is *net purchases*. Since retailers often return merchandise to vendors—just as customers return merchandise to retailers—a purchase returns and allowances figure is often used. Thus, gross purchases less returns and allowances equal net purchases.

Another possible difference involves certain classes of merchandise that need some work performed before they can be delivered to the customer. For example, it is still traditional in most "quality" stores for alterations on men's clothing to be performed at no cost to the customer. If it costs the store $5 to alter a man's suit, this increases the cost of goods sold by a like amount. Furniture or appliances often need minor touch-ups before delivery, and expensive jewelry items may be engraved at no cost to the customer. The performance of any alteration or workroom costs in excess of any charges paid by customers for the performance of these tasks increases the cost of goods sold figure.

Taking into consideration these factors mentioned above, an alternative form for the cost of goods sold section might look like this:

```
Less: Cost of goods sold
   Beginning inventory Jan. 1, 197X                    $ 60,000
   Gross purchases                        $116,000
   Less: Returns and allowances              8,000
   Net purchases                                       108,000
   Transportation                                        3,000
   Total merchandise available for sale               $171,000
   Less: Ending inventory Dec. 31, 197X                 40,000
   Gross cost of goods sold                           $131,000
   Less: Cash discounts                                  3,000
   Plus: Alterations and workroom costs                  2,000
Cost of goods sold                                              $130,000
```

GROSS MARGIN

As you probably recognize by now, gross margin expressed as a percentage of sales is equivalent to the maintained markup percentage for a class of merchandise or a particular item of merchandise. Thus the target gross margin percentage serves as a guide to the merchant in computing the initial markup on various classes or items of merchandise.

Volume of sales alone will not tell the retailer whether he will make a profit. Only by considering costs of goods sold in relation to sales—that is, gross margin—and comparing this figure to expenses can the retailer determine profitability.[2]

EXPENSES

A brief consideration of expenses is included here because of their importance as a major component of the income statement. Total expenses as a percentage of sales vary widely depending upon the type of retail store under consideration. For labor-intensive types of service establishments such as beauty shops and dry cleaners, expenses may run from 75 to 90 percent of sales. For other retailers such as automobile dealers, grocery stores, liquor stores, and lumber and building materials stores, expenses as a percent of sales may be less than 20 percent.[3] Most types of stores fall between these figures, with 25 to 40 percent being fairly typical.

Financial Statements **457**

Just as a merchandise budget is desirable for merchandise control, the preparation of an expense budget is extremely helpful for expense control. Normally, certain expenses are relatively fixed and remain constant regardless of the amount of business generated. For example, when rent is a fixed amount, the retailer knows that he will pay so many dollars per month. Based upon past experience, the utilities expense will remain fairly constant from year to year. Administrative salaries and insurance are also relatively fixed.

Variable expenses are largely determined by the level of sales achieved. Just as the preparation of the merchandise budget is dependent upon projected sales, so too is the preparation of the variable expenses portion of the expense budget determined by anticipated sales. However, variable expenses should be budgeted as target figures.

NET PROFIT BEFORE TAXES

Net profit before taxes is a residual; it is what remains after expenses are deducted from gross margin. Net profit before taxes determines the amount of *income taxes* to be paid by the retail operation. Certain license fees and taxes—payroll taxes, sales taxes, inventory and property taxes, and excise taxes—are listed as expenses. Thus, net profit before taxes indicates that only the various income taxes applicable—federal, state, and city—are to be deducted to arrive at net profit. Since these taxes are based upon the profitability of the firm, they cannot be computed until profitability is determined.

Net profit as a percent of sales differs widely among retail businesses. The nature and size of the business as well as location and managerial acumen are the primary reasons for this variance. For example, net profit for family shoe stores ranges from 9.2 percent for stores with less than $50,000 in annual business to 4.9 percent for stores with $100,000 to $149,999 in annual sales.[4] Net profit before taxes averages from less than 5 percent for appliance outlets, radio and TV stores, automobile dealers, and office supply stores to more than 15 percent for beauty salons, children's and infants' wear stores, jewelry stores, and music stores. Of course, these are averages and are subject to wide differences for individual stores.

For tax purposes, profit from a sole proprietorship (which represents most small businesses) is treated as income on the owner's income tax return. In many cases the amount of this business income is less than the owner could earn working for someone else. Still, many small business owners are willing to engage in business because of the non-monetary benefits. The freedom to be one's own boss, to set one's own hours, and to operate one's business as one sees fit is often worth some sacrifice in money income. The psychic income provided by the greater amount of freedom often offsets the lesser amount of money income. Viewed objectively, and discounting the psychic income, the small business owner should receive a business income equal to what could be earned working for someone else *plus* a profit on his business investment as compensation for the risks inherent in operating a business.

SPOTLIGHT

Can a super-growth company show concern for employees and stockholders? Lowe's Companies, Inc., of North Wilkesboro, North Carolina, shares its profits and financial information freely and continues to grow and prosper.

A retailer, with operations confined largely to the southeastern part of the United States, Lowe's qualifies by almost any measuring rod as a super-growth company, which explains why its OTC-traded stock normally sells at anywhere from fifty to sixty times earnings. Sales have spurted from $39 million to $234 million over the past ten years. Profits over the same span have grown from $1.2 million to $9.1 million. Not a single acquisition was made, so these spectacular performance figures represent internal growth entirely—growth stemming from an expanding network of stores that might best be described as combination lumber yards and hard goods discount houses.

Aside from its ability to grow and make money, Lowe's is a notable company in at least two other respects. First, every year it puts out an annual report that many financial observers believe to be the best issued by a U.S. corporation, bar none. Second, it has a profit-sharing plan that probably also ranks as the best in U.S. industry, bar none—from the standpoint of employee benefits.

The hallmarks of a good annual report are clarity and ample disclosure of pertinent financial information. The Lowe's reports pass these tests with room to spare. They provide not only a detailed picture of company operations, but an overall look at the entire markets in which Lowe's sells, including useful comparisons with other retailers. The Lowe's annual report is virtually an accountant's dream come true. It carries the financial review back sixteen years, breaks down sales by seven product categories, shows sales per store, sales per square foot of selling space, sales per employee. It gives a state-by-state breakdown of shareholders. Tucked into each annual report is a questionnaire inviting shareholders to rate the report.

Lowe's has integrated the interests of employees into the well-being of the company through a profit-sharing plan that has enabled many employees to retire rich. For example, thirteen store managers, salesmen, warehousemen, and office workers who retired in 1971 collected a total of $17.5 million.

The spectacular performance of the profit-sharing fund—it had a compound annual growth rate of 36.5 percent between 1961 and 1971—results from its ownership of Lowe's stock, a spectacular performer in its own right. The employee trust owns 2.5 million of 8.5 million outstanding shares. These shares represent 90 percent of the fund's assets. The 3.8 million shares owned by the trust in 1961 were then worth $7.3 million. The 2.5 million shares now owned by the trust were worth $168 million at the end of 1972.

The Lowe's profit-sharing fund ranks as one of the ten largest in the nation. In relation to number of employees (the plan has 1,600 members), it is *the* largest. And the average individual account balance is the largest of any profit-sharing fund.

Source: "Lowe's Companies, Inc., North Wilkesboro, N.C.," in Company Performance Roundup, *Business and Society Review/Innovation*, Summer 1973, pp. 94–95.

> **REVIEW BOX 19:2**
>
> 1. The two major financial statements of a firm are the _____ and the _____.
> 2. Two primary components of a balance sheet are assets and liabilities. The third is _____.
> 3. Two of the five major components of an income statement are _____ and _____.
> 4. Two primary means of increasing profits of a retail firm besides increasing sales are _____ and _____.
> 5. Theoretically, _____ include all monies paid for obtaining merchandise and getting it to the store, while _____ are monies paid to facilitate the movement of merchandise to the consumer.
> 6. Both _____ and _____ are residual figures.

INVENTORY VALUATION

The value of present inventory is extremely important in determining profit. This figure is often one of the most elusive in retailing, but unless it is accurately determined, profit for an accounting period may be easily misstated. Since operating efficiency is judged on profits and since income taxes must be paid on profits, the net profit figure is of utmost importance.

You may recall that beginning and ending inventory figures are necessary in determining cost of goods sold. If the ending inventory is undervalued, the cost of goods sold figure is inflated, and both gross margin and net profit are understated. Conversely, if the ending inventory is overvalued, the cost of goods sold is understated, and both gross margin and net profit are inflated. To clarify this situation, let us examine Figures 19-6 and 19-7. All figures are the same down to the values of the ending inventory. In Figure 19-6, the value of the ending inventory is understated by $10,000, as shown in the right-hand portion of the abbreviated income statement. Note that as a result, cost of goods sold is overstated by $10,000. This causes the gross margin to be understated, with the result that the firm shows no profit.

In Figure 19-7, the value of the ending inventory is overstated by $10,000, with the result that cost of goods sold is understated by an equal amount. Thus, both gross margin and net profit before taxes are overstated. The effect of improper inventory valuation should immediately become clear.

The careful reader with some accounting knowledge will recognize that the situation *may* correct itself during the following accounting period. Let us

	Ending inventory properly valued	Ending inventory undervalued
Net sales	$110,000	$110,000
Less: Cost of goods sold:		
Beginning inventory	$ 30,000	$ 30,000
Purchases	90,000	90,000
Total merchandise available	$120,000	$120,000
Less: Ending inventory	50,000	40,000
Cost of goods sold	70,000	80,000
Gross margin	$ 40,000	$ 30,000
Expenses	30,000	30,000
Net profit before taxes	$ 10,000	0

FIGURE 19-6

The results of undervaluing ending inventory

examine how this could happen and then look at some of the implications. If our misstated ending inventory figure is used as the beginning inventory figure for the next accounting period, then the beginning inventory figure is also in error. If the value of the inventory was understated, and *if* the next inventory figure is correct, then the error is corrected by understating the cost of goods sold and overstating the gross margin and net profit figures for the second year. The error thus resolves itself at the end of the second accounting period *if* the ending inventory for the second period is *correct*.

	Ending inventory Properly valued	Ending inventory overvalued
Net sales	$110,000	$110,000
Less: Cost of goods sold:		
Beginning inventory	$ 30,000	$ 30,000
Purchases	90,000	90,000
Total merchandise available	$120,000	$120,000
Less: Ending inventory	50,000	60,000
Cost of goods sold	70,000	60,000
Gross margin	$ 40,000	$ 50,000
Expenses	30,000	30,000
Net profit before taxes	$ 10,000	$ 20,000

FIGURE 19-7

The results of overvaluing ending inventory

The same situation exists if the ending inventory figure was originally overstated. The result, though, is that at the end of the second accounting period the correction results in $10,000 less profit being shown for that year. You may be thinking "okay, what's the big deal?" if the error is corrected and no one is really hurt. Suppose you are an employee of this firm who gets a bonus or participates in a profit-sharing plan. If the inventory is undervalued at the end of the first accounting period, the firm makes zero profit and you get no bonus. You may get disgusted and quit. Or suppose that the ending inventory is overvalued and you receive a substantial bonus. You count on approximately the same bonus the second year, but at the end of the second year when the error is corrected, the firm shows no profit. You get no bonus and may decide to look for another job.

Where store managers are paid a percentage of the profits, some have been known to manipulate the inventory figures to overvalue the ending inventory. They then collect an unearned percentage of profits and leave the store before the error is detected. Perhaps now it is even more evident why the value of an inventory is so important.

So far we have said nothing about how the inventory figure is determined. Essentially there are two ways of ascertaining this figure: the cost method and the retail method of inventory valuation. We shall examine each of these in turn.

The Cost Method

The *only* method of determining cost of goods sold is by obtaining the values of the beginning and ending inventories *at cost*. Thus all components of the cost of goods sold section of the income statement must be cost values, rather than retail values, a necessity that can present the retailer with some problems. For example, a physical inventory must be taken before profitability can be ascertained under the cost method of inventory valuation, and conducting a physical inventory is time-consuming, tedious work. In fact, most merchants find that conducting a physical count of all merchandise on hand more than once or twice a year is nearly impossible. As a result, most retailers using the cost method of inventory valuation determine their profit situation only once or twice a year.

Before a physical inventory can be taken at cost values, some method of ascertaining these cost values must be instituted. For an appliance retailer, or similar type of retailer, this may be no problem. Frequently, these retailers maintain a perpetual inventory system, recording all needed information on cards kept in a card file. But for a retailer such as a hardware store that handles numerous small items, this kind of system involves too much work.

For small-item retailers a more common method is to record the cost price on all price tags affixed to merchandise. Normally a number or letter code, known only to store employees, is used. When cost prices are not coded onto price tickets, the retailer is forced to refer back to merchandise invoices to determine the cost of an item contained in the inventory. When the inventory is relatively large, this task is very time consuming and frequently leads to guessing or other short cuts which result in a "sloppy" total inventory figure.

Under either method, transportation changes are normally not included in the cost price of individual merchandise items. Since transportation costs are a part of the cost of goods sold figure, some provision for them should be made in the cost value of the inventory. A common method is to determine the percentage of all transportation costs to total merchandise costs for the period under consideration. Applying this percentage figure to the ending inventory indicates how many dollars should be added to the ending inventory to cover transportation. Granted such a procedure is not very exact, but it is much better than ignoring transportation costs completely.

In addition to the problems of infrequent profit determination and handling of transportation charges, one other problem is inherent under the cost method. Merchandise is sold at retail prices which are recorded as sales. Inventory figures and purchases are recorded at cost prices. Using this system, there is no way to know the value of inventory which *should be* on hand. A physical inventory reveals how much merchandise *is* on hand, but there is nothing with which to compare this figure to determine shrinkage or shortages. This limitation of the cost method has become more pronounced with increasing merchandise shrinkage.

Despite its shortcomings, the cost method of inventory valuation is used by a majority of retailers, especially smaller ones. The retail inventory method, to be covered next, overcomes some difficulties of the cost method, but it also contains some problems of its own.

REVIEW BOX 19:3

1. If the ending inventory is undervalued, both gross margin and net profit are _____.
2. The result of overvaluing an ending inventory is to _____ cost of goods sold.
3. In order to obtain cost of goods sold, the retailer must ascertain the values of beginning and ending inventories at _____.
4. Undoubtedly the greatest single shortcoming of the cost method of inventory valuation is _____.

Inventory Valuation

The Retail Method

Many retailers, especially larger ones and those handling fashion merchandise, find that the cost method of inventory valuation does not provide them with the information they need. Particularly, they desire more frequent measures of profitability than can be easily obtained under the cost method, and they also want information on stock shortages. The retail method overcomes these deficiencies and provides other advantages.

While the retail inventory method is relatively simple in practice, it may seem somewhat complex initially. Therefore, we shall investigate the operations one at a time.

PROCEDURE The total effort involved in using the retail method is somewhat greater than with the cost method. It does, however, provide more information than is available under the cost method. There is also a transfer of effort, with some additional bookkeeping effort offsetting the problems involved in taking a physical inventory.

Determining Values of Merchandise Available for Sale. The first step in converting to the retail method is to determine the value of the beginning inventory at both cost and retail. In effect, we must initially conduct a dual inventory — one at cost and one at retail. Second, all purchases must be recorded on the books at both cost and at retail prices. Third, any additional markups taken must be recorded.

Thus, to determine the values of merchandise available for sale during an accounting period *at cost* and *at retail*, the following procedure is followed:

	Cost Value	Retail Value
Beginning inventory	$20,000	$ 30,000
Net purchases	60,000	90,000
Transportation	300	
Net additional markups		100
Total merchandise available	$80,300	$120,100

Note that the beginning inventory is listed in both the cost and the retail columns. The same is true for purchases. Since net purchases are shown, we know that any purchase returns and allowances have been deducted from both values, indicating both the cost value and the retail value of any merchandise returned to the vendor. Any transportation charges paid are listed only under the cost column. No listing is made in the retail column, since transportation costs would have been included in total merchandise costs when determining the markup to be applied. Therefore, transportation costs are in effect already included in the net purchases at retail.

Additional markups may be taken on merchandise after it is placed on the selling floor. These additional markups affect only the retail value of the goods and are thus recorded only in the retail column. The fact that the label "net additional markups" is used indicates that any *cancellations* of additional markups have been deducted to arrive at the net markup figure.

Thus far we have calculated that a total of $80,300 in merchandise *at cost* and $120,100 in merchandise *at retail* was available for sale in the store during the period under consideration. Thus, at any point throughout the year, we can obtain from our records both the cost and retail value of merchandise available for sale up to that point without taking a physical inventory.

Determining the Cost Complement. The next step involves determining the relationship which exists between the cost value and the retail value of the total goods available for sale. We do this by dividing the total value of merchandise at cost by the total value at retail:

$$\$80{,}300 \div \$120{,}100 = 66.86\%$$

To understand what the cost complement means, we need to investigate further. We can determine the cumulative markup on all this merchandise by subtracting the total cost value from the total retail value and dividing that figure by the total retail value:

$$\$120{,}100 - \$80{,}300 = \$39{,}800 \div 120{,}100 = 33.14\%$$

If the cumulative markup is 33.14 percent of retail, then since cost + markup = retail, 100 percent − 33.14 percent = 66.86 percent, the cost complement. The value of determining the cumulative markup figure is to allow comparison of the actual cumulative markup with planned markup.

Reductions in Merchandise Values at Retail. Hopefully not all of the merchandise value that was available for sale remains at intervals throughout the year. Common reductions in the retail value are as follows:

	Retail Value
Net sales	$80,000
Net markdowns	2,000
Employee discounts	1,000
Estimated shortages	2,000
Total retail reductions	$85,000

The net sales figure indicates that sales returns have been taken into consideration. Any customer allowances as well as merchandise marked down are included in the net markdown figure. If any goods were marked down for a special promotion and not all of them sold, a markdown cancellation would have been recorded. Thus the net markdown figure includes those markdowns on goods presently available for sale at marked down prices.

Since any discounts allowed employees also reduce the retail value of merchandise sold, this figure must be recorded. Although employee discounts are a form of markdown, most merchants desire to keep this figure separate in order to measure the dollar volume of these discounts. Also, keeping this figure separate prevents "contaminating" the net markdown figure. The general purposes of markdowns are for promotion, to clear out merchandise, and to allow for customer adjustments.

Estimated shortages are used to reduce the retail value of the inventory to cover shoplifting, employee theft, and clerical errors. An estimate is used when a physical inventory is not taken and an interim estimate of profit is needed. This figure is based upon past experience. For example, if an interim estimate of profit is to be made at the end of three months, and if experience indicates that shortages usually amount to $100 per month, then $300 would represent the estimated shortage for the three-month period. A more accurate shortage figure requires a physical inventory.

Determining Ending Inventory at Retail and at Cost. Under the retail method, the physical inventory is recorded at retail prices. This greatly simplifies the taking of a physical inventory, since like items are counted and multiplied by the retail price shown on the items. If the items have received additional markups or markdowns, this is of no concern to those taking the inventory. They record whatever retail prices are shown on the merchandise.

When the inventory is completed, the retail value of the physical inventory is compared to the retail book inventory figure. If the book inventory figure is greater, as is usually the case, a shortage exists. In this case the book inventory figure is adjusted to equal the physical inventory figure. This adjustment is made by indicating the actual stock shortage instead of an estimated shortage. For example:

Closing book inventory at retail	$36,600
Physical inventory at retail	35,100
Actual stock shortage	$ 1,500

The book inventory figure is adjusted downward by showing the $1,500 stock shortage as a reduction in the retail value of merchandise available for sale.

Regardless of whether a physical inventory is taken at retail or the book inventory figure at retail is obtained, we are unable to arrive at profits using this figure. We must obtain an ending inventory figure at cost before we can ascertain cost of goods sold, and for this reason the cost complement figure was computed. By multiplying the book ending inventory figure at retail by the cost complement, we can obtain the ending inventory at cost.

The book ending inventory figure is obtained by subtracting total retail reductions for the period from the total retail value of merchandise available for sale. The retail value of the total merchandise available for sale during the period was $120,100, while total retail reductions were $85,000. Thus the retail value of the book ending inventory is $35,100. Multiplying this value by the cost complement of 66.86 percent, we find the cost value of the ending inventory is $23,467.86.

Determining Cost of Goods Sold and Gross Margin. Once we compute the cost value of the ending inventory, we have the information necessary to complete an income statement. The cost value of total merchandise available for sale minus the cost value of the ending inventory gives us cost of goods sold:

Cost value of total merchandise available for sale	$80,300.00
Cost value of ending inventory	23,467.86
Cost of goods sold	$56,832.14

Now we can subtract cost of goods sold from net sales to obtain the gross margin:

Net sales	$80,000.00
Cost of goods sold	56,832.14
Gross margin	$23,167.86

Summary of the Procedure. Figure 19-8 summarizes the computational steps in using the retail inventory method:

1. Determine total merchandise available for sale at both cost and retail values for the period under consideration.
2. Determine the cost complement by dividing total merchandise available at cost by the total merchandise available at retail.
3. Determine total retail reductions during the period by adding net sales, net markdowns, employee discounts, and actual or estimated stock shortages.
4. Determine the ending book inventory at retail by subtracting total retail reductions from total retail value of merchandise available for sale. Determine the value of the ending inventory at cost by multiplying the ending inventory at retail times the cost complement.
5. Determine cost of goods sold by subtracting the ending inventory at cost from the total cost value of merchandise available for sale. Determine gross margin by subtracting cost of goods sold from net sales.

	Cost	Retail
1. Beginning inventory	$20,000.00	$ 30,000.00
Net purchases	60,000.00	90,000.00
Transportation	300.00	
Net additional markups		100.00
Total merchandise available	$80,300.00	$120,100.00
2. Cost complement		
$80,300 ÷ $120,100 = 66.86%		
3. Net sales		$ 80,000.00
Net markdowns		2,000.00
Employee discounts		1,000.00
Estimated shortage		2,000.00
Total reductions		85,000.00
4. Ending inventory at retail		$ 35,100.00
Ending inventory at cost		
$35,100 × .6686 =	$23,467.86	
5. Cost of goods sold	$56,832.14	
Net sales		$80,000.00
Cost of goods sold		56,832.14
Gross margin		$23,167.86

FIGURE 19-8

Computational procedure using the retail method

Following this ordered sequence ensures that the necessary figures are available as they are needed. Once gross margin has been obtained, net profit before taxes can be determined by subtracting expenses.

BENEFITS OF THE RETAIL METHOD

Retail inventory valuation has several benefits, the major one being the provision for interim profit estimates. Between physical inventories, reliable estimates of profitability under the cost method are exceedingly difficult, if not impossible. Retailers need feedback on their operations throughout the year. Certainly, sales volume provides some of this feedback, but it lacks the proper emphasis on gross margin and expense control. Periodic income statements provide information necessary for the continuous review of various merchandising activities. Since a perpetual book inventory figure is maintained, figures needed for dollar merchandise control are readily available. Thus the retail method provides the retailer with a continuous flow of information rather than a once or twice a year set of figures.

Under the retail method the necessity for cost coding all price tickets or locating cost prices on invoices is eliminated. The retail method greatly simplifies taking physical inventories, and it makes for speedier and probably more accurate inventories.

Under the cost method some adjustment in the inventory figures may be necessary to arrive at a conservative figure (cost or market, whichever is lower). Under the retail method, no such problem exists. If markdowns are taken as justified and are properly recorded, the retail value of the inventory is automatically adjusted downward. When the cost complement is applied to the ending inventory at retail, the cost value of the inventory is also adjusted downward. The net effect is very similar to cost or market, whichever is lower.

The retail method has become widely accepted as a means of inventory valuation. Where accurate records are kept, this method is satisfactory to the Internal Revenue Service for taxing purposes, to lending institutions as a basis for loans, and to insurance companies in connection with casualty losses.

PROBLEMS WITH THE RETAIL METHOD

The retail method is not entirely satisfactory for all types of stores or in all situations. The major problem involves use of the cost complement. The underlying assumption is that the relationship between cost price and selling price is the same in the ending inventory as it was in the total merchandise available for sale. If a standard markup is applied to all merchandise purchased, then no problem exists. However, the use of such uniform pricing is relatively infrequent. Often, different types of merchandise carry different markup percentages. This is especially true over broad classifications of merchandise.

This limitation can be turned into an advantage. Stores using the retail method usually find it necessary to departmentalize for proper merchandise planning and control, and departmentalization typically results in the division of merchandise into fairly homogeneous classes. The result is usually less variation in the markup applied within a generic class of merchandise than across generic classes. Departmentalization is thus an aid in overcoming the problem of widely varying markups, while at the same time facilitating merchandise planning and control. Of course, even within a given department, a standard markup is not usually applied to all merchandise.

Since the retail inventory method rests on the assumption that merchandise in the ending inventory exists in approximately the same proportion as when the cost complement was calculated, caution is necessary when this condition does not exist and when there are substantial differences in markups applied.

Although it may be viewed as either an advantage or a limitation, additional record keeping is required with the retail method. Figures on purchases must be maintained at both cost and retail, and records on all price changes (additional markups, markdowns, and employee discounts) must be maintained. Keeping such records is more time consuming but does supply managers with more information than is available under the cost system.

Inventory Valuation

> **REVIEW BOX 19:4**
>
> 1. The first step to be taken when initiating the retail method of inventory valuation is to _____.
> 2. In addition to net sales and employee discounts, other reductions in merchandise values at retail are _____ and _____.
> 3. When the value of the book inventory is greater than the value of a physical inventory, a _____ exists.
> 4. The _____ multiplied by the ending inventory at retail provides _____.
> 5. The underlying assumption of using the cost complement is that the same relationship between _____ exists in the ending inventory as in the total merchandise available for sale.

CHAPTER SUMMARY

- The primary steps in effectively securing and using financial resources are to (1) identify financial needs, (2) develop a financial plan, (3) identify alternative sources of funds, (4) obtain funds, (5) manage assets efficiently, and (6) evaluate financial performance.
- Long-term financing involves the use of funds for ten years or more and is normally limited to the acquisition of land and buildings. Debt financing involves borrowing of funds, while equity financing means that ownership rights are exchanged for funds.
- Intermediate-term financing ranges from one to ten years and is normally used for equipment, furniture, and fixtures.
- Short-term financing is for less than a year and is used primarily to meet seasonal needs or other temporary cash shortages. Trade credit, sale of accounts receivable, commercial bank loans, and floor planning are the major types of short-term credit used by retailers.
- The balance sheet, which shows the financial *condition* of a firm, is comprised of three major sections: assets, liabilities, and net worth.
- The income statement, which indicates the *performance* of a firm for some specified period of time, is comprised of five major components: sales, cost of goods sold, gross margin, expenses, and net profit before taxes.
- Increased profits can occur with an increase in sales, a decrease in cost of goods sold, a reduction in expenses, or some combination of these factors. Both gross margin and net profit are residuals.
- Almost every retail firm suffers from some impermanence of sales

revenues. Sales returns and allowances reveal the degree of this impermanence.
- Accurate inventory valuation is crucial, since inaccurate inventory figures result in misstated net profit.
- In order to arrive at a cost of goods sold figure, beginning and ending inventory figures *at cost* must be obtained.
- Under the cost method of inventory valuation, no interim estimates of profit can be made without taking a physical inventory. This is the greatest shortcoming of the cost method. Despite its limitations, this method is the most widely used type of inventory valuation.
- In addition to providing interim estimates of profitability, the retail method provides more information than the cost method. Proper use of the retail method automatically results in a conservative inventory valuation.
- The five steps involved in using the retail method are:
  1. determine values of merchandise available for sale
  2. compute the cost complement
  3. determine total reductions in merchandise values at retail
  4. determine ending inventory at retail and at cost
  5. determine cost of goods sold and gross margin
- A major assumption of the retail method is that the relationship between cost and selling prices (markup) which exists when the cost complement is computed is the same in the ending inventory. When this relationship does not hold, the ending inventory at cost may be improperly valued.

CHAPTER NOTES

[1] "Sales Will Brighten a Dimmer Christmas," *Business Week*, December 1, 1973, p. 23.
[2] The term gross margin has been used consistently rather than the term gross profit, which some use. It is the authors' opinion that the term gross profit is misleading in that only a small portion of gross margin typically results in profit.
[3] For expense percentages in various types of retail business, see *Expenses in Retail Business*, a pamphlet of the Marketing Services Department, The National Cash Register Company, Dayton, Ohio, no date shown.
[4] Ibid., p. 38.

QUESTIONS AND ASSIGNMENTS

1. Explain the steps that a retailer should take in securing and using financial resources. How often should these steps be taken?
2. Assume that you are going to open a Tots-to-Teens Clothing Shop. Indicate the different types of financing you may need, the purpose of the financing, and where you might obtain the funds.

3. Distinguish between debt and equity financing.
4. Explain why the cash needs of a retail firm are typically not steady throughout the year.
5. Explain the difference between a balance sheet and an income statement. What does each one show?
6. Suppose a retail firm's current liabilities exceed current assets. You are a potential supplier for the firm. Would you sell to this retailer? Why or why not?
7. Indicate some ways a retail firm may increase profits.
8. Both gross margin and net profit before taxes are residuals. Why might a retailer want to set goals for attaining these figures and then plan the other major components of the income statement from these figures?
9. A retailer finds that his sales returns and allowances are a much higher percentage of sales than experienced by other similar types of businesses. How should he begin an investigation to find the cause of these high returns?
10. Explain the consequences of overvaluing or undervaluing an ending inventory. Are these consequences serious enough to warrant increased effort to assure an accurate inventory? Explain.
11. Given the following information, compute the ending inventory at cost, cost of goods sold, and gross margin.
    Beginning inventory: Cost $10,000, retail $15,000
    Net purchases: Cost $30,000, retail $45,000
    Transportation: $100
    Additional markups: $200
    Net sales: $50,000
    Markdowns and employee discounts: $2,000
    Estimated shortage: $1,000
12. Summarize the advantages and limitations of the retail method of inventory valuation.

ANSWERS TO REVIEW BOX QUESTIONS

Box 19:1

1. equity; debt
2. intermediate-term
3. floor planning

Box 19:2

1. balance sheet; income or operating statement
2. net worth
3. Any two of the following: sales, cost of goods sold, gross margin, expenses, net profit before taxes
4. decrease cost of goods sold; reduce expenses
5. costs; expenses
6. gross margin; net profit before taxes

Box 19:3
1. understated
2. understate
3. cost
4. the lack of frequent estimates of profitability of the firm

Box 19:4
1. take a beginning inventory at both cost and retail
2. net markdowns; estimated shortages
3. shortage
4. the cost value of the ending inventory
5. cost and selling prices

Expense Control

20

Ever hear of an expense control contest? Ridiculous, you may say. But it's true. The National Retail Merchants' Association sponsored one in 1973.[1] The thought behind the contest was relatively simple. During this period, retailers were faced with rising expenses in almost every category and with increasing costs for merchandise. However, because of price controls, the obvious alternative of passing on increased costs to consumers was limited. The contest was designed to elicit suggested solutions that would be publicized to the Association's membership. (You will recall that decreasing expenses is *one* possible way of increasing profit.)

Expense control is usually viewed as minimizing expenses that are incurred in selling products or services. Obviously, most retailers incur expenses which could be substantially reduced. The danger, of course, is that minimizing expenses can lead to a reduction in sales and, possibly, in profits. Consider, for example, the retailer who decides to eliminate all advertising and to reduce his sales force substantially. Certainly he has cut expenses, but in a very short time he may also experience a loss in sales proportionately greater than the amount of reduced expenses.

Another retailer may find that *increasing* advertising, an expense, boosts sales and profits. Across-the-board cuts are not always the answer. The ideal is an *optimum level* of expenses—not necessarily a minimum level—which will allow the firm to achieve its objective.

The problem, however, is that retailers typically have more than one objective. For example, a retailer may want to maximize long-run profit but also want to provide fast, efficient service to customers. Although these two objectives are not contradictory, they may not be entirely compatible. Providing fast, efficient service may require expenditures (a greater number of

salespeople, for example) that will reduce the likelihood of *maximum* long-run profit. In this case, the service objective acts as a constraint upon the achievement of the profit objective. The result will be suboptimization (somewhat less than optimization) of the primary objective. Thus the *best* level of expenses is higher (to meet the service objective) than desirable to achieve the profit objective.

In the remainder of the chapter we will often think in terms of reducing expenses. The rationale is that retailers typically incur more expenses than are necessary to achieve their objectives. We shall define *expenses* as all money paid or obligations incurred for purposes *other than* for merchandise and its transportation, items that are reflected in the cost of goods sold section of the income statement.

Normally a substantial portion of each sales dollar goes to cover expenses in most retail firms. With this in mind, we will examine expense classification, budgets, allocation, and management in the following sections.

CLASSIFICATION OF EXPENSES

Every retail store, regardless of size, nature of its business, or number of employees, incurs expenses. In order to control expenses effectively, the manager must develop a classification system so that expenses can be summarized periodically. This provides decision-making information that is essential to expense control.

No single classification system works best for all businesses. A small, one-man retail operation typically needs a less complete expense classification system than does a large department store. Although various trade associations and the National Retail Merchants' Association have encouraged standardization of expense classification categories, it is doubtful whether any single system or even a select few systems will ever be totally accepted. There are simply too many differences in individual retail outlets for all to use any particular system.

Three primary expense classification systems are in use. They are natural classification, functional classification, and expense center classification.

Natural Classification

The natural classification of expenses assigns expenses to categories according to the nature of the expenditure. Such a classification system is very similar in nature to one that would be developed intuitively by a person with some bookkeeping or accounting knowledge. Obviously, the number of accounts needed varies among different sizes and types of stores. Larger stores typically utilize more accounts than smaller stores. Some larger stores even find it desirable to subdivide the categories.

Table 20-1 indicates a typical natural classification system and the general types of expenses which are often included in each classification. It is important that consistency be maintained in charging expenses to the proper account. Essentially this involves providing the bookkeeper or accountant with enough information (if such is not indicated on a bill) to facilitate proper classification.

Many small stores find natural classification entirely satisfactory for charging expenses. In some cases the natural accounts may be condensed

TABLE 20-1

A Natural Expense Classification System

Classification	Types of expenses included
Payroll	All forms of payment to all levels of employees
Property rental	All amounts paid for land and buildings rented or leased for business operation. Income from property subleased to another business is deducted from this account
Advertising	All those expenses associated with placement of advertising in any advertising medium
Taxes	All taxes paid to city, county, state, and federal governments except income taxes
Services purchased	Payment of any non-professional services, including utilities, repairs, cleaning, and any other payments made for performance of a non-professional service
Supplies	All consumable items purchased for the operation of the business—office supplies and cleaning and maintenance items are examples
Travel	All expenses for all employees traveling on company business
Communications	All expenses for telephones, telegrams, postage, and rental of communication equipment
Pensions	Payments made to retired employees and to pension funds
Insurance	Payments made for all types of insurance coverage
Depreciation	Value of the decline (approved by taxing authorities) in value of major furniture, fixture, equipment, and buildings. No money actually paid out but rather "held" in reserve for depreciation account
Professional services	Fees and payments made for professional services—legal, accounting, medical, and advertising
Bad debt loss	Uncollectable bills, bad checks, and fraudulent purchases
Equipment rental	Payments made for rental or lease of all equipment except communication equipment
Interest	All amounts paid for use of borrowed capital for business purposes
Donations	All contributions made to non-profit organizations
Unclassified	All expenses not included in other natural divisions

into as few as eight or ten classifications and still provide enough detail for effective decision making. In larger stores, however, the system of natural accounts may conceal details needed for decision making. The functional classification system overcomes many of these problems.

Functional Classification

A functional classification system identifies the activity or function to which each expense applies. While the natural classification is concerned with the basic *nature* of the expenditure, the functional classification centers on the general *purpose* of the expenditure.

The five major functions which have been used for classification are (1) administration, (2) occupancy, (3) publicity, (4) buying, and (5) selling. A frequently used approach is to subdivide natural expenses according to functions, as shown in Figure 20-1. The first row total would indicate total payroll expenditures, the second row, total property rental expenses, and so on. *Row* totals indicate amounts expended according to the natural accounts, while *column* totals show amounts spent by function. Such a two-way expenditure classification enables a retail manager to determine precisely the nature of expenditures and locate troublesome areas.

Suppose, for example, a manager notes that the supplies total for a particular accounting period seems to have risen inordinately. With natural accounts only, it might be impossible to determine why such an increase occurred. However, a two-way classification system may indicate that one of the functional areas accounts for most of the increase. If the store had earlier made the decision to buy a new, fancier type of bag with the store's name and advertising logo on both sides, the results of such a decision might be easily spotted by the increase in selling supplies.

In the small store, functional expense classification is probably unnecessary. The store owner-manager has day-to-day contact with all areas of the business. In addition, total expense transactions are few enough in number that an examination of the books may reveal unusual expense activity.

Functional expense classification probably makes the greatest contribution in a medium-size store. Most large stores no longer use a functional classification system. The major shortcoming of the functional classification system is that major responsibilities in a large store do not always correspond with the functions designated. In most large stores today, expense center accounting is deemed more appropriate.

Expense Center Accounting

The use of expense center accounting requires grouping expenses necessary to the performance of a particular kind of store service or job task.[2] The basic

	Administration	Occupancy	Publicity	Buying	Selling	Total
Payroll						
Property Rental						
Advertising						
Taxes						
Services Purchased						
Supplies						
Traveling						
Communications						
Pension						
Insurance						
Depreciation						
Professional Services						
Bad Debt Loss						
Equipment Rental						
Interest						
Donations						
Unclassified						
TOTAL						

FIGURE 20-1

Expense summary form combining natural
and functional expense classifications

expense centers recommended by the National Retail Merchants' Association and the numbering system are shown in Table 20-2. Note that these centers are really an expansion of the functional accounts previously discussed.

The same type of expense summary form as shown in Figure 20-1 can be developed for expense centers. Rather than present such a summary, let us simply examine one expense center to see how a natural classification system

TABLE 20-2

Basic Expense Figures

110	Management
120	Property and equipment
210	Accounting and data processing
310	Accounts receivable
320	Credit and collections
410	Sales promotion
510	Service and operation
550	Telephone and other utilities
570	Cleaning
580	Maintenance and repairs
610	Personnel
630	Supplementary benefits
720	Maintenance of reserve stock
740	Receiving and marking
750	Shuttle service
810	Selling supervision
820	Direct selling
830	Customer services
860	Wrapping and packing
880	Delivery
910	Merchandising
920	Buying
930	Merchandise control

Source: Retail Accounting Manual (New York: National Retail Merchants Association, 1962), p. IV-1.

"fits" into the expense center to reveal a great deal more about expenses than could be obtained by using each separately.

The credit and collections department is one of the basic expense centers. Numerous "natural" expenses are incurred in operating such a department. The primary responsibility of the department (expense center) is to open new accounts, approve credit purchases, and collect overdue accounts. Table 20-3 presents the classification of natural expenses within the credit and collections department. Certainly this breakdown is more useful than would be a simple total expense figure of $55,400 for the operation of the department. In this case a major portion of the expenses was for payroll, but other expense centers might have more balanced expenses. It is very helpful for a manager to be able to pinpoint the exact nature of various expenses in an operation. The credit manager knows that turning uncollectable accounts over to an attorney or an outside collection agency accounted for part of the services purchased, while the remainder was spent to obtain credit information from the local credit bureau. He knows, too, that having his collectors call in person on slow-paying accounts shows up as traveling expense. Thus,

Classification of Expenses

TABLE 20-3

Expense Center 320—Credit and Collections with Natural Classifications

Payroll	$50,000
Supplies	1,500
Services purchased	2,000
Traveling	500
Bad debts	1,250
Equipment costs	50
Unclassified	100
	$55,400

expense center accounting coupled with a natural classification of accounts provides much needed information in a large retail operation.

In extremely large retail stores, even the above system may be inadequate. For example, a credit manager may desire more specific information for each accounting period on the breakdown of the payroll account. Fortunately, the expense center system readily allows for further subdivision of activities into more detailed functions. This can be done by means of a "fan-out" principle. For example, in an extremely large store the credit and collection functions may be separated and subdivided even further as follows:

Credit
    Credit promotion
    Credit granting
    Authorization (approving purchases on account)

Collection
    Collection efforts (in store)
    Outside collectors
    P and L section (bad debt write-offs)

Each of these subdivisions may then carry natural expense divisions as in Table 20-3. When relatively large numbers of departments and employees are involved, such an arrangement may be entirely logical.

Despite the possible increase in accounting efforts (by having more accounts), the increased control over expense activities may be warranted, since detailed breakdowns provided by expense center accounting offer other advantages. A major benefit is that widespread acceptance of the expense center concept makes it possible for stores to compare their experience with those of other stores. Table 20-4 presents average expenses as a percent of sales for various sizes of department and specialty stores. Note that this is a general breakdown by nine expense centers. Comparison of an individual store's percentages with those shown may indicate expense centers which are out of line with the averages for their group of stores.[3] Although deviations from average figures are obviously permissible because of differences in emphasis or methods of operation, the average figures do call attention to such departures.

> **REVIEW BOX 20:1**
>
> 1. Expense control is concerned with determining the _____ _____ level of expenses.
> 2. In order to control expenses properly, retailers need a _____ _____ system so that expenses can be summarized periodically.
> 3. A small retailer is most likely to use the _____ classification of expenses.
> 4. The _____ classification system is simply an expanded version of the _____ classification system.

TABLE 20-4

Expenses of Typical Expense Centers as Percent of Total Sales for Department Stores and Specialty Stores

		Department Stores by Sales Volume (millions of dollars)						Specialty Stores	
		All companies[a]	$1–$2	$2–$5	$5–$10	$10–$20	$20–$50	Over $50	$1–$5	Over $5
EXPENSE CENTER										
100	Fixed and policy expenses	5.52	6.60	6.31	6.65	5.81	5.64	5.35	8.34	7.07
200	Control and accounting	0.90	1.51	1.30	1.09	0.99	0.85	0.87	1.38	1.22
300	Accounts receivable and credit	1.61	1.77	1.42	1.60	1.51	1.69	1.60	2.08	1.99
400	Sales promotion	3.54	3.53	3.72	3.81	3.73	3.67	3.46	3.81	4.22
500	Superintendency and building operations	2.84	2.90	2.65	2.95	2.95	2.83	2.83	3.14	3.37
600	Personnel and employee benefits	2.09	1.55	2.00	1.91	1.91	1.88	2.19	1.71	2.11
700	Material handling	1.36	0.85	0.73	0.89	1.19	1.21	1.47	0.90	0.99
800	Direct and general selling	10.57	10.09	9.41	9.77	9.33	10.10	10.95	9.01	9.96
900	Merchandising	3.30	3.70	3.58	3.99	3.58	3.36	3.20	3.27	3.73
Gross operating expense		32.01	32.68	31.12	32.97	31.21	31.91	32.11	33.98	34.88
Less: Accounts receivable handling charges		1.84	0.97	1.10	1.43	1.34	1.94	1.93	1.21	1.23
Net operating expense		29.96	31.71	30.02	31.49	29.56	29.79	29.96	32.77	33.65

[a] A weighted average is used for the "All Companies" figure. A "typical" figure is used for each volume classification.
Source: Controller's Congress, National Retail Merchants' Association, as shown in *Expenses in Retail Business* (Dayton, Ohio: The National Cash Register Company, no date), pp. 12–13.

EXPENSE ALLOCATION

Although expense center classifications are extremely helpful in *controlling* the expenses of performing various functions, the primary purpose of each expense center is to *support* the primary revenue-producing units (for example, selling departments within a store, various stores within a chain, or branch stores). By allocating expenses to these units, the retail manager can attempt to measure the "value" of each unit.

Since revenue-producing units need to have expense functions performed, it is generally thought that such units should be evaluated on their ability to cover these expenses. For example, a branch store may contribute a substantial sales volume to overall company sales, but it may contribute little or nothing to company profitability because of the high expense associated with its operations. The same type of situation can exist with respect to departments within a store.

The primary purpose of allocating expenses to selling departments is to allow management to judge the effectiveness of each department. A measure of selling department effectiveness is necessary as a basis for deciding:

Whether to expand, reduce, or perhaps eliminate a particular department

To divide a selling department or combine it with another department

To relocate the department

Whether the department manager is doing a good job

Whether a certain department needs more or fewer services (which would affect expenses)

No consensus exists as to which kind of allocation plan is best. The usefulness of any plan to a particular retail operation depends upon business philosophy, the particular store situation, and the type of accounting records maintained. Before discussing specific allocation plans, we will examine a problem common to all types of plans.

Types of Expenses

The major problem involved in allocating expenses concerns the two recognized types of expenses, direct and indirect. *Direct* (or *controllable*) expenses are those under the complete control of a particular department. They would be eliminated if the department were discontinued. An example of a direct expense is the payroll for sales personnel in a department. These expenses are direct in that they are unquestionably related to a specific department, and they are controllable in that the department manager can regulate their *level.* In the case of payroll expenses, more people or fewer people can be hired.

Some other expenses that can usually be attributed to a specific department are those related to the travel of buyers and department managers and those having to do with the maintenance of departmental stock. Of course, problems of allocation will arise when a buyer has responsibility for obtaining merchandise for more than one department, when a manager supervises two or more departments, and when stock maintenance covers the merchandise of several departments. In such cases, an appropriate portion of the expenses will be charged to each department involved.

The greatest problem of allocation is caused by *indirect* (or *uncontrollable*) expenses. These expenses are ones that have no direct relation to a specific selling department and would continue even if a department were eliminated. Institutional advertising, salaries of top administrators, and contributions to charities are examples of indirect expenses.

Some expenses that appear to be indirect are actually treated as direct expenses when there is some equitable basis for charging them to various departments. Such expenses are then labeled *semidirect.* This is often done in medium-size or large department stores for window display and interior display; for the advertising of merchandise, including catalogs and brochures as well as newspaper, radio, and television ads; and for promotion events such as fashion shows, grand openings, and receptions.

With this discussion as a basis, we now turn to an examination of the various allocation methods.

Methods of Allocating Expenses

The basic philosophy underlying the *net profit* plan is that *all* expenses are allocated to selling departments. In theory, then, each selling department is viewed much as an independent business and is judged upon its ability to produce a profit. The argument in favor of the net profit plan is that it is the best single indicator of a department manager's ability and that it determines the worth of the department to the store. Proponents of the plan also maintain that it makes department managers more conscious of expenses. While this may be true, it is also possible that department managers may feel it is fruitless to attempt to control expenses since there are so many uncontrollable expenses charged to their departments.

NET PROFIT PLAN

In order to develop and maintain sound bases for allocating indirect expenses to departments, rather expensive and complex calculations are necessary. Even then, there are some expenses for which no sound basis for allocation seems to exist. Table 20-5 indicates the bases for distributing some expenses from expense centers to departments.

The problems associated with determining a satisfactory basis for

TABLE 20-5

Bases Used for Allocating Common Expenses

Expenses	Basis for allocation
Credit authorization	Number of credit sales
Accounts payable	Number of invoices processed
Sales audit	Total sales transactions
Accounts receivable	Total credit sales transactions
Delivery	Total pieces delivered
Security office (protection)	Weighted floor space
Receiving and marking	Number of pieces checked & marked
Personnel	Number of employees
Accounting	Net sales
Collections	Total credit sales
General administration	Net sales
Cleaning and maintenance	Weighted floor space
Cash office	Net sales

allocating rental (or real estate) expenses merit mention. First, it is normally assumed that the value of floor space decreases with each higher floor level. Also, on a particular floor the value of the floor space varies from one area to another. The difficulty then entails determining a square footage rental value for various store areas. In most cases the final value per square foot is rather arbitrarily decided upon. Further complicating the matter is the fact that some departments expand or contract seasonally. For example, a bathing suit department in a Chicago store might exist only during the summer and during the "cruise season." Thus there are problems not only of equitably allocating floor space expenses but also of continually updating the amount of floor space occupied by a particular department.

Even greater questions arise in the allocation of general administrative expenses. Commonly, these expenses are allocated on the basis of net sales. While such a basis may make little sense, it is difficult to find a more equitable one. If such expenses are distributed according to the amount of management time devoted to each department, conflicts may develop. For example, a merchandise manager may spend a disproportionate amount of time with a new department manager. If the new department is charged with this time, and the result is lower profits, then the new manager will be justifiably unhappy.

Probably the most severe criticism leveled at the net profit plan is that department managers are charged with some expenses over which they have absolutely no control. Because of the rather arbitrary basis for charging some indirect expenses, there is the question of whether any given departmental net profit is a true or actual profit.

CONTRIBUTION MARGIN PLAN

The contribution margin plan (sometimes called simply the contribution plan) was initiated largely because of dissatisfaction with the net profit plan. Essentially, the contribution margin plan allocates all direct (or controllable) expenses to selling departments. After cost of goods sold and direct expenses are deducted from sales, the remainder is contribution margin rather than net profit. Table 20-6 should clarify the differences between the net profit plan and the contribution margin plan.

Allocating all expenses under the net profit plan results in a net profit figure for the department. Under the contribution margin plan, there exists, after the allocation of all those expenses deemed to be direct, an amount that represents net profit plus an amount to contribute toward the covering of all indirect store expenses. This amount is a department's contribution (or controllable) margin.

Some retailing specialists argue that the effectiveness of a selling department manager and the worth of a department are more fairly judged on the basis of contribution than on net profit. Such reasoning emphasizes the responsibility of selling department managers for the control of direct expenses. It is felt that psychologically this is much better than holding managers responsible for expenses over which they have absolutely no control. Managers who know that they will be charged with precisely the amount of supplies used and exactly the number of payroll dollars expended will carefully control the level of these expenses. When managers know they will be charged for indirect expenses as well, and perhaps on a less than logical basis, they may become discouraged and pay relatively little attention to controlling direct expenses.

Another advantage of the contribution plan is simplicity and ease of understanding by all concerned. There are no complex formulas for allocating indirect expenses as may be used under the net profit plan. Proponents of the contribution method emphasize that only those expenses that are unquestionably controllable should be charged as direct expenses.

The contribution method is not above criticism. One drawback is that selling department managers may contribute substantially to an increased

TABLE 20-6

A Comparison of the Net Profit and Contribution Margin Plans

Net profit plan		*Contribution margin plan*	
Net sales	$100,000	Net sales	$100,000
Cost of goods sold	60,000	Cost of goods sold	60,000
Gross margin	$ 40,000	Gross margin	$ 40,000
Less: Direct and indirect expenses	35,000	Less direct expenses	20,000
Net profit before taxes	$ 5,000	Contribution margin	$ 20,000

level of some indirect expenses if they suffer no penalties for doing so. Efforts to increase sales and thus contribution margin may place inordinate demands upon "free" services provided by the store. For example, if selling departments are not charged any portion of credit or delivery expenses, the temptation might be to utilize these activities to increase sales. Salespeople may thus try to please customers by encouraging them to charge very inexpensive items and to have small packages delivered. Such actions increase total store expenses and negatively affect overall store profit.

One other major criticism is that the amount of planned initial markup required to break even or to produce a profit remains unknown. Recall that the amount of markup should be sufficient to cover expenses plus profit plus reductions. When departmental expenses are unknown, as under the contribution margin plan, there is no way to determine how much the planned initial markup should be.

COMBINATION PLAN

Successful stores can be found using each of the above methods. Some retailers, however, are dissatisfied with both methods, and they frequently use a combination of the two to minimize the shortcomings of each. One such combination plan is as follows:

Net sales	$100,000
Less: Cost of goods sold	60,000
Gross margin	$ 40,000
Less: Direct expenses	20,000
Contribution margin	$ 20,000
Less: Indirect expenses	15,000
Net profit	$ 5,000

Performance of the selling department manager and worth of the department can be evaluated on the basis of contribution margin. Since all indirect expenses are also distributed, the information necessary to provide a basis for initial markup is also available.

One modification is the situation in which expenses are subdivided into three categories of expenses:

Direct expenses: those which are incurred by a particular department.
Indirect expenses: those expenses that admit of no measurable relationship with any one department.
Semidirect expenses: those expenses which are not direct, but for which some equitable basis of allocation exists or can be devised. Examples of semidirect expenses include billing, which may be distributed on the basis of orders; credit supervision, which may be allocated on the basis of the number of customers; and so forth.[4]

The result of using such a plan might look like this:

Net sales	$100,000
Less: Cost of goods sold	60,000
Gross margin	$ 40,000
Less: Direct expenses	10,000
Contribution margin	$ 30,000
Less: Semidirect expenses	12,000
Contribution after semidirect expenses	$ 18,000
Less: Indirect expenses	13,000
Net profit	$ 5,000

The major value of this allocation method is that more total information is available than with the previously mentioned methods. Note that the various expenses are subtracted in descending order of control by the selling department manager.

REVIEW BOX 20:2

1. Expense _____ refers to the charging of expenses to the various revenue-producing departments.
2. _____ expenses are those under the complete control of a particular department manager. These expenses would be eliminated if the department were discontinued.
3. All expenses are allocated to revenue-producing units under the _____ plan of allocation.
4. Under the contribution margin plan of expense allocation, only the _____ expenses are allocated.
5. Those expenses which are not direct but for which some equitable means of allocation exists are called _____ expenses.

EXPENSE BUDGETS

Just as a merchandise budget sets forth a plan for merchandise requirements, the expense budget details a plan for expenditures other than those made to acquire merchandise. The expense budget may be viewed as a forecast of expenditures for a proposed period of time. Like other budgets prepared by a retail establishment, it is based on the sales budget, and the total amount to be expended is largely dependent upon the sales level to be achieved. Thus the aim of the expense budget is to spend money in order to achieve stated objectives, namely the desired level of sales and profits.

The time interval involved is largely dependent upon the sales budget and the merchandise budget. If these budgets are prepared for a six-month period, the expense budget normally covers the same period.

There are those who strongly object to the preparation and use of an expense budget. Objections seem to fall into three main categories. First, some objectors maintain that the time and effort spent on expense budget preparation are wasteful. Admittedly, a well-prepared expense budget is time consuming. However, it does force a manager to plan and anticipate expenses rather than be "surprised" at large expense outlays.

Second, there are those who maintain that expense budgets limit a firm's flexibility in meeting unexpected conditions. While this criticism may have some merit, it is not the budget or the budgeting process that is at fault. If a serious economic downturn occurs and sales decline, astute management should immediately revise the expense budget downward. If an unanticipated economic "boom" occurs, a manager should not hold the line on a budget prepared for a lower level of sales. Thus, judicious retail managers modify the expense budget when unexpected events warrant changes.

The third group of dissenters argue that expense budgets cause the retail firm to be "penny wise but pound foolish." Largely, this criticism suggests that retail managers may become so enamored with controlling expenses that they neglect other, more important opportunities for profit growth. While it is true that a manager *could* become overly involved in controlling expenses, it is doubtful that many successful retail managers fall into this trap.

Expense budgets should be viewed as an aid to effective expense management and certainly not a substitute for it. Expenses must be incurred in effectively moving merchandise off the shelves and into the consumers' hands. Effective control of these expenses through an expense budget makes good economic sense.

The Purpose of Expense Budgeting

Essentially the expense budgeting procedure is a system for planning and controlling expenses. As with other budgets, management sets objectives it wishes to achieve and makes plans to reach these objectives. Figure 20-2 illustrates how the total budgeting procedure fits into a management system.

Once the budget is constructed, actual results can be compared with planned results. Where no differences are found, corrective actions are not needed. However, the reasons for any differences found must be investigated. Feedback is thus necessary to provide information for revising the budget. This is represented by the feedback loop on the left side of the figure. Where differences occur on the basis of performance, corrective actions are taken to improve performance. This is indicated by the feedback loop on the right side.

It can be seen that the budgeting process represents an ongoing planning and control system. It is important that this perspective be maintained with respect to expense budgets. Too often, budgets are viewed primarily as

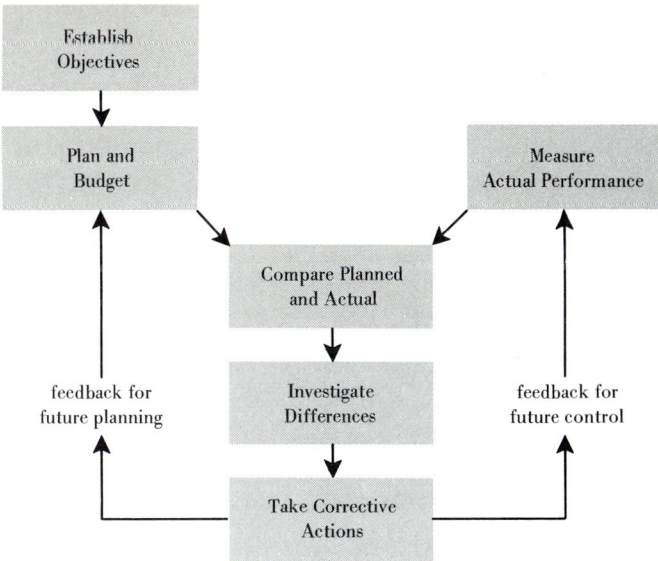

FIGURE 20-2

Budgeting as a management system

Source: Carl L. Moore and Robert K. Jaedicke, *Managerial Accounting*, 2nd ed. (Cincinnati: South-Western Publishing Company, 1967), p. 459

constraining devices aimed at inhibiting expenditures. When this view prevails, a budget's value as a planning device is largely lost. The prime value of an expense budget is to balance planned expenditures with planned income in order to achieve a satisfactory level of profits.

Expense Budgets in Smaller Stores

Unfortunately, many smaller retail establishments do not prepare expense budgets. Some smaller stores do not maintain accounting records that are adequate enough to allow a detailed analysis of past expenses. More frequently, though, small retailers view expense budgets as a nicety that they just do not have time to prepare.

Although there are different ways a small retailer could approach expense budgeting, the following example illustrates a common-sense approach. Consider the owner of a small (less than $100,000 per year in sales) family shoe store. Through his trade association, the retailer has found average expenses, as a percentage of sales, for similar shoe retailers. He then computed his store's last year's expenses and expressed them as a percentage of net

TABLE 20-7

Comparison of Individual Store Expenses with Industry Averages

	Industry averages	Store's figures
Sales	100.0	100.0
Cost of goods sold	63.0	60.0
Gross margin	37.0	40.0
Expenses:		
Rent	3.5	4.0
Owner's salary	8.9	10.0
Employees' salaries	7.7	9.2
Advertising	2.4	3.5
Freight in	1.3	
All other expenses	6.4	8.2
Total expenses	30.2	35.0
Net operating profit	6.8	5.0
Purchase discounts	1.4	
Net income before taxes	8.2	5.0

Source of industry averages: Expenses in Retail Business (Dayton, Ohio: National Cash Register Company, no date given).

sales. The chart in Table 20-7 is the result of this study. A comparison reveals that net income before taxes is lower than average for this retailer. Further analysis is needed to indicate whether this difference is an acceptable deviation from the average or is reflective of a problem the retailer can correct.

Note that industry average figures show freight as an expense rather than as a part of cost of goods sold. In addition, purchase discounts are shown as additional income rather than as a reduction in cost of goods sold. Although the overall result is the same, if these items had been included in the cost of goods sold figure, it would have amounted to 62.9 percent rather than 63.0 percent $(63.0 + 1.3 - 1.4 = 62.9)$. The store's gross margin is thus 2.9 percent greater than the industry average.

An investigation of expenses reveals that total expenses of 35 percent exceed the industry average of 28.9 percent (excluding freight in) by 6.1 percent. Obviously, the store's lower profit is due to this higher level of expenses. Apparently the most acceptable way of increasing profits is for the store owner to attempt to bring the various expenses more in line with the industry average. However, the expense categories that must be reduced cannot be known until the competitive situation facing the retailer is known.

If expenses were reduced, sales might fall drastically and net profit would be even lower. The essential point is that decision making can take place only with full knowledge of an individual retailer's situation. Even the retailer involved may have to engage in some experimenting to achieve the firm's objectives. For example, in the above situation, an increase in advertising or in employees' salaries (by adding personnel) might result in substantial increases in sales, causing total expenses as a percent of sales to decline. By carefully examining the target market and competitive situation, a retailer may be able to judge the course of action he should follow.

It is important for small retailers to compare their expenses with similar retail operations. Unless this is done, retailers have no real idea of how efficiently they are operating. Store managers may feel that net profit is too low (most small retailers feel this way), but unless they know something about the profit of other similar retailers, they have no benchmarks for comparison.

Suppose a small retailer knows that average total expenses for a similar store amount to 30 percent of net sales. He projects sales of $100,000 for the period and a gross margin of 40 percent. There are two possible approaches to planning expenses. First he can determine total expenses and profits for the period given an expense figure of 30 percent of $100,000. The computations might look something like this:

Sales	$100,000
Cost of goods sold (60% of $100,000)	60,000
Gross margin (40% of sales)	$ 40,000
Expenses (30% of sales)	30,000
Net profit before taxes	$ 10,000

Clearly, if sales are as projected and the gross margin percentage and expense percentage figures are achieved, gross margin will be $40,000, and total expenses must be limited to $30,000. If actual figures are the same as these planned figures, the retailer will have a net profit before taxes of $10,000. Again note that net profit is a residual—what remains after expenses are deducted from gross margin.

The second approach that the retailer might use is to set a net profit objective on the basis of sales and gross margin and determine the dollar amount of expenses that can be incurred. The computations, if the goal is $10,000 net profit before taxes, would look like this:

Sales	$100,000
Cost of goods sold (60% of $100,000)	60,000
Gross margin (40% of $100,000)	$ 40,000
Less: Net profit before taxes (desired)	10,000
Expenses	$ 30,000

Note that in this latter case, the total expense figure allowable is determined by other planned objectives of the firm. If these other planned figures are set unrealistically, the amount remaining for expenses may be equally unrealistic.

		Jan.	Feb.	Mar.	Apr.	May	June	July	Aug.	Sept.	Oct.	Nov.	Dec.	Total
Rent	Plan	330	330	330	330	330	330	330	330	330	330	330	330	3960
	Actual													
Owner's Salary	Plan	835	835	835	835	835	835	835	835	835	835	835	835	10020
	Actual													
Employees' Salary	Plan	675	675	1025	675	675	675	675	925	675	675	675	1175	9200
	Actual													
Advertising	Plan	100	200	500	200	100	100	100	500	200	100	150	200	2450
	Actual													
Utilities	Plan	110	110	90	90	90	120	120	120	100	100	110	130	1290
	Actual													
Miscellaneous	Plan	500	400	400	400	400	400	400	400	400	500	600	700	5500
	Actual													
Total	Plan	2550	2550	3180	2530	2430	2460	2460	3110	2540	2540	2700	3370	32420
	Actual													

FIGURE 20-3

A sample budget

In the first situation, the net profit that resulted was largely determined by the level of expenses normally encountered by other similar type firms. In practice, the retailer probably should use both methods as a check on the accuracy of the budgeting process.

Once a total expense figure is budgeted, the task then becomes one of dividing this figure into expense classes and dividing each of these figures among time periods. Let's examine how a retailer might do this. Assume that the $30,000 expense figure was for a year. Dividing that figure into expense classes and over time can be accomplished simultaneously. The first step is normally to consider the fixed expenses, those that are inescapable and do not vary over time. Using a budget sheet as shown in Figure 20-3, expenses for the coming year are planned.

Rent is fixed by an existing lease on the building and amounts to $330 per month. The owner has, in the past, drawn a stable salary at $835 per month. Past experience has indicated the need for one full-time employee and two part-time employees during normal periods. Peak sales periods are December, when slippers and boots are often bought for Christmas presents; March, with high levels of children's and ladies' shoes purchased for Easter; and August, when back-to-school business is especially large. Thus, additional sales help must be scheduled during these periods. Even though plans should be made for specific days of the week and hours of the day, at this point we will not get that detailed.

An advertising budget must also be set. As you can see in Figure 20-3, this retailer believes there are two major shoe seasons: spring and fall, the Easter and back-to-school periods. Therefore, advertising is concentrated during these times. Additional funds are provided for Christmas and end-of-season sales.

Past experience indicates that utilities, including telephone, are fairly constant throughout the year. After determining that none of the utility companies plans a rate increase for the coming year, the retailer uses the past year's utility expense as a guide and allocates this expense as shown.

Experience has shown this retailer that miscellaneous expenses also remain relatively constant from year to year. Rather than taking the time to plan these remaining expenses in detail, the retailer lumps them together into a miscellaneous category: all supplies (bags, signs, pencils, sales books, cleaning supplies), interest on loans, donations, building maintenance, insurance, bad debts, licenses, and membership in various organizations. Whether it makes good sense, as shown in Figure 20-3, to have a miscellaneous category as the third largest expense classification is questionable. However, if the retailer feels comfortable with such a budget and feels that it provides adequate information and control, then perhaps it is sufficient. As sketchy as this expense budget is, it is certainly better than no expense planning at all.

Expense Budgets in Large Stores

In a large retail store with its greater degree of specialization, preparation of expense budgets is more fragmented than in the small store. Typically the controller or chief fiscal officer handles most of the budgeting procedure. The preparation of individual expense budgets is usually delegated to heads of departments or various expense centers. Preparation of the budgets begins with the lowest supervisory level. The maker of each budget then defends it to his or her immediate superior. This superior usually combines all budgets of subordinate departments or levels and defends the result to the next person up the line. This procedure is repeated until the controller eventually receives expense budgets from each major division of the store. At any of the several review points, an individual budget may be returned to its originator for revision (usually downward). By following this procedure, responsibility for preparing and meeting budgeted figures is pushed downward to the organizational level where day-to-day control is vested. In other words, those responsible for "living with the budget" have major input into its preparation.

A major problem in large retail stores concerns the method to be followed in arriving at a total store expense figure. The method indicated above was a *bottom-up* approach. That is, the total expense budget was determined by adding together all of the expense center budgets.

A different approach is the so-called *top-down* method. Under this procedure, a total expense figure is determined (often as a percentage of budgeted sales) and is then allocated among the various expense centers. However, this approach may apportion too much money to some expense centers and too little to others.

Many stores therefore combine the two approaches. The controller provides general guidelines to each expense center manager in the form of a target figure. Often this figure is arrived at by projecting last year's figures adjusted for anticipated sales increases or decreases. The expense center manager is also informed of the percentage sales increase or decrease anticipated so the workload can be planned accordingly. Figure 20-4 indicates the degree of detail for payroll expenses during a six-month season. Even before this budget is prepared, the manager has probably planned the number of people (full-time and part-time) in terms of forty-hour equivalents. By knowing the weekly and hourly salary for the various employees, the manager can then determine the payroll dollars which will be required each week.

Note that some months contain four weeks while others are five-week months. Such a procedure is fairly common in order to achieve a balanced 52-week year. Although some weeks overlap into the next month, planning is easier than it would be if parts of weeks were included in a month.

Payroll		Jan.	Feb.	Mar.	Apr.	May	June	Season Total
Week 1	Plan	2,000	1,950	2,100	2,000	2,000	2,100	
	Actual							
Week 2	Plan	2,000	1,950	2,100	2,000	2,000	2,100	
	Actual							
Week 3	Plan	1,950	1,950	2,100	2,000	1,900	2,300	
	Actual							
Week 4	Plan	2,100	2,000	2,100	2,100	1,900	2,300	
	Actual							
Week 5	Plan	2,100		2,100				
	Actual							
Month Total	Plan	10,150	7,850	10,500	8,100	7,800	8,800	53,200
	Actual							

FIGURE 20-4

Illustration of expense planning detail

SPOTLIGHT

How much can a store's choice of lighting affect its expenses?

By using 400-watt metalarc lamps in its Washington, D.C., department store, Woodward & Lothrop is providing more than three times the illumination level at about one-third the operating cost.

Installed in the jewelry department last June during a routine remodeling, the light sources have already helped reduce the 80-year-old flagship store's electric bill, which annually costs $700,000.

General lighting on the 21-foot-high first floor is provided by incandescents set in box-like structures. To light the area with incandescents cost $5,647 for one year and resulted in an illumination level of 10 footcandles.

To have replaced this light source with fluorescents would have been too expensive, explains Arno P. Herzer, director of construction, due to extra wiring, fixtures and labor required. However, by using metalarcs that fit into the same format, it was possible to avoid the extra cost of wiring and labor. And the illumination level jumped to 32 footcandles and the operating cost dropped to $1,738.

This does not include the savings in maintenance and bulb replacement, since incandescents have a life of less than 1,000 hours and the metalarcs are rated at 10,500 hours, adds Herzer.

The fixtures contain lenses and reflectors. "The gold-tinted lens together with the color-corrected lamp seems to give the truest and most acceptable light tone for the jewelry department," says John Seipp, Woodward & Lothrop's manager of utilities.

The high-intensity source lends itself to a high ceiling level, he adds. Because the metalarc, a version of the mercury vapor lamp, is a point-source, there is little light dispersion; the crossover for the four fixtures, where the beam from one lamp intersects the beam of another, is at 12 feet above the floor.

This results in completely uniform illumination, only varying directly under the lamp, says Seipp.

In a recently remodeled department, where fluorescents totaling 1,300 watts per day had been installed, there was a wide range of illumination, from a low of 18 footcandles to a high of 76 directly under the fixture.

In a store with a high ceiling, there would be too much light dispersion to make it feasible to use fluorescents, says Seipp. "The metalarcs have a strong vertical drive and penetrate before dropping off in efficiency."

In an area with a low or normal ceiling height, there would probably be little difference in power requirements, it was felt. As for cost of fixtures, for an eight-lamp fluorescent unit the list price is about $33.60, compared to $28.75 for a 400-watt metalarc bay. The fluorescents have a rated life of about 15,500 hours, greater than the 10,500 hours for the metalarc.

"Two main points tipped the balance toward the high-intensity source," stresses Herzer, "the 21-foot ceiling height and the fact that installation was during the remodeling of an older building."

Source: "Triples Light, Cuts Cost 66%," *Chain Store Age*, March 1971, p. E32.

The same procedure as illustrated for payroll is followed for categories such as supplies, services purchased, advertising, and travel for a selling department. For expense centers the categories would likely be different. The primary advantages of having department managers prepare expense budgets are (1) the department manager should be more knowledgeable than any other single individual about the level of expenses necessary to provide the desired level of service, and (2) if the department manager has a strong voice in preparation of the budget, it is reasonable that he or she will put forth every effort to adhere to the budgeted figures.

A major advantage of using a form such as the one illustrated in Figure 20-4 is that periodic reports for control purposes can be issued by simply entering actual figures as they are compiled. In essence, the planning form becomes the detailed budget and the control form. This greatly reduces the labor and waste of preparing individual weekly, monthly, and seasonal reports.

REVIEW BOX 20:3

1. A forecast of expenditures (other than for merchandise) is called an _____.
2. The first step in preparing an expense budget is to _____.
3. In preparing an expense budget, the first type of expense usually considered is _____ expenses.
4. When the total expense budget is determined by adding together all of the individual expense center budgets (which have been prepared independently) the method used is the _____ _____ method.

CHAPTER SUMMARY

- Expense control is concerned with optimizing expenses to allow the retailer to achieve objectives.
- Expenses include all monies paid or obligations incurred for items not included in the cost of goods section of an income statement.
- An expense classification system is necessary to summarize expenses periodically as an aid to decision making. The three primary classification systems in use are the natural, functional, and expense center.
- The natural classification system, widely used by small retailers, classifies expenses according to the nature of the expenditure.

- A functional classification system utilizes the firm's major activities for classification purposes. The five major functions most frequently used are (1) administration, (2) occupancy, (3) publicity, (4) buying, and (5) selling.
- Expense center classification represents an expansion of functional classifications into more specific expense activities for larger stores. Expense centers exist to aid buying and selling activities.
- Expenses in retailing are of two basic types. Direct expenses are those under the complete control of a revenue-producing unit and occasioned by the existence of such a unit. Indirect expenses are not directly related to a particular revenue-producing department and are often called uncontrollable expenses, since the revenue-producing manager has no direct control over them.
- Expense allocation refers to the distribution of expenses to various revenue-producing units, necessary in judging the effectiveness of these units and their managers.
- Under the net profit plan of expense allocation, *both* direct and indirect expenses are allocated to selling units.
- Under the contribution margin plan of expense allocation, only direct expenses are charged to selling units.
- An expense budget details proposed expense items by category over a future period of time. Expense budgets aid effective management of expenses but are not a substitute for management decisions.
- Although many small retailers do not prepare expense budgets, they might improve their profits by doing so. Comparison of individual store expense categories with similar stores can indicate areas needing attention.
- Expense budgets in larger stores are usually constructed by each expense center manager. The method used may be either a build-up or a break-down approach or a combination of the two.

CHAPTER NOTES

[1] "An Expense Control Contest," *Stores*, October 1973, p. 22.
[2] *Retail Accounting Manual* (New York: National Retail Merchants Association, Controllers' Congress, 1962) has extended its former functional classification into the widely accepted expense center accounting. The following discussion draws heavily upon this source.
[3] For a more detailed expense center classification for department and specialty stores, see *Financial Operating Results of Department and Specialty Stores* (New York: National Retail Merchants Association, Controllers' Congress) published annually. This source also includes a natural classification within each expense center.
[4] Ronald E. Gist, *Retailing: Concepts and Decisions* (New York: John Wiley and Sons, Inc., 1968), pp. 500–01.

QUESTIONS AND ASSIGNMENTS

1. Explain what results might be expected if a retailer concentrated upon minimizing expenses.
2. Discuss why multiple objectives by a retailer may result in an increased level of expenses.
3. Set up what you believe would be an adequate expense classification system for a restaurant with approximately $200,000 in annual sales. Explain what type of classification system you used and why.
4. What is the difference between services purchased and professional services in a natural classification system.
5. Explain how the "fan-out" principle may be used to expand the number of expense centers in a store.
6. Distinguish between the net profit plan and the contribution margin plan of expense allocation. Indicate the advantages and disadvantages of each plan.
7. Explain the differences in direct, indirect, and semidirect expenses.
8. Assume you are a selling department manager in a large department store who is evaluated on the basis of contribution margin. You are aggressive and want to build a good reputation for yourself. How would you proceed?
9. You are the president of a chain of 15 women's apparel stores. What method would you use to evaluate each store manager?
10. Suppose you are the proprietor of an independent bookstore located in a college town. How would you proceed with an analysis of your expenses for the past year?
11. Why should expense budgets be viewed as an aid to effective management rather than as a substitute?
12. If you are the controller of a large store and are responsible for the preparation of a total store expense budget, how would you proceed?

ANSWERS TO REVIEW BOX QUESTIONS

Box 20:1
1. optimum
2. classification
3. natural
4. expense center; functional

Box 20:2
1. allocation
2. direct
3. net profit
4. direct
5. semidirect

Box 20:3
1. expense budget
2. establish objectives
3. fixed
4. build-up

Questions and Assignments

RETAILING DECISION
Ace Hardware

Ace Hardware is owned and managed by Ray Peoples. Mr. Peoples bought the store in 1951 and since that time has operated it successfully in the same location. However, since 1972 he has noticed an alarming trend of declining sales. In an attempt to analyze the situation, he has made the following observations:

Many of his regular customers of 5, 10, and 15 years ago no longer come to his store.

He has lost sales when prospective customers have requested lower-priced merchandise than he carries. Mr. Peoples has always prided himself on the high quality of his offerings.

In the neighborhood shopping center in which he is located, a fast-food hamburger restaurant has replaced a family style, sit-down restaurant and, for the first time that he can remember, two of the eight storefronts are vacant.

1. What problem(s) do these symptoms suggest?
2. What information should Mr. Peoples collect to analyze the situation?

RETAILING DECISION

The Newton Store

David Wilbanks, a department manager in The Newton Store, opened the morning mail, looked at his monthly operating statement from the Controller's Office, and flew into a rage. He then rushed toward the Divisional Merchandise Manager's office. As he entered the DMM's office he said: "Jim, what the - - - is going on here? My department has the highest sales of any department in the division. I operate on an extremely low, competitive markup. You know I've been working to improve the profitability of my department and now you hit me with this!" (David pointed at two figures he had circled in red on his monthly operating statement.)

"Simmer down, Dave," replied Jim Largent. "I know you've been doing a good job. Just last month I told the General Merchandise Manager what a terrific job you're doing. Your sales are up 28% over last year and the department has never run more smoothly."

"It's sure not going to run smoothly if this continues. What the devil is this charge of $1,800 for supervision and $2,200 for rent? You know my charges for these items have always been $500 for each."

"Look, Dave, the president has changed the method of allocating indirect expenses. Charges for supervision and rent are now based on net sales. Those departments with large sales volume are better able to absorb overhead expenses. You've got no reason for complaint."

"Yes, but look what happens," replied Dave. "My department shows a loss for the month because of these increased charges. My salary is based on performance, and now I look like a bum."

1. Do you agree with the new method of allocating expenses? Why or why not?
2. Does David Wilbanks have a legitimate complaint? Explain.

PART SEVEN

Special Topics

The Impact of Consumerism

Although the term *consumerism* achieved the status of a household word in the late 1960s and early 1970s, it still has a vague meaning to many people. You have only to ask consumers what the term means to see how hazy or indistinct it really is. They may talk about Ralph Nader, an organized effort, about consumer protection, or even about government regulations. Rarely, though, will they respond with a clear, concise definition. The reason, of course, is that this broad term covers a host of activities, efforts, and problems between business and consumers with the government often in the middle.

Writers on the subject of consumerism sometimes differ in their emphasis. Consider the following:

> [Consumerism is] the organized efforts of consumers seeking redress, restitution and remedy for dissatisfaction they have accumulated in the acquisition of their standard of living.[1]

> Consumerism is a social movement seeking to augment the rights and powers of buyers in relation to sellers.[2]

> Consumerism is the term that describes the efforts by organized groups to call attention to business activities that are seen to be detrimental to the best interests of the consumer groups they represent.[3]

> Consumerism may be defined as (1) the reaction—and an increasingly organized reaction—of consumers to their dissatisfactions and unrealized expectations and (2) their efforts to have these perceived injustices remedied.[4]

These definitions indicate that consumers are often dissatisfied with their present relationship with business, are willing to voice this dissatisfaction, and are even willing, in some cases, to engage in actions to remedy the cause of their dissatisfaction. The last definition presented above best fits the authors' perception of consumerism.

THE EVOLUTION OF CONSUMERISM

Although the term consumerism is relatively new, consumer dissatisfaction is by no means a recent occurrence. Throughout recorded history one can find reference to questionable marketing practices by businessmen and evidence that consumers have been disenchanted with shoddy products and practices. In 1727, for example, Daniel Defoe said:

> Hence comes the common saying among some people, who perhaps want charity more than they want knowledge, that all tradesmen are knaves; and 'tis absolutely necessary they should be so; that it cannot be otherwise; that 'tis impossible they should be honest men; and if they were not all rogues, they would break, and be undone; they could not live or get their bread; and the like.[5]

Caveat emptor (let the buyer beware) is certainly not a recently coined phrase; nor are consumer concerns about misrepresentation, inferior quality of goods, and other attempts at deception newly evolved.

In this century there have been two periods of widespread consumer unrest prior to the one beginning in the 1960s.[6] In each period consumers faced a decline in purchasing power brought about by rising prices. The first unrest, in the early 1900s, climaxed with the publication of Upton Sinclair's book *The Jungle*, in 1906. Sinclair's book was an exposé of conditions within the meat-packing industry and aroused enough public sentiment to force Congress to act. The result was passage of the Pure Food and Drug Act and the Meat Inspection Act.

In the 1930s, consumers again suffered from falling incomes and were upset by exposés such as *Your Money's Worth* and *100,000,000 Guinea Pigs* and by the death of more than 100 people from a patent medicine. Congress reacted by passing the Food, Drug and Cosmetic Act and the Wheeler-Lea Act. The former act strengthened and extended the Pure Food and Drug Act, while the latter brought the advertising of foods, drugs, and cosmetics under the jurisdiction of the Federal Trade Commission. An additional outcome was the establishment of various independent testing agencies—the best known of which are Consumers' Research and Consumers Union.[7] These organizations were formed primarily to test products and inform consumers of the results of such tests.

In both earlier eras of consumer unrest, widespread consumer concern and outcry aided by shocking publications brought pressure to bear on Congress for protective legislation. However, these consumer movements were relatively short-lived, and the protective legislation provided only stop-gap measures and was not broad enough to give the consumer complete protection.

Initially, the current consumer uprising followed much the same pattern as the earlier ones. However, as it has matured there seem to be several differences. First, the present consumer movement gathered speed very slowly before it was translated into positive action. Second, consumerism shows no signs of declining. Last, current consumer concern is much broader in scope. Today consumers are perturbed not only about lack of product information and safety but also with a broad range of business practices: illegal, unethical, and inefficient marketing practices; any action which adversely affects the physical environment; and actions that are perceived by consumers as putting them at a disadvantage, while putting business and industry in a profitable position.

REVIEW BOX 21:1

1. Consumerism indicates _____.
2. *Caveat emptor* means _____.
3. In all three eras of consumer unrest, consumers were faced with a decline in purchasing power brought about by _____.

THE PRESENT CONSUMER MOVEMENT

Americans today are better educated, more affluent, and more knowledgeable about products than any other group of consumers in the world. Still, these consumers are calling for help. Barraged with a constant flow of new products and product information, consumers today are faced with more difficult buying decisions than those who were faced with a limited choice of products 25 or 50 years ago.

We will examine first some of the changes in retailing that have contributed to consumer dissatisfaction and will go on to look at government's responses to consumer woes.

The Role of Retailing

Retailers can operate under either of two distinct philosophies: they can view themselves as purchasing agents *for* consumers or as sellers of merchandise *to* consumers. A retail operation that adopts the first philosophy is making the consumer the focal point of all its activities, the justification for its existence.

The wants and needs of the consumer dictate the kinds of merchandise the firm should handle as well as its methods of operation. This philosophy is based on the *marketing concept:* determining the wants and needs of consumers and then striving to satisfy those wants in order to produce a reasonable profit for the firm.

The second philosophy, on the other hand, requires merely that the retailer act as a linking pin in the channel of distribution between the manufacturer and the consumer. The retailer is, in effect, a disposer of goods.

As firms adopt the second philosophy, the relationship between retailer and consumer is depersonalized. Consumers often do not get what they want, because the retailer is not concerned primarily with their wants. Consumer dissatisfaction is not dealt with, because the retailer is more interested in "moving goods" than in filling customer needs.

Another area of depersonalization is in the buyer-customer relationship. Before large-scale, multi-store retailing, retail buyers were usually also responsible for the selling function. They were in constant contact with customers and were well aware of their wants and needs. However, with the trend toward separation of buying and selling in many multi-unit stores, buyers have little if any face-to-face contact with consumers. In the latter situation, buyers tend to buy goods that might have some kind of mass appeal, while in the former situation they view themselves as purchasing agents for the consumer, seeking out merchandise that specifically fills the needs of their customers.

Accompanying this separation of buying and selling has been a growing trend toward self-service, an approach that moves buying decisions even further from a consideration of customers' wants and needs. The buyer is unable to discover customers' needs from sales personnel, and the customer is unable to register a complaint about merchandise selection and quality.

Retailers are aware of these problems, and many firms are making serious attempts to solve them. Meanwhile, the government has become involved in consumerism.

The Role of Government

Recognizing some of the complexities facing consumers in 1962, President Kennedy presented Congress with his program on consumer protection. He "pointed out that two-thirds of all spending in our economy is by consumers; that we cannot afford waste in consumption any more than we can afford inefficiency in business and industry; and that the problems consumers face today are greater than they have ever been in history, and are likely to become more complex as time goes on."[8] In addition, he enumerated four basic consumer rights which by now are relatively well known. They are:

>The right to safety
>The right to be informed

The right to choose
The right to be heard

Presidents Johnson and Nixon also encouraged more consumer protection. As a result, consumers began to feel that they could make themselves heard—that someone, namely the federal government, really did care about their problems. Because of this government concern, consumers are voicing complaints such as the following:

Inadequate information. As products have become more technologically complicated, price and quality comparisons have become more difficult.

Lack of complete honesty. Consumers want honesty in advertising, sales presentations packaging, and point-of-purchase information.

Poor service. Consumers feel they are entitled to prompt, efficient service, and such service is normally dependent upon concerned, conscientious people.

Unsafe products. Consumers want and even demand protection from products which are, or can be, dangerous.

Products that perform below expectation. Consumers are tired of buying products which do not adequately perform the function for which they were purchased.

Complicated warranties. These are often designed primarily to limit manufacturers' and retailers' liability. Consumers want the warranty to benefit them, and they want it spelled out in clear, precise language which can be understood without the aid of an attorney.

Lack of durability. Consumers complain that products are not built to last.

The preceding complaints fall within the four basic consumer rights and are deserving of the immediate attention of business. The impact of these complaints upon retailers is examined in the following section.

REVIEW BOX 21:2

1. The business philosophy that involves determining the wants and needs of consumers and attempting to satisfy those wants while producing a reasonable profit is known as the _____.
2. The trends toward separation of buying and selling functions and increased self-service make it difficult for a retail store buyer to view himself as a _____ for the consumer.
3. The four basic consumer rights are: _____, _____, _____, and _____.

RETAILING AND THE CHALLENGE OF CONSUMERISM

Many retailers feel that they are faced with an awkward situation. More than any other group of businessmen, they are affected by the consumer movement, yet many problems confronting consumers are not of the retailer's making. For example, a department store salesperson persuades a young couple to spend the extra money necessary to purchase a well-known, nationally advertised brand of carpet. The couple agrees, and arrangements are made to have the carpet installed. On the appointed day, the couple moves all the furniture out of the room and the husband goes off to work expecting to return to a beautifully carpeted room. The carpet installers arrive, unroll the carpet, and begin to install it. The vigilant wife, who has been watching the progress, notices a severe flaw in the carpet. Pointing it out, she voices her dissatisfaction. At this point the installers agree. The manufacturer's tufting machine apparently skipped several stitches, and the quality control inspectors overlooked the resulting flaw.

The customer is not particularly interested in the cause of the flaw. She is unhappy with the retailer, since she either has to wait for another roll to be ordered, select another color, or take the flawed carpet. In any case the retailer bears the brunt of the irate woman's wrath, even though the store was not responsible for the problem.

Many retailers thus feel that they are wedged between "a rock and a hard place"—between producers and consumers. Retailers are on the firing line, almost daily receiving complaints about products, warranties, labeling, high prices, and misleading advertising. In many cases they have no control over the alleged unfair treatment. Yet invariably the consumer registers his complaint with the retailer. Faced with this situation, how should the retailer respond? Let's examine some actions open to the retailer.

Be Honest With the Consumer

Since honesty is generally accepted to be related to legality, some businesspeople have taken the position that any activity that is not illegal is therefore honest. For the consumer, however, this jump in logic is not satisfactory. Consumers have the right to expect merchants to be completely accurate and fair in their advertising, in sales presentations, and in all other interactions with their customers and potential customers. Consider for a moment those retail stores which you believe are the "best" stores in which to shop. In all probability, those stores have an outstanding reputation for fair and honest dealings with their customers. They put their customers first and generally practice "the golden rule." Obviously these stores are concerned with more than just the legality of their actions.

Examples of practices which are legal but perhaps less than honest are plentiful. Some supermarkets package meat so that fat or bone is hidden by the meat tray and the see-through portion of the package shows only lean meat. Other stores price products at six for a dollar or 15 cents each. In this instance it is more economical to purchase individual units, but consumers have been led to expect lower prices on multiple units and may not notice the difference. Placing a "sale" sign above a "prices marked" sign, and then including both regular-price items as well as markdown items on the racks is a questionable practice.

Youthful consumers are particularly insistent that advertising should "tell it like it is." Youth often feel they have been "tricked" by businesses and often hold a sour attitude toward businesspeople and business in general. It is imperative that merchants adopt a fair and honest approach to youth, since they will mature and become tomorrow's major consumers.[9]

Provide Adequate Information

Consumers need full information to make sound buying decisions. Retailers can cooperate in this endeavor by ensuring that salespeople are knowledgeable about the offerings they sell and that manufacturers provide relatively complete information on packages and tags and in promotional literature. Strong pressures for adequate information can be exerted on suppliers by refusing to handle products which do not meet minimum information standards. Consumers have the right to be informed, and it is the retailer's responsibility to ensure that this right is protected. Retailers should lead the way in implementing the doctrine of *doceatur emptor:* let the buyer be informed.[10]

Listen to Customers

A frequent consumer complaint is that no one is listening. Sources of constant frustration are computers that ignore written complaints about incorrect billings, unanswered phones in service departments, delays in deliveries or service calls and rude and inattentive salespeople. Generally, consumers feel there is no effective feedback system operating in the marketplace. Ideally, consumers feel they should be able to take a problem to the retailer for a quick and effective solution.

Sophisticated computer technology often serves to widen the communications gap between retailers, especially the larger ones, and their customers. There are many incidents on record that would be funny if the experiences were not so frustrating. Generally, they concern billing errors and attempts to get these errors corrected.

For whatever reason, it appears that some retailers erect barriers that separate them from their customers. For example, consider some self-service stores. If a customer returns merchandise to the store because it is defective or is the wrong size or color, the normal procedure is to take the merchandise immediately to a customer service desk located near the entrance. In many cases the service desk is the information booth, the returned goods desk, the credit office, the adjustment department, the parcel check room, the paging service, and the check-approval office. As a result, there is often a long line at this desk. In addition, employees who work at this desk are not always well trained, so that any unusual requests or complaints result in the paging of a department manager or the store manager for assistance and a longer wait for the shopper.

At the same time, the service desk often does not handle complaints about a rude employee, an advertised item that is not found in the store, or a discrepancy in price. The store manager or his assistant is often inaccessible. The customer feels that there is no one to listen and, more importantly, *do* something to remedy the situation. In essence, what is needed are concerned employees and management who are accessible to customers, who will *listen*, and who will take corrective action.

A consumer who apparently could not get anyone to listen *and* take corrective action is Eddie Campos of Whittier, California. In October 1969, Campos purchased a $10,300 Lincoln Continental Mark III. His trouble began when he had driven the car seven miles. One problem after another cropped up, and he was unable to obtain satisfaction from his dealer. Finally in desperation Mr. Campos parked his car on the front lawn of a Ford assembly plant. He sprinkled it liberally with five gallons of gasoline and ceremoniously burned it to a crisp—even though he still owed $1812 on the car. Granted, few consumers go to such lengths to demonstrate their dissatisfaction, but many undoubtedly share Mr. Campos' feelings.[11]

REVIEW BOX 21:3

1. Some businesspeople equate honesty with _____.
2. Consumers need full _____ so that they can make sound buying decisions.
3. Consumers want someone who will _____ and take corrective action.

LEGISLATIVE AND JUDICIAL EFFECTS OF CONSUMERISM

A generally recommended solution to consumer unrest is for government bodies to pass laws that prohibit certain acts or require adherence to specified minimum standards. The United States Congress has responded by passing several laws designed to protect consumers. In some cases many business firms have actively supported such legislative efforts. Two laws and a special type of court action that have widespread implications for retailers will be covered here.[12]

Truth-in-Packaging

The Truth-in-Packaging, or Fair Packaging and Labeling Act, is largely due to the efforts of Senator Philip Hart of Michigan. The Senator became concerned when he found that the net weight of packaged cereal had been reduced with no significant change in the package other than shape and with no change in price. The fact that consumers might not realize they were getting less for their money convinced the Senator of the need for protecting them against such tactics. Not until 1965, five years later, did his proposal become a law.

The long series of House and Senate committee hearings produced evidence which suggested that, indeed, some manufacturers were using deceptive packaging. This included oversize packages to create the impression of more contents, use of fractionalized weights to make price comparisons difficult, and statements concerning the number of servings contained without indicating the size of a serving. Nevertheless, legislators were unable to muster enough support to pass the bill.

In early 1966 President Johnson asked Congress to pass a truth-in-packaging law. With respect to the bill, Senator Hart stated:

> The bill is specifically concerned with practices developed in the course of the great growth in the prepackaging of consumable items during recent years. A great number of varying goods and items have been taken off the scale and put into a package during this period. As a result, the package and not the product has become the measure of comparison. It is important that the package present the basic quantity offered in a way that will facilitate per unit comparison and make readily apparent on a per unit basis the price that a person is paying. The bill will facilitate the making of price comparisons.[13]

The final legislation, although a step in the right direction, did not make it easy for the shopper to make price-per-unit comparisons across different brands. In the final bill, a provision requiring standardization of package sizes was omitted, and standardization was left purely voluntary:

> The act says that when the Secretary of Commerce determines "there is undue proliferation of weights, measures or quantities" that "impairs the reasonable ability of consumers to make value comparisons," then he can ask industry to develop voluntary standards. If industry fails to do so within a year, he can ask Congress for further legislation.[14]

The Federal Trade Commission, in charge of enforcing the act, requires the following labeling information:

1. Identification of the contents
2. The name and address of the manufacturer, packer, or distributor
3. A statement of the net quantity of the contents[15]

Truth-in-Lending

In 1968 the Consumer Credit Protection Act, usually referred to as the federal Truth-in-Lending law, was passed. The intent of this legislation paralleled the Truth-in-Packaging law—that is, to aid the consumer in decision-making.

"Looks like they're really putting teeth in the 'Truth-in-Lending' law."

Essentially, the law requires that the creditor make full disclosure of the rate of finance charges and other details of a consumer credit transaction. Such disclosures would supposedly allow a consumer to compare various credit terms which are available to him, since the finance charges must be stated in terms of simple interest per annum.

The law does not reduce or put any ceiling on interest rates. Neither does it prohibit the strong-arm practices which are employed by a limited number of unscrupulous collectors. However, the full-disclosure stipulation applies to any retailer who offers credit.

There have been criticisms that the law does not really aid those who most need it. There is evidence that middle-class buyers had already discovered where credit is the cheapest, so the bill was passed too late to be of any great benefit to them. For poverty-area consumers, the bill has been largely ineffective, since in many cases these consumers cannot qualify for lower interest rates even if they are aware of them.[16]

Class Action Suits

One way in which consumers can seek redress from a business firm is through class action. Class action suits allow one plaintiff to bring suit on behalf of others in the same situation. In effect, rather than several individuals having to file separate suits against a business for some alleged wrong, one suit represents all the plaintiffs.

The present status of class action suits is uncertain. In December 1973 the United States Supreme Court decided that it would not allow an "aggregate claims" test to determine whether a minimum of $10,000 damage had resulted. Since that decision, federal courts will consider class action suits only when individual claims amount to $10,000 per person.

Despite the Supreme Court decision, there is much pressure to liberalize the conditions under which class actions will be allowed. Some have advocated allowing suits as small as $10 to be filed. If approved, such legislation might allow suits:

- Against the manufacturer of a product involved in an accident, even though no negligence was charged
- Against advertisers who ran ads containing misrepresentations, even without a claim that a buyer was tricked
- Demanding repayments for such practices as short-weighting
- Charging the violation of an implied warranty if a product wore out significantly sooner than the average[17]

Unless some restrictions are set forth, such legislation could result in thousands of nuisance suits against retailers.

VOLUNTARY ACTIONS BY RETAILERS

Consumer advocates would like further legislation designed specifically to protect consumers. Given all the laws proposed, more laws would, in many experts' opinions, so stifle business that there would be little latitude for effective competition. Some retailers have responded by voluntarily providing the consumer with more information.

Unit Pricing

A shopper at a supermarket is faced with the difficult task of obtaining the most value for her dollar. Faced with approximately 8,000 items in the typical supermarket, including multiple brands and sizes of individual products, the shopper is easily bewildered. The difficulty of making price comparisons between two packages — for example, $10\frac{3}{4}$ ounce for $1.29 versus $9\frac{2}{3}$ ounce for $1.09 — further complicates shopping. One frustrated shopper reacted by saying, "Most of us are simply too busy or too tired or too harassed to take a computer, a slide rule and an M.I.T. graduate to market...."[18]

Although some consumerists have suggested federal legislation to correct this problem, many grocery retailers have already introduced unit pricing. This form of pricing involves showing the price for some standard unit of measure, such as cents per ounce, dollars per pound, or cents per quart. See Figure 21-1 for an example of Jewel Food Company's unit pricing. By early

FIGURE 21-1

Unit pricing as practiced by Jewel Food Stores

SPOTLIGHT

Was she a turncoat?

Mrs. Esther Peterson represented the consumer's interest at the White House under two presidents. She was known as a militant consumer advocate, outspoken in her criticisms of businesses that took advantage of consumers. With such a background why would she ever join the ranks of business executives? How did Giant Food, Inc., a large supermarket chain, ever persuade her to become an employee? Such questions are best answered in Mrs. Peterson's own words:

"After I left the White House, Giant's president, Joseph Danzansky, asked me to help him develop a corporate consumer program based on a totally new concept. A company's consumer representative has traditionally served as its ambassador to the consumer. Under this new concept, the consumer adviser would serve as the consumer's ambassador to the company's top councils—a crucial difference.

"I turned Mr. Danzansky's offer down repeatedly over the next few months; I didn't want to chance becoming a publicity gimmick. Finally, he asked me to write my own ticket. My conditions were stiff. I had to have complete freedom to speak out according to my convictions, both publicly and within the company. I had to have a hand at the levers of corporate power—to participate in decision making in the top councils of the company, in a role not limited to so-called "consumer matters." Finally, the company had to commit itself to try some of the programs I believed in. I wanted to make a reality of the recommendations of the President's Committee on Consumer Interests, the White House Conference on Food, Nutrition, and Health, the Food Marketing Commission reports, and other studies that the taxpayers had paid for. When he readily agreed to my demands, I accepted the job."

Esther Peterson, "Consumerism as a Retailer's Asset," *Harvard Business Review*, May-June 1974, pp. 92–94.

You can imagine the chagrin of many consumers and Giant Food executives alike at Mrs. Peterson's new job. Probably both groups thought she had been "bought."

Mrs. Peterson's record with Giant speaks for itself. Among Giant Food's responses to consumerism have been unit pricing, open-dating, nutritional labeling, use of "shatter Guard" bottles for Giant soft drinks, and straightforward advertising. Many other programs aimed at protecting and enhancing consumers' rights are underway at Giant. Both Giant Food executives and consumers have learned that Mrs. Peterson is capable of serving the interests of both groups objectively and fairly.

1972, seventy-five supermarket chains had adopted some form of unit pricing.[10]

An early experiment in unit pricing was begun in 1970 by Jewel Food Stores, a Chicago-based food chain. Jewel's unit pricing program, called Compar-A-Buy, covered 3,027 items in all of its 258 stores. After seven months, 63 percent of Jewel's customers were aware of the program, and 45 percent had used the pricing system one or more times.[20] Although customers apparently liked the additional information, there was no evidence of widespread brand switching or movement to larger sizes or private labels as a result of better information. The general conclusion was that unit pricing was a good marketing tool, since it created customer satisfaction. It was not, however, an essential service (based on product movement studies), and its cost could not be justified on that basis. Despite this, Jewel has continued to offer unit pricing in all of its stores.

Various estimates of installing unit pricing in supermarkets indicate that the initial cost is $300 to $500 per store, and costs of operating the program run as high as $800 to $1,300 per year. In spite of these costs, and the fact that most consumers do not use the information continuously, there seems to be a trend toward more unit pricing programs. The mere fact that additional information is available provides a certain amount of customer satisfaction. They seem to trust the store that appears to have nothing to hide.

Open Dating

Many food manufacturers use freshness codes on their products. Originally these codes combined letters and numbers to indicate when products were no longer fresh enough to be sold. These codes were not revealed to the consumer, however.

Open dating takes the secrecy out of freshness coding. Although there is no uniform practice, these dates typically indicate when products should be removed from the supermarket shelf to assure freshness at time of use after normal home storage. Many bakery companies now color code bread wrapper closure devices. A different color represents each day of the week, indicating the day the bread was delivered.

In early 1972 some 59 major grocery chains had some form of open dating, especially for their own products.[21] Jewel Food Stores' form is shown in Figure 21-2. The date indicated is the last day on which the product is to be sold. Before open dating, many stores provided a code book to allow the customer to interpret codes that were prestamped by manufacturers on their products. The difficulty with the method was that it involved extra trouble for the customer, since the code books were usually kept at the customer service counter.

Jewel was the first major food chain in the country to begin widespread

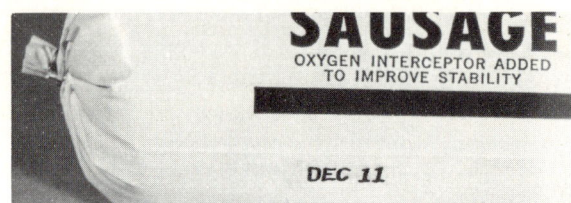

FIGURE 21-2

Sampling of open code dated packaged meat products

open dating together with an educational program for its customers. In addition to open coding its own brand labels, Jewel began encouraging manufacturers to standardize coding procedures.

Once customers know that open dating is being practiced, they may pay relatively little attention to the dates, assuming that store personnel will automatically remove any products that might become stale before the customer used them. It is equally likely that consumers like to shop at stores using open dating since this is again evidence of fair, open, and honest business practice.

REVIEW BOX 21:4

1. The easiest solution to the consumer unrest problem is for the government to _____.
2. The _____ law requires a statement of the net quantity of the contents of a package.
3. The Truth-in-Lending Law requires _____ of credit terms.
4. _____ shows the price for some standard unit of measure for products.
5. Freshness coding in terms the consumer can understand is called _____.

---

518   Ch. 21 The Impact of Consumerism

THE ANSWER TO CONSUMERISM

Because of their unique role in linking manufacturers and consumers, retailers probably possess more power to deal with consumer problems than any other single group—including the federal government. By viewing themselves as purchasing agents for the consumer, retailers try to understand consumers and their wants and needs. This also requires that retailers have empathy for the consumer—the ability to put themselves in consumers' "shoes," to feel as they feel.

A retailer with empathy will *initiate* action designed to satisfy consumers rather than merely *react* to complaints. As the consumer movement progressed in the late 1960s, retailers as well as other businesses were extremely defensive and tended to deny the allegations of consumer activists. In the 1970s, however, evidence suggests that more retailers are initiating actions, anticipating possible sources of consumer dissatisfaction. Unit pricing and open dating by supermarkets, covered above, generally fall into this category. There are further indications that retailers are becoming more perceptive concerning consumers' needs. The next section describes one such action by a retailer.

Posting of Prescription Prices

Traditionally, prescription drug prices have been quite "hush-hush," keeping the consumer unaware of the price until the prescription is filled. Largely through pharmaceutical associations' efforts, drug price advertising has been banned in many states as "adverse to the public interest." In 1972 several retail drug stores challenged this type of thinking by publicly displaying the prices of their leading prescription drug items. Most notable among these was the Osco Drug chain with 186 stores in 17 states. Despite court action or Pharmacy Board rebukes against the chain in eight of those states, the price posting continued.

Osco began by displaying price lists of the 100 most frequently prescribed drugs in each of its stores. In addition, Osco's customers were encouraged to ask for any prices not displayed. Osco also began including the name, strength, and quantity on all prescription drug labels, unless otherwise directed by the physician.

Osco believed that this action would allow consumers to be better informed and would strengthen the relationship between Osco's registered pharmacists and their customers. Despite pressures from state regulatory boards, Osco persisted. Eventually its actions were ratified by President

Nixon's Phase II economic guidelines requiring all pharmacies to post prescription prices or otherwise make them available to consumers.

Other Initiating Actions

As purchasing agents for consumers, retailers are in a unique position to educate and protect consumers. A New York supermarket firm dropped the facial tissues of a manufacturer who reduced the number of tissues per box while maintaining the same price. The manufacturer contended that its only alternative was to raise prices. However, the supermarket informed its customers that the manufacturer's plan was deceptive since all competing manufacturers continued with the same number of tissues at the same price.

A mass merchandiser shipped back the remaining stock of a children's toy when it found that the plaything was extremely dangerous and could conceivably damage an unsuspecting child's eye. A hardware store discontinued a line of hand tools when it found that the manufacturer's warranty was not honored to the extent implied.

Each of these actions was taken independently; none was the result of any unified action by retailers. In each case the retail firm initiated the action as soon as the discrepancy came to its attention. They all indicated that they were primarily interested in their customers' welfare—even at the expense of short-run profits.

Other opportunities for achieving customer satisfaction—and thereby avoiding the ill effects of consumerism—abound. As an example, merchants should open communication channels with consumers, making it easy for consumers to complain about merchandise, advertisements, or other business practices that bother them. Setting up a special complaint counter does not mean the retailer will be inundated with complaints. It will mean, however, that consumers know they can receive speedy action on a complaint.

Retailers have a great deal of power, and they should use that power to help achieve consumer satisfaction.

REVIEW BOX 21:5

1. Retailers should _____ action designed to satisfy the consumer rather than _____ to consumer complaints.
2. The posting of prescription drug prices aids the consumer by providing him additional _____ upon which to base his buying decision.

CHAPTER SUMMARY

- Consumerism is the reaction of consumers to their dissatisfactions and unrealized expectations and their efforts to have these perceived injustices remedied.
- In recent history there have been three periods of consumer unrest, but the most recent one differs from the others in that it gathered speed slowly, shows no signs of decline, and is much broader in scope.
- Retailers should view themselves as purchasing agents *for* consumers rather than as sellers *to* consumers.
- The consumer should be the primary justification for the existence of retailers.
- The separation of buying and selling activities and the increase in self-service stores have widened the communications gap between consumers and retail store buyers.
- The four basic rights of consumers are the right to safety, the right to be informed, the right to choose, and the right to be heard.
- Retailers should be honest with consumers, provide them adequate information, and listen to them.
- Truth-in-packing requires identification of the package contents, name and address of the manufacturer, packer, or distributor, and a statement of the net quantity of the contents of the package.
- Unit pricing involves indicating the price for some standard unit of measure.
- Open dating reveals the freshness of the product to the consumer.
- Retailers should *initiate* action to satisfy consumers rather than respond defensively to their complaints.

CHAPTER NOTES

[1] Richard H. Buskirk and James T. Rothe, "Consumerism—An Interpretation," *Journal of Marketing*, October 1970, p. 62.

[2] Philip Kotler, "What Consumerism Means for Marketers," *Harvard Business Review*, May–June 1972, p. 49.

[3] David J. Rachman, *Marketing Strategy and Structure* (Englewood Cliffs, N. J.: Prentice-Hall, Inc., 1974), p. 69.

[4] William J. Stanton, *Fundamentals of Marketing*, 3rd ed. (New York: McGraw-Hill Book Company, 1971), pp. 657–58.

[5] Daniel Defoe, *The Compleat English Tradesman* (London: Printed for Charles Rivington at the Bible and Crown in St. Paul's Churchyard, 1727), p. 31. Reprinted by Augustus M. Kelley, New York, 1969.

[6] Identification of these three eras and an interesting discussion may be found in Robert O. Herrmann, "Consumerism: Its Goals, Organizations and Future," *Journal of Marketing*,

October 1970, pp. 55–60. Also see: Ralph M. Gaedeke, "The Movement for Consumer Protection: A Century of Mixed Accomplishments," *University of Washington Business Review*, Spring 1970, pp. 31–40.

[7] Consumers' Research, Inc. publishes *Consumer Bulletin*, and Consumers Union of the United States, Inc., publishes *Consumer Reports*. Both are monthly publications aimed at providing information to aid consumers in buying decisions.

[8] David A. Swankin, "Consumer Activism," in *The Challenge of Consumerism* (New York: The Conference Board Record, 1971), p. 37.

[9] See Don L. James, *Youth, Media, and Advertising* (Austin, Texas: University of Texas, Bureau of Business Research, 1971) for a more thorough treatment of the attitudes of youth toward advertising.

[10] For recommendations applicable to repair service firms, see Michael J. Etzel and Don L. James, "Can Government Regulation Replace Marketing Orientation?" *Journal of Retailing*, Winter 1970–71, pp. 14–23.

[11] Jay Sharbutt, "Man Who Burned New Car Is Now Folk Hero to Many," The Associated Press, carried in Houston *Chronicle*, September 26, 1971; reprinted in Betsy D. Gelb and Ben M. Enis, eds., *Marketing is Everybody's Business* (Pacific Palisades, California: Goodyear Publishing Co., Inc., 1974), p. 104.

[12] There are a host of other laws which have been passed for the protection of the consumer. They include, for example, the Cigarette Labeling Act, Wholesome Poultry Products Act, Child Protection and Safety Act of 1969, the Fair Credit Reporting Act, and Consumer Product Safety Act.

[13] Senator Philip Hart as quoted in Irving Scher, "Legal Briefs," *Stores*, September 1969, p. 37.

[14] Jeremy Main, "Industry Still Has Something to Learn About Congress," in David A. Aaker and George S. Day, eds., *Consumerism* (New York: The Free Press, 1971), p. 78.

[15] Scher, *op. cit.*, p. 38.

[16] For a stimulating presentation of the limitations of Truth-in-Lending, see Homer Kripke, "Gesture and Reality in Consumer Credit Reform," in David A. Aaker and George S. Day, eds., *Consumerism* (New York: The Free Press, 1971), pp. 160–68.

[17] "Are Class Action Suits Worth the Cost?", *Business Week*, June 3, 1972, p. 22.

[18] E. B. Weiss, "Marketers Fiddle While Consumers Burn," *Harvard Business Review*, July–August 1968, p. 48.

[19] Ronald G. Shafer, "A Food Chain Recruits a Consumer Advocate to Shape its Policies," *The Wall Street Journal*, January 1, 1972, p. 1.

[20] Press release, Jewel Food Stores (Melrose Park, Ill.: October 11, 1970).

[21] Ronald G. Shafer, *op. cit.*, p. 1.

QUESTIONS AND ASSIGNMENTS

1. Define consumerism, and indicate what you believe will be the primary consumer concern in coming years.
2. Give some current examples of how increasingly complex products can and do contribute to consumer dissatisfaction.
3. What is your greatest dissatisfaction with retailers today? Have you communicated this dissatisfaction to those retailers?
4. Talk to two or three retailers in your community to see what, if any, responses they have made to the consumerism movement.
5. What are the advantages of a retailer viewing himself as a purchasing agent for the consumer?
6. How have the division of buying and selling responsibilities and the increase in self-service contributed to consumers' problems? Can you offer any solutions to these problems?
7. If American consumers today are better educated, more affluent, and more

knowledgeable about products than consumers in other parts of the world, why aren't they more satisfied than other consumers?
8. In what ways can retailers respond to the challenge of consumerism?
9. What is the effect of the Truth-in-Lending law upon retailers?
10. Do you think retailers should be responsible for helping to educate consumers in how to get more value for their dollar? Why or why not?
11. How can retailers act as watchdogs for consumers?

ANSWERS TO REVIEW BOX QUESTIONS

Box 21:1
1. consumer dissatisfaction
2. let the buyer beware
3. rising prices

Box 21:2
1. marketing concept
2. purchasing agent
3. the right to safety; the right to be informed; the right to choose; the right to be heard

Box 21:3
1. legality
2. information
3. listen

Box 21:4
1. pass laws
2. Truth-in-Packaging
3. full disclosure
4. unit pricing
5. open dating

Box 21:5
1. initiate; react
2. information

Retailing and Racial Minorities

This chapter investigates racial minorities as consumers and as retailers. Focusing primarily on blacks, Spanish-Americans, and American Indians, the chapter has been written for several reasons. First, racial minorities make up over 12 percent of the population in this country; thus, as a group they account for a significant amount of buying power. Second, retailing has traditionally been the most common area of business ownership for minorities. Finally, during the last few years both government and business have shown an increased interest in economic and social inequities of minorities in the United States. More will be said about each of these points later, but for now they indicate an increasingly important relationship between retailing and members of minority groups.

The chapter is divided into two major parts: retailing *to* minorities and retailing *by* minorities. In the first part we will discuss the characteristics of minorities relevant to retailing, the nature of minority markets, and the problems of minority consumers. In the second part of the chapter we will look at minority successes, failures, and opportunities as retailers.

RETAILING TO MINORITIES

The first point to make clear is that this discussion will be concerned with low-income consumers. This emphasis does not mean that low-income and minorities are synonymous. It means simply that the minority group members who do have relatively low incomes are the people who experience the most consumer problems.

In order to analyze minorities as potential markets, it is first necessary to develop a general picture of the people who make up these groups. This section will profile major racial minorities—black Americans, Spanish-Americans (including Mexican-Americans, Puerto Ricans, and Cubans), and American Indians.

General Characteristics of Minority Groups

BLACK AMERICANS

Accounting for 11 percent of the total U.S. population, or over 22 million people, blacks are by far the largest racial minority group.[1] Over the last 10 years a large proportion of the black population has migrated from the South to cities in the North and West. In 1970, 60 percent of the blacks in the United States lived in the central city of major metropolitan areas. In fact, at least one-third of the residents in four of the seven largest United States cities are blacks.

Family income for black Americans has increased significantly over the last 20 years, but it still remains well below that of white families. In 1970 it was 65 percent of the average for whites, or about $6,520. In the same year, 24 percent of black families had incomes over $10,000, while the proportion of white families with this income was over 49 percent. About one-third of all black families have incomes below the poverty level.

The level of education for blacks has improved substantially in the last decade. In 1960 only 38 percent of young adult blacks had completed high school, as compared to 56 percent in 1970. Finally, black families tend to be larger than white families and are much more likely to have a female household head.

SPANISH-AMERICANS

The Spanish-American population amounted to 10.5 million people in 1973, or about 5 percent of the U.S. population.[2] The largest portion of these are Mexican-Americans (60 percent), followed by Puerto Ricans (15 percent), and Cubans (7 percent). The remaining 18 percent trace their origin to a wide variety of Central and South American countries.

Combining all Spanish-Americans even at this general level can be somewhat misleading, since there are significant differences among subgroups. For example, 80 percent of the Mexican-Americans reside in the five southwestern states of Arizona, California, Colorado, New Mexico, and Texas. In contrast, Puerto Ricans and Cubans have settled along the eastern seaboard, particularly concentrating in New York and Florida. In addition, the groups differ widely in age. The median age for Mexican-Americans and Puerto Ricans is nineteen, while the Cuban median age, reflecting the greater migration of adults, is thirty-five.

To a greater extent than the Mexican-Americans, the Puerto Ricans and Cubans have concentrated in central city areas, although large enclaves of

Retailing to Minorities

Mexican-Americans can be found in Los Angeles, San Antonio, San Diego, San Francisco, El Paso, Phoenix, and Tucson.

The most common feature of all Spanish-American groups is the importance of their language. Because of a constant flow of immigrants and frequent visits to the "old country" (especially by Mexican-Americans), Spanish remains the principal language for a high percentage of this segment of our population.

The average family income in 1973 for all Spanish-American families was $8,180, or about $2,000 less than the average for white families. A total of 20 percent of Mexican-Americans and 18 percent of Puerto Ricans and Cuban families have incomes below $4,000.

The level of education for Spanish-Americans has improved dramatically but remains substandard. In 1973, 50 percent of Spanish-Americans between twenty-five and twenty-nine had completed high school, while only 25 percent of those forty-five to sixty-four had done so. The subgroup with the lowest educational attainment is Mexican-Americans, while Cubans have the highest.

The family is very important to the Spanish-American. It can be generalized that the Spanish-American family is: large, with 57 percent having four or more members and 12 percent seven or more; relatively young, with an average of two persons under age eighteen per family; and usually headed by a male. It is interesting that only 4 percent of Spanish-Americans over fourteen years old live alone.

AMERICAN INDIANS

The third largest racial minority group in the United States is the American Indian. Numbering about 800,000, or less than one-half of 1 percent of the total population, this group is the most disadvantaged of the three discussed.

The Indian population is quite highly concentrated in the Southwest, with 50 percent of the total in Oklahoma, Arizona, California, and New Mexico.[3] However, Indians have not migrated in large numbers to major metropolitan areas. A possible explanation for this is the existence of 55 million acres of land set aside for them. Although much of this reservation land is of little value—37 percent of the 19.5 million acres of reservation in Arizona is semi-arid grazing land—it has resulted in a large portion of the Indian population remaining in rural areas.

In a speech to Congress in 1968, President Lyndon Johnson pointed out several of the problems of Indians:[4]

> Fifty percent of the Indian families have incomes of less than $2,000 a year, and 75 percent have incomes below $3,000.
> Indian educational achievement and literacy rates are among the lowest in the nation. Ten percent of the Indians over fourteen have no schooling. Nearly 60 percent have less than an eighth grade education.

Unemployment among the Indians is 10 times that of the national average.

The infant mortality rate among Indians is one-third higher than the national average.

That these problems continue to exist is reflected in a statement of Richard Nixon to Congress in 1970:

> The first Americans—the Indians—are the most deprived and the most isolated minority group in our nation. On virtually every scale of measurement—employment, income, education, health—the conditions of the Indian people rank at the bottom.[5]

SUMMARY

Taking all these facts and figures into consideration, what can we say that generally applies to all racial minorities? First, they tend to be geographically concentrated either in central cities or regions of the country. Second, they have family incomes considerably below the national average. Third, they have higher birth rates and larger average families than the total U.S. population. Finally, the level of education is below average for all the groups and very much below average for Indians. With these things in common, the question is whether or not these groups constitute markets for retailers. The next section explores this issue.

REVIEW BOX 22:1

1. The three major racial minority groups in the United States in order of size are _____, _____, and _____.
2. The most common feature of all Spanish-American groups is the importance of their _____.
3. The most disadvantaged minority group is the _____.

Is There a Minority Market?

Retailers disagree on the existence of racially defined markets. Regarding blacks, a Houston merchant says, "We serve the whole community, not just part of it. Blacks need the same thing everyone else does."[6] A similar reaction came from a Los Angeles supermarket operator who said "Promotions which single out blacks are considered humiliating, and we avoid that kind of overkill."

RETAILERS' VIEWS

In contrast, some retailers are aggressively going after what they see as a real market. For example, some Detroit retailers stock cosmetics for blacks, Afro dresses and wigs, high style clothing popular among blacks, and novelty items adorned with African symbols. In addition to black-oriented products, these same retailers provide shelf space for black-manufactured merchandise. In Charlotte, North Carolina, several stores have hired black sales personnel, use black models in ads, advertise in the black media, and display black mannequins. Although these comments and reactions only reflect retailers' responses to blacks as a market, the same variety of opinions exists for all other minorities.

RESEARCHERS' FINDINGS

Authors and researchers are also divided on the question. In the recent past there was a tendency to lump all low-income consumers into a single group and generalize along such lines as: They lack mobility to shop outside their immediate residential areas; they prefer to shop at stores within the confines of their neighborhoods; and they are suspicious of supermarkets. Reports of recent research support some of these general conclusions, challenge others, and disagree on still others. For example, studying the buying behavior of low-income Mexican-Americans in East Los Angeles, Frederick Sturdivant concluded that they sought cultural reinforcement in shopping. He says, "In spite of certain advantages to be gained by shopping outside the retailing community servicing his immediate area, the Mexican-American generally prefers to shop in nearby stores where Spanish is spoken."[7] Similarly, in a study of blacks in St. Louis, Carl Block found that 42 percent limited their grocery shopping to within walking distance of their homes.[8] In direct contrast, other researchers found that the majority of Mexican-Americans in a Denver-based study shopped for food at large supermarkets outside or on the perimeter of the Mexican-American community.[9] In still another study of low-income black consumers in Philadelphia, Charles Goodman concluded that for grocery purchases they go outside their residence areas to seek lower prices and higher quality.[10]

These differences can be partially explained by the various settings and times in which these studies were done. However, we might also suspect that there are some real behavioral differences in racial groups:

> Perhaps one of the most important implications of this study is that the findings strongly support the need for caution in making generalizations concerning low-income consumer behavior. . . . One must be careful in assuming that low-income consumers, regardless of race, are more similar than different.[11]

The question of whether minority groups differ from whites has also been investigated. In Houston the purchasing behaviors of whites and blacks from a variety of income classes were compared.[12] Many differences in purchases in five product categories—food, soft drinks, liquor, personal hygiene products, and major appliances—were explained by differences in income. However, two products, butter and Scotch, were purchased more heavily by blacks than by whites at all income levels. Since the authors could not explain the difference economically, they attributed it to behavioral differences between blacks and whites.

In another study comparing blacks and whites in Chicago, differences were found in store choice, the amount of shopping between stores, and choices of certain private-brand goods.[13]

These studies suggest two conclusions. First, all racial minorities cannot be lumped together, nor can the members of any particular minority group be assumed to be homogeneous. Second, racial minorities, whether because of race or some other factor, do shop and purchase differently from white consumers.

MARKET OPPORTUNITY

Differences exist between and within racial minority groups, and just as the white market has been segmented geographically, demographically, and behaviorally, so must the minority market. Several operating areas should be considered.

Special Merchandise. This is probably of little concern for products like furniture or appliances in which needs and tastes are not related to race. However, in supermarkets, drug stores, and variety stores, this is an important area of consideration. For example, in 1972 a Los Angeles rack jobber specializing in health and beauty aid items for Blacks did $1.25 million in business through discount houses and supermarkets.[14] This clearly indicates that a distinct market exists for the right products. In the case of Mexican-Americans it has been established that they purchase more flour, spices, fresh fruits and vegetables, and dry cereal and less frozen foods and expensive cuts of meat than typical white consumers. Collecting information like this in a particular minority market area can help retailers develop a tailored merchandise mix.

Special Services. Because of shopping and buying constraints, minority consumers may be attracted by special services that many retailers could provide. For example, in some areas, delivery of items usually transported by the buyer could be a valuable selling tool. Another appealing service would be credit programs for low-income consumers. Although frequently unable to meet traditional credit requirements involving income, length of employment, credit references, and home ownership, low-income consumers may still be good credit risks. The challenge is to discover new indicators of credit worthiness or design special plans with initially low credit limits to allow consumers an opportunity to develop a sound credit standing.

Personnel. Customers prefer to buy from salespeople they consider knowledgeable. For products designed for minorities, potentially the most knowledgeable salesperson would be another minority group member. In addition, the presence of minority group members on a retailer's payroll can contribute to a favorable attitude among minority customers. The problem here is the appearance of tokenism. Both employees and customers will quickly see through the use of a minority salesperson who is simply a showpiece to demonstrate the store's broadmindedness. Minority employees should be evaluated like any other employee and make normal progress in an organization.

SPOTLIGHT

Can a retailer make it in the inner city? Jewel Companies thinks so.

This company began selling food door-to-door in 1899. Today it still operates a home-delivery food service, but by diversification and expansion it has risen to become the tenth-largest retailer in the nation. And it has done so by emphasizing what the company calls a "merchants of empathy" philosophy. Donald S. Perkins, chairman of Jewel, describes this as meaning that "we had to be leaders in responding to the growing expectations of consumers."

Especially notable has been Jewel's determination to serve the inner city rather than retreat to the suburbs. While A&P and National were pulling stores out of Chicago's black and Hispanic neighborhoods during the late 1960s, Jewel was closing eleven old stores and opening sixteen new and larger supermarkets. As a result, it has become the leading food chain in the inner city of Chicago. It pursued the same course when it invaded Milwaukee with thirteen stores in 1972. "We could have ringed Milwaukee with new stores," said Mr. Perkins. "But we needed a few key stores in older areas. We were willing to invest where Kroger was not."

This policy did not entail a sacrifice of earnings. Jewel is one of the most profitable retailers in the country, with a return on sales that is one of the best in this low-margin industry.

Jewel increased its minority employee ratio from 2.5 percent to more than 7.5 percent from 1966 to 1973: at the Jewel Food Stores division the proportion is 13 percent. The Jewel supermarket chain also last year doubled its purchases of goods and services from minority suppliers to reach the level of $5.5 million.

Jewel was the first food retailer in the nation to place a black on its board, having named Jewel Stradford Lafontant as a director in 1971. After Mrs. Lafontant resigned to become deputy solicitor general of the United States, Jewel elected to its board another black woman, Barbara Scott Preiskel, the legislative counsel for the Motion Picture Association of America. Also serving as a director is Dr. Helen Le Baron Hilton, who is dean of the college of home economics at Iowa State University.

Source: "Company Performance Roundup," *Business and Society Review/Innovation*, Summer 1974, p. 102.

Advertising. The growing availability of ethnic media, especially local newspapers and radio stations, provides excellent ways of reaching minority markets. It is interesting that in his study of black consumers, Block found newspapers and television were the most helpful sources of product information for both blacks and whites. However, advice from friends was ranked third by blacks and only sixth by whites.[15] This points out the importance of word-of-mouth communication among minority consumers and the care a retailer must take to achieve and then protect a favorable image. Word-of-mouth communication combined with the often justified criticism and publicity of inequities and inefficiencies in marketing to minorities make it very important that retailers deal in complete honesty.

Summary. Minority markets are real. However, simply recognizing their existence does not guarantee success. It is up to the interested retailer to identify the areas of unique interest and taste in minority markets and translate these into profitable retailing strategies.

Problems of Minority Consumers

A special problem of the low-income, minority consumer is stretching a limited income as far as possible. This section discusses some of the reasons why low-income consumers' dollars may not go as far as those of the more affluent. The problems low-income minority consumers face in the marketplace are the result of structural factors and unethical practices. Structural factors are economic circumstances or human characteristics that put the low-income consumer at a disadvantage and are beyond the control of the individual retailer or consumer. Unethical practices are activities of retailers designed to take advantage of consumers. Some examples of each type are discussed below.

STRUCTURAL FACTORS

Inefficiencies and High Operating Costs. Most retail outlets located in predominantly low-income neighborhoods are small, inefficient operations. Because of their size, the retailers tend to purchase small amounts of merchandise and therefore pay higher prices. Add to this the costs of vandalism and shoplifting and the higher-than-average insurance premiums, and it is clear why retailers in these areas frequently charge higher prices.

Though the circumstances differ on Indian reservations, the results are the same. The population is so geographically dispersed that large retail operations are impractical. Thus, small stores, often located in remote areas pay high prices to get merchandise. In addition, reservation retailers sometimes engage in bartering merchandise for Indian handicrafts and assume the role of middlemen in finding markets for these Indian goods. This, of course, is an added cost that gets passed on to the consumer.

Consumer Characteristics. Among some minorities, particularly Spanish-Americans and Indians, language is often a problem. Unable to explain their needs to white retailers or to read advertisements and labels, these consumers are at a distinct disadvantage in comparing prices and product features.

For some low-income consumers, lack of adequate refrigeration facilities and the absence of financial reserves make it impossible to take advantage of specials or to stock up on sale items. Thus, they always pay the "regular" price. Another consumer problem is the inability of many minority individuals to qualify for credit. The traditional criteria for credit worthiness, like credit references and home ownership, cannot be satisfied. As a result, credit is generally unavailable to the segment of the population that most needs it.

UNETHICAL PRACTICES

Although the structural factors are common for retailers of all kinds of merchandise, the unethical practices seem to apply mostly to sellers of durable goods such as automobiles, furniture, and appliances.

The Markups. As pointed out in the preceding section, many retailers in low-income areas charge higher prices. However, some artificially inflate their prices well beyond fair markups, assuming consumers will be too naive or not have the means to shop around to compare prices between outlets. One method of doing this is not putting prices on merchandise and then "adjusting" the price, based on the apparent sophistication of the potential purchaser.[16]

Advertising. One tactic employed by unethical retailers is called "bait and switch" advertising. This involves advertising a product at an unusually low price to attract consumers to the store. Once the consumer is in the store, the retailer either claims to be "fresh out" of the advertised item or emphasizes its limitations and attempts to convince the customer to buy a higher priced product. Fast-talking, hard sell retailers have found this to be an effective method for taking advantage of some consumers.

Installment Credit. Probably the most common area of unethical retailer practices is in installment credit. Low-income consumers need credit for major purchases. A Federal Trade Commission study reported that 93 percent of the sales made by low-income area furniture and appliance merchants involved credit, while in higher income areas only 27 percent of the sales are made on credit.[17] Since low-income minority consumers often find it difficult to obtain credit from major retailers, they resort to the credit offered by low-income area merchants. Although higher credit charges to cover the greater risk would be expected, several studies have reported exorbitant and illegal charges. In Watts and East Los Angeles, black and Mexican-American areas, respectively, credit charges as high as 82 percent of the price of merchandise were found.[18]

Certainly, not all retailers in low-income areas are unethical. In fact, many are not only honest but have been extremely helpful to low-income consumers. It has been pointed out that several retail establishments were left untouched during the Watts riots of 1963, while stores all around were vandalized and burned. Unfortunately, however, dishonest and unethical practices are much more common in low-income areas than elsewhere.

REVIEW BOX 22:2

1. There is considerable disagreement among retailers and researchers over the existence of _____ _____.
2. Four areas to consider in segmenting minority markets are the merchandise mix, special services, personnel, and _____.
3. Minority consumer problems can be categorized as resulting from _____ factors and _____ practices.

RETAILING BY MINORITIES

Historical Perspective

A brief history of black business development provides a useful perspective for discussing the current situation in minority retailing. Prior to emancipation, few blacks had established successful businesses in America. During the early 1800s the most successful area was Philadelphia, where by 1820 the black population of 12,000 owned about $250,000 worth of property.[19]

During the next 100 years, black business investment continued to grow slowly. In 1920 there were 26,000 black-owned businesses dealing primarily in personal services, such as restaurants, beauty parlors, barber shops, and funeral parlors.[20] The size of these businesses is reflected in a 1928 National Negro Business League study. Of a total of 1,534 businesses in 33 cities, less than 10 percent had annual gross incomes of $10,000, and the majority did less than $5,000 worth of business a year.

Black businesses, concentrated in the service industries, were severely hit by the Great Depression. In the early 1930s the number of black-owned banks dropped from 56 to 11 and insurance companies from 110 to 30. Following World War II the economic situation improved slightly. More blacks were acquiring educations, and returning servicemen had new skills to apply in a peacetime economy. The primary areas of new business growth were cosmetics, newspapers *(The Pittsburgh Courier, Chicago Defender)*, magazines (the *Negro Digest, Ebony*), and various service enterprises aimed at black consumers. These advancements, although reflecting the success of only a few, were a significant improvement over earlier years.

Through the 1950s and 1960s, blacks in limited numbers continued to become more economically involved. President John Kennedy, in an attempt to stimulate the employment of blacks, sought the voluntary agreement of business to provide equal opportunities. This program was moderately successful and led to antidiscriminatory hiring legislation. Note, however, that black economic involvement has been primarily as employees rather than business owners.

The Current Scope

In 1969, minority group members owned just 4 percent of all U.S. business, although they made up over 15 percent of the population. Even worse, these 322,000 firms had total sales that accounted for only 0.7 percent of the sales of all U.S. firms.[21] A further indication of the size of these establishments is that only 5 percent employed 10 or more people, while the figure for all other businesses was nearly 20 percent.

Table 22-1, which shows the most important categories of product and service minority retailers, illustrates several points. First, blacks account for the greatest number of minority-owned businesses, followed by Spanish-Americans. Second, the largest number of businesses are in the personal services category (such as barber shops, dry cleaners, and restaurants). Finally, the greatest volume of sales is produced by food stores.

TABLE 22-1

Retail Categories of Minority-Owned Businesses Ranked by Total Receipts, 1969
(receipts in millions of dollars)

Industry	All Minority-Owned Firms		Black		Spanish-Speaking		Other Minorities	
	No. of firms	Receipts	No. of firms	Receipts	No. of firms	Receipts	No. of firms	Receipts
Food stores	22,492	$1,493	11,268	$438	6,378	$373	4,846	$682
Car dealers and service stations	12,086	1,181	6,380	631	4,087	315	1,619	235
Eating and drinking places	27,318	953	14,125	360	7,518	265	5,675	328
Retail stores	13,527	584	6,412	278	3,800	125	3,315	181
Personal services	53,252	532	33,960	288	10,701	123	8,645	121

Source: U.S. Bureau of the Census, *Statistical Abstract of the United States: 1972*, 93rd ed. (Washington, D.C.: U.S. Government Printing Office, 1972), p. 472.

Efforts to Increase Minority Involvement

In the 1960s, it was realized that the best approach to improving the economic situation of minorities is through the ownership of businesses. The basic rationale is that ownership, as opposed to working for someone else, gives a person greater control over the future and the opportunity to grow economically according to one's skills and effort. This approach, often called "Black Capitalism" since blacks constitute the majority of minorities, received official support in a recommendation of the National Advisory Commission on Civil Disorders which in 1968 stated, "special encouragement [should be given] to Negro ownership of business in the ghetto area."[22]

Efforts by many organizations—including the Black Economic League, Urban Coalition, Small Business Administration, and the Department of Commerce—to increase the number of minority-owned businesses are sometimes successful, and at other times they meet with frustration. For example, Uplands, Inc., organized in 1969 to help rural Indians and Mexican-Americans in the Southwest Four Corners area (where Colorado, Utah, Arizona, and New Mexico meet) has proven very successful.[23] The federally funded corporation works with minority individuals in processing loan applications and provides management assistance to new businesses. Of the 68 businesses, mostly retail and service firms, which have received significant aid from Uplands, 63 appear likely to succeed. Among the firms are a retail outlet selling Indian handcrafted textiles, a motel and community center, and a combined general store-gas station cooperative.

Although a number of minority business interests have been successful, the failure rate is much higher and the profitability for the successes are usually much lower than for white-owned businesses. For example, lack of site selection expertise has been very costly to one predominantly black shopping center on Chicago's south side. The State and Fifty-First Medical-Shopping Center, costing $2.2 million to construct and consisting of 17 stores, has been hit by continued theft and vandalism. Because it is located between a string of high-rise public housing apartments and the neighborhood schools, 5,000 young people pass through the center each day. Every window in the center has been broken at least once, and $8,000 in shrubbery and landscaping was destroyed in two months. Many stores now have bricked fronts and, due to repeated burglaries, several stores refuse to carry floor models of TVs, radios, and appliances, forcing customers to order from catalogs.[24]

Several factors have contributed to minority retailing failures. First, most minority-owned retail outlets are located in predominantly minority areas with mostly low-income residents. As a result, the area from which a minority enterprise must draw its customers has very limited spending power. Second, in the case of shopping centers, it is difficult to get a large "name" store to locate in a predominantly minority shopping area. Simple economics indicates that companies can locate stores in more prosperous neighborhoods and make more money.

Third, costs in the form of insurance, vandalism, and theft must be covered by higher prices which, of course, do not appeal to customers. Fourth, though they may be eager and hardworking, many minority entrepreneurs have not had the opportunity to learn how to operate a business. Finally, the shortage of investment and operating capital for these relatively high risk businesses make it difficult for the minority retailer to compete.

To help solve the last two of these problems, the Office of Minority Business Enterprise (OMBE) was created as an agency of the Commerce Department. This organization has been directed by the President to "create conditions in the Federal and private marketplace which will allow significant minority business success and profit."[25]

To help minority business acquire investment funds, OMBE created the Minority Enterprise Small Business Investment Company (MESBIC). These companies are licensed, regulated, and partially funded by the federal government. As of June 1973, the 51 MESBICs in operation had generated $43.5 million in investment capital for minority businesses.

Another important government source of minority business support is the Small Business Administration (SBA). In fiscal 1972, the SBA made it possible for minority businesses to get $352.9 million in loans and credit, principally by guaranteeing loans made by private business.

Help in providing minority businesses with the needed skills to operate is coming from both government and private enterprise. OMBE has provided financial support to colleges, franchisors, and other firms to help them establish management training programs for minority enterprises. In 1973, basic business management courses were being offered by 37 institutions under this program.

In the private sector, General Motors has established a training program in which 25 minority dealers will undergo 18 months of training. Upon successful completion of the course, the trainees are guaranteed a franchised dealership. Menswear Retailers Association and the International Council of Shopping Centers are offering help to minority retailers in such areas as selling methods, inventory management, and services control. These, of course, are only a few of the things that are happening, but they are indicative of the efforts being undertaken.

Prospects for the Future

Unquestionably, the involvement of minorities in retailing is going to continue to grow. It is not a question of whether change will occur, but when and how. Minority business ownership programs have experienced many problems. Several reasons have been offered for their shortcomings.[26]

First, the programs expected too much. They expected new businesses to spring up and become profitable overnight and old businesses to be rejuvenated and grow by leaps and bounds. Such goals would probably be unrealistic in any area and certainly were unjustified in a situation where the owner-managers were untrained and inexperienced. Second, the goals created false hopes in the minds of minority entrepreneurs, who quickly became disappointed when results were not forthcoming. Finally, the programs assumed that the key to solving the problem was providing the money, when a large portion of the problem was actually a lack of skills and abilities. Loans were probably too easy for minority businessmen to get. What they lacked was the ability to plan, organize, and control a business. In short, they were not skilled managers, and money alone could not make them successful.

The current programs, based on experience and extensive planning, seem to have much more potential in bringing racial minorities into the mainstream of economic life.

REVIEW BOX 22:3

1. The largest number of minority businesses are in the _____ industry.
2. Common reasons for minority business failure are location, lack of "name" stores, operating costs, lack of skills, and _____.
3. Business ownership programs for minorities have experienced only limited success in the past because of their concentration on _____ and failure to develop _____.

CHAPTER SUMMARY

- Minorities are important to retailing because: (1) they make up 15 percent of the population; (2) retailing is the most common type of business owned by minority group members; and (3) government and business have shown a growing concern over economic inequities that exist for minority groups in the United States.
- Retailers seem to disagree about the existence of minority markets, and researchers have suggested the presence of a wide variety of different characteristics. A retailer who is interested in selling to minorities should consider providing special merchandise and special services, and should think about hiring minority employees and advertising in minority-oriented media.

- Minority consumers have been subjected to numerous problems that can be classified as structural factors and unethical practices.
- The history of minority business in the United States shows ownership to be concentrated in the service industries. In addition, minority-owned businesses have never been a significant force in the U.S. economy.
- The chief reasons for minority business failures have been a lack of managerial and marketing skills, the economic weaknesses of the areas in which minority businesses tend to operate, costs, lack of training, and inadequate capital.
- Black capitalism, the name given to attempts to improve the economic situation of minorities through the ownership of business, has met with mixed success. One explanation for the limited success of programs aimed at increasing minority business ownership suggests that the goals have been too high, false hopes have been created among minority businessmen, and the programs have concentrated on providing capital and ignored the need for managerial training.
- Under the guidance of the Office of Minority Business Enterprise (OMBE), the efforts of government and private industry to raise capital and provide managerial training are beginning to show significant results.

CHAPTER NOTES

[1] The information in this section comes from U.S. Bureau of the Census, *Current Population Reports*, P-23, No. 394, "The Social and Economic Status of Negroes in the United States, 1970" (Washington, D.C.: U.S. Government Printing Office, 1971).

[2] The information in this section comes from U.S. Bureau of the Census, *Current Population Reports*, P-20, No. 364, "Persons of Spanish Origin in the United States: March, 1973" (Washington, D.C.: U.S. Government Printing Office, 1974).

[3] *The World Almanac*, 1974 Edition, George E. Delury, ed. (New York: Newspaper Enterprise Association, 1974), p. 149.

[4] Lyndon B. Johnson, Address to Congress, March 6, 1968.

[5] Richard M. Nixon, Special Message to Congress, July 8, 1970.

[6] This and the following comments on the retailers' view are taken from Thayer C. Taylor, "In the Bigger Cities, Dig Black," *Sales Management*, November 15, 1971, pp. 71–73.

[7] Frederick D. Sturdivant, "Business and the Mexican-American Community," *California Management Review*, Spring 1969, p. 74.

[8] Carl E. Block, "Prepurchase Search Behavior of Low-Income Households," *Journal of Retailing*, Spring 1972, p. 4.

[9] Leonard L. Berry and Paul J. Solomon, "Generalizing about Low-Income Food Shoppers: A Word of Caution," *Journal of Retailing*, Summer 1971, p. 44.

[10] Charles S. Goodman, "Do the Poor Pay More?" *Journal of Marketing*, January 1968, p. 24.

[11] Berry and Solomon, *op.cit.*, p. 49.

[12] James E. Stafford, Keith K. Cox, and James B. Higgenbotham, "Some Consumption Pattern Differences Between Urban Whites and Negroes," *Social Science Quarterly*, December 1968, pp. 619–30.

[13] Donald E. Sexton, Jr., "Differences in Food Shopping Habits by Area of Residence, Race and Income," *Journal of Retailing*, Spring 1974, pp. 37–48.
[14] Glenn H. Snyder, "'Black Is Beautiful' Market Bringing New Dollars to Supers," *Progressive Grocer*, April 1972, pp. 142–50.
[15] Block, *op.cit.*, p. 9.
[16] This and other unethical practices are described in David Caplovitz, *The Poor Pay More* (New York: Free Press, 1963).
[17] Federal Trade Commission, *Economic Report on Installment Credit*, undated, p. IX.
[18] Frederick D. Sturdivant and Walter T. Wilhelm, "Poverty, Minorities, and Consumer Exploitation," in *The Ghetto Marketplace*, Frederick D. Sturdivant, ed. (New York: Free Press, 1969), p. 115.
[19] Berkeley G. Burrell and John Seder, *Getting It Together* (New York: Harcourt Brace Jovanovich, 1971), p. 12.
[20] The remainder of this historical summary is based on Alvin C. Puryear and Charles A. West, *Black Enterprise, Inc.* (Garden City, N.Y.: Anchor Press, 1973), pp. 20–29.
[21] U.S. Bureau of the Census, *Statistical Abstract of the United States, 1972*, 93rd ed. (Washington, D.C.: U.S. Government Printing Office, 1972).
[22] Report of the National Advisory Commission on Civil Disorders (Washington, D.C.: U.S. Government Printing Office, 1968), p. 236.
[23] "Business Development Uplands Style," *Access*, May–June 1973, pp. 9–10.
[24] Burt Schorr, "Black Leaders' Plans to Build Ghetto Stores Often End in Defeat," *Wall Street Journal*, May 1, 1972, pp. 1, 13.
[25] This quote and the comments on OMBE that follow come from U.S. Department of Commerce, "Progress Report: The Minority Business Enterprise Program, 1972" (Washington, D.C.: U.S. Government Printing Office, 1972).
[26] Richard N. Farmer, "The Pros of Black Capitalism," *Business Horizons*, February 1970, pp. 37–40.

QUESTIONS AND ASSIGNMENTS

1. Why are minorities an important area of study in retailing?
2. Explain why any minority group (Blacks, Mexican-Americans, American Indians, etc.) cannot be considered a single market.
3. In your school library, find the percentages of population in Los Angeles, Chicago, and Omaha that were minority group members in 1950, 1960, and 1970. Of what value is this information to retailers in these cities?
4. Visit a drug store or variety store located in a predominantly minority neighborhood and look for merchandise that might be aimed specifically at the minority market. What proportion of this store's total merchandise do these items make up? What does that tell you about the similarity in the white and minority markets?
5. Why has minority business ownership concentrated primarily in the service industries?
6. What reasons have been offered for the limited success of economic programs aimed at increasing the number of minority-owned businesses?
7. Do you think college students trained in business could help a minority businessman? In what areas of business do you feel they could offer the most help?
8. What are the two primary areas of emphasis in current government and private enterprise programs designed to increase the number of minority-owned businesses?

ANSWERS TO REVIEW BOX QUESTIONS

Box 22:1

1. black Americans, Spanish-Americans, American Indians
2. language
3. American Indians

Box 22:2

1. minority markets
2. advertising
3. structural; unethical

Box 22:3

1. services
2. lack of capital
3. capital; managerial skills

Franchise Operations

> Nowhere in America do the twin ideals of democracy and free enterprise come together more closely and more successfully than in the franchising industry.... Franchising makes it possible for *any* enterprising American to become an independent, self-sufficient businessman.
>
> *Senator Edward W. Brooke*[1]

> All too often, the franchisee finds himself working long hours with little to show for his efforts.
>
> *Harold Brown, franchising lawyer*[2]

Although somewhat difficult to imagine, both statements refer to the same subject, franchising. This method of doing business consists of "a continuing relationship in which a franchisor provides a licensed privilege to do business plus assistance in organizing, training, merchandising, and management in return for a consideration from the franchisee."[3] Thus a *franchisor* (sometimes called franchise system) is the parent company, a *franchisee* owns the individual business unit, and what a franchisor sells to a franchisee is a *franchise*.

As the introductory statements suggest, franchising has been both praised and criticized. Of course, many forms of business receive mixed reactions. Besides the fact that it is somewhat controversial, you should become familiar with franchising because of its magnitude as well as its substantial impact on various parties involved in retailing, on numerous categories of product and service offerings, and on certain retailing methods.

This chapter is intended to familiarize you with the various dimensions of franchising. The first two major sections provide the "big picture" by looking at franchising's present significance, what it actually is, the various types, and how it grew and then experienced growing pains. The other three sec-

541

tions examine this method of doing business from three different viewpoints: those of the franchisor, the franchisee, and the retail manager.

THE DEVELOPMENT OF FRANCHISING

Present Significance

According to 1973 data, sales of products and services through franchises reached $150 billion in 1974, up 24 percent from 1972. The number of franchised establishments such as McDonald's, Chevrolet dealerships, and Exxon service stations was about 482,000 in 1974, an increase of 8 percent from 1972.[4] More than 1,200 corporations have franchise operations,[5] mostly in the field of retailing. Most franchise systems have company-owned outlets in addition to franchised outlets.

Franchising has been most significant in automotive-related fields. For example, a consumer may buy the family car from a Ford dealership, gas at a Standard station, and have the muffler replaced a few years later at a Midas Muffler shop. On a family vacation, they stay at Holiday Inn and eat breakfast at International House of Pancakes, lunch at Burger King, and dinner at Mr. Steak. However, franchising's impact has spread across most retail offerings, as shown in Table 23-1. In fact, franchises literally extend from A (airplane-leasing agencies) to Z (miniature zoos in shopping centers). Because franchising essentially is a method of distribution, as is discussed in the next section, "virtually anything can be sold by franchise."[6]

Franchising has had an impact on consumers as well as retail executives, managers of independent outlets, and entrepreneurs. Because of the attractiveness of various franchises, many consumers have altered their frequency of purchasing certain offerings (such as take-out foods) or their shopping patterns.

Franchising has had an impact on retailing methods, both with respect to how customers are attracted and retained through a retailing mix and how daily, internal operations are carried out. For instance, diverse franchise systems such as Holiday Inns and 7-Eleven Food Stores have been successful with highly standardized offerings. Consumers evidently appreciate knowing that quality and price are essentially the same from one unit to the next. Because of its successful application in franchise operations, standardization has become more of a "must" for all retail firms with multiple outlets.

Types of Franchising

Two quite different kinds of franchising are found in the business world. Governments grant telephone companies and electric power producers the

TABLE 23-1

Franchising in 1974:
Number of Establishments and Sales Volume

Selected Categories	Number of franchised establishments	Sales volume (in thousands) of franchised establishments	Percent changes, 1972–1974	
			Estab.	Sales
Automobile and Truck Dealers	32,652	$ 89,465,000	0.2%	22.6%
Automotive Products and Services**	43,918	3,577,050	20.4%	20.3%
Construction, Home Improvements, Maintenance, and Cleaning Services*	13,216	807,659	36.6%	33.7%
Convenience Food Marts*	5,177	1,293,000	30.8%	24.2%
Fast Food Restaurants (All Types)*	31,488	6,722,391	24.2%	40.5%
Gasoline Service Stations	168,800	29,458,000	−4.1%	18.6%
Hotels and Motels*	4,714	3,697,831	41.8%	44.1%
Campgrounds*	1,495	72,981	63.3%	102.2%
Recreation, Entertainment, and Travel*	4,412	195,723	55.2%	61.8%
Rental Services (Auto-Truck-Aircraft-Boats)*	7,460	390,500	10.2%	23.3%
Retailing (Non-Food)**	46,593	6,114,768	24.7%	21.4%
Retailing (Food, Other Than Convenience Food Marts)**	12,042	702,044	19.2%	27.8%
Soft Drink Bottlers	2,520	6,381,000	−4.7%	23.2%
Total: All Categories	398,924	$150,891,438	8.2%	23.5%

* Signifies that category *ordinarily* involves service sponsor-retailer type of franchise.
** Signifies that category *sometimes* involves service sponsor-retailer type.
Source: Adapted from *Franchising in the Economy, 1972–1974, op. cit.*, p. 45.

right to operate a *public utility* as a monopoly. The other kind is called *free-enterprise franchising*, in which a business firm (not the government) grants the operating rights. This is the general kind in which we are interested. As the definition at the chapter's beginning suggests, the key ingredient in franchising is a *continuing relationship* between franchisor and franchisee.

When franchises are classified according to the business firms entering into the agreement, four types can be identified. In one type, wholesalers grant franchises to independent retailers. This type of franchise, most often found in the grocery and hardware field, provides small retailers with the benefits of volume buying power and other operating efficiencies. Currently using the wholesaler-retailer type of franchise are Associated Grocers, Ace Hardware stores, Super Valu supermarkets, Western Auto outlets, and Walgreen drug stores.

A second type involves manufacturers and wholesalers. The best example is found in the soft drink industry, most prominently Coca-Cola and

The Development of Franchising

TABLE 23-2

Samples of Successful Service Sponsor-Retailer Franchises

Franchise and basic offering to consumers	*Main elements of franchise package*	*Financial requirements*
Shakey's Pizza Parlor: pizza, beverages, and "fun"	Complete instruction at "Shakey's University" for owner-manager and key employees. Proven operations pattern and operations manual. Continuing supervision and assistance from field staff.	Total investment of $220,000 for full-size parlor (land and building, $170,000, often are leased; dealers who purchase land and building usually can finance 70% of cost) Approximately $35,000 cash required. Franchisee pays a royalty of $5\frac{1}{2}\%$ on monthly food sales.
Holiday Inn: food, lodging, swimming, and service	Complete instruction at Holiday Inn University for innkeeper and key employees. Year-round innkeepers conferences to continually update key personnel in the "Holiday Inn Way." Everything needed to create and operate a Holiday Inn. Promotional and operational services.	Total investment for a 120-room inn between $1,080,000 and $1,800,000, plus land. Franchisee pays royalties of 3% of gross room revenue or 15¢ per room per night, whichever is greater.
Baskin-Robbins: at least 31 flavors of quality ice cream	Completely equipped store facilities. Standardized operating procedure. Continuing arrangement for large volume warehousing and supply facilities. Continuing merchandising and advertising program.	Minimum cash requirement between $14,000 and $20,000 for inventory, deposits, and down payment on the equipment, the lease-hold improvements, and remodeling. Franchisee pays rent.
AAMCO: automatic transmissions and repairs	AAMCO's customary training and indoctrination course. Original equipment, supplies, and inventory.	Franchise fee of 8% weekly gross receipts. Sign rental at $200 per year.
McDonald's: hamburgers and French fries	Complete training at Hamburger University and regional seminars. Comprehensive operations manual and other training materials. Regional field service staff.	Total investment $140,000 including $75,000 cash requirement. Franchisee pays service fee of 3% monthly net gross sales and rental of 8.5% monthly net gross sales.

Source: Franchise sales literature.

PepsiCo. These syrup manufacturers franchise local bottlers, who in turn sell the finished products to retailers and non-profit institutions.

Manufacturer-retailer franchises, the third type, may cover a line of products or an entire business. Manufacturers such as Magnavox, Whirlpool, and other appliance and television producers grant franchises covering their line of products in order to strengthen working relationships with dealers. A franchised or "authorized" dealer selects the name of his business firm rather than having to use the franchise name. Also, the dealer can have several manufacturers' franchises. Finally, in contrast to franchisees of entire outlets, an authorized dealer does not receive as much support from franchisors, a manufacturer in this case, but has greater freedom of operation.

Manufacturer-retailer franchises covering the entire outlet are most evident in the petroleum and automobile industries. Prominent examples of manufacturers using franchising for retail distribution include General Motors and the other auto makers plus most petroleum refiners such as Exxon, Shell, and Mobil. When the total business is franchised, the manufacturer primarily determines the outlet's retailing strategies and operating methods. The franchise owner runs the outlet on a daily basis in return for a salary and any net profits.

Until the 1950s a franchise ordinarily linked business firms at different levels in a distribution channel. This is evident in the three types just described. In the last 25 years, some successful retailers (and a few manufacturers) have expanded by establishing franchises at the same level of business. For example, the original McDonald's fast-food outlet opened additional outlets through franchising. In this type, known as a *service sponsor-retailer franchise*, the franchisor (service sponsor) sells the franchisee (retailer) a proven method for operating an entire business.

All service sponsor-retailer franchises have certain common features: not only a continuing relationship and a proven method of operating an entire outlet but also the same trade name on all outlets and standardized operations through a contract and perhaps an operations manual. Still, service sponsor-retailer franchises vary according to the basic offering to consumers and specific operating features. The list of service sponsor-retailer operations seems almost endless: Kampgrounds of America, Burger King, 7-Eleven convenience grocery stores, Hertz, Howard Johnson restaurants, Dunkin' Donuts, Midas Muffler shops, and United Rent-All centers, among others. Table 23-2 outlines the major features of several established service sponsor-retailer franchises.

The term service sponsor does not mean that only services can be marketed through this type. On the contrary, many different products *and* services are sold through service sponsor-retailer franchises. Looking back at Table 23-1, note how most categories involve this type. Because it accounts for a substantial proportion of retail franchising, has grown so rapidly in the last two decades, and is somewhat controversial, the service sponsor-retailer type receives primary coverage in this chapter.

The Development of Franchising

> **REVIEW BOX 23:1**
>
> 1. In 1974, sales of products and services through franchises reached about $_____.
> 2. Of the various product and service categories, franchising has been most significant in _____ fields.
> 3. In basic terms, franchising can be defined as _____.

The Boom and Bust

Free-enterprise franchising represents an American "invention." Apparently the Singer Sewing Machine Company initiated the franchise method of distribution around 1863.[7] General Motors and Rexall adopted it around 1900. Only since 1950, however, has franchising grown substantially. The growth of retail franchises in this period can be traced to their attractiveness to various parties: as a method of distributing products, from a manufacturer's standpoint; as a way of owning and operating a business, from the standpoints of entrepreneurs and small businessmen; and as a supplier of desired products and services, from the standpoint of consumers.

There are two particular reasons why large numbers of consumers have patronized franchises in recent years. One reason is that franchises have been conveniently located where potential customers live, shop, and travel. A second reason is that the product or service offering is pretty much the same at all outlets in the system, especially attractive to the highly mobile U.S. population.

Franchising's growth has not only been recent; it has also been rapid. In fact, franchising, especially the service sponsor-retailer type, expanded so greatly during the 1960s that it was labeled a "boom." In 1970, an editor of *Fortune* magazine estimated that "about 90 percent of the franchise companies now in operation have started since 1954."[8] Likewise, the variety of offerings sold through franchises multiplied. In addition to the fast-food field, franchise systems were established "in a bewildering array of fields ranging from carpet shops and rent-a-car outlets to income-tax advisory services, business colleges, community greeting organizations, and high-rise combined one-stop mausoleum-funeral homes."

This rapid growth eventually created an assortment of problems for franchisors and franchisees alike. In fact, many individual franchisees and total franchise systems went "belly up" during the 1969–1972 period. Consider one field, day-care centers:

> But most of the dozen or so companies . . . failed. Some of the others have had to take over the day-care centers they franchised out. Other centers went bankrupt.[9]

In particular, Mary Moppet's franchise system has experienced a bundle of problems, although it has survived them. Chief among the problems have been complaints and some lawsuits by disgruntled franchisees who charge that promised assistance from the parent company never materialized.

What factors contributed to the franchise "bust," as it has been called? Three stand out: inept management, fraudulent activities of some businesspeople calling themselves franchisors, and saturation in some areas of retailing. Regarding inept management, some new franchisors simply did not have the finances necessary to set up a solid business organization *and* to establish themselves in the marketplace. Other franchisors failed when consumers rejected their retailing mix. Some systems experienced initial success but were unable to handle their growth because of a lack of management controls. Also, some franchisees began operations with less capital than needed to survive the rough introductory period.

The illusion of easy profits attracted more than a few fraudulent or "fly-by-night" operators to franchising. Some scheming franchisors sold unsound or unproven franchises to ignorant buyers. Others obtained excessive income from franchisees through an unfair contract.

Many celebrity-backed franchises also flopped. Among others, Mickey Mantle attached his name to clothing stores and restaurants, Eva Gabor was connected with wig salons, and Joe Namath backed restaurant franchises. None has been successful. Some persons purchased a celebrity franchise because of the name involved without considering whether it was a sound retailing operation. When some of these systems collapsed, franchisees lost their initial investments and sometimes much more.

Some systems encountered difficulties because the growth of franchising created too many competitors. In other words, their field became saturated. Relatively speaking, the fast-food area has been the most saturated of the various fields in which franchising is common. There are hundreds of *different* restaurant franchises, and many cities contain rows of what some people call "fast-food joints." Two other areas of franchising which perhaps reached a saturation point during the early 1970s were motels and movie theaters.

Despite its growing pains, franchising remains a major force in retailing. We will examine this force from the point of view of the franchisor, the franchisee, and other retailers.

FRANCHISOR'S VIEWPOINT

This section considers franchising from the standpoint of *prospective franchisors*—the retail firm contemplating expansion or the entrepreneur looking for a way to retail an appealing product or service—and from the viewpoint of *current franchisors*.

Relative Merits of Retailing Through Franchises

When a retail firm desires to increase the number of its outlets, the alternatives are company-owned outlets and franchises. The relative merits of each determine which method is adopted. From a franchisor's point of view, there are major *advantages* to retailing through franchises:

1. Rapid expansion is facilitated, since franchisees provide capital when they purchase franchises.
2. Because they own the business and their income depends on the outlets' profits, franchisees should be highly motivated to do a good job.
3. A franchise system often can make additional profits by selling franchisees needed products or services. In most situations, a franchisor cannot legally require franchisees to buy supplies from the parent company. Still, many franchisees willingly make various purchases in this way.

Rather than sell franchises, many retailers expand by opening company-owned outlets. That is, they establish a corporate chain. Also, some franchise systems own some outlets in addition to their franchise units. The advantages of company-owned outlets are actually the *drawbacks* of franchising:

1. According to many businessmen, company-owned units are more profitable than franchises to the parent company. Several years ago, the head of Kentucky Fried Chicken stated: "We'll make more profit from 300 company-owned stores than we will from 2,100 franchise outlets."[10]
2. Corporate chains control individual units' advertising, pricing, personnel practices, and so on. This is advantageous because standardization, especially with respect to product or service quality, is a key to success for a group of retail outlets operating under the same name. Furthermore, a company manager can be fired or transferred if necessary, whereas a franchisee can be terminated only if he violates the franchise contract.

Major Feature of Franchise Operations

As noted earlier, franchising involves a continuing relationship between a franchisor and a franchisee. This working relationship, especially close in the service sponsor-retailer type, distinguishes retail franchises from other retail firms. A non-franchised retail firm obtains its merchandise, supplies, and support services such as accounting and advertising from a variety of sources. Usually these working relationships between retailer and supplier are intermittent rather than continuing.

SPOTLIGHT

Can franchising and company ownership of outlets be combined?

The franchising of additional outlets has some attractive features for a large firm that wants to expand. But company-owned outlets may provide greater profits and control for the parent company. It would seem to be ideal if the better features of the two could be combined. Can this be done?

Sambo's Restaurants, headquartered in California, thinks so. The firm has developed a "manager-partner" plan for its more than 300 limited-menu restaurants, a plan that combines certain features of franchises and company-owned outlets. Here's how it works: Fifty percent of the ownership of each restaurant is retained by Sambo's Restaurants, Inc. The new manager-partner purchases a 20-percent interest, and the other 30 percent goes into an investment pool with similar interests in the other Sambo's restaurants. Managers and supervisors throughout the chain are allowed to purchase 5-percent units from the pool. Each 5-percent unit costs $5,000, so the manager's original investment is $20,000.

Because of the 20-percent equity plus 5-percent units purchased from the pool, the manager of a Sambo's restaurant is not just an ordinary employee. Each manager profits from the success of both the individual outlet and the chain as a whole. Still, Sambo's retains management control through its 50-percent ownership. In a sense, "the prospective manager-partner actually only 'buys' himself a job, a job from which he can be dismissed if he doesn't meet company requirements." And the parent company definitely makes the strategic decisions: "The manager-partner has little to say, even as to where the operation will be."

Another benefit to Sambo's is that the managers are motivated to run a profitable operation by their partial ownership of the restaurant. Their investments in other members of the chain also seems to stimulate cooperation among the manager-partners. For example, the managers refer traveling customers to other Sambo's restaurants along their route and mention effective new operating methods to each other. To the manager-partner, the arrangement involving 20-percent ownership in one restaurant and 5-percent units in others means that all his eggs are *not* in one basket; rather, the risk of loss is spread across a number of outlets.

Like any business arrangement, the manager-partner plan includes some potential problems. *Business Week* has noted, "The most obvious is the need to keep growing rapidly. Unless more restaurants are added, there can be no new pool units with which to reward managers."

Another problem is the occasional gripes, like the following from a manager who quit the company: "They're getting a lot of cheap labor, if you ask me, and they seem to be looking for people with money to buy investment units, not people with management ability."

These potential problems notwithstanding, the manager-partner plan shows impressive results. Management turnover is unusually low, and Sambo's is not only profitable but one of the most rapidly expanding restaurant chains in the country.

Sources: Charles Berrisford, "Sambo's Manager-Partners," *Fast Food*, February 1970, pp. 95–96; and "Sambo's Serves Its Managers an Extra Slice," *Business Week*, January 26, 1974, p. 82.

The nature of a franchisor-franchisee relationship is determined for the most part by the franchisor, ordinarily the more powerful of the two parties. Hence, the continuing relationship is discussed in this section.

Basically, a franchisor provides a franchisee with various kinds of support (or help) in the operation of a retail business. The total support provided, called a franchise package, covers not only a retailing mix but also financial and personnel management. In return, an owner-manager runs the business under certain controls established by the franchisor and under a financial arrangement which provides revenue to the parent company. McDonald's arrangement with its licensees (their term for franchisees) has been described as follows:

> The licensee must lay out an average of $150,000, at least half of it in cash. For that, he gets to lead a life regimented by Ray Kroc, chairman of the board, and subordinates. To begin with, the licensee has little choice of where he will operate. Headquarters executives pick out all the sites, buy (or sometimes lease) the land, arrange for construction of the store, and rent it with equipment to the licensee for 8.5% of gross, plus a 3% annual franchise fee. . . . In return for their money and submission to headquarters, the licensees get to use the McDonald's real estate, name and formula.[11]

Thus the continuing relationship can be thought of as a two-way flow of certain items which are specified in a contract.

As noted earlier, it appears that today's mobile consumers expect a particular offering to be very similar in quality and price across all outlets of the same name. Obviously, various outlets' offerings cannot be standardized when each franchisee is "doing his own thing." Thus, while some systems give franchisees much operating freedom, most control franchise operations very tightly.

When he was still active in Kentucky Fried Chicken, Colonel Sanders was the leading enforcer of controls over franchisees—especially with respect to the chicken gravy. During his travels, he often paid surprise visits to KFC outlets to inspect the kitchen and sample the gravy. When the gravy quality did not meet his expectations, he often would shout at the franchisee: "How do you serve this *!#%*&#! slop? With a straw?" Besides the Colonel's personal efforts, KFC has long relied on various controls: "From the day a franchisee gets his franchise until the day he dies or sells out, he is nagged about doing things the KFC way."[12] The controls begin with "KFC University," the training program for new owners, and continue with periodic visits from field supervisors and occasional seminars on operating procedures.

However, some franchisees may resent stringent controls. Thus, a franchisor must be careful about the amount of control he exercises.

A franchise arrangement is structured so that both parties might make a profit. Ordinarily, a franchise owner-manager receives a reasonable salary *and* any net profits from the business.

A franchisor's operating revenue comes from payments made by franchisees. The initial fee, usually non-refundable, sometimes exceeds $10,000.

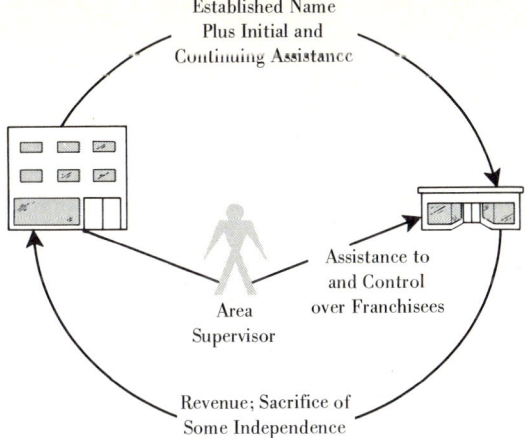

Various tangible and intangible items flow between franchisor and franchisee.

In addition, franchisees buy or rent certain equipment, supplies, materials—even their building and land—from their parent company.

Finally, a royalty payment is included in most franchise agreements. The royalty usually consists of a percentage of sales, often around 5 percent. In return, a franchisee most often benefits from advertising assistance and managerial advice from area supervisors who periodically visit all outlets.

The franchisor-franchisee relationship is set forth in a contract which specifies the rights and obligations of both parties, the length of the agreement, the conditions under which a franchisee can be terminated, and other legal details. Some authorities criticize the typical franchise contract and the resulting relationship as being too one-sided in the franchisor's favor. After reviewing more than 100 franchise contracts, two researchers concluded that "the basic franchise document imposes far more obligations on the franchisee than on the franchisor."[13] Also, one lawyer blasted it as an "instrument of repression."[14] Franchisors, on the other hand, contend that a tight contract is necessary to achieve standardized operations, which in turn benefit both parties.

REVIEW BOX 23:2

1. One of the two specific reasons why many franchises have achieved substantial sales volume is _____.
2. Three particular factors were primarily responsible for the franchise "bust" around 1969–1972. One of these is _____.
3. From the franchisor's standpoint, an advantage of franchising is _____; a reported disadvantage is _____.
4. The major feature of retail franchises is _____.

FRANCHISEE'S VIEWPOINT

The first part of this section again looks at franchising's relative merits, but this time through the eyes of the other party to the arrangement — current and prospective owner-managers. The second part contains some guidelines on a substantial and risky decision, buying a franchise.

Relative Merits of Business Ownership Through Franchising

Franchises have one common attraction to people who want to own a business: Generally speaking, the complete business connected with a franchise is superior to the business an individual could put together on his own. As one writer explained:

> The most important advantage of franchising can be summarized in one word: *Help!* Most people who have been successful in franchising can attribute their success to the assistance they have received from their parent companies; and, in this regard, the most important assistance has been in the form of advice which could not otherwise be obtained except through long and often hardwon experience.[15]

Thus the likelihood of success is increased by a complete, tested franchise package. One prime cause of retailing failures, lack of business knowledge and competence, is greatly reduced.

While various kinds of help are franchising's major advantage, many franchisees apparently feel that their franchisors could be providing much better support in some areas. For example, in a recent study, franchisees of fast-food restaurants had mixed feelings about the quality of franchisors' assistance:

> Over half the franchisees rated their franchisors' assistance to be of average quality or better. However, substantial discontent exists in the areas of local advertising, national advertising, day-to-day advice, field supervisors, bookkeeping and pricing assistance.[16]

The situation described by the franchisee of a United Rent-All equipment center in the Denver area reflects the experiences of some, perhaps many, franchise owner-managers:

> "At first I didn't get the help I was told I'd get," he says. "The coordinator they sent to help me get started was completely inept." The company failed to deliver all the items for his inventory by the time the store opened, Moberly complains.

He finds United Rent-All better to work with now. "They have an excellent system for keeping track of what is in stock and how much is earned on each item, and their public image is good," he says. "Knowing what I know today, I'd open up as an independent rental store. Knowing as little as I did when I opened, I think I'd go with the franchise again."[17]

Apparently, numerous franchisees recognize the value of a franchise package but have been disgruntled at some point in their dealings with the franchisor.

The principal disadvantages of a franchise pertain to the franchisee's reduced freedom of operations. In actuality, a franchisee is not truly his own boss. Recent findings suggest, however, that franchisees do *not* feel they have sacrificed much freedom. Over half the franchisees surveyed felt they had almost complete responsibility for most areas of operations. Interestingly, the franchisees perceived much greater freedom in making these decisions than their franchisors felt the owner-managers actually had.[18]

Other disadvantages of business ownership through franchising have been mentioned. These include high royalties or fees charged by franchisor; higher costs on equipment, supplies, or merchandise to be resold; higher rental or lease rates; and mandatory participation in promotional programs or purchases of support services.

As you can see, franchisees actually are neither independent entrepreneurs nor regular store managers. Rather, they really are *semi-independent* businessmen. To some franchisees this semi-independence means a loss of operating freedom; they thus consider it a disadvantage. To others, any disadvantage is out-weighed by the help provided by the franchisor.

Am I to assume, Thorndyke, that you've decided to buy that franchised business you've been considering?

Guidelines on Purchasing a Franchise

When considering a major purchase, you naturally shop around and evaluate different sellers' offerings. You want good quality, a reasonable price, and so on. Surprisingly, numerous persons have bought franchises, certainly a major purchase, without adequate information and evaluation of alternatives. Recall that franchising has had its share of fraudulent franchisors. A combination of these two factors has resulted in a sizeable number of franchisees being stuck with "lemons."

Since about 1970, more institutions have tried to assist persons interested in purchasing a franchise. In particular, banks, the National Association of Franchised Businessmen, and the International Franchise Association (the franchisors' trade association) have urged prospective franchisees to "investigate before you invest." They have also suggested procedures for evaluating franchise opportunities. Several states and Congress have either enacted or proposed laws requiring *full disclosure* by franchisors. Full disclosure is intended to provide prospects with various facts and figures which permit an informed decision on whether to buy a franchise, and if so, which would be the best buy.

Let us assume that you are interested in becoming a franchisee. A suitable procedure to follow involves three distinct steps. First, you should learn about franchising in general. You should be aware of such factors as the nature of the franchisee position and the investment ordinarily required in terms of both capital and hours of work each week.

The second step consists of a self-evaluation—comparing your own capabilities, interests, and personality with the demands of franchising. Questions to ask yourself include:

> Are my finances sufficient for getting into the kind of franchise in which I am interested?
> Am I willing to work long hours and as many as six days a week? Also, am I willing to have other family members (most likely, my spouse) involved in the business as a bookkeeper, sales clerk, or assistant manager?
> Am I willing to risk an investment in order to acquire semi-independence and the possibility of making substantial profits?
> Am I willing to follow directions on how to operate a business?

If you are still qualified and interested, the third step is to evaluate various systems' franchises. You probably have a particular field in mind, such as automotive services or restaurants. This would reduce the alternatives to some extent. Relying on a franchise directory,[19] you can develop a list of franchise systems in your areas of interest and write for information.

When you receive a company's promotional material and then eventually talk with their representative, you must evaluate the potential of the franchise. The task is to appraise the franchise company itself, the product or service to be sold, the geographic territory (or sales area) covered by the franchise, the contract, and the nature of continuing assistance. A detailed checklist of factors which should be evaluated is in Figure 23-1.

Admittedly, obtaining objective information is very difficult. Still, careful evaluation is *crucial* in locating a sound franchise. Possible sources of additional information include: banks and the franchisors' or franchisees' association, as noted; your attorney, for advice regarding the contract's intricacies; existing franchisees, for insights about the franchisee position or about their particular system; and the local Better Business Bureau, for a list of franchises shown to be unsound or about which complaints have been received.

The best guideline on purchasing a franchise remains: *Caveat emptor!*

RETAIL MANAGER'S VIEWPOINT

The growing number of franchise systems and franchised outlets has brought about new patterns of competition in some fields of retailing. The greatest impact has been on *small, independent merchants*. Retail franchises' economies of scale, advertising muscle, and standardized offerings have made profitability—even survival—very difficult for many small independents. As a result, some have closed down. Other independents, recognizing the wisdom of "If you can't lick 'em, join 'em," have purchased a franchise.

Consider one field, pet stores. The title of one article noted: "Sophisticated merchandisers taking over mom-and-pop pet business with franchises."[20] Specifically, two franchise systems, Puppy Palace and Docktor's Pet Centers, entered this field around 1970. The franchises compete with each other, of course. But more significantly, they represent formidable competition for independent stores, which are especially prevalent in this field.

Franchising's impact on *retail chains* also is visible. Basically, the retailing mixes and operating methods of some franchise systems have proven so successful that chains have been forced into improvements and innovations in order to remain competitive.

The rise of franchised convenience stores in the grocery industry provides a good illustration. The success of 7-Eleven stores, in particular, was noticed by supermarket chains. The differential advantage of convenience grocery stores has been neighborhood locations and long store hours. Recently, fast service has also been featured by some firms in this field. Some supermarket chains have retaliated with longer hours of operation and Sunday openings where permitted by state and local laws. Furthermore, at least a few supermarket chains have opened company-owned or franchised convenience grocery outlets. These actions indicate how retail chains might use franchising to diversify.

The Franchisor

1. How long has the firm been involved in franchising?
2. How strong is the franchisor financially? (This question is best answered by a banker or Dun & Bradstreet.)
3. How many franchises and company-owned units are affiliated with the franchisor?
4. How many of the firm's franchisees have failed in the last three years, and for what underlying reasons?
5. What is the franchisor's reputation among its franchisees? (This question requires talking with a sample of franchisees near the proposed location.)

The Offering

6. How long has this merchandise or these services been successfully sold through franchises?
7. Will there be a relatively stable or these services been successfully sold through franchises? tors is this evaluation based?
8. Will you be permitted to sell any offerings other than the franchisor's?
9. Will you be required or permitted to sell all of the franchisor's offerings?
10. What is the offering's advantage(s) over competitive merchandise or services?

Finances

11. What is the total cost of purchasing and opening the franchise, including franchise fee, purchase or lease of building and equipment, initial inventory, and working capital?
12. Does the franchisor assist in financing a franchisee's initial outlay?
13. What royalty or other continuing payments (such as for advertising) must be made for advertising?
14. What levels of sales and profits can a franchisee expect? What is the basis for these projections?

Franchise Location and Territory

15. How will a suitable location for the franchise business be selected?

FIGURE 23-1

Checklist for evaluating a franchise offer.

REVIEW BOX 23:3

1. The _____ represents the major advantage of franchising from the franchise owner-manager's standpoint.
2. Franchisees are neither independent entrepreneurs nor regular store managers, but really are _____ businessmen.
3. A suitable procedure in considering purchase of a franchise involves three steps, with the third step being: _____.
4. The rise of franchises has had the greatest competitive impact on _____.

16. What is the present and future potential of this location? What is the basis for these assessments?
17. How strong is the competition for the franchisee's merchandise or services in the territory covered by the franchise?
18. Does the franchise give you an exclusive territory, meaning that the franchisor cannot open additional units in the territory covered by the franchise?

Initial and Continuing Assistance

19. What training, in terms of length and topics covered, does the franchisor provide a franchisee prior to opening the business?
20. What types of continuing marketing, personnel, accounting, and financial assistance does the franchisor provide? Are these free or on a fee basis?
21. What is the nature and extent of the franchisor's current and planned advertising program?
22. Does the franchisor have field supervisors who assist with the grand opening and provide continuing consultation?
23. Does the franchisor provide an arrangement whereby a franchisee can save money by purchasing equipment, inventory, and/or supplies from the firm rather than an outside supplier?

The Contract

24. Does the contract impose any undue restraints or obligations on a franchisee?
25. Is the franchise contract complete? (The preceding two questions should be answered in counsel with a lawyer.)
26. Does a franchisee have sufficient operating freedom under the contract?
27. Under what conditions can a franchise be terminated or repurchased by the franchisor or renewed, terminated, or sold by a franchisee? When any of the preceding occur, how much is the franchisee compensated?
28. Does the owner have to serve as full-time manager of the franchise?
29. Is a successful franchisee permitted to purchase additional units?

CHAPTER SUMMARY

- Franchising is defined as a continuing relationship in which a franchisor (the parent company) provides a licensed privilege to do business plus assistance in organizing, training, merchandising, and management in return for a consideration from the franchisee (the owner of the individual unit).
- Franchises are most significant in automotive-related fields but are used in retailing a wide variety of products and services. In 1973 an estimated 1,200 corporations had 385,000 franchised outlets which accounted for $134 billion in sales.
- The fastest-growing type of franchise is the service sponsor-retailer,

in which a franchisor (service sponsor) sells the franchisee (retailer) a proven method for operating an entire business.
- Retail franchises have become widespread in the last two decades because they have advantages as a distribution method, as a way of owning and operating a smaller business, and as suppliers of products and services to consumers. In the late 1960s, franchising's "boom" turned into a "bust" because of inept management, fraudulent activities of some businessmen calling themselves franchisors, and saturation in some areas of retailing.
- From a franchisor's viewpoint, two primary advantages of franchising are that expansion capital is obtained and franchisees are more highly motivated than regular store managers. The disadvantage most often mentioned is that franchises are less profitable to a parent company than company-owned outlets.
- The feature which distinguishes retail franchises from other retail firms is the close relationship between the parties (franchisor and franchisee). This working relationship is especially close in the service sponsor-retailer type.
- From a franchisee's viewpoint, franchising main attraction is the varied assistance supplied by a franchisor in starting and operating a business; the major drawback is reduced freedom of operations.
- A suitable procedure in considering the purchase of a franchise involves three steps: learning about franchising in general, evaluating oneself in relation to the demands of franchising, and evaluating various systems' franchises.
- The rise of franchises has meant formidable competition for independent retailers, forcing some out of business, and has pushed some retail chains into improvements and innovations in order to remain competitive.

CHAPTER NOTES

[1] Charles L. Vaughn and David B. Slater, eds., *Franchising Today—1966–1967* (Albany, N.Y.: Matthew Bender & Co., 1967), p. v.
[2] Harold Brown, *Franchising: Trap for the Trusting* (Boston: Little, Brown, 1969), p. 1.
[3] "Franchising: The Modern System of Distribution" (Chicago: International Franchise Association, not dated), p. 1.
[4] *Franchising in the Economy, 1972–1974* (Washington, D.C.: U.S. Department of Commerce, 1974), p. 1.
[5] Charles G. Burck, "Franchising's Troubled Dream World," *Fortune*, March 1970, p. 118.
[6] *Ibid.*, p. 17.
[7] Robert Rosenberg and Madelon Bedell, *Profits From Franchising* (New York: McGraw-Hill Book Company, 1969), p. 9.
[8] This quote and the following one come from Burck, *op. cit.*, p. 117.
[9] The quote and the description of Mary Moppet's are drawn from Joann S. Lublin, "Day-Care Franchises, Beset with Problems, Find Allure Is Fading," *Wall Street Journal*, November 29, 1972, p. 1.

[10] Burck, *op. cit.*, p. 121.
[11] "The Burger That Conquered the Country," *Time*, September 17, 1973, pp. 89–90.
[12] As described in William Whitworth, "Profiles: Kentucky-Fried," *The New Yorker*, February 14, 1970, pp. 40, 48, and 51.
[13] U. B. Ozanne and Shelby D. Hunt, *The Economic Effects of Franchising* (Madison, Wis.: Graduate School of Business, University of Wisconsin, 1971), p. 8-6.
[14] Brown, *op. cit.*, p. 103.
[15] Harry Kursh, *The Franchise Boom*, rev. ed. (Englewood Cliffs, N.J.: Prentice-Hall, 1968), p. 41.
[16] Ozanne and Hunt, *op. cit.*, p. 2-16.
[17] Michael Creedman, "A Franchise Is a Hard Way to Get Rich," *Money*, September 1973, p. 36.
[18] Ozanne and Hunt, *op. cit.*, p. 2-14.
[19] For example, the International Franchise Association membership roster or Frank Reynolds, ed., *The Annual—A Franchise Directory*, 1970 ed. (Lewiston, N.Y.: International Franchise Opportunities, 1970).
[20] In *Marketing Insights*, March 30, 1970, pp. 12–13.

QUESTIONS AND ASSIGNMENTS

1. After reading about retail franchise operations, what one or two words do you think best describes them? Explain.
2. Contact the owner-manager of a fast-food restaurant franchise and show him the two quotes at the beginning of the chapter. Which does he feel is more accurate? Discuss his reasons with him.
3. a. Define franchising.
   b. Is the company which *sells* a franchise called franchisor or franchisee?
   c. What is the key ingredient in a true franchise?
4. Which is the fastest-growing type of franchise? How is it different from the other three types?
5. Which areas of retailing do not involve franchising to any degree? In which area do you feel franchising could be used successfully? Why do you think this area might be ripe for franchising?
6. In the last year or two, what area of franchising has been most publicized, either favorably or unfavorably? Specifically, what has been written or said about this area?
7. What successful celebrity-backed franchises are located in your community? Do you know of any celebrity franchises which failed in your community? Can you pinpoint any differences in the retailing mixes of the successful and unsuccessful franchises which might partially explain the failures?
8. Let's review franchising's relative merits. What are *two*:
   a. advantages of franchising, from a franchisor's standpoint?
   b. disadvantages, from a franchisor's standpoint?
   c. advantages, from a franchisee's standpoint?
   d. disadvantages, from a franchisee's standpoint?
9. Would you like to own a franchise? Why or why not? If yes, in what field?
10. Talk with an independent retailer about the extent to which franchises compete with his retail outlet. Has he changed his operations in order to be more competitive with franchises?
11. Select a franchise, and write the parent company for information and brochures on this franchise opportunity. Look over the material you are sent. Assuming you had sufficient finances, did you receive enough information on the franchise to decide whether to purchase it? If yes, what

makes this particular franchise an attractive opportunity? If no, what other information do you need?

ANSWERS TO REVIEW BOX QUESTIONS

Box 23:1

1. $151 billion
2. automotive-related
3. Something along the following line: A business deal in which a big company permits and helps a smaller company operate a business in return for various money payments.

Box 23:2

1. Either of the following: conveniently located where people live, shop, and travel; product or service offering is same at all outlets in system
2. One of the following: inept management on the part of franchisors or franchisees, fraudulent activities of some persons calling themselves franchisors, saturation in some areas of retailing
3. One of the following as an *advantage:* possible expansion with franchisee's capital, greater motivation of franchisees, additional profits from selling franchisees needed products or services
   One of the following as a *disadvantage:* less profitable than company-owned units, less control over individual unit's operations than with company-owned outlets
4. a continuing business relationship

Box 23:3

1. franchise package or help
2. semi-independent
3. evaluation of various systems' franchises
4. small, independent retailers

Retailing of Primary Services

24

Although to many people retailing suggests the sale of *products* to consumers, retailing actually involves the sale of *both products and services*. Consequently, services have been discussed as appropriate throughout the text. Why, then, do *primary services* deserve a separate chapter? Basically, for two reasons: First, primary services continue to increase in significance in the U.S. economy. Second, as compared to products retailing, effective services retailing requires changes in some retailing mix elements.

THE NATURE AND GROWTH OF PRIMARY SERVICES

A Definition and Some Distinctions

Our purpose in this section is to clarify the meaning of the term *primary services* and to identify the main sellers of these offerings. Although primary services such as hair care, mass transportation, television and radio repair, and lodging are diverse, they do have one common feature: each is intangible in nature. That is, they do not have physical characteristics.

We can define primary services as want-satisfying intangibles which are the object of a transaction between a business firm and either an ultimate consumer, another business firm, or an institution. Being intangible, primary services are distinguishable from products. As the object of a transaction, they are distinguishable from supplementary services (such as gift wrapping or credit) designed to stimulate sales.

561

Primary services are sold chiefly by *retail service establishments*. This kind of retailer may also sell products, but the majority of its sales volume comes from services. For example, a barber shop typically sells hair-care products such as shampoo and maybe even hand-held hair dryers. But most of its revenue results from services performed, such as hair cuts and shaves.

On the other hand, according to the terminology of retailing, products are sold chiefly by *retail stores*. This type of business concentrates on products but also may retail services to a lesser extent. For instance, department stores often include beauty salons and automotive service departments.

Thus, retail stores and service establishments overlap in terms of their offerings to consumers and thereby compete with each other. One writer identified this trend some years ago:

> . . . Either as part of general merchandise stores, or as separate stores, low-margin retailers will move strongly into service retailing. We already see this happening. . . . They are entering the automatic laundry and dry cleaning fields. . . . A number offer banking facilities. And, of course, most discount department stores include the various service departments that operate in other types of outlets — optical, beauty shop, etc.[1]

Most primary services are sold on an in-store basis. Some services, such as transportation and lawn-care, however, are sold on a non-store basis, which means consumers do not come to an outlet to purchase them. In addition, some service establishments operating out of an outlet also "deliver" their service. For example, most radio and TV repair shops make service calls to residences as well as repair sets brought to their outlets.

Growth of Services

Economists tell us that as an economy prospers and matures, the emphasis shifts from agriculture and manufacturing to service industries. This shift has been very pronounced for the U.S. economy. Since the end of World War II, more and more of every dollar spent by consumers has been on services. In 1947 about 31 cents of every consumer dollar went for services, whereas the 1973 figure was 42 cents.[2] Actually, the proportion first reached 42 percent in 1969, which suggests a leveling off in the relative amount spent on services.

Numerous factors fueled the surge in spending on services. One factor already touched upon is the economic advancement of the United States. Most persons' disposable income (earnings after taxes) and discretionary income (money remaining after essential and fixed expenditures) have been improving steadily. Consequently, consumers have been able to buy non-essentials (even luxuries), many of which are services such as intercity transportation and entertainment.

Along with incomes, life styles have changed. Ownership of products has been de-emphasized, while "going places and doing your own thing" has been emphasized. An activities-oriented life style involves purchases of educational, personal care, and recreational services, in particular. Also, the decreased importance of ownership has stimulated the growth of rental services.

Another factor is inflation. Specifically, the prices of most services have risen more than the prices of products in recent years, especially during the 1970s. Because of inflation, consumers have to spend an increasing proportion of every dollar to obtain the same amount of services. Apparently, consumers value services enough that they have been willing to do so.

As more women work outside the home, spending on services is increased in two ways. First, working wives have less time to perform homemaking tasks. Hence, they hire service establishments for child care (nursery schools), ironing and alterations (dry-cleaning outlets), and so on. Second, their earnings supplement family income, making these and other service purchases possible.

Finally, new services have been developed, either in response to or in anticipation of consumer desires. For example, recreational vehicles, especially motor homes and pickup campers, became very popular around 1970. The result: "To accommodate them, a host of auxiliary services have sprung up."[3] Specifically, campgrounds have been opened for the vehicles, "land marinas" where big motor homes can be stored and serviced between trips have been designed, and rentals of recreational vehicles have grown tremendously—all new services.

Some new services are more "far out." As one example, personal color consultants advise clients about colors to feature in their clothing and their homes. The price for a personal color consultation: $35 or more. Far out or not, "consultants around the nation say business is booming."[4]

To complete this background on services retailing, Table 24-1 lists

TABLE 24-1

Kinds of Service Establishments

Barber shops	Nursery schools
Equipment rental agencies	Truck and car rental agencies
Car washes	Savings and loan associations
Banks	Beauty salons
Health spas and gyms	Automotive maintenance and repair shops (as well as the more specialized muffler shops and transmission centers)
Radio, TV, and appliance repair shops	
Amusement parks	
Laundry/dry-cleaning outlets (full service or self-service)	
	Country clubs
Movie theaters	Tax preparation services
Hotels and motels	Shoe-repair shops
Massage parlors	Dance studios
Campgrounds	Film processing outlets
Photo studios	

different kinds of retail service establishments. Although the range of operations is striking, all are similar in that they are engaged primarily in retailing intangibles.

SHORTCOMINGS IN SERVICES RETAILING

Seeing the tremendous growth in services, we may be tempted to conclude that all is well for service establishments. But this in fact is not true.

Several shortcomings, each of which can hurt individual service establishments, are very noticeable in the retailing of various services. These shortcomings have proven fatal to some service outlets. For others, the shortcomings discussed below have reduced profits. Considering service industries in general rather than as individual establishments, it is quite possible that these shortcomings have prevented even more growth in purchases of services.

Incompetent Performance

One problem plaguing some service fields is that unqualified persons perform the service sold to consumers. A California state agency which polices the retailing of automotive services has pointed to such incompetency as "the worst thing about the industry."[5]

Incompetency is rather widespread because anyone with a limited amount of capital can open almost any kind of service establishment. All that is needed is a building and the necessary equipment and tools, all of which usually can be rented. Entry into some service fields is more difficult because a license is necessary. Still, licensing does not ensure that the person is more than minimally competent or that the skills will be maintained or improved as needed to serve customers adequately.

Another type of incompetency relates to running a business. Some persons are skilled in performing a particular service but are unskilled as businessmen. This can lead to poor treatment of customers, mismanagement of personnel (which in turn can lower service quality), and general inefficiency of operations. Lacking business skills, some service establishment operators either do not attempt or are unable to engage in retail operations planning.

Misapplication of the Marketing Concept

For years, writers have emphasized the importance of consumer orientation by service establishments: "In today's competitive atmosphere, the planning of business activities associated with consumer services must start at the consumption end of the stream of activities, rather than at the production end."⁶

However, many service establishments remain unaware of the marketing concept and its significance in modern retailing; others are simply misapplying it. Two mistakes have been common. First, the factor of consumer orientation has been ignored or confused. Banks have been criticized frequently for this: "At the philosophical level, banks evidently have mistaken friendliness for true customer-orientation."⁷ Second, at the other extreme, attempts to satisfy consumers have been exaggerated to the point where profit is disregarded.

The Communications Gap

Poor communications hinder the relationship not only between parents and teenagers, between politicians and constituents, but also between service establishments and consumers. This communications gap, the paramount shortcoming in services retailing, has two elements: not obtaining from consumers information needed in developing an effective retailing mix, which suggests a lack of research; and not providing consumers with useful, factual information about the firm's offerings, which represents promotion deficiencies. Of course, consumers sometimes contribute to the communications gap by failing to explain exactly what is wanted, by not inquiring in advance about prices or time schedules, or by requesting "extras" after an agreement has been reached, to cite several possibilities.

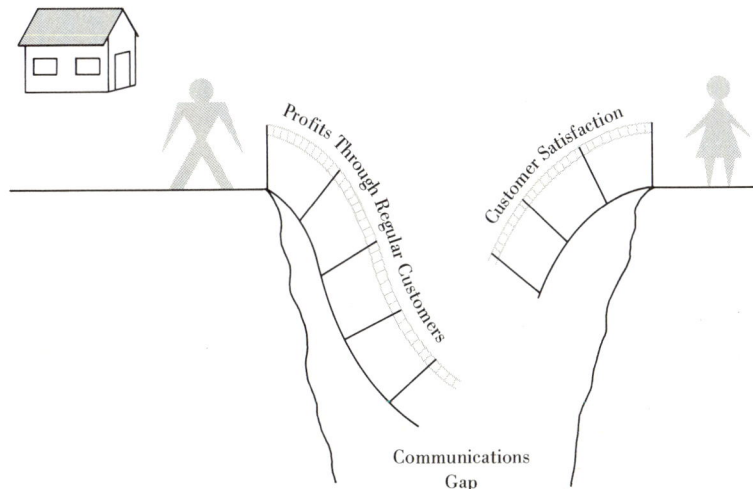

The communications gap hurts both businessmen and consumers.

"What's this little item?—'install and adjust new watchamacallit—$34.95'."

FIGURE 24-1

Consumers desire full explanation of services performed.

LACK OF RESEARCH

Even though research can be uncomplicated and inexpensive, many service establishments do little or none. As a result, they do not fully know important things such as what consumer needs their offerings could satisfy, the shopping patterns of potential customers, what customers think about the firm's offerings, and whether loyal customers are being developed.

Lack of research leads to a service establishment's "stabbing in the dark" in attempts to develop an effective retailing mix. One illustration should underscore the perils of too little research. To boost its percentage of under-thirty customers, a bank decided to organize a "youth club." The bank staged expensive parties on its premises, featuring golf exhibitions and go-go girls. But the idea flopped; few new under-thirty customers were attracted, while older customers might have been driven away. Basically, the youth club failed because the bank had not studied the motivations of young people with respect to banking services. As a bank executive explained, "The bank's key mistake was that it assumed young people would respond the same way they do to an ad for blue jeans."[8]

PROMOTION DEFICIENCIES

Shortcomings in this area are connected with both major forms of promotion, advertising and personal selling. Basically, the problem is one of not providing enough useful, factual information to consumers before, during, or after a service purchase.

Misleading advertising has occurred in some service fields. For example, leading firms in the tax preparation and automotive repair businesses have been charged by the Federal Trade Commission with misrepresenting their actual offerings in advertising. Deceiving consumers may, in fact, produce short-term gains. But misleading advertising is a serious error because of its potential long-term consequences. When consumers eventually learn that they have been deceived, the resulting backlash in terms of lost customers and negative word-of-mouth promotion ordinarily more than offsets any short-term gains.

Another frequent shortcoming consists of salespersons' insufficient explanation of the "what, why, and how much" of services which will be or have been performed. Whereas misleading advertising is usually intentional, insufficient explanation is often unintentional. Service personnel or sales clerks may not realize that customers want specific information about a service, or they may forget to mention an important item. Insufficient explanation can create customer dissatisfaction. For example, after checking into a motel room, you may find that it's smaller or not as clean as you expected. If you are angry enough, the motel may have just lost a customer. Your anger could have been avoided if the desk clerk told you when you checked in about the convention or maids' strike that was temporarily creating problems—a logical reason which you probably would have accepted. The key point is that the quality of a salesman's explanation during and after, as well as before, a service is performed can significantly affect customer satisfaction with the service purchase.

REVIEW BOX 24:1

1. Although they range from dry cleaning of clothing to lawn care, all primary services have one common feature: _____.
2. One error in attempting to apply the marketing concept is to disregard the profitability factor; another error is to _____.
3. The paramount shortcoming in services retailing is _____; it has two elements: _____ and _____.

DISTINCTIVE FEATURES OF SERVICES RETAILING

Insight into the reasons for the shortcomings just described can be gained by considering various distinctive features of services retailing and also retail service establishments. Furthermore, the difficulties connected with services retailing should become apparent as we proceed through this discussion.

Characteristics of Services

Several characteristics of services themselves affect the retailing requirements for these kinds of offerings: intangibility, discretionary nature of expenditure, desire for convenience, and close seller-customer relationship.

INTANGIBILITY The fact that services are intangible is their most significant characteristic. This intangibility complicates services retailing in a variety of ways. The utility or want satisfaction of a service resides in an activity, whereas the utility of a product is derived from its physical characteristics. For example, the benefits which tennis shoes yield — protection and comfort — are physical. This is quite different from, say, recreation services where the benefit is in an activity. As one researcher explained, "Pride and prestige of ownership by consumers do not apply to services as they do for commodities [products]."[9] Thus, intangibility's first effect is that service establishments must sell potential customers on the idea of doing something or having something done for them rather than on owning something.

A second effect is that services cannot be produced at one time and place and then stored for sale at another time or shipped to a place of greater demand. This is especially troublesome when demand varies greatly depending upon time of day, day of the week, or season of the year. Consider movie theaters and lawn care service as two examples. Because services cannot be stored or shipped, efficient utilization of facilities and personnel are especially important. Maintenance and repair firms, for example, must avoid having too few repairmen but cannot afford to have idle repairmen on the payroll either.

A third effect of intangibility is that consumers have difficulty judging quality and value of some services. This is true not only before a transaction but also, in many cases, after the service is performed. If you have used a tax preparation service, for instance, did you wonder whether they did a good job? Did the thought cross your mind that the tax service might have overcharged you?

People can get by without getting their cars washed, without patronizing an amusement park or campground, or without having a family portrait taken at a photo studio. Products, on the other hand, more often are essential—food, clothing, furniture, and health care products, in particular. Because many service purchases are discretionary, they can be postponed. If the money situation is tight, you can wait a little longer before going on a vacation. This means a delay in the likely purchases of automotive services, lodging, food, and perhaps recreation services.

DISCRETIONARY EXPENDITURE

As an alternative to postponing the purchase, consumers may substitute their own efforts or purchased products for the primary service, as, for example, when an amateur photographer develops film at home. One report suggested when substitution is greatest: "During periods of economic uncertainty, people tend to substitute products for services—otherwise known as do-it-yourselfism."[10]

The substitution alternative really hurts service establishments since revenue is reduced. Thus, the selling task for many service establishments is twofold: (1) convincing consumers of the benefits of spending money to have something done or to do something and (2) indicating why the purchase should be made *now*.

In services retailing, two forms of convenience are important to consumers: convenience of performance and convenience of purchase. Convenience of performance represents a basic reason for the purchase of primary services:

DESIRE FOR CONVENIENCE

> In spite of the growth of 'do-it-yourself' activities, many people prefer the convenience of hiring service firms to wash their automobiles, shine and repair their shoes, repair their appliances, shampoo and curl their hair, and clean and mend their clothing rather than perform those services for themselves."[11]

Of course, consumers also must have the spending power to purchase these primary services.

Convenience of purchase, the other form, has three components: location, time, and payment. To compete successfully, a service establishment ordinarily must be located close to potential customers, be open when consumers want to purchase the service, and offer credit so that payment is easy. Thus primary services provide a consumer with convenient performance, which usually must be accompanied by convenience of purchase.

As contrasted with the retailing of most products, services retailing *requires* a close relationship between seller and customer. The relationship is close in that the customer often plays a part in production, while the seller personally can affect the amount of satisfaction provided by the offering.

CLOSE SELLER-CUSTOMER RELATIONSHIP

Several factors account for this close relationship. First, one person often is both producer and marketer (or at least salesperson) for a primary

Distinctive Features of Services Retailing

service. Second, a service is frequently produced and sold simultaneously. Third, in many cases, performance of the service is carried out in the buyer's presence. Finally, in some service transactions the consumer "figuratively or literally places himself 'in the hand' of the seller."[12]

Consider instructional services, such as dancing or pilot lessons, in terms of the factors above. The instructor does the teaching (the production task), of course, usually informs the student of further needs, schedules additional lessons, and often rings up the customer's payment (the selling tasks). Because the customer often is present when the service is performed, he becomes involved in the process—directly or indirectly. For example, a dance student gives the instructor information on previous dancing experience; a laundromat customer does some of the work. Customer involvement suggests two "musts" for a service establishment. First, the outlet's atmosphere must be attractive and suitable to the nature of the service. Second, the service establishment's representative must ask the customer for information that may help in performing the service well.

The most important consequence of this close relationship is that the producer-seller has a very demanding role. To carry out this dual role effectively requires technical skills connected with production of the service *and* understanding and communicating with people. These abilities largely determine how much satisfaction the customer receives.

Characteristics of Service Establishments

Two particular characteristics help explain why many service establishments operate as they do. These characteristics are their generally small size, in terms of both capital and sales volume, and the labor-intensive nature of the business.

SMALL SIZE

A small firm cannot afford much research, substantial advertising, or managers who are specialists in different business operations. This means that service establishments generally rely on intuitive decisions or experience, rather simple retailing mixes and word-of-mouth promotion, and the skills of the owner-manager and perhaps key employees in the dual roles of producer-seller. As a result, many service establishments are hard pressed to compete profitably with retail chains which sell services in their stores.

LABOR-INTENSIVE OPERATIONS

Service establishments are more "people" oriented than are manufacturers or product retailers. That is, relatively large numbers of employees and small amounts of machinery, specialized equipment, and fixtures are required. While merchandise retailing is quite labor-intensive compared to manufacturing, services retailing is even more so.

Quite simply, some services—such as repairs and taking care of children—cannot be performed by machines. Even when mechanization is possible, people are needed to operate the machines and to run the business.

A labor-intensive business faces control and cost problems. First, since they have minds of their own, people often are hard to satisfy and reluctant to follow directions. This can make life difficult for a service establishment manager. Second, in times of rising prices, the cost of employees (their wages) ordinarily goes up faster than the cost of machinery or equipment. This is another headache for the manager of a service establishment.

REVIEW BOX 24:2

1. Intangibility is the most important characteristic of primary services; another characteristic discussed is _____.
2. Post-purchase doubt is especially common after purchase of a primary service because _____.
3. Generally, service establishments are (a) small in size and (b) _____, which means that _____.

IMPROVEMENTS IN SERVICES RETAILING

Thus far, we have looked at certain shortcomings in services retailing and at the distinctive features of services and service establishments which partially explain the shortcomings and suggest the difficulties connected with services retailing. Now the question becomes: What has been done or can be done to improve services retailing? Any such improvement should increase customer satisfaction or efficiency of the service firm. Ideally, both would be achieved.

Elimination of Shortcomings

Earlier, four specific shortcomings in services retailing were discussed: incompetent performance, misapplication of the marketing concept, lack of research, and promotion deficiencies. Steps to overcome these problems cover four basic areas:

1. An emphasis on consumer orientation *and* profitability. The marketing concept, which these two dimensions represent, should guide a service establishment's operations. Note that the concept is a blend of two dimensions, not just the notion of "The Customer Is King" or a goal of "Profits at Any Cost." In banking, for example, the following approach has been recommended: "We must deal with customers in a warm and human way and be attuned to their needs, but we must also keep our attention focused on their potential profitability."[13]

SPOTLIGHT

Does the government have to run the automotive repair industry?

When their cars developed trouble between Las Vegas and Los Angeles, many motorists stopped at a particular gas station in the desert. Quite often, the owner or his mechanic diagnosed the trouble as a faulty alternator or regulator, important parts in a car but unrelated to the common desert driving problem of overheating. The usual repair bill: around $100. Eventually, a motorist who knew the only thing wrong with her car was one loose sparkplug wire drove into the station and said she had engine problems. The mechanic installed a used alternator, telling the customer it was a new one, and billed her $99.75.

The catch was that this particular motorist worked for a relatively new California state agency charged with controlling fraud in the auto repair business. As a result, both the owner and his mechanic were fined on fraud and other charges, and the station owner faced a ban from the auto repair business in California.

According to many observers, "rip-offs" of motorists by auto repair firms occur countless times each day. In 1972, for instance, Senator Philip Hart of Michigan estimated that the American public was being cheated out of $8 billion to $10 billion a year on car repairs. Besides creating obvious problems for consumers, the fraud uncovered in the auto repair business has made life difficult for the many skilled, honest auto repairmen. They have to deal with potential customers who not only are aggravated because of the need for repairs but also have stereotyped repairmen as crooks or bunglers—or both.

To protect consumers and the skilled, honest repair firms from the "bad eggs," California has established a Bureau of Automotive Repair. It apparently met a real need, as it was swamped with more than 17,000 complaints in its first eight months. When it finds sufficient cause, the bureau can suspend or revoke a repair firm's license or go to court seeking penalties of up to six months in jail and a $1,000 fine. According to the bureau's first director, the agency is more interested in compliance with the law than in prosecution. Therefore, it often functions as a "marriage counselor," bringing the repair firm and customer back together to work out a settlement. In some cases, the director noted, the bureau's investigation establishes that the customer was in error or was trying to "rip off" the firm.

To restore consumer confidence and establish satisfying transactions as the rule rather than exception in the auto repair field, improved retailing efforts, self-regulation among repair firms, and—for the time being, apparently—governmental supervision are needed.

Source: Adapted from James E. Bylin, "If California Garage Bills You $90 for Flat, It's in Trouble, Too," reprinted with permission of *The Wall Street Journal,* © Dow Jones & Company, Inc., 1973. Senator Hart's estimate was contained in Lynne Olson, "Senate Investigator Is Coauthor of Book on 'Auto Repair Robbery'," *Sunday Herald-Leader,* Lexington, Ky., October 1, 1972.

2. Conducting informal or formal research, as practical. A bank that had been burned by too little research began to conduct some research. For example, a thorough study of the youth market indicated that these customers were irritated by high minimum balances on checking accounts and what they thought to be unrealistic credit standards for loans and credit cards. Armed with these facts, the bank modified its youth market strategy, and it now offers low-cost checking plus easier loan and credit arrangements. The bank estimates that its share of the youth market has risen substantially as a result of the modifications suggested by research.[14]

   Research is appropriate—necessary, in fact—for new or soon-to-open service firms as well as successful ones. Persons planning to start a service establishment have special information needs. According to one article, the major cause of business failure, improper planning, "can be overcome by a detailed appraisal of alternative available retail sites, a proper estimation of the total market potential of a given trading area, and a realistic division of the potential among the existing competitive structure."[15]

3. Periodic employee training. New employee training, a must, should cover the *how* and *why* of performing the service and dealing with customers. Periodically, all employees of a service establishment should receive training which checks their necessary skills and upgrades them.

4. Honesty in dealings, with no exceptions. Although this step obviously is essential to long-term success, abuses in certain fields dictate that it be mentioned. Repair fraud has become prevalent enough that some states have enacted specific laws and established agencies aimed at curbing these abuses. For example, California has two agencies charged with overseeing TV-radio-phonograph repairmen and auto repair outlets.

   Because consumers have become aware of the presence of dishonest businessmen, service firms must be completely honest with customers to avoid acquiring a reputation as being dishonest or "shady." Also, they should report dishonest competitors to the appropriate agency. Dishonest firms not only make consumers reluctant to spend money on services but also, in essence, steal sales and profits away from honest firms.

AGGRESSIVE MEASURES

Beyond the basic steps above, a service establishment can move aggressively to improve its operations. Being aggressive in retailing means doing two things: actively seeking, rather than waiting for, new opportunities for profitably satisfying present and potential customers; and making, rather than meeting, competition in the sense of being innovative. This means being the first or one of the first firms to adopt a new service offering or operating method.

Four particular measures are aggressive, in the above sense. Although the following improvements are "easier said than done," they deserve serious consideration by service establishments.

1. Market segmentation. As we have discussed, no retailer can satisfy all consumers. It is more realistic to identify a group of consumers not fully satisfied with present offerings and then put together a more satisfying retailing mix for them. This is known as market segmentation.

   The Marriott Corporation has applied this technique: "The company has crowded the highways with a variety of eating places in much the same way that detergent makers crowd supermarket shelves with a host of products, each aimed at a specific type of buyer."[16] Thus, Marriott's restaurants along the East Coast range from the classy Joshua Tree Steak House to Jr. Hot Shoppes with their low-price hamburgers. Similarly, banks have identified segments with special desires—such as college students or retired persons—and then tailored retailing mixes to their needs.

2. Development of a differential advantage. This should follow market segmentation. Recall that a retail firm must distinguish itself from competitors by offering consumers some benefit or set of benefits not available from other retailers. Among the possibilities are low prices, extremely convenient location, and helpful sales personnel. Having come up with a differential advantage, the firm should promote it to consumers.

   These two techniques are neither new nor highly sophisticated. However, they have often been overlooked in services retailing. When applied properly, they can make a major contribution.

3. Mechanization. In some situations, greater efficiencies or customer satisfaction will result if machines are substituted for labor in services retailing. This result is most likely if employees are not performing well or if they become very expensive.

   Various machines which aid in the production of services have been developed. Machines can wax cars, vacuum clipped hair, or develop film, to cite several examples. It is possible, however, to go too far or too fast with mechanization. For once thing, consumers may get less satisfaction from being served by a machine than by a person. Or consumers may feel that machines do not perform the service as well.

4. Franchise operations. Services retailing can be improved through franchising basically because the owner-manager of the establishment receives help in developing a retailing mix and in financial and personnel management. For instance, the manager and perhaps key

employees receive training in how to perform the service and conduct an efficient business. The franchisee is also supplied with forms and procedures for carrying out specialized functions such as inventory control, purchasing, and bookkeeping. Franchisors even perform some functions for franchisees for a fee.

Besides reducing personnel inadequacies, a franchise package can reduce the communications gap. The franchisor conducts necessary research and then develops a suitable retailing mix for franchisees. A franchisee's training prior to opening the establishment ordinarily covers personal selling techniques as well as methods for training employees in customer relations.

By no means is franchising a "can't miss" way of improving services retailing—some service franchises have faltered or totally failed. But since franchising can, in fact, minimize various shortcomings connected with services retailing, many small firms have purchased franchises. At the same time, service firms or chains of some size have utilized franchising to open additional outlets.

Many kinds of primary services are retailed through franchises. Holiday Inns of America, H & R Block tax preparation, AAMCO transmission repair shops, Weight Watchers International, 60 Minute Systems dry-cleaning outlets, and Postal Instant Press printing shops are among the numerous franchise systems in the services field. Others include Budget Rent-a-Car, Kampgrounds of America, Duraclean carpet and upholstery cleaning, United Rent-All rental centers, Putt-Putt Golf Courses, and Lawn-a-Mat lawn and garden care.

It is no coincidence that franchising has grown tremendously at the same time that consumers are spending larger sums on primary services. There is a natural "marriage" between services retailing and franchising in that franchise operations can increase customer satisfaction and efficiency of the service firm.

REVIEW BOX 24:3

1. One step that can be taken to overcome problems connected with services retailing is to emphasize consumer orientation *and* profitability; another is _____.
2. One way in which a service establishment can move aggressively to improve its operations is to use _____.
3. Various shortcomings common in services retailing can be eliminated or avoided through franchise operations because the franchisee receives _____.

CHAPTER SUMMARY

- Primary services are want-satisfying intangibles which are the object of a transaction between a business firm and either an ultimate consumer, another business firm, or an institution.
- Various kinds of retail firms sell primary services. A retail outlet which gets the majority of its sales volume from primary services is called a retail service establishment.
- Since the end of World War II, consumers have substantially increased their relative expenditures on services. In 1973, more than 40 cents of every consumer dollar was spent on services.
- The following shortcomings have hampered the effective retailing of various services: incompetent performance, misapplication of the marketing concept, and a communications gap. The gap means that service establishments often do not obtain from consumers the information needed to develop a retailing mix, or they do not provide consumers with enough information about the firm's offerings.
- Several characteristics of services affect the retailing requirements for them: intangibility, discretionary nature of expenditure, the desire for convenience, and the close seller-customer relationship. Two characteristics of service establishments help explain why they operate as they do: their generally small size and the labor-intensive nature of the business.
- Among the steps service firms have taken to overcome shortcomings are: emphasizing consumer orientation *and* profitability, conducting research as practical, training employees periodically, and being honest in their dealings.
- Besides trying to overcome shortcomings, a service establishment can take more aggressive measures to improve operations: market segmentation, development of a differential advantage, and mechanization.
- Franchise operations are another possible means of improving services retailing in that the service franchisee receives a package of help in developing a retailing mix and also in financial and personnel management.

CHAPTER NOTES

[1] E. B. Weiss, "The Next Wave of Discount Mavericks," *Advertising Age*, March 19, 1962, p. 92.
[2] The 1947 figure is from *Business Statistics: 1969* (a biennial supplement to *Survey of Current Business*), p. 1; the 1969 and 1973 figures are from *Survey of Current Business*, February 1970, p. 8 and February 1974, p. 12.
[3] "Motor-Home Sales Build Up Speed," *Business Week*, April 29, 1972, p. 46.
[4] Marcy Kates, "Do You Look Good in Purple and Puce?" *Wall Street Journal*, August 6, 1973, p. 1.
[5] James E. Bylin, "If California Garage Bills You $90 for Flat, It's in Trouble, Too," *Wall Street Journal*, March 29, 1973, p. 10.
[6] Donald D. Parker, *The Marketing of Consumer Services* (Seattle: Bureau of Business Research, University of Washington, 1960), p. 137.
[7] Richard H. Brien and James E. Stafford, "The Myth of Marketing in Banking," *Business Horizons*, Spring 1967, p. 72.
[8] "Now Banks Are Turning to the Hard Sell," *Business Week*, June 24, 1972, p. 82.
[9] Parker, *op. cit.*, p. 33.
[10] This point and other insights regarding the services boom and related problems are contained in "Services Grow While the Quality Shrinks," *Business Week*, October 30, 1971, pp. 50–51ff.
[11] Parker, *op. cit.*, p. 137.
[12] John M. Rathmell, "What Is Meant by Services?" *Journal of Marketing*, October 1966, p. 34.
[13] "Banking Calls for Realism: Interview," *Banking*, June 1966, p. 69.
[14] "Now Banks Are Turning to the Hard Sell," *Business Week*, June 24, 1972, p. 82.
[15] Charles T. Moore and Joseph B. Mason, "What Is the Market for Your Services?" *Journal of Small Business Management*, April 1970, p. 25.
[16] "Marriott Tries Its Trick on New Ventures," *Business Week*, June 17, 1972, p. 61.

QUESTIONS AND ASSIGNMENTS

1. a. What are a retail firm's three possible offerings to consumers?
   b. Can a retailer offer a combination of all three offerings? If no, explain. If yes, cite two actual retailers who do this.
2. Explain specifically why you agree or disagree with the following statement: "Services are services—all of them are pretty similar to each other. For instance, hair styling is basically the same type of offering as clothing alterations provided by a clothing store. And both of these are similar to repairs of, say, appliances."
3. When a firm adopts the marketing concept, what two factors are emphasized? Explain the two shortcomings of some service firms with respect to the marketing concept. Can you point to any service establishments in your community that you feel have made these errors?
4. "Service establishments are relatively small businesses; research is expensive; therefore, service establishments can't conduct research." True or false? Explain.
5. a. What is intangibility?
   b. Describe at least two ways in which intangibility affects how services are retailed.

6. How would you respond to the following statement: "Running a small service establishment is tough indeed because of employee problems. But I've come up with a solution—I'm going to replace most of them with machines. The way I figure it, most of my problems will leave with the employees."
7. Talk with the manager of a service establishment in your community about the techniques of market segmentation and differential advantage (which the manager may call by different names). Have these measures been attempted in this business? If not, why not? If they have, what does the manager consider to be the establishment's differential advantage? Do you agree? If the manager has used the technique of market segmentation, are there any plans for modifying the target markets or retailing mix in the near future?
8. Discuss franchising with the manager of an independent service firm. Does the manager feel that retailing efforts would be improved by a franchise? If not, what are the advantages of independent operation for this manager? If so, what improvements would result *and* why hasn't a franchise been purchased?

ANSWERS TO REVIEW BOX QUESTIONS

Box 24:1

1. intangibility
2. ignore or confuse the factor of consumer orientation
3. the communications gap; lack of research and promotion deficiencies

Box 24:2

1. One of the following: discretionary nature of expenditure, desire for convenience, close seller-customer relationship
2. consumers have difficulty judging quality and value due to the intangibility characteristic
3. labor-intensive operations; relatively large numbers of employees but small amounts of machinery, specialized equipment, and fixtures are involved

Box 24:3

1. One of the following: to conduct research as practical, to conduct periodic employee training, to be honest in dealings
2. One of the following: market segmentation, development of a differential advantage, or mechanization
3. help in developing a retailing mix and in financial and personnel management

RETAILING DECISION
Friendly Supermarkets, Inc.

Jan Imes is quickly glancing through the morning mail, a daily ritual with an eye-opener cup of coffee. Jan manages a Friendly Supermarket in a community of 60,000, which is the home of a growing 15,000-student university. There is another Friendly store across town, and a third on the drawing board.

The following memo from Bob Angin, president of Friendly Supermarkets, catches Jan's eye:

FRIENDLY SUPERMARKETS, INC.
Fine quality . . . Fair prices . . . and the familiar, fast Friendly service

TO: Jan Imes and Troy Harris
FROM: Bob Angin
SUBJECT: Proposed strategy change

As we have discussed, I'm concerned about whether our present merchandising strategy will work for us in the future. I wonder whether our unmatched assortment of quality groceries and competitive prices will be effective, considering changing market conditions. The consumerism movement — concern about nutrition, trading stamps, freshness, inflation, and so forth — seems to particularly affect grocery retailing.

The article I've enclosed suggests a new Friendly strategy that I'd like your reaction to. We already offer open dating and nutritional labeling, and I propose that we begin to offer the other nine services listed here.

Please give some serious thought to this matter, and we'll discuss it at our regular Monday meeting.

Jan skims the article, making mental notes of the 11 services discussed:

1. Case lots of produce at one-third off.
2. Wholesale meat, cut to the customer's needs, at discount prices.
3. A home economist in the store to answer questions on nutrition, cooking, new products — over coffee.
4. Nutritional labeling that includes explanations of all additives.
5. Open dating on all foods.
6. No price increases for items already on the shelves.
7. Discounts for senior citizens.
8. Free pamphlets on nutrition, cooking, best buys, meal planning, food storage.
9. A choice of foods with or without certain chemical additives.
10. Computerized checkout systems.
11. A consumer board to provide a line of communication between shoppers and store management.

Jan jots down a few other relevant facts presented: First, each of these services is already available in one or more supermarkets or chains of markets. Second, while some consumer services are still experimental, others — for example, unit pricing, open dating, and uniform meat labeling — are becoming standard practices, and nutritional labeling is required by law as of January 1, 1975.

The article referred to is "Consumerism Coming to Market" by Marilynn Marter of Knight Newspapers, *Sunday Herald-Leader*, Lexington, Ky., August 4, 1974, p. D-14.

1. In Jan Imes' position, what would you recommend to Mr. Angin?
2. What other information would you want, if you had to decide whether to offer the new services?

RETAILING DECISION
TLC Auto Repair

With 14 full-time mechanics, TLC Auto Repair was the largest, or perhaps second largest, auto maintenance and repair firm in the city of Los Arcos. The owner, Vincent Luston, took great pride in the growth of his firm and also in his efforts to provide his customers' cars with TLC (tender lovin' care). But he was concerned that with 22 employees (3 service advisors, 2 cashiers, 2 janitor/drivers, and a newly hired business manager in addition to the mechanics), TLC would be harder to provide than it had been when the firm consisted of himself and six mechanics.

Because of his worries over the effects of growth on the TLC that had produced many regular customers, Luston was very receptive to the suggestion of Manuel Tember, the new business manager, that they discuss the matter of customer service. A recent business school graduate, Tember had been hired to handle the financial and marketing aspects of the business. This permitted Luston to supervise the mechanics and to oversee personnel matters and customer relations (primarily, responding to complaints). Tember had this to say:

"Recently, I've noticed more customers griping about their bills when they get them from the cashier. For example, one guy about my age said, 'Well you could've expected it would be higher than the unofficial estimate.' Also, it seems that more people are calling with questions about their bills after they get home. Overall, our customers don't show many signs of being satisfied with our work.

"I think we need some follow-up with our customers to assure them of our interest in doing the repairs or maintenance work to their full satisfaction. For customers with bills of less than $50, I propose we send them a letter the day after they pick up their car. The letter would be individually addressed and typed but would follow a standard format—basically thanking them for their patronage, reminding them about our extra TLC steps, and giving them the name and phone number of a service advisor to call if they're not completely satisfied. When the bill is over $50, I propose that you or I phone them the day after and say the same things contained in the standard letter. If customers feel the TLC has disappeared, they just may not come back."

1. Should Luston use Tember's follow-up plan? If he should, which of the two suggested forms of follow-up do you feel will be more effective in assuring customers of the firm's quality work? If not, what are the problems with the proposal?
2. In either case, what changes should be made before a follow-up plan is implemented? Are there any other possible forms of follow-up?

PART EIGHT

Beyond In-Store Retailing Today

Non-Store Retailing

The emphasis in this book is on the institution that comes to most people's minds when the word retailing is mentioned—the retail store However, many final sales of products and services are made in places other than stores: over the telephone, through the mail, in buyers' homes, and from machines. These retailing methods account for such a large volume of retail sales that they deserve consideration in a separate chapter.

To begin with, non-store retailing must be defined. *Non-store retailing* is any purchase of goods or services for personal consumption that takes place beyond the premises of the seller. Thus, the purchase of gasoline at a service station would be classified as in-store retailing, since the pumps are on the seller's premises. On the other hand, buying cigarettes from a vending machine would be non-store retailing if the machine is owned by a vending company.

For our discussion, non-store retailing will be divided into *personal, non-store*, which includes telephone sales and in-home sales, and *non-personal, non-store* which includes mail order, catalog sales, and machine vending. There are other types of non-store retailing, for example, a roasted chestnut vendor on a street corner or a souvenir salesman outside a football stadium, but the types discussed here account for the majority of sales.

PERSONAL, NON-STORE RETAILING

Personal, non-store retailing includes telephone sales and sales made in a buyer's home. The key word, of course, is *personal*. There is face-to-face or at least voice contact between buyer and seller, even though the purchase does not occur in a store.

Telephone Sales

Telephone sales can be made by retailers who have an outlet or by firms that do not have an outlet. In the first case, the retailer is attempting to generate additional sales from potential customers who for some reason cannot or do not want to visit the store. The telephone salesman without a store, the second case, does not account for a large volume of retail sales, but since this may be the forerunner of an important retailing development, it is worth noting.

FROM A RETAIL STORE

For a retailer with a store, telephone sales can be generated three ways: (1) through advertising; (2) as a result of customer experience and confidence in the store; and (3) by salespeople calling special customers when there is slack time on the sales floor. (Do not confuse this with *telephone sales promotion* in which a salesperson makes calls in the hope of attracting customers to the store with such information as the arrival of new merchandise or an upcoming sale.)

Generated by Advertising. Retailers frequently include the note "telephone orders accepted" in local advertising. This offer makes the advertised product available to customers who are not able to visit the store. The popularity of telephone orders is apparent in the fact that many retailers point out in their advertising for special sales that telephone sales will not be accepted due to the limited quantities of merchandise or the additional burden it places on sales personnel.

The credit card has greatly increased the opportunity for telephone sales. By having a customer read the account number over the phone, a store can verify the purchaser's identity and credit status. When the merchandise is sent to the address recorded for the account, there is little chance of the credit card's being fraudulently used. In addition, it makes customer's purchases easy, since the transaction is simply added to the credit account.

Generated by Experience. Some consumers prefer to buy standardized merchandise by telephone. For example, rather than visit a grocery store, some people prefer to call their orders in and have the groceries delivered. Although the cost is usually higher (since only small stores with higher average prices handle such sales) and the customer pays a delivery charge, the convenience outweighs the cost for some people. Other types of retailing in which telephone orders frequently combined with delivery are common include florists, drug stores, and carry-out restaurants such as pizza parlors.

Generated by Salespeople. Many retailers, especially exclusive specialty stores, expect their salespeople to maintain a list of preferred customers and their needs. When something the customer has been looking for comes in, or when the salesperson sees an item the customer might like, the salesperson calls and offers to send the merchandise out "on approval." On receiving the merchandise, the customer either agrees with the salesperson's selection and pays for it or returns it.

This can be an effective way of increasing sales, but it must be done very carefully. First, the store should have the customer's advance approval for such calls. Second, the salesperson must use discretion in sending merchandise, since too much returned merchandise becomes expensive for the store and an irritation to the customer. In most cases, this procedure would be appropriate for only a small number of customers with whose taste the salesperson is very familiar.

There are several reasons why consumers may prefer buying by phone rather than visiting a retail store. Among the most common are:

1. Lack of transportation to and from the store
2. Illness or physical disability
3. Lack of time or the desire for convenience
4. Dislike of congestion, shopping, or waiting to be served

From a retailer's standpoint, telephone orders are attractive first because the majority of them are additional sales. That is, if not made by telephone, the sale would not have occurred. Second, individual telephone orders may be larger than sales floor orders. In the case of a department store, the customer consolidates several items into one call that would involve several individual purchases if they were made in the store. This reduces paperwork and therefore saves money for the retailer.

WITHOUT A RETAIL STORE Telephone sales made by retailers without stores presently account for only a small percentage of all sales but have excellent growth potential. Currently this type of retailing is limited to undifferentiated goods (like milk or eggs) or branded goods (like golf or tennis balls) for which there is repeat demand.

This kind of retailer usually advertises locally, possibly using classified newspaper ads, then responds to calls by interested consumers. The only investments are a telephone, advertising, the stock of merchandise, and a means of delivery.

Growth of this type of retailing depends upon technological developments in the areas of picturephones, which would enable consumers to see a seller and the merchandise, and cable television, which may provide commercial channels on which such a retailer could advertise locally. Since this type of operation requires little overhead, consumers can be offered a considerable price savings. The biggest handicap is the image of instability or a "fly-by-night" operation. As consumers see more and more of this type of retailing, this problem should become less significant.

To contrast these two methods, the major differences between telephone selling by retailers with stores and by those without stores are summarized in Table 25-1. Note that even though both use the telephone for selling, the characteristics are quite different from the consumer's viewpoint and from the retailer's.

TABLE 25-1

Characteristics of Telephone Sales

	From stores	*Not from stores*
Proportion of sales	Additional sales	Total sales
Prices	Sometimes higher than in store	Lower than in store
Image	Tied to store	Uncertain
Investment	Low	Low
Future	Growth depends on retailers' efforts	Growth depends on technological developments

In-Home Retailing

A surprising number of retail transactions take place in or at consumers' homes. Included in this category are door-to-door sales, party selling, custom selling, and route sales.

Door-to-door sales (D-T-D) include all types of product and service transactions in which a seller calls on a consumer at home and attempts to make the sale there. The variety of goods and services in this category is very broad, including insurance, mutual funds, cosmetics, encyclopedias, vacuum cleaners, and many others. Such well-known firms as Electrolux, Fuller Brush, Stanley Products, and Avon use D-T-D as their sole or major method of distribution.

One approach in D-T-D sales is to have a salesperson visit homes within a prescribed area on a random basis hoping to find an individual with a need and relying on his ability to convince the consumer that the company's product or service will fill the need. This is called "cold canvassing." Another approach is to have salespeople call on individuals who have been referred or who have indicated an interest in the product or service through responses to ads or requests for information.

Two types of products seem to be best suited for D-T-D selling. First are

DOOR-TO-DOOR SALES

Personal, Non-Store Retailing

"Our ad said no *salesman* would call — I am a consumer Advisory Consultant!"

© Wall Street Journal, 1974

FIGURE 25-1

products that require extensive demonstration because they have benefits that may not be immediately obvious (cookware, cosmetics), or they are complex and therefore difficult for a consumer to appreciate (vacuum cleaners, sewing machines). Second are unsought goods or products for which consumers do not recognize a need (reference books, insurance, mutual funds). In both cases a concentrated, uninterrupted selling effort is needed. The home usually provides an ideal setting for such an effort.

D-T-D selling has developed an unsavory reputation in recent years as a result of the unscrupulous tactics of some firms and the behavior of particular salespeople. Some salespeople deceive consumers and "get a foot in the door" by introducing themselves as market researchers collecting information. After asking a few meaningless questions, they begin the sales pitch. Other firms use brand names on their product similar to the names of well-known, reputable brands. Thus, the consumer thinks he is getting the established quality brand but ends up with an inferior product. Some D-T-D salesmen have contributed to the negative image of the industry by using "hard sell" tactics, unsubstantiated claims about product quality or guarantees, and misleading statements. Though these tactics are limited to only a small segment of the industry, the bad publicity has negatively affected all D-T-D distributors. Figure 25-1 depicts the unscrupulous salesman — and the expression on the lady's face reflects the reaction of most consumers to this type of practice.

CUSTOM SELLING

Some products and services are custom made at a consumer's home. This includes all types of home decorating and home improvement products and services, carpet vans (a truck filled with carpet samples that comes to the consumer's home), home roofing and storm gutters, heating and air conditioning, and lawn care, among others.

Firms in these types of businesses generate sales in several ways. One way is simply responding to the requests of potential customers who see the firm's ad in a newspaper or telephone book yellow pages. A second source of business is referrals from satisfied customers. Finally, for firms dealing in products or services visible from outside the home (gutters, roofs, lawns), simply driving or walking through neighborhoods and calling on homeowners obviously in need of the service or product is a third method.

Again, the opportunity for abuses exist in this type of selling. For example, in product areas where consumers have little knowledge (roofing, furnaces), some firms offer "free inspections" and invariably "find" something that needs repair or replacing. These few dishonest businesses have damaged the entire industry's reputation.

ROUTE SALES

Route salespeople travel a specified itinerary either selling merchandise on a scheduled basis (dairy products) or on a demand basis (bakery goods). Besides dairy products and bakery goods, other types of products sold on routes include potato chips, spices and condiments, and services such as laundry and dry cleaning. Because a consumer usually pays a slightly higher price for the convenience of buying this way, major ingredients of success are constant quality and reliable availability. If customers cannot be assured that the bread or pastry will be fresh or that the milkman will always arrive before a certain time in the morning, they will not continue to want these services.

Because of the personnel and operating equipment costs associated with route sales, many companies have discontinued this method of retailing and rely entirely on in-store sales. Others have responded to the increased costs by redefining their objective. For example, the president of H. P. Hood and Sons, Inc., the country's largest regional dairy, describes the milkman as potentially a "major marketing vehicle for all kinds of goods and services."[1] In line with this definition, Hood milkmen have distributed Jewel Co. catalogs, margarine samples for Lever Bros., and candy bars for Quaker Oats. Another firm, Foremost Dairy Products, has had its San Francisco "milkmen" selling panty hose, garbage pails, laundry detergent, toys, and candy in addition to their traditional products.

PARTY SELLING

In this type of in-home selling, a person invites several friends to his or her home to listen to a sales presentation. The party atmosphere is encouraged by party games, door prizes, and refreshments as well as the normal small talk and socializing. As an incentive, the hostess receives a gift for having

SPOTLIGHT

Are there opportunities left in non-store retailing?

As the following example quoted from *Business Week* illustrates, the future seems limited only by the imagination of the seller.

To most motorists, stopping at a gas station is a pain. The tank inevitably runs low when you are running late. Now a new company called North American Suburban Corp. has begun bringing the service station to the car.

For no more than a motorist pays at a gas station, a North American service truck will visit his company parking lot and — going by a coded bumper sticker — will gas up his car with regular or premium, check the oil, tire wear and pressure, battery, and radiator, clean the headlights and windshield and even fill the windshield washer tank. By acting as both distributor and retailer and chopping out the overhead of gas stations and attendants, North American claims that it can match station prices of the larger oil companies and turn an even tidier profit.

Something extra. At the same time, North American, which projects a gross volume of $800,000 this year, offers something else. "Industry is more and more concerned about the good and welfare of its employees," says Richard B. April, North American's president and chief operating officer. "Now we offer the company a new fringe benefit which it can promote as a special service and convenience. And it doesn't cost the company a cent."

The key is volume. "If we can get about 15 cars in a single lot," says Stuart D. Baker, North American's chairman, "then we can make money on that particular operation."

In Greensboro, N. C., where North American just wound up a test run, the company started out with only six or eight cars in each of two company parking lots. Today, North American is up to 25% to 30% of each lot — or about 100 cars — and has expanded into 30 or so additional lots with a total of more than 550 customers. This week, the company is lining up customers for a move into the metropolitan New York market.

Eventually, North American plans to go nationwide. "But you have to pick your markets carefully," says April. "It takes much more than simply heavy concentrations of industry and parking lots to make our business. The gas market has to be just right. Take Detroit. The margins are extremely thin there, and we would think long and hard before tackling that area." In the meantime, plenty of other markets beckon.

Source: "Bringing the Gas Station to the Car" Reprinted from the October 31, 1971 issue of *Business Week* by special permission. © 1971 by McGraw-Hill, Inc.

the party and often receives additional merchandise if a certain number of people come to the party or if a minimum level of sales is made. In party selling a salesperson uses a well-planned, often humorous (to fit the party atmosphere) presentation. Because scheduling future parties depends upon referrals from those at the party, a "soft sell" technique is usually employed.

Miracle Maid, a cookware firm, believes its products must be "seen in action" to be properly appreciated. Thus, their salespeople are trained to prepare and serve a complete meal and clean up afterwards in order to demonstrate the merchandise and also provide an incentive for the hostess.

It is interesting that party selling is aimed predominantly at women and is generally limited to kitchen products or jewelry. Other potential markets, including teenagers (clothing, records, jewelry) and men (golf and tennis equipment, lawn care products), have been virtually ignored. Possibly some entrepreneur will come along with the right product and a party selling approach as a method of competing in one of these markets.

REVIEW BOX 25:1

1. The two types of personal, non-store retailing are telephone sales and _____.
2. Telephone sales for a retail store can be generated through advertising, salespeople, and _____.
3. The four types of in-home retailing are door-to-door, custom selling, party selling, and _____.

NON-PERSONAL, NON-STORE RETAILING

The term *non-personal, non-store* means that the sale takes place somewhere other than in a retailer's store and there is no direct contact between seller and customer. The three types of retailing in this category are mail order, catalog, and vending.

Mail Order Sales

Mail order selling is a retailing technique in which the contact between the seller and the consumer is by means of the mail or a combination of mail and some common carrier. The buyer orders and pays for the merchandise by mail, and the seller ships the goods to him. Mail order should not be confused with *direct mail advertising* in which a seller solicits business by mailing advertisements to potential customers. Although mail order firms use direct mail advertising, so do all other types of retailers, including department and specialty stores, supermarkets, and discount houses.

WHAT MAIL ORDER OFFERS

Mail order selling has several distinct differences from other types of retailing. The most significant are:

Convenience. A buyer can select a product, pay for it, and receive it without ever leaving home. Thus, the problems of getting to the store, parking, shopping, and congestion are all avoided.

Novelty. Many mail order items are unique. A person interested in custom-made items or personalized objects (engraved or monogrammed) will often find the offerings of mail order firms very attractive.

Lower Prices. Since mail order eliminates the overhead expenses of the retail store and sales personnel, prices including postage are frequently lower than in retail stores.

MAIL ORDER PRODUCTS

Because a seller does not have direct contact with a buyer and since the merchandise must be mailed or transported in some fashion, there are certain constraints on the types of products appropriate for this retailing. Generally, a mail order firm would consider the following in selecting products:

Advertisability. The seller must be able to describe the product and explain its use completely in a brief amount of time or space. Since the advertisement must do the entire selling job, it is important that the product have an attractive advertisable feature.

Exclusiveness. Ordinary or common products can be seen, handled, and bought in retail stores. Mail order products need to be unique or special in some way, possibly through personalization (putting the buyer's name on the product) or through being unavailable anywhere else.

Reliability. A mail order firm cannot afford the cost and confusion associated with the return of defective or unsatisfactory products.

Simplicity. Complex products with many working parts are difficult to advertise and often difficult for the buyer to operate, resulting in complaints and dissatisfaction.

Mailable. Lightweight, durable products that are not too bulky or perishable are ideal for mail order business.

Regularly Purchased. Repeat purchases are important for mail order firms that rely on customer experience and their good reputation for many sales. Certain items like pens and pencils, cigars, and toys are frequently purchased and can result in many repeat sales to satisfied customers.

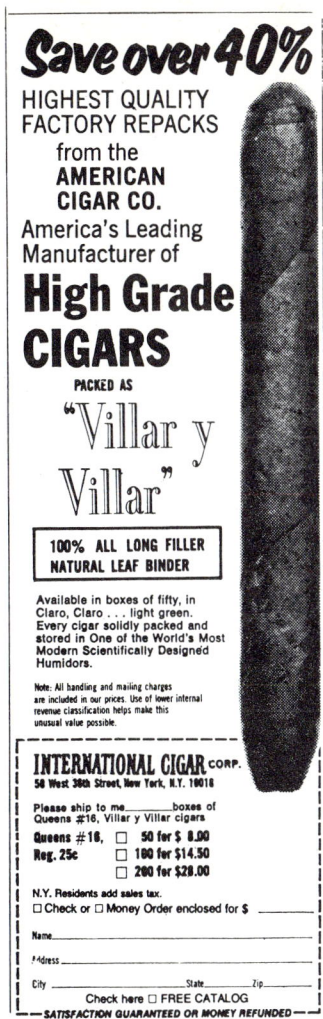

FIGURE 25-2

Typical newspaper ads for mail order products

It should be noted that these are not strict rules. In fact, some exceptions have proven highly successful. For example, the sale of fresh fruit by mail (an exception to the mailable rule) and mail order, ready-to-wear men's clothing (contradicts the exclusiveness rule) might have been rejected if these criteria were always followed. Mail order retailers should evaluate alternative products carefully, because even products meeting all the rules will not always be successful when sold this way.

Non-Personal, Non-Store Retailing

PLANNING MAIL ORDER ADVERTISING

As mentioned above, a critical aspect of mail order selling is advertising. Because a mail order firm must rely *entirely* on advertising to make sales, developing highly effective messages is critical.

Mail order advertisements can be found in most media. Whether on television, radio, in some publication, or mailed directly to consumers, this kind of advertising must combine brevity with a strong selling message. Figure 25-2 illustrates a newspaper ad for a mail order product. Although a wide range of form and sophistication is possible, this is not a project for an inexperienced individual. It requires talented writers and artists. To find the type and quality of work desired, a mail order firm can get in touch with advertising agencies and request proposals, review the advertising of other mail order firms for ideas, and ask non-competing mail order firms to identify reputable and skilled advertising agencies.

Mail order firms advertise in two ways: either through some mass medium (magazines, newspapers, and more recently radio and television) or by direct mail. Since placement of advertising in mass media was discussed in Chapter 16, the comments here are limited to direct mail advertising.

Direct mail advertising is a promotion method in which the seller sends potential customers a letter or circular advertising the merchandise. A principal advantage of direct mail is that more information can be transmitted than through advertising in mass media. It is not uncommon for a direct mail piece to include four or five pages of information. As with all advertising, to be effective, direct mail must get into the hands of potential buyers. Thus, the first task is to decide who the most likely potential buyers are.

Coincidentally with defining the target audience, the seller must develop, rent, or purchase a mailing list. Many mail order firms develop their own lists based upon past sales. However, maintaining quality lists is an expensive, time-consuming job. Thus, especially if they wish to identify special or unique groups, direct mail advertisers frequently rely on *list suppliers*, firms that specialize in providing mailing lists. An amazing number and variety of lists are available for rental. For example, a trade publication, *Direct Marketing*, recently included ads for the following lists: new and expectant mothers, aircraft pilots, new home buyers in Baltimore County, paint-by-the-numbers mail order buyers, mail order grapefruit buyers, mail order garden buyers, and college students, among many others. There are also *list brokers* who seek out the best lists available given a description of the seller's target market. Lists usually can be rented for one to three cents per name for printed mailing labels.

A problem for mail-order retailers has been complaints by consumers over the amount of direct mail advertising they receive. To help solve this problem, the Direct Mail Marketing Association provides a form consumers can request and complete. The completed forms are circulated to the 1800 Association members who delete the consumers' names from their mailing lists. Interestingly, in three years only 29,000 forms have been submitted. A possible reason, suggested by the Association, is that individuals requesting the delisting form are warned that they will probably receive fewer contest offers, product samples, coupons, and catalogs.[2]

Basic components of a direct mail offering include the mailing envelope, the letter, an order form, and incentives. Each serves a distinct purpose important to the success of this promotion method.

Mailing Envelope. Today's consumer often feels swamped by direct mail advertising, most of which gets thrown away unopened. To overcome this problem, a mailing envelope must arouse sufficient interest or curiosity to get the consumer to open it. One method is to make the envelope look like personal mail by using a handwritten or individually typed name and address. Another method is using a "teaser" on the outside of the envelope. Such statements as "free offer inside," "you may already be a winner," or "you owe it to your children to read this" can be sufficient inducements to get the envelope opened.

The Message. Once the recipient opens the envelope, the enclosed message, usually in letter form, must obtain and hold attention. Letters are sometimes two to four pages long, detailing the nature and advantages of the product. Quality of printing and layout and, of course, the message's style and content are critical features. It is in this area where professional copywriters and printers can be of valuable aid. Figure 25-3 illustrates an effective direct mail message.

Because mail order buyers cannot see the actual product prior to purchase, direct mail ads always offer return privileges and guarantees. Many also offer "free home trial." That is, the consumer is allowed to order the merchandise and use it for a short time, usually 7 to 10 days, and then either remit payment or return it.

Order Forms. Since the mail is the only contact the seller has with the potential customer, some method must be available for the consumer to make a purchase. The primary requirement for the order form is that it should be easy for the consumer to use. Self-addressed, postage-paid postcards or envelopes make ordering easy and therefore more likely.

Samples and Incentives. To aid consumers, some mail pieces include samples, and some offer premiums for ordering. A mail order firm selling greeting cards or stationery can include a few samples for a customer's scrutiny. Clothing mail order houses often enclose material swatches so the consumer can get a better feel for the color and fabric. Although samples add to the cost of direct mail, they help convince prospects and reduce the number of returns from customers with incorrect expectations.

Premiums are frequently offered as an inducement to purchases. For example, a menswear mail order firm may allow a customer to choose a belt or tie free with an order of $20 or more. A premium is of little value, however,

The Gasoline Shortage Is No Problem.

It's an opportunity to solve a problem. And that's how we got started. Just a year ago, a group of college students in Fresno, California, began to experiment with a new mode of automobile propulsion.

We designed and constructed a device that actually converts chicken manure and other organic waste materials into methane gas, an efficient, non-polluting and cheap fuel. We've used our own methane gas to power a car, a gas cooking stove and a power lawn mower.

Our experiments and research uncovered some interesting facts and we'd like to pass them along.

There is a huge supply of solid organic waste material in the U.S. One reliable estimate is that 17 trillion cubic feet of methane gas could be produced each year if just half the available feedlot manure in this country were collected and processed.

Smog producing emissions of the gasoline powered engine can be reduced between 72 and 95% by using fuel containing 85% methane gas, according to a recent press release by the Southern California Gas Company.

The conversion process is quite simple. No particular mechanical skill is needed to make a safe, workable automobile conversion. Harold Bate, the British developer of the original Chicken-Powered car estimates the cost at less than $100.00. Our original pilot project cost $83.00.

Motoring on methane offers the economy of converting the equivalent of one gallon of regular gasoline at a cost of 3 cents per gallon.

Well, that's our story in just a few words. As part of our project, we've published the results of our experiments in a book titled *Chicken Doodle*. This is a fully illustrated, highly readable manual written for people who would like to make their own methane conversion or those who would just like to learn more about the subject. The price per copy is $2.25.

Hoping you'll agree that there's no stopping an idea whose time has come, we thank you for your time and interest.

Fresno Methane Systems
811 East Dennett Avenue
Fresno, California 93728

FIGURE 25-3

This well-designed mail order message is interesting, informative, and persuasive.

unless it is (1) something a customer wants (thus, it must be tailored to the needs of the market) and (2) considered significantly valuable by a customer.

Catalog Sales

Catalog selling does not fit perfectly into the classification of non-store retailing as either personal or non-personal since it can be both. It could also be considered a type of in-store retailing because some firms send catalogs to consumers and orders are placed in the store. For example, all Sears stores have catalog desks. Although catalog selling overlaps the categories established for this discussion, it is included in this subsection because it began as a non-personal method of retailing. It is given separate treatment because of its growing importance as a retailing method. As an indication of this growth, Sears' catalog sales have increased 100 percent over the last ten years and account for approximately 20 percent of the firm's sales.[3] Another giant retailer, Montgomery Ward, has more catalog stores than conventional retail outlets, and the 1972 catalog sales of $622 million amounted to 26 percent of total sales.[4]

At its inception over 150 years ago, catalog selling was aimed primarily at rural consumers who found it very difficult or impossible to visit large general merchandise stores. Catalog buying's recent popularity can be explained in terms of its time savings and convenience. A shopper does not have to leave home or deal with traffic problems or crowded stores. He or she can make a decision any time, call or mail in an order, and have the merchandise delivered. To add to the convenience, many large retailers now operate catalog departments 24 hours a day, 7 days a week.

For a retailer, catalog selling offers the prime benefits of sales without sales personnel and with no merchandise displays. Also, customers serve as a final assembly station for many products that are packaged and shipped unassembled by the manufacturer.

The chief disadvantage for catalog retailing for both consumer and seller is returned merchandise. For a customer it is an inconvenience; for a seller it is costly. Catalog sales always have a higher return rate than in-store retailing because the customer cannot see the product and must rely on a description and picture to evaluate color, structure, size, and other features. To reduce this problem, sellers are constantly working to develop explicit descriptions of products and produce true color pictures.

There are basically three types of catalog sellers: general merchandisers, specialty, and seasonal.

TYPES OF CATALOG RETAILING

General Merchandisers. Catalogs produced by major retailing chains like J. C. Penney, Sears, and Montgomery Ward best exemplify this type. They contain a full assortment of merchandise and may be 1,000 or more pages long. General merchandisers frequently produce two catalogs a year: a fall-winter version and a spring-summer edition. Although catalogs are available to anyone requesting them, they are usually sent without request to customers who made a certain minimum amount of purchases from the previous year's catalog. The Sears catalogs are circulated to over 16,000,000 homes.

Specialty Catalogs. These catalogs concentrate on limited lines of merchandise and are aimed at specific market segments. For example, a catalog of guns or stereo equipment would be of interest only to selected people. An interesting example of a specialty catalog is the one sent to Ford Mustang owners offering a line of more than 40 leisuretime products from tennis apparel to golf clubs, most monogrammed with the Mustang II emblem, and priced from 20 to 35 percent below retail store prices.[5] Sears has over 15 specialty catalogs, including home improvement, organic health foods, and apparel for tall women.

These catalogs tend to be short, usually less than 50 pages. They are very selectively mailed to previous and potential customers who meet certain specific criteria.

Seasonal Catalogs. This third type attempts to capitalize on the time of year, the most popular season being Christmas. Catalogs describing gift packages of cheese, fruit, or candy in various combinations of size and price abound in the fall. A well-known seasonal catalog produced by a department store is the Neiman-Marcus Christmas catalog. In addition to the normal array of gifts, this catalog always offers a special gift for the man or woman "who has everything." In 1973 it was an $80,000 12 × 15 foot, egg-shaped enclosure for "the man who has everything and wants some privacy in which to enjoy it."[6]

THE NATURE OF CATALOG RETAILING

Necessary components of an effective catalog sales operation are similar to those required for successful mail order retailing: well-designed advertising (in this case, a well-designed catalog), an efficient order-handling system, and meticulous buying and inventory control. As with mail order sales, the opportunities for errors, confusion, and dissatisfaction are great, due to the fact that the customer does not actually see the merchandise before the sale.

Although a certain amount of returned merchandise and some customer complaints are inevitable, these problems can be minimized when an efficient, knowledgeable staff is receiving and filling orders. Familiarity with the product line, awareness of possible substitutes should a product be out of stock, and the ability to fill orders quickly and accurately are essential.

One advantage of catalog selling is not having to display merchandise and, in many cases, not carrying inventory. Frequently a catalog seller can have merchandise shipped directly from the manufacturer to the buyer. In other cases, when an inventory must be maintained, it should be kept small; this is possible, of course, only if suppliers provide speedy delivery.

FUTURE OF CATALOG SALES

Almost certainly catalog selling will continue to grow. Quality of catalogs in portraying merchandise and the convenience such buying affords the consumer virtually guarantee the future of catalogs. One concern, however, is that consumers must be taught how to shop efficiently using the catalog. For example, a shopper who orders four different lamps in order to see them all, but intends to purchase only one, adds to the cost of selling and eventually to the price of the merchandise sold through catalogs.

REVIEW BOX 25:2

1. The primary differences between buying at a retail store and buying mail order items are convenience, novelty, and _____.
2. The three major types of catalogs are general merchandise, specialty, and _____.
3. A major problem for a firm making sales through a catalog is _____.

Vending

In this last type of non-personal, non-store retailing, products or services are sold through a machine with no personal contact between the buyer and the seller.

GROWTH OF VENDING

In 1972, vending sales amounted to $6.9 billion, more than double the 1962 amount. The growth of vending seems to continue no matter what goes on in the economy. There are several possible explanations for this phenomenon. First, the advancing technology of vending equipment makes it possible to sell more and more offerings this way. Second, consumers are becoming accustomed to buying from vending machines and are more confident that quality can be maintained with this method of retailing. Finally, American consumers, seemingly always on the go, find the convenience provided by vending very attractive.

In Table 25-2, some selected vending sales data and the number of vending machines are presented. These figures suggest the vending industry's growing significance. From 1960 to 1972 every category except ice cream at least doubled in sales, while some nearly tripled. During the same period the number of machines in each category increased at a much slower rate.

Three factors have made vending operations possible. First, some locations are not appropriate for normal retailing either because the space is inadequate or the setting is inappropriate (for example, on the floor of a factory). Second, the time at which merchandise is desired may not be conducive to traditional retailing. In plants that operate night shifts or in states in which "blue laws" prohibit Sunday retailing, vending machines make it possible for people to enjoy products that would not be available otherwise. Third, the volume of sales in many areas could not support a retail counter

TABLE 25-2

Selected Vended Sales Volume and Number
of Vending Machines, Selected Years

Product	1960	1964	1968	1972
Packaged confections	$304,647,000 585,400	$392,205,000 688,110	$554,668,000 805,969	$707,000,000 853,000
Cigarettes	$1,141,920,000 793,000	$1,399,780,000 883,700	$1,811,539,000 930,340	$2,315,000,000 937,200
Soft drinks (cups)	$132,338,000 122,300	$236,045,000 166,900	$358,768,000 203,300	$517,000,000 216,900
Hot drinks	$142,900,000 149,800	$268,920,000 199,200	$412,702,000 244,840	$533,000,000 258,000
Ice cream	$25,550,000 36,500	$29,694,000 42,300	$37,192,000 48,548	$42,000,000 49,000

Source: Vend Magazine. Reprinted from *Vending and Food Service Management Review, 1973* with permission of National Automatic Merchandising Association.

operation. Table 25-3 shows the average annual sales by type of machine. With figures this low—none over $3,000 per year, and the lowest being only $730—it is quite clear that vending machines seldom replace traditional retailing. They simply provide products in locations where traditional retailers could not survive.

WHAT VENDING INVOLVES

A vending operation involves a wide variety of tasks that require multiple skills. Among the activities are:

Selecting and purchasing vending machines
Securing locations for machines
Purchasing or preparing items to be sold in machines
Maintaining a fresh stock of merchandise in the machines
Maintaining the machines in good working order

In particular, vending personnel must be able to evaluate alternative locations and be convincing salespeople in order to secure prime locations.

Location decisions involve four steps. First, the need or needs the vended product or service satisfies must be identified, and the number of people experiencing the need at or near particular sites must be determined. Second, the presence of competing vending equipment at potential locations must be investigated. Third, since the owners of most potential locations are paid a commission, arrangements must be made for the amount and payment

TABLE 25-3

Average Sales per Machine

Product	1972
Packaged confections	$1,054
Cigarettes	$2,095
Soft drinks (cups)	$2,162
Hot drinks	$2,938
Ice cream	$ 730
Sandwiches, salads, pastry	$2,071
Milk	$2,112

Source: Vending and Food Service Management Review, 1973. Reprinted with permission of National Automatic Merchandising Association.

method. Finally, to protect the equipment and the merchandise, the potential site should be evaluated for security and protection from vandalism.

Selecting locations is not an easy task. It should be done with considerable care since a bad location can create a wide variety of problems including lost income, the cost of moving the equipment, and ill will that may be produced by installing the machine and then moving it.

THE FUTURE FOR VENDING

Prospects for vending are bright. When consumers now buy flight insurance, make banking transactions, and handle postal business using vending machines, it is clear that vending has become an accepted part of our culture. This acceptance, combined with the improvements in the quality of machines and merchandise vended and the desire for convenience by consumers, assures a strong future. The primary challenge to the vending operator lies in identifying new products and services that can be sold through this method of non-store retailing. The future is limited only by the imagination of the vending firm.

REVIEW BOX 25:3

1. The product with the largest dollar volume of sales sold through vending machines is _____.
2. In selecting a location for vending machines, the primary considerations are identifying needs, competition, commissions, and _____.

Non-Personal, Non-Store Retailing

CHAPTER SUMMARY

- Besides in-store retailing, there are personal, non-store retailing—final sales made away from a retail store in which there is direct contact between buyer and seller—and non-personal, non-store retailing—final sales made away from a retail store and in which there is *no* direct contact between buyer and seller.
- Personal, non-store retailing includes two types: telephone sales and in-home sales.
- Telephone sales can be made from a retail store or by a seller without a store. Those made from a retail store are generated by salespeople, advertising, and experience. At the present time, telephone sales without a retail store account for a small portion of retail sales. However, the development of picture phones and cable television may greatly increase this type of retailing.
- In-home selling methods include door-to-door sales, custom selling, route sales, and party selling.
- Non-personal, non-store retailing includes mail order, catalog, and vending sales.
- Mail order can offer the consumer added convenience, novel products, and lower prices. Products most easily sold by mail are advertisable, exclusive, reliable, simple, mailable, and regularly purchased.
- An important aspect of mail order selling is direct mail advertising. The components of direct mail advertisements are mailing envelope, message, order form, samples, and incentives. Catalog retailing includes general merchandise catalogs, specialty catalogs, and seasonal catalogs. Catalog sales are becoming increasingly important in retailing primarily because of the convenience they offer consumers.
- Vending is a fast-growing industry made possible by the inability of traditional retailing forms to respond to consumer needs because of space, time, or volume limitations. Critical to vending success is the selection of prime locations. The chief considerations in location choice are identifying needs and competition, determining commissions, and evaluating security.
- Major problem areas in vending are securing and maintaining good equipment, theft and vandalism, and commissions.
- The future for all types of non-store retailing is good because each offers the consumer special advantages, the most important being convenience.

CHAPTER NOTES

[1] "Hood Broadens the Milkman's Line," *Business Week*, August 5, 1972, p. 74.
[2] "Receptive Recipients?," *Wall Street Journal*, June 6, 1974, p. 1.
[3] "How Giant Sears Grows and Grows," *Business Week*, December 16, 1972, p. 52.
[4] Marcor, Annual Report, 1972.
[5] "To Help Build Customer Loyalty," *Business Week*, November 3, 1973, p. 90.
[6] "The Neiman-Marcus Christmas Catalog," *Business Week*, November 24, 1973, p. 54.

QUESTIONS AND ASSIGNMENTS

1. Define non-store retailing. What is the difference between personal, non-store retailing and non-personal, non-store retailing?
2. In using salespeople to generate telephone sales from a retail store, what two things must the store be careful about? Give an example of the type of store where this kind of retailing might occur.
3. What are four reasons consumers may prefer to purchase by telephone rather than visit a retail store?
4. How would a picture phone help a telephone seller who does not have a retail store? From the consumer's viewpoint, what is the biggest difference between telephone sellers with stores and those without stores?
5. What are the features of products that are generally sold door-to-door?
6. What has hurt the reputation of door-to-door sellers?
7. As the costs of operating a route sales program increase, what options does the firm have in reacting to the increases?
8. On what market segment has party selling been concentrated? Why?
9. Find three mail order advertisements for products that do not meet one or more of the rules in the chapter for products appropriate for this type of retailing. Does finding such products mean the "rules" are of no value?
10. The three factors in direct mail advertising are who receives it, when and where it is received, and what is received. Describe the types of professional help the advertiser can get in these decision areas.
11. What kinds of information could you use in determining how often to send a direct mail advertisement to customers?
12. Why is catalog selling growing in importance? What is the biggest problem in catalog selling?
13. People sometimes think vending only involves keeping machines filled with merchandise. What other activities must be carried out in a vending operation?
14. Assume you have two ice cream vending machines to place in your community. Describe your decision-making process in selecting specific locations.
15. What kinds of developments in the consumer, the economy, and the environment could interrupt the continuing growth of non-store retailing? (The answer to this question is not in the chapter. It is designed to stretch your thinking a little.)

ANSWERS TO REVIEW BOX QUESTIONS

Box 25:1

1. in-home retailing
2. experience
3. route sales

Box 25:2

1. lower price
2. seasonal
3. returns

Box 25:3

1. cigarettes
2. security

Retailing Tomorrow

26

In looking toward a future in retailing, you might have two questions. The first deals with a rather immediate concern: How does a person go about starting a career in retailing? The second is a more long-run issue: What will retailing be like in the future? This chapter looks at these two related but quite different topics. The first, careers in retailing, is rather straightforward and factual. The second, the future of retailing, is an exercise in speculation, as you will see.

CAREERS IN RETAILING

At this point in the book it should be clear to you that retailing is largely a "people-oriented" industry. It is people (retailers, retail employees) helping other people (consumers) satisfy their needs and wants through the sale of products and services. In some cases this involves personal contact between buyer and seller, while in others a machine comes between them. However the exchange takes place, there will always be a need for qualified people to identify what consumers want, and where and when they want it, and to develop the program for meeting these needs.

To investigate what a career in retailing involves, we will first look at the difference between entrepreneurship and employment. Then, since most people begin retail careers as employees, we will look at how a career as a retail manager gets started.

Entrepreneur or Employee

There are two routes a person going into retailing can take. One is as an entrepreneur, opening and running a business. The other is to become an employee in someone else's business. These two routes put quite different demands on an individual.

THE ENTREPRENEUR

Owning and managing a business sounds very appealing to many people. The "rags to riches" stories of such retailers as J. C. Penney, who started out with a dry goods store in Kemmerer, Wyoming, and Rowland Macy, who began with a thread and needle shop in Boston, further encourage a person with independent notions.

What does it take to be a successful retailer (though maybe not so successful as the above retailing giants)? In the absence of blind luck, the three key ingredients are sufficient capital, knowledge of retailing, and experience.

Capital. A common rule of thumb is that to start a business a person should have enough money to operate for one full year without any revenue. That includes money to pay for inventory, advertising and promotion, utilities, salaries, rent or mortgage, insurance, supplies, and equipment. Of course, the assumption of no revenue is a drastic one. However, until a retailer establishes a reputation and develops a following of loyal customers, business is typically slow. In addition, unanticipated expenses like the need for a delivery van or minor remodeling have a way of coming up in a new business. Thus, starting on a "shoestring" with only enough capital to open a store almost always results in failure.

Knowledge of Retailing. In a conversation with an individual untrained in retailing, one of the authors was told that retailing consists of "putting razor blades by the cash register and saying 'thank you and come back soon.'" This notion, that retailing is simply common sense, is unfortunately rather widespread. Since most people see retailing only from the consumer's side, their knowledge of it is very superficial. As a result, successful retailing looks easy.

After reading this book, you know that there is much to learn in the field of retailing. Although it is far from an exact science, retailing does require a working knowledge of merchandising methods, promotional techniques, and pricing strategies. Of course, one book does not nearly exhaust the field. For example, there are several books devoted entirely to the subjects of store location and design.

Experience. The ingredient a young, potential entrepreneur is least likely to possess is retailing experience. Knowledge can be gained in school, and capital may be provided by parents, an inheritance, or a co-signed loan, but experience is something that no one else can provide. No classroom explanation can substitute for making a sale, satisfying an irate customer, or helping to make buying decisions.

There are many ways of gaining experience, including summer employment, part-time jobs, cooperative retailing programs, or full-time employment after graduation. Experience can be gained in a large or small store; however, a small store may offer the opportunity to participate in a broader range of decisions. The objective of the prospective entrepreneur should be to learn as much as possible about every aspect of retailing.

We should note that there is considerable disagreement over the relative merits of experience and education, and whether they are substitutable. On the side of experience is the notion of "learning by doing." No one would deny that actually making decisions (even minor ones), working with experienced retailers, and being around customers can result in a lot of learning. Education, on the other hand, should provide better-organized learning. Starting with basic concepts and working toward more sophisticated and specific notions, the student develops an appreciation of the entire retailing process. In addition, education exposes a student to all types of retailing, whereas the individual who gains experience, for example, in a small clothing store, has knowledge limited to one firm in one category of merchandise.

The ideal situation is to combine the two. Schools and retailers, through cooperative programs, are doing this. For example, Shillito's in Cincinnati (a division of Federated Department Stores) has an internship program for college juniors interested in retailing careers. Figure 26-1 describes the Shillito program. Of course, less formal experience can also pay dividends. Part-time or weekend jobs in retail firms may not provide as formalized or varied experience as an internship program, but they are still valuable.

THE EMPLOYEE

The person seeking employment in a retail firm faces a set of circumstances different from those faced by the entrepreneur. Because he or she will be working for someone else, the success ingredients are somewhat different. For example, in this case, capital is not necessary, but knowledge of retailing and a creditable background are.

Knowledge. Because an employee will be trained in the firm after being hired, often in a formal training program, education and experience can be somewhat less important. This is not to say that a marketing or retailing background is not valuable to a new retail employee, but the amount of education necessary to launch a career depends on the individual and the job. Some training programs, for example, require that all trainees have a college degree. On the other hand, there are many successful retailers who ended their formal education with a high school diploma.

Education has its primary impact on the starting position. A graduate degree may make it possible to move into a corporate executive training pro-

FOR COLLEGE JUNIORS INTERESTED IN A FUTURE CAREER IN DEPARTMENT STORE MANAGEMENT

SHILLITO'S, SOUTHERN OHIO'S LARGEST DEPARTMENT STORE, one of 18 divisions of Federated Department Stores — America's largest with sales close to $2 billion last year — offers a summer program of on-the-job work experience and classroom seminars to a limited number of success-minded young men and women.

IF YOU ARE:

- In your junior year now
- Majoring in marketing, business administration, economics, retailing or related fields
- Maintaining a record of achievement in class work and in extracurricular activities
- Interested in people and in a position offering a challenge, creativity and a variety of duties

. . . We'd Like to Meet You!

OUR SUMMER INTERN PROGRAM CONSISTS OF:

- A formal program for a 10-week period from mid-June through August, providing an opportunity to earn up to $1500 this summer.
- Initial 2 to 3 weeks' orientation to selling and supervision by planned rotation in selected departments.
- Subsequent in-depth training in supervision and administration by assignment in one department, gaining valuable experience in all areas of department store management.
- Seminars led by top executives in subjects selected to give complete overview of department store management.
- Job counseling and job evaluation interviews with Personnel executives to discuss your training and progress.

QUALIFIED STUDENTS, INVESTIGATE THIS OPPORTUNITY NOW

Contact your Placement Office for additional information. A Shillito's representative will be on campus to interview on:

If this date is not convenient, send a complete resume to Executive Recruiting and Development Office, Shillito's, 7th and Race Streets, Cincinnati, Ohio 45202

FIGURE 26-1 Internship program for college students

gram, while an associate degree may mean starting in a store management training program. One point, however, is very important. After securing the job it is performance that counts:

> A college diploma or a graduate school degree helps put you on the payroll at a good starting salary, but your financial growth and your progress thereafter are totally unrelated to your academic portfolio.[1]

Personal Background. Retailers are interested in an applicant's maturity, motivation, personality, intelligence, health, communication skills, leadership ability, and integrity. Some of these things can be determined by tests administered during job interviews, while others are inferred from an individual's past. For example, an interviewer for a retail firm would be interested in whether the applicant has held any positions of trust or confidence; has been selected by peers to a leadership position; is neat and clean; is capable of speaking well; has shown an interest in other people or has engaged in activities such as volunteer work, sports, or the school debate team; and has done some thinking about the future.

The Road to the Executive Suite

There are essentially two tracks of employment in retailing. One is non-executive retail employment. This track includes jobs for checkers, stockers, receiving and marking personnel, salespeople, and so forth. Although the jobs and pay may differ, the one thing they have in common is that they are all at a non-managerial level. The other type of jobs are management or executive positions. Since most people who continue their education beyond high school and are interested in retailing aspire to such positions, the remainder of our discussion will be limited to this level.

An individual seeking a managerial position in retailing can initially contact firms in three ways: through a college placement service, through a private placement agency, or directly. Whichever route a person chooses, two important preparatory tasks are producing a resume and preparing for interviews.

JOB HUNTING

Job applicants' resumes are used by a firm as an initial screening device. There are almost always many more applicants than available positions; as an extreme example, a campus recruiter interviewing for a particularly attractive retail firm recently told one of the authors that the firm would consider 2,500 applicants for 70 positions. Hence, a large number of prospects must be quickly eliminated from consideration. This is why a well thought out, carefully prepared resume is very important. Your college placement director can assist you in developing a resume, or you may wish to make use of some of the helpful publications in this area.[2]

Careers in Retailing

For an applicant who survives the initial screening, a preliminary interview is usually arranged. During this 30 minutes to an hour, the firm's representative is looking for indications of traits discussed earlier and not always found on a resume. Self-evaluation and knowledge about the company involved are helpful preparation for this interview. The college placement service can usually provide company information; self-evaluation, of course, depends upon the individual.

Following these two screenings, the remaining candidates normally proceed through a series of interviews and often tests, usually at the retailer's headquarters. Here the applicant talks to a number of executives, and their collective judgment will determine whether or not a job offer will be forthcoming.

Assuming the applicant is offered a job and accepts, what comes next? Most large retail firms place new employees in a management training program.

MANAGEMENT TRAINING

Individual differences in how they operate plus the need of most young employees for experience has led most large firms to establish management training programs. Figure 26-2 describes such a training program at Gimbels. As you can see from the description, the training serves two purposes. First,

---

Executive Training and Development at Gimbels begins with an intensive introductory program to the retailing field of up to ten weeks duration. The program is designed to prepare the individual for immediate executive responsibilities in the Merchandise Division, Operations Division or the Control Division.

Limited in number, but not in importance are career opportunities in other Divisions within Gimbels — such as Personnel or Sales Promotion.

The Executive Training Program is chiefly an on-the-job controlled learning experience combined with classroom theory and assigned projects. After a brief introductory exposure to sales and management, each Trainee is assigned to two merchandising assignments — one is hard goods and one in soft goods. This enables the individual to determine his or her interests. Under the direction of a Buyer, the young executive is exposed in an actual work situation to the elements of effective merchandising presentation, promotion and control. Where appropriate, additional assignments or special projects are given to selected trainees.

Each Executive Trainee's performance is evaluated and discussed with the individual several times during the introductory program. Ample opportunity is given to the trainee for "give and take" sessions with his or her own appointed counselor. This review process is instrumental in placing the individual in his or her first permanent executive position. Individual interests and abilities determine the area of placement wherever possible.

FIGURE 26-2

Gimbels executive training program

Source: "Executive Development," Gimbels Executive Training Program.

BURDINE'S JUNIOR EXECUTIVE TRAINING PROGRAM

Ours is basically an On-The-Job training approach. We believe strongly in extending responsibility early in a trainee's experience, and we practice this philosophy by placing trainees in positions that offer just that. Match this day-to-day growing process with periodic development classes in systems and procedures, and seminars with management representatives, and you have a formal, yet flexible, growth program.

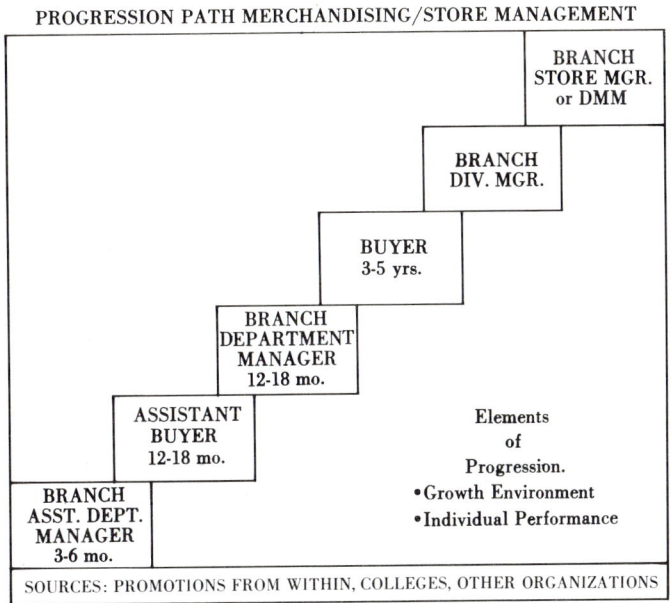

ASSISTANT DEPARTMENT MANAGER: Initial placement as an Assistant Department Manager exposes the trainee to basic management techniques and responsibilities. You will get your first experiences in managing people, time, and merchandise. It will be your first taste of being deeply involved in running a piece of a business.

ASSISTANT BUYER: As an Assistant Buyer you will work in a buying office. You will learn the skills and techniques of a Buyer. How to buy—What to buy; Merchandise Planning and Presentation, How to coordinate many separate businesses into one total business. You will learn merchandise classification philosophy and how to apply it. *You'll learn how to run a business with our money.*

DEPARTMENT MANAGER: At this stage, you will really begin to polish the rough edges. You'll have major independent responsibilities for running a business in one of our branch stores. You'll be in a position to really apply the things you have learned to date, and see the results mirrored in success. Your success—your ability to plan and manage will finally be brought to its greatest clarity. And as you exhibit the ability to apply what you have learned, you will be just around the corner from being a Buyer.

BUYER: This is the person who really decides what our customers have to choose from. You will be totally responsible for a multi-million dollar business. You will go into domestic and foreign market places and buy goods for Burdine's. You will make the decisions that make our business grow.

Beyond Buyers are the positions of Branch Divisional Managers, Branch Store Managers, and Divisional Merchandise Managers. The growth and development of people is an on-going process in Burdine's.

FIGURE 26-3

Source: Reprinted from "Burdine's-Creative Merchandisers," Burdine's Department Stores, 1974.

through classroom training and on-the-job experience, it familiarizes the new employee with how the firm operates. Second, it provides feedback to the firm about the individual's potential.

Training programs range in length from a few weeks to a year or more. They generally include a wide variety of experiences from the stock room to the accounting office in virtually every phase of the business.

ADVANCEMENT

What is likely to happen to the young executive after completion of a training program? The answer to that question is, it depends. It depends upon the organization's structure, the individual's performance, and the availability of opportunities. Rather than try to describe a general plan of advancement, we will use an example to suggest what a person might expect.

Figure 26-3 shows the ideal advancement plan for an executive at Burdine's Department Store chain in Florida. After an initial on-the-job training program, the new employee becomes a branch store assistant department manager. Two points in the Burdine's program should be noted. First, progress in the program results from a growth environment provided by the firm and the performance of the individual. Second, three sources are used to produce managers: the company's present employees, colleges, and other retail organizations.

Prospects for beginning a career in retailing look promising, but what are the prospects for the industry? The next section takes a look at the challenges the retail executive of the future will face.

REVIEW BOX 26:1

1. Three things a prospective retail entrepreneur should possess are capital, knowledge, and _____.
2. In contrast to an entrepreneur, an individual seeking a managerial position with an existing firm should have a knowledge of retailing and _____.
3. The first screening device firms use in recruiting is the _____. The next screening is done at the initial _____.

THE FUTURE OF RETAILING

What's in store for retailing in the future? A field of business that has responded so vigorously to the changes in the social and economic environment during its 200-year history in this country certainly will continue to prosper.

New needs will develop and will be fulfilled; new technology will become available and will be used; new products will be invented and will be sold; and new methods of distribution will be discovered and put into operation.

To discuss the future of retailing, we have divided this section into two parts. First, we will consider external changes, or changes in the environment, that will affect retailing. Second, internal changes, or the things retailers are planning for the future, will be discussed.

External Changes

The population through 1980 is expected to grow at a rate of about 1 percent per year. Although this is considerably below the rate we have experienced since World War II, the total U.S. population will probably reach 230 million by 1980. That will be an increase of 25 million people in 10 years. Besides simply growing, the population will also experience significant changes, several of which are discussed below.

CHANGES IN THE CONSUMER

Income. The amount of income people receive depends upon the rate of growth of the economy. Assuming an average 4.3 percent annual growth rate, income in 1980 will be 50 percent greater than it was in 1970. Translating that into dollars, about 15 percent of the families in the United States had incomes over $10,000 in 1967. By 1980, 55 percent of all families should earn that much, and 68 percent will earn more than $10,000.[3] Increased income, if it is not eaten up by inflation, means more spending power. But what will the consumer be like?

Age Distribution. Because of fluctuations in the birth rate, the age distribution of consumers is shifting. Most important over the next ten years will be the increase in the percentage of the population between the ages of twenty and thirty-five. Because these are the years of family formation and child bearing, the demand for housing, furniture, appliances, and other home furnishings should be excellent.

During this same period, the number of people over fifty-five will grow at a faster rate than the overall population. Since many of these people will be retired or without children at home, the demand for leisure-time products and services aimed at this market should expand.

Education. The educational level of the population has steadily increased since World War II, and it will continue to do so. In 1968, 20 percent of adults had some college; by 1980, 25 percent of a much larger population will have attended college. More education means better prepared, more thoughtful consumers who will evaluate products, prices, and selling terms. The gullible consumer, easily convinced by the fast talking salesman, may soon be a thing of the past.

Status of Women. The role of women in society is undergoing drastic revision. Of course, the most visible reflection of change is the "Women's Lib" movement. The change goes much deeper than a small number of activists, however, which means that the impact on retailing will be significant. For example, there is a trend toward later marriage and a decline in the marriage rate of young people. Young women no longer look to a husband and family as inevitable. One effect of this increased independence will be a growing demand for rental housing and household furnishings.

A corresponding development is the increase of women in the labor force. For the first time in our history, a majority of women (52 percent) from age eighteen to age sixty-four are employed, and more will be in the future. What are the implications of this development for retailing? First, working women spend a greater share of income on clothes, cosmetics, and convenience foods. Second, shopping habits are revised to conform to work schedules. Evening and weekend shopping will grow in importance. Third, media exposure changes. No longer at home during the daytime to see television or listen to the radio, the working woman spends less time in contact with all forms of mass media and limits exposure to non-working hours.

Changes in attitudes and behavior have an impact on how women view themselves and how they want to be viewed. For example, a *Good Housekeeping* panel felt that 40 percent of television commercials are offensive to women.[4] A finding like this suggests that retail advertisers should completely re-evaluate the approach used in promoting products and services to women.

CHANGES IN LIVING AND WORK PATTERNS

As people change, the way they live also changes. Several alterations in our social structure either going on now or about to begin will affect the future of retailing. Four of these will be discussed: where people live, the mobility of Americans, the changing work week, and leisure time.

The Location of the Population. We have witnessed the growth of cities, the flight to the suburbs, the growth of suburban retailing, and the decay of the inner city. What will be next?

The suburban dweller is heavily dependent on the automobile. However, gasoline shortages, congestion, pollution, and other problems associated with cars are making suburban living less attractive. With downtown areas being cleaned up and decent living and shopping facilities being provided, we may see a move back from the suburbs. Such a move would be disconcerting to many retailers who followed consumers to the suburbs and virtually ignored their older, downtown stores. If downtown areas begin to show a resurgence, retailers may be forced to redirect their efforts to improving downtown stores. In what may prove to be a forerunner of this development, Broadway Plaza in the heart of downtown Los Angeles has opened with 30 stores, a hotel, an office building, and a Broadway-Hale department store.

Mobility. Our society is surely the most mobile in history. Americans change homes once every five years on the average. Young couples often reside hundreds of miles away from their parents as family ties become less important.

Increased mobility is both helpful and upsetting for retailers. It is helpful because it creates additional demand. Each time a family moves and establishes a new household, many essential items must be purchased. On the other hand, this mobility makes it difficult to predict what the composition of a particular market area will be a few years in the future.

Working Hours. The number of hours in the average work week will continue to decline in the future. In addition to being shorter, the structure of the work week is changing. In response to demand, more and more retail outlets are operating beyond "normal" working hours. Some banks open at 7 A.M., many bowling alleys and supermarkets stay open all night, and most retail operations are experimenting with Sunday openings where they are permitted by law. These changes create staffing and scheduling problems for retailers and may lead to increased automation in retailing. For example, automated bank tellers already exist, and coin-operated bowling alleys are not too far-fetched.

Retailers will also be forced to respond to changes in the work schedules of customers. One such change is called "flex-time." Flex-time is a work-scheduling system in which employees determine their own starting and quitting time as long as they work the prescribed number of hours per day. Thus, an early riser may start work at 6:00 A.M. and finish early enough for a round of golf. On the other hand, the "night owl" can sleep in and work well into the evening. At the present, flex-time is being experimented with in certain blue collar and white collar jobs in which such scheduling is not disruptive. If it spreads, what implications might it have for retailing? First, it would free people to shop at non-traditional times, creating new demands on retailers. Second, it suggests the need for retailers to be more attentive to changes in shopping patterns as this and other innovations spread shopping hours all over the clock and calendar.

Leisure Time. Another effect of a shorter work week is more leisure time. One way consumers will use this time is to consume more, particularly in the areas of education, recreation, and travel. Another likelihood is that shopping will once again become a social activity, satisfying in itself. That means retailers will be faced with consumers who want more facts and information, more time to decide, and more alternatives to choose from.

CHANGES IN THE ECONOMY

The majority of economic forecasts in the early 1970s painted a rosy picture of more income, more leisure, and a better life style for everyone. Although this may prove to be true, it is only half the picture. Associated with all of these increases are some costs. We first began experiencing them in terms of serious shortages during 1973, when supplies of certain foods ran dangerously low and the government came close to rationing fuel. In addition, high rates of inflation and serious recession damaged the economy in 1974. These events caused many to consider the possible situation of retailing in an economy of scarcity. Both prospects are briefly discussed below.

A Society of Abundance. In 1969, a National Industrial Conference Board publication, *The Consumer of the Seventies*, observed:

> The changing patterns of American life, and more particularly the explosive growth in the population of the upper income brackets, has made for an unparalleled prosperity for a wide range of industries, especially those catering to the fancies of the relatively affluent.[5]

Based on consumer behavior over the past ten years and an anticipated growth in the nation's economy in the future, the greatest growth in the economy was projected for entertainment, personal care products, foreign travel, and education—mostly non-essential items.

Clearly, in 1970 the prospects for the future were bright. Higher levels of education, a greater proportion of the population at the household formation age, growing incomes, and increasing leisure all suggested good times. However, by mid-1973 the outlook was revised.

A Society of Scarcity. In the face of shortages, talk of rationing, empty store shelves, "brownouts," and rising prices resulting from inflation, retailers were forced to consider strategy revisions. Some of the reactions in late 1973 are described below.[6] Montgomery Ward reduced the consumption of electricity in its corporate headquarters by 20.4 percent. Bloomingdale's cut merchandise transportation costs between stores by using larger trucks and fewer trips. Other stores reduced display lights, lowered thermostats, and offered consumers energy crisis products. The Hecht Company in Washington created a special department in its store to handle such "crisis type" items as candles, blankets, comforters, fireplace equipment, and bicycles.

The branch and suburban stores that rely on automobile traffic may face special problems.[7] Some possible alternatives include using buses financed by the shopping center, encouraging customers to car pool, increasing the desirability of carrying merchandise home, and reducing store hours.

The role of advertising in an unabundant economy may be to get people to change their habits as well as to convince them to buy products and services:

> Getting people to modify their habits [preserving rather than wasting resources] will be an extremely difficult task. They will need to be persuaded that accepting change or substitutes in products is not only proper behavior, but socially desirable and necessary.[8]

Among the messages advertising may carry in the future will be an emphasis on value and utility rather than on status and pleasure. Advertising may educate consumers on how to get the greatest use from products and services and encourage the use of less socially expensive substitutes (for example, buses rather than cars).

There are two conclusions that can be drawn from recent economic events. First, developments can be unpredictable and rapid. All the signs in 1970 pointed to unprecedented prosperity. By 1974, although few were willing to despair, enough problems had arisen to bring retailers "down to earth" and cause them to rethink their strategies. This leads to the second point. A retailer should remain in touch with local, regional, and national economic behavior in order to respond correctly.

CHANGES IN THE LEGAL ENVIRONMENT

There are several areas of retailing in which the government is likely to further intervene in the future. Certainly the rights of consumers will be an important concern of legislators. In the future, additional regulations overseeing the relationship between buyer and seller are likely in personal selling, the wording of advertising, statement of terms of sale, and return privileges.

As the government continues its attempt to eliminate poverty, a negative income tax or some form of greater support for the poor may be forthcoming. This would force retailers to re-evaluate market segmentation based on income.

Another area in which the government is likely to intervene is growth through acquisition. As big retailers get bigger, antitrust action will force retailers to develop alternative methods of growing, including diversification into other areas.

CHANGES IN TECHNOLOGY

Probably the most intriguing area of the future, especially in a society as oriented toward gadgets as ours, is technology. Tremendous strides have been made in recent years, for obvious reasons. Ninety percent of all scientists who have ever lived are alive today, and one-half of all the energy consumed by man in the last 2,000 years has been consumed in the last 100 years.[9]

Could the future include underground pipelines for sending merchandise directly to consumers' homes as we now send water and natural gas? What other prospects are there in the future? How about advertising through extrasensory perception? A business society that operates without cash? Consumers purchasing electronic stimulation that produces the same effect as a relaxing vacation, or a pill that tremendously improves learning and retention? Although these ideas do not sound very realistic, they have all been suggested by various imaginative writers. However, rather than deal with flights of the imagination, we will look at two important technological developments.

Cable Television. Cable television, with its many potential channels, offers a fantastic marketing tool. Experiments are already being conducted in which two-way communication can occur between a viewer and a sender. By tuning to a particular channel and dialing a special number on an attached phone, a consumer can see advertisements for a selected class of products. Other channels might offer supermarket advertising or newly introduced consumer products. This exposure to advertising by choice will offer consumers unprecedented convenience and reduce shopping time, while giving the seller the undivided attention of an interested potential customer.

Neiman-Marcus has implemented a forerunner of this system. The firm has distributed a cable television "catalog" to 50 cable TV systems throughout the country. The videotape catalog runs for 30 minutes and displays 30 items from pillows to pantsuits. The stations agree to play the tape three times a day in return for a percentage on the mail order sales Neiman-Marcus receives from customers in their viewing area.[10]

Cable television is currently faced with technical problems in some areas. For example, the cost of laying underground cable in large cities has been a stumbling block. However, the problems do not appear to be insurmountable, and the flexibility of cable television should result in it becoming an important advertising medium of the future.

Picture Phones. For several years the Bell System has been investigating the potential of picture phones. By permitting users to see each other as well as talk, a picture phone has the potential of becoming a major selling medium. Customers will be able to call stores and see merchandise, and telephone sellers will be able to improve their credibility by allowing potential customers to see them and their merchandise. Could this contribute to the obsolescence of the traditional retail store?

Thus far we have described changes and developments that are occurring outside of retailing but which directly affect retail operations. The next section looks at some of the responses taking place within retailing that should have major importance in the foreseeable future.

REVIEW BOX 26:2

1. Among the expected changes in consumers are income, age distribution, education level, and _____.
2. Two potentially important technological developments for retailers of the future are _____ and _____.

Internal Changes

With about one store for every 125 Americans, there are 1,657,600 retail stores in the United States. However, there was a decline of 19,000 in the number of outlets from 1972 to 1973. This decrease can be attributed to the continuing rise in the cost of doing business and the associated profit squeeze.[11] Because costs are not likely to decline, and the factors described in the preceding section will add even more pressure, retailers have responded with a number of innovations that will play an increasingly significant role in the future. The most important are discussed below.

DISCOUNTING

No one would call discount retailing a new development. In fact, its growth over the last 20 years has been described as "perhaps the most important retailing phenomenon of the century."[12] Since its appearance shortly after World War II, the term has evolved over the years to describe a high-volume, low-service retailer with prices below those of full-service retailers. What is important for the future is the growth in discounting.

The major general merchandise discounters such as Woolworth's with Woolco, J. C. Penney with Treasure Island Stores, and Kresge with K-Mart continue to expand at a rate far exceeding conventional retailers. In addition, food chains are moving into discounting following the success of such discounters as K-Mart. The reason? Discounters have been able to make up for the lower prices with greater volume.

Will discounting continue to grow? Let's look at some reasons for its past growth and the prospects for these factors in the future. In recent years many consumers have become more price-conscious. With rising prices, shoppers spend more time evaluating and comparing in order to get the best buy. At the same time, consumer protection agencies are carrying on mass media campaigns to educate consumers in more judicious buying. Are higher prices and better prepared consumers likely in the future? The answer is surely yes. Thus, discounters are likely to prosper and grow as they continue to satisfy the needs of price-conscious consumers.

CATALOG SHOWROOMS

A recent, rapidly growing retail innovation is the catalog showroom. Basically it involves pre-shopping from a mailed catalog and then visiting an outlet to make a purchase. Among the major firms in the industry are Kellmer's in Philadelphia, F. C. Dahnken in Salt Lake City, and Best Products Co. in Virginia. Presently, catalog showrooms are concentrating on traditionally high markup items such as jewelry, luggage, and small appliances.

This method of retailing has a variety of potential advantages for the retailer.[13] Because of the nature of the merchandise and the limited display area, shoplifting is virtually eliminated. Since consumers have pre-shopped with the catalog, fewer salespeople are needed. In addition, many catalog showrooms accept only bank credit cards to avoid financing credit purchases, and most do not deliver. Finally, a large number have joined buying syndicates like Creative Merchandising Inc. and Jewelcor, giving them the ability to buy in volume at lower prices. As a result of all these factors, the customers pay a significantly lower price for the merchandise. Recognizing its potential, several conventional retailers—Dayton-Hudson, Grand Union, and May Department Stores—are moving into catalog showroom retailing.

Variations on the basic catalog showroom are also being developed. Cities Service Oil Company has opened Citgo Mart.[14] The firm offers a catalog showroom incorporated into a service station building and a 500-page catalog that includes a wide variety of items from toys to electronic equipment. Because Citgo service stations are located in high traffic areas, the company feels they have an advantage over typical catalog showrooms.

Another firm, Tel-E-Gift Center Showrooms in San Diego, has combined small showrooms with a magazine-format catalog.[15] The catalog, in addition to presenting over 1,000 items, also contains buying tips and product news. Only one unit of each item is kept in the showroom for display purposes. Thus, the problem of shoplifting is eliminated, and the number of employees necessary is significantly reduced.

The catalog showroom reflects a shift in shopping behavior. Consumers are becoming more confident of their ability to judge merchandise quality. As a result, they are less dependent on retail salesmen. Second, consumers are placing less value on post-purchase service, possibly because of a growing sentiment that it is of generally low quality, and more value on a low initial price. These are not good omens for conventional retailers.

WAREHOUSE SHOWROOMS

This version of furniture retailing combines a showroom to display merchandise with a giant warehouse containing an extensive inventory to bring consumers discount prices and immediate availability of merchandise. Offering a deep selection of medium-priced, brand name furniture, retailers such as Levitz Furniture Corporation and Wickes have taken a large share of the furniture business away from conventional outlets.

Several steps are taken to keep costs down and make the discount prices possible. First, the outlets are located on inexpensive land, usually near a freeway and railroad siding. This keeps rental costs down and makes it possible to order full carloads of merchandise. Second, the stores are all on one level, reducing unloading and handling costs. In a conventional store, 90 percent of the personnel work in the back room. In a warehouse showroom, automation and carefully planned design reduces this to 65 percent. Third, salespeople are paid lower commissions. However, higher sales volume produces incomes at least equivalent to those earned in conventional stores. When all these savings are added together, the warehouse showroom typically has 10 percent less overhead than furniture stores.

In the Levitz outlets the consumers make their selections from merchandise marked with two prices. The first price is comparable to that of local furniture retailers. The second price, which is 15 to 25 percent lower, is the price consumers pay if they want to carry the merchandise out. For an additional 4 to 5 percent, the warehouse showroom operator will provide delivery and set up.

Big department stores such as Federated and Rich's, seeing the inroads being made by warehouse showrooms in furniture sales, are moving into the business. The next few years are likely to see several thousand outlets of this type opening, and this method of retailing spreading to other types of merchandise.

SUPER STORES

A recent development that is quickly spreading is a store designed to satisfy all the consumer's needs for routine purchases, including those now served by supermarkets. *Progressive Grocer* defines a super store as having at least 30,000 square feet of space and $100,000 in weekly sales (compared to $45,000 for the average supermarket).[16]

The typical merchandise in a super store includes food for home preparation, fast foods, health and beauty aids, alcoholic beverages and tobacco, standard apparel, housewares and hardware, lawn and garden products, stationery and sewing supplies, and household services such as laundry and shoe repair.[17] Some super stores also include fresh flowers, meeting rooms, and customer advisors.

The super store concept is the outgrowth of increased competitive pressure among food retailers and the resulting search for a differential advantage, consumers' continued desire for greater shopping convenience, and the success of super stores that have annual sales of $65 million. The success of the initial super stores, including Giant Food Stores in the Midwest and Handy Andy's in Houston, gives rise to speculation that many food chains will be moving in this direction in the near future.

PRIMARY SERVICES

Services retailing continues to grow as a proportion of total retail sales. The increase in products that require professional maintenance and service, plus consumers' desire for greater freedom and pleasure, and ability to afford more luxury, have led to the rapid and continuing growth of services retailing. Indicative of the growth is E. B. Weiss's prediction that Sears Roebuck will soon derive over 50 percent of its net profit from the sale of services.[18] Already Sears gets almost 25 percent of its net profit from the sale of Allstate Insurance.

The forecast that services will become more important in retailing is only half the point. As retailers see opportunities in services, they will break out of traditional merchandise lines and move into new areas. Weiss has already chided retailers for not moving more quickly.[19] In addition he offers numerous examples of primary services retailers could offer. Among them are spa facilities in department stores (in Tokyo, a department store has installed showers for customers), tennis facilities on store roofs, child care centers tied in with the sale of children's clothing, travel services, courses in plant care and flower arranging, cooking lessons tied in with merchandise, and home catering service.

SPOTLIGHT

Where should U.S. retailers look for innovations? In the case of the super store, it was Europe.

Whether you call it a hypermarket, supercenter, or hypermarché, it still adds up to a significant retailing development. Begun in Europe in the early 1960s, these giant retail stores typically cover an area of 5 to 6 acres, sell 20,000 to 50,000 brand name groceries, soft goods, and durable items at discount prices, and have sales 2 to 3 times that of conventional U.S. discount stores.

One of the most successful superstore chains is Paris-based Carrefour. Sales in the sparsely decorated Carrefour stores are made up of 60% food items, 27% durables, and 13% soft goods. The firm's success (34 outlets with $539.5 million in sales and $13.3 million in profits in 1972) stems from fast turnover, margins as low as half those of competitors, and low overhead. Reflecting the concern for cost saving, forklift trucks move up and down the aisles stacking cases of merchandise on pipe racks rising as high as 10 feet in the air. Carrefour concentrates on volume selling of the highest turnover items such as meat and produce and actually offers fewer different grocery items than the typical U.S. supermarket.

The first North American super store is the Hypermarché Laval outside Montreal. This store contains almost 150,000 square feet of selling space (compared to 20,000 for the typical supermarket), cost $11 million to build and stock, provides parking for 3,000 cars, and has over 60 checkout registers. The projected $35 million in annual sales will be made up of 55% food items and 45% general merchandise. Like Carrefour, success is based on low prices and one-stop shopping. In addition, the Hypermarché has added wand scanning for 90% of the general merchandise to speed up checkout and electronic point-of-sales systems to provide almost immediate access to sales data to improve the speed and efficiency of decision making.

What's in store for the future? Preliminary reports are encouraging. Average purchases per visit are over $20 compared to about $9 for U.S. discounters, and total sales volume has been high. A super store needs a market area of about 450,000 to succeed. Since there are many of these in the U.S., we may soon see the super store concept spread across the country as rapidly as it has in Germany, where there are over 350 such stores.

Data Sources: "Carrefour: A Superdiscounter Eyes the U.S.," *Business Week*, December 15, 1973, p. 78. Robert E. O'Neill, "Inside the Hypermarket," *Progressive Grocer*, May 1974, pp. 43–50. E. B. Weiss, "Let Me Put It This Way: Department Stores and Hypermarché Competition," *Stores*, June 1974, p. 40.

Traditional merchandise retailers seem to resist a move into services retailing, but the opportunities will likely overcome their resistance. Thus, future consumers will probably find fewer distinctions between service and merchandise retailers.

In addition to new operating methods, the package of supplementary services retailers offer appears to be in for some changes in the future. Among the more interesting are credit and telephone shopping.

SUPPLEMENTARY SERVICES

Retail Credit. In recent years there has been much talk about a "cashless-checkless" society, in which cash and checks would be eliminated from our payment system. Consumers' paychecks would be deposited directly in their bank accounts. Through electronic hookups, all purchases would be made with some type of credit card. The amount of purchases would simply be transferred from a consumer's account to the accounts of retailers from whom purchases were made. Limited versions of this system already exist in some areas for insurance premium payments and utility bills. Eventually, according to the forecasts, this will expand to all purchases.

Although such a system may be some distance in the future, it seems inevitable that the relatively inefficient transaction devices of cash and checks will be replaced by electronic funds transfer. For retailers, this move has both favorable and unfavorable implications. On the favorable side, it will mean fewer problems with bad checks, less paperwork to process, and immediate availability of funds. On the negative side, it will require retailers to overcome any consumer resistance and make relatively large investments in electronic sensing equipment.

Telephone Shopping. A development of the mid-1970s that is destined to grow at a rapid rate is a telephone shopping plan for buying convenience goods.[20] Under such a plan, consumers are provided with a list of grocery, non-prescription drug, and cosmetic items, and for a small membership fee, they can call in orders and have merchandise delivered. The advantages include the elimination of shopping trips, monthly billing, and guaranteed satisfaction (so the consumer does not have to worry about getting inferior cuts of meat or low-quality produce).

Although this sounds like the kind of special service small grocery stores and drug stores have long offered preferred customers, the retailers here are quite different. They operate highly automated warehouses, with few employees in low-cost locations. This method of selling convenience goods has been described as the "next revolution in retailing" that will drastically affect the structure of distribution of groceries, toiletries, sundries, and standard household supplies.[21]

Our forecasts for the future are not sensational. They are a result of looking at hard facts and composite estimates of what is likely to happen in the next 10 years. What may be more important than the specific forecasts is the realization that retailing is truly a dynamic industry.

REVIEW BOX 26:3

1. An internal response by retailers that has been around since World War II but will also have a significant impact in the future is _____.
2. A catalog showroom can offer the retailer reduced shoplifting, no credit financing, freedom from delivery, low-cost locations, and _____.
3. A new method of distribution described as the "next revolution in retailing" is _____.

CHAPTER SUMMARY

- Two important concerns of a person interested in retailing are how to get started and what retailing will be like in the future.
- A retailing career can involve entrepreneurship or being employed by an organization. Critical ingredients of success in the first case are capital, knowledge, and experience. For the employee, knowledge and a creditable background are important.
- The initial hurdle for a prospective retail manager is getting the right job. To do that, a person must prepare a convincing resume and perform well in interviews.
- Most organizations have some type of formal training program for potential executives. Advancement depends upon the way a firm is organized and the individual's performance.
- The future of retailing can be described in terms of external changes affecting retailing and internal responses by retailers to the environment.
- The major external changes will be found in consumers, the social structure, the economy, the legal environment, and technology.
- Internal responses are many and varied. Some of the most significant are in the areas of discounting, catalog showrooms, warehouse showrooms, super stores, primary services, and supplementary services. Although this is certainly not an exhaustive list of internal changes in retailing, it suggests the dynamic nature of this industry.

CHAPTER NOTES

[1] Harriet Wilinsky, *Careers and Opportunities in Retailing* (New York: E. P. Dutton and Co., 1970), p. 32. This book is an excellent introduction to retailing careers. It offers insights into preparing and searching for jobs, what to expect on the job, and where a job might lead.

[2] Two handbooks on job hunting are C. Randall Powell, *Business Career Guide* (Dubuque, Iowa: Kendall/Hunt Publishing Co., 1971); and *College Placement Annual*, a yearly publication of the College Placement Council which is available free of charge at most college placement services. Another very helpful booklet, *Making the Most of Your Job Interview*, is available from New York Life Insurance Company.

[3] Figures on income, age, and education are based upon forecasts in Fabian Linden, *The Consumer of the Seventies* (New York: National Industrial Conference Board, 1969).

[4] "A Marketing-Eye View of Women's Lib," *Grey Matter*, Grey Advertising, Inc., February, 1973.

[5] *The Consumer of the Seventies* (New York: National Industrial Conference Board, 1969), p. 67.

[6] "Sales Will Brighten a Dimmer Christmas," *Business Week*, December 1, 1973, pp. 23–24.

[7] E. B. Weiss, "The Branch Store and the Energy Crisis," *Stores*, January 1974, p. 40.

[8] "Advertising: New Role in 'Unabundant' Economy," *Grey Matter*, Grey Advertising, Inc., February 1974.

[9] Alvin Toffler, *Future Shock* (New York: Random House, 1970), pp. 23 and 27.

[10] "Sales from a T.V. Catalog," *Business Week*, March 2, 1974, pp. 34–35.

[11] "19,000 U.S. Retail Outlets Lost, Store: People Ratio at Record 1-125," *Marketing News*, December 15, 1973, p. 2.

[12] Leo Bogart, "The Future of Retailing," *Harvard Business Review*, November–December 1973, p. 27.

[13] "Discount Catalogues: A New Way to Sell," *Business Week*, April 29, 1972, pp. 72–74; and Stanley H. Slom, "The Catalog Showroom Booms, Reduces Costs, Makes Shopping Easier," *Wall Street Journal*, July 5, 1972, pp. 1 and 13.

[14] "Tricky Currents in Retailing Challenge Marketers," *Grey Matter*, Grey Advertising, Inc., November 1973.

[15] "Marketing Briefs," *Marketing News*, January 15, 1974, p. 2.

[16] "Anatomy of the U.S. Super Store," *Progressive Grocer*, May 1973, pp. 45–59.

[17] Walter J. Salmon, Robert D. Buzzell, and Stanton G. Cort, "Today the Shopping Center, Tomorrow the Superstore," *Harvard Business Review*, January–February 1974, pp. 89–98.

[18] E. B. Weiss, "Let Me Put It This Way," *Stores*, July 1973, p. 64.

[19] E. B. Weiss, "Let Me Put It This Way," *Stores*, September 1972, pp. 47–48.

[20] For an article describing this type of shopping, see William G. Nickels, "Central Distribution Facilities Challenge Traditional Retailing," *Journal of Retailing*, Spring 1973, pp. 45–50.

[21] Alton F. Doody and William R. Davidson, "Next Revolution in Retailing," *Harvard Business Review*, May–June 1967, pp. 4–20.

QUESTIONS AND ASSIGNMENTS

1. Make up a list of the expense categories an entrepreneur might expect during the first year of operating a small clothing store.
2. Discuss the relative advantages and disadvantages of learning about retailing through education and experience. If you had to choose one over the other, which would you select and why?
3. If your school has a cooperative retailing program or distributive education

program, interview the professor in charge and describe the program to the class.
4. If your school has a placement director, invite him and a retailing recruiter to class to describe the process of job hunting and employee selection.
5. Develop a resume for yourself. On a separate sheet, describe the major strengths and weaknesses in your background that a retailing recruiter might notice.
6. What are the major external changes the chapter forecast for the next 10 years? Can you think of any others?
7. Talk to three retailers in your community and ask them what they think will be the most important development affecting their business in the next 10 years; 5 years; 2 years. After talking to them, do you think businessmen are very "future-oriented"? Why or why not?
8. Why is discounting growing in popularity? What other types of products or services can you visualize being sold at discount prices in the future?
9. If there is a warehouse showroom in your area, visit it and then compare the similarities and differences between it and a traditional furniture store in your community.
10. Several primary services that traditional product retailers could offer are suggested in the chapter. In thinking about your community, what do you think are some other services retailers could offer?

ANSWERS TO REVIEW BOX QUESTIONS

Box 26:1

1. experience
2. creditable background
3. resume; interview

Box 26:2

1. status of women
2. cable TV; picture phones

Box 26:3

1. discounting
2. fewer salespeople
3. telephone shopping

Glossary

above-the-market strategy A retailer's plan of pricing offerings higher than competitors' (Ch. 12)

adaptive formula selling A somewhat flexible sales approach in which an employee adapts a general six-step procedure to specific shoppers and situations (Ch. 15)

additional markup An increase in the original (or previous) price of an offering (Ch. 13)

advertising One of the three forms of promotion, consisting of activities that communicate to consumers a paid, nonpersonal, and sponsored message (Ch. 16)

AIDA The fundamental tasks that must be accomplished for promotion to be effective: attract Attention, generate Interest, create Desire, and obtain Action (Ch. 14)

announcements The type of institutional advertising intended to inform target consumers about basic facts or changes concerning a firm or its operations (Ch. 16)

anticipation A form of discount allowed if an invoice is paid prior to the expiration of a stated cash discount period (Ch. 9)

assortment breadth (breadth of offering) The variety or number of different non-competing product lines carried by a store (Ch. 8)

assortment consistency The degree to which different products offered by a store are related (Ch. 8)

assortment depth (depth of offering) The number of alternative brands or styles within a product line or generic class carried by a store (Ch. 8)

assortment display An interior display that presents a complete merchandise assortment (Ch. 14)

at-the-market strategy A retailer's plan of marking most items with prices comparable to competitors' (Ch. 12)

automatic markdowns The reduction of prices according to a predetermined time schedule (Ch. 13)

available approach An approach to the first personal selling step that emphasizes letting the shopper know assistance is available when needed (Ch. 15)

back order A situation in which a supplier who cannot fill a complete order makes a partial shipment and arranges to send the rest of the order when available (Ch. 9)

bait-and-switch pricing An unethical retail tactic of advertising a bargain and then trying to induce shoppers to buy a higher-priced, more profitable item instead; a deceptive variation on leader offerings (Ch. 12)

balance sheet A statement of assets, liabilities, and net worth that indicates the financial position of a firm at a particular point in time (Ch. 19)

basic stock list A list of staple items to be carried in stock, usually indicating the minimum quantity to maintain on hand and the quantity to reorder (Ch. 8)

below-the-market strategy A retailer's plan of pricing offerings below prevailing market levels (Ch. 12)

books The accounting records maintained by a firm (Ch. 19)

boutique A store layout that consolidates in one area a complete or nearly complete offering for a particular market. For example, a ladies' fashion boutique might include dresses, slacks, blouses, shoes, and accessories. (Ch. 5)

breadth of offering The number of different, non-competing product lines offered by a retailer (Ch. 1)

break-down approach A procedure for allocating the advertising budget by lines of offerings that begins with a total budget that is then subdivided by the promotion director (Ch. 16); compare *"build-up" approach*

build-up approach A procedure for allocating the advertising budget by lines of offerings that begins with tentative departmental budgets that are then adjusted as necessary and combined by the promotion or advertising director (Ch. 16); compare *"breakdown" approach*

buyer An individual who buys merchandise for resale. In situations where one individual is responsible for both buying and selling activities, the terms buyer and department manager are often used interchangeably (Ch. 6)

buying error A retailer's failure to match purchases with demand; one cause of markdowns (Ch. 13)

buying theme The benefits a firm says consumers will receive from shopping at an outlet and/or from purchasing an advertised offering; identified by the firm in its advertising program (Ch. 16)

cash discount A deduction off the invoice price of goods granted if the bill is paid within a specified period of time before the net amount of the bill is due (Ch. 9)

catalog retailing Offering products or services to consumers in a catalog from which selections are made and orders placed (Ch. 1)

catalog sales A form of non-store retailing in which the consumer makes selections and places orders from a catalog supplied by the retailer (Ch. 25)

catalog showroom A retail outlet that relies on consumers preshopping from a mailed catalog and then visiting the outlet to make purchases (Ch. 26)

caveat emptor "Let the buyer beware." (Ch. 21)

central business district (CBD) The downtown area of a city or town (Ch. 4)

central market A large collection of merchandise vendors concentrated in one geographic area (Ch. 9)

centralized buying A type of buying for multistore organizations whereby buying authority is centralized outside of individual stores (Ch. 6)

centralized training Training conducted by a department other than that in which the individual will work, usually by the training department of the personnel division; compare *decentralized training* (Ch. 7)

chain store A retail organization consisting of two or more units with common ownership (Ch. 1)

charter objectives Statements of a business' general scope (Ch. 2)

clearance-sale advertising Promotional advertising that features lower than normal prices on merchandise that is out of style or out of season, odd sizes or colors, remnants, or merchandise that has been around too long and will be less saleable in the future (Ch. 16); compare *regular-price* and *reduced-price advertising*

cluster An unplanned group of small specialty stores located in a high-density living area (Ch. 4)

combination advertising A planned blend of the institutional and promotional approaches in the same piece of advertising (Ch. 16)

committee buying A group of individuals who make buying decisions for a retail organization; most often found in chain store retailing (Ch. 9)

communications gap A deficient flow of information between retailers and consumers, especially prevalent in services retailing (Ch. 24)

community shopping center A shopping center with 15 to 30 tenants, usually including both a small department store and a supermarket (Ch. 4)

comparison shopper A retail employee who checks prices on designated offerings in competitors' outlets (Ch. 12)

competitive differential The way(s), favorable and/or unfavorable, in which a retail firm differs from competing firms (Ch. 2)

consignment buying A method of buying in which title to the merchandise remains with the vendor, relieving the buyer from risks other than damage or shoplifting. The retailer pays the vendor only for those goods sold. (Ch. 9)

consumer rights The right to safety, the right to be informed, the right to choose, and the right to be heard. Originally enumerated by President John F. Kennedy (Ch. 21)

consumerism Consumers' reactions toward business resulting from dissatisfaction and unrealized expectations, and their efforts to remedy these perceived injustices (Ch. 21)

contribution margin plan of expense allocation Charging only direct expenses to various selling departments (Ch. 20)

control division A functional division of a department store usually headed by a controller, who serves as the store's chief fiscal and accounting officer (Ch. 6)

convenience shopping center A shopping center consisting of 3 to 6 outlets, frequently located along a heavily traveled street (Ch. 4)

cooperative buying Group buying by independent, non-competing stores (Ch. 9)

cost complement A decimal figure indicating the relationship between cost value and retail value of total merchandise available for sale during a stated period of time; determined by dividing cost value by retail value (Ch. 19)

cost method of inventory valuation Determination of the value of a physical inventory according to prices paid for merchandise (Ch. 15)

cost of merchandise (cost of merchandise sold) Base invoice for merchandise plus any transportation charges less any applicable quantity, trade, and/or cash discounts (Ch. 11)

cost per thousand (CPM) A dollar figure that indicates how expensive an advertising medium or vehicle is in reaching a specified group of consumers (Ch. 16)

costs Expenditures made to obtain merchandise for resale and to transport it to the store (Ch. 19)

counter-cyclical advertising A method of timing advertising in which much advertising is run when sales normally do *not* occur and is reduced during normally big-volume months (Ch. 16)

couponing A supportive promotion method that involves distributing certificates that entitle a consumer to buy a particular offering at a reduced price (Ch. 14)

creative selling The most demanding type of personal selling, characterized by the need for all six selling steps, the acquisition and use of various types of information, the ability to demonstrate items, and persuasive skills (Ch. 15)

custom selling A form of in-home retailing in which the product or service is at least partially custom-made for the consumer (Ch. 25)

customary prices Those prices expected by consumers as a result of experience (Ch. 3)

customer discounts Selective or across-the-board price reductions granted to special classes of consumers, such as senior citizens or students, by some retail outlets (Ch. 13)

dating A specification of the amount of time allowed for the payment of an invoice (Ch. 9)

debt financing Financing by borrowing funds, primarily by means of mortgages or corporate bonds (Ch. 19)

decentralized training Training conducted by those outside a training department—often on-the-job (Ch. 7); compare *centralized training*

demand-oriented pricing An approach to price-setting that reflects the nature of consumer demand for the offering (Ch. 11); compare *cost-oriented pricing*

department store A retail store with more than 25 employees organized into separate departments for the purposes of accounting, control, and promotion, that carries several merchandise lines such as (1) furniture, home furnishings, and major appliances; (2) family ready-to-wear and accessories; and (3) piece goods, dry goods, and housewares (Ch. 6)

depth of offering (assortment depth) The number of competing alternatives within a product line offered by a retailer (Ch. 1)

differential advantage A feature (or features) that causes target consumers to shop at a particular retail outlet rather than at competitors (Ch. 2)

differential disadvantage A feature (or features) of a retail outlet that tends to repel consumers (Ch. 2)

direct expenses Those controllable expenses that can be related directly to a particular selling department and that would disappear if the selling department were eliminated (Ch. 20); compare *indirect expenses*

direct mail advertising A promotion method in which the prospective seller sends potential customers letters, circulars, or catalogs advertising offerings (Ch. 16)

discount retailing (discounting) A retailer that uses price as a major selling point by combining below-the-market prices and reduced costs of doing business; usually offers broad but relatively shallow assortments and incorporates self-service techniques (Ch. 1)

discounts Deductions allowed off list or published prices (Ch. 9)

discretionary personal income The amount of income left after essential purchases (food, clothing, utilities) and fixed payments (rent or mortgage, installment purchases, insurance) (Ch. 2)

display The in-store presentation of merchandise and information to shoppers; a supportive promotion method (Ch. 14)

display window The presentation of merchandise and information in a store window (Ch. 14); compare with interior display

disposable personal income The amount of income available for spending or saving after tax and nontax payments to the government are deducted (Ch. 2)

divisional merchandise manager Person responsible for implementing merchandising policies under the direction of the general merchandise manager and for supervising department managers in related departments (Ch. 6)

doceatur emptor "Let the buyer be informed" (Ch. 21)

dollar control Regulation of the amount of money invested in inventory to achieve desired sales (Ch. 10)

dollar markdown The dollar size of a price reduction; obtained by subtracting markdown price from previous retail price (Ch. 13)

door-to-door sales All types of product or service transactions in which a seller contacts a consumer at home and attempts to make a sale (Ch. 25)

economic order quantity (EOQ) The number of units of merchandise to order that minimizes total ordering and carrying costs (Ch. 8)

80-20 principle 80 percent of dollar sales are generated by 20 percent of stocked goods (Ch. 10)

electronic cash register (ECR) A sophisticated cash register that provides a large volume of usable information (Ch. 18)

electronic point-of-sale system (POS) The combination of an electronic cash register with a computer that mechanizes most retail checkout activities and provides a large volume of managerial information (Ch. 18)

employee discounts Across-the-board price reductions granted to employees as a fringe benefit by most retail outlets (Ch. 13)

enabling elements Those aspects of a retail firm, including financial resources and information for decision making, that indirectly affect a firm's efforts to satisfy target consumers at a profit (Ch. 2)

end-of-the-month dating (EOM) Terms under which cash discount and net credit period begin with the end of the month (Ch. 9)

equity financing Financing through funds furnished by owners of a business (Ch. 19)

expense allocation Distribution of expenses to various revenue-producing units so as to judge the "value" of selling departments (Ch. 20)

expense budget A detailed plan for expenditures other than those made to acquire merchandise; a system for planning and controlling expenses (Ch. 20)

expense center accounting Grouping those expenses necessary to the performance of a particular kind of store service or task (Ch. 20)

expense control Achieving an optimum level of expenses consistent with the firm's objectives (Ch. 20)

expenses All expenditures except for the acquisition of merchandise for resale and its transportation to a store (Ch. 19)

external credit Retail credit in which some firm other than the retailer finances the accounts receivable (Ch. 17); compare *internal credit*

external forces Forces beyond the control of the retailer (for example, societal, economic, technological, and governmental) that influence the firm's operations (Ch. 1)

extra dating Terms under which extra time is allowed before cash discount and net credit periods expire; often shown as 3/10 net 30, 60X (Ch. 9)

extras People on-call willing to work on an irregular basis (Ch. 7)

fashion goods Merchandise of a style that is generally popular. Fashion items tend to have shorter life spans than staples, depend less on utilitarian functions, and are usually offered in deeper assortments. (Ch. 8)

floor planning Short-term financing by a commercial bank or sales financing company in which money is loaned against high unit value merchandise in the retailer's inventory until the goods are sold (Ch. 19)

formal organization Organization in which there is a hierarchy of responsibility for achieving the firm's goals; most commonly depicted by an organization chart (Ch. 6)

formula selling A sales approach in which the employee proceeds through a six-step procedure in dealing with a shopper (Ch. 15)

franchise A licensed privilege to operate a particular business plus the initial and continuing assistance that a franchisor sells to a franchisee (Ch. 23)

franchise contract A legal document that specifies the rights and obligations of both franchisor and franchisee, the length of the agreement, the conditions under which a franchise can be terminated, and other legal details (Ch. 23)

franchise fee A one-time payment, usually non-refundable, that a franchisee pays a franchisor upon signing a franchise contract; covers such services as site selection and initial training (Ch. 23)

franchise package The total support provided a franchisee by a franchisor, covering not only a retailing mix but also assistance in financial and personnel management (Ch. 23)

franchise system The network of retail outlets licensed by a franchisor and individually owned by franchisees, as well as the franchisor's and franchisees' combined activities in planning and operating the outlets (Ch. 23)

franchisee A businessperson who purchases a franchise from a franchisor and then manages the franchised business or hires a full-time manager to do so (Ch. 23)

franchisor The parent company in franchise operations that provides another firm with a license to do business and various forms of initial and continuing assistance (Ch. 23)

free flow layout A retail store layout with no distinguishable pattern, designed to allow customer movement in virtually any direction (Ch. 5)

free-standing location A single retail store standing alone; most often found along a major highway or street (Ch. 4)

full disclosure Legislation enacted in several states and proposed at the federal level that requires franchisors to provide prospective franchisees with the information needed to make an informed decision as to whether to buy a particular franchise (Ch. 23)

full-service retailing A retailing approach that offers many salespeople to assist shoppers as well as a variety of supplementary services (Ch. 1); compare *self-service*

full-service wholesaler A wholesaler that buys merchandise in anticipation of re-

functional classification of expenses Assignment of expenses to categories according to the activity or function to which the expense applies (Ch. 20)

functional organization Division of responsibilities in a store on the basis of activities or functions. The most common break down consists of five functions: (1) merchandising division, (2) store operations division, (3) control division, (4) promotion division, and (5) personnel division (Ch. 6)

general area analysis The evaluation of a community or a general location within a city as a potential retail location; precedes specific site analysis (Ch. 4)

general merchandise manager The top policy-maker for merchandise offerings of a large store. He or she normally reports to the store president and is responsible for coordinating total merchandising efforts (Ch. 6)

general store An early U.S. retailer offering a full line of staple goods (Ch. 1)

grid The traditional retail store layout, with tables and counters set at right angles and a major traffic aisle through the center of the store (Ch. 5)

gross margin A residual left after cost of goods sold is subtracted from net sales (Ch. 19)

growth sales managers Managers who supervise the selling activities of several departments; typically found in branch stores (Ch. 6)

hard goods Durable goods such as hardware, appliances, and housewares (Ch. 6)

hierarchy of needs The five levels of needs — psychological, safety, social, esteem, and self-actualization — that act to motivate behavior (Ch. 3)

horizontal cooperative advertising An arrangement in which a group of retailers sponsors advertising and shares costs (Ch. 16); compare *vertical cooperative* or *individual advertising*

image advertising Institutional advertising intended to build or strengthen a favorable picture of the firm in target customers' minds (Ch. 16)

image components Those factors that make up a retail firm's image — price, quality and assortment of offerings, sales personnel, store atmosphere, and location (Ch. 2)

income statement (operating statement, profit and loss statement) A financial statement that summarizes the results of operations for a given period of time; consists of five major components: sales, cost of goods sold, gross margin, expenses, and net profit before taxes (Ch. 19)

independent retailer A single retail outlet unaffiliated with other retail units in the same or similar lines of trade (Ch. 1)

indirect expenses Those expenses not having a direct measurable relationship to specific selling departments; often called uncontrollable expenses since selling departments have no direct control over their level (Ch. 20); compare *direct expenses*

individual advertising Advertising paid for entirely by a retailer (Ch. 16); compare *horizontal* or *vertical cooperative advertising*

informal organization The relationship of individuals within a formal organization that arises to expedite work. Informal organization allows circumvention of the strict hierarchical structure of the formal organization. (Ch. 6)

in-home retailing Retailing in which the transaction takes place in a consumer's home (Ch. 1)

initial markup The difference between cost of merchandise and original retail price (Ch. 11); compare *maintained markup*

installment credit A form of consumer credit in which purchase price is divided into equal parts, payment is spread over time, and interest is charged on the unpaid balance (Ch. 17)

institutional advertising A form of advertising that promotes aspects of the retail firm itself or other information that the retailer wants to communicate (Ch. 16); compare *promotional* and *combination advertising*

institutional display A display window or interior display highlighting some feature of the store itself other than its products or services (Ch. 14)

in-store retailing A form of retailing in which the consumer visits the seller's place of business to make a purchase (Ch. 1)

intangibility The quality of not having physical attributes; the most significant characteristic of primary services (Ch. 24)

interior display A presentation of merchandise and information in a store's selling area (Ch. 14); compare *display window*

intermediate-term financing Financing for one to ten years (Ch. 19)

internal credit Retail credit in which the retailer finances the accounts receivable (Ch. 17)

internally generated information Decision-oriented information gathered from employees or from machines in the retail outlet (Ch. 18)

job analysis A study of a specific job to identify significant activities performed (Ch. 7)

job enlargement Increasing the number of different tasks an employee is to perform. The aim is to make the employee's job more interesting through despecialization (Ch. 6)

job enrichment Changing the nature of an employee's job to allow more opportunity for advancement and individual growth (Ch. 6)

job description Written summary of specific duties, responsibilities, and relationships of a particular job (Ch. 7)

job specification An enumeration of the traits or abilities necessary to the performance of a specific job (Ch. 7)

joint promotion A special sale sponsored by a group of firms, such as merchants in a shopping center, rather than by a single retailer (Ch. 14)

labor-intensive An operation requiring a relatively large number of employees and small amounts of machinery, specialized equipment, and fixtures; particularly characteristic of retail-service establishments (Ch. 24)

leader offerings (loss leader) A retail policy of sometimes placing relatively low, less profitable prices on selected products or services in order to attract shoppers (Ch. 12)

life cycle The various stages of life a person passes through from childhood to retirement (Ch. 3)

limited-service retailer A retailer that offers fewer services than other retailers in the same line of trade; usually offset by lower prices (Ch. 1)

limited-service wholesaler A wholesaler that provides fewer services than a full-service wholesaler; often eliminates credit, delivery, and salesmen (Ch. 9)

list suppliers Firms that specialize in preparing and providing names and addresses of defined groups of people to direct mail advertisers (Ch. 25)

long-term financing Financing for more than ten years (Ch. 19)

mail order retailing A non-store retailing technique in which the placing of orders, payment, and delivery of merchandise are carried out by mail or some common carrier (Ch. 1)

maintained markup The difference between cost of merchandise and actual selling price, expressed as either a dollar figure or a percentage (Ch. 11)

markdown A reduction in the original (or previous) price of an offering (Ch. 13)

markdown price The price of an offering after a reduction; obtained by subtracting dollar markdown from previous retail price (Ch. 13)

Glossary **633**

market A group of people with needs to satisfy, money to spend, and a willingness to purchase (Ch. 2)

market analysis A study of consumers in terms of population characteristics, income levels and distribution, and buying behavior; the first step in identifying target markets (Ch. 2)

market segmentation The second step in identifying target markets; involves identifying a reasonably similar group of consumers who are not fully satisfied with present offering and then developing a more satisfying retailing mix for them (Ch. 2)

markup (markon) The difference between retail price and cost of merchandise sold; the amount intended to cover operating expenses and some profit (Ch. 11)

mechanization The substitution of machines for labor; one possible way of improving services retailing (Ch. 24)

memorandum buying Title to merchandise passes to the retailer at time of purchase but retailer retains privilege of returning any unsold goods for full refund (Ch. 9)

merchandise approach A way of handling the first personal selling step in which emphasis is placed on aiding a shopper in making a selection (Ch. 15)

merchandise budget A plan of the amount of merchandise to have on hand during specified times in order to achieve planned sales (Ch. 8)

merchandise display A display window that features the store's products (Ch. 14)

merchandise mart A large permanent building for the continuous display of merchandise by vendors; normally located in large cities (Ch. 9)

merchandise mix The full range of merchandise offered by a retailer (Ch. 1)

merchandise resources Sources of supply for merchandise (Ch. 9)

merchandise shrinkage The difference between dollar value of inventory that should be on hand and the amount actually on hand (Ch. 10)

middle-of-month dating (MOM) Terms under which cash discount and net credit periods begin with the 15th of the month if merchandise is purchased in the first half of the month, and with the end of the month if purchased during the second half of the month (Ch. 9)

Minority Enterprise Small Business Investment Company (MESBIC) A creation of the Office of Minority Business Enterprise designed to help minority businesses acquire investment funds (Ch. 22)

model stock plan A planned dollar breakdown of fashion merchandise according to characteristics deemed important for classification (for example, by type, color, size, etc.) (Ch. 8)

money income The actual cash or checks received as personal income (Ch. 2); compare *real income*

multiple-unit pricing Offering a special price when two or more units of the same product or service are purchased together (Ch. 3)

natural classification of expenses Assignment of expenses to categories according to the nature or objective of the expenditures (Ch. 20)

negotiated-price system A retail policy of adjusting prices as necessary—and as feasible—to close a sale with an individual customer (Ch. 12); compare *one-price system*

neighborhood center A shopping center with 6 to 10 outlets and a large supermarket as the major tenant (Ch. 4)

net dating Terms under which no cash discount is allowed and the net invoice price is due within a specified time (Ch. 9)

net profit plan of expense allocation The practice of charging all expenses, controllable and uncontrollable, to selling departments (Ch. 20)

non-merchandising areas Sales supportive activities designed to assist merchandising divisions (Ch. 6)

Non-personal, non-store retailing Retailing that takes place away from the seller's premises and in which there is no direct contact between seller and customer (for example, mail order retailing) (Ch. 25)

non-store retailing Retail sales that take place without consumers visiting the store or premises of the seller (Ch. 1)

normal margin retailer A retail store that offers merchandise at prices comparable to the majority of competitors and that does not use price as a primary selling point (Ch. 1)

objective (goal) A desired result that represents an organization's reasons for being in existence (Ch. 2)

observation A consumer research method that involves watching and recording consumer behavior (Ch. 18)

odd-ending prices Prices that end in a number other than zero so as to suggest low prices or bargains; one type of psychological price (Ch. 12)

offerings The products and/or services presented for sale by a retailer (Ch. 2)

Office of Minority Business Enterprise (OMBE) An agency of the U.S. Commerce Department charged with creating conditions in the federal and private marketplace that will encourage significant minority business success and profit (Ch. 22)

off-retail percentage One measure of the size of a markdown; obtained by dividing dollar markdown by previous retail price (Ch. 13)

one-price system A retail policy of charging every purchaser of a particular item the same price (Ch. 12); compare *negotiated-price system*

open dating Freshness dating of perishable merchandise, typically indicating the date products should be removed from the shelf (Ch. 21)

open-to-buy The amount of money available during a month to spend on purchases; the difference between planned purchases for the month and merchandise on hand plus merchandise on order (Ch. 8)

operations planning A firm's complete strategy, produced by a four-step process: assessing the environment, identifying target market(s), formulating desired image and differential advantage, and designing the retailing mix (Ch. 2)

ordinary dating Terms under which cash discount and net credit periods begin with the date of the invoice (Ch. 9)

organization A group of people cooperating to achieve specified objectives; the product of organizing efforts (Ch. 6)

organization chart A framework or skeleton of an organization showing how the workload has been divided into divisions, departments, or other subdivisions, and how the hierarchical structure is arranged (Ch. 6)

organizational manual A document that spells out in specific detail the job responsibilities of employees; normally supplements an organization chart (Ch. 6)

organizing The activity of arranging individual effort through systematic planning and coordination. Organizing is a process. (Ch. 6)

original retail price The first price placed on an offering, not necessarily the price at which the item will be sold (Ch. 11)

overorganizing Defining employee responsibilities so specifically through extreme job specialization that employees have little latitude in their jobs. Overorganizing is most likely to occur in large retail stores. (Ch. 6)

part-timers Employees who work on a continuing basis but for fewer hours per day or per week than regular employees (Ch. 7)

party selling A form of non-store, in-home retailing in which the salesperson makes a presentation to a group of people invited by the host or hostess (Ch. 25)

patronage motive An indication of a consumer's desire to buy from a particular retailer (Ch. 3)

percentage cost markup Dollar markup (retail price minus cost) divided by cost of merchandise (Ch. 11)

percentage-of-sales approach A simple, but

Glossary **635**

unrealistic, advertising budgeting method that establishes the ratio of advertising to sales in the past and then applies this ratio to the sales volume estimate (Ch. 16)

percentage (retail) markup Dollar markup (retail price minus cost) divided by retail price; the common way of expressing the differences between retail price and cost of merchandise sold as a percentage (Ch. 11)

performance objectives Desired financial performance for a specified time period; usually stated in terms of profits (Ch. 2)

personal selling One of the three forms of promotion, consisting of retail employees' activities in directly helping shoppers to buy satisfying offerings (Ch. 15)

personnel division A functional division of a store responsible for attracting, selecting, hiring, and training store employees (Ch. 6)

planned initial markup A figure, usually stated as a percentage, that shows the average difference between merchandise cost and retail prices necessary to cover operating expenses, reductions, and desired profit (Ch. 12)

point-of-purchase display (POP) A special type of interior display that presents an arrangement of merchandise and/or information close to the full display of an item (Ch. 14)

point scoring A system of evaluating credit applications in which points are allocated according to characteristics of the applicant, and the applicant must achieve a minimum total number of points to be eligible for credit (Ch. 17)

policies Guidelines that indicate appropriate methods in different situations (Ch. 2)

post-purchase doubt Common occurrence of a consumer questioning the wisdom of his choice after making a purchase (Ch. 3)

potential trading area A circle drawn with a potential site at the center and with a radius equal to the distance customers can be expected to travel to visit the outlet; a preliminary step in retail site selection (Ch. 4)

practical trading area The portion of the potential trading area from which the bulk of the outlet's potential customers can be expected to come (Ch. 4)

prestige pricing A situation in which a higher price indicates greater quality or status, and thus larger quantities may be sold at higher prices than at lower prices (Ch. 11)

price The amount of money and perhaps something else of value necessary to purchase a seller's offering of merchandise and/or services (Ch. 11)

price-aura effect The relationship of the price of other merchandise in an outlet to the perception of quality of a particular product, or the relationship of the price of one salient product to the perception of an entire outlet (Ch. 3)

price level strategy A retailer's plan as to whether prices will be generally above, at, or below market price levels (Ch. 12)

price lining A retail tactic of setting up distinct price points or zones and then pricing all offerings in a category at these points or within these zones (Ch. 12)

pricing decision sequence The series of eight steps through which an original retail price is established (Ch. 12)

pricing errors Selection of a price at which the offering does not sell well; one cause of markdowns (Ch. 13)

primary service A want-satisfying intangible that is the object of a transaction between a business firm and an ultimate consumer, another business firm, or an institution (Ch. 24); compare *product* and *supplementary service*

private brands Items carrying a store's or a wholesaler's name or label rather than a manufacturer's (Ch. 12)

probabilistic sample A subset of a population selected in such a manner that every member of the population has an equal chance of being included (Ch. 18)

profit The amount of money left after costs and expenses are deducted from a firm's total revenue (Ch. 11)

premium offer A supportive promotion method in which a product or service is given free or at a greatly reduced price with the purchase of another designated offering (Ch. 14)

product life cycle The five phases most products go through from birth to death: introduction, growth, maturity, saturation, and decline (Ch. 8)

programmed merchandising Integrated planning between a retail store and selected key merchandise resources; involves the development of a specific merchandise plan (Ch. 8)

promotion Communication from a retailer or, in other situations, communication between a retailer's salespeople and shoppers (Ch. 14)

promotion blend That combination of methods used by a retailer to communicate with consumers (Ch. 14)

promotion division A functional division of a department store responsible for creation of desired store image and attraction of customers; sometimes called sales promotion or publicity division (Ch. 6)

promotional advertising Advertising that features specific offerings of the retail firm (Ch. 16); compare *combination* and *institutional advertising*

promotional discount A deduction allowed off list price to compensate retailers for their assistance in promoting merchandise (Ch. 9)

psychological prices Certain prices, including odd-ending, multiple-unit, and quality-related prices, that supposedly have special psychological effects on shoppers, in particular to encourage or discourage purchases (Ch. 12)

public service advertising The type of institutional advertising that promotes an idea or a cause, often unrelated to the firm's business, that a merchant feels is in the public's best interest (Ch. 16)

public service display A display window that features a community event, organization, or charity, rather than a display pertaining to the store (Ch. 14)

publicity Supportive promotion activities with no out-of-pocket costs to a retailer; personal appearances and news stories are the most common forms. (Ch. 14)

purchasing agent An individual who buys all items for a store except merchandise for resale (supplies and equipment) (Ch. 9)

push money (PMs, spiffs) A payment received by a salesperson for selling a unit of a designated brand or model (Ch. 15)

quality discount A deduction from list price allowed to encourage buyers to purchase larger quantities (Ch. 9)

quality-related price A higher than normal price used when the quality of an offering is quite important to consumers and when consumers judge quality from price; one type of psychological price (Ch. 3)

questioning A consumer research method that involves directly asking individuals for information (Ch. 18)

rack jobber A specialized wholesaler that typically provides a merchandise display unit, selects merchandise for the unit, and keeps the rack well stocked (Ch. 9)

real income The purchasing power of personal income after inflation has been taken into account (Ch. 2)

receipt of goods dating (ROG) Terms under which cash discount and net credit periods begin with the receipt of goods or arrival of goods; also called arrival of goods dating, or AOG (Ch. 9)

recruiting Those activities used to attract applicants for positions in a firm (Ch. 7)

reduced-price advertising Promotional advertising that features lower than normal prices on offerings that are reasonably attractive even without large price reductions (Ch. 16); compare *regular-price* and *clearance-sale advertising*

regional shopping center A shopping center with a large number of tenants (50 or more) drawing customers from a wide geographic area (Ch. 4)

regular-price advertising The type of promotional advertising that emphasizes the merits of an offering itself (Ch. 16); com-

Glossary **637**

pare *reduced-price* and *clearance-sale advertising*

resale price maintenance laws A combination of federal and state legislation, found in many states, that permits manufacturers or wholesalers to establish retail prices for their brands; called "fair trade" laws by backers (Ch. 12)

research process A plan for conducting research that includes defining the problem, setting objectives, and facilitating the performance of research and the use of results (Ch. 18)

resident buying office Market specialists located in market centers who serve as "eyes and ears" of retailers in the market (Ch. 9)

retail method of inventory valuation Determining the value of a physical inventory according to retail price marked on merchandise. This value must then be converted to a cost value to determine cost of goods sold for an income statement (Ch. 19)

retail organization An establishment of relationships among people and other productive resources to accomplish the objective of satisfying consumers' wants and needs at a profit (Ch. 6)

retail sales manager An employee, common to only a few retail firms, whose primary responsibility is to manage the sales force (Ch. 15)

retail store A retailer that chiefly sells products (merchandise) through a physical outlet but may also sell some primary services and provide various supplementary services (Ch. 24); compare *service establishment*

retail system The large arena in which a retail firm operates, consisting of consumers and uncontrollable factors as well as the firm's operating strategies, policies, methods, and enabling elements (Ch. 2)

retailer A firm engaged primarily in retailing (Ch. 1)

retailing All the activities associated with the sale of offerings for final consumption (Ch. 1)

retailing mix A combination of offerings, physical facilities, prices, and promotion used by a retailer in an attempt to satisfy target consumers and to achieve performance objectives (Ch. 2)

revolving credit A credit plan that allows a customer to continuously make credit purchases as long as a stated minimum is paid on the outstanding balance and the total outstanding balance remains below some specified maximum (Ch. 17)

route sales A form of non-store retailing in which the salesman travels a specified route selling merchandise on a scheduled or demand basis (Ch. 25)

routine selling A type of personal selling that may require all six selling steps but does not require specialized information and skills (Ch. 15)

royalty A periodic payment, usually a percentage of sales, that a franchisee makes to a franchisor under most franchise arrangements, particularly the service sponsor-retailer type (Ch. 23)

sales budget A forecast in dollars of sales anticipated for a stated period of time (Ch. 8)

sales forecasting A prediction of sales for a specified time period that takes into consideration the retailer's operating plan and external factors that may influence sales (Ch. 18)

sample A subset of a defined group or population; in consumer research, the group from whom data are collected (Ch. 18)

sampling A supportive promotion method whereby shoppers are given a free unit of a product or service with the aim of turning them into regular customers (Ch. 14)

scheduling The decision as to how many salespeople will be on duty at each time period of the sales week, as well as the hours that each salesperson will work (Ch. 15)

scrambled merchandising Stocking products or product lines not traditionally carried by a particular type of store (Ch. 8)

seasonal catalogs Catalogs containing merchandise designed for a particular season or holiday such as the Christmas season (Ch. 25)

seasonal discount A deduction allowed off list price for ordering and sometimes taking delivery in the off-season (Ch. 9)

section manager A retail employee responsible for personal selling activities in a specified part of a store, usually several departments (Ch. 15)

selection Determination of which job applicants will be hired (Ch. 7)

self-concept How an individual views himself and how he thinks others view him (Ch. 3)

self-service An approach to retailing in which shoppers examine various offerings without assistance from a salesperson and then take their selection to a check-out area (Ch. 15); compare *full service retailing*

selling area The area in the store in which merchandise is displayed and transactions take place (Ch. 5)

selling errors Careless or negligible attempts at adequate display and personal selling technique and/or incorrect decisions concerning personal selling; one cause of markdowns (Ch. 13)

selling price (actual selling price) The price at which an offering is sold (Ch. 11); compare *original retail price*

service approach A way of handling the first personal selling step in which the emphasis is on closing the sale (Ch. 15)

service establishment A business that chiefly sells primary services but may also sell some products (Ch. 24); compare *retail store*

service sponsor-retailer One of the four types of franchises, in which the franchisor (service sponsor) sells the franchisee (retailer) a proven method for operating an entire business (Ch. 23)

setting display The type of interior display that shows merchandise in surroundings similar to those in which it is to be used (Ch. 14)

shoplifting Theft of merchandise by persons other than store employees (Ch. 10)

shopping center A planned grouping of retail stores in a multi-unit structure, usually with the physical facility under single ownership, that provides a coordinated variety of outlets (Ch. 4)

short-term financing Financing for one year or less (Ch. 19)

short-timers Employees hired to work, usually full-time, for brief periods such as the Christmas and back-to-school seasons (Ch. 7)

small store A retailer with an annual volume of less than $1,000,000 and/or fewer than 15 employees (Ch. 6)

social class A grouping of people in a society according to certain demographic characteristics. Members of a particular social class are generally believed to have similar ambitions, values, and behavior patterns. (Ch. 3)

soft goods Nondurable goods such as textiles and apparel (Ch. 6)

space productivity The ability of selling space to produce revenue or sales (Ch. 5)

special sale A supportive promotion method in which merchandise with reduced prices is promoted vigorously, especially through advertising, for a limited time (Ch. 14)

specialty catalogs Catalogs presenting limited lines of merchandise and aimed at specific market segments (Ch. 25)

specialty good A brand that a consumer insists upon and will not accept a substitute for (Ch. 11)

specific site analysis The evaluation of a specific site as a potential retail location (Ch. 4)

specification buying A type of buying that ranges from private labeling to having merchandise manufactured exactly to a retailer's specifications (Ch. 9)

spectacular A very elaborate, expensive supportive promotion activity, such as a parade (Ch. 14)

split shipment An order broken into two or more shipments when all merchandise is not available for shipping (Ch. 9)

staffing All activities concerned with acquiring employees and bringing them to a peak level of performance; includes recruit-

Glossary

ing, selection, training, compensation, and supervision (Ch. 7)

staple goods Merchandise for which style is relatively unimportant to the consumer. Such items tend to change very slowly, are fairly standardized, and are often viewed as necessities (Ch. 8)

stock count books One means of unit control whereby stock counts are periodically made and recorded (Ch. 10)

stock turnover (stockturn) The number of times an average inventory is sold during a stated period of time (usually a year); may be computed in physical units, dollars at cost, or dollars at retail (Ch. 8)

store design The exterior and interior physical appearance of a retail store, including walls, ceiling, lighting, windows, fixtures, and signs (Ch. 5)

store image From a retailer's standpoint, the overall picture a firm tries to project to target consumers; from a consumer's standpoint, his or her set of attitudes toward a particular outlet (Ch. 2)

store layout The way in which merchandise is presented to consumers, including placement of display counters and tables, location of various types of merchandise in the outlet, allocation of space to selling and nonselling areas, and the proportion of selling area allocated to specific items (Ch. 5)

store location The physical site of a retail business (Ch. 4)

store operations division A functional division of a department store responsible for the physical aspects of maintenance. Responsibilities typically include housekeeping, repairs, security, receiving, checking, and marking. (Ch. 6)

strategy A general way in which a firm's resources are deployed in order to surprise and surpass competitors or to seize opportunities (Ch. 2)

string location A grouping of retail outlets developed over time in an unplanned fashion along a major thoroughfare (Ch. 4)

super stores Giant retail outlets designed to offer products and services to satisfy all the consumer's needs for routine purchases (Ch. 26)

supplementary service A service offered to customers and intended to facilitate the sale of a product or primary service (Ch. 17)

supportive promotion methods Ways of communicating with consumers other than advertising and personal selling; includes display, special sales, publicity, trading stamps, premium offers, and couponing (Ch. 14)

tactical markdowns Markdowns planned as part of a pricing approach or at least recognized as a necessary evil (Ch. 13)

tactics Specific policies and methods that follow from strategies and are used by a retailer to achieve objectives (Ch. 2)

target market That portion of a total group of consumers, who possess money and a willingness to spend, on which a firm concentrates its efforts (Ch. 2)

task-and-factors approach A desirable, but difficult, advertising budgeting method that involves estimating the advertising level and approach necessary to reach a sales objective and then considering the tentative budget in relation to specific factors in the competitive situation (Ch. 16)

telephone sales Non-store retail sales in which the transaction is conducted by telephone (Ch. 1)

terms of sale Statement of transportation charges, discounts, and amount of time allowed for payment of invoices; subject to negotiation between a retailer and a supplier (Ch. 9)

30-day single-payment credit A convenient form of credit in which the customer charges a purchase and pays the total amount when billed, usually within 30 days (Ch. 17)

tracking A procedure in which the dollar amounts, percentages, and probable causes of markdowns are recorded and analyzed in order to aid future pricing and merchandise buying decisions (Ch. 13)

trade association A non-profit organization

supported by member firms that provides information on legal, environmental, and business developments affecting the industry and acts as an industry spokesman (Ch. 18)

trade credit Any credit terms, other than strict cash on delivery, extended by vendors (Ch. 19)

trade discount (functional discount) A deduction allowed to compensate buyers for the performance of certain marketing functions (Ch. 9)

trading area The geographic area from which the bulk of an outlet's customers come (Ch. 4)

trading stamps Certificates given by some retailers with each purchase that customers can accumulate and then trade for merchandise; a supportive promotion method (Ch. 14)

transaction processing A type of personal selling that requires few selling steps other than closing the sale (Ch. 15)

uncontrollable environmental factors Factors over which the retailer has no control, such as abnormal weather, that cause markdowns (Ch. 13)

underorganizing Failure to assign specific duties and responsibilities on a continuing basis, most prevalent in small retail firms (Ch. 6)

unfair sales practices acts (sales-below-cost laws) State laws that specify minimum legal retail prices in relation to costs; applicable to specific items in some states and to most kinds of merchandise in other states (Ch. 12)

unit control Regulating the number of units of merchandise on hand necessary to achieve desired sales (Ch. 10)

unit pricing Displaying the price for some standard unit of measure, such as cents per ounce or dollars per pound (Ch. 21)

vending A form of non-store retailing in which products or primary services are sold through a machine with no personal contact between the buyer and seller (Ch. 1)

vertical cooperative advertising An arrangement in which part or all of the cost of specific advertising done by a retailer is paid by a supplier (Ch. 16); compare *horizontal cooperative* or *individual advertising*

walk-ins Applicants for jobs who voluntarily call on a store seeking a position (Ch. 7)

walk-outs Customers who leave a store without purchasing because they were unable to find merchandise to meet their needs (Ch. 9)

want slip A form completed by a salesperson that indicates a customer's request for merchandise not handled by a department or store (Ch. 8)

warehouse showrooms A combination showroom-warehouse selling primarily furniture and appliances that provides discount prices and immediate availability of merchandise (Ch. 26)

welcoming organizations Business representatives that visit newcomers and provide information about the community as well as promotional material, gifts, and coupons from participating merchants; one supportive promotion method (Ch. 14)

wholesale price The amount of money a retail firm must pay for merchandise it will resell (Ch. 12)

word-of-mouth publicity What consumers, suppliers, and other businessmen say about a retail firm; a type of publicity that a retailer cannot control directly (Ch. 14)

Page	Picture Credits
2	Harbrace—Robin Forbes
5	(top) Sybil Shackman—Monkmeyer (bottom) De Wys, Inc.
15	Seemen—ROTHCO
18	NCR Corp. photo
23	Library of Congress
25	(top) F. W. Woolworth Co. (bottom) Frank Tsikitas
29	Frank Tsikitas
43	Sybil Shelton—Monkmeyer
54	Guidance Associates/Martin, © 1973 by Guidance Associates
70,	
79	Frank Tsikitas
80	(top) Larimer Square Associates (bottom) Leviton, Atlanta, Ga.
94	Courtesy *Progressive Grocer*
95	Jay Hoops—De Wys, Inc.
96	*Architectural Record*, May 1954
105	Frank Tsikitas
106	Byck's Speciality Shops, Louisville, Ky.
107	Roy "Scotty" Morris for J. Mangin & Co.
140	Courtesy *Progressive Grocer*
148	Harbrace
154,	
155	Courtesy The Higbee Co., Cleveland, Ohio
159	Harbrace
192	Courtesy *Progressive Grocer*
199	Frank Tsikitas
204	Photo by Karl Nemecek, *TEMPO*, Vol. 20, No. 1, 1974; reprinted by permission of Touche Ross & Co.
206	(left) Harbrace (right) National Retail Merchants Assn.
216	Courtesy *Progressive Grocer*
236	Frank Tsikitas
238	Courtesy Shopper's Choice Supermarket, Lexington, Ky.
247	Courtesy The Governor's Office, State of Illinois
254	Guidance Associates/Szkodzinsky, © 1972 by Guidance Associates
278	Courtesy *Progressive Grocer*
287	Courtesy Allied Supermarkets, Inc., Cleveland, Ohio
299,	
302	Frank Tsikitas
304	Courtesy Filene's, Boston, Mass.
314	Erich Hartmann—Magnum
326	All photos by Frank Tsikitas
328	Courtesy *Progressive Grocer*
329	Courtesy Lehn & Fink Products Co., Division of Sterling Drug, Inc.
337	Courtesy Schaffer Diversified Corp., Retail Services Group
370	Courtesy Brody Bros., Inc., Indiana, Pa.
372	Courtesy Abraham & Straus, Brooklyn, N.Y.
373	Courtesy Henri's Fashions, Lexington, Ky.
374	Courtesy Diamond's, Phoenix, Ariz.
375	Courtesy Salkin & Linoff, Inc., Minneapolis, Minn.
377	Courtesy Central Kentucky Allied Florists Assn., Lexington, Ky.
389,	
390	Courtesy True Value Hardware Stores, Cotter & Co., Chicago, Ill.
397,	
408	Frank Tsikitas
412	Courtesy Motivational Systems, Inc., New York, N.Y.
422	Peat, Marwick, Mitchell & Co.
439	Harbrace
474	National Retail Merchants Assn.
502	Mark Godfrey—Magnum
511	ROTHCO
515, 518, 526	Courtesy Turn Style, A. Jewel Co., Franklin Park, Ill.
526	Frank Tsikitas
553	Courtesy *Insight, Management and Marketing*, formerly *Franchise Journal*
582	A. T. & T. Photo Center
587	Avon Products, Inc.
593	(left) Courtesy International Cigar Corp., New York, N.Y. (right) Courtesy Henniker's, San Francisco, Calif.
596	Courtesy FMS, Belvedere, Calif.
598	American Archives Catalog Division, Meriden, Conn.
608	Courtesy, Federated Department Stores, Inc.
618	A. T. & T. Photo Center

Index

A & P Food Stores, 10, 25, 133, 205, 269, 281
AAMCO, 544
Above-the-market pricing strategy, 279
Accounting, expense center, 477–81
Accounting concepts, *see* Financial statements; Financing; Inventory valuation
Adaptive formula selling, 349–51
Additional markups, 298
Advertising, 48, 366–96, 531
   assessment, 392–93
   budget, 381–84
   buying theme, 380–81
   changes in, 616–17
   combination, 376
   consumer expectations and, 73
   the economy and, 616–17
   expenditures, 367–68
   horizontal cooperative, 376–77
   institutional, 373–76
   limitations, 367
   magazines, 386
   mail order, 13, 24, 387, 592, 594–96
   national, 59
   nature of, 366–69
   newspapers, 385–86, 391
   organizational arrangements, 368–69
   outdoor, 388
   payment arrangements, 376–78
   preparation, 392
   primary services, 567
   process of determining, 388–91
   program development, 379–80
   promotional, 371–73
   purpose of, 367
   racial minorities and, 532
   radio, 386–87, 391
   target audience and, 391–92
   telephone sales generated by, 585
   television, 387, 391
   timing of, 383–84
   vertical cooperative, 377–78
   "yellow pages," 388
Advertising allowance, 217–18
Age Discrimination in Employment Act of 1967, 145
Agent middlemen, 204
Allied Supermarkets, 17
American Indians, *see* Racial minorities
Anticipation, 220
Antimonopoly laws, 20
Antitrust laws, 20
Aptitude tests, 145
Arby's, 9
Arlen Corporation, 29
Arrival of goods (AOG), 221
Arrival patterns, 355
Assets, defined, 451
Assistant manager, 354
Associated Credit Bureaus, Inc., 412–14
Associated Merchandising Corporation (AMC), 208
Associated resident buying office, 208
Assortment display, 327
Assortments, merchandise, 170–72
At-the-market pricing strategy, 281
Automatic markdowns, 305
Automobile Information Disclosure Act of 1958, 20
Automobile traffic, 86–87
Average inventory, 181–82
Averaging markups, 269
Avon Products, Inc., 12

Back orders, 224
Bait-and-switch pricing, 286, 532
Balance sheet, 450–51
Basic stock list, 176, 178
Basic stock method, 186–87
Baskin-Robbins, 279, 544
Below-the-market pricing strategy, 281
Best Products Co., 619
Billboards, 388
Billing, credit accounts, 414–15
Bird Cage shopping center, 81
Black Americans, *see* Racial minorities
Black capitalism, 535
Bloomingdale's, 258
Bonuses, 157–58
Bottom-up method, 184, 494
Boutiques, 96
Broadcast media advertising, 386, 387, 391
Broadway-Hale Stores, Inc., 66, 79
Budgets:
   advertising, 381–84
   expense, 487–96
      in large stores, 493–94, 496
      purpose of, 488–89
      in small stores, 489–93
   merchandise, 186–92
      open-to-buy, 191–92
      purchases, 190–91
      reductions, 189–90
      stocks, 186–89
   personnel, 143
   sales, 184–86
Bullock's, 19
Burdine's Department Store, 611, 612
Buying, 198–227
   centralized, 121, 125, 127, 210
   committee, 210–11
   consignment, 211, 277
   cooperative, 209–10
   errors, 302
   leased departments, 212
   memo, 211
   merchandise pricing by resources, 212–21
      dating, 220–21
      discounts, 215–20

Buying *(Cont.)*
   negotiating, 213
   terms of sale, 213–21
   transportation terms, 214–15
   relationships with resources, 222–24
     back orders, 224
     cooperation, 224
     order cancellations and returns, 223–24
     split shipments, 224
     store order, 222–23
   selection of resources, 203–08
   selling separated from, 132
   store policies and, 202
   task of, 198–202
   vs. purchasing, 200
   See also Merchandise resources
Byck's Specialty Shop, 108

Cable television, 617–18
Capital, to start business, 606
Career in retailing, 605–12
   advancement, 612
   as employee, 607, 609
   as entrepreneur, 606–07
   job hunting, 609–10
   management training, 610–12
Cash discounts, 218
Cash registers, 431
   electronic, 431–32
   errors at, 244
Cash theft, by employees, 241–42
Cash-and-carry wholesaler, 203–04
Cashiers, 352
Catalog sales, 13, 596–99
Catalog showrooms, 619–20
Census of Business, 435
Central business district (CBD), 79
Central markets, 205–06
Centralized buying, 121, 125, 127, 210
Chain discounts, 215–16
Chain Store Age, 436
Chain stores, 10
   buying by, 125, 127, 210
   evolution of, 25
   organization of, 121–22, 125–27
Charter objectives, 30–31
Check-out clerks, 352
Cities Service Oil Company, 620

City Stores, 10
Civil Rights Act of 1964, 144–45
Class action suits, 514
Classroom training, 154–55
Clayton Act of 1914, 20
Clearance sales, 373
Clearance-sale advertising, 373
Closed assortment display, 327
Clusters, 82
Cognitive dissonance, 74
Collection, credit accounts, 415–16
Commerce, Department of, 535
Commission, 157–58
Committee buying, 210–11
Community center, 81
Community size, 38
Comparison shopping, 177
Compensation, 156–57, 356–57, 360–61
Competition, 16
   pricing and, 277–78
   store location and, 84
   supplementary services, 400–01
Competitive differential, 41–42
Complementary outlet, 87
Computer, 18–19
   buyer training and, 200
   credit and, 416
   store location analysis with, 89
Consignment buying, 211, 277
Consistency of assortment, 171
Consultants, 442
Consumer behavior, 36, 56–77
   expected benefits, 73–74
   life cycle, 66–69
     application of concept of, 68–69
     free years, 68
     middle years, 67–68
     senior citizens, 68
     teenagers, 66
     young adulthood, 67
   loyalty, 72–73
   post-purchase doubt, 74
   and prices, 69–72; *see also* Pricing
   self-concept, 60, 62–63
   social class, 63–66
Consumer Credit Protection Act of 1968, 20, 513–14
Consumer needs, 57–60
   hierarchy of, 57–58
   identification of, 58–59
   strength of, 59–60

Consumerism, 292–93, 504–23
   defined, 504–05
   evolution of, 505–06
   government, role of, 507–08
   judicial effects of, 514
   legislative effects of, 512–14
   responding to, 509–11, 519–20
   retailing, role of, 506–07
   voluntary actions by retailers, 515–18
Consumers, 5–6
   changes in, 613–15
   communication gap, 565
   convenience, desire for, 569
   discounts for, 299
   discretionary expenditure, 569
   as information source, 437–41; *see also* Information
   intangibility of services and, 568
   merchandise planning for, 170–80; *see also under* Merchandise planning
   price-conscious, 258–59
   racial minorities as, 524–40
   seller-customer relationship, 569–70
   and services retailing, 571
Consumers' Research, 505
Consumers Union, 505
Contests, 356–57
Contribution margin plan, 485–86
Control division, 129, 130
Convenience center, 79, 81
"Cooling-off" legislation, 21
Cooperative advertising programs, 218
Cooperative buying, 209–10
Cooperative chain, 210
Cost:
   as markup base, 265–66
   promotional, 319
   store location and, 88–89
Cost of goods sold:
   determination of, 264, 467
   in expense budgeting, 490–91
   on income statement, 456–57
Cost method of inventory valuation, 462–63
Counters, 106
County Business Patterns, 435
Coupons, 338–39
CPM (cost per thousand), 392
Creative Merchandising Inc., 619

Creative selling, 352–53
Creativity, promotion and, 319–20
Credit, retail, *see* Retail credit
Credit, trade, 448
Credit bureaus, 411–14
Cumulative quantity discounts, 217
Current assets, 451
Current liabilities, 451
Curtis Supermarkets, 42
Custom selling, 589
Customary prices, 289
Customer patronage motives, 72–73
Customer services, 11–12

Daily newspapers, 385
Data collection methods, 439–40
Data sources, store location analysis, 89–91
Dating, 220–21
　open, 517–18
Dayton-Hudson Corporation, 11, 620
Dayton's, 24
Debt financing, 447
Decision making:
　pricing, 272–75, 300–02
　programming operations, 30–33
　See also Information
Decorations, 328
Deep assortments, 171
Demand-oriented pricing, 260–61
Demographic characteristics, 37
Department stores:
　advertising, 368
　bad debts, 415
　boutiques, 96
　buyers, 201
　comparison shoppers, 177
　employees, 141, 142
　evolution of, 24–25
　images, 40
　layout, 95, 96
　maintenance, 104
　organizational structure, 118–25, 127–31
　routine selling, 352
　sales activity fluctuations, 141
Design, store, *see* Store design
Differential advantage, 41–42, 398–99, 574
Differential disadvantage, 42

Direct Marketing, 594
Discount houses:
　employees, 141, 142
　evolution of, 25–26
　sales activity fluctuations, 141
Discount pricing, 11, 281
Discounts:
　anticipation, 220
　cash, 218–20
　customer, 299
　employee, 299
　merchandise buying, 215–20
　promotional, 217–18
　quantity, 216–17
　seasonal, 218
　trade or functional, 215–16
　unauthorized, 241–42
Discretionary personal income, 36
Discrimination, laws concerning, 144–45
Display, 325–30
　interior, 327–29
　point-of-purchase, 329–30
　price cards, 330
　selection of merchandise for, 330
　types of, 525–30
　use considerations, 330
Display cases, 106, 237
Display windows, 104, 326–27
Disposable personal income, 36
Docktor's Pet Centers, 555
Dollar markups, 263–64, 266–67
Dollar merchandise control, 229–30
Door-to-door sales (D-T-D), 587–88

Economic conditions:
　changes in, 615–17
　markup and, 293
　store location and, 83
Economic order quantity (EOQ), 183
Educational institutions, as recruiting source, 147
Electronic cash registers, 431–32
Electronic point-of-scale systems, 432–34
Electronic signal devices, 238
Elevators, 106–07
Employee errors, 243–45
Employee feedback, 430–31

Employee motivation, *see* Motivation of employees
Employee recruitment, 143–47, 355
　determining requirements, 143–44
　laws concerning, 144–45
　sources, 146–47
Employee theft, 240–43
　of cash, 241–42
　controlling, 242–43
　hiring practices and, 242
　of merchandise, 241
　prosecution, 248
　rewards to deter, 242–43
　training and, 242, 246
　unauthorized discounts, 241–42
Employee training, 150–56, 242, 246, 573
　centralized or decentralized, 151
　classroom, 154–55
　on-the-job, 152–54
　salespeople, 355, 360, 361
　self-teaching, 155–56
Employees:
　advancement, 612
　control of, 357–58
　difficulties in finding, 138–43
　　profit squeeze, 139–40
　　retailing's reputation, 140–41
　　sales activity fluctuations, 141–42
　discounts for, 299
　education, 607, 609
　executive, 609–12
　hiring, 150, 242
　LNOs, 142
　motivating, *see* Motivation of employees
　part-timers, 141–42
　personal background, 609
　racial minorities, 529–30
　recruiting, *see* Employee recruitment
　sales, *see* Personal selling
　shoplifting control by, 239–40, 246
　short-timers, 141
　supervision of, 357–58
　training, *see* Employee training
　unionization, 16–17
　working hours, 16–17, 615
Employment agencies, 147
End-of-month dating (EOM), 221

Index **645**

Entrepreneurs, 606–07
Environment, assessing, 34–35
Equal Employment Opportunity Commission, 145
Equal Pay Act of 1963, 144
Equity financing, 447
Escalators, 106–07
Ethan Allen Inc., 325, 352–53
Expansion decisions, 427
Expense control, 474–501
   allocation methods, 483–87
   types of expenses, 482–83
Expense budgets, 487–96
   in large stores, 493–94, 496
   purpose of, 488–89
   in small stores, 489–93
Expense classification, 475–81
   expense center accounting, 477–81
   functional, 477
   natural, 475–77
Experience, sales space allocation and, 98
Exxon Corporation, 11, 542

Face-to-face interviews, 439
Fair Packaging and Labeling Act of 1966, 20, 339
Families, mobile, 38–39
Fashion merchandise, 174, 176
Fashion-wear stores, 175
Fast food restaurants, 9, 81
Federal Aviation Agency (FAA), 20
Federal Communications Commission (FCC), 20
Federal Trade Commission (FTC), 20, 217, 339, 378, 505, 532, 567
Federal Trade Commission Act of 1914, 20
Federated Department Stores, 10, 11, 208, 441, 626
Filene's, 24, 288, 304–05
Financial statements, 450–58
   balance sheet, 450–51
   income statement, 452–58
Financing, 445–49
   debt, 447
   equity, 447
   importance of, 449
   intermediate-term, 447
   long-term, 446–47

   short-term, 447–48
Five-function organization, 118
Fixed assets, 451
Fixed liabilities, 451
Fixtures, shoplifting control and, 237
Fluorescent lighting, 104–05
FOB terms, 214
Food, Drug and Cosmetic Act, 505
Food and Drug Administration (FDA), 20, 339
Ford Motor Company, 73
Forecasting, sales, 426–27
Foremost Dairy Products, 589
Formal organization, see Organizational structure
Formula selling, 349
Forward integration, 16
Franchising, 10, 541–60, 574–75
   advertising, 369
   development of, 542–47
   franchisee's viewpoint, 552–53
   franchisor's viewpoint, 547–51
   guidelines on purchasing, 554–57
   merits of, 548, 552–53
   retail manager's viewpoint, 555, 557
   types of, 542–45
Franklin Stores Corporation, 432
Free flow layout, 95–96
Free-enterprise franchising, 543
Free-standing locations, 82
Fringe benefits, 158–59
Full disclosure, 554
Full-service outlets, see Personal selling
Full-service wholesalers, 203
Functional discounts, 215–16
Functions, organizing according to, 118

General Electric Company, 291, 292
General Motors Corporation, 536, 546
General store, 23–24
Giant Food Stores, 621
Gift wrapping, 403
Gimbels, 10, 610
Government:
   automotive repair industry and, 572

   as information source, 435–36
   regulation, 19–21
   role in consumerism, 507–08
Grand Union, 620
Grid layout, 94–95
Gross margin:
   determining, 467
   in expense budgeting, 490–91
   on income statement, 457
Gross sales, 455
Growth, store location and, 84

Handling cost, 289–90
Handy Andy's, 629
Hard goods, defined, 121
Hecht Company, 616
Help-wanted advertisements, 147
Higbee Company, The, 360
Hiring, 150, 242
Holder-in-due-course doctrine, 21
Holiday Inns, 10, 101, 542, 544, 575
Home planner, 352–353
Honesty, 509–510, 573
Horizontal cooperative advertising, 376–77
Hudson, J. L., Co., 17

Ideal self, 60
Image of a retail firm, 39–46
   components, 40
   creating, 43
   design and, 101
   differential advantage, 41–42
   enhancing, 43–44
   evaluating, 45–46
   promotion and, 319
Income statement, 452–58
   cost of goods sold, 456–57
   expenses, 457–58
   gross margin, 457
   net profit before taxes, 458
   sales, 455–56
Income taxes, 458
Incompetency, in services retailing, 564
Independent buying offices, 207
Independent retail operation, 10
Indirect competitors, 87
Individual advertising, 376
Informal organization, 115
Information, 424–43

coordination, 422–28
  evaluating, 425, 428
  external sources, 434–41
  internal sources, 430–34
  knowing customers, 428
  management, 441–42
  operation, 425, 427–28
  planning, 425, 426–27
  research, 428–29, 437–39, 441–42
  sales forecasting, 426–27
  value of, 424–25
In-home retailing, 12, 587–89, 591
Initial markup, 266, 288–90
  planned, 274–75, 282–83
Installment credit, 409, 532–33
Institutional advertising, 373–76
Institutional display windows, 326–27
In-store retailing, 7–14
  merchandise mix, 8–9
  organizational structure, 10
  pricing strategy, 10–11
  supplementary customer services, 11–12
Insurance plans, 159
Intangibility concept, primary services, 568
Interior lighting, 104–05
Interior displays, 327–29
Intermediate-term financing, 447
International Council of Shopping Centers, 536
Interviews, employee, 148, 439
Inventory:
  average, 181–82
  perpetual, 181, 232
  physical mistakes, 243–44
  See also Inventory control; Inventory valuation; Merchandise control
Inventory control, 228–32
  dollar control, 229–30
  unit control, 230–32
Inventory valuation, 460–69
  cost method, 462–63
  retail method, 464–69
    benefits of, 468–69
    problems with, 469
    procedure, 464–68
Involvement selling, 361

Jantzen, Inc., 291

Jewel Company, 432–34
Jewel Food Stores, 515, 517–18, 530
Jewelcor, 102–03, 619
JGE discount stores, 291
Job analysis, 144
Job descriptions, 143–44
Job security, 17
Job specification, 144
Joseph Magnin Department Stores, 105, 108

Kellmer's, 619
Kentucky Fried Chicken, 548, 550
K-Mart, 82, 281, 286, 287, 373, 403, 619
Korvettes, 29, 82, 281, 373
Kresge, 11, 25, 82, 402–03, 619
Kroger's, 10

Labeling, private, 205
Large store organization, 117–22
Larimer Square, 79, 80
Layout of store, *see* Store layout
Leader offerings, 286, 287
Leaders, 261
Leadership style, 161–62
Leased departments, 212
Legislation, 19–21
  changes in, 617
  consumer protection, 20–21, 512–14
  pricing, 291–92
  recruiting, 144–45
Leisure time, changes in, 615
Levitz Furniture Corporation, 620
Liabilities, defined, 451
Licensing, 564
Lie detectors, 149–50
Lighting, interior, 104–05
Limited-service wholesalers, 203–04
List brokers, 594
List suppliers, 594
LNOs, 142
Loans, bank, 448
Location of business, *see* Store location
Long-term financing, 446–47
Looking-glass self, 60
Lord and Taylor, 16
Loss leaders, 286

Lowe's Companies, Inc., 459
Loyalty, consumer, 72–73

Magazines:
  advertising in, 386
  as information source, 436–37
  merchandise planning and, 180
Mail order sales, 13, 24, 591–96
Mail surveys, 439–40
Mailing envelopes, 595
Maintained markup, 266–67
Management training, 610–12
Manpower planning and recruiting, 143–47, 354–55
  determining requirements, 143–44
  laws concerning, 144–45
  sources, 146–47
Manufacturer-retailer franchises, 545
Manufacturers, 204–05
  price control by, 276–77
  retailing and, 6
Manufacturing center, 207
Markdowns, 290, 299–309
  automatic, 305
  causes of, 302–03
  decision sequence, 300–02
  defined, 299
  establishing price, 306–07
  planned, 189–90, 302–03
  size, 305–06
  timing, 305–06
  tracking, 307–09
Market segmentation, 36–39, 173, 574
Marketing concept, 507
  misapplication of, 564–65
Markets:
  central, 205–06
  defined, 35
  income factors, 35–36
  population characteristics, 35
  racially defined, 527–31
  target, 35–36
Marking, improper, 244–45
Markups, 256, 263–69
  additional, 298
  average, 269
  bases for, 265–66
  basic relationship, 263–66
  cost of merchandise sold, 264
  distinctions, 266–67

Markups *(Cont.)*
  dollar, 263–64, 266–67
  formulas, summary, 268
  initial, 266, 274–75, 282–83, 288–90
  maintained, 266–67
  nature of offering and, 288–90
  percentage, 265–66, 267
Marriott Corporation, 574
Marts, 206–07
Mass production, 6
Mathematics aptitude test, 145, 146
Matsushita Electric, 292
May Company, 357
May Department Stores, 620
McDonald's, 9, 41, 86, 101, 369, 542, 544, 545, 550
Meat Inspection Act, 505
Mechanization, 574
Meier and Frank's, 24
Memo buying, 211
Men's Wear, 436
Menswear Retailers Association, 536
Merchandise:
  fashion, 174, 176
  placement, 100
  private-brand, 281–82
  special, for racial minorities, 529
  staple, 174, 176
Merchandise brokers, 207–208
Merchandise budget, 186–92
  open-to-buy, 191–92
  purchases, 190–91
  reductions, 189–90
  stock planning, 186–89
    basic stock method, 186–87
    percentage variation method, 188
    stock-sales ratio method, 188–89
    weeks' supply method, 189
Merchandise control, 228–53
  educating customers, 246
  employee errors, 243–45
  employee theft, *see* Employee theft
  inventory, *see* Inventory control
  obsolescence, 245
  shoplifting, *see* Shoplifting
  spoilage, 245
Merchandise management, 123–27

buying and selling responsibilities, 123–25
  centralized buying, 125, 127
Merchandise marts and shows, 206–07
Merchandise mix, 8–9
Merchandise planning, 170–97
  basic stock list, 176, 178
  budgeting, *see* Merchandise budget
  comparison shopping, 177
  for consumer wants, 170–80
  customer complaints, 177
  customer requests, 177
  historical sales data, 174, 176
  market segmentation, 173
  merchandise assortments, 170–72
  model stock plan, 176–77, 179
  product life cycle, 172–73
  sales budget, 183–92
  stock turnover, 180–83
    ascertaining turnover rate, 181–82
    defined, 180
    profitability and, 182–83
    trade papers and magazines, 180
  See also Buying
Merchandise resources:
  pricing by, *see under* Pricing
  relationships with, 222–24
    back orders, 224
    cooperation, 224
    order cancellations and returns, 223–24
    split shipments, 224
    store order, 222–23
  selection of, 203–08
    central markets, 205–06
    manufacturers, 204–05
    manufacturing center, 207
    merchandise marts and shows, 206–07
    resident buying offices, 207–08
    wholesalers, 203–04
Merchandising:
  programmed, 193–94
  scrambled, 16, 171
Merchandising and Operating Results, 98
Mexican-Americans, *see* Racial minorities

Midas Muffler, 10
Middle-of-the-month dating (MOM), 221
Mini-malls, 81
Minority Enterprise Small Business Investment Company (MESBIC), 536
Minority groups, *see* Racial minorities
Miracle Maid, 591
Mobile families, 38–39
Model stock plan, 176–77, 179
Montgomery Ward & Company, 11, 16, 63, 82, 200, 205, 281, 386, 404, 453, 597, 616
Motivation of employees, 156–62
  combination plans, 157–58
  compensation, 156–57, 356–57, 360–61
  fringe benefits, 158–59
  managers and, 159–62
  straight commission, 157
  straight salary, 157
Multiple-unit pricing, 71, 285

Narrow assortments, 171
Natick Mall, 19
National advertising themes, 59
National Retail Merchants Association (NRMA), 98, 434–35, 474
Natural classification of expenses, 475–77
Needs, consumer, 57–60
  hierarchy of, 57–58
  identification of, 58–59
  strength of, 59–60
Negotiated-price system, 285
Neighborhood center, 81
Neiman-Marcus Co., 44, 118, 173, 258, 279, 304, 598, 618
Net dating, 220
Net income, in expense budgeting, 490–91
Net profit plan, 483–84, 485
Net sales, 455
Net worth, 451
Never outs, 176
Newspapers:
  advertising in, 385–86, 391
  as information source, 435–36
Noncumulative quantity discounts, 217

Non-store retailing, 12–14, 584–604
 non-personal, 591–601
  catalog sales, 13, 596–99
  mail order sales, 13, 24, 591–96
  vending, 13, 599–601
 personal, 584–91
  in-home, 12, 587–89, 591
  telephone sales, 585–87
Nordstrom-Best, 10
Normal-margin pricing, 11
North American Suburban Corp., 590

Objectives, setting, 30–31
Observation of consumers, 437–38
Obsolescence, merchandise, 245
Odd-ending prices, 70, 285
Offerings, 47
Office of Minority Business Enterprise (OMBEE), 536
One-price system, 284–85
On-the-job training, 152–54
One-way mirrors, 237–38
Open assortment display, 327
Open dating, 517–18
Open-to-buy figure, 191–92
Open-to-buy form, 229–30
Operations division, 128–29
Operations planning, 29–53
 defined, 29
 programming, 30–33
  methods development, 32
  planning strategies, 32
  policy development, 32–33
  setting objectives, 30–31
 relating price to, 276
 steps in, 33–50
  desired image formulation, 39–46
  environment assessment, 34–35
  market segmentation, 36–39
  retailing mix design, 46–50
  target market identification, 35–36
Order cancellation and returns, 223–24
Order forms, 595
Organization, defined, 111
Organization manual, 115

Organizational structure, 10, 111–37
 chain stores, 121–22, 125–27
 current trends, 132–34
 customer relations, 134
 department stores, 118–25, 127–31
 formal, 114–15
 informal, 115
 merchandise management, 123–27
 need for, 112
 small stores, 116–17
 top management, 133–34
Original price, 293–94
Osco Drug, 519
Outdoor advertising, 388
Oxmoor Shopping Center, 108

Pacific Stereo Shops, 285
Parking, 87–88
Part-timers, 141–42
Party selling, 589, 591
Pathmark, 205
Patronage, 72–73
Patronage discounts, 217
Peck & Peck, 318
Pedestrian traffic, 86–87
Pendleton sportswear, 291
Penney, J. C., Co., Inc., 25, 35, 63, 205, 360, 369, 597, 619
Percentage markups, 265–66, 267
Percentage variation method, stocks, 188
Performance objectives, 31
Perpetual inventory, 181, 232
Personal income, 36
Personal non-store retailing, 584–91
 in home, 12, 587–89, 591
 telephone sales, 585–87
Personal selling, 48, 344–65
 adaptive formula selling, 349–51
 basic procedure, 349
 creative selling, 352–53
 criticism of, 345
 defined, 344–45
 fundamentals, 348–53
 importance of, 345–47
 nature of, 344–48
 routine selling, 352
 sales management, 353–62

 self-service operations and, 347–48
 transaction processing, 352
 types of, 352–53
Personnel, *see* Employees; Staffing
Personnel budget, 143
Personnel division, 130, 131
Physical examinations, employee, 148–49, 150
Physical facilities, *see* Store location
Physical inventory mistakes, 243–44
Physiological needs, 57
Picture phones, 618
Pizza Hut, 335
Planned initial markup, 274–75, 282–83
PMs, 357
Point scoring, in credit approval, 411, 412
Point-of-purchase displays, 329–30
Point-of-purchase terminal, 19, 199, 232, 432–34
Policy, *see* Store policies
Polygraph tests, 149–50
Population:
 changes in, 14–15, 35, 614
 store location and, 83–84
Post-purchase doubt, 74
Potential trading area, 85
Practical trading area, 85
Preference, consumer, 72
Premium offers, 337–38, 595–96
Prescription prices, posting of, 519–20
Price adjustments, 298–313
 additional markups, 298
 employee and customer discounts, 299
 markdowns, *see* Markdowns
 See also Pricing
Price cards, 330
Price disadvantage, 42
Price lining, 286, 288
Price-aura effect, 71
Price-level strategy, 278–79, 281–82
Prices:
 customary, 70–71
 multiple-unit, 71, 285
 odd-ending, 70, 285

Index **649**

Prices (Cont.)
  price-aura effect, 71
  quality related, 70
  See also Pricing
Pricing, 256–71
  as an art, 260
  behavioral meanings of, 69–72
  defined, 257
  demand-oriented, 260–61
  determining range of feasible prices, 260–61
  errors, 302
  markups, see Markups
  normal-margin, 11
  profits and, 261–63
  purchase decisions and, 257–59
  within retailing mix, 257
  unit, 21, 292–93, 515, 517
  See also Price adjustments; Prices; Pricing methods
Pricing methods, 262–97
  above-the-market strategy, 279
  at-the-market strategy, 281
  bait-and-switch pricing, 286, 532
  below-the-market strategy, 281
  competition and, 277–78
  consumerism and, 292–93
  control of prices, 276–77
  decision sequence, 272–75
  economic climate and, 293
  leader offerings, 286, 287
  legislation and, 291–92
  nature of offerings, 288–90
  one-price system, 284–85
  operations planning and, 276
  original price, establishing, 293–94
  planned initial markup, 274–75, 282–83
  price lining, 286, 288
  price-level strategy, 278–79, 281–82
  private brands, 281–82
  store policies and, 284–88
Primary services, 47, 561–79
  changes in, 621, 623
  characteristics of, 568–71
  defined, 397, 561
  growth of, 563–64
  improvements in, 571, 573–75
  nature of, 561–62
  shortcomings, 564–67
Private labeling, 205

Private-brand merchandise, 281–82
Probabilistic sample, 440
Product life cycle, 172–73
Profit:
  defined, 261
  net, 458
  pricing and, 261–63
  stockturn and, 182–83
Profit squeeze, staffing and, 139–40
Programmed instruction, 155–56
Programmed merchandising, 193–94
Programming retail operations, 30–33
  methods development, 32
  planning strategies, 32
  policy development, 32–33
  setting objectives, 30–31
Progressive Grocer, 436
Promotion, 43–44, 48, 316–43
  coupons, 338–39
  defined, 317
  developing blend of, 322–24
  display, 325–30
  fundamental tasks, 320–21
  premium offers, 337–38, 595–96
  prerequisites, 318–20
  publicity, 334, 336
  purposes of, 317–18
  responsibility for, 321–22
  special sales, 331–33
  trading stamps, 336–37
  See also Advertising; Personal selling; Supplementary services
Promotion division, 130, 131
Promotional advertising, 371–73
Promotional discounts, 217–18
Prune Yard, 81
Psychological needs, 36
Psychological prices, 70–71, 285
Psychological tests, 145, 149
Public service advertising, 376
Public service display, 327
Public utility, 543
Publicity, 334, 336
Puppy Palace, 555
Purchasing:
  buying vs., 200
  planning, 190–91
  pricing and, 257–59
Pure Food and Drug Act, 505

Push money, 357

Quality-related prices, 70, 285
Quantity discounts, 216–17
Questioning of consumers, 438–39

Racial minorities, 524–40
  general characteristics, 525–27
  problems, 531–33
  racially defined markets, 527–31
  retailing by, 533–37
Rack jobbers, 204, 211
Radio advertising, 386–87, 391
Random sample, 440
Real income, 36
Receipt of goods (ROG), 221
Receiving errors, 244
Recruiting, 143–47, 355
  determining requirements, 143–44
  laws concerning, 144–45
  sources, 146–47
Reduced-price advertising, 373
Reductions, planning, 189–90
Regional center, 81
Resale price maintenance laws, 291–92
Resident buying offices, 207–08
Resources, see Merchandise resources
Retail credit, 11, 405–16
  approval, 411–14
  billing, 414–15
  collection, 415–16
  computer and, 416
  decision to offer, 410–11
  external, 405, 408
  installment, 409, 532–33
  internal, 405, 411–16
  management, 411–16
  payment schedules, 408–10
  racial minorities and, 532–33
  records, 414
  revolving, 409–10
  state and local government regulation, 21
Retail method of inventory valuation, 464–69
  benefits of, 468–69
  problems with, 469
  procedure, 464–68

Retail operations planning, *see* Operations planning
Retail sales manager, 354
Retailers:
  classification of, 7–14
  consumerism and, 515–18
  economic forces affecting, 16–17
  governmental forces affecting, 19–21
  prospective, 31
  retailing distinguished from, 4–5
  societal forces affecting, 14–16
  technological forces affecting, 18–19
Retailing:
  careers in, 605–12
    advancement, 612
    as employee, 607, 609
    as entrepreneur, 606–07
    job hunting, 609–10
    management training, 610–12
  defined, 4–5
  evolution of, 23–26
  future of, 612–24
  in-home, 12–13, 587–89, 591
  in-store, *see* In-store retailing
  manufacturers and, 6
  need for, 5–6
  non-store, *see* Non-store retailing
  role in consumerism, 506–07
  scope of, 6–7
Retailing mix:
  components, 47–48
  defined, 46
  nature of, 46–47
  position within retail system, 49–50
Return privileges, 11
Revolving credit, 409–10
Rexall, 546
Richman Brothers, 35
Rich's, 16, 626
Riverfront Plaza, 79
Robinson-Patman Act of 1936, 213, 217, 378
Route sale, 589
Routine selling, 352

Safety needs, 57
Safeway, 10, 16
Saks Fifth Avenue, 118, 279, 304
Salary:
  as employee motivation, 157
  laws concerning, 144
  profit squeeze and, 139–40
  straight, 157
Sales:
  in expense budgeting, 490–91
  fluctuations, employees and, 141–42
  on income statement, 455–56
  non-personal, 13–14
  personal, 12–13
  special, 331–33
Sales budget, 184–86
Sales consultants, 352
Sales data, historical, 174
Sales forecasting, 426–27
Sales management, 353–62
  compensation, 356–57
  control, 357–58
  initial tasks, 358–59
  manpower planning, 354–55
  motivation, 360–62
  raising productivity, 359
  responsibility for, 354
  scheduling, 355–56
  supervision, 357–58
  training, 355, 360, 361
Sales Management, 35, 436
Sales recording system, 231–32
Sales slips, 431
Sales space, 98–99
Sales volume, 355–56
Sambo's Restaurants, 549
Samples:
  information, 440–41
  mail order houses, 595
Scheduling, 355–56
Scrambled merchandising, 16, 171
Sears, Roebuck and Co., 11, 13, 63, 82, 205, 369, 385, 386, 404, 433, 597, 626
Seasonal catalogs, 598
Seasonal discounts, 218
Section managers, 354
Security force, 238–39
Self-actualization needs, 57
Self-concept, consumer, 60, 62–63
Self-liquidating loans, 448
Self-service operations, 142, 347–48
Self-teaching, 155–56

Selling, *see* Personal selling
Selling area, 97
Selling costs, 289–90
Selling errors, 302
Senior citizens, 68
Seniority, 17
Service sponsor-retailer franchise, 545
Service times, 355
Services, *see* Primary services; Supplementary services
Setting display, 327
7-Eleven Food Stores, 542, 555
Shakey's Pizza Parlor, 544
Shell Oil Company, 11
Sherman Antitrust Act of 1890, 20
Sherwin-Williams, 16
Shillito's, 104
Shoplifting, 16, 19, 106, 233–40, 348
  defined, 233
  educating consumers, 246
  employee control of, 239–40, 246
  forms of, 233–34
  identifying, 234–36
  prosecution, 248
  security, 236–40
  severity, 234
Shoppers' news, 385
Shopping centers, 25, 79, 81
Short-term financing, 447–48
Short-timers, 141
Showrooms, catalog, 619–20
Shows, merchandise, 206–07
Shrinkage, *see* Merchandise control
Signs, 107–08, 237, 327
Singer Sewing Machine Company, 546
Small Business Administration (SBA), 435, 535, 536
Small stores organization, 116–17
Social class, 63–66
Social needs, 57
Societal forces, 14–16
Soft goods, defined, 121
Sony Corporation of America, 292
Southland Corporation, 280
Space allocation, 96–100
  sales space, 98–99
  selling vs. nonselling areas, 97
  space productivity, 99

Index **651**

Spanish-Americans, *see* Racial minorities
Special sales, 331–33
Special-audience papers, 385
Specialty catalogs, 598
Specialty shops, 23
Specification buying, 204–05
Spiffs, 357
Split shipments, 224
Spoilage, merchandise, 245
Staffing, 138–67
  difficulties, 138–43
    profit squeeze, 139–40
    retailing's reputation, 140–41
    sales activity fluctuations, 141–42
  hiring, 150, 242
  motivation, *see* Motivating employees
  planning and recruiting, 143–47
    determining requirements, 143–44
    laws concerning, 144–45
    sources, 146–47
  selection, 147–50
  training, *see* Employee training
Staple merchandise, 174, 176
State and local government regulation, 21
STEM ("Shoplifters Take Everybody's Money"), 246
Stephen Crane Associates, 153
Stock list, basic, 176–78
Stock method, basic, 186–87
Stock plan, model, 176–77, 179
Stock planning, 186–89
  basic stock method, 186–87
  percentage variation method, 188
  stock-sales ratio method, 188–89
  weeks' supply method, 189
Stock turnover, 180–83
  ascertaining turnover rate, 181–82
  defined, 180
  profitability and, 182–83
Stock-count books, 231
Stock-sales ratio method, 188–89
Store design, 48, 93, 100–08
  counters, 106
  display cases, 106
  display windows, 104
  elevators, 106–07
  entrance, 102–03
  equipment, 105–08
  escalators, 106–07
  interior lighting, 104–05
  objectives, 101, 104
  signs, 107–08
  store dividers, 108
Store layout, 93–100
  alternatives, 94–96
    boutique, 96
    free flow, 95–96
    grid, 94–95
  merchandise placement, 100
  shoplifting control, 237
  space allocation, 96–100
    of sales space, 98–99
    selling vs. nonselling areas, 97
    space productivity, 99
Store location, 47–48, 78–91
  factors in, 78–82
  objectives, 82
  types of, 79–82
  See also Store location analysis
Store location analysis, 83–91
  area changes, 88
  competition, 84
  complementary outlets, 87
  cost, 88–89
  data sources for, 89–91
  economic conditions, 83
  general area, 83–84
  growth, 84
  indirectly competing outlets, 87
  parking, 87–88
  pedestrian and auto traffic, 86–87
  population, 83–84
  specific site, 84–87
  surroundings, 88
  trading area, 84–85
  vulnerability, 87
Store operations division, 128–29
Store order, 222–23
Store policies:
  buying and, 202
  developing, 32–33
  price and, 284–88
Stores, 436
Straight commission, 157
Straight salary, 157
Strategy, planning, 32, 33–34
Strikes, 17
String locations, 81
Suburban shopping areas, evolution of, 25
Sunbeam, 291
Supermarkets:
  advertising, 368, 385
  competition and, 16
  consumerism and, 292–93
  evolution of, 25
  grid layout, 95
  image, 42
  shoplifting control, 234
  in shopping centers, 81
  specification buying, 205
Superstores, 621, 622
Supplementary services, 11–12, 47, 48, 397–421
  attraction of, 398–99
  changes in, 623–24
  credit, *see* Retail credit
  decision to offer, 399–401
  development of, 398–402
  life cycle of, 401–02
  management of, 402–04
    charging, 403–04
    customer misuse, 404
    periodic evaluation, 402–03
Surroundings, store location and, 88
Surveillance, 16
"Survey of Buying Power," 35
Syndicate resident buying office, 208

Target audience, 391–92
Target discount chain, 11
Target markets, 35–36
Technology:
  changes in, 617–18
  external, 19
  internal, 18–19
Teenagers, 65
Tel-E-Gift Center Showrooms, 620
Telephone sales, 12–13, 585–87
Telephone shopping, 623–24
Telephone surveys, 440
Television:
  advertising and, 387, 391
  cable, 617–18
  shoplifting control and, 237–38
Tests, employee, 145, 146
Theft, *see* Employee theft; Shoplifting

Top management, 133–34
Top-down method, 184, 494
Trade associations:
   as information source, 434–35
   sales space allocation and, 98
Trade credit, 448
Trade discounts, 215–16
Trade papers and magazines, 180
Trading area, 84–85
Trading stamps, 336–37
Training:
   buyers, 200
   centralized or decentralized, 151
   classroom, 154–55
   employee, 150–56, 242, 246
   management, 610–12
   on-the-job, 152–54
   salespeople, 355, 360, 361
   self-teaching, 155–56
Transaction processing, 352
Transit advertising, 388
Transportation terms, merchandise buying, 214–15
Truth-in-Lending law, 20, 513–14

Truth-in-Packaging law, 512–13
Tupperware, 12

Underground Atlanta, 79, 80
Underorganizing, 112, 114
Unfair sales practices acts, 292
Unionization, 16–17
Unit control, 230–32
Unit pricing, 21, 292–93, 515, 517
Urban Coalition, 535

Value shifts, 15–16
Vandalism, 16
Variety stores, 16, 347
Vending, 13, 599–601
Vertical cooperative advertising, 377–78
Video playback units, 155
Vulnerability, 87

Walgreen's, 16
Walk-ins, 146

Wanamaker's, 24
Want slip, 177
Warehouse showrooms, 620–21
Weeks' supply method, stocks, 189
Western Auto, 35
Wheeler-Lea Act, 505
Wholesale price, 289
Wholesalers, 203–04, 276–77
Wickes, 620
Wide Area Telephone Service (WATS), 440
Women, status of, 614
Woodward & Lothrop, 495
Woolco, 281
Woolworth's, 25, 619
Working hours, 16–17, 615

"Yellow pages," advertising in, 388

Zenith Radio Corporation, 292